Dear West Customer:

West Academic Publishing has changed the look of its American Casebook Series®.

In keeping with our efforts to promote sustainability, we have replaced our former covers with book covers that are more environmentally friendly. Our casebooks will now be covered in a 100% renewable natural fiber. In addition, we have migrated to an ink supplier that favors vegetable-based materials, such as soy.

Using soy inks and natural fibers to print our textbooks reduces VOC emissions. Moreover, our primary paper supplier is certified by the Forest Stewardship Council, which is testament to our commitment to conservation and responsible business management.

The new cover design has migrated from the long-standing brown cover to a contemporary charcoal fabric cover with silver-stamped lettering and black accents. Please know that inside the cover, our books continue to provide the same trusted content that you've come to expect from West.

We've retained the ample margins that you have told us you appreciate in our texts while moving to a new, larger font, improving readability. We hope that you will find these books a pleasing addition to your bookshelf.

Another visible change is that you will no longer see the brand name Thomson West on our print products. With the recent merger of Thomson and Reuters, I am pleased to announce that books published under the West Academic Publishing imprint will once again display the West brand.

It will likely be several years before all of our casebooks are published with the new cover and interior design. We ask for your patience as the new covers are rolled out on new and revised books knowing that behind both the new and old covers, you will find the finest in legal education materials for teaching and learning.

Thank you for your continued patronage of the West brand, which is both rooted in history and forward looking towards future innovations in legal education. We invite you to be a part of our next evolution.

Best regards,

Louis H. Higgins
Editor in Chief, West Academic Publishing

CASES AND MATERIALS ON
THE LAW AND POLICY OF SENTENCING AND CORRECTIONS

Eighth Edition

. . .

By
Lynn S. Branham
Visiting Professor of Law
St. Louis University School of Law
and
Michael S. Hamden, Esq.

AMERICAN CASEBOOK SERIES®

WEST®
A Thomson Reuters business

Mat #40775918

American Casebook Series is a trademark registered in the U.S. Patent and Trademark Office.

COPYRIGHT © 1997 WEST PUBLISHING CO.
© West, a Thomson business, 2002, 2005
© 2009 Thomson Reuters

    610 Opperman Drive
    St. Paul, MN 55123
    1–800–313–9378

Printed in the United States of America

ISBN: 978–0–314–19943–0

Dedicated

to

My son
Jordan.

Always
Blessed and a blessing
Ever
In my heart

*

PREFACE

The eighth edition of this book, like its predecessors, focuses on two areas of law and policy that are hotbeds of controversy: sentencing and corrections. For those who wish to practice criminal law proficiently and effectively, learning about these key components of the criminal-justice system is a must. But, as will become evident when reading the materials in this book, sentencing and correctional law and policy affect not just those who work in the criminal-justice system or are processed through it. They affect us all, with each of us having a stake in the legality and cost-effectiveness of sentencing and corrections-related decisions. Learning more about sentencing and corrections will redound then, most assuredly, to the benefit of all.

This casebook will enable law schools and criminal-justice programs to ensure that their course offerings include these cutting-edge areas of law and policy. The book can be used in two discrete courses, one on sentencing law and policy and the other on correctional law and policy, or in a blended course that provides a broader overview of these subjects. When I teach sentencing law and policy, the assignments span the first nine chapters of the book, while the last ten chapters of the book typically are the focus of a separate class on correctional law and policy.

Like earlier editions of this book, the current edition includes seminal Supreme Court cases bearing on the subjects of correctional and sentencing law and highlights significant issues percolating in the lower courts. Interwoven into the book are statutes, court rules, sentencing guidelines, article excerpts, model standards, policy statements, statistics, and problems that are designed not only to impart knowledge, but to provoke thought, discussion, and debate about how the law and policy of sentencing and corrections should evolve.

Within the book, footnotes and citations to secondary materials and some section headings in cases have been omitted without so specifying. When footnotes have been included, the numbers from the original sources have been retained. All letter footnotes contain information added by the author.

In 1973, Sheldon Krantz wrote the precursor to this book, reflecting what has become our shared commitment to inform the discussion of, and debate on, issues about sentencing and correctional law and policy. I am grateful to Sheldon for the confidence he placed in me by "passing the torch"—the responsibility for writing earlier and future editions of this book—to me. And I was fortunate to receive assistance in completing the last edition of this book from Michael Hamden, a lawyer with unparalleled expertise in correctional law and policy.

I would like to express my appreciation to the publishers and authors who granted permission to reprint the book and article excerpts whose inclusion in the book has greatly enhanced its pedagogical value. I am also deeply indebted to Lori Owens, whose word-processing skills and equanimity in the face of deadlines enabled me to complete this "labor of love" for others. David Kullman, a librarian at the St. Louis University School of Law, is also to be credited for his assistance in procuring materials I needed to complete this book and for bringing levity to tasks of such gravitas. And I am particularly thankful to Dean Jeff Lewis for his words of encouragement and unflagging support during my sojourn at St. Louis University School of Law.

Finally, I would be remiss were I not to reiterate the comments Sheldon made in an earlier edition of this book, for truly it can be said that "much of the inspiration for preparing this casebook and its previous editions has come from knowing and working with those in the correctional field who labor constantly for reform, who often suffer for their efforts, but who never give up."

LYNN S. BRANHAM

June 2009

SUMMARY OF CONTENTS

TABLE OF CONTENTS

TABLE OF CASES

The principal cases are in bold type. Cases cited or discussed in the text are in roman type. References are to pages. Cases cited in principal cases and within other quoted materials are not included.

CASES AND MATERIALS ON
THE LAW AND POLICY OF SENTENCING AND CORRECTIONS

Eighth Edition

*

PART 1

THE LAW AND POLICY OF SENTENCING

■ ■ ■

CHAPTER 1

INTRODUCTION TO SENTENCING

■ ■ ■

A. SENTENCING: YESTERDAY AND TODAY

Winston Churchill once said that "[t]he mood and temper of the public with regard to the treatment of crime and criminals is one of the most unfailing tests of the civilization of any country." Marvin E. Frankel, Criminal Sentences: Law without Order 9 (1973). We should at times, therefore, stop and ask ourselves, "How civilized is our country's system of punishing criminals? And, from a practical perspective, how effective are our efforts to punish and control crime and to hold offenders accountable for the harm they have caused individuals and their communities?"

It is obvious, when comparing the punishment system of today in our country with the modes of punishment employed in earlier years, that punishment practices have changed dramatically. In colonial times, for example, individuals who had committed such offenses as not observing the Sabbath and being in the company of drunkards often had their legs immobilized in stocks, which were set up in a public place. Pillories, wooden frames used to immobilize individuals' heads and hands, were also frequently used as a form of punishment, and as an added touch, offenders sometimes had their ears nailed to the wood on either side of the holes through which their heads were stuck. Members of the community often gathered at the site of stocks and pillories to ridicule the hapless offenders and throw objects such as stale eggs, potatoes, and excrement at them.

Public humiliation was a common element of other types of punishment as well. Many offenders were required to wear letters sewn on their clothes or branded on their bodies publicizing their malefactions. An "A" signified that an individual had committed adultery, a "B" that the individual had uttered blasphemous words, and a "D" that the individual had been drunk.

During these times, women, particularly women who scolded their husbands, often were singled out for punishment. A type of stick that pinched the tongue sometimes was affixed to the tongue of a scolding wife, or the wife was placed in a ducking stool and then immersed in water. The ducking stool was used for other purposes as well. Married couples who

2

quarreled too much or too loudly, for example, were tied back to back at times and dunked in the water together.

Whipping was another popular form of punishment during the early years of this country, one employed for such offenses as stealing a loaf of bread, lying, and name-calling. Other forms of physical punishment were common as well. Offenders sometimes had their ears cut off, their nostrils slit, a hole bored through their tongues, or their cheeks, foreheads, or other parts of their bodies branded as punishment for an assortment of crimes. For more information about punishment practices in earlier years in this country, see The Oxford History of the Prison (Norval Morris & David J. Rothman eds., 1995) and Alice M. Earle, Curious Punishments of Bygone Days (1968).

Penitentiaries came into use in this country in the late 1700s as part of a reform movement designed to alleviate the harshness of some of the forms of punishment described above. Penitentiaries were viewed, as their name suggests, as places where offenders could contemplate the error of their ways, become penitent, and seek God's forgiveness for their sins. This reform process, it was felt, could be accomplished through a regimen of compulsory Bible reading and enforced silence to protect prisoners from bad influences exerted by other prisoners. John W. Roberts, Reform and Retribution: An Illustrated History of American Prisons 26–27, 31–33 (1997).

We now have moved into another punishment phase in this country. Although prisons today are hardly characterized by pervasive silence and Bible reading, imprisonment is still a very popular form of punishment in the United States. In fact, the United States incarcerates more people than any other country in the world, including countries that are much more heavily populated. The Pew Center on the States, One in 100: Behind Bars in America 2008, at 5 (2008) (hereinafter Pew Center Report). And the per-capita incarceration rate in this country is the highest in the world, far eclipsing the rate in other industrialized nations. Id. at 5, 35 (reporting that 750 of every 100,000 residents in the United States were incarcerated in 2008 compared, for example, to 148 in England and Wales, 93 in Germany, and 85 in France).

The reliance on incarceration as a criminal sanction, however, still continues to increase, straining prison and jail resources and government budgets. The nation's prison population in 2007 was almost triple the size it was twenty years earlier. Id. at 5. The per-capita incarceration rate in the nation (a figure which includes jails) climbed from 458 inmates per every 100,000 residents in 1990 to 750 inmates per every 100,000 residents in 2008. Id.; Bureau of Justice Statistics, U.S. Dep't of Justice, Prisoners in 2001, at 2 (2002). Since reported per-capita incarceration rates typically include residents who are children and since most children are not incarcerated, these statistics somewhat mask the prevalence of incarceration in the United States. Statistics considering only adults in the calculus reveal that more than one in every 100 adults in this country are confined in prisons or jails. Pew Center Report, at 5.

At the same time, probation is imposed widely in the United States as a criminal sanction, far more frequently than imprisonment. Bureau of Justice Statistics, U.S. Dep't of Justice, Probation and Parole in the United States, 2006, at 1, 2 (2007) (4,237,023 adults on probation at the end of 2006 compared to 1,492,973 in prison and 766,010 in jail). The total number of people under correctional supervision in the country, whether on probation or parole, in jail, or in prison, reached over 7.2 million in 2006, approximately one of every thirty-one adults. Id. at 2. In addition, other community-based sanctions, such as fines, restitution, community service, home confinement, and day-reporting centers are being used with increasing frequency as criminal-justice policymakers and practitioners strive to find the most appropriate criminal sanctions to impose on criminal offenders—cost-effective sanctions that are neither overly lenient nor overly punitive.

B.   THE PURPOSES OF CRIMINAL SENTENCES

1.   TRADITIONAL SENTENCING PURPOSES

In assessing the soundness and efficacy of the present criminal-sanctioning system in this country and in determining whether it is, as it purports to be, a criminal-"justice" system, a number of questions must be addressed, including the following: First, for what purpose or purposes is punishment to be imposed? Second, what types of conduct should be subject to criminal sanctions? Third, what form or forms of punishment should be employed as criminal sanctions? Fourth, what constraints should be placed on the use of these sanctions in terms of amount, duration, and other conditions? And fifth, what steps should be taken and procedural safeguards put in place to ensure that an appropriate penalty is imposed on a particular individual? After answering all of these questions, a sixth question then must be addressed: Are we willing to pay the costs of the criminal-justice system we are contemplating? For if we are not, then we must reexamine our answers concerning the direction to be taken by our nation's criminal-justice system.

Set forth below are some of Professor Wayne LaFave's observations regarding the first question set forth above: What are the purposes of punishment? Then follows a case, United States v. Bergman, 416 F.Supp. 496 (S.D.N.Y.1976), in which the court considered these purposes in deciding the appropriate penalty to impose on a defendant.

WAYNE R. LAFAVE, CRIMINAL LAW

(4th ed. 2003). Reprinted with permission of Thomson Reuters/West

* * *

Purposes of the Criminal Law—Theories of Punishment

The broad purposes of the criminal law are, of course, to make people do what society regards as desirable and to prevent them from doing what society considers to be undesirable. Since criminal law is framed in terms of imposing punishment for bad conduct, rather than of granting rewards for good conduct, the emphasis is more on the prevention of the undesirable than on the encouragement of the desirable.

In determining what undesirable conduct should be punished, the criminal law properly aims more to achieve a minimum standard of conduct than to bring about ideal conduct (say, the conduct of a highly-principled, selfless, heroic person). It is a fine thing for a man, at the risk of his own life, to enter a blazing building in order to rescue a stranger trapped therein; but the law does not (and should not) punish a failure to live up to such a heroic standard of behavior. It is a virtuous thing for an engaged man and woman to refrain from engaging in sexual intercourse until they are married; but it does not follow that the law should punish a failure to adhere to such a highly moral standard of conduct.

* * *

The criminal law is not, of course, the only weapon which society uses to prevent conduct which harms or threatens to harm these important interests of the public. Education, at home and at school, as to the types of conduct that society thinks good and bad, is an important weapon; religion, with its emphasis on distinguishing between good and evil conduct, is another. The human desire to acquire and keep the affection and respect of family, friends and associates no doubt has a great influence in deterring most people from conduct which is socially unacceptable. The civil side of the law, which forces one to pay damages for the harmful results which his undesirable conduct has caused to others, or which in appropriate situations grants injunctions against bad conduct or orders the specific performance of good conduct, also plays a part in influencing behavior along desirable lines.

(a) Theories of Punishment. How does the criminal law, with its threat of punishment to violators, operate to influence human conduct away from the undesirable and toward the desirable? There are a number of theories of punishment, and each theory has or has had its enthusiastic adherents. Some of the theories are concerned primarily with the particular offender, while others focus more on the nature of the offense and the general public. These theories are:

(1) Prevention. By this theory, also called *intimidation,* or, when the deterrence theory is referred to as general deterrence, *particular deter-*

rence,[a] criminal punishment aims to deter the criminal himself (rather than to deter others) from committing further crimes, by giving him an unpleasant experience he will not want to endure again. The validity of this theory has been questioned by many, who point out the high recidivism rates of those who have been punished. On the other hand, it has been observed that our attempts at prevention by punishment may enjoy an unmeasurable degree of success, in that without punishment for purposes of prevention the rate of recidivism might be much higher. This assumption is not capable of precise proof, nor is the assertion that in some instances punishment for prevention will fill the prisoner with feelings of hatred and desire for revenge against society and thus influence future criminal conduct.

(2) Restraint. The notion here, also expressed as *incapacitation, isolation,* or *disablement,* is that society may protect itself from persons deemed dangerous because of their past criminal conduct by isolating these persons from society. If the criminal is imprisoned or executed, he cannot commit further crimes against society. Some question this theory because of doubts that those who present a danger of continuing criminality can be accurately identified. It has also been noted that resort to restraint without accompanying rehabilitative efforts is unwise, as the vast majority of prisoners will ultimately be returned to society. The restraint theory is sometimes employed to justify execution or life imprisonment without chance of parole for those offenders believed to be beyond rehabilitation.

(3) Rehabilitation. Under this theory, also called *correction* or *reformation,* we "punish" the convicted criminal by giving him appropriate treatment, in order to rehabilitate him and return him to society so reformed that he will not desire or need to commit further crimes. It is perhaps not entirely correct to call this treatment "punishment," as the emphasis is away from making him suffer and in the direction of making his life better and more pleasant. The rehabilitation theory rests upon the belief that human behavior is the product of antecedent causes, that these causes can be identified, and that on this basis therapeutic measures can be employed to effect changes in the behavior of the person treated. Even when there has been more of a commitment to the "rehabilitative ideal" than to other theories of punishment, much of what is done by way of post-conviction disposition of offenders is not truly rehabilitative. Perhaps this is why the theory of reformation has not as yet shown very satisfactory results in practice.

* * *

(4) Deterrence. Under this theory, sometimes referred to as *general prevention,* the sufferings of the criminal for the crime he has committed are supposed to deter others from committing future crimes, lest they suffer the same unfortunate fate. The extent to which punishment actually has this effect upon the general public is unclear; conclusive empirical

---

a. This penological purpose also is referred to commonly as "specific deterrence."

research on the subject is lacking, and it is difficult to measure the effectiveness of fear of punishment because it is but one of several forces that restrain people from violating the law.

It does seem fair to assume, however, that the deterrent efficacy of punishment varies considerably, depending upon a number of factors. Those who commit crimes under emotional stress (such as murder in the heat of anger) or who have become expert criminals through the training and practice of many years (such as the professional safebreaker and pickpocket) are less likely than others to be deterred. Even apart from the nature of the crime, individuals undoubtedly react differently to the threat of punishment, depending upon such factors as their social class, age, intelligence, and moral training. The magnitude of the threatened punishment is clearly a factor, but perhaps not as important a consideration as the probability of discovery and punishment.

(5) Education. Under this theory, criminal punishment serves, by the publicity which attends the trial, conviction and punishment of criminals, to educate the public as to the proper distinctions between good conduct and bad—distinctions which, when known, most of society will observe. While the public may need no such education as to serious *malum in se* crimes, the educational function of punishment is important as to crimes which are not generally known, often misunderstood, or inconsistent with current morality.

(6) Retribution. This is the oldest theory of punishment, and the one which still commands considerable respect from the general public. By this theory, also called *revenge* or *retaliation,* punishment (the infliction of suffering) is imposed by society on criminals in order to obtain revenge, or perhaps (under the less emotional concept of retribution) because it is only fitting and just that one who has caused harm to others should himself suffer for it. Typical of the criticism is that this theory "is a form of retaliation, and as such, is morally indefensible."

However, the retribution theory, when explained on somewhat different grounds, continues to draw some support. Some contend that when one commits a crime, it is important that he receive commensurate punishment in order to restore the peace of mind and repress the criminal tendencies of others. In addition, it is claimed that retributive punishment is needed to maintain respect for the law and to suppress acts of private vengeance. For this reason, even some critics of the retribution theory acknowledge that it must occupy a "minor position" in the contemporary scheme.

Although retribution was long the theory of punishment least accepted by theorists, it "is suddenly being seen by thinkers of all political persuasions as perhaps the strongest ground, after all, upon which to base a system of punishment." Today it is commonly put forward under the rubric of "deserts" or "just deserts":

The offender may justly be subjected to certain deprivations because he deserves it; and he deserves it because he has engaged in wrongful conduct—conduct that does or threatens injury and that is prohibited by law. The penalty is thus not just a means of crime prevention but a merited response to the actor's deed, "rectifying the balance" in the Kantian sense and expressing moral reprobation of the actor for the wrong.[43]

Those who favor the theory claim it "provides an important check against tyranny, for a person is punished only when he deserves it; and the opposite is also true—that he is not punished if he does not deserve it." They are also likely to reject utilitarian approaches to punishment because of the view that punishment may not be inflicted upon a person in order to benefit the collective interests of others.

(b) Conflict Between the Theories. For many years most of the literature on the subject of punishment was devoted to advocacy of a particular theory to the exclusion of others. Those who espoused the rehabilitation theory condemned the rest, those who favored the deterrence theory denied the validity of all others, and so on. But in recent years the "inclusive theory of punishment" has gained considerable support; there is now general agreement that all (or, at least most) of the theories described above deserve some consideration.

This has given rise to another difficult problem, namely, what the priority and relationship of these several aims should be. This problem must be confronted, as it is readily apparent that the various theories tend to conflict with one another at several points. The retribution, deterrence, and prevention theories call for presenting the criminal with an unpleasant experience; but the chances for rehabilitation are often defeated by harsh treatment. The rehabilitation theory would let the criminal go when (and perhaps *only* when) he had been reformed. This may be a substantially shorter period of time (or a substantially *longer* period of time) than can be justified under the deterrence and retribution theories, which would vary the punishment in accordance with the seriousness of the crime. Because of such conflicts, the legislators who enact the punishment clauses (generally with minimum and maximum provisions) for the various crimes, the judges (or, in some states as to some crimes, the juries) who must sentence the convicted defendant within the limits set forth in legislation, and the administrative officials (parole and pardoning authorities) who are empowered to release convicted criminals from imprisonment, must determine priorities.

It is undoubtedly true that the thinking of legislators, judges and juries, and administrative officers who have a part in fixing punishment, as well as the thinking of the expert criminologist and non-expert layman whose views tend to influence those officials, varies from situation to

---

43. A. von Hirsch, Doing Justice 51 (1976). It "is likely to include two princip[al] assertions. First, the primary object of criminal sanctions is to punish culpable behavior. Although punishment may result in certain utilitarian benefits, notably the reduction of criminal behavior, the justification of punishment does not require such a showing; for it is moral and just that culpable behavior be punished. Second, the severity of the sanctions visited on the offender should be proportioned to the degree of his culpability." F. Allen, The Decline of the Rehabilitative Ideal 66 (1981).

situation. Sometimes the retribution theory will predominate; most of us share the common feeling of mankind that a particularly shocking crime should be severely punished. Where, for example, a son, after thoughtfully taking out insurance on his mother's life, places a time bomb in her suitcase just before she boards a plane, which device succeeds in killing the mother and all forty-two others aboard the plane, we almost all feel that he deserves a severe punishment, and we reach this result with little reflection about influencing future conduct. Likewise, when a less serious crime is involved and it was committed by a young person who might be effectively reformed, the rehabilitation theory rightly assumes primary importance. And the deterrence theory may be most important when the crime is not inherently wrong or covered by moral prohibition. Illustrative are income tax violations, as to which deterrence is especially important because of our reliance on a system of self-assessment.

Although allowance must be made for such variables, it is fair to say, as a general proposition, that for much of the twentieth century the pendulum was swinging away from retribution and deterrence and in the direction of rehabilitation as the chief goal of punishment; or, to put it differently, away from the philosophy that the punishment should fit the crime toward one that the punishment should fit the criminal. The tendency was to move away from backward-looking and negative theories to the positive goal of influencing future conduct along desirable lines. * * *

* * *

But skepticism regarding the rehabilitative model began developing in the mid–1960's, and about ten years later there came "an explosion of criticism * * * calling for restructuring of the theoretical underpinnings of the criminal sanction." This rejection of rehabilitation, usually in favor of a "just deserts" theory, was prompted by several considerations. One was the concern with the wide disparity in sentencing which resulted from giving judges broad sentencing discretion to act according to the perceived rehabilitative needs in the particular case. The "just deserts" model was seen as necessary "to counter the capricious and irresponsible uses of state power." The existing system was perceived by many as being arbitrary because rehabilitative efforts were often unsuccessful. When confidence was "lost in the rehabilitative capacities of penal programs and in the ability of parole boards and correctional officers to determine when reformation has been achieved, the rehabilitationist rationale for treatment differentials no longer serves, and the differences are seen as irrational and indefensible." Finally, the retribution or "just deserts" theory, precisely because it "operates from a consensus model of society where the community * * * is acting in the right" and "the criminal is acting in the wrong," had appeal because it seemed to reaffirm our moral values at a time when they were under frequent attack.

UNITED STATES v. BERGMAN

United States District Court, Southern District of New York, 1976.
416 F.Supp. 496.

FRANKEL, DISTRICT JUDGE.

Defendant is being sentenced upon his plea of guilty to two counts of an 11–count indictment. The sentencing proceeding is unusual in some respects. It has been the subject of more extensive submissions, written and oral, than this court has ever received upon such an occasion. The court has studied some hundreds of pages of memoranda and exhibits, plus scores of volunteered letters. A broad array of issues has been addressed. Imaginative suggestions of law and penology have been tendered. A preliminary conversation with counsel, on the record, preceded the usual sentencing hearing. Having heard counsel again and the defendant speaking for himself, the court postponed the pronouncement of sentence for further reconsideration of thoughts generated during the days of studying the briefs and oral pleas. It seems fitting now to report in writing the reasons upon which the court concludes that defendant must be sentenced to a term of four months in prison.[1]

I. *Defendant and His Crimes*

Defendant appeared until the last couple of years to be a man of unimpeachably high character, attainments, and distinction. A doctor of divinity and an ordained rabbi, he has been acclaimed by people around the world for his works of public philanthropy, private charity, and leadership in educational enterprises. Scores of letters have come to the court from across this and other countries reporting debts of personal gratitude to him for numerous acts of extraordinary generosity. (The court has also received a kind of petition, with fifty-odd signatures, in which the signers, based upon learning acquired as newspaper readers, denounce the defendant and urge a severe sentence. Unlike the pleas for mercy, which appear to reflect unquestioned facts inviting compassion, this document should and will be disregarded.) In addition to his good works, defendant has managed to amass considerable wealth in the ownership and operation of nursing homes, in real estate ventures, and in a course of substantial investments.

Beginning about two years ago, investigations of nursing homes in this area, including questions of fraudulent claims for Medicaid funds, drew to a focus upon this defendant among several others. The results that concern us were the present indictment and two state indictments. After extensive pretrial proceedings, defendant embarked upon elaborate plea negotiations with both state and federal prosecutors. A state guilty

---

1. The court considered, and finally rejected, imposing a fine in addition to the prison term. Defendant seems destined to pay hundreds of thousands of dollars in restitution. The amount is being worked out in connection with a state criminal indictment. Apart from defendant's further liabilities for federal taxes, any additional money exaction is appropriately left for the state court.

plea and the instant plea were entered in March of this year. (Another state indictment is expected to be dismissed after defendant is sentenced on those to which he has pled guilty.) As part of the detailed plea arrangements, it is expected that the prison sentence imposed by this court will comprise the total covering the state as well as the federal convictions.

For purposes of the sentence now imposed, the precise details of the charges, and of defendant's carefully phrased admissions of guilt, are not matters of prime importance. Suffice it to say that the plea on Count One (carrying a maximum of five years in prison and a $10,000 fine) confesses defendant's knowing and willful participation in a scheme to defraud the United States in various ways, including the presentation of wrongfully padded claims for payments under the Medicaid program to defendant's nursing homes. Count Three, for which the guilty plea carries a theoretical maximum of three more years in prison and another $5,000 fine, is a somewhat more "technical" charge. Here, defendant admits to having participated in the filing of a partnership return which was false and fraudulent in failing to list people who had bought partnership interests from him in one of his nursing homes, had paid for such interests, and had made certain capital withdrawals.

The conspiracy to defraud, as defendant has admitted it, is by no means the worst of its kind; it is by no means as flagrant or extensive as has been portrayed in the press; it is evidently less grave than other nursing-home wrongs for which others have been convicted or publicized. At the same time, the sentence, as defendant has acknowledged, is imposed for two federal felonies including, as the more important, a knowing and purposeful conspiracy to mislead and defraud the Federal Government.

II. The Guiding Principles of Sentencing

Proceeding through the short list of the supposed justifications for criminal sanctions, defense counsel urge that no licit purpose could be served by defendant's incarceration. Some of these arguments are plainly sound; others are not.

The court agrees that this defendant should not be sent to prison for "rehabilitation." Apart from the patent inappositeness of the concept to this individual, this court shares the growing understanding that no one should ever be sent to prison *for rehabilitation*. That is to say, nobody who would not otherwise be locked up should suffer that fate on the incongruous premise that it will be good for him or her. Imprisonment is punishment. Facing the simple reality should help us to be civilized. It is less agreeable to confine someone when we deem it an affliction rather than a benefaction. If someone must be imprisoned—for other, valid reasons—we should seek to make rehabilitative resources available to him or her. But the goal of rehabilitation cannot fairly serve in itself as grounds for the sentence to confinement.[2]

Equally clearly, this defendant should not be confined to incapacitate him. He is not dangerous. It is most improbable that he will commit similar, or any, offenses in the future. There is no need for "specific deterrence."

Contrary to counsel's submissions, however, two sentencing considerations demand a prison sentence in this case:

First, the aim of *general deterrence,* the effort to discourage similar wrongdoing by others through a reminder that the law's warnings are real and that the grim consequence of imprisonment is likely to follow from crimes of deception for gain like those defendant has admitted.

Second, the related, but not identical, concern that any lesser penalty would, in the words of the Model Penal Code, § 7.01(1)(c), "depreciate the seriousness of the defendant's crime."

Resisting the first of these propositions, defense counsel invoke Immanuel Kant's axiom that "one man ought never to be dealt with merely as a means subservient to the purposes of another."[4] * * *

As for Dr. Kant, * * * we take the widely accepted stance that a criminal punished in the interest of general deterrence is not being employed "*merely* as a means * * *." Reading Kant to mean that every man must be deemed *more* than the instrument of others, and must "always be treated as an end in himself," the humane principle is not offended here. Each of us is served by the enforcement of the law—not least a person like the defendant in this case, whose wealth and privileges, so long enjoyed, are so much founded upon law. * * *

But the whole business, defendant argues further, is guesswork; we are by no means certain that deterrence "works." The position is somewhat overstated; there is, in fact, some reasonably "scientific" evidence for the efficacy of criminal sanctions as deterrents, at least as against some kinds of crimes. Moreover, the time is not yet here when all we can "know" must be quantifiable and digestible by computers. The shared wisdom of generations teaches meaningfully, if somewhat amorphously, that the utilitarians have a point; we do, indeed, lapse often into rationality and act to seek pleasure and avoid pain. It would be better, to be sure, if we had more certainty and precision. Lacking these comforts, we continue to include among our working hypotheses a belief (with some concrete evidence in its support) that crimes like those in this case— deliberate, purposeful, continuing, non-impulsive, and committed for profit—are among those most likely to be generally deterrable by sanctions most shunned by those exposed to temptation.

The idea of avoiding depreciation of the seriousness of the offense implicates two or three thoughts, not always perfectly clear or universally

---

2. This important point, correcting misconceptions still widely prevalent, is developed more fully by Dean Norval Morris in *The Future of Imprisonment* (1974).

4. Quoting from I. Kant, *Philosophy of Law* 1986 (Hastie Trans.1887).

agreed upon, beyond the idea of deterrence. It should be proclaimed by the court's judgment that the offenses are grave, not minor or purely technical. Some attention must be paid to the demand for equal justice; it will not do to leave the penalty of imprisonment a dead letter as against "privileged" violators while it is employed regularly, and with vigor, against others. There probably is in these conceptions an element of retributiveness, as counsel urge. And retribution, so denominated, is in some disfavor as a reason for punishment. It remains a factor, however, * * * as is known to anyone who talks to judges, lawyers, defendants, or people generally. It may become more palatable, and probably more humanely understood, under the rubric of "deserts" or "just deserts." However the concept is formulated, we have not yet reached a state, supposing we ever should, in which the infliction of punishments for crime may be divorced generally from ideas of blameworthiness, recompense, and proportionality.

III. An Alternative, "Behavioral Sanction"

Resisting prison above all else, defense counsel included in their thorough memorandum on sentencing two proposals for what they call a "constructive," and therefore a "preferable" form of "behavioral sanction." One is a plan for Dr. Bergman to create and run a program of Jewish vocational and religious high school training. The other is for him to take charge of a "Committee on Holocaust Studies," again concerned with education at the secondary school level.

A third suggestion was made orally at yesterday's sentencing hearing. It was proposed that Dr. Bergman might be ordered to work as a volunteer in some established agency as a visitor and aide to the sick and the otherwise incapacitated. The proposal was that he could read, provide various forms of physical assistance, and otherwise give comfort to afflicted people.

No one can doubt either the worthiness of these proposals or Dr. Bergman's ability to make successes of them. But both of the carefully formulated "sanctions" in the memorandum involve work of an honorific nature, not unlike that done in other projects to which the defendant has devoted himself in the past. It is difficult to conceive of them as "punishments" at all. The more recent proposal is somewhat more suitable in character, but it is still an insufficient penalty. The seriousness of the crimes to which Dr. Bergman has pled guilty demands something more than "requiring" him to lend his talents and efforts to further philanthropic enterprises. It remains open to him, of course, to pursue the interesting suggestions later on as a matter of unforced personal choice.

IV. "Measuring" the Sentence

In cases like this one, the decision of greatest moment is whether to imprison or not. As reflected in the eloquent submissions for defendant, the prospect of the closing prison doors is the most appalling concern; the feeling is that the length of the sojourn is a lesser question once that threshold is passed. Nevertheless, the setting of a term remains to be accomplished. And in some respects it is a subject even more perplexing, unregulated, and unprincipled.

Days and months and years are countable with a sound of exactitude. But there can be no exactitude in the deliberations from which a number emerges. Without pretending to a nonexistent precision, the court notes at least the major factors.

The criminal behavior, as has been noted, is blatant in character and unmitigated by any suggestion of necessitous circumstance or other pressures difficult to resist. However metaphysicians may conjure with issues about free will, it is a fundamental premise of our efforts to do criminal justice that competent people, possessed of their faculties, make choices and are accountable for them. In this sometimes harsh light, the case of the present defendant is among the clearest and least relieved. Viewed against the maxima Congress ordained, and against the run of sentences in other federal criminal cases, it calls for more than a token sentence.[14]

On the other side are factors that take longer to enumerate. Defendant's illustrious public life and works are in his favor, though diminished, of course, by what this case discloses. This is a first, probably a last, conviction. Defendant is 64 years old and in imperfect health, though by no means so ill, from what the court is told, that he could be expected to suffer inordinately more than many others of advanced years who go to prison.

Defendant invokes an understandable, but somewhat unworkable, notion of "disparity." He says others involved in recent nursing home fraud cases have received relatively light sentences for behavior more culpable than his. He lays special emphasis upon one defendant whose frauds appear indeed to have involved larger amounts and who was sentenced to a maximum of six months' incarceration, to be confined for that time only on week nights, not on week days or weekends. This court has examined the minutes of that sentencing proceeding and finds the case distinguishable in material respects. But even if there were a threat of such disparity as defendant warns against, it could not be a major weight on the scales.

Our sentencing system, deeply flawed, is characterized by disparity. We are to seek to "individualize" sentences, but no clear or clearly agreed standards govern the individualization. The lack of meaningful criteria does indeed leave sentencing judges far too much at large. But the result, with its nagging burdens on conscience, cannot be meaningfully alleviated by allowing any handful of sentences in a short series to fetter later judgments. The point is easy, of course, where Sentence No. 1 or Sentences 1–5 are notably harsh. It cannot be that a later judge, disposed to

---

14. Despite Biblical teachings concerning what is expected from those to whom much is given, the court has not, as his counsel feared might happen, held Dr. Bergman to a higher standard of responsibility because of his position in the community. But he has not been judged under a lower standard either.

more leniency, should feel in any degree "bound." The converse is not identical, but it is not totally different. The net of this is that this court has considered and has given some weight to the trend of the other cited sentences (though strict logic might call for none), but without treating them as forceful "precedents" in any familiar sense.

How, then, the particular sentence adjudged in this case? As has been mentioned, the case calls for a sentence that is more than nominal. Given the other circumstances, however—including that this is a first offense, by a man no longer young and not perfectly well, where danger of recidivism is not a concern—it verges on cruelty to think of confinement for a term of years. We sit, to be sure, in a nation where prison sentences of extravagant length are more common than they are almost anywhere else. By that light, the term imposed today is not notably long. For this sentencing court, however, for a nonviolent first offense involving no direct assaults or invasions of others' security (as in bank robbery, narcotics, etc.), it is a stern sentence. For people like Dr. Bergman, who might be disposed to engage in similar wrongdoing, it should be sufficiently frightening to serve the major end of general deterrence. For all but the profoundly vengeful, it should not depreciate the seriousness of his offenses.

V. *Punishment in or for the Media*

Much of defendant's sentencing memorandum is devoted to the extensive barrage of hostile publicity to which he has been subjected during the years before and since his indictment. He argues, and it appears to be undisputed, that the media (and people desiring to be featured in the media) have vilified him for many kinds of evildoing of which he has in fact been innocent. Two main points are made on this score with respect to the problem of sentencing.

First, as has been mentioned, counsel express the concern that the court may be pressured toward severity by the force of the seeming public outcry. That the court should not allow itself to be affected in this way is clear beyond discussion. Nevertheless, it is not merely permissible, but entirely wholesome and responsible, for counsel to bring the expressed concern out in the open. Whatever our ideals and mixed images about judges, it would be naive to doubt that judges have sometimes been swept by a sense of popular demand toward draconian sentencing decisions. It cannot hurt for the sentencing judge to be reminded of this and cautioned about it. There can be no guarantees. The sentencer must confront and regulate himself. But it bears reaffirmance that the court must seek to discount utterly the fact of notoriety in passing its judgment upon the defendant.

* * *

Defendant's second point about his public humiliation is the frequently heard contention that he should not be incarcerated because he "has been punished enough." The thought is not without some initial appeal. If punishment were wholly or mainly retributive, it might be a weighty factor. In the end, however, it must be a matter of little or no force. Defendant's notoriety should not in the last analysis serve to lighten, any more than it may be permitted to aggravate, his sentence. The fact that he has been pilloried by journalists is essentially a consequence of the prestige and privileges he enjoyed before he was exposed as a wrongdoer. The long fall from grace was possible only because of the height he had reached. The suffering from loss of public esteem reflects a body of opinion that the esteem had been, in at least some measure, wrongly bestowed and enjoyed. It is not possible to justify the notion that this mode of nonjudicial punishment should be an occasion for leniency not given to a defendant who never basked in such an admiring light at all. The quest for both the appearance and the substance of equal justice prompts the court to discount the thought that the public humiliation serves the function of imprisonment.

Writing, as judges rarely do, about a particular sentence concentrates the mind with possibly special force upon the experience of the sentencer as well as the person sentenced. Consigning someone to prison, this defendant or any other, "is a sad necessity." There are impulses of avoidance from time to time—toward a personally gratifying leniency or toward an opposite extreme. But there is, obviously, no place for private impulse in the judgment of the court. The course of justice must be sought with such objective rationality as we can muster, tempered with mercy, but obedient to the law, which, we do well to remember, is all that empowers a judge to make other people suffer.

* * *

QUESTIONS AND POINTS FOR DISCUSSION

1. Do you agree with the sentence imposed by the court in *Bergman*? Why or why not?

2. If you were the sentencing judge, what sentence would you impose in the following four cases? Explain your conclusions in light of what you consider the appropriate purposes of criminal punishment.

    a. When driving while intoxicated, the defendant ran through two red lights, hit a car, and killed two passengers in the car. Before getting into his car, the defendant had been warned by a police officer not to drive because of his apparent drunkenness. At the time of the accident, the defendant was twenty years old and was employed as a delivery driver. He had no prior felony convictions or any convictions for reckless driving or driving while intoxicated. However, he had received seven traffic tickets in the past three years, one of which was for leaving the scene of an accident after running into a car in a parking lot.

    The defendant was willing to plead guilty to voluntary manslaughter, but refused to plead guilty to second-degree murder as the prosecutor insisted. A state statute defined second-degree murder to include "intentionally perform[ing] an act that results in the death of another person under circumstances manifesting an extreme indifference to the value of human life." A jury found the defendant guilty of two counts of second-degree murder and one count of assault. See Pears v. Alaska, 698 P.2d 1198 (Alaska 1985).

b.　During a three-month period, the defendant, a former college and professional football player, a member of the state legislature, and an alcoholic, wrote seventy-six checks on a closed account to pay for $8,000 worth of goods and services. He pled guilty to one count of theft over $250. By the time of the sentencing hearing, he had paid back the money owed for the bad checks. See Minnesota v. Staten, 390 N.W.2d 914 (Minn.App.1986).

c.　A jury found the defendant guilty on all counts of an indictment charging him with defrauding investors of millions of dollars. The convictions were the defendant's first, and he never had expressed any remorse for his crimes.

After the defendant's trial, he had a stroke, which left him unable to speak and the right side of his body paralyzed. After participating in an intensive therapy program conducted both in Colorado and New York, he regained much of his ability to speak. He still, however, had curtailed use of his right arm and leg and had difficulty thinking clearly. He also continued to periodically suffer what were described as small strokes.

At the sentencing hearing, five defense witnesses—three neurologists and two rehabilitation specialists—described the defendant's physical progress since the stroke. They also testified that this progress might be halted or reversed if the defendant's physical-therapy program was stopped or its quality reduced and that subsequent therapy might not be able to undo this damage. See United States v. King, 442 F.Supp. 1244 (S.D.N.Y.1978).

d.　The defendant pled guilty to conspiracy to distribute and possess with intent to distribute cocaine base after police officers found 191.8 grams of cocaine base in a bag she was carrying. The defendant had no prior criminal record and no history of substance abuse. She was a single mother with three children ages three, thirteen months, and three months, and she was breastfeeding the infant. See United States v. Dyce, 91 F.3d 1462 (D.C. Cir. 1996).

3.　The deterrent objective of criminal sanctions has met with controversy in recent years. Of particular concern has been the failure of the prison experience to deter many prisoners from committing further crimes after they have been released from prison. One study of the recidivism rates of prisoners, for example, revealed that 68% of released prisoners were rearrested for a felony or serious misdemeanor within three years of their release. Bureau of Justice Statistics, U.S. Dep't of Justice, Recidivism of Prisoners Released in 1994, at 1, 3 (2002). See also Bureau of Justice Statistics, U.S. Dep't of Justice, Examining Recidivism 1 (1985) (61% of the inmates surveyed had previously been incarcerated).

One of the reasons that has been postulated why the possibility of incarceration has a limited deterrent effect on many criminal offenders is that many of them are under the influence of drugs, alcohol, or both at the time of their crimes, making it unlikely that they can and will coolly assess the costs and benefits of a crime before its commission. See Bureau of Justice Statistics, U.S. Dep't of Justice, Drug Use and Dependence, State and Federal Prisoners, 2004, at 1, 5 (2006) (32% of state prisoners and 26% of federal prisoners were under the influence of drugs when they committed the crimes for which they were incarcerated); Bureau of Justice Statistics, U.S. Dep't of Justice, Correctional Populations in the United States, 1997, at 61 (2000) (52% of state prisoners and 34% of federal prisoners were under the influence of alcohol or drugs at the time of their crimes). In addition, many crimes are committed impulsively, and often in anger, without any reflection on the part of the offender about the potential consequences of the criminal activity. Joan Petersilia, California's Prison Policy: Causes, Costs, and Consequences, 72 Prison J. 8, 28 (1993). What other factors can you identify that might limit the deterrent impact of incarceration?

4. Many people cite incapacitation as the principal reason for incarcerating more criminal offenders. These people argue that by incarcerating more offenders, public safety will be enhanced as offenders are physically disabled from preying on the public. Set forth below are excerpts from a report of the Sentencing Project recounting a different perspective and citing some of what are believed to be overlooked limits and complexities of incapacitation:

Limits of Incarceration's Impact on Criminal Behavior

For many people, the relationship between incarceration and crime rates seems intuitive. "If you lock people up, they can't commit more crime." However, the dynamics of both crime and imprisonment challenge this seemingly commonsense notion. Among the reasons for incarceration's limited impact on crime rates are:

Diminishing Returns—Expanding the use of imprisonment inevitably results in diminishing returns in crime control. This is because high-rate and serious or violent offenders will generally be incarcerated even at modest levels of imprisonment, but as prison systems expand, new admissions will increasingly draw in lower-rate offenders. This growth in lower-rate and lower-level offenders shifts the cost-to-benefit ratio, as an equal amount of resources are spent per offender, but the state receives less return on its investment in terms of declining crime rates. * * *

Limited Drug Offender Effects—Drug offenders have represented the most substantial source of growth in incarceration in recent decades * * *. Compared to other offenses, the effect of sentencing and incarceration on drug offenses is quite limited since drug selling is subject to a "replacement effect." For example, if an armed robber is convicted and sentenced to prison, the effect of incapacitation removes that person's crime potential during the period of imprisonment. But street-level drug sellers are often replaced quickly by other sellers seeking to make profits from the drug market. As criminologist Alfred Blumstein has noted," . . . drug markets are inherently demand driven. As long as the demand is there, a supply network will emerge to satisfy that demand. While efforts to assault the supply-side may have some disruptive effects in the short term, the ultimate need is to reduce the demand in order to have an effect on drug abuse in the society.

* * *

Negative Impacts on Family and Community—The rapid growth of incarceration has had profoundly disruptive effects that radiate into other spheres of society. The persistent removal of persons from the community to prison and their eventual return has a destabilizing effect that has been demonstrated to fray family and community bonds, and contribute to an increase in recidivism and future criminality.[21] More-over, these trends are exacerbated as prisoners are increasingly incarcer-ated in facilities hundreds of miles from their homes. Research by the Urban Institute in a number of cities indicates that a critical predictor of success for persons returning to the community is family connections, and prospects for employment are strengthened for persons who are able to maintain some degree of attachment to their former networks of contacts. However, as the use of incarceration continues to grow, there is a resultant decline in these contacts, and a harmful impact on the individual, the family, and the community at large.

Impact of Incarceration Compared to Other Interventions

Estimates that about one-quarter of the drop in crime during the 1990s can be attributed to incarceration do not inform us about whether reliance upon incarceration was the *most* effective way to achieve these results. A variety of research demonstrates that investments in drug treatment, interventions with at-risk families, and school completion programs are more cost-effective than expanded incarceration as crime control measures. Regarding drug use, a RAND analysis concluded that the expenditure of $1 million to expand mandatory minimum sentencing would result in a national decrease in drug consumption of 13 kilograms, while dedicating those funds to drug treatment would reduce consump-tion by 100 kilograms.[24] * * *

In terms of prevention, an analysis of a wide range of national programs aimed at school completion and addressing the needs of at-risk youth found similar returns on taxpayer investments, in terms of in-creased productivity and decreased crime * * *.[27] * * *

Sentencing Project, Incarceration and Crime: A Complex Relationship 6–8 (2005).

5.   Researchers have identified other limits on the cost-effectiveness of the incapacitative function of incarceration. One problem of grounding incar-ceration on predictions of future criminal activity is that it leads to the confinement of what are called "false positives," people incorrectly identified

21. Clear, T., Rose, D.R., Waring, E., and Scully, K. (2003). "Coercive Mobility and Crime: A Preliminary Examination of Concentrated Incarceration and Social Disorganization," *Justice Quarterly*, Vol. 20, (1), pp. 33–64.

24. Caulkins, J.P., Rydell, C.P., Scwabe, W.L., Chiesa, J. (1997). *Mandatory Minimum Drug Sentences: Throwing Away The Key or The Taxpayers' Money?* Santa Monica, CA: RAND. (pp. xvii–xviii).

27. Aos, S., Phipps, P., Barnoski, R., & Lieb, R. (2001). *The Comparative Costs and Benefits of Programs to Reduce Crime*. Olympia, WA: Washington State Institute for Public Policy.

as posing high risks to the community. Franklin E. Zimring & Gordon Hawkins, Incapacitation 68–70 (1995). The economic and human costs of incarcerating these individuals are very high, since they would pose no or little risk to others if they were sanctioned within the community.

There is another frequently cited fact that curtails the capacity of incarceration to curb crime, whether through incapacitation or deterrence: Most crimes are not solved, so many offenders never will be apprehended or expect to be apprehended. See Marc Mauer, Race to Incarcerate 114–17 (2006) (noting that more than half of crimes never are reported to police and that only one-sixth of the crimes reported to police and for which national statistics are tabulated—murder and non-negligent homicide, rape, robbery, aggravated assault, burglary, larceny-theft, motor-vehicle theft, and arson— culminate in an arrest and the filing of a criminal charge). Can you postulate any other factors that might bear on the crime-control costs and benefits of incarceration? See Alex R. Piquero & Alfred Blumstein, Does Incapacitation Reduce Crime, 23 J. Quantitative Criminology 267, 279–83 (2007).

6. Research on the association between the crime rate and the rate of incarceration provides further evidence that the increased incarceration of criminal offenders will not lead to a proportionate increase in the public's safety. While the nation's incarceration rate has climbed steadily for over thirty years, the national crime rate has fluctuated greatly, sometimes rising and sometimes falling. Sentencing Project, Incarceration and Crime: A Complex Relationship 3 (2005). Statistics at the state level further confirm two complexities about crime and incarceration rates. First, the correlation between the incarceration rate and the crime rate varies greatly from state to state, with some studies finding that an increase in the incarceration rate can reach a point that exacerbates the level of crime. See Don Stemen, Vera Inst. of Justice, Reconsidering Incarceration: New Directions for Reducing Crime 3–7 (2007) (reporting widely varying research findings on the relationship between incarceration and crime rates). And second, a multitude of factors other than incarceration, such as the rate of unemployment, the high-school graduation rate, and the number of young people in the population, affect the crime rate far more than incarceration. Id. at 9–13.

7. The retributive theory of punishment is not new. The Bible verse importuning that "life *shall go* for life, eye for eye, tooth for tooth, hand for hand, foot for foot" is known to all. *Deuteronomy* 19:21 (King James) (emphasis in the original). Do you subscribe to the retributive theory? If so, how do we determine what punishment is "deserved" for a crime, and how can a consensus be reached on this question?

8. The American Correctional Association's "Public Correctional Policy on Use of Appropriate Sanctions and Controls" embraces what is known as the "least-restrictive-alternative principle" or "parsimony principle." The policy, which is set forth below, defines the boundaries that should be placed on punishment:

> The sanctions and controls imposed by courts and administered by corrections should be the least restrictive, consistent with public and individual safety and the maintenance of social order. Selection of the least restrictive sanctions and punishments in specific cases inherently

requires balancing several important objectives—individual dignity, fiscal responsibility, effective correctional operations, the interest of the victim, and severity of the crime. To meet these objectives, correctional agencies should:

A. Advocate to all branches of government and to the public at large the development and appropriate use of a wide range of sanctions, punishments, programs, and facilities;

B. Recommend the use of the least restrictive appropriate dispositions in judicial decisions;

C. Classify persons under correctional jurisdiction to the least restrictive appropriate programs/facilities; and

D. Employ only the level of regulation and control necessary for the safe and efficient operation of programs, services, and facilities.

American Correctional Association, Public Correctional Policy on Use of Appropriate Sanctions and Controls (2003).

The American Bar Association also has called for the integration of the least-restrictive-alternative principle into sentencing systems and decisions: "Sentences authorized and imposed, taking into account the gravity of the offenses, should be no more severe than necessary to achieve the societal purposes for which they are authorized." ABA Standards for Criminal Justice: Sentencing, Standard 18–2.4 (3d ed. 1994). The least-restrictive-alternative principle has been described as both "utilitarian and humanitarian." Norval Morris, The Future of Imprisonment 61 (1974). Do you agree? If so, how can this general principle be given practical effect when drafting sentencing statutes and guidelines and making sentencing decisions?

9. For additional information about the traditional purposes of criminal sanctions, read pages 471–73.

2. A NEW PARADIGM: RESTORATIVE JUSTICE

Dissatisfaction with present criminal-justice systems that are premised on retributive and utilitarian theories has spurred calls for a new criminal-justice model, one that is founded on what is called restorative justice. The principal purpose of restorative justice is to repair the injuries to victims and the community caused by crimes, as well as the harm that criminal offenders have inflicted on themselves and their families.

Victim-offender mediation programs are one of the means through which the objectives of restorative justice may be realized. In these programs, a victim and an offender typically meet face to face with a trained mediator to discuss the offender's crime. During the meeting or meetings, the victim is afforded the opportunity to discuss the crime's impact on the victim and to ask the offender questions that may have been troubling the victim, such as why the offender chose the victim's home to burglarize. The offender is also given an opportunity to discuss the effects of, and reasons for, committing the crime, and this discussion often culminates in an expression of remorse for the harm the offender has caused. The parties then attempt to identify what they consider an appropriate resolution of the case. The agreement reached may require the offender to pay restitution to the victim, to do work for the victim, to perform community-service work, or to participate in programs, such as a substance-abuse treatment program, to address problems that may have contributed to the offender's criminal behavior.

Proponents of victim-offender mediation programs argue that one of their chief benefits is that they humanize the criminal-justice process. By bringing criminal offenders together face-to-face with their victims, it is thought that it becomes more difficult for offenders to rationalize their criminal behavior. As they face the individual they have victimized, the harm caused by their crime is no longer an abstraction, but very real.

Mediation sessions, it is said, also bring a human face to the person who is otherwise abstractly and impersonally known as "the offender." During such sessions, a victim may gain a better understanding of who the offender is and of the circumstances that may have contributed to the offender's criminal behavior.

Finally, supporters of victim-offender mediation programs cite the research results confirming the many benefits of victim-offender mediation programs. See Mark S. Umbreit, The Handbook of Victim Offender Mediation 163–77, 183–92, 206–14, 224–33, 243–52 (2001). These documented benefits include, among others, victims' high level of satisfaction with the programs and a significant increase in the likelihood that offenders who participate in them will pay restitution as compared to offenders who are ordered by a court to pay restitution. In addition, many, though not all, studies of victim-offender mediation programs have found that offenders participating in them had lower recidivism rates. See Mark S. Umbreit et al., Restorative Justice in the Twenty–First Century: A Social Movement Full of Opportunities and Pitfalls, 89 Marq. L.Rev. 251, 284–86 (2005).

Despite the cited benefits of victim-offender mediation programs, what concerns might they raise? Do the program requirements set forth below, promulgated by the American Bar Association, a proponent of victim-offender mediation programs, adequately address those concerns?

AMERICAN BAR ASSOCIATION, "VICTIM–OFFENDER MEDIATION/DIALOGUE PROGRAM REQUIREMENTS"

Appendix to Rep. 101B, Summary of Action of the
House of Delegates, 1994 Annual Meeting

1. Participation in a program by both the offender and victim must be voluntary.

2. Program goals are specified in writing and procedures are established to meet those goals.

3. A plan exists for ongoing evaluation and review of goals and the steps taken to reach such goals.

4. Before participating in such programs, victims and offenders are appropriately screened on a case-by-case basis, are fully informed orally and in writing about the mediation-dialogue process, procedures and goals, and are specifically told that their participation in the process is voluntary.

5. Refusal to participate in a program in no way adversely affects an offender, and procedural safeguards are established to ensure that there are no systemic negative repercussions because of an offender's refusal to participate in the program.

6. A face-to-face meeting is encouraged.

7. When agreements are reached between victims and offenders, which may include restitution, a process is established to monitor and follow up on the agreements reached.

8. The statements made by victims and offenders and documents and other materials produced during the mediation/dialogue process are inadmissible in criminal or civil court proceedings.

9. Properly trained mediator-facilitators are used in the mediation/dialogue process.

10. The programs are adequately funded and staffed.

11. Mediator-facilitators are selected from a cross-section of the community to ensure that they reflect the diversity of their community in terms of race, ethnicity, and gender.

12. Criminal justice professionals and the public are educated about these programs, and these programs are fully integrated with other components of the criminal justice system.

13. Participation in a program that occurs prior to an adjudication of guilt takes place only with the consent of the prosecutor and with the victim's and offender's informed consent, obtained in writing, or orally in court. If the offender is represented by an attorney, the offender's consent should be given only after the offender has had the chance to discuss with the attorney the advisability of participating in the victim-offender mediation/dialogue program. Participation in a program that occurs after an adjudication of guilt takes place only after notification to the prosecutor and defense attorney, if any.

QUESTIONS AND POINTS FOR DISCUSSION

1. Restorative justice can be implemented through other means in addition to victim-offender mediation programs. For example, during what is called family group conferencing, family members and friends, as well as the victim and the offender, attend and participate in the mediation session or sessions. See Mark S. Umbreit, U.S. Dep't of Justice, Family Group Conferencing: Implications for Crime Victims (2000).

A "peacemaking circle," also known as a "sentencing circle," includes an even broader array of participants. Criminal-justice officials, as well as other members of the community, participate in the circle, which often is facilitated by a trained member of the community. Each person in the circle is allowed to speak as a "talking piece," whether a stick or feather, is passed around the circle. A commitment to treating each member of the circle with respect and "speaking from the heart" suffuses the circle, which is grounded on Native–American precepts. Howard Zehr, The Little Book of Restorative Justice 51 (2002). While the agreement reached within the circle may be transmitted as a sentencing recommendation to the court, the ultimate goals of the circle, which may meet multiple times, are broader. Examples of these goals include the promotion of healing for victims, families, offenders, and the community and the averting of future crimes through "holistic" reintegration of the offender. Gordon Bazemore & Mark Umbreit, U.S. Dep't of Justice, A Comparison of Four Restorative Conferencing Models 6 (2001) (hereinafter Bazemore & Umbreit). For additional information on peacemaking circles, see Kay Pranis et al., Peacemaking Circles: From Crime to Community (2003).

Community reparative boards are another restorative-justice tool. In communities that utilize these boards, the offender appears before a small group of specially trained citizens who discuss the impact of the offender's crime with the offender. The board then develops a sanctioning agreement with the offender and monitors the offender's compliance with the agreement. See Bazemore & Umbreit, at 3–5.

If a victim or offender refuses to participate in a mediation session, family group conferencing, or peace circle, victim-offender panels can be used for reparative purposes. For example, several victims of drunk drivers can appear before a group of offenders convicted of drunk driving to discuss the harm drunk drivers inflicted on the victims and their families. See Daniel Van Ness & Karen Heetderks Strong, Restoring Justice 74–76 (1997).

2. As the American Bar Association has recommended, some states have begun to integrate restorative justice into their criminal-justice systems. Restorative justice can be incorporated into multiple levels of those systems. For example, a Vermont statute directs that mechanisms for implementing restorative-justice principles be included in court-diversion programs (programs where prosecutors refer individuals to a restorative-justice program in lieu of processing their criminal cases through the court system), in the sentencing process, and in programs for persons in the custody of the department of corrections. Vt. Stat. Ann. tit. 28, § 2a.

3. Howard Zehr has graphed some of the key distinctions between the current retributive-justice norm and restorative justice. Those distinctions are set forth below:

Retributive Justice	**Restorative Justice**
1. Crime defined as violation of the state	1. Crime defined as violation of one person by another
2. Focus on establishing blame, on guilt, on past (did he/she do it?)	2. Focus on problem solving, on liabilities and obligations, on future (what should be done?)

Retributive Justice	Restorative Justice
3. Adversarial relationship and process normative	3. Dialogue & negotiation normative
4. Imposition of pain to punish and deter/prevent	4. Restitution as a means of restoring both parties' goal of reconciliation/restoration
5. Justice defined by intent & process: right rules	5. Justice defined as right relationships and outcomes
6. Interpersonal, conflictual nature of crime obscured, repressed; conflict seen as individual vs. the state	6. Crime recognized as interpersonal conflict; value of conflict is recognized
7. One social injury replaced by another	7. Focus on repair of social injury
8. Community on sideline, represented abstractly by state	8. Community as facilitator in restorative process
9. Encouragement of competitive, individualistic values	9. Encouragement of mutuality
10. Action directed from state to offender • victim ignored • offender passive	10. Victim & offender engaged in the process • victim rights/needs recognized • offender encouraged to take responsibility
11. Offender accountability defined as taking punishment	11. Offender accountability defined as understanding impact of action and helping decide how to make things right
12. Offense defined in purely legal terms, devoid of moral, social, economic, and political dimensions	12. Offense understood in whole context—moral, social, economic, and political dimensions
13. "Debt" owed to state and society in the abstract	13. Debt/liability to victim recognized
14. Response focused on offender's past behavior	14. Response focused on harmful consequences of offender's behavior
15. Stigma of crime irreparable	15. Stigma of crime reparable through restorative action
16. No encouragement for repentance & forgiveness	16. Possibilities for repentance & forgiveness
17. Dependence upon proxy professionals	17. Direct involvement by participants

Howard Zehr, Restorative Justice, Retributive Justice, New Perspectives on Crime and Justice 18 (1985) (reprinted with the permission of the Mennonite Central Committee).

Do you subscribe to the precepts of restorative justice? How do you believe the criminal-justice system would change if restorative justice became the centerpiece of the system?

C. CALIBRATING THE USE OF INCARCERATION: A LOOK TOWARDS THE FUTURE

As mentioned earlier, the number of prisoners and the rate at which people are incarcerated in this country have increased substantially in recent years. As a result, many prisons are literally full to the brim with inmates. Bureau of Justice Statistics, U.S. Dep't of Justice, Prisoners in 2007, at 7 (2008) (reporting that the federal prison system and the prison systems in nineteen states were operating at more than 100% of their highest capacity in 2007). There is undoubtedly a link between, on the one hand, the heavy reliance on incarceration in the United States and the prison crowding problem and, on the other hand, prosecution and sentencing policies.

The declaration of a "war on drugs," which has spawned the increased prosecution and confinement of drug offenders, is but one illustration of this interconnection. In recent years, for example, the number of federal drug prosecutions has escalated dramatically, culminating in federal prisons holding more than twenty times as many drug offenders in 2009 as they did in 1980. Compare Fed. Bureau of Prisons, Quick Facts (February 21, 2009) available at http://www.bop.gov/news/quick.jsp (98,373 drug offenders, comprising approximately 52% of the federal prison population, in federal prisons in 2009) with Bureau of Justice Statistics, U.S. Dep't of Justice, Sourcebook of Criminal Justice Statistics 2003, at 519 (2005) (4,749 drug offenders, comprising approximately 25% of the federal prison population, in federal prisons in 1980). In addition, the length of federal prisoners' sentences has increased significantly in recent years, with the average length of imprisonment for drug offenders, for example, more than tripling between 1984 and 2008, increasing from twenty-seven to eighty-two months. U.S. Sentencing Comm'n, 2008 Sourcebook of Federal Sentencing Statistics, Fig. E (2009); U.S. Sentencing Comm'n, 1991 Annual Report 148 (1992). But while the Federal Bureau of Prisons has responded to the increase in the size of its prison population with a massive prison construction program, federal prisons are still grossly overcrowded. Bureau of Justice Statistics, U.S. Dep't of Justice, Prisoners in 2007, at 7 (2008) (federal prison population in 2006 exceeded prison capacity by 36%).

Set forth below are several proposals expressing views on what can be done to better calibrate the use of incarceration so as to minimize its human and economic costs, maximize its crime-control benefits, and avoid prison and jail crowding. Do you agree or disagree with the views expressed?

ALVIN J. BRONSTEIN, A RESPONSE TO PRISON OVERCROWDING

7 The GAO Journal 29 (Fall, 1989). Reprinted with the permission of The GAO Journal

[The author begins by discussing three traditional responses to crowding in state and federal prisons: prison construction, the expanded use of community sanctions, and doing nothing. The author first dismisses prison construction as a means of redressing prison overcrowding, citing huge increases in the nation's prison population despite massive construction programs costing billions of dollars. The author also believes that community sanctions will not alone relieve overcrowding, as evidenced by the experiences of states that have expanded the use of community sanctions but have experienced large increases in their prison populations. Finally, the author lambasts jurisdictions that do nothing in the face of an overcrowding problem, charging that riots, like the one at the Attica State Prison in 1971 that left forty-three dead, and the one in 1980 at the New Mexico State Penitentiary, which resulted in thirty-six deaths, are the tragic result of this do-nothing stance.]

None of the * * * responses addresses what is causing prison overcrowding: changed sentencing practices * * *, which require longer sentences and mandatory minimum sentences, and the so-called "war on drugs." * * *

Although admittedly difficult to implement given the current mood of the country, my proposed responses have the advantage at least of directly addressing the causes of prison overcrowding.

● **Sentence as many people as we are now, perhaps more, but for shorter periods of time.** We must begin to consider prison space as a scarce resource, reserving it for short prison terms for those offenders who we feel must be punished by incarceration. Bankrupting the future of this country by building more prisons will have no significant impact on the number of crimes committed. The public is confused into thinking that locking up more criminals is the same thing as reducing crime rates. * * *

Consequently, we should eliminate most mandatory minimum sentences, eliminate most repeat-offender enhanced sentences, and shorten sentences to lengths comparable to those in other industrial democracies. Faced with the decision of how to use one prison bed over a three-year period, I would rather use it to sentence 12 burglars to three months each than to sentence one burglar for all 36 months.

● **Make the drug problem a public health and social welfare problem, not a criminal justice problem.** * * * We are seeing rising levels of corruption in federal, state, and local criminal justice systems

* * * because of the powerful allure of illicit drug dollars. We are seeing more and more drug-related crime. We are seeing the greatest benefits of our current anti-drug strategy going to drug traffickers. In other words, our absurd drug policies are proving costly, ineffective, and counterproductive—just as Prohibition did 60 years ago.

Adopting rational new drug policies would have a huge impact on prison overcrowding. We should remove drugs from the criminal justice system and, as with alcohol and tobacco, deal with drugs as a public health problem. The huge sums of money now going into ineffective law enforcement efforts should be diverted into education, treatment, and other social welfare programs.

ALFRED BLUMSTEIN, PRISONS, IN CRIME

(James Q. Wilson & Joan Petersilia eds., 1995). Reprinted with
the permission of the Institute for Contemporary Studies

* * *

States that are facing severe prison congestion and that feel compelled to avoid overcrowding—usually because they are required to do so by court order—need to find some means of allocating their limited number of cells. Obviously, it would be desirable if that allocation could be in terms of maximizing the protection of public safety, by keeping in prison those who represent the greatest current threat to public safety, and releasing those for whom the risk is least. * * *

* * *

The best example of a planned policy sensitive to prison capacity is the sentencing guidelines matrix developed by the Minnesota Sentencing Guidelines Commission or the recent one developed in North Carolina. The Minnesota commission's initial work followed from an explicit legislative mandate to "take account of prison capacity" in developing its guidelines, and used prison capacity as a specific constraint on the sentencing schedule that emerged. Thus, if some commission member wanted to increase the prescribed sentence for robbery, he had to identify the offenses for which he would like to reduce the sentences in exchange. Such a procedure requires a technology (such as some kind of simulation or impact-estimation model) that enables the policy group to calculate for each possible sentencing schedule the prison capacity it would consume. * * *

The existence of this prison capacity constraint imposes a rare discipline on the policy debate. In most settings where sanction policies are debated, advocates of tougher sentences gain political benefits without having to consider the costs of their actions. But the availability of this discipline has undoubtedly contributed to making Minnesota the state with the second lowest incarceration rate in the nation * * *.[b] * * *

---

b. By 2007, the imprisonment rate in Minnesota was still the second lowest in the country, with 181 out of every 100,000 residents imprisoned. Bureau of Justice Statistics, U.S. Dep't of

* * *

For the longer term, it seems essential that we get at some of the major factors that are contributing to important and large segments of our nation's population having no stake in legitimate conformity, and so having greatly diminished sensitivity to the sanctions available to the criminal justice system. That problem is a direct consequence of the erosion of family structure and the associated abandonment in far too many cases of the obligation of socialization of growing children. The society will have to consider how the inadequate efforts in these families may be augmented, whether that is done merely by the widespread introduction of day-care centers in the schools (to enable the teenage mothers to finish school, to begin socializing their children, and to teach those mothers basic parenting skills) or by a massive array of boarding schools to which mothers might send their children. Any such efforts, of course, are likely to be expensive, perhaps enormously so, and the benefits are still very uncertain; but, even if successful, they are not likely to be realized for at least ten years * * *.

* * *

AMERICAN BAR ASSOCIATION, RECOMMENDATIONS ON PRISON AND JAIL IMPACT STATEMENTS

Summary of Action of the House of Delegates—
1990 Midyear Meeting 12

BE IT RESOLVED, that the American Bar Association, recognizing the severe problem with overcrowding in the nation's prisons and jails, recommends the following:

1. The states and the federal government should adopt procedures ensuring that a prison and jail impact statement be prepared for and considered by a state legislature or Congress before the passage of laws involving the sentencing of convicted criminals, parole policies, and other issues whose resolution may directly lead to an increase in the number of persons incarcerated in correctional facilities or the length of their incarceration.
2. The prison and jail impact statement should include, at a minimum, the following information:
    (a) an estimate of the number of individuals who will annually be incarcerated in or remain incarcerated in prisons or jails as a result of the contemplated legislation being enacted;
    (b) an estimate of the amount of additional prison or jail space needed to accommodate the increase in the size of the prison or jail populations;
    (c) an estimate of the cost of building additional prisons or jails or of taking other steps to make the space available for the anticipated greater number of incarcerated persons; and

---

Justice, Prisoners in 2007, at 18 (2008). By contrast, the national imprisonment rate was 506 of every 100,00 residents. Id.

(d) an estimate of the amount by which the expected increase in the number of persons incarcerated in prisons or jails or the duration of their confinement will increase operating expenses, which are the sums incurred when paying for staff, food, supplies, medical care, and the other costs stemming from the supervision, treatment, and care of inmates.

3. Congress and the state legislatures should not enact legislation that will increase the number of persons incarcerated in correctional facilities or the length of their confinement without taking steps to ensure that either:

(a) the resources, including space and money for increased operating expenses, are already available to handle the increase in the size of the prison or jail populations; or

(b) money is appropriated to cover the costs of implementing the legislation; or

(c) other counterbalancing steps are taken to decrease the size of the prison or jail populations.

QUESTIONS AND POINTS FOR DISCUSSION

1. Prison and jail impact statements can serve several purposes. First, by informing legislators of the direct monetary costs of expanding the use of incarceration for a particular crime or in certain other circumstances, the impact statements can prompt legislators to assess whether a proposed change is advisable. Legislators can, for example, consider whether there are other correctional sanctions that would more cost-effectively serve the intended purpose or purposes of the expanded use of incarceration. Second, the impact statements can avert the problem of the government's money not following "its mouth"—of statutes authorizing or mandating the increased use of incarceration not accompanied by enough funds to pay for the additional staff, programming, space, and other needs generated by that increase.

The American Bar Association now has recognized that impact statements yield similar benefits whenever a proposed law will increase the use of any criminal sanction, including those other than incarceration. Consequently, the ABA has called for the preparation of "correctional fiscal impact statements" and their consideration by legislators and the governor or president before the enactment of legislation that would increase the number of people subject to a particular sanction or increase the potential length of their sentence. See American Bar Association, Blueprint for Cost–Effective Pretrial Detention, Sentencing, and Corrections Systems, at 1, Appendix to Rep. 107, Summary of Action of the House of Delegates, 2002 Annual Meeting, available at http://www.abanet.org/crimjust/policy/cjpol.html. (setting forth twenty recommendations designed to make corrections and sentencing systems more cost-effective). The ABA goes still further by recommending that laws that increase the number of incarcerated persons or the length of their confinement be subject to a sunset provision when the legislature fails to appropriate the funds needed to pay for the projected increase in the size of the jurisdiction's prison or jail population. Id.

2.   Correctional impact statements report the direct financial costs of expanding the use of a particular criminal sanction. In determining whether a contemplated change in a sentencing system would be cost-effective, what other costs and benefits, in your opinion, should be included in the economic calculus? Consider the methodological problems of measuring these costs and benefits. How would these problems affect the way in which you conduct your assessment of cost-effectiveness?

Professor William Spelman has argued that the cost-effectiveness of increased incarceration should not be weighed in a vacuum, in other words, by considering just the costs and any crime-control benefits of incarceration. He has reasoned:

> [W]hether more prisons reduce crime matters less than how much. Crime is not the only problem the American public is grappling with. Policy makers may decide to spend taxpayer dollars on child care, college educations, jobs programs, or (for that matter) childhood immunization, infrastructure for decaying cities, subsidies to tobacco farmers, or B2 stealth bombers. (Occasionally, they even decide that the best use of the money is to give it back to taxpayers.) It is not enough to have a small effect on the crime problem if that means forgoing a big effect on an equally thorny social problem.
>
> And prisons are no longer the only way to fight crime. Policy makers may decide to spend money on other agencies in the criminal justice system (e.g., more judges, better-managed police, or better-trained probation officers); on changes in the physical environment that make it more difficult to commit a crime; on community organizing and education efforts that improve the public's capacity to intervene; on education and jobs programs that reduce would-be offenders' motivations to commit crimes; and on a host of other equally plausible alternatives.
>
> With few exceptions, we have been unable to determine the benefit-cost ratios associated with these policies and programs. Nevertheless, we can be fairly sure that most do more good than harm * * *. Thus it is no longer sufficient, if it ever was, to demonstrate that prisons are better than nothing. Instead, they must be better than the next-best use of the money.

William Spelman, What Recent Studies Do (and Don't) Tell Us About Imprisonment and Crime, 27 Crime & Just. 419, 420 (2000).

3.   In addition to incarceration rates unrivaled by other nations, crowded prisons and jails, and costly, though still often underfunded, institutional and community-based correctional programs, another distinguishing feature of the sentencing and correctional systems in this country is the disproportionate involvement of racial and ethnic minorities in those systems. In 2006, one out of every fifteen African–American men aged eighteen or older was confined in prison or jail, compared to one out of every 106 white men of that age. The Pew Center on the States, One in 100: Behind Bars in America 2008, at 6 (2008). And a study issued in 1995 by the Sentencing Project revealed that one out of every three African–American men aged twenty through twenty-nine was, on any given day, in prison or jail or on probation or parole. Marc Mauer & Tracy Huling, Young Black Americans and the Criminal Justice

System: Five Years Later 1 (1995). By contrast, one out of every fifteen white men in that age group was under correctional supervision. Id. at 5.

Researchers have identified multiple causes for this disparity, including discrimination in the operations of the criminal-justice system and the disproportionate involvement of African–American men in certain types of crime. See Michael Tonry, Malign Neglect: Race, Crime, and Punishment in America 49–123 (1995). Assuming that both discrimination and a disproportionate involvement in some crimes explain the disparity in the percentage of young black men, compared to white men, under correctional supervision, what steps, in your opinion, can and should be taken, and by whom, to reduce this disparity? For a list of recommendations regarding steps that police officers, prosecutors, defense attorneys, judges, probation officers, and other officials in the criminal-justice system can take to diminish racial disparity in the criminal-justice system, see Sentencing Project, Reducing Racial Disparity in the Criminal Justice System: A Manual for Practitioners and Policymakers 25–61 (2008).

In the succeeding chapters of this book, you will learn about sentencing policies in this country, the sentencing process, and the rights of criminal offenders during and after sentencing. As you read these materials, consider what changes need to be made in sentencing, correctional, and other governmental policies to ensure that the system for controlling crime in this country is effective, humane, nondiscriminatory, and affordable.

CHAPTER 2

GUILTY PLEAS AND PLEA BARGAINING

■ ■ ■

An individual charged with a crime can enter one of several different pleas to the charge. The individual can plead guilty or not guilty. In some jurisdictions, a third alternative exists: the individual charged with a crime can enter a plea of *nolo contendere,* which means "no contest." See, e.g., Fed.R.Crim.P. 11(a)(1) (defendant can, with the court's consent, enter a plea of *nolo contendere*). With one exception, such a plea generally has the same consequences as entering a plea of guilty. The person who pleads "no contest" can be sentenced as if he or she had pled guilty to the crime, even to a period of incarceration. The principal distinction between a plea of *nolo contendere* and a guilty plea is that evidence of the former type of plea is inadmissible in civil lawsuits, which most often would be brought by victims of the crime in question.

The vast majority of criminal convictions are obtained through guilty pleas. In 2004, for example, 95% of the individuals convicted of felonies in the state courts pled guilty. Bureau of Justice Statistics, U.S. Dep't of Justice, Felony Sentences in State Courts, 2004, at 1 (2007). This statistic underscores the central role that guilty pleas presently play in the operation of the criminal-justice system.

There are two main types of guilty pleas—what are called "blind" pleas and negotiated pleas. A "blind" plea is a plea that is uninduced by any commitment made by a prosecutor or judge. The defendant simply acknowledges his or her guilt and awaits the imposition of a sentence by the court. By contrast, when a defendant enters a negotiated plea, the defendant has been promised a benefit in return for his or her guilty plea. That benefit may come in many forms. The defendant, for example, may be permitted to plead guilty to a crime that is less serious than the crime with which he or she was originally charged. Even if the defendant does not plead guilty to a reduced charge, other criminal charges may be dismissed or not filed in return for the plea of guilty. Or the defendant may plead guilty upon the condition that the prosecutor recommends, or the court imposes, a particular sentence.

In recent years, the practice of plea bargaining has come under attack. Chief among the criticisms of plea bargaining include the following: (1) that favorable plea offers induce innocent defendants to plead guilty; (2) that because of plea agreements, the unconstitutional actions of law-enforcement officers are often concealed; (3) that plea bargaining results in more favorable dispositions for defendants who forgo their constitutional right to trial, in effect punishing other defendants who invoke this constitutional right; (4) that plea bargaining results in dispositions that compromise public safety and fail to meet the objectives of criminal sentences; and (5) that behind-the-scenes negotiations invite abuse by the participants in the negotiation process, who labor under conflicts of interest. The latter criticism is prompted in part by the fact that in order to maintain a high conviction rate, some prosecutors are more willing to enter into a plea agreement when their case against a defendant is weak, thereby enhancing the risk of an innocent person being convicted. Stephen J. Schulhofer, Plea Bargaining as Disaster, 101 Yale L.J. 1979, 1987 (1992); Albert W. Alschuler, The Prosecutor's Role in Plea Bargaining, 36 U.Chi.L.Rev. 50, 58 (1968). Public defenders, who are often overburdened with very heavy caseloads, also have a strong incentive to resolve cases through plea bargaining rather than trials. Stephanos Bibas, Plea Bargaining Outside the Shadow of Trial, 117 Harv. L. Rev. 2463, 2479 (2004). In addition, some private defense attorneys maximize their profits on a case by simply "copping a plea" and then collecting their fee, without fully exploring whether entry of a guilty plea and the terms of a plea agreement are in their client's best interests. See, e.g., Albert W. Alschuler, Personal Failure, Institutional Failure, and the Sixth Amendment, 14 N.Y.U.Rev.L. & Soc.Change 149 (1986). For a list of articles calling for the abolition of plea bargaining, see Oren Gazal–Ayal, Partial Ban on Plea Bargains, 27 Cardozo L.Rev. 2295, 2297 n. 4 (2006).

Plea bargaining, however, has many defenders. See, e.g., ABA Standards for Criminal Justice, Pleas of Guilty, Standard 14–3.1(a) (3d ed. 1999); U.S. President's Commission on Law Enforcement and Administration of Justice, Task Force Report: The Courts 10 (1967). Many of these plea-bargaining proponents candidly acknowledge the abuses that can attend plea bargaining. Yet they contend that these abuses can be limited and that the retention of plea bargaining is good for, and in fact essential to, the effective operation of the criminal-justice system.

Some of the primary argued benefits of plea bargaining include the following: (1) that without plea bargaining, the criminal-justice system would simply break down, particularly in the urban areas of this country, since the system lacks the resources to provide trials for many more criminal defendants; (2) that plea bargains can relieve victims, other witnesses, defendants, and the families of victims and defendants from the uncertainty and financial and psychological burdens that attend litigation while also reducing the costs to taxpayers of prosecuting criminal cases; (3) that plea bargains can forestall the imposition of unduly harsh sentences, particularly under mandatory-minimum sentencing laws; (4) that plea bargaining can facilitate law enforcement, since in exchange for leniency, defendants can be persuaded to provide officials with information needed to apprehend and convict other criminals; and (5) that because of plea bargains, the amount of time that defendants who cannot post bail must spend in jail while awaiting trial can be reduced, to the benefit not only of the defendants, but also the public that must pay for the costs of their confinement.

The defenders of plea bargaining also charge its opponents with exaggerating its drawbacks, including the risk it purportedly creates of convicting innocent persons. Some of these plea-bargaining proponents argue that the abolition of plea bargaining would decrease the time available for trials and trial preparation, leading to truncated trials that actually enhance the risk of innocent persons being convicted. See Robert E. Scott & William J. Stuntz, Plea Bargaining as Contract, 101 Yale L.J. 1909, 1950 (1992). Others argue that plea bargaining is at least as effective, and possibly more effective, than trials in differentiating innocent and guilty people, in part because prosecutors are more adept than jurors in assessing the probative value of evidence, particularly eyewitness testimony. See Frank H. Easterbrook, Plea Bargaining as Compromise, 101 Yale L.J. 1969, 1970–72 (1992).

Many of the cases and materials set forth below focus on the constraints placed by the Constitution on plea bargaining. However, even though the Constitution may permit plea bargaining and some plea-bargaining practices that have been contested by defendants, fundamental policy questions about plea bargaining, as well as the process for entering guilty pleas, remain. While some of these policy questions are interspersed throughout the chapter, you will be asked to address several of them at the end of the chapter: whether plea bargaining should be abolished and if not, the extent to which and ways in which it should be controlled. As you read about the constitutional constraints that apply to guilty pleas and plea negotiations, you should keep these questions in mind.

A. THE DUE PROCESS REQUIREMENT OF AN INTELLIGENT AND VOLUNTARY PLEA

BOYKIN v. ALABAMA

Supreme Court of the United States, 1969.
395 U.S. 238, 89 S.Ct. 1709, 23 L.Ed.2d 274.

MR. JUSTICE DOUGLAS delivered the opinion of the Court.

[In 1966, the petitioner was charged with, and pled guilty to, five armed robberies that had occurred in Mobile, Alabama. At the time, these crimes were punishable by death. The record did not reflect that the judge asked the petitioner any questions when he entered his guilty pleas, nor did the petitioner apparently address the court when his pleas were entered.

The petitioner was sentenced to death for each of the robberies to which he had pled guilty. On appeal, the Alabama Supreme Court affirmed, and the United States Supreme Court then granted certiorari.]

It was error, plain on the face of the record, for the trial judge to accept petitioner's guilty plea without an affirmative showing that it was intelligent and voluntary. * * *

* * * The requirement that the prosecution spread on the record the prerequisites of a valid waiver is no constitutional innovation. In *Carnley v. Cochran,* 369 U.S. 506, 516, we dealt with a problem of waiver of the right to counsel, a Sixth Amendment right. We held: "Presuming waiver from a silent record is impermissible. The record must show, or there must be an allegation and evidence which show, that an accused was offered counsel but intelligently and understandingly rejected the offer. Anything less is not waiver."

We think that the same standard must be applied to determining whether a guilty plea is voluntarily made. For, as we have said, a plea of guilty is more than an admission of conduct; it is a conviction.[4] * * *

Several federal constitutional rights are involved in a waiver that takes place when a plea of guilty is entered in a state criminal trial. First, is the privilege against compulsory self-incrimination guaranteed by the Fifth Amendment and applicable to the States by reason of the Fourteenth. Second, is the right to trial by jury. Third, is the right to confront one's accusers. We cannot presume a waiver of these three important federal rights from a silent record.

What is at stake for an accused facing death or imprisonment demands the utmost solicitude of which courts are capable in canvassing the matter with the accused to make sure he has a full understanding of what the plea connotes and of its consequence. When the judge discharges that function, he leaves a record adequate for any review that may be later sought and forestalls the spin-off of collateral proceedings that seek to probe murky memories.[7]

* * *

MR. JUSTICE HARLAN, whom MR. JUSTICE BLACK joins, dissenting. [Opinion omitted.]

QUESTIONS AND POINTS FOR DISCUSSION

1. The Supreme Court distinguished *Boykin v. Alabama* in Parke v. Raley, 506 U.S. 20, 113 S.Ct. 517 (1992). In *Parke,* the defendant had been sentenced as a "persistent felony offender" under a Kentucky statute because he had two previous convictions for burglary in addition to his current

---

4. "A plea of guilty is more than a voluntary confession made in open court. It also serves as a stipulation that no proof by the prosecution need be advanced.... It supplies both evidence and verdict, ending controversy." *Woodard v. State,* 171 So.2d 462, 469.

7. "A majority of criminal convictions are obtained after a plea of guilty. If these convictions are to be insulated from attack, the trial court is best advised to conduct an on the record examination of the defendant which should include, inter alia, an attempt to satisfy itself that the defendant understands the nature of the charges, his right to a jury trial, the acts sufficient to constitute the offenses for which he is charged and the permissible range of sentences." *Commonwealth ex rel. West v. Rundle,* 237 A.2d 196, 197–198 (1968).

conviction for robbery. The defendant contended that his two previous burglary convictions, obtained through guilty pleas, were invalid under *Boykin* since there were no transcripts of the plea proceedings that confirmed that the defendant's guilty pleas were knowing and voluntary. Under the law in Kentucky, however, a presumption existed that prior convictions were valid, and a defendant had the burden of producing evidence that rebutted this presumption. Only after producing some evidence that a right was infringed during a prior proceeding culminating in a conviction did the burden shift to the government to prove by a preponderance of the evidence that the conviction was obtained in conformance with the law.

One of the questions before the Supreme Court was whether the presumption that a prior conviction was valid violated due process. In the course of holding that this presumption of regularity was constitutional, the Court distinguished *Boykin*. In *Boykin*, the Court noted, the defendant was challenging his conviction on appeal, while in this case, the defendant was challenging his prior convictions in a collateral proceeding. The Court held that in such a collateral proceeding, it is constitutional to apply a presumption of regularity, at least to the extent that the burden of production on the issue of a prior conviction's validity is placed on a defendant.

The Supreme Court furthermore held that it was constitutional for Kentucky to allow the government to prove the validity of a prior conviction by only a preponderance of the evidence. The Court did not resolve, because it did not need to, the question whether it would be constitutional to place the entire burden of proof on a defendant.

2.　The Supreme Court has amplified the constitutional requirements for a valid guilty plea, holding that a defendant must be apprised of the elements of the crime to which the defendant is pleading guilty. Bradshaw v. Stumpf, 545 U.S. 175, 183, 125 S.Ct. 2398, 2405 (2005). See also Henderson v. Morgan, 426 U.S. 637, 96 S.Ct. 2253 (1976) (guilty plea to second-degree murder vacated because defendant was not aware that intent to kill was an element of the crime). Providing the defendant with a copy of the indictment creates a presumption, though a rebuttable one, that the defendant has received the requisite notice. Bousley v. United States, 523 U.S. 614, 618, 118 S.Ct. 1604, 1609 (1998). But according to the Supreme Court, a judge need not explain the elements of the crime to the defendant on the record. The requirements of due process are met as long as the record reflects that the defendant's attorney informed the defendant of the nature of the charge and the elements of the crime to which the defendant is pleading guilty. In addition, the record generally does not have to include the details of the information relayed by defense counsel to the defendant. In *Bradshaw*, the Supreme Court stated that "[w]here a defendant is represented by competent counsel, the court usually may rely on that counsel's assurance that the defendant has been properly informed of the nature and elements of the charge to which he is pleading guilty." Id. at 183, 125 S.Ct. at 2406.

Do you agree that defense counsel's statement on the record that she has apprised her client of the nature of the charge and the elements of the crime generally satisfies due process? See Julian A. Cook, III, Crumbs from the Master's Table: The Supreme Court, Pro Se Defendants and the Federal

Guilty Plea Process, 81 Notre Dame L.Rev. 1895, 1910 (2006) (criticizing *Bradshaw* for allowing "blanket and largely unsubstantiated assertions of extra-judicial explanations" of the nature and elements of the crime).

3.　Ismael Ramirez was a permanent legal resident from Mexico living in the United States. He had married a woman who was a United States citizen, and their four children, three-year-old twins and two siblings, ages five and six, were also U.S. citizens. Under a plea agreement, Ramirez pled guilty to the crime of possessing a controlled substance with intent to deliver. He received a suspended prison sentence of ten years and was placed on probation. Only after he entered his plea and was sentenced did Ramirez discover that his conviction would result in his mandatory deportation from the United States. Should the court's failure to ensure that Ramirez was aware of the deportation consequences of entering his plea invalidate the guilty plea? See State v. Ramirez, 636 N.W.2d 740, 743 (Iowa 2001) (due process does not require a court to apprise a defendant of the collateral consequences of a guilty plea, including mandatory deportation).

4.　Deportation has been described as "a life sentence of exile." Jordan v. De George, 341 U.S. 223, 243, 71 S.Ct. 703, 714 (1951) (Jackson, J., dissenting). Nonetheless, courts generally have concurred that the failure to apprise a defendant of the immigration consequences of a guilty plea does not violate due process. See Santos–Sanchez v. United States, 548 F.3d 327, 336–37 (5th Cir. 2008). These holdings have rested on the distinction the courts have drawn between the "direct" and "collateral" consequences of a conviction. In United States v. Gonzalez, 202 F.3d 20 (1st Cir. 2000), the First Circuit Court of Appeals explained this distinction:

> What renders [a] plea's immigration effects "collateral" is not that they arise "virtually by operation of law," but the fact that deportation is "not the sentence of the court which accept[s] the plea but of another agency over which the trial judge has no control and for which he [or she] has no responsibility."

Id. at 27.

In your opinion, is the distinction described above between the direct and collateral consequences of a conviction relevant in determining what information due process requires a court to provide a defendant before accepting a guilty plea? If the courts are correct that due process generally does not require a court to inform a defendant about collateral consequences that may ensue from a conviction, should statutes and court rules still require a court to relay this information to a defendant tendering a guilty plea? If so, what exactly should a court be required to tell a defendant?

As you contemplate these questions, consider the alternative approach outlined in the ABA Standards for Criminal Justice: Collateral Sanctions and Discretionary Disqualification of Convicted Persons (3d ed. 2004), pertinent portions of which are set forth on pages 447–53. These standards differentiate between "collateral sanctions" and "discretionary disqualifications." A "collateral sanction" includes any "legal penalty, disability or disadvantage" that automatically follows from a conviction, such as mandatory deportation. A "discretionary disqualification" is an authorized, though not mandatory, penalty, disability, or disadvantage that can be imposed following a conviction.

Standard 19–1.1. According to Standard 19–2.3(a), a defendant pleading guilty must be apprised of the collateral sanctions—the automatic sanctions—that will be triggered by the plea. This notification can come from the defendant's attorney, however, unless the law or court rules require notification of the defendant by the court. For a list of states requiring that courts notify defendants that their guilty pleas may have immigration consequences, see Attila Bogdan, Guilty Pleas by Non–Citizens in Illinois: Immigration Consequences Reconsidered, 53 DePaul L. Rev. 19, 49–50 (2003).

5. When an uncounselled defendant is entering a guilty plea, the court must take steps to ensure not only that the guilty plea is otherwise voluntary and intelligent, but that the defendant is validly waiving his or her right to counsel. In order for the waiver of the Sixth Amendment right to counsel at a plea hearing to be valid, a defendant needs to be apprised of the "nature" of the pending charges, of the right to have counsel provide advice regarding the tendering of a plea, and of the range of penalties that might be imposed if the defendant enters a plea of guilty. Iowa v. Tovar, 541 U.S. 77, 81, 124 S.Ct. 1379, 1383 (2004). The judge need not elaborate further and highlight the potential adverse consequences of forgoing counsel's assistance, such as the risk that the defendant will unwittingly relinquish a viable defense to the criminal charges. Id. at 91–92, 124 S.Ct. at 1389.

Arguing in an amicus brief in *Iowa v. Tovar* that additional warnings are needed in order for the waiver of the constitutional right to counsel to be knowing, intelligent, and voluntary, the National Association of Criminal Defense Lawyers cited several examples of the impact a lawyer's advice can have on a defendant's decision whether, and to what, to plead guilty:

> The defendant pleads guilty to driving while intoxicated without realizing that the results of his breathalyzer test are suppressible. An innocent defendant pleads guilty without realizing that he has an entrapment defense, a duress defense, or that his intoxication negates the specific intent required by the crime. The defendant pleads guilty to what he thinks is a nonserious theft without realizing that the consideration of his relevant conduct, including uncharged or acquitted conduct, will likely lead to a sentence at the high end of the statutory range. The defendant pleads guilty to a minor felony to resolve the case quickly and get on with his life without realizing that the conviction will lead to his deportation.

Brief for National Ass'n of Criminal Defense Lawyers as Amici Curiae Supporting Respondent at 7, *Tovar* (No. 02–1541), 2003 WL 23051967. In your opinion, are the warnings specified by the Supreme Court in *Iowa v. Tovar* adequate to safeguard a defendant's Sixth Amendment right to counsel at a plea hearing? If not, how should the warnings be augmented to meet the requirements of the Constitution?

6. Apart from the constitutional requirements that must be met in order for a guilty plea to be valid are the requirements which must be met under federal and state statutes and court rules. Rule 11 of the Federal Rules of Criminal Procedure, which governs the rendering and acceptance of guilty pleas in federal courts, is an example of one such court rule. That rule is set forth below:

Rule 11. Pleas

(a) Entering a Plea.

(1) In General. A defendant may plead not guilty, guilty, or (with the court's consent) nolo contendere.

(2) Conditional Plea. With the consent of the court and the government, a defendant may enter a conditional plea of guilty or nolo contendere, reserving in writing the right to have an appellate court review an adverse determination of a specified pretrial motion. A defendant who prevails on appeal may then withdraw the plea.

(3) Nolo Contendere Plea. Before accepting a plea of nolo contendere, the court must consider the parties' views and the public interest in the effective administration of justice.

(4) Failure to Enter a Plea. If a defendant refuses to enter a plea or if a defendant organization fails to appear, the court must enter a plea of not guilty.

(b) Considering and Accepting a Guilty or Nolo Contendere Plea.

(1) Advising and Questioning the Defendant. Before the court accepts a plea of guilty or nolo contendere, the defendant may be placed under oath, and the court must address the defendant personally in open court. During this address, the court must inform the defendant of, and determine that the defendant understands, the following:

(A) the government's right, in a prosecution for perjury or false statement, to use against the defendant any statement that the defendant gives under oath;

(B) the right to plead not guilty, or having already so pleaded, to persist in that plea;

(C) the right to a jury trial;

(D) the right to be represented by counsel—and if necessary have the court appoint counsel—at trial and at every other stage of the proceeding;

(E) the right at trial to confront and cross-examine adverse witnesses, to be protected from compelled self-incrimination, to testify and present evidence, and to compel the attendance of witnesses;

(F) the defendant's waiver of these trial rights if the court accepts a plea of guilty or nolo contendere;

(G) the nature of each charge to which the defendant is pleading;

(H) any maximum possible penalty, including imprisonment, fine, and term of supervised release;

(I) any mandatory minimum penalty;

(J) any applicable forfeiture;

(K) the court's authority to order restitution;

(L) the court's obligation to impose a special assessment;

(M) in determining a sentence, the court's obligation to calculate the applicable sentencing-guideline range and to consider that range, possible departures under the Sentencing Guidelines, and other sentencing factors under 18 U.S.C. § 3553(a); and

(N) the terms of any plea-agreement provision waiving the right to appeal or to collaterally attack the sentence.

(2) Ensuring That a Plea Is Voluntary. Before accepting a plea of guilty or nolo contendere, the court must address the defendant personally in open court and determine that the plea is voluntary and did not result from force, threats, or promises (other than promises in a plea agreement).

(3) Determining the Factual Basis for a Plea. Before entering judgment on a guilty plea, the court must determine that there is a factual basis for the plea.

(c) Plea Agreement Procedure.

(1) In General. An attorney for the government and the defendant's attorney, or the defendant when proceeding pro se, may discuss and reach a plea agreement. The court must not participate in these discussions. If the defendant pleads guilty or nolo contendere to either a charged offense or a lesser or related offense, the plea agreement may specify that an attorney for the government will:

(A) not bring, or will move to dismiss, other charges;

(B) recommend, or agree not to oppose the defendant's request, that a particular sentence or sentencing range is appropriate or that a particular provision of the Sentencing Guidelines, or policy statement, or sentencing factor does or does not apply (such a recommendation or request does not bind the court); or

(C) agree that a specific sentence or sentencing range is the appropriate disposition of the case, or that a particular provision of the Sentencing Guidelines, or policy statement, or sentencing factor does or does not apply (such a recommendation or request binds the court once the court accepts the plea agreement).

(2) Disclosing a Plea Agreement. The parties must disclose the plea agreement in open court when the plea is offered, unless the court for good cause allows the parties to disclose the plea agreement in camera.

(3) Judicial Consideration of a Plea Agreement.

(A) To the extent the plea agreement is of the type specified in Rule 11(c)(1)(A) or (C), the court may accept the agreement, reject it, or defer a decision until the court has reviewed the presentence report.

(B) To the extent the plea agreement is of the type specified in Rule 11(c)(1)(B), the court must advise the defendant that the defendant has no right to withdraw the plea if the court does not follow the recommendation or request.

(4) Accepting a Plea Agreement. If the court accepts the plea agreement, it must inform the defendant that to the extent the plea agreement is of the type specified in Rule 11(c)(1)(A) or (C), the agreed disposition will be included in the judgment.

(5) Rejecting a Plea Agreement. If the court rejects a plea agreement containing provisions of the type specified in Rule 11(c)(1)(A) or (C), the court must do the following on the record and in open court (or, for good cause, in camera):

(A) inform the parties that the court rejects the plea agreement;

(B) advise the defendant personally that the court is not required to follow the plea agreement and give the defendant an opportunity to withdraw the plea; and

(C) advise the defendant personally that if the plea is not withdrawn, the court may dispose of the case less favorably toward the defendant than the plea agreement contemplated.

(d) Withdrawing a Guilty or Nolo Contendere Plea. A defendant may withdraw a plea of guilty or nolo contendere:

(1) before the court accepts the plea, for any reason or no reason; or

(2) after the court accepts the plea, but before it imposes sentence if:

(A) the court rejects a plea agreement under Rule 11(c)(5); or

(B) the defendant can show a fair and just reason for requesting the withdrawal.

(e) Finality of a Guilty or Nolo Contendere Plea. After the court imposes sentence, the defendant may not withdraw a plea of guilty or nolo contendere, and the plea may be set aside only on direct appeal or collateral attack.

(f) Admissibility or Inadmissibility of a Plea, Plea Discussions, and Related Statements. The admissibility or inadmissibility of a plea, a plea discussion, and any related statement is governed by Federal Rule of Evidence 410.

(g) Recording the Proceedings. The proceedings during which the defendant enters a plea must be recorded by a court reporter or by a suitable recording device. If there is a guilty plea or a nolo contendere plea, the record must include the inquiries and advice to the defendant required under Rule 11(b) and (c).

(h) Harmless Error. A variance from the requirements of this rule is harmless error if it does not affect substantial rights.

How, if at all, should Rule 11 be modified? Contrast the information that Rule 11(b)(1) requires be relayed to a defendant pleading guilty or *nolo contendere* with that prescribed by Standard 14–1.4 of the ABA Standards for Criminal Justice: Pleas of Guilty (3d ed. 1999):

Standard 14–1.4. Defendant to be advised

(a) The court should not accept a plea of guilty or nolo contendere from a defendant without first addressing the defendant personally in open court and determining that the defendant understands:

(i) the nature and elements of the offense to which the plea is offered, and the terms and conditions of any plea agreement;

(ii) the maximum possible sentence on the charge, including that possible from consecutive sentences, and the mandatory minimum sentence, if any, on the charge, or any special circumstances affecting probation or release from incarceration;

(iii) that, if the defendant has been previously convicted of an offense and the offense to which the defendant has offered to plead is one for which a different or additional punishment is authorized by reason of the previous conviction or other factors, the fact of the previous conviction or other factors may be established after the plea, thereby subjecting the defendant to such different or additional punishment;

(iv) that by pleading guilty the defendant waives the right to a speedy and public trial, including the right to trial by jury; the right to insist at a trial that the prosecution establish guilt beyond a reasonable doubt; the right to testify at a trial and the right not to testify at a trial; the right at a trial to be confronted by the witnesses against the defendant, to present witnesses in the defendant's behalf, and to have compulsory process in securing their attendance;

(v) that by pleading guilty the defendant generally waives the right to file further motions in the trial court, such as motions to object to the sufficiency of the charging papers to state an offense or to evidence allegedly obtained in violation of constitutional rights; and

(vi) that by pleading guilty the defendant generally waives the right to appeal, except the right to appeal a motion that has been made, ruled upon and expressly reserved for appeal and the right to appeal an illegal or unauthorized sentence.

(b) If the court is in doubt about whether the defendant comprehends his or her rights and the other matters of which notice is required to be supplied in accordance with this standard, the defendant should be asked to repeat to the court in his or her own words the information about such rights and the other matters, or the court should take such other steps as may be necessary to assure itself that the guilty plea is entered with complete understanding of the consequences.

(c) Before accepting a plea of guilty or nolo contendere, the court should also advise the defendant that by entering the plea, the defendant may face additional consequences including but not limited to the forfeiture of property, the loss of certain civil rights, disqualification from certain governmental benefits, enhanced punishment if the defendant is convicted of another crime in the future, and, if the defendant is not a United States citizen, a change in the defendant's immigration status. The court should advise the defendant to consult with defense counsel if the defendant needs additional information concerning the potential consequences of the plea.

(d) If the defendant is represented by a lawyer, the court should not accept the plea where it appears the defendant has not had the effective assistance of counsel.

7. If a court accepts a defendant's guilty plea, the defendant's statements, including incriminating admissions, made at the Rule 11 hearing are admissible against the defendant at later proceedings, such as a sentencing hearing. Mitchell v. United States, 526 U.S. 314, 324, 119 S.Ct. 1307, 1313 (1999) (*dictum*). But invoking the Fifth Amendment privilege against self-incrimination at a Rule 11 hearing poses a risk to a defendant: the court may then decide not to accept the plea because the factual basis for it has not been adequately established. Id.

Federal Rule of Evidence 410(4) provides that a defendant's statements made during plea negotiations are generally inadmissible at trial if the negotiations do not culminate in a guilty plea. In United States v. Mezzanatto, 513 U.S. 196, 115 S.Ct. 797 (1995), the Supreme Court held that a defendant can waive the protection afforded by this exclusionary provision. The waiver at issue in *Mezzanatto*, which was extracted from the defendant before the prosecutor would enter into what proved to be unsuccessful plea negotiations, permitted the defendant's statements during the negotiations to be admitted for impeachment purposes—in other words, to contradict the defendant's testimony at trial. Three of the Justices who joined the seven-person majority in the case—Justices Ginsberg, O'Connor, and Breyer—emphasized in a concurring opinion that the case did not involve or resolve the question whether a waiver of the exclusionary rule can encompass statements of the defendant introduced in the prosecution's case-in-chief to prove the defendant's guilt.

Since *Mezzanatto*, federal prosecutors frequently have refused to enter into plea negotiations unless defendants agree that any statements they make during plea discussions can be used to impeach their contradictory testimony at trial. Some "proffer letters," the documents which spell out the government's conditions for entering into plea discussions, go even further, providing that the defendant's statements during plea negotiations can be used to rebut any evidence offered or elicited at any stage of the criminal prosecution or any factual assertions made on the defendant's behalf. See, e.g., United States v. Barrow, 400 F.3d 109, 120–122 (2d Cir. 2005) (interpreting proffer agreement to allow government to introduce defendant's admissions of drug dealing, made during plea negotiations, after counsel argued in his opening statement at trial that someone else perpetrated the drug crimes); United States v. Velez, 354 F.3d 190, 195–96 (2d Cir. 2004) (holding a waiver provision enforceable when a defendant's plea-related statements are introduced for rebuttal purposes, whether or not the defendant testifies).

As a policy matter, should court rules permit the use of a defendant's statements during plea negotiations for impeachment purposes? What are the competing arguments for and against enforcing a waiver when the defendant's statements are used, not to impeach the defendant's testimony, but to rebut other contradictory evidence introduced by the defendant as part of his defense or to refute arguments made by defense counsel? Finally, should court rules allow, and does the Constitution permit, statements made by a defendant during plea negotiations to be admitted in the prosecution's case-in-chief? For a discussion of proffer agreements and their enforceability, see David P. Leonard, Waiver of Protections Against the Use of Plea Bargains and Plea Bargaining Statements after *Mezzanatto*, 23 Crim. Just. 8 (Fall 2008).

8.   Rule 11(d)(2)(B) of the Federal Rules of Criminal Procedure provides that before sentencing, a defendant can withdraw a guilty plea upon showing a "fair and just reason" for the plea withdrawal. In United States v. Hyde, 520 U.S. 670, 117 S.Ct. 1630 (1997), a defendant pleaded guilty as part of a plea agreement under which the government agreed to dismiss other pending charges and refrain from bringing certain criminal charges in the future. The court accepted the defendant's guilty plea but deferred consideration of the plea agreement until a presentence report had been prepared.

A month after the court had accepted his guilty plea, the defendant sought to withdraw it. The court refused to let him do so because he had not established that there was a "fair and just reason" for his plea withdrawal. The court then accepted the plea agreement and sentenced the defendant to two and a half years in prison.

The defendant contended that the requirement that there be a "fair and just reason" for a plea withdrawal does not apply until the court accepts a tendered plea agreement. The Supreme Court disagreed, holding that acceptance of the guilty plea alone triggers the requirement. Otherwise, the Court observed, in the many cases in which a court accepts a plea agreement and then imposes the sentence in the same proceeding, the limitation on plea withdrawals would only apply during the short period of time between the acceptance of the plea agreement and the imposition of the sentence.

9.   Of the requirements that must be met in order for a guilty plea to be valid under Rule 11, which do you believe are also required by the Constitution? Consider the extent to which the following case has a bearing on the answer to that question.

NORTH CAROLINA v. ALFORD

Supreme Court of the United States, 1970.
400 U.S. 25, 91 S.Ct. 160, 27 L.Ed.2d 162.

Mʀ. Jᴜꜱᴛɪᴄᴇ Wʜɪᴛᴇ delivered the opinion of the Court.

On December 2, 1963, Alford was indicted for first-degree murder, a capital offense under North Carolina law. The court appointed an attorney to represent him, and this attorney questioned all but one of the various witnesses who appellee said would substantiate his claim of innocence. The witnesses, however, did not support Alford's story but gave statements that strongly indicated his guilt. Faced with strong evidence of guilt and no substantial evidentiary support for the claim of innocence, Alford's attorney recommended that he plead guilty, but left the ultimate decision to Alford himself. The prosecutor agreed to accept a plea of guilty to a charge of second-degree murder, and on December 10, 1963, Alford pleaded guilty to the reduced charge.

Before the plea was finally accepted by the trial court, the court heard the sworn testimony of a police officer who summarized the State's case. Two other witnesses besides Alford were also heard. Although there was no eyewitness to the crime, the testimony indicated that shortly before the killing Alford took his gun from his house, stated his intention to kill the victim, and returned home with the declaration that he had carried out the killing. After the summary presentation of the State's case, Alford took the stand and testified that he had not committed the murder but that he was pleading guilty because he faced the threat of the death penalty if he did not do so.[2] In response to the questions of his counsel, he acknowledged that his counsel had informed him of the difference between second- and first-degree murder and of his rights in case he chose to go to trial. The trial court then asked appellee if, in light of his denial of guilt, he still desired to plead guilty to second-degree murder and appellee answered, "Yes, sir. I plead guilty on—from the circumstances that he [Alford's attorney] told me." After eliciting information about Alford's prior criminal record, which was a long one, the trial court sentenced him to 30 years' imprisonment, the maximum penalty for second-degree murder.

* * *

If Alford's statements were to be credited as sincere assertions of his innocence, there obviously existed a factual and legal dispute between him and the State. Without more, it might be argued that the conviction entered on his guilty plea was invalid, since his assertion of innocence negatived any admission of guilt, which * * * is normally "[c]entral to the plea and the foundation for entering judgment against the defendant. . . . "

---

2.   After giving his version of the events of the night of the murder, Alford stated:

"I pleaded guilty on second degree murder because they said there is too much evidence, but I ain't shot no man, but I take the fault for the other man. We never had an argument in our life and I just pleaded guilty because they said if I didn't they would gas me for it, and that is all."

In response to questions from his attorney, Alford affirmed that he had consulted several times with his attorney and with members of his family and had been informed of his rights if he chose to plead not guilty. Alford then reaffirmed his decision to plead guilty to second-degree murder:

"Q [by Alford's attorney]. And you authorized me to tender a plea of guilty to second degree murder before the court?

"A. Yes, sir.

"Q. And in doing that, that you have again affirmed your decision on that point?

"A. Well, I'm still pleading that you all got me to plead guilty. I plead the other way, circumstantial evidence; that the jury will prosecute me on—on the second. You told me to plead guilty, right. I don't—I'm not guilty but I plead guilty."

In addition to Alford's statement, however, the court had heard an account of the events on the night of the murder, including information from Alford's acquaintances that he had departed from his home with his gun stating his intention to kill and that he had later declared that he had carried out his intention. Nor had Alford wavered in his desire to have the trial court determine his guilt without a jury trial. Although denying the charge against him, he nevertheless preferred the dispute between him and the State to be settled by the judge in the context of a guilty plea proceeding rather than by a formal trial. Thereupon, with the State's telling evidence and Alford's denial before it, the trial court proceeded to convict and sentence Alford for second-degree murder.

State and lower federal courts are divided upon whether a guilty plea can be accepted when it is accompanied by protestations of innocence and hence contains only a waiver of trial but no admission of guilt. Some courts, giving expression to the principle that "[o]ur law only authorizes a conviction where guilt is shown," require that trial judges reject such pleas. But others have concluded that they should not "force any defense on a defendant in a criminal case," particularly when advancement of the defense might "end in disaster...." They have argued that, since "guilt, or the degree of guilt, is at times uncertain and elusive," "[a]n accused, though believing in or entertaining doubts respecting his innocence, might reasonably conclude a jury would be convinced of his guilt and that he would fare better in the sentence by pleading guilty...." As one state court observed nearly a century ago, "[r]easons other than the fact that he is guilty may induce a defendant to so plead, ... [and] [h]e must be permitted to judge for himself in this respect." *State v. Kaufman,* 51 Iowa 578, 580, 2 N.W. 275, 276 (1879) (dictum).[7]

This Court has not confronted this precise issue, but prior decisions do yield relevant principles. * * *

The issue in *Hudson v. United States,* 272 U.S. 451 (1926), was whether a federal court has power to impose a prison sentence after accepting a plea of *nolo contendere,* a plea by which a defendant does not expressly admit his guilt, but nonetheless waives his right to a trial and authorizes the court for purposes of the case to treat him as if he were guilty. The Court held that a trial court does have such power * * *. Implicit in the *nolo contendere* cases is a recognition that the Constitution does not bar imposition of a prison sentence upon an accused who is unwilling expressly to admit his guilt but who, faced with grim alternatives, is willing to waive his trial and accept the sentence.

* * *

Nor can we perceive any material difference between a plea that refuses to admit commission of the criminal act and a plea containing a protestation of innocence when, as in the instant case, a defendant

---

7. A third approach has been to decline to rule definitively that a trial judge must either accept or reject an otherwise valid plea containing a protestation of innocence, but to leave that decision to his sound discretion.

intelligently concludes that his interests require entry of a guilty plea and the record before the judge contains strong evidence of actual guilt. Here the State had a strong case of first-degree murder against Alford. Whether he realized or disbelieved his guilt, he insisted on his plea because in his view he had absolutely nothing to gain by a trial and much to gain by pleading. Because of the overwhelming evidence against him, a trial was precisely what neither Alford nor his attorney desired. Confronted with the choice between a trial for first-degree murder, on the one hand, and a plea of guilty to second-degree murder, on the other, Alford quite reasonably chose the latter and thereby limited the maximum penalty to a 30–year term. When his plea is viewed in light of the evidence against him, which substantially negated his claim of innocence and which further provided a means by which the judge could test whether the plea was being intelligently entered,[10] its validity cannot be seriously questioned. In view of the strong factual basis for the plea demonstrated by the State and Alford's clearly expressed desire to enter it despite his professed belief in his innocence, we hold that the trial judge did not commit constitutional error in accepting it.[11]

MR. JUSTICE BRENNAN, with whom MR. JUSTICE DOUGLAS and MR. JUSTICE MARSHALL join, dissenting.

* * * *[W]ithout reaching the question whether due process permits the entry of judgment upon a plea of guilty accompanied by a contemporaneous denial of acts constituting the crime, I believe that at the very least such a denial of guilt is also a relevant factor in determining whether the plea was voluntarily and intelligently made. With these factors in mind, it is sufficient in my view to state that the facts set out in the majority opinion demonstrate that Alford was "so gripped by fear of the death penalty" that his decision to plead guilty was not voluntary but was "the product of duress as much so as choice reflecting physical constraint." * * *

QUESTIONS AND POINTS FOR DISCUSSION

1. At least two purposes are served by requiring a factual basis for a guilty plea. First, the existence of a factual basis helps to ensure that the defendant is not unknowingly pleading guilty to a crime that he or she did not or could not have committed. McCarthy v. United States, 394 U.S. 459, 467, 89 S.Ct. 1166, 1171 (1969). Second, the factual basis for the plea helps to

---

10. Because of the importance of protecting the innocent and of insuring that guilty pleas are a product of free and intelligent choice, various state and federal court decisions properly caution that pleas coupled with claims of innocence should not be accepted unless there is a factual basis for the plea, and until the judge taking the plea has inquired into and sought to resolve the conflict between the waiver of trial and the claim of innocence.

11. Our holding does not mean that a trial judge must accept every constitutionally valid guilty plea merely because a defendant wishes so to plead. A criminal defendant does not have an absolute right under the Constitution to have his guilty plea accepted by the court, although the States may by statute or otherwise confer such a right. Likewise, the States may bar their courts from accepting guilty pleas from any defendants who assert their innocence. We need not now delineate the scope of that discretion.

ensure that the defendant's plea is in fact voluntary and not the result of impermissible threats, promises, or other pressures. Libretti v. United States, 516 U.S. 29, 42, 116 S.Ct. 356, 364 (1995).

Most courts have concluded that in the absence of a protestation of innocence by the defendant or some other special circumstances, due process does not require that a factual basis for a guilty plea be established before the plea is accepted. See State ex rel. Farmer v. Trent, 551 S.E.2d 711, 718 (W.Va. 2001). Some courts have gone further, holding that even when a defendant tendering a guilty plea steadfastly refuses to admit guilt or affirmatively professes his or her innocence, the Constitution does not require a strong factual basis or, according to several of these courts, any factual basis at all. See State v. Edgar, 127 P.3d 986, 996 (Kan. 2006) (listing cases). Consequently, in states with no statutes or court rules requiring factual bases for guilty pleas, a court generally may accept a guilty plea without any evidence or information being tendered to the court that would support the conclusion that the defendant is culpable of the offense to which he or she is pleading guilty. The absence of a factual basis or strong factual basis for the guilty plea simply is one of a number of factors bearing on the question whether the defendant's guilty plea is intelligent and voluntary.

In your opinion, when, if ever, is a factual basis for a guilty plea constitutionally required?

2.   The Notes of the Advisory Committee on Rules, which drafted Rule 11 of the Federal Rules of Criminal Procedure, state that the factual basis for a guilty plea can be established in a variety of ways. A defendant may, when entering the plea, make inculpatory admissions in court which establish the defendant's guilt of the crime to which a guilty plea is being entered. Alternatively, the prosecutor or defense attorney may recite details about the defendant's crime on the record as a way of establishing the factual basis. The Advisory Committee Notes also suggest that the factual-basis requirement might be satisfied by a presentence report or by other undefined means.

3.   Most jurisdictions remit the decisions whether to accept a guilty plea or a plea agreement to the court's discretion. While most courts have underscored the breadth of the trial judge's discretion to accept or reject a guilty plea, some federal courts have held that the trial judge has no authority to reject an unconditional guilty plea if the plea meets the requirements of Rule 11. See In re Vasquez–Ramirez, 443 F.3d 692, 695–96 (9th Cir. 2006).

Defendants sometimes challenge a trial judge's decision to reject a guilty plea or plea agreement on the grounds that the rejection constituted an abuse of discretion. After the rejection of their guilty pleas, these defendants generally have gone to trial, been found guilty, and received a more severe sentence than would have been imposed under a proffered plea agreement. Courts usually have found no abuse of discretion when a guilty plea was rejected because the defendant professed innocence or there was an inadequate factual basis to support the plea. See, e.g., France v. Artuz, 1999 WL 1251817, at *7 (E.D.N.Y.1999) (no abuse of discretion to reject guilty plea to manslaughter when the defendant, whom the jury later convicted of murder, contended he was innocent); Elsten v. State, 698 N.E.2d 292, 295 (Ind.1998) (no abuse of discretion in rejecting plea of "guilty but mentally ill" of defendant, who was later convicted of murder, when two court-ordered psychological evaluations found no evidence that the defendant was mentally ill when he shot his wife). Examples of other decisions in which no abuse of discretion was found in the trial court's rejection of a guilty plea or plea agreement include: Hoskins v. Maricle, 150 S.W.3d 1, 25 (Ken. 2004) (no abuse of discretion to reject, because unduly lenient, plea agreement under which defendants charged with capital murder would have received a ten-year prison sentence for manslaughter); Newsome v. State, 797 N.E.2d 293, 298 (Ind. Ct. App. 2003) (no abuse of discretion in rejecting guilty plea to two counts of molestation and incest when the court believed the plea was tendered to avert the introduction of evidence in the defendant's trial for rape that he had fathered the child of the victim he had molested and later raped); United States v. Severino, 800 F.2d 42, 46–47 (2d Cir.1986) (no abuse of discretion where the judge thought the defendant had lied during his plea allocution); United States v. Escobar Noble, 653 F.2d 34, 36–37 (1st Cir.1981) (no abuse of discretion where judge rejected plea to a misdemeanor so that prerogative to impose a more severe sentence upon conviction of a felony could be preserved); United States v. David E. Thompson, Inc., 621 F.2d 1147, 1150–51 (1st Cir.1980) (no abuse of discretion to reject *nolo contendere* plea that would have denied victims bringing civil actions against the defendant of the benefit of the government's prosecutorial efforts).

On occasion, but infrequently, an appellate court will find that a trial court abused its discretion in rejecting a guilty plea or plea agreement. See, e.g., United States v. Washington, 969 F.2d 1073, 1077–79 (D.C.Cir.1992) (improper to reject guilty plea because defendant would not inculpate his codefendant). The courts are split on whether the refusal to accept a plea agreement because it was tendered after a court-imposed deadline constitutes an abuse of discretion. See State v. Brown, 689 N.W.2d 347, 351–52 (Neb. 2004) (listing cases). For example, in United States v. Gamboa, 166 F.3d 1327, 1331 (11th Cir.1999), the Eleventh Circuit Court of Appeals found no abuse of discretion when the trial judge refused to accept plea agreements submitted forty minutes after the court's deadline, while in State v. Hager, 630 N.W.2d 828, 837 (Iowa 2001), the Iowa Supreme Court held that the trial court had abused its discretion when it automatically rejected a plea agreement because it was tendered the morning of the trial. What competing policy considerations underlie this disagreement amongst the courts, and how would you balance them?

BRADY v. UNITED STATES

Supreme Court of the United States, 1970.
397 U.S. 742, 90 S.Ct. 1463, 25 L.Ed.2d 747.

MR. JUSTICE WHITE delivered the opinion of the Court.

In 1959, petitioner was charged with kidnaping in violation of 18 U.S.C. § 1201(a).[1] Since the indictment charged that the victim of the

---

1. "Whoever knowingly transports in interstate or foreign commerce, any person who has been unlawfully seized, confined, inveigled, decoyed, kidnapped, abducted, or carried away and held for ransom or reward or otherwise, except, in the case of a minor, by a parent thereof, shall be punished (1) by death if the kidnapped person has not been liberated unharmed, and if the

kidnaping was not liberated unharmed, petitioner faced a maximum penalty of death if the verdict of the jury should so recommend. Petitioner, represented by competent counsel throughout, first elected to plead not guilty. * * * Upon learning that his codefendant, who had confessed to the authorities, would plead guilty and be available to testify against him, petitioner changed his plea to guilty. His plea was accepted after the trial judge twice questioned him as to the voluntariness of his plea.[2] Petitioner was sentenced to 50 years' imprisonment, later reduced to 30.

In 1967, petitioner sought relief under 28 U.S.C. § 2255, claiming that his plea of guilty was not voluntarily given because § 1201(a) operated to coerce his plea * * *.

After a hearing, the District Court for the District of New Mexico denied relief. * * * The court held that § 1201(a) was constitutional and found that petitioner decided to plead guilty when he learned that his codefendant was going to plead guilty: petitioner pleaded guilty "by reason of other matters and not by reason of the statute" or because of any acts of the trial judge. The court concluded that "the plea was voluntarily and knowingly made."

The Court of Appeals for the Tenth Circuit affirmed * * *. * * *

I

In *United States v. Jackson* [,390 U.S. 570 (1968)], the defendants were indicted under § 1201(a). The District Court dismissed the § 1201(a) count of the indictment, holding the statute unconstitutional because it permitted imposition of the death sentence only upon a jury's recommendation and thereby made the risk of death the price of a jury trial. This Court held the statute valid, except for the death penalty provision; with respect to the latter, the Court agreed with the trial court "that the death penalty provision ... imposes an impermissible burden upon the exercise of a constitutional right...." * * *

---

verdict of the jury shall so recommend, or (2) by imprisonment for any term of years or for life, if the death penalty is not imposed."

2. Eight days after petitioner pleaded guilty, he was brought before the court for sentencing. At that time, the court questioned petitioner for a second time about the voluntariness of his plea:

"THE COURT: ... Having read the presentence report and the statement you made to the probation officer, I want to be certain that you know what you are doing and you did know when you entered a plea of guilty the other day. Do you want to let that plea of guilty stand, or do you want to withdraw it and plead not guilty?

"DEFENDANT BRADY: I want to let that plea stand, sir.

"THE COURT: You understand that in doing that you are admitting and confessing the truth of the charge contained in the indictment and that you enter a plea of guilty voluntarily, without persuasion, coercion of any kind? Is that right?

"DEFENDANT BRADY: Yes, your Honor.

"THE COURT: And you do do that?

"DEFENDANT BRADY: Yes, I do.

"THE COURT: You plead guilty to the charge?

"DEFENDANT BRADY: Yes, I do."

Since the "inevitable effect" of the death penalty provision of § 1201(a) was said by the Court to be the needless encouragement of pleas of guilty and waivers of jury trial, Brady contends that *Jackson* requires the invalidation of every plea of guilty entered under that section, at least when the fear of death is shown to have been a factor in the plea. Petitioner, however, has read far too much into the *Jackson* opinion.

* * *

Plainly, it seems to us, *Jackson* ruled neither that all pleas of guilty encouraged by the fear of a possible death sentence are involuntary pleas nor that such encouraged pleas are invalid whether involuntary or not. *Jackson* prohibits the imposition of the death penalty under § 1201(a), but that decision neither fashioned a new standard for judging the validity of guilty pleas nor mandated a new application of the test theretofore fashioned by courts and since reiterated that guilty pleas are valid if both "voluntary" and "intelligent."

II

* * *

The voluntariness of Brady's plea can be determined only by considering all of the relevant circumstances surrounding it. One of these circumstances was the possibility of a heavier sentence following a guilty verdict after a trial. It may be that Brady, faced with a strong case against him and recognizing that his chances for acquittal were slight, preferred to plead guilty and thus limit the penalty to life imprisonment rather than to elect a jury trial which could result in a death penalty. But even if we assume that Brady would not have pleaded guilty except for the death penalty provision of § 1201(a), this assumption merely identifies the penalty provision as a "but for" cause of his plea. That the statute caused the plea in this sense does not necessarily prove that the plea was coerced and invalid as an involuntary act.

* * *

Of course, the agents of the State may not produce a plea by actual or threatened physical harm or by mental coercion overbearing the will of the defendant. But nothing of the sort is claimed in this case; nor is there evidence that Brady was so gripped by fear of the death penalty or hope of leniency that he did not or could not, with the help of counsel, rationally weigh the advantages of going to trial against the advantages of pleading guilty. Brady's claim is of a different sort: that it violates the Fifth Amendment to influence or encourage a guilty plea by opportunity or promise of leniency and that a guilty plea is coerced and invalid if influenced by the fear of a possibly higher penalty for the crime charged if a conviction is obtained after the State is put to its proof.

Insofar as the voluntariness of his plea is concerned, there is little to differentiate Brady from (1) the defendant, in a jurisdiction where the judge and jury have the same range of sentencing power, who pleads guilty because his lawyer advises him that the judge will very probably be more lenient than the jury; (2) the defendant, in a jurisdiction where the judge alone has sentencing power, who is advised by counsel that the judge is normally more lenient with defendants who plead guilty than with those who go to trial; (3) the defendant who is permitted by prosecutor and judge to plead guilty to a lesser offense included in the offense charged; and (4) the defendant who pleads guilty to certain counts with the understanding that other charges will be dropped. In each of these situations,[8] as in Brady's case, the defendant might never plead guilty absent the possibility or certainty that the plea will result in a lesser penalty than the sentence that could be imposed after a trial and a verdict of guilty. We decline to hold, however, that a guilty plea is compelled and invalid under the Fifth Amendment whenever motivated by the defendant's desire to accept the certainty or probability of a lesser penalty rather than face a wider range of possibilities extending from acquittal to conviction and a higher penalty authorized by law for the crime charged.

* * *

[W]e cannot hold that it is unconstitutional for the State to extend a benefit to a defendant who in turn extends a substantial benefit to the State and who demonstrates by his plea that he is ready and willing to admit his crime and to enter the correctional system in a frame of mind that affords hope for success in rehabilitation over a shorter period of time than might otherwise be necessary.

A contrary holding would require the States and Federal Government to forbid guilty pleas altogether, to provide a single invariable penalty for each crime defined by the statutes, or to place the sentencing function in a separate authority having no knowledge of the manner in which the conviction in each case was obtained. In any event, it would be necessary to forbid prosecutors and judges to accept guilty pleas to selected counts, to lesser included offenses, or to reduced charges. The Fifth Amendment does not reach so far.

* * *

* * * Brady first pleaded not guilty; prior to changing his plea to guilty he was subjected to no threats or promises in face-to-face encounters with the authorities. He had competent counsel and full opportunity to assess the advantages and disadvantages of a trial as compared with those attending a plea of guilty; there was no hazard of an impulsive and improvident response to a seeming but unreal advantage. His plea of guilty was entered in open court and before a judge obviously sensitive to the requirements of the law with respect to guilty pleas. Brady's plea * * * was voluntary.

---

8. We here make no reference to the situation where the prosecutor or judge, or both, deliberately employ their charging and sentencing powers to induce a particular defendant to tender a plea of guilty. In Brady's case there is no claim that the prosecutor threatened prosecution on a charge not justified by the evidence or that the trial judge threatened Brady with a harsher sentence if convicted after trial in order to induce him to plead guilty.

The standard as to the voluntariness of guilty pleas must be essentially that defined by Judge Tuttle of the Court of Appeals for the Fifth Circuit:

> " '[A] plea of guilty entered by one fully aware of the direct consequences, including the actual value of any commitments made to him by the court, prosecutor, or his own counsel, must stand unless induced by threats (or promises to discontinue improper harassment), misrepresentation (including unfulfilled or unfulfillable promises), or perhaps by promises that are by their nature improper as having no proper relationship to the prosecutor's business (e.g. bribes).' 242 F.2d at page 115."

Under this standard, a plea of guilty is not invalid merely because entered to avoid the possibility of a death penalty.

III

The record before us also supports the conclusion that Brady's plea was intelligently made. He was advised by competent counsel, he was made aware of the nature of the charge against him, and there was nothing to indicate that he was incompetent or otherwise not in control of his mental faculties; once his confederate had pleaded guilty and became available to testify, he chose to plead guilty, perhaps to ensure that he would face no more than life imprisonment or a term of years. Brady was aware of precisely what he was doing when he admitted that he had kidnapped the victim and had not released her unharmed.

It is true that Brady's counsel advised him that § 1201(a) empowered the jury to impose the death penalty and that nine years later in *United States v. Jackson,* the Court held that the jury had no such power as long as the judge could impose only a lesser penalty if trial was to the court or there was a plea of guilty. But these facts do not require us to set aside Brady's conviction.

Often the decision to plead guilty is heavily influenced by the defendant's appraisal of the prosecution's case against him and by the apparent likelihood of securing leniency should a guilty plea be offered and accepted. Considerations like these frequently present imponderable questions for which there are no certain answers; judgments may be made that in the light of later events seem improvident, although they were perfectly sensible at the time. The rule that a plea must be intelligently made to be valid does not require that a plea be vulnerable to later attack if the defendant did not correctly assess every relevant factor entering into his decision. A defendant is not entitled to withdraw his plea merely because he discovers long after the plea has been accepted that his calculus misapprehended the quality of the State's case or the likely penalties attached to alternative courses of action. More particularly, absent misrepresentation or other impermissible conduct by state agents, a voluntary plea of guilty intelligently made in the light of the then applicable law does not become vulnerable because later judicial decisions indicate that the plea rested on a faulty premise. A plea of guilty triggered by the expectations of a competently counseled defendant that the State will have a strong case against him is not subject to later attack because the defendant's lawyer correctly advised him with respect to the then existing law as to possible penalties but later pronouncements of the courts, as in this case, hold that the maximum penalty for the crime in question was less than was reasonably assumed at the time the plea was entered.

The fact that Brady did not anticipate *United States v. Jackson* does not impugn the truth or reliability of his plea. We find no requirement in the Constitution that a defendant must be permitted to disown his solemn admissions in open court that he committed the act with which he is charged simply because it later develops that the State would have had a weaker case than the defendant had thought or that the maximum penalty then assumed applicable has been held inapplicable in subsequent judicial decisions.

This is not to say that guilty plea convictions hold no hazards for the innocent or that the methods of taking guilty pleas presently employed in this country are necessarily valid in all respects. This mode of conviction is no more foolproof than full trials to the court or to the jury. * * * We would have serious doubts about this case if the encouragement of guilty pleas by offers of leniency substantially increased the likelihood that defendants, advised by competent counsel, would falsely condemn themselves. But our view is to the contrary and is based on our expectations that courts will satisfy themselves that pleas of guilty are voluntarily and intelligently made by competent defendants with adequate advice of counsel and that there is nothing to question the accuracy and reliability of the defendants' admissions that they committed the crimes with which they are charged. In the case before us, nothing in the record impeaches Brady's plea or suggests that his admissions in open court were anything but the truth.

Although Brady's plea of guilty may well have been motivated in part by a desire to avoid a possible death penalty, we are convinced that his plea was voluntarily and intelligently made and we have no reason to doubt that his solemn admission of guilt was truthful.

MR. JUSTICE BRENNAN, with whom MR. JUSTICE DOUGLAS and MR. JUSTICE MARSHALL join, concurring in the result.

* * *

An independent examination of the record in the instant case convinces me that the conclusions of the lower courts are not clearly erroneous. Although Brady was aware that he faced a possible death sentence, there is no evidence that this factor alone played a significant role in his decision to enter a guilty plea. Rather, there is considerable evidence, which the District Court credited, that Brady's plea was triggered by the confession and plea decision of his codefendant and not by any substantial fear of the death penalty. * * * Furthermore, Brady's plea was accepted by a trial judge who manifested some sensitivity to the seriousness of a guilty plea and questioned Brady at length concerning his guilt and the voluntariness of the plea before it was finally accepted.

In view of the foregoing, I concur in the result reached by the Court in the *Brady* case.

QUESTIONS AND POINTS FOR DISCUSSION

1. In McMann v. Richardson, 397 U.S. 759, 90 S.Ct. 1441 (1970), several defendants claimed that the constitutional requirement that their guilty pleas be "intelligent" was not satisfied because their attorneys had failed to recognize that their confessions were involuntary and could not have been introduced in evidence had they gone to trial. The Supreme Court rejected this argument for the reasons set forth below:

> That a guilty plea must be intelligently made is not a requirement that all advice offered by the defendant's lawyer withstand retrospective examination in a post-conviction hearing. Courts continue to have serious differences among themselves on the admissibility of evidence, both with respect to the proper standard by which the facts are to be judged and with respect to the application of that standard to particular facts. That this Court might hold a defendant's confession inadmissible in evidence, possibly by a divided vote, hardly justifies a conclusion that the defendant's attorney was incompetent or ineffective when he thought the admissibility of the confession sufficiently probable to advise a plea of guilty.

> In our view a defendant's plea of guilty based on reasonably competent advice is an intelligent plea not open to attack on the ground that counsel may have misjudged the admissibility of the defendant's confession. Whether a plea of guilty is unintelligent and therefore vulnerable when motivated by a confession erroneously thought admissible in evidence depends as an initial matter, not on whether a court would retrospectively consider counsel's advice to be right or wrong, but on whether that advice was within the range of competence demanded of attorneys in criminal cases.

Id. at 770–71, 90 S.Ct. at 1448–49. For an overview of the information of which a defense attorney should be aware and the steps the attorney should take to effectively represent a defendant who wishes to plead guilty or enter into plea negotiations, see 2 David Rossman, Criminal Law Advocacy (2007).

2. In Hill v. Lockhart, 474 U.S. 52, 106 S.Ct. 366 (1985), the Supreme Court expanded upon its holding in *McMann v. Richardson*, ruling that even if an attorney's advice given to a defendant deciding whether to plead guilty is palpably deficient, the defendant's guilty plea is not necessarily invalid. The Court in *Hill* held that a two-part test previously adopted by the Court in Strickland v. Washington, 466 U.S. 668, 104 S.Ct. 2052 (1984) should be applied when determining whether a defendant received ineffective assistance of counsel during the plea process, rendering the guilty plea invalid. Under the first part of this test, a defendant must establish that the attorney acted unreasonably under "prevailing professional norms" when advising the defen-

dant and acting on his or her behalf. Id. at 688, 104 S.Ct. at 2065. To satisfy this part of the test, the defendant must rebut a "strong presumption" that the attorney acted within "the wide range of reasonable professional assistance." Id. at 689, 104 S.Ct. at 2065. Even if the attorney acted unreasonably, however, the defendant must still establish that he or she was prejudiced by counsel's deficient performance. In the plea context, this means that the defendant must demonstrate that there is a "reasonable probability" that had the attorney rendered reasonable professional assistance, the defendant would not have pled guilty and would instead have gone to trial. *Hill,* 474 U.S. at 59, 106 S.Ct. at 370.

In *Hill* itself, the defendant alleged that he had received ineffective assistance of counsel, in violation of his Sixth Amendment right to counsel, when he decided to plead guilty after his attorney apprised him that he would have to serve only one-third of his sentence before becoming eligible for parole. He later learned that he would actually have to serve one-half of his sentence before becoming eligible for parole. The Supreme Court held that the defendant had failed to establish that he had received ineffective assistance of counsel; he had not satisfied the second prong of the *Strickland* test because he had failed to allege that he would have gone to trial had he received accurate advice about his eligibility for parole.

By contrast, in Meyers v. Gillis, 142 F.3d 664, 667–70 (3d Cir.1998), the Third Circuit Court of Appeals held that the defendant had received ineffective assistance of counsel, thereby invalidating his guilty plea, when counsel had erroneously apprised the defendant that he would be eligible for parole if he pleaded guilty to second-degree murder. In *Meyers,* unlike *Hill,* the defendant had asserted, in testimony that the district court found credible, that he would not have pleaded guilty if his attorney had accurately apprised him that his plea would subject him to a life sentence without the possibility of parole.

3. Consider again the facts of State v. Ramirez, 636 N.W.2d 740 (Iowa 2001) recounted in note 3 on page 38. Should an attorney's failure to advise a client of the deportation consequences of entering a guilty plea be considered the ineffective assistance of counsel that requires the vacating of the guilty plea if the defendant was prejudiced by this failure?

The courts are divided on this question. Most have held that defense attorneys have no duty to apprise their clients of the collateral consequences of a conviction, including deportation. See, e.g., Santos–Sanchez v. U.S., 548 F.3d 327, 334–36 (5th Cir. 2008). Some of these courts have subscribed to this general rule but carved out an exception when counsel affirmatively misrepresents the impact of a guilty plea on the defendant's immigration status. See Rubio v. State, 194 P.3d 1224, 1230–31 (Nev. 2008) (listing cases); United States v. Couto, 311 F.3d 179, 188 (2d Cir. 2002) (attorney told the defendant there were steps she could take to avoid deportation when, in fact, she faced automatic and mandatory deportation if she pled guilty). Finally, some courts have held that lack of advice, not just misadvice, about the deportation consequences of a guilty plea satisfies the first prong of the *Strickland* test. See, e.g., State v. Paredez, 101 P.3d 799, 804–05 (N.M. 2004) (attorneys render deficient performance if they fail to ascertain a client's immigration status or to inform the client of the "specific immigration consequences" of a guilty plea, including whether deportation is "virtually certain"). For information about the immigration consequences of criminal convictions, see Robert James McWhirter, The Criminal Lawyer's Guide to Immigration Law: Questions and Answers (2d ed. 2006).

4. In Roe v. Flores–Ortega, 528 U.S. 470, 120 S.Ct. 1029 (2000), the Supreme Court considered when a defense attorney's failure to file a notice of appeal following the entry of a guilty plea constitutes ineffective assistance of counsel. The Court noted that the threshold query was whether the defense attorney had consulted with the defendant about taking an appeal, apprising the defendant of the advantages and disadvantages of appealing and then determining whether the defendant wanted to do so. If this consultation had occurred and the defendant had asked the attorney to file an appeal, the failure to do so constituted unconstitutional ineffectiveness. On the other hand, if the defendant had indicated, after this consultation, that he did not want to pursue an appeal, the failure to file a notice of appeal did not abridge the defendant's Sixth Amendment right to the effective assistance of counsel.

The Supreme Court then turned to the specific question before it: Did a defense attorney who failed to even consult with a defendant about taking an appeal render unreasonable professional assistance, thereby satisfying the first prong of the *Strickland* test for constitutional ineffectiveness? In answering that question, the Court acknowledged that in the "vast majority of cases," an attorney's failure to consult with his or her client about the prospect of taking an appeal would be professionally unreasonable. Id. at 481, 120 S.Ct. at 1037. But the Court refused to hold that such a failure should be considered deficient performance in all circumstances, instead requiring that courts engage in a "circumstance-specific reasonableness inquiry":

> We cannot say, as a *constitutional* matter, that in every case counsel's failure to consult with the defendant about an appeal is necessarily unreasonable, and therefore deficient. Such a holding would be inconsistent with both our decision in *Strickland* and common sense. For example, suppose that a defendant consults with counsel; counsel advises the defendant that a guilty plea probably will lead to a 2 year sentence; the defendant expresses satisfaction and pleads guilty; the court sentences the defendant to 2 years' imprisonment as expected and informs the defendant of his appeal rights; the defendant does not express any interest in appealing, and counsel concludes that there are no nonfrivolous grounds for appeal. Under these circumstances, it would be difficult to say that counsel is "professionally unreasonable," as a constitutional matter, in not consulting with such a defendant regarding an appeal. Or, for example, suppose a sentencing court's instructions to a defendant about his appeal rights in a particular case are so clear and informative as to substitute for counsel's duty to consult. In some cases, counsel might then reasonably decide that he need not repeat that information. We therefore reject a bright-line rule that counsel must always consult with the defendant regarding an appeal.

> We instead hold that counsel has a constitutionally-imposed duty to consult with the defendant about an appeal when there is reason to think

either (1) that a rational defendant would want to appeal (for example, because there are nonfrivolous grounds for appeal), or (2) that this particular defendant reasonably demonstrated to counsel that he was interested in appealing. In making this determination, courts must take into account all the information counsel knew or should have known. Although not determinative, a highly relevant factor in this inquiry will be whether the conviction follows a trial or a guilty plea, both because a guilty plea reduces the scope of potentially appealable issues and because such a plea may indicate that the defendant seeks an end to judicial proceedings. Even in cases when the defendant pleads guilty, the court must consider such factors as whether the defendant received the sentence bargained for as part of the plea and whether the plea expressly reserved or waived some or all appeal rights. Only by considering all relevant factors in a given case can a court properly determine whether a rational defendant would have desired an appeal or that the particular defendant sufficiently demonstrated to counsel an interest in an appeal.

Id. at 479–80, 120 S.Ct. at 1036.

The Supreme Court underscored that a finding that counsel's failure to consult with the defendant about an appeal was unreasonable does not necessarily mean that the defendant's right to the effective assistance of counsel was violated, entitling the defendant to now take an appeal. To prevail on the ineffectiveness claim, the defendant also has to establish that there is a "reasonable probability" that an appeal would have been timely filed had that consultation occurred. Id. at 484, 120 S.Ct. at 1038. Two particularly relevant factors to consider when determining whether the defendant has met this burden are whether the defendant had nonfrivolous grounds for appealing and whether the defendant had "promptly" expressed an interest in filing an appeal. Id. at 485, 120 S.Ct. at 1039.

The Supreme Court emphasized that while the defendant's showing that there were nonfrivolous grounds for an appeal would give credence to the argument that an appeal would have been filed had the attorney properly consulted with the defendant, a defendant does not have to demonstrate that he or she would have prevailed on the appeal to successfully assert a claim of ineffective assistance of counsel. The Court noted that it would be "unfair" to require a defendant, often proceeding without the assistance of counsel, to identify the claims that would have been asserted on appeal and to prove their legal merit. Id. at 486, 120 S.Ct. at 1040.

5. Tollett v. Henderson, 411 U.S. 258, 93 S.Ct. 1602 (1973) involved a defendant who sought to set aside his plea of guilty to murder on the grounds that African Americans unconstitutionally had been excluded from the grand jury that had indicted him. The defendant contended that his guilty plea was not rendered intelligently because he was unaware when he pled guilty of the constitutional infirmity in the grand-jury selection procedures.

The Supreme Court concluded that the principles set forth in earlier Supreme Court cases, including *McMann v. Richardson*, foreclosed the defendant's claim that his lack of knowledge of the constitutional violation was enough to automatically invalidate his guilty plea:

[A] guilty plea represents a break in the chain of events which has preceded it in the criminal process. When a criminal defendant has solemnly admitted in open court that he is in fact guilty of the offense with which he is charged, he may not thereafter raise independent claims relating to the deprivation of constitutional rights that occurred prior to the entry of the guilty plea. He may only attack the voluntary and intelligent character of the guilty plea by showing that the advice he received from counsel was not within the standards set forth in *McMann.*

A guilty plea, voluntarily and intelligently entered, may not be vacated because the defendant was not advised of every conceivable constitutional plea in abatement he might have to the charge, no matter how peripheral such a plea might be to the normal focus of counsel's inquiry.

Id. at 267, 93 S.Ct. at 1608. The Court then remanded the case for consideration of the question whether the defendant's guilty plea was invalid because of his attorney's failure to apprise him of the unconstitutionality of the methods through which the grand jury had been selected.

The Supreme Court distinguished its decision in *Tollett* in the succeeding case of Menna v. New York, 423 U.S. 61, 96 S.Ct. 241 (1975) (per curiam). In that case, the defendant was held in criminal contempt of court and sentenced to thirty days in jail after he refused to answer questions posed by a grand jury. He also was indicted for his refusal to cooperate with the grand jury. After unsuccessfully moving to dismiss the indictment on double-jeopardy grounds, the defendant pled guilty to the indictment, but then appealed, claiming his conviction was barred by the Double Jeopardy Clause in the Fifth Amendment. The state responded that the defendant had waived this claim by pleading guilty.

The Supreme Court sided with the defendant, holding that "[w]here the State is precluded by the United States Constitution from haling a defendant into court on a charge, federal law requires that a conviction on that charge be set aside even if the conviction was entered pursuant to a counseled plea of guilty." Id. at 62, 96 S.Ct. at 242. In a footnote, the Court explained the distinction between the case before it and *Tollett*:

Neither *Tollett v. Henderson* nor our earlier cases on which it relied, e.g., *Brady v. United States* and *McMann v. Richardson,* stand for the proposition that counseled guilty pleas inevitably "waive" all antecedent constitutional violations. * * * The point of these cases is that a counseled plea of guilty is an admission of factual guilt so reliable that, where voluntary and intelligent, it *quite validly* removes the issue of factual guilt from the case. In most cases, factual guilt is a sufficient basis for the State's imposition of punishment. A guilty plea, therefore, simply renders irrelevant those constitutional violations not logically inconsistent with the valid establishment of factual guilt and which do not stand in the way of conviction, if factual guilt is validly established. Here, however, the claim is that the State may not convict petitioner no matter how validly his factual guilt is established. The guilty plea, therefore, does not bar the claim.

> We do not hold that a double jeopardy claim may never be waived. We simply hold that a plea of guilty to a charge does not waive a claim that—judged on its face—the charge is one which the State may not constitutionally prosecute.

Id. at 62–63 n. 2, 96 S.Ct. at 242 n. 2.

In United States v. Broce, 488 U.S. 563, 109 S.Ct. 757 (1989), the Supreme Court confirmed that not all double-jeopardy claims can be asserted by a defendant following entry of a guilty plea. The defendants in that case had pled guilty to two counts of conspiracy. They later sought to vacate their sentence on one of the two counts on the grounds that they had really participated in only one overarching conspiracy and that to punish them for two contravened the Double Jeopardy Clause.

The Supreme Court responded by invoking the general rule that collateral attacks on guilty pleas are barred. The exception to that rule discussed in *Menna v. New York* was inapplicable here, according to the Court, because that exception was limited to those instances where "on the face of the record the court had no power to enter the conviction or impose the sentence." Id. at 569, 109 S.Ct. at 762. Since a reviewing court would have to go beyond the record to determine whether the defendants had been involved in one or two conspiracies and since the defendants did not allege that they had received ineffective assistance of counsel, their guilty pleas to, and sentences for, two separate conspiracies would remain in effect.

Do you agree with the Supreme Court's decisions in *McMann, Tollett, Menna,* and *Broce*? Under what circumstances should a defendant be able to get a guilty plea set aside because of a constitutional violation? Can and should a defendant be able to challenge a guilty plea on the grounds that the defendant's right to a speedy trial was violated? See United States v. Pierre, 120 F.3d 1153, 1155 (11th Cir.1997) (speedy-trial claim involves a nonjurisdictional defect in the court's proceedings and can therefore only be preserved through entry of a conditional guilty plea reserving the right to assert the claim on appeal).

6. Defendants who go to trial have a constitutional right, grounded in due process, to be informed by the prosecutor of any material evidence that points to the defendant's innocence or would mitigate the defendant's punishment. Brady v. Maryland, 373 U.S. 83, 87, 83 S.Ct. 1194, 1197 (1963). This right to be apprised of exculpatory evidence before trial includes certain impeachment evidence—evidence that discredits the credibility of a prosecution witness. Giglio v. United States, 405 U.S. 150, 154, 92 S.Ct. 763, 766 (1972). In United States v. Ruiz, 536 U.S. 622, 122 S.Ct. 2450 (2002), the Supreme Court considered whether the refusal to disclose impeachment evidence or evidence supporting an affirmative defense to a defendant invalidates a guilty plea. The Court rejected the defendant's claim that the withholding of such exculpatory information renders a guilty plea involuntary. While the Court acknowledged that the disclosure of this information would make the defendant's plea decision "wiser," it emphasized that "the Constitution does not require the prosecutor to share all useful information with the defendant." Id. at 629, 122 S.Ct. at 2455. The Court also cited the adverse consequences that might ensue from the disclosure of the exculpatory evi-

dence in question: the revelation of informants' identities might interfere with ongoing criminal investigations and jeopardize witnesses' safety. In addition, requiring the government to ferret out impeachment evidence and evidence supporting affirmative defenses would place a burden on the government, substantially diminishing one of plea bargaining's principal advantages—the conservation of government resources.

The Supreme Court in *Ruiz* did not resolve whether the failure to disclose other kinds of *Brady* material, such as the fact that someone else had admitted committing the crime or that DNA evidence pointed to someone else's guilt, invalidates a guilty plea. How would you resolve this question and why? See McCann v. Mangialardi, 337 F.3d 782, 787–88 (7th Cir. 2003) (explaining why it is "highly likely" the Supreme Court would hold that due process requires the government to reveal to a defendant evidence of factual innocence of which it is aware before the defendant enters a guilty plea).

7. Although a defendant may not have a constitutional right to assert certain constitutional claims following the entry of a guilty plea, a state retains the prerogative to permit a defendant to later assert these claims on appeal. See, e.g., N.Y.Crim.Proc.Law § 710.70(2) (defendant who has pled guilty can still challenge denial of a motion to suppress evidence on appeal). In addition, many jurisdictions allow a defendant to enter a conditional guilty plea, preserving the right to appeal an adverse ruling of the trial court and then withdraw the guilty plea if the ruling is reversed on appeal. See, e.g., Rule 11(a)(2) of the Federal Rules of Criminal Procedure, on page 40, which allows for the entry of such a conditional plea provided that both the court and the prosecutor consent.

B. BREACHES OF PLEA AGREEMENTS

SANTOBELLO v. NEW YORK

Supreme Court of the United States, 1971.
404 U.S. 257, 92 S.Ct. 495, 30 L.Ed.2d 427.

MR. CHIEF JUSTICE BURGER delivered the opinion of the Court.

We granted certiorari in this case to determine whether the State's failure to keep a commitment concerning the sentence recommendation on a guilty plea required a new trial.

The facts are not in dispute. The State of New York indicted petitioner in 1969 on two felony counts, Promoting Gambling in the First Degree, and Possession of Gambling Records in the First Degree. Petitioner first entered a plea of not guilty to both counts. After negotiations, the Assistant District Attorney in charge of the case agreed to permit petitioner to plead guilty to a lesser-included offense, Possession of Gambling Records in the Second Degree, conviction of which would carry a maximum prison sentence of one year. The prosecutor agreed to make no recommendation as to the sentence.

On June 16, 1969, petitioner accordingly withdrew his plea of not guilty and entered a plea of guilty to the lesser charge. * * * The court accepted the plea and set a date for sentencing. * * *

* * *

At this appearance, another prosecutor had replaced the prosecutor who had negotiated the plea. The new prosecutor recommended the maximum one-year sentence. In making this recommendation, he cited petitioner's criminal record and alleged links with organized crime. Defense counsel immediately objected on the ground that the State had promised petitioner before the plea was entered that there would be no sentence recommendation by the prosecution. He sought to adjourn the sentence hearing in order to have time to prepare proof of the first prosecutor's promise. The second prosecutor, apparently ignorant of his colleague's commitment, argued that there was nothing in the record to support petitioner's claim of a promise, but the State, in subsequent proceedings, has not contested that such a promise was made.

The sentencing judge ended discussion, with the following statement, quoting extensively from the presentence report:

"Mr. Aronstein [Defense Counsel], I am not at all influenced by what the District Attorney says, so that there is no need to adjourn the sentence, and there is no need to have any testimony. It doesn't make a particle of difference what the District Attorney says he will do, or what he doesn't do.

"I have here, Mr. Aronstein, a probation report. I have here a history of a long, long serious criminal record. I have here a picture of the life history of this man. . . .

" 'He is unamenable to supervision in the community. He is a professional criminal.' This is in quotes. 'And a recidivist. Institutionalization?'; that means, in plain language, just putting him away, 'is the only means of halting his anti-social activities,' and protecting you, your family, me, my family, protecting society. 'Institutionalization.' Plain language, put him behind bars.

"Under the plea, I can only send him to the New York City Correctional Institution for men for one year, which I am hereby doing."

The judge then imposed the maximum sentence of one year.

[The petitioner's conviction was affirmed on appeal, and the Supreme Court then granted the petition for certiorari.]

Disposition of charges after plea discussions is not only an essential part of the process but a highly desirable part for many reasons. It leads to prompt and largely final disposition of most criminal cases; it avoids much of the corrosive impact of enforced idleness during pretrial confinement for those who are denied release pending trial; it protects the public from those accused persons who are prone to continue criminal conduct even while on pretrial release; and, by shortening the time between charge and disposition, it enhances whatever may be the rehabilitative prospects of the guilty when they are ultimately imprisoned.

However, all of these considerations presuppose fairness in securing agreement between an accused and a prosecutor. * * *

This phase of the process of criminal justice, and the adjudicative element inherent in accepting a plea of guilty, must be attended by safeguards to insure the defendant what is reasonably due in the circumstances. Those circumstances will vary, but a constant factor is that when a plea rests in any significant degree on a promise or agreement of the prosecutor, so that it can be said to be part of the inducement or consideration, such promise must be fulfilled.

On this record, petitioner "bargained" and negotiated for a particular plea in order to secure dismissal of more serious charges, but also on condition that no sentence recommendation would be made by the prosecutor. It is now conceded that the promise to abstain from a recommendation was made, and at this stage the prosecution is not in a good position to argue that its inadvertent breach of agreement is immaterial. The staff lawyers in a prosecutor's office have the burden of "letting the left hand know what the right hand is doing" or has done. That the breach of agreement was inadvertent does not lessen its impact.

We need not reach the question whether the sentencing judge would or would not have been influenced had he known all the details of the negotiations for the plea. He stated that the prosecutor's recommendation did not influence him and we have no reason to doubt that. Nevertheless, we conclude that the interests of justice and appropriate recognition of the duties of the prosecution in relation to promises made in the negotiation of pleas of guilty will be best served by remanding the case to the state courts for further consideration. The ultimate relief to which petitioner is entitled we leave to the discretion of the state court, which is in a better position to decide whether the circumstances of this case require only that there be specific performance of the agreement on the plea, in which case petitioner should be resentenced by a different judge, or whether, in the view of the state court, the circumstances require granting the relief sought by petitioner, *i.e.,* the opportunity to withdraw his plea of guilty.[2]
* * *

* * *

Mr. Justice Douglas, concurring.

* * *

I join the opinion of the Court and favor a constitutional rule for this as well as for other pending or oncoming cases. Where the "plea bargain" is not kept by the prosecutor, the sentence must be vacated and the state court will decide in light of the circumstances of each case whether due

---

2. If the state court decides to allow withdrawal of the plea, the petitioner will, of course, plead anew to the original charge on two felony counts.

process requires (a) that there be specific performance of the plea bargain or (b) that the defendant be given the option to go to trial on the original charges. One alternative may do justice in one case, and the other in a different case. In choosing a remedy, however, a court ought to accord a defendant's preference considerable, if not controlling, weight inasmuch as the fundamental rights flouted by a prosecutor's breach of a plea bargain are those of the defendant, not of the State.

MR. JUSTICE MARSHALL, with whom MR. JUSTICE BRENNAN and MR. JUSTICE STEWART join, concurring in part and dissenting in part.

I agree with much of the majority's opinion, but conclude that petitioner must be permitted to withdraw his guilty plea. This is the relief petitioner requested, and, on the facts set out by the majority, it is a form of relief to which he is entitled.

* * *

QUESTIONS AND POINTS FOR DISCUSSION

1. While the prosecutor in *Santobello* had agreed as part of the plea bargain to refrain from making a sentencing recommendation, prosecutors often agree to make a particular sentencing recommendation as part of a plea agreement. In United States v. Benchimol, 471 U.S. 453, 105 S.Ct. 2103 (1985), for example, the parties had agreed that the prosecutor would recommend probation in return for the defendant's guilty plea. The court nonetheless sentenced the defendant to prison for six years.

The defendant later moved to vacate his guilty plea or to be resentenced because the prosecutor, according to the defendant, had not enthusiastically recommended a sentence of probation to the court at the sentencing hearing and had not explained the government's reasons for recommending probation. The Supreme Court held that a defendant may bargain for a commitment by the prosecutor to enthusiastically make a particular recommendation to the court or to explain the reasons for the government's recommendation. No such agreements were made between the parties in this case, however, and the Court refused to imply such terms into their agreement.

2. Assume that a defendant, who was charged with first-degree murder, entered into a plea agreement under which he agreed to plead guilty to second-degree murder in return for the prosecutor's promise not to recommend a life sentence. At the defendant's sentencing hearing, the prosecutor recommended a prison sentence of seventy to one hundred years, and the court sentenced the defendant to prison for thirty-five to fifty-five years. Did the prosecutor breach the plea agreement in violation of due process? See Smith v. Stegall, 385 F.3d 993 (2004).

3. The Supreme Court distinguished *Santobello* in Mabry v. Johnson, 467 U.S. 504, 104 S.Ct. 2543 (1984). In *Mabry,* the defendant, who was already serving concurrent sentences of twenty-one and twelve years for burglary and assault, was facing a murder charge. The prosecutor offered to recommend a twenty-one-year sentence, to be served concurrently with the defendant's other sentences, if he agreed to plead guilty to being an accessory

after a felony murder. The defendant's attorney then called the prosecutor, accepting the offer. The prosecutor, however, said that he had made a mistake in making the offer to the defendant and retracted the offer. The prosecutor instead offered to recommend a twenty-one-year sentence, to be served consecutively with the defendant's other sentences, if he pled guilty. The defendant eventually accepted this offer and received a twenty-one-year consecutive sentence.

The defendant then filed a habeas corpus petition, contending that his due-process rights were violated when the prosecutor refused to abide by the terms of his original plea offer. The Supreme Court unanimously disagreed. Noting that at the time the defendant pled guilty he knew fully well that the prosecutor would recommend a consecutive sentence, the Court concluded that the defendant's plea simply was not induced by the prosecutor's original plea offer. Consequently, the original plea offer, even though "accepted" by the defendant, was "without constitutional significance." Id. at 510, 104 S.Ct. at 2548.

4.   Plea agreements may be breached, of course, not only by prosecutors, but by defendants. The Supreme Court case of Ricketts v. Adamson, 483 U.S. 1, 107 S.Ct. 2680 (1987) reveals the potentially severe consequences that can ensue from such a breach by a defendant. That case involved a defendant who was charged with first-degree murder. The prosecutor and the defendant entered into a plea agreement under which the defendant agreed to plead guilty to second-degree murder and to testify "when requested" against two other people involved in the murder. In return, the defendant would receive a prison sentence of forty-eight to forty-nine years. The trial court accepted this plea agreement.

The defendant then testified in the trials of his two codefendants, as he had agreed to do, and they were convicted of first-degree murder. Their convictions, however, were reversed on appeal and their cases remanded for retrial. At this point, the defendant, believing that he had fulfilled the terms of the plea agreement, balked at testifying again on the government's behalf unless the government agreed to release him from prison after the retrials. The state informed the defendant that he was in breach of the plea agreement and once again charged him with first-degree murder. Following a trial, the defendant was convicted of first-degree murder and sentenced to death.

The defendant contended that his right not to be subjected to double jeopardy barred his prosecution for first-degree murder, but the Supreme Court held that the terms of the plea agreement foreclosed that claim. The agreement specifically provided that " '[s]hould the defendant refuse to testify or should he at any time testify untruthfully * * * then this entire agreement is null and void and the original charge will be automatically reinstated.' " Id. at 4, 107 S.Ct. at 2682. According to the Court, when the defendant decided to unilaterally pursue his own interpretation of the meaning of the plea agreement, he assumed the risk that he would be found in breach of the agreement and subject to a first-degree murder prosecution. Even if he had acted in good faith, the defendant had taken a calculated gamble, exposing himself to the risk of a death sentence. Id. at 10–11, 107 S.Ct. at 2686.

The defendant, in the end, did not lose his life as the price for his miscalculation. On remand from the Supreme Court, the Ninth Circuit Court of Appeals reversed the defendant's conviction for other reasons. Adamson v. Ricketts, 865 F.2d 1011, 1017–19 (9th Cir.1988). The prosecutor and the defendant then eventually agreed to reinstate the original plea agreement requiring the defendant to testify against his two codefendants. State v. Dunlap, 930 P.2d 518, 525 (Ariz.Ct.App.1996).

C. CONSTRAINTS ON THE GOVERNMENT IN OFFERING INCENTIVES TO PLEAD GUILTY

BORDENKIRCHER v. HAYES

Supreme Court of the United States, 1978.
434 U.S. 357, 98 S.Ct. 663, 54 L.Ed.2d 604.

MR. JUSTICE STEWART delivered the opinion of the Court.

The question in this case is whether the Due Process Clause of the Fourteenth Amendment is violated when a state prosecutor carries out a threat made during plea negotiations to reindict the accused on more serious charges if he does not plead guilty to the offense with which he was originally charged.

The respondent, Paul Lewis Hayes, was indicted by a Fayette County, Ky., grand jury on a charge of uttering a forged instrument in the amount of $88.30, an offense then punishable by a term of 2 to 10 years in prison. After arraignment, Hayes, his retained counsel, and the Commonwealth's Attorney met in the presence of the Clerk of the Court to discuss a possible plea agreement. During these conferences the prosecutor offered to recommend a sentence of five years in prison if Hayes would plead guilty to the indictment. He also said that if Hayes did not plead guilty and "save the court the inconvenience and necessity of a trial," he would return to the grand jury to seek an indictment under the Kentucky Habitual Criminal Act, which would subject Hayes to a mandatory sentence of life imprisonment by reason of his two prior felony convictions. Hayes chose not to plead guilty, and the prosecutor did obtain an indictment charging him under the Habitual Criminal Act. It is not disputed that the recidivist charge was fully justified by the evidence, that the prosecutor was in possession of this evidence at the time of the original indictment, and that Hayes' refusal to plead guilty to the original charge was what led to his indictment under the habitual criminal statute.

A jury found Hayes guilty on the principal charge of uttering a forged instrument and, in a separate proceeding, further found that he had twice before been convicted of felonies. As required by the habitual offender statute, he was sentenced to a life term in the penitentiary. * * *

[On appeal, the Kentucky Court of Appeals rejected Hayes's argument that his enhanced sentence was unconstitutional, as did the federal district court to which Hayes later applied for a writ of habeas corpus. The Sixth Circuit Court of Appeals, however, reversed the district court's judgment.]

It may be helpful to clarify at the outset the nature of the issue in this case. While the prosecutor did not actually obtain the recidivist indictment until after the plea conferences had ended, his intention to do so was clearly expressed at the outset of the plea negotiations. Hayes was thus fully informed of the true terms of the offer when he made his decision to plead not guilty. This is not a situation, therefore, where the prosecutor without notice brought an additional and more serious charge after plea negotiations relating only to the original indictment had ended with the defendant's insistence on pleading not guilty. As a practical matter, in short, this case would be no different if the grand jury had indicted Hayes as a recidivist from the outset, and the prosecutor had offered to drop that charge as part of the plea bargain.

The Court of Appeals nonetheless drew a distinction between "concessions relating to prosecution under an existing indictment," and threats to bring more severe charges not contained in the original indictment—a line it thought necessary in order to establish a prophylactic rule to guard against the evil of prosecutorial vindictiveness.[6] Quite apart from this chronological distinction, however, the Court of Appeals found that the prosecutor had acted vindictively in the present case since he had conceded that the indictment was influenced by his desire to induce a guilty plea. The ultimate conclusion of the Court of Appeals thus seems to have been that a prosecutor acts vindictively and in violation of due process of law whenever his charging decision is influenced by what he hopes to gain in the course of plea bargaining negotiations.

* * *

This Court held in *North Carolina v. Pearce,* 395 U.S. 711, 725, that the Due Process Clause of the Fourteenth Amendment "requires that vindictiveness against a defendant for having successfully attacked his first conviction must play no part in the sentence he receives after a new trial."[a] The same principle was later applied to prohibit a prosecutor from reindicting a convicted misdemeanant on a felony charge after the defen-

---

6. "Although a prosecutor may in the course of plea negotiations offer a defendant concessions relating to prosecution under an existing indictment . . . he may not threaten a defendant with the consequence that more severe charges may be brought if he insists on going to trial. When a prosecutor obtains an indictment less severe than the facts known to him at the time might permit, he makes a discretionary determination that the interests of the state are served by not seeking more serious charges. . . . Accordingly, if after plea negotiations fail, he then procures an indictment charging a more serious crime, a strong inference is created that the only reason for the more serious charges is vindictiveness. Under these circumstances, the prosecutor should be required to justify his action." 547 F.2d, at 44–45.

a. In *North Carolina v. Pearce,* the defendant successfully appealed his conviction for assault with intent to commit rape. He then was retried, convicted again, and sentenced to prison for an amount of time that exceeded his original sentence. The Court held that to impose a greater sentence on the defendant to retaliate against him for having taken an appeal violated due process of law, and that under the circumstances, there was a presumption that the increased sentence was due to proscribed judicial vindictiveness. This presumption could be rebutted by the prosecution, but in *Pearce,* was not.

dant had invoked an appellate remedy, since in this situation there was also a "realistic likelihood of 'vindictiveness.'" *Blackledge v. Perry,* 417 U.S., at 27.[b]

In those cases the Court was dealing with the State's unilateral imposition of a penalty upon a defendant who had chosen to exercise a legal right to attack his original conviction—a situation "very different from the give-and-take negotiation common in plea bargaining between the prosecution and defense, which arguably possess relatively equal bargaining power." The Court has emphasized that the due process violation in cases such as *Pearce* and *Perry* lay not in the possibility that a defendant might be deterred from the exercise of a legal right, but rather in the danger that the State might be retaliating against the accused for lawfully attacking his conviction.

To punish a person because he has done what the law plainly allows him to do is a due process violation of the most basic sort, and for an agent of the State to pursue a course of action whose objective is to penalize a person's reliance on his legal rights is "patently unconstitutional." But in the "give-and-take" of plea bargaining, there is no such element of punishment or retaliation so long as the accused is free to accept or reject the prosecution's offer.

Plea bargaining flows from "the mutuality of advantage" to defendants and prosecutors, each with his own reasons for wanting to avoid trial. Defendants advised by competent counsel and protected by other procedural safeguards are presumptively capable of intelligent choice in response to prosecutorial persuasion, and unlikely to be driven to false self-condemnation. * * *

While confronting a defendant with the risk of more severe punishment clearly may have a "discouraging effect on the defendant's assertion of his trial rights, the imposition of these difficult choices [is] an inevitable"—and permissible—"attribute of any legitimate system which tolerates and encourages the negotiation of pleas." It follows that, by tolerating and encouraging the negotiation of pleas, this Court has necessarily accepted as constitutionally legitimate the simple reality that the prosecutor's interest at the bargaining table is to persuade the defendant to forgo his right to plead not guilty.

It is not disputed here that Hayes was properly chargeable under the recidivist statute, since he had in fact been convicted of two previous felonies. In our system, so long as the prosecutor has probable cause to believe that the accused committed an offense defined by statute, the decision whether or not to prosecute, and what charge to file or bring

---

b. In *Blackledge,* the defendant was charged with, and convicted of, the misdemeanor of assault with a deadly weapon in a district court in North Carolina. He received a six-month prison sentence. As he was entitled to do under a state statute, he then filed a notice of appeal, seeking a trial *de novo* in a superior court. Following the filing of this notice of appeal, the prosecutor obtained an indictment charging the defendant with felony assault. The defendant pled guilty to this charge and was sentenced to prison for five to seven years. The Court held that, under the circumstances, there was a presumption that the enhanced charge was the product of prosecutorial vindictiveness and hence violative of the defendant's due-process rights.

before a grand jury, generally rests entirely in his discretion.[8] Within the limits set by the legislature's constitutionally valid definition of chargeable offenses, "the conscious exercise of some selectivity in enforcement is not in itself a federal constitutional violation" so long as "the selection was [not] deliberately based upon an unjustifiable standard such as race, religion, or other arbitrary classification." To hold that the prosecutor's desire to induce a guilty plea is an "unjustifiable standard," which, like race or religion, may play no part in his charging decision, would contradict the very premises that underlie the concept of plea bargaining itself. Moreover, a rigid constitutional rule that would prohibit a prosecutor from acting forthrightly in his dealings with the defense could only invite unhealthy subterfuge that would drive the practice of plea bargaining back into the shadows from which it has so recently emerged.

There is no doubt that the breadth of discretion that our country's legal system vests in prosecuting attorneys carries with it the potential for both individual and institutional abuse. And broad though that discretion may be, there are undoubtedly constitutional limits upon its exercise. We hold only that the course of conduct engaged in by the prosecutor in this case, which no more than openly presented the defendant with the unpleasant alternatives of forgoing trial or facing charges on which he was plainly subject to prosecution, did not violate the Due Process Clause of the Fourteenth Amendment.

* * *

MR. JUSTICE BLACKMUN, with whom MR. JUSTICE BRENNAN and MR. JUSTICE MARSHALL join, dissenting.

I feel that the Court * * * is departing from, or at least restricting, the principles established in *North Carolina v. Pearce,* 395 U.S. 711 (1969), and in *Blackledge v. Perry,* 417 U.S. 21 (1974). * * *

* * *

* * * In this case vindictiveness is present to the same extent as it was thought to be in *Pearce* and in *Perry;* the prosecutor here admitted that the sole reason for the new indictment was to discourage the respondent from exercising his right to a trial. Even had such an admission not been made, when plea negotiations, conducted in the face of the less serious charge under the first indictment, fail, charging by a second indictment a more serious crime for the same conduct creates "a strong inference" of vindictiveness. * * *

Prosecutorial vindictiveness, it seems to me, in the present narrow context, is the fact against which the Due Process Clause ought to protect. I perceive little difference between vindictiveness after what the Court describes as the exercise of a "legal right to attack his original convic-

---

8.   This case does not involve the constitutional implications of a prosecutor's offer during plea bargaining of adverse or lenient treatment for some person *other* than the accused, which might pose a greater danger of inducing a false guilty plea by skewing the assessment of the risks a defendant must consider.

tion," and vindictiveness in the " 'give-and-take negotiation common in plea bargaining.' " Prosecutorial vindictiveness in any context is still prosecutorial vindictiveness. The Due Process Clause should protect an accused against it, however it asserts itself. * * *

It might be argued that it really makes little difference how this case, now that it is here, is decided. The Court's holding gives plea bargaining full sway despite vindictiveness. A contrary result, however, merely would prompt the aggressive prosecutor to bring the greater charge initially in every case, and only thereafter to bargain. The consequences to the accused would still be adverse, for then he would bargain against a greater charge, face the likelihood of increased bail, and run the risk that the court would be less inclined to accept a bargained plea. Nonetheless, it is far preferable to hold the prosecution to the charge it was originally content to bring and to justify in the eyes of its public.[2]

MR. JUSTICE POWELL, dissenting. [Opinion omitted.]

QUESTIONS AND POINTS FOR DISCUSSION

1. In United States v. Goodwin, 457 U.S. 368, 102 S.Ct. 2485 (1982), the Supreme Court addressed a question left open in *Bordenkircher*—whether due process is violated when unsuccessful plea negotiations are followed by the bringing, without notice, of additional and more serious charges by the prosecutor. *Goodwin* involved a defendant who had been stopped for speeding and then fled in his car after the police officer noticed a plastic bag under the armrest of the car and asked the defendant to lift up the armrest. While trying to flee, the defendant struck the police officer with his car.

The defendant was charged with multiple misdemeanor and petty offenses. Although the defendant and the prosecutor initially engaged in plea negotiations, the defendant ultimately decided that he wanted a jury trial. A few weeks later, the defendant was indicted for the felony of forcibly assaulting a federal officer and three other crimes stemming from the incident at the scene of the traffic stop. The defendant was convicted of the felony as well as one misdemeanor.

---

2. That prosecutors, without saying so, may sometimes bring charges more serious than they think appropriate for the ultimate disposition of a case, in order to gain bargaining leverage with a defendant, does not add support to today's decision, for this Court, in its approval of the advantages to be gained from plea negotiations, has never openly sanctioned such deliberate overcharging or taken such a cynical view of the bargaining process. Normally, of course, it is impossible to show that this is what the prosecutor is doing, and the courts necessarily have deferred to the prosecutor's exercise of discretion in initial charging decisions.

Even if overcharging is to be sanctioned, there are strong reasons of fairness why the charges should be presented at the beginning of the bargaining process, rather than as a filliped threat at the end. First, it means that a prosecutor is required to reach a charging decision without any knowledge of the particular defendant's willingness to plead guilty; hence the defendant who truly believes himself to be innocent, and wishes for that reason to go to trial, is not likely to be subject to quite such a devastating gamble since the prosecutor has fixed the incentives for the average case.

Second, it is healthful to keep charging practices visible to the general public, so that political bodies can judge whether the policy being followed is a fair one. Visibility is enhanced if the prosecutor is required to lay his cards on the table with an indictment of public record at the beginning of the bargaining process, rather than making use of unrecorded verbal warnings of more serious indictments yet to come.

The defendant moved to set aside the jury's verdict on the grounds that the prosecutor, in violation of due process of law, had charged the defendant with a felony to retaliate against him for having invoked his right to a jury trial. The prosecutor responded by citing a number of reasons why he had sought the felony indictment, including his belief that the defendant was trafficking in drugs when his car was stopped, the number of violent crimes committed by the defendant in the past, and the fact that the defendant had fled from the jurisdiction for three years following his initial arrest and arraignment.

The Supreme Court considered whether a presumption of vindictiveness is warranted when new and more serious charges are brought before trial following a defendant's decision to stand trial. According to the Court, for such a presumption to exist, there would have to be a "reasonable likelihood" that in such circumstances, the government's actions are due to proscribed vindictiveness. Id. at 373, 102 S.Ct. at 2488. The Court noted that such a presumption was warranted in Blackledge v. Perry, 417 U.S. 21, 94 S.Ct. 2098 (1974), where the new charge was brought after the defendant was convicted in one court but then exercised his statutory right to a trial *de novo* in a different court. The Court, however, distinguished the pretrial setting in which the new charges were brought in this case:

> There is good reason to be cautious before adopting an inflexible presumption of prosecutorial vindictiveness in a pretrial setting. In the course of preparing a case for trial, the prosecutor may uncover additional information that suggests a basis for further prosecution or he simply may come to realize that information possessed by the State has a broader significance. At this stage of the proceedings, the prosecutor's assessment of the proper extent of prosecution may not have crystallized. In contrast, once a trial begins—and certainly by the time a conviction has been obtained—it is much more likely that the State has discovered and assessed all of the information against an accused and has made a determination, on the basis of that information, of the extent to which he should be prosecuted. Thus, a change in the charging decision made after an initial trial is completed is much more likely to be improperly motivated than is a pretrial decision.

* * *

Thus, the timing of the prosecutor's action in this case suggests that a presumption of vindictiveness is not warranted. A prosecutor should remain free before trial to exercise the broad discretion entrusted to him to determine the extent of the societal interest in prosecution. An initial decision should not freeze future conduct. As we made clear in *Bordenkircher,* the initial charges filed by a prosecutor may not reflect the extent to which an individual is legitimately subject to prosecution.

* * *

* * * Moreover, unlike the trial judge in *Pearce,* no party is asked "to do over what it thought it had already done correctly." A prosecutor has no "personal stake" in a bench trial and thus no reason to engage in "self-vindication" upon a defendant's request for a jury trial. Perhaps

most importantly, the institutional bias against the retrial of a decided question that supported the decisions in *Pearce* and *Blackledge* simply has no counterpart in this case.

457 U.S. at 381–83, 102 S.Ct. at 2493–94.

Although defendants charged before trial with additional and more serious charges following their insistence on going to trial cannot avail themselves of the benefits of a presumption of vindictiveness, the Supreme Court in *Goodwin* did leave open the possibility that a defendant could prevail on a due-process claim by showing that the prosecutor's charging decision was actually prompted by vindictiveness. Can you reconcile this statement with the decision in *Bordenkircher,* where the Court acknowledged that the prosecutor had charged the defendant with being a habitual offender because of his decision to plead not guilty, but found no due-process violation?

Concurring in the judgment in *Goodwin,* Justice Blackmun stated that when a defendant elects to go to trial and the prosecutor then files additional and more serious charges, there should be a presumption of vindictiveness, whether or not the new charges are filed before or after trial. He found, however, that the prosecutor had rebutted the presumption of vindictiveness in this case. Justice Brennan, joined by Justice Marshall, dissented, noting that the evidence of a due-process violation was even more compelling in this case, where the increased punishment followed the defendant's exercise of his constitutional right to a jury trial, than in *Blackledge*, where the increased punishment followed the defendant's invocation of his statutory right to a trial *de novo.*

2. In Alabama v. Smith, 490 U.S. 794, 109 S.Ct. 2201 (1989), the Supreme Court once again refused to permit a defendant to invoke a presumption of vindictiveness. In that case, the defendant pled guilty to burglary and rape in return for the state's dismissal of a sodomy charge. The trial court then sentenced the defendant to thirty years in prison for each conviction, with his sentences to be served concurrently.

The defendant successfully appealed his convictions on the grounds that his guilty pleas were invalid because he had not been sufficiently apprised of the penalties that could be imposed if he pled guilty. The government then reinstated the sodomy charge, and the case went to trial before a jury. The same judge who had initially sentenced the defendant presided at the trial.

Following the defendant's conviction on all three counts, the judge sentenced him to life imprisonment for the burglary, a concurrent life term for the sodomy, and 150 years in prison for the rape, with the latter sentence to be served consecutively with the other two sentences. In imposing these sentences, the trial judge noted that the trial had revealed additional facts about the defendant's crimes of which the judge was previously unaware, including that the defendant had raped the victim five times, forced her to have oral sex with him, and threatened her with a knife.

The defendant contended that the increased sentences were imposed by the judge in order to retaliate against him for getting his guilty plea set aside. The question before the Supreme Court was whether the defendant could avail himself of a presumption of vindictiveness or whether he would instead have to prove actual vindictiveness to prevail on his due-process claim.

Answering this question, according to the Court, required an assessment of whether there was a "reasonable likelihood" that sentences imposed after trial that are greater than those imposed following guilty pleas are the product of judicial vindictiveness. The Court answered this question in the negative:

> [W]hen a greater penalty is imposed after trial than was imposed after a prior guilty plea, the increase in sentence is not more likely than not attributable to the vindictiveness on the part of the sentencing judge. Even when the same judge imposes both sentences, the relevant sentencing information available to the judge after the plea will usually be considerably less than that available after a trial.

* * *

> As this case demonstrates, in the course of the proof at trial the judge may gather a fuller appreciation of the nature and extent of the crimes charged. The defendant's conduct during trial may give the judge insights into his moral character and suitability for rehabilitation. See United States v. Grayson, 438 U.S. 41, 53 (1978) (sentencing authority's perception of the truthfulness of a defendant testifying on his own behalf may be considered in sentencing). Finally, after trial, the factors that may have indicated leniency as consideration for the guilty plea are no longer present. Here, too, although the same Judge who sentenced following the guilty plea also imposes sentence following trial, in conducting the trial the court is not simply "do[ing] over what it thought it had already done correctly."

Id. at 801–02, 109 S.Ct. at 2205–06.

What might be the likely effect of the Court's decision on defendants' willingness to challenge the validity of their guilty pleas?

3. Consider the facts of the following case. The defendant was charged with a number of crimes, including murder and multiple counts of rape. His mother, father, brother, two sisters, and sister-in-law were charged with a number of crimes stemming from their alleged attempts to cover up the defendant's crimes. The first trial, that of the defendant's brother, resulted in criminal convictions for which the brother was sentenced to prison for four and a half years. The prosecutor then promised the defendant that if he pled no contest to the murder charge and two counts of first-degree criminal sexual penetration, his brother would be released from prison, criminal charges against his sisters and sister-in-law would be dropped, and his parents would be permitted to plead no contest to a conspiracy charge and placed on probation. In addition, thirty other felony charges pending against the defendant would be dropped. The defendant agreed to this proposal. Was his guilty plea valid? Why or why not? See Miles v. Dorsey, 61 F.3d 1459, 1468–69 (10th Cir.1995).

4. In Newton v. Rumery, 480 U.S. 386, 107 S.Ct. 1187 (1987), the Supreme Court considered the validity of what are called release-dismissal agreements. In that case, Bernard Rumery was charged with the felony of

tampering with a witness. After his attorney threatened to sue certain police and other government officials for having brought unfounded charges against Rumery, the prosecutor agreed to dismiss the criminal charge in return for Rumery's agreement not to bring a civil suit against any government officials. Rumery acquiesced, and the criminal charge was dismissed.

Ten months later, Rumery brought a § 1983 civil-rights suit against the city and various local officials, claiming, among other things, that his arrest was unlawful. In a motion to dismiss, the defendants argued that the release-dismissal agreement barred the lawsuit. Rumery responded that the agreement was contrary to public policy and consequently void.

In a 5–4 decision, the Supreme Court held that the release-dismissal agreement at issue in the case was valid and enforceable. The Court acknowledged that the prospect of obtaining such agreements might induce prosecutors to file frivolous criminal charges as a way of pressuring individuals to forgo plans to sue government officials. In addition, such agreements might lead to the abandonment of criminal prosecutions when the interests of the public favor prosecution. Finally, such agreements might permit constitutional violations to go unremedied. Nonetheless, the Court concluded that such agreements are not *per se* invalid. The circumstances surrounding an agreement instead have to be examined to determine its validity and enforceability.

Justice O'Connor wrote a concurring opinion in *Newton* to emphasize that the burden is upon government officials sued under § 1983 to establish that a release-dismissal agreement was "voluntarily made, not the product of prosecutorial overreaching, and in the public interest." Id. at 401, 107 S.Ct. at 1197 (O'Connor, J., concurring). She identified some of the factors relevant to these questions:

> Many factors may bear on whether a release was voluntary and not the product of overreaching, some of which come readily to mind. The knowledge and experience of the criminal defendant and the circumstances of the execution of the release, including, importantly, whether the defendant was counseled, are clearly relevant. The nature of the criminal charges that are pending is also important, for the greater the charge, the greater the coercive effect. The existence of a legitimate criminal justice objective for obtaining the release will support its validity. And, importantly, the possibility of abuse is clearly mitigated if the release-dismissal agreement is executed under judicial supervision.

Id. at 401–02, 107 S.Ct. at 1197.

Even the four dissenters in this case—Justices Stevens, Brennan, Marshall, and Blackmun—acknowledged that in certain circumstances, release-dismissal agreements might be valid. The dissenters felt, however, that the government officials sued in this case had not established the validity of the release-dismissal agreement at issue in the case. By contrast, the majority of the Court felt that the release-dismissal agreement was valid, particularly because there was evidence that the prosecutor entered into the agreement largely to avoid trauma to the witness with whom Rumery had allegedly tampered and who might be called as a witness in the civil suit.

5.   Can a prosecutor condition a plea agreement on the defendant's agreement to refrain from interviewing a witness, such as the victim of a sex crime with which the defendant is charged? In State v. Draper, 784 P.2d 259, 264 (Ariz. 1989), the Arizona Supreme Court held that conditioning a plea agreement on a defendant's surrender of his right to interview witnesses violates due process unless the record demonstrates a "special reason" that makes the condition reasonable. The court also held that such a condition violates the defendant's right to the effective assistance of counsel unless the attorney has access to other information that would enable the attorney to effectively represent the defendant without interviewing the witness.

6.   Can and should a prosecutor be able to extract, as a condition of a plea agreement, a waiver by the defendant of his or her right to appeal? Is the waiver, for example, of the right to appeal a sentence enforceable when a sentencing court erroneously concluded that it could not impose concurrent sentences on the defendant but must impose consecutive sentences? See United States v. Hahn, 359 F.3d 1315, 1329 (10th Cir. 2004) (holding a waiver enforceable in such circumstances).

The majority of the courts, thus far, have held that conditioning a plea agreement on the defendant's waiver of the right to appeal generally is permissible provided the waiver is knowing and voluntary. See, e.g., Creech v. State, 887 N.E.2d 73, 74 (Ind. 2008). Some of these courts have carved out exceptions to this general rule. Some of the more common exceptions allow an appeal when a defendant claims that the sentence exceeded the statutory maximum, that racial discrimination tainted the sentencing process, or that the defendant received ineffective assistance of counsel. See, e.g., United States v. Novosel, 481 F.3d 1288, 1289 (10th Cir. 2007). Other courts have held that such a waiver is unenforceable. See, e.g., State v. Ethington, 592 P.2d 768, 769–70 (Ariz. 1979). See also David E. Carney, Note, Waiver of the Right to Appeal Sentencing in Plea Agreements with the Federal Government, 40 Wm. & Mary L. Rev. 1019, 1044–51 (1999) (arguing that in order for waiver-of-appeal provisions to be enforceable in federal prosecutions, plea agreements should have to specify the sentence to be imposed, thereby permitting the plea to be withdrawn under what is now Rule 11(c)(5) of the Federal Rules of Criminal Procedure if the court does not impose that sentence).

Proponents of appeal waivers maintain that they have many benefits. Among the cited benefits are that they save the courts and the parties the time and money that would be expended on appeals, benefit defendants by giving them a bargaining chip, and help bring closure to victims, the defendant, and the government. Critics of these waivers, on the other hand, argue that they enable illegal sentences and convictions to remain in effect, insulate the misconduct of trial judges, defense attorneys, and prosecutors from judicial review, and exacerbate sentencing disparity. This latter argument is grounded in part on the premise that appellate review diminishes sentencing disparity. In addition, researchers have found significant differences in the frequency with which waiver-of-appeal clauses are inserted into plea agreements. See Nancy J. King & Michael E. O'Neill, Appeal Waivers and the Future of Sentencing Policy, 55 Duke L.J. 209, 231–32 (2005) (reporting that including a waiver clause in a plea agreement is the norm in some federal circuits and the exception in others).

What additional arguments could be propounded in favor of and against enforcing waivers of the right to appeal that are incorporated into plea agreements? If, as a general rule, these appeal waivers are enforceable, what exceptions, if any, should apply to this rule?

7. Not only the Constitution, but statutes, court rules, and prosecution policies may limit what a prosecutor can do to induce a defendant to plead guilty. The National Advisory Commission on Criminal Justice Standards and Goals, Report on Courts (1973) recommended that the following limitations be placed on prosecutors during plea bargaining:

STANDARD 3.6

PROHIBITED PROSECUTORIAL INDUCEMENTS TO ENTER A PLEA OF GUILTY

No prosecutor should, in connection with plea negotiations, engage in, perform, or condone any of the following:

1. Charging or threatening to charge the defendant with offenses for which the admissible evidence available to the prosecutor is insufficient to support a guilty verdict.

2. Charging or threatening to charge the defendant with a crime not ordinarily charged in the jurisdiction for the conduct allegedly engaged in by him.

3. Threatening the defendant that if he pleads not guilty, his sentence may be more severe than that which ordinarily is imposed in the jurisdiction in similar cases on defendants who plead not guilty.

4. Failing to grant full disclosure before the disposition negotiations of all exculpatory evidence material to guilt or punishment.

Are there any other prosecutorial inducements that you would consider improper, if not unconstitutional? See, e.g., Arizona v. Horning, 761 P.2d 728 (Ariz.Ct.App.1988) (plea involuntary when entered in return for prosecutor's agreement not to interfere with defendant's attempts to secure conjugal visits with his wife in jail).

8. The Supreme Court case of Corbitt v. New Jersey, 439 U.S. 212, 99 S.Ct. 492 (1978) dealt with the constitutionality, not of prosecutorial inducements to plead guilty, but of legislative inducements. The defendant in that case had been charged with first-degree murder. If convicted of first-degree murder following a jury trial, he faced a mandatory sentence of life imprisonment. If the jury instead found him guilty of second-degree murder, he could be sentenced to up to thirty years in prison. Although guilty pleas to murder were prohibited in New Jersey, a defendant could plead *nolo contendere* to a murder indictment. If a defendant entered such a plea, and the plea was accepted by the court, the judge could impose either a life sentence or the sentence for second-degree murder, *i.e.*, a maximum of thirty years.

The defendant in *Corbitt* opted to go to trial and was found guilty of first-degree murder by a jury. He was then sentenced to life in prison as required by the New Jersey statute. On appeal, he claimed that New Jersey unconstitutionally penalized defendants charged with first-degree murder who pursued their constitutional right to a jury trial. The Supreme Court disagreed:

> [N]ot every burden on the exercise of a constitutional right, and not every pressure or encouragement to waive such a right, is invalid. Specifically, there is no *per se* rule against encouraging guilty pleas. We have squarely held that a State may encourage a guilty plea by offering substantial benefits in return for the plea. The plea may obtain for the defendant "the possibility or certainty ... [not only of] a lesser penalty than the sentence that could be imposed after a trial and a verdict of guilty ...," but also of a lesser penalty than that *required* to be imposed after a guilty verdict by a jury.
>
> [The Court here cited and discussed *Bordenkircher v. Hayes*.]
>
> * * *
>
> * * * There is no doubt that those homicide defendants who are willing to plead *non vult* may be treated more leniently than those who go to trial, but withholding the possibility of leniency from the latter cannot be equated with impermissible punishment as long as our cases sustaining plea bargaining remain undisturbed. Those cases, as we have said, unequivocally recognize the constitutional propriety of extending leniency in exchange for a plea of guilty and of not extending leniency to those who have not demonstrated those attributes on which leniency is based.

Id. at 218–20, 223–24, 99 S.Ct. at 497–98, 500.

In *Corbitt,* the Supreme Court distinguished United States v. Jackson, 390 U.S. 570, 88 S.Ct. 1209 (1968), discussed on page 51, a case where the Court had held the sentencing provisions of the Federal Kidnapping Act to be unconstitutional. Under that statute, a defendant found guilty by a jury of violating the Act could receive the death penalty. By contrast, the maximum penalty that could be imposed on a defendant tried in a bench trial or who pled guilty was life in prison. The Supreme Court in *Corbitt* highlighted the following distinctions between *Jackson* and the case before it:

> The principal difference is that the pressures to forgo trial and to plead to the charge in this case are not what they were in *Jackson*. First, the death penalty, which is "unique in its severity and irrevocability," is not involved here. Although we need not agree with the New Jersey court that the *Jackson* rationale is limited to those cases where a plea avoids any possibility of the death penalty's being imposed, it is a material fact that under the New Jersey law the maximum penalty for murder is life imprisonment, not death. Furthermore, in *Jackson,* any risk of suffering the maximum penalty could be avoided by pleading guilty. Here, although the punishment when a jury finds a defendant guilty of first-degree murder is life imprisonment, the risk of that punishment is not completely avoided by pleading *non vult* because the judge accepting the plea has the authority to impose a life term. New Jersey does not reserve the maximum punishment for murder for those who insist on a jury trial.

439 U.S. at 217, 99 S.Ct. at 496.

9.   In his concurring opinion in Brady v. United States, 397 U.S. 742, 90 S.Ct. 1463 (1970), Justice Marshall noted that threats or promises made by a trial judge to induce a guilty plea may render that plea involuntary. See, e.g., United States v. Anderson, 993 F.2d 1435, 1437–38 (9th Cir.1993) (guilty plea tendered after judge's statements at the arraignment that he would not accept a plea after that date to fewer than all thirty counts of the indictment was involuntary). Because of the risk that judicial participation in plea bargaining will place undue pressure on a defendant to plead guilty, a number of jurisdictions have barred the involvement of judges in plea discussions. See, e.g., Fed.R.Crim.P. 11(c)(1).

The American Bar Association at one point supported an intermediate approach to the issue of judicial involvement in plea negotiations, permitting judges to participate in such discussions, but limiting where those discussions could occur and what trial judges could say during them. Under Standard 14–3.3 of the American Bar Association Standards for Criminal Justice: Pleas of Guilty (2d ed. 1980 & Supp. 1986), parties unable to conclude a plea agreement could ask the judge to moderate their plea discussions. Absent "good cause" for meeting in chambers, the parties would appear before the judge in open court and present their differing perspectives on a plea agreement. The judge would then either identify charge or sentencing concessions the judge would consider acceptable if the defendant pled guilty or order the preparation of a preplea report to facilitate the making of that decision. Even if the parties had not requested the judge's intervention in plea discussions, a judge could ask the parties whether they had attempted to negotiate the case and could order an adjournment to enable the parties to engage in such negotiations.

The third edition of the ABA Standards for Criminal Justice curtail judicial participation in plea negotiations much more:

Standard 14–3.3. Responsibilities of the judge

* * *

(c) The judge should not through word or demeanor, either directly or indirectly, communicate to the defendant or defense counsel that a plea agreement should be accepted or that a guilty plea should be entered.

(d) A judge should not ordinarily participate in plea negotiation discussions among the parties. Upon the request of the parties, a judge may be presented with a proposed plea agreement negotiated by the parties and may indicate whether the court would accept the terms as proposed and if relevant, indicate what sentence would be imposed. * * *

* * *

ABA Standards for Criminal Justice: Pleas of Guilty, Standard 14–3.3 (3d ed. 1999). What constraints would you place on the participation of judges in plea negotiations? For examples of judges placing strong pressure on defendants to plead guilty, see Richard Klein, Due Process Denied: Judicial Coercion in the Plea Bargaining Process, 32 Hofstra L. Rev. 1349 (2004).

10. *Class Exercise:* Discuss and debate the following questions:

1. Should plea bargaining be abolished? If so, should the prohibition extend to some or all crimes? See, e.g., Fla. Stat. Ann. § 316.656(2) (prohibiting judges from accepting a guilty plea to a lesser offense when a person charged with driving while under the influence of alcohol had a blood or breath alcohol content of .20 or more or caused property damage or personal injury at the time of the crime).

2. What restrictions should be placed on plea bargaining in jurisdictions that retain it? Can and should any other steps be taken to curtail plea-bargaining abuses? For several proposals designed to prevent or limit the problems that can attend plea bargaining, see Susan R. Klein, Enhancing the Judicial Role in Criminal Plea and Sentence Bargaining, 84 Tex. L.Rev. 2023 (2006); Stephanos Bibas, Plea Bargaining Outside the Shadow of Trial, 117 Harv. L. Rev. 2463, 2531–45 (2004).

CHAPTER 3

THE SENTENCING PROCESS

■ ■ ■

A. RIGHTS DURING SENTENCING

Defendants who are charged with crimes are protected by an array of constitutional rights if their cases proceed to trial. They have the right, for example, to the assistance of an attorney, a right bestowed by the Sixth Amendment, and if they are indigent, they have the right, in certain circumstances, to appointed counsel. Gideon v. Wainwright, 372 U.S. 335, 344, 83 S.Ct. 792, 796 (1963). They have the right to a jury trial when charged with a non-petty offense. Duncan v. Louisiana, 391 U.S. 145, 158–59, 88 S.Ct. 1444, 1452 (1968). They have the right to present witnesses who will testify on their behalf, Washington v. Texas, 388 U.S. 14, 18–19, 87 S.Ct. 1920, 1923 (1967), and the right to confront and cross-examine adverse witnesses. Coy v. Iowa, 487 U.S. 1012, 1019–20, 108 S.Ct. 2798, 2802 (1988). Defendants are also presumed innocent unless and until the government rebuts this presumption and establishes their guilt beyond a reasonable doubt. In re Winship, 397 U.S. 358, 364, 90 S.Ct. 1068, 1072 (1970).

The procedural safeguards that must attend the guilt-innocence stage of a criminal prosecution should be contrasted with the more limited rights that the courts have recognized during the sentencing stage of criminal prosecutions. The succeeding subsections discuss some of the rights defendants have claimed they have during the sentencing process and courts' responses to those claims.

1. RIGHTS TO CONFRONTATION, CROSS-EXAMINATION, AND REBUTTAL

The Sixth Amendment provides that "[i]n all criminal prosecutions, the accused shall enjoy the right ... to be confronted with the witnesses against him." As mentioned earlier, defendants have the related right to cross-examine adverse witnesses at trial. In the case that follows, the Supreme Court considered whether the rights to confront and cross-examine witnesses extend to sentencing proceedings.

WILLIAMS v. NEW YORK

Supreme Court of the United States, 1949.
337 U.S. 241, 69 S.Ct. 1079, 93 L.Ed. 1337.

MR. JUSTICE BLACK delivered the opinion of the Court.

A jury in a New York state court found appellant guilty of murder in the first degree. The jury recommended life imprisonment, but the trial judge imposed [a] sentence of death. In giving his reasons for imposing the death sentence the judge discussed in open court the evidence upon which the jury had convicted stating that this evidence had been considered in the light of additional information obtained through the court's "Probation Department, and through other sources." * * *

* * * The evidence proved a wholly indefensible murder committed by a person engaged in a burglary. * * *

About five weeks after the verdict of guilty with recommendation of life imprisonment, and after a statutory pre-sentence investigation report to the judge, the defendant was brought to court to be sentenced. Asked what he had to say, appellant protested his innocence. After each of his three lawyers had appealed to the court to accept the jury's recommendation of a life sentence, the judge gave reasons why he felt that the death sentence should be imposed. He narrated the shocking details of the crime as shown by the trial evidence, expressing his own complete belief in appellant's guilt. He stated that the pre-sentence investigation revealed many material facts concerning appellant's background which though relevant to the question of punishment could not properly have been brought to the attention of the jury in its consideration of the question of guilt. He referred to the experience appellant "had had on thirty other burglaries in and about the same vicinity" where the murder had been committed. The appellant had not been convicted of these burglaries although the judge had information that he had confessed to some and had been identified as the perpetrator of some of the others. The judge also referred to certain activities of appellant as shown by the probation report that indicated appellant possessed "a morbid sexuality" and classified him as a "menace to society." The accuracy of the statements made by the judge as to appellant's background and past practices was not challenged by appellant or his counsel, nor was the judge asked to disregard any of them or to afford appellant a chance to refute or discredit any of them by cross-examination or otherwise.

* * * Within limits fixed by statutes, New York judges are given a broad discretion to decide the type and extent of punishment for convicted defendants. Here, for example, the judge's discretion was to sentence to life imprisonment or death. To aid a judge in exercising this discretion intelligently the New York procedural policy encourages him to consider information about the convicted person's past life, health, habits, conduct, and mental and moral propensities. The sentencing judge may consider such information even though obtained outside the courtroom from per-

sons whom a defendant has not been permitted to confront or cross-examine. * * *

Appellant urges that the New York statutory policy is in irreconcilable conflict with the underlying philosophy of a second procedural policy grounded in the due process of law clause of the Fourteenth Amendment. That policy * * * is in part that no person shall be tried and convicted of an offense unless he is given reasonable notice of the charges against him and is afforded an opportunity to examine adverse witnesses. * * *

Tribunals passing on the guilt of a defendant always have been hedged in by strict evidentiary procedural limitations. But both before and since the American colonies became a nation, courts in this country and in England practiced a policy under which a sentencing judge could exercise a wide discretion in the sources and types of evidence used to assist him in determining the kind and extent of punishment to be imposed within limits fixed by law. Out-of-court affidavits have been used frequently, and of course in the smaller communities sentencing judges naturally have in mind their knowledge of the personalities and backgrounds of convicted offenders. * * *

In addition to the historical basis for different evidentiary rules governing trial and sentencing procedures there are sound practical reasons for the distinction. In a trial before verdict the issue is whether a defendant is guilty of having engaged in certain criminal conduct of which he has been specifically accused. Rules of evidence have been fashioned for criminal trials which narrowly confine the trial contest to evidence that is strictly relevant to the particular offense charged. These rules rest in part on a necessity to prevent a time-consuming and confusing trial of collateral issues. They were also designed to prevent tribunals concerned solely with the issue of guilt of a particular offense from being influenced to convict for that offense by evidence that the defendant had habitually engaged in other misconduct. A sentencing judge, however, is not confined to the narrow issue of guilt. His task within fixed statutory or constitutional limits is to determine the type and extent of punishment after the issue of guilt has been determined. Highly relevant—if not essential—to his selection of an appropriate sentence is the possession of the fullest information possible concerning the defendant's life and characteristics. * * *

* * *

Under the practice of individualizing punishments, investigational techniques have been given an important role. Probation workers making reports of their investigations have not been trained to prosecute but to aid offenders. Their reports have been given a high value by conscientious judges who want to sentence persons on the best available information rather than on guesswork and inadequate information. * * * We must recognize that most of the information now relied upon by judges to guide them in the intelligent imposition of sentences would be unavailable if information were restricted to that given in open court by witnesses subject to cross-examination. And the modern probation report draws on information concerning every aspect of a defendant's life. The type and extent of this information make totally impractical if not impossible open court testimony with cross-examination. Such a procedure could endlessly delay criminal administration in a retrial of collateral issues.

The considerations we have set out admonish us against treating the due process clause as a uniform command that courts throughout the Nation abandon their age-old practice of seeking information from out-of-court sources to guide their judgment toward a more enlightened and just sentence. New York criminal statutes set wide limits for maximum and minimum sentences. * * * In determining whether a defendant shall receive a one-year minimum or a twenty-year maximum sentence, we do not think the Federal Constitution restricts the view of the sentencing judge to the information received in open court. * * *

* * *

MR. JUSTICE RUTLEDGE dissents. [Opinion omitted.]

MR. JUSTICE MURPHY, dissenting. [Opinion omitted.]

QUESTIONS AND POINTS FOR DISCUSSION

1. Since the Supreme Court decided *Williams v. New York,* courts generally have rejected defendants' claims that they have a right under the Sixth Amendment's Confrontation Clause or due process to cross-examine witnesses at sentencing hearings. See United States v. Paull, 551 F.3d 516, 527–28 (6th Cir. 2009) (listing cases). The courts are divided, however, on whether defendants have a constitutional right to confront and cross-examine witnesses at a sentencing hearing in a capital case. See United States v. Brown, 441 F.3d 1330, 1361 n.12 (11th Cir. 2006) (listing cases). If you were representing a defendant in a capital case raising this question, how would you distinguish *Williams v. New York*? What additional arguments would you make in support of your position that defendants have a constitutional right to confront and cross-examine witnesses at death-penalty hearings? See Penny J. White, "He Said," "She Said," and Issues of Life and Death: The Right to Confrontation at Capital Sentencing Proceedings, 19 Regent U.L. Rev. 387 (2007). After reading Gardner v. Florida, 430 U.S. 349, 97 S.Ct. 1197 (1977) on page 93, consider once again the arguments you might make on your client's behalf.

2. The adoption of the federal sentencing guidelines highlighted the significance of the question whether the Constitution affords a defendant the right to confront and cross-examine adverse witnesses at sentencing hearings. Under these guidelines, the sentence imposed under the often broad sentencing range established by statute depends in part on the defendant's "offense conduct." Federal Sentencing Guidelines Manual § 1B1.2(a) (2008). The "base offense level" for the crime of which the defendant was convicted then is raised to reflect other "relevant conduct," including other crimes with

which the defendant has not been charged that were related to the offense of conviction. Id. §§ 1B1.2(b), 1B1.3. Although, as discussed later in this book, the Supreme Court has ruled that the federal sentencing guidelines are only advisory, they still are factored into a court's sentencing decision. See United States v. Booker, 543 U.S. 220, 125 S.Ct. 738 (2005) on page 131 and pages 216–17.

United States v. Silverman, 976 F.2d 1502 (6th Cir.1992) illustrates the potential significance of "relevant conduct" to a defendant's sentence. In that case, the defendant pled guilty to one count of possession with intent to distribute drugs after he was arrested for selling a quarter of an ounce of cocaine to a confidential government informant. The base offense level for this crime, coupled with his criminal-history level, would have yielded a maximum prison sentence of two years and three months. At the sentencing hearing, however, the probation officer who had prepared the presentence investigation report and a Drug Enforcement Agency (DEA) agent testified that several individuals had reported that the defendant had sold a kilogram of cocaine the previous year. The defendant was not told the names of these individuals or given an opportunity to cross-examine them. Based on the "relevant conduct" disclosed in these hearsay statements, the district court imposed a sentence more than five years higher than the base offense level. On appeal, the Sixth Circuit Court of Appeals concluded that the defendant had no right to confront and cross-examine the witnesses whose statements had led to the increase in his sentence. Do you agree with this holding?

3. To assist you in your analysis of the question whether the Constitution accords a defendant the right to confront and cross-examine adverse witnesses during the sentencing stage of a criminal prosecution, an example of a presentence investigation report is set forth on the next page. The report, written about a defendant who pled guilty to criminal sexual conduct in the first degree, is reprinted here with the permission of the Probation Office of the Ingham County Circuit Court, Ingham County, Michigan. Names and other identifying information in the report have been changed or deleted.

MICHIGAN DEPARTMENT OF CORRECTIONS
PRESENTENCE INVESTIGATION REPORT

Honorable Andrew Lopez   County Ingham   Sentence Date 7-24-95

Docket 54154   Attorney Ann Witt   Appt. _____ Restrained xx

Defendant Fred Jones   Age 46   D.O.B 9-19-48

CURRENT CONVICTION(S) $50,000 Surety

Final Charge(s)   Max.   Jail Credit   Bond

1. CT. II. CSC 1st Degree   LIFE   2   days yes
2. _____   _____   _____ days _____
3. _____   _____   _____ days _____

Convicted by: Plea X Jury ___ Judge ___ Plea Under Advisement ___ Nolo Contendere
Conviction Date 6-26-95   Plea Agreement nolle pross Cts. I. II. & IV
Pending Charges none   Where _____

PRIOR RECORD

Convictions: Felonies 1   Misdemeanors 1   Juvenile Record: Yes ___ No X
Probation: Active ___   Former yes   Pending Violation _____
Parole: Active ___   Former ___   Pending Violation _____
Current Michigan Prisoner: Yes ___ No x   Number _____
Currently Under Sentence: Offense _____   Sentence _____

PERSONAL HISTORY

(Self-employed)
Education 12th   Employed yes Where Fred's Automotive Diagnostics, Inc.
Psychiatric History: Yes ___ No XX Physical Handicaps: Yes ___ No XX Marital Status divorced
Substance Abuse History: Yes X No ___ What alcohol   How Long _____

RECOMMENDATION

1. 30 to 45 years with the Michigan Corrections Commission.
2. Mental Health therapy for sex offenders.

Agent Marie Franklin   Date 7-22-95
Signature _____   Supervisor's Approval _____

EVALUATION AND PLAN:

Fred Jones age 46 is before the court for his second felony conviction. His other felony conviction occurred in 1979 and it was Accosting Children for Immoral Purposes. He was given three days in jail and two years probation.

The defendant has resided in Lansing almost all of his life. After graduating from Eastern High School in 1967 he entered the United States Army. He was honorably discharged after serving three years.

The defendant is self-employed. He owns and operates Fred's Automotive Diagnostics Inc., 2308 Curry Street. He began operating this business on the date of his arrest for this offense, May 10, 1995. Respondent has worked in the automotive field four years, and he previously owned his own shop between 88 and 93. It was then located at 400 Northampton Street.

Mr. Jones is also the State Commissioner for the American Bicycle Association's BMX Racing Program. The American Bicycle Association is out of Phoenix, Arizona. As commissioner, the defendant traveled to various tracks in the state, set up promotional activities, and got tracks going as well as directed the local BMX Race Program.

Right after leaving the military the defendant was employed by Spartan Oil, and managed a station before opening his mechanic shop in 1988.

Respondent admits to a history of heavy drinking. He said that after the breakup of his first marriage he, "Got into drinking constantly. I was drinking all day. I filed bankruptcy. I finally woke up and started seeing Jane (second wife)." He said he then went back to drinking heavily in 1988 or 1989 when his business was going bad. He said, "I started drinking heavy again around 1992 or 93. I had gotten into hanging out all night and running with people who were smoking pot." Mr. Jones has never participated in an alcohol or drug program. He denies selling marijuana to children in his former neighborhood, contrary to the statements given to police by some of the youngsters. Jones does admit to "occasionally" arranging for adults to purchase marijuana.

The defendant reports no physical problems. He does indicate that his left leg and foot are smaller than the right. He believes this is the result of a mild case of polio.

Since his arrest for the instant offense the defendant has gone into mental health therapy with Dr. Gilbert Riler of the Community Mental Health Program. Respondent is seeing Dr. Riler once per week. Dr. Riler said that he would provide an evaluation to the court, prior to the defendant's sentencing. When I spoke with the Doctor on July 8, 1995, he said the defendant's MMPI test shows subject is essentially a personality disorder, characterized by "Hedonistic" and "Pleasure Oriented" manifestation. Dr. Riler states the defendant's positive qualities are the fact that he is acknowledging his guilt in the instant offense. Also, he has been open and candid with the doctor, advising the doctor that he has been involved with 40 to 50 different boys. Also, Mr. Jones has displayed no indication of psychopathic or manipulative behavior in therapy.

Mr. Jones notes the following liabilities, Ingham County Friend of the Court $1500 in arrearages (at $40 per month), Mr. Donald Smith (Holder of defendant's land contract) $135,000 at $1700 per month, Ronald Gorman (Business associate) $9000 at $400 per month, Bank of Lansing $1900 (executive credit) at $100 per month, Master Charge/VISA $200 at $40 per month, American Express $500 at $150 per month, June Wiler (ex-wife) $2000, Attorney fees $1300.

He reports the following assets: Fred's Automotive Diagnostics Inc. $150,000 ($15,000 equity), 1983 Chrysler $600, 1986 Cadillac $3000.

In summation, before the court is an intelligent individual with marketable skills, who has functioned as a productive member of society. He has, however, been plagued with substance abuse for many years. Also, Mr. Jones has displayed a propensity toward sexual involvement with pre-adolescent boys for well over a decade. His tendency toward pedophilic behavior has left emotional scars not only on the instant offense victim, but the uncharged victims as well as their families. The community deserves to be protected from Mr. Jones. In the defendant's favor, he does acknowledge his guilt, but also acknowledges that his behavior is some-thing over which he has little in the way of control.

Placement in a structured setting where he will not have access to pre-adolescent teenage boys is strongly recommended. Mr. Jones should be provided treatment in an effort to help him overcome his illness. Howev-er, the main issue in sentencing, in my opinion, is protecting other potential victims from the defendant.

INVESTIGATOR'S VERSION OF OFFENSE:

According to Lansing Police Department complaint #95–05592: On or about April 12 or 19th, 1995, the defendant Fred Jones engaged in sexual penetration with Greg Daley, dob: 5–23–82, a person under 13 years of age. Daley told investigating officers that on that occasion he had spent the night at Fred Jones's residence in Lansing, Michigan. Daley was asleep on a couch in the living room. He awoke to find Jones crawling underneath the sheet and pulling Daley's undershorts off. When asked by officers, what Jones did next, Daley said, "He gave me a blow job". Upon further questioning, Daley revealed the defendant had given him a glass of beer earlier in the evening. Daley also told officers that this same type of incident had happened, "Maybe five or six times."

Daley upon further questioning told officers that on one occasion Fred Jones was performing oral sex upon him, while two other adult males were also in the room performing fellatio on each other.

Lansing Police Officers became aware of Daley's situation as well as the assault upon numerous other early adolescent boys via an anonymous tip that was phoned into the police department on May 7, 1995. The tipster told officers that Jones was involving himself sexually with a number of children at the Jones residence. Four names were provided by the tipster. Investigating officers James Martin and Alex Finch went to the schools that the various boys attended and after getting permission from their parents, interviewed several of them. All of the boys acknowledged that they had been to Jones's home and they were aware that he was sexually involved with numerous young boys. Some of the boys interviewed said they were not sexually involved with Jones, while others admitted to the officers that Jones had been engaging in sexual activities with them. They also told the officers Jones had been providing beer, as well as marijuana, to the boys while at his home. The boys also told the officers that Jones had been showing them numerous pornographic movies, most of which involved homosexual activity between males. The boys had also been shown numerous items of sexual paraphernalia including magazines, pictures and various other sexual paraphernalia.

Based on the information gathered through interviewing the boys, a search warrant was requested and granted by Judge Claude R. Thomas of Lansing District Court, on May 10, 1995.

At approximately 4:15 p.m. May 10, 1995, the defendant was arrested at his place of work. He was served with a four count felony warrant for Criminal Sexual Conduct. Fifteen minutes later four officers of the Lansing Police Department Criminal Intelligence Unit executed a search warrant at the defendant's residence. A large quantity of evidence was seized and transported to the Police Department Evidence Room. Attached to this report is the list of items seized during the search. The items include numerous pictures of some of his victims in sexually provocative poses. I viewed the photographs at the Lansing Police Department. There were photographs of the victims performing and having oral sex performed upon them. There were photographs of boys sitting on the defendant's lap, kissing him on the mouth, there was a photograph of the defendant in bed with one of the victims, engaging in anal intercourse, there were a number of photographs taken at a "Birthday Party" where there were a number of joints placed on the cake so as to resemble candles.

As noted above, the defendant was arrested on May 10, 1995, and was released on bond the following day. He remains free awaiting sentence. Officers James Martin and Alex Finch, who investigated this case and interviewed the victims, both recommend life imprisonment. Martin pointed out that there was a total of 19 counts against the defendant. The officers spoke with 13 different children who acknowledged they had been sexually involved with the defendant, and who were willing to press charges. Further, Martin and Finch stressed the devastating emotional effect Jones has had on the children in arriving at their recommendation for sentencing. Daley, for instance, was a straight 'A' student at Otto Junior High School, but dropped out of school after the instant offense became publicized for fear of being ridiculed by his fellow students. Another young man, Gordon Taylor, a student at Waverly West Junior High said he felt like a monster, and he also said he would commit suicide if his fellow students were to find out about his involvement with Jones. Finally, the officers said a number of the children involved had started to display acting out behavior; they had started dropping out of school and were getting involved with drinking and drugs, all of which the officers feel is related to their experiences with the defendant.

I spoke to the mother of Greg Daley (the victim that the defendant has pled guilty to assaulting), on July 12, 1995. Mrs. Daley is very bitter about the whole incident. She said that she and her family have known the defendant approximately seven years. She said he always presented himself as a "nice neighbor" who was always interested in the kids' well-being. She said the defendant often said, "Let's do things for the kids." She went on to say that he professed to wanting to get the kids involved in BMX Racing as a way of, "Keeping them off the street."

Mrs. Daley said her child's experience with the defendant has changed his personality. She said previously Greg, "Was usually a quiet easy-going person, but now he is very closed. He just doesn't want to talk about the incident. He gets very angry. He used to be very easy-going, but now he flies off the handle. I feel this has really screwed him up." Mrs. Daley said Jones had also been involved with Greg's older brother Mark, though Mark refuses to discuss his involvement with the defendant. Mark is learning disabled and has always been involved in special education.

When asked for a recommendation for sentencing, Mrs. Daley responded, "I think he should go natural life. No parole. Don't let him get to no one else. I am not a person with a lot of hate, but I know that if he were to walk and I saw him on the street, I wouldn't hesitate to run him down."

I spoke with Gordon Taylor's mother on July 18, 1995. Mrs. Taylor said, "We trusted Fred. Fred had become a real good friend of ours. He was in our home. We had him in our home for dinner. If I had a chance, I would have killed Fred. I just wanted to kill him. My husband feels the same way. My son Gordon does too. I am very hostile."

Mrs. Taylor went on to explain to me just how devastated her entire family is as the result of learning that the defendant was engaging in sexual activity with Gordon. She said that both she and her husband are in counseling with Gordon. She also said immediately after they were told of what was going on between Fred Jones and their son, her husband went to Jones's home with a gun. He was sitting outside of Jones's home. Mrs. Taylor called Lansing Police because she was afraid there would be trouble. The police officers arrived and told Mr. Taylor to go home, and at that point he broke down and cried because he was so devastated.

Mrs. Taylor continued, "Fred bought Gordon a $160 bow for a birthday present. Fred was buying Gordon everything. He was going on vacation with him, going fishing and on vacation. It was like Fred was a big brother. I just don't know why I didn't see through it."

When asked how her son had been affected, Mrs. Taylor said, "Gordon is a straight 'A' student in school. When this happened he didn't go to school, see his friends, or go outside." Mrs. Taylor said during the summer of 1994, Gordon has now related to her, on one occasion Fred chased a young man out of his (Fred's) residence with a gun. Gordon was present. Fred told Gordon if Gordon told anyone about what was going on he would kill him. It was at that point that Gordon developed an ulcer. Gordon is 14 years of age.

Mrs. Taylor continued, "I blame myself for not being able to see it. I will never trust anybody again, I don't care if it is a baseball coach, or a teacher. Whenever an adult is friends with my kid I won't have it." I asked Mrs. Taylor her recommendation for sentencing. She said, "I want him to pay for what he did to my son. I want him to hurt like we hurt. I want him to think about this for a long, long time. This hurt is the most hurt we have ever had.... I just pray to God Fred doesn't come around us any time again. I hope the law can make us happy by putting him away and not letting him out. Fred is a sick man and he needs lots of help."

OFFENDER'S VERSION OF OFFENSE:

"Greg Daley and I have known each other for about five years. We have basically been good friends. He has stayed with me and come with me on many occasions over the five years. Greg's been a boy that always wanted fatherly attention. He has climbed in bed with me and cuddled and everything. Over the last six months he started sexually maturing and things happen."

The defendant admits to having sexual relations with Greg Daley dob: 5–23–82, Gordon Taylor dob: 4–30–81, Allen Freeman dob: 1–18–80, and Michael Cook dob: 11–16–80. Mr. Jones admits to being sexually involved with boys he has met through BMX, over the past four to five years. He went on to say he would sometimes feel "guilty" after going "all the way" with the boys. He stated, "I would discuss personal problems with the boys, when they were having them." He said he discussed the dangers of becoming involved in drugs with them.

Jones continued, "I think it started out as a kind of father/son and I let it go too far. I wouldn't always have sex with them. We spent a lot of time together fishing, bowling and spending time on the BMX track. But I would feel guilty afterwards. I don't feel like I took advantage of them, but I did let it go too far. But, the boys were aggressive in the sex acts and I feel they kept coming back because they enjoyed visiting."

Over the past four years Jones estimates he has worked with "about 400 youngsters," "but there has not always been the sexual activity." Finally, Jones stated, "I have gotten back involved with my own sons and I am trying to get my business back together. It was not my intention to hurt anybody. At that time I felt I was doing something I hadn't ought to be doing. I hadn't any intention of doing any harm or hurting anybody. I tried to help them, by helping with their home life and school problems. We discussed lives and I was trying to help them. I know I went too far, but what's the old saying hindsight is better than foresight. I guess sometimes when you are alone and lonely, and the aggressiveness is there and everything and especially if you are getting high you let everything go to the wind."

PREVIOUS CRIMINAL HISTORY:

Juvenile: None

Adult:

1–2–67—Lansing—Larc/Bldg.—final charge: Larc/U/$100—sentenced 1–3–67—3 months probation—$30 fine.

6–27–79—Lansing—Indecent Liberties with a Child—final charge: Accosting Children for Immoral Purposes—sentenced 9–19–79—2 yrs. probation 3 days jail—$200 costs.

PERSONAL HISTORY:

Lorraine Jones—Mother—age 65—Daytona Beach, Florida.

Willis Jones—Stepfather—age 68—Daytona Beach, Florida.

Oliver Cartwright—Father—deceased (defendant knows nothing about him).

Richard Jones—Brother—age 48—Lansing.

Donald Jones—Brother—age 43—Daytona Beach, Florida.

James Jones—Son—age 23—attends Western Michigan University.

David Jones—Son—age 20—attends MSU.

The defendant was born and raised in Lansing. Until age 11 he resided with his mother and grandparents. Subject's mother married Willis Jones when the defendant was 11 years of age.

Mr. Jones adopted the defendant and his siblings. The elder Jones was employed by the United States Postal Service while the defendant's mother was pretty much a dental office receptionist. As a teenager, respondent reports a very poor relationship with his stepfather. He describes it as, "He (stepfather) was a Navy man. He [would] strike first and maybe ask questions later." At about age 16 the defendant ran away from home and lived above a store in downtown Lansing. He said he supported himself by managing a bowling alley on South Washington. After living on his own at the apartment, and briefly at the YMCA he "begged" the principal at Eastern High School to let him return. He said he did return and graduated in 1967.

Respondent reports becoming involved in homosexual activities in his late teens.

Jones reports a good relationship with his mother, and a satisfactory relationship with his stepfather. He said he and his brothers have never been close. Jones goes on to say he attempted to talk with his mother as well as his minister about his homosexual inclinations in his teens, but Jones said, "They just kind of said it would go away, they didn't want to deal with it."

MARITAL HISTORY:

The defendant married the former June Takahisha in 1970 while serving with the United States Army in Tokyo, Japan. She returned to his country with him, and two sons were born to their union. They were married 8 or 9 years, but he said his long work hours and the strain of having children caused the breakdown in their relationship. He said after a while, "It seemed like I was just a paycheck to her."

Respondent states that he and his former wife rarely communicate, however, she did loan him $2000 of the necessary money to post bond.

The defendant married the former Jane Francis in 1980. The marriage lasted five years. There were no children born to the union. This was Jones's second marriage. Respondent said, "I turned into a workaholic, alcoholic and dopeaholic, and conflicts with our children and then my gay activities started flaring up," leading to the demise of this marriage.

4. As is apparent from the presentence investigation report set forth above, presentence investigation reports, upon which sentencing courts frequently rely when imposing sentences, often are filled with references to the

hearsay statements of witnesses. Whether defendants have a constitutional right to have access to these reports and to respond to information contained within them were issues in the following case.

GARDNER v. FLORIDA

Supreme Court of the United States, 1977.
430 U.S. 349, 97 S.Ct. 1197, 51 L.Ed.2d 393.

MR. JUSTICE STEVENS announced the judgment of the Court and delivered an opinion, in which MR. JUSTICE STEWART and MR. JUSTICE POWELL joined.

Petitioner was convicted of first-degree murder and sentenced to death. When the trial judge imposed the death sentence he stated that he was relying in part on information in a presentence investigation report.[a] Portions of the report were not disclosed to counsel for the parties. Without reviewing the confidential portion of the presentence report, the Supreme Court of Florida, over the dissent of two justices, affirmed the death sentence. We conclude that this procedure does not satisfy the constitutional command that no person shall be deprived of life without due process of law.

* * *

* * * [W]e consider the justifications offered by the State for a capital-sentencing procedure which permits a trial judge to impose the death sentence on the basis of confidential information which is not disclosed to the defendant or his counsel.

The State first argues that an assurance of confidentiality to potential sources of information is essential to enable investigators to obtain relevant but sensitive disclosures from persons unwilling to comment publicly about a defendant's background or character. The availability of such information, it is argued, provides the person who prepares the report with greater detail on which to base a sentencing recommendation and, in turn, provides the judge with a better basis for his sentencing decision. But consideration must be given to the quality, as well as the quantity, of the information on which the sentencing judge may rely. Assurances of secrecy are conducive to the transmission of confidences which may bear no closer relation to fact than the average rumor or item of gossip, and may imply a pledge not to attempt independent verification of the information received. The risk that some of the information accepted in confidence may be erroneous, or may be misinterpreted, by the investigator or by the sentencing judge, is manifest.

If, as the State argues, it is important to use such information in the sentencing process, we must assume that in some cases it will be decisive in the judge's choice between a life sentence and a death sentence. * * *

---

a. In imposing the death sentence, the trial judge rejected a jury recommendation that the defendant be sentenced to life in prison. The jury had no access to the presentence investigation report that was prepared after the jury had returned its advisory verdict.

[I]f it is the basis for a death sentence, the interest in reliability plainly outweighs the State's interest in preserving the availability of comparable information in other cases.

The State also suggests that full disclosure of the presentence report will unnecessarily delay the proceeding. We think the likelihood of significant delay is overstated because we must presume that reports prepared by professional probation officers * * * are generally reliable.[10] In those cases in which the accuracy of a report is contested, the trial judge can avoid delay by disregarding the disputed material. Or if the disputed matter is of critical importance, the time invested in ascertaining the truth would surely be well spent if it makes the difference between life and death.

The State further urges that full disclosure of presentence reports, which often include psychiatric and psychological evaluations, will occasionally disrupt the process of rehabilitation. The argument, if valid, would hardly justify withholding the report from defense counsel. Moreover, whatever force that argument may have in noncapital cases, it has absolutely no merit in a case in which the judge has decided to sentence the defendant to death. * * *

Finally, Florida argues that trial judges can be trusted to exercise their discretion in a responsible manner, even though they may base their decisions on secret information. * * * The argument rests on the erroneous premise that the participation of counsel is superfluous to the process of evaluating the relevance and significance of aggravating and mitigating facts. Our belief that debate between adversaries is often essential to the truth-seeking function of trials requires us also to recognize the importance of giving counsel an opportunity to comment on facts which may influence the sentencing decision in capital cases.

Even if it were permissible to withhold a portion of the report from a defendant, and even from defense counsel, pursuant to an express finding of good cause for nondisclosure, it would nevertheless be necessary to make the full report a part of the record to be reviewed on appeal. Since the State must administer its capital-sentencing procedures with an even hand, it is important that the record on appeal disclose to the reviewing court the considerations which motivated the death sentence in every case in which it is imposed. * * *

* * *

We conclude that petitioner was denied due process of law when the death sentence was imposed, at least in part, on the basis of information which he had no opportunity to deny or explain.

* * *

THE CHIEF JUSTICE concurs in the judgment.

---

10. Our presumption that the reports are normally reliable is, of course, not inconsistent with our concern about the possibility that critical unverified information may be inaccurate and determinative in a particular case.

MR. JUSTICE WHITE, concurring in the judgment.

* * *

* * * Here the sentencing judge indicated that he selected petitioner Gardner for the death penalty in part because of information contained in a presentence report which information was not disclosed to petitioner or to his counsel and to which petitioner had no opportunity to respond. A procedure for selecting people for the death penalty which permits consideration of such secret information relevant to the "character and record of the individual offender" fails to meet the "need for reliability in the determination that death is the appropriate punishment". This conclusion stems solely from the Eighth Amendment's ban on cruel and unusual punishments and my conclusion is limited to cases in which the death penalty is imposed. I thus see no reason to address in this case the possible application to sentencing proceedings—in death or other cases—of the Due Process Clause, other than as the vehicle by which the strictures of the Eighth Amendment are triggered in this case. For these reasons, I do not join the plurality opinion but concur in the judgment.

MR. JUSTICE BLACKMUN, concurring in the judgment. [Opinion omitted.]

MR. JUSTICE BRENNAN.

[Justice Brennan concurred that due process is violated when a defendant in a capital case is not apprised of the contents of the presentence investigation report provided to the sentencing judge.]

MR. JUSTICE MARSHALL, dissenting. [Opinion omitted.]

MR. JUSTICE REHNQUIST, dissenting. [Opinion omitted.]

QUESTIONS AND POINTS FOR DISCUSSION

1. *Gardner* concerned the constitutional rights of a defendant in a capital case to have access to a presentence investigation report and to explain or rebut information in it before sentencing. The Supreme Court has yet to definitively resolve whether these rights extend to defendants in noncapital cases. The Sixth Circuit Court of Appeals has capsulized the law's uncertainty: "The upshot is this: while a defendant may not have the constitutional right to *confront* the witnesses against him at sentencing, it remains unclear under modern sentencing practices what due process right he has to *know* who these witnesses are and what they have said, to *respond* meaningfully to the accusations or otherwise to *ensure* that the accusations are accurate." United States v. Hamad, 495 F.3d 241, 247 (6th Cir. 2007).

As is discussed later in this chapter, basing a sentence on materially false information can abridge a defendant's due-process rights. See notes 6 and 7 on pages 156–57. Does this constitutional limitation on the information on which a sentence can be grounded have a bearing on the question whether the constitutional rights recognized in *Gardner* extend to defendants in noncapital cases? The Sixth Circuit has queried, " 'How can a due process guarantee against a sentence predicated on misinformation be viable, and not rendered meaningless, if the defendant has no way of determining that the sentencing judge was misadvised?' " Stewart v. Erwin, 503 F.3d 488, 498 (6th Cir. 2007) (quoting Baker v. United States, 388 F.2d 931, 935 n.1 (4th Cir. 1968) (Winter, J., concurring)).

2. When determining whether due process accords a right to a particular procedural safeguard, the Supreme Court typically applies what has come to be known as the *Mathews* balancing test. Mathews v. Eldridge, 424 U.S. 319, 335, 96 S.Ct. 893, 903 (1976). Three factors are balanced under this test. The first factor is the "private interest" at stake. The more weighty the interest the more likely it is that the procedural safeguard in question is constitutionally mandated. The second factor focuses on the risk that the individual will be deprived erroneously of this private interest under current procedures and the "probable value" of the additional safeguard in averting this erroneous deprivation. The greater the benefits of the procedural safeguard in preventing erroneous deprivations of the private interest the more likely it is that there is a due-process right to this procedural safeguard. The third and final factor is the impact on governmental interests if the safeguard were required. To the extent that the safeguard would advance a governmental interest this factor points towards finding the procedural safeguard to be part of due process. On the other hand, if providing the safeguard would adversely affect a governmental interest, this factor points against finding the safeguard subsumed within due process.

Under the *Mathews* balancing test, do defendants convicted of noncapital crimes have the constitutional rights, in your opinion, to have access to information in a presentence investigation report and the opportunity to deny or explain that information? Explain your reasoning.

2. THE RIGHT TO COUNSEL

a. Retained and Appointed Counsel

In Mempa v. Rhay, 389 U.S. 128, 88 S.Ct. 254 (1967), the Supreme Court concluded that the Sixth Amendment right to counsel extends to sentencing hearings. Noting the "critical nature of sentencing in a criminal case," the Court observed that an attorney could assist "in marshaling the facts, introducing evidence of mitigating circumstances and in general aiding and assisting the defendant to present his case as to sentence." Id. at 134–35, 88 S.Ct. at 256–57.

The holding of the Supreme Court in *Mempa* must be read against the backdrop of the Court's subsequent decision in Scott v. Illinois, 440 U.S. 367, 99 S.Ct. 1158 (1979), a case that concerned the right to be represented by appointed counsel at trial. In *Scott,* the Court held, in a 5–4 decision, that whether an indigent defendant has the right to appointed counsel at trial depends on the sanction ultimately imposed on the defendant. The Court noted that an indigent defendant has no such right to appointed counsel unless the sanction imposed includes some period of incarceration.

The language of *Scott v. Illinois* was all-encompassing, seeming to suggest that whether there is a Sixth Amendment right to appointed counsel at trial depends in every case on the actual penalty imposed in that case. *Scott* itself, however, involved a defendant who had been convicted of a misdemeanor. In a subsequent case, Nichols v. United States, 511 U.S. 738, 743 n. 9, 114 S.Ct. 1921, 1925 n. 9 (1994), the Supreme Court, in *dictum,* indicated that the actual-incarceration standard does not apply in a felony case, observing: "In felony cases, in contrast to misdemeanor charges, the Constitution requires that an indigent defendant be offered appointed counsel unless that right is intelligently and competently waived."

In Alabama v. Shelton, 535 U.S. 654, 122 S.Ct. 1764 (2002), the Supreme Court added another limitation to the actual-incarceration standard. In that case, the Court, in another 5–4 decision, held that the right to appointed counsel in a misdemeanor case exists even if a court suspends a prison or jail sentence and places the defendant on probation. A question not resolved by the Court in *Shelton* was whether a defendant has a right to appointed counsel in a misdemeanor case that results in a stand-alone sentence to probation—one not coupled with an actual or suspended term of incarceration. Some courts have concluded that the right to appointed counsel does not apply in that situation while acknowledging that the failure to appoint counsel might foreclose incarceration of a defendant whose probation is later revoked. See, e.g., United States v. Pollard, 389 F.3d 101, 104–06 (4th Cir. 2004); United States v. Perez–Macias, 335 F.3d 421, 426–28 (5th Cir. 2003).

If the Sixth Amendment right to appointed counsel at a sentencing hearing tracks the right to appointed counsel at trial, then all indigent defendants convicted of felonies apparently have the right to assistance from an appointed attorney during the sentencing process. In addition, indigent defendants convicted of misdemeanors have a Sixth Amendment right to the assistance of appointed counsel at a sentencing hearing when the penalty imposed involved some period of incarceration, whether suspended or not. Do you agree with this method of differentiating between misdemeanants who do and do not have the right to the assistance of appointed counsel at sentencing?

Separate and apart from questions concerning the right to the assistance of counsel at sentencing hearings is the question whether the defendant has the Sixth Amendment right to the assistance of counsel at certain interviews during which information is gathered from the defendant that will be considered at the sentencing hearing. The Supreme Court addressed this question in Estelle v. Smith, 451 U.S. 454, 101 S.Ct. 1866 (1981). In that case, the defendant was charged with murder. When the state disclosed that it intended to seek imposition of the death penalty, the trial judge directed that the defendant be examined by a psychiatrist to determine his competency to stand trial.

After the defendant was convicted of murder, the state called the psychiatrist as a witness at the sentencing hearing. The psychiatrist testified that the defendant was a sociopath for whom treatment would be unavailing. This testimony bore on the question of the defendant's future dangerousness, an issue which, if resolved against the defendant, could, and in this case did, lead to the imposition of the death penalty.

The Supreme Court unanimously concluded that the interviewing of the defendant by the psychiatrist without prior notification to the defendant's attorney that the interview would cover the subject of future dangerousness, as well as competency to stand trial, violated the defendant's Sixth Amendment right to counsel. Without such notice, the defendant was deprived of the opportunity to make a knowing decision as to whether to participate in the interview. The Supreme Court, however, added a caveat to its opinion, emphasizing that the defendant did not claim that he had the right to have his attorney actually present during the interview with the psychiatrist; he only claimed that his attorney should have received advance notice of the scope of topics that would be considered during the psychiatric examination. With seeming approval, the Court then quoted from the opinion of the court of appeals, which had stated that " 'an attorney present during the psychiatric interview could contribute little and might seriously disrupt the examination.' " Id. at 470 n. 14, 101 S.Ct. at 1877 n. 14.

When faced with the question whether a defendant has a Sixth Amendment right to have counsel present when being interviewed by a probation officer conducting a presentence investigation, most lower courts have distinguished *Estelle v. Smith*. In re Carter, 848 A.2d 281, 299 (Vt. 2004) (listing cases). United States v. Jackson, 886 F.2d 838 (7th Cir.1989) is a case in point. In that case, the Seventh Circuit Court of Appeals observed:

> A district judge's use of a defendant's statement to a probation officer in applying the Sentencing Guidelines is markedly unlike the *prosecutor's* adversarial use of a defendant's pretrial statement to a psychiatrist to carry the state's burden of proof before a jury. A federal probation officer is an extension of the court and not an agent of the government. The probation officer does not have an adversarial role in the sentencing proceedings. In interviewing a defendant as part of the presentence investigation, the probation officer serves as a neutral information gatherer for the sentencing judge. The interview of a defendant is but one of many aspects of the presentence investigation conducted by a probation officer.

* * *

> The pretrial statement made by the defendant in *Estelle* became a factor satisfying an element of the burden of proof borne by the prosecution in seeking the death penalty in a trial before a jury. *Estelle* is simply inapplicable on its facts and legal theory to a federal district judge's discretionary use of a defendant's postconviction statement made to a federal probation officer carrying out a nonadversarial presentence investigation.

Id. at 844–45.

Do you find the reasoning of the court in *Jackson* persuasive? Consider the facts of In re Carter, 848 A.2d 281 (Vt. 2004). The defendant in that case had been convicted of aggravated sexual assault of a former girlfriend. When two probation officers preparing his presentence investigation report approached the defendant to interview him, he said that he did not want to talk to them without his attorney present. The two probation officers, however, proceeded with the interview.

During the interview, the defendant talked about his hatred of the victim and his unwillingness to participate in sex-offender treatment:

> I've got a lot of hate for this girl. She didn't say no, she put the rubber on me and everything. . . . She knows she lied. I didn't do anything. I'm not doing no sex offender shit. I'll max my sentence. I'll do violent offender, but no sex shit. I have a lot of hate for her and frustrated anger. I could have killed her and been looking at the same amount of time I'm facing now.

These statements were quoted in the presentence report and cited in support of the recommendation in the report that the defendant be sentenced to thirty years to life. The sentencing judge referred to and relied upon these statements when imposing a prison sentence of forty-five years to life. Pointing to the defendant's lack of remorse for his actions and his denial of criminal responsibility, the judge explained that such a long sentence was necessary because the defendant posed a serious threat to the victim and others.

In concluding that a presentence interview by a probation officer is a critical stage of the prosecution to which the Sixth Amendment right to counsel attaches, the Supreme Court of Vermont proffered a different perspective that that shared by the majority of the courts:

> "The presentence interview plays a crucial role in determining the probation officer's recommended sentence. . . . [A] single finding by the probation officer can significantly affect the ultimate sentencing range." At a presentence interview, a defendant is likely to address matters that were not raised at trial and that will likely have a significant impact on sentencing. Moreover, a defendant's statements during a presentence interview can even have an impact on later prosecutions—of both the defendant and others. * * *

> The facts of this case are a clear example of the importance of the presentence investigation and a criminal defendant's participation in the development of the report. It is not an overstatement to say that petitioner committed sentencing suicide in his PSI interview. His criminal conduct warranted a long sentence of incarceration, but in a single paragraph he ensured that he would spend virtually all of his adult life in jail. * * *

* * *

* * * [A] criminal defendant, who testifies that he is innocent of the charged conduct, is unlikely to understand the need to admit responsibility for that conduct to improve his prospects at sentencing. On the other hand, admission of responsibility will constitute a waiver of defendant's self-incrimination right and could be the basis for a perjury prosecution.* * *

* * * [N]o Supreme Court decision supports the rationale of *Jackson* and other circuit court decisions that conclude that the right to counsel is limited to proceedings with an "adversary character." Further, this assertion is contrary to the long line of Supreme Court cases holding that a defendant's right to counsel under the Sixth Amendment depends primarily on the possibility of prejudice and unfairness in the proceedings and the ability of the presence of counsel to protect against such prejudice and unfairness.

Id. at 296–97, 299–300.

Do you believe that a probation officer's interview with a defendant during a presentence investigation is a critical stage of the prosecution to which the Sixth Amendment right to counsel attaches? Does your answer hinge on whether the presentence interview is conducted in a capital or a noncapital case? See Hoffman v. Arave, 236 F.3d 523, 540 (9th Cir.2001) (defendant, who received a death sentence, had a Sixth Amendment right to have counsel present at the presentence interview during which the defendant admitted being present at two other murders and doing nothing to stop them).

b.   Right to the Effective Assistance of Counsel

The Sixth Amendment right to the assistance of counsel at a sentencing hearing includes the right to the effective assistance of counsel. Strickland v. Washington, 466 U.S. 668, 104 S.Ct. 2052 (1984). In *Strickland,* the Supreme Court outlined the test to be applied when determining whether a defendant at a sentencing hearing for a capital crime received the effective assistance of counsel. To prevail on an ineffectiveness claim under the *Strickland* test, the defendant must prove two things: first, that his or her attorney acted unreasonably, in contravention of "prevailing professional norms," and second, that the defendant was prejudiced by this deficient performance. Id. at 687–88, 104 S.Ct. at 2064–65. To establish prejudice, the defendant must prove that there is a "reasonable probability" that the death penalty would not have been imposed if the defense attorney had performed competently. Id. at 694, 104 S.Ct. at 2068. Even when the defendant meets this burden, however, the prejudice requirement will not always be satisfied, as Lockhart v. Fretwell, 506 U.S. 364, 113 S.Ct. 838 (1993) makes clear.

In *Lockhart,* the defendant's attorney had failed at the sentencing hearing to make an objection that, based on the case law in existence at the time of the hearing, was meritorious and would have prevented imposition of a death sentence. The case upon which an objection could have been founded, however, was later overruled. While the Supreme Court seemed to recognize that the defendant would not have received the death sentence had his attorney made the appropriate objection at the sentencing hearing, the Court noted that the probable effect of counsel's deficient performance on the outcome of the sentencing process was not the end of the prejudice inquiry. A court also had to determine whether the deficient performance had led to a result that was "fundamentally unfair or unreliable." Id. at 369, 113 S.Ct. at 842. And in this case, the Court noted, the result was neither unfair nor unreliable because counsel's mistake only had deprived the defendant of "the chance to have the state court make an error in his favor." Id. at 371, 113 S.Ct. at 843.

In Williams v. Taylor, 529 U.S. 362, 120 S.Ct. 1495 (2000), the Supreme Court clarified that *Lockhart* did not supplant the two-part *Strickland* test for ineffective assistance of counsel with a three-pronged test. The Court noted that the *Strickland* test applies to "virtually all" claims of ineffective assistance of counsel. Id. at 391, 120 S.Ct. at 1512. Only in " 'unusual' " cases—when it would be "unjust" to treat the difference in outcome as "prejudice"—will the inept performance of counsel that likely affected the outcome of the proceeding not lead to a finding of unconstitutional ineffectiveness. Id. at 391–92, 393 n. 18, 120 S.Ct. at 1512, 1513 n.18 (quoting Lockhart v. Fretwell, 506 U.S. 364, 373, 113 S.Ct. 838, 845 (1993) (O'Connor, J., concurring)). Put in other words, "prejudice" under the *Strickland* test exists when counsel's deficient representation deprived the defendant of a "substantive or procedural right to which the law entitles him." Id. at 392–93 & n. 17, 120 S.Ct. at 1513 & n.17.

In Glover v. United States, 531 U.S. 198, 121 S.Ct. 696 (2001), a noncapital case, the Supreme Court further defined the contours of the prejudice prong of the *Strickland* test. In that case, the defendant's attorneys failed, both at the sentencing hearing and on appeal, to contest an alleged error in the sentencing court's calculation of the defendant's sentence under the federal sentencing guidelines. That error led to an increase in the defendant's sentence by six to twenty-one months.

The lower courts held that this increase in the sentence length was not long enough to constitute the requisite "prejudice" under the *Strickland* test. The Supreme Court disagreed, noting that any increase in the length of incarceration due to counsel's deficient performance can constitute the prejudice needed to sustain a claim for ineffective assistance of counsel. The Court's decision was driven in part by pragmatic considerations, with the Court observing that there is no "obvious dividing line" between sentence increases that cause "substantial" prejudice and those that do not. Id. at 204, 121 S.Ct. at 700.

3. THE RIGHTS TO PRESENT EVIDENCE AND MAKE A STATEMENT TO THE SENTENCER

Defendants have claimed that they not only have a right to speak to the court through their attorneys on the subject of their sentence, but that they also have a constitutional right to address the court themselves. The right that the defendants are invoking is known as the right of allocution.

The lower courts are split on the question whether defendants have a constitutionally-based right of allocution. Compare United States v. Biagon, 510 F.3d 844, 847 (9th Cir. 2007) (recognizing a due-process right of allocution) with United States v. Reyna, 358 F.3d 344, 349 (5th Cir. 2004) (holding that there is no constitutional right of allocution).The courts concluding that there is no constitutional right of allocution have relied heavily on the Supreme Court's decision in Hill v. United States, 368 U.S. 424, 82 S.Ct. 468 (1962). In *Hill,* however, the Court emphasized some special facts about the case. First, the Court noted that the sentencing court simply had failed to ask the defendant if he had anything to say before the court imposed sentence; the court had not forbidden a defendant who expressed his desire to address the court from doing so. Second, the Court underscored that the defendant had not claimed that the sentencing judge misunderstood, or was unaware of, relevant facts in sentencing the defendant. And finally, the Court emphasized that the defendant in *Hill* was represented by an attorney at the sentencing hearing.

Should this latter fact have any bearing on the question whether a defendant has a constitutional right of allocution? See Green v. United States, 365 U.S. 301, 304, 81 S.Ct. 653, 655 (1961), a case in which the Supreme Court, when discussing the right of allocution under Rule 32 of the Federal Rules of Criminal Procedure, stated: "The most persuasive counsel may not be able to speak for a defendant as the defendant might, with halting eloquence, speak for himself." Is it relevant to the constitutional question whether the defendant will be sentenced by a judge or a jury? See United States v. Hall, 152 F.3d 381, 393 (5th Cir.1998) (noting that a jury, unlike a judge, may not recognize that a defendant's unsworn statements may be less credible). Does it matter whether the sentencing hearing is in a capital or a noncapital case? See State v. Colon, 864 A.2d 666, 793–95 (Conn. 2004) (holding that defendant had no constitutional right to make an unsworn statement to a capital sentencing jury).

Though a defendant may or may not have a constitutional right of allocution, it is clear that at least in some circumstances, the defendant has a constitutional right to present evidence at a sentencing hearing. For example, in Green v. Georgia, 442 U.S. 95, 99 S.Ct. 2150 (1979) (per curiam), the Supreme Court held that the defendant's due-process rights were violated when he was not permitted to call a witness to testify at a sentencing hearing in a capital case because the witness's testimony, under the state's evidentiary rules, would be hearsay. The witness apparently would have testified that a codefendant had admitted to the witness that he was the one who had actually shot the victim whom the defendant was convicted of murdering. In concluding that the defendant's due-process rights were violated when he was not allowed to call the witness to testify at the sentencing hearing, the Court emphasized both that the witness's testimony was "highly relevant" to a "critical issue" in the sentencing hearing and that there were "substantial reasons" for believing that the testimony was reliable. The reasons mentioned by the Court included the following: the codefendant was a close friend of the witness; the codefendant had made a declaration against penal interest; there was evidence that corroborated the codefendant's admission; and the state had considered the admission reliable enough to use against the codefendant during his own trial for capital murder. See also Ake v. Oklahoma, 470 U.S. 68, 83–84, 86–87, 105 S.Ct. 1087, 1096–98 (1985) (indigent defendant convicted of capital murders had a due-process right to be afforded access to a psychiatrist to help the defendant prepare and present evidence on the question of his future dangerousness, a question that was a "significant factor" at his sentencing hearing).

The Supreme Court distinguished *Green v. Georgia* in Oregon v. Guzek, 546 U.S. 517, 126 S.Ct. 1226 (2006). In *Guzek*, the Court held that the defendant in that case had no constitutional right to present evidence at his capital sentencing hearing that he was innocent of the crime of which he had been convicted. The Court cited three factors that underlay its conclusion that the Eighth and Fourteenth Amendments afforded the defendant no such right: one, sentencing hearings traditionally have focused on how, not whether, the defendant committed the crime; two, the parties already had litigated the question of the defendant's guilt; and three, a state statute permitted the defendant to introduce at the sentencing hearing any evidence of his innocence adduced at the original trial, mitigating the adverse effects of the bar on the introduction at the sentencing hearing of new evidence of innocence, such as new evidence supporting an alibi defense.

4. RIGHT TO A STATEMENT OF REASONS FOR THE SENTENCE IMPOSED

According to the courts, defendants generally do not have a constitutional right to be apprised, whether orally or in writing, of the reasons why a particular sentence was imposed by a sentencer. United States v. Golomb, 754 F.2d 86, 90 (2d Cir.1985). Do you concur with this conclusion? Does the *Mathews* balancing test point towards or against the existence of a constitutional right to this statement of reasons?

In some exceptional circumstances, courts have found a statement of reasons required by, or linked to, the Constitution. For example, in North Carolina v. Pearce, 395 U.S. 711, 726, 89 S.Ct. 2072, 2081 (1969), the

Supreme Court held that the reasons for a higher sentence imposed on a defendant who successfully had appealed his first conviction and been convicted again after a second trial had to "affirmatively appear" on the record. The Court's rationale was that in these circumstances, there was too high a risk that the increased sentence was imposed, in violation of due process, to retaliate against the defendant for having exercised his right to appeal his conviction.

In subsequent cases, the Supreme Court has described the *Pearce* rule as a " 'judicially created means' " of effectuating a constitutional right, in this case the right not to have a sentence increased for vindictive reasons. Texas v. McCullough, 475 U.S. 134, 138, 106 S.Ct. 976, 978 (1986) (quoting Stone v. Powell, 428 U.S. 465, 482, 96 S.Ct. 3037, 3046 (1976)). Consequently, the Court has limited the application of the *Pearce* rule to circumstances where the risk of an increased sentence being imposed is sufficiently high to create a presumption of vindictiveness. Thus, in *Texas v. McCullough*, the Court ruled that the risk of vindictiveness is not great enough when the sentence was imposed by a "different sentencer" the second time around. 475 U.S. at 140, 106 S.Ct. at 979. Nor does a presumption of vindictiveness necessitating a statement of reasons for an increased sentence exist when the second sentence was imposed even by the same sentencer, but following the granting of a motion for a new trial. Id. at 138–39, 106 S.Ct. at 979. In these circumstances, according to the Court, the fact that the trial judge acknowledged the need for a new trial, instead of being ordered by the appellate court to hold one, sufficiently reduces the risk that the increased sentence was due to proscribed vindictiveness. Finally, as was discussed in Chapter 2, no presumption of vindictiveness exists when a defendant's guilty plea was set aside on appeal and the increased sentence was imposed following the defendant's trial on the reinstated charges. See the discussion of Alabama v. Smith, 490 U.S. 794, 109 S.Ct. 2201 (1989) on page 73.

5. STANDARD OF PROOF/RIGHT TO JURY TRIAL

When deciding what sentence to impose on a defendant, a court typically will consider a number of facts, including facts about the defendant, facts about the defendant's crime, and facts about the impact of a particular sentence on others. The constitutional rights that apply during sentencing proceedings hinge in part on whether a fact affecting a sentencing outcome is a sentencing factor or is, in actuality, an element of the crime. The Supreme Court has wrestled with the distinction between sentencing factors and elements of a crime, as the cases in this subsection confirm.

McMILLAN v. PENNSYLVANIA
Supreme Court of the United States, 1986.
477 U.S. 79, 106 S.Ct. 2411, 91 L.Ed.2d 67.

MR. JUSTICE REHNQUIST delivered the opinion of the Court.

We granted certiorari to consider the constitutionality, under the Due Process Clause of the Fourteenth Amendment and the jury trial guarantee of the Sixth Amendment, of Pennsylvania's Mandatory Minimum Sentencing Act.

I

The Act was adopted in 1982. It provides that anyone convicted of certain enumerated felonies is subject to a mandatory minimum sentence of five years' imprisonment if the sentencing judge finds, by a preponderance of the evidence, that the person "visibly possessed a firearm" during the commission of the offense. At the sentencing hearing, the judge is directed to consider the evidence introduced at trial and any additional evidence offered by either the defendant or the Commonwealth.[1] The Act operates to divest the judge of discretion to impose any sentence of less than five years for the underlying felony; it does not authorize a sentence in excess of that otherwise allowed for that offense.

* * *

II

Petitioners argue that under the Due Process Clause, * * * if a state wants to punish visible possession of a firearm it must undertake the burden of proving that fact beyond a reasonable doubt. We disagree. [*In re*] *Winship*[, 397 U.S. 358 (1970)] held that "the Due Process Clause protects the accused against conviction except upon proof beyond a reasonable doubt of every fact necessary to constitute the crime with which he is charged." * * * But in *Patterson* [*v. New York,* 432 U.S. 197 (1977)], we rejected the claim that whenever a State links the "severity of punishment" to "the presence or absence of an identified fact" the State must prove that fact beyond a reasonable doubt. * * * In particular, we upheld against a due process challenge New York's law placing on defendants charged with murder the burden of proving the affirmative defense of extreme emotional disturbance.

1.　Section 9712 provides in full:

"(a) Mandatory sentence.—Any person who is convicted in any court of this Commonwealth of murder of the third degree, voluntary manslaughter, rape, involuntary deviate sexual intercourse, robbery * * *, aggravated assault * * * or kidnapping, or who is convicted of attempt to commit any of these crimes, shall, if the person visibly possessed a firearm during the commission of the offense, be sentenced to a minimum sentence of at least five years of total confinement notwithstanding any other provision of this title or other statute to the contrary.

"(b) Proof at sentencing.—Provisions of this section shall not be an element of the crime and notice thereof to the defendant shall not be required prior to conviction, but reasonable notice of the Commonwealth's intention to proceed under this section shall be provided after conviction and before sentencing. The applicability of this section shall be determined at sentencing. The court shall consider any evidence presented at trial and shall afford the Commonwealth and the defendant an opportunity to present any necessary additional evidence and shall determine, by a preponderance of the evidence, if this section is applicable.

"(c) Authority of court in sentencing.—There shall be no authority in any court to impose on an offender to which this section is applicable any lesser sentence than provided for in subsection (a) or to place such offender on probation or to suspend sentence. Nothing in this section shall prevent the sentencing court from imposing a sentence greater than that provided in this section."

* * * [I]n determining what facts must be proved beyond a reasonable doubt the state legislature's definition of the elements of the offense is usually dispositive * * *. * * *

* * * [T]he Pennsylvania Legislature has expressly provided that visible possession of a firearm is not an element of the crimes enumerated in the mandatory sentencing statute, but instead is a sentencing factor that comes into play only after the defendant has been found guilty of one of those crimes beyond a reasonable doubt. Indeed, the elements of the enumerated offenses, like the maximum permissible penalties for those offenses, were established long before the Mandatory Minimum Sentencing Act was passed. While visible possession might well have been included as an element of the enumerated offenses, Pennsylvania chose not to redefine those offenses in order to so include it, and *Patterson* teaches that we should hesitate to conclude that due process bars the State from pursuing its chosen course in the area of defining crimes and prescribing penalties.

As *Patterson* recognized, of course, there are constitutional limits to the State's power in this regard; in certain limited circumstances *Winship*'s reasonable-doubt requirement applies to facts not formally identified as elements of the offense charged. * * * While we have never attempted to define precisely * * * the extent to which due process forbids the reallocation or reduction of burdens of proof in criminal cases, and do not do so today, we are persuaded by several factors that Pennsylvania's Mandatory Minimum Sentencing Act does not exceed those limits.

* * * Responding to the concern that its rule would permit States unbridled power to redefine crimes to the detriment of criminal defendants, the *Patterson* Court advanced the unremarkable proposition that the Due Process Clause precludes States from discarding the presumption of innocence * * *. Nor does [§ 9712] relieve the prosecution of its burden of proving guilt; § 9712 only becomes applicable after a defendant has been duly convicted of the crime for which he is to be punished.

* * * Section 9712 neither alters the maximum penalty for the crime committed nor creates a separate offense calling for a separate penalty; it operates solely to limit the sentencing court's discretion in selecting a penalty within the range already available to it without the special finding of visible possession of a firearm. Section 9712 "ups the ante" for the defendant only by raising to five years the minimum sentence which may be imposed within the statutory plan.[4] The statute gives no impression of having been tailored to permit the visible possession finding to be a tail which wags the dog of the substantive offense. Petitioners' claim that visible possession under the Pennsylvania statute is "really" an element of the offenses for which they are being punished—that Pennsylvania has in effect defined a new set of upgraded felonies—would have at least more

---

4. By prescribing a mandatory minimum sentence, the Act incidentally serves to restrict the sentencing court's discretion in setting a maximum sentence. Pennsylvania law provides that a minimum sentence of confinement "shall not exceed one-half of the maximum sentence imposed." Thus, the shortest maximum term permissible under the Act is 10 years.

superficial appeal if a finding of visible possession exposed them to greater or additional punishment, but it does not.

Finally, we note that the specter raised by petitioners of States restructuring existing crimes in order to "evade" the commands of *Winship* just does not appear in this case. As noted above, § 9712's enumerated felonies retain the same elements they had before the Mandatory Minimum Sentencing Act was passed. The Pennsylvania Legislature did not change the definition of any existing offense. It simply took one factor that has always been considered by sentencing courts to bear on punishment—the instrumentality used in committing a violent felony—and dictated the precise weight to be given that factor if the instrumentality is a firearm. Pennsylvania's decision to do so has not transformed against its will a sentencing factor into an "element" of some hypothetical "offense."

Petitioners seek support for their due process claim by observing that many legislatures have made possession of a weapon an element of various aggravated offenses. But the fact that the States have formulated different statutory schemes to punish armed felons is merely a reflection of our federal system, which demands "[t]olerance for a spectrum of state procedures dealing with a common problem of law enforcement" * * *.

* * *

III

Having concluded that States may treat "visible possession of a firearm" as a sentencing consideration rather than an element of a particular offense, we now turn to petitioners' subsidiary claim that due process nonetheless requires that visible possession be proved by at least clear and convincing evidence. Like the court below, we have little difficulty concluding that in this case the preponderance standard satisfies due process. Petitioners do not and could not claim that a sentencing court may never rely on a particular fact in passing sentence without finding that fact by "clear and convincing evidence." Sentencing courts have traditionally heard evidence and found facts without any prescribed burden of proof at all. Pennsylvania has deemed a particular fact relevant and prescribed a particular burden of proof. We see nothing in Pennsylvania's scheme that would warrant constitutionalizing burdens of proof at sentencing.[8]

* * *

---

8. *Addington v. Texas,* 441 U.S. 418 (1979), and *Santosky v. Kramer,* 455 U.S. 745 (1982), which respectively applied the "clear and convincing evidence" standard where the State sought involuntary commitment to a mental institution and involuntary termination of parental rights, are not to the contrary. Quite unlike the situation in those cases, criminal sentencing takes place only after a defendant has been adjudged guilty beyond a reasonable doubt. Once the reasonable-doubt standard has been applied to obtain a valid conviction, "the criminal defendant has been constitutionally deprived of his liberty to the extent that the State may confine him." *Meachum v. Fano,* 427 U.S. 215, 224 (1976). As noted in text, sentencing courts have always operated without constitutionally imposed burdens of proof; embracing petitioners' suggestion that we apply the clear-and-convincing standard here would significantly alter criminal sentencing, for we see no

IV

In light of the foregoing, petitioners' final claim—that the Act denies them their Sixth Amendment right to a trial by jury—merits little discussion. Petitioners again argue that the jury must determine all ultimate facts concerning the offense committed. Having concluded that Pennsylvania may properly treat visible possession as a sentencing consideration and not an element of any offense, we need only note that there is no Sixth Amendment right to jury sentencing, even where the sentence turns on specific findings of fact. See *Spaziano v. Florida,* 468 U.S. [447,] 459 [1984].

* * *

JUSTICE MARSHALL, with whom JUSTICE BRENNAN and JUSTICE BLACKMUN join, dissenting. [Opinion omitted.]

JUSTICE STEVENS, dissenting.

Petitioner Dennison, a 73–year–old man, committed an aggravated assault upon a neighborhood youth whom he suspected of stealing money from his house. After a trial at which the Commonwealth proved the elements of the offense of aggravated assault beyond a reasonable doubt, the trial judge imposed a sentence of imprisonment of 11½ to 23 months. Because he had concluded that Pennsylvania's recently enacted Mandatory Minimum Sentencing Act was unconstitutional, the trial judge refused to impose the 5–year minimum sentence mandated by that Act whenever the Commonwealth proves—by a preponderance of the evidence—that the defendant "visibly possessed a firearm during the commission of the offense."

* * *

It would demean the importance of the reasonable-doubt standard— indeed, it would demean the Constitution itself—if the substance of the standard could be avoided by nothing more than a legislative declaration that prohibited conduct is not an "element" of a crime. A legislative definition of an offense named "assault" could be broad enough to encompass every intentional infliction of harm by one person upon another, but surely the legislature could not provide that only that fact must be proved beyond a reasonable doubt and then specify a range of increased punishments if the prosecution could show by a preponderance of the evidence that the defendant robbed, raped, or killed his victim "during the commission of the offense."

Appropriate respect for the rule of *In re Winship* requires that there be some constitutional limits on the power of a State to define the elements of criminal offenses. The high standard of proof is required because of the immense importance of the individual interest in avoiding both the loss of liberty and the stigma that results from a criminal

---

way to distinguish the visible possession finding at issue here from a host of other express or implied findings sentencing judges typically make on the way to passing sentence.

conviction. It follows, I submit, that if a State provides that a specific component of a prohibited transaction shall give rise both to a special stigma and to a special punishment, that component must be treated as a "fact necessary to constitute the crime" within the meaning of our holding in *In re Winship*.

Pennsylvania's Mandatory Minimum Sentencing Act reflects a legislative determination that a defendant who "visibly possessed a firearm" during the commission of an aggravated assault is more blameworthy than a defendant who did not. A judicial finding that the defendant used a firearm in an aggravated assault places a greater stigma on the defendant's name than a simple finding that he committed an aggravated assault. And not to be overlooked, such a finding with respect to petitioner Dennison automatically mandates a punishment that is more than twice as severe as the *maximum* punishment that the trial judge considered appropriate for his conduct.

It is true, as the Court points out, that the enhanced punishment is within the range that was authorized for any aggravated assault. That fact does not, however, minimize the significance of a finding of visible possession of a firearm whether attention is focused on the stigmatizing or punitive consequences of that finding. The finding identifies conduct that the legislature specifically intended to prohibit and to punish by a special sanction. In my opinion the constitutional significance of the special sanction cannot be avoided by the cavalier observation that it merely "ups the ante" for the defendant. No matter how culpable petitioner Dennison may be, the difference between 11½ months and 5 years of incarceration merits a more principled justification than the luck of the draw.

I respectfully dissent.

QUESTIONS AND POINTS FOR DISCUSSION

1. *McMillan* did not resolve, because it did not have to, whether the government must prove the existence of aggravating sentencing factors by at least a preponderance of the evidence. In your opinion, if the Pennsylvania statute at issue in *McMillan* had not required the sentencing judge to find, by a preponderance of the evidence, that the defendant "visibly possessed a firearm" in order to impose the mandatory-minimum sentence of five years, would due process require the government to meet this standard of proof?

2. Whatever the government's burden of proof with respect to aggravating facts that do not constitute elements of the crime, due process is not violated when the burden of proving mitigating circumstances by a preponderance of the evidence is placed on a defendant, even in a death-penalty case. Walton v. Arizona, 497 U.S. 639, 650, 110 S.Ct. 3047, 3055 (1990). Courts have reasoned that it is fundamentally fair to place the burden on a defendant of proving the facts about such things as family stability, educational background, and employment history of which the defendant, but not the government, is readily aware.

3. In Almendarez–Torres v. United States, 523 U.S. 224, 118 S.Ct. 1219 (1998), the Supreme Court once more confronted the question whether a statutory provision described an element of a crime or a sentencing factor. Under the statute before the Court, a deported alien who later illegally returned to the United States was subject to a maximum prison sentence of two years. But if the deportation had followed a conviction for an "aggravated felony," a prison sentence of up to twenty years could be imposed.

The Fifth Amendment requires that a federal indictment spell out the elements of a felony with which a defendant has been charged. But in a 5–4 decision in *Almendarez–Torres*, the Supreme Court held that the deported alien's prior conviction was a sentencing factor, not an element. As a result, the prior conviction did not have to be alleged in the indictment. The Court observed that traditionally, recidivism has been treated as a sentencing factor. In addition, the Court noted that a mandatory-minimum sentence, like the one to which the defendant was subject in *McMillan*, will often disadvantage a defendant more than an enhanced maximum sentence, since a judge is not bound to impose the maximum sentence.

Justice Scalia, in a dissenting opinion joined by Justices Stevens, Souter, and Ginsburg, argued that there is " 'serious doubt' whether the Constitution permits a defendant's sentencing exposure to be increased tenfold on the basis of a fact that is not charged, tried to a jury, and found beyond a reasonable doubt." Id. at 260, 118 S.Ct. at 1238. In order to avoid resolving what he described as a "difficult constitutional issue," Justice Scalia therefore construed the statute as setting forth an element of the crime rather than a sentencing factor.

4. In Monge v. California, 524 U.S. 721, 118 S.Ct. 2246 (1998), the Supreme Court considered another issue stemming from the imposition of a sentencing enhancement. The defendant in that case was convicted of using a minor to sell marijuana. Under California law, a defendant's sentence had to be doubled when the defendant had been convicted previously of a "serious felony." An assault conviction was considered a serious felony if the defendant had inflicted great bodily harm or had used a dangerous or deadly weapon during the assault. After the prosecutor produced a prison record at trial indicating that the defendant had been convicted previously of assault with a deadly weapon, the sentencing judge doubled the defendant's prison sentence from five to ten years.

On appeal, the state admitted that it had not, as required by the state statute, proven beyond a reasonable doubt that the defendant either had inflicted great bodily injury or used a deadly weapon during the prior assault of which he had been convicted. The state therefore requested that the case be remanded so that the state could attempt to meet its burden of proof by introducing evidence regarding the circumstances surrounding the assault.

The defendant responded that a retrial would violate his constitutional right not to be subjected to double jeopardy. The defendant based his double-jeopardy argument on the Supreme Court's decision in Bullington v. Missouri, 451 U.S. 430, 101 S.Ct. 1852 (1981). In that case, which involved a capital crime, the defendant was sentenced to life in prison by the original sentencing jury. After his conviction was reversed on appeal, the state announced that it, once again, would seek the death penalty.

The Supreme Court held in *Bullington* that the Fifth Amendment's double-jeopardy prohibition foreclosed further pursuit of the death penalty. The Court cited the longstanding rule that a state cannot reprosecute a person for a crime of which he or she was acquitted. The Court concluded that this rule should be extended to cases where the original sentencing jury had decided not to impose the death penalty after a trial-like sentencing proceeding in which the state had had to prove beyond a reasonable doubt the aggravating factors warranting imposition of the death penalty.

The defendant in *Monge* pointed out that his prior conviction of a "serious felony" had been considered during a trial in which he, like the defendant in *Bullington*, had a number of rights. Under California law, he had the right to a jury trial on the prior-conviction issue, the right to confront witnesses, and the privilege against self-incrimination. In addition, the state had to prove the prior conviction beyond a reasonable doubt.

Emphasizing the uniqueness of the death penalty, the Supreme Court, however, refused to extend the ruling in *Bullington* to a noncapital case. Thus, when a state fails to introduce enough evidence in the original sentencing proceeding to support an enhanced sentence, the state may be given, as far as double jeopardy is concerned, "another bite at the apple" in a noncapital case. See also North Carolina v. Pearce, 395 U.S. 711, 718–21, 89 S.Ct. 2072, 2077–79 (1969) (holding, in a noncapital case, that double jeopardy places only one constraint on sentencing: a defendant resentenced for a crime must be given credit for time served on the initial sentence).

While Justice Scalia agreed, in a dissenting opinion in *Monge* in which Justices Souter and Ginsburg joined, that the Double Jeopardy Clause does not apply to noncapital sentencing proceedings, he disagreed that this case involved only sentencing. Resolving the question that he had discussed, but not decided, a few months earlier in *Almendarez–Torres v. United States*, Justice Scalia concluded that so-called sentencing enhancements that increase the maximum sentence for a crime are actually elements of that crime. Therefore, according to Justice Scalia, because insufficient evidence was originally introduced regarding the defendant's prior conviction, the state could not constitutionally be given a second chance to prove the aggravated crime of which the defendant, in effect, had been acquitted.

Consider whether the Supreme Court's decisions in *Almendarez–Torres* and *Monge* can be reconciled with the case that follows.

APPRENDI v. NEW JERSEY

Supreme Court of the United States, 2000.
530 U.S. 466, 120 S.Ct. 2348, 147 L.Ed.2d 435.

JUSTICE STEVENS delivered the opinion of the Court.

A New Jersey statute classifies the possession of a firearm for an unlawful purpose as a "second-degree" offense. Such an offense is punishable by imprisonment for "between five years and 10 years." A separate statute, described by that State's Supreme Court as a "hate crime" law, provides for an "extended term" of imprisonment if the trial judge finds, by a preponderance of the evidence, that "[t]he defendant in committing the crime acted with a purpose to intimidate an individual or group of individuals because of race, color, gender, handicap, religion, sexual orientation or ethnicity." The extended term authorized by the hate crime law for second-degree offenses is imprisonment for "between 10 and 20 years."

The question presented is whether the Due Process Clause of the Fourteenth Amendment requires that a factual determination authorizing an increase in the maximum prison sentence for an offense from 10 to 20 years be made by a jury on the basis of proof beyond a reasonable doubt.

I

At 2:04 a.m. on December 22, 1994, petitioner Charles C. Apprendi, Jr., fired several .22–caliber bullets into the home of an African–American family that had recently moved into a previously all-white neighborhood in Vineland, New Jersey. Apprendi was promptly arrested and, at 3:05 a.m., admitted that he was the shooter. After further questioning, at 6:04 a.m., he made a statement—which he later retracted—that even though he did not know the occupants of the house personally, "because they are black in color he does not want them in the neighborhood."

A New Jersey grand jury returned a 23–count indictment charging Apprendi with four first-degree, eight second-degree, six third-degree, and five fourth-degree offenses. The charges alleged shootings on four different dates, as well as the unlawful possession of various weapons. None of the counts referred to the hate crime statute, and none alleged that Apprendi acted with a racially biased purpose.

The parties entered into a plea agreement, pursuant to which Apprendi pleaded guilty to two counts (3 and 18) of second-degree possession of a firearm for an unlawful purpose and one count (22) of the third-degree offense of unlawful possession of an antipersonnel bomb. * * * As part of the plea agreement, however, the State reserved the right to request the court to impose a higher "enhanced" sentence on count 18 (which was based on the December 22 shooting) on the ground that that offense was committed with a biased purpose * * *. Apprendi, correspondingly, reserved the right to challenge the hate crime sentence enhancement on the ground that it violates the United States Constitution.

* * * Because the plea agreement provided that the sentence on the sole third-degree offense (count 22) would run concurrently with the other sentences, the potential sentences on the two second-degree counts were critical. If the judge found no basis for the biased purpose enhancement, the maximum consecutive sentences on those counts would amount to 20 years in aggregate; if, however, the judge enhanced the sentence on count 18, the maximum on that count alone would be 20 years and the

maximum for the two counts in aggregate would be 30 years, with a 15–year period of parole ineligibility.

After the trial judge accepted the three guilty pleas, the prosecutor filed a formal motion for an extended term. The trial judge thereafter held an evidentiary hearing on the issue of Apprendi's "purpose" for the shooting on December 22. Apprendi adduced evidence from a psychologist and from seven character witnesses who testified that he did not have a reputation for racial bias. He also took the stand himself, explaining that the incident was an unintended consequence of overindulgence in alcohol, denying that he was in any way biased against African–Americans, and denying that his statement to the police had been accurately described. The judge, however, found the police officer's testimony credible, and concluded that the evidence supported a finding "that the crime was motivated by racial bias." Having found "by a preponderance of the evidence" that Apprendi's actions were taken "with a purpose to intimidate" as provided by the statute, the trial judge held that the hate crime enhancement applied. Rejecting Apprendi's constitutional challenge to the statute, the judge sentenced him to a 12–year term of imprisonment on count 18, and to shorter concurrent sentences on the other two counts.

* * *

III

* * *

At stake in this case are constitutional protections of surpassing importance: the proscription of any deprivation of liberty without "due process of law" and the guarantee that "[i]n all criminal prosecutions, the accused shall enjoy the right to a speedy and public trial, by an impartial jury."[3] Taken together, these rights indisputably entitle a criminal defendant to "a jury determination that [he] is guilty of every element of the crime with which he is charged, beyond a reasonable doubt."

* * * [T]he historical foundation for our recognition of these principles extends down centuries into the common law. "[T]o guard against a spirit of oppression and tyranny on the part of rulers," and "as the great bulwark of [our] civil and political liberties," trial by jury has been understood to require that *the truth of every accusation*, whether preferred in the shape of indictment, information, or appeal, should afterwards be confirmed by the unanimous suffrage of twelve of [the defendant's] equals and neighbors. . . . "

---

3. Apprendi has not here asserted a constitutional claim based on the omission of any reference to sentence enhancement or racial bias in the indictment. He relies entirely on the fact that the "due process of law" that the Fourteenth Amendment requires the States to provide to persons accused of crime encompasses the right to a trial by jury, *Duncan v. Louisiana*, 391 U.S. 145 (1968), and the right to have every element of the offense proved beyond a reasonable doubt, *In re Winship*, 397 U.S. 358 (1970). That Amendment has not, however, been construed to include the Fifth Amendment right to "presentment or indictment of a Grand Jury" that was implicated in our recent decision in *Almendarez–Torres v. United States*, 523 U.S. 224 (1998). We thus do not address the indictment question separately today.

Equally well founded is the companion right to have the jury verdict based on proof beyond a reasonable doubt. * * *

* * *

[W]ith respect to the criminal law of felonious conduct, "the English trial judge of the later eighteenth century had very little explicit discretion in sentencing. The substantive criminal law tended to be sanction-specific; it prescribed a particular sentence for each offense. The judge was meant simply to impose that sentence * * *." * * *

This practice at common law held true when indictments were issued pursuant to statute. Just as the circumstances of the crime and the intent of the defendant at the time of commission were often essential elements to be alleged in the indictment, so too were the circumstances mandating a particular punishment. "Where a statute annexes a higher degree of punishment to a common-law felony, if committed under particular circumstances, an indictment for the offence, in order to bring the defendant within that higher degree of punishment, must expressly charge it to have been committed under those circumstances, and must state the circumstances with certainty and precision. [2 M. Hale, Pleas of the Crown *170]." * * *

We should be clear that nothing in this history suggests that it is impermissible for judges to exercise discretion—taking into consideration various factors relating both to offense and offender—in imposing a judgment *within the range* prescribed by statute. * * *

The historic link between verdict and judgment and the consistent limitation on judges' discretion to operate within the limits of the legal penalties provided highlight the novelty of a legislative scheme that removes the jury from the determination of a fact that, if found, exposes the criminal defendant to a penalty *exceeding* the maximum he would receive if punished according to the facts reflected in the jury verdict alone.[10]

We do not suggest that trial practices cannot change in the course of centuries and still remain true to the principles that emerged from the Framers' fears "that the jury right could be lost not only by gross denial, but by erosion." But practice must at least adhere to the basic principles undergirding the requirements of trying to a jury all facts necessary to constitute a statutory offense, and proving those facts beyond reasonable doubt. As we made clear in *Winship*, the "reasonable doubt" requirement "has a vital role in our criminal procedure for cogent reasons." Prosecu-

---

10. * * * The evidence we describe that punishment was, by law, tied to the offense (enabling the defendant to discern, barring pardon or clergy, his punishment from the face of the indictment), and the evidence that American judges have exercised sentencing discretion within a legally prescribed range (enabling the defendant to discern from the statute of indictment what maximum punishment conviction under that statute could bring), point to a single, consistent conclusion: The judge's role in sentencing is constrained at its outer limits by the facts alleged in the indictment and found by the jury. Put simply, facts that expose a defendant to a punishment greater than that otherwise legally prescribed were by definition "elements" of a separate legal offense.

tion subjects the criminal defendant both to "the possibility that he may lose his liberty upon conviction and ... the certainty that he would be stigmatized by the conviction." We thus require this, among other, procedural protections in order to "provid[e] concrete substance for the presumption of innocence," and to reduce the risk of imposing such deprivations erroneously. If a defendant faces punishment beyond that provided by statute when an offense is committed under certain circumstances but not others, it is obvious that both the loss of liberty and the stigma attaching to the offense are heightened; it necessarily follows that the defendant should not—at the moment the State is put to proof of those circumstances—be deprived of protections that have, until that point, unquestionably attached.[13]

* * *

* * * *Almendarez–Torres v. United States*, 523 U.S. 224 (1998), represents at best an exceptional departure from the historic practice that we have described. In that case, we considered a federal grand jury indictment, which charged the petitioner with "having been 'found in the United States ... after being deported,'" in violation of 8 U.S.C. § 1326(a)—an offense carrying a maximum sentence of two years. Almendarez–Torres pleaded guilty to the indictment, admitting at the plea hearing that he had been deported, that he had unlawfully reentered this country, and that "the earlier deportation had taken place 'pursuant to' three earlier 'convictions' for aggravated felonies." The Government then filed a presentence report indicating that Almendarez–Torres' offense fell within the bounds of § 1326(b) because, as specified in that provision, his original deportation had been subsequent to an aggravated felony conviction; accordingly, Almendarez–Torres could be subject to a sentence of up to 20 years. Almendarez–Torres objected, contending that because the indictment "had not mentioned his earlier aggravated felony convictions," he could be sentenced to no more than two years in prison.

Rejecting Almendarez–Torres' objection, we concluded that sentencing him to a term higher than that attached to the offense alleged in the indictment did not violate the strictures of *Winship* in that case. Because Almendarez–Torres had *admitted* the three earlier convictions for aggravated felonies—all of which had been entered pursuant to proceedings with substantial procedural safeguards of their own—no question concerning the right to a jury trial or the standard of proof that would apply to a contested issue of fact was before the Court. * * * [T]he specific question decided concerned the sufficiency of the indictment. More important, * * * our conclusion in *Almendarez–Torres* turned heavily upon the fact that the additional sentence to which the defendant was subject was "the prior commission of a serious crime." Both the certainty that procedural

---

13. The principal dissent accuses us of today "overruling *McMillan*." We do not overrule *McMillan*. We limit its holding to cases that do not involve the imposition of a sentence more severe than the statutory maximum for the offense established by the jury's verdict—a limitation identified in the *McMillan* opinion itself. Conscious of the likelihood that legislative decisions may have been made in reliance on *McMillan*, we reserve for another day the question whether *stare decisis* considerations preclude reconsideration of its narrower holding.

safeguards attached to any "fact" of prior conviction, and the reality that
Almendarez–Torres did not challenge the accuracy of that "fact" in his
case, mitigated the due process and Sixth Amendment concerns otherwise
implicated in allowing a judge to determine a "fact" increasing punishment beyond the maximum of the statutory range.[14]

Even though it is arguable that *Almendarez–Torres* was incorrectly
decided and that a logical application of our reasoning today should apply
if the recidivist issue were contested, Apprendi does not contest the
decision's validity and we need not revisit it for purposes of our decision
today to treat the case as a narrow exception to the general rule we
recalled at the outset. Given its unique facts, it surely does not warrant
rejection of the otherwise uniform course of decision during the entire
history of our jurisprudence.

* * * Other than the fact of a prior conviction, any fact that increases
the penalty for a crime beyond the prescribed statutory maximum must be
submitted to a jury, and proved beyond a reasonable doubt. * * *[16]

V

The New Jersey statutory scheme that Apprendi asks us to invalidate
allows a jury to convict a defendant of a second-degree offense based on its

---

14. The principal dissent's contention that our decision in *Monge v. California*, 524 U.S. 721
(1998), "demonstrates that *Almendarez–Torres* was" something other than a limited exception to
the jury trial rule is both inaccurate and misleading. *Monge* was another recidivism case in which
the question presented and the bulk of the Court's analysis related to the scope of double
jeopardy protections in sentencing. * * * Most telling of *Monge*'s distance from the issue at stake
in this case is that the double jeopardy question in *Monge* arose because the State had failed to
satisfy its own statutory burden of proving beyond a reasonable doubt that the defendant had
committed a prior offense (and was therefore subject to an enhanced, recidivism-based sentence).
524 U.S., at 725 ("According to California law, a number of procedural safeguards surround the
assessment of prior conviction allegations: Defendants may invoke the right to a jury trial . . .;
the prosecution must prove the allegation beyond a reasonable doubt; and the rules of evidence
apply"). The Court thus itself warned against a contrary double jeopardy rule that could "create
disincentives that would diminish these important procedural protections."

16. The principal dissent would reject the Court's rule as a "meaningless formalism," because
it can conceive of hypothetical statutes that would comply with the rule and achieve the same
result as the New Jersey statute. While a State could, hypothetically, undertake to revise its
entire criminal code in the manner the dissent suggests, extending all statutory maximum
sentences to, for example, 50 years and giving judges guided discretion as to a few specially
selected factors within that range—this possibility seems remote. Among other reasons, structural democratic constraints exist to discourage legislatures from enacting penal statutes that expose
every defendant convicted of, for example, weapons possession, to a maximum sentence exceeding
that which is, in the legislature's judgment, generally proportional to the crime. * * *

In all events, if such an extensive revision of the State's entire criminal code were enacted for
the purpose the dissent suggests, or if New Jersey simply reversed the burden of the hate crime
finding (effectively assuming a crime was performed with a purpose to intimidate and then
requiring a defendant to prove that it was not), we would be required to question whether the
revision was constitutional under this Court's prior decisions.

Finally, the principal dissent ignores the distinction the Court has often recognized between
facts in aggravation of punishment and facts in mitigation. If facts found by a jury support a
guilty verdict of murder, the judge is authorized by that jury verdict to sentence the defendant to
the maximum sentence provided by the murder statute. If the defendant can escape the statutory
maximum by showing, for example, that he is a war veteran, then a judge that finds the fact of
veteran status is neither exposing the defendant to a deprivation of liberty greater than that
authorized by the verdict according to statute, nor is the judge imposing upon the defendant a
greater stigma than that accompanying the jury verdict alone. Core concerns animating the jury
and burden-of-proof requirements are thus absent from such a scheme.

finding beyond a reasonable doubt that he unlawfully possessed a prohibited weapon; after a subsequent and separate proceeding, it then allows a judge to impose punishment identical to that New Jersey provides for crimes of the first degree based upon the judge's finding, by a preponderance of the evidence, that the defendant's "purpose" for unlawfully possessing the weapon was "to intimidate" his victim on the basis of a particular characteristic the victim possessed. In light of the constitutional rule explained above, and all of the cases supporting it, this practice cannot stand.

* * *

* * * Despite what appears to us the clear "elemental" nature of the factor here, the relevant inquiry is one not of form, but of effect—does the required finding expose the defendant to a greater punishment than that authorized by the jury's guilty verdict?[19]

* * *

The New Jersey procedure challenged in this case is an unacceptable departure from the jury tradition that is an indispensable part of our criminal justice system. * * *

JUSTICE SCALIA, concurring.

I feel the need to say a few words in response to Justice Breyer's dissent. * * *

* * * I think it not unfair to tell a prospective felon that if he commits his contemplated crime he is exposing himself to a jail sentence of 30 years—and that if, upon conviction, he gets anything less than that he may thank the mercy of a tenderhearted judge (just as he may thank the mercy of a tenderhearted parole commission if he is let out inordinately early, or the mercy of a tenderhearted governor if his sentence is commuted). Will there be disparities? Of course. But the criminal will never get *more* punishment than he bargained for when he did the crime, and his guilt of the crime (and hence the length of the sentence to which he is exposed) will be determined *beyond a reasonable doubt by the unanimous vote of 12 of his fellow citizens.*

* * *

JUSTICE THOMAS, with whom JUSTICE SCALIA joins as to Parts I and II, concurring.

I join the opinion of the Court in full. I write separately to explain my view that the Constitution requires a broader rule than the Court adopts.

* * *

---

19. This is not to suggest that the term "sentencing factor" is devoid of meaning. The term appropriately describes a circumstance, which may be either aggravating or mitigating in character, that supports a specific sentence *within the range* authorized by the jury's finding that the defendant is guilty of a particular offense. On the other hand, when the term "sentence enhancement" is used to describe an increase beyond the maximum authorized statutory sentence, it is the functional equivalent of an element of a greater offense than the one covered by the jury's guilty verdict. * * *

* * * A long line of essentially uniform authority addressing accusations, and stretching from the earliest reported cases after the founding until well into the 20th century, establishes that the original understanding of which facts are elements was even broader than the rule that the Court adopts today.

This authority establishes that a "crime" includes every fact that is by law a basis for imposing or increasing punishment (in contrast with a fact that mitigates punishment). Thus, if the legislature defines some core crime and then provides for increasing the punishment of that crime upon a finding of some aggravating fact—of whatever sort, including the fact of a prior conviction—the core crime and the aggravating fact together constitute an aggravated crime, just as much as grand larceny is an aggravated form of petit larceny. The aggravating fact is an element of the aggravated crime. Similarly, if the legislature, rather than creating grades of crimes, has provided for setting the punishment of a crime based on some fact—such as a fine that is proportional to the value of stolen goods—that fact is also an element. * * *

* * *

* * * [O]ne of the chief errors of *Almendarez–Torres*—an error to which I succumbed—was to attempt to discern whether a particular fact is traditionally (or typically) a basis for a sentencing court to increase an offender's sentence. * * * What matters is the way by which a fact enters into the sentence. If a fact is by law the basis for imposing or increasing punishment—for establishing or increasing the prosecution's entitlement—it is an element. * * *

* * * I think it clear that the common-law rule would cover the *McMillan* situation of a mandatory minimum sentence * * *. No doubt a defendant could, under such a scheme, find himself sentenced to the same term to which he could have been sentenced absent the mandatory minimum. The range for his underlying crime could be 0 to 10 years, with the mandatory minimum of 5 years, and he could be sentenced to 7. (Of course, a similar scenario is possible with an increased maximum.) But it is equally true that his expected punishment has increased as a result of the narrowed range and that the prosecution is empowered, by invoking the mandatory minimum, to require the judge to impose a higher punishment than he might wish. The mandatory minimum "entitl[es] the government" to more than it would otherwise be entitled (5 to 10 years, rather than 0 to 10 and the risk of a sentence below 5). * * *

* * *

JUSTICE O'CONNOR, with whom THE CHIEF JUSTICE, JUSTICE KENNEDY, and JUSTICE BREYER join, dissenting.

* * *

Our Court has long recognized that not every fact that bears on a defendant's punishment need be charged in an indictment, submitted to a jury, and proved by the government beyond a reasonable doubt. Rather, we have held that the "legislature's definition of the elements of the offense is usually dispositive." * * *

In one bold stroke the Court today casts aside our traditional cautious approach and instead embraces a universal and seemingly bright-line rule limiting the power of Congress and state legislatures to define criminal offenses and the sentences that follow from convictions thereunder. The Court states: "Other than the fact of a prior conviction, any fact that increases the penalty for a crime beyond the prescribed statutory maximum must be submitted to a jury, and proved beyond a reasonable doubt." * * *

* * *

* * * *Almendarez–Torres* constituted a clear repudiation of the rule the Court adopts today. My understanding is bolstered by *Monge v. California*, a decision relegated to a footnote by the Court today. In *Monge*, in reasoning essential to our holding, we reiterated that "the Court has rejected an absolute rule that an enhancement constitutes an element of the offense any time that it increases the maximum sentence to which a defendant is exposed." At the very least, *Monge* demonstrates that *Almendarez–Torres* was not an "exceptional departure" from "historic practice."

* * *

* * * [A]pparently New Jersey could cure its sentencing scheme, and achieve virtually the same results, by drafting its weapons possession statute in the following manner: First, New Jersey could prescribe, in the weapons possession statute itself, a range of 5 to 20 years' imprisonment for one who commits that criminal offense. Second, New Jersey could provide that only those defendants convicted under the statute who are found by a judge, by a preponderance of the evidence, to have acted with a purpose to intimidate an individual on the basis of race may receive a sentence greater than 10 years' imprisonment.

* * *

* * * [C]onsistent with our decision in *Patterson*, New Jersey could achieve virtually the same results, by drafting its weapons possession statute in the following manner: First, New Jersey could prescribe, in the weapons possession statute itself, a range of 5 to 20 years' imprisonment for one who commits that criminal offense. Second, New Jersey could provide that a defendant convicted under the statute whom a judge finds, by a preponderance of the evidence, *not* to have acted with a purpose to intimidate an individual on the basis of race may receive a sentence no greater than 10 years' imprisonment.

The rule that Justice Thomas advocates in his concurring opinion embraces this precise distinction between a fact that increases punishment and a fact that decreases punishment. * * * [I]t is difficult to understand, and neither the Court nor Justice Thomas explains, why the Constitution would require a state legislature to follow such a meaningless and formalistic difference in drafting its criminal statutes.

* * *

JUSTICE BREYER, with whom CHIEF JUSTICE REHNQUIST joins, dissenting.

* * *

* * * [T]he majority, in support of its constitutional rule, emphasizes the concept of a statutory "maximum." * * *

* * * [A]s a practical matter, a legislated mandatory "minimum" is far more important to an actual defendant. A judge and a [sentencing] commission, after all, are legally free to select any sentence below a statute's maximum, but they are not free to subvert a statutory minimum. * * * I do not understand why, when a legislature authorizes a judge to impose a higher penalty for bank robbery (based, say, on the court's finding that a victim was injured or the defendant's motive was bad), a new crime is born; but where a legislature requires a judge to impose a higher penalty than he otherwise would (within a pre-existing statutory range) based on similar criteria, it is not.

* * * [B]y leaving mandatory minimum sentences untouched, the majority's rule simply encourages any legislature interested in asserting control over the sentencing process to do so by creating those minimums. That result would mean significantly less procedural fairness, not more.

* * *

QUESTIONS AND POINTS FOR DISCUSSION

1. In Walton v. Arizona, 497 U.S. 639, 110 S.Ct. 3047 (1990), a case decided before *Apprendi*, the Supreme Court had held that the sentencing structure for imposing the death penalty in Arizona was constitutional. Under an Arizona statute, a judge decided whether to sentence a defendant to death after a jury had found a defendant guilty of first-degree murder. A death sentence required a finding by the judge of at least one aggravating factor enumerated in the statute. In Ring v. Arizona, 536 U.S. 584, 122 S.Ct. 2428 (2002), the Supreme Court concluded that *Apprendi* and *Walton* were irreconcilable. In overruling *Walton*, the Court observed: "The right to trial by jury guaranteed by the Sixth Amendment would be senselessly diminished if it encompassed the factfinding necessary to increase a defendant's sentence by two years, but not the factfinding necessary to put him to death." Id. at 609, 122 S.Ct. at 2443.

2. Although *Apprendi* led to the overruling of *Walton*, the Supreme Court, in a 5–4 decision, later reaffirmed its decision in *McMillan*. To a plurality of the Justices in Harris v. United States, 536 U.S. 545, 122 S.Ct. 2406 (2002), the distinguishing feature of *McMillan* and the case before them was that the judicial factfinding that led to the imposition of a mandatory-minimum sentence did not culminate in a sentence that exceeded the statuto-

ry maximum. Writing for the plurality, Justice Kennedy noted: "That a fact affects the defendant's sentence, even dramatically so, does not by itself make it an element." Id. at 566, 122 S.Ct. at 2419.

Interestingly, a majority of the Court in *Harris*—the four dissenters (Justices Thomas, Stevens, Souter, and Ginsburg) and Justice Breyer, who wrote a concurring opinion—found *McMillan* difficult to distinguish from *Apprendi*. But because Justice Breyer disagreed with *Apprendi*, he refused to extend its scope even further.

Set forth below is another closely divided decision in which the Supreme Court once again addressed the implications of *Apprendi*.

BLAKELY v. WASHINGTON

Supreme Court of the United States, 2004.
542 U.S. 296, 124 S.Ct. 2531, 159 L.Ed.2d 403.

JUSTICE SCALIA delivered the opinion of the Court.

* * *

Petitioner married his wife Yolanda in 1973. He was evidently a difficult man to live with, having been diagnosed at various times with psychological and personality disorders including paranoid schizophrenia. His wife ultimately filed for divorce. In 1998, he abducted her from their orchard home in Grant County, Washington, binding her with duct tape and forcing her at knifepoint into a wooden box in the bed of his pickup truck. In the process, he implored her to dismiss the divorce suit and related trust proceedings.

When the couple's 13–year–old son Ralphy returned home from school, petitioner ordered him to follow in another car, threatening to harm Yolanda with a shotgun if he did not do so. Ralphy escaped and sought help when they stopped at a gas station, but petitioner continued on with Yolanda to a friend's house in Montana. He was finally arrested after the friend called the police.

The State charged petitioner with first-degree kidnapping. Upon reaching a plea agreement, however, it reduced the charge to second-degree kidnapping involving domestic violence and use of a firearm. Petitioner entered a guilty plea admitting the elements of second-degree kidnapping and the domestic-violence and firearm allegations, but no other relevant facts.

The case then proceeded to sentencing. In Washington, second-degree kidnapping is a class B felony. State law provides that "[n]o person convicted of a [class B] felony shall be punished by confinement ... exceeding ... a term of ten years." Other provisions of state law, however, further limit the range of sentences a judge may impose. Washington's Sentencing Reform Act specifies, for petitioner's offense of second-degree kidnapping with a firearm, a "standard range" of 49 to 53 months. A judge may impose a sentence above the standard range if he finds "substantial and compelling reasons justifying an exceptional sentence."

The Act lists aggravating factors that justify such a departure, which it recites to be illustrative rather than exhaustive. Nevertheless, "[a] reason offered to justify an exceptional sentence can be considered only if it takes into account factors other than those which are used in computing the standard range sentence for the offense." When a judge imposes an exceptional sentence, he must set forth findings of fact and conclusions of law supporting it. A reviewing court will reverse the sentence if it finds that "under a clearly erroneous standard there is insufficient evidence in the record to support the reasons for imposing an exceptional sentence."

Pursuant to the plea agreement, the State recommended a sentence within the standard range of 49 to 53 months. After hearing Yolanda's description of the kidnapping, however, the judge rejected the State's recommendation and imposed an exceptional sentence of 90 months—37 months beyond the standard maximum. He justified the sentence on the ground that petitioner had acted with "deliberate cruelty," a statutorily enumerated ground for departure in domestic-violence cases.

Faced with an unexpected increase of more than three years in his sentence, petitioner objected. The judge accordingly conducted a 3–day bench hearing featuring testimony from petitioner, Yolanda, Ralphy, a police officer, and medical experts. After the hearing, he issued 32 findings of fact * * *. The judge adhered to his initial determination of deliberate cruelty.

Petitioner appealed, arguing that this sentencing procedure deprived him of his federal constitutional right to have a jury determine beyond a reasonable doubt all facts legally essential to his sentence. The State Court of Appeals affirmed * * *. * * *

This case requires us to apply the rule we expressed in *Apprendi v. New Jersey,* 530 U.S. 466, 490 (2000): "Other than the fact of a prior conviction, any fact that increases the penalty for a crime beyond the prescribed statutory maximum must be submitted to a jury, and proved beyond a reasonable doubt." * * *[6]

* * *

In this case, petitioner was sentenced to more than three years above the 53–month statutory maximum of the standard range because he had acted with "deliberate cruelty." The facts supporting that finding were neither admitted by petitioner nor found by a jury. The State nevertheless contends that there was no *Apprendi* violation because the relevant "statutory maximum" is not 53 months, but the 10–year maximum for class B felonies * * *. Our precedents make clear, however, that the "statutory maximum" for *Apprendi* purposes is the maximum sentence a judge may impose *solely on the basis of the facts reflected in the jury*

---

6.   * * * It bears repeating that the issue between us is not *whether* the Constitution limits States' authority to reclassify elements as sentencing factors (we all agree that it does); it is only which line * * * the Constitution draws. * * * Justice O'Connor does not even provide a coherent alternative meaning for the jury-trial guarantee, unless one considers "whatever the legislature chooses to leave to the jury, so long as it does not go too far" coherent.

verdict or admitted by the defendant. See *Ring* [*v. Arizona*, 536 U.S. 584,] 602 (2002). In other words, the relevant "statutory maximum" is not the maximum sentence a judge may impose after finding additional facts, but the maximum he may impose *without* any additional findings. When a judge inflicts punishment that the jury's verdict alone does not allow, the jury has not found all the facts "which the law makes essential to the punishment," and the judge exceeds his proper authority.

The judge in this case could not have imposed the exceptional 90–month sentence solely on the basis of the facts admitted in the guilty plea. * * * Had the judge imposed the 90–month sentence solely on the basis of the plea, he would have been reversed. * * *

The State defends the sentence by drawing an analogy to those we upheld in *McMillan v. Pennsylvania,* 477 U.S. 79 (1986), and *Williams v. New York,* 337 U.S. 241 (1949). Neither case is on point. *McMillan* involved a sentencing scheme that imposed a statutory *minimum* if a judge found a particular fact. We specifically noted that the statute "does not authorize a sentence in excess of that otherwise allowed for [the underlying] offense." *Williams* involved an indeterminate-sentencing regime that allowed a judge (but did not compel him) to rely on facts outside the trial record in determining whether to sentence a defendant to death. The judge could have "sentenced [the defendant] to death giving no reason at all." Thus, neither case involved a sentence greater than what state law authorized on the basis of the verdict alone.

* * *

Because the State's sentencing procedure did not comply with the Sixth Amendment, petitioner's sentence is invalid.

Our commitment to *Apprendi* in this context reflects not just respect for longstanding precedent, but the need to give intelligible content to the right of jury trial. That right is no mere procedural formality, but a fundamental reservation of power in our constitutional structure. Just as suffrage ensures the people's ultimate control in the legislative and executive branches, jury trial is meant to ensure their control in the judiciary. *Apprendi* carries out this design by ensuring that the judge's authority to sentence derives wholly from the jury's verdict. Without that restriction, the jury would not exercise the control that the Framers intended.

Those who would reject *Apprendi* are resigned to one of two alternatives. The first is that the jury need only find whatever facts the legislature chooses to label elements of the crime, and that those it labels sentencing factors—no matter how much they may increase the punishment—may be found by the judge. This would mean, for example, that a judge could sentence a man for committing murder even if the jury convicted him only of illegally possessing the firearm used to commit it— or of making an illegal lane change while fleeing the death scene. Not even *Apprendi*'s critics would advocate this absurd result. The jury could not function as circuitbreaker in the State's machinery of justice if it were relegated to making a determination that the defendant at some point did something wrong, a mere preliminary to a judicial inquisition into the facts of the crime the State *actually* seeks to punish.[10]

The second alternative is that legislatures may establish legally essential sentencing factors *within limits*—limits crossed when, perhaps, the sentencing factor is a "tail which wags the dog of the substantive offense." *McMillan,* 477 U.S., at 88. What this means in operation is that the law must not go *too far*—it must not exceed the judicial estimation of the proper role of the judge.

The subjectivity of this standard is obvious. Petitioner argued below that second-degree kidnapping with deliberate cruelty was essentially the same as first-degree kidnapping, the very charge he had avoided by pleading to a lesser offense. The court conceded this might be so but held it irrelevant. Petitioner's 90–month sentence exceeded the 53–month standard maximum by almost 70%; the Washington Supreme Court in other cases has upheld exceptional sentences 15 times the standard maximum. See *State v. Oxborrow,* 723 P.2d 1123, 1125, 1128 (1986) (15–year exceptional sentence; 1–year standard maximum sentence); *State v. Branch,* 919 P.2d 1228, 1235 (1996) (4–year exceptional sentence; 3–month standard maximum sentence). Did the court go *too far* in any of these cases? There is no answer that legal analysis can provide. With *too far* as the yardstick, it is always possible to disagree with such judgments and never to refute them.

Whether the Sixth Amendment incorporates this manipulable standard rather than *Apprendi*'s bright-line rule depends on the plausibility of the claim that the Framers would have left definition of the scope of jury power up to judges' intuitive sense of how far is *too far*. We think that claim not plausible at all, because the very reason the Framers put a jury-trial guarantee in the Constitution is that they were unwilling to trust government to mark out the role of the jury.

By reversing the judgment below, we are not, as the State would have it, "find[ing] determinate sentencing schemes unconstitutional." This case is not about whether determinate sentencing is constitutional, only about how it can be implemented in a way that respects the Sixth Amendment. Several policies prompted Washington's adoption of determinate sentencing, including proportionality to the gravity of the offense and parity among defendants. Nothing we have said impugns those salutary objectives.

Justice O'Connor argues that, because determinate sentencing schemes involving judicial factfinding entail less judicial discretion than indeterminate schemes, the constitutionality of the latter implies the

---

10. Justice O'Connor believes that a "built-in political check" will prevent lawmakers from manipulating offense elements in this fashion. But the many immediate practical advantages of judicial factfinding suggest that political forces would, if anything, pull in the opposite direction. In any case, the Framers' decision to entrench the jury-trial right in the Constitution shows that they did not trust government to make political decisions in this area.

constitutionality of the former. This argument is flawed on a number of levels. First, the Sixth Amendment by its terms is not a limitation on judicial power, but a reservation of jury power. It limits judicial power only to the extent that the claimed judicial power infringes on the province of the jury. Indeterminate sentencing does not do so. It increases judicial discretion, to be sure, but not at the expense of the jury's traditional function of finding the facts essential to lawful imposition of the penalty. Of course indeterminate schemes involve judicial factfinding, in that a judge (like a parole board) may implicitly rule on those facts he deems important to the exercise of his sentencing discretion. But the facts do not pertain to whether the defendant has a legal *right* to a lesser sentence—and that makes all the difference insofar as judicial impingement upon the traditional role of the jury is concerned. In a system that says the judge may punish burglary with 10 to 40 years, every burglar knows he is risking 40 years in jail. In a system that punishes burglary with a 10–year sentence, with another 30 added for use of a gun, the burglar who enters a home unarmed is *entitled* to no more than a 10–year sentence—and by reason of the Sixth Amendment the facts bearing upon that entitlement must be found by a jury.

But even assuming that restraint of judicial power unrelated to the jury's role is a Sixth Amendment objective, it is far from clear that *Apprendi* disserves that goal. Determinate judicial-factfinding schemes entail less judicial power than indeterminate schemes, but more judicial power than determinate *jury*-factfinding schemes. Whether *Apprendi* increases judicial power overall depends on what States with determinate judicial-factfinding schemes would do, given the choice between the two alternatives. * * * When the Kansas Supreme Court found *Apprendi* infirmities in that State's determinate-sentencing regime * * *, the legislature responded not by reestablishing indeterminate sentencing but by applying *Apprendi*'s requirements to its current regime. See Kan. Stat. Ann. § 21–4718.[b] The result was less, not more, judicial power.

Justice Breyer argues that *Apprendi* works to the detriment of criminal defendants who plead guilty by depriving them of the opportunity to argue sentencing factors to a judge. But nothing prevents a defendant from waiving his *Apprendi* rights. When a defendant pleads guilty, the State is free to seek judicial sentence enhancements so long as the defendant either stipulates to the relevant facts or consents to judicial factfinding. If appropriate waivers are procured, States may continue to offer judicial factfinding as a matter of course to all defendants who plead guilty. Even a defendant who stands trial may consent to judicial factfind-

---

    b. This Kansas statute requires a prosecutor seeking an upward durational departure in a defendant's sentence to file a pretrial motion, generally thirty days before trial. The court then decides whether the facts supporting the departure will be presented at trial or, alternatively, to the jury following the adjudication of the defendant's guilt or innocence. Absent a waiver of the jury-trial right, a jury must find beyond a reasonable doubt the fact or facts (other that facts regarding the defendant's prior convictions) justifying an upward departure.

ing as to sentence enhancements, which may well be in his interest if relevant evidence would prejudice him at trial. * * *12

* * *

Ultimately, our decision cannot turn on whether or to what degree trial by jury impairs the efficiency or fairness of criminal justice. One can certainly argue that both these values would be better served by leaving justice entirely in the hands of professionals; many nations of the world, particularly those following civil-law traditions, take just that course. There is not one shred of doubt, however, about the Framers' paradigm for criminal justice: not the civil-law ideal of administrative perfection, but the common-law ideal of limited state power accomplished by strict division of authority between judge and jury. * * *

* * *

Petitioner was sentenced to prison for more than three years beyond what the law allowed for the crime to which he confessed, on the basis of a disputed finding that he had acted with "deliberate cruelty." The Framers would not have thought it too much to demand that, before depriving a man of three more years of his liberty, the State should suffer the modest inconvenience of submitting its accusation to "the unanimous suffrage of twelve of his equals and neighbors."

* * *

JUSTICE O'CONNOR, with whom JUSTICE BREYER joins, and with whom THE CHIEF JUSTICE and JUSTICE KENNEDY join as to all but Part IV–B, dissenting.

The legacy of today's opinion, whether intended or not, will be the consolidation of sentencing power in the State and Federal Judiciaries. The Court says to Congress and state legislatures: If you want to constrain the sentencing discretion of judges and bring some uniformity to sentencing, it will cost you—dearly. Congress and States, faced with the burdens imposed by the extension of *Apprendi* to the present context, will either trim or eliminate altogether their sentencing guidelines schemes and, with them, 20 years of sentencing reform. * * * Because I find it implausible that the Framers would have considered such a result to be required by the Due Process Clause or the Sixth Amendment, and because the practical consequences of today's decision may be disastrous, I respectfully dissent.

---

12. Justice Breyer responds that States are not *required* to give defendants the option of waiving jury trial on some elements but not others. True enough. But why would the States that he asserts we are coercing into hard-heartedness—that is, States that *want* judge-pronounced determinate sentencing to be the norm but we won't let them—want to prevent a defendant from *choosing* that regime? Justice Breyer claims this alternative may prove "too expensive and unwieldy for States to provide," but there is no obvious reason why forcing defendants to choose between contesting all elements of his hypothetical 17–element robbery crime and contesting none of them is less expensive than also giving them the third option of pleading guilty to some elements and submitting the rest to judicial factfinding. * * *

One need look no further than the history leading up to and following the enactment of Washington's guidelines scheme to appreciate the damage that today's decision will cause. Prior to 1981, Washington, like most other States and the Federal Government, employed an indeterminate sentencing scheme. Washington's criminal code separated all felonies into three broad categories: "class A," carrying a sentence of 20 years to life; "class B," carrying a sentence of 0 to 10 years; and "class C," carrying a sentence of 0 to 5 years. Sentencing judges, in conjunction with parole boards, had virtually unfettered discretion to sentence defendants to prison terms falling anywhere within the statutory range, including probation—*i.e.,* no jail sentence at all.

This system of unguided discretion inevitably resulted in severe disparities in sentences received and served by defendants committing the same offense and having similar criminal histories. Indeed, rather than reflect legally relevant criteria, these disparities too often were correlated with constitutionally suspect variables such as race.

To counteract these trends, the state legislature passed the Sentencing Reform Act of 1981. * * * The Act neither increased any of the statutory sentencing ranges for the three types of felonies * * *, nor reclassified any substantive offenses. It merely placed meaningful constraints on discretion to sentence offenders within the statutory ranges, and eliminated parole. * * *

Far from disregarding principles of due process and the jury trial right, as the majority today suggests, Washington's reform has served them. Before passage of the Act, a defendant charged with second degree kidnapping, like petitioner, had no idea whether he would receive a 10–year sentence or probation. The ultimate sentencing determination could turn as much on the idiosyncrasies of a particular judge as on the specifics of the defendant's crime or background. A defendant did not know what facts, if any, about his offense or his history would be considered relevant by the sentencing judge or by the parole board. After passage of the Act, a defendant charged with second degree kidnapping knows what his presumptive sentence will be; he has a good idea of the types of factors that a sentencing judge can and will consider when deciding whether to sentence him outside that range; he is guaranteed meaningful appellate review to protect against an arbitrary sentence. Criminal defendants still face the same statutory maximum sentences, but they now at least know, much more than before, the real consequences of their actions.

Washington's move to a system of guided discretion has served equal protection principles as well. Over the past 20 years, there has been a substantial reduction in racial disparity in sentencing across the State. * * *

* * * While not a constitutional prohibition on guidelines schemes, the majority's decision today exacts a substantial constitutional tax.

The costs are substantial and real. Under the majority's approach, any fact that increases the upper bound on a judge's sentencing discretion is an element of the offense. Thus, facts that historically have been taken into account by sentencing judges to assess a sentence within a broad range—such as drug quantity, role in the offense, risk of bodily harm—all must now be charged in an indictment and submitted to a jury, simply because it is the legislature, rather than the judge, that constrains the extent to which such facts may be used to impose a sentence within a pre-existing statutory range.

While that alone is enough to threaten the continued use of sentencing guidelines schemes, there are additional costs. For example, a legislature might rightly think that some factors bearing on sentencing, such as prior bad acts or criminal history, should not be considered in a jury's determination of a defendant's guilt—such "character evidence" has traditionally been off limits during the guilt phase of criminal proceedings because of its tendency to inflame the passions of the jury. If a legislature desires uniform consideration of such factors at sentencing, but does not want them to impact a jury's initial determination of guilt, the State may have to bear the additional expense of a separate, full-blown jury trial during the penalty phase proceeding.

* * *

* * * A rule of deferring to legislative labels * * * would be easier to administer than the majority's rule, inasmuch as courts would not be forced to look behind statutes and regulations to determine whether a particular fact does or does not increase the penalty to which a defendant was exposed.

The majority is correct that rigid adherence to such an approach *could conceivably* produce absurd results * * *. The pre-*Apprendi* rule of deference to the legislature retains a built-in political check to prevent lawmakers from shifting the prosecution for crimes to the penalty phase proceedings of lesser included and easier-to-prove offenses—*e.g.,* the majority's hypothesized prosecution of murder in the guise of a traffic offense sentencing proceeding. * * *

* * *

The consequences of today's decision will be as far reaching as they are disturbing. Washington's sentencing system is by no means unique. Numerous other States have enacted guidelines systems, as has the Federal Government. Today's decision casts constitutional doubt over them all * * *.

* * *

JUSTICE KENNEDY, with whom JUSTICE BREYER joins, dissenting. [Opinion omitted.]

JUSTICE BREYER, with whom JUSTICE O'CONNOR joins, dissenting.

* * *

* * * As a result of the majority's rule, sentencing must now take one of three forms, each of which risks either impracticality, unfairness, or harm to the jury trial right the majority purports to strengthen. This circumstance shows that the majority's Sixth Amendment interpretation cannot be right.

A

A first option for legislators is to create a simple, pure or nearly pure "charge offense" or "determinate" sentencing system. In such a system, an indictment would charge a few facts which, taken together, constitute a crime, such as robbery. Robbery would carry a single sentence, say, five years' imprisonment. And every person convicted of robbery would receive that sentence—just as, centuries ago, everyone convicted of almost any serious crime was sentenced to death.

Such a system assures uniformity, but at intolerable costs. First, simple determinate sentencing systems impose identical punishments on people who committed their crimes in very different ways. When dramatically different conduct ends up being punished the same way, an injustice has taken place. * * *

Second, in a world of statutorily fixed mandatory sentences for many crimes, determinate sentencing gives tremendous power to prosecutors to manipulate sentences through their choice of charges. * * *

B

A second option for legislators is to return to a system of indeterminate sentencing * * *.

* * *

Returning to such a system * * * would do little to "ensur[e] [the] control" of what the majority calls "the peopl[e,]" *i.e.,* the jury, "in the judiciary," since "the peopl[e]" would only decide the defendant's guilt, a finding with no effect on the duration of the sentence. While "the judge's authority to sentence" would formally derive from the jury's verdict, the jury would exercise little or no control over the sentence itself. * * *

C

A third option is that which the Court seems to believe legislators will in fact take. That is the option of retaining structured schemes that attempt to punish similar conduct similarly and different conduct differently, but modifying them to conform to *Apprendi*'s dictates. Judges would be able to depart *downward* from presumptive sentences upon finding that mitigating factors were present, but would not be able to depart *upward* unless the prosecutor charged the aggravating fact to a jury and proved it beyond a reasonable doubt. * * *

This option can be implemented in one of two ways. The first way would be for legislatures to subdivide each crime into a list of complex crimes, each of which would be defined to include commonly found sentencing factors such as drug quantity, type of victim, presence of violence, degree of injury, use of gun, and so on. * * *

* * * The prosecutor, through control of the precise charge, controls the punishment, thereby marching the sentencing system directly away from, not toward, one important guideline goal: rough uniformity of punishment for those who engage in roughly the same *real* criminal conduct. The artificial (and consequently unfair) nature of the resulting sentence is aggravated by the fact that prosecutors must charge all relevant facts about the way the crime was committed before a presentence investigation examines the criminal conduct, perhaps before the trial itself, *i.e.*, before many of the facts relevant to punishment are known.

This "complex charge offense" system also prejudices defendants who seek trial, for it can put them in the untenable position of contesting material aggravating facts in the guilt phases of their trials. Consider a defendant who is charged, not with mere possession of cocaine, but with the specific offense of possession of more than 500 grams of cocaine. Or consider a defendant charged, not with murder, but with the new crime of murder using a machete. Or consider a defendant whom the prosecution wants to claim was a "supervisor," rather than an ordinary gang member. How can a Constitution that guarantees due process put these defendants, as a matter of course, in the position of arguing, "I did not sell drugs, and if I did, I did not sell more than 500 grams" or, "I did not kill him, and if I did, I did not use a machete," or "I did not engage in gang activity, and certainly not as a supervisor" to a single jury? * * *

* * * States may very well decide that they will *not* permit defendants to carve subsets of facts out of the new, *Apprendi*-required 17–element robbery crime, seeking a judicial determination as to some of those facts and a jury determination as to others. Instead, States may simply require defendants to plead guilty to all 17 elements or proceed with a (likely prejudicial) trial on all 17 elements.

* * *

The second way to make sentencing guidelines *Apprendi*-compliant would be to require at least two juries for each defendant whenever aggravating facts are present: one jury to determine guilt of the crime charged, and an additional jury to try the disputed facts that, if found, would aggravate the sentence. Our experience with bifurcated trials in the capital punishment context suggests that requiring them for run-of-the-mill sentences would be costly, both in money and in judicial time and resources. * * *

* * *

D

* * * The simple fact is that the design of any fair sentencing system must involve efforts to make practical compromises among competing

goals. The majority's reading of the Sixth Amendment makes the effort to find those compromises—already difficult—virtually impossible.

* * *

[O]ur modern, pre-*Apprendi* cases made clear that legislatures could, within broad limits, distinguish between "sentencing facts" and "elements of crimes." See *McMillan,* 477 U.S., at 85–88, 106 S.Ct. 2411. * * *

Is there a risk of unfairness involved in permitting Congress to make this labeling decision? Of course. As we have recognized, the "tail" of the sentencing fact might "wa[g] the dog of the substantive offense." Congress might permit a judge to sentence an individual for murder though convicted only of making an illegal lane change. But that is the kind of problem that the Due Process Clause is well suited to cure. * * *

* * *

QUESTIONS AND POINTS FOR DISCUSSION

1. In United States v. Booker, 543 U.S. 220, 125 S.Ct. 738 (2005), the Supreme Court held that there was "no distinction of constitutional significance" between the federal sentencing guidelines and the sentencing structure in the state of Washington deemed unconstitutional in *Blakely.* Id. at 748. The defendant in *Booker* was charged with a drug offense punishable by up to life in prison. The jury found that the defendant had possessed 92.5 grams of crack cocaine. In the absence of any additional factual findings, the jury's verdict would have required the judge to impose a prison sentence under the federal sentencing guidelines falling between 210 and 262 months. However, the sentencing judge found by a preponderance of the evidence that the defendant had possessed an additional 566 grams of crack cocaine and had obstructed justice. The guidelines therefore required the judge to choose a sentence from a higher sentencing range: 360 months to life imprisonment. The judge imposed a thirty-year sentence on the defendant.

Because the defendant's sentence exceeded the maximum sentence authorized by the facts reflected in the jury's verdict, the Supreme Court held that the sentence violated the defendant's Sixth Amendment right to a jury trial. Turning to the question of how to remedy the Sixth Amendment problem with the federal guidelines, the Court concluded that the guidelines would remain in effect but would be advisory, rather than mandatory. In other words, federal judges would consult the guidelines when deciding what sentence to impose on a defendant but would not be bound by them.

The Court furthermore found that this modified sentencing structure necessitated changes in the standards applied by federal appellate courts when reviewing sentences on appeal. In 2003, Congress had enacted legislation requiring appellate courts to conduct a *de novo* review of a sentence when a sentencing judge had departed from the presumptive sentencing range set forth in the sentencing guidelines. See Prosecutorial Remedies and Other Tools to End the Exploitation of Children Today Act of 2003, Pub.L. No. 108–21, § 401(d)(1), 117 Stat. 670. The purpose of this legislation was to curtail judicial discretion when sentencing federal defendants, a purpose that the Court in *Booker* considered at odds with what were now advisory guidelines. Consequently, the Court announced that federal sentences henceforth would be reviewed on appeal for "unreasonable[ness]." 543 U.S. at 261, 125 S.Ct. at 765. For a discussion of subsequent Supreme Court cases addressing questions regarding how to apply federal sentencing guidelines that are only advisory, see pages 216–18.

2. In Cunningham v. California, 549 U.S. 270, 127 S.Ct. 856 (2007), the Supreme Court ruled that California's determinate-sentencing law violated the constitutional right to have a jury find a fact beyond a reasonable doubt when it will subject a defendant to an elevated sentence—one beyond that authorized by the jury's verdict at trial or the defendant's factual admissions to the court. That law had directed the sentencing judge to impose the middle of three potential imprisonment terms unless the court identified aggravating circumstances warranting imposition of the elevated sentence (or mitigating circumstances justifying imposition of the "lower term"). In response to *Cunningham*, the California legislature amended the sentencing statute, placing the choice of which of the three imprisonment terms to impose on a defendant "within the sound discretion of the court." See Cal. Penal Code § 1170(b). The legislature indicated that it adopted this change in order to prevent havoc in the state's criminal-justice system while a full review of the state's sentencing structure was being conducted.

3. When a defendant is convicted of multiple crimes, the sentences will be served either consecutively or concurrently. If the judge imposes consecutive sentences, the defendant will serve the first sentence and then the second. For example, if the defendant receives two ten-year sentences to be served consecutively, the defendant will be imprisoned for twenty years. By contrast, if the ten-year sentences are concurrent, the defendant will serve them at the same time and be confined for ten years.

Assume that a state statute prohibits the imposition of consecutive sentences for crimes committed in a "single course of conduct" unless one of the crimes was a Class X or Class 1 felony and the defendant caused "severe bodily injury" to someone during the crime. Assume also that a defendant was convicted of first-degree murder and armed robbery. At the sentencing hearing, the judge found that the defendant had inflicted severe bodily injury during the armed robbery, a Class X felony. Consequently, the judge imposed a 29–year sentence for the murder and a ten-year sentence for the armed robbery, with the sentences to run consecutively. In your opinion, were the defendant's constitutional rights abridged by this judicial fact-finding?

In Oregon v. Ice, 129 S.Ct. 711 (2009), the Supreme Court held, in a 5–4 decision, that there is no Sixth Amendment right to have a jury find beyond a reasonable doubt a fact necessary for the imposition of consecutive sentences. The Court underscored that historically judges have had full discretion to impose either concurrent or consecutive sentences. The Court further observed: "All agree that a scheme making consecutive sentences the rule, and concurrent sentences the exception, encounters no Sixth Amendment shoal. To hem in States by holding that they may not equally choose to make concurrent sentences the rule, and consecutive sentences the exception, would make scant sense." Id. at 719.

Because the defendant in *Oregon v. Ice* received consecutive, not concurrent, sentences, he was sentenced to prison for 340 months, as opposed to ninety. If you had been charged with writing the dissenting opinion in that case, what arguments would you have made? Compare your arguments with those of Justice Scalia, who, you may not be surprised to hear, wrote the dissenting opinion in *Ice*.

4. How would you differentiate between sentencing factors and elements of a crime? Under your approach, would the outcomes in *McMillan*, *Almendarez–Torres*, *Apprendi*, *Blakely*, *Booker*, or *Oregon v. Ice* have been different?

5. As is true for most constitutional violations, a *Blakely* error will not lead automatically to the reversal of a conviction. Washington v. Recuenco, 548 U.S. 212, 126 S.Ct. 2546 (2006). Instead, the harmless-error rule applies; if the government proves beyond a reasonable doubt that the *Blakely* error was harmless—that the jury would have found that the fact in question existed, the conviction will not be set aside.

6. NONCONSTITUTIONAL SOURCES OF SENTENCING RIGHTS

Apart from the procedural safeguards required by the United States Constitution during the sentencing process, additional rights may be bestowed by state constitutions, statutes, court rules, and sentencing guidelines. An example of one such source of additional rights is Rule 32 of the Federal Rules of Criminal Procedure, which governs sentencing proceedings in the federal courts. Pertinent excerpts from Rule 32 are set forth below. As you review the rule, consider how, if at all, you would revise it.

Rule 32. Sentencing and Judgment

* * *

(b) Time of Sentencing.

(1) In General. The court must impose sentence without unnecessary delay.

(2) Changing Time Limits. The court may, for good cause, change any time limits prescribed in this rule.

(c) Presentence Investigation.

(1) Required Investigation.

(A) In General. The probation officer must conduct a presentence investigation and submit a report to the court before it imposes sentence unless:

(i) 18 U.S.C. § 3593(c) or another statute requires otherwise; or

(ii) the court finds that the information in the record enables it to meaningfully exercise its sentencing authority under 18 U.S.C. § 3553, and the court explains its finding on the record.

(B) Restitution. If the law requires restitution, the probation officer must conduct an investigation and submit a report that contains sufficient information for the court to order restitution.

(2) Interviewing the Defendant. The probation officer who interviews a defendant as part of a presentence investigation must, on request, give the defendant's attorney notice and a reasonable opportunity to attend the interview.

(d) Presentence Report.

(1) Applying the Sentencing Guidelines. The presentence report must:

(A) identify all applicable guidelines and policy statements of the Sentencing Commission;

(B) calculate the defendant's offense level and criminal history category;

(C) state the resulting sentencing range and kinds of sentences available;

(D) identify any factor relevant to:

(i) the appropriate kind of sentence, or

(ii) the appropriate sentence within the applicable sentencing range; and

(E) identify any basis for departing from the applicable sentencing range.

(2) Additional Information. The presentence report must also contain the following:

(A) the defendant's history and characteristics, including:

(i) any prior criminal record;

(ii) the defendant's financial condition; and

(iii) any circumstances affecting the defendant's behavior that may be helpful in imposing sentence or in correctional treatment;

(B) information that assesses any financial, social, psychological, and medical impact on any victim;

(C) when appropriate, the nature and extent of nonprison programs and resources available to the defendant;

(D) when the law provides for restitution, information sufficient for a restitution order;

(**E**) if the court orders a study under 18 U.S.C. § 3552(b),[c] any resulting report and recommendation; and

(**F**) any other information that the court requires, including information relevant to the factors under 18 U.S.C. § 3553(a).

(**3**) **Exclusions.** The presentence report must exclude the following:

(**A**) any diagnoses that, if disclosed, might seriously disrupt a rehabilitation program;

(**B**) any sources of information obtained upon a promise of confidentiality; and

(**C**) any other information that, if disclosed, might result in physical or other harm to the defendant or others.

(**e**) **Disclosing the Report and Recommendation.**

(**1**) **Time to Disclose.** Unless the defendant has consented in writing, the probation officer must not submit a presentence report to the court or disclose its contents to anyone until the defendant has pleaded guilty or nolo contendere, or has been found guilty.

(**2**) **Minimum Required Notice.** The probation officer must give the presentence report to the defendant, the defendant's attorney, and an attorney for the government at least 35 days before sentencing unless the defendant waives this minimum period.

(**3**) **Sentence Recommendation.** By local rule or by order in a case, the court may direct the probation officer not to disclose to anyone other than the court the officer's recommendation on the sentence.

(**f**) **Objecting to the Report.**

(**1**) **Time to Object.** Within 14 days after receiving the presentence report, the parties must state in writing any objections, including objections to material information, sentencing guideline ranges, and policy statements contained in or omitted from the report.

(**2**) **Serving Objections.** An objecting party must provide a copy of its objections to the opposing party and to the probation officer.

(**3**) **Action on Objections.** After receiving objections, the probation officer may meet with the parties to discuss the objections. The probation officer may then investigate further and revise the presentence report as appropriate.

(**g**) **Submitting the Report.** At least 7 days before sentencing, the probation officer must submit to the court and to the parties the presentence report and an addendum containing any unresolved objections, the

---

c.   18 U.S.C. § 3552(b) authorizes a sentencing judge who wants more information about a defendant before imposing sentence to order a study of the defendant by "qualified consultants" within the community or, where there is a "compelling reason," by the Bureau of Prisons.

grounds for those objections, and the probation officer's comments on them.

(h) Notice of Possible Departure from Sentencing Guidelines. Before the court may depart from the applicable sentencing range on a ground not identified for departure either in the presentence report or in a party's prehearing submission, the court must give the parties reasonable notice that it is contemplating such a departure. The notice must specify any ground on which the court is contemplating a departure.

(i) Sentencing.

    (1) In General. At sentencing, the court:

        (A) must verify that the defendant and the defendant's attorney have read and discussed the presentence report and any addendum to the report;

        (B) must give to the defendant and an attorney for the government a written summary of—or summarize in camera— any information excluded from the presentence report under Rule 32(d)(3) on which the court will rely in sentencing, and give them a reasonable opportunity to comment on that information;

        (C) must allow the parties' attorneys to comment on the probation officer's determinations and other matters relating to an appropriate sentence; and

        (D) may, for good cause, allow a party to make a new objection at any time before sentence is imposed.

    (2) Introducing Evidence; Producing a Statement. The court may permit the parties to introduce evidence on the objections. If a witness testifies at sentencing, Rule 26.2(a)–(d) and (f) applies.[d] If a party fails to comply with a Rule 26.2 order to produce a witness's statement, the court must not consider that witness's testimony.

    (3) Court Determinations. At sentencing, the court:

        (A) may accept any undisputed portion of the presentence report as a finding of fact;

        (B) must—for any disputed portion of the presentence report or other controverted matter—rule on the dispute or determine that a ruling is unnecessary either because the matter will not affect sentencing, or because the court will not consider the matter in sentencing; and

        (C) must append a copy of the court's determinations under this rule to any copy of the presentence report made available to the Bureau of Prisons.

---

    d. Rule 26.2(a) of the Federal Rules of Criminal Procedure requires the court to direct a party who has called a witness, other than the defendant, to testify to provide a party, upon motion, with any statements of that witness bearing on the witness's testimony. Other sections of the rule further delineate the scope of this requirement.

(4) Opportunity to Speak.

(A) By a Party. Before imposing sentence, the court must:

(i) provide the defendant's attorney an opportunity to speak on the defendant's behalf;

(ii) address the defendant personally in order to permit the defendant to speak or present any information to mitigate the sentence; and

(iii) provide an attorney for the government an opportunity to speak equivalent to that of the defendant's attorney.

(B) By a Victim. Before imposing sentence, the court must address any victim of the crime who is present at sentencing and must permit the victim to be reasonably heard.

(C) In Camera Proceedings. Upon a party's motion and for good cause, the court may hear in camera any statement made under Rule 32(i)(4).

(j) Defendant's Right to Appeal.

(1) Advice of a Right to Appeal.

(A) Appealing a Conviction. If the defendant pleaded not guilty and was convicted, after sentencing the court must advise the defendant of the right to appeal the conviction.

(B) Appealing a Sentence. After sentencing—regardless of the defendant's plea—the court must advise the defendant of any right to appeal the sentence.

(C) Appeal Costs. The court must advise a defendant who is unable to pay appeal costs of the right to ask for permission to appeal in forma pauperis.

(2) Clerk's Filing of Notice. If the defendant so requests, the clerk must immediately prepare and file a notice of appeal on the defendant's behalf.

* * *

B. FACTORS CONSIDERED AT SENTENCING

UNITED STATES v. GRAYSON

Supreme Court of the United States, 1978.
438 U.S. 41, 98 S.Ct. 2610, 57 L.Ed.2d 582.

MR. CHIEF JUSTICE BURGER delivered the opinion of the Court.

We granted certiorari to review a holding of the Court of Appeals that it was improper for a sentencing judge, in fixing the sentence within the statutory limits, to give consideration to the defendant's false testimony observed by the judge during the trial.

I

In August 1975, respondent Grayson was confined in a federal prison camp under a conviction for distributing a controlled substance. In October, he escaped but was apprehended two days later by FBI agents in New York City. He was indicted for prison escape * * *.

During its case in chief, the United States proved the essential elements of the crime, including his lawful confinement and the unlawful escape. In addition, it presented the testimony of the arresting FBI agents that Grayson, upon being apprehended, denied his true identity.

Grayson testified in his own defense. He admitted leaving the camp but asserted that he did so out of fear: "I had just been threatened with a large stick with a nail protruding through it by an inmate that was serving time at Allenwood, and I was scared, and I just ran." He testified that the threat was made in the presence of many inmates by prisoner Barnes who sought to enforce collection of a gambling debt and followed other threats and physical assaults made for the same purpose. Grayson called one inmate, who testified: "I heard [Barnes] talk to Grayson in a loud voice one day, but that's all. I never seen no harm, no hands or no shuffling whatsoever."

Grayson's version of the facts was contradicted by the Government's rebuttal evidence and by cross-examination on crucial aspects of his story. For example, Grayson stated that after crossing the prison fence he left his prison jacket by the side of the road. On recross, he stated that he also left his prison shirt but not his trousers. Government testimony showed that on the morning after the escape, a shirt marked with Grayson's number, a jacket, and a pair of prison trousers were found outside a hole in the prison fence.[1] Grayson also testified on cross-examination: "I do believe that I phrased the rhetorical question to Captain Kurd, who was in charge of [the prison], and I think I said something if an inmate was being threatened by somebody, what would ... he do? First of all he said he would want to know who it was." On further cross-examination, however, Grayson modified his description of the conversation. Captain Kurd testified that Grayson had never mentioned in any fashion threats from other inmates. Finally, the alleged assailant, Barnes, by then no longer an inmate, testified that Grayson had never owed him any money and that he had never threatened or physically assaulted Grayson.

The jury returned a guilty verdict, whereupon the District Judge ordered the United States Probation Office to prepare a presentence report. At the sentencing hearing, the judge stated:

"I'm going to give my reasons for sentencing in this case with clarity, because one of the reasons may well be considered by a Court of Appeals to be impermissible; and although I could come into this Court Room and sentence this Defendant to a five-year prison term

---

1. The testimony regarding the prison clothing was important for reasons in addition to the light it shed on quality of recollection. Grayson stated that after unpremeditatedly fleeing the prison with no possessions and crossing the fence, he hitchhiked to New York City—a difficult task for a man with no trousers. The United States suggested that by prearrangement Grayson met someone, possibly a woman friend, on the highway near the break in the fence and that this accomplice provided civilian clothes. It introduced evidence that the friend visited Grayson often at prison, including each of the three days immediately prior to his penultimate day in the camp.

without any explanation at all, I think it is fair that I give the reasons so that if the Court of Appeals feels that one of the reasons which I am about to enunciate is an improper consideration for a trial judge, then the Court will be in a position to reverse this Court and send the case back for re-sentencing.

"In my view a prison sentence is indicated, and the sentence that the Court is going to impose is to deter you, Mr. Grayson, and others who are similarly situated. Secondly, *it is my view that your defense was a complete fabrication without the slightest merit whatsoever. I feel it is proper for me to consider that fact in the sentencing, and I will do so.*" (Emphasis added.)

He then sentenced Grayson to a term of two years' imprisonment, consecutive to his unexpired sentence.

On appeal, a divided panel of the Court of Appeals for the Third Circuit directed that Grayson's sentence be vacated and that he be resentenced by the District Court without consideration of false testimony.
* * *

* * *

II

In *Williams v. New York*, 337 U.S. 241, 247 (1949), Mr. Justice Black observed that the "prevalent modern philosophy of penology [is] that the punishment should fit the offender and not merely the crime," and that, accordingly, sentences should be determined with an eye toward the "[r]eformation and rehabilitation of offenders." * * *

* * *

A defendant's truthfulness or mendacity while testifying on his own behalf, almost without exception, has been deemed probative of his attitudes toward society and prospects for rehabilitation and hence relevant to sentencing. Soon after *Williams* was decided, the Tenth Circuit concluded that "the attitude of a convicted defendant with respect to his willingness to commit a serious crime [perjury] ... is a proper matter to consider in determining what sentence shall be imposed within the limitations fixed by statute." *Humes v. United States*, 186 F.2d 875, 878 (1951). * * *

Only one Circuit has directly rejected the probative value of the defendant's false testimony in his own defense. In *Scott v. United States*, 135 U.S.App.D.C. 377, 382, 419 F.2d 264, 269 (1969), the court argued that

"the peculiar pressures placed upon a defendant threatened with jail and the stigma of conviction make his willingness to deny the crime an unpromising test of his prospects for rehabilitation if guilty. It is indeed unlikely that many men who commit serious offenses would balk on principle from lying in their own defense. The guilty man may quite sincerely repent his crime but yet, driven by the urge to remain free, may protest his innocence in a court of law.''

The *Scott* rationale rests not only on the realism of the psychological pressures on a defendant in the dock—which we can grant—but also on a deterministic view of human conduct that is inconsistent with the underlying precepts of our criminal justice system. A "universal and persistent" foundation stone in our system of law, and particularly in our approach to punishment, sentencing, and incarceration, is the "belief in freedom of the human will and a consequent ability and duty of the normal individual to choose between good and evil." Given that long-accepted view of the "ability and duty of the normal individual to choose," we must conclude that the defendant's readiness to lie under oath—especially when, as here, the trial court finds the lie to be flagrant—may be deemed probative of his prospects for rehabilitation.

III

Against this background we evaluate Grayson's constitutional argument that the District Court's sentence constitutes punishment for the crime of perjury for which he has not been indicted, tried, or convicted by due process. A second argument is that permitting consideration of perjury will "chill" defendants from exercising their right to testify on their own behalf.

A

In his due process argument, Grayson does not contend directly that the District Court had an impermissible purpose in considering his perjury and selecting the sentence. Rather, he argues that this Court, in order to preserve due process rights, not only must prohibit the impermissible sentencing practice of incarcerating for the purpose of saving the Government the burden of bringing a separate and subsequent perjury prosecution but also must prohibit the otherwise *permissible* practice of considering a defendant's untruthfulness for the purpose of illuminating his need for rehabilitation and society's need for protection. He presents two interrelated reasons. The effect of both permissible and impermissible sentencing practices may be the same: additional time in prison. Further, it is virtually impossible, he contends, to identify and establish the impermissible practice. We find these reasons insufficient * * *.

First, the evolutionary history of sentencing * * * demonstrates that it is proper—indeed, even necessary for the rational exercise of discretion—to consider the defendant's whole person and personality, as manifested by his conduct at trial and his testimony under oath, for whatever light those may shed on the sentencing decision. The "parlous" effort to appraise "character," degenerates into a game of chance to the extent that a sentencing judge is deprived of relevant information concerning "every aspect of a defendant's life." The Government's interest, as well as the offender's, in avoiding irrationality is of the highest order. That interest more than justifies the risk that Grayson asserts is present when a sentencing judge considers a defendant's untruthfulness under oath.

Second, in our view, *Williams* fully supports consideration of such conduct in sentencing. There the Court permitted the sentencing judge to consider the offender's history of prior antisocial conduct, including burglaries for which he had not been duly convicted. This it did despite the risk that the judge might use his knowledge of the offender's prior crimes for an improper purpose.

Third, the efficacy of Grayson's suggested "exclusionary rule" is open to serious doubt. No rule of law, even one garbed in constitutional terms, can prevent improper use of firsthand observations of perjury. The integrity of the judges, and their fidelity to their oaths of office, necessarily provide the only, and in our view adequate, assurance against that.

B

Grayson's argument that judicial consideration of his conduct at trial impermissibly "chills" a defendant's statutory right, 18 U.S.C. § 3481 (1976 ed.), and perhaps a constitutional right to testify on his own behalf is without basis. The right guaranteed by law to a defendant is narrowly the right to testify truthfully in accordance with the oath. * * * Assuming, *arguendo,* that the sentencing judge's consideration of defendants' untruthfulness in testifying has any chilling effect on a defendant's decision to testify falsely, that effect is entirely permissible. There is no protected right to commit perjury.

Grayson's further argument that the sentencing practice challenged here will inhibit exercise of the right to testify truthfully is entirely frivolous. That argument misapprehends the nature and scope of the practice we find permissible. Nothing we say today requires a sentencing judge to enhance, in some wooden or reflex fashion, the sentences of all defendants whose testimony is deemed false. Rather, we are reaffirming the authority of a sentencing judge to evaluate carefully a defendant's testimony on the stand, determine—with a consciousness of the frailty of human judgment—whether that testimony contained willful and material falsehoods, and, if so, assess in light of all the other knowledge gained about the defendant the meaning of that conduct with respect to his prospects for rehabilitation and restoration to a useful place in society. Awareness of such a process realistically cannot be deemed to affect the decision of an accused but unconvicted defendant to testify truthfully in his own behalf.

* * *

Mʀ. Jᴜsᴛɪᴄᴇ Sᴛᴇᴡᴀʀᴛ, with whom Mʀ. Jᴜsᴛɪᴄᴇ Bʀᴇɴɴᴀɴ and Mʀ. Jᴜsᴛɪᴄᴇ Mᴀʀsʜᴀʟʟ join, dissenting.

The Court begins its consideration of this case with the assumption that the respondent gave false testimony at his trial. But there has been no determination that his testimony was false. This respondent was given a greater sentence than he would otherwise have received—how much greater we have no way of knowing—solely because a single judge *thought* that he had not testified truthfully. In essence, the Court holds today that *whenever* a defendant testifies in his own behalf and is found guilty, he opens himself to the possibility of an enhanced sentence. Such a sentence is nothing more or less than a penalty imposed on the defendant's exercise of his constitutional and statutory rights to plead not guilty and to testify in his own behalf.

It does not change matters to say that the enhanced sentence merely reflects the defendant's "prospects for rehabilitation" rather than an additional punishment for testifying falsely. The fact remains that all defendants who choose to testify, and only those who do so, face the very real prospect of a greater sentence based upon the trial judge's unreviewable perception that the testimony was untruthful. The Court prescribes no limitations or safeguards to minimize a defendant's rational fear that his truthful testimony will be perceived as false.[4] Indeed, encumbrance of the sentencing process with the collateral inquiries necessary to provide such assurance would be both pragmatically unworkable and theoretically inconsistent with the assumption that the trial judge is merely considering one more piece of information in his overall evaluation of the defendant's prospects for rehabilitation. But without such safeguards I fail to see how the Court can dismiss as "frivolous" the argument that this sentencing practice will "inhibit exercise of the right to testify truthfully."

* * * Other witnesses risk punishment for perjury only upon indictment and conviction in accord with the full protections of the Constitution. Only the defendant himself, whose testimony is likely to be of critical importance to his defense, faces the additional risk that the disbelief of a single listener will itself result in time in prison.

The minimal contribution that the defendant's possibly untruthful testimony might make to an overall assessment of his potential for rehabilitation cannot justify imposing this additional burden on his right to testify in his own behalf. I do not believe that a sentencing judge's discretion to consider a wide range of information in arriving at an appropriate sentence allows him to mete out additional punishment to the defendant simply because of his personal belief that the defendant did not testify truthfully at the trial.

* * *

---

4. For example, the dissenting judge in the Court of Appeals in this case suggested that a sentencing judge "should consider his independent evaluation of the testimony and behavior of the defendant only when he is convinced beyond a reasonable doubt that the defendant intentionally lied on material issues of fact ... [and] the falsity of the defendant's testimony [is] necessarily established by the finding of guilt." 550 F.2d 103, 114 (Rosenn, J., dissenting). Contrary to Judge Rosenn, I do not believe that the latter requirement was met in this case. The jury could have believed Grayson's entire story but concluded, in the words of the trial judge's instructions on the defense of duress, that "an ordinary man" would *not* "have felt it necessary to leave the Allenwood Prison Camp when faced with the same degree of compulsion, coercion or duress as the Defendant was faced with in this case."

QUESTIONS AND POINTS FOR DISCUSSION

1.   In United States v. Dunnigan, 507 U.S. 87, 113 S.Ct. 1111 (1993), the Supreme Court reaffirmed its holding in *Grayson* when it held that a court constitutionally can increase a defendant's offense level under the federal sentencing guidelines for "willfully obstructing or impeding proceedings" by committing perjury at trial. After Blakely v. Washington, 542 U.S. 296, 124 S.Ct. 2531 (2004) and United States v. Booker, 543 U.S. 220, 125 S.Ct. 738 (2005), would such judicial factfinding necessarily violate the Sixth Amendment right to a jury trial and due-process right to have an element of a crime established beyond a reasonable doubt if the federal sentencing guidelines had remained mandatory? In answering this question, consider the comments of Justice Stevens in *Booker*:

> * * * To be clear, our holding * * * that *Blakely* applies to the Guidelines does not establish the "impermissibility of judicial factfinding." Instead, judicial factfinding to support an offense level determination or an enhancement is *only unconstitutional when that finding raises the sentence beyond the sentence that could have lawfully been imposed by reference to facts found by the jury or admitted by the defendant.* This distinction is crucial to a proper understanding of why the Guidelines could easily function as they are currently written.

> Consider, for instance, a case in which the defendant's initial sentencing range under the Guidelines is 130–to–162 months, calculated by combining a base offense level of 28 and a criminal history category of V. Depending upon the particular offense, the sentencing judge may use her discretion to select any sentence within this range, even if her selection relies upon factual determinations beyond the facts found by the jury. If the defendant described above also possessed a firearm, the Guidelines would direct the judge to apply a two-level enhancement * * *, which would raise the defendant's total offense level from 28 to 30. That, in turn, would raise the defendant's eligible sentencing range to 151–to–188 months. That act of judicial factfinding would comply with the Guidelines and the Sixth Amendment so long as the sentencing judge then selected a sentence between 151–to–162 months—the lower number (151) being the bottom of offense level 30 and the higher number (162) being the maximum sentence under level 28, which is the upper limit of the range supported by the jury findings alone. This type of overlap between sentencing ranges is the rule, not the exception, in the Guidelines as currently constituted. * * * The interaction of these various Guidelines provisions demonstrates the fallacy in the assumption that judicial factfinding can never be constitutional under the Guidelines.

Id. at 278–79, 125 S.Ct. at 775–76 (Stevens, J., dissenting in part).

2.   In Witte v. United States, 515 U.S. 389, 115 S.Ct. 2199 (1995), the Supreme Court held that a defendant's Fifth Amendment right not to be subjected to double jeopardy was not violated when uncharged criminal conduct was used to increase the defendant's offense level and the defendant later was convicted of a crime based on the same conduct. In that case, the

defendant pled guilty to one count of attempting to possess marijuana with intent to distribute it. While the indictment charged the defendant with being involved in a drug transaction that occurred in early 1991, the judge considered the defendant's alleged involvement in the importation of large quantities of cocaine and marijuana into the country in 1990 as "relevant conduct" bearing on the defendant's offense level under the federal sentencing guidelines. Consideration of these uncharged crimes increased the defendant's offense level over sixteen years.

When the defendant subsequently was charged with, and convicted of, crimes stemming from the 1990 drug transactions, he argued that he unconstitutionally was being punished twice for the same crimes. The Supreme Court rejected that claim, noting that the defendant previously had been punished only for the 1991 crime. The 1990 conduct had been considered solely to determine what would be an appropriate penalty for that crime. Do you agree with the Court's reasoning?

3. United States v. Watts, 519 U.S. 148, 117 S.Ct. 633 (1997) perhaps best illustrates the breadth of information that can be considered by courts when sentencing a criminal defendant. In a *per curiam* opinion (one rendered without briefing and arguments by the parties), the Supreme Court in that case held that the Double Jeopardy Clause does not prohibit the consideration during the sentencing process of conduct underlying charges of which a defendant has been acquitted "so long as that conduct has been proved by a preponderance of the evidence." Id. at 156, 117 S.Ct. at 638. In that case, after police found cocaine base and two loaded guns and ammunition in the defendant's house, he was charged with two crimes—possession of cocaine base with intent to distribute and use of a firearm in relation to a drug offense. A jury found the defendant guilty of the first crime but not guilty of the second. When sentencing the defendant though, the judge found, by a preponderance of the evidence, that the guns related to the drug crime, a finding that raised the offense level under the federal sentencing guidelines used to calculate the defendant's sentence. As a result, the defendant received a longer prison sentence, though one that still fell within the statutory maximum for the drug crime.

After *Blakely*, what constitutional limits exist on the procedures governing consideration of conduct underlying a criminal charge of which a defendant was acquitted when sentencing the defendant under mandatory sentencing guidelines? From a policy perspective, do you support or oppose the consideration of such conduct during the sentencing process?

4. Statutes and sentencing guidelines often delineate the factors to be considered by a judge when sentencing a defendant. The mitigating and aggravating factors outlined in the Illinois statutes set forth below exemplify the variety of factors that may enter into the sentencing decision:

730 Ill. Comp. Stat. 5/5–5–3.1 Factors in Mitigation

§ 5–5–3.1. Factors in Mitigation. (a) The following grounds shall be accorded weight in favor of withholding or minimizing a sentence of imprisonment:

(1) the defendant's criminal conduct neither caused nor threatened serious physical harm to another;

(2) the defendant did not contemplate that his criminal conduct would cause or threaten serious physical harm to another;

(3) the defendant acted under a strong provocation;

(4) there were substantial grounds tending to excuse or justify the defendant's criminal conduct, though failing to establish a defense;

(5) the defendant's criminal conduct was induced or facilitated by someone other than the defendant;

(6) the defendant has compensated or will compensate the victim of his criminal conduct for the damage or injury that he sustained;

(7) the defendant has no history of prior delinquency or criminal activity or has led a law-abiding life for a substantial period of time before the commission of the present crime;

(8) the defendant's criminal conduct was the result of circumstances unlikely to recur;

(9) the character and attitudes of the defendant indicate that he is unlikely to commit another crime;

(10) the defendant is particularly likely to comply with the terms of a period of probation;

(11) the imprisonment of the defendant would entail excessive hardship to his dependents;

(12) the imprisonment of the defendant would endanger his or her medical condition;

(13) the defendant was mentally retarded as defined in Section 5–1–13 of this Code.

(b) If the court, having due regard for the character of the offender, the nature and circumstances of the offense and the public interest finds that a sentence of imprisonment is the most appropriate disposition of the offender, or where other provisions of this Code mandate the imprisonment of the offender, the grounds listed in paragraph (a) of this subsection shall be considered as factors in mitigation of the term imposed.

730 Ill. Comp. Stat. 5/5–5–3.2 Factors in Aggravation

§ 5–5–3.2. Factors in Aggravation. (a) The following factors shall be accorded weight in favor of imposing a term of imprisonment or may be considered by the court as reasons to impose a more severe sentence under Section 5–8–1:

(1) the defendant's conduct caused or threatened serious harm;

(2) the defendant received compensation for committing the offense;

(3) the defendant has a history of prior delinquency or criminal activity;

(4) the defendant, by the duties of his office or by his position, was obliged to prevent the particular offense committed or to bring the offenders committing it to justice;

(5) the defendant held public office at the time of the offense, and the offense related to the conduct of that office;

(6) the defendant utilized his professional reputation or position in the community to commit the offense, or to afford him an easier means of committing it;

(7) the sentence is necessary to deter others from committing the same crime;

(8) the defendant committed the offense against a person 60 years of age or older or such person's property;

(9) the defendant committed the offense against a person who is physically handicapped or such person's property;

(10) by reason of another individual's actual or perceived race, color, creed, religion, ancestry, gender, sexual orientation, physical or mental disability, or national origin, the defendant committed the offense against (i) the person or property of that individual; (ii) the person or property of a person who has an association with, is married to, or has a friendship with the other individual; or (iii) the person or property of a relative (by blood or marriage) of a person described in clause (i) or (ii). * * *;

(11) the offense took place in a place of worship or on the grounds of a place of worship, immediately prior to, during or immediately following worship services. * * *;

(12) the defendant was convicted of a felony committed while he was released on bail or his own recognizance pending trial for a prior felony and was convicted of such prior felony, or the defendant was convicted of a felony committed while he was serving a period of probation, conditional discharge, or mandatory supervised release * * * for a prior felony;

(13) the defendant committed or attempted to commit a felony while he was wearing a bulletproof vest. * * *;

(14) the defendant held a position of trust or supervision such as, but not limited to, family member as defined in Section 12–12 of the Criminal Code of 1961, teacher, scout leader, baby sitter, or day care worker, in relation to a victim under 18 years of age, and the defendant committed [one of several specified sexual crimes] * * * against that victim;

(15) the defendant committed an offense related to the activities of an organized gang. * * *;

(16) the defendant committed an offense in violation of [certain specified statutory provisions that prohibit an array of crimes, including sexual abuse and assault, kidnapping, aggravated assaults and batteries, juvenile prostitution, armed robbery, armed violence, and "compelled organization membership"] while in a school, regardless of the time of day or time of year; on any conveyance owned, leased, or contracted by a school to transport students to or from school or a school-related activity;

on the real property of a school; or on a public way within 1,000 feet of the real property comprising any school;

(16.5) the defendant committed an offense in violation of one of [the specified statutory provisions proscribing certain sex crimes] while in a day care center, regardless of the time of day or time of year; on the real property of a day care center, regardless of the time of day or time of year; or on a public way within 1,000 feet of the real property comprising any day care center, regardless of the time of day or time of year * * *;

(17) the defendant committed the offense by reason of any person's activity as a community policing volunteer or to prevent any person from engaging in activity as a community policing volunteer. * * *;

(18) the defendant committed the offense in a nursing home or on the real property comprising a nursing home. * * *;

(19) the defendant was a federally licensed firearm dealer and was previously convicted of a violation of subsection (a) of Section 3 of the Firearm Owners Identification Card Act and has now committed either a felony violation of the Firearm Owners Identification Card Act or an act of armed violence while armed with a firearm.

(20) the defendant (i) committed the offense of reckless homicide * * * or the offense of driving under the influence of alcohol, other drug or drugs, intoxicating compound or compounds or any combination thereof * * * and (ii) was operating a motor vehicle in excess of 20 miles per hour over the posted speed limit * * *;

(21) the defendant (i) committed the offense of reckless driving or aggravated reckless driving * * * and (ii) was operating a motor vehicle in excess of 20 miles per hour over the posted speed limit * * *;

(22) the defendant committed the offense against a person that the defendant knew, or reasonably should have known, was a member of the Armed Forces of the United States serving on active duty. * * *; or

(23) the defendant committed the offense against a person who was elderly, disabled, or infirm by taking advantage of a family or fiduciary relationship with the elderly, disabled, or infirm person.

Are there any additional aggravating or mitigating factors that should be added to the lists? Are there any, in your opinion, that should be deleted?

5.   In Roberts v. United States, 445 U.S. 552, 100 S.Ct. 1358 (1980), the Supreme Court concluded that a defendant's failure to cooperate with authorities investigating other individuals' criminal activities of which the defendant had knowledge could be considered by a sentencing judge. The defendant in that case, both before and after being indicted for several drug-distribution offenses, repeatedly refused to name his drug suppliers. The sentencing court later cited this failure to cooperate as one reason for the prison sentences imposed on the defendant.

The Supreme Court noted that a defendant's cooperation with criminal investigators suggests that the defendant is willing to abandon his or her criminal lifestyle. According to the Court, it followed that "[u]nless a different explanation is provided, a defendant's refusal to assist in the investigation of ongoing crimes gives rise to an inference that these laudable attitudes are lacking." Id. at 557, 100 S.Ct. at 1362.

The defendant in *Roberts* argued that there was indeed a "different explanation" for his refusal to name his suppliers—his fear for his safety if he betrayed his criminal associates as well as his desire not to relinquish his privilege against self-incrimination. The Supreme Court acknowledged that these arguments might have had merit if they had been presented to the sentencing judge. The judge could have assessed whether the defendant's fears of retaliation and self-incrimination were well-founded. But just because there may have been legitimate reasons for the defendant's lack of cooperation was not enough to make inappropriate or unconstitutional the sentencing judge's consideration of the defendant's lack of cooperation when the defendant had failed to assert these reasons at the time of sentencing.

6. Mitchell v. United States, 526 U.S. 314, 119 S.Ct. 1307 (1999) involved a defendant who pled guilty to four federal drug crimes. When entering her plea, the defendant reserved her right to contest the amount of drugs involved in the conspiracy count to which she was pleading guilty, a factor that would affect the length of her sentence. The judge warned the defendant that by entering the plea, she was agreeing to relinquish a number of rights, including her right to remain silent at trial. The judge then described the factual basis for the plea and asked the defendant, "Did you do that?" "Some of it," the defendant replied.

At the defendant's sentencing hearing, the prosecution introduced evidence about the frequency with which the defendant sold drugs and the amount of drugs that she sold. The defendant did not take the stand to rebut this testimony. The judge then found that the amount of drugs the defendant had conspired to sell exceeded the five kilograms needed to trigger a ten-year minimum term of imprisonment under the statute in question. The court acknowledged that this finding was predicated in part on the defendant's failure to testify and refute the government's evidence regarding the quantity of drugs.

The threshold question before the Supreme Court was whether a defendant who pleads guilty to a crime waives the protection of the privilege against self-incrimination at the sentencing hearing. The Court observed that by entering a plea of guilty, a defendant is expressing a willingness to forgo a trial and the rights that accompany a trial, including the privilege against self-incrimination. The Court held that the entry of the guilty plea and the defendant's statements made during the plea colloquy though do not constitute a relinquishment of the privilege at the sentencing hearing, typically the most important stage of the criminal prosecution for defendants who plead guilty.

The Supreme Court then turned to the question whether a court constitutionally can draw an adverse inference against a defendant because of his or her failure to testify at the sentencing hearing. The Court cited the general rule set forth in Griffin v. California, 380 U.S. 609, 614, 85 S.Ct. 1229, 1232–33 (1965) prohibiting the drawing of a negative inference from a defendant's failure to testify at trial. The Court held that this rule extends to sentencing hearings as well, at least to the extent of prohibiting a defendant's failure to testify regarding "the circumstances and details of the crime" to give rise to a negative inference about those circumstances, such as the amount of drugs involved in a drug crime. 526 U.S. at 328, 119 S.Ct. at 1315. The Supreme Court left open the question whether a court can take the defendant's silence into account when resolving other issues at the sentencing hearing, such as whether the defendant's sentence should be lowered for accepting responsibility for his or her crimes.

Assuming, *arguendo*, that *Mitchell* was correctly decided, should the "no inference" rule extend to other issues at sentencing, such as the defendant's future dangerousness and whether the defendant is repentant? See id. at 340–41, 119 S.Ct. at 1320–21 (Scalia, J., dissenting).

7. The Supreme Court's decision in Dawson v. Delaware, 503 U.S. 159, 112 S.Ct. 1093 (1992) illustrates another limitation that the Constitution places on the factors that may be taken into account at the time of sentencing. In that case, the Court considered whether the introduction of evidence in a capital sentencing hearing that the defendant was a member of a prison gang of white racists violated the defendant's rights under the First and Fourteenth Amendments. The Court first rejected the defendant's broad argument that all evidence regarding a defendant's beliefs or activities that are protected by the First Amendment must be excluded from consideration at sentencing. Sometimes, the Court observed, such beliefs or activities will be relevant to the issues considered at sentencing. For example, if a defendant were a member of a group that advocates killing certain individuals, evidence of that membership would help to show that the defendant could endanger the public in the future.

The Court proceeded to conclude, however, that introduction of the evidence of the defendant's gang membership at the sentencing hearing in this case violated his constitutional rights. This evidence was presented to the jury in the form of a stipulation that basically said that the Aryan Brotherhood, whose name was tattooed on the defendant's hand, was a "white prison gang" organized to respond to gangs comprised of racial minorities. According to the Court, this stipulation was too narrow to make evidence of the defendant's gang membership admissible. At most, the evidence revealed that the defendant was racist, which, according to the Court, was irrelevant in this case since his murder victim was white. The Court intimated, however, that had the stipulation been broader, going beyond the defendant's "abstract beliefs" and mentioning the Aryan Brotherhood's involvement in drugs, violent prison escapes, and murders, introducing evidence of the defendant's membership in the gang would not have violated the Constitution.

The Supreme Court's decision in *Dawson* can be contrasted with its decision in Wisconsin v. Mitchell, 508 U.S. 476, 113 S.Ct. 2194 (1993). In *Mitchell*, the Court upheld a statute under which the penalty for battery was increased when the victim was selected because of his or her race. While the defendant contended that he was being punished for his beliefs and speech in violation of the First Amendment, the Court underscored that the statute was directed at conduct—a criminal battery—that was unprotected by the First Amendment. In holding that examination at the sentencing hearing of the motive behind that conduct was constitutionally permissible, the Court added that the motive for committing a crime traditionally has been a factor of central importance to the sentencing decision.

As a matter of policy, do you believe that penalties should be enhanced because a crime was motivated by the victim's race? If so, should crimes against any other categories of victims trigger enhanced penalties under hate-crime laws? For contrasting views on the advisability of enacting hate-crime laws, see Frederick M. Lawrence, Punishing Hate: Bias Crimes under American Law (1999) and James B. Jacobs & Kimberly Potter, Hate Crimes: Criminal Law & Identity Politics (1998).

8. Separate and apart from the questions whether hate crimes can and should be punished more severely because of a defendant's motive in committing a crime is the question of the procedures that must be followed in determining whether the facts supporting an enhanced penalty exist. In Apprendi v. New Jersey, 530 U.S. 466, 120 S.Ct. 2348 (2000), supra page ___, the Supreme Court considered this latter question in a case in which the defendant's racially motivated crime increased the statutory maximum sentence to which he was subject.

9. United States v. Tucker, 404 U.S. 443, 92 S.Ct. 589 (1972) involved the validity of a sentence imposed on a defendant who had been found guilty of an armed bank robbery. Having been apprised that the defendant had three prior felony convictions, the sentencing judge imposed the maximum sentence for the armed robbery—25 years. Only later was it determined that two of the defendant's three prior convictions had been obtained unconstitutionally, in violation of his Sixth Amendment right to counsel.

While acknowledging the breadth of the information that can be considered by a sentencing court when imposing sentence, the Supreme Court held that the defendant's sentence in this case was invalid because it was based "at least in part upon misinformation of constitutional magnitude." Id. at 447, 92 S.Ct. at 591–92. The defendant therefore had to be resentenced, since his original sentence "might have been different" had the sentencing judge been aware that the defendant already had spent ten years of his life unconstitutionally locked up in prison. Id. at 448, 92 S.Ct. at 592.

In the case which follows, the Supreme Court considered whether *Tucker* means that defendants generally have a constitutional right at a sentencing hearing to challenge the constitutionality of prior convictions introduced to increase their sentences.

CUSTIS v. UNITED STATES

Supreme Court of the United States, 1994.
511 U.S. 485, 114 S.Ct. 1732, 128 L.Ed.2d 517.

CHIEF JUSTICE REHNQUIST delivered the opinion of the Court.

The Armed Career Criminal Act, 18 U.S.C. § 924(e) (ACCA), raises the penalty for possession of a firearm by a felon from a maximum of 10 years in prison to a mandatory minimum sentence of 15 years and a maximum of life in prison without parole if the defendant "has three previous convictions ... for a violent felony or a serious drug offense."

[After a jury convicted Daniel J. Custis in 1991 of possession of a firearm and possession of cocaine, a federal prosecutor moved to have Custis's sentence enhanced under § 924(e) based on three prior felony convictions—state convictions in 1985 for robbery and burglary and a state conviction in 1989 for attempted burglary. Custis, however, claimed that two of those convictions had been obtained in violation of his constitutional rights—his Sixth Amendment right to the effective assistance of counsel and his due-process right to have judgment entered on a guilty plea only when it is knowing and intelligent.

The federal district court concluded that Custis had no statutory or constitutional right to challenge, at the time of sentencing, the constitutionality of prior convictions supporting an enhanced sentence under § 924(e), and the Fourth Circuit Court of Appeals affirmed. The Supreme Court agreed with the lower courts that there was no statutory right under § 924(e) to mount a collateral attack on the constitutionality of prior convictions upon which an enhanced sentence might otherwise be based. The Court then turned to the question whether Custis had a constitutional right to challenge the constitutionality of the predicate convictions during the sentencing proceeding under § 924(e).]

Custis argues that regardless of whether § 924(e) permits collateral challenges to prior convictions, the Constitution requires that they be allowed. He relies upon our decisions in *Burgett v. Texas,* 389 U.S. 109 (1967), and *United States v. Tucker,* 404 U.S. 443 (1972), in support of this argument. Both of these decisions relied upon our earlier decision in *Gideon v. Wainwright,* 372 U.S. 335 (1963), holding that the Sixth Amendment of the United States Constitution required that an indigent defendant in state court proceedings have counsel appointed for him.
* * *

Following our decision in *Gideon,* the Court decided *Burgett v. Texas.* There the defendant was charged under a Texas recidivist statute with having been the subject of four previous felony convictions. The prosecutor introduced certified records of one of the defendant's earlier convictions in Tennessee. The defendant objected to the admission of this conviction on the ground that he had not been represented by counsel and had not waived his right to counsel, but his objection was overruled by the trial court. This Court reversed, finding that the certified records of the Tennessee conviction on their face raised a "presumption that petitioner was denied his right to counsel . . ., and therefore that his conviction was void." The Court held that the admission of a prior criminal conviction which is constitutionally infirm under the standards of *Gideon* is inherently prejudicial and to permit use of such a tainted prior conviction for sentence enhancement would undermine the principle of *Gideon.*

* * *

Custis invites us to extend the right to attack collaterally prior convictions used for sentence enhancement beyond the right to have appointed counsel established in *Gideon.* We decline to do so. We think that since the decision in *Johnson v. Zerbst*[, 304 U.S. 458 (1938)] more than half a century ago, and running through our decisions in *Burgett* and *Tucker,* there has been a theme that failure to appoint counsel for an indigent defendant was a unique constitutional defect. Custis attacks his previous convictions claiming the denial of the effective assistance of counsel, that his guilty plea was not knowing and intelligent, and that he had not been adequately advised of his rights in opting for a "stipulated facts" trial. None of these alleged constitutional violations rises to the level of a jurisdictional defect resulting from the failure to appoint counsel at all.

Ease of administration also supports the distinction. As revealed in a number of the cases cited in this opinion, failure to appoint counsel at all will generally appear from the judgment roll itself, or from an accompanying minute order. But determination of claims of ineffective assistance of counsel, and failure to assure that a guilty plea was voluntary, would require sentencing courts to rummage through frequently nonexistent or difficult to obtain state court transcripts or records that may date from another era, and may come from any one of the 50 States.

The interest in promoting the finality of judgments provides additional support for our constitutional conclusion. As we have explained, "[i]nroads on the concept of finality tend to undermine confidence in the integrity of our procedures" and inevitably delay and impair the orderly administration of justice. * * * By challenging the previous conviction, the defendant is asking a district court "to deprive [the] [state court judgment] of [its] normal force and effect in a proceeding that ha[s] an independent purpose other than to overturn the prior judgmen[t]." These principles bear extra weight in cases in which the prior convictions, such as one challenged by Custis, are based on guilty pleas, because when a guilty plea is at issue, "the concern with finality served by the limitation on collateral attack has special force."

We therefore hold that § 924(e) does not permit Custis to use the federal sentencing forum to gain review of his state convictions. Congress did not prescribe and the Constitution does not require such delay and protraction of the federal sentencing process. We recognize, however, as did the Court of Appeals, that Custis, who was still "in custody" for purposes of his state convictions at the time of his federal sentencing under § 924(e), may attack his state sentences in Maryland or through federal habeas review. If Custis is successful in attacking these state sentences, he may then apply for reopening of any federal sentence enhanced by the state sentences. We express no opinion on the appropriate disposition of such an application.

* * *

JUSTICE SOUTER, with whom JUSTICE BLACKMUN and JUSTICE STEVENS join, dissenting.

[Justice Souter concluded that Congress had accorded defendants a statutory right to challenge, at a sentencing hearing, the constitutionality of prior convictions offered in support of an enhanced sentence under § 924(e). He therefore criticized the majority for unnecessarily deciding what he termed "a difficult constitutional question."]

This is a difficult question, for one thing, because the language and logic of *Burgett* and *Tucker* are hard to limit to claimed violations of the right, recognized in *Gideon v. Wainwright,* to have a lawyer appointed if necessary. * * * *Tucker* made it clear that "the real question" before the Court was whether the defendant's sentence might have been different if the sentencing judge had known that the defendant's "previous convictions had been unconstitutionally obtained."

Even if, consistently with principles of *stare decisis, Burgett* and *Tucker* could be read as applying only to some class of cases defined to exclude claimed violations of *Strickland* or *Boykin,* the question whether to confine them so is not easily answered. *Burgett* and *Tucker* deal directly with claimed violations of *Gideon,* and distinguishing for these purposes between violations of *Gideon* and *Strickland* would describe a very fine line. To establish a violation of the Sixth Amendment under *Strickland,* a defendant must show that "counsel's performance was deficient," and that "the deficient performance prejudiced the defense" in that "counsel's errors were so serious as to deprive the defendant of a fair trial, a trial whose result is reliable." It is hard to see how such a defendant is any better off than one who has been denied counsel altogether, and why the conviction of such a defendant may be used for sentence enhancement if the conviction of one who has been denied counsel altogether may not. The Sixth Amendment guarantees no mere formality of appointment, but the "assistance" of counsel, and whether the violation is of *Gideon* or *Strickland,* the defendant has been denied that constitutional right.

It is also difficult to see why a sentencing court that must entertain a defendant's claim that a prior conviction was obtained in violation of the Sixth Amendment's right to counsel need not entertain a defendant's claim that a prior conviction was based on an unknowing or involuntary guilty plea. That claim, if meritorious, would mean that the defendant was convicted despite invalid waivers of at least one of two Sixth Amendment rights (to trial by jury and to confront adverse witnesses) or of a Fifth Amendment right (against compulsory self-incrimination). It is, to be sure, no simple task to prove that a guilty plea was the result of "[i]gnorance, incomprehension, coercion, terror, inducements, [or] subtle or blatant threats," but it is certainly at least a difficult question whether a defendant who can make such a showing ought to receive less favorable treatment than the defendants in *Burgett* and *Tucker.*

* * *

The Court invokes "[e]ase of administration" to support its constitutional holding. * * * [T]he burden argument here is not a strong one. The burdens of allowing defendants to challenge prior convictions at sentencing are not so severe, and are likely less severe than those associated with the alternative avenues for raising the very same claims.

* * * [T]he Court sees administrative burdens arising because "sentencing courts [would be required] to rummage through frequently nonexistent or difficult to obtain state-court transcripts or records that may date from another era, and may come from any of the 50 States." It would not be sentencing courts that would have to do this rummaging, however, but defendants seeking to avoid enhancement, for no one disagrees that the burden of showing the invalidity of prior convictions would rest on the defendants.

Whatever administrative benefits may flow from insulating sentencing courts from challenges to prior convictions will likely be offset by the administrative costs of the alternative means of raising the same claims. The Court acknowledges that an individual still in custody for a state conviction relied upon for enhancement may attack that conviction through state or federal habeas review and, if successful, "may ... apply for reopening any federal sentence enhanced by the state sentence." * * * From the perspective of administrability, it strikes me as entirely sensible to resolve any challenges to the lawfulness of a predicate conviction in the single sentencing proceeding, especially since defendants there will normally be represented by counsel, who bring efficiency to the litigation (as well as equitable benefits).

* * *

QUESTIONS AND POINTS FOR DISCUSSION

1.   Federal prisoners in custody under a sentence imposed in violation of the Constitution or federal laws can file a petition under 28 U.S.C. § 2255 to have the sentence vacated or corrected. In Daniels v. United States, 532 U.S. 374, 121 S.Ct. 1578 (2001), the Supreme Court considered whether a defendant imprisoned under the Armed Career Criminal Act can challenge the federal sentence under § 2255 on the grounds that the sentence was enhanced because of a prior unconstitutional conviction. In a 5–4 decision, the Supreme Court answered that question in the negative. Writing for the majority, Justice O'Connor explained that the same factors that propelled the Court's decision in Custis v. United States—the difficulty of unearthing state records needed to adjudicate the constitutional claim and the interest in preserving the finality of state-court judgments—at least generally foreclose collateral attacks on prior convictions in § 2255 proceedings.

The Court in Daniels emphasized that defendants have many opportunities to challenge the constitutionality of their state convictions—on appeal, in state postconviction proceedings, and in federal habeas corpus actions brought under 28 U.S.C. § 2254. If defendants fail, however, to avail themselves of these opportunities or do so unsuccessfully, they generally have no right to "another bite at the apple" simply because an allegedly unconstitutional conviction augmented their federal sentence. Id. at 383, 121 S.Ct. at 1584.

In a dissenting opinion, Justice Souter countered that oftentimes defendants do not appeal a conviction because the light penalty imposed does not warrant the bringing of an appeal. In addition, they may refrain from challenging the conviction in a state postconviction proceeding because they have no attorney to assist them in collaterally attacking the conviction. To the argument that defendants may have little or no reason to challenge a conviction until it results in the imposition of an enhanced sentence, the majority responded:

> [T]he fact remains that avenues of redress are generally available if sought in a timely manner. If a person chooses not to pursue those remedies, he does so with the knowledge that the conviction will stay on his record. This knowledge should serve as an incentive not to commit a subsequent crime and risk having the sentence for that crime enhanced under a recidivist sentencing statute.

Id. at 381 n. 1, 121 S.Ct. at 1583 n. 1.

The Supreme Court in *Daniels* did carve out what Justice Souter described as "a textually untethered exception to its own rule." Id. at 390, 121 S.Ct. at 1588 (Souter, J., dissenting). According to the Court, a § 2255 petition can be a vehicle for challenging a prior conviction that resulted in an enhanced federal sentence if the prior conviction was the by-product of an unconstitutional failure to appoint counsel to represent the defendant, at least if the *Gideon* challenge was raised at the time the court imposed the enhanced federal sentence. In addition, a plurality of the Court (Justice Scalia did not join this portion of Justice O'Connor's opinion) alluded to the possibility that there might be other "rare cases" when a constitutional challenge to a prior conviction can be mounted in a § 2255 proceeding. Id. at 383, 121 S.Ct. at 1584. In a companion case decided the same day as *Daniels*, Lackawanna County Dist. Attorney v. Coss, 532 U.S. 394, 121 S.Ct. 1567 (2001), the same plurality described two situations when a defendant might be able to challenge a prior conviction in such a proceeding. First, a defendant might introduce "compelling evidence" that could not have been timely discovered and that demonstrates the defendant's innocence of the crime of which he or she previously was convicted. Id. at 405, 121 S.Ct. at 1575. Second, the failure to obtain an earlier review of the validity of the prior conviction may have been the government's, not the defendant's, fault. According to the plurality, the second scenario might arise, for example, when a state court had previously refused, for no reason, to adjudicate the constitutional claim.

2.   State prisoners in custody in violation of the Constitution or federal laws can seek release from their illegal confinement by filing a petition in federal court under 28 U.S.C. § 2254 for a writ of habeas corpus. In *Lackawanna County Dist. Attorney v. Coss*, the companion case to *Daniels* discussed above, the Supreme Court extended its holding in *Daniels* to state prisoners attempting to challenge in a habeas corpus proceeding the constitutionality of prior convictions that resulted in the imposition of an augmented sentence. Holding that prior state convictions are "conclusively valid" once those convictions can no longer be directly or collaterally attacked, id. at 403, 121 S.Ct. at 1574, the Court once again recognized a *Gideon* exception to this rule. In addition, a plurality of the Court observed, but did not decide, that the

general rule might not apply in the two situations described earlier: when, as a practical matter, the habeas corpus proceeding might be "the first and only forum" for challenging the constitutionality of the prior conviction. Id. at 406, 121 S.Ct. at 1575.

3. Johnson v. Mississippi, 486 U.S. 578, 108 S.Ct. 1981 (1988) involved a defendant who was sentenced to death for murder in Mississippi. One of the aggravating circumstances relied upon in imposing the death penalty was the defendant's prior conviction in New York for assault with intent to commit rape. That conviction, however, was set aside by a New York court after the death-penalty hearing in Mississippi. The Supreme Court concluded that since the defendant's death sentence was predicated on an invalid conviction, it violated the Eighth Amendment's prohibition of cruel and unusual punishments.

4. As discussed earlier in this chapter, the Supreme Court has held that an indigent defendant who was unrepresented by counsel at trial cannot, if convicted, be sentenced to any period of incarceration for the crime of which he or she was convicted. See pages 96–97. But according to the Court, a misdemeanor conviction obtained when the defendant was not represented by counsel can be used to increase the prison sentence imposed for a subsequent crime. See Nichols v. United States, 511 U.S. 738, 114 S.Ct. 1921 (1994) (reliance on uncounseled misdemeanor conviction in computing defendant's criminal-history score increased his prison sentence by over two years). The Court reasoned in *Nichols* that a conviction that is initially valid does not suddenly become invalid when used for enhancement purposes. In a dissenting opinion, Justice Blackmun, joined by Justices Stevens and Ginsburg, objected that a conviction which is too unreliable, because it was obtained without the assistance of counsel, to permit incarceration in the first place is too unreliable to be used subsequently to increase the amount of time that a defendant will be incarcerated.

5. The Federal Rules of Evidence are inapplicable in sentencing hearings. Fed.R.Evid. 1101(d)(3). Thus, although hearsay statements are generally inadmissible in federal trials, the rules do not preclude judges from considering hearsay statements at the time of sentencing. An example of such a statement would be a presentence investigation report's reference to the remark of a witness that the defendant had committed a certain crime in the past for which he was neither arrested nor convicted.

Hearsay statements are generally inadmissible at trial because of the risk that they are untruthful or inaccurate. Some commentators consequently have derided the concept of "reliable hearsay" for purposes of sentencing as an "oxymoron." See, e.g., Deborah Young, Fact–Finding at Federal Sentencing: Why the Guidelines Should Meet the Rules, 79 Cornell L.Rev. 299, 342, 362 (1994) (advocating the extension of the Federal Rules of Evidence to federal sentencing hearings).

6. In Townsend v. Burke, 334 U.S. 736, 68 S.Ct. 1252 (1948), the Supreme Court was confronted with questions about when a judge's reliance on false information when sentencing a defendant violates due process of law. In that case, a defendant, who was unrepresented by counsel, was sentenced to prison for ten to twenty years for burglary and robbery. At the sentencing

hearing, the judge recited the defendant's criminal record. In fact, however, the defendant had been acquitted, or the criminal charges dismissed, in three of the cited cases. On these facts, the Supreme Court concluded that the defendant's right to due process of law had been violated:

> It is not the duration or severity of this sentence that renders it constitutionally invalid; it is the careless or designed pronouncement of sentence on a foundation so extensively and materially false, which the prisoner had no opportunity to correct by the services which counsel would provide, that renders the proceedings lacking in due process.

> Nor do we mean that mere error in resolving a question of fact on a plea of guilty by an uncounseled defendant in a non-capital case would necessarily indicate a want of due process of law. Fair prosecutors and conscientious judges sometimes are misinformed or draw inferences from conflicting evidence with which we would not agree. But even an erroneous judgment, based on a scrupulous and diligent search for truth, may be due process of law.

Id. at 741, 68 S.Ct. at 1255.

7. As *Townsend v. Burke* makes clear, due process is violated only when the sentencing judge actually relies on certain false information when imposing a sentence. Consequently, Rule 32(i)(3)(B), which can be found on page 136, provides a judge with two options when faced with a defendant's challenge to the accuracy of information included in a presentence investigation report. The judge either must resolve the factual dispute or confirm that the disputed information was not considered when sentencing the defendant or did not otherwise affect the sentence.

Even when a judge considers demonstrably false information when sentencing a defendant, the defendant's due-process rights are not necessarily violated. Due process, for example, is not violated if the mistake involved an immaterial fact. See, e.g., United States v. Addonizio, 442 U.S. 178, 99 S.Ct. 2235 (1979) (sentencing judge's expectations about the defendant's parole-release date were not enforceable against the parole board and therefore the judge's erroneous prediction when sentencing the defendant as to when the defendant would be released on parole did not involve "misinformation of constitutional magnitude" that would entitle the defendant to be resentenced). Are there any other instances, in your opinion, when a sentencing judge's actual reliance on false information when sentencing a defendant would not violate the defendant's due-process rights?

8. Just because evidence was obtained unconstitutionally and is inadmissible at trial does not necessarily mean that the evidence is also inadmissible during a sentencing hearing. For example, assume that during an unconstitutional warrantless search of the home of a murder suspect, the police find a diary revealing the deliberateness with which the defendant had planned the murder. Although the diary will be inadmissible at trial because of the violation of the defendant's Fourth Amendment rights, if he is nonetheless convicted, most lower courts have held that such illegally seized evidence can be considered by the sentencing judge, at least when the purpose of the search was not to find evidence to enhance the defendant's sentence. See, e.g., United States v. Acosta, 303 F.3d 78, 84–85 (1st Cir. 2002) (listing cases).

Seventh Circuit Judge Frank Easterbrook has sharply criticized both the prevailing rule that illegally seized evidence is admissible at sentencing and the exception courts have carved out to that rule:

> [S]uch an exception is chimerical. Police do not mull over the potential uses of evidence, fix on *a* use, and then seize the evidence for that purpose. Officers have multiple purposes—they want to close down drug operations (even if no prosecution ensues), they want to get the goods that will help turn a dope peddler against his supplier, they want to facilitate convictions, they want to maximize sentences when convictions occur. It is inconceivable that any defendant will be able to show that the police had only one of these purposes in mind when making a seizure. * * *
>
> It is awfully hard to see why motive should matter on either prudential or doctrinal grounds. Is the seizure less offensive to the Constitution, or is deterrence less important, when the police drain their minds of the possibility that the seizure will contribute to a conviction? As for doctrine: the fourth amendment establishes an objective standard. *Graham v. Connor*, 490 U.S. 386, 397 (1989). I think it most unlikely that the Supreme Court will admit intent through the back door in deciding whether to apply the exclusionary rule. Application is categorical: the exclusionary rule applies, or it doesn't, to one or another juncture of litigation. * * *

* * *

* * *Today prosecutors often present at trial only a small fraction of the defendant's provable conduct. The rest is reserved for sentencing. * * * In drug cases the guidelines require the court to take into consideration all quantities sold or under negotiation as "part of the same course of conduct or common scheme or plan as the offense of conviction". U.S.S.G. § 1B1.3(a)(2). Our case is the norm: the prosecutor charged the defendants with distributing slightly more than 5 kilograms of drugs but asked for a sentence based on more than 50 (and the court imposed a sentence based on more than 15). Where once courts sentenced the offender and not the conduct, now courts sentence for crimes that were the subject of neither charge nor conviction. In proving such additional crimes, illegally seized evidence may play a central role—the same sort of role it used to play in supporting convictions on additional counts.

* * * The crime of which Jewel and Jackson were convicted, selling more than 5 kilograms of a mixture containing a detectable amount of cocaine, carries a minimum of 10 years and a maximum of life. Parole has been abolished. If the police seize 5 kilograms legally and another 46 illegally, this statute, coupled with § 1B1.3(a)(2), allows the court to impose a sentence of life imprisonment, just as if all of the drugs had been seized in compliance with the Constitution. * * *

Judge Silberman recognized that to allow the use of unconstitutionally seized evidence in sentencing is to take "a big bite out of the exclusionary rule", [*United States v.*] *McCrory*, 930 F.2d at 72 [D.C. Cir. 1991]. * * * [I]f we do not apply the exclusionary rule in sentencing under the guidelines, the constitutional ban on unreasonable searches and seizures will become a parchment barrier.

United States v. Jewel, 947 F.2d 224, 238–40 (7th Cir.1991) (Easterbrook, J., concurring). Do you agree with Judge Easterbrook's comments?

According to the Supreme Court, when resolving questions concerning the applicability of the Fourth Amendment exclusionary rule, the benefits of excluding the evidence during the stage of the criminal prosecution in question must be weighed against the costs of such exclusion. United States v. Calandra, 414 U.S. 338, 349, 94 S.Ct. 613, 620 (1974) (Fourth Amendment exclusionary rule does not apply to grand-jury proceedings). How would you assess the costs and benefits of applying the Fourth Amendment exclusionary rule during sentencing hearings? For a discussion of the applicability of the exclusionary rule in parole-revocation hearings, see Pennsylvania Bd. of Probation and Parole v. Scott, 524 U.S. 357, 118 S.Ct. 2014 (1998) on page 395.

———

In recent years, crime victims have mobilized to ensure that they are not overlooked by the criminal-justice system. As a result, a number of jurisdictions have enacted legislation authorizing or requiring consideration of victim-impact statements during the sentencing stage of criminal prosecutions. See, e.g., Mich.Comp.Laws § 771.14(2)(b); Va.Code Ann. § 19.2–299.1. In the case which follows, the Supreme Court considered the constitutionality of introducing such statements at a sentencing hearing in a capital case.

PAYNE v. TENNESSEE

Supreme Court of the United States, 1991.
501 U.S. 808, 111 S.Ct. 2597, 115 L.Ed.2d 720.

CHIEF JUSTICE REHNQUIST delivered the opinion of the Court.

* * *

Petitioner, Pervis Tyrone Payne, was convicted by a jury on two counts of first-degree murder and one count of assault with intent to commit murder in the first degree. He was sentenced to death for each of the murders and to 30 years in prison for the assault.

The victims of Payne's offenses were 28–year–old Charisse Christopher, her 2–year–old daughter Lacie, and her 3–year–old son Nicholas. The three lived together in an apartment in Millington, Tennessee, across the hall from Payne's girlfriend, Bobbie Thomas. On Saturday, June 27, 1987, Payne visited Thomas' apartment several times in expectation of her return from her mother's house in Arkansas, but found no one at home. * * *

Payne passed the morning and early afternoon injecting cocaine and drinking beer. * * * Sometime around 3 p.m., Payne returned to the apartment complex, entered the Christophers' apartment, and began making sexual advances towards Charisse. Charisse resisted and Payne became violent. A neighbor who resided in the apartment directly beneath the Christophers heard Charisse screaming, " 'Get out, get out,' as if she were telling the children to leave." The noise briefly subsided and then began, " 'horribly loud.' " The neighbor called the police after she heard a "blood curdling scream" from the Christopher's apartment.

When the first police officer arrived at the scene, he immediately encountered Payne, who was leaving the apartment building, so covered with blood that he appeared to be " 'sweating blood.' " * * *

Inside the apartment, the police encountered a horrifying scene. Blood covered the walls and floor throughout the unit. Charisse and her children were lying on the floor in the kitchen. Nicholas, despite several wounds inflicted by a butcher knife that completely penetrated through his body from front to back, was still breathing. Miraculously, he survived, but not until after undergoing seven hours of surgery and a transfusion of 1,700 cc's of blood—400 to 500 cc's more than his estimated normal blood volume. Charisse and Lacie were dead.

Charisse's body was found on the kitchen floor on her back, her legs fully extended. She had sustained 42 direct knife wounds and 42 defensive wounds on her arms and hands. * * *

Lacie's body was on the kitchen floor near her mother. She had suffered stab wounds to the chest, abdomen, back, and head. The murder weapon, a butcher knife, was found at her feet. * * *

* * *

At trial, Payne took the stand and, despite the overwhelming and relatively uncontroverted evidence against him, testified that he had not harmed any of the Christophers. * * * The jury returned guilty verdicts against Payne on all counts.

During the sentencing phase of the trial, Payne presented the testimony of four witnesses: his mother and father, Bobbie Thomas, and Dr. John T. Hutson, a clinical psychologist specializing in criminal court evaluation work. * * *

* * *

The State presented the testimony of Charisse's mother, Mary Zvolanek. When asked how Nicholas had been affected by the murders of his mother and sister, she responded:

"He cries for his mom. He doesn't seem to understand why she doesn't come home. And he cries for his sister Lacie. He comes to me many times during the week and asks me, Grandmama, do you miss my Lacie. And I tell him yes. He says, I'm worried about my Lacie."

In arguing for the death penalty during closing argument, the prosecutor commented on the continuing effects of Nicholas' experience, stating:

"But we do know that Nicholas was alive. And Nicholas was in the same room. Nicholas was still conscious. His eyes were open. He responded to the paramedics. He was able to follow their directions. He was able to hold his intestines in as he was carried to the ambulance. So he knew what happened to his mother and baby sister."

* * *

"Somewhere down the road Nicholas is going to grow up, hopefully. He's going to want to know what happened. And he is going to know what happened to his baby sister and his mother. He is going to want to know what type of justice was done. He is going to want to know what happened. With your verdict, you will provide the answer."

In the rebuttal to Payne's closing argument, the prosecutor stated:

"You saw the videotape this morning. You saw what Nicholas Christopher will carry in his mind forever. When you talk about cruel, when you talk about atrocious, and when you talk about heinous, that picture will always come into your mind, probably throughout the rest of your lives. . . .

* * *

". . . No one will ever know about Lacie Jo because she never had the chance to grow up. Her life was taken from her at the age of two years old. So, no there won't be a high school principal to talk about Lacie Jo Christopher, and there won't be anybody to take her to her high school prom. And there won't be anybody there—there won't be her mother there or Nicholas' mother there to kiss him at night. His mother will never kiss him good night or pat him as he goes off to bed, or hold him and sing him a lullaby.

* * *

"[Petitioner's attorney] wants you to think about a good reputation, people who love the defendant and things about him. He doesn't want you to think about the people who love Charisse Christopher, her mother and daddy who loved her. The people who loved little Lacie Jo, the grandparents who are still here. The brother who mourns for her every single day and wants to know where his best little playmate is. He doesn't have anybody to watch cartoons with him, a little one. These are the things that go into why it is especially cruel, heinous, and atrocious, the burden that that child will carry forever."

The jury sentenced Payne to death on each of the murder counts.

The Supreme Court of Tennessee affirmed the conviction and sentence. * * *

* * *

We granted certiorari to reconsider our holdings in *Booth* [*v. Maryland*, 482 U.S. 496 (1987)] and [*South Carolina v.*] *Gathers*[, 490 U.S. 805 (1989)] that the Eighth Amendment prohibits a capital sentencing jury from considering "victim impact" evidence relating to the personal characteristics of the victim and the emotional impact of the crimes on the victim's family.

In *Booth,* the defendant robbed and murdered an elderly couple. As required by a state statute, a victim impact statement was prepared based on interviews with the victims' son, daughter, son-in-law, and granddaughter. The statement, which described the personal characteristics of the victims, the emotional impact of the crimes on the family, and set forth the family members' opinions and characterizations of the crimes and the defendant, was submitted to the jury at sentencing. The jury imposed the death penalty. * * *

This Court held by a 5–to–4 vote that the Eighth Amendment prohibits a jury from considering a victim impact statement at the sentencing phase of a capital trial. * * * In *Gathers,* decided two years later, the Court extended the rule announced in *Booth* to statements made by a prosecutor to the sentencing jury regarding the personal qualities of the victim.

* * *

Booth and *Gathers* were based on two premises: that evidence relating to a particular victim or to the harm that a capital defendant causes a victim's family do not in general reflect on the defendant's "blameworthiness," and that only evidence relating to "blameworthiness" is relevant to the capital sentencing decision. However, the assessment of harm caused by the defendant as a result of the crime charged has understandably been an important concern of the criminal law, both in determining the elements of the offense and in determining the appropriate punishment. Thus, two equally blameworthy criminal defendants may be guilty of different offenses solely because their acts cause differing amounts of harm. "If a bank robber aims his gun at a guard, pulls the trigger, and kills his target, he may be put to death. If the gun unexpectedly misfires, he may not. His moral guilt in both cases is identical, but his responsibility in the former is greater." * * *

* * *

We have held that a State cannot preclude the sentencer from considering "any relevant mitigating evidence" that the defendant proffers in support of a sentence less than death. * * * *Booth* has, we think, unfairly weighted the scales in a capital trial; while virtually no limits are placed on the relevant mitigating evidence a capital defendant may introduce concerning his own circumstances, the State is barred from either offering "a quick glimpse of the life" which a defendant "chose to extinguish" or demonstrating the loss to the victim's family and to society which has resulted from the defendant's homicide.

The *Booth* Court reasoned that victim impact evidence must be excluded because it would be difficult, if not impossible, for the defendant to rebut such evidence without shifting the focus of the sentencing hearing away from the defendant, thus creating a " 'mini-trial' on the victim's character." In many cases the evidence relating to the victim is already before the jury at least in part because of its relevance at the guilt phase of the trial. But even as to additional evidence admitted at the sentencing phase, the mere fact that for tactical reasons it might not be prudent for the defense to rebut victim impact evidence makes the case no different than others in which a party is faced with this sort of a dilemma. * * *

Payne echoes the concern voiced in *Booth*'s case that the admission of victim impact evidence permits a jury to find that defendants whose victims were assets to their community are more deserving of punishment than those whose victims are perceived to be less worthy. As a general matter, however, victim impact evidence is not offered to encourage comparative judgments of this kind—for instance, that the killer of a hardworking, devoted parent deserves the death penalty, but that the murderer of a reprobate does not. It is designed to show instead *each* victim's "uniqueness as an individual human being," whatever the jury might think the loss to the community resulting from his death might be. The facts of *Gathers*[e] are an excellent illustration of this: The evidence showed that the victim was an out of work, mentally handicapped individual, perhaps not, in the eyes of most, a significant contributor to society, but nonetheless a murdered human being.

* * *

* * * In the majority of cases, and in this case, victim impact evidence serves entirely legitimate purposes. In the event that evidence is introduced that is so unduly prejudicial that it renders the trial fundamentally unfair, the Due Process Clause of the Fourteenth Amendment provides a mechanism for relief. * * *

We are now of the view that a State may properly conclude that for the jury to assess meaningfully the defendant's moral culpability and blameworthiness, it should have before it at the sentencing phase evidence of the specific harm caused by the defendant. "[T]he State has a legitimate interest in counteracting the mitigating evidence which the defendant is entitled to put in, by reminding the sentencer that just as the murderer should be considered as an individual, so too the victim is an individual whose death represents a unique loss to society and in particular to his family." By turning the victim into a "faceless stranger at the penalty phase of a capital trial," *Booth* deprives the State of the full moral force of its evidence and may prevent the jury from having before it all the

---

e. During closing arguments to the jury in the death-penalty hearing in *Gathers,* the prosecutor had mentioned a Bible and voter's registration card that the victim was carrying when the defendant murdered him. The prosecutor then argued that these items revealed that the victim cared about God and the United States.

information necessary to determine the proper punishment for a first-degree murder.

The present case is an example of the potential for such unfairness. The capital sentencing jury heard testimony from Payne's girlfriend that they met at church; that he was affectionate, caring, and kind to her children; that he was not an abuser of drugs or alcohol; and that it was inconsistent with his character to have committed the murders. Payne's parents testified that he was a good son, and a clinical psychologist testified that Payne was an extremely polite prisoner and suffered from a low IQ. None of this testimony was related to the circumstances of Payne's brutal crimes. In contrast, the only evidence of the impact of Payne's offenses during the sentencing phase was Nicholas' grandmother's description—in response to a single question—that the child misses his mother and baby sister. * * * [T]he testimony illustrated quite poignantly some of the harm that Payne's killing had caused; there is nothing unfair about allowing the jury to bear in mind that harm at the same time as it considers the mitigating evidence introduced by the defendant. * * *

* * *

We thus hold that if the State chooses to permit the admission of victim impact evidence and prosecutorial argument on that subject, the Eighth Amendment erects no *per se* bar. * * *

* * *

[W]e conclude, for the reasons heretofore stated, that [*Booth* and *Gathers*] were wrongly decided and should be, and now are, overruled.[2]

JUSTICE O'CONNOR, with whom JUSTICE WHITE and JUSTICE KENNEDY join, concurring.

* * *

* * * "Murder is the ultimate act of depersonalization." It transforms a living person with hopes, dreams, and fears into a corpse, thereby taking away all that is special and unique about the person. The Constitution does not preclude a State from deciding to give some of that back.

* * *

JUSTICE SOUTER, with whom JUSTICE KENNEDY joins, concurring.

* * *

* * * Murder has foreseeable consequences. When it happens, it is always to distinct individuals, and, after it happens, other victims are left

---

2. Our holding today is limited to the holdings of *Booth v. Maryland* and *South Carolina v. Gathers* that evidence and argument relating to the victim and the impact of the victim's death on the victim's family are inadmissible at a capital sentencing hearing. *Booth* also held that the admission of a victim's family members' characterizations and opinions about the crime, the defendant, and the appropriate sentence violates the Eighth Amendment. No evidence of the latter sort was presented at the trial in this case.

behind. Every defendant knows, if endowed with the mental competence for criminal responsibility, that the life he will take by his homicidal behavior is that of a unique person, like himself, and that the person to be killed probably has close associates, "survivors," who will suffer harms and deprivations from the victim's death. Just as defendants know that they are not faceless human ciphers, they know that their victims are not valueless fungibles; and just as defendants appreciate the web of relationships and dependencies in which they live, they know that their victims are not human islands, but individuals with parents or children, spouses or friends or dependents. Thus, when a defendant chooses to kill, or to raise the risk of a victim's death, this choice necessarily relates to a whole human being and threatens an association of others, who may be distinctly hurt. The fact that the defendant may not know the details of a victim's life and characteristics, or the exact identities and needs of those who may survive, should not in any way obscure the further facts that death is always to a "unique" individual, and harm to some group of survivors is a consequence of a successful homicidal act so foreseeable as to be virtually inevitable.

That foreseeability of the killing's consequences imbues them with direct moral relevance, and evidence of the specific harm caused when a homicidal risk is realized is nothing more than evidence of the risk that the defendant originally chose to run despite the kinds of consequences that were obviously foreseeable. It is morally both defensible and appropriate to consider such evidence when penalizing a murderer, like other criminals, in light of common knowledge and the moral responsibility that such knowledge entails. * * *

* * *

I do not, however, rest my decision to overrule wholly on the constitutional error that I see in the cases in question. I must rely as well on my further view that *Booth* sets an unworkable standard of constitutional relevance that threatens, on its own terms, to produce such arbitrary consequences and uncertainty of application as virtually to guarantee a result far diminished from the case's promise of appropriately individualized sentencing for capital defendants. * * *

A hypothetical case will illustrate these facts and raise what I view as the serious practical problems with application of the *Booth* standard. Assume that a minister, unidentified as such and wearing no clerical collar, walks down a street to his church office on a brief errand, while his wife and adolescent daughter wait for him in a parked car. He is robbed and killed by a stranger, and his survivors witness his death. What are the circumstances of the crime that can be considered at the sentencing phase under *Booth*? The defendant did not know his victim was a minister, or that he had a wife and child, let alone that they were watching. Under *Booth*, these facts were irrelevant to his decision to kill, and they should be barred from consideration at sentencing. Yet evidence of them will surely be admitted at the guilt phase of the trial. The widow will testify to what she saw, and, in so doing, she will not be asked to pretend that she was a mere bystander. She could not succeed at that if she tried. The daughter may well testify too. The jury will not be kept from knowing that the victim was a minister, with a wife and child, on an errand to his church. This is so not only because the widow will not try to deceive the jury about her relationship, but also because the usual standards of trial relevance afford factfinders enough information about surrounding circumstances to let them make sense of the narrowly material facts of the crime itself. No one claims that jurors in a capital case should be deprived of such common contextual evidence, even though the defendant knew nothing about the errand, the victim's occupation, or his family. And yet, if these facts are not kept from the jury at the guilt stage, they will be in the jurors' minds at the sentencing stage.

Booth thus raises a dilemma with very practical consequences. If we were to require the rules of guilt-phase evidence to be changed to guarantee the full effect of *Booth*'s promise to exclude consideration of specific facts unknown to the defendant and thus supposedly without significance in morally evaluating his decision to kill, we would seriously reduce the comprehensibility of most trials by depriving jurors of those details of context that allow them to understand what is being described. If, on the other hand, we are to leave the rules of trial evidence alone, *Booth*'s objective will not be attained without requiring a separate sentencing jury to be empaneled. This would be a major imposition on the States, however, and I suppose that no one would seriously consider adding such a further requirement.

But, even if *Booth* were extended one way or the other to exclude completely from the sentencing proceeding all facts about the crime's victims not known by the defendant, the case would be vulnerable to the further charge that it would lead to arbitrary sentencing results. In the preceding hypothetical, *Booth* would require that all evidence about the victim's family, including its very existence, be excluded from sentencing consideration because the defendant did not know of it when he killed the victim. Yet, if the victim's daughter had screamed "Daddy, look out," as the defendant approached the victim with drawn gun, then the evidence of at least the daughter's survivorship would be admissible even under a strict reading of *Booth,* because the defendant, prior to killing, had been made aware of the daughter's existence, which therefore became relevant in evaluating the defendant's decision to kill. Resting a decision about the admission of impact evidence on such a fortuity is arbitrary.

* * *

* * * *Booth* promises more than it can deliver, given the unresolved tension between common evidentiary standards at the guilt phase and *Booth*'s promise of a sentencing determination free from the consideration of facts unknown to the defendant and irrelevant to his decision to kill. An extension of the case to guarantee a sentencing authority free from the influence of information extraneous under *Booth* would be either an unworkable or a costly extension of an erroneous principle and would itself create a risk of arbitrary results. * * * Therefore, I join the Court in its partial overruling of *Booth* and *Gathers*.

JUSTICE MARSHALL, with whom JUSTICE BLACKMUN joins, dissenting.

Power, not reason, is the new currency of this Court's decisionmaking. Four Terms ago, a five-Justice majority of this Court held that "victim impact" evidence of the type at issue in this case could not constitutionally be introduced during the penalty phase of a capital trial. * * * Neither the law nor the facts supporting *Booth* and *Gathers* underwent any change in the last four years. Only the personnel of this Court did.

* * * Because I believe that this Court owes more to its constitutional precedents in general and to *Booth* and *Gathers* in particular, I dissent.

* * *

JUSTICE STEVENS, with whom JUSTICE BLACKMUN joins, dissenting.

* * *

Until today our capital punishment jurisprudence has required that any decision to impose the death penalty be based solely on evidence that tends to inform the jury about the character of the offense and the character of the defendant. Evidence that serves no purpose other than to appeal to the sympathies or emotions of the jurors has never been considered admissible. Thus, if a defendant, who had murdered a convenience store clerk in cold blood in the course of an armed robbery, offered evidence unknown to him at the time of the crime about the immoral character of his victim, all would recognize immediately that the evidence was irrelevant and inadmissible. Evenhanded justice requires that the same constraint be imposed on the advocate of the death penalty.

* * *

* * * The fact that each of us is unique is a proposition so obvious that it surely requires no evidentiary support. * * * Evidence offered to prove such differences can only be intended to identify some victims as more worthy of protection than others. Such proof risks decisions based on the same invidious motives as a prosecutor's decision to seek the death penalty if a victim is white but to accept a plea bargain if the victim is black.

* * *

QUESTIONS AND POINTS FOR DISCUSSION

1. Courts have been grappling with the question whether they can and should permit a videotape about a murder victim's life, including video clips of the victim when he or she was alive, to be played at a sentencing hearing. See People v. Kelly, 171 P.3d 548, 555–57 (Cal. 2008) (listing cases permitting and

forbidding the playing of a videotape about the victim). If you represented the defendant in a case raising this question, what arguments would you make in opposition to the introduction of this kind of victim-impact evidence? If you were the prosecutor, how would you respond? And if you were the judge, would you allow the showing of such videotapes? If so, what limitations would you place on this kind of victim-impact evidence? For one such videotape, which was narrated by the victim's mother and showed the victim interacting with her family and friends, riding a horse, and singing "You Light Up My Life," see http://www.supremecourtus.gov/opinions/video/kelly_v_california. html.

2.   Recommended procedures to govern the introduction of written and oral victim-impact statements are outlined in Office for Victims of Crime, U.S. Dep't of Justice, Victims of Crime: Proposed Model Legislation II–1–3 (1986). Section 105(B) of the proposed model legislation leaves to the victim the decision whether to make an oral statement at the sentencing hearing in addition to, or in lieu of, a written victim-impact statement prepared by the victim or the probation officer submitting a presentence investigation report in the case. By contrast, under Guideline 11 of the ABA Guidelines for the Fair Treatment of Crime Victims and Witnesses (1983), the court decides whether the victim or the victim's representative will be permitted to make an oral statement at the time of sentencing, balancing "the conflicting considerations, on the one hand, of citizen participation, public confidence in law enforcement, and the victim's understandable interest; and on the other, the potentially inflammatory impact in some matters of the victim's court-room statement and appearance." Which do you believe is the preferable approach and why?

3.   Another point of contention concerning victims' rights at sentencing is whether a victim's oral statement made at a sentencing hearing should or must be under oath. Compare Uniform Victims of Crime Act, § 216(a) (1992) (oral statement should be under oath) with ABA Standards for Criminal Justice on Sentencing Alternatives and Procedures and Appellate Review of Sentences, Standard 18–5.12 (3d ed. 1993) (oral statement need not be under oath, but unsworn statement cannot serve as the basis for any findings of fact by the sentencing court). See also Buschauer v. Nevada, 804 P.2d 1046, 1048 (1990) (due process requires that victim testifying at sentencing hearing be under oath). How should this issue, in your opinion, be resolved?

CHAPTER 4

SENTENCING STATUTES AND GUIDELINES

■ ■ ■

A. "PURE" SENTENCING MODELS

Two critical decisions must be made in the course of sentencing a criminal defendant. First, what is known as the in-out decision must be made—the decision as to whether the defendant will be incarcerated. Once this decision has been made, the duration, amount, and terms of the defendant's sentence then must be determined—in other words, the length of any community-based or incarcerative sentence, the amount of any fine or restitution to be paid by the defendant, and other requirements to which the defendant will be subject, such as mandatory drug treatment. Set forth below is a description of three different ways of allocating the authority to make these important sentencing decisions.

ALAN M. DERSHOWITZ, BACKGROUND PAPER FROM FAIR AND CERTAIN PUNISHMENT: REPORT OF THE TWENTIETH CENTURY FUND TASK FORCE ON CRIMINAL SENTENCING

(1976). Reprinted with the permission of The Twentieth Century Fund, Inc., © by The Twentieth Century Fund, New York.

* * *

The history of criminal sentencing in the United States has been a history of shift in institutional power and in the theories that have guided the exercise of such power. In each period, one of three sentencing models has predominated, either the legislative, judicial, or administrative model. These are so called in recognition of the institution or the group of policy makers [that] exercises the power to imprison and to determine the length of imprisonment. Although incarcerative powers usually are shared by several persons or agencies, it is nevertheless possible to postulate pure sentencing models.

In the *legislatively fixed model,* the legislature determines that conviction for a given crime warrants a given term of imprisonment. For example, a first offender convicted of armed robbery must be sentenced to five years' imprisonment. There is no judicial or administrative discretion under this model; the legislature has authorized but one sentence.

* * *

In the *judicially fixed model,* the legislature determines the general range of imprisonment for a given crime. For example, a first offender convicted of armed robbery shall be sentenced to no less than 1 and no more than 10 years' imprisonment. The sentencing judge must fix a determinate sentence within that range: "I sentence the defendant to five years' imprisonment." Once this sentence is fixed, it cannot be increased or reduced by any parole board or adult authority; the defendant must serve for five years. (This model does not consider good-time provisions or other relatively automatic reductions, nor does it consider commutation or pardon.)

Under this model, discretion is vested in the sentencing judge; how much is vested depends on the range of imprisonment authorized by the legislature. On the day he is sentenced, however, the defendant knows precisely how long he will serve; there is no discretion vested in the parole board or prison authorities.

In the *administratively fixed model,* the legislature sets an extremely wide permissible range of imprisonment for a given crime. A first-offense armed robber, for example, shall be sentenced to a term of one day to life. The sentencing judge must—or may—impose the legislatively determined sentence: "You are sentenced to one day to life." The actual duration of the sentence is decided by an administrative agency while the prisoner is serving his sentence. For example, after five years of imprisonment, the adult authority decides that the prisoner is ready for release.

Under this model, vast discretion is vested in the administrative agency and in the prison authorities. On the day he is sentenced, the defendant does not know how long he will have to serve, although he probably can make an educated guess based on past practices.

* * *

QUESTIONS AND POINTS FOR DISCUSSION

1. What are the advantages and disadvantages of each of the three sentencing models described above? Can you construct a sentencing model that incorporates most or many of the advantages of the three "pure" sentencing models, but not their disadvantages?

2. The "pure" legislative sentencing model purports to eliminate judicial and administrative discretion in the sentencing process. Are there any reasons why this aim of eliminating the exercise of discretion as to the sentence to be served by a defendant might be frustrated in a jurisdiction adopting this model? See note 5 on page 179.

B.　SENTENCING STATUTES

1.　INDETERMINATE SENTENCING STATUTES

Most of the sentencing systems in this country are hybrids of the "pure" legislative, judicial, and administrative sentencing models described earlier. Sentencing statutes generally are divided into two categories: indeterminate and determinate. When an indeterminate sentence is imposed, as its name suggests, the offender does not know how much time he or she actually will spend in prison. The legislature, typically in conjunction with the sentencing judge, defines the minimum period of incarceration, if there is one, and the maximum term of confinement. A parole board, however, decides in the future when the inmate should be released from prison.

In practice, here is how an indeterminate sentencing structure might work. Assume that a legislature authorizes a sentence of from one to thirty years for a particular crime. The sentencing judge then imposes a sentence falling within this range, sentencing the defendant to a minimum of ten years in prison and a maximum of thirty. The parole board then decides when to actually release the defendant from prison, whether after ten years, thirty years, or some time in between.

The Iowa statutory provisions set forth below further exemplify the way in which an indeterminate sentencing system can operate:

IOWA CODE ANN. § 902.3 Indeterminate sentence

When a judgment of conviction of a felony other than a class "A" felony is entered against a person, the court, in imposing a sentence of confinement, shall commit the person into the custody of the director of the Iowa department of corrections for an indeterminate term, the maximum length of which shall not exceed the limits as fixed by section 902.9, unless otherwise prescribed by statute, nor shall the term be less than the minimum term imposed by law, if a minimum sentence is provided. * * *

IOWA CODE ANN. § 902.8 Minimum sentence—habitual offender

An habitual offender is any person convicted of a class "C" or a class "D" felony, who has twice before been convicted of any felony in a court of this or any other state, or of the United States. * * * A person sentenced as an habitual offender shall not be eligible for parole until the person has served the minimum sentence of confinement of three years.

IOWA CODE ANN. § 902.9 Maximum sentence for felons

The maximum sentence for any person convicted of a felony shall be that prescribed by statute or, if not prescribed by statute, if other than a class "A" felony[a] shall be determined as follows:

* * *

2. A class "B" felon shall be confined for no more than twenty-five years.

3. An habitual offender shall be confined for no more than fifteen years.

4. A class "C" felon, not an habitual offender, shall be confined for no more than ten years, and in addition shall be sentenced to a fine of at least one thousand dollars but not more than ten thousand dollars.

5. A class "D" felon, not an habitual offender, shall be confined for no more than five years, and in addition shall be sentenced to a fine of at least seven hundred fifty dollars but not more than seven thousand five hundred dollars. * * *

QUESTIONS AND POINTS FOR DISCUSSION

1. The provisions of indeterminate sentencing statutes vary widely from state to state. For example, statutes may differ as to whether a minimum period of incarceration is prescribed, what that minimum is, and what the maximum penalty is.

There are several ways in which a legislature can define the minimum prison sentence to be imposed or served for a particular crime. A state, for example, may do what Iowa does with habitual offenders, specifying a certain number of years that offenders must spend in prison before they can be considered for release on parole. Alternatively or in addition, a state can require that the minimum sentence be no more or no less than a certain percentage of the maximum sentence imposed on a defendant. See, e.g., N.Y. Penal Law § 70.00(3)(b) (McKinney) (minimum prison sentence for most felonies shall be no less than one year, but no more than one-third of the maximum sentence imposed); Wyo.Stat. § 7–13–201 (minimum should be no greater than 90% of the maximum sentence). Why would a legislature limit a minimum sentence to a certain percentage of the maximum sentence?

2. One of the chief criticisms of indeterminate sentencing statutes is that they lead to disparity in sentencing. This problem with sentencing disparity was highlighted by statistics gathered when indeterminate sentences were imposed by the federal district courts, before adoption of the federal sentencing guidelines. These statistics, gathered during a study of the federal district courts, revealed gross differences in the sentencing decisions of the various district courts. For example, while 84% of the individuals convicted in the District of Minnesota of larceny or theft during the year before June 30, 1977 were sentenced to prison, only 8% of those convicted of these crimes in the District of Colorado were imprisoned. Legislation to Revise and Recodify

---

     a. Under Iowa Code Ann. § 902.1, a defendant convicted of a class "A" felony must be sentenced to life in prison and cannot be released on parole unless the governor commutes the sentence to a term of years.

Federal Criminal Laws: Hearings Before the Subcomm. on Criminal Justice of the House Comm. on the Judiciary, 95th Cong., 1st & 2d Sess. 2459 (1978) (statement of William J. Anderson). In addition to differences in the percentage of offenders incarcerated, the study revealed stark contrasts in the average length of prison sentences imposed by the courts. For example, in the Southern District of New York, the average sentence for bank robbery was seven years during the time of the study; in the District of South Carolina, by contrast, the average sentence was eighteen years. Id.

Judges working on the same court or in the same judicial district also treat offenders differently. The report of the President's Commission on Law Enforcement and the Administration of Justice, for example, discussed the results of a study of the Detroit Recorder's Court that revealed considerable differences in the sentencing decisions of judges who worked in that court. One of the ten judges studied sentenced 75 to 90% of the offenders who appeared before him to prison, while another judge imposed a prison sentence in only 35% of the cases. The President's Comm'n on Law Enforcement & the Admin. of Justice, Task Force Report: The Courts 23 (1967).

Such disparity in sentencing not only contravenes basic notions of fairness and equality, but creates practical problems as well. Offenders who have received much more severe sentences than other offenders who have similar backgrounds and committed similar crimes are naturally resentful. This resentment can breed hostility and contempt for the law which in turn makes the offenders more difficult for correctional officials to control and less amenable to rehabilitative efforts. In addition, the different sentencing practices of judges can lead to logjams in the courts as defense attorneys whose cases are scheduled before more punitive judges try to stall the cases in hopes of getting them transferred to a more lenient judge.

3. At least some of the disparity caused by indeterminate sentencing statutes can be alleviated through the use of parole guidelines. Parole guidelines establish the release date for prisoners in "ordinary" cases based on specified factors, such as the offense of conviction and criminal history. An inmate, however, can be released earlier or later than this presumptive release date when the parole board explains in writing why the inmate does not fit the prototypical case. While parole guidelines can help ensure that similar offenders spend about the same amount of time in prison, they have no effect on the disparity that can result when judges are making the in-out decision—the decision whether to imprison an offender. Some offenders may be sentenced to prison while similar offenders are punished in the community.

4. In recent years, a number, though not all, of the states with indeterminate sentencing systems have abolished discretionary parole release completely or eliminated it for prisoners convicted of violent or other specified crimes. See Bureau of Justice Statistics, U.S. Dep't of Justice, Trends in State Parole, 1990–2000, at 1, 3 (2001). This movement away from discretionary parole release has sparked controversy and debate, prompting a call by some for the retention or restoration of this back-end release mechanism. What arguments would you propound in favor of, and in opposition to, discretionary parole release? See Kevin R. Reitz, Questioning the Conventional Wisdom of Parole Release Authority, in The Future of Imprisonment 199 (Michael Tonry

ed., 2004). If you were a policy maker, what data would help to inform your decision on whether to preserve or restore indeterminate sentencing? Remember that the issue you are addressing is not whether released prisoners will be subject to supervision in the community for a period of time after their release from prison; the issue is who should decide how long an individual will be confined in prison.

2. DETERMINATE SENTENCING STATUTES

As mentioned above, many states have abandoned their indeterminate sentencing systems, supplanting them with determinate sentencing laws. Determinate sentencing statutes differ from indeterminate sentencing statutes in that offenders, after receiving a determinate sentence, generally know how much time they will spend in prison; they will be incarcerated for the amount of time designated in the sentencing order minus any good-time credits that they earn for their good behavior or participation in rehabilitative programs while in prison.

Determinate sentencing statutes can take many different forms. Set forth below are three examples of determinate sentencing statutes. The Illinois and Indiana statutes exemplify two of the varied ways to structure what is known as a determinate-discretionary sentencing system. And the Michigan felony-firearm statute is an example of a mandatory sentencing statute.

a. Determinate–Discretionary Sentencing

730 ILL. COMP. STAT. 5/5–8–1. Sentence of Imprisonment for Felony.

(a) Except as otherwise provided in the statute defining the offense, a sentence of imprisonment for a felony shall be a determinate sentence set by the court under this Section, according to the following limitations:

(1) for first degree murder,

(a) a term shall be not less than 20 years and not more than 60 years, or [The statute then describes when a person convicted of first-degree murder can or must be sentenced to life in prison.];

(1.5) for second degree murder, a term shall be not less than 4 years and not more than 20 years;

(2) for a person adjudged a habitual criminal * * *, the sentence shall be a term of natural life imprisonment;

* * *

(3) except as otherwise provided in the statute defining the offense, for a Class X felony, the sentence shall be not less than 6 years and not more than 30 years;

(4) for a Class 1 felony other than second degree murder, the sentence shall be not less than 4 years and not more than 15 years;

(5) for a Class 2 felony, the sentence shall be not less than 3 years and not more than 7 years;

(6) for a Class 3 felony, the sentence shall be not less than 2 years and not more than 5 years;

(7) for a Class 4 felony, the sentence shall be not less than 1 year and not more than 3 years.

(b) The sentencing judge in each felony conviction shall set forth his reasons for imposing the particular sentence he enters in the case* * *. Those reasons may include any mitigating or aggravating factors specified in this Code,[b] or the lack of any such circumstances, as well as any other such factors as the judge shall set forth on the record that are consistent with the purposes and principles of sentencing set out in this Code.

* * *

(d) Except where a term of natural life is imposed, every sentence shall include as though written therein a term in addition to the term of imprisonment. For those sentenced under the law in effect prior to February 1, 1978, such term shall be identified as a parole term. For those sentenced on or after February 1, 1978, such term shall be identified as a mandatory supervised release term. Subject to earlier termination under Section 3–3–8, the parole or mandatory supervised release term shall be as follows:

(1) for first degree murder or a Class X felony * * *, 3 years;

(2) for a Class 1 felony or a Class 2 felony * * *, 2 years;

(3) for a Class 3 felony or a Class 4 felony, 1 year;

(4) for defendants who commit the offense of predatory criminal sexual assault of a child, aggravated criminal sexual assault, or criminal sexual assault, * * * the term of mandatory supervised release shall range from a minimum of 3 years to a maximum of the natural life of the defendant;

(5) if the victim is under 18 years of age, for a second or subsequent offense of aggravated criminal sexual abuse or felony criminal sexual abuse, 4 years, at least the first 2 years of which the defendant shall serve in an electronic home detention program * * *.

* * *

IND. CODE ANN. § 35–50–2–3. Murder

(a) A person who commits murder shall be imprisoned for a fixed term of between forty-five (45) and sixty-five (65) years, with the advisory sentence being fifty-five (55) years. In addition, the person may be fined not more than ten thousand dollars ($10,000).

---

b.   A list of these mitigating and aggravating factors can be found on pages 144–47.

(b) Notwithstanding subsection (a), a person who was:

(1) at least eighteen (18) years of age at the time the murder was committed may be sentenced to:

(A) death; or

(B) life imprisonment without parole; and

(2) at least sixteen (16) years of age but less than eighteen (18) years of age at the time the murder was committed may be sentenced to life imprisonment without parole;

* * * unless a court determines under IC 35–36–9 that the person is an individual with mental retardation.

IND. CODE ANN. § 35–50–2–4. Class A felony

A person who commits a class A felony shall be imprisoned for a fixed term of between twenty (20) and fifty (50) years, with the advisory sentence being thirty (30) years. In addition, the person may be fined not more than ten thousand dollars ($10,000).

IND. CODE ANN. § 35–50–2–5. Class B felony

A person who commits a class B felony shall be imprisoned for a fixed term of between six (6) and twenty (20) years, with the advisory sentence being ten (10) years. In addition, the person may be fined not more than ten thousand dollars ($10,000).

IND. CODE ANN. § 35–50–2–6(a). Class C felony

(a) A person who commits a class C felony shall be imprisoned for a fixed term of between two (2) and eight (8) years, with the advisory sentence being four (4) years. In addition, the person may be fined not more than ten thousand dollars ($10,000).

IND. CODE ANN. § 35–50–2–7(a). Class D felony

(a) A person who commits a class D felony shall be imprisoned for a fixed term of between six (6) months and three (3) years, with the advisory sentence being one and one-half (1 1/2) years. In addition, the person may be fined not more than ten thousand dollars ($10,000).

b. Mandatory Sentences

MICH. COMP. LAWS § 750.227b. Possession of firearm at time of commission or attempted commission of felony; additional sentence, punishment

(1) A person who carries or has in his or her possession a firearm when he or she commits or attempts to commit a felony * * * is guilty of a felony, and shall be imprisoned for 2 years. Upon a second conviction under this section, the person shall be imprisoned for 5 years. Upon a third or subsequent conviction under this section, the person shall be imprisoned for 10 years.

(2) A term of imprisonment prescribed by this section is in addition to the sentence imposed for the conviction of the felony or the attempt to commit the felony, and shall be served consecutively with and preceding

any term of imprisonment imposed for the conviction of the felony or attempt to commit the felony.

(3) A term of imprisonment imposed under this section shall not be suspended. The person subject to the sentence mandated by this section is not eligible for parole or probation during the mandatory term imposed pursuant to subsection (1).

* * *

QUESTIONS AND POINTS FOR DISCUSSION

1. Determinate sentencing statutes, as well as indeterminate ones, that outline the possible prison sentences that can be imposed on convicted felons must be considered in conjunction with other statutes that often provide judges with the option of sentencing offenders to probation or imposing some other community sanction. An example of one such statute is set forth below:

730 ILL. COMP. STAT. 5/5–6–1. Sentences of Probation and of Conditional Discharge[c] and Disposition of Supervision

* * *

(a) Except where specifically prohibited by other provisions of this Code,[d] the court shall impose a sentence of probation or conditional discharge upon an offender unless, having regard to the nature and circumstance of the offense, and to the history, character and condition of the offender, the court is of the opinion that:

(1) his imprisonment or periodic imprisonment is necessary for the protection of the public; or

(2) probation or conditional discharge would deprecate the seriousness of the offender's conduct and would be inconsistent with the ends of justice; or

(3) a combination of imprisonment with concurrent or consecutive probation when an offender has been admitted into a drug court program * * * is necessary for the protection of the public and for the rehabilitation of the offender.

* * *

(b) The court may impose a sentence of conditional discharge for an offense if the court is of the opinion that neither a sentence of imprisonment nor of periodic imprisonment nor of probation supervision is appropriate.

* * *

---

c. 730 Ill. Comp. Stat. 5/5–1–4 defines conditional discharge as "a sentence or disposition of conditional and revocable release without probationary supervision but under such conditions as may be imposed by the court."

d. Examples of some of the crimes for which a sentence to probation or conditional discharge cannot be imposed include first-degree murder, some drug offenses, residential burglary, aggravated battery of a senior citizen, and a second or subsequent conviction for institutional vandalism when the property damage exceeded $300. 730 Ill. Comp. Stat. 5/5–5–3(c)(2).

(c) The court may, upon a plea of guilty or a stipulation by the defendant of the facts supporting the charge or a finding of guilt, defer further proceedings and the imposition of a sentence, and enter an order for supervision[e] of the defendant, if the defendant is not charged with [certain specified Class A misdemeanors, such as domestic battery and resisting a police officer] or [a] felony. If the defendant is not barred from receiving an order for supervision as provided in this subsection, the court may enter an order for supervision after considering the circumstances of the offense, and the history, character and condition of the offender, if the court is of the opinion that:

(1) the offender is not likely to commit further crimes;

(2) the defendant and the public would be best served if the defendant were not to receive a criminal record; and

(3) in the best interests of justice an order of supervision is more appropriate than a sentence otherwise permitted under this Code.
* * *

2. As was mentioned earlier, even when an offender receives a determinate prison sentence, the amount of time that the offender spends in prison may be reduced if the offender is awarded good-time credits for good behavior or participation in rehabilitative programs while in prison. An example of a good-time-credit statute is 730 Ill. Comp. Stat. 5/3–6–3. This statute provides for what is called day-for-day good time for many, though not all, prisoners; for every day of good behavior while in prison, the offender's sentence is reduced by one day. An Illinois prisoner who is sentenced to prison for six years and is eligible for day-for-day good-time credits therefore may be released in three years if the prisoner, while incarcerated, complies with all institutional rules and regulations. In addition, the amount of good-time credits awarded may be further increased when the prisoner successfully completes an educational program, correctional-industry assignment, or substance-abuse program to which he or she is assigned full time. Id. § 5/3–6–3(a)(4).

3. Convicted offenders also often are given credit for time spent incarcerated while awaiting trial or sentencing. For example, 18 U.S.C. § 3585(b) provides that a federal offender sentenced to prison must be given credit for time spent in "official detention" before the prison sentence began. In Reno v. Koray, 515 U.S. 50, 115 S.Ct. 2021 (1995), the Supreme Court held that 24–hour-a-day confinement in a community-treatment center while awaiting sentencing did not constitute the "official detention" for which credit must be given under § 3585(b). Because the convicted offender in that case had been released on bail pending sentencing, although subject to the condition that he stay in the community-treatment center at all times of the day, he was not subject, according to the Court, to "official detention" within the meaning of the statute. In your opinion, should convicted offenders ever receive credit for

---

e. In many ways, a sentence to court supervision is like a conditional-discharge sentence; the defendant is not subject to probationary supervision, but the court may impose various restrictions as conditions of the court-supervision sentence. The difference between the two types of sentences is that following successful completion of a period of court supervision, the charges against a defendant will be dismissed, which means that the defendant can avoid the onus of a criminal conviction. 730 Ill. Comp. Stat. 5/5–1–21.

time spent awaiting trial or sentencing if they are not incarcerated in jail or prison during that time? If so, under what circumstances?

4. When a convicted offender is sentenced to prison, the decision as to what prison to confine the offender in typically is remitted to the department of corrections. In your opinion, should that placement authority include the discretion to assign the offender to what is commonly known as a halfway house, a community residential facility from which offenders may be released for certain portions of the day and for limited purposes, such as to work? If so, should the discretion to place an offender in a halfway house extend throughout the duration of the confinement sentence or be limited to a defined portion of the back end of the sentence?

The American Bar Association supports granting correctional officials the discretion to designate a halfway house or other community residential facility as the place where an offender will serve a sentence to incarceration, subject to the caveat that the exercise of the discretion comport with the public's safety. See Amer. Bar Ass'n, Blueprint for Cost–Effective Pretrial Detention, Sentencing, and Corrections Systems, at 3, Appendix to Rep. 107, Summary of Action of the House of Delegates, 2002 Annual Meeting. A federal statute, by contrast, affirmatively directs the Bureau of Prisons to ensure "to the extent practicable" that prisoners serve a portion, but not more than a year, of the final part of their prison sentences in a community correctional facility or in other "conditions" that provide them with a "reasonable opportunity" to adapt to and prepare for reentry into the community. 18 U.S.C. § 3624(c)(1). If home confinement is chosen as the means to implement this requirement governing the tail end of federal prison sentences, that confinement cannot exceed six months or ten percent of the prisoner's sentence, whichever time period is shortest. Id. § 3624(c)(2).

5. In response to public demands to "get tough on crime," legislatures across the country have enacted mandatory sentencing statutes, requiring that a designated prison or jail sentence be imposed for certain crimes regardless of any mitigating circumstances surrounding the crime or the criminal offender. Mandatory sentencing statutes often apply to such crimes as murder, aggravated rape, drug offenses, and felonies in which firearms were used, as well as to persons found to be habitual offenders. Michael Tonry, Sentencing Matters 146–47 (1996).

Researchers have found that the purpose of mandatory sentencing laws— to ensure that a particular sentence is imposed for a particular crime—is often thwarted by police officers, prosecutors, and judges. Id. at 147. See also Barbara S. Vincent & Paul J. Hofer, Fed. Judicial Ctr., The Consequences of Mandatory Minimum Prison Terms: A Summary of Recent Findings 17–18 (1994) (studies conducted by the U.S. Sentencing Commission, Federal Judicial Center, and General Accounting Office found, respectively, that 40%, 46%, and 34% of convicted offenders subject to certain mandatory-minimum sentences received sentences lower than the statutory minimum). Police officers, for example, may not arrest an individual for a crime for which the offender, if convicted, would have to be incarcerated for a defined period of time. Or prosecutors, for the same reason, may refrain from filing charges or file charges for a related offense for which there is not a mandatory penalty. Even judges may attempt to circumvent what they consider unduly harsh mandatory sentencing statutes by dismissing charges or finding defendants not guilty. In cases where a mandatory sentence is imposed because of particular conduct of the defendant during the course of a felony, such as using a firearm, a judge also may nullify the mandatory penalty, in effect, by decreasing the sentence for the underlying felony by the amount by which the sentence then will be increased under the mandatory sentencing statute.

Studies also have found that the uneven application of mandatory-minimum sentences is having disparate adverse effects on minorities. The United States Sentencing Commission, for example, has reported that white offenders are able to avoid mandatory-minimum sentences much more often than African Americans and Hispanics guilty of comparable conduct. U.S. Sentencing Comm'n, Special Report to the Congress: Mandatory Minimum Penalties in the Federal Criminal Justice System 76, 80–82 (1991). See also Meierhoefer, supra, at 20–21 (1992). Excerpts of an article in which Professor Stephen J. Schulhofer describes some additional effects of mandatory minimums are set forth below.

STEPHEN J. SCHULHOFER, RETHINKING MANDATORY MINIMUMS

28 Wake Forest Law Review 199 (1993).
Reprinted with the permission of the Wake Forest Law Review.

* * * Real-world mandatories may be truly mandatory or merely discretionary, and the great majority of mandatory minimum statutes fall squarely in the latter category. * * *

A. DISCRETIONARY MANDATORIES

Mandatories require the judge to impose a given minimum sentence upon conviction under a specified charge, but they do not necessarily obligate prosecutors to bring such a charge just because the facts support it. Therefore, the most important question in any mandatory minimum statute concerns the prosecutor's role: Does the statute entail a *mandate to prosecute* or merely an *option to bargain*? Legislatures rarely address this crucial threshold issue explicitly. Rather, they in effect delegate to prosecutors the power to decide whether the statute is really a mandate to impose a minimum sentence or instead is only a source of discretion. Prosecutors, in turn, often assume that the statute imposes no mandate *on them*. Mandatories then become little more than a bargaining chip, a "hammer" which the prosecutor can invoke at her option, to obtain more guilty pleas under more favorable terms. Bargaining-chip mandatories help avoid the high process costs of the additional trials that real mandatories can generate, and they may even *reduce* process costs because potentially severe penalties can induce pleas that would not otherwise be forthcoming. Bargaining-chip mandatories also have two important crime-control benefits. Though they do not constrain prosecutors, they do constrain judges, who are sometimes perceived as more likely than prosecutors to be "soft" on crime. Even when bargained away, the mandatories have crime-control value because they tend to increase the severity of sentences that guilty plea defendants will accept. Yet, the deterrence value of both severity effects is undercut by the uncertainty that mandatories will be applied and by the perception among offenders that the mandatory can be manipulated. Moreover, bargaining-chip mandatories tend to increase rather than reduce disparity because their application depends so much on low-visibility prosecutorial choices and because their most severe effects fall not on flagrantly guilty repeat offenders (who avoid the mandatory by their guilty pleas), but rather on first offenders in borderline situations (who may have plausible defenses and are more likely to insist upon trial).

These potential effects of the bargaining-chip approach are dramatically illustrated by recent experience in the Arizona state courts. Prosecutors there have treated mandatories primarily as a bargaining tool and have made clear their willingness, in return for a guilty plea, to drop counts carrying stiff minimum penalties. As a result, the trial rate in Arizona has fallen dramatically, from ten percent in the period just before introduction of mandatories to only four percent currently. Average sentences, prison populations, and, of course, the correctional budget have all risen substantially, but the deterrence pay-off from these effects remains speculative because of the perception that anyone willing to "cop a plea" can avoid the mandatory sentence. At the same time, mandatories have produced severe punishments for offenders of marginal culpability who showed the poor judgment to insist on trial.

* * *

C. MANDATORY MANDATORIES

When mandatories are actually applied to all fact situations falling within their scope, predictable and severe sentences are achieved. The results are longer prison terms, increased correctional costs, and enhanced deterrence. Because mandatories prevent judges from awarding a discount for a guilty plea * * *, the percentage of defendants going to trial will rise sharply. Finally, mandatory-prosecution mandatories insure equal treatment of similarly situated offenders. However, this virtue of mandatories is also a central vice because equal treatment is achieved through inflexibility and deliberate inattention to context.

* * * [T]here are four common effects of inattention to context: cliffs, mistakes, misplaced equality, and the cooperation paradox. All four effects undermine the perceived fairness of mandatory minimum schemes. As a result, prosecutors and judges are less willing to apply mandatories with the consistency that the mandatory-prosecution model assumes. When that happens, bargaining-chip features tend to reappear.

1. Cliffs

Cliffs result when an offender's conduct just barely brings him within the terms of a mandatory minimum. For example, a first offender who helps sell 495 grams of cocaine might be thought to deserve anywhere from two to four years of imprisonment. Under the sentencing guidelines, his presumptive sentence (after allowance for his acceptance of responsibility and minimal role in the offense) would fall in the range of twenty-seven to thirty-three months, or about two and one-half years. For an identical offender who sold just five grams more, the sentence would double, because the five-year mandatory minimum applicable to sales of 500 grams would kick in. Conversely, an offender facing the five-year minimum can obtain a dramatic decrease in his sentence if he can establish a very small reduction in the quantity for which he is held responsible. The cliff effect means that small drug quantities have enormous importance, while all other factors bearing on culpability and dangerousness have no importance at all.

* * *

2. Mistakes

Mistakes occur when mandatory provisions are badly drafted or poorly coordinated with other statutes. [The author then cites examples of what he considers "obvious bloopers," such as the required imposition under one statute of a mandatory-minimum sentence that is disproportionately severe compared to the maximum sentence authorized by another statute.]

* * *

Of course, mistakes can be fixed. * * * But Congress can never foresee the full range of circumstances to which a mandatory might apply or the full scope of interconnections to other pertinent federal and state criminal statutes. *Mistakes are inevitable.* Anomalies and injustices will arise in any system that attempts to establish severe minimum sentences triggered by just one or two circumstances of a case.

3. Misplaced equality

Misplaced equality occurs even if all outright mistakes can be eliminated. Ensuring equal treatment of like offenders prevents one form of disparity, but the resulting equal treatment of *unlike* offenders creates another serious problem—*excessive uniformity.* Excessive uniformity is inevitable under mandatories because the statutes necessarily single out just one or a very small number of factors to determine the minimum sentence. Offenders who differ in a host of crucial respects receive inappropriately equal treatment.

For example, a common problem associated with mandatories is the equal treatment of offenders who played sharply different roles in the offense. The ringleader faces the same sentence as a moderately important underling, who in turn gets the same sentence as a young messenger or secretary who had little responsibility or control over the events. Parties who were pressured to provide minor assistance face the same sentence as the most violent and abusive leaders. Since mandatories are usually stated as minimums, they could, in theory, incorporate such factors by permitting an offender's role in the offense to aggravate the applicable sentence. However, this approach would require setting the mandatory penalty at the level appropriate for the least culpable offender, and such a statute would hardly "send a message" in the way that legislators intend. Instead, mandatories are invariably pegged at a level that the legislature considers appropriate for a highly culpable participant. In fact, in some of the federal mandatories, the "minimum" sentence is life imprisonment without parole. Just punishment for lesser roles is inevitably precluded.

A comparable problem is the absence of differentiation on the basis of a prior criminal record. Some mandatories do not consider an offender's prior record at all. Many of the federal mandatories do provide higher minimums for a subsequent offense, but the enhancement is invariably crude, failing to account for the recency of the prior offense or its similarity to the present misconduct. As with the variations in an offender's role, variations found in prior records are too complex to be captured in just one or a few factors. * * *

Other types of misplaced equality could be catalogued, but such a list would obscure the main point. Important differences among offenders are by nature difficult to anticipate and categorize. Hence, uniform treatment through mandatories invariably produces unfairness and generates systemic pressure for evasion. Mandatory-prosecution mandatories can be grossly unjust if faithfully applied, but (perhaps fortunately) they become difficult to sustain in practice because the misplaced equality such mandatories engender produces powerful resistance to their enforcement.

4. The cooperation paradox

The cooperation paradox provides a final example of the serious distortions that result from inattention to context. One universally recognized exception to a mandatory minimum requirement is the situation in which a defendant offers to testify against confederates or to provide leads in other investigations. Informal mechanisms for avoiding mandatories, in federal courts and elsewhere, insure that sentence concessions will be available to those defendants who provide the most information at the earliest possible point in an investigation, thus guaranteeing that mandatories will not choke the flow of cooperation. Indeed, mandatories coupled with an exception for cooperation provide powerful inducements for assistance that might not otherwise be forthcoming. This practice is formalized in 18 U.S.C. § 3553(e), which renders all federal mandatories inoperable and authorizes the judge to impose a sentence below the mandatory minimum, if the government makes a motion for a lower sentence on the basis of a defendant's substantial assistance in the investigation or prosecution of others.

Yet, the escape hatch for cooperation creates a paradox. Defendants who are most in the know, and thus have the most "substantial assistance" to offer, are often those who are most centrally involved in conspiratorial crimes. The highly culpable offender may be the best placed to negotiate a big sentencing break. Minor players, peripherally involved and with little knowledge or responsibility, have little to offer and thus can wind up with far more severe sentences than the boss.[69]

Of course, sentence concessions for helping the government have always been part of American sentencing systems and always will be. The vice of an escape hatch for "substantial assistance" stems from its interaction with the unqualified rigidity that mandatories otherwise impose. The quantity-driven drug mandatories pose this problem in its most acute form. Normal principles holding defendants accountable for the acts of their co-conspirators, even if carefully applied, can leave low-level dealers, middlemen and more important distributors responsible for the same quantity of drugs flowing through the conspirational network. * * * Thus, the inflexibility of mandatories means that all participants tend to face the same high sentence, regardless of their limited role in the offense or any mitigating personal circumstances. The "big fish" and the "minnows" wind up in the same sentencing boat. Enter the statutory escape hatch, with sentence concessions that tend to increase with the knowledge and responsibility of the offender. The big fish get the big breaks, while the minnows are left to face severe and sometimes draconian penalties.

This result makes nonsense of the intuitively plausible scale of punishments that Congress and the ordinary person envisage when they think of sentences linked to drug quantity or other hallmarks of the most serious criminal responsibility. Instead of a pyramid of liability with long sentences for leaders at the top of the organizational ladder, the mandatory system can become an inverted pyramid with stiff sentences for minor players and modest punishments for knowledgeable insiders who can cut favorable deals.

D. SUMMARY

A mandatory minimum is not a discrete policy instrument; rather, it is a label for two different and partially opposed concepts. Mandatory mandatories constrain both judges and prosecutors. Discretionary mandatories are mandatory for judges, but not for prosecutors, and are largely used as bargaining chips for plea negotiation. * * *

Whichever element predominates in a particular statutory scheme brings with it drawbacks that undercut much of a mandatory minimum's expected benefits. Discretionary mandatories can enhance sentence severity for offenders convicted on the mandatory count, but the deterrent value of this effect is undermined by the uncertainty of its application to any

---

69.   Thus, in United States v. Brigham, 977 F.2d 317 (7th Cir.1992), a low-level driver received a 120–month sentence, while the organization's kingpin received only an 84–month sentence because of his "substantial assistance." Reluctantly affirming the sentence, the court, per Easterbrook, J., wrote: "Mandatory minimum penalties, combined with a power to grant exemptions, create a prospect of inverted sentencing. The more serious the defendant's crimes, the lower the sentence—because the greater his wrongs, the more information and assistance he has to offer to a prosecutor." Id. at 318. See also United States v. Evans, 970 F.2d 663, 676–78 & n. 19 (10th Cir.1992) (underlings received terms of 210 months, 292 months, 295 months and life, while more responsible organizers received sentences of mere probation or supervised release).

particular case. At the same time, discretionary mandatories undermine the perceived fairness of the prescribed sentence as a just punishment because the penalty is haphazardly invoked and because the most culpable offenders can escape its impact by waiving their right to trial.

Truly mandatory mandatories avoid both of these difficulties while provoking new ones. Because real mandatories leave little room for plea incentives, trial rates and process costs are likely to rise sharply. At the same time, true mandatories present acute problems of inequitable punishment because of cliff effects, mistakes, misplaced equality and the cooperation paradox. These inequities, together with the process costs of true mandatories, make deterrence and "equal treatment" benefits costly to realize even when true mandatories are fully implemented in practice. Perhaps more important, these inequities and process costs generate powerful pressure for avoidance. Discretionary mandatories reemerge, though in less visible forms, and often with some of the acute process costs of true mandatories. The result, as with New York's Rockefeller drug law,[f] may be the worst of both worlds.

QUESTIONS AND POINTS FOR DISCUSSION

1. What is known as the "safety-valve provision" in 18 U.S.C. § 3553(f) mitigates, at least somewhat, the effects of mandatory-minimum sentences for low-level offenders convicted of certain federal drug crimes. This provision authorizes federal judges to impose sentences below the statutory minimum if the following conditions are met: (1) the defendant has no more than one criminal-history point under the federal sentencing guidelines; (2) the defendant did not use or threaten violence or possess a firearm or other dangerous weapon while committing the crime; (3) the crime did not lead to someone's death or serious bodily harm; (4) the defendant did not act as an organizer, leader, manager, or supervisor in committing the crime or engage in a "continuing criminal enterprise"; and (5) the defendant has provided the government with all the information the defendant has about the crime and other related crimes. In your opinion, is the safety-valve provision an effective means of redressing the problems of mandatory minimums highlighted by Professor Schulhofer and others? How, if at all, would you modify the safety-valve provision? See Virginia G. Villa, Retooling Mandatory Minimum Sentencing: Fixing the Federal "Statutory Safety Valve" to Act as an Effective Mechanism for Clemency in Appropriate Cases, 21 Hamline L.Rev. 109, 122–26 (1997); Jane L. Froyd, Comment, Safety Valve Failure: Low–Level Drug Offenders and the Federal Sentencing Guidelines, 94 Nw. U.L. Rev. 1471, 1498–1506 (2000).

2. The "three strikes and you're out" laws currently in effect in many states are an example of one type of mandatory sentencing statute. Under these laws, certain three-time felons must be sentenced to prison for a very

---

f. This law restricted plea bargaining for certain drug crimes triggering severe mandatory minimums. After the law's enactment, the rate of indictment after arrest, the rate of conviction after indictment, and the number of arrests for the drug crimes declined, while trial rates and case-processing times increased dramatically See Professor Schulhofer's article at 207–08.

lengthy, statutorily-prescribed period of time—under some laws, to life in prison without possibility of parole. See, e.g., Wash.Rev.Code § 9.94A.570. The crimes that will trigger a strike vary substantially from state to state. See Linda S. Beres & Thomas D. Griffith, Do Three Strikes Laws Make Sense? Habitual Offender Statutes and Criminal Incapacitation, 87 Georgetown L.J. 103, 110–11 (1998) (listing examples of variations). In some states, only violent felonies, like murder, rape, armed robbery, and kidnapping, can count as strikes. In other states, convictions for nonviolent felonies can constitute strikes, including convictions for petty theft prosecuted as a felony because the defendant had a prior felony conviction. See Scott Ehlers et al., Justice Policy Inst., Still Striking Out: Ten Years of California's Three Strikes 8 (2004) (reporting that in September 2003, the "third strike" for 354 of the prisoners serving sentences of twenty years to life under California's three-strikes law was a petty-theft offense prosecuted as a felony); Lisa E. Cowart, Comment, Legislative Prerogative vs. Judicial Discretion: California's Three Strikes Law Takes a Hit, 47 DePaul L.Rev. 615, 624 n. 37 (1998) (recounting the cases of two men in California who received life sentences under the state's three-strikes law, one after being convicted of stealing two packs of cigarettes and the other after being convicted of stealing a slice of pizza). For a discussion of the constitutionality of prison sentences imposed under California's three-strikes law, see notes 3 through 5 on pages 353–54.

If you were drafting a state's habitual-offender law, what would be its key provisions? Would research findings that criminal activity peaks when individuals are in their late teens and early twenties and that most people refrain from committing crimes by the time they reach forty have any effect on the way in which you would draft such a law? Beres & Griffith, supra, at 135–37. Would research findings revealing substantial differences, by county, in prosecutors' enforcement of California's three-strikes law have a bearing on the statute you draft? See John Clark et al., U.S. Dep't of Justice, "Three Strikes and You're Out": A Review of State Legislation 4 (1997). Is there any other information you would want to obtain before making the final policy choices reflected in the statute? For analyses of the practical effects of California's three-strikes law, see Ehlers et al., supra; Franklin E. Zimring et al., Punishment and Democracy: Three Strikes and You're Out in California (2001).

3. Another offshoot of the get-tough-on-crime movement is what is called "truth in sentencing." Truth-in-sentencing laws require certain criminal offenders, typically violent offenders, to serve most of their prison sentences—usually eighty-five percent of the sentence imposed—before becoming eligible for release. The time served in prison by these targeted offenders is increased by restricting their eligibility for parole and by restricting or eliminating the good-time credits they can accumulate.

Truth-in-sentencing laws are, in part, a response to concerns that prisoners, as a whole, have been serving a fraction of the prison sentences imposed on them. See Bureau of Justice Statistics, U.S. Dep't of Justice, Truth in Sentencing in State Prisons 1 (1999) (prisoners released in 1996 had, on average, served 44% of their sentences). The enactment of such laws has been further spurred by federal legislation conditioning the awarding of grants to build or expand correctional facilities on the adoption of truth-in-sentencing laws for certain violent offenders. Id. at 3. See 42 U.S.C. §§ 13703–13704.

Would you advise a state legislature to incorporate "truth in sentencing" into its sentencing structure? If so, how? Consider these questions in light of the materials that follow.

C. SENTENCING GUIDELINES

Sentencing guidelines differ from sentencing statutes in that they generally are developed by judges or by a sentencing commission established by the legislature, rather than by the legislature itself. Sentencing-guideline systems have been held constitutional despite arguments that they are the product of an excessive delegation of legislative power and violate separation-of-powers principles. See, e.g., Mistretta v. United States, 488 U.S. 361, 109 S.Ct. 647 (1989). In part, this is because the legislature still plays a role in a sentencing process governed by guidelines—defining the ranges of punishment within which the guidelines will operate and often approving the guidelines formulated by the sentencing commission. For example, a state statute might state that a convicted burglar can be sentenced to probation or anywhere from one to five years in prison. Sentencing guidelines then can provide further guidance as to whether a convicted burglar should be imprisoned and, if imprisoned, the length of the term of imprisonment.

Sentencing guidelines can be presumptive, which means that the sentence outlined in the guidelines must be imposed unless facts are established justifying a departure from the guidelines. Or guidelines may be advisory only, leaving to individual judges the decision whether to comply with them, subject to limited appellate review for an abuse of sentencing discretion. Some examples of these two kinds of guidelines are discussed below.

1. PRESUMPTIVE GUIDELINES

Minnesota was the first state to establish a sentencing commission to draft presumptive sentencing guidelines. These guidelines were approved by the legislature in 1980 and have since served as a model for other jurisdictions contemplating the adoption of sentencing guidelines. Portions of these guidelines and the commentary explaining them are set forth below.

MINNESOTA SENTENCING GUIDELINES
AND COMMENTARY
Revised August 1, 2008

I. STATEMENT OF PURPOSE AND PRINCIPLES

The purpose of the sentencing guidelines is to establish rational and consistent sentencing standards which reduce sentencing disparity and ensure that sanctions following conviction of a felony are proportional to the severity of the offense of conviction and the extent of the offender's criminal history. Equity in sentencing requires (a) that convicted felons similar with respect to relevant sentencing criteria ought to receive similar sanctions, and (b) that convicted felons substantially different from a typical case with respect to relevant criteria ought to receive different sanctions.

The sentencing guidelines embody the following principles:

1.   Sentencing should be neutral with respect to the race, gender, social, or economic status of convicted felons.

2.   While commitment to the Commissioner of Corrections is the most severe sanction that can follow conviction of a felony, it is not the only significant sanction available to the sentencing judge. Development of a rational and consistent sentencing policy requires that the severity of sanctions increase in direct proportion to increases in the severity of criminal offenses and the severity of criminal histories of convicted felons.

3.   Because the capacities of state and local correctional facilities are finite, use of incarcerative sanctions should be limited to those convicted of more serious offenses or those who have longer criminal histories. To ensure such usage of finite resources, sanctions used in sentencing convicted felons should be the least restrictive necessary to achieve the purposes of the sentence.

4.   While the sentencing guidelines are advisory to the sentencing judge, departures from the presumptive sentences established in the guidelines should be made only when substantial and compelling circumstances exist.

II.   DETERMINING PRESUMPTIVE SENTENCES

The presumptive sentence for any offender convicted of a felony * * * is determined by locating the appropriate cell of the Sentencing Guidelines Grids.[g] The grids represent the two dimensions most important in current sentencing and releasing decisions—offense severity and criminal history.

A.   Offense Severity: The offense severity level is determined by the offense of conviction. When an offender is convicted of two or more felonies, the severity level is determined by the most severe offense of conviction. * * *

Felony offenses * * * are arrayed into eleven levels of severity, ranging from low (Severity Level I) to high (Severity Level XI). * * * First degree murder and [certain specified sex offenses] are excluded from the sentencing guidelines, because by law the sentence is mandatory imprisonment for life. Offenses listed within each level of severity are deemed to be generally equivalent in severity. The severity level for each felony offense is governed by Section V: Offense Severity Reference Table. * * *

---

g.   A copy of the grid that governs most felonies can be found on page 206. The guidelines also include a separate guidelines grid for sex offenses.

Comment

II.A.01. Offense severity is determined by the offense of conviction. The Commission thought that serious legal and ethical questions would be raised if punishment were to be determined on the basis of alleged, but unproven, behavior, and prosecutors and defenders would be less accountable in plea negotiation. It follows that if the offense of conviction is the standard from which to determine severity, departures from the guidelines should not be permitted for elements of offender behavior not within the statutory definition of the offense of conviction. Thus, if an offender is convicted of simple robbery, a departure from the guidelines to increase the severity of the sentence should not be permitted because the offender possessed a firearm or used another dangerous weapon.

* * *

B. Criminal History: A criminal history index constitutes the horizontal axis of the Sentencing Guidelines Grids. The criminal history index is comprised of the following items: (1) prior felony record; (2) custody status at the time of the offense; (3) prior misdemeanor and gross misdemeanor record; and (4) prior juvenile record for young adult felons.

* * *

Comment

II.B.01. The sentencing guidelines reduce the emphasis given to criminal history in sentencing decisions. Under past judicial practice, criminal history was the primary factor in dispositional decisions. Under sentencing guidelines, the offense of conviction is the primary factor, and criminal history is a secondary factor in dispositional decisions. In the past there were no uniform standards regarding what should be included in an offender's criminal history, no weighting format for different types of offenses, and no systematic process to check the accuracy of the information on criminal history.

II.B.02. The guidelines provide uniform standards for the inclusion and weighting of criminal history information. The sentencing hearing provides a process to assure the accuracy of the information in individual cases. These improvements will increase fairness and equity in the consideration of criminal history.

* * *

The offender's criminal history index score is computed in the following manner:

1. Subject to the conditions listed below, the offender is assigned a particular weight for every extended jurisdiction juvenile conviction and for every felony conviction for which a felony sentence was stayed or

imposed before the current sentencing or for which a stay of imposition[h] of sentence was given before the current sentencing. Multiple offenses are sentenced in the order in which they occurred. For purposes of this section, prior extended jurisdiction juvenile convictions are treated the same as prior felony sentences.

* * *

a. * * * [T]he weight assigned to each prior felony sentence is determined according to its severity level, as follows:

Severity Level I–II = ½ point;

Severity Level III–V = 1 point;

Severity Level VI–VIII = 1½ points;

Severity Level IX–XI = 2 points; and

Murder 1st Degree = 2 points * * *.

* * *

f. Prior felony sentences or stays of imposition following felony convictions will not be used in computing the criminal history score if a period of fifteen years has elapsed since the date of discharge from or expiration of the sentence, to the date of the current offense.

The felony point total is the sum of these weights; no partial points are given.

Comment

II.B.101. The basic rule for computing the number of prior felony points in the criminal history score is that the offender is assigned a particular weight for every felony conviction for which a felony sentence was stayed or imposed before the current sentencing or for which a stay of imposition of sentence was given for a felony level offense, no matter what period of probation is pronounced, before the current sentencing. * * * The felony point total is the sum of these

---

h. In Minnesota, there is a distinction between what is called a stay of imposition and a stay of execution. The distinction is explained in the definitional section of the guidelines as follows:

Stay of Imposition/Stay of Execution—There are two steps in sentencing: the imposition of a sentence, and the execution of the sentence which was imposed. The imposition of sentence consists of pronouncing the sentence to be served in prison (for example, three years imprisonment). The execution of an imposed sentence consists of transferring the felon to the custody of the Commissioner of Corrections to serve the prison sentence. A stayed sentence may be accomplished by either a stay of imposition or a stay of execution.

If a stay of imposition is granted, the imposition (or pronouncement) of a prison sentence is delayed to some future date, provided that until that date the offender comply with conditions established by the court. If the offender does comply with those conditions until that date, the case is discharged, and for civil purposes (employment applications, etc.) the offender has a record of a misdemeanor rather than a felony conviction.

If a stay of execution is granted, a prison sentence is pronounced, but the execution (transfer to the custody of the Commissioner of Corrections) is delayed to some future date, provided that until that date the offender comply with conditions established by the court. If the offender does comply with those conditions, the case is discharged, but the offender continues to have a record of a felony conviction.

weights. No partial points are given—thus, a person with less than a full point is not given that point. For example, an offender with a total weight of 2½ would have 2 felony points.

II.B.102. The Commission determined that it was important to establish a weighting scheme for prior felony sentences to assure a greater degree of proportionality in the current sentencing. Offenders who have a history of serious felonies are considered more culpable than those offenders whose prior felonies consist primarily of low severity, nonviolent offenses.

* * *

II.B.110. The decision to stay execution of sentence rather than to stay imposition of sentence as a means to a probationary term following a felony conviction is discretionary with the judge. Considerable disparity appears to exist in the use of these options. In the case of two similar offenders it is not uncommon for one to receive a stay of execution and another to receive the benefit of a stay of imposition. * * * As a result of the disparity that exists in the use of stays of imposition, the Commission determined that stays of execution and stays of imposition shall be treated the same with respect to criminal history point accrual. Similar treatment has the additional advantage of a simplified procedure for computing criminal history scores.

* * *

II.B.113. Under Minn.Stat. § 260B.130, a child alleged to have committed a felony offense under certain circumstances may be prosecuted as an extended jurisdiction juvenile. If the prosecution results in a guilty plea or finding of guilt and the court imposes a disposition according to Minn.Stat. § 260B.130, subd. 4(a), the extended jurisdiction juvenile conviction shall be treated in the same manner as an adult felony sentence for purposes of calculating the prior felony record component of the criminal history score. All of the policies under sections II.B.1.a–f, and corresponding commentary apply to extended jurisdiction juvenile convictions. * * *

2.   One point is assigned if the offender:

a.   was on probation, parole, supervised release, conditional release, or confined in a jail, workhouse, or prison pending sentencing, following a guilty plea, guilty verdict, or extended jurisdiction juvenile conviction in a felony, non-traffic gross misdemeanor or gross misdemeanor driving while impaired or refusal to submit to a chemical test case; or

b.   was released pending sentencing at the time the felony was committed for which he or she is being sentenced * * *; or

c.   committed the current offense within the period of the initial probationary sentence. * * * This policy applies to a prior felony,

gross misdemeanor or an extended jurisdiction juvenile conviction.
* * *

* * *

Comment

II.B.201. The basic rule assigns offenders one point if they were under some form of criminal justice custody when the offense was committed for which they are now being sentenced. * * *

II.B.202. * * * Probation, parole, and supervised release will be the custodial statuses that most frequently will result in the assignment of a point.

II.B.203. It should be emphasized that the custodial statuses covered by this policy are those occurring after conviction of a felony or gross misdemeanor. Thus, a person who commits a new felony while on pre-trial diversion or pre-trial release on another charge would not get a custody status point. Likewise, persons serving a misdemeanor sentence at the time the current offense was committed would not receive a custody status point * * *.

* * *

3.   Subject to the conditions listed below, the offender is assigned one unit for each misdemeanor conviction and for each gross misdemeanor conviction included on the *Misdemeanor and Gross Misdemeanor Offense List* and for which a sentence was stayed or imposed before the current sentencing or for which a stay of imposition of sentence was given before the current sentencing. * * * Four such units shall equal one point on the criminal history score, and no offender shall receive more than one point for prior misdemeanor or gross misdemeanor convictions. * * *

* * *

c.   A prior misdemeanor or gross misdemeanor sentence or stay of imposition following a misdemeanor or gross misdemeanor conviction shall not be used in computing the criminal history score if a period of ten years has elapsed since the offender was adjudicated guilty for that offense, to the sentencing date for the current offense.
* * *

Comment

II.B.301. The Commission established a measurement procedure based on units for misdemeanor and gross misdemeanor sentences which are totaled and then converted to a point value. The purpose of this procedure is to provide different weightings for convictions of felonies, gross misdemeanors, and misdemeanors. Under this procedure, misdemeanors and gross misdemeanors are assigned one unit. An offender must have a total of four units to receive one point on the criminal history score. No partial points are given—thus, a person with three units is assigned no point value.

* * *

II.B.305. The Commission placed a limit of one point on the consideration of misdemeanors or gross misdemeanors in the criminal history score. This was done because with no limit on point accrual, persons with lengthy, but relatively minor, misdemeanor records could accrue high criminal history scores and, thus, be subject to inappropriately severe sentences upon their first felony conviction. The Commission limited consideration of misdemeanors to particularly relevant misdemeanors under existing state statute[s]. * * * Offenders whose criminal record includes at least four prior sentences for misdemeanors and gross misdemeanors contained in the *Misdemeanor and Gross Misdemeanor Offense List,* are considered more culpable and are given an additional criminal history point under the guidelines.

* * *

4. The offender is assigned one point for every two offenses committed and prosecuted as a juvenile that are felonies under Minnesota law, provided that:

a. Findings were made by the juvenile court pursuant to an admission in court or after trial;

b. Each offense represented a separate behavioral incident or involved separate victims in a single behavioral incident;

c. The juvenile offenses occurred after the offender's fourteenth birthday;

d. The offender had not attained the age of twenty-five at the time the felony was committed for which he or she is being currently sentenced; and

e. Generally, an offender may receive only one point for offenses committed and prosecuted as a juvenile. This point limit does not apply to offenses committed and prosecuted as a juvenile for which the sentencing guidelines would presume imprisonment. The presumptive disposition of the juvenile offense is considered to be imprisonment if the presumptive disposition for that offense under the sentencing guidelines is imprisonment. This determination is made regardless of the criminal history score and includes those offenses that carry a mandatory minimum prison sentence and other presumptive imprisonment offenses described in section II.C. Presumptive Sentence.

Comment

* * *

II.B.406. The Commission decided that, provided the above conditions are met, it would take two juvenile offenses to equal one point on the criminal history score, and generally, an offender may not receive more than one point on the basis of prior juvenile offenses. This point limit does not apply to offenses committed and prosecuted as a juvenile for which the guidelines would presume imprisonment. The presumptive disposition for a prior juvenile offense is considered to be imprisonment if the presumptive disposition for that offense under the sentencing guidelines is imprisonment regardless of criminal history. * * * The criminal history record is not used to determine whether the juvenile offense carries a presumptive imprisonment sentence because of the difficulty in applying criminal history score computations to prior juvenile offenses. Two juvenile offenses are required for each additional point. Again, no partial points are allowed, so an offender with only one juvenile offense meeting the above criteria would receive no point on the criminal history score. * * *

* * *

5. The designation of out-of-state convictions as felonies, gross misdemeanors, or misdemeanors shall be governed by the offense definitions and sentences provided in Minnesota law. * * *

* * *

6. When determining the criminal history score for a current offense that is a felony solely because the offender has previous convictions for similar or related misdemeanor and gross misdemeanor offenses, the prior gross misdemeanor conviction(s) upon which the enhancement is based may be used in determining custody status, but the prior misdemeanor and gross misdemeanor conviction(s) cannot be used in calculating the remaining components of the offender's criminal history score. * * *

Comment

II.B.601. There are a number of instances in Minnesota law in which misdemeanor or gross misdemeanor behavior carries a felony penalty as a result of the offender's prior record. The Commission decided that in the interest of fairness, a prior misdemeanor or gross misdemeanor offense that elevated the misdemeanor or gross misdemeanor behavior to a felony should not also be used in criminal history points other than custody status. * * *

* * *

7. The criminal history score is the sum of points accrued under items one through four above.

C. Presumptive Sentence: The offense of conviction determines the appropriate severity level on the vertical axis of the appropriate grid. The offender's criminal history score * * * determines the appropriate location on the horizontal axis of the appropriate grid. The presumptive fixed sentence for a felony conviction is found in the Sentencing Guidelines Grid cell at the intersection of the column defined by the criminal history score and the row defined by the offense severity level. The offenses within the Sentencing Guidelines Grids are presumptive with respect to the duration of the sentence and whether imposition or execution of the felony sentence should be stayed.

The shaded areas on the Sentencing Guidelines Grids demarcate those cases for whom the presumptive sentence is stayed from those for whom the presumptive sentence is executed. For cases contained in cells outside of the shaded areas, the sentence should be executed. For cases contained in cells within the shaded areas, the sentence should be stayed, unless the conviction offense carries a mandatory minimum sentence.

* * *

Every cell in the Sentencing Guidelines Grid provides a fixed duration of sentence. For cells above the solid line, the guidelines provide both a presumptive prison sentence and a range of time for that sentence. Any prison sentence duration pronounced by the sentencing judge which is outside the range of the presumptive duration is a departure from the guidelines, regardless of whether the sentence is executed or stayed, and requires written reasons from the judge pursuant to Minn.Stat. § 244.10, subd. 2, and section II. D of these guidelines.

Comment

II.C.01. The guidelines provide sentences which are presumptive with respect to (a) disposition—whether or not the sentence should be executed, and (b) duration—the length of the sentence. For cases outside the shaded areas of the grids, the guidelines create a presumption in favor of execution of the sentence. For cases in cells within the shaded areas, the guidelines create a presumption against execution of the sentence, unless the conviction offense carries a mandatory minimum sentence.

The dispositional policy adopted by the Commission was designed so that scarce prison resources would primarily be used for serious person offenders and community resources would be used for most property offenders. The Commission believes that a rational sentencing policy requires such trade-offs, to ensure the availability of correctional resources for the most serious offenders. * * *

II.C.02. * * * In the cells outside of the shaded areas of the grids, the guidelines provide a fixed presumptive sentence length, and a range of time around that length. Presumptive sentence lengths are shown in months, and it is the Commission's intent that months shall be computed by reference to calendar months. Any sentence length given that is within the range of sentence length shown in the appropriate cell of the Sentencing Guidelines Grids is not a departure from the guidelines, and any sentence length given which is outside that range is a departure from the guidelines. In the cells in the shaded areas of the grids, the guidelines provide a single fixed presumptive sentence length.

II.C.03. The presumptive duration listed on the grids, when executed, includes both the term of imprisonment and the period of supervised release. According to M.S. § 244.101, when the court sentences an offender to an executed sentence * * *, the sentence consists of two parts: a specified minimum term of imprisonment equal to two-thirds of the total executed sentence; and a specified maximum supervised release term equal to one-third of the total executed sentence. A separate table following the Sentencing Guidelines Grids illustrates how executed sentences are broken down into their two components.

The Commissioner of Corrections may extend the amount of time an offender actually serves in prison if the offender violates disciplinary rules while in prison or violates conditions of supervised release. This extension period could result in the offender's serving the entire executed sentence in prison.

* * *

D. Departures From The Guidelines: The sentence ranges provided in the Sentencing Guidelines Grids are presumed to be appropriate for the crimes to which they apply. Thus, the judge shall pronounce a sentence within the applicable range unless there exist identifiable, substantial, and compelling circumstances to support a sentence outside the range on the grids. A sentence outside the applicable range on the grids is a departure from the sentencing guidelines and is not controlled by the guidelines, but rather, is an exercise of judicial discretion constrained by case law and appellate review. However, in exercising the discretion to depart from a presumptive sentence, the judge must disclose in writing or on the record the particular substantial and compelling circumstances that make the departure more appropriate than the presumptive sentence.

Furthermore, if an aggravated departure is to be considered, the judge must afford the accused an opportunity to have a jury trial on the additional facts that support the departure and to have the facts proved beyond a reasonable doubt. If the departure facts are proved beyond a reasonable doubt, the judge may exercise the discretion to depart from the presumptive sentence. In exercising that discretion, it is recommended that the judge pronounce a sentence that is proportional to the severity of the crime for which the sentence is imposed and the offender's criminal history, and take into consideration the purposes and underlying principles of the sentencing guidelines. Because departures are by definition exceptions to the sentencing guidelines, the departure factors set forth in II.D are advisory only, except as otherwise established by settled case law.
* * *

Comment

II.D.01. The guideline sentences are presumed to be appropriate for every case. However, there will be a small number of cases where substantial and compelling aggravating or mitigating factors are present. When such factors are present, the judge may depart from the presumptive disposition or duration provided in the guidelines, and stay or impose a sentence that is deemed to be more appropriate than the presumptive sentence. A defendant has the right to a jury trial to determine whether or not aggravating factors are proved beyond a reasonable doubt.

II.D.02. Decisions with respect to disposition and duration are logically separate. Departures with respect to disposition and duration also are logically separate decisions. A judge may depart from the presumptive disposition without departing from the presumptive duration, and vice-versa. A judge who departs from the presumptive disposition as well as the presumptive duration has made two separate departure decisions, each requiring written reasons.

II.D.03. The aggravating or mitigating factors and the written reasons supporting the departure must be substantial and compelling to overcome the presumption in favor of the guideline sentence. The purposes of the sentencing guidelines cannot be achieved unless the presumptive sentences are applied with a high degree of regularity. Sentencing disparity cannot be reduced if judges depart from the guidelines frequently. Certainty in sentencing cannot be attained if departure rates are high. Prison populations will exceed capacity if departures increase imprisonment rates significantly above past practice.

* * *

1. *Factors that should not be used as reasons for departure*: The following factors should not be used as reasons for departing from the presumptive sentences provided in the Sentencing Guidelines Grids:

    a. Race

    b. Sex

    c. Employment factors, including:

        (1) occupation or impact of sentence on profession or occupation;

        (2) employment history;

        (3) employment at time of offense;

        (4) employment at time of sentencing.

    d. Social factors, including:

        (1) educational attainment;

        (2) living arrangements at time of offense or sentencing;

(3) length of residence;

(4) marital status.

e.   The exercise of constitutional rights by the defendant during the adjudication process.

Comment

II.D.101. The Commission believes that sentencing should be neutral with respect to offenders' race, sex, and income levels. Accordingly, the Commission has listed several factors which should not be used as reasons for departure from the presumptive sentence, because these factors are highly correlated with sex, race, or income levels. Employment is excluded as a reason for departure not only because of its correlation with race and income levels, but also because this factor is manipulable—offenders could lessen the severity of the sentence by obtaining employment between arrest and sentencing. While it may be desirable for offenders to obtain employment between arrest and sentencing, some groups (those with low income levels, low education levels, and racial minorities generally) find it more difficult to obtain employment than others. It is impossible to reward those employed without, in fact, penalizing those not employed at time of sentencing. The use of the factors "amenable to probation (or treatment)" or "unamenable to probation" to justify a dispositional departure, could be closely related to social and economic factors. The use of these factors, alone, to explain the reason for departure is insufficient and the trial court shall demonstrate that the departure is not based on any of the excluded factors.

* * *

II.D.103. It follows from the Commission's use of the conviction offense to determine offense severity that departures from the guidelines should not be permitted for elements of alleged offender behavior not within the definition of the offense of conviction. Thus, if an offender is convicted of simple robbery, a departure from the guidelines to increase the severity of the sentence should not be permitted because the offender possessed a firearm or used another dangerous weapon.

2.   *Factors that may be used as reasons for departure*: The following is a *nonexclusive* list of factors which may be used as reasons for departure:

a.   Mitigating Factors:

(1) The victim was an aggressor in the incident.

(2) The offender played a minor or passive role in the crime or participated under circumstances of coercion or duress.

(3) The offender, because of physical or mental impairment, lacked substantial capacity for judgment when the offense was

committed. The voluntary use of intoxicants (drugs or alcohol) does not fall within the purview of this factor.

(4) The offender's presumptive sentence is a commitment to the commissioner but not a mandatory minimum sentence, and either of the following exist:

(a) The current conviction offense is at severity level I or II and the offender received all of his or her prior felony sentences during less than three separate court appearances; or

(b) The current conviction offense is at severity level III or IV and the offender received all of his or her prior felony sentences during one court appearance.

(5) Other substantial grounds exist which tend to excuse or mitigate the offender's culpability, although not amounting to a defense.

(6) Alternative placement for offender with serious and persistent mental illness.

b. Aggravating Factors:

(1) The victim was particularly vulnerable due to age, infirmity, or reduced physical or mental capacity, which was known or should have been known to the offender.

(2) The victim was treated with particular cruelty for which the individual offender should be held responsible.

(3) The current conviction is for a Criminal Sexual Conduct offense or an offense in which the victim was otherwise injured and there is a prior felony conviction for a Criminal Sexual Conduct offense or an offense in which the victim was otherwise injured.

(4) The offense was a major economic offense, identified as an illegal act or series of illegal acts committed by other than physical means and by concealment or guile to obtain money or property, to avoid payment or loss of money or property, or to obtain business or professional advantage. The presence of two or more of the circumstances listed below are aggravating factors with respect to the offense:

(a) the offense involved multiple victims or multiple incidents per victim;

(b) the offense involved an attempted or actual monetary loss substantially greater than the usual offense or substantially greater than the minimum loss specified in the statutes;

(c) the offense involved a high degree of sophistication or planning or occurred over a lengthy period of time;

(d) the defendant used his or her position or status to facilitate the commission of the offense, including positions of trust, confidence, or fiduciary relationships; or

(e) the defendant has been involved in other conduct similar to the current offense as evidenced by the findings of civil or administrative law proceedings or the imposition of professional sanctions.

(5) The offense was a major controlled substance offense, identified as an offense or series of offenses related to trafficking in controlled substances under circumstances more onerous than the usual offense. The presence of two or more of the circumstances listed below are aggravating factors with respect to the offense:

(a) the offense involved at least three separate transactions wherein controlled substances were sold, transferred, or possessed with intent to do so; or

(b) the offense involved an attempted or actual sale or transfer of controlled substances in quantities substantially larger than for personal use; or

(c) the offense involved the manufacture of controlled substances for use by other parties; or

(d) the offender knowingly possessed a firearm during the commission of the offense; or

(e) the circumstances of the offense reveal the offender to have occupied a high position in the drug distribution hierarchy; or

(f) the offense involved a high degree of sophistication or planning or occurred over a lengthy period of time or involved a broad geographic area of disbursement; or

(g) the offender used his or her position or status to facilitate the commission of the offense, including positions of trust, confidence or fiduciary relationships (e.g., pharmacist, physician or other medical professional).

(6) The offender committed, for hire, a crime against the person.

(7) Offender is sentenced according to Minn.Stat. § 609.3455, subd. 3a (Mandatory sentence for certain engrained [sexual] offenders).

(8) Offender is a "dangerous offender who commits a third violent crime" (See Minn.Stat. § 609.1095, subd. 2).

(9) Offender is a "career offender" (See Minn.Stat. § 609.1095, subd. 4).

(10) The offender committed the crime as part of a group of three or more persons who all actively participated in the crime.

(11) The offender intentionally selects the victim or the property against which the offense is committed, in whole or in part, because of the victim's, the property owner's or another's actual or perceived race, color, religion, sex, sexual orientation, disability, age or national origin.

(12) The offender's use of another's identity without authorization to commit a crime. This aggravating factor may not be used when the use of another's identity is an element of the offense.

Comment

II.D.201. The Commission provided a non-exclusive list of reasons which may be used as reasons for departure. The factors are intended to describe specific situations involving a small number of cases. * * * Some of these factors may be considered in establishing conditions of stayed sentences, even though they may not be used as reasons for departure. For example, whether or not a person is employed at time of sentencing may be an important factor in deciding whether restitution should be used as a condition of probation, or in deciding on the terms of restitution payment.

II.D.202. The Commission recognizes that the criminal history score does not differentiate between the crime spree offender who has been convicted of several offenses but has not been previously sanctioned by the criminal justice system and the repeat offender who continues to commit new crimes despite receiving previous consequences from the criminal justice system. The Commission believes the nonviolent crime spree offender should perhaps be sanctioned in the community at least once or twice before a prison sentence is appropriate. At this time, the Commission believes that the judge is best able to distinguish these offenders and can depart from the guidelines accordingly.

* * *

F. Concurrent/Consecutive Sentences:[i] Generally, when an offender is convicted of multiple current offenses, or when there is a prior felony sentence which has not expired or been discharged, concurrent sentencing is presumptive. In certain situations consecutive sentences are presumptive; there are other situations in which consecutive sentences are permissive. These situations are outlined below. The use of consecutive sentences in any other case constitutes a departure from the guidelines and requires written reasons pursuant to Minn.Stat. § 244.10, subd. 2 and section II. D of these guidelines.

---

i. When concurrent sentences are imposed, an offender serves several sentences at the same time. When consecutive sentences are imposed, the offender first serves one sentence and then the other.

[The guidelines then specify when consecutive sentences are presumptively to be imposed and when they are otherwise permissible.]

* * *

III.   RELATED POLICIES

A.   Establishing Conditions of Stayed Sentences:

1. *Method of Granting Stayed Sentences*: When the appropriate cell of the Sentencing Guidelines Grids provide a stayed sentence, and when the judge chooses to grant that stay by means of a stay of execution, the duration of prison sentence shown in the appropriate cell is pronounced, but its execution is stayed. When the judge chooses to grant the stay by means of a stay of imposition, the duration of the prison sentence in the appropriate cell is not pronounced and the imposition of the sentence is stayed. The judge would then establish conditions which are deemed appropriate for the stayed sentence, including establishing a length of probation, which may exceed the duration of the presumptive prison sentence.

The Commission recommends that stays of imposition be used as the means of granting a stayed sentence for felons convicted of lower severity offenses with low criminal history scores. The Commission further recommends that convicted felons be given one stay of imposition, although for very low severity offenses, a second stay of imposition may be appropriate.

Comment

III.A.101. When the presumptive sentence is a stay, the judge may grant the stay by means of either a stay of imposition or a stay of execution. The use of either a stay of imposition or stay of execution is at the discretion of the judge. The Commission has provided a non-presumptive recommendation regarding which categories of offenders should receive stays of imposition, and has recommended that convicted felons generally should receive only one stay of imposition. The Commission believes that stays of imposition are a less severe sanction, and ought to be used for those convicted of less serious offenses and those with short criminal histories. Under current sentencing practices, judges use stays of imposition most frequently for these types of offenders.

III.A.102. When a judge grants a stayed sentence, the duration of the stayed sentence may exceed the presumptive sentence length indicated in the appropriate cell of the Sentencing Guidelines Grids, and may be as long as the statutory maximum for the offense of conviction. Thus, for an offender convicted of Theft over $5,000 (severity level III), with a criminal history score of 1, the duration of the stay could be up to ten years. The 13 month sentence shown in the guidelines is the presumptive sentence length and, if imposed, would be executed if (a) the judge departs from the dispositional recommendation and decides to execute the sentence, or (b) if the stay is later revoked and the judge decides to imprison the offender.

2. *Conditions of Stayed Sentences*: The Commission has chosen not to develop specific guidelines relating to the conditions of stayed sentences. The Commission recognizes that there are several penal objectives to be considered in establishing conditions of stayed sentences, including, but not limited to, retribution, rehabilitation, public protection, restitution, deterrence, and public condemnation of criminal conduct. The Commission also recognizes that the relative importance of these objectives may vary with both offense and offender characteristics and that multiple objectives may be present in any given sentence. The development of principled standards for establishing conditions of stayed sentences requires that judges first consider the objectives to be served by a stayed sentence and, second, consider the resources available to achieve those objectives. When retribution is an important objective of a stayed sentence, the severity of the retributive sanction should be proportional to the severity of the offense and the prior criminal record of the offender, and judges should consider the availability and adequacy of local jail or correctional facilities in establishing such sentences. The Commission urges judges to utilize the least restrictive conditions of stayed sentences that are consistent with the objectives of the sanction. When rehabilitation is an important objective of a stayed sentence, judges are urged to make full use of local programs and resources available to accomplish the rehabilitative objectives. The absence of a rehabilitative resource, in general, should not be the basis for enhancing the retributive objective in sentencing and, in particular, should not be the basis for more extensive use of incarceration than is justified on other grounds. The Commission urges judges to make expanded use of restitution and community work orders as conditions of a stayed sentence, especially for persons with short criminal histories who are convicted of property crimes, although the use of such conditions in other cases may be appropriate. Supervised probation should continue as a primary condition of stayed sentences. To the extent that fines are used, the Commission urges the expanded use of day fines, which standardizes the financial impact of the sanction among offenders with different income levels.

Comment

III.A.201. The judge may attach any conditions to a stayed sentence which are permitted by law and which he or she deems appropriate. The guidelines neither enlarge nor restrict the conditions that judges may attach to a stayed sentence. Laws 1978, Chapter 723 permits, but does not require, the Commission to establish guidelines covering conditions of stayed sentences. The Commission chose not to develop such guidelines during their initial guideline development effort. The Commission has provided some language in the above section of the guidelines which provides general direction in the use of conditions of stayed sentences.

III.A.202. While the Commission has resolved not to develop guidelines for nonimprisonment sanctions at this time, the Commission believes it is important for the sentencing judge to consider proportionality when pronouncing a period of local confinement as a condition of probation. * * * The period of local confinement should be proportional to the severity of the conviction offense and the prior criminal history score of the offender. Therefore, the period of local confinement should not exceed the term of imprisonment that would be served if the offender were to have received an executed prison sentence according to the presumptive guidelines duration.

B. Revocation of Stayed Sentences: The decision to imprison an offender following a revocation of a stayed sentence should not be undertaken lightly and, in particular, should not be a reflexive reaction to technical violations of the conditions of the stay. Great restraint should be exercised in imprisoning those violating conditions of a stayed sentence who were convicted originally of low severity offenses or who have short prior criminal histories. Rather the Commission urges the use of more restrictive and onerous conditions of a stayed sentence, such as periods of local confinement. Less judicial forbearance is urged for persons violating conditions of a stayed sentence who were convicted of a more severe offense or who had a longer criminal history. Even in these cases, however, imprisonment upon a technical violation of the conditions of a stayed sentence should not be reflexive.

The Commission would view commitment to the Commissioner of Corrections following revocation of a stayed sentence to be justified when:

    1. The offender has been convicted of a new felony for which the guidelines would recommend imprisonment; or

    2. Despite prior use of expanded and more onerous conditions of a stayed sentence, the offender persists in violating conditions of the stay.

Comment

III.B.01. The guidelines are based on the concept that the severity of the sanction ought to depend primarily on the severity of the current offense and the criminal history of the offender. Therefore, great restraint should be used when considering increasing the severity of the sanction based upon non-criminal technical violations of probationary conditions.

C. Jail Credit: * * * [W]hen a convicted felon is committed to the custody of the Commissioner of Corrections, the court shall assure that the record accurately reflects all time spent in custody in connection with the offense, * * * which time shall be deducted by the Commissioner of Corrections from the sentence imposed by subtracting the time from the specified minimum term of imprisonment and if there is any remaining time, subtracting such time from the specified maximum period of supervised release. * * * Jail credit shall reflect time spent in confinement as a condition of a stayed sentence when the stay is later revoked and the offender is committed to the custody of the Commissioner of Corrections. Such credit is limited to time spent in jails, workhouses, and regional correctional facilities. * * *

* * *

Comment

III.C.01. In order to promote the goals of the sentencing guidelines, it is important to ensure that jail credit is consistently applied to reflect all time spent in custody in connection with the offense. Granting jail credit to the time served in custody in connection with an offense ensures that a defendant who cannot post bail because of indigency will serve the same amount of time that a person in identical circumstances who is able to post bail would serve. Also, the total amount of time a defendant is incarcerated should not turn on irrelevant concerns such as whether the defendant pleads guilty or insists on his right to trial. * * *

* * *

III.C.04. The Commission also believes that jail credit should be awarded for time spent in custody as a condition of a stay of imposition or stay of execution when the stay is revoked and the offender is committed to the Commissioner of Corrections. The primary purpose of imprisonment is punishment, and the punishment imposed should be proportional to the severity of the conviction offense and the criminal history of the offender. If, for example, the presumptive duration in a case is 18 months, and the sentence was initially executed, the specified minimum term of imprisonment would be 12 months. If the execution of the sentence had initially been stayed and the offender had served four months in jail as a condition of the stay, and later the stay was revoked and the sentence executed, the offender would be confined for 16 months rather than 12 without awarding jail credit. By awarding jail credit for time spent in custody as a condition of a study of imposition or execution, proportionality is maintained.

Credit for time spent in custody as a condition of a stay of imposition or stay of execution is limited to time spent in jails, workhouses, and regional correctional facilities. Credit should not be extended for time spent in residential treatment facilities or on electronic monitoring as a condition of a stay of imposition or stay of execution.

* * *

F. Modifications: Modifications to the Minnesota Sentencing Guidelines and associated commentary will be applied to offenders whose date of offense is on or after the specified modification effective date. * * *

IV. SENTENCING GUIDELINES GRID
Presumptive Sentence Lengths in Months

Italicized numbers within the grid denote the range within which a judge may sentence without the sentence being deemed a departure. Offenders with non-imprisonment felony sentences are subject to jail time according to law.

SEVERITY LEVEL OF CONVICTION OFFENSE (Common offenses listed in italics)		CRIMINAL HISTORY SCORE						
		0	1	2	3	4	5	6 or more
Murder, 2nd Degree (intentional murder; drive-by-shootings)	XI	306 261-367	326 278-391	346 295-415	366 312-439	386 329-463	406 346-480	426 363-480
Murder, 3rd Degree Murder, 2nd Degree (unintentional murder)	X	150 128-180	165 141-198	180 153-216	195 166-234	210 179-252	225 192-270	240 204-288
Assault, 1st Degree Controlled Substance Crime, 1st Degree	IX	86 74-103	98 84-117	110 94-132	122 104-146	134 114-160	146 125-175	158 135-189
Aggravated Robbery, 1st Degree Controlled Substance Crime, 2nd Degree	VIII	48 41-57	58 50-69	68 58-81	78 67-93	88 75-105	98 84-117	108 92-129
Felony DWI	VII	36	42	48	54 46-64	60 51-72	66 57-79	72 62-84
Controlled Substance Crime, 3rd Degree	VI	21	27	33	39 34-46	45 39-54	51 44-61	57 49-68
Residential Burglary Simple Robbery	V	18	23	28	33 29-39	38 33-45	43 37-51	48 41-57
Nonresidential Burglary	IV	12[1]	15	18	21	24 21-28	27 23-32	30 26-36
Theft Crimes (Over $5,000)	III	12[1]	13	15	17	19 17-22	21 18-25	23 20-27
Theft Crimes ($5,000 or less) Check Forgery ($251-$2,500)	II	12[1]	12[1]	13	15	17	19	21 18-25
Sale of Simulated Controlled Substance	I	12[1]	12[1]	12[1]	13	15	17	19 17-22

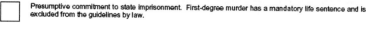

Presumptive commitment to state imprisonment. First-degree murder has a mandatory life sentence and is excluded from the guidelines by law.

Presumptive stayed sentence; at the discretion of the judge, up to a year in jail and/or other non-jail sanctions can be imposed as conditions of probation. * * *

1 One year and one day

Effective August 1, 2008

Examples of Executed Sentences (Length in Months) Broken Down by: Specified Minimum Term of Imprisonment and Specified Maximum Supervised Release Term

Offenders committed to the Commissioner of Corrections * * * will no longer earn good time. In accordance with Minn.Stat. § 244.101, offenders will receive an executed sentence pronounced by the court consisting of two parts: a specified minimum term of imprisonment equal to two-thirds of the total executed sentence and a supervised release term equal to the remaining one-third. This provision requires that the court pronounce the total executed sentence and explain the amount of time the offender will serve in prison and the amount of time the offender will serve on supervised release, assuming the offender commits no disciplinary offense in prison that results in the imposition of a disciplinary confinement period. The court shall also explain that the amount of time the offender actually serves in prison may be extended by the Commissioner if the offender violates disciplinary rules while in prison or violates conditions of supervised release. This extension period could result in the offender's serving the entire executed sentence in prison. The court's explanation is to be included in a written summary of the sentence.

Executed Sentence	Term of Imprisonment	Supervised Release Term	Executed Sentence	Term of Imprisonment	Supervised Release Term
12 and 1 day	8 and 1 day	4	78	52	26
13	8 2/3	4 1/3	86	57 1/3	28 2/3
15	10	5	88	58 2/3	29 1/3
17	11 1/3	5 2/3	98	65 1/3	32 2/3
18	12	6	108	72	36
19	12 2/3	6 1/3	110	73 1/3	36 2/3
21	14	7	122	81 1/3	40 2/3
23	15 1/3	7 2/3	134	89 1/3	44 2/3
24	16	8	146	97 1/3	48 2/3
27	18	9	150	100	50
28	18 2/3	9 1/3	158	105 1/3	52 2/3
30	20	10	165	110	55
33	22	11	180	120	60
36	24	12	190	126 2/3	63 1/3
38	25 1/3	12 2/3	195	130	65
39	26	13	200	133 1/3	66 2/3
42	28	14	210	140	70
43	28 2/3	14 1/3	220	146 2/3	73 1/3
45	30	15	225	150	75
48	32	16	230	153 1/3	76 2/3
51	34	17	240	160	80
54	36	18	306	204	102
57	38	19	326	217 1/3	108 2/3
58	38 2/3	19 1/3	346	230 2/3	115 1/3
60	40	20	366	244	122
66	44	22	386	257 1/3	128 2/3
68	45 1/3	22 2/3	406	270 2/3	135 1/3
72	48	24	426	284	142

[Additional tables and lists, including the "Sex Offender Grid," table identifying the offense severity level for numerous felonies, and list of misdemeanors and gross misdemeanors used to compute units in the criminal-history score, have been omitted.]

QUESTIONS AND POINTS FOR DISCUSSION

1. How, if at all, would you modify the Minnesota sentencing guidelines?

2. Some of the sentencing guidelines adopted in other states are more expansive in scope than Minnesota's. For example, North Carolina's "punishment charts" establish presumptive sentences for misdemeanors as well as

felonies and for nonincarcerative as well as incarcerative punishments. See N.C. Gen. Stat. §§ 15A–1340.10 to 1340.23. The North Carolina guidelines also define presumptive sentencing ranges for aggravated and mitigated sentences as well as standard sentences. For information on the ways in which other states have structured their sentencing guidelines and a discussion of some of the questions to be addressed and resolved when devising sentencing guidelines, see Richard S. Frase, State Sentencing Guidelines: Diversity, Consensus, and Unresolved Policy Issues, 105 Colum. L.Rev. 1190 (2005).

3.   Assume that the Minnesota sentencing guidelines apply in each of the following cases. Before referring to the guidelines, consider what sentence you believe would be appropriate in each case and why. Is there any additional information you would want to know in order to identify the appropriate sentence?

Now apply the guidelines to these cases. Do you need any additional information to properly apply the guidelines? How did the presumptive sentences under the guidelines differ from your initial views about the appropriate penalty? Upon reflection, which penalty is most appropriate?

Case #1

The defendant has been convicted of aggravated robbery. In Minnesota, aggravated robbery is defined as a robbery committed while armed with a dangerous weapon or during which the perpetrator inflicts bodily harm upon another. The defendant is twenty-one. He has no immediate family, limited work skills, and a bad employment record. He also has a severe drug problem. The defendant has three prior convictions, two for burglary and one for robbery. He spent eighteen months in prison on the last conviction and received probation on each of the first two. The defendant was a juvenile when he committed the burglaries. In the robbery for which the defendant is awaiting sentencing, the victim was assaulted and received a laceration on his skull which required surgical care.

Case #2

Defendant Patty Hearst has been convicted of aggravated robbery. She is in her early 20s, comes from a wealthy family, is well-educated, and has no prior convictions. The defendant was kidnapped by a group of self-proclaimed revolutionaries and later participated with them in the bank robbery for which she was convicted. Her defense was that she committed the crime out of fear for her safety since she was under the control of the kidnappers. The jury did not believe her.

Case #3

The defendant has been convicted of embezzlement of $5,000 from a bank where he is employed. The defendant took the money to pay off gambling and loansharking debts. He is in his late 20s, is married, and has two young children. He is also a college graduate, has been employed at the bank for eight years, is reasonably well-paid, and has no prior criminal record.

4. Under the Minnesota sentencing guidelines, a judge cannot impose a sentence that departs upwards from the presumptive sentence unless a jury has found beyond a reasonable doubt the facts on which the aggravated departure rests and the judge has explained the reasons why the departure is justified. See Minn. Sentencing Guidelines § II.D. (2008). When applying the guidelines to the three cases described above, did the extra steps that need to be taken in order to depart upwards from the guidelines affect what sentence you imposed under the guidelines? Should the need to take those procedural steps factor, in your opinion, into the judge's sentencing decision?

5. The Minnesota sentencing guidelines have succeeded, to some extent, in achieving two of their objectives—reducing sentencing disparity and ensuring that the punishment meted out in a particular case is proportionate to the severity of the crime committed. During the first three years after the guidelines were adopted, judges adhered to the dispositional prescriptions of the guidelines, which govern the "in-out decision," in over 90% of the cases covered by the guidelines. Michael H. Tonry, U.S. Dep't of Justice, Sentencing Reform Impacts 61 (1987). Compliance with the durational prescriptions of the guidelines was also quite high. Id. at 61–62. In addition, the use of the imprisonment sanction for nonviolent offenders dramatically decreased as prison resources were directed more towards punishing violent offenders. During the first year in which the guidelines were in effect, for example, only 15% of offenders convicted of minor property crimes were sentenced to prison, 72% less than were imprisoned before the guidelines were adopted. Id. at 68. On the other hand, 78% of the offenders with no criminal-history or low criminal-history scores who were convicted of serious, violent crimes were imprisoned, 73% more than before implementation of the guidelines. Id. For additional information on the effects of the Minnesota sentencing guidelines, see Richard S. Frase, Sentencing Guidelines in Minnesota, 1978–2003, 32 Crime & Just. 131 (2005).

North Carolina witnessed some of the same changes in the profile of persons receiving prison sentences after the enactment of its sentencing "guidelines." (North Carolina did not call its punishment charts "guidelines" in an attempt to distance itself from the widely criticized federal sentencing guidelines. Michael Tonry, Sentencing Matters 11–12 (1996)). For example, the percentage of felons convicted of property crimes who were sentenced to prison dropped from 45% in 1993–94 to 28% in 1999–2000. Ronald F. Wright, Counting the Cost of Sentencing in North Carolina, 1980–2000, 29 Crime & Just. 39, 87 (2002). During the same time period, the average length of the prison sentences served by violent offenders increased from twenty-one to sixty-seven months. Id. at 88.

6. The initial success of the Minnesota sentencing guidelines was somewhat tempered in later years by attempts to circumvent the guidelines through charging decisions and plea negotiations. Displeasure with what many prosecutors considered the too lenient treatment of property offenders under the guidelines led them to file more charges against such offenders and to require guilty pleas to more such charges than in the past. Michael H. Tonry, U.S. Dep't of Justice, Sentencing Reform Impacts 71–73 (1987). For example, while in pre-guidelines days prosecutors might agree to entry of a plea of guilty to one count of theft by a defendant charged with several thefts,

after adoption of the guidelines, prosecutors often insisted on a plea of guilty to several of the thefts to increase an offender's criminal-history score. Prosecutors also took steps to skirt guidelines sentences that they considered too severe. For example, because the offense-severity level is based on the offense of conviction, charge reductions were used to avoid what was considered too stringent a penalty.

The Minnesota Sentencing Commission has continually monitored the implementation of the guidelines and made modifications to them to modulate the effects of charging and negotiation decisions on the realization of the guidelines' goals. For example, while the guidelines originally assigned one point to the criminal-history score for each prior felony conviction, the Sentencing Commission moved to weighing felony convictions based on their severity, with more serious felony convictions assigned a higher score. This change was designed to dissipate the effects of the stacking of criminal-history convictions by prosecutors, which in turn was resulting in the increased incarceration of property offenders and reduction in the resources available to punish violent offenders. Minnesota Sentencing Guidelines § II.C. cmt. II. C.01 (2008).

Other jurisdictions also have taken steps to try to impede circumvention of their sentencing guidelines. The state of Washington, for example, has adopted, in conjunction with sentencing guidelines, guidelines to govern prosecutorial charging and bargaining practices. Wash.Rev.Code §§ 9.94A.401–.470. The federal sentencing guidelines, on the other hand, have taken a different approach to limit, to a certain extent, the effects of plea bargaining on the operation of the guidelines, adopting a modified version of what is called "real-offense" sentencing. As § 1B1.2(a), (c) of the guidelines, which is set forth below, illustrates, the offense-severity level under the guidelines is not determined exclusively by the offense of conviction.

(a) Determine the offense guideline section in Chapter Two (Offense Conduct) applicable to the offense of conviction (*i.e.*, the offense conduct charged in the count of the indictment or information of which the defendant was convicted). However, in the case of a plea agreement (written or made orally on the record) containing a stipulation that specifically establishes a more serious offense than the offense of conviction, determine the offense guideline section in Chapter Two applicable to the stipulated offense. * * *

* * *

(c) A plea agreement (written or made orally on the record) containing a stipulation that specifically establishes the commission of additional offense(s) shall be treated as if the defendant had been convicted of additional count(s) charging those offense(s).

U.S. Sentencing Comm'n, Federal Sentencing Guidelines Manual, § 1B1.2(a), (c) (2008).

The federal sentencing guidelines reflect real-offense sentencing in other ways. Under the federal guidelines, for example, the offense level for certain crimes, such as those involving an amount of drugs or money, is based not only on the offense of conviction but on other "relevant conduct." Id. § 1B1.3.

Thus, if a defendant was charged with and convicted of distributing five grams of cocaine but the judge determined that the defendant had sold five kilograms as part of the "same course of conduct" or "common scheme or plan," the judge would adjust the defendant's offense level to reflect this higher amount. Under the federal guidelines, however, the sentence imposed on a defendant cannot exceed the maximum penalty that could be imposed under the applicable statute for the crime of which the offender actually was convicted. Id. § 5G1.1(a), (c)(1). In addition, after United States v. Booker, 543 U.S. 220, 125 S.Ct. 738 (2005), discussed on page 131, the sentencing adjustments prescribed by the federal guidelines to reflect the defendant's "real offense" are advisory rather than mandatory.

7. Real-offense sentencing has sparked heated controversy, and that controversy remains even after Blakely v. Washington, 542 U.S. 296, 124 S.Ct. 2531 (2004) and United States v. Booker, 543 U.S. 220, 125 S.Ct. 738 (2005). For example, in an indeterminate sentencing system, a judge might be accorded the discretion to sentence a defendant based on the defendant's "real offense," with the caveat that the sentence not exceed the maximum sentence for the crime of which the defendant was convicted. Alternatively, a defendant's "real offense" might be a factor when sentencing the defendant under a set of advisory sentencing guidelines or when sentencing the defendant, in a jurisdiction with presumptive sentencing guidelines, within the sentencing range that reflects the facts established by the jury's verdict or admitted in the defendant's guilty plea. Consequently, the soundness, from a policy perspective, of real-offense sentencing needs to be considered.

In an article, excerpts of which are set forth below, Professor Julie R. O'Sullivan defended real-offense sentencing:

> The use of this subset of relevant nonconviction conduct reflects sentencers' longstanding belief that "few things could be so relevant [to sentence] as other criminal activity of the defendant." Reference to just deserts and crime control considerations underscores the reasonableness of this historical estimation. Thus, for example, assume that a defendant is convicted on a single count of possessing a quantity of cocaine with the intent to distribute that drug. Assume further that the defendant in fact acted as the leader of a sophisticated and large-scale drug cartel and that the count of conviction was simply one act in furtherance of the defendant's ongoing business.

> Information about the true scope of the defendant's and his accomplices' related criminal activity informs our assessment of the defendant's just deserts for the offense of conviction in so far as it illuminates the defendant's motivation and purposefulness in engaging in this criminal act. Certainly the "real" facts regarding the extent of the defendant's related criminal activity are essential to meaningful crime control judgments regarding the real danger the defendant's act poses to society, his likelihood of recidivism, and the likely deterrent effect of any particular sanction. In short, we may not be able to determine with certainty the precise sentence that would further the goals of sentencing in light of this information, but we certainly know that its exclusion must compromise the sentencing judge's ability to impose a sentence that will reflect the

true seriousness of the offense of conviction, the defendant's danger to the community, and the deterrent effect that a significant sanction may have upon the defendant's and his co-conspirator's ongoing appetite for drug smuggling.

* * *

If consideration of nonconviction offense conduct were eliminated and a charge-offense sentencing scheme adopted, the prosecutor would essentially select the sentence by choosing the applicable charge. The system itself would not require uniform treatment of offenders based upon penologically relevant offense and offender characteristics. Rather, it would defer to prosecutorial decisions as to who should be treated alike and who should not. To illustrate, suppose that Congress created grades of fraud distinguished by elements relating to the amount of monetary loss flowing from the offense, the degree of planning that went into the fraud, and the number of victims affected by it. Under existing law and practice, a prosecutor who had evidence that a particular crime satisfied the highest grade of fraud would have the discretion to charge that grade or any grade beneath it. In a pure charge-offense system, the prosecutor's choice of the charge would determine the sentence. A defendant whose conduct is worthy of more severe punishment, then, would at the prosecutor's election be treated for sentencing purposes the same as a defendant of lesser culpability.

Such a system would necessarily create unwarranted sentencing disparities * * *.

Julie R. O'Sullivan, In Defense of the U.S. Sentencing Guidelines' Modified Real–Offense System, 91 Nw. U.L.Rev. 1342, 1369–70, 1401 (1997) (Reprinted by special permission of Northwestern University School of Law, *Law Review*). See also Frank O. Bowman, III, The Quality of Mercy Must Be Restrained, and Other Lessons in Learning to Love the Federal Sentencing Guidelines, 1996 Wis. L.Rev. 679, 702–04 (1996).

Critics of real-offense sentencing have charged that it is "incompatible with the basic values of our legal system" and "antithetical to basic notions of individual worth and liberty." Michael H. Tonry, Real Offense Sentencing: The Model Sentencing and Corrections Act, 72 J.Crim.L. & Criminology 1550, 1564 (1981). Professor Kevin R. Reitz has explained the underpinnings of this charge and expressed other concerns about real-offense sentencing:

> [A]ssume that defendant Smith has been convicted of one count of armed robbery, for which the maximum statutory penalty is ten years in prison. Smith is a first offender and, under normal circumstances, the sentencing judge would select a sentence of two years. In this case, however, the judge has been persuaded during sentencing proceedings (perhaps by hearsay in the presentence report) that Smith probably committed a second armed robbery for which he has not been tried. Based on this conclusion, the judge imposes a term of four years rather than two, which is the same sentence she would have chosen if Smith had been convicted of both robberies.

* * * [T]he sentencing court has acted improperly in imposing an extra two years for the second robbery. The increment of punishment for the nonconviction offense bypasses all trial safeguards that should precede an independent guilt determination. Indeed, the judge has done something just as unwarranted as sending Smith to prison for the initial two-year term in the absence of any conviction at all, based only on an informal judicial finding that Smith "probably" committed the first robbery.

A real-offense advocate might find this case too hastily made. If it is likely that Smith was a two-time armed robber, why should the state be foreclosed from responding to this probable reality? The answer is that the state is not foreclosed. Implementation of a conviction-offense system places a burden on prosecutors to file and prove, or bargain for, conviction charges that reflect the seriousness of an offenders' criminal behavior. If, with respect to certain nonconviction crimes, this is an obligation they cannot discharge, then we should have grave doubts that the imposition of punishment is justified.

* * * In a slight alteration of the illustration above, suppose that a jury has acquitted Smith of one robbery while convicting him of the other. The sentencing judge, however, disagrees with the jury's verdict of acquittal or, more precisely, finds that she can reach a contrary factual conclusion when freed of the reasonable doubt standard and other trial constraints. Accordingly, the judge's sentence reflects two crimes.

In this scenario, the judge effectively has entered a judgment of guilt notwithstanding the verdict, which she would not be permitted to do explicitly. Indeed, the procedural anomaly goes further. Presumably, if we were to abolish the jury-trial guarantee to allow judgments n.o.v. of guilt, we would still require judges to find that no reasonable jury could have discerned reasonable doubt as to the nonconviction charge. Moreover, we would insist that such a conclusion be based on evidence admitted at trial, under the rules of evidence and other applicable safeguards. Real-offense practice, in contrast, allows courts to override the jury without satisfying such imposing requirements and, in most jurisdictions, without entering findings or an explanation on the record. Thus, at sentencing, an acquittal is overturned quite easily in comparison with the forbidden judgment n.o.v., and is subject to little or no appellate review.

The consideration of acquittal offenses is unique among real-offense practices because it involves the redetermination of factual disputes fully litigated at trial. On a symbolic level, this carries at least two effects. It would be excusable for members of the jury to conclude that their hard work, and careful parsing of the allegations, was for naught. From the perspective of the public, the message conveyed is that criminal trials, expensive as they are, determine little more than raw guilt or innocence. Beyond symbolism, the relitigation of acquittal counts at sentencing adds a substantial burden on defendants convicted of some charges and acquitted of others. Acquittal charges must be defended twice, and the defense must be more vigorous the second time around because the available procedures are more spare. On policy grounds, we should question the wisdom of requiring those accused of crime to "run the gauntlet" of successive proceedings, apart from the unseemliness of ignoring the jury's decision.

* * *

* * * There may also be special reason to bar the real-offense use of dismissed charges, or charges not brought, under the terms of plea bargains, as a basis for increased sentences. This practice, when anticipated by offenders, can discourage settlement. Aside from affecting incentives to plea bargain, real-offense consideration of dismissed charges raises ethical questions of permitting the government to strike meaningless bargains. Particularly when defense counsel is deficient, defendants may be deceived into thinking that a sizable charge concession will have a meaningful impact on sentence. The waiver of important trial rights, supposedly allowed only when "intelligent and voluntary," should not be premised on such a misunderstanding.

* * *

* * * Some have argued that real-offense sentencing diminishes prosecutors' abilities to influence sentencing through the selection of charges. This claim centers on the distorting effect of the charging decision as one filter between factual and legal guilt. It contends that sentence decisions will bear closer resemblance to "reality," and will be less marked by the prosecutor's stamp, if the boundaries of formal conviction can be overlooked.

* * *

[I]t is exceedingly strange to cast real-offense sentencing as a brake on prosecutorial power when the great force of its impact is in the opposite direction. Real-offense practice gives the government two opportunities to establish criminal conduct: once at trial or by plea, and again at sentencing. Indeed, the second bite at the apple is a dramatic addition to the state's arsenal because so many trial protections have fallen by the wayside. This creates the temptation, if not the practice, of undercharging or underbargaining on the part of prosecutors, who can wait for sentencing to make out their full case. Also, in tried cases that are not fully successful for the government, real-offense rules allow the state to recoup its losses.

Kevin R. Reitz, Sentencing Facts: Travesties of Real–Offense Sentencing, 45 Stan. L.Rev. 523, 550–53, 563–64 (1993) (Republished with the permission of the Stanford Law Review).

What do you believe is the appropriate focus when determining the offense-severity level when sentencing a defendant—the offense of conviction or the "real offense"?

2.　ADVISORY GUIDELINES

a.　The Federal Sentencing Guidelines: Several Key Distinctions

As a result of the Supreme Court's decision in United States v. Booker, 543 U.S. 220, 125 S.Ct. 738 (2005), the federal sentencing guidelines are advisory only, not presumptive like those in Minnesota. The federal guidelines differ from the Minnesota guidelines in a number of other ways. The federal guidelines, for example, contain forty-three offense levels, as compared to the eleven offense levels in Minnesota, and include detailed rules for the raising and lowering of sentences by prescribed increments. The complexity of the federal sentencing guidelines has provoked complaints from many federal judges and practitioners frustrated with what Second Circuit Judge Jose A. Cabranes has described as "a byzantine system of rules." Bowman, supra note 7 above, at 705 n. 104. See also Albert W. Alschuler, The Failure of Sentencing Guidelines: A Plea for Less Aggregation, 58 U. Chi. L.Rev. 901, 950 (1991) ("The 258–box federal sentencing grid * * * should be relegated to a place near the Edsel in a museum of twentieth-century bad ideas.").

Many of the differences between the Minnesota guidelines and the federal guidelines are attributable to the sentencing commissions' differing views about the appropriate kinds and amount of punishment for certain types of crimes. Of particular importance are the different opinions as to what constitutes a proportionate penalty for nonviolent criminals and what is an appropriate use of prison resources. The Minnesota Sentencing Commission believed that most nonviolent offenders can and should be punished effectively in the community and that prisons generally should be reserved for violent offenders. In addition, the Commission believed that the guidelines should not lead to a substantial increase in the size of the state's prison population. The guidelines reflect these beliefs. The vast majority of felony offenders in Minnesota are presumptively subject to community sanctions under the guidelines, although judges have the option of imposing or not imposing a jail term as a condition of probation. See Richard S. Frase, Sentencing Guidelines in Minnesota, 1978–2003, 32 Crime & Just. 131, 136, 195 (2005) (reporting that the rate—typically between 20 and 24%—with which felons are sentenced to prison under the Minnesota guidelines consistently has remained below the national average, although the proportion of felons sentenced to jail has escalated, far exceeding the national rate).

By contrast, although a federal statute, 28 U.S.C. § 994(g), directed the U.S. Sentencing Commission to draft the guidelines in a way that would "minimize the likelihood that the federal prison population will exceed the capacity of the federal prisons," the federal prisons are some of the most crowded in the country. See Bureau of Justice Statistics, U.S. Dep't of Justice, Prisoners in 2007, at 7 (2008) (federal prisons were operating at 136% of their capacity in 2007). In addition, the Commission disagreed with the past practice of generally imposing community-based sanctions for such economic crimes as theft, tax evasion, antitrust offenses, insider trading, fraud, and embezzlement. U.S. Sentencing Comm'n, Federal Sentencing Guidelines Manual, Ch. 1, Pt. A, § 4(d) (2008). The Commission believed that these crimes are usually "serious," therefore warranting some mandatory period of confinement or detention. Id. Consequently, under the federal guidelines, the vast majority of offenders are now subject to some period of confinement, either in prison or elsewhere. Only under the first eight, out of a total of forty-three, offense levels is a first offender eligible for probation without any attending confinement or detention. Id. at § 5B1.1(a). See also U.S. Sentencing Comm'n, 2008 Annual Report 34 (2009) (89% of the federal offenders sentenced in 2008 received prison sentences).

To what extent do your views correspond with those of the United States Sentencing Commission? To what extent do they mirror those of the Minnesota Sentencing Commission? For more information about the federal sentencing guidelines and practical tips for litigating under the guidelines, see Practice Under the Federal Sentencing Guidelines (Phylis Skloot Bamberger & David J. Gottlieb eds., 4th ed. 2008).

b. Application of the Advisory Federal Guidelines at Sentencing

The Supreme Court and the lower courts have struggled, and continue to struggle, with the import of the Supreme Court's holding in *Booker* that the federal sentencing guidelines are advisory only. One question is how the federal guidelines can factor into sentencing decisions. In Gall v. United States, 128 S.Ct. 586, 596 (2007), the Supreme Court said that the guidelines are the "starting point"—the "initial benchmark"—for the sentencing judge. But the judge cannot presume that a sentence within the guidelines range is reasonable. Instead, in determining the appropriate sentence, the judge must consider the sentencing factors outlined in 18 U.S.C. § 3553(a), such as the need to protect the public from future crimes committed by the defendant and the need to provide the defendant with necessary educational services, vocational training, medical care, and other treatment in the "most effective manner." (See footnote b on page 228 of the casebook for a list of the sentencing factors set forth in § 3553(a).) If the judge then decides that a sentence outside the guidelines is warranted, the judge must make sure that the reason for this variance from the guidelines is "sufficiently compelling" to justify a variance of that amount. Id. at 597. And the sentencing judge must provide a "more significant justification" for a "major" deviation from the guidelines than for a "minor" one. Id.

Gall illustrates the wider variation in sentences for a crime that can ensue when sentencing guidelines are advisory rather than mandatory. The lowest sentence under the guidelines range for the crime to which the defendant pled guilty in that case—conspiracy to distribute several controlled substances—was thirty months in prison. Citing the defendant's voluntary withdrawal from the conspiracy over four years before his indictment, his subsequent securing of a college degree and employment, and other facts, the district judge sentenced the defendant to probation for thirty-six months. Giving "due deference" to this decision, the Supreme Court found that the district judge had not abused his discretion in rendering this sentence. Id. at 602. See also Kimbrough v. United States, 128 S.Ct. 558 (2007) (upholding a sentence for drug-related crimes that was over four years lower than the bottom sentence in the guidelines range). Is this greater variation in sentences for a crime, in your opinion, a positive or negative repercussion of the Court's holding that the federal sentencing guidelines are no longer mandatory?

c. Appellate Review of Federal Sentences

In *Booker*, the Supreme Court held that when a federal sentence is challenged on appeal the appellate court should determine whether the sentence was "unreasonable." 543 U.S. at 261, 125 S.Ct. at 765. When making this determination, the appellate court is to apply a "deferential abuse-of-discretion standard." Gall v. United States, 128 S.Ct. at 591.

Federal appellate courts can apply, but are not required to apply, a presumption that a sentence falling within the range set forth in the federal sentencing guidelines is reasonable. The Supreme Court reasoned in Rita v. United States, 551 U.S. 338, 127 S.Ct. 2456 (2007) that such a presumption is permissible since both the Sentencing Commission, through the crafting of the guideline range within whose parameters the sentence fell, and the district court, through the imposition of a sentence in line with the guidelines, have concurred that the within-the-guidelines sentence comports with the sentencing factors set forth in 18 U.S.C. § 3553(a).

The Supreme Court emphasized in *Rita* that the rebuttable presumption that a within-the-guidelines sentence is reasonable is an *"appellate court presumption"*; the sentencing judge, as noted earlier, cannot invoke such a presumption. Id. at 2465. But the Court conceded that an appellate presumption that a within-the-guidelines sentence is reasonable might exert what Justice Souter, in dissent, described as a "gravitational pull" on federal district judges to adhere to the guidelines when imposing sentences. Id. at 2487 (Souter, J., dissenting). Justice Souter believed that the presumption condoned by the Court would undermine *Apprendi* and the constitutional rights it protects. Do you agree?

While a federal appellate court can apply a presumption of reasonableness when reviewing a sentence that fell within the guidelines range, the court cannot apply a presumption of unreasonableness when reviewing a sentence falling outside that range. According to the Supreme Court in *Gall*, a presumption of unreasonableness would give too much weight to the federal sentencing guidelines, conflicting with the Court's attempt in *Booker* to remedy the Sixth Amendment problem with the guidelines by treating them as advisory in nature. To avoid undermining *Booker*, an appellate court also cannot require that there be "extraordinary circumstances" to justify a substantial variance from the guidelines. 128 S.Ct. at 595. But the extent to which the sentence imposed varies from the recommended sentence under the guidelines is, according to the Supreme Court, a relevant factor to be considered by an appellate court deciding whether the sentence was unreasonable and an abuse of the sentencing judge's discretion.

Justice Thomas has charged that the Supreme Court's decision to remedy the Sixth Amendment by treating the federal sentencing guidelines as advisory has forced the Court to perform the "legislative role" of creating a new sentencing structure. Kimbrough v. United States, 128 S.Ct. 558, 578 (2007) (Thomas, J., dissenting). Do you agree? If so, do you concur with his conclusion that the Court should rectify its mistake by interpreting the guidelines as mandatory but requiring that a jury resolve factual questions bearing on a sentence when the Sixth Amendment so dictates? Or is "[t]he ball," as the Court observed in *Booker*, now "in Congress' court"? 543 U.S. at 265, 125 S.Ct. at 768.

D. *EX POST FACTO* LIMITATIONS ON SENTENCING STATUTES AND GUIDELINES

Guideline III.F. of the Minnesota sentencing guidelines, which limits the application of guideline modifications to offenders who commit their crimes on or after the date a modification goes into effect, is designed to avoid *ex post facto* problems with the guidelines. Article I, § 10 of the United States Constitution prohibits the states from enacting any *ex post facto* laws, and Article I, § 9 prohibits Congress from enacting such laws. A law which increases the punishment for a crime after the crime has been committed falls within this *ex post facto* prohibition. Lindsey v. Washington, 301 U.S. 397, 401 57 S.Ct. 797, 799 (1937).

The Supreme Court has interpreted the *Ex Post Facto* Clause as prohibiting the imposition of the presumptive sentence set forth in sentencing guidelines in effect at the time of sentencing that was higher than the presumptive sentence under the guidelines in effect at the time of a defendant's crime. Miller v. Florida, 482 U.S. 423, 107 S.Ct. 2446 (1987). Reducing the good-time or other sentencing credits that could be earned under the law in effect at the time of the crime also violates the *ex post facto* prohibition. See Lynce v. Mathis, 519 U.S. 433, 117 S.Ct. 891 (1997) (statute revoking sentencing credits to which the prisoner was entitled under a statute in effect at the time of his crime, which provided for the awarding of such credits when the state's prison system reached a certain level of crowding, violated the Constitution's *ex post facto* prohibition); Weaver v. Graham, 450 U.S. 24, 101 S.Ct. 960 (1981) (law enacted after the date of the defendant's crime and sentencing, which decreased the rate that good-time credits accumulate, is an unconstitutional *ex post facto* law).

In California Dep't of Corrections v. Morales, 514 U.S. 499, 115 S.Ct. 1597 (1995), however, the Supreme Court held that a state statute that increased the length of time between parole-suitability hearings for certain offenders did not constitute an *ex post facto* law. The statute in question authorized the parole board to defer the parole-suitability hearing of a prisoner with two or more homicide convictions for up to three years if the board found that it was "not reasonable to expect" that parole would be granted during the intervening years and explained the reason for this conclusion. The statute in effect at the time of the murder for which the prisoner in this case was imprisoned had provided, by contrast, for annual parole-suitability hearings. The prisoner argued that the new statute unconstitutionally increased the punishment to which he was subjected since it eliminated the possibility that he might be released on parole during the three-year period between his parole-suitability hearings. The Supreme Court responded that the risk that the statute enhanced the punishment of the prisoner was too remote and speculative to give rise to a constitutional violation. The Court emphasized both that the statute applied to a category of prisoners whose release on parole was extremely unlikely and that the board had to follow certain procedures to ensure that parole-suitability hearings were deferred only in appropriate cases.

In Garner v. Jones, 529 U.S. 244, 120 S.Ct. 1362 (2000), the Supreme Court went beyond *Morales*, holding that a change in a parole board's rules lengthening the period of time before parole reconsideration from three years to up to eight years for prisoners serving life sentences did not necessarily violate the constitutional prohibition on *ex post facto* laws. The Court concluded that the new rules, on their face, did not create a "significant risk" of prolonged confinement for prisoners with life sentences because, under the board's procedures, a prisoner could be afforded expedited reconsideration for parole based on a "change in circumstances." Id. at 251, 255, 120 S.Ct. at 1368, 1370. The Court added though that while the new rules were not unconstitutional on their face, an individual prisoner must be afforded the opportunity to show that the way in which the rules actually have been applied to him or her has created a significant risk of increased punishment.

In a separate opinion concurring, in part, in the judgment, Justice Scalia objected to giving a prisoner the chance to demonstrate that the board's new procedures have significantly increased the risk, to that particular prisoner, of prolonged incarceration. Underscoring that parole is "a matter of grace" and not an entitlement—an opportunity for "mercy" remitted to the parole board's discretion, Justice Scalia contended:

> It makes no more sense to freeze in time the Board's discretion as to procedures than it does to freeze in time the Board's discretion as to substance. Just as the *Ex Post Facto* Clause gives respondent no cause to complain that the Board in place at the time of his offense has been replaced by a new, tough-on-crime Board that is much more parsimo-

nious with parole, it gives him no cause to complain that it has been replaced by a new, big-on-efficiency Board that cuts back on reconsiderations without cause.

Id. at 259, 120 S.Ct. at 1372 (Scalia, J., concurring in part in judgment).

In your opinion, under what circumstances, if any, does a change in the time interval before parole consideration or reconsideration violate the *Ex Post Facto* Clause?

CHAPTER 5

COMMUNITY-BASED SANCTIONS

■ ■ ■

A. MULTI-TIERED SENTENCING STRUCTURES

Until recently, the sentencing options available to judges were limited. Generally, judges either fined criminal offenders, placed them on probation, with very minimal supervision, or sentenced them to jail or prison. When convicted criminals violated the conditions of their probation, judges often felt that they had no other choice but to send the violators to prison or jail.

Although other criminal sanctions have now been developed and are being imposed on increasing numbers of criminal offenders in some jurisdictions, the two-tiered sentencing system described above, under which judges are forced to choose between incarceration and perfunctory supervision, if any, of criminal offenders, is still prevalent throughout much of the county. See Bureau of Justice Statistics, U.S. Dep't of Justice, Felony Sentences in State Courts, 2004, at 2–3 (2007) (reporting that in 2004, state courts sentenced 70% of convicted felons to prison or jail and 28% to probation with no additional jail or prison time). This simplistic system has proven to be both ineffectual and costly. If simply fined or placed on "straight probation," many offenders will not receive the supervision or treatment that might lead them to refrain from committing future crimes. As a result, the public's interest in combating crime will be thwarted and the safety of the public perhaps jeopardized. On the other hand, in many instances, incarcerating an offender may not be needed to serve the government's penological goals and in fact, may undermine those goals. If incarcerated, an offender may lose his or her job, and family ties may be broken, diminishing the prospects of rehabilitation. Exposure to criminogenic influences during incarceration may further reduce the chances that the offender will, in the future, abide by the law. And incarceration is extremely costly, straining budgets at the local, state, and federal levels.

Government decisionmakers have begun to realize that judges need a range of sentencing options from which to choose to respond to the wide range of criminal behavior. Set forth below is a proposal for one kind of multi-tiered sentencing structure.

PIERRE S. DU PONT IV, EXPANDING SENTENCING OPTIONS: A GOVERNOR'S PERSPECTIVE

National Institute of Justice (1985).*

* * *

* * * Despite its great cost, and the promise of more increases to come, the present [corrections] system might be largely acceptable if it were working properly. But it isn't. We traditionally rely on incarceration as the primary method of punishing criminals, but—as numerous studies have demonstrated—there is no evidence that higher incarceration rates have any impact on the crime rate. For one thing, prison overcrowding limits whatever chances exist for success in rehabilitative programs.

Despite the evidence that change is imperative, we seem unable to break out of our present pattern of dealing with criminals. It is as if our corrections system is a prisoner, too.

* * *

* * * In Delaware, we are beginning to consider an alternative program developed by the Delaware Sentencing Reform Commission. That alternative program stresses accountability—accountability of the offender to the victim and the State, and accountability of the corrections system to the public and other criminal justice agencies. The accountability concept could create an ordered yet flexible system of sentencing and corrections. This system would be based on the belief that an offender should be sentenced to the least restrictive (and least costly) sanction available, consistent with public safety. * * *

A system built on accountability would structure the movement of offenders into and out of the corrections system, making it fairer and more cost-efficient. It would provide incentives for offenders to work at rehabilitation, since this would permit them to move into less restrictive (and less expensive) forms of control. At the same time accountability would strengthen the safeguards against violent offenders, who could be held in prison as long as necessary, or at least as long as their sentences ran.

* * *

It is not [an] overstatement to say that the proposals of the Delaware Sentencing Reform Commission would completely overhaul our sentencing and corrections laws. They would establish a range of sanctions available

---

* This document was originally published in 1985 by the National Institute of Justice, U.S. Department of Justice, Washington D.C. Points of view or opinions expressed in the publication are those of the author and do not necessarily represent the official position or policies of the U.S. Department of Justice.

to a judge over 10 "levels of accountability." The table displays these 10 levels. [See page 224.]

Level I is unsupervised probation; Level X is maximum-security imprisonment. Moving from probation, there is a full range of alternatives, each more restrictive than the last, until the judge—and the criminal—reach a sentence of maximum-security incarceration.

Within each level there are degrees of control and accountability. These involve the offender's freedom of action within the community, the amount of supervision he or she is subject to, and what privileges are to be withheld or what other special conditions are to be attached to the sentence. In addition, the system provides for a range of possible financial sanctions to be imposed, including victims' compensation. Through such flexible controls, we would be able to control the offender's choice of job, choice of residence, ability to drive, ability to drink, ability to travel, and even ability to make telephone calls.

And to all of this we would add the probation fee concept. Successfully used in Georgia and Florida, the $10– to $50–per–month fee is charged to probationers to offset the cost of their supervision. Like the sanctions, the fee could be increased depending on the level of supervision required.

What is so attractive about this idea of accountability is that it applies not only to sentencing offenders, but also to controlling them following sentencing. And the same level of flexibility available to judges would be available to corrections officials responsible for probation.

Let's look at two hypothetical cases to see how the flexible sentencing and control system might work in practice.

First, let's take a drug offender with a minimal prior record but unstable employment record. He might be sentenced in Level II to supervised probation for 2 years, with restrictions on his place of residence, his association with certain individuals, and/or his right to visit high-drug/crime locations. And we might charge him a $10–per–month fee to offset some of the costs of keeping him straight.

If he observes these conditions for the first year of his probation, he could move down the sanctions scale into Level I. This level involves unsupervised probation and levies no fees, but holds out the possibility of certain restrictions on mobility and personal associations to minimize the chance of the offender slipping back into the drug scene and its associated crime. If our hypothetical drug offender violates the terms of his probation, he could be moved on to Level III, with heightened supervision, a curfew, and an increased monthly fee. Thus, the offender has a clear incentive to comply with his sentence. And, equally important, the sentencing judge has available options other than prison when probation is violated. Having and using these options will increase the certainty of appropriate punishment.

Restrictions	Level I	Level II	Level III	Level IV	Level V	Level VI	Level VII	Level VIII	Level IX	Level X
Mobility in the community [1]	100 percent (unrestricted)	100 percent (unrestricted)	90 percent (restricted 0-10 hours/week)	80 percent (restricted 10-30 hours/week)	60 percent (restricted 30-40 hours/week)	30 percent (restricted 50-100 hours/week)	20 percent (restricted 100-140 hours/week)	10 percent (90 percent of time incarcerated)	Incarcerated	Incarcerated
Amount of supervision	None	Monthly written report	1-2 face-to-face/month; 1-2 weekly phone contact	3-6 face-to-face/month; weekly phone contact	2-6 face-to-face/week; daily phone contact; weekly written reports	Daily phone contact; daily face-to-face; weekly written reports	Daily onsite supervision 8-16 hours/day	Daily onsite supervision 24 hours/day	Daily onsite supervision 24 hours/day	Daily onsite supervision 24 hours/day
Privileges withheld or special conditions [2]	100 percent (same as prior conviction)	100 percent (same as prior conviction)	1-2 privileges withheld	1-4 privileges withheld	1-7 privileges withheld	1-10 privileges withheld	1-12 privileges withheld	5-15 privileges withheld	15-19 privileges withheld	20 or more privileges withheld
Financial obligations [3]	Fine, court costs may be applied (0- to 2-day fine)	Fine, court costs, restitution; probation (supervisory fee may be applied; 1- to 3-day fine)	Same (increase probation fee by $5-10/month; 2- to 4-day fine)	Same (increase probation fee by $5-10/month; 3- to 5-day fine)	Same (pay partial cost of food/lodging/supervision fee; 4- to 7-day fine)	Same as Level V (8- to 10-day fine)	Same as Level V (11- to 12-day fine)	Fine, court costs, restitution payable upon release to Level VII or lower (12- to 15-day fine)	Same as Level VIII	Same as Level VIII
Examples (Note: many other scenarios could be constructed meeting the requirements at each level)	$50 fine, court costs; 6 months unsupervised probation	$50 fine, court costs, restitution; 6 months supervised probation; $10 monthly fee; written report	Fine, court costs, restitution; 1 year probation; weekend community service; no drinking	Weekend community service or mandatory treatment 5 hours/day; $30 month probation fee; no drinking; no out-of-State trips	Mandatory rehabilitation skills program 8 hours/day; restitution; $40/month probation fee; no drinking; curfew	Work release; pay portion of food/lodging; restitution; no kitchen privileges outside mealtimes; no drinking; no sex; weekends home	Residential treatment program; pay portion of program costs; limited privileges	Minimum-security prison	Medium-security prison	Maximum-security prison

1. Restrictions on freedom structure an offender's time, controlling his or her schedule, whereabouts, and activities for a designated period. To the extent that monitoring is not standard or consistent or to the extent that no sanctions accrue for failure on the part of the offender, the time is *not* structured. It could consist of residential, part-time residential, community service, or other specific methods for meeting the designated hours. The judge could order that the hours be met daily (e.g., 2 hours/day) or in one period (e.g., weekend in jail).

2. Privileges/conditions; choice of job, choice of residence, mobility within setting, driving, drinking (possible use of Antabuse), out-of-State trips, phone calls, curfew, mail, urinalysis, associates, areas off limits.

3. As a more equitable guide to appropriate fines, the amount would be measured in units of equivalent daily income, such as 1 day's salary = "1-day fine."

The second example is near the other end of the offense spectrum. This time our hypothetical offender is a twice-convicted armed robber. He was sentenced to 20 years, with the sentence to begin at Level X, or a maximum-security prison. After serving 2 years, and adhering to all the rules, the man might be moved to Level IX, a medium-security facility, where he might be able to take advantage of expanded rehabilitative programs.

Two years later, with continued good behavior, the offender again could move down the scale, this time to a minimum-security facility with still greater opportunities for rehabilitation. By the same token, if the prisoner's action at Level IX was disruptive and uncooperative, he could be returned to Level X.

Later, at a parole hearing, some appropriate program at Level VI might be selected instead of releasing the offender to a fuller freedom in the streets or leaving him in prison.

When the Sentencing Reform Commission applied the concept of accountability levels to the present offender population in Delaware, it found that only 21 percent of that population fell within Levels IX and X. But that medium- and maximum-security population accounted for 87 percent of the total corrections budget in Delaware. The Commission also found that roughly 70 percent of the corrections population fell between Levels I and III. Less than 10 percent filled the middle ground, and most of these were in some sort of alcohol or drug abuse program. Analysis showed that many in prison could be safely released if the programs were available to restrict their activities properly and closely supervise their rehabilitation. That analysis also showed that many in probation were undersupervised. Many of these men and women clearly needed to be moved into a middle level where they would be subject to stronger, more restrictive programs.

Let me sum up by shifting the focus from corrections mechanics to corrections philosophy. In this regard, I think it reasonable to consider two important goals of sentencing reform. The first is to reverse the long-established trend of growing prison populations and skyrocketing corrections budgets. The second is to redirect the system so that it guides offenders toward a useful life within the law.

Don't expect miracles from the reform proposals I am suggesting. Even with a sophisticated accountability system, we may not be able to reverse quickly the growth of corrections populations and spending. But we reasonably can expect to slow growth in spending and, ultimately, to stabilize costs. A hallmark of the accountability concept is cost avoidance—that is, developing and using less costly alternatives in our corrections programs. And, optimally, the effect of the accountability concept, as the offender moves through the system, will be to help reduce recidivism.

* * *

Delaware ultimately adopted a streamlined and diluted version of the du Pont plan. The Delaware sentencing system includes five "accountability levels,'' and judges' adherence to the system is recommended, but not mandated''. Del. Code Ann. tit. 11, § 4204(c).

How, if at all, would you modify the du Pont plan? See Norval Morris & Michael Tonry, Between Prison and Probation 68 (1990). Consider also how the accountability levels former governor du Pont proposed could be integrated with sanctioning units and exchange rates, which are discussed at the end of this chapter, and reentry courts, which are described on pages 454–57.

B. SENTENCING OPTIONS

In the article written by former governor du Pont, he discussed the need for the development of a wide range of sentencing options to ensure that criminal sanctions are cost-effective and meet the purposes for which they are imposed. Set forth below is a discussion of some of the sanctions that can be imposed in lieu of incarceration. As you read these materials, consider what other community-based sanctions could be developed and what can be done to make the community-based sanctions that presently exist more effective.

1. PROBATION

In the United States, probation is one of the most common penalties imposed on criminal offenders. At the end of 2007, 4,215,361 adults were on probation, and another 799,058 were on parole. Bureau of Justice Statistics, U.S. Dep't of Justice, Probation and Parole in the United States, 2007 Statistical Tables, tbls. 2 & 3 (2008). When added to the over two million adults incarcerated in prisons or jails in that year, 3.2% of the nation's adult population—one out of every thirty-one adults—was under correctional supervision. Press Release, Bureau of Justice Statistics, U.S. Dep't of Justice, One in Every 31 U.S. Adults Were in Prison or Jail or on Probation or Parole in 2007 (Dec. 11, 2008).

Probation is a generic term used to describe a variety of ways of controlling, treating, and supervising criminal offenders during their probationary period. In terms of the constraints placed on probationers, probation may consist of little more than a requirement that the probationers refrain from criminal activity and talk with their probation officers, either in person or on the telephone, once a month or even more infrequently. Probationers may, on the other hand, be placed on what is called intensive supervision probation. These probationers may be required to meet with their probation officers several times a week or even every day and may be subject to a number of other conditions and controls, such as curfews and frequent drug testing. Examples of some of the types of restrictions that may be placed on probationers can be found in 18 U.S.C. § 3563, which is set forth below.

18 U.S.C. § 3563. CONDITIONS OF PROBATION

(a) **Mandatory conditions.**—The court shall provide, as an explicit condition of a sentence of probation—

(1) for a felony, a misdemeanor, or an infraction, that the defendant not commit another Federal, State, or local crime during the term of probation;

(2) for a felony, that the defendant also abide by at least one condition set forth in subsection (b)(2) or (b)(12), unless the court has imposed a fine under this chapter, or unless the court finds on the record that extraordinary circumstances exist that would make such a condition plainly unreasonable, in which event the court shall impose one or more of the other conditions set forth under subsection (b);

(3) for a felony, a misdemeanor, or an infraction, that the defendant not unlawfully possess a controlled substance;

(4) for a domestic violence crime as defined in section 3561(b) by a defendant convicted of such an offense for the first time that the defendant attend a public, private, or private nonprofit offender rehabilitation program that has been approved by the court, in consultation with a State Coalition Against Domestic Violence or other appropriate experts, if an approved program is readily available within a 50–mile radius of the legal residence of the defendant; and

(5) for a felony, a misdemeanor, or an infraction, that the defendant refrain from any unlawful use of a controlled substance and submit to one drug test within 15 days of release on probation and at least 2 periodic drug tests thereafter (as determined by the court) for use of a controlled substance, but the condition stated in this paragraph may be ameliorated or suspended by the court for any individual defendant if the defendant's presentence report or other reliable sentencing information indicates a low risk of future substance abuse by the defendant;

(6) that the defendant—

(A) make restitution in accordance with sections 2248, 2259, 2264, 2327, 3663, 3663A, and 3664; and

(B) pay the assessment imposed in accordance with section 3013;[a]

(7) that the defendant will notify the court of any material change in the defendant's economic circumstances that

---

a. Title 18 U.S.C. § 3013(a) requires a court to impose a "[s]pecial assessment" on each person convicted of a crime. The amount of the assessment imposed on individual defendants ranges from five dollars for an infraction or class C misdemeanor to one hundred dollars for a felony.

might affect the defendant's ability to pay restitution, fines, or special assessments;

(8) for a person required to register under the Sex Offender Registration and Notification Act, that the person comply with the requirements of that Act; and

(9) that the defendant cooperate in the collection of a DNA sample from the defendant if the collection of such a sample is authorized pursuant to section 3 of the DNA Analysis Backlog Elimination Act of 2000.

If the court has imposed and ordered execution of a fine and placed the defendant on probation, payment of the fine or adherence to the court-established installment schedule shall be a condition of the probation.

(b) Discretionary conditions.—The court may provide, as further conditions of a sentence of probation, to the extent that such conditions are reasonably related to the factors set forth in section 3553(a)(1) and (a)(2)[b] and to the extent that such conditions involve only such deprivations of liberty or property as are reasonably necessary for the purposes indicated in section 3553(a)(2), that the defendant—

(1) support his dependents and meet other family responsibilities;

(2) make restitution to a victim of the offense * * *;

---

b. Section 3553(a)(1)–(2) provides as follows:

(a) Factors to be considered in imposing a sentence.—The court shall impose a sentence sufficient, but not greater than necessary, to comply with the purposes set forth in paragraph (2) of this subsection. The court, in determining the particular sentence to be imposed, shall consider—

(1) the nature and circumstances of the offense and the history and characteristics of the defendant;

(2) the need for the sentence imposed—

(A) to reflect the seriousness of the offense, to promote respect for the law, and to provide just punishment for the offense;

(B) to afford adequate deterrence to criminal conduct;

(C) to protect the public from further crimes of the defendant; and

(D) to provide the defendant with needed educational or vocational training, medical care, or other correctional treatment in the most effective manner.

(3) the kinds of sentences available;

(4) the kinds of sentence and the sentencing range established for—

(A) the applicable category of offense committed by the applicable category of defendant as set forth in the guidelines * * * issued by the Sentencing Commission * * *; or

(B) in the case of a violation of probation or supervised release, the applicable guidelines or policy statements issued by the Sentencing Commission * * *;

(5) any pertinent policy statement * * * issued by the Sentencing Commission * * *;

(6) the need to avoid unwarranted sentence disparities among defendants with similar records who have been found guilty of similar conduct; and

(7) the need to provide restitution to any victims of the offense.

(3) give to the victims of the offense the notice ordered pursuant to the provisions of section 3555;[c]

(4) work conscientiously at suitable employment or pursue conscientiously a course of study or vocational training that will equip him for suitable employment;

(5) refrain, in the case of an individual, from engaging in a specified occupation, business, or profession bearing a reasonably direct relationship to the conduct constituting the offense, or engage in such a specified occupation, business, or profession only to a stated degree or under stated circumstances;

(6) refrain from frequenting specified kinds of places or from associating unnecessarily with specified persons;

(7) refrain from excessive use of alcohol, or any use of a narcotic drug or other controlled substance * * * without a prescription by a licensed medical practitioner;

(8) refrain from possessing a firearm, destructive device, or other dangerous weapon;

(9) undergo available medical, psychiatric, or psychological treatment, including treatment for drug or alcohol dependency, as specified by the court, and remain in a specified institution if required for that purpose;

(10) remain in the custody of the Bureau of Prisons during nights, weekends, or other intervals of time, totaling no more than the lesser of one year or the term of imprisonment authorized for the offense, during the first year of the term of probation or supervised release;

(11) reside at, or participate in the program of, a community corrections facility * * * for all or part of the term of probation;

(12) work in community service as directed by the court;

(13) reside in a specified place or area, or refrain from residing in a specified place or area;

(14) remain within the jurisdiction of the court, unless granted permission to leave by the court or a probation officer;

(15) report to a probation officer as directed by the court or the probation officer;

(16) permit a probation officer to visit him at his home or elsewhere as specified by the court;

---

c. Section 3555 authorizes a court to require a defendant convicted of fraud or "other intentionally deceptive practices" to notify victims of the crime of his or her conviction.

(17) answer inquiries by a probation officer and notify the probation officer promptly of any change in address or employment;

(18) notify the probation officer promptly if arrested or questioned by a law enforcement officer;

(19) remain at his place of residence during nonworking hours and, if the court finds it appropriate, that compliance with this condition be monitored by telephonic or electronic signaling devices, except that a condition under this paragraph may be imposed only as an alternative to incarceration;

(20) comply with the terms of any court order or order of an administrative process * * * requiring payments by the defendant for the support and maintenance of a child or of a child and the parent with whom the child is living;

(21) be ordered deported by a United States district court, or United States magistrate judge, pursuant to a stipulation entered into by the defendant and the United States * * *, except that, in the absence of a stipulation, the United States district court or a United States magistrate judge, may order deportation as a condition of probation, if, after notice and hearing pursuant to such section, the Attorney General demonstrates by clear and convincing evidence that the alien is deportable;

(22) satisfy such other conditions as the court may impose; or

(23) if required to register under the Sex Offender Registration and Notification Act, submit his person, and any property, house, residence, vehicle, papers, computer, other electronic communication or data storage devices or media, and effects to search at any time, with or without a warrant, by any law enforcement or probation officer with reasonable suspicion concerning a violation of a condition of probation or unlawful conduct by the person, and by any probation officer in the lawful discharge of the officer's supervision functions.

(c) Modifications of conditions.—The court may modify, reduce, or enlarge the conditions of a sentence of probation at any time prior to the expiration or termination of the term of probation, pursuant to the provisions of the Federal Rules of Criminal Procedure relating to the modification of probation and the provisions applicable to the initial setting of the conditions of probation.

(d) Written statement of conditions.—The court shall direct that the probation officer provide the defendant with a written statement that sets forth all the conditions to which the sentence is subject, and that is sufficiently clear and specific to serve as a guide for the defendant's conduct and for such supervision as is required.

* * *

QUESTIONS AND POINTS FOR DISCUSSION

1. The preceding sections of the Federal Probation Act exemplify the types of conditions that can be imposed as conditions of probation, supervised release, or parole. Judges traditionally have been accorded broad discretion when imposing probation and supervised-release conditions, as have parole boards when imposing parole conditions. As long as the conditions are reasonably related to one or more of the penological goals served by probation or parole and meet any other statutory or constitutional requirements, the conditions generally have been upheld. See, e.g., United States v. Jeremiah, 493 F.3d 1042, 1045–46 (9th Cir. 2007) (condition requiring defendant, who "willfully" had failed to make restitution payments, to incur no credit charges without probation officer's prior approval was reasonably related to monitoring his ability to pay restitution); United States v. Rearden, 349 F.3d 608, 620–21 (9th Cir. 2003) (supervised-release condition prohibiting defendant, who had been convicted of shipping child pornography over the Internet, from possessing or using a computer with Internet access without prior approval of the probation officer was reasonably related to the goals of deterrence, rehabilitation, and protection of the public).

Some courts have applied variants of this reasonable-relationship test. For example, in some states, the probation or parole condition must be reasonably related to the crime of which the person was convicted. See, e.g., Boyd v. State, 749 So.2d 536 (Fla.Dist.Ct.App.2000) (probation conditions prohibiting the defendant from possessing or consuming alcohol, frequenting bars, and associating with persons who consume alcohol were not reasonably related to the crime for which he was sentenced—solicitation or delivery of cocaine). See also Andrew Horwitz, Coercion, Pop–Psychology, and Judicial Moralizing: Some Proposals for Curbing Judicial Abuse of Probation Conditions, 57 Wash. & Lee L. Rev. 75, 90–95 (2000) (describing different formulations of the reasonable-relationship test).

The application of the reasonable-relationship test or its variants typically leads to the same result—the upholding of a probation or parole condition. See, e.g., United States v. Rodriguez, 558 F.3d 408, 413–14 (5th Cir. 2009) (upholding supervised-release condition prohibiting defendant, who had been convicted of assaulting a federal officer and had a state charge for sexual assault of a minor pending against him, from "associating with" a child under the age of eighteen unless an adult designated in writing by the probation officer was present and supervising); United States v. Mills, 959 F.2d 516, 519 (5th Cir.1992) (supervised-release condition prohibiting used-car salesman convicted of odometer tampering from working in car-sales business was valid); People v. Meyer, 661 N.E.2d 526, 528 (Ill.App.Ct.1996) (reasonable to require defendant convicted of battery, as a condition of his probation, to place a sign at his property entrances reading, "WARNING! A Violent Felon lives here. Enter at your own Risk!''); Todd v. State, 911 S.W.2d 807, 817–18 (Tex.Ct.App.1995) (not an abuse of discretion to require defendant convicted of negligent homicide, as conditions of his probation, to perform one hundred hours of community service in a place where he would see the aftermath of automobile accidents and to write letters of apology to the victim's girlfriend and family on the first and second anniversaries of the crime and when his probation term ends).

On occasion, an appellate court will find a probation or parole condition to be unconstitutional or its imposition an abuse of discretion. For example, in United States v. Crume, 422 F.3d 728, 733 (8th Cir. 2005), the Eight Circuit Court of Appeals vacated a supervised-release condition that barred the defendant, who had been convicted of knowingly receiving and knowingly possessing child pornography, from accessing a computer and the Internet without first obtaining written consent from his probation officer. Concluding that this condition impinged on the defendant's First Amendment rights more than "reasonably necessary," the court mentioned a more narrow alternative: prohibiting the defendant from accessing certain websites and kinds of information on the Internet, and monitoring compliance with this condition through a combination of software filters and random searches. In striking down the supervised-release condition, the court also emphasized that the defendant had used his computer and the Internet "merely" to possess child pornography and not, for example, to transmit pornographic images to others. Id. at 733. For examples of other cases invalidating a condition of probation, parole, or supervised release, see State v. Muhammad, 43 P.3d 318, 325 (Mont. 2002) (probation condition requiring defendant convicted of a sex crime involving a fourteen-year-old to post a sign at every entrance of his residence stating, "CHILDREN UNDER THE AGE OF 18 ARE NOT ALLOWED BY COURT ORDER," not reasonably related to the goals of rehabilitating the defendant or protecting the victim and the public); People v. Letterlough, 655 N.E.2d 146, 149–51 (N.Y.1995) (probation condition requiring defendant convicted of drunk driving to affix fluorescent sign stating "convicted dwi" to any vehicle he drives not reasonably related to defendant's rehabilitation, as required by state statute); State v. Qualey, 906 P.2d 835, 837–38 (Or.Ct.App.1995) (abuse of discretion to require defendant convicted of assault to refrain from drinking intoxicants for three years when there was no evidence that alcohol played a role in defendant's crime or that he had a history of alcohol abuse); State v. Mosburg, 768 P.2d 313 (Kan.Ct.App.1989) and the cases cited therein (requiring that defendants convicted of child abuse or neglect not become pregnant while on probation or parole violated their constitutional right to privacy); Wiggins v. State, 386 So.2d 46 (Fla.Dist.Ct. App.1980) (probation condition prohibiting defendants, who claimed they had committed forgeries and burglary so they could feed their illegitimate children, from having sexual intercourse with anyone with whom they were not married was invalid); Inman v. State, 183 S.E.2d 413 (Ga.Ct.App.1971) (unconstitutional to require defendant, who was convicted of marijuana possession, to keep his hair short as a condition of probation). For an in-depth analysis of whether a "shame sentence" imposed on a defendant was authorized by statute and was constitutional, see United States v. Gementera, 379 F.3d 596 (9th Cir. 2004), on page 358.

2. As 18 U.S.C. § 3563 demonstrates, legislatures can mandate or authorize courts to impose certain probation conditions. Legislatures also can prohibit the imposition of certain probation conditions. In your opinion, should legislatures prohibit a court from requiring any defendants, as a condition of probation, to utilize birth control? See 730 Ill. Comp. Stat. 5/5–5–3(k) (prohibiting courts from requiring defendants "to be implanted or injected with or to use any form of birth control"). Or should legislatures specifically authorize or require imposition of such a probation condition in certain circumstances? If so, what are those circumstances? After reading the ensuing note, consider how, if at all, your opinions on these questions have changed.

3. State v. Kline, 963 P.2d 697 (Or.Ct.App.1998) involved a defendant whose parental rights were terminated after he abused his son, breaking his arm. Several years later, the defendant and his wife had a daughter, whom he also abused, both physically and emotionally, when he was high on methamphetamine. Holding the baby up to his face, the defendant would scream obscenities at her. He also would leave the baby sometimes in her crib all day and not let his wife check on her. And when his wife and her parents discovered bruises on the baby's chest and back, the defendant threatened to kill anyone who called the Children's Services Division.

One day, when the defendant went to retrieve the baby from her crib, she began screaming. Although the defendant's wife noticed a few minutes later that the baby appeared to have a leg injury, the defendant would not let her take the baby to a doctor for three days. When she did, X-rays revealed that the baby's leg had been fractured.

The defendant was convicted of criminal mistreatment in the first degree and placed on probation for thirty-six months. As a condition of probation, he was prohibited from "fathering a child" unless he first obtained the court's written approval and successfully completed a drug-treatment and anger-management program. If you were on the appellate court, would you uphold this probation condition? Would you uphold a condition, imposed on a defendant convicted of intentionally refusing to pay child support for the nine children he had had with four different women, prohibiting him from having another child unless he demonstrated that he would support the child and his other nine children? See State v. Oakley, 629 N.W.2d 200 (Wis. 2001).

4. As a condition of probation or parole or as a condition of being eligible for certain privileges in prison, offenders with substance-abuse problems have been required to attend Alcoholics Anonymous (AA) or Narcotics Anonymous (NA) meetings. The twelve steps to recovery prescribed by AA and NA and recited at their meetings include numerous references to God. For example, meeting attendees acknowledge that they have "made a decision to turn our will and our lives over to the care of God as we understood Him." Most courts have held that requiring offenders to attend AA or NA meetings violates the First Amendment's proscription of governmental "establishment of religion." Inouye v. Kemna, 504 F.3d 705, 715 (9th Cir. 2007) (listing cases). To avoid an Establishment Clause problem, offenders must be advised of, and if they wish afforded, a "meaningful" secular alternative to AA or NA. Bausch v. Sumiec, 139 F.Supp.2d 1029, 1033 n. 4, 1036 (E.D.Wis.2001). The

location, cost, and frequency of a secular alternative's meetings may bear on whether the choice offered the offender is, in truth, a meaningful one. See Michael G. Honeymar, Jr., Note, Alcoholics Anonymous as a Condition of Drunk Driving Probation: When Does It Amount to Establishment of Religion, 97 Colum. L. Rev. 437, 465–67 (1997) (listing factors that may lead to "de facto compulsory Alcoholics Anonymous").

5. Some probation and parole conditions prohibit offenders from entering or remaining in a particular geographical area during a probation or parole period. See, e.g., United States v. Crume, 422 F.3d 728, 733–34 (8th Cir. 2005) (upholding probation condition prohibiting defendant, who had been convicted of receiving and possessing child pornography, from "places where minor children under the age of 18 congregate," including schools, parks, pools, daycare centers, and certain residences). Most courts have invalidated conditions banishing an offender from the state, finding them to be unconstitutional abridgements on the right to interstate travel and not reasonably related to sentencing goals. Commonwealth v. Pike, 701 N.E.2d 951, 960 (Mass. 1998). In striking down such a probation condition, the Supreme Judicial Court of Massachusetts observed that making other states a " 'dumping ground' " for the state's criminals would contravene public policy and invite retaliation from other states. Id. (quoting State v. Doughtie, 74 S.E.2d 922, 924 (N.C. 1953)).

Courts, on the other hand, sometimes have upheld, and other times have stricken, more limited geographical restrictions. Compare Terry v. Hamrick, 663 S.E.2d 256, 258–60 (Ga. 2008) (probation condition banishing defendant, who had been convicted of aggravated stalking of his wife and other crimes, from 158 of the state's 159 counties was valid) and Parrish v. State, 355 S.E.2d 682, 683–84 (Ga.Ct.App.1987) (probation condition banning defendant, who had been convicted of assault, obstruction of officers, possession of marijuana, and tampering with evidence, from judicial circuit for six-year probation period upheld) with State v. Stewart, 713 N.W.2d 165, 170–71 (Wis.Ct.App. 2006) (probation condition banning defendant, who had been convicted of felony bail jumping and felony fleeing, from township for five years was overbroad; since most of his criminal conduct, which included abuse of his wife and children and masturbating in public, was directed towards his family and neighbors, the court could have imposed a "more narrowly drawn condition," banning the defendant from his house and the immediate neighborhood) and People v. Beach, 195 Cal.Rptr. 381, 386–87 (Cal.Ct.App.1983) (probation condition requiring defendant, who had been found guilty of involuntary manslaughter, to leave the community where she had lived for twenty-four years unconstitutionally impinged on her right to intrastate travel and to possess and enjoy her personal property). In your opinion, would a probation or parole condition prohibiting a defendant who had been convicted of prostitution from entering portions of the city where prostitution was prevalent be constitutional? Compare State v. Morgan, 389 So.2d 364 (La. 1980) with In re White, 158 Cal.Rptr. 562 (Cal.Ct.App.1979).

Set forth below is a proposal for what the authors describe as a "new paradigm" in the structuring and operations of probation. As you read this proposal, consider its tenability and soundness and identify what other or different steps you would propose to enhance the cost-effectiveness of this criminal sanction.

FRANCIS T. CULLEN, JOHN E. ECK, & CHRISTOPHER T. LOWENKAMP, ENVIRONMENTAL CORRECTIONS— A NEW PARADIGM FOR EFFECTIVE PROBATION AND PAROLE SUPERVISION

66 Federal Probation 28 (Sept. 2002). Reprinted with the permission of Federal Probation.

* * *

The Need to Reinvent Community Supervision

At present, American criminologists hold two incompatible views of probation and parole. First, most criminologists—representing a liberal or progressive position—see community supervision as the lesser of two evils: at least it is better than incarceration! There is no agenda as to how probation and parole might be accomplished more effectively. Rather, value inheres in community supervision only—or mainly—because it is not prison. In this scenario, prisons are depicted as costly and inhumane. They are seen as causing crime in two ways: by making those placed behind bars more criminogenic and by so disrupting communities—especially minority communities that lose high percentages of young males to incarceration—as to exacerbate crime's root causes (e.g., increase institutional disorganization). * * *

Second, a minority of criminologists—representing a conservative position—sees community supervision as an evil. John DiIulio is perhaps most noted for warning about the risks of failing to incarcerate offenders. For DiIulio, probation and premature parole are dangerous policies that allow not only petty offenders but also chronic and potentially violent offenders to continue their criminality. * * *

* * *

Where, then, do these various considerations leave us? First, in contrast to the desires of conservative commentators, the stubborn reality is that most offenders will not be incarcerated but will be placed under community supervision. And among those who are locked up, a high proportion will reenter society in a reasonably short period of time—and perhaps more criminogenic than they were before being imprisoned. Second, in contrast to the implicitly rosy portrait that liberals often paint of the criminally wayward, many of these offenders placed in the community will be occasional, if not high-rate, offenders. In short, we are left with the inescapable necessity of supervising many potentially active, if not dangerous, offenders in the community.

In this light, it is odd how little liberal commentators have had to say about the "technology" of offender supervision—that is, how to do it more effectively. They have remained silent for 30 years on methods of improving community-based supervision. In part, this silence represents a larger rejection of the social welfare role in corrections and the belief that the two sides of the probation/parole officer role—treatment and control—are in inherent conflict and render officers ineffective in their efforts to improve offenders. * * *

In contrast, beginning in the 1980s, conservative commentators had much to say about how to "reform" community supervision: purge it of its social welfare functions and increase its policing and deterrence functions. We will revisit this matter soon, but we will give advance notice that this prescription has been detrimental to the practice of community supervision. It is a failed model.

* * *[T]he purpose of the current paper is to suggest a new paradigm or strategy for improving the community supervision of offenders. * * * In developing a different paradigm or way of thinking for probation and parole, we hope to provide advice where liberals have offered none and provide better advice than that furnished by conservatives.

The main premise of this enterprise is that effective correctional intervention must be based on effective criminological research and theory. * * *

* * *

Crime in the Making—Propensity and Opportunity

For a criminal event to occur, two ingredients must converge in time and space: first, there must be a "motivated offender"—a person who has the propensity to commit the criminal act. Second, the person harboring a criminal propensity must have the opportunity to commit a crime. This simple idea—that the recipe for making a criminal act is propensity and opportunity—holds potentially profound and complex implications for how to reduce crime. These implications have seldom been systematically or scientifically explored within corrections.

What Works with Propensity

Following the publication of Robert Martinson's (1974) classic review of research suggesting that treatment programs had "no appreciable effect" on recidivism, it became widely believed that "nothing works" in corrections. Fortunately, this position is no longer tenable. Research from available meta-analysis is now incontrovertible that correctional intervention programs—especially in the community—reduce recidivism. These programs are especially effective in reducing reoffending when they are consistent with certain principles of effective intervention. Such principles include: 1) using cognitive-behavioral interventions within the context of multi-modal programs; 2) targeting for change the known predictors of recidivism; 3) focusing on higher-risk offenders; 4) applying a sufficient dosage of treatment; and 5) providing appropriate aftercare.

* * *

What Does Not Work with Opportunity

From the beginning period in which community supervision was invented, it was understood that "supervision" involved both trying to change offenders for the better and acting as an external source of control that, backed up by the threat of revocation, tried to keep offenders away from "trouble." When placed in the community, offenders often were given lists of "conditions" that spelled out the kind of situations they must avoid, including, for example, not frequenting bars, not having contact with criminal associates, and not carrying a weapon. There were also prescriptions of what offenders could do, such as staying employed and attending school. Embedded within these probation and parole "conditions" was the assumption that "going straight" was facilitated by offenders avoiding situations where opportunities for crime were present and frequenting situations where opportunities for crime were absent. Unfortunately, this core insight was never fully developed to its logical conclusion: the idea that a fundamental goal of community supervision was to plan systematically with each offender on how precisely to reduce his or her opportunities for wayward conduct.

* * * [O]pportunity reduction involves, among other factors, problem solving—that is, figuring out how to keep offenders away from situations in which trouble inheres. This approach requires, fundamentally, changing the nature of supervision. In contrast, efforts from the 1980s to the present to "intensively supervise" offenders—the deterrence-oriented "reform" advocated by conservatives—have sought mainly to change the amount of supervision. This strategy is akin to a police crackdown on crime in hopes of increasing the risk of detection or arrest as opposed to using police resources to solve the problems fostering neighborhood crime; even if the crackdown works for a specific period or for specific offenders, the effects tend to wear off over time because the underlying problems are not addressed. In any event, whether the literature involves narrative reviews, meta-analyses, or randomized experimental evaluations, the results are clear in showing that deterrence-oriented intensive supervision simply does not reduce recidivism. * * *

The weakness in the intensive supervision approach—the "pee 'em and see 'em" model as some officers call it—is that it is based on a crude understanding of crime. Efforts to specifically deter offenders through uncertain and distant threats of punishment are notoriously ineffective. It may seem like good "common sense" that more intense monitoring would increase the deterrent capacity of community supervision. But its effects are diminished by two factors: it does not do much to change the underlying propensity to offend and it does not do much to change the structure of opportunities that induce "motivated offenders" to recidivate.

In short, the two key ingredients to making crime—propensity and opportunity—are not transformed by increasing the amount of supervision. A new theory of supervision is needed—one that shows how to change the nature of supervision. * * *

* * *

A New Paradigm for Correctional Supervision

Probation and Parole Officers as Problem Solvers

Recidivism is due to offenders' retaining criminogenic motivation or propensity and their having access to opportunities for crime. Thus, to reduce reoffending, an important task for a probation or parole agency is to provide or place offenders into treatment programs, based on the principles of effective rehabilitation, that diminish their propensity for crime. The other task, however, is for probation and parole officers to reduce offenders' access to crime opportunities. In many agencies, this challenge will involve reconceptualizing the very nature of what offender supervision entails.

* * *

In this context, we are proposing that probation and parole officers reconceptualize their supervision function as involving not only watching and busting offenders but also problem solving. The key problem to solve, of course, is how to reduce offenders' access to criminal opportunities. * * *

* * *

Working with Offenders. * * * [O]fficers would focus on three tasks. First, with individual supervisees, they would try to disrupt routine activities that increase crime opportunities. As opposed to broad supervision conditions, such as "not associating with known felons," officers would seek to prohibit contact with specific people (e.g., past co-offenders), traveling on specific streets (e.g., outlined on a map given to offenders), and access to specific establishments (e.g., bars where trouble often ensues). Second, behavioral change involves not only extinguishing inappropriate conduct, but also replacing it with preferred alternatives. Officers thus might work with offenders to develop daily "activity calendars" scheduling prosocial activities. This process might involve officers "brokering" prosocial activities—that is, developing rosters of "things to do" in the community or at home to lead offenders away from crime opportunities. Third, officers would see themselves not exclusively as "enforcing supervision conditions" but as handlers of offenders. Although the threat of revocation—a formal sanction—would necessarily loom in the background, the goal would be to exercise informal social control over offenders. This would entail using positive reinforcements for prosocial routine activities and building a "bond" with offenders. * * *

Working with Family Members and the Community. Ideally, officers would also attempt to enlist an offender's family, prosocial friends, and community members (e.g., minister, teacher) to assist in designing an opportunity reduction plan. * * * One strategy would be to have a "problem-solving conference" in which offenders and those in their intimate circle would jointly identify problematic routines and places and decide how these might be avoided. * * *

* * *

[A] new paradigm—a new way of thinking—is needed to replace the failed paradigm that, in large part, has tried to use scare tactics to keep offenders away from crime opportunities. The purpose of this paper has been to sketch the components of this new approach to community supervision—a paradigm that we have called environmental corrections.

* * *

We recognize that translating theory into practice is fraught with a host of difficulties, not the least of which is that our ideas on reducing crime opportunities are likely to be labor intensive. In practical terms, this approach is likely to be cost effective primarily with high-risk offenders, who already often receive more intensive supervision. * * *

QUESTIONS AND POINTS FOR DISCUSSION

1. Note one of the central premises of the preceding article—that criminal sanctions should be structured and continually refined to reflect research findings on "what works" and "what doesn't work" in corrections. As a practical matter, what steps can be taken so that the policymakers authorizing the imposition of particular criminal sanctions are well-informed about their relative efficacy or inefficacy? What steps can be taken so that corrections professionals are well-informed about the effectiveness of the varied ways in which to implement those sanctions and of different treatment modalities? For additional information on intensive supervision probation, see Betsy Fulton et al., The State of ISP: Research and Policy Implications, 61 Fed. Probation 65 (Dec. 1997); Michael Tonry, Sentencing Matters 114–17 (1996).

2. As 18 U.S.C. § 3563 demonstrates, many of the sanctions that are discussed subsequently in this chapter, such as fines, restitution, community service, and home confinement, can be included as conditions of an offender's probation. Probation also can be combined with an incarcerative sanction when a defendant is sentenced. When what is known as a "split sentence" is imposed on a defendant, the defendant is sentenced to prison or jail for a specified period of time, to be followed by a period of probation.

Another hybrid sanction is known as "shock incarceration." In a shock-incarceration program, which usually is called a boot camp, an offender is subjected to a short, but intensive, incarceration program. The program generally has military-type features—a highly structured regimen, strict discipline, physical exercise, hard labor, and drills and ceremonies. What has been described as the "in your face" approach that typifies boot-camp programs is reflected in the following introduction of boot-camp participants to one such program:

> You are nothing and nobody, fools, maggots, dummies, motherf____ s___, and you have just walked into the worst nightmare you ever dreamed. I don't like you. I have no use for you, and I don't give a f___ who you are on the street. This is my acre, hell's half acre, and it matters not one damn to me whether you make it here or get tossed out into the general prison population, where, I promise you, you won't last three minutes before you're somebody's wife. Do you know what that means, tough guys?

Doris Layton MacKenzie & Claire Souryal, A "Machiavellian" Perspective on the Development of Boot Camp Prisons: A Debate, 2 U.Chi.L. Sch. Roundtable 435, 447 (1995). If an offender successfully completes a boot-camp program, which usually lasts three to six months, the offender will be resentenced to probation and avoid confinement in prison.

Researchers have concluded that boot camps generally do not result in lower recidivism compared to other sanctions, whether community penalties or incarceration. Nat'l Inst. of Just., U.S. Dep't of Justice, Correctional Boot Camps: Lessons from a Decade of Research 4, 7 (2003); Doris Layton MacKenzie et al., Effects of Correctional Boot Camps on Offending, 578 Annals Am. Acad. Pol. & Soc. Sci. 126, 137–39 (2001). Evaluation studies have suggested several reasons for the lack of success of boot camps in affecting participants' criminal behavior. These reasons include the brevity of the programs, the absence of treatment services in many boot-camp programs, and the failure to afford participants the programming and support that will facilitate their successful reentry into society following their graduation from a boot-camp program. Can you postulate any other reasons why these programs might be unsuccessful in reducing recidivism? For more information on shock-incarceration programs, see Doris L. MacKenzie & Gaylene S. Armstrong, Correctional Boot Camps: Basic Training or a Model for Corrections? (2004).

2.   DAY REPORTING CENTERS

As an independent sanction or as a condition of probation, offenders may be sentenced to a day reporting center (DRC), which is also sometimes called a "day incarceration center." During the parts of the day that offenders are at a day reporting center, they may have to participate in programs designed to redress some of the problems that may have contributed to their criminal behavior. For example, offenders who dropped out of school may have to go to classes and work towards obtaining a GED. Alternatively or in addition, offenders may have to undergo vocational training, participate in counseling or other treatment programs, and get tested for signs of drug or alcohol use.

During designated parts of the day, offenders may leave the DRC to work, attend school, or participate in other treatment programs, or they may be sent into the community to perform public-service work. The offenders usually must complete daily itineraries apprising DRC staff where they will be when they are not at the day reporting center. The staff members then confirm the offenders' whereabouts by periodically placing calls to them throughout the day. In some jurisdictions, the individuals placed in day reporting programs are legally classified as inmates, leading to a heightened number of contacts each day between the individuals and DRC staff. For examples of the array of day reporting centers in the country, see Sudipto Roy & Jennifer N. Grimes, Adult Offenders in a Day Reporting Center—A Preliminary Study, 66 Fed. Probation 44, 44–45 (June 2002); 1 Dale G. Parent et al., U.S. Dep't of Justice, Day Reporting Centers (1995).

3. HOME CONFINEMENT AND ELECTRONIC MONITORING

In the search for intermediate sanctions falling between the extremes of standard probation and incarceration, government officials have increasingly turned to a sanction known as home confinement. As the name of the sanction suggests, offenders sentenced to home confinement must remain in their homes or apartments at certain times. The conditions of their home confinement, however, may vary. For example, offenders may be required to be in their homes only a few designated hours a day, or they may have to stay in their homes up to twenty-four hours a day. Probation officers, police officers, and other individuals may monitor offenders' compliance with their home-confinement sentences through visits or phone calls to their homes, or electronic monitoring devices (EMDs) can be used to ensure that offenders are in their homes when they are supposed to be.

In developing standards to govern the use of home confinement, with or without electronic monitoring, as a criminal sanction, policymakers, judges, and others have had to grapple with a number of questions, including the following:

1. Which offenders should be subject to these sanctions? Should only offenders who would otherwise be sentenced to prison or jail be confined in their homes? Should only offenders convicted of nonviolent crimes be sentenced to home confinement?

2. Under what circumstances should offenders sentenced to home confinement be permitted to leave their homes? Should the yard of an offender's home be considered part of the home into which he or she can venture? If so, what should be done about offenders who have no homes and are confined in their apartments?

3. How long should home-confinement sentences be?

4. Should offenders sentenced to home confinement be required to pay fees to defray the expenses of EMDs? If so, how should the fees be calculated?

How would you resolve these questions?

A variety of EMDs have been developed to assist in the enforcement of the home-confinement sanction, and new innovations are constantly being placed on the market. With one type of device, involving what is called programmed contact, a computer is programmed to periodically call offenders at their homes or elsewhere. The offenders do not know when these calls will be made. When called, the offenders must confirm their presence in the home or other place, such as the workplace, where they are authorized to be, either by placing a wristlet they are required to wear in a verifier box attached to the phone, through a voice-verification process, through visual confirmation if a visual telephone is being used, or through other means.

Another type of EMD uses a radio transmitter worn by the offender. This radio transmitter continually sends a signal to a receiving device in the home, which in turn apprises a central computer of the offender's presence in the home. If an offender leaves the home at a time when he or she is not authorized to do so or attempts to tamper with or remove the device, the central computer alerts officials, who then can investigate the offender's whereabouts. Hybrid electronic monitoring systems also have been developed which utilize both programmed contacts and radio transmitters to monitor offenders in their homes.

Some jurisdictions are also beginning to use Global Positioning System (GPS) satellite monitoring to monitor offenders' whereabouts twenty-four hours a day. GPS technology can be used to monitor an offender's presence in "inclusion zones," areas where the offender must be at prescribed times, or "exclusion zones," areas into which the offender is prohibited from entering. When an offender leaves an inclusion zone or enters an exclusion zone, the GPS can alert authorities and any victim on the notification list programmed into the system. Cecil E. Greek, Tracking Probationers in Space and Time: The Convergence of GIS and GPS Systems, 66 Fed. Probation 51 (June 2002).

EMDs can be used for purposes other than to confirm an offender's presence in the home or elsewhere. Some devices, for example, can analyze an offender's breath to determine whether the offender has, in violation of the conditions of a sentence, consumed any alcohol. After a positive reading has been verified by the monitoring computer, a probation officer can be sent to the home to administer a breathalyzer test. The technology also exists that would enable live video feeds of an offender to be funneled continuously or periodically to authorities. Another tool in the technological arsenal being developed to monitor convicted offenders more closely is a microchip that can be implanted in an offender's body, making it possible to know where the offender is at all times and even whether the offender has ingested drugs or alcohol in contravention of the court's sentencing order. Do you favor the incorporation of these emerging technologies into criminal sentences? If so, under what circumstances, and if not, why not? For additional information on electronic monitoring technology, see Isaac B. Rosenberg, Involuntary Endogenous RFID Compliance Monitoring as a Condition of Federal Supervised Release—Chips Ahoy?, 10 Yale J.L. & Tech. 331 (2008); Darren Gowen, Remote Location Monitoring—A Supervision Strategy to Enhance Risk Control, 65 Fed. Probation 38 (Sept. 2001); Tony Fabelo, U.S. Dep't of Justice, "Technocorrections": The Promises, the Uncertain Threats 2 (2000).

4. FINES

One way to punish criminal offenders is to require them to pay a fine. Constitutional questions have arisen, however, when indigent defendants sentenced to pay a fine have been jailed because of their failure to do so. In Williams v. Illinois, 399 U.S. 235, 90 S.Ct. 2018 (1970), the Supreme Court addressed one of these constitutional questions. In that case, the defendant, who had been convicted of petty theft, had been sentenced to one year in jail and to pay a $500 fine and five dollars in court costs. The defendant, however, was unable to pay the fine and court costs because he was indigent and, due to his incarceration, unemployed. In this type of situation, a state statute authorized a criminal offender's continued detention in jail until he had "worked off" his overdue fine at the rate of five dollars a day. The end result was that the defendant was required to remain in jail 101 days longer than the maximum jail sentence authorized for the crime of which he had been convicted.

The Supreme Court concluded that keeping an indigent person unable to pay a fine in jail for a period exceeding the maximum sentence that could be imposed on a nonindigent person violated the indigent defendant's right under the Fourteenth Amendment to be afforded equal protection of the law. At the same time, the Court emphasized that indigent defendants need not necessarily receive the same sentences as those who are not indigent:

> The State is not powerless to enforce judgments against those financially unable to pay a fine; indeed, a different result would amount to inverse discrimination since it would enable an indigent to avoid both the fine and imprisonment for nonpayment whereas other defendants must always suffer one or the other [penalty].

Id. at 244, 90 S.Ct. at 2024.

The Supreme Court found *Williams* to be controlling in the later case of Tate v. Short, 401 U.S. 395, 91 S.Ct. 668 (1971). That case involved a defendant who had been fined for a series of traffic offenses, none of which were punishable by incarceration. He too was unable to pay the fines because of his indigency, so he was sentenced to a prison farm to "work off" the fines at the rate of five dollars a day. The Court held that the defendant had been discriminated against, in violation of the Equal Protection Clause, when he received a sentence exceeding the maximum penalty for the traffic offenses and imposed on him "solely because of his indigency." Id. at 398, 91 S.Ct. at 670.

In Bearden v. Georgia, 461 U.S. 660, 103 S.Ct. 2064 (1983), the case which follows, the Supreme Court once again explored the effect that indigency constitutionally can have on the criminal sanction imposed on a defendant.

BEARDEN v. GEORGIA

Supreme Court of the United States, 1983.
461 U.S. 660, 103 S.Ct. 2064, 76 L.Ed.2d 221.

JUSTICE O'CONNOR delivered the opinion of the Court.

The question in this case is whether the Fourteenth Amendment prohibits a State from revoking an indigent defendant's probation for failure to pay a fine and restitution. * * *

In September 1980, petitioner was indicted for the felonies of burglary and theft by receiving stolen property. He pleaded guilty, and was sentenced on October 8, 1980. Pursuant to the Georgia First Offender's Act, the trial court did not enter a judgment of guilt, but deferred further proceedings and sentenced petitioner to three years on probation for the burglary charge and a concurrent one year on probation for the theft charge. As a condition of probation, the trial court ordered petitioner to pay a $500 fine and $250 in restitution. Petitioner was to pay $100 that day, $100 the next day, and the $550 balance within four months.

Petitioner borrowed money from his parents and paid the first $200. About a month later, however, petitioner was laid off from his job. Petitioner, who has only a ninth-grade education and cannot read, tried repeatedly to find other work but was unable to do so. The record indicates that petitioner had no income or assets during this period.

Shortly before the balance of the fine and restitution came due in February 1981, petitioner notified the probation office he was going to be late with his payment because he could not find a job. In May 1981, the State filed a petition in the trial court to revoke petitioner's probation because he had not paid the balance. After an evidentiary hearing, the trial court revoked probation for failure to pay the balance of the fine and restitution, entered a conviction, and sentenced petitioner to serve the remaining portion of the probationary period in prison. * * *

* * *

The question presented here is whether a sentencing court can revoke a defendant's probation for failure to pay the imposed fine and restitution, absent evidence and findings that the defendant was somehow responsible for the failure or that alternative forms of punishment were inadequate. The parties, following the framework of *Williams* [*v. Illinois*] and *Tate* [*v. Short*], have argued the question primarily in terms of equal protection, and debate vigorously whether strict scrutiny or rational basis is the appropriate standard of review. There is no doubt that the State has treated the petitioner differently from a person who did not fail to pay the imposed fine and therefore did not violate probation. To determine whether this differential treatment violates the Equal Protection Clause, one must determine whether, and under what circumstances, a defendant's indigent status may be considered in the decision whether to revoke probation. This is substantially similar to asking directly the due process question of whether and when it is fundamentally unfair or arbitrary for the State to revoke probation when an indigent is unable to pay the fine. Whether analyzed in terms of equal protection or due process,[8] the issue cannot be resolved by resort to easy slogans or pigeonhole analysis, but rather requires a careful inquiry into such factors as "the nature of the individual interest affected, the extent to which it is affected, the rationality of the connection between legislative means and purpose, [and] the existence of alternative means for effectuating the purpose...."

* * *

The rule of *Williams* and *Tate* is that the State cannot " 'impos[e] a fine as a sentence and then automatically conver[t] it into a jail term solely because the defendant is indigent and cannot forthwith pay the fine in full.' " In other words, if the State determines a fine or restitution to be the appropriate and adequate penalty for the crime, it may not thereafter imprison a person solely because he lacked the resources to pay it. Both *Williams* and *Tate* carefully distinguished this substantive limitation on the imprisonment of indigents from the situation where a defendant was at fault in failing to pay the fine. * * *

This distinction, based on the reasons for nonpayment, is of critical importance here. If the probationer has willfully refused to pay the fine or restitution when he has the means to pay, the State is perfectly justified in using imprisonment as a sanction to enforce collection. Similarly, a probationer's failure to make sufficient bona fide efforts to seek employment or borrow money in order to pay the fine or restitution may reflect an insufficient concern for paying the debt he owes to society for his crime. In such a situation, the State is likewise justified in revoking probation and using imprisonment as an appropriate penalty for the offense. But if the probationer has made all reasonable efforts to pay the fine or restitution, and yet cannot do so through no fault of his own, it is fundamentally unfair to revoke probation automatically without considering whether adequate alternative methods of punishing the defendant are available. * * *

The State, of course, has a fundamental interest in appropriately punishing persons—rich and poor—who violate its criminal laws. A defendant's poverty in no way immunizes him from punishment. * * *

---

8. A due process approach has the advantage in this context of directly confronting the intertwined question of the role that a defendant's financial background can play in determining an appropriate sentence. When the court is initially considering what sentence to impose, a defendant's level of financial resources is a point on a spectrum rather than a classification. Since indigency in this context is a relative term rather than a classification, fitting "the problem of this case into an equal protection framework is a task too Procrustean to be rationally accomplished." The more appropriate question is whether consideration of a defendant's financial background in setting or resetting a sentence is so arbitrary or unfair as to be a denial of due process.

The decision to place the defendant on probation, however, reflects a determination by the sentencing court that the State's penological interests do not require imprisonment. A probationer's failure to make reasonable efforts to repay his debt to society may indicate that this original determination needs reevaluation, and imprisonment may now be required to satisfy the State's interests. But a probationer who has made sufficient bona fide efforts to pay his fine and restitution, and who has complied with the other conditions of probation, has demonstrated a willingness to pay his debt to society and an ability to conform his conduct to social norms. The State nevertheless asserts three reasons why imprisonment is required to further its penal goals.

First, the State argues that revoking probation furthers its interest in ensuring that restitution be paid to the victims of crime. A rule that imprisonment may befall the probationer who fails to make sufficient bona fide efforts to pay restitution may indeed spur probationers to try hard to pay, thereby increasing the number of probationers who make restitution. Such a goal is fully served, however, by revoking probation only for persons who have not made sufficient bona fide efforts to pay. Revoking the probation of someone who through no fault of his own is unable to make restitution will not make restitution suddenly forthcoming. Indeed, such a policy may have the perverse effect of inducing the probationer to use illegal means to acquire funds to pay in order to avoid revocation.

Second, the State asserts that its interest in rehabilitating the probationer and protecting society requires it to remove him from the temptation of committing other crimes. This is no more than a naked assertion that a probationer's poverty by itself indicates he may commit crimes in the future and thus that society needs for him to be incapacitated. * * * This would be little more than punishing a person for his poverty.

Third, and most plausibly, the State argues that its interests in punishing the lawbreaker and deterring others from criminal behavior require it to revoke probation for failure to pay a fine or restitution. The State clearly has an interest in punishment and deterrence, but this interest can often be served fully by alternative means. * * * For example, the sentencing court could extend the time for making payments, or reduce the fine, or direct that the probationer perform some form of labor or public service in lieu of the fine. * * *

We hold, therefore, that in revocation proceedings for failure to pay a fine or restitution, a sentencing court must inquire into the reasons for the failure to pay. If the probationer willfully refused to pay or failed to make sufficient bona fide efforts legally to acquire the resources to pay, the court may revoke probation and sentence the defendant to imprisonment within the authorized range of its sentencing authority. If the probationer could not pay despite sufficient bona fide efforts to acquire the resources to do so, the court must consider alternative measures of punishment other than imprisonment. Only if alternative measures are not adequate to meet the State's interests in punishment and deterrence may the court imprison a probationer who has made sufficient bona fide efforts to pay. To do otherwise would deprive the probationer of his conditional freedom simply because, through no fault of his own, he cannot pay the fine. Such a deprivation would be contrary to the fundamental fairness required by the Fourteenth Amendment.[12]

* * *

JUSTICE WHITE, with whom THE CHIEF JUSTICE, JUSTICE POWELL, and JUSTICE REHNQUIST join, concurring in the judgment.

* * *

Poverty does not insulate those who break the law from punishment. When probation is revoked for failure to pay a fine, I find nothing in the Constitution to prevent the trial court from revoking probation and imposing a term of imprisonment if revocation does not automatically result in the imposition of a long jail term and if the sentencing court makes a good-faith effort to impose a jail sentence that in terms of the State's sentencing objectives will be roughly equivalent to the fine and restitution that the defendant failed to pay.

The Court holds, however, that if a probationer cannot pay the fine for reasons not of his own fault, the sentencing court must at least consider alternative measures of punishment other than imprisonment, and may imprison the probationer only if the alternative measures are deemed inadequate to meet the State's interests in punishment and deterrence. There is no support in our cases or, in my view, the Constitution, for this novel requirement.

* * *

In this case, in view of the long prison term imposed, the state court obviously did not find that the sentence was "a rational and necessary trade-off to punish the individual who possesse[d] no accumulated assets." Accordingly, I concur in the judgment.

QUESTIONS AND POINTS FOR DISCUSSION

1. Assume that a defendant is convicted of a crime for which the maximum penalty is six months in jail and/or a $500 fine. The court sentences the defendant under this statute to either pay a $300 fine or spend 30 days in jail. If the sentence remains in effect, the defendant will have to go to jail because he has no resources with which to pay the fine. Is the sentence valid?

---

12. As our holding makes clear, we agree with Justice White that poverty does not insulate a criminal defendant from punishment or necessarily prevent revocation of his probation for inability to pay a fine. We reject as impractical, however, the approach suggested by Justice White. He would require a "good-faith effort" by the sentencing court to impose a term of imprisonment that is "roughly equivalent" to the fine and restitution that the defendant failed to pay. Even putting to one side the question of judicial "good faith," we perceive no meaningful standard by which a sentencing or reviewing court could assess whether a given prison sentence has an equivalent sting to the original fine.

What if the judge, aware of the defendant's indigency and inability to pay the fine, simply imposes the 30–day jail sentence? Is there any constitutional basis for challenging this sentence?

2. In Black v. Romano, 471 U.S. 606, 105 S.Ct. 2254 (1985), the Supreme Court considered whether, in all cases in which a defendant's probation is revoked, the court must state on the record that there are no sentencing alternatives, other than incarceration, that would meet the government's penological objectives. The Court held that although *Bearden v. Georgia* indicated that such a statement is needed when the failure to comply with a condition of probation is due to the probationer's indigency, due process normally does not require such a statement. The Court explained its conclusion:

> We do not question the desirability of considering possible alternatives to imprisonment before probation is revoked. Nonetheless, incarceration for violation of a probation condition is not constitutionally limited to circumstances where that sanction represents the only means of promoting the State's interest in punishment and deterrence. The decision to revoke probation is generally predictive and subjective in nature, and the fairness guaranteed by due process does not require a reviewing court to second-guess the factfinder's discretionary decision as to the appropriate sanction. * * * We believe that a general requirement that the factfinder elaborate upon the reasons for a course not taken would unduly burden the revocation proceeding without significantly advancing the interests of the probationer.

Id. at 613, 105 S.Ct. at 2258.

The Court in *Black* emphasized that one reason why probationers would not benefit that much from a specific statement that other sentencing alternatives had been found unsatisfactory is because of the number of procedural safeguards that already must attend probation-revocation proceedings. See Gagnon v. Scarpelli, 411 U.S. 778, 93 S.Ct. 1756 (1973), infra page 378. When probation is revoked, for example, probationers are entitled to a written statement outlining the evidence relied on in revoking their probation and the reasons for the revocation decision. This procedural safeguard as well as others, according to the Court, will adequately protect probationers from unfounded probation revocations.

Even if a finding that incarceration is the only appropriate response to a probation violation is not constitutionally required before a probationer can be confined in prison or jail for the violation, should a legislature require such a court finding? Why or why not?

————

In a thought-provoking report on the results of a study conducted for the National Institute of Justice, researchers Sally Hillsman, Barry Mahoney, and Joyce Sichel discussed the potential that fines have as a meaningful form of punishment, even for defendants who are poor. Set forth below are some excerpts from this study, whose findings still have relevance today.

SALLY T. HILLSMAN, JOYCE L. SICHEL, & BARRY MAHONEY, FINES IN SENTENCING: A STUDY OF THE USE OF THE FINE AS A CRIMINAL SANCTION (EXECUTIVE SUMMARY)

National Institute of Justice (1984).*

* * *

There is a striking contrast between American and Western European theory with respect to the use of the fine as a criminal sentence. In the United States during most of the twentieth century, scholarly thought and legislative policy have tended to discourage broad use of the fine, except for minor offenses and crimes involving pecuniary gain. * * * [F]ines have not become recognized as an effective form of punishment or as a potential alternative to incarceration. Sentencing statutes passed by American states in recent years have generally attempted to establish longer prison terms and provide for mandatory minimum periods of incarceration, but have seldom sought to increase fine ceilings, strengthen fine enforcement practices, or address the difficult problem of imposing meaningful (and enforceable) monetary sanctions upon offenders with limited means. Even when monetary penalties have been written into law, they have usually been intended for use as supplements to other sentences, and the emphasis has been more on restitution than on fines.

By contrast, legislators and other policymakers in Britain, Sweden, and West Germany have taken a more affirmative stance with respect to the use of fines as criminal penalties. Broad use of fines has become explicit national policy in these countries, with the express aim of reducing reliance upon short-term custodial sentences. About two-thirds of all offenders sentenced for crimes against a person in West Germany are fined, as are about half of all such offenders in England and Sweden. The fine is the sentence of choice for most criminal offenses and the primary alternative to short-term incarceration in the criminal justice systems of each of these countries. * * *

The emphasis upon use of the fine in Western Europe springs from a clear objective of sentencing policy: punishment of the offender. Fines are regarded as "unequivocally *punitive*." It is also thought that they may have some deterrent value and that they are less likely to produce harmful effects on subsequent behavior than is a jail or prison sentence.

* * *

Most criminal court defendants are poor, but some are not. The heart of the problem, with respect to the use of the fine as a sanction, is how to set fine amounts at a level which will reflect the seriousness of an offense yet also be within the ability of the offender to pay. Courts vary widely in

---

* Points of view or opinions expressed in the study are those of the authors and do not necessarily represent the official position or policies of the U.S. Department of Justice.

how they deal with this problem. One approach is to use a kind of "tariff" system. The judges who follow this approach make sentencing judgments more or less across the board for defendants convicted of particular offenses, after developing a presumption about their "typical" defendants' degree of poverty and the fine amount most are likely to be able to pay. Similar offenses result in fines of similar amounts and little or no inquiry is made into the financial situation of individual defendants. For instance, the presumption among many New York City judges seems to be that few defendants have money to pay fines and that almost no one will be able to pay a substantial fine. Therefore, they limit the amounts of most of the fines they impose in Criminal Court and seldom use fines at all in felony cases. In contrast, some courts visited in Georgia use fines extensively in felony cases. They tend to assume that defendants, however poor, will be able to pay substantial fines and to make restitution payments as well, if given the duration of a probation sentence to pay and pressure from probation officers to do so. Only when default occurs do they seem to consider seriously the offender's actual ability to pay.

At the other end of the spectrum, some judges inquire carefully into the economic situations of convicted defendants for whom a fine is a possible sentence. This approach is consistent with the ability-to-pay concept that has been incorporated into many state statutes. For example, New Jersey's statutes provide that:

> In determining the amount and method of payment of a fine, the court shall consider the financial resources of the defendant and the nature of the burden that its payment will impose (New Jersey Revised Statutes, 2C–44–2).

This statutory directive is followed by judges who ask offenders questions about the reality of their day-to-day living. For example, one judge in the Newark Municipal Court typically asks defendants such questions as: "Do you have a car? Do you buy gas? Do you smoke?"

Many of the judges interviewed during this study, when asked how they determined whether a defendant would be likely to pay a fine, tended to talk about a "feel" for the individual defendant's financial condition based on whether he was working, his age, his personal appearance, and his address of residence. Some of them would ask the defendant what he could afford (sometimes directly and sometimes through the defense attorney) and would then tailor the fine to that amount. And when court papers showed that a defendant failed to raise even a low bail, judges sometimes used this information as a basis for setting a low fine. Especially if the offense was minor and the fine set was relatively small, judges appeared to be comfortable with these "soft data." When they were contemplating a high fine or restitution in a more major case, they would be more likely to rely on presentence reports prepared by probation staffs.

The principal problem with a tariff system is that its impacts upon defendants convicted of similar offenses can be grossly inequitable. Some poverty-stricken defendants are fined more than they can possibly pay, while some relatively affluent defendants are given fines that are meaningless as punishment. Both results undermine the fine's effectiveness as a sanction. But an approach centered on the defendant's ability to pay also has conceptual and practical difficulties. If poor defendants are given very low fines (and no other punishment), there is a risk that the public will perceive such sentences as unduly lenient. On the other hand, if a judge's inquiry into the defendant's ability to pay indicates that the defendant is seriously impoverished, the sentencing decision may be jail instead of a fine.

Data from Western European countries, as well as our own findings on the rather widespread use of fines in American courts, suggest that in fact the poor *are* being fined in many courts. Moreover, there is evidence that a high proportion of these offenders—on both sides of the Atlantic— are paying their fines. It seems apparent that some degree of poverty does not necessarily preclude imposition of a fine or payment of it, but there is an obvious need to develop effective ways of tailoring fines to both the seriousness of the offense and the financial circumstances of the offender.

* * *

The "day-fine" is a Swedish innovation which is now also firmly entrenched in West German sentencing practice. It is designed to enable a sentencing judge to impose a level of punishment which is commensurate to the seriousness of the offense and the prior record of the offender, while at the same time taking account of his or her poverty or affluence.

In a day-fine system, the amount of the fine is established in two stages. The first involves setting of the number of units of punishment to be imposed, taking account of the seriousness of the offense (and perhaps the defendant's prior history, too), but without regard to the means of the offender. In the second stage, the monetary value of each unit of punishment is set in light of information about the offender's financial circumstances. Thus, at least theoretically, the degree of punishment should be in proportion to the gravity of the offense, and roughly equivalent (in terms of severity of impact on the individual) across defendants of differing means.

* * *

In West Germany, the day-fine system was adopted at about the same time that legislation was enacted providing that custodial terms of less than six months were to be replaced by fines or probation in all but exceptional cases. Together, these innovations appear to have produced significant changes in sentencing patterns. * * * [M]ore than 113,000 sentences to custodial terms of less than six months were imposed by West German courts in 1968, the year before the legislation was passed. By 1976, this number had dropped to less than 11,000 (1.8% of all sentences). During the same period, the proportion of fine sentences rose from 63% of the total to 83%.

* * *

QUESTIONS AND POINTS FOR DISCUSSION

1.   Do you agree that day fines will have a "roughly equivalent" impact on the offenders on whom they are imposed? Would a fine equal to one week's salary have a "roughly equivalent" effect on a person of Bill Gates's means and a person employed as a hotel maid? For additional information on day fines, see Bureau of Justice Assistance, U.S. Dep't of Justice, How to Use Structured Fines (Day Fines) as an Intermediate Sanction (1996).

2.   Fines continue to be the preferred criminal sanction in Germany, with fines imposed in more than 80% of the cases in which offenders are convicted. Bernd–Dieter Meier, Alternatives to Imprisonment in the German Criminal Justice System, 16 Fed. Sent. R. 222, 224 (2004). Even when offenders are sentenced to imprisonment in Germany, their prison sentences are suspended in two thirds of the cases. Id. These policies account, in part, for the low incarceration rate in Germany compared to the rate in the United States. Id. at 222 (reporting an incarceration rate of 73.7 per every 100,000 inhabitants in Germany in 2002 compared to an incarceration rate of 701 in the United States).

Other countries, in addition to those highlighted in the NIJ study, have employed fines widely as criminal sanctions. See Hans–Jörg Albrecht, Post–Adjudication Dispositions in Comparative Perspective, in Sentencing and Corrections in Western Countries 306–14 (Michael Tonry & Richard S. Frase eds., 2001) (discussing "major role" of fines in sentencing structures through-out Western Europe). For example, in the Netherlands, fines are presumed under the law to be the most appropriate penalty, and when judges impose a different sanction, they must explain why they did not impose a fine. Peter J. Tak, Sentencing and Punishment in The Netherlands, in Sentencing and Corrections in Western Countries, supra, at 161.

3.   For a discussion of the constraints the Eighth Amendment places on the imposition of fines and the forfeiture of property—a type of "in-kind fine," see note 2 on page 352.

5. RESTITUTION, FEES, AND DENIAL OF GOVERNMENT BENEFITS

A restitution order, like a fine, imposes a financial burden on a criminal offender. The difference between the two sanctions is that restitution is paid to the victim of a crime, while a fine is paid to the government. Restitution is designed to compensate the victim for at least some of the losses sustained by the victim because of the crime committed by the defendant.

Restitution, like a fine, may be the sole sanction imposed on an offender. Or the offender may be placed on probation with restitution ordered as one of the conditions of that probation. Restitution also may be ordered in conjunction with other sanctions, such as a prison sentence. Set forth below are portions of the Victim and Witness Protection Act (VWPA), 18 U.S.C. §§ 3663–64, which reflects one approach to implement-ing the restitution sanction:

18 U.S.C. § 3663. ORDER OF RESTITUTION

(a)(1)(A) The court, when sentencing a defendant convicted of [certain specified crimes] may order, in addition to or, in the case of a misdemeanor, in lieu of any other penalty authorized by law, that the defendant make restitution to any victim of such offense, or if the victim is deceased, to the victim's estate. The court may also order, if agreed to by the parties in a plea agreement, restitution to persons other than the victim of the offense.

(B)(i) The court, in determining whether to order restitution under this section, shall consider—

(I) the amount of the loss sustained by each victim as a result of the offense; and

(II) the financial resources of the defendant, the financial needs and earning ability of the defendant and the defendant's dependents, and such other factors as the court deems appropriate.

(ii) To the extent that the court determines that the complication and prolongation of the sentencing process resulting from the fashioning of an order of restitution under this section outweighs the need to provide restitution to any victims, the court may decline to make such an order.

(2) For the purposes of this section, the term "victim" means a person directly and proximately harmed as a result of the commission of an offense for which restitution may be ordered * * *.

(3) The court may also order restitution in any criminal case to the extent agreed to by the parties in a plea agreement.

(b) The order may require that such defendant—

(1) in the case of an offense resulting in damage to or loss or destruction of property of a victim of the offense—

(A) return the property to the owner of the property or someone designated by the owner; or

(B) if return of the property under subparagraph (A) is impossible, impractical, or inadequate, pay an amount equal to the greater of—

(i) the value of the property on the date of the damage, loss, or destruction, or

(ii) the value of the property on the date of sentencing, less the value (as of the date the property is returned) of any part of the property that is returned;

(2) in the case of an offense resulting in bodily injury to a victim * * *—

(A) pay an amount equal to the cost of necessary medical and related professional services and devices relating to physical, psychiatric, and psychological care, including nonmedical care and treatment rendered in accordance with a method of healing recognized by the law of the place of treatment;

(B) pay an amount equal to the cost of necessary physical and occupational therapy and rehabilitation; and

(C) reimburse the victim for income lost by such victim as a result of such offense;

(3) in the case of an offense resulting in bodily injury [that] also results in the death of a victim, pay an amount equal to the cost of necessary funeral and related services;

(4) in any case, reimburse the victim for lost income and necessary child care, transportation, and other expenses related to participation in the investigation or prosecution of the offense or attendance at proceedings related to the offense;

(5) in any case, if the victim (or if the victim is deceased, the victim's estate) consents, make restitution in services in lieu of money, or make restitution to a person or organization designated by the victim or the estate; and

(6) in the case of an offense [involving specified forms of identity theft], pay an amount equal to the value of the time reasonably spent by the victim in an attempt to remediate the intended or actual harm incurred by the victim from the offense.

(c)(1) Notwithstanding any other provision of law (but subject to the provisions of subsections (a)(1)(B)(i)(II) and (ii)), when sentencing a defendant convicted of [certain drug offenses] in which there is no identifiable victim, the court may order that the defendant make restitution in accordance with this subsection.

(2)(A) An order of restitution under this subsection shall be based on the amount of public harm caused by the offense, as determined by the court in accordance with guidelines promulgated by the United States Sentencing Commission.

(B) In no case shall the amount of restitution ordered under this subsection exceed the amount of the fine which may be ordered for the offense charged in the case.

(3) Restitution under this subsection shall be distributed as follows:

(A) 65 percent of the total amount of restitution shall be paid to the State entity designated to administer crime victim assistance in the State in which the crime occurred.

(B) 35 percent of the total amount of restitution shall be paid to the State entity designated to receive Federal substance abuse block grant funds.

(4) The court shall not make an award under this subsection if it appears likely that such award would interfere with a forfeiture under chapter 46 of this title or under the Controlled Substances Act (21 U.S.C. 801 et seq.).

(5) Notwithstanding section 3612(c) or any other provision of law, a penalty assessment under section 3013 or a fine under subchapter C of chapter 227 shall take precedence over an order of restitution under this subsection.

* * *

18 U.S.C. § 3664. PROCEDURE FOR ISSUANCE AND ENFORCEMENT OF ORDER OF RESTITUTION

(a) For orders of restitution under this title, the court shall order the probation officer to obtain and include in its presentence report, or in a separate report, as the court may direct, information sufficient for the court to exercise its discretion in fashioning a restitution order. The report shall include, to the extent practicable, a complete accounting of the losses to each victim, any restitution owed pursuant to a plea agreement, and information relating to the economic circumstances of each defendant. If the number or identity of victims cannot be reasonably ascertained, or other circumstances exist that make this requirement clearly impracticable, the probation officer shall so inform the court.

(b) The court shall disclose to both the defendant and the attorney for the Government all portions of the presentence or other report pertaining to the matters described in subsection (a) of this section.

* * *

(d)(1) Upon the request of the probation officer, but not later than 60 days prior to the date initially set for sentencing, the attorney for the Government, after consulting, to the extent practicable, with all identified victims, shall promptly provide the probation officer with a listing of the amounts subject to restitution.

(2) The probation officer shall, prior to submitting the presentence report under subsection (a), to the extent practicable—

(A) provide notice to all identified victims of—

(i) the offense or offenses of which the defendant was convicted;

(ii) the amounts subject to restitution submitted to the probation officer;

(iii) the opportunity of the victim to submit information to the probation officer concerning the amount of the victim's losses;

(iv) the scheduled date, time, and place of the sentencing hearing;

(v) the availability of a lien in favor of the victim pursuant to subsection (m)(1)(B); and

(vi) the opportunity of the victim to file with the probation officer a separate affidavit relating to the amount of the victim's losses subject to restitution; and

(B) provide the victim with an affidavit form to submit pursuant to subparagraph (A)(vi).

(3) Each defendant shall prepare and file with the probation officer an affidavit fully describing the financial resources of the defendant, including a complete listing of all assets owned or controlled by the defendant as of the date on which the defendant was arrested, the financial needs and earning ability of the defendant and the defendant's dependents, and such other information that the court requires relating to such other factors as the court deems appropriate.

(4) After reviewing the report of the probation officer, the court may require additional documentation or hear testimony. The privacy of any records filed, or testimony heard, pursuant to this section shall be maintained to the greatest extent possible, and such records may be filed or testimony heard in camera.

(5) If the victim's losses are not ascertainable by the date that is 10 days prior to sentencing, the attorney for the Government or the probation officer shall so inform the court, and the court shall set a date for the final determination of the victim's losses, not to exceed 90 days after sentencing. If the victim subsequently discovers further losses, the victim shall have 60 days after discovery of those losses in which to petition the court for an amended restitution order. Such order may be granted only upon a showing of good cause for the failure to include such losses in the initial claim for restitutionary relief.

(6) The court may refer any issue arising in connection with a proposed order of restitution to a magistrate judge or special master for proposed findings of fact and recommendations as to disposition, subject to a de novo determination of the issue by the court.

(e) Any dispute as to the proper amount or type of restitution shall be resolved by the court by the preponderance of the evidence. The burden of demonstrating the amount of the loss sustained by a victim as a result of the offense shall be on the attorney for the Government. The burden of demonstrating the financial resources of the defendant and the financial needs of the defendant's dependents, shall be on the defendant. The burden of demonstrating such other matters as the court deems appropriate shall be upon the party designated by the court as justice requires.

(f)(1)(A) In each order of restitution, the court shall order restitution to each victim in the full amount of each victim's losses as determined by the court and without consideration of the economic circumstances of the defendant.

(B) In no case shall the fact that a victim has received or is entitled to receive compensation with respect to a loss from insurance or any other source be considered in determining the amount of restitution.

(2) Upon determination of the amount of restitution owed to each victim, the court shall * * * specify in the restitution order the manner in which, and the schedule according to which, the restitution is to be paid, in consideration of—

(A) the financial resources and other assets of the defendant, including whether any of these assets are jointly controlled;

(B) projected earnings and other income of the defendant; and

(C) any financial obligations of the defendant, including obligations to dependents.

(3)(A) A restitution order may direct the defendant to make a single, lump-sum payment, partial payments at specified intervals, in-kind payments, or a combination of payments at specified intervals and in-kind payments.

(B) A restitution order may direct the defendant to make nominal periodic payments if the court finds from facts on the record that the economic circumstances of the defendant do not allow the payment of any amount of a restitution order, and do not allow for the payment of the full amount of a restitution order in the foreseeable future under any reasonable schedule of payments.

(4) An in-kind payment described in paragraph (3) may be in the form of—

(A) return of property;

(B) replacement of property; or

(C) if the victim agrees, services rendered to the victim or a person or organization other than the victim.

(g)(1) No victim shall be required to participate in any phase of a restitution order.

(2) A victim may at any time assign the victim's interest in restitution payments to the Crime Victims Fund in the Treasury without in any way impairing the obligation of the defendant to make such payments.

(h) If the court finds that more than 1 defendant has contributed to the loss of a victim, the court may make each defendant liable for payment of the full amount of restitution or may apportion liability among the defendants to reflect the level of contribution to the victim's loss and economic circumstances of each defendant.

(i) If the court finds that more than 1 victim has sustained a loss requiring restitution by a defendant, the court may provide for a different payment schedule for each victim based on the type and amount of each victim's loss and accounting for the economic circumstances of each victim. In any case in which the United States is a victim, the court shall ensure that all other victims receive full restitution before the United States receives any restitution.

(j)(1) If a victim has received compensation from insurance or any other source with respect to a loss, the court shall order that restitution be paid to the person who provided or is obligated to provide the compensation, but the restitution order shall provide that all restitution of victims required by the order be paid to the victims before any restitution is paid to such a provider of compensation.

(2) Any amount paid to a victim under an order of restitution shall be reduced by any amount later recovered as compensatory damages for the same loss by the victim in—

(A) any Federal civil proceeding; and

(B) any State civil proceeding, to the extent provided by the law of the State.

(k) A restitution order shall provide that the defendant shall notify the court and the Attorney General of any material change in the defendant's economic circumstances that might affect the defendant's ability to pay restitution. The court may also accept notification of a material change in the defendant's economic circumstances from the United States or from the victim. The Attorney General shall certify to the court that the victim or victims owed restitution by the defendant have been notified of the change in circumstances. Upon receipt of the notification, the court may, on its own motion, or the motion of any party, including the victim, adjust the payment schedule, or require immediate payment in full, as the interests of justice require.

(l) A conviction of a defendant for an offense involving the act giving rise to an order of restitution shall estop the defendant from denying the essential allegations of that offense in any subsequent Federal civil proceeding or State civil proceeding, to the extent consistent with State law, brought by the victim.

(m)(1)(A)(i) An order of restitution may be enforced by the United States in the manner provided for in subchapter C of chapter 227 and subchapter B of chapter 229 of this title; or

(ii) by all other available and reasonable means.

(B) At the request of a victim named in a restitution order, the clerk of the court shall issue an abstract of judgment certifying that a judgment has been entered in favor of such victim in the amount specified in the restitution order. Upon registering, recording, docketing, or indexing such abstract in accordance with the rules and requirements relating to judgments of the court of the State where the district court is located, the abstract of judgment shall be a lien on the property of the defendant located in such State in the same manner and to the same extent and under the same conditions as a judgment of a court of general jurisdiction in that State.

(2) An order of in-kind restitution in the form of services shall be enforced by the probation officer.

(n) If a person obligated to provide restitution, or pay a fine, receives substantial resources from any source, including inheritance, settlement, or other judgment, during a period of incarceration, such person shall be required to apply the value of such resources to any restitution or fine still owed.

* * *

QUESTIONS AND POINTS FOR DISCUSSION

1. The Mandatory Victims Restitution Act (MVRA), 18 U.S.C. § 3663A, mandates the payment of restitution to victims of certain crimes, such as violent crimes. Do you favor mandatory restitution? Why or why not?

2. The Seventh Amendment to the United States Constitution provides in part that "[i]n suits at common law, where the value in controversy shall exceed twenty dollars, the right of trial by jury shall be preserved. * * *" Some defendants have challenged the constitutionality of the federal restitution statutes on the grounds that they violate this right to a jury trial. The lower courts generally have rejected these claims, holding that the statutes exact a criminal penalty and not a civil one, even though the penalty is paid to the victim. See United States v. Dubose, 146 F.3d 1141, 1148 (9th Cir.1998) (listing cases); United States v. Rochester, 898 F.2d 971, 982 (5th Cir.1990) (convicted offender ordered to pay over seven million dollars in restitution under the VWPA had no right to a jury trial on the amount of restitution owed). See also Kelly v. Robinson, 479 U.S. 36, 52–53, 107 S.Ct. 353, 362–63 (1986) (restitution obligation is penal and is ordered for the state's benefit, rather than to provide "compensation for actual pecuniary loss" within the meaning of the bankruptcy statute, and the obligation therefore is not dischargeable in a bankruptcy proceeding).

3. Assume that a defendant, who fled the state with her child in violation of a court order awarding custody to her former husband, is convicted of "childnapping" under a state statute. A probation officer states in the presentence investigation report that the husband incurred $20,000 in expenses to locate the child. This statement is based on remarks of the husband made during an interview with the probation officer. The court then places the defendant on probation for five years and orders her, as a condition of probation, to pay restitution in the amount of $20,000 to her ex-husband. Is there any basis, constitutional or otherwise, for potentially challenging this restitution order?

4. Under many restitution statutes, the defendant's financial resources and financial obligations to others may reduce or forestall a restitution award. This limitation on the amount of restitution ordered is due to a concern that unduly high restitution awards may impede offenders' rehabilitation and literally cause them to "rob Peter to pay Paul."

An alternative approach to this problem can be found in the American Bar Association Guidelines Governing Restitution to Victims of Criminal Conduct (1988). Under these guidelines, a court can order restitution in the full amount, but then stay payment of all or part of the restitution awarded. Guideline 1.5(a). If the offender's financial situation later changes, making it feasible for the offender to pay more of the restitution award, the victim then can file a motion to remove the stay. Guideline 1.11(a). For additional information on restitution mechanisms and steps to expand the use, and improve the enforcement, of this sanction, see Victims Comm., Am. Bar Ass'n, Restitution for Crime Victims: A National Strategy (2004).

5. In addition to requiring convicted offenders to pay fines and restitution, jurisdictions often levy fees and special assessments against offenders to help defray the costs of certain criminal-justice operations and correctional programs. The types of fees that offenders are required to pay are varied and include: court costs; bail-investigation fees to cover some of the costs of determining individuals' suitability for release from jail while awaiting trial; presentence-investigation-report fees; mediation fees; residential fees for offenders staying in work-release centers or other correctional facilities in the community; fees to defray the costs of a public defender or other court-appointed attorney; restitution-collection fees; substance-abuse-assessment fees for offenders evaluated for alcohol or drug problems; substance-abuse-treatment fees; urinalysis fees; driver-education fees; counseling fees; probation-supervision fees; parole-supervision fees; community-service fees; home-confinement fees; and jail fees for offenders incarcerated before or after their convictions. Fahy G. Mullaney, U.S. Dep't of Justice, Economic Sanctions in Community Corrections 3–4 (1988). Failure to coordinate the imposition of these fees can lead to financial obligations being placed on offenders that are almost impossible for them to meet. In addition, fulfilling these fee obligations may prevent offenders from meeting other court-imposed financial obligations, such as fines and restitution.

The American Bar Association has responded to these potential problems by calling for the coordination of economic sanctions and assessments. ABA Standards for Criminal Justice, Sentencing Alternatives and Procedures and

Appellate Review of Sentences, Standard 18–3.22(d) (3d ed. 1993). In addition, under the ABA standards, assessed costs and fees, unlike fines and restitution, are not considered part of the criminal sentence. Standard 18–3.22(a). The failure to pay these costs and fees therefore cannot lead to revocation proceedings. Instead, the court's assessment order must be enforced through other means, such as those utilized when enforcing a civil judgment.

6. In recent years, governments have crafted other criminal penalties that have financial repercussions on offenders, including the denial of certain government benefits. One federal statute, for example, authorizes, and in certain circumstances requires, the denial of benefits as part of the criminal sentence imposed on a drug offender. See 21 U.S.C. § 862. Some of the benefits that a convicted drug offender can lose include student loans, agricultural subsidies, housing loans, and federal contracts. The statute grants judges the discretion to include a ban on these benefits when sentencing offenders convicted of possessing or distributing a controlled substance, but the sentence must include such a ban when the defendant has been convicted of drug trafficking three or more times. The ineligibility period varies depending on whether the offender was convicted of trafficking or possession and whether, and how many times, the offender has been previously convicted of that kind of drug crime. In addition, the ban on benefits cannot include certain benefits exempted by the statute, including retirement, welfare, Social Security, health, disability, public housing, and veterans' benefits.

Convicted offenders can be barred from receiving certain government benefits even when the bar is not included as part of the criminal sentence. These and other "collateral consequences" of a conviction are discussed in Chapter 9.

6. COMMUNITY SERVICE

Requiring criminal offenders to perform certain services for the community without pay is another criminal sanction. In a sense, community service is a form of restitution. Instead of paying their debts to crime victims, however, offenders pay society as a whole for the harm caused by their crimes.

Proponents of community-service sentences tout their many advantages. Rather than sitting around in a prison or jail as so many inmates do, offenders sentenced to community-service programs are involved in productive work—planting trees, picking up litter in parks and next to roads, refurbishing public buildings, renovating neighborhoods ravaged by crime, and performing other services from which the public benefits. Community-service programs also cost much less than incarceration, and if offenders are sentenced to perform community service, they can avoid the criminogenic influences that prevail in prisons and jails. In addition, they can maintain ties with family members.

Despite these benefits, community service remains, in Professor Michael Tonry's words, "the most underused intermediate sanction in the United States." Michael Tonry, Sentencing Matters 121 (1996). One of the impediments that curbs the widespread use of this criminal sanction is that there is no central agency in many jurisdictions that is responsible for ensuring both that community-service programs are readily available as a sentencing option and that they are meeting their objectives. Even when a sentence to community service could feasibly be imposed on an offender, presentence investigators and defense attorneys often fail to apprise judges of the viability of this sentencing option. The community-service sentencing option also faces union opposition and raises concerns about liability for injuries incurred when offenders are performing community-service work. See, e.g., Arriaga v. County of Alameda, 892 P.2d 150 (1995) (person injured when performing community-service work is entitled to workers' compensation benefits). For additional information on community-service programs, see Gordon Bazemore & David R. Karp, A Civic Justice Corps: Community Service as a Means of Reintegration, 1 Just. Pol'y J. 1 (2004); Michael Tonry, Sentencing Matters 121–24 (1996).

7. IMPOSITION OF THE APPROPRIATE SENTENCE

United States District Judge John Kane expressed the views of many trial judges when he said, "I know of no more excruciating decision for a judge to make than whether to confine and, if so, for how long and under what terms and conditions." United States v. O'Driscoll, 586 F.Supp. 1486, 1486 (D.Colo.1984). Having reviewed information about some of the many sentencing options that may be available to a sentencing judge, what sentence would you impose in the two cases set forth below if you were the sentencing judge and all penalty options were available to you?[d] In addition, reconsider what the appropriate penalty would be in the cases described in note 2 on pages 16–17.

1.   Samuel E. Cole has pled guilty to two counts of Distribution of a Controlled Substance—Cocaine. Cole is twenty-six. His father is a former Marine who is presently self-employed as an insurance agent. His mother is a homemaker.

Cole has been described as having been hyperactive when growing up, but he never received medication or counseling for his hyperactivity. His academic skills were above average, but he was not interested in school and eventually dropped out of high school six months before graduation. Over the next six years, Cole worked at a variety of different jobs—as a horse groomer, salesman, construction carpenter apprentice, van and moving assistant, aluminum siding installer, and a waiter. Few of these jobs, however, appealed to him, but he did receive his G.E.D. by attending night classes during this time period.

---

d. Information about the two cases was drawn from sentencing proposals prepared by the National Center on Institutions and Alternatives (NCIA). NCIA, a private, nonprofit agency, was founded in 1977 by Dr. Jerome Miller and Herbert J. Hoeltner for the purpose of promoting the use of safe and effective alternative sanctions to prisons and jails.

Six years ago, Cole was involved in a car accident. According to Cole, the occupants of the car came up to him after the accident and began hitting him. In self-defense, he struck back, slapping one of his assailants. He was later charged with assault and battery. Though he insisted he was not guilty, Cole followed his attorney's advice and pled guilty. The court then placed Cole on what is called "Probation Before Judgment."

Three years ago, Cole began working at a restaurant where he met people who regularly used cocaine. Cole also began to use the drug two to three times a week. Eventually, his cocaine use escalated, and he began losing weight and working only sporadically. Within a few months, he was in financial trouble, and about this time, he was also arrested for drunk driving.

When a police informant contacted Cole and asked him if he knew of a cocaine dealer from whom the informant could buy cocaine, Cole bought some cocaine from a dealer and sold it to the informant three different times. One sale involved a half-ounce of cocaine, one involved one ounce, and one involved two ounces. Cole was arrested for these three drug transactions and released on his own recognizance. Since Cole's arrest ten months ago, he has worked full-time as a restaurant employee. His manager has described Cole as "one of the restaurant's best employees."

2. Nathan Forester is a 32–year–old dentist who was raised by religious and hardworking parents. His father has worked for Ford Motor Company for the last twenty-seven years, but sometimes worked two or three jobs at a time to support his family. His mother is a salesclerk in a men's clothing store.

Nathan was an above-average student and extremely athletic. He lettered in basketball, baseball, and football while in high school and played on the college baseball team.

After taking graduate courses in biology for several years, Nathan decided to become a dentist, and he acquired his D.D.S. in three years. He then entered two post-doctoral programs, one of which was in orthodontics. He also began working in two dental clinics five days a week for half-days.

The consequences of Nathan's extensive commitments soon became evident. His grades dropped, he fell behind in his research, and he could not meet deadlines. He began to feel desperate, incompetent, and depressed. It was during this time that Nathan attended the annual convention of the American Association of Orthodontists. On the first day of the convention, he felt "inexplainable anxiety" and skipped the meetings. Instead, he went and sat on a knoll near a bank. When he saw a woman enter the bank to use the automatic teller machine, he went in after her, threatened her, and then sexually assaulted her. During the assault, which was recorded on film by the bank's security camera, he was unable to have an erection.

After the assault, Nathan, who was extremely distraught, went to find one of his professors, and she accompanied him to his room. She described him as disoriented, incoherent, and suicidal. While she was in the room, he was crying and tried several times to jump out of the tenth-floor window.

Nathan was convicted of second-degree forcible rape. His dental license has been suspended, and it appears as though it soon will be revoked.

C. COMPREHENSIVE AND INTEGRATED CORRECTIONS SYSTEMS

It would seem self-evident that public safety can best be protected and correctional goals met when corrections systems within a state offer a comprehensive set of sentencing options and work in close partnership together to ensure the cost-effective sanctioning of criminal offenders. In reality, however, most corrections systems in this country are fragmented and not only fail to collaborate in the sanctioning of criminal offenders, but often work at cross-purposes. Set forth below are two proposals designed to help make corrections systems within a state more comprehensive and integrated. Former governor du Pont's article at the beginning of this chapter contains a third proposal, and a fourth, on reentry courts, can be found in chapter 9 on pages 454–57. As you review these proposals, consider how, if at all, they should be changed and what other steps can and should be taken to integrate corrections systems and diversify the sentencing and supervision options for convicted offenders.

1. COMPREHENSIVE COMMUNITY CORRECTIONS ACTS

To help ensure that the most appropriate sentence is imposed on a criminal offender, the American Bar Association has called on each state and United States territory to adopt what is known as a "comprehensive community corrections act." The ABA has prepared the following "Model Adult Community Corrections Act" to provide guidance to the states and territories as they adopt their own acts. As you review the Act, consider how, if at all, you would modify it. For information on different ways to structure a community corrections act, see M. Kay Harris, Key Differences Among Community Corrections Acts in the United States: An Overview, 76 Prison J. 192 (June 1996).

MODEL ADULT COMMUNITY CORRECTIONS ACT

Approved by the American Bar Association House of Delegates—February, 1992. Reprinted with the permission of the American Bar Association.

I. OVERVIEW

A. Goals and Objectives

   (1) To enhance public safety and achieve economies by encouraging the development and implementation of community sanctions as a sentencing option;

   (2) To enhance the value of criminal sanctions and ensure that the criminal penalties imposed are the most appropriate ones by encouraging the development of a wider array of criminal sanctions;

   (3) To increase the community's awareness of, participation in, and responsibility for the administration of the corrections system;

   (4) To ensure that the offender is punished in the least restrictive setting consistent with public safety and the gravity of the crime;

   (5) To provide offenders with education, training and treatment to enable them to become fully functional members of the community upon release from criminal justice supervision;

   (6) To make offenders accountable to the community for their criminal behavior, through community service programs, restitution programs, and a range of locally developed sanctions; and

   (7) To foster the development of policies and funding for programs that encourage jurisdictions to minimize the use of incarceration where other sanctions are appropriate.

B. Definitions

   (1) Community. Any local jurisdiction, or any combination of jurisdictions, the government(s) of which undertake(s) joint efforts and shared responsibilities for purposes of providing community corrections options in the jurisdiction(s) in accordance with the purposes and requirements of this Act.

   (2) Community Corrections. Any of a number of sanctions which are served by the offender within the community in which the offender committed the offense or in the community in which the offender resides.

   (3) Incarceration. Any sanction which involves placement of the offender in a prison, jail, boot camp, or other secure facility.

II. SANCTIONS

A. This Model Community Corrections Act provides for local implementation of the following community-based sanctions (the list is not intended to be exclusive of other community-based sanctions):

   (1) Standard probation;

   (2) Intensive supervision probation;

   (3) Community service;

(4) Home confinement with or without electronic monitoring;

(5) Electronic surveillance (including telephone monitoring);

(6) Community-based residential settings offering structure, supervision, surveillance, drug/alcohol treatment, employment counseling and/or other forms of treatment or counseling;

(7) Outpatient treatment;

(8) Requirement of employment and/or education/training;

(9) Day reporting centers;

(10) Restitution; and

(11) Means-based fines.

B. Definitions

   (1) <u>Standard Supervised Probation</u>. A judicially imposed criminal sanction permitting court supervision of the offender within the community.

   (2) <u>Intensive Supervision Probation</u>. An organized program of probation which includes a combination of conditions such as training, community service, home confinement, or counseling and treatment, and is characterized by frequent and close monitoring of the offender.

   (3) <u>Community Service</u>. A program of specific work assigned to the offender which substantially benefits the community in which the offense was committed.

   (4) <u>Home Confinement</u>. A judicially or administratively imposed condition requiring an offender to remain at home for some portion of the day. There are three types of home confinement:

     (a) <u>Curfew</u>. A type of home confinement requiring the offender to be home during established hours;

     (b) <u>Home Detention</u>. A type of home confinement requiring offenders to remain at home except during periods of work or study or other permitted absence; and

     (c) <u>Home Incarceration</u>. A type of home confinement requiring the offender to remain at home at virtually all times.

   (5) <u>Electronic Surveillance</u>. A means of utilizing telephonic or telemetry technology to monitor the presence or absence of an individual at a particular location from a remote location.

   (6) <u>Community-based residential settings offering structure, supervision, surveillance, drug/alcohol treatment, employment counseling and/or other forms of treatment or counseling</u>. A program of organized treatment or counseling designed to assist the offender in overcoming any psychological and/or physical conditions which may have contributed to his or her prior criminal behavior while also providing structure, supervision and/or surveillance.

   (7) <u>Outpatient Treatment</u>. This option is identical to subsection (6) above with the exception that such treatment would be offered on an outpatient basis.

   (8) <u>Requirement of Employment and/or Education/Training</u>. A judicially imposed requirement that the offender remain employed

or participate in an educational training course as a condition of his or her sentence.

(9) Day Reporting Centers. A center where an offender serving a community-based sentence in a community corrections setting would be required to report as a condition of his or her sentence.

(10) Restitution. Reparation by the offender for personal or property damages incurred by the victim as a result of the offense.

(11) Means-based Fines. A monetary sanction imposed on an offender which is proportional to the crime(s) committed and the offender's ability to pay within a reasonable period of time.

III. STATE CRIMINAL JUSTICE COUNCIL

A. The Community Corrections Act shall be administered by a State Criminal Justice Council that has oversight responsibility for state criminal justice policies and programs. The Council shall be responsible for ensuring that policies and activities undertaken by state or local governmental units or other organizations in furtherance of the purposes of the Act are consistent with those purposes and with the statewide community corrections plan required under Section III(D)(1) of this Act.

B. Not later than 90 days after the effective date of this Act, the governor shall appoint, and the legislature shall confirm, the 15 members of the Council as follows:

(1) One member shall be a county sheriff;

(2) One member shall be a chief of a city police department;

(3) One member shall be a judge of a general jurisdiction trial court;

(4) One member shall be a judge from an appellate level court;

(5) One member shall be a county commissioner or county board head;

(6) One member shall be a city government official;

(7) One member shall represent an existing community corrections program;

(8) One member shall be the director of the department of corrections or his or her designee;

(9) One member shall be a county prosecutor;

(10) One member shall be a criminal defense attorney;

(11) One member shall be the head of a probation department; and

(12) Four members shall be representatives of the general public.

C. The governor shall ensure that there is a fair geographic representation on the State board and that minorities and women are fairly represented.

D. The Council shall:

(1) Develop a plan for statewide implementation of the Act that incorporates the purposes and objectives of the Act; ensures consistency of community corrections programs and requirements with other applicable State laws and regulations; and establishes goals, criteria, timetables, and incentives for initiation of community corrections programs;

(2) Establish standards and guidelines for community development of plans to implement the Act in local jurisdictions, as described in Section IV of this Act;

(3) Review initial community plans, require revisions as necessary, and monitor implementation of approved plans to ensure consistency with the statewide plan;

(4) Award, administer, and monitor grants, loans, or other State funding mechanisms that the State Legislature establishes for assisting communities in implementing their community corrections plans, as provided in Section VI of this Act;

(5) Review community plans and their implementation at least annually to ensure consistency with the statewide plan and require modification of plans as necessary to ensure compliance with the objectives of this Act;

(6) Evaluate annually the effectiveness of policies and programs carried out under the Act and report to the Legislature on evaluation findings;

(7) Monitor and evaluate the effect of the Act's implementation on offenders of different races;

(8) Take steps to ensure that the community corrections program is adequately funded by the Legislature;

(9) Provide technical assistance and training to provide community corrections services in local jurisdictions;

(10) Provide guidance to local Community Corrections Boards, as defined in Section IV(A) of the Act, in educating the public concerning the purposes of the Act, the types of programs and activities to be undertaken under the Act, the possible impacts of the Act on local jurisdictions, and other matters that may assist the local Boards in establishing and carrying out their community corrections programs;

(11) Maintain records on the number of offenders who met the eligibility criteria in Section V(A)(1)(a) through V(A)(1)(c) but who were incarcerated;

(12) Monitor the results of appeals of offenders who met the eligibility criteria in Section V(A)(1)(a) through V(A)(1)(c) but who were incarcerated;

(13) Assess user fees against communities that incarcerate eligible offenders based on the per-inmate incarceration cost formula described in Section VI(C)(1); and

(14) Hire an executive director, who shall serve at the pleasure of the Council.

E. The Legislature shall appropriate such funds as are necessary for the Council to carry out its responsibilities under the Act, including funds to hire an executive director and necessary staff to implement the program. Appropriations shall be provided in a way and an amount to ensure program continuity and stability.

COMMENTARY

* * *

Although some states currently operate community corrections programs through established entities, such as probation and parole departments or departments of corrections, the objectives of a community corrections program are broader, and in some instances different from those of other criminal justice departments or agencies in a state. An entity that is separate from those departments or agencies would therefore generally be most able to coordinate implementation of a community corrections program among all affected departments and agencies. In addition, a Criminal Justice Council would be able to handle funding administration, training and education, local program oversight, and other responsibilities that often would not fall within the purview of other departments or agencies, but that are essential to the operation of a successful community corrections program.

It is possible, however, that in some states, existing bodies might be able to assume the implementation, administrative, coordinating, and oversight functions for a statewide community corrections program. Minnesota and Oregon, for example, administer community corrections programs through their Departments of Corrections. Oregon's community corrections program is actually a hybrid model. It allows for varying levels of local participation, ranging from local administration of all community corrections sanctions and supervision programs to centralized state administration of those sanctions and programs with local advisory input.

* * *

IV. COMMUNITY CORRECTIONS BOARDS

A. Every city and county in the State shall establish a community corrections program by applying individually or as part of a grouping designated as a "community," as defined in Section I of this Act, to participate in programs and activities, including grant and other financial assistance programs, authorized by this Act and the state-wide plan described in Section III(D)(1) of this Act.

B. Each community shall establish a local Community Corrections Board that shall be responsible for developing and implementing a community corrections plan for the community (including locating suitable sites for community correctional programs). Each Board shall be comprised, at minimum, of representatives of the following categories:

(1) Local prosecutor;

(2) Local public defender;

(3) Local member of the criminal defense bar;

(4) Local judges from limited and general jurisdiction courts including courts with jurisdiction over criminal matters;

(5) Local law enforcement official;

(6) Local corrections official;

    (7) Local representative from the probation department;

    (8) Local government representative;

    (9) Local health, education, and human services representatives;

    (10) Nonprofit community corrections services provider; and

    (11) Three or more representatives of the general public.

C. Each community shall ensure that minorities and women are fairly represented on the Community Corrections Board.

D. In accordance with such rules, regulations, or other policies as the State Council establishes under Section III(D) of this Act, each Board shall develop a comprehensive community corrections plan that, consistent with the objectives and requirements of the Act:

    (1) Offers programs for the placement of offenders in the community rather than in correctional institutions; specifies the type(s) and scope of community-based sentencing options to be offered and the type(s) of offenders to be included in the program; describes the community's capacity to carry out the specified community-based sanction; and identifies the means by which the Board intends to provide the sentencing option;

    (2) Addresses projected program costs and identifies sources of funds, including grants, loans, or other financial assistance available through the Council, to meet those costs;

    (3) Provides for monitoring and annual reporting of program results to the Council;

    (4) Provides for annual review of the plan and for its revision, as necessary or desirable;

    (5) Includes a commitment to carry out the plan in cooperation and coordination with other governmental entities and to conduct the program in a manner designed to ensure public safety and the program's efficacy;

    (6) Addresses the need for involvement and education of the community regarding the purposes and objectives of the Act generally and the local community corrections program specifically; and

    (7) Identifies the extent to which its plan will affect the number of individuals who are incarcerated.

E. Each Board shall submit its plan to the State Council for review. An approved plan shall serve as the basis for subsequent Board activity and for the Council's determination of the extent of funding assistance to be provided for community corrections in that Board's community.

V. PROGRAM CRITERIA

A. Offender Eligibility

    (1) The following offender groups shall be eligible for sentencing to community-based sanctions:

        (a) misdemeanants;

        (b) nonviolent felony offenders, including drug abusers and other offenders with special treatment needs;

        (c) parole, probation, and community corrections condition violators whose violation conduct is either non-criminal or would meet either criterion (a) or (b) above had it been charged as a criminal violation;

(d) offenders who, although not eligible under criteria (a) through (c) above, are found by the court to be the type of individuals for whom such a sentence would serve the goals of this Act. In making such a determination, the judge shall consider factors that bear on the danger posed and likelihood of recidivism by the offender, including but not limited to the following:

   (i) that the offender has a sponsor in the community;

   (ii) that the offender either has procured employment or has enrolled in an educational or rehabilitative program; and

   (iii) that the offender has not demonstrated a pattern of violent behavior and does not have a criminal record that indicates a pattern of violent offenses.

VI. FUNDING MECHANISM

A. Eligibility: A community will apply for State funding by submitting a community corrections plan to the State Criminal Justice Council. The plan will provide information on a community's demonstrated need for community corrections. The plan also will establish program criteria consistent with this Act. Once the Council has approved a proposed corrections plan, that community will be eligible to receive a grant payment for part of the plan's cost.

B. Funding

   (1) Communities will be allocated grant funds to ensure program continuity and stability.

   (2) To allocate funds appropriated by the State to implement the Community Corrections Act, the Council will equitably apportion funds to communities.

   (3) The Council will redetermine periodically each community's appropriate level of funding, taking into account the community's proven commitment to the implementation of this Act.

   (4) The funds provided under this Act shall not supplant current spending by the local jurisdiction for any existing community corrections program.

[C. Chargeback Provision

   (1) Commencing two years after the approval of a community's corrections plan, the Criminal Justice Council will charge each community a user fee equivalent to 75 percent of the per-inmate cost of incarceration for each offender who has met the eligibility criteria in Sections V(A)(1)(a) through V(A)(1)(c) but who has been either:

   (a) Committed to a State correctional facility by a sentencing authority in the community; or

   (b) Committed by a sentencing authority in the community to a county or regional jail facility.

(2) The amount charged to a community under this Section shall not exceed the amount of financial aid received under Section VI(B).]

D. Audit: Every two years, the state's general auditor will audit all community financial reports related to Community Corrections Act projects.

E. Continual Grant Funding: To receive aid, communities must comply with the requirements established by this Act and the standards promulgated by the State Criminal Justice Council under it. A community corrections program will be evaluated two years after the approval of the community's correction plan and every year thereafter.

F. Notice: If a community fails to meet the standards of the Act, the Council shall notify the community that it has 60 days to comply or funding will be discontinued. The community shall have the opportunity to respond within 30 days after receipt of such notice.

COMMENTARY

* * *

The chargeback provisions of Section VI(C) are a means of encouraging the development and use of community-based sanctions and of further ensuring that an offender for whom a community-based sanction or sanctions is appropriate will be so sentenced. The figure of 75% of the cost of incarceration as a charge to a community that fails to use community-based sanctions for eligible offenders is high enough to provide communities with a substantial incentive to punish those offenders within the community. The actual amount of the fee would be calculated by multiplying 75% of the cost of incarcerating the inmate in a correctional institution by the length of the incarcerative sentence imposed. The fee would not be assessed against the community if, because of the results of an appeal, an offender sentenced to a period of incarceration is not actually incarcerated.

The chargeback provision provides communities with an incentive to develop and implement effective community corrections programs. The potentially harsh effect of the provision is ameliorated by the limit on the amount that may be charged back to the community under Section VI(C)(2). In addition, the chargeback provision does not apply until after communities have had time to develop their community corrections programs.

Some jurisdictions, notably Oregon, have avoided the use of a chargeback provision by adopting sentencing guidelines to ensure that community-based sanctions are imposed on offenders who fall within the target population. Sentencing guidelines that govern the imposition of community-based sanctions can help ensure their appropriate use while avoiding the criticism often leveled at chargeback provisions that they penalize city and county governments for decisions made by judges over whom they have little or no control. * * * If those guidelines include community-based sanctions, as is recommended by Section VII(D)(1) of this Act, reliance on the chargeback provisions of Section VI(C) would be unnecessary, which is why that section has been placed in brackets.

VII. SENTENCING DETERMINATIONS

A. Presentence Report

    (1) All presentence reports shall be required to specifically address whether a community-based sanction is a viable sentencing option.

B. Judicial Sentencing Statement

    (1) The sentencing judge must consider the community-based sanctions set out in this statute before sentencing any eligible offender as defined in Section V(A).

    (2) Where the judge has decided that a community-based sanction is inappropriate, the judge must state on the record at the time of sentencing that the court considered community correction sentencing options and must explain why such sentencing options were rejected.

C. Appellate Review

    (1) All individuals sentenced under this State's criminal statutes shall have a right of review of their sentence for conformity with the provisions of this Act, provided that such grounds for appeal are raised on direct appeal of the conviction.

D. Relationship Between Community Corrections Sanctions and Sentencing Guidelines in Jurisdictions with Sentencing Guidelines

    (1) The [State legislature] in those jurisdictions with sentencing guidelines shall appoint a committee for the purpose of fashioning sentencing guidelines that incorporate community corrections sentences in a manner consistent with the provisions of this Act.

    (2) Under guidelines drafted pursuant to Section VII(D)(1), non-incarceration sanctions will be the presumptively appropriate sentence for offenders meeting the criteria of Section V(A)(1)(a)–V(A)(1)(c).

VIII. ENABLING PROVISION

A. Judges with jurisdiction over misdemeanors and felonies are authorized to sentence eligible offenders as defined by Section V(A)(1) of this Act.

B. Judges with jurisdiction over misdemeanors and felonies are authorized to use the sentencing options set out in Section II of this Act.

QUESTIONS AND POINTS FOR DISCUSSION

1. One of the premises of the Model Adult Community Corrections Act is that community sanctions can be punishing. This premise is supported by surveys of offenders in multiple states in which the offenders ranked certain community sanctions as more punishing than prison. Joan Petersilia, Reforming Probation and Parole in the 21st Century 71 (2002). This premise is buttressed further by research revealing that some offenders, when given the choice between serving a prison sentence or being subjected to intensive

supervision in the community, have opted for incarceration. See, e.g., id. (approximately one third of the offenders involved in a study in Oregon and who were eligible for intensive supervision probation chose instead to go to prison); Joan Petersilia, When Probation Becomes More Dreaded Than Prison, 54 Fed. Probation 23 (March 1990) (15% of prisoners in New Jersey who applied for placement in the intensive-supervision program withdrew their applications when apprised of the demands of the program).

2.   Another premise of the Model Adult Community Corrections Act is that the risks to the public safety posed by offenders in the community can be limited, though admittedly never eliminated, through an appropriately constructed comprehensive community-punishment system. Some researchers in fact have concluded that the incarceration of certain offenders actually exacerbates risks to the public safety. For example, one study conducted by the RAND Corporation found that community-based drug treatment of cocaine dealers is seven times more effective than arrest and incarceration in reducing consumption of cocaine and fifteen times more effective in reducing the "social costs" of cocaine use—crime and lost productivity. C. Peter Rydell & Susan S. Everingham, Controlling Cocaine: Supply Versus Demand Programs xvi (1994).

These research findings have prompted voters in a few states, including California, to approve initiatives requiring community-based drug treatment in lieu of incarceration for certain drug offenders. See Judith Greene & Vincent Schiraldi, Justice Policy Inst., Cutting Correctly: New Prison Policies for Times of Fiscal Crisis 13 (2002). Many other jurisdictions have established "drug courts" for the processing of certain drug cases. Defendants charged with drug-related crimes who are eligible for drug court must adhere to a strict treatment regimen that typically includes meetings every week or even every day with treatment providers, urinalysis tests at least once a week, and frequent status hearings where the drug-court judge reviews the offender's progress and modulates the constraints to which the offender is subject based on that progress. If the offender successfully completes the treatment program, the criminal charges, in many jurisdictions, are dismissed.

Although some of the many evaluations of drug courts have been marked by methodological problems, most of the evaluations have concluded that the courts reduce recidivism. U.S. Gov't Accountability Office, Adult Drug Courts: Evidence Indicates Recidivism Reductions and Mixed Results for Other Outcomes 44–56 (2005). Besides recidivism reduction, what other outcome measures and factors would you consider when deciding whether to integrate drug courts into sentencing and corrections systems? See id. at 57–71.

Drawing upon the drug-court model, jurisdictions are establishing, with increasing frequency, other specialized courts with a treatment and problem-solving orientation. Mental-health courts, through which offenders with mental illnesses can be processed, are a notable example. For an overview of mental-health courts and recommendations to improve their operations, see Robert Bernstein & Tammy Seltzer, Criminalization of People with Mental Illnesses: The Role of Mental Health Courts in System Reform, 7 U.D.C.L. Rev. 143 (2002). For additional information on drug courts, see Drug Courts Program Office, U.S. Dep't of Justice, Looking at a Decade of Drug Courts

(1999); Drug Courts Program Office, U.S. Dep't of Justice, Defining Drug Courts: The Key Components (1997).

3. One of the particularly critical features of the Model Adult Community Corrections Act is its requirement that a broad array of criminal-justice officials be involved, at both the state and local levels, in the development and implementation of comprehensive community corrections plans. Researchers and officials have found that without such broad participation in the development of community corrections policies, community corrections programs are much more likely to fail. See, e.g., Bureau of Justice Assistance, U.S. Dep't of Justice, Critical Elements in the Planning, Development, and Implementation of Successful Correctional Options 5–6 (1998); Joan Petersilia, Conditions that Permit Intensive Supervision Programs to Survive, 36 Crime & Delinquency 126, 138 (Jan. 1990).

4. One of the primary responsibilities of the local community corrections boards established under the Model Adult Community Corrections Act is to educate the public about community-based sanctions—about what they are; about their costs compared to those of incarceration; about how punishing, if necessary, they can be; about how they can be structured to reduce, though not eliminate, risks to the public safety; and about the possibility that incarcerating nonviolent offenders may jeopardize the safety of the public by increasing recidivism rates. Studies have shown that when members of the public are informed about community sanctions, their support for them shifts dramatically. For example, in a study in Alabama, 422 adults were told about twenty-three hypothetical offenders whose crimes ranged from shoplifting, selling drugs, drunk driving, burglary, and embezzlement to rape and armed robbery. When first given the choice of either sentencing the offenders to prison or probation, the respondents opted to incarcerate the offenders in eighteen of the twenty-three cases. When later instructed about five other sentencing options—"strict probation," which entailed meeting with a probation officer up to five times a week for up to two years; strict probation plus restitution; strict probation combined with community service; house arrest for up to one year; and boot camp for three to six months—the respondents chose imprisonment in only four of the cases. Significantly, many of the offenders for whom the respondents preferred an alternative sanction had been convicted of quite serious crimes, including embezzling $250,000, dealing drugs for a third time, and committing an unarmed burglary for the second time. See John Doble & Josh Klein, Punishing Criminals: The Public's View—An Alabama Survey (1989). See also John Doble et al., Punishing Criminals: The People of Delaware Consider the Options (1991) (findings of the Alabama study essentially replicated). Obviously, the kinds of details shared with the public about standard probation, intermediate sanctions, and incarceration, including their relative costs and impact on recidivism, may affect the public's level of support for the imposition of a particular community sanction in lieu of incarceration. Francis T. Cullen et al., Public Opinion About Punishment and Corrections, 27 Crime & Just. 1, 43–45 (2000).

2. INCORPORATING COMMUNITY SANCTIONS INTO SENTENCING GUIDELINES

The need for a continuum of sanctions—a wide range of criminal sanctions of differing severity—was discussed in the beginning of this chapter. But with community-based sanctions, as with penalties involving incarceration, there is a concern about inequitable treatment of criminal offenders—a concern that the ad hoc exercise of discretion by sentencing judges will lead to the imposition of much more onerous community-based sanctions on some criminal offenders than on others who are similarly situated. A monograph written by Professor Michael Tonry, excerpts of which are set forth below, discusses some ways of structuring a comprehensive sentencing system to address this concern and limit disparity in the imposition of community-based sanctions.

MICHAEL TONRY, INTERMEDIATE SANCTIONS IN SENTENCING GUIDELINES

National Institute of Justice (1997).*

* * *

Incorporation of intermediate sanctions into sentencing guidelines is in its earliest days. There are, nonetheless, a number of techniques that have been developed and ideas that have been examined.

* * *

Zones of Discretion

Most guidelines commissions that have tried to expand their guidelines' coverage to include nonconfinement sentences have altered the traditional guidelines format to include more zones of discretion. The first guidelines in Minnesota, Pennsylvania, and Washington divided their grids into two zones. One contained confinement cells setting presumptive ranges for prison sentences, and the other contained nonconfinement cells that gave the judge unfettered discretion to impose any other sentence, often including an option of jail sentences of up to one year. Minnesota's guidelines, for example, contained a bold black line that separated the confinement and nonconfinement zones.

New North Carolina, revised Pennsylvania, and proposed Massachusetts guidelines, by contrast, have four or more zones. The details vary but they follow a common pattern. Sentences other than those authorized by the applicable zone are departures for which reasons must be given which are subject to review on appeal. One zone contains cells in which only prison sentences are presumed appropriate. A second might contain cells

* This document was originally published in 1997 by the National Institute of Justice, U.S. Department of Justice, Washington, D.C. Points of view or opinions expressed in the publication are those of the author and do not necessarily represent the official position or policies of the U.S. Department of Justice.

in which judges may choose between restrictive intermediate sanctions, such as residential drug treatment, house arrest with electronic monitoring, and a day-reporting center, and a prison sentence up to a designated length. A third might contain cells in which judges may choose among restrictive intermediate punishments. A fourth might authorize judges to choose between restrictive intermediate sanctions and a less restrictive penalty like community service or standard probation. A fifth might authorize sentencing choices only among less restrictive community penalties.

Punishment Units

A second approach that Oregon adopted and several other States considered is to express punishment in generic "punishment units" into which all sanctions can be converted. A hypothetical system might provide, for example, for the following conversion values:

- One year's confinement　　　　　　　　100 units
- One year's partial confinement　　　　　50 units
- One year's house arrest　　　　　　　　50 units
- One year's standard probation　　　　　20 units
- 25 days' community service　　　　　　50 units
- 30 days' intensive supervision　　　　　5 units
- 90 days' income (day fines)　　　　　　100 units
- 30 days' electronic monitoring　　　　　5 units

That is by no means a complete list; such things as drug testing, treatment conditions, and restitution might or might not be added. The values could be divided or multiplied to obtain values for other periods (for example, 75 days' confinement equals 20 units).

If guidelines, for example, set "120 punishment units" as the presumptive sentence for a particular offender, a judge could impose any combination of sanctions that represented 120 units. One year's confinement (100 units) plus 60 subsequent days' intensive supervision (10 units) on electronic monitoring (10 units) would be appropriate. So would a 90-unit day fine (100 units) plus one year's standard probation (20 units). So would 25 days' community service (50 units) and six months' intensive supervision (30 units), followed by two years' standard probation (40 units).

In practice, the punishment unit approach has proven too complicated to be workable.

* * *

Exchange Rates

Another approach is simply to specify equivalent custodial and noncustodial penalties and to authorize judges to impose them in the alternative. Washington's commission did this in a modest way and later proposed a more extensive system, which the legislature did not adopt.

Partial confinement and community service were initially authorized as substitutes for presumptive prison terms on the basis of 1 day's partial confinement or 3 days' community service for 1 day of confinement. The partial confinement/confinement exchange is probably workable (for short sentences; house arrest, assuming that to count as partial confinement, is seldom imposed for more than a few months), but the community service exchange rate is not.

* * *

The difficulty is that community service programs, to be credible, must be enforced, and experience in this country and elsewhere instructs that they must be short. That is why the best-known American program in New York set 70 hours as a standard, and the national policies in England and Wales, Scotland, and the Netherlands set 240 hours as the upper limit.

* * *

Exchange rates are limited in their potential uses for the same reason punishment units are. For so long as prevailing views require that imprisonment be considered the normal punishment and that substitutes for imprisonment be comparably burdensome and intrusive, exchange rates are unlikely to play a significant role in sentencing guidelines.

* * *

Future sentencing commissions will probably develop current ideas in new ways. None of the commissions that have adopted a zones-of-discretion approach, for example, has attempted to provide guidance to judges on how to choose *among* authorized intermediate sanctions or community penalties or between intermediate sanctions and authorized confinement or community sanctions. This could easily be done by setting policies that particular kinds of sanctions are appropriate for particular kinds of offenders: an obvious example would be a policy that residential drug treatment be presumed appropriate for a drug-dependent chronic property offender. Depending on how convinced the commission was about the wisdom of the policy, it could be made presumptive (and thus require a "departure" with reasons given for any other sentence) or only advisory.

* * *

QUESTIONS AND POINTS FOR DISCUSSION

1. Do you agree that punishment units and exchange rates are not viable ways to channel judges' discretion in the imposition of community sanctions? If you developed a sentencing system utilizing exchange rates for custodial and noncustodial penalties, what exchange rates would you adopt and why?

2. For another thought-provoking discussion of sanction exchange rates, see Norval Morris & Michael Tonry, Between Prison and Probation: Intermediate Punishments in a Rational Sentencing System 37–108 (1990).

CHAPTER 6

THE DEATH PENALTY

■ ■ ■

Few criminal-justice issues have engendered as much controversy as the questions whether the death penalty can and should be imposed on certain criminal offenders. The divergent opinions on these subjects have been reflected in the decisions of the Supreme Court, which often are characterized by 5–4 holdings and a confusing mix of plurality, concurring, and dissenting opinions.

Since 1972, when the Supreme Court decided the seminal case of Furman v. Georgia, 408 U.S. 238, 92 S.Ct. 2726 (1972), the Court has been grappling constantly with questions concerning the constitutionality of the death penalty. In *Furman,* the Court held that two death-penalty statutes that left the decision whether to impose the death penalty to the unconfined discretion of the judge or jury violated the Eighth Amendment's prohibition of cruel and unusual punishment. These statutes had resulted in such arbitrary and haphazard imposition of the death penalty that, in the words of Justice White, there was "no meaningful basis for distinguishing the few cases in which it is imposed from the many cases in which it is not." Id. at 313, 92 S.Ct. at 2764 (White, J., concurring).

It was evident from *Furman* that other death-penalty statutes across the country were also unconstitutional. A number of state legislatures responded by enacting new death-penalty statutes that they hoped would pass constitutional muster. In several cases decided in 1976, one of which is set forth below, and another of which can be found on page 295, the Supreme Court considered the constitutionality of some of these statutes.

GREGG v. GEORGIA

Supreme Court of the United States, 1976.
428 U.S. 153, 96 S.Ct. 2909, 49 L.Ed.2d 859.

Judgment of the Court, and opinion of MR. JUSTICE STEWART, MR. JUSTICE POWELL, and MR. JUSTICE STEVENS, announced by MR. JUSTICE STEWART.

The issue in this case is whether the imposition of the sentence of death for the crime of murder under the law of Georgia violates the Eighth and Fourteenth Amendments.

I

The petitioner, Troy Gregg, was charged with committing armed robbery and murder. In accordance with Georgia procedure in capital cases, the trial was in two stages, a guilt stage and a sentencing stage. The evidence at the guilt trial established that on November 21, 1973, the petitioner and a traveling companion, Floyd Allen, while hitchhiking north in Florida were picked up by Fred Simmons and Bob Moore. * * * A short time later the four men interrupted their journey for a rest stop along the highway. The next morning the bodies of Simmons and Moore were discovered in a ditch nearby.

* * * The next afternoon, the petitioner and Allen, while in Simmons' car, were arrested in Asheville, N.C. * * * Allen recounted the events leading to the slayings. His version of these events was as follows: After Simmons and Moore left the car, the petitioner stated that he intended to rob them. The petitioner then took his pistol in hand and positioned himself on the car to improve his aim. As Simmons and Moore came up an embankment toward the car, the petitioner fired three shots and the two men fell near a ditch. The petitioner, at close range, then fired a shot into the head of each. He robbed them of valuables and drove away with Allen.

A medical examiner testified that Simmons died from a bullet wound in the eye and that Moore died from bullet wounds in the cheek and in the back of the head. * * * Although Allen did not testify, a police detective recounted the substance of Allen's statements about the slayings and indicated that directly after Allen had made these statements the petitioner had admitted that Allen's account was accurate. The petitioner testified in his own defense. He confirmed that Allen had made the statements described by the detective, but denied their truth or ever having admitted to their accuracy. He indicated that he had shot Simmons and Moore because of fear and in self-defense, testifying they had attacked Allen and him, one wielding a pipe and the other a knife.[1]

* * * The jury found the petitioner guilty of two counts of armed robbery and two counts of murder.

At the penalty stage, * * * [t]he trial judge instructed the jury that it could recommend either a death sentence or a life prison sentence on each count. The judge further charged the jury that in determining what sentence was appropriate the jury was free to consider the facts and circumstances, if any, presented by the parties in mitigation or aggravation.

Finally, the judge instructed the jury that it "would not be authorized to consider [imposing] the penalty of death" unless it first found beyond a reasonable doubt one of these aggravating circumstances:

---

1. On cross-examination the State introduced a letter written by the petitioner to Allen entitled, "[a] statement for you," with the instructions that Allen memorize and then burn it. The statement was consistent with the petitioner's testimony at trial.

"One—That the offense of murder was committed while the offender was engaged in the commission of two other capital felonies, to-wit the armed robbery of [Simmons and Moore].

"Two—That the offender committed the offense of murder for the purpose of receiving money and the automobile described in the indictment.

"Three—The offense of murder was outrageously and wantonly vile, horrible and inhuman, in that they [sic] involved the depravity of [the] mind of the defendant."

Finding the first and second of these circumstances, the jury returned verdicts of death on each count.

The Supreme Court of Georgia affirmed the convictions and the imposition of the death sentences for murder. * * *

* * *

III

We address initially the basic contention that the punishment of death for the crime of murder is, under all circumstances, "cruel and unusual" in violation of the Eighth and Fourteenth Amendments of the Constitution. * * *

* * *

A

* * *

[T]he Court has not confined the prohibition embodied in the Eighth Amendment to "barbarous" methods that were generally outlawed in the 18th century. Instead, the Amendment has been interpreted in a flexible and dynamic manner. The Court early recognized that "a principle to be vital must be capable of wider application than the mischief which gave it birth." Thus the Clause forbidding "cruel and unusual" punishments "is not fastened to the obsolete but may acquire meaning as public opinion becomes enlightened by a humane justice."

* * *

* * * As Mr. Chief Justice Warren said, in an oft-quoted phrase, "[t]he Amendment must draw its meaning from the evolving standards of decency that mark the progress of a maturing society." *Trop v. Dulles,* [356 U.S.] at 101 [(1958)]. Thus, an assessment of contemporary values concerning the infliction of a challenged sanction is relevant to the application of the Eighth Amendment. As we develop below more fully, this assessment does not call for a subjective judgment. It requires, rather, that we look to objective indicia that reflect the public attitude toward a given sanction.

But our cases also make clear that public perceptions of standards of decency with respect to criminal sanctions are not conclusive. A penalty also must accord with "the dignity of man," which is the "basic concept underlying the Eighth Amendment." This means, at least, that the punishment not be "excessive." When a form of punishment in the abstract (in this case, whether capital punishment may ever be imposed as a sanction for murder) rather than in the particular (the propriety of death as a penalty to be applied to a specific defendant for a specific crime) is under consideration, the inquiry into "excessiveness" has two aspects. First, the punishment must not involve the unnecessary and wanton infliction of pain. Second, the punishment must not be grossly out of proportion to the severity of the crime.

B

Of course, the requirements of the Eighth Amendment must be applied with an awareness of the limited role to be played by the courts. This does not mean that judges have no role to play, for the Eighth Amendment is a restraint upon the exercise of legislative power. * * * *[19]

But, while we have an obligation to insure that constitutional bounds are not overreached, we may not act as judges as we might as legislators. * * *

Therefore, in assessing a punishment selected by a democratically elected legislature against the constitutional measure, we presume its validity. We may not require the legislature to select the least severe penalty possible so long as the penalty selected is not cruelly inhumane or disproportionate to the crime involved. And a heavy burden rests on those who would attack the judgment of the representatives of the people.

This is true in part because the constitutional test is intertwined with an assessment of contemporary standards and the legislative judgment weighs heavily in ascertaining such standards. "[I]n a democratic society legislatures, not courts, are constituted to respond to the will and consequently the moral values of the people." * * *

C

* * * We now consider specifically whether the sentence of death for the crime of murder is a *per se* violation of the Eighth and Fourteenth Amendments to the Constitution. * * *

The imposition of the death penalty for the crime of murder has a long history of acceptance both in the United States and in England. The common-law rule imposed a mandatory death sentence on all convicted murderers. And the penalty continued to be used into the 20th century by most American States, although the breadth of the common-law rule was

---

19. Although legislative measures adopted by the people's chosen representatives provide one important means of ascertaining contemporary values, it is evident that legislative judgments alone cannot be determinative of Eighth Amendment standards since that Amendment was intended to safeguard individuals from the abuse of legislative power. * * *

diminished, initially by narrowing the class of murders to be punished by death and subsequently by widespread adoption of laws expressly granting juries the discretion to recommend mercy.

It is apparent from the text of the Constitution itself that the existence of capital punishment was accepted by the Framers. At the time the Eighth Amendment was ratified, capital punishment was a common sanction in every State. Indeed, the First Congress of the United States enacted legislation providing death as the penalty for specified crimes. The Fifth Amendment, adopted at the same time as the Eighth, contemplated the continued existence of the capital sanction by imposing certain limits on the prosecution of capital cases:

> "No person shall be held to answer for a capital, or otherwise infamous crime, unless on a presentment or indictment of a Grand Jury ...; nor shall any person be subject for the same offense to be twice put in jeopardy of life or limb; ... nor be deprived of life, liberty, or property, without due process of law...."

And the Fourteenth Amendment, adopted over three-quarters of a century later, similarly contemplates the existence of the capital sanction in providing that no State shall deprive any person of "life, liberty, or property" without due process of law.

* * *

* * * Despite the continuing debate, dating back to the 19th century, over the morality and utility of capital punishment, it is now evident that a large proportion of American society continues to regard it as an appropriate and necessary criminal sanction.

The most marked indication of society's endorsement of the death penalty for murder is the legislative response to *Furman*. The legislatures of at least 35 States have enacted new statutes that provide for the death penalty for at least some crimes that result in the death of another person. And the Congress of the United States, in 1974, enacted a statute providing the death penalty for aircraft piracy that results in death. * * *

In the only statewide referendum occurring since *Furman* and brought to our attention, the people of California adopted a constitutional amendment that authorized capital punishment, in effect negating a prior ruling by the Supreme Court of California * * * that the death penalty violated the California Constitution.[25]

The jury also is a significant and reliable objective index of contemporary values because it is so directly involved. The Court has said that "one of the most important functions any jury can perform in making ... a selection [between life imprisonment and death for a defendant convicted in a capital case] is to maintain a link between contemporary community values and the penal system." It may be true that evolving standards have influenced juries in recent decades to be more discriminating in imposing

---

25. * * * A December 1972 Gallup poll indicated that 57% of the people favored the death penalty, while a June 1973 Harris survey showed support of 59%.

the sentence of death. But the relative infrequency of jury verdicts imposing the death sentence does not indicate rejection of capital punishment *per se*. Rather, the reluctance of juries in many cases to impose the sentence may well reflect the humane feeling that this most irrevocable of sanctions should be reserved for a small number of extreme cases. Indeed, the actions of juries in many States since *Furman* are fully compatible with the legislative judgments, reflected in the new statutes, as to the continued utility and necessity of capital punishment in appropriate cases. At the close of 1974 at least 254 persons had been sentenced to death since *Furman,* and by the end of March 1976, more than 460 persons were subject to death sentences.

As we have seen, however, the Eighth Amendment demands more than that a challenged punishment be acceptable to contemporary society. The Court also must ask whether it comports with the basic concept of human dignity at the core of the Amendment. Although we cannot "invalidate a category of penalties because we deem less severe penalties adequate to serve the ends of penology," the sanction imposed cannot be so totally without penological justification that it results in the gratuitous infliction of suffering.

The death penalty is said to serve two principal social purposes: retribution and deterrence of capital crimes by prospective offenders.[28]

In part, capital punishment is an expression of society's moral outrage at particularly offensive conduct. This function may be unappealing to many, but it is essential in an ordered society that asks its citizens to rely on legal processes rather than self-help to vindicate their wrongs. * * * "Retribution is no longer the dominant objective of the criminal law," but neither is it a forbidden objective nor one inconsistent with our respect for the dignity of men.[30] * * *

Statistical attempts to evaluate the worth of the death penalty as a deterrent to crimes by potential offenders have occasioned a great deal of debate. The results simply have been inconclusive. As one opponent of capital punishment has said:

> "[A]fter all possible inquiry, including the probing of all possible methods of inquiry, we do not know, and for systematic and easily visible reasons cannot know, what the truth about this 'deterrent' effect may be. . . .

---

28. Another purpose that has been discussed is the incapacitation of dangerous criminals and the consequent prevention of crimes that they may otherwise commit in the future.

30. Lord Justice Denning, Master of the Rolls of the Court of Appeal in England, spoke to this effect before the British Royal Commission on Capital Punishment:

"Punishment is the way in which society expresses its denunciation of wrong doing: and, in order to maintain respect for law, it is essential that the punishment inflicted for grave crimes should adequately reflect the revulsion felt by the great majority of citizens for them. It is a mistake to consider the objects of punishment as being deterrent or reformative or preventive and nothing else. . . . The truth is that some crimes are so outrageous that society insists on adequate punishment, because the wrong-doer deserves it, irrespective of whether it is a deterrent or not." Royal Commission on Capital Punishment, Minutes of Evidence, Dec. 1, 1949, p. 207 (1950).

"The inescapable flaw is . . . that social conditions in any state are not constant through time, and that social conditions are not the same in any two states. If an effect were observed (and the observed effects, one way or another, are not large) then one could not at all tell whether any of this effect is attributable to the presence or absence of capital punishment. A 'scientific'—that is to say, a soundly based—conclusion is simply impossible, and no methodological path out of this tangle suggests itself." C. Black, Capital Punishment: The Inevitability of Caprice and Mistake 25–26 (1974).

Although some of the studies suggest that the death penalty may not function as a significantly greater deterrent than lesser penalties, there is no convincing empirical evidence either supporting or refuting this view. We may nevertheless assume safely that there are murderers, such as those who act in passion, for whom the threat of death has little or no deterrent effect. But for many others, the death penalty undoubtedly is a significant deterrent. There are carefully contemplated murders, such as murder for hire, where the possible penalty of death may well enter into the cold calculus that precedes the decision to act. And there are some categories of murder, such as murder by a life prisoner, where other sanctions may not be adequate.

The value of capital punishment as a deterrent of crime is a complex factual issue the resolution of which properly rests with the legislatures. * * *

In sum, we cannot say that the judgment of the Georgia Legislature that capital punishment may be necessary in some cases is clearly wrong. Considerations of federalism, as well as respect for the ability of a legislature to evaluate, in terms of its particular State, the moral consensus concerning the death penalty and its social utility as a sanction, require us to conclude, in the absence of more convincing evidence, that the infliction of death as a punishment for murder is not without justification and thus is not unconstitutionally severe.

Finally, we must consider whether the punishment of death is disproportionate in relation to the crime for which it is imposed. There is no question that death as a punishment is unique in its severity and irrevocability. * * * But we are concerned here only with the imposition of capital punishment for the crime of murder, and when a life has been taken deliberately by the offender, we cannot say that the punishment is invariably disproportionate to the crime. * * *

We hold that the death penalty is not a form of punishment that may never be imposed, regardless of the circumstances of the offense, regardless of the character of the offender, and regardless of the procedure followed in reaching the decision to impose it.

IV

* * *

Furman mandates that where discretion is afforded a sentencing body on a matter so grave as the determination of whether a human life should be taken or spared, that discretion must be suitably directed and limited so as to minimize the risk of wholly arbitrary and capricious action.

* * *

While some have suggested that standards to guide a capital jury's sentencing deliberations are impossible to formulate, the fact is that such standards have been developed * * *.[44] While such standards are by necessity somewhat general, they do provide guidance to the sentencing authority and thereby reduce the likelihood that it will impose a sentence that fairly can be called capricious or arbitrary. Where the sentencing authority is required to specify the factors it relied upon in reaching its decision, the further safeguard of meaningful appellate review is available to ensure that death sentences are not imposed capriciously or in a freakish manner.

In summary, the concerns expressed in *Furman* that the penalty of death not be imposed in an arbitrary or capricious manner can be met by

---

44. The Model Penal Code proposes the following standards:

"(3) Aggravating Circumstances.

"(a) The murder was committed by a convict under sentence of imprisonment.

"(b) The defendant was previously convicted of another murder or of a felony involving the use or threat of violence to the person.

"(c) At the time the murder was committed the defendant also committed another murder.

"(d) The defendant knowingly created a great risk of death to many persons.

"(e) The murder was committed while the defendant was engaged or was an accomplice in the commission of, or an attempt to commit, or flight after committing or attempting to commit robbery, rape or deviate sexual intercourse by force or threat of force, arson, burglary or kidnapping.

"(f) The murder was committed for the purpose of avoiding or preventing a lawful arrest or effecting an escape from lawful custody.

"(g) The murder was committed for pecuniary gain.

"(h) The murder was especially heinous, atrocious or cruel, manifesting exceptional depravity.

"(4) Mitigating Circumstances.

"(a) The defendant has no significant history of prior criminal activity.

"(b) The murder was committed while the defendant was under the influence of extreme mental or emotional disturbance.

"(c) The victim was a participant in the defendant's homicidal conduct or consented to the homicidal act.

"(d) The murder was committed under circumstances which the defendant believed to provide a moral justification or extenuation for his conduct.

"(e) The defendant was an accomplice in a murder committed by another person and his participation in the homicidal act was relatively minor.

"(f) The defendant acted under duress or under the domination of another person.

"(g) At the time of the murder, the capacity of the defendant to appreciate the criminality [wrongfulness] of his conduct or to conform his conduct to the requirements of law was impaired as a result of mental disease or defect or intoxication.

"(h) The youth of the defendant at the time of the crime." ALI Model Penal Code § 210.6 (Proposed Official Draft 1962).

a carefully drafted statute that ensures that the sentencing authority is given adequate information and guidance.[46] * * *

* * *

We now turn to consideration of the constitutionality of Georgia's capital-sentencing procedures. In the wake of *Furman,* Georgia amended its capital punishment statute. * * *

Georgia did act * * * to narrow the class of murderers subject to capital punishment by specifying 10 statutory aggravating circumstances, one of which must be found by the jury to exist beyond a reasonable doubt before a death sentence can ever be imposed. In addition, the jury is authorized to consider any other appropriate aggravating or mitigating circumstances. The jury is not required to find any mitigating circumstance in order to make a recommendation of mercy that is binding on the trial court, but it must find a *statutory* aggravating circumstance before recommending a sentence of death.

These procedures require the jury to consider the circumstances of the crime and the criminal before it recommends sentence. No longer can a Georgia jury do as Furman's jury did: reach a finding of the defendant's guilt and then, without guidance or direction, decide whether he should live or die. Instead, the jury's attention is directed to the specific circumstances of the crime: Was it committed in the course of another capital felony? Was it committed for money? Was it committed upon a peace officer or judicial officer? Was it committed in a particularly heinous way or in a manner that endangered the lives of many persons? In addition, the jury's attention is focused on the characteristics of the person who committed the crime: Does he have a record of prior convictions for capital offenses? Are there any special facts about this defendant that mitigate against imposing capital punishment (*e.g.,* his youth, the extent of his cooperation with the police, his emotional state at the time of the crime). As a result, while some jury discretion still exists, "the discretion to be exercised is controlled by clear and objective standards so as to produce non-discriminatory application."

As an important additional safeguard against arbitrariness and caprice, the Georgia statutory scheme provides for automatic appeal of all death sentences to the State's Supreme Court. That court is required by statute to review each sentence of death and determine whether it was imposed under the influence of passion or prejudice, whether the evidence supports the jury's finding of a statutory aggravating circumstance, and whether the sentence is disproportionate compared to those sentences imposed in similar cases.

* * * On their face these procedures seem to satisfy the concerns of *Furman.* No longer should there be "no meaningful basis for distinguish-

---

46. A system could have standards so vague that they would fail adequately to channel the sentencing decision patterns of juries with the result that a pattern of arbitrary and capricious sentencing like that found unconstitutional in *Furman* could occur.

ing the few cases in which [the death penalty] is imposed from the many cases in which it is not."

The petitioner contends, however, that the changes in the Georgia sentencing procedures are only cosmetic, that the arbitrariness and capriciousness condemned by *Furman* continue to exist in Georgia—both in traditional practices that still remain and in the new sentencing procedures adopted in response to *Furman*.

First, the petitioner focuses on the opportunities for discretionary action that are inherent in the processing of any murder case under Georgia law. He notes that the state prosecutor has unfettered authority to select those persons whom he wishes to prosecute for a capital offense and to plea bargain with them. Further, at the trial the jury may choose to convict a defendant of a lesser included offense rather than find him guilty of a crime punishable by death, even if the evidence would support a capital verdict. And finally, a defendant who is convicted and sentenced to die may have his sentence commuted by the Governor of the State and the Georgia Board of Pardons and Paroles.

The existence of these discretionary stages is not determinative of the issues before us. At each of these stages an actor in the criminal justice system makes a decision which may remove a defendant from consideration as a candidate for the death penalty. *Furman,* in contrast, dealt with the decision to impose the death sentence on a specific individual who had been convicted of a capital offense. Nothing in any of our cases suggests that the decision to afford an individual defendant mercy violates the Constitution. *Furman* held only that, in order to minimize the risk that the death penalty would be imposed on a capriciously selected group of offenders, the decision to impose it had to be guided by standards so that the sentencing authority would focus on the particularized circumstances of the crime and the defendant.[50]

* * *

The petitioner next argues that the requirements of *Furman* are not met here because the jury has the power to decline to impose the death penalty even if it finds that one or more statutory aggravating circumstances are present in the case. * * * Since the proportionality requirement on review is intended to prevent caprice in the decision to inflict the penalty, the isolated decision of a jury to afford mercy does not render unconstitutional death sentences imposed on defendants who were sen-

---

50. The petitioner's argument is nothing more than a veiled contention that *Furman* indirectly outlawed capital punishment by placing totally unrealistic conditions on its use. In order to repair the alleged defects pointed to by the petitioner, it would be necessary to require that prosecuting authorities charge a capital offense whenever arguably there had been a capital murder and that they refuse to plea bargain with the defendant. If a jury refused to convict even though the evidence supported the charge, its verdict would have to be reversed and a verdict of guilty entered or a new trial ordered, since the discretionary act of jury nullification would not be permitted. Finally, acts of executive clemency would have to be prohibited. Such a system, of course, would be totally alien to our notions of criminal justice.

* * *

tenced under a system that does not create a substantial risk of arbitrariness or caprice.

* * *

For the reasons expressed in this opinion, we hold that the statutory system under which Gregg was sentenced to death does not violate the Constitution. * * *

* * *

MR. JUSTICE WHITE, with whom THE CHIEF JUSTICE and MR. JUSTICE REHNQUIST join, concurring in the judgment.

* * *

Petitioner * * * argues that decisions made by the prosecutor—either in negotiating a plea to some lesser offense than capital murder or in simply declining to charge capital murder—are standardless and will inexorably result in the wanton and freakish imposition of the penalty condemned by the judgment in *Furman*. I address this point separately because the cases in which no capital offense is charged escape the view of the Georgia Supreme Court and are not considered by it in determining whether a particular sentence is excessive or disproportionate.

Petitioner's argument that prosecutors behave in a standardless fashion in deciding which cases to try as capital felonies is unsupported by any facts. Petitioner simply asserts that since prosecutors have the power not to charge capital felonies they will exercise that power in a standardless fashion. This is untenable. Absent facts to the contrary, it cannot be assumed that prosecutors will be motivated in their charging decision by factors other than the strength of their case and the likelihood that a jury would impose the death penalty if it convicts. * * * Thus defendants will escape the death penalty through prosecutorial charging decisions only because the offense is not sufficiently serious; or because the proof is insufficiently strong. This does not cause the system to be standardless any more than the jury's decision to impose life imprisonment on a defendant whose crime is deemed insufficiently serious or its decision to acquit someone who is probably guilty but whose guilt is not established beyond a reasonable doubt. * * *

Petitioner's argument that there is an unconstitutional amount of discretion in the system which separates those suspects who receive the death penalty from those who receive life imprisonment, a lesser penalty, or are acquitted or never charged, seems to be in [the] final analysis an indictment of our entire system of justice. * * * Mistakes will be made and discriminations will occur which will be difficult to explain. However, one of society's most basic tasks is that of protecting the lives of its citizens and one of the most basic ways in which it achieves the task is through criminal laws against murder. I decline to interfere with the manner in which Georgia has chosen to enforce such laws on what is simply an assertion of lack of faith in the ability of the system of justice to operate in a fundamentally fair manner.

* * *

MR. JUSTICE BLACKMUN, concurring in the judgment. [Opinion omitted.]

MR. JUSTICE BRENNAN, dissenting.

* * *

The fatal constitutional infirmity in the punishment of death is that it treats "members of the human race as nonhumans, as objects to be toyed with and discarded. [It is] thus inconsistent with the fundamental premise of the Clause that even the vilest criminal remains a human being possessed of common human dignity." As such it is a penalty that "subjects the individual to a fate forbidden by the principle of civilized treatment guaranteed by the [Clause]." I therefore would hold, on that ground alone, that death is today a cruel and unusual punishment prohibited by the Clause. "Justice of this kind is obviously no less shocking than the crime itself, and the new 'official' murder, far from offering redress for the offense committed against society, adds instead a second defilement to the first."

* * *

MR. JUSTICE MARSHALL, dissenting.

* * *

Since the decision in *Furman,* the legislatures of 35 States have enacted new statutes authorizing the imposition of the death sentence for certain crimes, and Congress has enacted a law providing the death penalty for air piracy resulting in death. I would be less than candid if I did not acknowledge that these developments have a significant bearing on a realistic assessment of the moral acceptability of the death penalty to the American people. But if the constitutionality of the death penalty turns, as I have urged, on the opinion of an *informed* citizenry, then even the enactment of new death statutes cannot be viewed as conclusive. In *Furman,* I observed that the American people are largely unaware of the information critical to a judgment on the morality of the death penalty, and concluded that if they were better informed they would consider it shocking, unjust, and unacceptable. A recent study, conducted after the enactment of the post-*Furman* statutes, has confirmed that the American people know little about the death penalty, and that the opinions of an informed public would differ significantly from those of a public unaware of the consequences and effects of the death penalty.[1]

Even assuming, however, that the post-*Furman* enactment of statutes authorizing the death penalty renders the prediction of the views of an informed citizenry an uncertain basis for a constitutional decision, the

---

1. Sarat & Vidmar, Public Opinion, The Death Penalty, and the Eighth Amendment: Testing the Marshall Hypothesis, 1976 Wis.L.Rev. 171.

enactment of those statutes has no bearing whatsoever on the conclusion that the death penalty is unconstitutional because it is excessive. An excessive penalty is invalid under the Cruel and Unusual Punishments Clause "even though popular sentiment may favor" it. The inquiry here, then, is simply whether the death penalty is necessary to accomplish the legitimate legislative purposes in punishment, or whether a less severe penalty—life imprisonment—would do as well.

The two purposes that sustain the death penalty as nonexcessive in the Court's view are general deterrence and retribution. In *Furman,* I canvassed the relevant data on the deterrent effect of capital punishment. The state of knowledge at that point, after literally centuries of debate, was summarized as follows by a United Nations Committee:

> "It is generally agreed between the retentionists and abolitionists, whatever their opinions about the validity of comparative studies of deterrence, that the data which now exist show no correlation between the existence of capital punishment and lower rates of capital crime."

The available evidence, I concluded in *Furman,* was convincing that "capital punishment is not necessary as a deterrent to crime in our society."

* * *

There remains for consideration, however, what might be termed the purely retributive justification for the death penalty—that the death penalty is appropriate, not because of its beneficial effect on society, but because the taking of the murderer's life is itself morally good. * * *

* * * It is this latter notion, in particular, that I consider to be fundamentally at odds with the Eighth Amendment. The mere fact that the community demands the murderer's life in return for the evil he has done cannot sustain the death penalty, for * * * "the Eighth Amendment demands more than that a challenged punishment be acceptable to contemporary society." To be sustained under the Eighth Amendment, the death penalty must "compor[t] with the basic concept of human dignity at the core of the Amendment" * * *. Under these standards, the taking of life "because the wrongdoer deserves it" surely must fall, for such a punishment has as its very basis the total denial of the wrongdoer's dignity and worth.

The death penalty, unnecessary to promote the goal of deterrence or to further any legitimate notion of retribution, is an excessive penalty forbidden by the Eighth and Fourteenth Amendments. I respectfully dissent from the Court's judgment * * *.

QUESTIONS AND POINTS FOR DISCUSSION

1.   Thirty-five states and the federal government authorize the death penalty in some circumstances. Death Penalty Information Center, Death

Penalty Policy By State, at http://www.deathpenaltyinfo.org/death-penalty-policy-state. Between 1977, after it had become apparent that the Supreme Court considered the death penalty constitutional in some cases, and the end of 2007, 1099 people sentenced to death were executed. Bureau of Justice Statistics, U.S. Dep't of Justice, Capital Punishment, 2007–Statistical Tables tbl.9 (2008), at http://ojp.usdoj.gov/bjs/pub/html/cp/2007/tables/cp07st09.htm. An additional 3220 prisoners were on death row at the end of 2007. Id. tbl.4.

Over forty-five percent of the executions since 1977 occurred between 2000 and 2007. Id. tbl.15. Approximately two-thirds of the executions during that time period were in five states—Texas, Virginia, Oklahoma, Missouri, and Florida, with Texas accounting for more than a third of the total executions. Id. tbl.9. In your opinion, is the disproportionate execution of death sentences in a few states in the country relevant to the question whether the death penalty violates the Eighth Amendment?

2.   The debate between social scientists regarding whether the death penalty deters murders continues to this day. See John J. Donohue & Justin Wolfers, Uses and Abuses of Empirical Evidence in the Death Penalty Debate, 58 Stan. L.Rev. 791, 793–94 (2005) (citing studies with conflicting findings and concluding that there is "profound uncertainty" whether the death penalty has a deterrent effect). Does the answer to this empirical question have a bearing on your own views regarding the constitutionality of the death penalty?

3.   In *Gregg v. Georgia,* the Supreme Court emphasized the critical role that the proportionality review conducted by the Georgia Supreme Court played in reducing the risk that the death penalty had been imposed arbitrarily. Since *Gregg* was decided, however, the Court has held that such a proportionality review, during which the death penalty imposed in the case before an appellate court is compared with the sanction imposed in other similar cases, is not necessarily required in order for a capital-punishment system to be constitutional. Pulley v. Harris, 465 U.S. 37, 104 S.Ct. 871 (1984). Whether a proportionality review ever would be constitutionally mandated would depend on what other checks against arbitrariness are included in the system adopted by a jurisdiction for imposing capital punishment. Id. at 51, 104 S.Ct. at 879. In *Pulley,* those checks, deemed adequate by the Court, included review by the trial judge and the state supreme court of a jury's verdict of death.

Virtually all of the states in which the death penalty is authorized provide for the automatic review of a death sentence, typically by the state's highest appellate court. Bureau of Justice Statistics, U.S. Dep't of Justice, Capital Punishment, 2005, at 3 (2006) (reporting that thirty-seven of thirty-eight states provide for the automatic review of death sentences). Even if the defendant is opposed to the review, states generally require that the review be conducted. Id.

4.   In *Gregg v. Georgia,* the Supreme Court also emphasized the role that the jury plays as an indicator of "contemporary community values" when deciding whether to impose the death penalty. Yet there is no constitutional requirement, according to the Court, that a death sentence be imposed by a jury. Spaziano v. Florida, 468 U.S. 447, 104 S.Ct. 3154 (1984). In *Spaziano,*

the Supreme Court therefore upheld the death sentence imposed by a judge despite an advisory jury's recommendation that the defendant be sentenced to life in prison. But while a defendant has no constitutional right to have a jury make the decision whether the defendant's crime warrants the penalty of death, the defendant does have the right to have a jury make the factual findings regarding the aggravating factors whose existence is, under state law, a prerequisite to the imposition of the death penalty. See Ring v. Arizona, 536 U.S. 584, 122 S.Ct. 2428 (2002), which is discussed in note 1 on page 120.

5. To guard against arbitrariness in the imposition of the death penalty, courts have scrutinized the language of death-penalty statutes to ensure that they are not unconstitutionally vague. In Maynard v. Cartwright, 486 U.S. 356, 108 S.Ct. 1853 (1988), for example, the Supreme Court struck down, on Eighth Amendment grounds, a provision of a death-penalty statute treating the fact that a murder was "especially heinous, atrocious, or cruel" as an aggravating circumstance. In concluding that this language was unconstitutionally vague, the Court noted that "an ordinary person could honestly believe that every unjustified, intentional taking of human life is 'especially heinous.'" Id. at 364, 108 S.Ct. at 1859. How might this statute be redrafted to pass constitutional muster?

The Supreme Court's decision in Walton v. Arizona, 497 U.S. 639, 654–55, 110 S.Ct. 3047, 3057–58 (1990) provides some helpful insights in answering that question. In that case, the Court upheld an Arizona death-penalty statute couched in language much like the wording of the statute held unconstitutional in *Maynard*; the Arizona statute listed the fact that a murder was committed in "an especially heinous, cruel or depraved manner" as an aggravating circumstance supporting the imposition of the death penalty. Nonetheless, the Supreme Court held that the Arizona Supreme Court's limiting construction of the statute eradicated any unconstitutional vagueness. The state supreme court had said that "a crime is committed in an especially cruel manner when the perpetrator inflicts mental anguish or physical abuse before the victim's death" and that "[m]ental anguish includes a victim's uncertainty as to his ultimate fate." Id. at 646, 110 S.Ct. at 3053. The state court had also clarified that a murder is "especially depraved" when the murderer "relishes the murder, evidencing debasement or perversion," or "shows an indifference to the suffering of the victim and evidences a sense of pleasure" in the victim's death. Id.

The Arizona Supreme Court, incidentally, found that these standards were met in *Walton* and that imposition of the death penalty on the defendant was appropriate. Walton and his two codefendants had accosted the victim at gunpoint and forced him into his car. They then drove him out into the desert where Walton shot him in the head. Returning to the car, Walton then commented to his codefendants that he had "never seen a man pee in his pants before." The victim's body was found a week later. An autopsy revealed that the victim had not died immediately after being shot. Instead, blinded by the shot, he struggled about in the desert for six days, dying from dehydration, starvation, and pneumonia the day before his body was found.

6. Despite the Supreme Court's holding in *Gregg v. Georgia* that Georgia's system for imposing the death penalty, on its face, provided enough

procedural safeguards to sufficiently avert arbitrariness and irrationality in the imposition of the death penalty, the Supreme Court later was confronted in McCleskey v. Kemp, 481 U.S. 279, 107 S.Ct. 1756 (1987) with the claim that the statutory framework, as applied, did not meet constitutional standards—that the system for imposing the death penalty in Georgia was suffused with arbitrariness. The defendant in *McCleskey,* a black man sentenced to death for the killing of a white police officer, produced statistics demonstrating that defendants in Georgia charged with killing white victims were 4.3 times more likely to be sentenced to death than defendants whose victims were black. In addition, a black defendant who killed a white victim was much more likely to receive the death penalty than a white defendant who killed a white victim. While 22% of the murder cases studied involving black defendants and white victims resulted in imposition of the death penalty, the death penalty was imposed in only 8% of the cases in which both the defendant and the victim were white. In cases involving black victims, 3% of the white defendants were sentenced to death, while only 1% of the black defendants received the death penalty.

The Supreme Court assumed that these statistics, drawn from what was known as the "Baldus study," were reliable, but nonetheless, in a 5–4 decision, upheld the constitutionality of the capital-punishment system in Georgia. Responding to the defendant's argument that the system violated his Fourteenth Amendment right to be afforded the equal protection of the law, the Court noted that the defendant had failed to prove, as required by the Equal Protection Clause, that he had been discriminated against intentionally. The Court refused to assume that the jury that had sentenced the defendant to death had done so because of his race or the race of his victim. In addition, the Court observed that there was no evidence that the Georgia legislature had enacted the death-penalty statute in order to discriminate against African Americans.

The Supreme Court also rejected the defendant's claim that his death sentence constituted cruel and unusual punishment, emphasizing, once again, that the statistical evidence adduced by the defendant did not demonstrate that race was actually a factor in the imposition of the death penalty in his case. Nor was the Court willing to conclude that the death penalty in Georgia was applied arbitrarily, in violation of the Eighth Amendment, because of the risk that racial bias entered into capital-sentencing decisions. The Court observed:

> At most, the Baldus study indicates a discrepancy that appears to correlate with race. Apparent disparities in sentencing are an inevitable part of our criminal justice system. The discrepancy indicated by the Baldus study is "a far cry from the major systemic defects identified in *Furman.*" As this Court has recognized, any mode for determining guilt or punishment "has its weaknesses and the potential for misuse." Specifically, "there can be 'no perfect procedure for deciding in which cases governmental authority should be used to impose death.'" Despite these imperfections, our consistent rule has been that constitutional guarantees are met when "the mode [for determining guilt or punishment] itself has been surrounded with safeguards to make it as fair as possible." Where the discretion that is fundamental to our criminal process is involved, we

decline to assume that what is unexplained is invidious. In light of the safeguards designed to minimize racial bias in the process, the fundamental value of jury trial in our criminal justice system, and the benefits that discretion provides to criminal defendants, we hold that the Baldus study does not demonstrate a constitutionally significant risk of racial bias affecting the Georgia capital sentencing process.

Id. at 312–13, 107 S.Ct. at 1777–78.

In a dissenting opinion, Justice Brennan, joined by Justices Marshall, Blackmun, and Stevens, objected to the majority's observation that the risk of racial bias when defendants are sentenced to death in Georgia is not "constitutionally significant." Justice Brennan noted that for every eleven defendants sentenced to death in the state for killing a white person, six would not have received the death penalty if their victims had been black. "Surely," Justice Brennan observed, "we would not be willing to take a person's life if the chance that his death was irrationally imposed is *more* likely than not." Id. at 328, 107 S.Ct. at 1786 (Brennan, J., dissenting). Interestingly, Justice Powell, who wrote the majority opinion in *McCleskey,* later rued that decision, stating after he was no longer on the Court that he wished he had voted differently in the case. John C. Jeffries, Jr., Justice Lewis F. Powell, Jr. 451 (1994).

7. Could a state substantially reduce the risk of racial prejudice affecting capital-sentencing decisions without abandoning the death penalty? In a separate dissenting opinion in *McCleskey v. Kemp,* Justice Stevens answered this question in the affirmative. Justice Stevens pointed to the results of the Baldus study, which revealed that there is a class of extremely egregious murders that result in the imposition of the death penalty regardless of the race of the victim or defendant. Justice Stevens suggested that constitutional problems could be averted if the death penalty were reserved for this limited category of murders.

Would mandating imposition of the death penalty in certain circumstances eliminate the problem of racial bias in the application of death-penalty statutes? Would such a death-penalty structure be constitutional? The Supreme Court addressed this latter question in Woodson v. North Carolina, 428 U.S. 280, 96 S.Ct. 2978 (1976), the case which follows.

WOODSON v. NORTH CAROLINA

Supreme Court of the United States, 1976.
428 U.S. 280, 96 S.Ct. 2978, 49 L.Ed.2d 944.

Judgment of the Court, and opinion of MR. JUSTICE STEWART, MR. JUSTICE POWELL, and MR. JUSTICE STEVENS, announced by MR. JUSTICE STEWART.

* * *

The petitioners were convicted of first-degree murder as the result of their participation in an armed robbery of a convenience food store, in the course of which the cashier was killed and a customer was seriously wounded. There were four participants in the robbery: the petitioners

James Tyrone Woodson and Luby Waxton and two others, Leonard Tucker and Johnnie Lee Carroll. * * *

The evidence for the prosecution established that the four men had been discussing a possible robbery for some time. On the fatal day Woodson had been drinking heavily. About 9:30 p.m., Waxton and Tucker came to the trailer where Woodson was staying. When Woodson came out of the trailer, Waxton struck him in the face and threatened to kill him in an effort to make him sober up and come along on the robbery. The three proceeded to Waxton's trailer where they met Carroll. Waxton armed himself with a nickel-plated derringer, and Tucker handed Woodson a rifle. The four then set out by automobile to rob the store. Upon arriving at their destination Tucker and Waxton went into the store while Carroll and Woodson remained in the car as lookouts. Once inside the store, Tucker purchased a package of cigarettes from the woman cashier. Waxton then also asked for a package of cigarettes, but as the cashier approached him he pulled the derringer out of his hip pocket and fatally shot her at point-blank range. Waxton then took the money tray from the cash register and gave it to Tucker, who carried it out of the store, pushing past an entering customer as he reached the door. After he was outside, Tucker heard a second shot from inside the store, and shortly thereafter Waxton emerged, carrying a handful of paper money. Tucker and Waxton got in the car and the four drove away.

The petitioners' testimony agreed in large part with this version of the circumstances of the robbery. It differed diametrically in one important respect: Waxton claimed that he never had a gun, and that Tucker had shot both the cashier and the customer.

* * *

The petitioners were found guilty on all charges, and, as was required by statute, sentenced to death. The Supreme Court of North Carolina affirmed. * * *

* * *

* * * In ruling on the constitutionality of the sentences imposed on the petitioners under this North Carolina statute, the Court now addresses for the first time the question whether a death sentence returned pursuant to a law imposing a mandatory death penalty for a broad category of homicidal offenses[7] constitutes cruel and unusual punishment within the meaning of the Eighth and Fourteenth Amendments. * * *

A

The Eighth Amendment stands to assure that the State's power to punish is "exercised within the limits of civilized standards." Central to

---

7. This case does not involve a mandatory death penalty statute limited to an extremely narrow category of homicide, such as murder by a prisoner serving a life sentence, defined in large part in terms of the character or record of the offender. We thus express no opinion regarding the constitutionality of such a statute.

the application of the Amendment is a determination of contemporary standards regarding the infliction of punishment. As discussed in *Gregg v. Georgia,* indicia of societal values identified in prior opinions include history and traditional usage, legislative enactments, and jury determinations.

* * * At the time the Eighth Amendment was adopted in 1791, the States uniformly followed the common-law practice of making death the exclusive and mandatory sentence for certain specified offenses. Although the range of capital offenses in the American Colonies was quite limited in comparison to the more than 200 offenses then punishable by death in England, the Colonies at the time of the Revolution imposed death sentences on all persons convicted of any of a considerable number of crimes, typically including at a minimum, murder, treason, piracy, arson, rape, robbery, burglary, and sodomy. * * * Almost from the outset jurors reacted unfavorably to the harshness of mandatory death sentences. The States initially responded to this expression of public dissatisfaction with mandatory statutes by limiting the classes of capital offenses.

This reform, however, left unresolved the problem posed by the not infrequent refusal of juries to convict murderers rather than subject them to automatic death sentences. In 1794, Pennsylvania attempted to alleviate the undue severity of the law by confining the mandatory death penalty to "murder of the first degree" encompassing all "willful, deliberate and premeditated" killings. Other jurisdictions, including Virginia and Ohio, soon enacted similar measures, and within a generation the practice spread to most of the States.

Despite the broad acceptance of the division of murder into degrees, the reform proved to be an unsatisfactory means of identifying persons appropriately punishable by death. * * * Juries continued to find the death penalty inappropriate in a significant number of first-degree murder cases and refused to return guilty verdicts for that crime.

The inadequacy of distinguishing between murderers solely on the basis of legislative criteria narrowing the definition of the capital offense led the States to grant juries sentencing discretion in capital cases. Tennessee in 1838, followed by Alabama in 1841, and Louisiana in 1846, were the first States to abandon mandatory death sentences in favor of discretionary death penalty statutes. This flexibility remedied the harshness of mandatory statutes by permitting the jury to respond to mitigating factors by withholding the death penalty. * * * [B]y the end of World War I, all but eight States, Hawaii, and the District of Columbia either had adopted discretionary death penalty schemes or abolished the death penalty altogether. By 1963, all of these remaining jurisdictions had replaced their automatic death penalty statutes with discretionary jury sentencing.

The history of mandatory death penalty statutes in the United States thus reveals that the practice of sentencing to death all persons convicted of a particular offense has been rejected as unduly harsh and unworkably rigid. The two crucial indicators of evolving standards of decency respecting the imposition of punishment in our society—jury determinations and legislative enactments—both point conclusively to the repudiation of automatic death sentences. * * *[29]

* * *

Still further evidence of the incompatibility of mandatory death penalties with contemporary values is provided by the results of jury sentencing under discretionary statutes. * * * Various studies indicate that even in first-degree murder cases juries with sentencing discretion do not impose the death penalty "with any great frequency."[31] * * *

* * *

Although it seems beyond dispute that, at the time of the *Furman* decision in 1972, mandatory death penalty statutes had been renounced by American juries and legislatures, there remains the question whether the mandatory statutes adopted by North Carolina and a number of other States following *Furman* evince a sudden reversal of societal values regarding the imposition of capital punishment. In view of the persistent and unswerving legislative rejection of mandatory death penalty statutes beginning in 1838 and continuing for more than 130 years until *Furman,* it seems evident that the post-*Furman* enactments reflect attempts by the States to retain the death penalty in a form consistent with the Constitution, rather than a renewed societal acceptance of mandatory death sentencing. * * *

* * *

* * * North Carolina's mandatory death penalty statute for first-degree murder departs markedly from contemporary standards respecting the imposition of the punishment of death and thus cannot be applied consistently with the Eighth and Fourteenth Amendments' requirement that the State's power to punish "be exercised within the limits of civilized standards."

B

A separate deficiency of North Carolina's mandatory death sentence statute is its failure to provide a constitutionally tolerable response to *Furman*'s rejection of unbridled jury discretion in the imposition of capital sentences. Central to the limited holding in *Furman* was the conviction

---

29. See unpublished Hearings on S. 138 before the Subcommittee on the Judiciary of the Senate Committee on the District of Columbia 19–20 (May 17, 1961) (testimony of Sen. Keating). Data compiled by a former United States Attorney for the District of Columbia indicated that juries convicted defendants of first-degree murder in only 12 of the 60 jury trials for first-degree murder held in the District of Columbia between July 1, 1953, and February 1960. The conviction rate was "substantially below the general average in prosecuting other crimes." The lower conviction rate was attributed to the reluctance of jurors to impose the harsh consequences of a first-degree murder conviction in cases where the record might justify a lesser punishment.

* * *

31. Data compiled on discretionary jury sentencing of persons convicted of capital murder reveal that the penalty of death is generally imposed in less than 20% of the cases.

that the vesting of standardless sentencing power in the jury violated the Eighth and Fourteenth Amendments. It is argued that North Carolina has remedied the inadequacies of the death penalty statutes held unconstitutional in *Furman* by withdrawing all sentencing discretion from juries in capital cases. But when one considers the long and consistent American experience with the death penalty in first-degree murder cases, it becomes evident that mandatory statutes enacted in response to *Furman* have simply papered over the problem of unguided and unchecked jury discretion.

* * * American juries have persistently refused to convict a significant portion of persons charged with first-degree murder of that offense under mandatory death penalty statutes. * * * North Carolina's mandatory death penalty statute provides no standards to guide the jury in its inevitable exercise of the power to determine which first-degree murderers shall live and which shall die. * * * Instead of rationalizing the sentencing process, a mandatory scheme may well exacerbate the problem identified in *Furman* by resting the penalty determination on the particular jury's willingness to act lawlessly. While a mandatory death penalty statute may reasonably be expected to increase the number of persons sentenced to death, it does not fulfill *Furman*'s basic requirement by replacing arbitrary and wanton jury discretion with objective standards to guide, regularize, and make rationally reviewable the process for imposing a sentence of death.

C

A third constitutional shortcoming of the North Carolina statute is its failure to allow the particularized consideration of relevant aspects of the character and record of each convicted defendant before the imposition upon him of a sentence of death. * * * It treats all persons convicted of a designated offense not as uniquely individual human beings, but as members of a faceless, undifferentiated mass to be subjected to the blind infliction of the penalty of death.

* * * While the prevailing practice of individualizing sentencing determinations generally reflects simply enlightened policy rather than a constitutional imperative, we believe that in capital cases the fundamental respect for humanity underlying the Eighth Amendment requires consideration of the character and record of the individual offender and the circumstances of the particular offense as a constitutionally indispensable part of the process of inflicting the penalty of death.

This conclusion rests squarely on the predicate that the penalty of death is qualitatively different from a sentence of imprisonment, however long. Death, in its finality, differs more from life imprisonment than a 100–year prison term differs from one of only a year or two. Because of that qualitative difference, there is a corresponding difference in the need for reliability in the determination that death is the appropriate punishment in a specific case.

For the reasons stated, we conclude that the death sentences imposed upon the petitioners under North Carolina's mandatory death sentence statute violated the Eighth and Fourteenth Amendments and therefore must be set aside. * * *

* * *

MR. JUSTICE BRENNAN, concurring in the judgment. [Opinion omitted.]

MR. JUSTICE MARSHALL, concurring in the judgment. [Opinion omitted.]

MR. JUSTICE WHITE, with whom THE CHIEF JUSTICE and MR. JUSTICE REHNQUIST join, dissenting. [Opinion omitted.]

MR. JUSTICE BLACKMUN, dissenting. [Opinion omitted.]

MR. JUSTICE REHNQUIST, dissenting.

* * *

There was undoubted dissatisfaction, from more than one sector of 19th century society, with the operation of mandatory death sentences. One segment of that society was totally opposed to capital punishment, and was apparently willing to accept the substitution of discretionary imposition of that penalty for its mandatory imposition as a halfway house on the road to total abolition. Another segment was equally unhappy with the operation of the mandatory system, but for an entirely different reason. As the plurality recognizes, this second segment of society was unhappy with the operation of the mandatory system, not because of the death sentences imposed under it, but because people obviously guilty of criminal offenses were *not* being convicted under it. Change to a discretionary system was accepted by these persons not because they thought mandatory imposition of the death penalty was cruel and unusual, but because they thought that if jurors were permitted to return a sentence other than death upon the conviction of a capital crime, fewer guilty defendants would be acquitted.

So far as the action of juries is concerned, the fact that in some cases juries operating under the mandatory system refused to convict obviously guilty defendants does not reflect any "turning away" from the death penalty, or the mandatory death penalty, supporting the proposition that it is "cruel and unusual." Given the requirement of unanimity with respect to jury verdicts in capital cases, * * * it is apparent that a single juror could prevent a jury from returning a verdict of conviction. * * * The fact that the presence of such jurors could prevent conviction in a given case, even though the majority of society, speaking through legislatures, had decreed that it should be imposed, certainly does not indicate that society as a whole rejected mandatory punishment for such offenders; it does not even indicate that those few members of society who serve on juries, as a whole, had done so.

* * *

The second constitutional flaw which the plurality finds in North Carolina's mandatory system is that it has simply "papered over" the problem of unchecked jury discretion. * * *

* * *

In Georgia juries are entitled to return a sentence of life, rather than death, for no reason whatever, simply based upon their own subjective notions of what is right and what is wrong.[a] * * * Why these types of discretion are regarded by the plurality as constitutionally permissible, while that which may occur in the North Carolina system is not, is not readily apparent. * * *

* * *

QUESTIONS AND POINTS FOR DISCUSSION

1. In Sumner v. Shuman, 483 U.S. 66, 107 S.Ct. 2716 (1987), the Supreme Court answered a question left open in *Woodson*—whether a statute that requires imposition of the death penalty when an inmate commits a murder while serving a life sentence without possibility of parole is constitutional. The Court held that such a mandatory death sentence violates the Eighth Amendment. The Court noted that even when an inmate serving a life sentence without possibility of parole commits a murder, there might be mitigating circumstances that contraindicate imposition of the death penalty. Circumstances surrounding the murder itself, for example, might diminish the inmate's culpability, even though those circumstances did not rise to the level of a legal defense to the charge of murder. Or there might have been circumstances surrounding the conduct underlying the conviction for which the defendant is serving a life sentence that might suggest to the sentencer that imposition of the death penalty is unwarranted. Finally, there might be other factors, such as the defendant's age, that point against imposition of a death sentence.

To the argument that a mandatory death sentence is necessary in order to deter murders by inmates serving life sentences with no possibility of parole and to provide a means of punishing such inmates, the Court responded that these purposes could be effectuated by retaining the death penalty, though not a mandatory one. If the inmates were not sentenced to die, they still could be punished for a murder, according to the Court, by withdrawing privileges from them that they otherwise would enjoy in the prison. See also Roberts v. Louisiana, 431 U.S. 633, 97 S.Ct. 1993 (1977) (mandatory death sentence for murdering a police officer violates the Eighth Amendment).

2. According to the Supreme Court, not every death-penalty statute that has a mandatory component in it violates constitutional strictures. In Blystone v. Pennsylvania, 494 U.S. 299, 110 S.Ct. 1078 (1990), the Court upheld the constitutionality of a death-penalty statute which required the jury to sentence a defendant to death if it found that aggravating circumstances in

---

a. In Gregg v. Georgia, 428 U.S. 153, 96 S.Ct. 2909 (1976), supra page 279, the Supreme Court upheld the Georgia death-penalty scheme alluded to above.

the case outweighed any mitigating circumstances. The Supreme Court distinguished *Woodson,* noting that in the case before it "[d]eath is not automatically imposed upon conviction for certain types of murder. It is imposed only after a determination that the aggravating circumstances outweigh the mitigating circumstances present in the particular crime committed by the particular defendant, or that there are no such mitigating circumstances." Id. at 305, 110 S.Ct. at 1082–83. The Eighth Amendment also permits statutes to mandate imposition of a death sentence when the jury finds that the aggravating and mitigating factors are "in equipoise"—in other words, evenly balanced. Kansas v. Marsh, 548 U.S. 163, 166, 126 S.Ct. 2516, 2520 (2006).

3. In applying the Eighth Amendment requirement, to which *Woodson* alluded, that a defendant in a death-penalty case be afforded an individualized sentencing determination, the Supreme Court has concluded that a sentencer must not be precluded from considering any relevant mitigating circumstances when deciding whether to sentence a defendant to death. See, e.g., Hitchcock v. Dugger, 481 U.S. 393, 107 S.Ct. 1821 (1987) (defendant has a right to introduce, and have the sentencer consider, evidence of mitigating circumstances not mentioned in the death-penalty statute); Skipper v. South Carolina, 476 U.S. 1, 106 S.Ct. 1669 (1986) (defendant should have been permitted to introduce evidence about how well he had adjusted to jail while awaiting trial); Eddings v. Oklahoma, 455 U.S. 104, 102 S.Ct. 869 (1982) (sentencing judge acted unconstitutionally in refusing to consider evidence of defendant's troubled childhood and his emotional problems). The Court has acknowledged that there is "some tension" between this Eighth Amendment requirement and the need, emphasized in *Gregg v. Georgia,* to place limits on the sentencer's exercise of discretion when decisions are being made regarding imposition of the death penalty. Tuilaepa v. California, 512 U.S. 967, 973, 114 S.Ct. 2630, 2635 (1994). Nonetheless, the Court has concluded that what the Eighth Amendment seeks to ensure, and can ensure, is that systems developed for imposing the death penalty are "at once consistent and principled but also humane and sensible to the uniqueness of the individual." Eddings v. Oklahoma, 455 U.S. at 110, 102 S.Ct. at 874.

Several Justices on the Supreme Court have lambasted this conclusion. Justice Scalia, for one, sees not only "tension" between the line of Supreme Court cases emphasizing the need for structured decision making in capital cases and the line of decisions underscoring the need for individualized sentencing in such cases, but finds them totally irreconcilable. He explained his views in a concurring opinion in Walton v. Arizona, 497 U.S. 639, 110 S.Ct. 3047 (1990):

> Shortly after introducing our doctrine *requiring* constraints on the sentencer's discretion to "impose" the death penalty, the Court began developing a doctrine *forbidding* constraints on the sentencer's discretion to "*decline* to impose" it. This second doctrine—counterdoctrine would be a better word—has completely exploded whatever coherence the notion of "guided discretion" once had.

* * *

> To acknowledge that "there perhaps is an inherent tension" between this line of cases and the line stemming from *Furman* is rather like

saying that there was perhaps an inherent tension between the Allies and the Axis Powers in World War II. And to refer to the two lines as pursuing "twin objectives" is rather like referring to the twin objectives of good and evil. They cannot be reconciled. Pursuant to *Furman,* and in order "to achieve a more rational and equitable administration of the death penalty," we require that States "channel the sentencer's discretion by 'clear and objective standards' that provide 'specific and detailed guidance.'" In the next breath, however, we say that "the State *cannot* channel the sentencer's discretion ... to consider any relevant [mitigating] information offered by the defendant" and that the sentencer must enjoy unconstrained discretion to decide whether any sympathetic factors bearing on the defendant or the crime indicate that he does not "deserve to be sentenced to death." The latter requirement quite obviously destroys whatever rationality and predictability the former requirement was designed to achieve.

* * * [T]he question remains why the Constitution demands that the aggravating standards and mitigating standards be accorded opposite treatment. It is impossible to understand why. Since the individualized determination is a unitary one (does this defendant deserve death for this crime?) once one says each sentencer must be able to answer "no" for whatever reason it deems morally sufficient (and indeed, for whatever reason any one of 12 jurors deems morally sufficient), it becomes impossible to claim that the Constitution requires consistency and rationality among sentencing determinations to be preserved by strictly limiting the reasons for which each sentencer can say "yes." * * *

* * *

* * * *Stare decisis* cannot command the impossible. Since I cannot possibly be guided by what seem to me incompatible principles, I must reject the one that is plainly in error.

* * *

* * * Accordingly, I will not, in this case or in the future, vote to uphold an Eighth Amendment claim that the sentencer's discretion has been unlawfully restricted.

Id. at 661, 664–66, 673, 110 S.Ct. at 3061, 3063–64, 3068.

In Callins v. Collins, 510 U.S. 1141, 114 S.Ct. 1127 (1994) (Blackmun, J., dissenting), Justice Blackmun agreed that the Eighth Amendment requirements expounded in the Supreme Court's opinions are in conflict:

Any statute or procedure that could effectively eliminate arbitrariness from the administration of death would also restrict the sentencer's discretion to such an extent that the sentencer would be unable to give full consideration to the unique characteristics of each defendant and the circumstances of the offense. By the same token, any statute or procedure that would provide the sentencer with sufficient discretion to consider fully and act upon the unique circumstances of each defendant would "thro[w] open the back door to arbitrary and irrational sentencing." All efforts to strike an appropriate balance between these conflicting constitutional commands are futile because there is a heightened need for both in the administration of death.

Id. at 1155, 114 S.Ct. at 1136. Justice Blackmun, however, balked at the idea of eliminating this conflict by reading the individualized-sentencing requirement out of the Eighth Amendment, as Justice Scalia proposed. Convinced that the need for individualized sentencing in capital cases is deeply embedded in American standards of decency, Justice Blackmun observed that "[t]he notion of prohibiting a sentencer from exercising its discretion 'to dispense mercy on the basis of factors too intangible to write into a statute,' is offensive to our sense of fundamental fairness and respect for the uniqueness of the individual." Id. at 1150, 114 S.Ct. at 1133. Concluding that it was simply impossible to administer a death-penalty system in which death sentences were imposed both fairly and consistently, Justice Blackmun announced that he would no longer "tinker with the machinery of death"—that he would henceforth vote to strike down, on constitutional grounds, all death sentences reviewed by the Court. Id. at 1145, 114 S.Ct. at 1130.

Although the acknowledged "tension" between the general rules adopted to ensure consistency in the imposition of the death penalty and the requirement that there be unconstrained consideration of mitigating circumstances in capital cases has not led to the invalidation of the death penalty, the Supreme Court has cited that "tension" as a reason to limit the death penalty's scope. See Kennedy v. Louisiana, 128 S.Ct. 2641, 2659 (2008) on page 316. With which view do you agree? With that of a majority of the Supreme Court that the twin Eighth Amendment goals of ensuring that imposition of the death penalty is both "consistent and principled" and "humane and sensible to the uniqueness of the individual" can be met but that the conflict between these goals should limit the kinds of cases in which a death sentence can be imposed? With Justice Scalia's view that this conflict should be eradicated by abandoning the individualized-sentencing requirement? Or with Justice Blackmun's view that death-penalty statutes cannot be administered constitutionally because of this conflict?

4. Precluding a defendant from introducing, in a capital-sentencing hearing, evidence suggesting that imposition of the death penalty is unwarranted may violate not only the Eighth Amendment, but due process as well. Simmons v. South Carolina, 512 U.S. 154, 114 S.Ct. 2187 (1994) is a case in point. In that case, the prosecutor urged the jury to sentence the defendant to death because he would continue to pose a danger to others in the future. The defendant, however, was barred from informing the jury, either through the arguments of his attorney or a court instruction, that if the defendant was not sentenced to death, he would be sentenced to life in prison without the possibility of parole. The Supreme Court reaffirmed that due process forbids imposing the death penalty based on information that a defendant had " 'no opportunity to deny or explain.' " Id. at 161, 114 S.Ct. at 2192–93 (quoting Gardner v. Florida, 430 U.S. 349, 362, 97 S.Ct. 1197, 1207 (1977), supra page 93). When a defendant's future dangerousness is an issue in a capital-sentencing hearing, the defendant therefore has a due-process right to inform the sentencing jury that a life sentence forecloses release on parole. Accord Kelly v. South Carolina, 534 U.S. 246, 122 S.Ct. 726 (2002); Shafer v. South Carolina, 532 U.S. 36, 121 S.Ct. 1263 (2001).

To counterbalance a defendant's argument in a capital case that a life sentence without the possibility of parole will adequately safeguard the public, a prosecutor may seek to have the jury instructed about the possibility that the exercise of executive clemency powers might lead to the defendant's release from prison in the future. In California v. Ramos, 463 U.S. 992, 103 S.Ct. 3446 (1983), the Supreme Court held, in a 5–4 decision, that there is no federal constitutional impediment to the submission of such an instruction to the jury. If you were going to oppose, on state constitutional or policy grounds, permitting such an instruction, what arguments would you make? See Blaine LeCesne, Tipping the Scales Toward Death: Instructing Capital Jurors on the Possibility of Executive Clemency, 65 U. Cin. L. Rev. 1051 (1997).

5. The mitigating circumstances that may lead a sentencing judge or jury to refrain from imposing a death sentence typically fall into two categories: facts about the defendant and facts about the crime itself. The question arises as to whether there are any mitigating facts about a defendant that, rather than just being weighed in the sentencing calculus, erect a *per se* bar to the imposition of the death penalty.

In Penry v. Lynaugh, 492 U.S. 302, 109 S.Ct. 2934 (1989), the Supreme Court held that while a defendant's mental retardation is a mitigating circumstance that should be considered by the sentencer when deciding whether to sentence the defendant to death, the defendant's mental impairment does not automatically preclude imposition of the death penalty. Thirteen years later, in Atkins v. Virginia, 536 U.S. 304, 122 S.Ct. 2242 (2002), the Court reversed its position, holding that executing a person who is mentally retarded constitutes cruel and unusual punishment. The Court noted that while only two states barred the execution of mentally retarded offenders at the time *Penry* was decided, eighteen states now generally prohibited such executions. The Court explained that it was the "consistency of the direction of change," more than the numerical count, that provided "powerful evidence" of a consensus view that had emerged since *Penry* that mentally retarded individuals are less culpable for their crimes. Id. at 315–16, 122 S.Ct. at 2249. The Court also opined that the mentally retarded are at "special risk of wrongful execution," in part because their mental deficiencies limit their effectiveness as witnesses and their ability to assist their attorneys in preparing their defense. Id. at 321, 122 S.Ct. at 2252. The Court left to the states the task of determining how to differentiate between defendants who are mentally retarded and those who are not.

The Supreme Court also has vacillated on the question whether the execution of individuals who were younger than eighteen at the time of their crimes violates the Eighth Amendment. The Supreme Court considered this question in the case that follows.

ROPER v. SIMMONS

Supreme Court of the United States, 2005.
543 U.S. 551, 125 S.Ct. 1183, 161 L.Ed.2d 1.

JUSTICE KENNEDY delivered the opinion of the Court.

* * *

At the age of 17, when he was still a junior in high school, Christopher Simmons, the respondent here, committed murder. * * * Before its commission Simmons said he wanted to murder someone. In chilling, callous terms he talked about his plan, discussing it for the most part with two friends, Charles Benjamin and John Tessmer, then aged 15 and 16 respectively. Simmons proposed to commit burglary and murder by breaking and entering, tying up a victim, and throwing the victim off a bridge. Simmons assured his friends they could "get away with it" because they were minors.

The three met at about 2 a.m. on the night of the murder, but Tessmer left before the other two set out. * * * Simmons and Benjamin entered the home of the victim, Shirley Crook, after reaching through an open window and unlocking the back door. * * *

Using duct tape to cover her eyes and mouth and bind her hands, the two perpetrators put Mrs. Crook in her minivan and drove to a state park. They reinforced the bindings, covered her head with a towel, and walked her to a railroad trestle spanning the Meramec River. There they tied her hands and feet together with electrical wire, wrapped her whole face in duct tape and threw her from the bridge, drowning her in the waters below.

[After his arrest, Simmons confessed to the murder. He was tried for murder as an adult, convicted, and sentenced to death. The Missouri Supreme Court eventually set the death sentence aside on the grounds that the Eighth Amendment prohibited the execution of a defendant who was younger than eighteen when the crime was committed. The Supreme Court then granted certiorari.]

* * *

In *Thompson v. Oklahoma,* 487 U.S. 815 (1988), a plurality of the Court determined that our standards of decency do not permit the execution of any offender under the age of 16 at the time of the crime. * * *

* * * With Justice O'Connor concurring in the judgment on narrower grounds,[b] the Court set aside the death sentence that had been imposed on the 15–year–old offender.

The next year, in *Stanford v. Kentucky,* 492 U.S. 361 (1989), the Court, over a dissenting opinion joined by four Justices, referred to contemporary standards of decency in this country and concluded the Eighth and Fourteenth Amendments did not proscribe the execution of juvenile offenders over 15 but under 18. * * *

* * *

---

b. In her concurring opinion in *Thompson,* Justice O'Connor noted that it was likely, though not entirely clear, that there was a national consensus against the death penalty for a crime committed when a defendant was fifteen years old or younger. She therefore considered imposition of the death penalty to be unconstitutional when a state, like Oklahoma, had not specifically authorized the execution of individuals who were younger than sixteen at the time of their crimes.

* * * [W]e now reconsider the issue decided in *Stanford*. The beginning point is a review of objective indicia of consensus, as expressed in particular by the enactments of legislatures that have addressed the question. * * * We then must determine, in the exercise of our own independent judgment, whether the death penalty is a disproportionate punishment for juveniles.

III

A

* * * [Thirty] States prohibit the juvenile death penalty, comprising 12 that have rejected the death penalty altogether and 18 that maintain it but, by express provision or judicial interpretation, exclude juveniles from its reach. * * * [E]ven in the 20 States without a formal prohibition on executing juveniles, the practice is infrequent. Since *Stanford,* six States have executed prisoners for crimes committed as juveniles. In the past 10 years, only three have done so * * *.

* * * Five States that allowed the juvenile death penalty at the time of *Stanford* have abandoned it in the intervening 15 years—four through legislative enactments and one through judicial decision.

Though less dramatic than the change from *Penry* [*v. Lynaugh*, 492 U.S. 302 (1989)] to *Atkins* [*v. Virginia*, 536 U.S. 304 (2002)] * * *, we still consider the change from *Stanford* to this case to be significant. * * * Since *Stanford,* no State that previously prohibited capital punishment for juveniles has reinstated it. * * * Any difference between this case and *Atkins* with respect to the pace of abolition is thus counterbalanced by the consistent direction of the change.

The slower pace of abolition of the juvenile death penalty over the past 15 years, moreover, may have a simple explanation. When we heard *Penry*, only two death penalty States had already prohibited the execution of the mentally retarded. When we heard *Stanford*, by contrast, 12 death penalty States had already prohibited the execution of any juvenile under 18, and 15 had prohibited the execution of any juvenile under 17. * * * "It would be the ultimate in irony if the very fact that the inappropriateness of the death penalty for juveniles was broadly recognized sooner than it was recognized for the mentally retarded were to become a reason to continue the execution of juveniles now that the execution of the mentally retarded has been barred."

* * *

As in *Atkins*, the objective indicia of consensus in this case—the rejection of the juvenile death penalty in the majority of States; the infrequency of its use even where it remains on the books; and the consistency in the trend toward abolition of the practice—provide sufficient evidence that today our society views juveniles, in the words *Atkins* used respecting the mentally retarded, as "categorically less culpable than the average criminal."

B

* * *

Because the death penalty is the most severe punishment, the Eighth Amendment applies to it with special force. Capital punishment must be limited to those offenders who commit "a narrow category of the most serious crimes" and whose extreme culpability makes them "the most deserving of execution." * * *

Three general differences between juveniles under 18 and adults demonstrate that juvenile offenders cannot with reliability be classified among the worst offenders. First, as any parent knows and as the scientific and sociological studies respondent and his *amici* cite tend to confirm, "[a] lack of maturity and an underdeveloped sense of responsibility are found in youth more often than in adults and are more understandable among the young. These qualities often result in impetuous and ill-considered actions and decisions." * * * In recognition of the comparative immaturity and irresponsibility of juveniles, almost every State prohibits those under 18 years of age from voting, serving on juries, or marrying without parental consent.

The second area of difference is that juveniles are more vulnerable or susceptible to negative influences and outside pressures, including peer pressure. * * *

The third broad difference is that the character of a juvenile is not as well formed as that of an adult. * * *

These differences render suspect any conclusion that a juvenile falls among the worst offenders. The susceptibility of juveniles to immature and irresponsible behavior means "their irresponsible conduct is not as morally reprehensible as that of an adult." Their own vulnerability and comparative lack of control over their immediate surroundings mean juveniles have a greater claim than adults to be forgiven for failing to escape negative influences in their whole environment. The reality that juveniles still struggle to define their identity means it is less supportable to conclude that even a heinous crime committed by a juvenile is evidence of irretrievably depraved character. From a moral standpoint it would be misguided to equate the failings of a minor with those of an adult, for a greater possibility exists that a minor's character deficiencies will be reformed. * * *

* * *

Once the diminished culpability of juveniles is recognized, it is evident that the penological justifications for the death penalty apply to them with lesser force than to adults. * * * Whether viewed as an attempt to express the community's moral outrage or as an attempt to right the balance for the wrong to the victim, the case for retribution is not as strong with a minor as with an adult. Retribution is not proportional if the law's most severe penalty is imposed on one whose culpability or blameworthiness is diminished, to a substantial degree, by reason of youth and immaturity.

As for deterrence, it is unclear whether the death penalty has a significant or even measurable deterrent effect on juveniles * * *. * * * [T]he absence of evidence of deterrent effect is of special concern because the same characteristics that render juveniles less culpable than adults suggest as well that juveniles will be less susceptible to deterrence. In particular, * * * "[t]he likelihood that the teenage offender has made the kind of cost-benefit analysis that attaches any weight to the possibility of execution is so remote as to be virtually nonexistent." To the extent the juvenile death penalty might have residual deterrent effect, it is worth noting that the punishment of life imprisonment without the possibility of parole is itself a severe sanction, in particular for a young person.

* * * Certainly it can be argued, although we by no means concede the point, that a rare case might arise in which a juvenile offender has sufficient psychological maturity, and at the same time demonstrates sufficient depravity, to merit a sentence of death. Indeed, this possibility is the linchpin of one contention pressed by petitioner and his *amici*. They assert that even assuming the truth of the observations we have made about juveniles' diminished culpability in general, jurors nonetheless should be allowed to consider mitigating arguments related to youth on a case-by-case basis, and in some cases to impose the death penalty if justified. * * *

We disagree. The differences between juvenile and adult offenders are too marked and well understood to risk allowing a youthful person to receive the death penalty despite insufficient culpability. An unacceptable likelihood exists that the brutality or cold-blooded nature of any particular crime would overpower mitigating arguments based on youth as a matter of course, even where the juvenile offender's objective immaturity, vulnerability, and lack of true depravity should require a sentence less severe than death. * * *

* * *

IV

Our determination that the death penalty is disproportionate punishment for offenders under 18 finds confirmation in the stark reality that the United States is the only country in the world that continues to give official sanction to the juvenile death penalty. This reality does not become controlling, for the task of interpreting the Eighth Amendment remains our responsibility. Yet * * * the Court has referred to the laws of other countries and to international authorities as instructive for its interpretation of the Eighth Amendment's prohibition of "cruel and unusual punishments."

As respondent and a number of *amici* emphasize, Article 37 of the United Nations Convention on the Rights of the Child, which every country in the world has ratified save for the United States and Somalia, contains an express prohibition on capital punishment for crimes committed by juveniles under 18. * * *

Respondent and his *amici* have submitted, and petitioner does not contest, that only seven countries other than the United States have executed juvenile offenders since 1990: Iran, Pakistan, Saudi Arabia, Yemen, Nigeria, the Democratic Republic of Congo, and China. Since then each of these countries has either abolished capital punishment for juveniles or made public disavowal of the practice. In sum, it is fair to say that the United States now stands alone in a world that has turned its face against the juvenile death penalty.

* * *

* * * It does not lessen our fidelity to the Constitution or our pride in its origins to acknowledge that the express affirmation of certain fundamental rights by other nations and peoples simply underscores the centrality of those same rights within our own heritage of freedom.

* * *

The Eighth and Fourteenth Amendments forbid imposition of the death penalty on offenders who were under the age of 18 when their crimes were committed. * * *

* * *

JUSTICE STEVENS, with whom JUSTICE GINSBURG joins, concurring.

Perhaps even more important than our specific holding today is our reaffirmation of the basic principle that informs the Court's interpretation of the Eighth Amendment. If the meaning of that Amendment had been frozen when it was originally drafted, it would impose no impediment to the execution of 7–year–old children today. See *Stanford v. Kentucky,* 492 U.S. 361, 368 (1989) (describing the common law at the time of the Amendment's adoption). The evolving standards of decency that have driven our construction of this critically important part of the Bill of Rights foreclose any such reading of the Amendment. * * *

JUSTICE O'CONNOR, dissenting.

* * *

In determining whether the juvenile death penalty comports with contemporary standards of decency, our inquiry begins with the "clearest and most reliable objective evidence of contemporary values"—the actions of the Nation's legislatures. As the Court emphasizes, the overall number of jurisdictions that currently disallow the execution of under–18 offenders is the same as the number that forbade the execution of mentally retarded offenders when *Atkins* was decided. * * *

While the similarities between the two cases are undeniable, the objective evidence of national consensus is marginally weaker here. Most importantly, in *Atkins* there was significant evidence of *opposition* to the execution of the mentally retarded, but there was virtually no countervailing evidence of affirmative legislative *support* for this practice. The States that permitted such executions did so only because they had not enacted any prohibitory legislation. Here, by contrast, at least eight States have current statutes that specifically set 16 or 17 as the minimum age at which commission of a capital crime can expose the offender to the death penalty. * * *

Moreover, the Court in *Atkins* made clear that it was "not so much the number of [States forbidding execution of the mentally retarded] that [was] significant, but the consistency of the direction of change." In contrast to the trend in *Atkins,* the States have not moved uniformly towards abolishing the juvenile death penalty. Instead, since our decision in *Stanford,* two States have expressly reaffirmed their support for this practice by enacting statutes setting 16 as the minimum age for capital punishment. Furthermore, * * * the pace of legislative action in this context has been considerably slower than it was with regard to capital punishment of the mentally retarded. In the 13 years between our decisions in *Penry* and *Atkins,* no fewer than 16 States banned the execution of mentally retarded offenders. By comparison, since our decision 16 years ago in *Stanford,* only four States that previously permitted the execution of under–18 offenders, plus the Federal Government, have legislatively reversed course, and one additional State's high court has construed the State's death penalty statute not to apply to under–18 offenders. * * *

* * *

* * * Without a clearer showing that a genuine national consensus forbids the execution of such offenders, this Court should not substitute its own "inevitably subjective judgment" on how best to resolve this difficult moral question for the judgments of the Nation's democratically elected legislatures.

JUSTICE SCALIA, with whom THE CHIEF JUSTICE and JUSTICE THOMAS join, dissenting.

In urging approval of a constitution that gave life-tenured judges the power to nullify laws enacted by the people's representatives, Alexander Hamilton assured the citizens of New York that there was little risk in this, since "[t]he judiciary ... ha[s] neither FORCE nor WILL but merely judgment." The Federalist No. 78, p. 465 (C. Rossiter ed.1961). But Hamilton had in mind a traditional judiciary, "bound down by strict rules and precedents which serve to define and point out their duty in every particular case that comes before them." Bound down, indeed. What a mockery today's opinion makes of Hamilton's expectation, announcing the Court's conclusion that the meaning of our Constitution has changed over the past 15 years—not, mind you, that this Court's decision 15 years ago was *wrong,* but that the Constitution *has changed.* The Court reaches this implausible result by purporting to advert, not to the original meaning of the Eighth Amendment, but to "the evolving standards of decency" of our national society. It then finds, on the flimsiest of grounds, that a national consensus which could not be perceived in our people's laws barely 15 years ago now solidly exists. * * *

* * *

* * * Now, the Court says a legislative change in four States is "significant" enough to trigger a constitutional prohibition.[4] It is amazing to think that this subtle shift in numbers can take the issue entirely off the table for legislative debate.

* * *

The Court's reliance on the infrequency of executions for under–18 murderers credits an argument that this Court considered and explicitly rejected in *Stanford*. That infrequency is explained, we accurately said, both by "the undisputed fact that a far smaller percentage of capital crimes are committed by persons under 18 than over 18" and by the fact that juries are required at sentencing to consider the offender's youth as a mitigating factor. Thus, "it is not only possible, but overwhelmingly probable, that the very considerations which induce [respondent] and [his] supporters to believe that death should *never* be imposed on offenders under 18 cause prosecutors and juries to believe that it should *rarely* be imposed."

* * *

Of course, the real force driving today's decision is not the actions of four state legislatures, but the Court's " ' "own judgment" ' " that murderers younger than 18 can never be as morally culpable as older counterparts. * * *

* * *

Today's opinion provides a perfect example of why judges are ill equipped to make the type of legislative judgments the Court insists on making here. To support its opinion that States should be prohibited from imposing the death penalty on anyone who committed murder before age 18, the Court looks to scientific and sociological studies, picking and choosing those that support its position. It never explains why those particular studies are methodologically sound; none was ever entered into evidence or tested in an adversarial proceeding. * * * In other words, all the Court has done today, to borrow from another context, is to look over the heads of the crowd and pick out its friends.

We need not look far to find studies contradicting the Court's conclusions. As petitioner points out, the American Psychological Association (APA), which claims in this case that scientific evidence shows persons under 18 lack the ability to take moral responsibility for their decisions, has previously taken precisely the opposite position before this very Court. In its brief in *Hodgson v. Minnesota*, 497 U.S. 417 (1990), the APA found

---

4. As the Court notes, Washington State's decision to prohibit executions of offenders under 18 was made by a judicial, not legislative, decision. * * * It is irrelevant to the question of changed national consensus.

a "rich body of research" showing that juveniles are mature enough to decide whether to obtain an abortion without parental involvement. The APA brief, citing psychology treatises and studies too numerous to list here, asserted: "[B]y middle adolescence (age 14–15) young people develop abilities similar to adults in reasoning about moral dilemmas, understanding social rules and laws, [and] reasoning about interpersonal relationships and interpersonal problems." Given the nuances of scientific methodology and conflicting views, courts—which can only consider the limited evidence on the record before them—are ill equipped to determine which view of science is the right one. Legislatures "are better qualified to weigh and 'evaluate the results of statistical studies in terms of their own local conditions and with a flexibility of approach that is not available to the courts.' "

Even putting aside questions of methodology, the studies cited by the Court offer scant support for a categorical prohibition of the death penalty for murderers under 18. At most, these studies conclude that, *on average,* or *in most cases,* persons under 18 are unable to take moral responsibility for their actions. Not one of the cited studies opines that all individuals under 18 are unable to appreciate the nature of their crimes.

* * *

That "almost every State prohibits those under 18 years of age from voting, serving on juries, or marrying without parental consent" is patently irrelevant * * *. * * * As we explained in *Stanford,* it is "absurd to think that one must be mature enough to drive carefully, to drink responsibly, or to vote intelligently, in order to be mature enough to understand that murdering another human being is profoundly wrong, and to conform one's conduct to that most minimal of all civilized standards." Serving on a jury or entering into marriage also involve decisions far more sophisticated than the simple decision not to take another's life.

Moreover, the age statutes the Court lists "set the appropriate ages for the operation of a system that makes its determinations in gross, and that does not conduct individualized maturity tests." The criminal justice system, by contrast, provides for individualized consideration of each defendant. * * * In other contexts where individualized consideration is provided, we have recognized that at least some minors will be mature enough to make difficult decisions that involve moral considerations. For instance, we have struck down abortion statutes that do not allow minors deemed mature by courts to bypass parental notification provisions. See, *e.g., Bellotti v. Baird,* 443 U.S. 622, 643–644 (1979) (opinion of Powell, J.); *Planned Parenthood of Central Mo. v. Danforth,* 428 U.S. 52, 74–75 (1976). It is hard to see why this context should be any different. Whether to obtain an abortion is surely a much more complex decision for a young person than whether to kill an innocent person in cold blood.

The Court concludes, however, that juries cannot be trusted with the delicate task of weighing a defendant's youth along with the other mitigating and aggravating factors of his crime. * * * This assertion is based on no evidence; to the contrary, the Court itself acknowledges that the execution of under–18 offenders is "infrequent" even in the States "without a formal prohibition on executing juveniles," suggesting that juries take seriously their responsibility to weigh youth as a mitigating factor.

Nor does the Court suggest a stopping point for its reasoning. If juries cannot make appropriate determinations in cases involving murderers under 18, in what other kinds of cases will the Court find jurors deficient? * * *

The Court's contention that the goals of retribution and deterrence are not served by executing murderers under 18 is also transparently false. The argument that "[r]etribution is not proportional if the law's most severe penalty is imposed on one whose culpability or blameworthiness is diminished," is simply an extension of the earlier, false generalization that youth *always* defeats culpability. The Court claims that "juveniles will be less susceptible to deterrence," because " '[t]he likelihood that the teenage offender has made the kind of cost-benefit analysis that attaches any weight to the possibility of execution is so remote as to be virtually nonexistent.' " The Court unsurprisingly finds no support for this astounding proposition, save its own case law. The facts of this very case show the proposition to be false. Before committing the crime, Simmons encouraged his friends to join him by assuring them that they could "get away with it" because they were minors. * * *

* * *

Though the views of our own citizens are essentially irrelevant to the Court's decision today, the views of other countries and the so-called international community take center stage.

* * *

* * * Foreign sources are cited today, *not* to underscore our "fidelity" to the Constitution, our "pride in its origins," and "our own [American] heritage." To the contrary, they are cited *to set aside* the centuries-old American practice * * * of letting a jury of 12 citizens decide whether, in the particular case, youth should be the basis for withholding the death penalty. What these foreign sources "affirm," rather than repudiate, is the Justices' own notion of how the world ought to be, and their diktat that it shall be so henceforth in America. * * *

* * *

QUESTIONS AND POINTS FOR DISCUSSION

1. In your opinion, of what significance, if any, are the following factors to the question whether the death penalty, in certain or all circumstances, constitutes cruel and unusual punishment: public-opinion polls, the views of professional organizations, the practices of other countries, and the results of

studies that bear on the question whether the death penalty effectuates penological goals?

2. The Supreme Court has identified another category of persons whose execution is barred by the Eighth Amendment: Prisoners who have been convicted of a capital crime and sentenced to death, but are now insane, cannot be executed unless and until their sanity is restored. In explaining why execution of an insane person would be cruel and unusual punishment, the Supreme Court in Ford v. Wainwright, 477 U.S. 399, 106 S.Ct. 2595 (1986) noted that for a number of reasons, not one state in the country permits an insane person to be executed. One of these reasons is that many people doubt that the death penalty could serve its retributive aim when the person being executed is incapable of understanding why he is being put to death. The Court also mentioned the religious roots of such execution bans—the belief that it would be unconscionable to kill individuals who are incapable of first seeking God's forgiveness for their sins.

Courts still must resolve when a prisoner is "insane" in the constitutional sense that bars his or her execution. A mentally ill prisoner whose case was before the Supreme Court in Panetti v. Quarterman, 551 U.S. 930, 127 S.Ct. 2842 (2007) claimed that what he recognized was the state's asserted reason for executing him—his commission of two brutal murders—was a "sham" and that he really was being put to death by "forces of the darkness" to keep him from preaching. The Supreme Court noted that even though a prisoner with a psychotic disorder is aware that he is being executed for a crime, he still might be incompetent to be executed. Holding that the Eighth Amendment also requires that a prisoner have a "rational understanding" of the reason for his execution, the Court left to the courts on remand to decide whether the prisoner in this case met this requirement.

3. A court's conclusion that a prisoner on death row, though mentally ill, is sane and therefore can be executed likely will be appealed. But by the time a round of appeals is completed, the prisoner's mental condition may have deteriorated to the point that the prisoner now is insane—to the point that the prisoner does not know, for example, why she is being executed or does not have a "rational understanding" of that reason. What, in your opinion, are the practical and constitutional implications, if any, of the fact that the gravity of a mental illness can fluctuate while courts adjudicate the question of the prisoner's sanity?

4. In Washington v. Harper, 494 U.S. 210, 227, 110 S.Ct. 1028, 1039–40 (1990), which is discussed on pages 636–39 and 757–62, the Supreme Court held that mentally ill prisoners can be forced to take antipsychotic drugs when they pose a danger to themselves or others and the administration of the medication is in their "medical interest." But the Supreme Court thus far has skirted the question whether the United States Constitution permits the government to force insane prisoners to take medication that will make them sane enough to be executed. Perry v. Louisiana, 498 U.S. 38, 111 S.Ct. 449 (1990). The Louisiana Supreme Court, on the other hand, has held that the compulsory administration of antipsychotic drugs for such a purpose violates both the right to privacy and the right not to be subjected to cruel, excessive,

or unusual punishments protected by the Louisiana Constitution. Louisiana v. Perry, 610 So.2d 746 (La.1992).

How would you resolve the federal constitutional question? As a constitutional matter, does it make any difference if the antipsychotic medication is administered involuntarily in order to protect the inmate or others from danger but has the collateral effect of making the prisoner competent for execution? See Singleton v. Norris, 319 F.3d 1018, 1026–27 (8th Cir. 2003) (involuntary administration of antipsychotic medication in conformance with the requirements of Washington v. Harper that had the side effect of making the prisoner competent to understand the nature of, and reason for, his execution did not violate due process or the Eighth Amendment).

––––––––

Consider the following facts, which were drawn from a real case: The defendant's girlfriend left her one-year-old baby with the defendant for thirty minutes while she drove to her cousin's house. When she returned, she found the baby crying. The baby's underwear was soaked with blood. The defendant unsuccessfully tried to persuade his girlfriend not to take the baby to the hospital. The physical examination at the hospital revealed that the baby's rectum had been torn and was bleeding. Following his arrest, the defendant told the police that he had been sleeping on the bed with the baby when she rolled on top of him. He claimed that in the dark and in his drowsy state, he thought the baby was his girlfriend, so he penetrated her with his penis. He denied having an ejaculation, but semen matching the defendant's type was found in the baby's underwear. The defendant was convicted of aggravated rape.

What arguments would you make in support of the constitutionality of a statute authorizing imposition of the death penalty in this case? What arguments would you make against the statute's constitutionality? Is there any additional information you would want or need in order to complete your constitutional analysis? Compare your answers to these questions with the arguments and analysis in the following case.

KENNEDY v. LOUISIANA

Supreme Court of the United States, 2008.
128 S.Ct. 2641, 171 L.Ed.2d 525.

JUSTICE KENNEDY delivered the opinion of the Court.

* * * This case presents the question whether the Constitution bars respondent from imposing the death penalty for the rape of a child where the crime did not result, and was not intended to result, in death of the victim. * * *

I

* * * At 9:18 a.m. on March 2, 1998, petitioner called 911 to report that his stepdaughter, referred to here as L. H., had been raped. He told

the 911 operator that L. H. had been in the garage while he readied his son for school. Upon hearing loud screaming, petitioner said, he ran outside and found L. H. in the side yard. Two neighborhood boys, petitioner told the operator, had dragged L. H. from the garage to the yard, pushed her down, and raped her. Petitioner claimed he saw one of the boys riding away on a blue 10–speed bicycle.

When police arrived at petitioner's home between 9:20 and 9:30 a.m., they found L. H. on her bed, wearing a T-shirt and wrapped in a bloody blanket. She was bleeding profusely from the vaginal area. Petitioner told police he had carried her from the yard to the bathtub and then to the bed. Consistent with this explanation, police found a thin line of blood drops in the garage on the way to the house and then up the stairs. Once in the bedroom, petitioner had used a basin of water and a cloth to wipe blood from the victim. This later prevented medical personnel from collecting a reliable DNA sample.

L. H. was transported to the Children's Hospital. An expert in pediatric forensic medicine testified that L. H.'s injuries were the most severe he had seen from a sexual assault in his four years of practice. A laceration to the left wall of the vagina had separated her cervix from the back of her vagina, causing her rectum to protrude into the vaginal structure. Her entire perineum was torn from the posterior fourchette to the anus. The injuries required emergency surgery.

At the scene of the crime, at the hospital, and in the first weeks that followed, both L. H. and petitioner maintained in their accounts to investigators that L. H. had been raped by two neighborhood boys. One of L. H.'s doctors testified at trial that L. H. told all hospital personnel the same version of the rape, although she reportedly told one family member that petitioner raped her. L. H. was interviewed several days after the rape by a psychologist. The interview was videotaped, lasted three hours over two days, and was introduced into evidence at trial. On the tape one can see that L. H. had difficulty discussing the subject of the rape. She spoke haltingly and with long pauses and frequent movement. Early in the interview, L. H. expressed reservations about the questions being asked:

> "I'm going to tell the same story. They just want me to change it … They want me to say my Dad did it … I don't want to say it … I tell them the same, same story."

She told the psychologist that she had been playing in the garage when a boy came over and asked her about Girl Scout cookies she was selling; and that the boy "pulled [her by the legs to] the backyard," where he placed his hand over her mouth, "pulled down [her] shorts," and raped her.

Eight days after the crime, and despite L. H.'s insistence that petitioner was not the offender, petitioner was arrested for the rape. * * * [T]he case for the prosecution, credited by the jury, was based upon the following evidence: An inspection of the side yard immediately after the assault was inconsistent with a rape having occurred there, the grass having been found mostly undisturbed but for a small patch of coagulated blood. Petitioner said that one of the perpetrators fled the crime scene on a blue 10–speed bicycle but gave inconsistent descriptions of the bicycle's features, such as its handlebars. Investigators found a bicycle matching petitioner and L. H.'s description in tall grass behind a nearby apartment, and petitioner identified it as the bicycle one of the perpetrators was riding. Yet its tires were flat, it did not have gears, and it was covered in spider webs. In addition police found blood on the underside of L. H.'s mattress. This convinced them the rape took place in her bedroom, not outside the house.

Police also found that petitioner made two telephone calls on the morning of the rape. Sometime before 6:15 a.m., petitioner called his employer and left a message that he was unavailable to work that day. Petitioner called back between 6:30 and 7:30 a.m. to ask a colleague how to get blood out of a white carpet because his daughter had " 'just become a young lady.' " At 7:37 a.m., petitioner called B & B Carpet Cleaning and requested urgent assistance in removing bloodstains from a carpet. Petitioner did not call 911 until about an hour and a half later.

About a month after petitioner's arrest L. H. was removed from the custody of her mother, who had maintained until that point that petitioner was not involved in the rape. On June 22, 1998, L. H. was returned home and told her mother for the first time that petitioner had raped her. And on December 16, 1999, about 21 months after the rape, L. H. recorded her accusation in a videotaped interview with the Child Advocacy Center.

The state charged petitioner with aggravated rape of a child * * * and sought the death penalty. * * *

* * *

The trial began in August 2003. L. H. was then 13 years old. She testified that she " 'woke up one morning and Patrick was on top of [her].' " * * * L. H. acknowledged that she had accused two neighborhood boys but testified petitioner told her to say this and that it was untrue.

The jury having found petitioner guilty of aggravated rape, the penalty phase ensued. The State presented the testimony of S. L., who is the cousin and goddaughter of petitioner's ex-wife. S. L. testified that petitioner sexually abused her three times when she was eight years old and that the last time involved sexual intercourse. She did not tell anyone until two years later and did not pursue legal action.

The jury unanimously determined that petitioner should be sentenced to death. The Supreme Court of Louisiana affirmed. * * *

* * *

II

* * *

Evolving standards of decency must embrace and express respect for the dignity of the person, and the punishment of criminals must conform to that rule. * * * When the law punishes by death, it risks its own sudden descent into brutality, transgressing the constitutional commitment to decency and restraint.

* * *

III

A

* * *

In 1925, 18 States, the District of Columbia, and the Federal Government had statutes that authorized the death penalty for the rape of a child or an adult. Between 1930 and 1964, 455 people were executed for those crimes. * * *

In 1972, *Furman* invalidated most of the state statutes authorizing the death penalty for the crime of rape; and in *Furman*'s aftermath only six States reenacted their capital rape provisions. * * * All six statutes were later invalidated under state or federal law.

Louisiana reintroduced the death penalty for rape of a child in 1995. Under the current statute, any anal, vaginal, or oral intercourse with a child under the age of 13 constitutes aggravated rape and is punishable by death. Mistake of age is not a defense, so the statute imposes strict liability in this regard. Five States have since followed Louisiana's lead * * *. Four of these States' statutes are more narrow than Louisiana's in that only offenders with a previous rape conviction are death eligible. Georgia's statute makes child rape a capital offense only when aggravating circumstances are present, including but not limited to a prior conviction.

* * *

The evidence of a national consensus with respect to the death penalty for child rapists * * * shows divided opinion but, on balance, an opinion against it. Thirty-seven jurisdictions—36 States plus the Federal Government—have the death penalty. As mentioned above, only six of those jurisdictions authorize the death penalty for rape of a child. Though our review of national consensus is not confined to tallying the number of States with applicable death penalty legislation, it is of significance that, in 45 jurisdictions, petitioner could not be executed for child rape of any kind. * * *

B

* * *

* * * In *Coker* [*v. Georgia*, 433 U.S. 584 (1977*)*], a four-Member plurality of the Court, plus Justice Brennan and Justice Marshall in concurrence, held that a sentence of death for the rape of a 16–year–old woman, who was a minor under Georgia law yet was characterized by the

Court as an adult, was disproportionate and excessive under the Eighth Amendment. (The Court did not explain why the 16–year–old victim qualified as an adult, but it may be of some significance that she was married, had a home of her own, and had given birth to a son three weeks prior to the rape.)

* * *

* * * The *Coker* plurality framed the question as whether, "with respect to rape of an adult woman," the death penalty is disproportionate punishment. The opinion does not speak to the constitutionality of the death penalty for child rape, an issue not then before the Court. * * *

* * *

We conclude * * * that there is no clear indication that state legislatures have misinterpreted *Coker* to hold that the death penalty for child rape is unconstitutional. The small number of States that have enacted this penalty, then, is relevant to determining whether there is a consensus against capital punishment for this crime.

C

Respondent insists that the six States where child rape is a capital offense, along with the States that have proposed but not yet enacted applicable death penalty legislation, reflect a consistent direction of change in support of the death penalty for child rape. Consistent change might counterbalance an otherwise weak demonstration of consensus. But whatever the significance of consistent change where it is cited to show emerging support for expanding the scope of the death penalty, no showing of consistent change has been made in this case.

Respondent and its *amici* identify five States where, in their view, legislation authorizing capital punishment for child rape is pending. It is not our practice, nor is it sound, to find contemporary norms based upon state legislation that has been proposed but not yet enacted. * * *

Aside from pending legislation, it is true that in the last 13 years there has been change towards making child rape a capital offense. This is evidenced by six new death penalty statutes, three enacted in the last two years.* * * Respondent argues the instant case is like *Roper* because, there, only five States had shifted their positions between 1989 and 2005, one less State than here. But in *Roper*, we emphasized that, though the pace of abolition was not as great as in *Atkins*, it was counterbalanced by the total number of States that had recognized the impropriety of executing juvenile offenders. * * * Here, the total number of States to have made child rape a capital offense after *Furman* is six. This is not an indication of a trend or change in direction comparable to the one supported by data in *Roper*.

D

There are measures of consensus other than legislation. Statistics about the number of executions may inform the consideration whether capital punishment for the crime of child rape is regarded as unacceptable in our society. These statistics confirm our determination from our review of state statutes that there is a social consensus against the death penalty for the crime of child rape.

Nine States * * * have permitted capital punishment for adult or child rape for some length of time between the Court's 1972 decision in *Furman* and today. Yet no individual has been executed for the rape of an adult or child since 1964, and no execution for any other nonhomicide offense has been conducted since 1963.

Louisiana is the only State since 1964 that has sentenced an individual to death for the crime of child rape; and petitioner and Richard Davis, who was convicted and sentenced to death for the aggravated rape of a 5–year–old child by a Louisiana jury, * * * are the only two individuals now on death row in the United States for a nonhomicide offense.

* * * [W]e conclude there is a national consensus against capital punishment for the crime of child rape.

IV

A

As we have said in other Eighth Amendment cases, objective evidence of contemporary values as it relates to punishment for child rape is entitled to great weight, but it does not end our inquiry. "[T]he Constitution contemplates that in the end our own judgment will be brought to bear on the question of the acceptability of the death penalty under the Eighth Amendment." * * *

* * *

* * * Evolving standards of decency that mark the progress of a maturing society counsel us to be most hesitant before interpreting the Eighth Amendment to allow the extension of the death penalty, a hesitation that has special force where no life was taken in the commission of the crime. * * *

* * *

Our concern here is limited to crimes against individual persons. We do not address, for example, crimes defining and punishing treason, espionage, terrorism, and drug kingpin activity, which are offenses against the State. As it relates to crimes against individuals, though, the death penalty should not be expanded to instances where the victim's life was not taken. * * *

* * *

Consistent with evolving standards of decency and the teachings of our precedents we conclude that, in determining whether the death penalty is excessive, there is a distinction between intentional first-degree murder on the one hand and nonhomicide crimes against individual persons, even including child rape, on the other. The latter crimes may be devastating in their harm, as here, but "in terms of moral depravity and of the injury to the person and to the public," they cannot be compared to murder in their "severity and irrevocability."

In reaching our conclusion we find significant the number of executions that would be allowed under respondent's approach. The crime of child rape, considering its reported incidents, occurs more often than first-degree murder. Approximately 5,702 incidents of vaginal, anal, or oral rape of a child under the age of 12 were reported nationwide in 2005; this is almost twice the total incidents of intentional murder for victims of all ages (3,405) reported during the same period. * * *

It might be said that narrowing aggravators could be used in this context, as with murder offenses, to ensure the death penalty's restrained application. We find it difficult to identify standards that would guide the decisionmaker so the penalty is reserved for the most severe cases of child rape and yet not imposed in an arbitrary way. Even were we to forbid, say, the execution of first-time child rapists or require as an aggravating factor a finding that the perpetrator's instant rape offense involved multiple victims, the jury still must balance, in its discretion, those aggravating factors against mitigating circumstances. In this context, which involves a crime that in many cases will overwhelm a decent person's judgment, we have no confidence that the imposition of the death penalty would not be so arbitrary as to be "freakis[h]." * * *

* * *

* * * [I]mprecision and the tension between evaluating the individual circumstances and consistency of treatment have been tolerated where the victim dies. It should not be introduced into our justice system, though, where death has not occurred.

* * *

B

* * *

The goal of retribution, which reflects society's and the victim's interests in seeing that the offender is repaid for the hurt he caused, does not justify the harshness of the death penalty here. * * *
* * *

There are, moreover, serious systemic concerns in prosecuting the crime of child rape that are relevant to the constitutionality of making it a capital offense. The problem of unreliable, induced, and even imagined child testimony means there is a "special risk of wrongful execution" in some child rape cases. * * *

* * *

With respect to deterrence, if the death penalty adds to the risk of non-reporting, that, too, diminishes the penalty's objectives. Underreporting is a common problem with respect to child sexual abuse. * * * [O]ne of the most commonly cited reasons for nondisclosure is fear of negative consequences for the perpetrator, a concern that has special force where the abuser is a family member. The experience of the *amici* who work with child victims indicates that, when the punishment is death, both the victim and the victim's family members may be more likely to shield the perpetrator from discovery, thus increasing underreporting. As a result, punishment by death may not result in more deterrence or more effective enforcement.

In addition, by in effect making the punishment for child rape and murder equivalent, a State that punishes child rape by death may remove a strong incentive for the rapist not to kill the victim. Assuming the offender behaves in a rational way, as one must to justify the penalty on grounds of deterrence, the penalty in some respects gives less protection, not more, to the victim, who is often the sole witness to the crime. * * *

Each of these propositions, standing alone, might not establish the unconstitutionality of the death penalty for the crime of child rape. Taken in sum, however, they demonstrate the serious negative consequences of making child rape a capital offense. These considerations lead us to conclude, in our independent judgment, that the death penalty is not a proportional punishment for the rape of a child.

V

* * *

* * * In most cases justice is not better served by terminating the life of the perpetrator rather than confining him and preserving the possibility that he and the system will find ways to allow him to understand the enormity of his offense. Difficulties in administering the penalty to ensure against its arbitrary and capricious application require adherence to a rule reserving its use, at this stage of evolving standards and in cases of crimes against individuals, for crimes that take the life of the victim.

* * *

JUSTICE ALITO, with whom THE CHIEF JUSTICE, JUSTICE SCALIA, and JUSTICE THOMAS join, dissenting.

The Court today holds that the Eighth Amendment categorically prohibits the imposition of the death penalty for the crime of raping a child. This is so, according to the Court, no matter how young the child, no matter how many times the child is raped, no matter how many children the perpetrator rapes, no matter how sadistic the crime, no matter how much physical or psychological trauma is inflicted, and no matter how heinous the perpetrator's prior criminal record may be. * * *

* * *

I turn first to the Court's claim that there is "a national consensus" that it is never acceptable to impose the death penalty for the rape of a child. * * * In assessing current norms, the Court relies primarily on the fact that only 6 of the 50 States now have statutes that permit the death penalty for this offense. But this statistic is a highly unreliable indicator of the views of state lawmakers and their constituents. * * * [D]icta in this Court's decision in *Coker* v. *Georgia*, 433 U.S. 584 (1977) * * * gave state legislators and others good reason to fear that any law permitting the imposition of the death penalty for this crime would meet precisely the fate that has now befallen the Louisiana statute that is currently before us, and this threat strongly discouraged state legislators—regardless of their own values and those of their constituents—from supporting the enactment of such legislation.

* * *

I do not suggest that six new state laws necessarily establish a "national consensus" or even that they are sure evidence of an ineluctable trend. In terms of the Court's metaphor of moral evolution, these enactments might have turned out to be an evolutionary dead end. But they might also have been the beginning of a strong new evolutionary line. We will never know, because the Court today snuffs out the line in its incipient stage.

The Court is willing to block the potential emergence of a national consensus in favor of permitting the death penalty for child rape because, in the end, what matters is the Court's "own judgment" regarding "the acceptability of the death penalty." * * *

* * *

A major theme of the Court's opinion is that permitting the death penalty in child-rape cases is not in the best interests of the victims of these crimes and society at large. * * *

These policy arguments, whatever their merits, are simply not pertinent to the question whether the death penalty is "cruel and unusual" punishment. The Eighth Amendment protects the right of an accused. It does not authorize this Court to strike down federal or state criminal laws on the ground that they are not in the best interests of crime victims or the broader society. * * *

The Court also contends that laws permitting the death penalty for the rape of a child create serious procedural problems. Specifically, the Court maintains that it is not feasible to channel the exercise of sentencing discretion in child-rape cases, and that the unreliability of the testimony of child victims creates a danger that innocent defendants will be convicted and executed. * * *

The Court's argument regarding the structuring of sentencing discretion is hard to comprehend. * * * Even assuming that the age of a child is not alone a sufficient factor for limiting sentencing discretion, the Court need only examine the child rape laws recently enacted in Texas, Oklahoma, Montana, and South Carolina, all of which use a concrete factor to limit quite drastically the number of cases in which the death penalty may be imposed. In those States, a defendant convicted of the rape of a child may be sentenced to death only if the defendant has a prior conviction for a specified felony sex offense.

Moreover, it takes little imagination to envision other limiting factors that a State could use to structure sentencing discretion in child rape cases. Some of these might be: whether the victim was kidnapped, whether the defendant inflicted severe physical injury on the victim, whether the victim was raped multiple times, whether the rapes occurred over a specified extended period, and whether there were multiple victims.

* * * [C]oncerns about limiting sentencing discretion provide no support for the Court's blanket condemnation of all capital child-rape statutes.

That sweeping holding is also not justified by the Court's concerns about the reliability of the testimony of child victims. * * * [I]f the Court's evidentiary concerns have Eighth Amendment relevance, they could be addressed by allowing the death penalty in only those child rape cases in which the independent evidence is sufficient to prove all the elements needed for conviction and imposition of a death sentence. * * *

* * *

The Court's final—and, it appears, principal—justification for its holding is that murder * * * is unique in its moral depravity and in the severity of the injury that it inflicts on the victim and the public. * * *

* * *

* * * I have little doubt that, in the eyes of ordinary Americans, the very worst child rapists—predators who seek out and inflict serious physical and emotional injury on defenseless young children—are the epitome of moral depravity.

With respect to the question of the harm caused by the rape of [a] child in relation to the harm caused by murder, it is certainly true that the loss of human life represents a unique harm, but that does not explain why other grievous harms are insufficient to permit a death sentence. And the Court does not take the position that no harm other than the loss of life is sufficient. The Court takes pains to limit its holding to "crimes against individual persons" and to exclude "offenses against the State," a category that the Court stretches—without explanation—to include "drug kingpin activity." But the Court makes no effort to explain why the harm caused by such crimes is necessarily greater than the harm caused by the rape of young children. * * *

The rape of any victim inflicts great injury, and "[s]ome victims are so grievously injured physically or psychologically that life *is* beyond repair." "The immaturity and vulnerability of a child, both physically and psychologically, adds a devastating dimension to rape that is not present when an adult is raped." * * *

* * *

The deep problems that afflict child-rape victims often become society's problems as well. Commentators have noted correlations between childhood sexual abuse and later problems such as substance abuse, dangerous sexual behaviors or dysfunction, inability to relate to others on an interpersonal level, and psychiatric illness. Victims of child rape are nearly 5 times more likely than nonvictims to be arrested for sex crimes and nearly 30 times more likely to be arrested for prostitution.

The harm that is caused to the victims and to society at large by the worst child rapists is grave. It is the judgment of the Louisiana lawmakers and those in an increasing number of other States that these harms justify the death penalty. The Court provides no cogent explanation why this legislative judgment should be overridden. * * *

QUESTIONS AND POINTS FOR DISCUSSION

1.   In Tison v. Arizona, 481 U.S. 137, 107 S.Ct. 1676 (1987), the Supreme Court concluded that it is not necessarily cruel and unusual punishment to impose the death penalty on a defendant who did not kill a murder victim and did not intend that the victim be killed. In that case, the defendants, who were brothers, smuggled guns into a prison and then used them to help their father and another prisoner escape. When they later had car trouble, one of the defendants flagged down a passing car whose passengers included a mother and father, their two-year-old son, and their fifteen-year-old niece. The defendants' father and the other escaped prisoner eventually shot and killed all four passengers. The defendants then were convicted of four counts of capital murder under the state's felony-murder statute and another statute holding certain felons responsible for crimes committed by their accomplices.

The Supreme Court, in a 5–4 decision, held that there is nothing cruel and unusual about executing a defendant whose participation in "the felony" was "major" and who had acted with "reckless indifference to human life." Id. at 158, 107 S.Ct. at 1691. The Court observed that a defendant's reckless disregard for human life can be inferred when a defendant "knowingly engag[es] in criminal activities known to carry a grave risk of death." Id. at 157, 107 S.Ct. at 1688.

Do you agree with the Court's holding in Tison? For a case holding, on state constitutional grounds, that a death sentence is a grossly disproportionate penalty when imposed on a defendant who had no intent to kill or knowledge that his actions would lead to someone's death, see Vernon Kills on Top v. State, 928 P.2d 182, 206 (Mont. 1996).

2.   In its opinion in Tison, the Supreme Court distinguished Enmund v. Florida, 458 U.S. 782, 102 S.Ct. 3368 (1982), a case in which the Court had ruled unconstitutional the imposition of the death penalty on a defendant who had driven the getaway car in an armed robbery, but had not killed the two murder victims. As the Court explained in Tison, the defendant's role in the

armed robbery and murders in *Enmund* was "minor," and there was no finding that he either had the intent to kill the victims or had acted with reckless indifference to human life. What if there had been a finding in *Enmund* that the defendant had acted with reckless disregard of the risk that the armed robbery could culminate in the death of the victims? Would imposition of the death penalty have been constitutional in those circumstances?

3. Sometimes a challenge is mounted, not against the constitutionality of executing a person falling within a certain category of individuals, but against the method of execution. The Supreme Court has upheld both the use of a firing squad and electrocution to implement a death sentence. Wilkerson v. Utah, 99 U.S. 130 (1878) (firing squad); In re Kemmler, 136 U.S. 436, 10 S.Ct. 930 (1890) (electrocution). In addition, in one case in which an effort to electrocute a prisoner failed to kill him, apparently because of a mechanical problem, the Court held that a second attempt to electrocute him would not subject him to cruel and unusual punishment. Louisiana ex rel. Francis v. Resweber, 329 U.S. 459, 67 S.Ct. 374 (1947).

Most states and the federal government employ lethal injection to implement the death penalty. Baze v. Rees, 128 S.Ct. 1520, 1526–27 (2008). The majority of these states use a three-drug regimen during the execution process. The first drug sedates the prisoner and, when administered properly, puts the prisoner in a comalike state. The second drug paralyzes the prisoner and, by paralyzing the diaphragm, prevents the prisoner from breathing. The third drug then stops the prisoner's heart from beating, inducing a cardiac arrest.

In *Baze v. Rees*, the Supreme Court considered whether the way in which the state of Kentucky was implementing this three-drug protocol when executing prisoners violated the Eighth Amendment. The prisoners on death row who raised this claim conceded that if the three drugs were administered properly, the end result would be a "humane death" comporting with the Constitution. But the prisoners contended that the state had adopted inadequate safeguards to prevent prisoners from being subjected to unnecessary and, in the words of the dissenters, "excruciating" pain. Id. at 1570 (Ginsburg, J., dissenting). One of the prisoners' chief concerns was that misadministration of the first drug, the sedative, could leave a prisoner conscious, though not visibly so. Due to the paralysis caused by the second drug, the prisoner then would have to endure what the dissent described as "the agony of conscious suffocation" and the "searing pain" caused by the third drug when it induced a cardiac arrest. Id. at 1571.

A majority of the Court rejected the constitutional challenge to the way in which Kentucky was following the three-drug protocol. The Justices were divided, however, on the standard to apply when assessing the constitutionality of a mode of execution. The plurality opinion, written by Justice Roberts and in which Justices Kennedy and Alito joined, stated that a threshold requirement must be met before a court need delve further into the Eighth Amendment claim: The means of execution must create a " 'substantial risk of serious harm' " apart from the pain that inevitably accompanies death. Id. at 1532 & n.3 (plurality opinion) (quoting Farmer v. Brennan, 511 U.S. 825,

842, 114 S.Ct. 1970, 1981 (1994)). If this requirement is met, a prisoner then has to demonstrate that an alternative execution method is "feasible, readily implemented, and in fact significantly reduce[s] a substantial risk of severe pain." 128 S.Ct. at 1532. And even if such an alternative exists, the execution method does not inflict cruel and unusual punishment if the state has a "legitimate penological justification" for not utilizing this alternative. Id.

In an opinion concurring in the judgment, Justice Thomas, joined by Justice Scalia, objected to this multi-pronged test. Justice Thomas argued that a method of execution violates the Eighth Amendment "only if it is deliberately designed to inflict pain"—when it is employed to cause "terror, pain, or disgrace," not just death. Id. at 1556, 1563 (Thomas, J., concurring in judgment). As support for this conclusion, Justice Thomas cited the kinds of penalties that had sparked the Eighth Amendment's adoption, such as burning at the stake, disemboweling convicted offenders while they were still alive, and hanging them in places where the public could view their bodies decomposing.

Three other Justices on the Court—Justices Ginsburg, Souter, and Breyer—opined that the pertinent inquiry is whether the execution method creates "an untoward, readily avoidable risk of inflicting severe and unnecessary pain." Id. at 1567 (Ginsburg, J., dissenting); id. at 1563 (Breyer, J., concurring in judgment). Three factors are considered when applying this test—one, the degree to which the execution method poses a risk of causing significant pain; two, the severity of the pain it risks causing; and three, the existence of a "readily available" alternative that will "materially increase" the probability that the mode of execution will not cause pain. Id. at 1569 (Ginsburg, J., dissenting). Unlike the plurality's approach, this "untoward risk" test does not require a threshold showing that an execution method creates a substantial risk of serious harm. Instead, all three factors are weighed, with a strong showing on one factor depreciating the significance of the other two.

The plurality maintained that this consideration at the outset of execution alternatives "would threaten to transform courts into boards of inquiry charged with determining 'best practices' for execution, with each ruling supplanted by another round of litigation touting a new and improved methodology." Id. at 1531 (plurality opinion). But Justice Thomas charged that the plurality's multi-pronged test also would embroil the courts in litigation as they were asked to determine whether a risk was "substantial," whether alternative procedures were "feasible," whether they could be "readily implemented," whether they would lead to a "significant" reduction in the risk, and whether a penological justification for adhering to a current execution protocol was "legitimate." Id. at 1562 (Thomas, J., concurring in judgment).

Which of the three Eighth Amendment tests propounded in *Baze* is, in your opinion, the most appropriate? Why? Is there a different test that you believe courts should apply when assessing the constitutionality of execution methods?

4. It behooves us to remember that the question of the test to be applied when resolving a constitutional issue is different from the question of what is the proper result when a particular test is applied. When the plurality in *Baze*

applied its multi-pronged test, it concluded that the three-drug protocol used in Kentucky was constitutional. The plurality found that the prisoners had failed to meet the threshold requirement of demonstrating that there was a substantial risk that an insufficient amount of the first drug, the sedative, would be administered during the execution process—that a prisoner would be conscious when he was asphyxiated and his heart was stopped.

The plurality had an additional response to concerns that the second drug, the one that paralyzes a prisoner, could mask signs that the prisoner was still conscious. The plurality asserted that this drug serves two legitimate purposes. First, it furthers the state's "interest in preserving the dignity of the procedure," since it suppresses involuntary movements that others might misconstrue as signs that the prisoner is conscious or distressed. Id. at 1535. And second, it expedites a prisoner's death by halting his breathing. Therefore, according to the plurality, the inclusion of this drug in the execution protocol did not render it unconstitutional.

In a concurring opinion, Justice Stevens spurned these rationales. Noting that Kentucky barred use of the second drug when euthanizing animals, he found it "unseemly—to say the least—that Kentucky may well kill petitioners using a drug that it would not permit to be used on their pets." Id. at 1543 (Stevens, J., concurring in judgment). But because Justice Stevens believed that inadequate facts were adduced at trial to support a finding that Kentucky's execution protocol was unconstitutional, he concurred, though reluctantly, in the judgment. At the same time, he emphasized that in future cases challenging the constitutionality of three-drug protocols utilized when executing prisoners via lethal injection, the outcome might be different.

Justice Stevens also confessed in *Baze* that he had come to the conclusion that the death penalty was unconstitutional, both because it, at best, only marginally advances any legitimate penological purposes and because arbitrariness in its application is unavoidable. But out of what he said was respect for precedent—prior Supreme Court cases upholding the constitutionality of the death penalty, Justice Stevens concurred in the Court's judgment.

5. In recent years, the death penalty has been the subject of increasing scrutiny and debate. A Columbia University study of 4,578 state capital cases between 1973 and 1995, for example, found that sixty-eight percent of the judgments imposing death sentences later were reversed. James S. Liebman et al., A Broken System: Error Rates in Capital Cases, 1973–1995, at 5 (2000). Eighty-two percent of the capital defendants whose death sentences were set aside and retried received a sentence less than death after being retried. Id. Seven percent were found not guilty. Id.

The case of Anthony Porter, who was sentenced to death in Illinois, illustrates how closely some individuals have come to being executed for crimes they had not committed. Only two days before Porter's execution date were his attorneys able to secure a stay to determine whether he was mentally competent to be executed. And it was only because of this stay that a Northwestern University journalism class then had the time to investigate Porter's case. During this investigation, the actual killer was found, and Porter was released. Ronald J. Tabak, Finality Without Fairness: Why We Are

Moving Towards Moratoria on Executions, and the Potential Abolition of Capital Punishment, 33 Conn. L. Rev. 733, 739 (2001).

In 2000, George Ryan, the governor of Illinois, declared a moratorium on executions, citing what he described as a "shameful record of convicting innocent people and putting them on death row." Liebman, supra, at 124 n.10. This decision helped spawn what has been described as "a tectonic shift in the politics of the death penalty," prompting other states to initiate studies of their capital-punishment systems. Id. at 2. Shortly before Governor Ryan left office, he pardoned four prisoners on death row and commuted the death sentences of the remaining 155 prisoners awaiting execution. Bureau of Justice Statistics, U.S. Dep't of Justice, Capital Punishment, 2003, at 8 (2004).

Justice Scalia has cited the setting aside of erroneous convictions and death sentences of persons on death row, whether by courts or through the exercise of executive clemency, as evidence of the "success" of the criminal-justice system, not its "failure." Kansas v. Marsh, 548 U.S. 163, 193, 126 S.Ct. 2516, 2536 (2006) (Scalia, J., concurring). Do you agree?

6. In *Kansas v. Marsh*, the Supreme Court acknowledged that "the criminal justice system does not operate perfectly" and stated that the death penalty would have to be abolished if its imposition had to be error-free. Id. at 181, 126 S.Ct. at 2529. In your opinion, does the possibility that an innocent person may be executed have a bearing on the death penalty's constitutionality? Can the errors made in imposing the death penalty be eliminated through measures short of abolishing capital punishment? If so, what are those measures? For one reform initiative enacted by Congress in 2004, see the Innocence Protection Act of 2004, Pub.L. No. 108–405, 118 Stat. 2278–93. For other reform proposals, see The Constitution Project, Mandatory Justice: Eighteen Reforms to the Death Penalty (2001); James S. Liebman, The Overproduction of Death, 100 Colum. L. Rev. 2030, 2143–54 (2000).

7. One of the problems contributing to erroneous convictions and death sentences in capital cases is the failure of some attorneys to afford capital defendants their constitutional right to the effective assistance of counsel. The quality of the assistance received by the defendant in Williams v. Taylor, 529 U.S. 362, 120 S.Ct. 1495 (2000) exemplifies what Judge David Bazelon has called "walking violations of the Sixth Amendment." David Bazelon, The Defective Assistance of Counsel, 42 U. Cin. L. Rev. 1, 2 (1973). In *Williams*, the defendant was sentenced to death after his attorney failed to introduce evidence of what the Supreme Court termed a "nightmarish childhood." Id. at 395, 120 S.Ct. at 1514. The jury was unaware, for example, that the defendant's parents had been imprisoned for child neglect after the defendant and his siblings were discovered living in the following conditions:

> The home was a complete wreck.... There were several places on the floor where someone had had a bowel movement. Urine was standing in several places in the bedrooms. There were dirty dishes scattered over the kitchen, and it was impossible to step any place on the kitchen floor where there was no trash.... The children were all dirty and none of them had on under-pants. Noah and Lula were so intoxicated, they could not find any clothes for the children, nor were they able to put the clothes

on them. . . . The children had to be put in Winslow Hospital, as four of them, by that time, were definitely under the influence of whiskey.

Id. at 395 n.19, 120 S.Ct. at 1514 n.19. The defendant's attorney also failed to disclose to the jury that the defendant's father often beat him severely and that the defendant was subjected to further abuse when living in a foster home while his parents were incarcerated. Nor was the jury apprised of other mitigating facts, including that the defendant was "borderline mentally retarded." Id. at 396, 120 S. Ct. at 1514.

Stephen Bright, the president of the Southern Center for Human Rights, has further highlighted the gravity of the problem of incompetent counsel in capital cases, some examples of which are set forth below:

> In the last forty-five years, judges in Houston, Texas have repeatedly appointed Joe Frank Cannon, known for hurrying through trials like "greased lightning," to defend indigent defendants despite his tendency to doze off during trial. Ten of Cannon's clients have been sentenced to death, one of the largest numbers among Texas attorneys. While representing Calvin Burdine at a capital trial, Cannon "dozed and actually fell asleep" during trial, "in particular during the guilt-innocence phase when the State's solo prosecutor was questioning witnesses and presenting evidence." The clerk of the court testified that "defense counsel was asleep on several occasions on several days over the course of the proceedings." Cannon's file on the case contained only three pages of notes. A law professor who later represented Carl Johnson, a previous Cannon client, in post-conviction proceedings found that Cannon's "ineptitude . . . jumps off the printed page" and that Cannon slept during the proceedings. Nevertheless, the death sentences in both cases were upheld. Carl Johnson has been executed.

* * *

> * * * An American Bar Association study found that "[i]n Tennessee . . . defense lawyers offered no evidence in mitigation in approximately one-quarter of all the death sentences affirmed by the Tennessee Supreme Court since the Tennessee legislature promulgated its current death penalty," and observed that "[d]efense representation is not necessarily better in other death penalty states."

> The consequences of not presenting such evidence is illustrated by the case of Horace Dunkins. The Alabama jury that sentenced him to death was never told that he was mentally retarded. Upon learning after the trial from newspaper reports that Dunkins was mentally retarded, one juror came forward and said she would not have voted for the death sentence if she had known of his condition. Nevertheless, Dunkins was executed.

* * *

> Some of those condemned to die in Texas could not have done any worse had they represented themselves than they did with the lawyers assigned to them by the Texas Court of Criminal Appeals. The court took over appointing counsel after the Texas Resource Center, which had

employed lawyers specializing in capital post-conviction litigation, was closed due to the elimination of federal funding * * *. * * *

* * *

The court assigned to Ricky Eugene Kerr an attorney who had been in practice for only two years, had never tried or appealed a capital case even as assistant counsel, and had suffered severe health problems that kept him out of his office in the months before he was to file a habeas corpus application on behalf of Kerr. The lawyer so misunderstood habeas corpus law that, as he later admitted, he thought he was precluded from challenging Kerr's conviction and sentence—the very purpose of a post-conviction petition. As a result, the lawyer filed a "perfunctory application" that failed to raise any issue attacking the conviction. After he and his family were unable to contact the lawyer, Kerr wrote a letter to the court complaining about the lawyer and asking the court to appoint another lawyer to prepare a habeas petition. Even though prosecutors did not object to a stay, the Court of Criminal Appeals denied Kerr's motion for a stay of execution and for the appointment of competent counsel. Judge Overstreet, warning that the court would have "blood on its hands" if Kerr was executed, dissented in order to "wash [his] hands of such repugnance" * * *.

* * *

Andrew Cantu finally resorted to representing himself after three different lawyers, appointed by the Criminal Court of Appeals to represent him over a period of eighteen months, failed even to file a petition. The first two lawyers withdrew, and the third never came to see him. At the hearing held five months after the third lawyer was appointed, that lawyer testified that he had not visited Cantu, claiming that he did not know where Cantu was housed in the prison system, had not contacted any investigator or expert witnesses, was not familiar with and had not read the Antiterrorism and Effective Death Penalty Act, which contains a one-year statute of limitations for filing a federal habeas petition, and was not aware of any ramifications of the Act for Cantu. Cantu had no state post-conviction review of his case and was barred from federal review of his case because the statute of limitations expired before any petition was filed. Cantu was executed on February 16, 1999.

Stephen B. Bright, Neither Equal Nor Just: The Rationing and Denial of Legal Services to the Poor When Life and Liberty Are at Stake, 1997 Ann. Surv. Am. L. 783, 789–90, 792, 802, 804–06 (1999) (Reprinted with the permission of the Annual Survey of American Law).

8. *Class Exercise:* Discuss and debate the following questions:

     a.   Is the death penalty, in your opinion, constitutional?

     b.   Assuming that, as the Supreme Court has concluded, the death penalty is not invariably unconstitutional, in what circumstances can the death penalty constitutionally be imposed by a state or the federal government?

c. Assuming that the death penalty is constitutional, should it be abolished on policy grounds? What factors should be incorporated into a policy analysis of the death penalty? Of what relevance, if any, is the fact that prisoners executed between 1977 and 2005 spent an average of over ten years in prison between the time they were sentenced to death and the time they were executed? Bureau of Justice Statistics, U.S. Dep't of Justice, Capital Punishment, 2005, at 10 (2006).

Consider the question whether capital punishment is advisable from a policy perspective against the backdrop of a real case in which the boyfriend of the mother of a four-year-old boy became irritated with his high-pitched voice and began beating him with his fists and sticks. These beatings continued over a period of months during which the boyfriend also burned the boy with cigarettes and an iron, stuck him with sewing needles, put his legs in scalding water, and hung him upside down in a locked, dark closet for hours at a time. The boy's mother never tried to intervene and protect her son.

One night, the boyfriend stuck a rag in the little boy's mouth, taped potato peelings over his eyes, and hung him in the closet overnight. The mother did not bother to check on her son the next morning, watching television instead. When the boyfriend finally released the boy from the closet, he pleaded for a drink of water. The boyfriend told the boy to get it himself, but the boy was too weak to walk across the room. The boyfriend then got angry and hit the boy on the head, killing him.

A newspaper columnist later wrote about this case and asked, "What possible justification could there be for permitting these two people to continue living among human beings?" How would you answer this question if you are or were an opponent of the death penalty?

d. Should the judge or jury members who sentence a defendant to death be required by statute to witness the execution? Should executions be televised?

CHAPTER 7

CRUEL AND UNUSUAL PUNISHMENT AND NONCAPITAL CASES

■ ■ ■

The previous chapter dealt with limitations the Eighth Amendment places on the imposition of a death sentence as a penalty for a crime. We turn now to a discussion of the application of the prohibition on cruel and unusual punishments in cases where some sentence other than the death penalty was imposed.

A. DISPROPORTIONALITY CLAIMS: CHALLENGES REGARDING THE LENGTH OR AMOUNT OF A CRIMINAL SANCTION

In 1980, the Supreme Court decided Rummel v. Estelle, 445 U.S. 263, 100 S.Ct. 1133 (1980), a case concerning the constitutionality of a life sentence imposed under a habitual-offender statute mandating life imprisonment for a third-time felon who had been imprisoned twice before. The defendant in that case had received a three-year prison sentence in 1964 after obtaining $80 worth of goods or services through the fraudulent use of a credit card. In 1969, he was convicted of a second felony—passing a forged check for $28.36—and sentenced to prison for four years. He then was convicted in 1973 of obtaining $120.75 through false pretenses, the felony that triggered the habitual-offender statute. In a 5–4 decision, the Supreme Court held that the defendant's life sentence, which included the possibility of parole, did not inflict the cruel and unusual punishment prohibited by the Eighth Amendment.

Two years later, in Hutto v. Davis, 454 U.S. 370, 102 S.Ct. 703 (1982) (per curiam), the Supreme Court held, in another 5–4 decision, that a 40–year prison sentence for possessing and distributing approximately nine ounces of marijuana that had a street value of about $200 did not constitute cruel and unusual punishment. Justice Powell, who had written the dissenting opinion in *Rummel*, in his words, "reluctantly" concurred in the Court's judgment in *Hutto* because in his opinion, *Rummel* was controlling. He noted that the defendant in *Rummel* had committed crimes "far less serious" than the crimes committed by this defendant and yet had suffered a much greater penalty than the 40–year sentence

334

imposed on the defendant in this case. Id. at 380, 102 S.Ct. at 708 (Powell, J., concurring).

The next year, the Supreme Court revisited the question whether a sentence was unconstitutionally disproportionate in Solem v. Helm, 463 U.S. 277, 103 S.Ct. 3001 (1983), the case which follows. This time, Justice Powell wrote the majority opinion for the Court.

SOLEM v. HELM

Supreme Court of the United States, 1983.
463 U.S. 277, 103 S.Ct. 3001, 77 L.Ed.2d 637.

JUSTICE POWELL delivered the opinion of the Court.

* * *

The issue presented is whether the Eighth Amendment proscribes a life sentence without possibility of parole for a seventh nonviolent felony.

I

By 1975 the State of South Dakota had convicted respondent Jerry Helm of six nonviolent felonies. In 1964, 1966, and 1969 Helm was convicted of third-degree burglary. In 1972 he was convicted of obtaining money under false pretenses. In 1973 he was convicted of grand larceny. And in 1975 he was convicted of third-offense driving while intoxicated. The record contains no details about the circumstances of any of these offenses, except that they were all nonviolent, none was a crime against a person, and alcohol was a contributing factor in each case.

In 1979 Helm was charged with uttering a "no account" check for $100. * * * Helm pleaded guilty.

Ordinarily the maximum punishment for uttering a "no account" check would have been five years' imprisonment in the state penitentiary and a $5,000 fine. As a result of his criminal record, however, Helm was subject to South Dakota's recidivist statute:

> "When a defendant has been convicted of at least three prior convictions [sic] in addition to the principal felony, the sentence for the principal felony shall be enhanced to the sentence for a Class 1 felony." S.D.Codified Laws § 22–7–8 (1979) (amended 1981).

The maximum penalty for a "Class 1 felony" was life imprisonment in the state penitentiary and a $25,000 fine. Moreover, South Dakota law explicitly provides that parole is unavailable: "A person sentenced to life imprisonment is not eligible for parole by the board of pardons and paroles." The Governor is authorized to pardon prisoners, or to commute their sentences, but no other relief from sentence is available even to a rehabilitated prisoner.

Immediately after accepting Helm's guilty plea, the South Dakota Circuit Court sentenced Helm to life imprisonment under § 22–7–8. * * *

The South Dakota Supreme Court, in a 3–2 decision, affirmed the sentence despite Helm's argument that it violated the Eighth Amendment.

After Helm had served two years in the state penitentiary, he requested the Governor to commute his sentence to a fixed term of years. Such a commutation would have had the effect of making Helm eligible to be considered for parole when he had served three-fourths of his new sentence. The Governor denied Helm's request in May 1981.

[Helm then filed a petition for a writ of habeas corpus in the United States District Court for the District of South Dakota, contending that his sentence constituted cruel and unusual punishment. The district court rejected this claim, but on appeal, the Eighth Circuit Court of Appeals reversed. The Supreme Court then granted certiorari.]

II

The Eighth Amendment declares: "Excessive bail shall not be required, nor excessive fines imposed, nor cruel and unusual punishments inflicted." The final clause prohibits not only barbaric punishments, but also sentences that are disproportionate to the crime committed.

* * *

There is no basis for the State's assertion that the general principle of proportionality does not apply to felony prison sentences. The constitutional language itself suggests no exception for imprisonment. We have recognized that the Eighth Amendment imposes "parallel limitations" on bail, fines, and other punishments, and the text is explicit that bail and fines may not be excessive. It would be anomalous indeed if the lesser punishment of a fine and the greater punishment of death were both subject to proportionality analysis, but the intermediate punishment of imprisonment were not. There is also no historical support for such an exception. * * *

* * * We agree * * * that, "[o]utside the context of capital punishment, *successful* challenges to the proportionality of particular sentences [will be] exceedingly rare." This does not mean, however, that proportionality analysis is entirely inapplicable in noncapital cases.

* * * Reviewing courts, of course, should grant substantial deference to the broad authority that legislatures necessarily possess in determining the types and limits of punishments for crimes, as well as to the discretion that trial courts possess in sentencing convicted criminals.[16] But no penalty is *per se* constitutional. * * *

---

16. Contrary to the dissent's suggestions, we do not adopt or imply approval of a general rule of appellate review of sentences. Absent specific authority, it is not the role of an appellate court to substitute its judgment for that of the sentencing court as to the appropriateness of a particular sentence; rather, in applying the Eighth Amendment the appellate court decides only whether the sentence under review is within constitutional limits. In view of the substantial deference that must be accorded legislatures and sentencing courts, a reviewing court rarely will be required to engage in extended analysis to determine that a sentence is not constitutionally disproportionate.

III

A

When sentences are reviewed under the Eighth Amendment, courts should be guided by objective factors that our cases have recognized. First, we look to the gravity of the offense and the harshness of the penalty. * * *

Second, it may be helpful to compare the sentences imposed on other criminals in the same jurisdiction. If more serious crimes are subject to the same penalty, or to less serious penalties, that is some indication that the punishment at issue may be excessive. * * *

Third, courts may find it useful to compare the sentences imposed for commission of the same crime in other jurisdictions. * * *

* * *

B

Application of these factors assumes that courts are competent to judge the gravity of an offense, at least on a relative scale. In a broad sense this assumption is justified, and courts traditionally have made these judgments—just as legislatures must make them in the first instance. Comparisons can be made in light of the harm caused or threatened to the victim or society, and the culpability of the offender. * * * For example, as the criminal laws make clear, nonviolent crimes are less serious than crimes marked by violence or the threat of violence.

There are other accepted principles that courts may apply in measuring the harm caused or threatened to the victim or society. The absolute magnitude of the crime may be relevant. Stealing a million dollars is viewed as more serious than stealing a hundred dollars—a point recognized in statutes distinguishing petty theft from grand theft. Few would dispute that a lesser included offense should not be punished more severely than the greater offense. Thus a court is justified in viewing assault with intent to murder as more serious than simple assault. It also is generally recognized that attempts are less serious than completed crimes. Similarly, an accessory after the fact should not be subject to a higher penalty than the principal.

Turning to the culpability of the offender, there are again clear distinctions that courts may recognize and apply. * * * Most would agree that negligent conduct is less serious than intentional conduct. South Dakota, for example, ranks criminal acts in ascending order of seriousness as follows: negligent acts, reckless acts, knowing acts, intentional acts, and malicious acts. A court, of course, is entitled to look at a defendant's motive in committing a crime. Thus a murder may be viewed as more serious when committed pursuant to a contract.

This list is by no means exhaustive. It simply illustrates that there are generally accepted criteria for comparing the severity of different crimes on a broad scale, despite the difficulties courts face in attempting to draw distinctions between similar crimes.

C

Application of the factors that we identify also assumes that courts are able to compare different sentences. This assumption, too, is justified. The easiest comparison, of course, is between capital punishment and noncapital punishments, for the death penalty is different from other punishments in kind rather than degree. For sentences of imprisonment, the problem is not so much one of ordering, but one of line-drawing. It is clear that a 25–year sentence generally is more severe than a 15–year sentence, but in most cases it would be difficult to decide that the former violates the Eighth Amendment while the latter does not. Decisions of this kind, although troubling, are not unique to this area. The courts are constantly called upon to draw similar lines in a variety of contexts.

* * *

IV

It remains to apply the analytical framework established by our prior decisions to the case before us. * * *

A

Helm's crime was "one of the most passive felonies a person could commit." It involved neither violence nor threat of violence to any person. The $100 face value of Helm's "no account" check was not trivial, but neither was it a large amount. One hundred dollars was less than half the amount South Dakota required for a felonious theft. It is easy to see why such a crime is viewed by society as among the less serious offenses.

Helm, of course, was not charged simply with uttering a "no account" check, but also with being a habitual offender. And a State is justified in punishing a recidivist more severely than it punishes a first offender. Helm's status, however, cannot be considered in the abstract. His prior offenses, although classified as felonies, were all relatively minor. All were nonviolent and none was a crime against a person. Indeed, there was no minimum amount in either the burglary or the false pretenses statutes, and the minimum amount covered by the grand larceny statute was fairly small.

Helm's present sentence is life imprisonment without possibility of parole. Barring executive clemency, Helm will spend the rest of his life in the state penitentiary. This sentence is far more severe than the life sentence we considered in *Rummel v. Estelle*. Rummel was likely to have been eligible for parole within 12 years of his initial confinement,[25] a fact on which the Court relied heavily. Helm's sentence is the most severe punishment that the State could have imposed on any criminal for any

---

25. We note that Rummel was, in fact, released within eight months of the Court's decision in his case.

crime. Only capital punishment, a penalty not authorized in South Dakota when Helm was sentenced, exceeds it.

We next consider the sentences that could be imposed on other criminals in the same jurisdiction. When Helm was sentenced, a South Dakota court was required to impose a life sentence for murder and was authorized to impose a life sentence for treason, first-degree manslaughter, first-degree arson, and kidnaping. No other crime was punishable so severely on the first offense. Attempted murder, placing an explosive device on an aircraft, and first-degree rape were only Class 2 felonies. Aggravated riot was only a Class 3 felony. Distribution of heroin and aggravated assault were only Class 4 felonies.

Helm's habitual offender status complicates our analysis, but relevant comparisons are still possible. Under [S.D.Codified Laws] § 22–7–7, the penalty for a second or third felony is increased by one class. Thus a life sentence was mandatory when a second or third conviction was for treason, first-degree manslaughter, first-degree arson, or kidnaping, and a life sentence would have been authorized when a second or third conviction was for such crimes as attempted murder, placing an explosive device on an aircraft, or first-degree rape. Finally, § 22–7–8, under which Helm was sentenced, authorized life imprisonment after three prior convictions, regardless of the crimes.

In sum, there were a handful of crimes that were necessarily punished by life imprisonment: murder, and, on a second or third offense, treason, first-degree manslaughter, first-degree arson, and kidnaping. There was a larger group for which life imprisonment was authorized in the discretion of the sentencing judge, including: treason, first-degree manslaughter, first-degree arson, and kidnaping; attempted murder, placing an explosive device on an aircraft, and first-degree rape on a second or third offense; and any felony after three prior offenses. Finally, there was a large group of very serious offenses for which life imprisonment was not authorized, including a third offense of heroin dealing or aggravated assault.

Criminals committing any of these offenses ordinarily would be thought more deserving of punishment than one uttering a "no account" check—even when the bad-check writer had already committed six minor felonies. * * *[26] In any event, Helm has been treated in the same manner as, or more severely than, criminals who have committed far more serious crimes.

Finally, we compare the sentences imposed for commission of the same crime in other jurisdictions. The Court of Appeals found that "Helm could have received a life sentence without parole for his offense in only one other state, Nevada," and we have no reason to doubt this finding. At the very least, therefore, it is clear that Helm could not have received such

---

26.   The State contends that § 22–7–8 is more lenient than the Texas habitual offender statute in *Rummel*, for life imprisonment under § 22–7–8 is discretionary rather than mandatory. Helm, however, has challenged only his own sentence. No one suggests that § 22–7–8 may not be applied constitutionally to fourth-time heroin dealers or other violent criminals. * * *

a severe sentence in 48 of the 50 States. But even under Nevada law, a life sentence without possibility of parole is merely authorized in these circumstances. We are not advised that any defendant such as Helm, whose prior offenses were so minor, actually has received the maximum penalty in Nevada. It appears that Helm was treated more severely than he would have been in any other State.

B

The State argues that the present case is essentially the same as *Rummel v. Estelle,* for the possibility of parole in that case is matched by the possibility of executive clemency here. The State reasons that the Governor could commute Helm's sentence to a term of years. We conclude, however, that the South Dakota commutation system is fundamentally different from the parole system that was before us in *Rummel.*

As a matter of law, parole and commutation are different concepts, despite some surface similarities. Parole is a regular part of the rehabilitative process. Assuming good behavior, it is the normal expectation in the vast majority of cases. The law generally specifies when a prisoner will be eligible to be considered for parole, and details the standards and procedures applicable at that time. Thus it is possible to predict, at least to some extent, when parole might be granted. Commutation, on the other hand, is an ad hoc exercise of executive clemency. A Governor may commute a sentence at any time for any reason without reference to any standards.

* * *

The Texas and South Dakota systems in particular are very different. * * * A Texas prisoner became eligible for parole when his calendar time served plus "good conduct" time equaled one-third of the maximum sentence imposed or 20 years, whichever is less. An entering prisoner earned 20 days good-time per 30 days served, and this could be increased to 30 days good-time per 30 days served. Thus Rummel could have been eligible for parole in as few as 10 years, and could have expected to become eligible, in the normal course of events, in only 12 years.

In South Dakota commutation is more difficult to obtain than parole. For example, the Board of Pardons and Paroles is authorized to make commutation recommendations to the Governor, but § 24–13–4 provides that "no recommendation for the commutation of . . . a life sentence, or for a pardon . . ., shall be made by less than the unanimous vote of all members of the board." In fact, no life sentence has been commuted in over eight years, while parole—where authorized—has been granted regularly during that period. Furthermore, even if Helm's sentence were commuted, he merely would be eligible to be considered for parole. Not only is there no guarantee that he would be paroled, but the South Dakota parole system is far more stringent than the one before us in *Rummel.* Helm would have to serve three-fourths of his revised sentence before he would be eligible for parole, and the provision for good-time credits is less generous.

The possibility of commutation is nothing more than a hope for "an *ad hoc* exercise of clemency." It is little different from the possibility of executive clemency that exists in every case in which a defendant challenges his sentence under the Eighth Amendment. Recognition of such a bare possibility would make judicial review under the Eighth Amendment meaningless.

V

The Constitution requires us to examine Helm's sentence to determine if it is proportionate to his crime. Applying objective criteria, we find that Helm has received the penultimate sentence for relatively minor criminal conduct. He has been treated more harshly than other criminals in the State who have committed more serious crimes. He has been treated more harshly than he would have been in any other jurisdiction, with the possible exception of a single State. We conclude that his sentence is significantly disproportionate to his crime, and is therefore prohibited by the Eighth Amendment.[32] * * *

CHIEF JUSTICE BURGER, with whom JUSTICE WHITE, JUSTICE REHNQUIST, and JUSTICE O'CONNOR join, dissenting.

The controlling law governing this case is crystal clear, but today the Court blithely discards any concept of *stare decisis,* trespasses gravely on the authority of the states, and distorts the concept of proportionality of punishment by tearing it from its moorings in capital cases. Only three Terms ago, we held in *Rummel v. Estelle* that a life sentence imposed after only a *third* nonviolent felony conviction did not constitute cruel and unusual punishment under the Eighth Amendment. Today, the Court ignores its recent precedent and holds that a life sentence imposed after a *seventh* felony conviction constitutes cruel and unusual punishment under the Eighth Amendment.[3] Moreover, I reject the fiction that all Helm's crimes were innocuous or nonviolent. Among his felonies were three burglaries and a third conviction for drunken driving. By comparison Rummel was a relatively "model citizen." Although today's holding can-

---

32. Contrary to the suggestion in the dissent, our conclusion today is not inconsistent with *Rummel v. Estelle.* The *Rummel* Court recognized—as does the dissent—that some sentences of imprisonment are so disproportionate that they violate the Eighth Amendment. * * * *Rummel* did reject a proportionality challenge to a particular sentence. But since the *Rummel* Court—like the dissent today—offered no standards for determining when an Eighth Amendment violation has occurred, it is controlling only in a similar factual situation. Here the facts are clearly distinguishable. Whereas Rummel was eligible for a reasonably early parole, Helm, at age 36, was sentenced to life with no possibility of parole.

3. Both *Rummel* and *Hutto v. Davis* leave open the possibility that in extraordinary cases—such as a life sentence for overtime parking—it might be permissible for a court to decide whether the sentence is grossly disproportionate to the crime. I agree that the Cruel and Unusual Punishments Clause might apply to those rare cases where reasonable men cannot differ as to the inappropriateness of a punishment. In all other cases, we should defer to the legislature's line-drawing. However, the Court does not contend that this is such an extraordinary case that reasonable men could not differ about the appropriateness of this punishment.

not rationally be reconciled with *Rummel,* the Court does not purport to overrule *Rummel.* I therefore dissent.

* * *

The *Rummel* Court categorically rejected the very analysis adopted by the Court today. * * *

First, it rejected the distinctions Rummel tried to draw between violent and nonviolent offenses, noting that "the absence of violence does not always affect the strength of society's interest in deterring a particular crime or in punishing a particular criminal." Similarly, distinctions based on the amount of money stolen are purely "subjective" matters of line drawing.

Second, the Court squarely rejected Rummel's attempt to compare his sentence with the sentence he would have received in other States—an argument that the Court today accepts. * * * [S]uch comparisons trample on fundamental concepts of federalism. Different states surely may view particular crimes as more or less severe than other states. Stealing a horse in Texas may have different consequences and warrant different punishment than stealing a horse in Rhode Island or Washington, D.C. Thus, even if the punishment accorded Rummel in Texas were to exceed that which he would have received in any other state,

> "that severity hardly would render Rummel's punishment 'grossly disproportionate' to his offenses or to the punishment he would have received in the other States.... *Absent a constitutionally imposed uniformity inimical to traditional notions of federalism, some State will always bear the distinction of treating particular offenders more severely than any other State.*"

Finally, we flatly rejected Rummel's suggestion that we measure his sentence against the sentences imposed by Texas for other crimes:

> "Other crimes, of course, implicate other societal interests, making any such comparison inherently speculative. * * * "

In short, *Rummel* held that the length of a sentence of imprisonment is a matter of legislative discretion * * *. * * *

* * *

_____

In Harmelin v. Michigan, 501 U.S. 957, 111 S.Ct. 2680 (1991), the case which follows, the Supreme Court once again considered a claim that a sentence was cruel and unusual because it was disproportionate to the severity of the crime committed.

HARMELIN v. MICHIGAN

Supreme Court of the United States, 1991.
501 U.S. 957, 111 S.Ct. 2680, 115 L.Ed.2d 836.

JUSTICE SCALIA announced the judgment of the Court and delivered the opinion of the Court with respect to Part IV, and an opinion with respect to Parts I, II, and III, in which THE CHIEF JUSTICE joins.

Petitioner was convicted of possessing 672 grams of cocaine and sentenced to a mandatory term of life in prison without possibility of parole. * * *

Petitioner claims that his sentence is unconstitutionally "cruel and unusual" for two reasons: first, because it is "significantly disproportionate" to the crime he committed; second, because the sentencing judge was statutorily required to impose it, without taking into account the particularized circumstances of the crime and of the criminal.

I

* * *

Solem based its conclusion principally upon the proposition that a right to be free from disproportionate punishments was embodied within the "cruell and unusual Punishments" provision of the English Declaration of Rights of 1689, and was incorporated, with that language, in the Eighth Amendment. There is no doubt that the Declaration of Rights is the antecedent of our constitutional text. * * *

* * *

* * * [T]he drafters of the Declaration of Rights did not explicitly prohibit "disproportionate" or "excessive" punishments. Instead, they prohibited punishments that were "cruel and unusual." The *Solem* Court simply assumed, with no analysis, that the one included the other. As a textual matter, of course, it does not: a disproportionate punishment can perhaps always be considered "cruel," but it will not always be (as the text also requires) "unusual." * * *

* * *

* * * [T]o use the phrase "cruel and unusual punishment" to describe a requirement of proportionality would have been an exceedingly vague and oblique way of saying what Americans were well accustomed to saying more directly. * * * Proportionality provisions had been included in several State Constitutions. See, e.g., Pa. Const., § 38 (1776) (punishments should be "in general more proportionate to the crimes"). * * * Both the New Hampshire Constitution, adopted 8 years before ratification of the Eighth Amendment, and the Ohio Constitution, adopted 12 years after, contain, in separate provisions, a prohibition of "cruel and unusual punishments" ("cruel *or* unusual," in New Hampshire's case) *and* a

requirement that "all penalties ought to be proportioned to the nature of the offence."

* * *

The actions of the First Congress, which are of course persuasive evidence of what the Constitution means, belie any doctrine of proportionality. * * * Shortly after proposing the Bill of Rights, the First Congress * * * punished forgery of United States securities, "running away with [a] ship or vessel, or any goods or merchandise to the value of fifty dollars," treason, and murder on the high seas with the same penalty: death by hanging. * * *

II

We think it enough that those who framed and approved the Federal Constitution chose, for whatever reason, not to include within it the guarantee against disproportionate sentences that some State Constitutions contained. It is worth noting, however, that there was good reason for that choice—a reason that reinforces the necessity of overruling *Solem*. While there are relatively clear historical guidelines and accepted practices that enable judges to determine which *modes* of punishment are "cruel and unusual," *proportionality* does not lend itself to such analysis. * * * This is not to say that there are no absolutes; one can imagine extreme examples that no rational person, in no time or place, could accept. But for the same reason these examples are easy to decide, they are certain never to occur.[11] The real function of a constitutional proportionality principle, if it exists, is to enable judges to evaluate a penalty that *some* assemblage of men and women has considered proportionate—and to say that it is not. For that real-world enterprise, the standards seem so inadequate that the proportionality principle becomes an invitation to imposition of subjective values.

This becomes clear, we think, from a consideration of the three factors that *Solem* found relevant to the proportionality determination: (1) the inherent gravity of the offense, (2) the sentences imposed for similarly grave offenses in the same jurisdiction, and (3) sentences imposed for the same crime in other jurisdictions. As to the first factor: Of course some offenses, involving violent harm to human beings, will always and everywhere be regarded as serious, but that is only half the equation. The issue is *what else* should be regarded to be *as serious* as these offenses, or even to be *more serious* than some of them. * * *

The difficulty of assessing gravity is demonstrated in the very context of the present case: Petitioner acknowledges that a mandatory life sen-

---

11. Justice White argues that the Eighth Amendment must contain a proportionality principle because otherwise legislatures could "mak[e] overtime parking a felony punishable by life imprisonment." * * * Justice White's argument has force only for those who believe that the Constitution prohibited everything that is intensely undesirable—which is an obvious fallacy, see Art. I, § 9 (implicitly permitting slavery). Nor is it likely that the horrible example imagined would ever in fact occur, unless, of course, overtime parking should one day become an arguably major threat to the common good, and the need to deter it arguably critical * * *.

tence might not be "grossly excessive" for possession of cocaine with intent to distribute, see *Hutto v. Davis*, 454 U.S. 370 (1982). But surely whether it is a "grave" offense merely to possess a significant quantity of drugs—thereby facilitating distribution, subjecting the holder to the temptation of distribution, and raising the possibility of theft by others who might distribute—depends entirely upon how odious and socially threatening one believes drug use to be. Would it be "grossly excessive" to provide life imprisonment for "mere possession" of a certain quantity of heavy weaponry? If not, then the only issue is whether the possible dissemination of drugs can be as "grave" as the possible dissemination of heavy weapons. Who are we to say no? The members of the Michigan Legislature, and not we, know the situation on the streets of Detroit.

The second factor suggested in *Solem* fails for the same reason. One cannot compare the sentences imposed by the jurisdiction for "similarly grave" offenses if there is no objective standard of gravity. Judges will be comparing what *they* consider comparable. Or, to put the same point differently: When it happens that two offenses judicially determined to be "similarly grave" receive significantly *dis*similar penalties, what follows is not that the harsher penalty is unconstitutional, but merely that the legislature does not share the judges' view that the offenses are similarly grave. Moreover, even if "similarly grave" crimes could be identified, the penalties for them would not necessarily be comparable, since there are many other justifications for a difference. For example, since deterrent effect depends not only upon the amount of the penalty but upon its certainty, crimes that are less grave but significantly more difficult to detect may warrant substantially higher penalties. * * * In fact, it becomes difficult, even to speak intelligently of "proportionality," once deterrence and rehabilitation are given significant weight. Proportionality is inherently a retributive concept * * *.

As for the third factor mentioned by *Solem*—the character of the sentences imposed by other States for the same crime—it must be acknowledged that that can be applied with clarity and ease. The only difficulty is that it has no conceivable relevance to the Eighth Amendment. That a State is entitled to treat with stern disapproval an act that other States punish with the mildest of sanctions follows *a fortiori* from the undoubted fact that a State may criminalize an act that other States do not criminalize *at all*. * * * Though the different needs and concerns of other States may induce them to treat simple possession of 672 grams of cocaine as a relatively minor offense, see Wyo. Stat. § 35–7–1031(c) (1988) (6 months); W.Va. Code § 60A–4–401(c) (1989) (6 months), nothing in the Constitution requires Michigan to follow suit. * * *

III

* * *

* * * In *Coker v. Georgia*, [433 U.S. 584 (1977)], the Court held that, because of the disproportionality, it was a violation of the Cruel and

Unusual Punishments Clause to impose capital punishment for rape of an adult woman. * * * Proportionality review is one of several respects in which we have held that "death is different," and have imposed protections that the Constitution nowhere else provides.

IV

Petitioner claims that his sentence violates the Eighth Amendment for a reason in addition to its alleged disproportionality. He argues that it is "cruel and unusual" to impose a mandatory sentence of such severity, without any consideration of so-called mitigating factors such as, in his case, the fact that he had no prior felony convictions. He apparently contends that the Eighth Amendment requires Michigan to create a sentencing scheme whereby life in prison without possibility of parole is simply the most severe of a range of available penalties that the sentencer may impose after hearing evidence in mitigation and aggravation.

* * * [T]his claim has no support in the text and history of the Eighth Amendment. Severe, mandatory penalties may be cruel, but they are not unusual in the constitutional sense, having been employed in various forms throughout our Nation's history. * * *

Petitioner's "required mitigation" claim, like his proportionality claim, does find support in our death penalty jurisprudence. We have held that a capital sentence is cruel and unusual under the Eighth Amendment if it is imposed without an individualized determination that that punishment is "appropriate"—whether or not the sentence is "grossly disproportionate." See *Woodson v. North Carolina.* Petitioner asks us to extend this so-called "individualized capital-sentencing doctrine" to an "individualized mandatory life in prison without parole sentencing doctrine." We refuse to do so.

Our cases creating and clarifying the "individualized capital sentencing doctrine" have repeatedly suggested that there is no comparable requirement outside the capital context, because of the qualitative difference between death and all other penalties.

> "The penalty of death differs from all other forms of criminal punishment, not in degree but in kind. It is unique in its total irrevocability. It is unique in its rejection of rehabilitation of the convict as a basic purpose of criminal justice. And it is unique, finally, in its absolute renunciation of all that is embodied in our concept of humanity." *Furman v. Georgia*, 408 U.S., at 306 (Stewart, J., concurring).

* * * In some cases, moreover, there will be negligible difference between life without parole and other sentences of imprisonment—for example, a life sentence with eligibility for parole after 20 years, or even a lengthy term sentence without eligibility for parole, given to a 65–year–old man. But even where the difference is the greatest, it cannot be compared with death. We have drawn the line of required individualized sentencing at capital cases, and see no basis for extending it further.

Justice Kennedy, with whom Justice O'Connor and Justice Souter join, concurring in part and concurring in the judgment.

I concur in Part IV of the court's opinion and in the judgment. I write this separate opinion because my approach to the Eighth Amendment proportionality analysis differs from Justice Scalia's. * * * *[S]tare decisis* counsels our adherence to the narrow proportionality principle that has existed in our Eighth Amendment jurisprudence for 80 years. * * *

I

* * *

* * * [C]lose analysis of our decisions yields some common principles that give content to the uses and limits of proportionality review.

The first of these principles is that the fixing of prison terms for specific crimes involves a substantive penological judgment that, as a general matter, is "properly within the province of legislatures, not courts." * * *

The second principle is that the Eighth Amendment does not mandate adoption of any one penological theory. * * * The federal and state criminal systems have accorded different weights at different times to the penological goals of retribution, deterrence, incapacitation, and rehabilitation. * * *

Third, marked divergences both in underlying theories of sentencing and in the length of prescribed prison terms are the inevitable, often beneficial, result of the federal structure. * * *

The fourth principle at work in our cases is that proportionality review by federal courts should be informed by " 'objective factors to the maximum possible extent.' " * * * Although "no penalty is per se constitutional," the relative lack of objective standards concerning terms of imprisonment has meant that " '[o]utside the context of capital punishment, successful challenges to the proportionality of particular sentences [are] exceedingly rare.' "

All of these principles—the primacy of the legislature, the variety of legitimate penological schemes, the nature of our federal system, and the requirement that proportionality review be guided by objective factors—inform the final one: The Eighth Amendment does not require strict proportionality between crime and sentence. Rather, it forbids only extreme sentences that are "grossly disproportionate" to the crime.

II

* * *

Petitioner's life sentence without parole is the second most severe penalty permitted by law. It is the same sentence received by the petitioner in *Solem*. Petitioner's crime, however, was far more grave than the crime at issue in *Solem*.

* * *

Petitioner was convicted of possession of more than 650 grams (over 1.5 pounds) of cocaine. This amount of pure cocaine has a potential yield of between 32,500 and 65,000 doses. * * * Petitioner's suggestion that his crime was nonviolent and victimless, echoed by the dissent, is false to the point of absurdity. To the contrary, petitioner's crime threatened to cause grave harm to society.

Quite apart from the pernicious effects on the individual who consumes illegal drugs, such drugs relate to crime in at least three ways: (1) A drug user may commit crime because of drug-induced changes in physiological functions, cognitive ability, and mood; (2) A drug user may commit crime in order to obtain money to buy drugs; and (3) A violent crime may occur as part of the drug business or culture. Studies bear out these possibilities and demonstrate a direct nexus between illegal drugs and crimes of violence. To mention but a few examples, 57 percent of a national sample of males arrested in 1989 for homicide tested positive for illegal drugs. The comparable statistics for assault, robbery, and weapons arrests were 55, 73, and 63 percent, respectively. * * *

* * *

The severity of petitioner's crime brings his sentence within the constitutional boundaries established by our prior decisions. In *Hutto v. Davis*, 454 U.S. 370 (1982), we upheld against proportionality attack a sentence of 40 years' imprisonment for possession with intent to distribute nine ounces of marijuana. Here Michigan could with good reason conclude that petitioner's crime is more serious than the crime in *Davis*. * * *

Petitioner and *amici* contend that our proportionality decisions require a comparative analysis between petitioner's sentence and sentences imposed for other crimes in Michigan and sentences imposed for the same crime in other jurisdictions. Given the serious nature of petitioner's crime, no such comparative analysis is necessary. Although *Solem* considered these comparative factors after analyzing "the gravity of the offense and the harshness of the penalty," it did not announce a rigid three-part test. In fact, *Solem* stated that in determining unconstitutional disproportionality, "no one factor will be dispositive in a given case."

On the other hand, one factor may be sufficient to determine the constitutionality of a particular sentence. Consistent with its admonition that "a reviewing court rarely will be required to engage in extended analysis to determine that a sentence is not constitutionally disproportionate," *Solem* is best understood as holding that comparative analysis within and between jurisdictions is not always relevant to proportionality review. The Court stated that "it *may* be helpful to compare sentences imposed on other criminals in the same jurisdiction," and that "courts *may* find it useful to compare the sentences imposed for commission of the same crime in other jurisdictions." It did not mandate such inquiries.

A better reading of our cases leads to the conclusion that intrajurisdictional and interjurisdictional analyses are appropriate only in the rare case in which a threshold comparison of the crime committed and the sentence imposed leads to an inference of gross disproportionality. * * *

* * *

III

* * * Reasonable minds may differ about the efficacy of Michigan's sentencing scheme, and it is far from certain that Michigan's bold experiment will succeed. The accounts of pickpockets at Tyburn hangings[a] are a reminder of the limits of the law's deterrent force, but we cannot say the law before us has no chance of success and is on that account so disproportionate as to be cruel and unusual punishment. * * *

Justice White, with whom Justice Blackmun and Justice Stevens join, dissenting.

The Eighth Amendment provides that "[e]xcessive bail shall not be required, nor excessive fines imposed, nor cruel and unusual punishments inflicted." * * *

The language of the Amendment does not refer to proportionality in so many words, but it does forbid "excessive" fines, a restraint that suggests that a determination of excessiveness should be based at least in part on whether the fine imposed is disproportionate to the crime committed. Nor would it be unreasonable to conclude that it would be both cruel and unusual to punish overtime parking by life imprisonment or, more generally, to impose any punishment that is grossly disproportionate to the offense for which the defendant has been convicted. * * *

Justice Scalia * * * asserts that if proportionality was an aspect of the restraint, it could have been said more clearly—as plain-talking Americans would have expressed themselves (as for instance, I suppose, in the Fifth Amendment's Due Process Clause or the Fourth Amendment's prohibition against unreasonable searches and seizures).

* * *

* * * Later in his opinion, however, Justice Scalia backtracks and appears to accept that the Amendment does indeed insist on proportional punishments in a particular class of cases, those that involve sentences of death. His fallback position * * * fails to explain why the words "cruel and unusual" include a proportionality requirement in some cases but not in others. * * *

* * *

---

a. Tyburn Hill was the site in England where raucous crowds used to gather in medieval times to watch executions. The Oxford History of the Prison 35, 58 (Norval Morris & David J. Rothman eds., 1995).

While Justice Scalia seeks to deliver a swift death sentence to *Solem*, Justice Kennedy prefers to eviscerate it, leaving only an empty shell. * * *

* * *

Justice Kennedy's abandonment of the second and third factors set forth in *Solem* makes an attempt at an objective proportionality analysis futile. The first prong of *Solem* requires a court to consider two discrete factors—the gravity of the offense and the severity of the punishment. A court is not expected to consider the interaction of these two elements and determine whether "the sentence imposed was grossly excessive punishment for the crime committed." Were a court to attempt such an assessment, it would have no basis for its determination that a sentence was—or was not—disproportionate, other than the "subjective views of individual [judges]," which is the very sort of analysis our Eighth Amendment jurisprudence has shunned. * * * Indeed, only when a comparison is made with penalties for other crimes and in other jurisdictions can a court begin to make an objective assessment about a given sentence's constitutional proportionality, giving due deference to "public attitudes concerning a particular sentence."

Because there is no justification for overruling or limiting *Solem*, it remains to apply that case's proportionality analysis to the sentence imposed on petitioner. * * *

* * *

The first *Solem* factor requires a reviewing court to assess the gravity of the offense and the harshness of the penalty. The mandatory sentence of life imprisonment without possibility of parole "is the most severe punishment that the State could have imposed on any criminal for any crime," for Michigan has no death penalty.

Although these factors are "by no means exhaustive," in evaluating the gravity of the offense, it is appropriate to consider "the harm caused or threatened to the victim or society," based on such things as the degree of violence involved in the crime and "[t]he absolute magnitude of the crime," and "the culpability of the offender," including the degree of requisite intent and the offender's motive in committing the crime.

Drugs are without doubt a serious societal problem. To justify such a harsh mandatory penalty as that imposed here, however, the offense should be one which will *always* warrant that punishment. Mere possession of drugs—even in such a large quantity—is not so serious an offense that it will always warrant, much less mandate, life imprisonment without possibility of parole. * * *

To be constitutionally proportionate, punishment must be tailored to a defendant's personal responsibility and moral guilt. Justice Kennedy attempts to justify the harsh mandatory sentence imposed on petitioner by focusing on the subsidiary effects of drug use, and thereby ignores this aspect of our Eighth Amendment jurisprudence. While the collateral consequences of drugs such as cocaine are indisputably severe, they are not unlike those which flow from the misuse of other, legal substances. * * *

The "absolute magnitude" of petitioner's crime is not exceptionally serious. Because possession is necessarily a lesser included offense of possession with intent to distribute, it is odd to punish the former as severely as the latter. Nor is the requisite intent for the crime sufficient to render it particularly grave. To convict someone under the possession statute, it is only necessary to prove that the defendant knowingly possessed a mixture containing narcotics which weighs at least 650 grams. There is no *mens rea* requirement of intent to distribute the drugs, as there is in the parallel statute. * * * Finally, this statute applies equally to first-time offenders, such as petitioner, and recidivists. * * *

* * *

The second prong of the *Solem* analysis is an examination of "the sentences imposed on other criminals in the same jurisdiction." As noted above, there is no death penalty in Michigan; consequently, life without parole, the punishment mandated here, is the harshest penalty available. It is reserved for three crimes: first-degree murder; manufacture, distribution, or possession with intent to manufacture or distribute 650 grams or more of narcotics; and possession of 650 grams or more of narcotics. Crimes directed against the persons and property of others—such as second-degree murder, rape, and armed robbery, do not carry such a harsh mandatory sentence, although they do provide for the possibility of a life sentence in the exercise of judicial discretion. It is clear that petitioner "has been treated in the same manner as, or more severely than, criminals who have committed far more serious crimes."

The third factor set forth in *Solem* examines "the sentences imposed for commission of the same crime in other jurisdictions." No other jurisdiction imposes a punishment nearly as severe as Michigan's for possession of the amount of drugs at issue here. Of the remaining 49 States, only Alabama provides for a mandatory sentence of life imprisonment without possibility of parole for a first-time drug offender, and then only when a defendant possesses *10 kilograms* or more of cocaine. * * *

Application of *Solem*'s proportionality analysis leaves no doubt that the Michigan statute at issue fails constitutional muster.[8] The statutorily mandated penalty of life without possibility of parole for possession of narcotics is unconstitutionally disproportionate in that it violates the Eighth Amendment's prohibition against cruel and unusual punishment. * * *

JUSTICE MARSHALL, dissenting. [Opinion omitted.]

---

8. Because the statute under which petitioner was convicted is unconstitutional under *Solem*, there is no need to reach his remaining argument that imposition of a life sentence without the possibility of parole necessitates the sort of individualized sentencing determination heretofore reserved for defendants subject to the death penalty.

JUSTICE STEVENS, with whom JUSTICE BLACKMUN joins, dissenting. [Opinion omitted.]

QUESTIONS AND POINTS FOR DISCUSSION

1. In People v. Bullock, 485 N.W.2d 866 (Mich. 1992), the Michigan Supreme Court held that the statute under which the defendant in *Harmelin* had been sentenced violated the Michigan Constitution. The court noted that the prohibition in the state constitution of "cruel *or* unusual" punishments encompassed more punishments than the more limited ban in the federal constitution of "cruel *and* unusual punishments." As a remedy, the court ordered that the no-parole provision in the Michigan statute be stricken, making defendants sentenced under the statute eligible for parole consideration after serving ten years of their sentences. To the argument that the court, by invalidating the statute, was encroaching undemocratically on the will of the people, as expressed through the enactments of the state legislature, the court responded: "The very purpose of a constitution is to subject the passing judgments of temporary legislative or political majorities to the deeper, more profound judgment of the people reflected in the constitution, the enforcement of which is entrusted to our judgment." Id. at 877.

2. The Eighth Amendment prohibits not only the infliction of cruel and unusual punishments, but also the imposition of "excessive fines." In United States v. Bajakajian, 524 U.S. 321, 118 S.Ct. 2028 (1998), the Supreme Court held that the same test applied when determining whether a punishment is cruel and unusual is to be applied when determining whether a fine is unconstitutionally "excessive." A court should assess whether the fine is "grossly disproportional to the gravity of a defendant's offense." Id. at 334, 118 S.Ct. at 2036.

Applying this test to the facts of the case before it, the Court concluded, in a 5–4 decision, that the forfeiture of $357,144 for failing to report, as required by law, that the defendant was transporting that amount of money out of the country would constitute an "excessive fine." The Court highlighted a number of factors in support of its conclusion: First, the defendant's only crime was failing to report certain information to the government. The actual transportation of the currency out of the country was legal. Second, the defendant's reporting crime was not related to any other crime. There was no evidence, for example, that the money had been obtained during illegal drug-dealing transactions. Third, the maximum sentence that could be imposed under the federal sentencing guidelines for the reporting crime—six months in prison and a $5,000 fine—confirmed that the defendant's criminal culpability was at the "minimal level." Id. at 339, 118 S.Ct. at 2038. And finally, the harm stemming from the defendant's crime was "minimal." Id., 118 S.Ct. at 2039. The government was the only party injured by the defendant's crime, and the harm was simply the loss of information about how much money was being taken out of the country.

Do you agree with the Court's analysis and conclusion? Do you discern any arguable inconsistency between *Bajakian* and *Harmelin*? See Pamela S. Karlan, "Pricking the Lines": The Due Process Clause, Punitive Damages, and Criminal Punishment, 88 Minn. L.Rev. 880, 900–02 (2004) (noting, for example, that while the Supreme Court in *Bajakian* focused solely on the harm caused by the defendant, Justice Kennedy factored into his analysis in *Harmelin* the harm caused generally by illegal drugs).

3. In Lockyer v. Andrade, 538 U.S. 63, 123 S.Ct. 1166 (2003), the defendant challenged the constitutionality of two lengthy prison sentences imposed under California's three-strikes law. That law mandates the imposition of a sentence of twenty-five years to life when a defendant has been convicted of a felony after previously having been convicted of two or more "serious" or "violent" felonies. The law was invoked against the defendant after he was convicted of shoplifting, in two separate incidents, a total of nine videotapes worth $153.54. Because the defendant had a prior theft conviction, though a misdemeanor, the prosecutor had the option, of which he availed himself, of prosecuting the defendant's petty thefts as felonies. The defendant also had prior convictions for several nonviolent felonies; he had been convicted twice of transporting marijuana and had pled guilty to three counts of residential burglary in one consolidated court hearing. In accordance with the terms of the three-strikes law, the 37–year–old defendant was sentenced to prison for twenty-five years to life for each theft, with the sentences to be served consecutively and with no possibility of parole before he had served the minimum 25–year sentence on each count.

Since the defendant in *Lockyer* was contesting the constitutionality of his sentence in a habeas corpus action, the technical question before the Supreme Court was whether the state appellate court's decision upholding the defendant's sentences was "contrary to, or an unreasonable application of, clearly established federal law." Id. at 66, 123 S.Ct. at 1169. The Court answered that question in the negative, in part because its decisions applying the Eighth Amendment to prison sentences have not, in its words, been "a model of clarity." Id. at 72, 123 S.Ct. at 1173. In your opinion, was the defendant in this case more like the defendant in *Rummel*, *Solem*, or *Harmelin*?

4. In Ewing v. California, 538 U.S. 11, 123 S.Ct. 1179 (2003), a companion case to *Lockyer*, the 38–year–old defendant was sentenced to prison for twenty-five years to life under California's three-strikes law, a sentence that a majority of the Court found did not violate the Eighth Amendment. The crime that triggered application of the three-strikes provision was the defendant's theft of three golf clubs priced at $399 apiece. The defendant also had an extensive criminal record, including prior convictions for several thefts, battery, possession of drug paraphernalia, possession of a firearm, four burglaries, and robbery.

What the Court in *Lockyer* aptly described as the Court-created "thicket of Eighth Amendment jurisprudence" was not eradicated in *Ewing*, another 5–4 decision. The plurality opinion, written by Justice O'Connor and in which Chief Justice Rehnquist and Justice Kennedy joined, followed the approach outlined in Justice Kennedy's concurring opinion in *Harmelin* in analyzing the defendant's Eighth Amendment claim. The concurring Justices, Scalia and Thomas, adhered to their position that there is no proportionality principle in the Eighth Amendment that constrains the length of prison sentences. Justice Stevens, in a dissenting opinion joined by Justices Souter, Ginsburg, and Breyer, stated that *Solem*'s three-part test was the most apropos, although Justice Breyer went ahead and applied the Kennedy test "for present purposes" in a separate dissenting opinion in which the other three dissenting Justices joined. Id. at 36, 123 S.Ct. at 1194 (Breyer, J., dissenting).

5. In his opinion concurring in the judgment in *Ewing v. California*, Justice Scalia skewered the idea, embraced by a majority of the Court, that a gross disproportionality principle applicable to prison sentences is embedded within the Eighth Amendment:

> Out of respect for the principle of *stare decisis*, I might nonetheless accept the contrary holding of *Solem v. Helm*—that the Eighth Amendment contains a narrow proportionality principle—if I felt I could intelligently apply it. This case demonstrates why I cannot.
>
> Proportionality—the notion that the punishment should fit the crime—is inherently a concept tied to the penological goal of retribution. "[I]t becomes difficult even to speak intelligently of 'proportionality,' once deterrence and rehabilitation are given significant weight," not to mention giving weight to the purpose of California's three strikes law: incapacitation. In the present case, the game is up once the plurality has acknowledged that "the Constitution does not mandate adoption of any one penological theory," and that a "sentence can have a variety of justifications, such as incapacitation, deterrence, retribution, or rehabilitation." That acknowledgment having been made, it no longer suffices merely to assess "the gravity of the offense compared to the harshness of the penalty"; that classic description of the proportionality principle (alone and in itself quite resistant to policy-free, legal analysis) now becomes merely the "first" step of the inquiry. Having completed that step (by a discussion which, in all fairness, does not convincingly establish that 25–years–to–life is a "proportionate" punishment for stealing three golf clubs), the plurality must then *add* an analysis to show that "Ewing's sentence is justified by the State's public-safety interest in incapacitating and deterring recidivist felons."
>
> Which indeed it is—though why that has anything to do with the principle of proportionality is a mystery. Perhaps the plurality should revise its terminology, so that what it reads into the Eighth Amendment is not the unstated proposition that all punishment should be reasonably proportionate to the gravity of the offense, but rather the unstated proposition that all punishment should reasonably pursue the multiple purposes of the criminal law. That formulation would make it clearer than ever, of course, that the plurality is not applying law but evaluating policy.

Id. at 31–32, 123 S.Ct. at 1190–91 (Scalia, J., concurring). Do you concur with Justice Scalia's view that the Eighth Amendment does not contain a proportionality principle applicable to noncapital sentences? Would it violate the Eighth Amendment to punish the crime of aggravated robbery less severely than the lesser-included offense of robbery?

6. Justice Stevens has found unpersuasive the argument that the difficulty of differentiating with exactitude between prison sentences that are grossly disproportionate and those that are not negates the existence of a

gross disproportionality principle applicable to prison sentences. In his rejoinder to Justice Scalia in *Ewing*, Justice Stevens noted that the law is replete with instances where "courts—faced with imprecise commands—must make difficult decisions." He cited the need for judges to determine, for example, whether an award of punitive damages in a case violated due process because the amount awarded was disproportionate to the defendant's wrongdoing; whether a defendant's Sixth Amendment right to a speedy trial was violated; whether a defendant's confession was coerced; whether the introduction at trial of illegally obtained evidence was a "harmless error"; and whether a defense attorney rendered unreasonable professional assistance and, if so, whether that deficiency prejudiced the defendant. Id. at 33–34, 123 S.Ct. at 1192 (Stevens, J. dissenting).

7. Punitive damages are awarded in civil cases to punish and deter certain opprobrious illegal conduct. The Due Process Clause places constraints on these awards, prohibiting awards that are "grossly excessive" or "arbitrary." State Farm Mut. Automobile Ins. Co. v. Campbell, 538 U.S. 408, 416, 123 S.Ct. 1513, 1519–20 (2003). While the Supreme Court has been extremely reticent to set aside prison sentences on the grounds that they are unconstitutionally disproportionate, the Court has manifested no such hesitancy in vacating punitive-damages awards. See, e.g., id. (finding $145 million punitive-damages award unconstitutional in insurance-fraud case where plaintiff was awarded $1 million in compensatory damages); BMW, Inc. v. Gore, 517 U.S. 559, 116 S.Ct. 1589 (1996) (vacating $2 million punitive-damages award in case in which plaintiff was awarded $4,000 in compensatory damages for defendant's fraud).

The Supreme Court also has applied a more exacting standard when assessing the constitutionality of punitive-damages awards in civil cases as opposed to prison sentences in criminal cases. Under this standard, three "guideposts" are factored into the analysis of whether a punitive-damages award is unconstitutionally excessive. A court first considers the reprehensibility of the defendant's conduct. Five facts bear on the extent to which the defendant's conduct is reprehensible: (1) whether the harm the defendant caused was physical or solely economic; (2) whether the defendant acted with indifference to the health or safety of others; (3) whether the victim was vulnerable financially; (4) whether the harmful conduct was recurrent or an "isolated incident"; and (5) whether the harm was caused accidentally or intentionally.

The second "guidepost" that a court considers when evaluating the constitutionality of a punitive-damages award is the ratio between the punitive damages and the harm caused by, and likely to ensue from, the defendant's illegal conduct. The Supreme Court has said that, as a general rule, a punitive-damages award that is ten or more times higher than the compensatory damages awarded in a case is unconstitutional. State Farm, 538 U.S. at 425, 123 S.Ct. at 1524.

The final "guidepost" in the constitutional analysis of a punitive-damages award focuses on the other penalties, both civil and criminal, that can be imposed for the kind of misconduct in which the defendant engaged. Notably, when discussing this "guidepost" in *BMW, Inc. v. Gore*, the Supreme Court said that a punitive-damages award "cannot be justified on the ground that it was necessary to deter future misconduct without considering whether less drastic remedies could be expected to achieve that goal." 517 U.S. at 584, 116 S.Ct. at 1603.

Some commentators have criticized the Supreme Court for its laxity when evaluating the constitutionality of the length of a prison sentence compared to its greater scrutiny of punitive-damages awards. See, e.g., Erwin Chemerinsky, The Constitution and Punishment, 56 Stan. L.Rev. 1049, 1079 (2004) ("There is something just wrong with a Court that has no problem with putting a person in prison for life, with no possibility of parole for fifty years, for stealing $153 worth of videotapes, but is outraged when too much is taken from a company in punitive damages when it defrauds its customers.") Do you believe that the analytical approach in the punitive-damages context warrants changes in the way in which courts evaluate claims that prison sentences are unconstitutionally disproportionate? Why or why not?

8. In your opinion, is the defendant's age at the time of sentencing relevant to the question whether a prison sentence constitutes cruel and unusual punishment because of its length? Compare Lockyer v. Andrade, 538 U.S. 63, 74 n.1, 123 S.Ct. 1166, 1174 n.1 (2003) (plurality opinion) (rejecting the proposition that two different sentences—a life sentence without parole and a life sentence with the possibility of parole in ten years—can become "materially indistinguishable" because of a defendant's age) with Crosby v. State, 824 A.2d 894, 910 (Del. 2003) (considering defendant's 45–year sentence, which would result in his imprisonment until he was at least eighty-two and possibly as old as ninety-one, a life sentence "in the literal sense").

9. Consider whether the sentence imposed in the following case violated the Eighth Amendment: The defendant, Grover Henderson, was convicted of delivering three "rocks" of crack cocaine weighing .238 grams, about a hundredth of an ounce. The drug sale was initiated by a government informant, who paid Henderson twenty dollars for the crack. Henderson, who had no prior convictions, was sentenced to life in prison. Only if the government later commuted his sentence to a term of years would he become eligible for parole. According to the state's records, Henderson was apparently the only first offender convicted in the state for selling this quantity of a controlled substance ever to receive a life sentence. In addition, state sentencing guidelines promulgated after the crime's commission and therefore not applicable to Henderson prescribed a presumptive sentence of three and a half years imprisonment for a crime like Henderson's. Only three states authorized a life sentence for a first offender convicted of delivering the amount of crack Henderson had sold, and in all but possibly one of those states, the offender was eligible for parole. See Henderson v. Norris, 258 F.3d 706 (8th Cir.2001).

10. Since the Supreme Court's decision in *Harmelin*, few defendants have prevailed on a claim that their sentences were unconstitutionally disproportionate under the Eighth Amendment. One of the notable exceptions occurred in State v. Bartlett, 830 P.2d 823 (Ariz. 1992). In that case, the defendant received two mandatory prison sentences totaling forty years, with no possibility of parole, for having had consensual sexual intercourse when he was twenty-three with two girls who were close to fifteen years old. In holding

that the defendant's sentences violated the Eighth Amendment, the Arizona Supreme Court emphasized, among other factors, the defendant's lack of any criminal record, the nonviolent nature of the crimes, and the "realities of adolescent life," namely the fact that so many teenagers are sexually active. Id. at 829. The court also noted that the mandatory minimum sentences for the defendant's crimes were the same as those to which he would have been subject if he had killed the girls and been convicted of second-degree murder.

In your opinion, should the prevalence of teenagers' involvement in sexual conduct have a bearing on the Eighth Amendment question? See also State v. Davis, 79 P.3d 64, 72 (Ariz. 2003) (citing this fact, among others, in finding that a 52–year prison sentence imposed on a 20–year–old defendant for having had sexual intercourse with two girls, one thirteen and one fourteen, was grossly disproportionate to his sexual-misconduct crimes).

11.   If a sentence is not disproportionate in the constitutional sense, appellate courts traditionally have been reluctant to set aside a sentence on the grounds that it is excessive. Dorszynski v. United States, 418 U.S. 424, 440 & n.14, 94 S.Ct. 3042, 3051 & n.14 (1974). A standard commonly applied when appellate courts are reviewing sentencing decisions is whether the sentence was the product of a "clear abuse of discretion." Hubbard v. State, 175 P.3d 625, 630 (2008). For additional discussion on the appeal and reversal of sentences for abuse of sentencing discretion, see pages 217–18.

12.   Defendants are not the only parties concerned about disproportionate sentences. Prosecutors too may be concerned that a sentence does not adequately reflect the seriousness of the crime committed or the culpability of the offender. Some legislatures have responded to this concern by enacting statutes under which prosecutors can, in limited circumstances, contest the leniency of a sentence on appeal. See, e.g., 18 U.S.C. § 3742(b) (providing for government appeals of sentences that (1) are imposed "in violation of law"; (2) are the product of an "incorrect application of the sentencing guidelines"; (3) are less than that specified in the guideline range; or (4) where no guidelines apply, are "plainly unreasonable").

In United States v. DiFrancesco, 449 U.S. 117, 101 S.Ct. 426 (1980), the Supreme Court held that imposing a greater sentence after a prosecutor successfully appeals a sentence under a statute authorizing such appeals does not violate the Double Jeopardy Clause of the Fifth Amendment. The Court reasoned that, in effect, the government had simply established a permissible "two-stage sentencing procedure." Id. at 140 n.16, 101 S.Ct. at 439 n.16.

13.   The American Bar Association has flip-flopped on the question whether prosecutors should be allowed to appeal sentences they consider too lenient. For years, the ABA opposed such appeals, in part because of the concern that prosecutors might in effect force defendants to forgo certain rights, such as the right to trial, by threatening to seek higher sentences on appeal if the defendants were convicted after a trial. See ABA Standards for Criminal Justice on Appellate Review of Sentences, Standard 20–1.1(d) (2d ed. 1978). This concern, however, was supplanted by the belief that fairness and equity demand that prosecutors be afforded the same opportunity as defendants to challenge a sentence. See ABA Standards for Criminal Justice,

Sentencing Alternatives and Procedures and Appellate Review of Sentences, Standard 18–8.3 (3d ed. 1993).

B. CHALLENGES REGARDING THE NATURE OF A CRIMINAL SANCTION

The imposition in recent years of seemingly novel criminal penalties—some actually have age-old-roots—has spawned claims of cruel and unusual punishment. These penalties fall within two general categories—shame sentences and medical interventions.

1. SHAME SENTENCES

"Scarlet letter" or shame sentences provoke legal challenges on several different grounds. The following case addressed two of the claims most frequently asserted against these kinds of sentences—that the judge had no statutory authority to impose this kind of penalty and that the sentence violated the Eighth Amendment's prohibition of cruel and unusual punishments.

UNITED STATES v. GEMENTERA

Court of Appeals, Ninth Circuit, 2004.
379 F.3d 596.

O'SCANNLAIN, CIRCUIT JUDGE:

* * *

I

Shawn Gementera pilfered letters from several mailboxes along San Francisco's Fulton Street on May 21, 2001. * * * After indictment, Gementera entered a plea agreement pursuant to which he pled guilty to mail theft, and the government dismissed a second count of receiving a stolen U.S. Treasury check.

The offense was not Gementera's first encounter with the law. Though only twenty-four years old at the time, Gementera's criminal history was lengthy for a man of his relative youth, and it was growing steadily more serious. At age nineteen, he was convicted of misdemeanor criminal mischief. He was twice convicted at age twenty of driving with a suspended license. At age twenty-two, a domestic dispute led to convictions for driving with a suspended license and for failing to provide proof of financial responsibility. By twenty-four, the conviction was misdemeanor battery. Other arrests and citations listed in the Presentence Investigation Report included possession of drug paraphernalia, additional driving offenses (most of which involved driving on a license suspended for his failure to take chemical tests), and, soon after his twenty-fifth birthday, taking a vehicle without the owner's consent.

On February 25, 2003, Judge Vaughn Walker of the United States District Court for the Northern District of California sentenced Gementera. The U.S. Sentencing Guidelines range was two to eight months incarceration; Judge Walker sentenced Gementera to the lower bound of the range, imposing two months incarceration and three years supervised release. He also imposed conditions of supervised release.

One such condition required Gementera to "perform 100 hours of community service," to consist of "standing in front of a postal facility in the city and county of San Francisco with a sandwich board which in large letters declares: 'I stole mail. This is my punishment.' " Gementera later filed a motion to correct the sentence by removing the sandwich board condition. *See* Fed.R.Crim.P. 35(a).

Judge Walker modified the sentence after inviting both parties to present "an alternative form or forms of public service that would better comport with the aims of the court." In lieu of the 100–hour signboard requirement, the district court imposed a four-part special condition in its stead. Three new terms, proposed jointly by counsel, mandated that the defendant observe postal patrons visiting the "lost or missing mail" window, write letters of apology to any identifiable victims of his crime, and deliver several lectures at a local school. It also included a scaled-down version of the signboard requirement:

> The defendant shall perform 1 day of 8 total hours of community service during which time he shall either (i) wear a two-sided sandwich board-style sign or (ii) carry a large two-sided sign stating, "I stole mail; this is my punishment," in front of a San Francisco postal facility identified by the probation officer. For the safety of defendant and general public, the postal facility designated shall be one that employs one or more security guards. Upon showing by defendant that this condition would likely impose upon defendant psychological harm or effect or result in unwarranted risk of harm to defendant, the public or postal employees, the probation officer may withdraw or modify this condition or apply to the court to withdraw or modify this condition. * * *[4]

II

We first address Gementera's argument that the eight-hour sandwich board condition violates the Sentencing Reform Act.

The Sentencing Reform Act affords district courts broad discretion in fashioning appropriate conditions of supervised release, while mandating that such conditions serve legitimate objectives. In addition to "any condition set forth as a discretionary condition of probation in [18 U.S.C.] section 3563(b)(1) through (b)(10) and (b)(12) through (b)(20)," the statute explicitly authorizes the court to impose *"any other condition it*

---

4. Gementera was ordered to surrender on March 31, 2003. On March 12, 2003, prior to his surrender, Gementera was arrested for possession of stolen mail, for which he was convicted and received a twenty-four month sentence.

considers to be appropriate." 18 U.S.C. § 3583(d)(emphasis added). Such special * * * condition must be "reasonably related" to "the nature and circumstances of the offense and the history and characteristics of the defendant." *See* 18 U.S.C. 3553(a)(1). Moreover, it must be both "reasonably related" to and "involve no greater deprivation of liberty than is reasonably necessary" to "afford adequate deterrence to criminal conduct," *see id.* at 3553(a)(2)(B), "protect the public from further crimes of the defendant," *see id.* at 3553(a)(2)(C), and "provide the defendant with needed educational or vocational training, medical care, or other correctional treatment in the most effective manner." *See id.* at 3553(a)(2)(D). Accordingly, the three legitimate statutory purposes of deterrence, protection of the public, and rehabilitation frame our analysis.

* * *

[T]he district court's discretion, while broad, is limited—most significantly here, by the statute's requirement that any condition reasonably relate to a legitimate statutory purpose. "This test is applied in a two-step process; first, this court must determine whether the sentencing judge imposed the conditions for permissible purposes, and then it must determine whether the conditions are reasonably related to the purposes." * * *

A

Gementera first urges that the condition was imposed for an impermissible purpose of humiliation. He points to certain remarks of the district court at the first sentencing hearing:

> [H]e needs to understand the disapproval that society has for this kind of conduct, and that's the idea behind the humiliation. And it should be humiliation of having to stand and be labeled in front of people coming and going from a post office as somebody who has stolen the mail.

According to Gementera, these remarks, among others, indicate that the district court viewed humiliation as an end in itself and the condition's purpose.

* * *

The court expressed particular concern that the defendant did not fully understand the gravity of his offense. Mail theft is an anonymous crime and, by "bring[ing] home to defendant that his conduct has palpable significance to real people within his community," the court aimed to break the defendant of the illusion that his theft was victimless or not serious. In short, it explained:

> While humiliation may well be—indeed likely will be—a feature of defendant's experience in standing before a post office with such a sign, the humiliation or shame he experiences should serve the salutary purpose of bringing defendant in close touch with the real significance of the crime he has acknowledged committing. Such an experience should have a specific rehabilitative effect on defendant

that could not be accomplished by other means, certainly not by a more extended term of imprisonment.

Moreover, "[i]t will also have a deterrent effect on both this defendant and others who might not otherwise have been made aware of the real legal consequences of engaging in mail theft."

Read in its entirety, the record unambiguously establishes that the district court imposed the condition for the stated and legitimate statutory purpose of rehabilitation and, to a lesser extent, for general deterrence and for the protection of the public. We find no error in the condition's purpose.

B

Assuming the court articulated a legitimate purpose, Gementera asserts, under the second prong of our test, that humiliation or so-called "shaming" conditions are not "reasonably related" to rehabilitation. In support, he cites * * * several state court decisions[9] * * *.

In evaluating probation and supervised release conditions, we have emphasized that the "reasonable relation" test is necessarily a "very flexible standard," and that such flexibility is necessary because of "our uncertainty about how rehabilitation is accomplished." * * *

* * *

---

9. In *People v. Hackler*, 16 Cal.Rptr.2d 681 (Cal.Ct.App.1993), a California court vacated a condition requiring a defendant during his first year of probation to wear a t-shirt whenever he was outside his home. The t-shirt read, "My record plus two-six packs equal four years," and on the back, "I am on felony probation for theft." Noting with disapproval the trial court's stated intention of "going back to some extent to the era of stocks" and transforming the defendant into "a Hester Prin [sic]," the court held that the t-shirt could not serve the rehabilitative purpose because it would render the defendant unemployable. By contrast, Gementera's condition was sharply limited temporally (eight hours) and spatially (one post office in a large city), eliminating any risk that its effects would similarly spill over into all aspects of the defendant's life. Indeed, the district court's imposition of the condition in lieu of lengthier incarceration enables Gementera to enter the private labor market.

People v. Johnson, 528 N.E.2d 1360 (1988), involved a condition that a DWI offender publish a newspaper advertisement with apology and mug shot. Interpreting the state supervision law as intended "to aid the defendant in rehabilitation and in avoiding future violations," and for no other purpose, the court held that the publication requirement "possibly, adds public ridicule as a condition" of supervision and could inflict psychological harm that disserves the goal of rehabilitation. *Id.* at 1362 (noting that the Illinois statute does not "refer to deterrent to others"). Relying on the fact that defendant was a young lady and a good student with no prior criminal record, had injured no one, and otherwise had no alcohol or drug problem, it found the condition impermissible, given the perceived mental health risk. By contrast, we have specifically held that mandatory public apology may be rehabilitative. Moreover, the condition specifically provided that the signboard requirement would be withdrawn if the defendant showed that the condition would inflict psychological harm.

The defendant's third case, *People v. Letterlough*, 655 N.E.2d 146 (1995), also involved a probation condition imposed upon a DWI offender. If he regained driving privileges, the offender was required to affix a fluorescent sign to his license plate, stating "CONVICTED DWI". The court imposed the condition under a catch-all provision of the New York law authorizing "any other conditions reasonably related to his [or her] rehabilitation." * * * Because the condition's "true design was not to advance defendant's rehabilitation, but rather to 'warn the public' of the threat presented by his presence behind the wheel," the court voided the condition. In contrast to the New York scheme, the district court made plain the rehabilitative purpose of the condition. We also note that in the federal system, unlike the New York system, rehabilitation is not the sole legitimate objective.

* * * [T]he district court concluded that public acknowledgment of one's offense—beyond the formal yet sterile plea in a cloistered court-room—was necessary to his rehabilitation.

* * *

Gementera and amicus contend that shaming conditions cannot be rehabilitative because such conditions necessarily cause the offender to withdraw from society or otherwise inflict psychological damage, and they would erect a per se bar against such conditions.[11] * * *

Criminal offenses, and the penalties that accompany them, nearly always cause shame and embarrassment. Indeed, the mere fact of conviction, without which state-sponsored rehabilitation efforts do not commence, is stigmatic. The fact that a condition causes shame or embarrassment does not automatically render a condition objectionable; rather, such feelings generally signal the defendant's acknowledgment of his wrongdoing. * * *

While the district court's sandwich board condition was somewhat crude, and by itself could entail risk of social withdrawal and stigmatization, it was coupled with more socially useful provisions, including lecturing at a high school and writing apologies, that might loosely be understood to promote the offender's social reintegration. *See* John Braithwaite, *Crime, Shame and Reintegration* 55 (1989) ("The crucial distinction is between shaming that is reintegrative and shaming that is disintegrative (stigmatization). Reintegrative shaming means that expressions of community disapproval, which may range from mild rebuke to degradation ceremonies, are followed by gestures of reacceptance into the community of law-abiding citizens."). We see this factor as highly significant. In short, here we consider not a stand-alone condition intended solely to humiliate, but rather a comprehensive set of provisions that expose the defendant to social disapprobation, but that also then provide an opportunity for Gementera to repair his relationship with society—first by seeking its forgiveness and then by making, as a member of the community, an independent contribution to the moral formation of its youth.[13] These

---

11. Even if shaming conditions were sometimes rehabilitative, Gementera also urges that the condition would be psychologically damaging in his specific case, given his "lack of coping skills, his substance abuse, and his unresolved personal issues with his father." * * * At the hearing, the court asked defense counsel, "is there some feature of his personality that makes him particularly vulnerable that you can substantiate?" The attorney replied, "I can't offer anything but my own personal observations and anecdotal observation based on my almost one-year representation of the defendant and his reaction and his family's reaction to what occurred in court." While not persuaded by the attorney's untutored lay psychological evidence, the district court nonetheless inserted a provision into the condition providing an avenue for Gementera to present more reliable evidence of psychological harm:

Upon showing by defendant that this condition would likely impose upon defendant psychological harm or effect or result in unwarranted risk of harm to defendant, the public or postal employees, the probation officer may withdraw or modify this condition or apply to the court to withdraw or modify this condition.

No such substantiation was presented. * * *

13. The dissent faults our analysis for looking beyond the signboard clause to other provisions of the four-part condition. * * * By acting in concert with others, a provision may reasonably

provisions,[14] tailored to the specific needs of the offender,[15] counsel in favor of concluding that the condition passes the threshold of being reasonably related to rehabilitation.

Finally, we are aware that lengthier imprisonment was an alternative available to the court. * * * The judge's reasoning that rehabilitation would better be served by means other than extended incarceration and punishment is plainly reasonable.

Accordingly, we hold that the condition imposed upon Gementera reasonably related to the legitimate statutory objective of rehabilitation.[16] * * *

III

* * *

We turn then to the Eighth Amendment, which forbids the infliction of "cruel and unusual punishments." "The basic concept underlying the Eighth Amendment was nothing less than the dignity of man." *Trop v. Dulles,* 356 U.S. 86, 100 (1958).

A particular punishment violates the Eighth Amendment if it constitutes one of "those modes or acts of punishment that had been considered cruel and unusual at the time that the Bill of Rights was adopted." Shaming sanctions of far greater severity were common in the colonial era, and the parties do not quarrel on this point.

The Amendment's prohibition extends beyond those practices deemed barbarous in the 18th century, however. "[T]he words of the Amendment are not precise, and [ ] their scope is not static. The Amendment must draw its meaning from the evolving standards of decency that mark the progress of a maturing society." * * *

The parties have offered no evidence whatsoever, aside from bare assertion, that shaming sanctions violate contemporary standards of decency. But the occasional imposition of such sanctions is hardly unusual, particularly in our state courts. Aside from a single case presenting concerns not at issue here,[17] we are aware of no case holding that

---

relate to rehabilitation, even though the relation existed primarily by virtue of its interaction with complementary provisions in an integrated program. A boot camp, for example, that operates by "breaking participants down" before "building them up again" is not rendered impermissible merely because the first step, standing alone, might be impermissible. Similarly, a program that emphasizes an offenders' separation from the community of law-abiding citizens, in order to generate contrition and an authentic desire to rejoin that community, need not be evaluated without reference to the program's affirmative provisions to reconcile the offender with the community and eventually to reintegrate him into it.

14. We do not pass here on the more difficult case of the district court's original 100–hour condition, which lacked significant reintegrative aspects.

15. We do acknowledge that one purpose of the Sentencing Guidelines was to promote greater uniformity in federal sentencing, and that permitting certain conditions of supervised release, as imposed here, may lead to less regularized sentences. * * *

16. In view of this holding, we do not reach the separate issue of whether the condition reasonably relates to the objectives of deterrence and protection of the public.

17. Gementera points to *Williams v. State,* 505 S.E.2d 816 (1998), in which a defendant convicted of soliciting sodomy was ordered to walk for ten days, between 7 p.m. and 11 p.m. each

contemporary shaming sanctions violate our Constitution's prohibition against cruel and unusual punishment.[18]

We do, however, note that *Blanton v. N. Las Vegas,* 489 U.S. 538 (1989), is instructive, if only indirectly. In *Blanton,* the Court considered whether a Nevada DUI defendant was entitled to a jury trial pursuant to the Sixth Amendment. The inquiry into whether the offense constituted a petty crime not subject to the Sixth Amendment trial provision required the Court to evaluate the severity of the maximum authorized penalty. The statute provided a maximum sentence of six months or, alternatively, forty-eight hours of community service while dressed in distinctive garb identifying the defendant as a DUI offender, payment of a $200–$1000 fine, loss of driving license, and attendance at an alcohol abuse course. The Court wrote:

> We are also unpersuaded by the fact that, instead of a prison sentence, a DUI offender may be ordered to perform 48 hours of community service dressed in clothing identifying him as a DUI offender. Even assuming the outfit is the source of some embarrassment during the 48–hour period, such a penalty will be less embarrassing and less onerous than six months in jail.

Id. at 544; *but see id.* at 544 n. 10 ("We are hampered in our review of the clothing requirement because the record from the state courts contains neither a description of the clothing nor any details as to where and when it must be worn."). Just as the Court concluded that 48 hours of service dressed in distinctive DUI garb was less onerous than six months imprisonment, it would stretch reason to conclude that eight hours with a signboard, in lieu of incarceration, constitutes constitutionally cruel and unusual punishment.

* * *

day, along that portion of the street where the solicitation occurred, holding a large sign stating, "BEWARE HIGH CRIME AREA." The police were to be notified in advance in order to monitor his performance and provide an appropriate level of safety. While the court commended the trial judge for his "initiative" in developing a "new and creative form of sentencing which might very well have a positive effect on [the defendant] and be beneficial to the public," and explained that shaming punishments are not forbidden, it nonetheless found that the condition exposed the defendant to a constitutionally impermissible danger.

* * * The condition in *Gementera* does not expose the defendant to any significant risk of danger. By contrast with *Williams,* the *Gementera* signboard is worn during eight hours of daylight during the business day, not at night; in front of a United States Post Office, not a "high crime" neighborhood where criminal solicitation occurs; and the sign's message does not provoke violence by threatening the criminal livelihood of those who illegally trade sex in a red light district, as the *Williams* sign might. Moreover, the district court in *Gementera* explicitly included a provision allowing for withdrawal of the condition upon a showing that the condition would impose a safety risk upon the defendant. Gementera made no such showing.

18. Numerous state courts have rejected Eighth Amendment challenges to shaming sanctions. *See, e.g., People v. Letterlough,* 613 N.Y.S.2d 687 (N.Y.App.Div.1994) ("CONVICTED DWI" sign on license plate); *Ballenger v. State,* 436 S.E.2d 793 (1993) (fluorescent pink DUI bracelet); *Lindsay v. State,* 606 So.2d 652, 656–57 (Fla.App.1992) (DUI advertisement in newspaper); *Goldschmitt v. State,* 490 So.2d 123, 125 (Fla.App.1986) ("Convicted DUI—Restricted License" bumper sticker); cf. *People v. McDowell,* 130 Cal.Rptr. 839 (Cal.App.1976) (tap shoes for purse thief who used tennis shoes to approach his victims quietly and flee swiftly).

HAWKINS, CIRCUIT JUDGE, dissenting:

Conditions of supervised release must be reasonably related to and "involve no greater deprivation of liberty than is reasonably necessary" to deter criminal conduct, protect the public, and rehabilitate the offender. Clearly, the shaming punishment at issue in this case was intended to humiliate Gementera. And that is all it will do. Any attempt to classify the goal of the punishment as anything other than humiliation would be disingenuous. Because humiliation is not one of the three proper goals under the Sentencing Reform Act, I would hold that the district court abused its discretion in imposing the condition.

* * *

* * *Admitting that the condition was "crude" and "could entail risk of social withdrawal and stigmatization," the majority nonetheless finds the condition acceptable because it was "coupled with more socially useful provisions." * * * The majority's position seems to be that even if one condition of a sentence manifestly violates the Sentencing Act, it can be cured by coupling the provision with other, proper ones. When such a novel proposition is put forward and no case law is cited to support it, there is usually a reason. At the end of the day, we *are* charged with evaluating a condition whose primary purpose is to humiliate, and that condition should simply not be upheld.

* * *

I would vacate the sentence and remand for re-sentencing, instructing the district court that public humiliation or shaming has no proper place in our system of justice.

QUESTIONS AND POINTS FOR DISCUSSION

1.   If you were on the court of appeals deciding this case, how, if at all, would your analysis and resolution of the two claims in the case be affected if the district court had retained the original requirement that the defendant display the sign attesting to his guilt for one hundred hours? What if the display time was limited to eight hours but the sentencing court did not order the defendant to write letters of apology to victims of his crime and to give speeches at high schools recounting his remorse for his crime? Would that change in the facts alter your disposition of the appeal?

2.   In recent years, courts have begun to impose "shame sentences" with increasing frequency. Examples of such sentences, in addition to those recounted in *Gementera*, include: requiring a man convicted of sexual abuse to place signs outside his home and on his car that said, "Dangerous Sex Offender–No Children Allowed," State v. Bateman, 771 P.2d 314 (Or.Ct.App. 1989); displaying on "John TV," a local television channel, the names and pictures of men convicted of soliciting prostitutes; and requiring a woman convicted of welfare fraud to wear a sign announcing, "I stole food from poor people." Dan Markel, Are Shaming Punishments Beautifully Retributive? Retributivism and the Implications for the Alternative Sanctions Debate, 54 Vand.L.Rev. 2157, 2171, 2175 (2001). (The latter defendant, incidentally,

opted to go to jail rather than wear the sign.) Other shame sentences have ordered offenders to get on their hands and knees and apologize to their victims, directed a defendant who killed two people when he drove while intoxicated to hang a picture of his victims in his prison cell, and required a man convicted of assaulting his ex-wife to let her spit in his face. Henry J. Reske, Scarlet Letter Sentences, 82 A.B.A. J. 16, 17 (Jan. 1996).

In your opinion, are any or all of the above sentences or those discussed in *Gementera* "cruel and unusual" within the meaning of the Eighth Amendment? Why or why not? Some courts have skirted this constitutional question, finding that the imposition of a particular shame punishment was not authorized by the state's sentencing statute. See, e.g., People v. Meyer, 680 N.E.2d 315, 320 (Ill. 1997) (state law did not authorize the trial judge to require the defendant, as a condition of his probation sentence for aggravated battery, to place a sign in his yard that said, "Warning! A Violent Felon lives here. Enter at your own Risk!").

3. Apart from questions regarding courts' authority to impose shame punishments and their constitutionality is the question of their efficacy. While there is very little empirical evidence regarding the effects of shame punishments on crime, Professor Toni Massaro has outlined five conditions that shame punishments need to meet in order to be "effective and meaningful":

> First, the potential offenders must be members of an identifiable group, such as a close-knit religious or ethnic community. Second, the legal sanctions must actually compromise potential offenders' group social standing. That is, the affected group must concur with the legal decision-maker's estimation of what is, or should be, humiliating to group members. Third, the shaming must be communicated to the group and the group must withdraw from the offender—shun her—physically, emotionally, financially, or otherwise. Fourth, the shamed person must fear withdrawal by the group. Finally, the shamed person must be afforded some means of regaining community esteem, unless the misdeed is so grave that the offender must be permanently exiled or demoted.

Toni M. Massaro, Shame, Culture, and American Criminal Law, 89 Mich. L.Rev. 1880, 1883 (1991). Do these conditions, assuming their validity, suggest that shame punishments would or would not be effectual in the United States? Are there any other considerations that should be factored into a decision whether to incorporate shame punishments into the country's sentencing structures?

4. Some commentators have distinguished between "shame punishments," which involve some kind of public debasement of the defendant, and "guilt punishments," which are designed to foster remorse for one's misdeeds without the public degradation that attends a shame punishment. See, e.g., Dan Markel, Are Shaming Punishments Beautifully Retributive? Retributivism and the Implications for the Alternative Sanctions Debate, 54 Vand. L. Rev. 2157, 2178–79, 2229 (2001). A classic example of a "guilt punishment" is a requirement that convicted drunk drivers hear victims of drunk drivers or victims' family members describe the injuries and losses they have suffered from this kind of crime.

Consider the case of a woman who, after being convicted of a traffic violation for failing to strap her three-year-old daughter in a child-safety seat, was ordered to write a fake obituary for her daughter recounting the cause of the child's death. Should the constitutionality of the defendant's sentence depend on whether she was forced to publicize the obituary, submit it to the court, or submit it to her probation officer? Should the soundness of the penalty from a policy perspective hinge on any of these distinctions?

2. MEDICAL INTERVENTIONS

Medical interventions can be incorporated into a defendant's sentence in ways that may give rise to claims of cruel and unusual punishment. For example, in State v. Brown, 326 S.E.2d 410 (S.C. 1985), the trial judge sentenced the defendants, who had been convicted of first-degree criminal sexual conduct, to thirty years in prison. The judge, however, announced that if the defendants agreed to be surgically castrated, he would suspend their prison sentences and place them on probation for five years. The Supreme Court of South Carolina summarily struck down this condition on the grounds that surgical castration, "a form of mutilation," was cruel and unusual punishment under the state's constitution. Id. at 411. Courts have also vacated sentences on statutory grounds when defendants elected to undergo surgical castration in lieu of incarceration or lengthier incarceration, finding that no state statute authorized surgical castration as a criminal penalty for the crime in question. See, e.g., Bruno v. State, 837 So.2d 521, 523 (Fla. Dist. Ct. App. 2003).

Through medical research, drugs now have been developed that can "chemically castrate" a man. Some of the men to whom such drugs are administered still can have erections, but the drugs eliminate or dramatically reduce libido and sexual activity. The effects of chemical castration on recidivism have not been determined definitively. Some studies of the effects of chemical castration have reported substantial decreases in the recidivism rates of paraphiliacs—sex offenders, such as pedophiles, whose compulsive sexual fantasies propel them to commit sex crimes. See Daniel L. Icenogle, Sentencing Male Sex Offenders to the Use of Biological Treatments, 15 J. Legal Med. 279, 282, 285 (1994) (reporting recidivism rates of 3 to 10% for treated paraphiliacs compared to recidivism rates of 54 to 85% for untreated sex offenders). Others have not. See John F. Stinneford, Incapacitation Through Maiming: Chemical Castration, the Eighth Amendment, and the Denial of Human Dignity, 3 U. St. Thomas L.J. 559, 575 (2006) (reporting recidivism rates ranging from 0 to 83% for paraphiliacs who were chemically castrated). In addition, chemical castration can have a number of adverse side effects. One of the most frequently administered drugs, medroxyprogesterone acetate, commonly known as Depo–Provera, can cause, among other effects, weight gain, high blood pressure, fatigue, nightmares, hot flashes, muscle aches, smaller testes, and a decrease in bone density. Other serious, though less common, side effects include blood clots, breathing difficulties, depression, and diverticulitis, an intestinal disorder.

Some state statutes authorize or require the chemical castration of certain sex offenders. In California, for example, a court, in its discretion, may order that Depo–Provera or a similar drug be administered when persons convicted for the first time of certain sex crimes involving children under the age of thirteen are paroled. Cal. Penal Code § 645(a). Persons convicted for the second time of such crimes must receive Depo–Provera treatments when they are released on parole. Id. § 645(b). Depo–Provera treatments continue until the Board of Prison Terms determines that the treatments are no longer necessary, although a sex offender can avoid the treatments by "voluntarily" undergoing surgical castration. Id. § 645(d), (e). For one variant of the California statute, see Iowa Code Ann. § 903B.10(1) (vesting both the court and the parole board with the authority to impose "hormonal intervention therapy" as a condition of release for certain sex offenders).

QUESTIONS AND POINTS FOR DISCUSSION

1. In your opinion, is the California statute constitutional? Do the Supreme Court's decisions in Washington v. Harper, 494 U.S. 210, 110 S.Ct. 1028 (1990) (holding constitutional the involuntary administration of psychotropic drugs to prisoners in certain circumstances), infra pages 636–39 and 757–62, and Kansas v. Hendricks, 521 U.S. 346, 117 S.Ct. 2072 (1997) (upholding the constitutionality of the indefinite civil confinement of certain sex offenders), infra page 429, have any bearing on this question?

Is the California statute wise from a policy perspective? How, if at all, would you modify the statute?

2. The American Civil Liberties Union (ACLU) of Florida has outlined certain conditions that, in its opinion, should be met in order for a defendant to be subjected to chemical castration in lieu of incarceration. Those conditions include the following:

a. A psychiatrist or psychologist must attest that the drug can effectively treat the defendant's sexual problem.

b. The drug must not pose "significant health risks" to the defendant.

c. The drug must not be experimental.

d. The drug's effects must end once the drug is no longer being administered.

e. The defendant must be provided psychotherapy in addition to the drug treatment.

f. The defendant must consent to the drug treatment.

g. Before this consent is obtained, the defendant must consult with counsel and must also be informed by a medical professional of the drug's potential side effects and of the psychotherapy component of the treatment regimen.

h. The state must pay for the consultations if the defendant is indigent.

i. At the sentencing hearing, the judge must: (a) ensure that the defendant understands what the drug treatment entails and that he has been provided the information considered a predicate to informed consent; (b) must identify what sentence the court will impose if the defendant does not undergo treatment; and (c) must apprise the defendant that he can withdraw his consent to the treatment at any time.

j. If the defendant later rescinds his authorization for the drug treatment, the judge should not automatically impose an incarcerative sentence at the resentencing hearing but should instead consider the defendant's reasons for withdrawing from the treatment.

Larry Helm Spalding, Florida's 1997 Chemical Castration Law: A Return to the Dark Ages, 25 Fla. St. U.L.Rev. 117, 137–38 (1998).

3. It is not too far-fetched to envision the time when criminal sentences could direct that a person be sentenced to a "coma-bay prison," where they would be placed in a coma for a prescribed period of time, whether days, weeks, months, or years. J.C. Oleson, The Punitive Coma, 90 Cal. L.Rev. 829 (2002). Would imposition of a "punitive coma" pass constitutional muster in your opinion? Under what circumstances? What would be the arguable advantages and disadvantages of such a penalty?

CHAPTER 8

PAROLE RELEASE AND PROBATION AND PAROLE REVOCATION

■ ■ ■

Parole boards determine inmates' suitability for release from prison so that they can serve the remainder of their sentences outside prison. In recent years, public demands to "get tough on crime" have led some legislatures to abolish their parole systems, adopting determinate sentencing statutes and, in some states, sentencing guidelines in their stead. See Bureau of Justice Statistics, U.S. Dep't of Justice, Trends in State Parole, 1990–2000, at 1 (2001) (reporting that by year-end 2000, sixteen states had eliminated discretionary parole release for all prisoners, and four states had abolished discretionary parole for certain violent offenders); Bureau of Justice Assistance, U.S. Dep't of Justice, 1996 National Survey of State Sentencing Structures 4–5 (1998). Under these structured sentencing systems, the amount of time that a convicted offender will be incarcerated for a crime is determined either exclusively by the legislature or by the legislature, the sentencing judge, and possibly a sentencing guidelines commission. See Chapter 4, pages 174–218. Often, however, the sentences in these jurisdictions must include a period of mandatory supervision in the community upon an offender's release from prison. See, e.g., 730 Ill. Comp. Stat. 5/5–8–1(d) on page 175. But because discretion as to when inmates will be released from prison is eliminated once their sentences are imposed, parole boards that determine prisoners' release dates are unnecessary. Administrative bodies, although perhaps not denominated parole boards, still may be utilized though to determine whether offenders have violated the conditions of their mandatory supervised-release term and should be required to serve some or all of the remainder of the supervision period in prison. See, e.g., 730 Ill. Comp. Stat. 5/3–3–9(a)(3).

Despite the abolition of parole in some states, many states have retained their parole systems. In the sections that follow, the constitutional standards that must be adhered to when deciding whether to release inmates on parole and whether to revoke their parole are discussed. Because the Supreme Court's decision in Morrissey v. Brewer, 408 U.S. 471, 92 S.Ct. 2593 (1972), which concerned parole-revocation proceedings, informed its later decisions concerning parole-release hearings, we will focus first on the subject of parole revocation.

A. PROBATION AND PAROLE REVOCATION

1. DUE PROCESS

MORRISSEY v. BREWER

Supreme Court of the United States, 1972.
408 U.S. 471, 92 S.Ct. 2593, 33 L.Ed.2d 484.

MR. CHIEF JUSTICE BURGER delivered the opinion of the Court.

We granted certiorari in this case to determine whether the Due Process Clause of the Fourteenth Amendment requires that a State afford an individual some opportunity to be heard prior to revoking his parole.

Petitioner Morrissey was convicted of false drawing or uttering of checks in 1967 pursuant to his guilty plea, and was sentenced to not more than seven years' confinement. He was paroled from the Iowa State Penitentiary in June 1968. Seven months later, at the direction of his parole officer, he was arrested in his home town as a parole violator and incarcerated in the county jail. One week later, after review of the parole officer's written report, the Iowa Board of Parole revoked Morrissey's parole, and he was returned to the penitentiary located about 100 miles from his home. Petitioner asserts he received no hearing prior to revocation of his parole.

The parole officer's report on which the Board of Parole acted shows that petitioner's parole was revoked on the basis of information that he had violated the conditions of parole by buying a car under an assumed name and operating it without permission, giving false statements to police concerning his address and insurance company after a minor accident, obtaining credit under an assumed name, and failing to report his place of residence to his parole officer. The report states that the officer interviewed Morrissey, and that he could not explain why he did not contact his parole officer despite his effort to excuse this on the ground that he had been sick. Further, the report asserts that Morrissey admitted buying the car and obtaining credit under an assumed name, and also admitted being involved in the accident. The parole officer recommended that his parole be revoked because of "his continual violating of his parole rules."

[The Court then discussed the claim of petitioner Booher, who also contended that his right to be afforded due process of law was violated when his parole was revoked without a hearing.]

* * *

I

* * *

During the past 60 years, the practice of releasing prisoners on parole before the end of their sentences has become an integral part of the penological system. Rather than being an *ad hoc* exercise of clemency, parole is an established variation on imprisonment of convicted criminals. Its purpose is to help individuals reintegrate into society as constructive individuals as soon as they are able, without being confined for the full term of the sentence imposed. It also serves to alleviate the costs to society of keeping an individual in prison. * * *

To accomplish the purpose of parole, those who are allowed to leave prison early are subjected to specified conditions for the duration of their terms. These conditions restrict their activities substantially beyond the ordinary restrictions imposed by law on an individual citizen. Typically, parolees are forbidden to use liquor or to have associations or correspondence with certain categories of undesirable persons. Typically, also they must seek permission from their parole officers before engaging in specified activities, such as changing employment or living quarters, marrying, acquiring or operating a motor vehicle, traveling outside the community, and incurring substantial indebtedness. Additionally, parolees must regularly report to the parole officer to whom they are assigned and sometimes they must make periodic written reports of their activities.

* * *

* * * In practice, not every violation of parole conditions automatically leads to revocation. Typically, a parolee will be counseled to abide by the conditions of parole, and the parole officer ordinarily does not take steps to have parole revoked unless he thinks that the violations are serious and continuing so as to indicate that the parolee is not adjusting properly and cannot be counted on to avoid antisocial activity. * * *

Implicit in the system's concern with parole violations is the notion that the parolee is entitled to retain his liberty as long as he substantially abides by the conditions of his parole. The first step in a revocation decision thus involves a wholly retrospective factual question: whether the parolee has in fact acted in violation of one or more conditions of his parole. Only if it is determined that the parolee did violate the conditions does the second question arise: should the parolee be recommitted to prison or should other steps be taken to protect society and improve chances of rehabilitation? The first step is relatively simple; the second is more complex. The second question involves the application of expertise by the parole authority in making a prediction as to the ability of the individual to live in society without committing antisocial acts. This part of the decision, too, depends on facts, and therefore it is important for the board to know not only that some violation was committed but also to know accurately how many and how serious the violations were. Yet this second step, deciding what to do about the violation once it is identified, is not purely factual but also predictive and discretionary.

If a parolee is returned to prison, he usually receives no credit for the time "served" on parole. Thus, the returnee may face a potential of substantial imprisonment.

II

We begin with the proposition that the revocation of parole is not part of a criminal prosecution and thus the full panoply of rights due a defendant in such a proceeding does not apply to parole revocations. Parole arises after the end of the criminal prosecution, including imposition of sentence. * * * Revocation deprives an individual, not of the absolute liberty to which every citizen is entitled, but only of the conditional liberty properly dependent on observance of special parole restrictions.

We turn, therefore, to the question whether the requirements of due process in general apply to parole revocations. * * * Whether any procedural protections are due depends on the extent to which an individual will be "condemned to suffer grievous loss." The question is not merely the "weight" of the individual's interest, but whether the nature of the interest is one within the contemplation of the "liberty or property" language of the Fourteenth Amendment. * * *

We turn to an examination of the nature of the interest of the parolee in his continued liberty. The liberty of a parolee enables him to do a wide range of things open to persons who have never been convicted of any crime. * * * Subject to the conditions of his parole, he can be gainfully employed and is free to be with family and friends and to form the other enduring attachments of normal life. Though the State properly subjects him to many restrictions not applicable to other citizens, his condition is very different from that of confinement in a prison. He may have been on parole for a number of years and may be living a relatively normal life at the time he is faced with revocation.[9] The parolee has relied on at least an implicit promise that parole will be revoked only if he fails to live up to the parole conditions. In many cases, the parolee faces lengthy incarceration if his parole is revoked.

We see, therefore, that the liberty of a parolee, although indeterminate, includes many of the core values of unqualified liberty and its termination inflicts a "grievous loss" on the parolee and often on others. It is hardly useful any longer to try to deal with this problem in terms of whether the parolee's liberty is a "right" or a "privilege." By whatever name, the liberty is valuable and must be seen as within the protection of the Fourteenth Amendment. Its termination calls for some orderly process, however informal.

Turning to the question what process is due, we find that the State's interests are several. The State has found the parolee guilty of a crime against the people. That finding justifies imposing extensive restrictions

---

9. See, *e.g., Murray v. Page,* 429 F.2d 1359 (C.A.10 1970) (parole revoked after eight years; 15 years remaining on original term).

on the individual's liberty. * * * Given the previous conviction and the proper imposition of conditions, the State has an overwhelming interest in being able to return the individual to imprisonment without the burden of a new adversary criminal trial if in fact he has failed to abide by the conditions of his parole.

Yet, the State has no interest in revoking parole without some informal procedural guarantees. * * *

* * * The parolee is not the only one who has a stake in his conditional liberty. Society has a stake in whatever may be the chance of restoring him to normal and useful life within the law. Society thus has an interest in not having parole revoked because of erroneous information or because of an erroneous evaluation of the need to revoke parole, given the breach of parole conditions. And society has a further interest in treating the parolee with basic fairness: fair treatment in parole revocations will enhance the chance of rehabilitation by avoiding reactions to arbitrariness.

* * *

III

We now turn to the nature of the process that is due, bearing in mind that the interest of both State and parolee will be furthered by an effective but informal hearing. In analyzing what is due, we see two important stages in the typical process of parole revocation.

(a) Arrest of Parolee and Preliminary Hearing. The first stage occurs when the parolee is arrested and detained, usually at the direction of his parole officer. The second occurs when parole is formally revoked. There is typically a substantial time lag between the arrest and the eventual determination by the parole board whether parole should be revoked. Additionally, it may be that the parolee is arrested at a place distant from the state institution, to which he may be returned before the final decision is made concerning revocation. Given these factors, due process would seem to require that some minimal inquiry be conducted at or reasonably near the place of the alleged parole violation or arrest and as promptly as convenient after arrest while information is fresh and sources are available. Such an inquiry should be seen as in the nature of a "preliminary hearing" to determine whether there is probable cause or reasonable ground to believe that the arrested parolee has committed acts that would constitute a violation of parole conditions.

In our view, due process requires that after the arrest, the determination that reasonable ground exists for revocation of parole should be made by someone not directly involved in the case. * * * The officer directly involved in making recommendations cannot always have complete objectivity in evaluating them.[14] * * *

---

14. This is not an issue limited to bad motivation. "Parole agents are human, and it is possible that friction between the agent and parolee may have influenced the agent's judgment."

This independent officer need not be a judicial officer. The granting and revocation of parole are matters traditionally handled by administrative officers. * * * It will be sufficient, therefore, in the parole revocation context, if an evaluation of whether reasonable cause exists to believe that conditions of parole have been violated is made by someone such as a parole officer other than the one who has made the report of parole violations or has recommended revocation. A State could certainly choose some other independent decisionmaker to perform this preliminary function.

With respect to the preliminary hearing before this officer, the parolee should be given notice that the hearing will take place and that its purpose is to determine whether there is probable cause to believe he has committed a parole violation. The notice should state what parole violations have been alleged. At the hearing the parolee may appear and speak in his own behalf; he may bring letters, documents, or individuals who can give relevant information to the hearing officer. On request of the parolee, a person who has given adverse information on which parole revocation is to be based is to be made available for questioning in his presence. However, if the hearing officer determines that an informant would be subjected to risk of harm if his identity were disclosed, he need not be subjected to confrontation and cross-examination.

The hearing officer shall have the duty of making a summary, or digest, of what occurs at the hearing in terms of the responses of the parolee and the substance of the documents or evidence given in support of parole revocation and of the parolee's position. Based on the information before him, the officer should determine whether there is probable cause to hold the parolee for the final decision of the parole board on revocation. Such a determination would be sufficient to warrant the parolee's continued detention and return to the state correctional institution pending the final decision. * * * "[T]he decision maker should state the reasons for his determination and indicate the evidence he relied on ..." but it should be remembered that this is not a final determination calling for "formal findings of fact and conclusions of law." No interest would be served by formalism in this process; informality will not lessen the utility of this inquiry in reducing the risk of error.

(b) The Revocation Hearing. There must also be an opportunity for a hearing, if it is desired by the parolee, prior to the final decision on revocation by the parole authority. This hearing must be the basis for more than determining probable cause; it must lead to a final evaluation of any contested relevant facts and consideration of whether the facts as determined warrant revocation. The parolee must have an opportunity to be heard and to show, if he can, that he did not violate the conditions, or, if he did, that circumstances in mitigation suggest that the violation does not warrant revocation. The revocation hearing must be tendered within a reasonable time after the parolee is taken into custody. A lapse of two months, as respondents suggest occurs in some cases, would not appear to be unreasonable.

* * * Our task is limited to deciding the minimum requirements of due process. They include (a) written notice of the claimed violations of parole; (b) disclosure to the parolee of evidence against him; (c) opportunity to be heard in person and to present witnesses and documentary evidence; (d) the right to confront and cross-examine adverse witnesses (unless the hearing officer specifically finds good cause for not allowing confrontation); (e) a "neutral and detached" hearing body such as a traditional parole board, members of which need not be judicial officers or lawyers; and (f) a written statement by the factfinders as to the evidence relied on and reasons for revoking parole. We emphasize there is no thought to equate this second stage of parole revocation to a criminal prosecution in any sense. It is a narrow inquiry; the process should be flexible enough to consider evidence including letters, affidavits, and other material that would not be admissible in an adversary criminal trial.

We do not reach or decide the question whether the parolee is entitled to the assistance of retained counsel or to appointed counsel if he is indigent.

We have no thought to create an inflexible structure for parole revocation procedures. The few basic requirements set out above, which are applicable to future revocations of parole, should not impose a great burden on any State's parole system. Control over the required proceedings by the hearing officers can assure that delaying tactics and other abuses sometimes present in the traditional adversary trial situation do not occur. Obviously a parolee cannot relitigate issues determined against him in other forums, as in the situation presented when the revocation is based on conviction of another crime.

* * *

MR. JUSTICE BRENNAN, with whom MR. JUSTICE MARSHALL joins, concurring in the result.

I agree that a parole may not be revoked, consistently with the Due Process Clause, unless the parolee is afforded, first, a preliminary hearing at the time of arrest to determine whether there is probable cause to believe that he has violated his parole conditions and, second, a final hearing within a reasonable time to determine whether he has, in fact, violated those conditions and whether his parole should be revoked. * * *

The Court, however, states that it does not now decide whether the parolee is also entitled at each hearing to the assistance of retained counsel or of appointed counsel if he is indigent. *Goldberg v. Kelly,* 397 U.S. 254 (1970),[a] nonetheless plainly dictates that he at least "must be allowed to retain an attorney if he so desires." As the Court said there, "Counsel can help delineate the issues, present the factual contentions in an orderly manner, conduct cross-examination, and generally safeguard

---

a.   *Goldberg v. Kelly* dealt with the procedural safeguards that must attend the termination of welfare benefits.

the interests of'' his client. The only question open under our precedents is whether counsel must be furnished the parolee if he is indigent.

MR. JUSTICE DOUGLAS, dissenting in part.

* * *

If a violation of a condition of parole is involved, rather than the commission of a new offense, there should not be an arrest of the parolee and his return to the prison or to a local jail.[8] Rather, notice of the alleged violation should be given to the parolee and a time set for a hearing. * * * Moreover, the parolee should be entitled to counsel. * * * "A hearing in which counsel is absent or is present only on behalf of one side is inherently unsatisfactory if not unfair. Counsel can see that relevant facts are brought out, vague and insubstantial allegations discounted, and irrelevancies eliminated."

The hearing required is not a grant of the full panoply of rights applicable to a criminal trial. But confrontation with the informer may * * * be necessary for a fair hearing and the ascertainment of the truth. * * *

* * *

QUESTIONS AND POINTS FOR DISCUSSION

1. In Young v. Harper, 520 U.S. 143, 117 S.Ct. 1148 (1997), the Supreme Court held that a "preparole conditional supervision program" under which certain prisoners were released from prison early in order to alleviate prison crowding was sufficiently like parole to give rise to a liberty interest. Under this program, when crowding in the prison system reached a certain level, the parole board could release on "preparole" prisoners who had served 15% of their prison sentences. After serving one third of their sentences, the preparolees then became eligible for parole. But except for what the Supreme Court considered minor differences, release on preparole was like release on parole. Both preparolees and parolees were subject to similar restrictions on their freedom, such as the requirement that they meet at regular intervals with their parole officer. Consequently, participants in the preparole program, according to the Court, could not be sent back to prison unless they were afforded the due-process protections set forth in Morrissey v. Brewer.

The prisoner who brought suit in Young was terminated from the preparole program and sent back to prison after the governor rejected the parole board's recommendation to release him on parole. The Supreme Court emphasized though that eligibility to continue participating in the preparole program was not conditioned on the governor's decision about parole. What if the preparole-program requirements were changed so that continued participation in the program was foreclosed if the governor denied parole? Under

---

8. * * * "Where serious violations of parole have been committed, the parolee will have been arrested by local or federal authorities on charges stemming from those violations. Where the violation of parole is not serious, no reason appears why he should be incarcerated before hearing. If, of course, the parolee willfully fails to appear for his hearing, this in itself would justify issuance of the warrant."

these circumstances, would a program participant be entitled to certain procedural safeguards before being removed from the program and reincarcerated?

2. In Gagnon v. Scarpelli, 411 U.S. 778, 93 S.Ct. 1756 (1973), the Supreme Court concluded that before individuals on probation can have their probation revoked, they must be afforded the procedural protections outlined in *Morrissey v. Brewer*. The Court in *Gagnon* also addressed a question left unanswered in *Morrissey*—whether indigent individuals have the right to be represented by appointed counsel during parole- or probation-revocation hearings. Pertinent portions of the Court's opinion discussing this issue are set forth below:

> [W]e think that the Court of Appeals erred in accepting respondent's contention that the State is under a constitutional duty to provide counsel for indigents in all probation or parole revocation cases. While such a rule has the appeal of simplicity, it would impose direct costs and serious collateral disadvantages without regard to the need or the likelihood in a particular case for a constructive contribution by counsel. In most cases, the probationer or parolee has been convicted of committing another crime or has admitted the charges against him. And while in some cases he may have a justifiable excuse for the violation or a convincing reason why revocation is not the appropriate disposition, mitigating evidence of this kind is often not susceptible of proof or is so simple as not to require either investigation or exposition by counsel.
>
> The introduction of counsel into a revocation proceeding will alter significantly the nature of the proceeding. If counsel is provided for the probationer or parolee, the State in turn will normally provide its own counsel; lawyers, by training and disposition, are advocates and bound by professional duty to present all available evidence and arguments in support of their clients' positions and to contest with vigor all adverse evidence and views. The role of the hearing body itself, aptly described in *Morrissey* as being "predictive and discretionary" as well as factfinding, may become more akin to that of a judge at a trial, and less attuned to the rehabilitative needs of the individual probationer or parolee. In the greater self-consciousness of its quasi-judicial role, the hearing body may be less tolerant of marginal deviant behavior and feel more pressure to reincarcerate than to continue nonpunitive rehabilitation. Certainly, the decisionmaking process will be prolonged, and the financial cost to the State—for appointed counsel, counsel for the State, a longer record, and the possibility of judicial review—will not be insubstantial.

> * * *

> We thus find no justification for a new inflexible constitutional rule with respect to the requirement of counsel. We think, rather, that the decision as to the need for counsel must be made on a case-by-case basis in the exercise of a sound discretion by the state authority charged with responsibility for administering the probation and parole system. Although the presence and participation of counsel will probably be both undesirable and constitutionally unnecessary in most revocation hearings, there will remain certain cases in which fundamental fairness—the

touchstone of due process—will require that the State provide at its expense counsel for indigent probationers or parolees.

It is neither possible nor prudent to attempt to formulate a precise and detailed set of guidelines to be followed in determining when the providing of counsel is necessary to meet the applicable due process requirements. The facts and circumstances in preliminary and final hearings are susceptible of almost infinite variation, and a considerable discretion must be allowed the responsible agency in making the decision. Presumptively, it may be said that counsel should be provided in cases where, after being informed of his right to request counsel, the probationer or parolee makes such a request, based on a timely and colorable claim (i) that he has not committed the alleged violation of the conditions upon which he is at liberty; or (ii) that, even if the violation is a matter of public record or is uncontested, there are substantial reasons which justified or mitigated the violation and make revocation inappropriate, and that the reasons are complex or otherwise difficult to develop or present. In passing on a request for the appointment of counsel, the responsible agency also should consider, especially in doubtful cases, whether the probationer appears to be capable of speaking effectively for himself. In every case in which a request for counsel at a preliminary or final hearing is refused, the grounds for refusal should be stated succinctly in the record.

Id. at 787–88, 790–91, 93 S.Ct. at 1762–63, 1763–64.

After *Gagnon,* the question still remains whether probationers and parolees have the right to be represented by a retained attorney in probation- and parole-revocation hearings where an indigent would have no right to appointed counsel. Id. at 783 n. 6, 93 S.Ct. at 1760 n. 6. How would you resolve this question?

3.   Since *Morrissey,* the Supreme Court has concluded that a parolee has no right to an initial preliminary hearing before being transferred back to prison for a suspected parole violation when he or she has already been convicted of the crime upon which the parole revocation is based. The conviction itself provides the requisite probable cause to believe the parolee has violated the terms and conditions of parole. Moody v. Daggett, 429 U.S. 78, 86 n. 7, 97 S.Ct. 274, 278 n. 7 (1976).

The Court in *Moody* also clarified the meaning of its observation in *Morrissey* that the opportunity for a final revocation hearing must be afforded a parolee "within a reasonable time after the parolee is taken into custody." The parolee in *Moody* had pled guilty to two crimes—manslaughter and second-degree murder—committed while he was on parole for rape. For these two homicides, he was sentenced to ten years in prison. Following his convictions, the United States Board of Parole issued, but did not execute, a parole-violator warrant. The issuance of the warrant simply held the parolee's rape sentence and parole term in abeyance while he served his other sentences.

Hoping that he could serve any imprisonment resulting from the revocation of his parole at the same time that he was serving the prison sentences for the homicides, the parolee asked the parole board to immediately execute the parole-violator warrant and decide whether to revoke his parole. The parole board refused. The parolee then filed a habeas corpus action contending that any revocation of his parole was barred by the board's failure to afford him the prompt parole-revocation hearing guaranteed by *Morrissey*.

The Supreme Court disagreed, holding that a parolee has no right to a parole-revocation hearing unless and until he is taken into custody as a parole violator. The Court also opined that delaying the parole-revocation hearing made sense in a case such as this one, because the parolee's conduct while in prison might be revealing to a parole board later deciding whether revocation of parole was warranted.

4.   According to most courts, the federal and state constitutions only require that probation and parole violations be established by a preponderance of the evidence. State v. Sylvester, 944 A.2d 909, 912 (Vt. 2007). In your opinion, should statutes mandate application of a higher standard of proof in revocation proceedings? Would a higher standard of proof necessarily benefit parolees and probationers? Cf. Young v. United States, 863 A.2d 804, 810 (D.C. 2004) (opining that judges would be less inclined to sentence defendants to probation if revocation had to be premised on clear and convincing evidence).

Most courts agree that an acquittal on criminal charges generally will not bar the revocation of probation or parole for the crime of which a probationer or parolee was acquitted. See, e.g., People v. Colon, 866 N.E.2d 207, 222–23 (Ill. 2007). The courts reason that even if the government was unable to prove the probationer's or parolee's guilt beyond a reasonable doubt, the government may be able to meet the lesser burden of proof applicable in revocation proceedings. Nor does the revocation of probation or parole following an acquittal violate the Fifth Amendment's double-jeopardy prohibition. A revocation proceeding is not considered a new criminal prosecution for the offense of which the probationer or parolee was acquitted but rather an adjunct to the original criminal prosecution that had led to the individual's placement on probation or parole. See also Johnson v. United States, 529 U.S. 694, 700–01, 120 S.Ct. 1795, 1800–01 (2000) (noting that reimprisonment after the revocation of supervised release is punishment for the original offense for which the individual was serving a term of supervised release, not punishment for the violation of release conditions).

Some people might think that if the government decides to proceed first with a revocation hearing and is unable to meet its burden of proof at that hearing, collateral-estoppel principles would bar a subsequent criminal prosecution based on the same alleged underlying conduct. Most, though not all, of the courts that have addressed this issue, however, have concluded that the outcome of a revocation hearing should not dictate whether a criminal prosecution can go forward. State v. Brunet, 806 A.2d 1007, 1010 (Vt. 2002) (listing cases). Some of these courts have reasoned that applying collateral-estoppel principles to foreclose a criminal prosecution would frustrate the government's interest in responding quickly to probation and parole violations. Krochta v. Commonwealth, 711 N.E.2d 142, 148 (Mass. 1999). In order to avoid a finding against the government at a revocation hearing that would have the effect of barring a future criminal prosecution, the government often might have to delay revocation proceedings.

Critics of the majority view, however, charge that it allows the government to use a revocation proceeding as a "fishing expedition" where it can obtain a preview of the defendant's defense before the criminal trial. State v. McDowell, 699 A.2d 987, 991 (Berdon, J., dissenting). These critics contend that permitting the government to treat revocation hearings as a " 'Heads I win, tails I flip again' proposition" will undermine the public's confidence in the justice system. Id. at 992 (quoting Lucido v. Superior Court, 795 P.2d 1223, 1243 (Cal. 1990) (Broussard, J., dissenting)). Nor, they add, is an immediate revocation hearing needed to protect the public's safety; if a probationer or parolee charged with criminal conduct poses a threat to the public's safety, that threat can be abated by denying release on bail or imposing appropriate pretrial-release conditions. State v. Brunet, 806 A.2d at 1018 (Johnson, J., dissenting).

In your opinion, do public-policy considerations support or oppose the barring of a criminal trial after a revocation hearing that resulted in factual findings inconsistent with the defendant's guilt?

5.   A parole-revocation proceeding may raise several issues, including the following: (1) Did the parolee violate a condition of his or her parole? See, e.g., Arciniega v. Freeman, 404 U.S. 4, 92 S.Ct. 22 (1971) (per curiam) (construing a condition that the parolee not associate with other ex-convicts as not encompassing contacts with ex-convicts employed at the same restaurant). (2) Did the parole board have the statutory authority to impose the condition? (3) Is the condition violated constitutional? (4) Does the violation of the condition warrant the revocation of parole and the parolee's return to prison? Similar questions may arise during probation-revocation proceedings except that a judge, rather than an administrative board or official, generally will decide whether probation should be revoked because of the violation of a condition of probation. For a discussion of statutory and constitutional constraints on probation and parole conditions, see notes 1 through 5 on pages 231–34 and Chapter 7, Section B.

6.   Sometimes the failure of an individual to abide by the conditions of probation or parole will warrant the modification of those conditions rather than the incarceration or reincarceration of the individual. The question is: When, if ever, does due process accord a right to certain procedural safeguards before the restrictions to which a person is subject as a condition of probation or parole are augmented? How would you answer this question? In doing so, consider the import, if any, of the Supreme Court decisions holding that transfers of inmates to prisons with more onerous conditions of confinement typically do not deprive them of a liberty interest, thereby triggering the protections of due process. See Meachum v. Fano, 427 U.S. 215, 96 S.Ct. 2532 (1976), on page 604, and the other cases in Section A of Chapter 14 discussing the due-process implications of prisoner transfers.

If you believe that the modification of probation or parole conditions can or does spark the protections of due process, what procedural safeguards, in your opinion, must attend that modification process? Most courts have held that a probationer has no due-process right to a court hearing or to the assistance of counsel before the conditions of probation are modified. State v. Smith, 769 A.2d 698, 704 (Conn. 2001) (listing cases). If you concur with this view, does it necessarily mean that a probation officer's directive that a probationer be subject to electronic monitoring or participate in a sex-offender treatment program comports with due process?

7.   Many inmates in the nation's prisons and jails are there because their probation or parole has been revoked. Bureau of Justice Statistics, U.S. Dep't of Justice, Prisoners in 2007, at 3 (2008) (parole violators comprised a third of the individuals admitted to prisons in 2007); Bureau of Justice Statistics, U.S. Dep't of Justice, Probation and Parole Violators in State Prison, 1991, at 3 (1995) (45% of state prison population in 1991 comprised of probation and parole violators, compared to 17% in 1974). The majority of these revocations are for nonviolent crimes or for technical violations of probation or parole conditions. Id. at 5. Technical violations are typically noncriminal violations, such as failing to report, as required, to a probation or parole officer.

The American Bar Association's Model Adult Community Corrections Act, which can be found on pages 265–73, calls for a different approach to probation and parole violations. The Act establishes a rebuttable presumption that a community-based sanction is the appropriate penalty for a violation of a condition of probation or parole that is either noncriminal or constitutes a misdemeanor or a nonviolent felony. Revocation guidelines could be a mechanism for implementing this presumption or for structuring in other ways the exercise of discretion in the revocation process, much like sentencing guidelines are used to channel the exercise of discretion when offenders initially are sentenced. Do you agree with the Model Act's recommended approach to probation and parole violations? How would you structure revocation guidelines if you were charged with the responsibility of drafting a set of model guidelines?

8.   Title 18 U.S.C. § 3583(e)(2)–(4), (h) is an example of a statute providing judges with a range of options when responding to a defendant's violation of a supervised-release condition. The judge can extend the period of supervised release if the defendant was not sentenced previously to the maximum supervised-release term, or the judge can modify the conditions of the supervised release. Alternatively, the judge can revoke the supervised-release term and require the defendant to serve some or all of the remainder of the term in prison, with no credit for the time already served under postrelease supervision. Finally, as an alternative to incarceration, the judge can order the defendant's confinement at home during nonworking hours, with the confinement monitored electronically or telephonically if the judge so orders.

2.   THE FIFTH AMENDMENT PRIVILEGE AGAINST SELF–INCRIMINATION

The Fifth Amendment to the United States Constitution provides in part that "[n]o person ... shall be compelled in any criminal case to be a witness against himself." This amendment, which directly constrains the federal government, also applies to the states via the Due Process Clause of the Fourteenth Amendment. Malloy v. Hogan, 378 U.S. 1, 6, 84 S.Ct. 1489, 1492 (1964).

Assume that a defendant is convicted of a sex offense, sentenced to probation, and as a condition of probation, required to participate in a sex-offender treatment program. For successful treatment to occur, experts who run the program agree that an offender must admit having committed the sex offense of which he or she was convicted. The defendant, however, refuses to admit criminal culpability or discuss the circumstances surrounding the offense. Can the defendant's probation constitutionally be revoked for failure to cooperate in the treatment program? Before answering this question, consider the Supreme Court's analysis in the following case of the Fifth Amendment claim of a prisoner who faced being transferred from a medium-security unit of a prison to a maximum-security unit if he refused to meet two of the requirements for participation in a sex-offender treatment program in the medium-security unit: that he discuss and accept responsibility for the sex crimes of which he had been convicted and that he reveal his sexual history, including uncharged sex-related crimes.

McKUNE v. LILE

Supreme Court of the United States, 2002.
536 U.S. 24, 122 S.Ct. 2017, 153 L.Ed.2d 47.

(This case can be found on page 639 of the casebook.)

QUESTIONS AND POINTS FOR DISCUSSION

1. In Minnesota v. Murphy, 465 U.S. 420, 104 S.Ct. 1136 (1984), the Supreme Court considered the admissibility in a criminal trial of incriminating statements made by the defendant during a meeting with his probation officer. At the time of the meeting, the defendant was on probation for the crime of false imprisonment, and one of the conditions of his probation was that he "be truthful" with his probation officer "in all matters." When questioned by his probation officer during the meeting about his suspected involvement in a rape and murder of a woman many years earlier, the defendant admitted committing the crimes.

The Supreme Court first rebuffed the defendant's argument that his incriminating statements should have been suppressed in his trial for murder because the probation officer failed to give him *Miranda* warnings before questioning him. The Court observed that when the defendant met with his probation officer in her office, he was not "in custody" within the meaning of *Miranda,* and therefore no *Miranda* warnings were necessary.

The defendant also argued that his incriminating statements should have been suppressed because when he was questioned by the probation officer, an unconstitutional burden had been placed on the exercise of his Fifth Amendment privilege against self-incrimination. He maintained that because of the probation condition requiring him to respond truthfully to his probation officer's questions, he faced a Hobson's choice: either respond to those questions, thereby providing evidence to be used against him in a criminal prosecution, or refuse to answer the questions and have his probation revoked. The Supreme Court, however, refused to construe the probation condition as requiring the defendant to answer questions when those answers might be incriminating in a criminal prosecution of the defendant. As the Court's discussion, set forth below, of some of the Fifth Amendment implications of probation interviews reveals, the result in the case would have been different had the Court found that the probation condition required the defendant, upon threat of revocation, to provide responses that could be used against him in a criminal prosecution:

> A State may require a probationer to appear and discuss matters that affect his probationary status; such a requirement, without more, does not give rise to a self-executing privilege. The result may be different if the questions put to the probationer, however relevant to his probationary status, call for answers that would incriminate him in a pending or later criminal prosecution. There is thus a substantial basis in our cases for concluding that if the State, either expressly or by implication, asserts that invocation of the privilege would lead to revocation of probation, it would have created the classic penalty situation, the failure to assert the privilege would be excused, and the probationer's answers would be deemed compelled and inadmissible in a criminal prosecution.[7]

* * *

> If Murphy did harbor a belief that his probation might be revoked for exercising the Fifth Amendment privilege, that belief would not have been reasonable. Our decisions have made clear that the State could not constitutionally carry out a threat to revoke probation for the legitimate exercise of the Fifth Amendment privilege.

Id. at 435 & n. 7, 438, 104 S.Ct. at 1146 & n. 7, 1148.

---

7. The situation would be different if the questions put to a probationer were relevant to his probationary status and posed no realistic threat of incrimination in a separate criminal proceeding. If, for example, a residential restriction were imposed as a condition of probation, it would appear unlikely that a violation of that condition would be a criminal act. Hence, a claim of the Fifth Amendment privilege in response to questions relating to a residential condition could not validly rest on the ground that the answer might be used to incriminate if the probationer was tried for another crime. Neither, in our view, would the privilege be available on the ground that answering such questions might reveal a violation of the residential requirement and result in the termination of probation. Although a revocation proceeding must comport with the requirements of due process, it is not a criminal proceeding. Just as there is no right to a jury trial before probation may be revoked, neither is the privilege against compelled self-incrimination available to a probationer. It follows that whether or not the answer to a question about a residential requirement is compelled by the threat of revocation, there can be no valid claim of the privilege on the ground that the information sought can be used in revocation proceedings.

Our cases indicate, moreover, that a State may validly insist on answers to even incriminating questions and hence sensibly administer its probation system, as long as it recognizes that the required answers may not be used in a criminal proceeding and thus eliminates the threat of incrimination. Under such circumstances, a probationer's "right to immunity as a result of his compelled testimony would not be at stake," and nothing in the Federal Constitution would prevent a State from revoking probation for a refusal to answer that violated an express condition of probation or from using the probationer's silence as "one of a number of factors to be considered by the finder of fact" in deciding whether other conditions of probation have been violated.

2.   In Ohio Adult Parole Authority v. Woodard, 523 U.S. 272, 118 S.Ct. 1244 (1998), a prisoner who had been sentenced to death contended that an interview in which he could participate as part of the clemency-review process impinged on his Fifth Amendment privilege against self-incrimination. By not affording him immunity for statements he made during the interview, the prisoner asserted that he was placed between the proverbial rock and a hard place. If he agreed to be interviewed and then made incriminating statements, he might doom his chances of obtaining postconviction relief from his conviction or death sentence. But if he refused to be interviewed, his silence might be used against him, thereby negating any prospect of obtaining a commutation of his sentence.

The Supreme Court rejected the prisoner's claim. Noting that the decision to participate in a clemency interview is a voluntary one, the Court held that the compulsion that would give rise to a Fifth Amendment violation was absent. According to the Court, the choice to participate or not in a clemency interview was no more difficult or constitutionally problematic than the choice faced by criminal defendants when deciding whether to testify at trial. Do you agree?

3.   Reconsider, in light of the Supreme Court decisions of which you have just read, the question posed earlier in this chapter: Would the revocation of the probation of an individual required, as a condition of probation, to participate in a sex-offender treatment program violate the Fifth Amendment privilege against self-incrimination when the revocation was based on the individual's refusal to discuss sex-related crimes? Does your answer depend at all on whether the defendant pleaded guilty to the crime for which he was sentenced to probation or was convicted following a trial? Does it matter whether the time for appealing his conviction had lapsed or his appeal had been denied? Is it constitutionally relevant whether eligibility for participation in the treatment program required the probationer to discuss sex crimes with which he had not been charged? For differing views on when eligibility for probation can be conditioned on the making of incriminating admissions as part of sex-offender treatment, see People v. Guatney, 183 P.3d 620, 626 (Colo. Ct. App. 2007) (absent a grant of immunity, revocation of probation violated Fifth Amendment when appeal of conviction was pending and defendant could be prosecuted for perjury for conflicting statements he made at trial) and State v. Pritchett, 69 P.3d 1278, 1285–87 (Utah 2003) (requiring defendant to admit committing the sex offense of which he was convicted to be eligible for probation and placement in a residential treatment center for sex offenders did not violate the privilege against self-incrimination).

3. THE FOURTH AMENDMENT

Not only are the rights of probationers and parolees limited because of the restrictions placed on them as conditions of probation or parole, but they are also limited because the Constitution affords them less protection than that afforded individuals not subject to probation or parole supervision. The following Supreme Court case is one of several that illustrate that the Fourth Amendment applies differently to probationers and parolees.

GRIFFIN v. WISCONSIN

Supreme Court of the United States, 1987.
483 U.S. 868, 107 S.Ct. 3164, 97 L.Ed.2d 709.

JUSTICE SCALIA delivered the opinion of the Court.

* * *

On September 4, 1980, Griffin, who had previously been convicted of a felony, was convicted in Wisconsin state court of resisting arrest, disorderly conduct, and obstructing an officer. He was placed on probation.

Wisconsin law puts probationers in the legal custody of the State Department of Health and Social Services and renders them "subject ... to ... conditions set by the court and rules and regulations established by the department." One of the Department's regulations permits any probation officer to search a probationer's home without a warrant as long as his supervisor approves and as long as there are "reasonable grounds" to believe the presence of contraband—including any item that the probationer cannot possess under the probation conditions. * * * Another regulation makes it a violation of the terms of probation to refuse to consent to a home search. And still another forbids a probationer to possess a firearm without advance approval from a probation officer.

On April 5, 1983, while Griffin was still on probation, Michael Lew, the supervisor of Griffin's probation officer, received information from a detective on the Beloit Police Department that there were or might be guns in Griffin's apartment. Unable to secure the assistance of Griffin's own probation officer, Lew, accompanied by another probation officer and three plainclothes policemen, went to the apartment. When Griffin answered the door, Lew told him who they were and informed him that they were going to search his home. During the subsequent search—carried out entirely by the probation officers under the authority of Wisconsin's probation regulation—they found a handgun.

Griffin was charged with possession of a firearm by a convicted felon, which is itself a felony. He moved to suppress the evidence seized during the search. The trial court denied the motion * * *. A jury convicted Griffin of the firearms violation, and he was sentenced to two years' imprisonment. The conviction was affirmed by the Wisconsin Court of Appeals.

On further appeal, the Wisconsin Supreme Court also affirmed. * * *

* * *

A probationer's home, like anyone else's, is protected by the Fourth Amendment's requirement that searches be "reasonable." Although we usually require that a search be undertaken only pursuant to a warrant (and thus supported by probable cause, as the Constitution says warrants must be), we have permitted exceptions when "special needs, beyond the normal need for law enforcement, make the warrant and probable-cause requirement impracticable." * * *

A State's operation of a probation system * * * presents "special needs" beyond normal law enforcement that may justify departures from the usual warrant and probable-cause requirements. * * * Probation is simply one point (or, more accurately, one set of points) on a continuum of possible punishments ranging from solitary confinement in a maximum-security facility to a few hours of mandatory community service. A number of different options lie between those extremes, including confinement in a medium- or minimum-security facility, work-release programs, "halfway houses," and probation—which can itself be more or less confining depending upon the number and severity of restrictions imposed. * * *

These restrictions are meant to assure that the probation serves as a period of genuine rehabilitation and that the community is not harmed by the probationer's being at large. These same goals require and justify the exercise of supervision to assure that the restrictions are in fact observed. * * * Supervision, then, is a "special need" of the State permitting a degree of impingement upon privacy that would not be constitutional if applied to the public at large. That permissible degree is not unlimited, however, so we next turn to whether it has been exceeded here.

* * *

A warrant requirement would interfere to an appreciable degree with the probation system, setting up a magistrate rather than the probation officer as the judge of how close a supervision the probationer requires. Moreover, the delay inherent in obtaining a warrant would make it more difficult for probation officials to respond quickly to evidence of misconduct and would reduce the deterrent effect that the possibility of expeditious searches would otherwise create. By way of analogy, one might contemplate how parental custodial authority would be impaired by requiring judicial approval for search of a minor child's room. And on the other side of the equation—the effect of dispensing with a warrant upon the probationer: Although a probation officer is not an impartial magistrate, neither is he the police officer who normally conducts searches against the ordinary citizen. He is an employee of the State Department of Health and Social Services who, while assuredly charged with protecting the public interest, is also supposed to have in mind the welfare of the probationer * * *. * * *

Justice Blackmun's dissent would retain a judicial warrant requirement, though agreeing with our subsequent conclusion that reasonableness of the search does not require probable cause. This, however, is a combination that neither the text of the Constitution nor any of our prior decisions permits. While it is possible to say that Fourth Amendment reasonableness demands probable cause without a judicial warrant, the reverse runs up against the constitutional provision that "no Warrants shall issue, but upon probable cause." Amdt. 4. * * *

We think that the probation regime would also be unduly disrupted by a requirement of probable cause. * * * First, even more than the requirement of a warrant, a probable-cause requirement would reduce the deterrent effect of the supervisory arrangement. The probationer would be assured that so long as his illegal (and perhaps socially dangerous) activities were sufficiently concealed as to give rise to no more than reasonable suspicion, they would go undetected and uncorrected. The second difference is * * * we deal with a situation in which there is an ongoing supervisory relationship—and one that is not, or at least not entirely, adversarial—between the object of the search and the decision-maker.

In such circumstances it is both unrealistic and destructive of the whole object of the continuing probation relationship to insist upon the same degree of demonstrable reliability of particular items of supporting data, and upon the same degree of certainty of violation, as is required in other contexts. In some cases—especially those involving drugs or illegal weapons—the probation agency must be able to act based upon a lesser degree of certainty than the Fourth Amendment would otherwise require in order to intervene before a probationer does damage to himself or society. * * *

* * *

The search of Griffin's residence was "reasonable" within the meaning of the Fourth Amendment because it was conducted pursuant to a valid regulation governing probationers. * * *

JUSTICE BLACKMUN, with whom JUSTICE MARSHALL joins and, as to Parts I–B and I–C, JUSTICE BRENNAN joins and, as to Part I–C, JUSTICE STEVENS joins, dissenting.[b]

In ruling that the home of a probationer may be searched by a probation officer without a warrant, the Court today takes another step that diminishes the protection given by the Fourth Amendment to the "right of the people to be secure in their persons, houses, papers, and effects, against unreasonable searches and seizures." In my view, petitioner's probationary status provides no reason to abandon the warrant requirement. The probation system's special law enforcement needs may justify a search by a probation officer on the basis of "reasonable suspicion," but even that standard was not met in this case.

* * *

---

b. Justice Brennan did not join the portion of Justice Blackmun's dissenting opinion asserting that a search of a probationer's home can be grounded on "reasonable suspicion," a level of suspicion lower than probable cause. Justice Brennan joined those portions of the dissenting opinion maintaining that a warrant is needed for this kind of search and concluding that there was no reasonable suspicion to support the search in this case. Justice Stevens agreed with this latter conclusion.

QUESTIONS AND POINTS FOR DISCUSSION

1. In United States v. Knights, 534 U.S. 112, 122 S.Ct. 587 (2001), the Supreme Court even more narrowly construed the scope of probationers' Fourth Amendment rights, upholding a warrantless search of a probationer's apartment conducted by a detective from the sheriff's office who had a reasonable suspicion that the apartment contained evidence of several crimes. In balancing the intrusiveness of these kinds of searches against the need for them, the Court emphasized that their intrusiveness is diminished because the liberty of probationers already is restricted. The Court also said that because probationers have such a high recidivism rate, there is a significant need to permit law-enforcement officials to conduct warrantless searches of their residences. See also People v. Johns, 795 N.E.2d 433, 444 (Ill. App. Ct. 2003) (Myerscough, J., dissenting) ("Law enforcement is armed and better equipped to conduct these searches.")

2. Because the search at issue in *Knights* was grounded on reasonable suspicion, the Court left open the question whether a search conducted without reasonable suspicion would pass constitutional muster. How would you resolve this question? However you resolve this question, would a suspicionless search, in any event, be constitutional if the defendant had agreed, as a condition of being placed on probation, to have his residence searched without a warrant or any reasonable suspicion?

In *United States v. Knights*, the Supreme Court left open two questions about such a probation condition: first, whether by agreeing to the condition, a probationer has validly (meaning "voluntarily") consented to suspicionless home searches; and second, whether such a condition eliminates, rather than just diminishes, the probationer's legitimate expectation of privacy in his home. The latter question is important because if an inspection does not intrude in an area where a person has a legitimate expectation of privacy, no "search" has occurred within the meaning of the Fourth Amendment. See the Supreme Court's decision in Hudson v. Palmer, 468 U.S. 517, 526, 104 S.Ct. 3194, 3200 (1984), on page 680, holding that the Fourth Amendment provides no protection to prisoners whose cells are searched, because prisoners have no legitimate expectation of privacy in their cells.

In the case that follows, the Supreme Court explored some of the Fourth Amendment ramifications of a condition predicating parole release on a prisoner's agreement to be searched by parole or police officers without a warrant and without cause. As you read this case, consider its implications for probationers.

SAMSON v. CALIFORNIA

Supreme Court of the United States, 2006.
547 U.S. 843, 126 S.Ct. 2193, 165 L.Ed.2d 250.

JUSTICE THOMAS delivered the opinion of the Court.

California law provides that every prisoner eligible for release on state parole "shall agree in writing to be subject to search or seizure by a parole officer or other peace officer at any time of the day or night, with or without a search warrant and with or without cause." Cal.Penal Code Ann. § 3067(a). We granted certiorari to decide whether a suspicionless search, conducted under the authority of this statute, violates the Constitution. * * *

In September 2002, petitioner Donald Curtis Samson was on state parole in California, following a conviction for being a felon in possession of a firearm. On September 6, 2002, Officer Alex Rohleder of the San Bruno Police Department observed petitioner walking down a street with a woman and a child. Based on a prior contact with petitioner, Officer Rohleder was aware that petitioner was on parole * * *.

* * * [P]ursuant to Cal.Penal Code Ann. § 3067(a) and based solely on petitioner's status as a parolee, Officer Rohleder searched petitioner. During the search, Officer Rohleder found a cigarette box in petitioner's left breast pocket. Inside the box he found a plastic baggie containing methamphetamine.

The State charged petitioner with possession of methamphetamine * * *. The trial court denied petitioner's motion to suppress the methamphetamine evidence * * *. A jury convicted petitioner of the possession charge and the trial court sentenced him to seven years' imprisonment.

The California Court of Appeal affirmed. Relying on *People v. Reyes,* 968 P.2d 445 ([Cal.] 1998), the court held that suspicionless searches of parolees are lawful under California law; that " '[s]uch a search is reasonable within the meaning of the Fourth Amendment as long as it is not arbitrary, capricious or harassing' "; and that the search in this case was not arbitrary, capricious, or harassing.

* * *

"[U]nder our general Fourth Amendment approach" we "examin[e] the totality of the circumstances" to determine whether a search is reasonable within the meaning of the Fourth Amendment. Whether a search is reasonable "is determined by assessing, on the one hand, the degree to which it intrudes upon an individual's privacy and, on the other, the degree to which it is needed for the promotion of legitimate governmental interests."

* * *

As we noted in *Knights,* parolees are on the "continuum" of state-imposed punishments. On this continuum, parolees have fewer expectations of privacy than probationers, because parole is more akin to imprisonment than probation is to imprisonment. * * * "In most cases, the State is willing to extend parole only because it is able to condition it upon compliance with certain requirements."

* * * The extent and reach of these conditions clearly demonstrate that parolees like petitioner have severely diminished expectations of privacy by virtue of their status alone.

Additionally, * * * the parole search condition under California law—requiring inmates who opt for parole to submit to suspicionless searches by a parole officer or other peace officer "at any time"—was "clearly expressed" to petitioner. He signed an order submitting to the condition and thus was "unambiguously" aware of it. In *Knights*, we found that acceptance of a clear and unambiguous search condition "significantly diminished Knights' reasonable expectation of privacy." Examining the totality of the circumstances pertaining to petitioner's status as a parolee, "an established variation on imprisonment," including the plain terms of the parole search condition, we conclude that petitioner did not have an expectation of privacy that society would recognize as legitimate.[3]

The State's interests, by contrast, are substantial. This Court has repeatedly acknowledged that a State has an "overwhelming interest" in supervising parolees because "parolees ... are more likely to commit future criminal offenses." Similarly, this Court has repeatedly acknowledged that a State's interests in reducing recidivism and thereby promoting reintegration and positive citizenship among probationers and parolees warrant privacy intrusions that would not otherwise be tolerated under the Fourth Amendment.

The empirical evidence presented in this case clearly demonstrates the significance of these interests to the State of California. * * * California's parolee population has a 68–to–70 percent recidivism rate. See California Attorney General, Crime in California 37 (Apr.2001) (explaining that 68 percent of adult parolees are returned to prison, 55 percent for a parole violation, 13 percent for the commission of a new felony offense). * * *

* * *

* * * Imposing a reasonable suspicion requirement, as urged by petitioner, would give parolees greater opportunity to anticipate searches and conceal criminality. This Court concluded that the incentive-to-conceal concern justified an "intensive" system for supervising probationers in *Griffin*. That concern applies with even greater force to a system of supervising parolees.

Petitioner observes that the majority of States and the Federal Government have been able to further similar interests in reducing recidivism and promoting re-integration, despite having systems that permit parolee searches based upon some level of suspicion. * * * Petitioner's reliance on the practices of jurisdictions other than California, however, is misplaced. That some States and the Federal Government require a level of individualized suspicion is of little relevance to our determination whether California's supervisory system is drawn to meet its needs and is reasonable, taking into account a parolee's substantially diminished expectation of privacy.

---

3. Because we find that the search at issue here is reasonable under our general Fourth Amendment approach, we need not reach the issue whether "acceptance of the search condition constituted consent in the * * * sense of a complete waiver of his Fourth Amendment rights." * * * Nor do we address whether California's parole search condition is justified as a special need under *Griffin v. Wisconsin*, 483 U.S. 868 (1987), because our holding under general Fourth Amendment principles renders such an examination unnecessary.

* * * The concern that California's suspicionless search system gives officers unbridled discretion to conduct searches, thereby inflicting dignitary harms that arouse strong resentment in parolees and undermine their ability to reintegrate into productive society, is belied by California's prohibition on "arbitrary, capricious or harassing" searches.[5] The dissent's claim that parolees under California law are subject to capricious searches conducted at the unchecked "whim" of law enforcement officers ignores this prohibition. * * *

Thus, we conclude that the Fourth Amendment does not prohibit a police officer from conducting a suspicionless search of a parolee. * * *

* * *

JUSTICE STEVENS, with whom JUSTICE SOUTER and JUSTICE BREYER join, dissenting.

Our prior cases have consistently assumed that the Fourth Amendment provides some degree of protection for probationers and parolees. The protection is not as robust as that afforded to ordinary citizens; we have held that probationers' lowered expectation of privacy may justify their warrantless search upon reasonable suspicion of wrongdoing. * * * But neither *Knights* nor *Griffin* supports a regime of suspicionless searches, conducted pursuant to a blanket grant of discretion untethered by any procedural safeguards, by law enforcement personnel who have no special interest in the welfare of the parolee or probationer.

* * *

The suspicionless search is the very evil the Fourth Amendment was intended to stamp out. The pre-Revolutionary "writs of assistance," which permitted roving searches for contraband, were reviled precisely because they "placed 'the liberty of every man in the hands of every petty officer.'" While individualized suspicion "is not an 'irreducible' component of reasonableness" under the Fourth Amendment, the requirement has been dispensed with only when programmatic searches were required to meet a " 'special need' . . . divorced from the State's general interest in law enforcement."

* * *

Ignoring just how "closely guarded" is that "category of constitutionally permissible suspicionless searches," the Court for the first time upholds an entirely suspicionless search unsupported by any special need. And it goes further: In special needs cases we have at least insisted upon programmatic safeguards designed to ensure evenhandedness in application; if individualized suspicion is to be jettisoned, it must be replaced with measures to protect against the state actor's unfettered discretion. Here, by contrast, there are no policies in place—no "standards, guide-

---

5. Under California precedent, we note, an officer would not act reasonably in conducting a suspicionless search absent knowledge that the person stopped for the search is a parolee.

lines, or procedures"—to rein in officers and furnish a bulwark against the arbitrary exercise of discretion that is the height of unreasonableness.

* * *

Nor is it enough, in deciding whether someone's expectation of privacy is "legitimate," to rely on the existence of the offending condition or the individual's notice thereof. * * * [T]he loss of a subjective expectation of privacy would play "no meaningful role" in analyzing the legitimacy of expectations, for example, "if the Government were suddenly to announce on nationwide television that all homes henceforth would be subject to warrantless entry."[4]

* * *

Had the State imposed as a condition of parole a requirement that petitioner submit to random searches by his parole officer, who is "supposed to have in mind the welfare of the [parolee]" and guide the parolee's transition back into society, the condition might have been justified either under the special needs doctrine or because at least part of the requisite "reasonable suspicion" is supplied in this context by the individual-specific knowledge gained through the supervisory relationship. Likewise, this might have been a different case had a court or parole board imposed the condition at issue based on specific knowledge of the individual's criminal history and projected likelihood of reoffending, or if the State had had in place programmatic safeguards to ensure evenhandedness. Under either of those scenarios, the State would at least have gone some way toward averting the greatest mischief wrought by officials' unfettered discretion. * * *[6]

The Court seems to acknowledge that unreasonable searches "inflic[t] dignitary harms that arouse strong resentment in parolees and undermine their ability to reintegrate into productive society." It is satisfied, however, that the California courts' prohibition against " 'arbitrary, capricious or harassing' " searches suffices to avert those harms * * *. I am unpersuaded. The requirement of individualized suspicion, in all its iterations, is the shield the Framers selected to guard against the evils of arbitrary action, caprice, and harassment. To say that those evils may be averted without that shield is, I fear, to pay lipservice to the end while withdrawing the means.

* * *

---

4. Likewise, the State's argument that a California parolee "consents" to the suspicionless search condition is sophistry. Whether or not a prisoner can choose to remain in prison rather than be released on parole, he has no "choice" concerning the search condition; he may either remain in prison, where he will be subjected to suspicionless searches, or he may exit prison and still be subject to suspicionless searches. Accordingly, "to speak of consent in this context is to resort to a manifest fiction, for the [parolee] who purportedly waives his rights by accepting such a condition has little genuine option to refuse."

6. The Court devotes a good portion of its analysis to the recidivism rates among parolees in California. * * * Of course, one cannot deny that the interest itself is valid. That said, though, it has never been held sufficient to justify suspicionless searches. If high crime rates were grounds enough for disposing of Fourth Amendment protections, the Amendment long ago would have become a dead letter.

Questions and Points for Discussion

1. Do you agree with the majority's conclusion that the search at issue in *Samson* comported with the Fourth Amendment? If not, would the alternative ways proffered by Justice Stevens to curtail officials' discretion in conducting searches of parolees obviate the Fourth Amendment problem?

2. Even if the Fourth Amendment permits suspicionless searches of parolees, at least when parole release is conditioned on a prisoner's agreement to be subjected to such searches, states and the federal government can place additional constraints on parolee searches. As a matter of policy, what restrictions would you place on parolee searches and why?

3. After being convicted of several federal crimes stemming from his armed robbery of a bank, Thomas Kincade was sentenced to prison for over eight years, to be followed by three years of supervised release. During this release term, Kincade's probation officer asked him to provide a blood sample from which DNA information would be extracted and then stored in a database maintained by the FBI. The probation officer's request was pursuant to a federal statute mandating that individuals who are convicted of certain crimes (primarily violent or sex-related crimes) and are incarcerated or on probation, parole, or supervised release provide a tissue, fluid, or "other bodily sample" from which DNA "identification information" can be obtained. 42 U.S.C. § 14135a. After Kincade refused to provide the requested sample, he was found in violation of the terms of his supervised release and sentenced to four months' imprisonment plus two years of supervised release.

If you were Kincade's attorney, what arguments would you make in support of your position that the DNA-testing requirement violates the Fourth Amendment? If you were representing the government, what arguments would you make in defending the statute's constitutionality? Are there additional facts that you need or want to know to complete your constitutional analysis? See the closely divided (6–5) decision of the Ninth Circuit Court of Appeals in which it joined the view of the majority of the courts that the mandatory DNA testing of prisoners and persons on probation, parole, or supervised release does not abridge Fourth Amendment rights. United States v. Kincade, 379 F.3d 813, 830–31 (9th Cir. 2004) (listing cases).

In 2004, Congress broadened the scope of the federal DNA-testing statute, extending the testing requirement to prisoners, parolees, probationers, or individuals on supervised release who had been convicted of any federal felony. 42 U.S.C. § 14135a(d). How, if at all, would your preceding analysis of the constitutionality of the DNA-testing requirement be changed if the person from whom a DNA sample was being obtained were serving a probation sentence for a nonviolent crime, such as aiding and abetting wire fraud? See United States v. Amerson, 483 F.3d 73 (2d Cir. 2007) (upholding the constitutionality of applying the DNA-collection statute to individuals on probation for nonviolent crimes). Notably, in 2006, Congress expanded the DNA-testing statute's scope even further. The amended statute, for example, authorizes the collection of DNA samples from individuals arrested for, charged with, or convicted of the crimes delineated in the statute, whether or not these individuals are imprisoned or on some form of conditional release. 42 U.S.C. § 14135a(a)(1)(A).

4. As a general rule, evidence obtained in violation of the Fourth Amendment is inadmissible in a criminal trial. Mapp v. Ohio, 367 U.S. 643, 655–60, 81 S.Ct. 1684, 1691–94 (1961). But in a 5–4 decision, the Supreme Court held in Pennsylvania Bd. of Prob. & Parole v. Scott, 524 U.S. 357, 118 S.Ct. 2014 (1998) that the Fourth Amendment exclusionary rule does not apply in parole-revocation hearings. As a result, the revocation of parole can be predicated partly or wholly on evidence procured in violation of the Fourth Amendment.

In determining whether the Fourth Amendment exclusionary rule applies in parole-revocation hearings, the Court, as it typically does when determining the exclusionary rule's scope, weighed the costs and benefits of applying the exclusionary rule in a particular context—in this case, during parole-revocation proceedings. The Court noted that since the government has an "overwhelming interest" in ensuring that parolees abide by the conditions of their parole and are returned to prison if they do not, the costs of excluding reliable and relevant evidence in parole-revocation hearings are quite high. In addition, the Court observed that importing the exclusionary rule into the parole-revocation context would transform the informal and, what the Court considered, largely nonadversarial revocation process into a "trial-like" proceeding not focused on what is in the parolee's and society's best interests. Id. at 366–67, 118 S.Ct. at 2021.

The Court then concluded that the costs of applying the Fourth Amendment exclusionary rule in parole-revocation proceedings were not counterbalanced by the benefits of deterring violations of the Fourth Amendment. The Court opined that since parole officers are not parolees' adversaries, they are less prone than police officers to violate the Fourth Amendment to find evidence of a crime or other violation of parole. And, according to the Court, even if parole officers were inclined sometimes to flout the Fourth Amendment, the potential prospect of being sued for damages or disciplined administratively would dissuade them from doing so.

The Court also was not persuaded that exempting parole-revocation hearings from application of the Fourth Amendment exclusionary rule would provide police offers with an incentive to ignore whatever constraints the Fourth Amendment places on parolee searches. The Court was confident that the knowledge that illegally seized evidence generally cannot be introduced at trial would propel police officers to comply with the Fourth Amendment. Suppression of the evidence at parole-revocation hearings, which are outside police officers' " 'zone of primary interest,' " therefore, would have little, if any, additional deterrent effects. Id. at 368, 118 S.Ct. at 2022.

In his dissenting opinion, Justice Souter disagreed with the majority's assessment of the impact that applying the Fourth Amendment exclusionary rule in parole-revocation hearings would have in deterring violations of the Fourth Amendment:

> As to the benefit of an exclusionary rule in revocation proceedings, the majority does not see that in the investigation of criminal conduct by someone known to be on parole, Fourth Amendment standards will have

very little deterrent sanction unless evidence offered for parole revocation is subject to suppression for unconstitutional conduct. It is not merely that parole revocation is the government's consolation prize when, for whatever reason, it cannot obtain a further criminal conviction, though that will sometimes be true. What is at least equally telling is that parole revocation will frequently be pursued instead of prosecution as the course of choice * * *.

The reasons for this tendency to skip any new prosecution are obvious. If the conduct in question is a crime in its own right, the odds of revocation are very high. Since time on the street before revocation is not subtracted from the balance of the sentence to be served on revocation, the balance may well be long enough to render recommitment the practical equivalent of a new sentence for a separate crime. And all of this may be accomplished without shouldering the burden of proof beyond a reasonable doubt; hence the obvious popularity of revocation in place of new prosecution.

The upshot is that without a suppression remedy in revocation proceedings, there will often be no influence capable of deterring Fourth Amendment violations when parole revocation is a possible response to new crime. Suppression in the revocation proceeding cannot be looked upon, then, as furnishing merely incremental or marginal deterrence over and above the effect of exclusion in criminal prosecution. Instead, it will commonly provide the only deterrence to unconstitutional conduct when the incarceration of parolees is sought, and the reasons that support the suppression remedy in prosecution therefore support it in parole revocation.

Id. at 378–79, 118 S.Ct. at 2027 (Souter, J., dissenting). What are the practical effects, from your perspective, of applying or not applying the Fourth Amendment exclusionary rule during parole-revocation proceedings?

B.   PAROLE RELEASE

In the case which follows, the Supreme Court considered the implications of *Morrissey v. Brewer* for parole-release decisions. The Court addressed two questions: first, does due process require that certain procedures be followed when determining whether an inmate should be released on parole, and second, if so, what procedural safeguards are constitutionally mandated?

GREENHOLTZ v. INMATES OF NEBRASKA PENAL AND CORRECTIONAL COMPLEX

Supreme Court of the United States, 1979.
442 U.S. 1, 99 S.Ct. 2100, 60 L.Ed.2d 668.

MR. CHIEF JUSTICE BURGER delivered the opinion of the Court.

* * *

I

Inmates of the Nebraska Penal and Correctional Complex brought a class action under 42 U.S.C. § 1983 claiming that they had been unconstitutionally denied parole by the Board of Parole. The suit was filed against the individual members of the Board. One of the claims of the inmates was that the statutes and the Board's procedures denied them procedural due process.

* * *

The procedures used by the Board to determine whether to grant or deny discretionary parole arise partly from statutory provisions and partly from the Board's practices. Two types of hearings are conducted: initial parole review hearings and final parole hearings. At least once each year initial review hearings must be held for every inmate, regardless of parole eligibility. At the initial review hearing, the Board examines the inmate's entire preconfinement and postconfinement record. Following that examination it provides an informal hearing; no evidence as such is introduced, but the Board interviews the inmate and considers any letters or statements that he wishes to present in support of a claim for release.

If the Board determines from its examination of the entire record and the personal interview that he is not yet a good risk for release, it denies parole, informs the inmate why release was deferred and makes recommendations designed to help correct any deficiencies observed. It also schedules another initial review hearing to take place within one year.

If the Board determines from the file and the initial review hearing that the inmate is a likely candidate for release, a final hearing is scheduled. The Board then notifies the inmate of the month in which the final hearing will be held; the exact day and time is posted on a bulletin board that is accessible to all inmates on the day of the hearing. At the final parole hearing, the inmate may present evidence, call witnesses and be represented by private counsel of his choice. It is not a traditional adversary hearing since the inmate is not permitted to hear adverse testimony or to cross-examine witnesses who present such evidence. However, a complete tape recording of the hearing is preserved. If parole is denied, the Board furnishes a written statement of the reasons for the denial within 30 days.

II

The District Court held that the procedures used by the Parole Board did not satisfy due process. It concluded that the inmate had the same kind of constitutionally protected "conditional liberty" interest, recognized by this Court in *Morrissey v. Brewer,* 408 U.S. 471 (1972), held that some of the procedures used by the Parole Board fell short of constitutional guarantees, and prescribed several specific requirements.

On appeal, the Court of Appeals for the Eighth Circuit agreed with the District Court that the inmate had a *Morrissey*-type, conditional liberty interest at stake and also found a statutorily defined, protectible interest in Neb.Rev.Stat. § 83–1,114 (1976). The Court of Appeals, however, modified the procedures required by the District Court as follows:

(a) When eligible for parole each inmate must receive a full formal hearing;

(b) the inmate is to receive written notice of the precise time of the hearing reasonably in advance of the hearing, setting forth the factors which may be considered by the Board in reaching its decision;

(c) subject only to security considerations, the inmate may appear in person before the Board and present documentary evidence in his own behalf. Except in unusual circumstances, however, the inmate has no right to call witnesses in his own behalf;

(d) a record of the proceedings, capable of being reduced to writing, must be maintained; and

(e) within a reasonable time after the hearing, the Board must submit a full explanation, in writing, of the facts relied upon and reasons for the Board's action denying parole.

* * *

III

* * *

There is no constitutional or inherent right of a convicted person to be conditionally released before the expiration of a valid sentence. * * * [T]he conviction, with all its procedural safeguards, has extinguished that liberty right: "[G]iven a valid conviction, the criminal defendant has been constitutionally deprived of his liberty."

Decisions of the Executive Branch, however serious their impact, do not automatically invoke due process protection; there simply is no constitutional guarantee that all executive decisionmaking must comply with standards that assure error-free determinations. This is especially true with respect to the sensitive choices presented by the administrative decision to grant parole release.

* * *

IV

Respondents suggest two theories to support their view that they have a constitutionally protected interest in a parole determination which calls for the process mandated by the Court of Appeals. First, they claim that a reasonable entitlement is created whenever a state provides for the *possibility* of parole. Alternatively, they claim that the language in Nebraska's statute, Neb.Rev.Stat. § 83–1,114(1) (1976), creates a legitimate expectation of parole, invoking due process protections.

A

In support of their first theory, respondents rely heavily on *Morrissey v. Brewer,* 408 U.S. 471 (1972), where we held that a parole-revocation determination must meet certain due process standards. See also *Gagnon v. Scarpelli,* 411 U.S. 778 (1973). They argue that the ultimate interest at stake both in a parole-revocation decision and in a parole determination is conditional liberty and that since the underlying interest is the same the two situations should be accorded the same constitutional protection.

The fallacy in respondents' position is that parole *release* and parole *revocation* are quite different. There is a crucial distinction between being deprived of a liberty one has, as in parole, and being denied a conditional liberty that one desires. The parolees in *Morrissey* (and probationers in *Gagnon*) were at liberty and as such could "be gainfully employed and [were] free to be with family and friends and to form the other enduring attachments of normal life." The inmates here, on the other hand, are confined and thus subject to all of the necessary restraints that inhere in a prison.

A second important difference between discretionary parole *release* from confinement and *termination* of parole lies in the nature of the decision that must be made in each case. As we recognized in *Morrissey,* the parole-revocation determination actually requires two decisions: whether the parolee in fact acted in violation of one or more conditions of parole and whether the parolee should be recommitted either for his or society's benefit. "The first step in a revocation decision thus involves a wholly retrospective factual question."

The parole-release decision, however, is more subtle and depends on an amalgam of elements, some of which are factual but many of which are purely subjective appraisals by the Board members based upon their experience with the difficult and sensitive task of evaluating the advisability of parole release. Unlike the revocation decision, there is no set of facts which, if shown, mandate a decision favorable to the individual. * * *

* * *

That the state holds out the *possibility* of parole provides no more than a mere hope that the benefit will be obtained. To that extent the general interest asserted here is no more substantial than the inmate's hope that he will not be transferred to another prison, a hope which is not protected by due process. *Meachum v. Fano,* 427 U.S., at 225.

B

Respondents' second argument is that the Nebraska statutory language itself creates a protectible expectation of parole. They rely on the section which provides in part:

"Whenever the Board of Parole considers the release of a committed offender who is eligible for release on parole, it shall order his release unless it is of the opinion that his release should be deferred because:

"(a) There is a substantial risk that he will not conform to the conditions of parole;

"(b) His release would depreciate the seriousness of his crime or promote disrespect for law;

"(c) His release would have a substantially adverse effect on institutional discipline; or

"(d) His continued correctional treatment, medical care, or vocational or other training in the facility will substantially enhance his capacity to lead a law-abiding life when released at a later date."[5]

* * *

* * * We can accept respondents' view that the expectancy of release provided in this statute is entitled to some measure of constitutional protection. However, we emphasize that this statute has unique structure and language and thus whether any other state statute provides a protectible entitlement must be decided on a case-by-case basis. We therefore turn to an examination of the statutory procedures to determine whether they provide the process that is due in these circumstances.

* * *

It is important that we not overlook the ultimate purpose of parole which is a component of the long-range objective of rehabilitation. * * * The objective of rehabilitating convicted persons to be useful, law-abiding members of society can remain a goal no matter how disappointing the progress. But it will not contribute to these desirable objectives to invite or encourage a continuing state of adversary relations between society and the inmate.

Procedures designed to elicit specific facts, such as those required in *Morrissey, Gagnon,* and *Wolff,*[c] are not necessarily appropriate to a Nebraska parole determination. Merely because a statutory expectation exists cannot mean that in addition to the full panoply of due process required to convict and confine there must also be repeated, adversary hearings in order to continue the confinement. However, since the Nebraska Parole Board provides at least one and often two hearings every year to each eligible inmate, we need only consider whether the additional procedures mandated by the Court of Appeals are required * * *.

Two procedures mandated by the Court of Appeals are particularly challenged by the Board:[6] the requirement that a formal hearing be held

---

5. The statute also provides a list of 14 explicit factors and one catchall factor that the Board is obligated to consider in reaching a decision.

c. In Wolff v. McDonnell, 418 U.S. 539, 94 S.Ct. 2963 (1974), the Supreme Court outlined procedural safeguards that due process requires during prison disciplinary proceedings that lead to the revocation of an inmate's good-time credits.

6. The Board also objects to the Court of Appeals' order that it provide written notice reasonably in advance of the hearing together with a list of factors that might be considered. At present the Board informs the inmate in advance of the month during which the hearing will be held, thereby allowing time to secure letters or statements; on the day of the hearing it posts

for every inmate, and the requirement that every adverse parole decision include a statement of the evidence relied upon by the Board.

The requirement of a hearing as prescribed by the Court of Appeals in all cases would provide at best a negligible decrease in the risk of error. When the Board defers parole after the initial review hearing, it does so because examination of the inmate's file and the personal interview satisfies it that the inmate is not yet ready for conditional release. * * * At the Board's initial interview hearing, the inmate is permitted to appear before the Board and present letters and statements on his own behalf. He is thereby provided with an effective opportunity first, to insure that the records before the Board are in fact the records relating to his case; and second, to present any special considerations demonstrating why he is an appropriate candidate for parole. Since the decision is one that must be made largely on the basis of the inmate's files, this procedure adequately safeguards against serious risks of error and thus satisfies due process.[7]

Next, we find nothing in the due process concepts as they have thus far evolved that requires the Parole Board to specify the particular "evidence" in the inmate's file or at his interview on which it rests the discretionary determination that an inmate is not ready for conditional release. The Board communicates the reason for its denial as a guide to the inmate for his future behavior. To require the parole authority to provide a summary of the evidence would tend to convert the process into an adversary proceeding and to equate the Board's parole-release determination with a guilt determination. The Nebraska statute contemplates, and experience has shown, that the parole-release decision is, as we noted earlier, essentially an experienced prediction based on a host of variables. The Board's decision is much like a sentencing judge's choice—provided by many states—to grant or deny probation following a judgment of guilt, a choice never thought to require more than what Nebraska now provides for the parole-release determination. The Nebraska procedure affords an opportunity to be heard, and when parole is denied it informs the inmate in what respects he falls short of qualifying for parole; this affords the process that is due under these circumstances. The Constitution does not require more.[8]

* * *

notice of the exact time. There is no claim that either the timing of the notice or its substance seriously prejudices the inmate's ability to prepare adequately for the hearing. The present notice is constitutionally adequate.

7. The only other possible risk of error is that relevant adverse factual information in the inmate's file is wholly inaccurate. But the Board has discretion to make available to the inmate any information "[w]henever the board determines that it will facilitate the parole hearing." Neb.Rev.Stat. § 83–1,112(1) (1976). Apparently the inmates are satisfied with the way this provision is administered since there is no issue before us regarding access to their files.

8. The Court of Appeals in its order required the Board to permit all inmates to appear and present documentary support for parole. Since both of these requirements were being complied with prior to this litigation, the Board did not seek review of those parts of the court's order and the validity of those requirements is not before us. The Court of Appeals also held that due process did not provide a right to cross-examine adverse witnesses or a right to present favorable

APPENDIX TO OPINION OF THE COURT

The statutory factors that the Board is required to take into account in deciding whether or not to grant parole are the following:

(a) The offender's personality, including his maturity, stability, sense of responsibility and any apparent development in his personality which may promote or hinder his conformity to law;

(b) The adequacy of the offender's parole plan;

(c) The offender's ability and readiness to assume obligations and undertake responsibilities;

(d) The offender's intelligence and training;

(e) The offender's family status and whether he has relatives who display an interest in him or whether he has other close and constructive associations in the community;

(f) The offender's employment history, his occupational skills, and the stability of his past employment;

(g) The type of residence, neighborhood or community in which the offender plans to live;

(h) The offender's past use of narcotics, or past habitual and excessive use of alcohol;

(i) The offender's mental or physical makeup, including any disability or handicap which may affect his conformity to law;

(j) The offender's prior criminal record, including the nature and circumstances, recency and frequency of previous offenses;

(k) The offender's attitude toward law and authority;

(l) The offender's conduct in the facility, including particularly whether he has taken advantage of the opportunities for self-improvement, whether he has been punished for misconduct within six months prior to his hearing or reconsideration for parole release, whether any reductions of term have been forfeited, and whether such reductions have been restored at the time of hearing or reconsideration;

(m) The offender's behavior and attitude during any previous experience of probation or parole and the recency of such experience; and

(n) Any other factors the board determines to be relevant. Neb.Rev. Stat. § 83–1,114(2) (1976).

MR. JUSTICE POWELL, concurring in part and dissenting in part.

[For the reasons set forth in Justice Marshall's dissenting opinion, Justice Powell opined that when a state sets up a system of parole, it creates a liberty interest in parole release protected by the Due Process Clause, regardless of the language of the parole-release statute. In addition, Justice Powell concluded that the notice provided Nebraska inmates

---

witnesses. The practice of taping the hearings also was declared adequate. Those issues are not before us and we express no opinion on them.

of their impending parole-release hearings did not comport with due process.]

MR. JUSTICE MARSHALL, with whom MR. JUSTICE BRENNAN and MR. JUSTICE STEVENS join, dissenting in part.

My disagreement with the Court's opinion extends to both its analysis of respondents' liberty interest and its delineation of the procedures constitutionally required in parole release proceedings. * * *

* * *

I

It is self-evident that all individuals possess a liberty interest in being free from physical restraint. Upon conviction for a crime, of course, an individual may be deprived of this liberty to the extent authorized by penal statutes. But when a State enacts a parole system, and creates the possibility of release from incarceration upon satisfaction of certain conditions, it necessarily qualifies that initial deprivation. In my judgment, it is the existence of this system which allows prison inmates to retain their protected interest in securing freedoms available outside prison. Because parole release proceedings clearly implicate this retained liberty interest, the Fourteenth Amendment requires that due process be observed, irrespective of the specific provisions in the applicable parole statute.

* * *

* * * [T]he Court discerns two distinctions between "parole *release* and parole *revocation*" * * *.

First, the Court finds a difference of constitutional dimension between a deprivation of liberty one has and a denial of liberty one desires. While there is obviously some difference, it is not one relevant to the established constitutional inquiry. Whether an individual currently enjoys a particular freedom has no bearing on whether he possesses a protected interest in securing and maintaining that liberty. The Court acknowledged as much in *Wolff v. McDonnell*[, 418 U.S. 539 (1974)] when it held that the loss of good-time credits implicates a liberty interest even though the forfeiture only deprived the prisoner of freedom he expected to obtain sometime hence. * * *

The Court's distinction is equally unrelated to the nature or gravity of the interest affected in parole release proceedings. * * * "[W]hether the immediate issue be release or revocation, the stakes are the same: conditional freedom versus incarceration."

The Court's second justification for distinguishing between parole release and parole revocation is based on the "nature of the decision that must be made in each case." The majority apparently believes that the interest affected by parole release proceedings is somehow diminished if the administrative decision may turn on "subjective evaluations." Yet the Court nowhere explains why the *nature of the decisional process* has even the slightest bearing in assessing the *nature of the interest* that this process may terminate. * * *

But even assuming the subjective nature of the decision-making process were relevant to due process analysis in general, this consideration does not adequately distinguish the processes of granting and revoking parole. Contrary to the Court's assertion that the decision to revoke parole is predominantly a " 'retrospective factual question,' " *Morrissey* recognized that only the first step in the revocation decision can be so characterized. * * * Moreover, to the extent parole release proceedings hinge on predictive determinations, those assessments are necessarily predicated on findings of fact.[8] Accordingly, the presence of subjective considerations is a completely untenable basis for distinguishing the interests at stake here from the liberty interest recognized in *Morrissey.*

* * *

II

A

I also cannot subscribe to the Court's assessment of the procedures necessary to safeguard respondents' liberty interest. Although the majority purports to rely on *Morrissey v. Brewer* and the test enunciated in *Mathews v. Eldridge,* 424 U.S. 319 (1976), its application of these standards is fundamentally deficient in several respects.

To begin with, the Court focuses almost exclusively on the likelihood that a particular procedure will significantly reduce the risk of error in parole release proceedings. Yet *Mathews* advances *three* factors to be considered in determining the specific dictates of due process:

> "First, the private interest that will be affected by the official action; second, the risk of an erroneous deprivation of such interest through the procedures used, and the probable value, if any, of additional or substitute procedural safeguards; and finally, the Government's interest, including the function involved and the fiscal and administrative burdens that the additional or substitute procedural requirement would entail."

By ignoring the other two factors set forth in *Mathews,* the Court skews the inquiry in favor of the Board. For example, the Court does not identify any justification for the Parole Board's refusal to provide inmates with specific advance notice of the hearing date or with a list of factors that may be considered. Nor does the Board demonstrate that it would be unduly burdensome to provide a brief summary of the evidence justifying the denial of parole. To be sure, these measures may cause some inconvenience, but "the Constitution recognizes higher values than speed and efficiency." Similarly lacking in the Court's analysis is any recognition of

---

8. The Nebraska statutes, in particular, demonstrate the factual nature of the parole release inquiry. One provision enumerates factual considerations such as the inmate's intelligence, family status, and employment history, which bear upon the four predictive determinations underlying the ultimate parole decision.

the private interest affected by the Board's action. Certainly the interest in being released from incarceration is of sufficient magnitude to have some bearing on the process due.

The second fundamental flaw in the Court's analysis is that it incorrectly evaluates the only factor actually discussed. The contribution that additional safeguards will make to reaching an accurate decision necessarily depends on the risk of error inherent in existing procedures. Here, the Court finds supplemental procedures to be inappropriate because it assumes existing procedures adequately reduce the likelihood that an inmate's files will contain incorrect information which could lead to an erroneous decision. No support is cited for this assumption, and the record affords none. In fact, researchers and courts have discovered many substantial inaccuracies in inmate files, and evidence in the instant case revealed similar errors.[15] * * *

Finally, apart from avoiding the risk of actual error, this Court has stressed the importance of adopting procedures that preserve the appearance of fairness and the confidence of inmates in the decisionmaking process. The Chief Justice recognized in *Morrissey* that "fair treatment in parole revocations will enhance the chance of rehabilitation by avoiding reactions to arbitrariness," a view shared by legislators, courts, the American Bar Association, and other commentators. This consideration is equally significant whether liberty interests are extinguished in parole release or parole revocation proceedings. * * *

B

Applying the analysis of *Morrissey* and *Mathews*, I believe substantially more procedural protection is necessary in parole release proceedings than the Court requires. The types of safeguards that should be addressed here, however, are limited by the posture of this case.[17] Thus, only three specific issues need be considered.

---

15. In this case, for example, the form notifying one inmate that parole had been denied indicated that the Board believed he should enlist in a self-improvement program at the prison. But in fact, the inmate was already participating in all such programs available. Such errors in parole files are not unusual. *E.g., Kohlman v. Norton,* 380 F.Supp. 1073 (Conn.1974) (parole denied because file erroneously indicated that applicant had used gun in committing robbery); *State v. Pohlabel,* 160 A.2d 647 (1960) (files erroneously showed that prisoner was under a life sentence in another jurisdiction); Hearings on H.R. 13118 et al. before Subcommittee No. 3 of the House Judiciary Committee, 92d Cong., 2d Sess., pt. VII–A, p. 451 (1972) (testimony of Dr. Willard Gaylin: "I have seen black men listed as white and Harvard graduates listed with borderline IQ's").

17. In accordance with the majority opinion, I do not address whether the Court of Appeals was correct in holding that the Nebraska Parole Board may not abandon the procedures it already provides. These safeguards include permitting inmates to appear and present documentary support at hearings, and providing a statement of reasons when parole is denied or deferred. Because the inmates failed to seek review of the Court of Appeals' decision, I also express no view on whether it correctly held that the Board's practice of allowing inmates to present witnesses and retain counsel for final parole hearings was not constitutionally compelled. Finally, it would be inappropriate to consider the suggestion advanced here for the first time that inmates should be allowed access to their files in order to correct factual inaccuracies.

Nevertheless, the range of protections currently afforded does affect whether additional procedures are constitutionally compelled. The specific dictates of due process, of course, depend on what a particular situation demands. Nebraska's use of formal hearings when the possibility of

While the question is close, I agree with the majority that a formal hearing is not always required when an inmate first becomes eligible for discretionary parole. * * *

The Court of Appeals directed the Parole Board to conduct such a formal hearing as soon as an inmate becomes eligible for parole, even where the likelihood of a favorable decision is negligible * * *. From a practical standpoint, this relief offers no appreciable advantage to the inmates. If the Board would not have conducted a final hearing under current procedures, inmates gain little from a requirement that such a hearing be held, since the evidence almost certainly would be insufficient to justify granting release. * * * The inmates' interest in this modification of the Board's procedures is thus relatively slight.[18] Yet the burden imposed on the Parole Board by the additional formal hearings would be substantial. Accordingly, I believe the Board's current practice of combining both formal and informal hearings is constitutionally sufficient.

However, a different conclusion is warranted with respect to the hearing notices given inmates. The Board currently informs inmates only that it will conduct an initial review or final parole hearing during a particular month within the next year. The notice does not specify the day or hour of the hearing. Instead, inmates must check a designated bulletin board each morning to see if their hearing is scheduled for that day. In addition, the Board refuses to advise inmates of the criteria relevant in parole release proceedings, despite a state statute expressly listing 14 factors the Board must consider and 4 permissible reasons for denying parole.

Finding these procedures insufficient, the District Court and the Court of Appeals ordered that each inmate receive written advance notice of the time set for his hearing, along with a list of factors the Board may consider.[19] Although the Board has proffered no justification for refusing to institute these procedures, the Court sets aside the relief ordered below on the ground that "[t]here is no claim that either the timing of the notice or its substance seriously prejudices the inmate's ability to prepare adequately for the hearing." But respondents plainly have contended throughout this litigation that reasonable advance notice is necessary to enable them to organize their evidence, call the witnesses permitted by the Board, and notify private counsel allowed to participate in the hearing * * *. Given the significant private interests at stake, and the importance of reasonable notice in preserving the appearance of fairness, I see no

---

granting parole is substantial and informal hearings in other cases, for example, combined with provision of a statement of reasons for adverse decisions, obviously reduces the need for supplemental procedures.

18. Although a formal hearing at the point of initial eligibility would reduce the risk of error and enhance the appearance of fairness, providing a summary of essential evidence and reasons, together with allowing inmates to appear at informal hearings, decreases the justification for requiring the Board to conduct formal hearings in every case.

19. The courts below found that 72 hours' advance notice ordinarily would enable prisoners to prepare for their appearances. The Court of Appeals further determined that the statutory criteria were sufficiently specific that the Board need only include a list of those criteria with the hearing notices or post such a list in public areas throughout the institution.

reason to depart here from this Court's longstanding recognition that adequate notice is a fundamental requirement of due process * * *.

Finally, I would require the Board to provide a statement of the crucial evidence on which it relies in denying parole. At present, the Parole Board merely uses a form letter noting the general reasons for its decision. In ordering the Board to furnish as well a summary of the essential facts underlying the denial, the Court of Appeals made clear that " 'detailed findings of fact are not required.' " The majority here, however, believes even this relief to be unwarranted, because it might render parole proceedings more adversary and equate unfavorable decisions with a determination of guilt.

* * * [I]t is difficult to believe that subsequently disclosing the factual justification for a decision will render the proceeding more adversary, especially when the Board already provides a general statement of reasons. And to the extent unfavorable parole decisions resemble a determination of guilt, the Board has no legitimate interest in concealing from an inmate the conduct or failings of which he purportedly is guilty.

While requiring a summation of the essential evidence might entail some administrative inconvenience, in neither *Morrissey v. Brewer, Gagnon v. Scarpelli,* nor *Wolff v. McDonnell* did the Court find that this factor justified denying a written statement of the essential evidence and the reasons underlying a decision. It simply is not unduly

> "burdensome to give reasons when reasons exist. Whenever an application . . . is denied . . . there should be some reason for the decision. It can scarcely be argued that government would be crippled by a requirement that the reason be communicated to the person most directly affected by the government's action." *Board of Regents v. Roth,* 408 U.S. 564, 591 (1972) (Marshall, J., dissenting).

And an inability to provide any reasons suggests that the decision is, in fact, arbitrary.

Moreover, considerations identified in *Morrissey* and *Mathews* militate in favor of requiring a statement of the essential evidence. Such a requirement would direct the Board's focus to the relevant statutory criteria and promote more careful consideration of the evidence. It would also enable inmates to detect and correct inaccuracies that could have a decisive impact.[23] And the obligation to justify a decision publicly would provide the assurance, critical to the appearance of fairness, that the Board's decision is not capricious. Finally, imposition of this obligation would afford inmates instruction on the measures needed to improve their

---

23. The preprinted list of reasons for denying parole is unlikely to disclose these types of factual errors. Out of 375 inmates denied parole during a 6–month period, the only reason given 285 of them was: "Your continued correctional treatment, vocational, educational, or job assignment in the facility will substantially enhance your capacity to lead a law-abiding life when released at a later date." Although the denial forms also include a list of six "[r]ecommendations for correcting deficiencies," such as "[e]xhibit some responsibility and maturity," the evidence at trial showed that all six items were checked on 370 of the 375 forms, regardless of the facts of the particular case.

prison behavior and prospects for parole, a consequence surely consistent with rehabilitative goals. Balancing these considerations against the Board's minimal interest in avoiding this procedure, I am convinced that the Fourteenth Amendment requires the Parole Board to provide inmates a statement of the essential evidence as well as a meaningful explanation of the reasons for denying parole release.[25]

* * *

QUESTIONS AND POINTS FOR DISCUSSION

1. In Board of Pardons v. Allen, 482 U.S. 369, 107 S.Ct. 2415 (1987), the Supreme Court held that the following parole statute in Montana created a liberty interest in parole of which a prisoner could not be divested without due process of law:

> Prisoners eligible for parole. (1) Subject to the following restrictions, the board shall release on parole * * * any person confined in the Montana state prison or the women's correctional center * * * when in its opinion there is reasonable probability that the prisoner can be released without detriment to the prisoner or to the community[.]

* * *

> (2) A parole shall be ordered only for the best interests of society and not as an award of clemency or reduction of sentence or pardon. A prisoner shall be placed on parole only when the board believes that he is able and willing to fulfill the obligations of a law-abiding citizen.

The Court refused to distinguish between parole statutes like Nebraska's that mandated parole release "unless" certain conditions were met and other parole statutes like Montana's that required release "if" or "when" certain conditions were met. The Court conceded that the standards governing parole release in Montana, which focused on whether release on parole would be detrimental to the prisoner or the community and in "the best interests of society," were more general than the Nebraska standards that were before the Court in *Greenholtz*. The Court, however, rejected the arguments of the three dissenting Justices—O'Connor, Rehnquist, and Scalia—that Montana prisoners had no more than a hope of being released on parole, rather than a protected liberty interest in such release, when the parole statute failed to specifically and "meaningfully" limit the discretion of the Montana parole board. Id. at 384, 107 S.Ct. at 2424.

2. Under the approach followed by the Supreme Court in *Greenholtz* and *Board of Pardons v. Allen* in determining whether a state has created a liberty interest in parole, would the following state statute create such an interest?

> No inmate shall be placed on parole until and unless the board shall find that there is reasonable probability that, if he is so released, he will live

---

25. This statement of reasons and the summary of essential evidence should be provided to all inmates actually eligible for parole, whether the adverse decision is rendered following an initial review or a final parole hearing.

and conduct himself as a respectable and law-abiding person and that his release will be compatible with his own welfare and the welfare of society. Furthermore, no person shall be released on pardon or placed on parole unless and until the board is satisfied that he will be suitably employed in self-sustaining employment or that he will not become a public charge.

See Sultenfuss v. Snow, 35 F.3d 1494, 1501–02 (11th Cir.1994). Would a liberty interest be created by a statute like the one set forth below?

A parole shall be ordered only for the best interest of society, not as an award of clemency; it shall not be considered to be a reduction of sentence or pardon. A prisoner shall be placed on parole only when arrangements have been made for his proper employment, or for his maintenance and care, and only when the Indiana parole board believes that he is able and willing to fulfill the obligations of a law-abiding citizen.

See Averhart v. Tutsie, 618 F.2d 479, 482 (7th Cir.1980).

3. In Sandin v. Conner, 515 U.S. 472, 115 S.Ct. 2293 (1995), infra page 610, the Supreme Court confronted the question whether the transfer of a prisoner to a disciplinary-segregation unit because of his violation of prison rules deprived him of a state-created liberty interest. In the course of answering that question, the Court expressed reservations about conditioning the finding of a state-created liberty interest on the existence of certain "mandatory language" in a prison regulation. Id. at 481–84, 115 S.Ct. at 2299–2300. The Court noted that this approach had the perverse effect of discouraging prison officials from adopting regulations that specifically dictated how prison officials should carry out their duties. The Court proceeded to articulate a new test to be applied when determining whether prison officials have deprived a prisoner of a state-created liberty interest. Under that test, a court examines whether the state has created an interest in "freedom from restraint which . . . imposes atypical and significant hardship on the inmate in relation to the ordinary incidents of prison life." Id. at 484, 115 S.Ct. at 2300.

Since *Sandin* was decided, most lower courts have concluded that application of the test it enunciated for state-created liberty interests is confined to decisions bearing on conditions of confinement and does not extend to assessments whether inmates in a particular state have a liberty interest in parole derived from state law. See, e.g., McQuillion v. Duncan, 306 F.3d 895, 903 (9th Cir. 2002). These holdings rest in part on the Supreme Court's reaffirmation in *Sandin* of its holding in *Board of Pardons v. Allen*. But in Wilkinson v. Austin, 545 U.S. 209, 229, 125 S.Ct. 2384, 2397 (2005), the Supreme Court said, though in *dictum* and in a case dealing with altered conditions of confinement, that "*Sandin* abrogated *Greenholtz's* . . . methodology for establishing the liberty interest."

In your opinion, should the Supreme Court modify the test it has applied when determining whether a state-created liberty interest in parole exists? If so, how? For an insightful discussion of the "mandatory language" approach of *Greenholtz* and *Board of Pardons v. Allen* and the Supreme Court's critique of that approach in *Sandin*, see Ellis v. District of Columbia, 84 F.3d 1413, 1417–18 (D.C. Cir. 1996).

4.   *Greenholtz* and *Board of Pardons v. Allen* should be contrasted with Connecticut Board of Pardons v. Dumschat, 452 U.S. 458, 101 S.Ct. 2460 (1981). In *Dumschat,* a prisoner who was serving a life sentence for murder contended that he was deprived of a liberty interest without due process of law when the Connecticut Board of Pardons denied his application for a commutation of his sentence. He argued that certain procedures should have been followed by the board when reviewing his commutation application.

Under the applicable Connecticut statute, the board was vested with unconfined discretion to commute sentences or grant pardons. The prisoner nonetheless contended that he had a legitimate expectation that his life sentence would be commuted, because the board commuted the vast majority—eighty-five to ninety percent—of the sentences of inmates serving life sentences. The Supreme Court rejected this argument:

> In terms of the Due Process Clause, a Connecticut felon's expectation that a lawfully imposed sentence will be commuted or that he will be pardoned is no more substantial than an inmate's expectation, for example, that he will not be transferred to another prison; it is simply a unilateral hope. A constitutional entitlement cannot "be created—as if by estoppel—merely because a wholly and *expressly* discretionary state privilege has been granted generously in the past." No matter how frequently a particular form of clemency has been granted, the statistical probabilities standing alone generate no constitutional protections; a contrary conclusion would trivialize the Constitution. The ground for a constitutional claim, if any, must be found in statutes or other rules defining the obligations of the authority charged with exercising clemency.

Id. at 465, 101 S.Ct. at 2464. See also Jago v. Van Curen, 454 U.S. 14, 102 S.Ct. 31 (1981) (rescission of parole-release decision that occurred before inmate's actual release and that was prompted by the discovery that the inmate had provided false information to the parole board did not implicate a liberty interest; inmate's understanding that he would be released on parole did not give rise to a liberty interest).

5.   In Ohio Adult Parole Authority v. Woodard, 523 U.S. 272, 118 S.Ct. 1244 (1998), the Supreme Court considered whether its holding in *Dumschat* should be extended to a capital case. The prisoner in *Woodard* contended that he was not afforded due process of law during clemency proceedings. In particular, he complained that he was told only ten days before of the impending clemency hearing, that he was given only three days notice of the option of being interviewed before the hearing, that his attorney was not permitted to be present during the interview, that he was not permitted to testify or to present documentary evidence at the clemency hearing, and that the decision whether to let his attorney participate in the hearing fell within the parole board's discretion.

A majority of the Court concluded that in a capital case, where life is at stake, clemency proceedings implicate due process. But in a splintered decision, a majority of the Justices concluded that the due-process rights of the prisoner in this case had not been violated.

Justice O'Connor, in an opinion joined by Justices Souter, Ginsburg, and Breyer, observed that the procedural safeguards incorporated into the state's clemency process, including the notice provisions and the opportunity afforded the prisoner to be interviewed before the clemency hearing, met the requirements of due process. While agreeing that clemency proceedings in capital cases trigger the protections of due process, Justice Stevens voted to remand the case back to the lower courts for an assessment of what procedural safeguards are required by due process in this context.

Four of the Justices—Justices Rehnquist, Scalia, Kennedy, and Thomas—took a more narrow view, asserting that clemency proceedings simply do not implicate due process. According to these Justices, it is during the trial and sentencing in a capital case, not the clemency process, that a person is deprived of his or her interest in life. If the prisoner sentenced to death is granted clemency, he receives "a benefit." Id. at 285, 118 S.Ct. at 1252. If not, he is "no worse off than he was before" under the sentence that was imposed after affording him the procedural safeguards required by due process. Id.

6. One of the questions left unresolved in *Greenholtz* was whether inmates have a constitutional right to have access to information in their parole files reviewed by parole boards. These files may include a presentence report; reports of disciplinary infractions; medical and psychiatric records; the prisoner's criminal record; reports about the inmate's adjustment while in prison; letters from the sentencing judge, police officers, victims, family members, and friends; and other materials.

The lower courts have divided on the question whether inmates have a right of access to their parole files when they are being considered for possible release on parole. Some courts have held that inmates simply have no such right. See, e.g., Worden v. Montana Bd. of Pardons and Parole, 962 P.2d 1157, 1166 (Mont.1998). Others have analyzed inmates' access demands on a case-by-case basis. See, e.g., Williams v. Ward, 556 F.2d 1143, 1160–61 (2d Cir.1977) (inmate had no right of access when he knew in advance of his parole hearing that the board might rely on allegedly false information, but took no steps to refute that information); Coralluzzo v. New York State Parole Bd., 566 F.2d 375, 380 (2d Cir.1977) (where parole board's statement of reasons for deferring parole consideration revealed that board had relied on information ordered stricken from the inmate's file by a state court, prisoner had a right of access to the file to confirm whether the information was still in his file). Still other courts have crafted more general rules providing for access to files or denying such access in defined circumstances. See, e.g., Ingrassia v. Purkett, 985 F.2d 987, 989 (8th Cir.1993) (prisoners have no right of access to parole files when they are denied parole because their release would deprecate the seriousness of their crimes); Walker v. Prisoner Review Bd., 694 F.2d 499, 503–04 (7th Cir.1982) (inmates have right of access to documents considered by the parole board); Williams v. Missouri Bd. of Probation and Parole, 661 F.2d 697, 700 (8th Cir.1981) (inmates up for parole have a general right to be apprised of information in their files that may adversely affect their parole prospects).

When, if ever, do you believe that inmates being considered for parole release have a constitutional right of access to their parole files?

7. Because of the many procedural safeguards already afforded prisoners being considered for parole in Nebraska, the Supreme Court in *Greenholtz* did

not have to decide whether those procedures were constitutionally mandated. In your opinion, which of the following procedures, if any, does due process require in a state where the denial of parole implicates a liberty interest? A right to appear before the parole board? A right to present documentary evidence? A right to call witnesses to testify on the inmate's behalf? A right to cross-examine adverse witnesses? A right to be represented by an attorney or to receive some other form of assistance? A right to receive a statement of the reason or reasons for a parole denial? A right to a "neutral and detached" decisionmaker?

8. Assuming that inmates have the right to a written statement outlining the reason or reasons why parole was denied, would a statement that release would deprecate the seriousness of the offense of which the inmate had been found guilty and engender disrespect for the law suffice? What would prevent a parole board from routinely reciting such reasons? How much more specific could the parole board be in relating its reasons for the parole denial?

9. As was mentioned at the beginning of this chapter, parole has been supplanted in some jurisdictions by what is called "supervised release." One of the key distinctions between parole and supervised release is that the supervised-release term is imposed by the court as part of the defendant's sentence. Sometimes statutes require that a period of supervised release be included as part of the sentence for a particular type of crime, and sometimes the decision whether to include a supervised-release term in a defendant's sentence is left to the court's discretion. See, e.g., 18 U.S.C. § 3583(a). Statutes also typically define the maximum length of supervised-release terms, providing for longer periods of supervision for offenders convicted of more serious crimes. See, e.g., id. § 3583(b) (no more than five years for Class A and B felonies, no more than three years for Class C and D felonies, and no more than one year for other crimes).

Another significant difference between parole and supervised release is that judges, rather than parole boards, often determine the conditions of defendants' supervised-release terms. These sentencing decisions must conform with the requirements of statutes outlining the permissible and mandatory conditions of supervised release. See, e.g., id. § 3583(c), (d).

10. A number of states and the federal government have developed special release mechanisms to enable terminally ill prisoners meeting defined criteria to be released early from prison. See, e.g., Cal. Penal Code § 1170(e)(2)(A)–(B) (authorizing the resentencing and release from prison of a prisoner with a terminal illness that a doctor employed by the department of corrections has determined will cause death within six months, provided the release will not jeopardize public safety and the prisoner was not sentenced to death or life in prison without possibility of parole). Should "compassionate release" statutes extend to prisoners other than those who are terminally ill? See, e.g., 18 U.S.C. § 3582(c)(1)(A)(ii) (upon motion of the director of the Bureau of Prisons, court can modify sentence of certain prisoners who are at least seventy years old, have served at least thirty years in prison on their current mandatory life sentences, and pose no danger to others). Should prisoners convicted of certain crimes be ineligible for compassionate release?

For proposed model legislation detailing the procedures and timelines for two different kinds of compassionate-release mechanisms—one implemented by courts and the other implemented administratively, whether by a parole board or the department of corrections, see ABA Working Group on Compassionate Release, Compassionate Release of Terminally Ill Prisoners, in 2 Prisoners and the Law 14B–3, 14B–24 to –28 (Ira P. Robbins ed., 2008).

CHAPTER 9

COLLATERAL SANCTIONS AND CONSEQUENCES

■ ■ ■

A. THE REINTEGRATION OF RELEASED PRISONERS INTO SOCIETY: PRACTICAL OBSTACLES

Each year, over 700,000 people are released from prison in this country. Bureau of Justice Statistics, U.S. Dep't of Justice, Prisoners in 2007, at 3 (2008). Eventually, almost all prisoners return to the community. See Bureau of Justice Statistics, U.S. Dep't of Justice, Felony Sentences in State Courts, 2004, at 3 (2007) (less than 1% of convicted felons sentenced to state prison in 2004 received life sentences).

Generally bereft of resources and money, many prisoners upon release are given, at most, a new change of clothing and a small amount of spending money and then sent on their way. Jeremy Travis et al., Urban Institute, From Prison to Home: The Dimensions and Consequences of Prisoner Reentry 19 (2001). Their prospects of finding a job with which to support themselves and any family members are dim. See Joan Petersilia, When Prisoners Return to Communities: Political, Economic, and Social Consequences, 65 Fed. Probation 3, 5 (June 2001) (sixty percent of former prisoners are not employed in the regular labor market one year after their release from prison). Many prisoners function at the two lowest literacy levels, with a large number of them unable to perform such mundane tasks as locating an intersection on a street map or determining the date of an appointment from an appointment slip. Elizabeth Greenberg et al., Nat'l Ctr. For Educ. Statistics, Literacy Behind Prison Bars: Results From the 2003 National Assessment of Adult Literacy Prison Survey 2–8, 13 (2007). In addition, the majority of prisoners do not receive vocational training while they are incarcerated or work in prison industry jobs. Bureau of Justice Statistics, U.S. Dep't of Justice, Education and Correctional Populations 4–5 (2003); Gen. Accounting Office, Prisoner Releases: Trends and Information on Reintegration Programs 4, 17 (2001). Few have been groomed on such basics as how to fill out a job-application form or dress for an interview, or even on the need to be punctual for an interview or job. And for those who are unable to procure a job, there is no unemployment compensation and often no welfare assistance upon which to fall back temporarily.

The prisoners who are fortunate enough to secure a job upon their release from prison generally find that the jobs are low-paying and often accompanied by poor working conditions. It is little wonder then that the impulse to return to a life of crime, where the financial remuneration may be high, frequently proves irresistible to a released prisoner. Studies have found that individuals who are unemployed following their release from prison are more likely to commit new crimes. Comm'n on Effective Criminal Sanctions, Am. Bar Ass'n, Second Chances in the Criminal Justice System: Alternatives to Incarceration and Reentry Strategies 27 (2007) (citing research findings that released prisoners who are unemployed are three times more likely to be reimprisoned than those who secure steady employment); Joan Petersilia, When Prisoners Come Home 112 (2003). Ex-offender unemployment may therefore explain, at least in part, the very high recidivism rates which presently prevail in this country. One study of released prisoners conducted by the Bureau of Justice Statistics revealed that 68% of them were rearrested for a felony or serious misdemeanor within three years of their release. Bureau of Justice Statistics, U.S. Dep't of Justice, Recidivism of Prisoners Released in 1994, at 1, 3 (2002). Recidivism studies have found, not surprisingly, that recidivism rates are highest during the first year after a prisoner's release from prison. Id. at 3.

Upon their release from prison, individuals face other challenges and problems that compound the difficulty of readjusting successfully to life outside prison. Substance-abuse problems are prevalent amongst prisoners, but most of them receive no treatment for those problems while they are in prison. Bureau of Justice Statistics, U.S. Dep't of Justice, Drug Use and Dependence, State and Federal Prisoners, 2004, at 9 (2006) (only 15% of surveyed state prisoners who were drug abusers or drug-dependent had received drug treatment since their admission to prison). In addition, incarceration exacts a psychological toll on inmates that can impede their adaptation to life outside prison. The tight controls exerted over prisoners make many of them highly dependent on others to make choices for them, leaving them poorly equipped to initiate the steps needed to reenter society as productive and law-abiding citizens. Other corrosive side effects of what is known as the "prisonization process" can include loss of trust in others, social withdrawal, feelings of degradation and low self-worth, a greater willingness and tendency to exploit others, and posttraumatic stress disorder. Craig Haney, The Psychological Impact of Incarceration: Implications for Postprison Adjustment, in Prisoners Once Removed: The Impact of Incarceration and Reentry on Children, Families, and Communities 40–46 (Jeremy Travis & Michelle Waul eds., 2003).

Finally, released prisoners typically return to fractured neighborhoods and communities plagued by unemployment, poverty, and high crime rates. These areas generally lack the jobs, resources, and family and other support systems that can foster prisoners' reentry into the society from which they have, in effect, been exiled. Amy L. Solomon et al., Urban Institute, From Prison to Work: The Employment Dimensions of Prisoner Reentry 1, 13 (2004).

B. THE REINTEGRATION OF RELEASED PRISONERS INTO SOCIETY: LEGAL OBSTACLES

1. EMPLOYMENT RESTRICTIONS

In addition to the practical obstacles that impede released prisoners' successful reintegration into the community, there are legal obstacles that stand in their way. Restrictions on the employment of convicted felons abound, with a number of federal and state statutes requiring or permitting the barring of certain ex-felons from specified jobs. In some states, for example, individuals with a felony conviction can be denied licenses to work as barbers or beauticians. See, e.g., 225 Ill. Comp. Stat. 410/4–7(1)(a) (barbers, cosmetologists, and manicurists). This kind of licensing restriction is particularly ironic, since many prison vocational-education programs provide inmates with training to work in these professions. Some statutes also exclude individuals convicted of particular types of official misconduct from many government jobs. See, e.g., Colo. Const. art. XII, § 4; Nev.Rev.Stat. 197.230. Others bar certain ex-felons from serving as union officers. See, e.g., 29 U.S.C. § 504(a) (2); N.D.Cent.Code § 34–01–16. See also De Veau v. Braisted, 363 U.S. 144, 157–60 80 S.Ct. 1146, 1153–55 (1960) (upholding the constitutionality of a state law that had the effect of disqualifying ex-felons from serving as officers of any waterfront labor union unless they had been pardoned or received a certificate of good conduct from the parole board). And convicted felons are barred from serving in the country's armed forces, although exceptions can be made in "meritorious cases." 10 U.S.C. § 504(a).

2. RESTRICTIONS ON GOVERNMENT BENEFITS

As was discussed in Chapter 5, judges may in some instances include a ban on the receipt of certain government benefits as part of a defendant's sentence. For example, individuals convicted of felony drug offenses can, and sometimes must, be barred by the sentence from receiving certain federal benefits, such as housing loans and student financial aid. 21 U.S.C. § 862. While this sentencing provision currently exempts some federal benefits from its scope, including retirement, welfare, Social Security, health, disability, public-housing, and veterans' benefits, convicted drug offenders can lose some of these exempted benefits under other federal statutes. For example, persons convicted of a felony drug crime are ineligible for food stamps and Temporary Assistance for Needy Families benefits, id. § 862a(a), although states can opt out of this exclusion or limit the length of the ineligibility period. Id. § 862a(d)(1)(A), (B). In addition, public-housing officials have broad discretion to evict or deny housing to persons whom they conclude are involved in criminal drug-related activity, and a drug-related conviction can be treated as evidence of such illegal activity. 42 U.S.C. § 1437d (l)(6).

Students convicted of possessing or selling a controlled substance and whose criminal conduct occurred when they were receiving federal financial aid for college are also ineligible for that aid, including student loans, for periods of time contingent on the nature and number of their drug convictions. 20 U.S.C. § 1091(r)(1) (ineligibility period for a first conviction for possession of a controlled substance is one year, two years for a second conviction, and an indefinite period for additional convictions; ineligibility period for a first conviction for selling a controlled substance is two years and an indefinite period for additional convictions). Students can regain their eligibility for financial aid by successfully completing a drug rehabilitation program. Id. § 1091(r)(2)(A).

Do you support the withholding of government benefits from certain criminal offenders, whether as part of their official sentence or as a collateral consequence of their conviction? Should the denial of benefits be automatic or discretionary upon conviction? If discretionary, to whom should be remitted the question whether a particular offender will be denied a government benefit, and what factors should be considered in determining whether to withhold that benefit?

3. RESTRICTIONS ON POLITICAL RIGHTS

Restrictions on political rights are another example of the legal impediments that make it difficult for ex-offenders to put their criminal pasts behind them. One of the most common forms of this kind of restriction curtails voting rights, the subject of the Supreme Court case which follows.

RICHARDSON v. RAMIREZ

Supreme Court of the United States, 1974.
418 U.S. 24, 94 S.Ct. 2655, 41 L.Ed.2d 551.

MR. JUSTICE REHNQUIST delivered the opinion of the Court.

The three individual respondents in this case were convicted of felonies and have completed the service of their respective sentences and paroles. They filed a petition for a writ of mandate in the Supreme Court of California to compel California county election officials to register them as voters. * * *

Article XX, § 11, of the California Constitution has provided since its adoption in 1879 that "[l]aws shall be made" to exclude from voting persons convicted of bribery, perjury, forgery, malfeasance in office, "or other high crimes." At the time respondents were refused registration, former Art. II, § 1, of the California Constitution provided in part that

"* * * no person convicted of any infamous crime * * * shall ever exercise the privileges of an elector in this State." Sections 310 and 321 of the California Elections Code provide that an affidavit of registration shall show whether the affiant has been convicted of "a felony which disqualifies [him] from voting." Sections 383, 389, and 390 direct the county clerk to cancel the registration of all voters who have been convicted of "any infamous crime * * *." Sections 14240 and 14246 permit a voter's qualifications to be challenged on the ground that he has been convicted of "a felony" * * *. California provides by statute for restoration of the right to vote to persons convicted of crime either by court order after the completion of probation, or, if a prison term was served, by executive pardon after completion of rehabilitation proceedings. California also provides a procedure by which a person refused registration may obtain judicial review of his disqualification.[8]

Each of the individual respondents was convicted of one or more felonies, and served some time in jail or prison followed by a successfully terminated parole. * * * All three respondents were refused registration because of their felony convictions.[9]

* * *

* * * The petition for a writ of mandate challenged the constitutionality of respondents' exclusion from the voting rolls on two grounds. First, it was contended that California's denial of the franchise to the class of ex-felons could no longer withstand scrutiny under the Equal Protection Clause of the Fourteenth Amendment. Relying on the Court's recent voting-rights cases, respondents argued that a compelling state interest must be found to justify exclusion of a class from the franchise, and that California could assert no such interest with respect to ex-felons. Second, respondents contended that application of the challenged California constitutional and statutory provisions by election officials of the State's 58 counties was so lacking in uniformity as to deny them due process and "geographical ... equal protection." They appended a report by respondent California Secretary of State, and the questionnaires returned by county election officials on which it was based. The report concluded that there was wide variation in the county election officials' interpretation of

---

8. * * * Respondents contended that pardon was not an effective device for obtaining the franchise, noting that during 1968–1971, 34,262 persons were released from state prisons but only 282 pardons were granted.

9. Respondent Ramirez was convicted in Texas of the felony of "robbery by assault" in 1952. He served three months in jail and successfully terminated his parole in 1962. In February 1972 the San Luis Obispo County Clerk refused to allow Ramirez to register to vote on the ground that he had been convicted of a felony and spent time in incarceration. Respondent Lee was convicted of the felony of heroin possession in California in 1955, served two years in prison, and successfully terminated his parole in 1959. In March 1972 the Monterey County Clerk refused to allow Lee to register to vote on the sole ground that he had been convicted of a felony and had not been pardoned by the Governor. Respondent Gill was convicted in 1952 and 1967 of second-degree burglary in California, and in 1957 of forgery. He served some time in prison on each conviction, followed by a successful parole. In April 1972 the Stanislaus County Registrar of Voters refused to allow Gill to register to vote on the sole ground of his prior felony convictions.

the challenged voting exclusions.[12] The Supreme Court of California upheld the first contention and therefore did not reach the second one.

* * *

Unlike most claims under the Equal Protection Clause, for the decision of which we have only the language of the Clause itself as it is embodied in the Fourteenth Amendment, respondents' claim implicates not merely the language of the Equal Protection Clause of § 1 of the Fourteenth Amendment, but also the provisions of the less familiar § 2 of the Amendment:

> "Representatives shall be apportioned among the several States according to their respective numbers, counting the whole number of persons in each State, excluding Indians not taxed. But when the right to vote at any election for the choice of electors for President and Vice President of the United States, Representatives in Congress, the Executive and Judicial officers of a State, or the members of the Legislature thereof, is denied to any of the male inhabitants of such State, being twenty-one years of age, and citizens of the United States, or in any way abridged, *except for participation in rebellion, or other crime,* the basis of representation therein shall be reduced in the proportion which the number of such male citizens shall bear to the whole number of male citizens twenty-one years of age in such State." (Emphasis supplied.)

Petitioner contends that the italicized language of § 2 expressly exempts from the sanction of that section disenfranchisement grounded on prior conviction of a felony. She goes on to argue that those who framed and adopted the Fourteenth Amendment could not have intended to prohibit outright in § 1 of that Amendment that which was expressly exempted from the lesser sanction of reduced representation imposed by § 2 of the Amendment. This argument seems to us a persuasive one * * *.

* * * The legislative history bearing on the meaning of the relevant language of § 2 is scant indeed * * *. Nonetheless, what legislative history there is indicates that this language was intended by Congress to mean what it says.

* * *

* * * [R]espondents argue that our recent decisions invalidating other state-imposed restrictions on the franchise as violative of the Equal Protection Clause * * * support the conclusions of the Supreme Court of California that a State must show a "compelling state interest" to justify

---

12. * * * The report concluded:

"2. Although the policy within most counties may be consistent, the fact that some counties have adopted different policies has created a situation in which there is a lack of uniformity across the state. It appears from the survey that a person convicted of almost any given felony would find that he is eligible to vote in some California counties and ineligible to vote in others.* * *"

exclusion of ex-felons from the franchise and that California has not done so here.

As we have seen, however, the exclusion of felons from the vote has an affirmative sanction in § 2 of the Fourteenth Amendment, a sanction which was not present in the case of the other restrictions on the franchise which were invalidated in the cases on which respondents rely. * * *

Pressed upon us by the respondents, and by *amici curiae,* are contentions that these notions are outmoded, and that the more modern view is that it is essential to the process of rehabilitating the ex-felon that he be returned to his role in society as a fully participating citizen when he has completed the serving of his term. We would by no means discount these arguments if addressed to the legislative forum which may properly weigh and balance them against those advanced in support of California's present constitutional provisions. But it is not for us to choose one set of values over the other. If respondents are correct, and the view which they advocate is indeed the more enlightened and sensible one, presumably the people of the State of California will ultimately come around to that view. And if they do not do so, their failure is some evidence, at least, of the fact that there are two sides to the argument.

We therefore hold that the Supreme Court of California erred in concluding that California may no longer, consistent with the Equal Protection Clause of the Fourteenth Amendment, exclude from the franchise convicted felons who have completed their sentences and paroles. The California court did not reach respondents' alternative contention that there was such a total lack of uniformity in county election officials' enforcement of the challenged state laws as to work a separate denial of equal protection, and we believe that it should have an opportunity to consider the claim * * *. * * *

* * *

MR. JUSTICE MARSHALL, with whom MR. JUSTICE BRENNAN joins, dissenting.

* * *

* * * The Court construes § 2 of the Fourteenth Amendment as an express authorization for the States to disenfranchise former felons. Section 2 does except disenfranchisement for "participation in rebellion, or other crime" from the operation of its penalty provision. As the Court notes, however, there is little independent legislative history as to the crucial words "or other crime"; the proposed § 2 went to a joint committee containing only the phrase "participation in rebellion" and emerged with "or other crime" inexplicably tacked on. * * *

* * *

It is clear that § 2 was not intended and should not be construed to be a limitation on the other sections of the Fourteenth Amendment.

Section 2 provides a special remedy—reduced representation—to cure a particular form of electoral abuse—the disenfranchisement of Negroes. There is no indication that the framers of the provisions intended that special penalty to be the exclusive remedy for all forms of electoral discrimination. * * *

* * *

* * * [D]isenfranchisement for participation in crime was not uncommon in the States at the time of the adoption of the Amendment. Hence, not surprisingly, that form of disenfranchisement was excepted from the application of the special penalty provision of § 2. But because Congress chose to exempt one form of electoral discrimination from the reduction-of-representation remedy provided by § 2 does not necessarily imply congressional approval of this disenfranchisement.[24] * * * There is no basis for concluding that Congress intended by § 2 to freeze the meaning of other clauses of the Fourteenth Amendment to the conception of voting rights prevalent at the time of the adoption of the Amendment. In fact, one form of disenfranchisement—one-year durational residence requirements—specifically authorized by the Reconstruction Act, one of the contemporaneous enactments upon which the Court relies to show the intendment of the framers of the Fourteenth Amendment, has already been declared unconstitutional by this Court in *Dunn v. Blumstein*, 405 U.S. 330 (1972).

* * *

In my view, the disenfranchisement of ex-felons must be measured against the requirements of the Equal Protection Clause of § 1 of the Fourteenth Amendment. That analysis properly begins with the observation that because the right to vote "is of the essence of a democratic society, and any restrictions on that right strike at the heart of representative government," voting is a "fundamental" right. * * * "[I]f a challenged statute grants the right to vote to some citizens and denies the franchise to others, 'the Court must determine whether the exclusions are *necessary* to promote a *compelling* state interest.'"

* * * The State has the heavy burden of showing, first, that the challenged disenfranchisement is necessary to a legitimate and substantial state interest; second, that the classification is drawn with precision—that it does not exclude too many people who should not and need not be excluded; and, third, that there are no other reasonable ways to achieve the State's goal with a lesser burden on the constitutionally protected interest.

---

24. To say that § 2 of the Fourteenth Amendment is a direct limitation on the protection afforded voting rights by § 1 leads to absurd results. If one accepts the premise that § 2 authorizes disenfranchisement for any crime, the challenged California provision could * * * require disenfranchisement for seduction under promise of marriage, or conspiracy to operate a motor vehicle without a muffler. Disenfranchisement extends to convictions for vagrancy in Alabama or breaking a water pipe in North Dakota, to note but two examples. Even a jaywalking or traffic conviction could conceivably lead to disenfranchisement, since § 2 does not differentiate between felonies and misdemeanors.

I think it clear that the State has not met its burden of justifying the blanket disenfranchisement of former felons presented by this case. There is certainly no basis for asserting that ex-felons have any less interest in the democratic process than any other citizen. Like everyone else, their daily lives are deeply affected and changed by the decisions of government. As the Secretary of State of California observed in his memorandum to the Court in support of respondents in this case:

> "It is doubtful ... whether the state can demonstrate either a compelling or rational policy interest in denying former felons the right to vote. The individuals involved in the present case are persons who have fully paid their debt to society. They are as much affected by the actions of government as any other citizens, and have as much of a right to participate in governmental decision-making. Furthermore, the denial of the right to vote to such persons is a hindrance to the efforts of society to rehabilitate former felons and convert them into law-abiding and productive citizens."

It is argued that disenfranchisement is necessary to prevent vote frauds. Although the State has a legitimate and, in fact, compelling interest in preventing election fraud, the challenged provision is not sustainable on that ground. First, the disenfranchisement provisions are patently both overinclusive and underinclusive. The provision is not limited to those who have demonstrated a marked propensity for abusing the ballot by violating election laws. Rather, it encompasses all former felons and there has been no showing that ex-felons generally are any more likely to abuse the ballot than the remainder of the population. In contrast, many of those convicted of violating election laws are treated as misdemeanants and are not barred from voting at all. It seems clear that the classification here is not tailored to achieve its articulated goal, since it crudely excludes large numbers of otherwise qualified voters.

Moreover, there are means available for the State to prevent voting fraud which are far less burdensome on the constitutionally protected right to vote. * * * [T]he State "has at its disposal a variety of criminal laws that are more than adequate to detect and deter whatever fraud may be feared." * * *

Another asserted purpose is to keep former felons from voting because their likely voting pattern might be subversive of the interests of an orderly society. * * *

Although, in the last century, this Court may have justified the exclusion of voters from the electoral process for fear that they would vote to change laws considered important by a temporal majority, I have little doubt that we would not countenance such a purpose today. The process of democracy is one of change. Our laws are not frozen into immutable form, they are constantly in the process of revision in response to the needs of a changing society. The public interest, as conceived by a majority of the voting public, is constantly undergoing re-examination. * * * Voters who opposed the repeal of prohibition could have disenfranchised those who advocated repeal "to prevent persons from being enabled by their votes to defeat the criminal laws of the country." Today, presumably those who support the legalization of marihuana could be barred from the ballot box for much the same reason. The ballot is the democratic system's coin of the realm. To condition its exercise on support of the established order is to debase that currency beyond recognition. * * *

* * *

* * * I think it clear that measured against the standards of this Court's modern equal protection jurisprudence, the blanket disenfranchisement of ex-felons cannot stand.

* * *

QUESTIONS AND POINTS FOR DISCUSSION

1. The Supreme Court distinguished *Richardson v. Ramirez* when holding a voting restriction unconstitutional in Hunter v. Underwood, 471 U.S. 222, 105 S.Ct. 1916 (1985). The restriction at issue in that case, set forth in the Alabama Constitution, precluded persons convicted of "any crime * * * involving moral turpitude" from voting. The Alabama Constitutional Convention of 1901 adopted this provision in order to disenfranchise African Americans whom, it was felt, were convicted of these types of crimes with greater frequency than white people. Because of the discriminatory intent which prompted the enactment of the disenfranchisement provision and because it continued to have a disproportionately adverse effect on African Americans, the Supreme Court, in a unanimous opinion written by Justice Rehnquist, struck down the provision on equal-protection grounds. The Court, however, left open the question whether the provision would have passed constitutional muster if it had been enacted without a discriminatory intent. But see McCleskey v. Kemp, 481 U.S. 279, 107 S.Ct. 1756 (1987) discussed on page 294 (right of defendant, a black man sentenced to death, to equal protection of the law was not violated by death-penalty statute that has a disproportionate impact on African Americans, because there was no evidence that the statute was enacted or applied to the defendant with discriminatory intent).

2. The decision of the Supreme Court of Canada in Sauvé v. Canada, 3 S.C.R. 519 (2002) stands in stark contrast with the United States Supreme Court's decision in *Richardson v. Ramirez*. At issue in *Sauvé* was the constitutionality of a statute that barred prisoners serving prison sentences of two years or longer from voting while they were incarcerated. The constitutional provision invoked by the Canadian Supreme Court in striking down this statute is worded quite differently than the Equal Protection Clause construed by the Supreme Court in *Richardson* in tandem with section 2 of the Fourteenth Amendment. Section 3 of the Canadian Charter of Rights and Freedoms specifically accords "[e]very citizen of Canada" the right to vote, subject to the caveat in section 1 that "reasonable limits" can be placed on a right when shown by the government to be "demonstrably justified in a free and democratic society."

The Supreme Court of Canada concluded that the government had failed to meet its burden of proving that the voting restriction was "demonstrably justified" in a democracy like Canada's. The Court rebuffed the government's argument that the disenfranchisement of certain prisoners served an educational purpose, teaching both inmates and the general public about the value of respecting the law. Describing disenfranchisement as, in fact, "bad pedagogy," the Court remonstrated that the denial of voting rights would have the opposite of its intended effect, promoting disrespect for the law and a disregard of civic responsibilities:

> Denying citizen law-breakers the right to vote sends the message that those who commit serious breaches are no longer valued as members of the community, but instead are temporary outcasts from our system of rights and democracy. More profoundly, it sends the unacceptable message that democratic values are less important than punitive measures ostensibly designed to promote order.

Id. at 548.

The government also asserted that allowing the disenfranchised prisoners to vote would "demean" the political process. But the Court found the notion that some people are less worthy to vote—whether because of their gender, their race, their socioeconomic status, or their conduct—to be an obsolete vestige of the past, one not in keeping with the respect for the dignity of each human being that is a core value of Canadian democracy.

The government furthermore argued that stripping prisoners serving prison sentences of two years or longer of their voting rights was a legitimate way of punishing them for their crimes. Writing for the majority of the Court, Chief Justice McLachlin dissected and ultimately rejected this asserted justification for disenfranchising prisoners:

> The argument, stripped of rhetoric, proposes that it is open to Parliament to add a new tool to its arsenal of punitive implements—denial of constitutional rights. I find this notion problematic. I do not doubt that Parliament may limit constitutional rights in the name of punishment, provided that it can justify the limitation. But it is another thing to say that a particular class of people for a particular period of time will completely lose a particular constitutional right. * * * Could Parliament justifiably pass a law removing the right of all penitentiary prisoners to be protected from cruel and unusual punishment? I think not. What of freedom of expression or religion? Why, one asks, is the right to vote different? * * *

Id. at 550, 552–53.

Other countries' higher courts have ruled that voting bans imposed on prisoners are unconstitutional. See, e.g., the decision of the South African Constitutional Court in Minister of Home Affairs v. Nat'l Inst. for Crime Prevention and the Re-integration of Offenders (NICRO) and Others, 2004 (5) BCLR 445 (CC). Courts have also found such bans in violation of certain international human-rights agreements. In Hirst v. United Kingdom, 38 E.H.R.R. 40 (Eur. Ct. H. R. 2004), for example, the European Court of Human Rights held that a statute in Great Britain prohibiting virtually all prisoners from voting contravened the European Convention on Human Rights. In some countries, such as Israel, polling places are located in prisons and detention centers to facilitate voting by prisoners and detainees. Pamela S. Karlan, Convictions and Doubts: Retribution, Representation, and the Debate Over Felon Disenfranchisement, 56 Stan.L.Rev. 1147, 1148 n.8 (2004).

3. Felon-disenfranchisement laws vary from state to state in this country. In 2008, forty-eight states barred prisoners convicted of a felony from voting, with only Maine and Vermont according inmates the right to vote. Thirty-five states excluded parolees from the franchise, while thirty disenfranchised felony probationers. Eleven states prohibited some or all felons who had completed serving their sentences from voting. The Sentencing Project, Felony Disenfranchisement Laws in the United States 1, 3 (2008). Approximately 5.3 million people—one out of every forty-one adults—were ineligible to vote in 2008 because of a felony conviction. This disenfranchised populace included 2.1 million people who had completed serving their sentences. Id. at 1. See also Jeff Manza & Christopher Uggen, Locked Out: Felon Disenfranchisement and American Democracy 77 (2006) (reporting that only a minority, roughly a quarter, of those disenfranchised because of a felony conviction are confined in prison or jail).

Felon-disenfranchisement laws have had a particularly significant impact on African–American males. In 2008, 1.4 million African–American men (13% of adult black males) were ineligible to vote because of a felony conviction. Sentencing Project, supra, at 1.

4. Some researchers have concluded that the disenfranchisement of convicted felons has affected the outcomes of elections, including the 2000 presidential election. The Democratic candidate in that election, Al Gore, won the popular vote, beating the Republican candidate, George W. Bush, by over a half a million votes. But Bush won the Electoral College after carrying the state of Florida by a very close margin—537 votes. At the time, Florida had more people disenfranchised because of felony convictions than any other state in the nation, with over 600,000 of the estimated 827,000 individuals in that state barred from voting having fully served their sentences. Manza & Uggen, supra note 3, at 192. After calculating the estimated turnout rate (27.2%) and the party preferences (68.9% Democratic) of the disenfranchised felons and ex-felons (persons whose sentences have been served), two prominent sociologists concluded that Gore would have defeated Bush by 80,000 votes in Florida and won the presidential election if these individuals had been eligible to vote. Id. Even if the estimated turnout rate was cut in half and only ex-felons had been permitted to vote, Gore reportedly would have carried the state of Florida by 30,000 votes. Id.

5. Like felon-disenfranchisement laws, other governmental policies pertaining to prisoners have political repercussions. These policies, which include those that affect how many and which people will be imprisoned, where they will be incarcerated, and the community they will be deemed residents of during the time they are incarcerated, have two particularly noteworthy effects. First, the Census Bureau counts prisoners as residents of the community in which they are incarcerated, not the community from which they came and typically will return following their release from prison. Since electoral

districts are based on population size and since most prisons are located far from the inner-city areas from where most prisoners come and will return, the end result is a tipping of political power towards more rural areas, where the nonprisoner population is predominantly white, and away from urban areas heavily populated by minorities.

Second, the amount of federal and state aid that a jurisdiction receives typically hinges on the size of its population as well as the median income of its residents. Since prisoners are counted as residents of the place they are imprisoned and since they make no or little money, urban areas lose vast sums of money when people from those areas are incarcerated elsewhere. See Pamela S. Karlan, Convictions and Doubts: Retribution, Representation, and the Debate Over Felon Disenfranchisement, 56 Stan.L.Rev. 1147, 1159–60 (2004) (reporting that the incarceration of approximately 26,000 people from Chicago in downstate prisons at the time of the 2000 census will result in a loss to the city of $88 million in federal and state aid over the ensuing decade).

The aggregate effects of the Census Bureau's residency rules, government funding formulas, the location of prisons, and the disenfranchisement of prisoners have been analogized by some commentators to the "Three-fifths Clause" that was part of the Constitution when it was first enacted. Id. at 1160. Under that provision, slaves, who had no right to vote, were counted as three-fifths of a person, thereby enhancing the political power of the slave states. U.S. Const. art. I, § 2, cl. 3. Do you find this analogy apposite? Where, in your opinion, should prisoners' domicile be for census purposes, which, as mentioned earlier, affects electoral districting and funding eligibility? If prisoners were accorded the right to vote, where should their domicile be for voting purposes? In the community where they resided before their incarceration? In the jurisdiction in which they are imprisoned? See Debra Parkes, Ballot Boxes Behind Bars: Toward the Repeal of Prisoner Disenfranchisement Laws, 13 Temp. Pol. & Civ. Rts. L. Rev. 71, 104–05 (2003) (positing the option of establishing a "default rule" under which prisoners' domicile, for voting purposes, is the place where they lived before their incarceration unless they change their domicile to the prison). What are the benefits and drawbacks of each domicile option?

6. Section 2 of the Voting Rights Act (VRA) of 1965, which Congress amended in 1982, provides as follows:

> No voting qualification or prerequisite to voting or standard, practice, or procedure shall be imposed or applied by any State or political subdivision in a manner which results in a denial or abridgement of the right of any citizen of the United States to vote on account of race or color * * *.

42 U.S.C. § 1973(a). The 1982 amendments to the VRA were designed to clarify that intent to discriminate in adopting a voting rule is not a prerequisite to a finding of a VRA violation. Farrakhan v. Washington, 338 F.3d 1009, 1014 (9th Cir. 2003).

The courts are divided about the applicability of the VRA to felon-disenfranchisement laws. Compare Hayden v. Pataki, 449 F.3d 305, 322–23 (2d Cir. 2006) (although felon-disenfranchisement laws fall within the literal scope of the VRA, Congress did not intend to extend the VRA to such laws) with Farrakhan v. Washington, 338 F.3d at 1015 (the VRA applies to such statutes). Those courts holding that felon-disenfranchisement laws may, in some circumstances, violate the VRA have concluded that Congress has the power, and intended through the VRA to exercise its power, to bar disenfranchisement laws that have racially disparate effects that can be linked to racial discrimination, including racial discrimination in the criminal-justice system. Such discrimination might occur, for example, when the race of a defendant influences charging and sentencing decisions. See id. at 1013–14 (noting that the district court found the plaintiffs' evidence of discrimination in the state's criminal-justice system and the disproportionate disenfranchisement of minorities ensuing from that discrimination to be "compelling").

7.   Under what circumstances, if any, do you believe that the conviction of a person of a crime should lead to his or her disenfranchisement? For a comparative analysis of the disenfranchisement of felons in Germany, see Nora V. Demleitner, Continuing Payment on One's Debt to Society: The German Model of Felon Disenfranchisement as an Alternative, 84 Minn. L. Rev. 753, 760–61 (2000) (deprivation of voting rights for a period of time ranging from two to five years following release from prison can be ordered, in the judge's discretion, as part of the sentence for election-related crimes, such as voting fraud, and crimes, like treason, that imperil the "foundation of the state").

8.   In addition to possibly losing the right to vote, released prisoners and other ex-felons may find that they are barred from serving on juries. See, e.g., Haw.Rev.Stat. § 612–4(b)(2) (unless pardoned, a person convicted of a state or federal felony cannot serve on a jury).

4.   RESTRICTIONS ON DRIVERS' LICENSES AND THE POSSESSION OF FIREARMS

A criminal conviction sometimes can trigger the suspension or revocation of a person's driver's license. States increasingly are restricting the driving privileges of individuals convicted of drug offenses, although some of these states authorize the issuance of restricted licenses that enable individuals with drug-related convictions to drive to work, school, or places where they will receive drug treatment. See Legal Action Center, After Prison: Roadblocks to Reentry 17 (2004) (reporting that twenty-seven states automatically suspend or revoke drivers' licenses for some or all drug-related convictions). When, in your opinion, should driving privileges be curtailed because of a criminal conviction?

Most states place some restrictions on the possession of firearms by convicted felons. Some states prohibit all convicted felons from possessing any type of firearm. See, e.g., Fla. Stat. Ann. § 790.23(1)(c). Other states limit firearms restrictions to those convicted of specified crimes, such as drug offenses or violent felonies. See, e.g., Ohio Rev. Code Ann. § 2923.13(A)(2)–(3).

Federal statutes also place restrictions on the possession of firearms by convicted felons. The interplay between state and federal firearms' restrictions can raise complex questions, as the Supreme Court's decision in Caron v. United States, 524 U.S. 308, 118 S.Ct. 2007 (1998) illustrates.

At issue in that case was a federal statute that provides for an enhanced sentence when a person who has three prior convictions for violent felonies or "serious" drug offenses possesses a firearm. 18 U.S.C. § 924(e). A prior conviction generally does not count, however, if the offender has had his or her civil rights restored for that offense. Only if the restoration of rights was limited, precluding the offender from possessing or otherwise dealing with firearms, would the prior conviction count towards imposition of an enhanced sentence under the federal statute. Id. § 921(a)(20).

The problem that the Court confronted in Caron stemmed from the fact that a state law had restored the right of the defendant, who had previously been convicted of several violent felonies, to possess most, but not all, firearms. Under that law, the defendant could not possess handguns outside his home or business. When rifles and shotguns were later seized from his house, the question was: Was he subject to an enhanced sentence because, under state law, he could not possess handguns in certain places, or was he not subject to an enhanced sentence because a state law had restored his right to possess the kinds of firearms—rifles and shotguns—that were found in his home?

The Supreme Court concluded that the defendant was subject to the enhanced sentence under federal law. Although most of his "gun rights" had been restored, state law still prohibited him from possessing at least some firearms. Consequently, his sentence was enhanced under the federal statute for possessing rifles and shotguns that, under state law, he was permitted to possess.

For a summary of federal statutes and regulations that impose civil disabilities on convicted offenders, see ABA Comm'n on Effective Criminal Sanctions & The Public Defender Serv. for the Dist. Of Columbia, Internal Exile: Collateral Consequences of Conviction in Federal Laws and Regulations (2009). For an overview of some of the civil rights lost in each state upon conviction of a felony, see Margaret Colgate Love, Relief from the Collateral Consequences of a Criminal Conviction: A State-by-State Resource Guide app. B (2006).

5. RESTRICTIONS ON SEX OFFENDERS: NOTIFICATION, REGISTRATION, AND CIVIL–COMMITMENT LAWS

In 1994, New Jersey enacted what is known as "Megan's Law," named after a seven-year-old girl who was raped and murdered by a man with two previous convictions for sexually assaulting children. N.J.Rev. Stat. §§ 2C:7–1 to –19. The law has two primary components: first, a requirement, backed up by criminal sanctions, that certain convicted sex offenders register at the local police department; and second, a requirement that local law-enforcement officials notify certain individuals and entities in the community about the offender's presence within the community.

The type of notification required under the community-notification provision depends upon the level of risk of reoffense posed by the sex offender, as determined by the county prosecutor in the county in which the offender was convicted, the prosecutor in the county in which the offender will reside, and any law-enforcement officials that the prosecutors pull into the assessment process. If the reoffense risk is low, only law-enforcement agencies likely to encounter the offender need to be notified. (Tier One notification) If the risk is moderate, agencies that supervise or provide care to children or women, such as schools and religious and youth organizations, must also be notified. (Tier Two notification) And if the reoffense risk is high, members of the public "likely to encounter" the sex offender must be notified as well. (Tier Three notification) As interpreted by the New Jersey Supreme Court, the latter group to be notified includes people in the offender's immediate neighborhood; all schools within the community, depending on its size; and schools in nearby communities, depending on how close they are to places where the offender lives, works, or goes to school. Doe v. Poritz, 662 A.2d 367, 385 (N.J.1995).

States across the country now have adopted sex-offender registration and community-notification laws. See Bureau of Justice Statistics, U.S. Dep't of Justice, Summary of State Sex Offender Registries, 2001, at 8–12 (2002). See also the Sex Offender Registration and Notification Act (SORNA), Pub. L. No. 109–248, 120 Stat. 587, which requires states to adopt sex-offender registration laws with community-notification provisions and mandates that information about registered sex offenders be available to the public on-line. 42 U.S.C. §§ 16912–16929. A corresponding criminal statute makes a sex offender's failure to comply with the Act's registration requirements a federal crime. 18 U.S.C. § 2250.

In your opinion, are these registration and community-notification laws sound or unsound from a policy perspective? Are they constitutional? In addressing the latter question, consider the import, if any, of the following Supreme Court case that discusses the constitutionality of another, and greater, restriction placed on certain sex offenders after they have served their criminal sentences.

KANSAS v. HENDRICKS

Supreme Court of the United States, 1997.
521 U.S. 346, 117 S.Ct. 2072, 138 L.Ed.2d 501.

JUSTICE THOMAS delivered the opinion of the Court.

* * *

I

A

The Kansas Legislature enacted the Sexually Violent Predator Act (Act) [Kan. Stat. Ann. § 59–29a01 *et seq.*] in 1994 to grapple with the problem of managing repeat sexual offenders. Although Kansas already had a statute addressing the involuntary commitment of those defined as "mentally ill," the legislature determined that existing civil commitment procedures were inadequate to confront the risks presented by "sexually violent predators." In the Act's preamble, the legislature explained:

"[A] small but extremely dangerous group of sexually violent predators exist who do not have a mental disease or defect that renders them appropriate for involuntary treatment pursuant to the [general involuntary civil commitment statute]. . . . In contrast to persons appropriate for civil commitment under the [general involuntary civil commitment statute], sexually violent predators generally have anti-social personality features which are unamenable to existing mental illness treatment modalities and those features render them likely to engage in sexually violent behavior. The legislature further finds that sexually violent predators' likelihood of engaging in repeat acts of predatory sexual violence is high. * * * The legislature further finds that the prognosis for rehabilitating sexually violent predators in a prison setting is poor * * *."

As a result, the Legislature found it necessary to establish "a civil commitment procedure for the long-term care and treatment of the sexually violent predator." The Act defined a "sexually violent predator" as: "any person who has been convicted of or charged with a sexually violent offense and who suffers from a mental abnormality or personality disorder which makes the person likely to engage in the predatory acts of sexual violence."

A "mental abnormality" was defined, in turn, as a "congenital or acquired condition affecting the emotional or volitional capacity which predisposes the person to commit sexually violent offenses in a degree constituting such person a menace to the health and safety of others."

As originally structured, the Act's civil commitment procedures pertained to: (1) a presently confined person who, like Hendricks, "has been convicted of a sexually violent offense" and is scheduled for release; (2) a person who has been "charged with a sexually violent offense" but has been found incompetent to stand trial; (3) a person who has been found "not guilty by reason of insanity of a sexually violent offense"; and (4) a person found "not guilty" of a sexually violent offense because of a mental disease or defect.

The initial version of the Act, as applied to a currently confined person such as Hendricks, was designed to initiate a specific series of procedures. The custodial agency was required to notify the local prosecutor 60 days before the anticipated release of a person who might have met the Act's criteria. The prosecutor was then obligated, within 45 days, to decide whether to file a petition in state court seeking the person's involuntary commitment. If such a petition were filed, the court was to determine whether "probable cause" existed to support a finding that the person was a "sexually violent predator" and thus eligible for civil commitment. Upon such a determination, transfer of the individual to a secure facility for professional evaluation would occur. After that evaluation, a trial would be held to determine beyond a reasonable doubt whether the individual was a sexually violent predator. If that determination were made, the person would then be transferred to the custody of the Secretary of Social and Rehabilitation Services (Secretary) for "control, care and treatment until such time as the person's mental abnormality or personality disorder has so changed that the person is safe to be at large."

In addition to placing the burden of proof upon the State, the Act afforded the individual a number of other procedural safeguards. In the case of an indigent person, the State was required to provide, at public expense, the assistance of counsel and an examination by mental health care professionals. The individual also received the right to present and cross-examine witnesses, and the opportunity to review documentary evidence presented by the State.

Once an individual was confined, the Act required that "[t]he involuntary detention or commitment . . . shall conform to constitutional requirements for care and treatment." Confined persons were afforded three different avenues of review: First, the committing court was obligated to conduct an annual review to determine whether continued detention was warranted. Second, the Secretary was permitted, at any time, to decide that the confined individual's condition had so changed that release was appropriate, and could then authorize the person to petition for release. Finally, even without the Secretary's permission, the confined person could at any time file a release petition. If the court found that the State could no longer satisfy its burden under the initial commitment standard, the individual would be freed from confinement.

B

In 1984, Hendricks was convicted of taking "indecent liberties" with two 13–year–old boys. After serving nearly 10 years of his sentence, he was slated for release to a halfway house. Shortly before his scheduled release, however, the State filed a petition in state court seeking Hendricks' civil confinement as a sexually violent predator. * * *

Hendricks subsequently requested a jury trial to determine whether he qualified as a sexually violent predator. During that trial, Hendricks' own testimony revealed a chilling history of repeated child sexual molestation and abuse, beginning in 1955 when he exposed his genitals to two young girls. At that time, he pleaded guilty to indecent exposure. Then, in 1957, he was convicted of lewdness involving a young girl and received a brief jail sentence. In 1960, he molested two young boys while he worked for a carnival. After serving two years in prison for that offense, he was paroled, only to be rearrested for molesting a 7–year–old girl. Attempts were made to treat him for his sexual deviance, and in 1965 he was considered "safe to be at large," and was discharged from a state psychiatric hospital.

Shortly thereafter, however, Hendricks sexually assaulted another young boy and girl—he performed oral sex on the 8–year–old girl and fondled the 11–year–old boy. He was again imprisoned in 1967, but refused to participate in a sex offender treatment program, and thus remained incarcerated until his parole in 1972. Diagnosed as a pedophile, Hendricks entered into, but then abandoned, a treatment program. He testified that despite having received professional help for his pedophilia, he continued to harbor sexual desires for children. Indeed, soon after his 1972 parole, Hendricks began to abuse his own stepdaughter and stepson. He forced the children to engage in sexual activity with him over a period of approximately four years. Then, as noted above, Hendricks was convicted of "taking indecent liberties" with two adolescent boys after he attempted to fondle them. As a result of that conviction, he was once again imprisoned, and was serving that sentence when he reached his conditional release date in September 1994.

Hendricks admitted that he had repeatedly abused children whenever he was not confined. He explained that when he "get[s] stressed out," he "can't control the urge" to molest children. Although Hendricks recognized that his behavior harms children, and he hoped he would not sexually molest children again, he stated that the only sure way he could keep from sexually abusing children in the future was "to die." Hendricks readily agreed with the state physician's diagnosis that he suffers from pedophilia and that he is not cured of the condition; indeed, he told the physician that "treatment is bull——."

The jury unanimously found beyond a reasonable doubt that Hendricks was a sexually violent predator. The trial court subsequently determined, as a matter of state law, that pedophilia qualifies as a "mental abnormality" as defined by the Act, and thus ordered Hendricks committed to the Secretary's custody.

Hendricks appealed, claiming, among other things, that application of the Act to him violated the Federal Constitution's Due Process, Double Jeopardy, and *Ex Post Facto* Clauses. * * *

* * *

II

A

Kansas argues that the Act's definition of "mental abnormality" satisfies "substantive" due process requirements. We agree. * * *

* * *

The challenged Act unambiguously requires a finding of dangerousness either to one's self or to others as a prerequisite to involuntary confinement. Commitment proceedings can be initiated only when a person "has been convicted of or charged with a sexually violent offense," and "suffers from a mental abnormality or personality disorder which makes the person likely to engage in the predatory acts of sexual violence." The statute thus requires proof of more than a mere predisposition to violence; rather, it requires evidence of past sexually violent behavior and a present mental condition that creates a likelihood of such conduct in the future if the person is not incapacitated. * * *

A finding of dangerousness, standing alone, is ordinarily not a sufficient ground upon which to justify indefinite involuntary commitment. We have sustained civil commitment statutes when they have coupled proof of dangerousness with the proof of some additional factor, such as a "mental illness" or "mental abnormality." These added statutory requirements serve to limit involuntary civil confinement to those who suffer from a volitional impairment rendering them dangerous beyond their control. * * *

Hendricks nonetheless argues that our earlier cases dictate a finding of "mental illness" as a prerequisite for civil commitment * * *. He then asserts that a "mental abnormality" is not equivalent to a "mental illness" because it is a term coined by the Kansas Legislature, rather than by the psychiatric community. * * *

[W]e have never required State legislatures to adopt any particular nomenclature in drafting civil commitment statutes. Rather, we have traditionally left to legislators the task of defining terms of a medical nature that have legal significance. As a consequence, the States have, over the years, developed numerous specialized terms to define mental health concepts. Often, those definitions do not fit precisely with the definitions employed by the medical community. The legal definitions of "insanity" and "competency," for example, vary substantially from their psychiatric counterparts.

To the extent that the civil commitment statutes we have considered set forth criteria relating to an individual's inability to control his dangerousness, the Kansas Act sets forth comparable criteria and Hendricks' condition doubtless satisfies those criteria. The mental health professionals who evaluated Hendricks diagnosed him as suffering from pedophilia, a condition the psychiatric profession itself classifies as a serious mental disorder. See, e.g., [American Psychiatric Association, Diagnostic and Statistical Manual of Mental Disorders], at 524–525, 527–528. Hendricks even conceded that, when he becomes "stressed out," he cannot "control the urge" to molest children. This admitted lack of volitional control, coupled with a prediction of future dangerousness, adequately distinguishes Hendricks from other dangerous persons who are perhaps more properly dealt with exclusively through criminal proceedings. Hendricks' diagnosis as a pedophile, which qualifies as a "mental abnormality" under the Act, thus plainly suffices for due process purposes.

B

We granted Hendricks' cross-petition to determine whether the Act violates the Constitution's double jeopardy prohibition or its ban on *ex post facto* lawmaking. The thrust of Hendricks' argument is that the Act establishes criminal proceedings; hence confinement under it necessarily constitutes punishment. He contends that where, as here, newly enacted "punishment" is predicated upon past conduct for which he has already been convicted and forced to serve a prison sentence, the Constitution's Double Jeopardy and *Ex Post Facto* Clauses are violated. We are unpersuaded by Hendricks' argument that Kansas has established criminal proceedings.

The categorization of a particular proceeding as civil or criminal "is first of all a question of statutory construction." We must initially ascertain whether the legislature meant the statute to establish "civil" proceedings. If so, we ordinarily defer to the legislature's stated intent. Here, Kansas' objective to create a civil proceeding is evidenced by its placement of the Sexually Violent Predator Act within the Kansas probate code, instead of the criminal code, as well as its description of the Act as creating a *"civil commitment procedure."* Kan. Stat. Ann., Article 29 (1994) ("Care and Treatment for Mentally Ill Persons"), § 59–29a01 (emphasis added). Nothing on the face of the statute suggests that the legislature sought to create anything other than a civil commitment scheme designed to protect the public from harm.

Although we recognize that a "civil label is not always dispositive," we will reject the legislature's manifest intent only where a party challenging the statute provides "the clearest proof" that "the statutory scheme [is] so punitive either in purpose or effect as to negate [the State's] intention" to deem it "civil." * * * Hendricks, however, has failed to satisfy this heavy burden.

As a threshold matter, commitment under the Act does not implicate either of the two primary objectives of criminal punishment: retribution or deterrence. The Act's purpose is not retributive because it does not affix culpability for prior criminal conduct. Instead, such conduct is used solely for evidentiary purposes, either to demonstrate that a "mental abnormality" exists or to support a finding of future dangerousness. * * * In addition, the Kansas Act does not make a criminal conviction a prerequisite for commitment—persons absolved of criminal responsibility may nonetheless be subject to confinement under the Act. * * *

* * *

Nor can it be said that the legislature intended the Act to function as a deterrent. Those persons committed under the Act are, by definition, suffering from a "mental abnormality" or a "personality disorder" that prevents them from exercising adequate control over their behavior. Such persons are therefore unlikely to be deterred by the threat of confinement. And the conditions surrounding that confinement do not suggest a punitive purpose on the State's part. The State has represented that an individual confined under the Act is not subject to the more restrictive conditions placed on state prisoners, but instead experiences essentially the same conditions as any involuntarily committed patient in the state mental institution. * * *

* * *

Finally, Hendricks argues that the Act is necessarily punitive because it fails to offer any legitimate "treatment." * * *

* * *

Accepting the Kansas court's apparent determination that treatment is not possible for this category of individuals does not obligate us to adopt its legal conclusions. We have already observed that, under the appropriate circumstances and when accompanied by proper procedures, incapacitation may be a legitimate end of the civil law. * * *

* * *

Although the treatment program initially offered Hendricks may have seemed somewhat meager, it must be remembered that he was the first person committed under the Act. That the State did not have all of its treatment procedures in place is thus not surprising. What is significant, however, is that Hendricks was placed under the supervision of the Kansas Department of Health and Social and Rehabilitative Services, housed in a unit segregated from the general prison population and operated not by employees of the Department of Corrections, but by other trained individuals. And, before this Court, Kansas declared "[a]bsolutely" that persons committed under the Act are now receiving in the neighborhood of "31.5 hours of treatment per week."[5]

Where the State has "disavowed any punitive intent"; limited confinement to a small segment of particularly dangerous individuals; provided strict procedural safeguards; directed that confined persons be segregated from the general prison population and afforded the same status as others who have been civilly committed; recommended treatment if such is possible; and permitted immediate release upon a showing that the individual is no longer dangerous or mentally impaired, we cannot say that it acted with punitive intent. We therefore hold that the Act does not establish criminal proceedings and that involuntary confinement pursuant to the Act is not punitive. Our conclusion that the Act is nonpunitive thus removes an essential prerequisite for both Hendricks' double jeopardy and *ex post facto* claims.

---

5. * * * [T]o the extent that treatment is available for Hendricks' condition, the State now appears to be providing it. By furnishing such treatment, the Kansas Legislature has indicated that treatment, if possible, is at least an ancillary goal of the Act, which easily satisfies any test for determining that the Act is not punitive.

1

The Double Jeopardy Clause provides: "[N]or shall any person be subject for the same offence to be twice put in jeopardy of life or limb." * * * Hendricks argues that, as applied to him, the Act violates double jeopardy principles because his confinement under the Act, imposed after a conviction and a term of incarceration, amounted to both a second prosecution and a second punishment for the same offense. We disagree.

Because we have determined that the Kansas Act is civil in nature, initiation of its commitment proceedings does not constitute a second prosecution. Moreover, as commitment under the Act is not tantamount to "punishment," Hendricks' involuntary detention does not violate the Double Jeopardy Clause, even though that confinement may follow a prison term. * * * If an individual otherwise meets the requirements for involuntary civil commitment, the State is under no obligation to release that individual simply because the detention would follow a period of incarceration.

* * *

2

Hendricks' *ex post facto* claim is similarly flawed. The *Ex Post Facto* Clause, which " 'forbids the application of any new punitive measure to a crime already consummated,' " has been interpreted to pertain exclusively to penal statutes. As we have previously determined, the Act does not impose punishment; thus, its application does not raise *ex post facto* concerns. * * *

III

We hold that the Kansas Sexually Violent Predator Act comports with due process requirements and neither runs afoul of double jeopardy principles nor constitutes an exercise in impermissible *ex post facto* law-making. * * *

JUSTICE KENNEDY, concurring.

* * *

* * * A law enacted after commission of the offense and which punishes the offense by extending the term of confinement is a textbook example of an *ex post facto* law. If the object or purpose of the Kansas law had been to provide treatment but the treatment provisions were adopted as a sham or mere pretext, there would have been an indication of the forbidden purpose to punish. * * *

* * * In this case, the mental abnormality—pedophilia—is at least described in the DSM–IV. American Psychiatric Association, Diagnostic and Statistical Manual of Mental Disorders 524–525, 527–528 (4th ed.1994).

* * *

On the record before us, the Kansas civil statute conforms to our precedents. If, however, civil confinement were to become a mechanism for retribution or general deterrence, or if it were shown that mental abnormality is too imprecise a category to offer a solid basis for concluding that civil detention is justified, our precedents would not suffice to validate it.

JUSTICE BREYER, with whom JUSTICES STEVENS and SOUTER join, and with whom JUSTICE GINSBURG joins as to Parts II and III, dissenting.

[In Part I of his dissenting opinion, Justice Breyer explained why he agreed with the majority of the Court that Kansas's Sexually Violent Predator Act does not violate due process.]

II

Kansas' 1994 Act violates the Federal Constitution's prohibition of "any . . . *ex post facto* Law" if it "inflicts" upon Hendricks "a greater punishment" than did the law "annexed to" his "crime[s]" when he "committed" those crimes in 1984. * * *

Certain resemblances between the Act's "civil commitment" and traditional criminal punishments are obvious. Like criminal imprisonment, the Act's civil commitment amounts to "secure" confinement and "incarceration against one's will." See Testimony of Terry Davis, SRS Director of Quality Assurance (confinement takes place in the psychiatric wing of a prison hospital where those whom the Act confines and ordinary prisoners are treated alike). In addition, a basic objective of the Act is incapacitation, which, as Blackstone said in describing an objective of criminal law, is to "depriv[e] the party injuring of the power to do future mischief." * * *

Moreover, the Act, like criminal punishment, imposes its confinement (or sanction) only upon an individual who has previously committed a criminal offense. And the Act imposes that confinement through the use of persons (county prosecutors), procedural guarantees (trial by jury, assistance of counsel, psychiatric evaluations), and standards ("beyond a reasonable doubt") traditionally associated with the criminal law.

These obvious resemblances by themselves, however, are not legally sufficient to transform what the Act calls "civil commitment" into a criminal punishment. Civil commitment of dangerous, mentally ill individuals by its very nature involves confinement and incapacitation. Yet "civil commitment," from a constitutional perspective, nonetheless remains civil. Nor does the fact that criminal behavior triggers the Act make the critical difference. The Act's insistence upon a prior crime, by screening out those whose past behavior does not concretely demonstrate the existence of a mental problem or potential future danger, may serve an important noncriminal evidentiary purpose. Neither is the presence of criminal law-type procedures determinative. Those procedures can serve an important purpose that in this context one might consider noncriminal, namely helping to prevent judgmental mistakes that would wrongly deprive a person of important liberty.

* * *

* * * I would place particular importance upon those features that would likely distinguish between a basically punitive and a basically nonpunitive purpose. * * *

* * *

* * * First, the State Supreme Court here * * * has held that treatment is not a significant objective of the Act. * * *

* * *

* * * Indeed, were we to follow the majority's invitation to look beyond the record in this case, an invitation with which we disagree, it would reveal that Hendricks, according to the commitment program's own director, was receiving "essentially no treatment." Dr. Charles Befort in State Habeas Corpus Proceeding, App. 393; 912 P.2d, at 131, 136.

* * *

Second, the Kansas statute insofar as it applies to previously convicted offenders, such as Hendricks, commits, confines, and treats those offenders after they have served virtually their entire criminal sentence.* * * But why, one might ask, does the Act not commit and require treatment of sex offenders sooner, say soon after they begin to serve their sentences?

* * * And it is particularly difficult to see why legislators who specifically wrote into the statute a finding that "prognosis for rehabilitating . . . in a prison setting is poor" would leave an offender in that setting for months or years before beginning treatment. This is to say, the timing provisions of the statute confirm the Kansas Supreme Court's view that treatment was not a particularly important legislative objective.

* * *

Third, the statute, at least as of the time Kansas applied it to Hendricks, did not require the committing authority to consider the possibility of using less restrictive alternatives, such as postrelease supervision, halfway houses, or other methods * * *. * * *

This Court has said that a failure to consider, or to use, "alternative and less harsh methods" to achieve a nonpunitive objective can help to show that [the] legislature's "purpose . . . was to punish." * * *

Fourth, the laws of other States confirm, through comparison, that Kansas' "civil commitment" objectives do not require the statutory features that indicate a punitive purpose. I have found 17 States with laws that seek to protect the public from mentally abnormal, sexually dangerous individuals through civil commitment or other mandatory treatment programs. * * * Only one State other than Kansas, namely Iowa, both delays civil commitment (and consequent treatment) and does not explicitly consider less restrictive alternatives. But the law of that State applies prospectively only, thereby avoiding *ex post facto* problems. See Iowa Code Ann. § 709C.12 (Supp.1997) (Iowa SVP act only "applies to persons convicted of a sexually violent offense on or after July 1, 1997"). * * *

* * *

* * * [A] State is free to commit those who are dangerous and mentally ill in order to treat them. Nor does my decision preclude a State from deciding that a certain subset of people are mentally ill, dangerous, and untreatable, and that confinement of this subset is therefore necessary * * *. But when a State decides offenders can be treated and confines an offender to provide that treatment, but then refuses to provide it, the refusal to treat while a person is fully incapacitated begins to look punitive.

* * *

* * * [T]he Act as applied to *Leroy Hendricks* (as opposed to others who may have received treatment or who were sentenced after the effective date of the Act), is punitive.

* * *

* * * This analysis, rooted in the facts surrounding Kansas' failure to treat Hendricks, cannot answer the question whether the Kansas Act, as it now stands, and in light of its current implementation, is punitive towards people other than he. And I do not attempt to do so here.

III

To find that the confinement the Act imposes upon Hendricks is "punishment" is to find a violation of the *Ex Post Facto* Clause. * * *

To find a violation of that Clause here, however, is not to hold that the Clause prevents Kansas, or other States, from enacting dangerous sexual offender statutes. A statute that operates prospectively, for example, does not offend the *Ex Post Facto* Clause. Neither does it offend the *Ex Post Facto* Clause for a State to sentence offenders to the fully authorized sentence, to seek consecutive, rather than concurrent, sentences, or to invoke recidivism statutes to lengthen imprisonment. Moreover, a statute that operates retroactively, like Kansas' statute, nonetheless does not offend the Clause *if the confinement that it imposes is not punishment*—if, that is to say, the legislature does not simply add a later criminal punishment to an earlier one.

The statutory provisions before us do amount to punishment primarily because, as I have said, the legislature did not tailor the statute to fit the nonpunitive civil aim of treatment * * *. * * *

* * *

QUESTIONS AND POINTS FOR DISCUSSION

1. Do you agree with the Supreme Court's constitutional analysis in *Hendricks*? If so, from a policy standpoint, do you support or oppose the enactment of sexually violent predator acts? For one critique of *Hendricks* and the soundness, from a policy perspective, of sexually violent predator acts, see Steven I. Friedland, On Treatment, Punishment, and the Civil Commitment of Sex Offenders, 70 U. Colo. L. Rev. 73 (1999).

2. In Kansas v. Crane, 534 U.S. 407, 122 S.Ct. 867 (2002), the Supreme Court elaborated on the nature of the mental abnormality needed for the civil confinement of a sexually violent predator to be constitutional. In addition to proving that the abnormality makes it likely that the defendant will commit acts of sexual violence in the future, the state must prove that the defendant has "serious difficulty," although not necessarily total incapacity, controlling his or her behavior. Id. at 413, 122 S.Ct. at 870. The genesis of this limitation on the mental abnormalities that will permit the civil confinement of sexually violent predators was the Court's obvious concern that because so many prisoners have mental disorders, civil commitments triggered solely by a finding of dangerousness and some kind of mental problem could be used as a matter of course to extend the confinement of vast numbers of prisoners. See id. at 412, 122 S.Ct. at 870 (citing one report that 40 to 60% of male prisoners have an antisocial personality disorder).

In a dissenting opinion, Justice Scalia, joined by Justice Thomas, excoriated the majority for concluding that due process requires a volitional impairment—a substantial inability to control one's behavior—before a person can be confined as a sexually violent predator. Justice Scalia objected:

> It is obvious that a person may be able to exercise volition and yet be unfit to turn loose upon society. The man who has a will of steel, but who delusionally believes that every woman he meets is inviting crude sexual advances, is surely a dangerous sexual predator.

Id. at 422, 122 S.Ct. at 875 (Scalia, J., dissenting). Do you agree or disagree with Justice Scalia's more limited construction of the requirements of due process?

3. Alcohol dependence and abuse are among the many mental disorders listed in the American Psychiatric Association's *Diagnostic and Statistical Manual of Mental Disorders* (4th ed., text rev. 2000). After *Hendricks* and *Crane*, would it be constitutional to civilly commit an inmate about to be released from prison for a fourth drunk-driving conviction under a state statute providing for the civil commitment of certain dangerous alcoholics who are unable to control their drinking? Why or why not?

4. In Seling v. Young, 531 U.S. 250, 121 S.Ct. 727 (2001), the Supreme Court considered a constitutional challenge to the implementation of the Washington statute after which the Kansas Sexually Violent Predator Act had been patterned. The petitioner in that case was committed as a sexually violent predator after serving a prison sentence for his sixth rape conviction. Placed in the custody of the state's social-services department, he was then

confined in a Special Commitment Center located on the grounds of a state prison.

In his petition for a writ of habeas corpus, the petitioner contended that the purportedly "civil" statute under which he had been committed was applied in such a punitive way that his rights under the Double Jeopardy and *Ex Post Facto* Clauses of the Constitution were violated. The petitioner cited the pervasive involvement of the Department of Corrections in the day-to-day operations of the Special Commitment Center and claimed that he was treated even more harshly than a prisoner.

The Supreme Court assumed that the Washington statute, like the Kansas Act, was civil in nature. The Court then rejected the petitioner's argument that a statute providing for the civil commitment of sexually violent predators can be challenged on double-jeopardy and *ex post facto* grounds because of the punitive way in which it is being implemented. Concluding that such "as applied" challenges would be unworkable because conditions of confinement constantly change, the Court observed: "The civil nature of a confinement scheme cannot be altered based merely on vagaries in the implementation of the authorizing statute." Id. at 263, 121 S. Ct. at 735.

The Supreme Court hastened to add that civilly committed sexually violent predators are not left remediless to challenge the conditions of their confinement. If those conditions do not comport with state law, such as a mandate to provide them with individualized treatment, they can seek enforcement of the state statute in a state court. Noting that due process requires that the conditions and length of a person's confinement bear a "reasonable relation" to the purpose for which the person was confined, the Supreme Court also seemed to suggest that sexually violent predators subject to civil confinement might mount, in some circumstances, a successful due-process challenge to their confinement conditions. Id. at 265, 121 S. Ct. at 736. Finally, the Court underscored that the Special Commitment Center itself was operating under an injunction issued in a different case brought under 42 U.S.C. § 1983 to enjoin certain unconstitutional conditions.

In *Seling*, the Supreme Court left open an issue that it said it had not yet "squarely addressed": the relevance of conditions of confinement to the threshold question whether a statute providing for the confinement of sexually violent predators is civil or punitive. Id. at 266–67, 121 S. Ct. at 736–37. In your opinion, how should this issue be resolved?

5.   The Supreme Court has adjudicated several questions concerning the constitutionality of sex-offender registration and notification laws, which were discussed earlier in this chapter. The question before the Court in Connecticut Dep't of Public Safety v. Doe, 538 U.S. 1, 123 S.Ct. 1160 (2003) was whether convicted sex offenders living in Connecticut had a due-process right to a hearing, at which it would be determined whether they were "currently dangerous," before information about them was included in a sex-offender registry that could be perused in certain state offices and on an Internet website. The state statute whose constitutionality was at issue in the case did not predicate the dissemination of information about convicted sex offenders, including their names, addresses, and photographs, on a finding that a registrant was currently dangerous. Instead, a conviction of certain crimes, by

itself, triggered the public-notification provisions of the statute. Consequently, the Supreme Court held, in a unanimous opinion, that the convicted sex offenders had no due-process right to a hearing on the question of the existence of a criterion—current dangerousness—that was irrelevant under the statute's public-notification provision. The offenders' right to procedural due process was satisfied by the plethora of procedural safeguards that attended the securing of the convictions that sparked the ensuing registration and notification requirements.

Would and should the outcome in this case have been different if under the statute, the inclusion of a sex offender's conviction in the sex-offender registry posted on the Internet hinged on his or her current dangerousness? Cf. Doe v. Poritz, 662 A.2d 367, 382–84, 421 (N.J. 1995) (convicted sex offenders have a right to a judicial hearing before being subject to community notification at the Tier–2 or Tier–3 levels).

In Smith v. Doe, 538 U.S. 84, 123 S.Ct. 1140 (2003), the Supreme Court considered another constitutional question about a sex-offender registration and public-notification law: whether Alaska's Sex Offender Registration Act violated the constitutional prohibition on *ex post facto* laws. The registration and notification provisions of that Act applied retroactively—to sex offenders convicted before the statute's enactment. Individuals convicted of a nonaggravated sex offense were subject to the statute's registration provisions for fifteen years, and they had to update the information provided to the Alaska Department of Public Safety, such as their place of employment and physical description, once a year. Individuals convicted of two or more sex offenses or of an aggravated sex offense were subject to the reporting requirements for life and had to update the registration information every three months. Most of this registration information was disseminated to the public via the Internet.

In an opinion written by Justice Kennedy, the Court found the registration and notification provisions to be nonpunitive measures designed to protect the public's safety rather than a punishment that cannot be imposed retrospectively. Unmoved by the fact that the registration provisions had been placed in the state's criminal code, the Court remarked: "The location and labels of a statutory provision do not by themselves transform a civil remedy into a criminal one." Id. at 94, 123 S.Ct. at 1148. Nor was the Court's conclusion that the restrictions were nonpunitive altered by the fact that Alaska's Rules of Criminal Procedure required courts to both apprise certain criminal offenders of the registration and notification provisions before accepting their guilty pleas and to spell out the provisions' requirements in the written judgments for specified crimes. Notifying offenders of the civil consequences of their convictions, observed the Court, did not make those consequences punitive. Such notification, the Court added, served the laudable, nonpunitive goal of ensuring that convicted offenders complied with the registration requirements.

In a dissenting opinion, Justice Stevens argued that the registration and notification provisions had all of the hallmarks of a criminal punishment. "[A] sanction that (1) is imposed on everyone who commits a criminal offense; (2) is not imposed on anyone else; and (3) severely impairs a person's liberty is punishment," he contended. Id. at 113, 123 S.Ct. at 1158. In discussing the latter component of a criminal punishment—how the registration provisions substantially curtailed the liberty of convicted sex offenders living in Alaska, Justice Stevens pointed out that the offenders could not take such mundane actions as changing the color of their hair, shaving their beards, or switching employers without notifying authorities.

In a separate dissenting opinion, Justice Ginsburg, joined by Justice Breyer, opined that the registration and notification requirements were simply modern counterparts to age-old shaming punishments like whipping, branding, the pillory, and banishment. But the majority, for two reasons, found the analogy inapposite: first, the colonial punishments involved either a "direct confrontation" between the offender and the public or the offender's expulsion from the community; and second, the primary purpose of these primeval punishments was to stigmatize the offender. Id. at 98, 123 S.Ct. at 1150. By contrast, the notification provision's purpose and "principal effect" were "to inform the public for its own safety, not to humiliate the offender." Id. at 99, 123 S.Ct. at 1150.

The Court did not consider this purpose belied by the fact that an offender's picture and other personal information were posted on an Internet website. The Court felt that utilizing the Internet was simply an efficient means through which the public could protect itself. The Court emphasized that this notification mechanism was "passive," since individuals had to visit the website to obtain the information they wanted or needed about convicted sex offenders. Id. at 105, 123 S.Ct. at 1153. In finding that this notification system was much more akin to visiting an archive to view criminal records than it was to the penalties designed to incite public opprobrium in colonial times, the Court stated: "Our system does not treat dissemination of truthful information in furtherance of a legitimate governmental objective as punishment." Id. at 98, 123 S.Ct. at 1150.

In your opinion, do registration and notification requirements for convicted sex offenders inflict punishment on them, raising *ex post facto* concerns if those requirements are applied retroactively? Was the result in *Smith v. Doe* dictated by the Court's earlier decision in *Kansas v. Hendricks*, or can you distinguish that case?

C.   RESTORATION OF RIGHTS AND OTHER STEPS TO LIMIT COLLATERAL SANCTIONS AND CONSEQUENCES

There are a number of ways in which the adverse collateral effects of criminal convictions can be dissipated. Several key mechanisms—pardons, restoration-of-rights procedures, the expungement or sealing of criminal records, and statutes restricting the collateral sanctions and consequences that can attend a conviction—are briefly discussed below. For additional information regarding these mechanisms and other steps jurisdictions have taken to dissipate the collateral effects of a criminal conviction, see Margaret Colgate Love, Relief from the Collateral Consequences of a Criminal Conviction: A State-by-State Resource Guide (2006).

1. PARDONS

All of the states and the federal government have procedures in place for issuing pardons to criminal offenders. See Clifford Dorne & Kenneth Gewerth, Mercy in a Climate of Retributive Justice: Interpretations From a National Survey of Executive Clemency Procedures, 25 New Eng. J. on Crim. & Civ. Confinement 413, 427–40 (1999) (describing different pardoning structures). In some states, the governor makes the pardoning decision; in others, the decision is made by the parole board or a board of pardons; and in still others, the decision is made by the governor in conjunction with, or after consultation with, the parole or pardon board. Id. at 427–28. In the federal system, the power to grant pardons is vested in the President. U.S. Const. art. II, § 2, cl. 1.

If the pardoning authority grants an unconditional pardon and the offender accepts the pardon, the offender will generally be relieved from at least most of the legal disabilities that attend a criminal conviction. The offender, for example, will be able to vote and sit on a jury.

In some jurisdictions, however, there are limitations on the ability of a pardon to fully restore the rights of individuals convicted of crimes. In accepting a pardon, convicted offenders are, according to some courts, implicitly acknowledging their guilt of the crimes for which they are being pardoned. See, e.g., Burdick v. United States, 236 U.S. 79, 94, 35 S.Ct. 267, 270 (1915). See also R.J.L. v. State, 887 So.2d 1268, 1281 (Fla. 2004) ("A pardon is the equivalent of forgiveness for a crime; it does not declare the pardoned individual innocent of the crime."); United States v. Noonan, 906 F.2d 952, 958–60 (3d Cir.1990) (presidential pardon does not mean that pardoned person is entitled to expungement of his or her criminal record). Consequently, in some jurisdictions, the conduct underlying a criminal conviction can be considered when an ex-convict applies for a position that requires that applicants meet certain character requirements. For example, in Hirschberg v. Commodity Futures Trading Comm'n, 414 F.3d 679, 682–84 (7th Cir. 2005), the Seventh Circuit Court of Appeals held that while it would violate the Pardons Clause to deny registration as a commodities broker (who acts as a fiduciary for others) because of a mail-fraud conviction for which a presidential pardon had been issued, denying the registration because of the conduct underlying that conviction would not. And criminal conduct resulting in a prior conviction may lead to a determination that an ex-convict is unfit to practice law, even though the ex-offender has been officially pardoned for his or her crime. See, e.g., Grossgold v. Supreme Court of Illinois, 557 F.2d 122, 125–26 (7th Cir.1977) (attorney can be suspended from practice of law, despite a presidential pardon, because the pardon "did not wipe out the moral turpitude inherent in the factual predicate" supporting the conviction).

One of the common criticisms of pardons is that the pardoning power is exercised so sparingly in most jurisdictions that it is an ineffectual means of restoring offenders' rights and reintegrating them into society. See Justice Kennedy Comm'n, Am. Bar Ass'n, Reports with Recommendations to the ABA House of Delegates 70 n. 9 (2004) (noting that President George W. Bush granted eleven pardons during the first three years of his presidency while denying 601 pardon applications in that time period). Political considerations, particularly a fear of appearing "soft on crime," suffuse the pardoning process, discouraging its use as a reintegration tool. In addition, many offenders lack the resources or knowledge needed to pursue a pardon or the political connections that often are needed to obtain a pardon in many jurisdictions. See Margaret Colgate Love, Starting Over With a Clean Slate: In Praise of a Forgotten Section of the Model Penal Code, 30 Fordham Urb.L.J. 1705, 1721 (2003), whose author served as the Pardon Attorney in the U.S. Department of Justice from 1990 to 1997.

2. RESTORATION–OF–RIGHTS PROCEDURES

A number of states have adopted statutes that enable certain or all convicted felons to get some or all of their civil rights lost as a result of their felony convictions restored. Margaret Colgate Love, Relief From the Collateral Consequences of a Criminal Conviction: A State-by-State Resource Guide app. B (2008). Many of these statutes provide for the automatic restoration of certain rights at a defined time after convicted felons have completed their sentences. See, e.g., N.H.Rev.Stat.Ann. § 607–A:5(I); Wis.Stat. § 304.078(2). Other statutes require that an application for restoration of rights be made to a court, administrative agency, or executive official. See, e.g., N.J. Stat. Ann. § 2A:167–5.

Restoration-of-rights statutes are often like pardons in the sense that even offenders whose civil rights, such as the right to vote or to serve on a jury, have been fully restored may be denied professional or occupational licenses because of the conduct that led to their criminal convictions. Margaret Colgate Love, Starting Over With a Clean Slate: In Praise of a Forgotten Section of the Model Penal Code, 30 Fordham Urb.L.J. 1705, 1719–20 (2003). In addition, ex-convicts whose rights have been restored, like some pardoned offenders, still may be obliged to reveal their criminal records on job-application forms. One of the differences between pardons and statutes providing for the automatic restoration of rights is that the former are discretionary while the latter are triggered automatically by the occurrence of a certain event.

3. EXPUNGEMENT AND SEALING
OF CRIMINAL RECORDS

The expungement or sealing of criminal records is another way of reducing or eliminating the adverse effects of a criminal conviction. If criminal records are expunged, they may be, but often are not, destroyed. See, e.g., Ark.Code Ann. § 16–90–901(a)(1)–(2) (expungement of criminal records means they are sealed and treated as confidential, but not destroyed). "Expunged" records that are not actually destroyed are typically available for use by law-enforcement officials and courts. If criminal records are sealed, access to them is also limited, but the records themselves are preserved. The advantage, from the offenders' perspective, of having criminal records expunged or sealed is that they may be entitled to refrain from mentioning their criminal records on job-application forms. See, e.g., Ark.Code Ann. § 16–90–902(b) ("Upon the entry of the uniform order to seal records of an individual, the individual's underlying conduct shall be deemed as a matter of law never to have occurred, and the individual may state that no such conduct ever occurred and that no such records exist.").

A study completed in 2002 revealed that forty states provided some mechanism for expunging or sealing conviction records. Bureau of Justice Statistics, U.S. Dep't of Justice, Compendium of State Privacy and Security Legislation: 2002 Overview 27, 29 (2003). State statutes vary, however, as to when expungement or sealing of criminal records is appropriate. Some, for example, apply only to individuals placed on probation or given a deferred sentence. See, e.g., Ark.Code Ann. § 16–93–303(b); Okla.Stat. tit. 22, § 991c(C). Others only apply to nonviolent offenders. See, e.g., R.I.Gen.Laws § 12–1.3–2(a). Still others permit or generally permit only first-time felony offenders to get records of their convictions expunged. See, e.g., Okla.Stat. tit. 22 § 991c(F); R.I.Gen.Laws § 12–1.3–2(a).

Commentators have pointed to some drawbacks in relying on the expungement and sealing of criminal records as means of enabling convicted offenders to put their criminal misdeeds behind them and move forward with their lives. The concealment of facts that occurs when criminal records are expunged or sealed and the ensuing license sometimes given offenders to deny the existence of their convictions, it has been argued, do not comport with a legal system grounded on a commitment to truth. In addition, with the evolution of technology, the expungement and sealing of records can be ineffectual in suppressing the circulation of information about a person's criminal history. See Margaret Colgate Love, Starting Over With a Clean Slate: In Pursuit of a Forgotten Section of the Model Penal Code 1705, 1726 (2003). Do you agree with these reservations about the appropriateness and efficacy of expunging and sealing criminal records? Under what circumstances, if any, do you believe that statutes should provide for the expungement or sealing of criminal records?

4. RESTRICTIONS ON COLLATERAL SANCTIONS AND CONSEQUENCES

Another way of mitigating the adverse effects of a criminal conviction is through statutes and court rules that limit the collateral sanctions and consequences that can ensue from a conviction. The ABA Standards for Criminal Justice: Collateral Sanctions and Discretionary Disqualification of Convicted Persons (3d ed. 2004) contain standards that can be incorporated in statutes and court rules to achieve this purpose. The ABA Standards are designed to diminish the adverse collateral effects of criminal convictions in three ways: one, by placing limits on the rights and privileges that can be lost because of a criminal conviction; two, by outlining certain procedures that must be followed when imposing a collateral sanction or what the Standards refer to as a "discretionary disqualification"; and three, by providing for the establishment of mechanisms to relieve individuals from the burdens of collateral sanctions and discretionary disqualifications. Some of these standards and portions of the commentary explaining them are set forth below:

STANDARDS FOR CRIMINAL JUSTICE: COLLATERAL SANCTIONS AND DISCRETIONARY DISQUALIFICATION OF CONVICTED PERSONS

INTRODUCTION

Persons convicted of a crime ordinarily expect to be sentenced to a term of probation or confinement, and perhaps to a fine and court costs. They also understand that they will bear the social stigma of a criminal conviction. But what they often do not appreciate is that their convictions will expose them to numerous additional legal penalties and disabilities, some of which may be far more onerous than the sentence imposed by the judge in open court. These "collateral consequences of conviction" include relatively traditional penalties such as disenfranchisement, loss of professional licenses, and deportation in the case of aliens, as well as newer penalties such as felon registration and ineligibility for certain public welfare benefits. They may apply for a definite period of time, or indefinitely for the convicted person's lifetime. To the extent they occur outside the sentencing process, they may take effect without judicial consideration of their appropriateness in the particular case, without notice at sentencing that the individual's legal status has dramatically changed, and indeed without any requirement that the judge, prosecutor, defense attorney or defendant even be aware that they exist.

* * *

These Standards proceed from a premise that it is neither fair nor efficient for the criminal justice system to label significant legal disabilities and penalties as "collateral" and thereby give permission to ignore them in the process of criminal sentencing, when in reality those disabilities and penalties can be the most important and permanent results of a criminal conviction.

* * *

The criminal justice system must also concern itself with unreasonable discrimination against convicted persons. "Discretionary disqualification" from benefits or opportunities on grounds related to [a] conviction, while not a "sanction" that must be considered at sentencing, may just as surely prevent or discourage convicted persons from successfully reentering the free community, and impose on the community the costs of their recidivism. * * *

* * *

PART I.
DEFINITIONS AND OBJECTIVES

Standard 19–1.1 Definitions

For purposes of this chapter:

(a) The term "collateral sanction" means a legal penalty, disability or disadvantage, however denominated, that is imposed on a person automatically upon that person's conviction for a felony, misdemeanor or other offense, even if it is not included in the sentence.

(b) The term "discretionary disqualification" means a penalty, disability or disadvantage, however denominated, that a civil court, administrative agency, or official is authorized but not required to impose on a person convicted of an offense on grounds related to the conviction.

Commentary

"Collateral sanctions" are those penalties that automatically become effective upon conviction even though not included in the court's judgment of conviction or identified on the record. The term signifies a direct and immediate change in an offender's legal status that does not depend upon some subsequent additional occurrence or administrative action, and that would not have occurred in the absence of a conviction. Examples include disenfranchisement, automatic loss of firearms privileges, per se disqualification from employment or public benefits, and mandatory felon registration. To the extent a non-citizen's immigration status changes as a result of a criminal conviction, so that the offender becomes automatically deportable without opportunity for discretionary exception or revision, deportation too must be regarded as a "collateral sanction."

* * *

"Collateral sanctions" are to be distinguished from discretionary penalties or disabilities based on conduct underlying a criminal conviction, which could occur whether or not the person has been convicted. These Standards deal with this more attenuated effect of conviction as a "discretionary disqualification." The disqualifying conduct might be established by the conviction, but it might also be established in some other way, such as by a civil action or administrative determination. An example of a discretionary disqualification is the law that excludes persons who engage

in "drug-related criminal activity" from federally funded housing benefits.
* * *

* * *

PART II.
COLLATERAL SANCTIONS

Standard 19–2.1 Codification of collateral sanctions

The legislature should collect, set out or reference all collateral sanctions in a single chapter or section of the jurisdiction's criminal code. The chapter or section should identify with particularity the type, severity and duration of collateral sanctions applicable to each offense, or to a group of offenses specifically identified by name, section number, severity level, or other easily determinable means.

Standard 19–2.2 Limitation on collateral sanctions

The legislature should not impose a collateral sanction on a person convicted of an offense unless it determines that the conduct constituting that particular offense provides so substantial a basis for imposing the sanction that the legislature cannot reasonably contemplate any circumstances in which imposing the sanction would not be justified.

Commentary

* * *

There are certain situations in which a collateral sanction will be so clearly appropriate given the nature of the offense that case-by-case evaluation at the time of sentencing would be pointless and inefficient. Examples might include exclusion of those convicted of sexual abuse from employment involving close contact with children, loss of public office upon conviction of bribery, denial of licensure where the offense involves the licensed activity, and prohibition of firearms to those convicted of violent crimes.

Examples of collateral sanctions that would not be justified under this Standard are denial of student aid and loss of a driver's license upon conviction of a drug offense. It might well be appropriate to provide for automatic suspension of a driver's license where the offense conduct is related to driving or motor vehicles, or to exclude from educational institutions those who sell drugs there. And, it may be appropriate to revoke a driver's license or exclude from aid on a case-by-case basis, subject to Standard 19–3.1. But it is unreasonable and counterproductive to deny all drug offenders access to the means of rehabilitating themselves and supporting their families, thereby imposing a cost upon the community with no evident corresponding benefit.

* * *

When the legislature identifies a close connection between the offense and the collateral sanction, the Standards provide that relief from the sanction should be available if warranted. Standard 19–2.5. * * *

Standard 19–2.4 Consideration of collateral sanctions at sentencing

(a) The legislature should authorize the sentencing court to take into account, and the court should consider, applicable collateral sanctions in determining an offender's overall sentence.

(b) The rules of procedure should require the court to ensure at the time of sentencing that the defendant has been informed of collateral sanctions made applicable to the offense or offenses of conviction under the law of the state or territory where the prosecution is pending, and under federal law. Except where notification by the court itself is otherwise required by law or rules of procedure, this requirement may be satisfied by confirming on the record that defense counsel has so advised the defendant.

* * *

Commentary

Standard 19–2.4(a) requires a sentencing court to take into account applicable collateral sanctions in fashioning a package of sanctions at sentencing. * * * [T]he sentencing court should ensure that the totality of the penalty is not unduly severe and that it does not give rise to undue disparity.

* * *

Standard 19–2.5 Waiver, modification, relief

(a) The legislature should authorize a court, a specified administrative body, or both, to enter an order waiving, modifying, or granting timely and effective relief from any collateral sanction imposed by the law of that jurisdiction.

(b) Where the collateral sanction is imposed by one jurisdiction based upon a conviction in another jurisdiction, the legislature in the jurisdiction imposing the collateral sanction should authorize a court, a specified administrative body, or both, to enter an order waiving, modifying, or granting timely and effective relief from the collateral sanction.

(c) The legislature should establish a process by which a convicted person may obtain an order relieving the person of all collateral sanctions imposed by the law of that jurisdiction.

* * *

Commentary

Standard 19–2.5(a) provides that collateral sanctions should be subject to waiver, modification, or "timely and effective relief" from a court or a specified administrative agency if the sanctions have become inappropriate or unfair based on the facts of the particular case. Jurisdictions could choose to allow the waiver authority to be exercised at the time of sentencing, or only at some later date. Waiver or modification of a collateral sanction under Standard 19–2.5, whether at the time of sentencing or at some later time, would not preclude a court or administrative agency from taking action based on the conduct underlying the conviction, pursuant to Standard 19–3.1.

* * *

Standard 19–2.5(c) differs from 19–2.5(a) and (b) insofar as it contemplates a judicial or administrative process for obtaining relief from *all* collateral sanctions imposed by the law of that jurisdiction. * * *

* * *

Standard 19–2.6 Prohibited collateral sanctions

Jurisdictions should not impose the following collateral sanctions:

(a) deprivation of the right to vote, except during actual confinement;

(b) deprivation of judicial rights, including the rights to:

(i) initiate or defend a suit in any court under one's own name under procedures applicable to the general public;

(ii) be eligible for jury service except during actual confinement or while on probation, parole, or other court supervision; and

(iii) execute judicially enforceable documents and agreements;

(c) deprivation of legally recognized domestic relationships and rights other than in accordance with rules applicable to the general public. Accordingly, conviction or confinement alone:

(i) should be insufficient to deprive a person of the right to contract or dissolve a marriage; parental rights, including the right to direct the rearing of children and to live with children except during actual confinement; the right to grant or withhold consent to the adoption of children; and the right to adopt children; and

(ii) should not constitute neglect or abandonment of a spouse or child, and confined persons should be assisted in making appropriate arrangements for their spouses or children;

(d) deprivation of the right to acquire, inherit, sell or otherwise dispose of real or personal property, except insofar as is necessary to preclude a person from profiting from his or her own wrong; and, for persons unable to manage or preserve their property by reason of confinement, deprivation of the right to appoint someone of their own choosing to act on their behalf;

(e) ineligibility to participate in government programs providing necessities of life, including food, clothing, housing, medical care, disability pay, and Social Security; provided, however, that a person may be suspended from participation in such a program to the extent that the purposes of the program are reasonably being served by an alternative program; and

(f) ineligibility for governmental benefits relevant to successful reentry into society, such as educational and job training programs.

Commentary

* * *

* * * Considering the very narrow circumstances in which a collateral sanction may be authorized, *see* Standard 19–2.2, and the availability of relief under Standard 19–2.5(a), a jurisdiction's ability to suspend a convicted person from a necessity of life program should be limited to cases presenting a clear risk to public safety and/or opportunity for recidivism.[57] * * *

PART III.
DISCRETIONARY DISQUALIFICATION OF
CONVICTED PERSONS

Standard 19–3.1 Prohibited discretionary disqualification

The legislature should prohibit discretionary disqualification of a convicted person from benefits or opportunities, including housing, employment, insurance, and occupational and professional licenses, permits and certifications, on grounds related to the conviction, unless engaging in the conduct underlying the conviction would provide a substantial basis for disqualification even if the person had not been convicted.

Commentary

* * *

[T]he line between a mandatory collateral sanction and discretionary disqualification is not always a bright one: * * * The key distinction is whether disqualification decisions are made on a bona fide case-by-case basis, taking into account the equitable merits of each case. If convicted persons are the *only* people disqualified, and if *all* convicted persons are disqualified without consideration of the merits, then under the principles of administrative law, the failure to exercise discretion might constitute an abuse of discretion that could be remedied on appeal or through judicial review.

---

57. For example, all persons who have been convicted of rape or sexual abuse of a minor could be automatically suspended from participation in a public housing program, but only so long as they have reasonable access to alternative low-cost housing. In the absence of alternative housing, individuals convicted of such crimes could be excluded from public housing upon case-by-case determinations that the conduct underlying their convictions constituted grounds for discretionary disqualification (see Standard 19–3.1).

Standard 19–3.2 Relief from discretionary disqualification

The legislature should establish a process for obtaining review of, and relief from, any discretionary disqualification.

Commentary

Standard 19–3.2 requires that some mechanism be available for obtaining review of, and relief from, any discretionary disqualification imposed by an administrative agency, civil court or other government official. On review, an individual might seek to argue that engaging in the conduct underlying the conviction is not a substantial basis for imposing the penalty; or that individuals who engage in the conduct but are not convicted are not subject to the same penalty. The procedures for review and the standard of review should be the same as those applied to review of other decisions by the decisionmaker.

Standard 19–3.3 Unreasonable discrimination

Each jurisdiction should encourage the employment of convicted persons by legislative and executive mandate, through financial incentives and otherwise. In addition, each jurisdiction should enact legislation prohibiting the denial of insurance, or a private professional or occupational license, permit or certification, to a convicted person on grounds related to the conviction, unless engaging in the conduct underlying the conviction would provide a substantial basis for denial even if the person had not been convicted.

QUESTIONS AND POINTS FOR DISCUSSION

1.   How, if at all, would you revise the ABA Standards?

Charging that the collateral consequences of a criminal conviction often serve no penological purpose and impede rehabilitation by relegating ex-offenders to the status of "second-class citizens" and "social outcasts," Professor Nora Demleitner has proposed the following restrictions on the imposition of collateral consequences: First, collateral consequences should only be imposed as part of a court-ordered sentence. Second, sentencing guidelines should guide courts' decisions regarding the inclusion of a collateral consequence as part of the sentence. Third, collateral consequences generally should be imposed only when necessary to prevent future crimes or, in limited situations, when needed to effectuate the retributive goals of the law or to communicate society's disapprobation. Fourth, laws imposing collateral consequences should contain sunset provisions, thereby necessitating legislative review of the laws' effectiveness. Nora V. Demleitner, Preventing Internal Exile: The Need for Restrictions on Collateral Sentencing Consequences, 11 Stan. L. & Pol'y Rev. 153, 154, 158 (1999). Do you concur or disagree with Professor Demleitner's recommendations?

2.   Convicted offenders face an array of employment barriers, including the unwillingness of employers to hire someone with a criminal record. Standard 19–3.3 of the ABA Standards set forth above calls for overcoming this unwillingness by offering employers financial or other incentives to hire individuals with prior convictions. Some states take a different tack, generally

barring employment discrimination because of prior convictions. See, e.g., Wis. Stat. § 111.321 (prohibiting employment discrimination based on "conviction record," subject to several exceptions found in Wis. Stat. § 111.335). To avert such discrimination, a Hawaii statute generally forbids an employer from inquiring about and considering a job applicant's criminal record until after the employer has tendered a conditional job offer to an applicant. Haw. Rev. Stat. § 378–2.5(b). And even then, the employer can withdraw the job offer only if the conviction has a "rational relationship" to the duties and responsibilities of the job. Id.

In your opinion, what steps should the government take to induce employers to hire persons with criminal records? For a proposal to limit the tort liability of employers for negligent hiring when their ex-offender employees injure others, see Leroy D. Clark, A Civil Rights Task: Removing Barriers to Employment of Ex–Convicts, 38 U.S.F.L. Rev. 193, 209–10 (2004).

3. In addition to statutory restrictions, the Constitution may sometimes constrain governments from denying government employment to individuals simply because of their criminal records. The Supreme Court has observed that due process requires at least a "rational connection" between the type of job for which the applicant applied and the criterion which led to the applicant's rejection. See, e.g., Schware v. Board of Bar Examiners, 353 U.S. 232, 239, 77 S.Ct. 752, 756 (1957). This rational-relationship test may not be met in certain circumstances when an applicant's criminal conviction serves as the basis for denial of a government job. In addition, state constitutions may prohibit public as well as private employers from denying a person a job because of a criminal conviction. See, e.g., Nixon v. Commonwealth, 839 A.2d 277, 288–90 (Pa. 2003) (statute prohibiting the hiring of certain individuals with convictions for specified crimes, including burglary, forgery, and felony drug crimes, at facilities providing care to senior citizens violated the state constitutional right to pursue an occupation).

D. THE REINTEGRATION OF RELEASED PRISONERS INTO SOCIETY: AN INTEGRATED APPROACH

To facilitate inmates' reintegration into the community upon their release from prison, Jeremy Travis, the former director of the National Institute for Justice, has advocated the creation of "reentry courts," which are patterned after drug courts. His description of one way in which reentry courts could operate follows:

JEREMY TRAVIS, BUT THEY ALL COME BACK: RETHINKING PRISONER REENTRY
National Institute of Justice (2000).*

* * *

Judges as reentry managers

If a new vision were written on a clean slate, the role of reentry management would best be assigned, in my view, to the sentencing judge,

* This document was originally published in 2000 by the National Institute of Justice, U.S. Department of Justice, Washington, D.C. Points of view or opinions expressed in the publication

whose duties would be expanded to create a "reentry court." At the time of sentencing, the judge would say to the offender, "John Smith, you are being sentenced to X years, Y months of which will be served in the community under my supervision. Our goal is to admit you back into our community after you pay your debt for this offense and demonstrate your ability to live by our rules. Starting today, we will develop, with your involvement, a plan to achieve that goal. The plan will require some hard work of you, beginning in prison and continuing—and getting harder—after you return to the community. It will also require that your family, friends, neighbors, and any other people interested in your welfare commit to the goal of your successful return. I will oversee your entire sentence to make sure the goal is achieved, including monitoring your participation in prison programs that prepare you for release. Many other criminal justice agencies—police, corrections, parole, probation, drug treatment, and others—will be part of a team committed to achieving the goal. If you do not keep up your end of the bargain, I will further restrict your liberty, although only in amounts proportionate to your failure. If you commit a crime again after your release, all bets are off. If you do keep up your end of the bargain, it is within my power to accelerate the completion of your sentence, to return privileges that might be lost (such as your right to hold certain kinds of jobs or your right to vote), and to welcome you back to the community."

At the time of sentencing, the judge would also convene the stakeholders who would be responsible for the offender's reentry. They would be asked to focus on that day, perhaps years in the future, when John returns home. How can he be best prepared for that day and for a successful reentry? What does his support network commit to doing to ensure that success? A "community justice officer" (who could be a police officer, probation officer, or parole officer) would also be involved, since there might be special conditions, geared to the neighborhood, that the offender would have to meet.

The judge-centered model described here obviously borrows heavily from the drug court experience. Both feature an ongoing, central role for the judge, a "contract" drawn up between court and offender, discretion on the judge's part to impose graduated sanctions for various levels of failure to meet the conditions imposed, the promise of the end of supervision as an occasion for ceremonial recognition.

---

are those of the author and do not necessarily represent the official position or policies of the U.S. Department of Justice.

Incarceration as a prelude to reentry

If John goes to prison, a significant purpose of his activities behind bars would be preparation for reentry. What does that mean? It depends on the type of offender and the offense, and could include sex offender treatment, job readiness, education and/or training, a residential drug treatment program, and anger management. These activities would also involve people, support systems, and social service and other programs based in John's neighborhood. Drug treatment in prison should be linked to drug treatment in the community, job training should be linked to work outside, and so forth. In other words, mirror support systems should be established so that John can move from one to the other seamlessly upon release.

Even while in prison, John would continue to pay restitution to his victim or to the community he has harmed—tangible, measurable restitution. A lot of time would be spent with John's family, to keep family ties strong and to talk about what John will be like when he returns home. As the release date approached, the circle would widen, as the support system was brought into the prison to discuss how to keep the offender on the straight and narrow after release. Buddy systems would be established and training in the early warning signs of relapse provided. Again, the community justice officer could broker this process. All the while, the judge would be kept apprised of progress.

Setting the terms of release

When released, John would be brought back to court, perhaps the same courtroom where he was sentenced. A public recognition ceremony would be held, before an audience of family and other members of the support team, and the judge would announce that John has completed a milestone in repaying his debt to society. Now, the judge would declare, the success of the next step depends on John, his support system, and the agencies of government represented by the community justice officer.

The terms of the next phase would be clearly articulated. If John's case were typical, he would have to remain drug free, make restitution to his victim and reparation to his community, work to make his community safer, participate in programs that began in prison (work, education, and the like), avoid situations that could trigger relapse, and refrain from committing crime. He would be required to appear in court every month to demonstrate how well the plan was working.

Making the contract work

The judge presiding over a reentry court would be responsible for making sure that John held up his end of the bargain and that the government agencies and the support system were doing their parts. As in drug courts, the court appearances need not be long, drawn-out affairs; the purpose of invoking the authority of the court would be to impress on John that he has important work to do and to mobilize the support network. The power of the court would be invoked sparingly when John failed to make progress. The court would view relapse in its broadest sense and would use the powers at its disposal (to impose prison sentences, greater restrictions on liberty, fines, and similar sanctions) to ensure that John toes the line. His family and other members of his support system would be encouraged to attend these court hearings. The community justice officer would keep the court apprised of neighborhood developments involving the offender. To the extent John became involved in programs that made his community safer, there would be occasion for special commendation. The judge would be empowered by statute to accelerate the end of the period of supervision, to remove such legal restrictions as the ban on voting, and to oversee John's "graduation" from the program—his successful reentry into the community.

This approach would have several benefits. It cuts across organizational boundaries, making it more likely that offenders are both held accountable and supported in fulfilling their part of the reentry bargain. By involving family members, friends, and other interested parties in the reentry plan, it expands the reach of positive influences upon the offender. By creating a supervisory role for judges, the approach gives them far greater capacity to achieve the purposes of sentencing. Most important, by focusing on the inexorable fact that the prison sentence will one day be completed and the offender will come back to live in the community, the approach directs private and public energies and resources toward the goal of successful reintegration.

* * *

QUESTIONS AND POINTS FOR DISCUSSION

1. Some jurisdictions have begun to utilize reentry courts, although their emergence has sparked some concerns. See, e.g., Eric J. Miller, The Therapeutic Effects of Managerial Reentry Courts, 20 Fed. Sent. R. 127 (2007). Do you support the use of reentry courts? Why or why not? If you favor the establishment of reentry courts, would you structure them in the way described above? As a practical matter, what obstacles might impede the development and operation of reentry courts?

2. Some jurisdictions have developed or begun to develop comprehensive plans to facilitate the reintegration of released prisoners into their communities. See the Michigan Prisoner ReEntry Initiative's website at http://www. michpri.com/index.php?page=home for information about one such endeavor. In 2008, Congress enacted the Second Chance Act of 2007, Pub. L. No. 110–199, 122 Stat. 657, which authorizes federal funding to spur the development of such reentry plans and programs.

What steps do you believe can and should be taken, both while prisoners are incarcerated and after their release, to facilitate their successful reentry back into society and reduce recidivism rates? After identifying these steps, compare your ideas with the thirty-five recommendations contained in the Report of the Re–Entry Policy Council: Charting the Safe and Successful

Return of Prisoners to the Community (2005), available at http://www. reentrypolicy.org/report/download. For additional information on the barriers hindering inmates' successful return to their communities and recommendations for overcoming those barriers, see Jeremy Travis & Michelle Waul, Prisoners Once Removed: The Impact of Incarceration and Reentry on Children, Families, and Communities (2003); Joan Petersilia, When Prisoners Come Home (2003); and Invisible Punishment: The Collateral Consequences of Mass Imprisonment (Marc Mauer & Meda Chesney–Lind eds., 2002).

PART 2

THE LAW AND POLICY OF CORRECTIONS

■ ■ ■

CHAPTER 10

PRISONERS' RIGHTS: AN INTRODUCTION

. . .

A. CONSTITUTIONAL RIGHTS FOR PRISONERS?

This section of the book focuses on the rights of prisoners and pretrial detainees. Pretrial detainees typically are individuals incarcerated while awaiting trial on criminal charges. The lower courts are divided on the question whether a person who has been convicted, but not yet sentenced, is to be considered a pretrial detainee or a prisoner when analyzing a claim contesting conditions or treatment within a jail during the time between entry of the judgment of conviction and the imposition of a sentence. Compare Tilmon v. Prator, 368 F.3d 521, 523–24 (5th Cir. 2004) (an inmate who has been convicted, but not yet sentenced, is like a sentenced prisoner, not a pretrial detainee, for purposes of determining his rights during disciplinary proceedings) with Fuentes v. Wagner, 206 F.3d 335, 341 & n. 7 (3d Cir. 2000) (a convicted, but not yet sentenced, inmate has the status of a pretrial detainee). But as for pretrial detainees awaiting trial, the starting point for defining their rights clearly is different because they retain a presumption of innocence on the charges filed against them. However, as will be seen in the materials that follow, the differences, in terms of the outcomes of lawsuits, between prisoners and pretrial detainees contesting the constitutionality of the conditions of their confinement are often illusory.

To many people, the phrase, "prisoners' rights," is an oxymoron, a combination of inherently contradictory words. The United States Supreme Court, thus far, has disagreed. According to the Court, "[t]here is no iron curtain drawn between the Constitution and the prisons of this country." Wolff v. McDonnell, 418 U.S. 539, 555–56, 94 S.Ct. 2963, 2974–75 (1974). Prisoners, no matter how incorrigible, no matter how despicable their crimes, do have rights. They have rights derived from the United States Constitution; they have rights under state constitutions; and they have rights under certain statutes and regulations. The basic premise that prisoners have rights under the United States Constitution is one, however, whose soundness should still be explored, because the force or lack of force of the reasons for concluding that prisoners have rights may affect the scope of those rights and the extent to which they are protected vigilantly by the courts and correctional officials.

Before reading the materials in this section of the book, consider these fundamental questions: (1) In your opinion, do and should prisoners have rights under the Constitution? (2) Why or why not? (3) Assuming that prisoners retain rights under the Constitution, what should be the scope of those rights?

The European Prison Rules are grounded on the premise that "[i]mprisonment is by the deprivation of liberty a punishment in itself." Committee of Ministers, Council of Europe, European Prison Rules, Recommendation No. 102.2 (2006). The rules therefore direct that prison conditions and practices not "aggravate the suffering" that inheres in incarceration. Do you agree with the premise underlying this rule: that people are sent to prison "as punishment, not for punishment"? Battle v. Anderson, 564 F.2d 388, 395 (10th Cir. 1977). Do you agree with the way in which the ABA Standard set forth below, Standard 23–1.1 of the American Bar Association's Standards for Criminal Justice: Legal Status of Prisoners (1981), defines the scope of prisoners' rights?

Standard 23–1.1 General Principle

Prisoners retain the rights of free citizens except:

(a) As specifically provided to the contrary in these standards; or

(b) When restrictions are necessary to assure their orderly confinement and interaction; or

(c) When restrictions are necessary to provide reasonable protection for the rights and physical safety of all members of the prison system and the general public.

B. HISTORY OF PRISONERS' RIGHTS— A GENERAL OVERVIEW

1. SLAVES OF THE STATE—THROUGH THE 1800s

RUFFIN v. THE COMMONWEALTH

Court of Appeals of Virginia, 1871.
62 Va. 790.

CHRISTIAN, J., delivered the opinion of the court.

[Woody Ruffin, an inmate in a Virginia penitentiary, killed a correctional officer while in Bath County, Virginia. Charged with murder, he was tried by a jury in Richmond, Virginia under a state statute directing that all criminal trials of inmates confined in a state penitentiary be held in Richmond. After being found guilty and sentenced to hang, Ruffin appealed. He contended that the failure to have his guilt adjudicated by a jury comprised of people from Bath County violated his state constitutional right to be tried by "an impartial jury of his vicinage."]

We have said that a reasonable and not a literal construction must be given to the clause under consideration, and a construction that is consistent with the other declarations of general principles in the same instrument. One of these declarations is, "that government is instituted for the common benefit, protection and security of the people." Now one of the most effectual means of promoting the common benefit and ensuring the protection and security of the people, is the certain punishment and prevention of crime. It is essential to the safety of society, that those who violate its criminal laws should suffer punishment. A convicted felon, whom the law in its humanity punishes by confinement in the penitentiary instead of with death, is subject while undergoing that punishment, to all the laws which the Legislature in its wisdom may enact for the government of that institution and the control of its inmates. For the time being, during his term of service in the penitentiary, he is in a state of penal servitude to the State. He has, as a consequence of his crime, not only forfeited his liberty, but all his personal rights except those which the law in its humanity accords to him. He is for the time being the slave of the State. He is *civiliter mortuus;* and his estate, if he has any, is administered like that of a dead man.

The bill of rights is a declaration of general principles to govern a society of freemen, and not of convicted felons and men civilly dead. Such men have some rights it is true, such as the law in its benignity accords to them, but not the rights of free men. * * *

When a convict in the penitentiary, while undergoing punishment for the crime of which he stands convicted, commits other offen[s]es, it is unquestionably in the power of the State, to which his penal servitude is due, to prescribe, through its Legislature, the mode of punishment as well as the manner of his trial. * * *

* * * If he has forfeited this right, which every freeman may claim, "a trial by a jury of his vicinage," that forfeiture is a consequence of his crime, and is one of the penalties which the law denounces against a convicted felon, as much one of the penalties attached to his crime, as the whipping post, the iron mask, the gag, or the dungeon, which is provided for offen[s]es other than felonies. He is for the time being a slave, in a condition of penal servitude to the State, and is subject to such laws and regulations as the State may choose to prescribe.

We are therefore of opinion, that there was no error in the refusal of the Circuit [C]ourt of Richmond either to remand the prisoner to the county of Bath for trial, or to send to said county for a jury to try him. * * *

Ruffin v. The Commonwealth reflected the general notion prevailing in the United States up through the 1800s that prisoners have no rights. As part of the penalty suffered for having committed a crime, a convict sentenced to prison lost the protection afforded by state and federal constitutions.

2. THE "HANDS–OFF DOCTRINE"— THE EARLY TO MID–1900s

The notion that prisoners have no rights gradually was displaced in the 1900s by a different approach to prisoners' claims asserting violations of their constitutional rights. The courts adopted what has become known as the "hands-off doctrine." Under this doctrine, the courts refused to adjudicate prisoners' constitutional claims, not necessarily because prisoners have no constitutional rights, but because, whatever their rights, the courts felt that they generally had neither the duty nor the power to define and protect those rights.

Although the court opinions dismissing prisoners' suits during this time were often cursory, some reasons for the "hands-off" approach can be gleaned from the cases. Those reasons include the following:

1. *Separation of Powers*—Some courts expressed the concern that judicial review of prisoners' complaints would usurp the authority of the legislative and executive branches of the government to supervise and operate prisons. See, e.g., Tabor v. Hardwick, 224 F.2d 526, 529 (5th Cir.1955) ("The control of federal penitentiaries is entrusted to the Attorney General of the United States and the Bureau of Prisons who, no doubt, exercise a wise and humane discretion in safeguarding the rights and privileges of prisoners so far as consistent with effective prison discipline. Unless perhaps in extreme cases, the courts should not interfere with the conduct of a prison or its discipline."); Banning v. Looney, 213 F.2d 771, 771 (10th Cir.1954) ("Courts are without power to supervise prison administration or to interfere with the ordinary prison rules or regulations.").

2. *Federalism*—Many courts believed that federal courts' consideration of the claims of state prisoners would encroach on an area falling within the states' domain—the punishment of individuals who have violated state criminal laws. See, e.g., United States ex rel. Morris v. Radio Station WENR, 209 F.2d 105, 107 (7th Cir.1953) ("Inmates of State penitentiaries should realize that prison officials are vested with wide discretion in safeguarding prisoners committed to their custody. Discipline reasonably maintained in State prisons is not under the supervisory discretion of federal courts."); Cullum v. California Dep't of Corrections, 267 F.Supp. 524, 525 (N.D.Cal.1967) ("[I]nternal matters in state penitentiaries are the sole concern of the state except under exceptional circumstances.").

3. *Maintenance of Institutional Security and Furtherance of Correctional Goals*—The courts were also concerned that judicial inter-

ference in the operation of prisons would cause security and discipline problems and frustrate the purposes of incarceration. Underlying this concern was the belief that judges, untrained in the complexities of prison administration, might not fully understand the need for certain prison rules and practices and, as a result, might render decisions adversely affecting prison security or the goals of incarceration. In addition, some courts were concerned that if prison officials knew that their actions were subject to judicial oversight, they might be dissuaded from taking the steps necessary to maintain order in the prisons out of fear that their actions would lead to lawsuits and possibly liability. See, e.g., id. at 525 ("[I]f every time a guard were called upon to maintain order he had to consider his possible tort liabilities it might unduly limit his actions. Such limitation may jeopardize his safety as well as the safety of other prisoners."). Finally, some courts were troubled by the complications and security problems that would attend the transporting of prisoners, whether parties or witnesses, to court. See, e.g., Tabor v. Hardwick, 224 F.2d 526, 529 (5th Cir.1955) ("[P]enitentiary wardens and the courts might be swamped with an endless number of unnecessary and even spurious lawsuits filed by inmates in remote jurisdictions in the hope of obtaining leave to appear at the hearing of any such case, with the consequent disruption of prison routine and concomitant hazard of escape from custody.").

4. *The Burdens of Processing Pro Se Inmates' Complaints*—This reason for dismissing the complaints of prisoners, who typically represented themselves and had little knowledge of the law and court procedures, was generally camouflaged in the courts' opinions. At most, some courts were willing to acknowledge a concern about being overrun by frivolous lawsuits filed by prisoners if the courts adjudicated their claims. See, e.g., Stroud v. Swope, 187 F.2d 850, 852 (9th Cir.1951) ("Aside from the purely legal aspects of this case very practical considerations militate against granting to appellant the relief for which he prays for to do so would open the door to a flood of applications from federal prisoners which would seriously hamper the administration of our prison system.").

3. THE PRISONERS' RIGHTS ERA—THE 1960s AND '70s

Even before the 1960s, a few courts were troubled by, and refused to apply, the "hands-off doctrine." See, e.g., Coffin v. Reichard, 143 F.2d 443 (6th Cir.1944). The idea that prisoners have rights that the courts are bound to protect, however, was not accepted by most courts until the 1960s and 1970s. During those decades, the "hands-off doctrine" was implicitly and sometimes expressly repudiated as courts, with increasing frequency, agreed to review claims of prisoners alleging violations of their constitutional rights. The movement to discard the "hands-off doctrine" reached its pinnacle when the Supreme Court, in a series of opinions, acknowledged that prisoners have constitutional rights for whose protection the courts have responsibility. See, e.g., Cruz v. Beto, 405 U.S. 319, 92 S.Ct. 1079 (1972) (freedom of religion); Wolff v. McDonnell, 418 U.S. 539, 94 S.Ct. 2963 (1974) (procedural due process); Pell v. Procunier, 417 U.S. 817, 94 S.Ct. 2800 (1974) (freedom of speech).

a. Reasons for the Abandonment of the "Hands–Off Doctrine"

Several explanations have been proffered for the courts' turnabout in the 1960s and 1970s. First, prisoners during this time became more outspoken, and even militant, as they clamored for recognition of their constitutional rights. During this time of civil-rights demonstrations, school integrations, Vietnam war protests, and ghetto riots, the nation's prisons, like the rest of the country, were marked by ferment and turmoil.

Second, in the 1960s and 1970s, more lawyers became concerned about civil rights and receptive to the idea of helping prisoners bring suits to vindicate their constitutional rights. With the development of a civil-liberties bar and the more effective presentation of prisoners' claims, it became more difficult for the courts to ignore some of the allegations about what was transpiring in the nation's prisons. Set forth below, for example, is an account of the conditions in Alabama prisons observed during a tour of the Alabama prison system in 1975 by attorneys from the American Civil Liberties Union's National Prison Project and expert witnesses hired to testify on the prisoners' behalf. The revelation of these conditions to the court led to the landmark decision in *James v. Wallace*, now known as Pugh v. Locke, 406 F.Supp. 318 (M.D. Ala. 1976), that conditions in the Alabama prison system violated both the Eighth and Fourteenth Amendments. The court consequently issued a comprehensive injunction to abate those unconstitutional conditions.

MATTHEW L. MYERS, THE ALABAMA CASE: 12 YEARS AFTER *JAMES v. WALLACE*

13 The National Prison Project Journal 8 (Fall 1987).
Reprinted with the permission of the National Prison Project.

* * *

As we approached the Atmore Prison Farm * * * in Southern Alabama, we saw a white man on a horse with a shotgun in his arms pointed at a small group of black men who were chained together, trudging out into a large farm field. Later, we discovered that virtually all of the guards were white men from rural Alabama, that the vast majority of the prisoners were black from urban Alabama, and that white prisoners were rarely assigned to work in the farm fields.

After two solid days of inspecting every corner of the Atmore Prison Farm and the nearby Holman Maximum Security Facility in sweltering heat, Ralph Knowles, Dr. Clements, and I thought that nothing new that we saw could have an impact on us. For two days we had been surrounded by prisoners crowded into filthy, unbearably hot, unsanitary dormitories so unsafe that the prison guards were afraid to go inside. Beds were stretched six across and stacked three high, only inches apart, and inches from exposed electrical wires hanging down from sockets where lights had once appeared. Only a few feet from this living area were leaking, non-functioning bathrooms with one or at most two functioning toilets for two to three hundred men from which smells emanated which defied description. Everywhere we went we were engulfed in a sea of humanity of men who endured unrelenting idleness, a constant fear of being raped or stabbed and virtually no hope that these conditions or their lives would ever improve.

We thought nothing could be worse that what we had already seen. We were wrong. I will never forget the fear we saw the next morning in the eyes of the young men—boys is a more apt description—crammed into the so-called modern classification center at Mt. Meigs, Alabama in conditions even more crowded than those we had seen at Atmore and Holman. Every available inch of floor space was occupied by prisoners waiting to be shipped to one of the other prisons. Many were forced to sleep beneath cracked and broken toilets and urinals which often leaked or overflowed because they no longer worked properly.

It didn't take long to understand what caused the fear. The dormitories were so dangerous that no guard dared venture inside. Even during our tour the warden warned us repeatedly that we were entering at our own risk. We later heard story after story of prisoners being raped and brutalized, including one retarded teenaged prisoner with the I.Q. of a five-year-old who was raped five times the first night he was at Mt. Meigs and brutally beaten the second night, after his pleas for help to the warden fell on deaf ears.

From Mt. Meigs we went to the Draper Correctional Center. Nothing we saw previously had prepared us for what we later encountered at Draper. It is hard to describe the reaction each of us felt as we climbed up to one second floor dormitory to find dozens upon dozens of old, helpless men, many in wheelchairs, incontinent or bedridden, unable to care for themselves and jammed into squalid, dilapidated living quarters which could only be described as a human death trap. But we had not yet witnessed the worst.

We had heard rumors of a segregation unit at Draper known as the "doghouse." Several hundred yards from the main prison facility, we found the infamous "doghouse." It was a concrete building with no windows and a solid front door with eight cells, each about the size of a small door. The windowless concrete building and the cells in it had no lights, no ventilation, no toilets, no furniture, no beds, no running water, and no sinks or showers. In each cell there was a single hole in the concrete floor for the men to use in place of a toilet. There was no guard in or near the building when we arrived. Prisoners in the doghouse received one meal a day, but were allowed no utensils. They were not permitted to leave their cell for any purpose. Two of the cells were empty, while each of the other four-foot by eight-foot cells contained either five or six prisoners. There wasn't room for them all to sit on the floor at the same time, let alone sleep.

What heinous act had these men committed to be condemned to such barbaric conditions? Several were there because they had been late to work. Several others were there for "talking back" to a prison guard. On the day we visited none were there for having committed an act of violence.

The risk of recounting these observations is that they give the impression that the Alabama prison system in 1975 was truly different from any other prison system in the United States. It wasn't. * * * [W]hile the conditions we found in Alabama were more visible than elsewhere, they were not qualitatively different. What we saw in Alabama in 1975—the overcrowding, the racial disparity and animosity between the guard staff and the prisoners, the unrelenting idleness, the constant fear of being raped or stabbed, the justifiable lack of hope, and the total irrationality of the treatment—has been seen in prison system after prison system all over the country.

A series of prison disturbances and riots were a third reason for the decline of the hands-off doctrine. The 1971 riot that resulted in forty-three deaths at the Attica State Prison in New York particularly jolted the nation, alerting the public, including judges, to the problems plaguing the nation's prisons. As knowledge about prison conditions and practices became more widespread, the courts' confidence that the executive and legislative branches would not abuse their authority to operate and supervise prisons became shaken, and it became more difficult for judges to say that the claims of prisoners, even those asserting flagrant constitutional violations and deprivations of basic human needs, were none of the courts' business.

Finally, with the advent of the "Warren Court" in 1953 came a commitment to protect the constitutional rights of disfavored minorities. The Warren Court, for example, expansively interpreted the rights of individuals accused of committing crimes, rendering such seminal decisions as Miranda v. Arizona, 384 U.S. 436, 86 S.Ct. 1602 (1966) (*Miranda* warnings and valid waiver must precede custodial interrogation); Mapp v. Ohio, 367 U.S. 643, 81 S.Ct. 1684 (1961) (Fourth Amendment exclusionary rule applicable to states through the Due Process Clause of the Fourteenth Amendment); and Katz v. United States, 389 U.S. 347, 88 S.Ct. 507 (1967) (Fourth Amendment protection not limited to physical intrusions). The same concern about protecting individuals from the abuse of governmental authority that underlay the Supreme Court's opinions involving the rights of the criminally accused also made the Court amenable to recognizing and protecting the rights of individuals incarcerated following their convictions.

For a discussion of the way in which the above events contributed to the abandonment of the "hands-off doctrine," see Michael B. Mushlin, 1 Rights of Prisoners 15–18 (3d ed. 2002).

b. The Role of Legal Developments in the Discarding of the "Hands–Off Doctrine"

Several developments in the law in the 1960s contributed to the abandonment of the "hands-off doctrine." Of central importance was the Supreme Court's decision in Monroe v. Pape, 365 U.S. 167, 81 S.Ct. 473 (1961). In that case, the plaintiffs brought suit after thirteen Chicago police officers allegedly entered the plaintiffs' home without a warrant and forced the plaintiffs to stand nude in the living room while their home was searched. The civil-rights statute under which the lawsuit was brought, 42 U.S.C. § 1983, provides in part as follows:

> Every person who, under color of any statute, ordinance, regulation, custom, or usage, of any State or Territory or the District of Columbia, subjects or causes to be subjected, any citizen of the United States or other person within the jurisdiction thereof to the deprivation of any rights, privileges, or immunities secured by the Constitution and laws, shall be liable to the party injured in an action at law, suit in equity, or other proper proceeding for redress * * *.

At issue in *Monroe v. Pape* was the meaning of the § 1983 requirement that the person sued must have acted "under color of" a state "statute, ordinance, regulation, custom, or usage" to be liable. The defendants in *Monroe* argued that this requirement had not been met, because the actions of the police officers were not authorized by any state laws or customs and in fact, were contrary to certain provisions of the Illinois Constitution and state statutes. In an opinion written by Justice Douglas, the Supreme Court responded that § 1983 was enacted in large part because of the failure of state governments in the south to control the lawlessness sparked by activities of the Ku Klux Klan following the Civil War. To Congress, it did not matter whether this failure was due to the reluctance of the state governments to rein in the Ku Klux Klan or simply to their inability to do so; what mattered was that, without this legislation providing a federal remedy for the violation of constitutional rights, the rights of citizens would remain unvindicated. Section 1983 therefore was directed against state officials whose "prejudice, passion, neglect, intolerance, or otherwise" caused the violation or nonenforcement of others' constitutional rights. Id. at 180, 81 S.Ct. at 480.

Congress's recognition that the availability of a state remedy in theory did not necessarily mean that a state remedy was available in practice influenced the Supreme Court's interpretation of § 1983 in *Monroe v. Pape*. The Court held that for activities to have been taken "under color of" state law, it was not necessary that the activities be authorized by state law. The statutory requirement would be satisfied as long as there was " '[m]isuse of power, possessed by virtue of state law and made possible only because the wrongdoer is clothed with the authority of state law.' " Id. at 184, 81 S.Ct. at 482 (quoting United States v. Classic, 313 U.S. 299, 326, 61 S.Ct. 1031, 1043 (1941)).

Monroe v. Pape therefore put to rest the notion that state officials did not act "under color of" state law, as required by § 1983, if they violated state law at the same time federal constitutional rights were allegedly violated. That notion had lent support to courts previously opting to refrain from adjudicating prisoners' constitutional claims. See, e.g., United States ex rel. Atterbury v. Ragen, 237 F.2d 953, 954–55 (7th Cir.1956).

A further development in the case law that facilitated review by the courts of prisoners' constitutional claims occurred when the Supreme Court in the 1960s held that a number of constitutional protections found in the Bill of Rights operated, through the Due Process Clause of the Fourteenth Amendment, as constraints on the states. Although there were numerous decisions during that decade in which the Court found that restrictions in the first ten amendments to the Constitution had been selectively incorporated into the Due Process Clause, the most important decision for prisoners wanting to challenge the conditions of their confinement or their treatment in state prisons was Robinson v. California, 370 U.S. 660, 82 S.Ct. 1417 (1962). In *Robinson,* the Court held that the Eighth Amendment right not to be subjected to cruel and unusual punishment was a right not to be infringed upon by the states as well as the federal government. In previous years, the Supreme Court had held that other rights of which prisoners frequently try to avail themselves, such as the First Amendment rights to freedom of speech and religious freedom and the Fourth Amendment right to be free from unreasonable searches and seizures, were applicable to the states through the Due Process Clause. See, e.g., Stromberg v. California, 283 U.S. 359, 368, 51 S.Ct. 532, 535 (1931) (freedom of speech); Cantwell v. Connecticut, 310 U.S. 296, 303, 60 S.Ct. 900, 903 (1940) (freedom of religion); Wolf v. Colorado, 338 U.S. 25, 27–28, 69 S.Ct. 1359, 1361 (1949) (Fourth Amendment).

4. PRISONERS' RIGHTS TODAY

The courts have now held that prisoners do have constitutional rights and that those rights are to be protected by the courts. For example, according to the Supreme Court, prisoners have First Amendment free-speech rights, the right to religious freedom, the right to marry, a right of access to the courts, the right to equal protection of the law, some procedural-due-process rights, and the right to be free from cruel and unusual punishment.

At the same time, as will be seen in subsequent chapters, vestiges of the "hands-off doctrine" remain. In a number of cases, the Supreme

Court, in rejecting prisoners' claims, has underscored the deference with which the courts should treat the judgments of correctional officials as to what is needed to protect institutional security and further correctional goals. The reasons given for this deference are many of the same reasons which underlay the "hands-off doctrine"—separation of powers, federalism, judges' lack of expertise in correctional matters, and a concern that judicial intervention will undermine institutional security and the purposes of incarceration and inundate the courts with prisoners' complaints.

In addition, the Supreme Court has excluded prisoners completely from the protections afforded by some constitutional provisions. For example, the Court held in Hudson v. Palmer, 468 U.S. 517, 104 S.Ct. 3194 (1984), infra page 680, that courts should not consider prisoners' claims asserting that searches of their cells contravened the Fourth Amendment. According to the Court, prisoners' cells simply are not protected by the Fourth Amendment.

Some observers of the Supreme Court, and even members of the Court, see the resurrection of the "hands-off doctrine" in these Supreme Court cases spurning prisoners' constitutional claims. Franklin A. Kaufman, Reflections of a Federal Judge, in 1 Prisoners and the Law 1–3, 1–7 (2008); Hudson v. Palmer, 468 U.S. 517, 555, 104 S.Ct. 3194, 3215 (1984) (Stevens J., concurring in part and dissenting in part) ("[T]he Court takes the 'hands off' approach to prison administration that I thought it had abandoned forever. . . ."). These individuals fear that prisoners' rights, as a practical matter, are becoming largely a legal and historical anachronism.

Others only see the Supreme Court giving effect to the common-sense proposition that the Constitution cannot apply fully in the prison setting. Kaufman, supra, at 1–7. Under this view, the Court is simply struggling to balance the imperatives of institutional security and the purposes of incarceration, on the one hand, against the interest of prisoners as well as the public in ensuring that all people in this country, including prisoners, receive the basic protection from arbitrary and oppressive governmental actions that the Constitution was designed to afford. As the Court attempts to reach the appropriate balance between these competing concerns, some constitutional rights will be excluded from the prison domain while others, although affording some protection to prisoners, will be applied in a diluted fashion.

Correctional attorney William Collins has opined that the Supreme Court has moved into the "one-hand-on, one-hand-off era" of prisoners' rights. William C. Collins, Correctional Law for the Correctional Officer 13 (4th ed. 2004). As you read in the ensuing chapters of this book the Supreme Court's decisions construing the scope of prisoners' constitutional rights, consider whether you concur with this description of the Court's approach to prisoners' rights. Consider also whether the Court in each decision accurately has interpreted the balance struck by the Constitution between the competing concerns alluded to above.

C. THE PURPOSES OF INCARCERATION

In cases analyzing prisoners' constitutional claims, the courts have repeatedly expressed a concern that their decisions not unduly interfere with the objectives purportedly served by incarcerating criminal offenders. The courts have obviously taken these objectives, as well as the governmental interests in maintaining prison security, order, and discipline, into account when defining the parameters of the rights of prisoners. A brief review of the primary purposes of imprisonment therefore seems in order.

When touting the benefits of imprisonment, commentators and government officials customarily point to at least four purposes of incarceration:

1. *Incapacitation*—What this benefit means is that while individuals are in prison, they will be physically "incapacitated" or unable to commit many crimes that they might otherwise commit. In the past, the focus of this penological objective primarily has been on protecting members of the public by limiting the physical mobility of convicted offenders. It is, though, common knowledge that the criminal activities of many prisoners persist while in prison. Prisoners, with disturbing frequency, steal from each other, sell drugs to each other, rape each other, and kill each other. Prisoners also assault, rape, maim, and kill correctional officers and other prison employees. To the extent that the purpose of confining convicted criminals is viewed to be the prevention of *any* crimes during the time of confinement and the protection of *all* persons from victimization, regardless of employment status or criminal record, the courts may condone even greater restrictions on the claimed rights of prisoners.

2. *Deterrence*—Incarceration is said to further two types of deterrence—specific and general. Specific deterrence refers to the effect that imprisonment is hoped to have on the particular individual imprisoned. This objective of incarceration is realized if the offender, upon release from prison, commits no further crimes because of the desire to avoid returning to prison.

General deterrence, as the name suggests, concerns the broader impact that the imprisonment sanction may have on society in general. This purpose of incarceration is served when members of the public refrain from criminal activity because of their fear of imprisonment.

3. *Rehabilitation*—The rehabilitative objective is somewhat similar to the goal of specific deterrence, at least in terms of the end result following the realization of either goal. Both penological objectives, when achieved, result in prisoners refraining from criminal activity after release from prison. One difference between the two objectives is in the reason why the released prisoners refrain from further crimes. Prisoners who spurn further criminal activity because

they have been deterred by what they experienced when previously imprisoned are motivated by an aversion to incarceration; by contrast, prisoners who abide by the law after release from prison because they are rehabilitated are reacting to an aversion, though newfound, to crime itself.

4. *Retribution*—What retribution basically means is that the individuals convicted of crimes are being incarcerated to punish them for their crimes. In other words, through incarceration, society is retaliating against, or exacting vengeance on, the prisoners for the crimes they have committed. This retributive aim of incarceration is purportedly, though it sometimes seems just theoretically, subject to a limiting principle known as "just deserts." Under this principle, prisoners are to be punished no more harshly than warranted by the severity of the crime of which they have been convicted. This principle, if properly applied, will place limits, for example, on the length of time that a person is imprisoned.

QUESTIONS AND POINTS FOR DISCUSSION

1. As noted above, to the extent that courts take into account penological goals when defining prisoners' rights, a broader interpretation of what the goal of incapacitation means may lead to a more restrictive interpretation of the scope of prisoners' rights. Would the other penological goals of deterrence, both specific and general, rehabilitation, and retribution support a more expansive or contracted definition of the rights of prisoners?

2. At least some of the goals of incarceration may be conflicting. For example, if the deprivation of freedom that attends incarceration is not, by itself, considered enough to meet the goal of retribution, additional steps taken to make imprisonment a sufficiently onerous and unpleasant experience to satisfy retributive aims may thwart attempts to rehabilitate the offender.

Any tension between the goals of retribution and rehabilitation would be of no concern if either goal were abandoned as a purpose of incarceration. Some commentators have urged that rehabilitation not be considered a reason for imprisonment. They have argued that to believe that prisoners can be forced to become penitent and regard with disdain a further life of crime is to engage in fantasy. See, e.g., Norval Morris, The Future of Imprisonment 14 (1974). Under this view, prisons are not, and cannot be, rehabilitative; prisoners are either incorrigible or will reform themselves because of internal forces rather than external pressures.

3. Even if the rehabilitation of prisoners, in the sense of forcing them to become "better," is an unrealistic goal, should one penological objective be to ensure that prisoners do not become "worse" or more criminally inclined because of their prison experiences? How would this goal of preventing any criminal propensities of an individual from being nurtured while the individual was in prison affect the balance for or against the recognition of prisoners' rights?

4. Retribution as an object of punishment has been attacked over the years. Opponents of retribution argue that for society to act out of revenge when imposing criminal sanctions is unseemly and uncivilized. See, e.g., Karl Menninger, The Crime of Punishment 190–218 (1968). Others respond that to deny that one purpose of these sanctions is to punish is delusive. See, e.g., Norval Morris, The Future of Imprisonment 58–60 (1974) (approving a retributive aim for punishment, but underscoring that the punishment imposed should be no more severe than what the offender deserves); K.G. Armstrong, The Retributivist Hits Back, Theories of Punishment 19–40 (Stanley E. Grupp ed. 1971).

5. Review pages 4–26 for additional information about the purposes of criminal sanctions, including prison sentences.

CHAPTER 11

FIRST AMENDMENT RIGHTS

■ ■ ■

A. FREEDOM OF SPEECH

The First Amendment to the United States Constitution provides in part that "Congress shall make no law ... abridging the freedom of speech." This constitutional provision serves as a restraint on the states as well, through operation of the Due Process Clause of the Fourteenth Amendment. 44 Liquormart, Inc. v. Rhode Island, 517 U.S. 484, 489 n.1, 116 S.Ct. 1495, 1501 n.1 (1996).

In a number of cases, the Supreme Court has considered the application of the First Amendment in the correctional setting. One of these cases is set forth below.

PROCUNIER v. MARTINEZ
Supreme Court of the United States, 1974.
416 U.S. 396, 94 S.Ct. 1800, 40 L.Ed.2d 224.

MR. JUSTICE POWELL delivered the opinion of the Court.

This case concerns the constitutionality of certain regulations promulgated by appellant Procunier in his capacity as Director of the California Department of Corrections. Appellees brought a class action on behalf of themselves and all other inmates of penal institutions under the Department's jurisdiction to challenge the rules relating to censorship of prisoner mail * * *.

* * *

* * * Under these regulations, correspondence between inmates of California penal institutions and persons other than licensed attorneys and holders of public office was censored for nonconformity to certain standards. * * * Rule 1201 directed inmates not to write letters in which they "unduly complain" or "magnify grievances." Rule 1205(d) defined as contraband writings "expressing inflammatory political, racial, religious or other views or beliefs...." Finally, Rule 2402(8) provided that inmates "may not send or receive letters that pertain to criminal activity; are lewd, obscene, or defamatory; contain foreign matter, or are otherwise inappropriate."

Prison employees screened both incoming and outgoing personal mail for violations of these regulations. No further criteria were provided to help members of the mailroom staff decide whether a particular letter contravened any prison rule or policy. When a prison employee found a letter objectionable, he could take one or more of the following actions: (1) refuse to mail or deliver the letter and return it to the author; (2) submit a disciplinary report, which could lead to suspension of mail privileges or other sanctions; or (3) place a copy of the letter or a summary of its contents in the prisoner's file, where it might be a factor in determining the inmate's work and housing assignments and in setting a date for parole eligibility.

The District Court held that the regulations relating to prisoner mail authorized censorship of protected expression without adequate justification in violation of the First Amendment and that they were void for vagueness. The court also noted that the regulations failed to provide minimum procedural safeguards against error and arbitrariness in the censorship of inmate correspondence. Consequently, it enjoined their continued enforcement.

* * *

Traditionally, federal courts have adopted a broad hands-off attitude toward problems of prison administration. * * * Prison administrators are responsible for maintaining internal order and discipline, for securing their institutions against unauthorized access or escape, and for rehabilitating, to the extent that human nature and inadequate resources allow, the inmates placed in their custody. The Herculean obstacles to effective discharge of these duties are too apparent to warrant explication. Suffice it to say that the problems of prisons in America are complex and intractable, and, more to the point, they are not readily susceptible of resolution by decree. Most require expertise, comprehensive planning, and the commitment of resources, all of which are peculiarly within the province of the legislative and executive branches of government. For all of those reasons, courts are ill equipped to deal with the increasingly urgent problems of prison administration and reform.[9] * * * Moreover, where state penal institutions are involved, federal courts have a further reason for deference to the appropriate prison authorities.

But a policy of judicial restraint cannot encompass any failure to take cognizance of valid constitutional claims whether arising in a federal or state institution. When a prison regulation or practice offends a fundamental constitutional guarantee, federal courts will discharge their duty to protect constitutional rights. * * *

* * *

---

9. * * * Moreover, the capacity of our criminal justice system to deal fairly and fully with legitimate claims will be impaired by a burgeoning increase of frivolous prisoner complaints. * * *

* * * In determining the proper standard of review for prison restrictions on inmate correspondence, we have no occasion to consider the extent to which an individual's right to free speech survives incarceration, for a narrower basis of decision is at hand. In the case of direct personal correspondence between inmates and those who have a particularized interest in communicating with them,[11] mail censorship implicates more than the right of prisoners.

* * * Whatever the status of a prisoner's claim to uncensored correspondence with an outsider, it is plain that the latter's interest is grounded in the First Amendment's guarantee of freedom of speech. And this does not depend on whether the nonprisoner correspondent is the author or intended recipient of a particular letter, for the addressee as well as the sender of direct personal correspondence derives from the First and Fourteenth Amendments a protection against unjustified governmental interference with the intended communication. * * * The wife of a prison inmate who is not permitted to read all that her husband wanted to say to her has suffered an abridgment of her interest in communicating with him as plain as that which results from censorship of her letter to him. In either event, censorship of prisoner mail works a consequential restriction on the First and Fourteenth Amendment rights of those who are not prisoners.

* * * We therefore turn for guidance, not to cases involving questions of "prisoners' rights," but to decisions of this Court dealing with the general problem of incidental restrictions on First Amendment liberties imposed in furtherance of legitimate governmental activities.

* * *

In *United States v. O'Brien,* 391 U.S. 367 (1968), the Court dealt with incidental restrictions on free speech occasioned by the exercise of the governmental power to conscript men for military service. O'Brien had burned his Selective Service registration certificate on the steps of a courthouse in order to dramatize his opposition to the draft and to our country's involvement in Vietnam. He was convicted of violating a provision of the Selective Service law that had recently been amended to prohibit knowing destruction or mutilation of registration certificates. O'Brien argued that the purpose and effect of the amendment were to abridge free expression and that the statutory provision was therefore unconstitutional, both as enacted and as applied to him. Although O'Brien's activity involved "conduct" rather than pure "speech," the Court did not define away the First Amendment concern, and neither did it rule that the presence of a communicative intent necessarily rendered O'Brien's actions immune to governmental regulation. Instead, it enunciated the following four-part test:

"[A] government regulation is sufficiently justified if it is within the constitutional power of the Government; if it furthers an important or

---

11. Different considerations may come into play in the case of mass mailings. No such issue is raised on these facts, and we intimate no view as to its proper resolution.

substantial governmental interest; if the governmental interest is unrelated to the suppression of free expression; and if the incidental restriction on alleged First Amendment freedoms is no greater than is essential to the furtherance of that interest.''

* * *

The case at hand arises in the context of prisons. One of the primary functions of government is the preservation of societal order through enforcement of the criminal law, and the maintenance of penal institutions is an essential part of that task. The identifiable governmental interests at stake in this task are the preservation of internal order and discipline,[12] the maintenance of institutional security against escape or unauthorized entry, and the rehabilitation of the prisoners. While the weight of professional opinion seems to be that inmate freedom to correspond with outsiders advances rather than retards the goal of rehabilitation, the legitimate governmental interest in the order and security of penal institutions justifies the imposition of certain restraints on inmate correspondence. Perhaps the most obvious example of justifiable censorship of prisoner mail would be refusal to send or deliver letters concerning escape plans or containing other information concerning proposed criminal activity, whether within or without the prison. Similarly, prison officials may properly refuse to transmit encoded messages. * * *

Applying the teachings of our prior decisions to the instant context, we hold that censorship of prisoner mail is justified if the following criteria are met. First, the regulation or practice in question must further an important or substantial governmental interest unrelated to the suppression of expression. Prison officials may not censor inmate correspondence simply to eliminate unflattering or unwelcome opinions or factually inaccurate statements. Rather, they must show that a regulation authorizing mail censorship furthers one or more of the substantial governmental interests of security, order, and rehabilitation. Second, the limitation of First Amendment freedoms must be no greater than is necessary or essential to the protection of the particular governmental interest involved. Thus a restriction on inmate correspondence that furthers an important or substantial interest of penal administration will nevertheless be invalid if its sweep is unnecessarily broad. This does not mean, of course, that prison administrators may be required to show with certainty that adverse consequences would flow from the failure to censor a particular letter. Some latitude in anticipating the probable consequences of allowing certain speech in a prison environment is essential to the proper discharge of an administrator's duty. But any regulation or practice that restricts inmate correspondence must be generally necessary to protect one or more of the legitimate governmental interests identified above.[14]

---

12. We need not and do not address in this case the validity of a temporary prohibition of an inmate's personal correspondence as a disciplinary sanction (usually as part of the regimen of solitary confinement) for violation of prison rules.

14. While not necessarily controlling, the policies followed at other well-run institutions would be relevant to a determination of the need for a particular type of restriction. * * *

On the basis of this standard, we affirm the judgment of the District Court. The regulations invalidated by that court authorized, *inter alia*, censorship of statements that "unduly complain" or "magnify grievances," expression of "inflammatory political, racial, religious or other views," and matter deemed "defamatory" or "otherwise inappropriate." These regulations fairly invited prison officials and employees to apply their own personal prejudices and opinions as standards for prisoner mail censorship. Not surprisingly, some prison officials used the extraordinary latitude for discretion authorized by the regulations to suppress unwelcome criticism. For example, at one institution under the Department's jurisdiction, the checklist used by the mailroom staff authorized rejection of letters "criticizing policy, rules or officials," and the mailroom sergeant stated in a deposition that he would reject as "defamatory" letters "belittling staff or our judicial system or anything connected with [the] Department of Corrections." Correspondence was also censored for "disrespectful comments," "derogatory remarks," and the like.

Appellants have failed to show that these broad restrictions on prisoner mail were in any way necessary to the furtherance of a governmental interest unrelated to the suppression of expression. * * * Appellants contend that statements that "magnify grievances" or "unduly complain" are censored "as a precaution against flash riots and in the furtherance of inmate rehabilitation." But they do not suggest how the magnification of grievances or undue complaining, which presumably occurs in outgoing letters, could possibly lead to flash riots, nor do they specify what contribution the suppression of complaints makes to the rehabilitation of criminals. And appellants defend the ban against "inflammatory political, racial, religious or other views" on the ground that "[s]uch matter clearly presents a danger to prison security...." The regulation, however, is not narrowly drawn to reach only material that might be thought to encourage violence nor is its application limited to incoming letters. In short, the Department's regulations authorized censorship of prisoner mail far broader than any legitimate interest of penal administration demands and were properly found invalid by the District Court.

We also agree with the District Court that the decision to censor or withhold delivery of a particular letter must be accompanied by minimum procedural safeguards. The interest of prisoners and their correspondents in uncensored communication by letter, grounded as it is in the First Amendment, is plainly a "liberty" interest within the meaning of the Fourteenth Amendment even though qualified of necessity by the circumstance of imprisonment. As such, it is protected from arbitrary governmental invasion. The District Court required that an inmate be notified of the rejection of a letter written by or addressed to him, that the author of that letter be given a reasonable opportunity to protest that decision, and that complaints be referred to a prison official other than the person who originally disapproved the correspondence. These requirements do not appear to be unduly burdensome, nor do appellants so contend. Accordingly, we affirm the judgment of the District Court with respect to the Department's regulations relating to prisoner mail.

[Justice Marshall, joined by Justice Brennan, concurred in the Court's judgment. Justice Douglas also wrote a concurring opinion. Both opinions are omitted here.]

QUESTIONS AND POINTS FOR DISCUSSION

1. Left unresolved by the Supreme Court in *Procunier v. Martinez* were the questions whether inmates retain free-speech rights while in prison and if so, to what extent. The Court addressed these questions in Pell v. Procunier, 417 U.S. 817, 94 S.Ct. 2800 (1974). The plaintiffs in that case, four California prison inmates and three journalists, had filed a § 1983 suit challenging the constitutionality of a regulation promulgated by the California Department of Corrections that prohibited media members from conducting face-to-face interviews with individual inmates of their choice. The inmate plaintiffs contended that the regulation violated their free-speech rights, while the media plaintiffs contended that the regulation violated the right to freedom of the press protected by the First and Fourteenth Amendments.

In addressing the inmates' claim, the Supreme Court observed that "a prison inmate retains those First Amendment rights that are not inconsistent with his status as a prisoner or with the legitimate penological objectives of the corrections system." Id. at 822, 94 S.Ct. at 2804. The penological objectives the Court mentioned that might validate a restriction on inmates' First Amendment interests were deterrence, incapacitation, rehabilitation, and the maintenance of institutional security within the prison.

The Court then concluded that the restriction on the inmates' First Amendment interests in this case was constitutional. In arriving at this conclusion, the Court balanced the burden that this restriction placed on the inmates' communicative interests against the governmental interests purportedly justifying the restriction. The Court found the burden on the inmates diminished by the fact that the inmates had alternative ways of communicating with the media—through the mail and through messages sent via family members, attorneys, clergy, and friends who had permission to visit the inmates. Although the Court acknowledged that communicating through the mail might not be a viable alternative for an illiterate inmate unless the inmate received some assistance from someone who was literate, the Court was untroubled by this fact because, in this particular case, there was no indication that inmates who needed assistance had been deprived of it. The Court also emphasized that the regulation was content-neutral—that its application did not hinge on the particular matters a member of the media wanted to discuss with an inmate.

To the extent that the restriction on press interviews did burden the First Amendment interests of inmates, the Supreme Court found this burden outweighed by the interest in institutional security it furthered. Permitting only those individuals with an existing personal or professional relationship to visit a prisoner would preserve institutional security by keeping the number of prison visits at a "manageable level." Id. at 827, 94 S.Ct. at 2806.

The Supreme Court rejected the media plaintiffs' claim grounded on the freedom of the press as well, holding that the press has no broader right of access to prisons than the general public. The Court furthermore noted that if members of the press could select inmates for interviews, the designated inmates might become power figures within the institution, exerting a disproportionate influence on other inmates. Availing themselves of this influence, the inmate power figures then might challenge the authority of prison officials and provoke disturbances. The regulation at issue in this case was designed to forestall this threat to prison security.

Four Justices—Justices Powell, Brennan, Marshall, and Douglas—dissented from the portion of the Court's opinion holding that the regulation prohibiting interviews with designated inmates did not abridge the freedom of the press. The dissenters' principal contention was that since the public is dependent on the press for information about prisons, the press has a right of access to prisons even when members of the public are not afforded the same access. "What is at stake here," observed Justice Powell in a companion case addressing the same issue, "is the societal function of the First Amendment in preserving free public discussion of governmental affairs." Saxbe v. Washington Post Co., 417 U.S. 843, 862, 94 S.Ct. 2811, 2821 (1974) (Powell, J. dissenting). Justice Powell also emphasized that there were less drastic means of achieving the government's objective of preserving institutional security. For example, to control what was denominated the "big wheel phenomenon," the number of interviews that any one inmate could have with members of the press during a certain time period could be limited. Id. at 866, 873, 94 S.Ct. at 2823, 2826 (Powell, J., dissenting). Justice Powell, incidentally, unlike the other three dissenters, concurred in the majority's disposition of the inmates' free-speech claim in *Pell*.

Do you agree with the Court's holdings in *Pell* and *Saxbe* that the media's right of access to prisons is no greater than the public's? Compare Daniel Bernstein, Comment, Slamming the Prison Doors on Media Interviews: California's New Regulations Demonstrate the Need for a First Amendment Right of Access to Inmates, 30 McGeorge L.Rev. 125, 163–64 (1998) (citing disclosures in media interviews with inmates about deficient medical care in prisons, the dearth of drug-treatment and job-training programs, and the intentional burning of an inmate by correctional officers as support for a broader right of media access to prisons than that afforded the general public). What are the potential practical repercussions of the Court's decisions? As a policy matter, what restrictions should be placed on media access to prisons and prisoners?

2. Should the interest in retribution be considered a "legitimate penological objective" that justifies the abridgement of inmates' First Amendment rights? Why or why not? See Hudson v. Palmer, 468 U.S. 517, 524, 104 S.Ct. 3194, 3199 (1984) (stating that restrictions on prisoners' rights serve as "reminders" of the retributive aim of criminal justice).

3. Amy Fisher, who was convicted of attempted murder after shooting her lover's wife, was paid two million dollars by a film-production company for the rights to her story. Orly Nosrati, Note, Son of Sam Laws: Killing Free Speech or Promoting Killer Profits, 20 Whittier L.Rev. 949, 949 (1999). To

prevent criminals like Fisher from reaping financial gains by capitalizing on the notoriety of their crimes, many states have enacted what commonly are called "Son of Sam" laws.

The issue of the constitutionality of the original "Son of Sam" law, which was enacted in New York, came before the Supreme Court in Simon & Schuster, Inc. v. Members of the New York State Crime Victims Bd., 502 U.S. 105, 112 S.Ct. 501 (1991). The statute in question governed certain contracts between members of the media and individuals who had been accused or convicted of a crime or admitted committing one. If, under the contract, the person's crime would be described in a book, magazine, film, or other communications medium, the statute directed that all contract payments be placed in an escrow account for five years. The money in the account then would be made available to pay the claims of crime victims and other creditors of the criminal.

A book publisher that had contracted with an organized-crime figure for a book about his life of crime brought suit challenging this statute on First Amendment grounds. The Supreme Court first noted that because the statute singled out certain speech based on its content, the statute had to be necessary to fulfill a compelling state interest and be narrowly drawn to achieve that purpose in order to survive constitutional scrutiny. The Court acknowledged that the statute in question served two compelling interests— ensuring that crime victims are compensated for the harm they have suffered and ensuring that criminals do not profit from their misdeeds. The Court found, however, that the statute was not narrowly tailored to achieve these objectives. The statute was written so broadly that it encompassed works that touched only tangentially on a person's crime. In addition, it extended to accounts of crimes that had occurred so long ago that the statute of limitations for filing a claim against the criminal had run. In concluding that New York's "Son of Sam" law abridged the First Amendment because it was overinclusive, the Court also cited well-known literary works that would have been subject to the law if it had been in effect at the time of their publication, including Thoreau's *Civil Disobedience* in which he discussed his refusal to pay taxes.

How would you draft a "Son of Sam" law to pass constitutional muster?

4. After *Pell v. Procunier*, the Supreme Court again addressed the First Amendment rights of prisoners in Jones v. North Carolina Prisoners' Labor Union, 433 U.S. 119, 97 S.Ct. 2532 (1977). The plaintiff in that case was a prisoners' labor union whose designated purpose was to improve, through collective bargaining, the working conditions of inmate laborers. A North Carolina statute, however, proscribed collective bargaining on behalf of inmates.

The plaintiff brought suit challenging the constitutionality of three rules promulgated by the North Carolina Department of Correction that inhibited the activities of the labor union in North Carolina prisons. The first rule prohibited inmates from trying to persuade other inmates to join the union. The second barred union meetings in the prison, and the third prohibited the bulk mailing of union materials into the prison. Despite these rules, authorities permitted inmates to be members of the union. In addition, the mailing of union materials to individual inmates was permitted, because individual mailings did not pose the same risk of contraband being smuggled into a prison as bulk mailings.

The prisoners' labor union contended that these three rules impinged upon its constitutional rights and those of its members. Specifically, the union claimed that all of the rules violated the First Amendment guarantee of freedom of speech and that the no-solicitation and no-meeting rules in addition contravened both the First Amendment right to freedom of association and the Fourteenth Amendment right to equal protection of the law. The latter claim was grounded on the fact that other organizations—the Jaycees and Alcoholics Anonymous—were permitted to hold meetings and distribute bulk mailings in the prisons.

State correctional officials defended the regulations, arguing that a prisoners' labor union posed dangers to institutional security. They contended that in furthering the goals of the union, certain union spokesmen could become power figures within the prison, commanding undue influence over other inmates. This influence might be misused, leading to general chaos within the institution, work stoppages, and even riots.

The district court credited this testimony, but noted that there was absolutely no evidence that the union had interfered in the past with the operations of the state's prisons. The court furthermore observed that since correctional officials permitted inmates to join the union, the ban on inmate-to-inmate solicitation to join the union made no sense and therefore violated the First Amendment. The district court also struck down the no-meeting and bulk-mailing rules on equal-protection grounds.

In an opinion written by Justice Rehnquist, the Supreme Court reversed:

> State correctional officials uniformly testified that the concept of a prisoners' labor union was itself fraught with potential dangers, whether or not such a union intended, illegally, to press for collective-bargaining recognition. * * * The District Court did not reject these beliefs as fanciful or erroneous. It, instead, noted that they were held "sincerely," and were arguably correct. Without a showing that these beliefs were unreasonable, it was error for the District Court to conclude that appellants needed to show more. In particular, the burden was not on appellants to show affirmatively that the Union would be "detrimental to proper penological objectives" or would constitute a "present danger to security and order." Rather, "[s]uch considerations are peculiarly within the province and professional expertise of corrections officials, and, in the absence of substantial evidence in the record to indicate that the officials have exaggerated their response to these considerations, courts should ordinarily defer to their expert judgment in such matters."

Id. at 126–28, 97 S.Ct. at 2538.

The Court also disagreed that the no-solicitation and no-meeting rules were unreasonable because inmate membership in the union was permissible. The Court explained: "It is clearly not irrational to conclude that individuals may believe what they want, but that concerted group activity, or solicitation therefor, would pose additional and unwarranted problems and frictions in the State's penal institutions." Id. at 129, 97 S.Ct. at 2539. The Court further observed:

> Appellant prison officials concluded that the presence, perhaps even the objectives, of a prisoners' labor union would be detrimental to order and security in the prisons. It is enough to say that they have not been conclusively shown to be wrong in this view. The interest in preserving order and authority in the prisons is self-evident. Prison life, and relations between the inmates themselves and between the inmates and prison officials or staff, contain the ever-present potential for violent confrontation and conflagration. Responsible prison officials must be permitted to take reasonable steps to forestall such a threat, and they must be permitted to act before the time when they can compile a dossier on the eve of a riot.

Id. at 132–33, 97 S.Ct. at 2541–42.

The Supreme Court therefore concluded that as far as the First Amendment was concerned, the rules were "reasonable" and "consistent with the inmates' status as prisoners and with the legitimate operational considerations of the institution." Id. at 130, 97 S.Ct. at 2540. At the same time, the Court emphasized that an internal grievance mechanism provided inmates with an alternative way of voicing complaints and that inmates could receive individual mailings of union materials.

The Supreme Court also rejected the union's argument that the proscription of bulk mailings of union materials and union meetings violated the right to equal protection of the law. According to the Court, the Equal Protection Clause required only that there be a "rational basis" for treating the union differently than the Jaycees and Alcoholics Anonymous. The Court found such a rational basis here, both because participation by inmates in the Jaycees and Alcoholics Anonymous was considered rehabilitative and because a central goal of the union, unlike the Jaycees and Alcoholics Anonymous, was to engage in an activity—collective bargaining—that was illegal under state law.

Justice Marshall, joined by Justice Brennan, dissented. The dissenters strongly objected to the reasonableness standard propounded by the majority, particularly to that portion of the Court's opinion condoning the curtailment of prisoners' associational activities whenever prison officials "reasonably conclude" that such activities pose the "likelihood" of causing a disruption within the prison or other adverse effects on the institution's legitimate penological objectives. Justice Marshall observed:

> The central lesson of over a half century of First Amendment adjudication is that freedom is sometimes a hazardous enterprise, and that the Constitution requires the State to bear certain risks to preserve our liberty. To my mind, therefore, the fact that appellants have not acted wholly irrationally in banning Union meetings is not dispositive. Rather, I believe that where, as here, meetings would not pose an immediate and substantial threat to the security or rehabilitative functions of the prisons, the First Amendment guarantees Union members the right to associate freely, and the Fourteenth Amendment guarantees them the right to be treated as favorably as members of other inmate organizations. The State can surely regulate the time, place, and manner of the

meetings, and perhaps can monitor them to assure that disruptions are not planned, but the State cannot outlaw such assemblies altogether.

Id. at 146, 97 S.Ct. at 2548.

5.   The Supreme Court's discussion in *Jones* stands in stark contrast to decisions of the Court involving the First Amendment rights of nonprisoners. One such decision is Tinker v. Des Moines Indep. Cmty. Sch. Dist., 393 U.S. 503, 89 S.Ct. 733 (1969), which was cited by Justice Marshall in his dissenting opinion in *Jones*. In that case, in which the Court held unconstitutional the disciplining of high-school and junior-high students who wore black armbands to protest the Vietnam War, the Court stated:

> The District Court concluded that the action of the school authorities was reasonable because it was based upon their fear of a disturbance from the wearing of the armbands. But, in our system, undifferentiated fear or apprehension of disturbance is not enough to overcome the right to freedom of expression. Any departure from absolute regimentation may cause trouble. Any variation from the majority's opinion may inspire fear. Any word spoken, in class, in the lunchroom, or on the campus, that deviates from the views of another person may start an argument or cause a disturbance. But our Constitution says we must take this risk.

Id. at 508, 89 S.Ct. at 737.

Would and should the outcome of *Tinker* have been the same if the persons wearing the black armbands to protest the war had been prisoners? What if prisoners wore black armbands to protest the failure of prison officials to provide adequate protection from assaults by other inmates? Or to protest the food they are fed? Or to protest the refusal of prison officials to provide each inmate with a television?

6.   Bell v. Wolfish, 441 U.S. 520, 99 S.Ct. 1861 (1979) was the next in a series of Supreme Court cases discussing the First Amendment rights of inmates. In *Bell,* the Court addressed the constitutionality of what it called the "publisher-only" rule, a rule in force at the Metropolitan Correctional Center, a federal custodial facility in New York City. Under this rule, prisoners and pretrial detainees only could receive books and magazines mailed to them by publishers, bookstores, and book clubs.

While the case was pending before the Supreme Court, the Bureau of Prisons informed the Court of its plans to amend its rules to permit inmates to receive paperback books and magazines from any source. The restriction with regard to the sources of hardbound books, however, would remain in effect because drugs, money, and other contraband could be hidden so easily in the book bindings and smuggled into the institution. Manually inspecting the pages and bindings of each hardbound book for contraband would be, according to the MCC warden, too time-consuming for the MCC staff.

The Supreme Court concluded that permitting inmates to receive hard-cover books from only publishers, bookstores, and book clubs was a "rational response" to "an obvious security problem." Id. at 550, 99 S.Ct. at 1880. The Court then noted several other factors contributing to its conclusion that the "publisher-only" rule did not violate the First Amendment:

The rule operates in a neutral fashion, without regard to the content of the expression. And there are alternative means of obtaining reading material that have not been shown to be burdensome or insufficient. "[W]e regard the available 'alternative means of [communication as] a relevant factor' in a case such as this where 'we [are] called upon to balance First Amendment rights against [legitimate] governmental ... interests.' " The restriction, as it is now before us, allows soft-bound books and magazines to be received from any source and hardback books to be received from publishers, bookstores, and book clubs. In addition, the MCC has a "relatively large" library for use by inmates. We are also influenced in our decision by the fact that the rule's impact on pretrial detainees is limited to a maximum period of approximately 60 days. See n. 3, supra.[a] In sum, considering all the circumstances, we view the rule, as we now find it, to be a "reasonable 'time, place and manner' regulatio[n that is] necessary to further significant governmental interests...."

Id. at 551–52, 99 S.Ct. at 1880–81.

When conducting its First Amendment analysis, the Court refused to distinguish between pretrial detainees and convicted inmates:

> Neither the Court of Appeals nor the District Court distinguished between pretrial detainees and convicted inmates in reviewing the challenged security practices, and we see no reason to do so. There is no basis for concluding that pretrial detainees pose any lesser security risk than convicted inmates. Indeed, it may be that in certain circumstances they present a greater risk to jail security and order. In the federal system, a detainee is committed to the detention facility only because no other less drastic means can reasonably assure his presence at trial. As a result, those who are detained prior to trial may in many cases be individuals who are charged with serious crimes or who have prior records. They also may pose a greater risk of escape than convicted inmates. This may be particularly true at facilities like the MCC, where the resident convicted inmates have been sentenced to only short terms of incarceration and many of the detainees face the possibility of lengthy imprisonment if convicted.

Id. at 547 n. 28, 99 S.Ct. at 1878 n. 28.

In a dissenting opinion, Justice Marshall objected to what he considered the Court's blunderbuss approach to the First Amendment. Emphasizing that pretrial detainees are presumed to be innocent and often are incarcerated only because they are too poor to post bail, he advocated the following approach to the First Amendment claims of pretrial detainees:

> When assessing the restrictions on detainees, * * * I believe the Government must bear a more rigorous burden of justification than the rational-basis standard mandates. At a minimum, I would require a

---

a. Footnote 3 to which the Court alluded stated:

This group of nondetainees may comprise, on a daily basis, between 40% and 60% of the MCC population. Prior to the District Court's order, 50% of *all* MCC inmates spent less than 30 days at the facility and 73% less than 60 days. However, of the unsentenced detainees, over half spent less than 10 days at the MCC, three-quarters were released within a month and more than 85% were released within 60 days.

showing that a restriction is substantially necessary to jail administration. Where the imposition is of particular gravity, that is, where it implicates interests of fundamental importance or inflicts significant harms, the Government should demonstrate that the restriction serves a compelling necessity of jail administration.

* * *

Simply stated, the approach I advocate here weighs the detainees' interests implicated by a particular restriction against the governmental interests the restriction serves. As the substantiality of the intrusion on detainees' rights increases, so must the significance of the countervailing governmental objectives.

Id. at 570–71, 99 S.Ct. at 1890–91.

Justice Marshall then concluded that the compelling-necessity test had to be applied in this case to the "publisher-only" rule because the rule interfered with the "fundamental" First Amendment right to receive information. Applying this test to the facts of the case before the Court, Justice Marshall concluded that the test was not met. He noted that while the "publisher-only" rule might be one rational way of curtailing the flow of contraband into a prison, less restrictive ways of achieving this objective existed. The number of hardbound books that any prisoner could receive, for example, could be limited, and books could be fluoroscoped for contraband.

Justice Stevens, joined by Justice Brennan, also dissented from the Court's opinion. Analyzing the constitutionality of the "publisher-only" rule under the Due Process Clause, Justice Stevens concluded that the across-the-board application of the rule to all pretrial detainees, regardless of the security risks posed by any particular detainee, inflicted punishment on them in violation of due process.

7. A prison regulation prohibits prisoners from receiving books, magazines, or other publications from a publisher unless the prisoner ordered the publication and paid for it out of her prison account. As a result, family members and friends of prisoners cannot purchase books as gifts to be sent by the publisher to the prisoner. If you represented the prison officials, what arguments would you make in support of the regulation's constitutionality? If you represented the prisoner challenging the publication ban's constitutionality, what arguments would you make in response? How would your arguments vary if prison officials permitted family members and friends to send money to be placed in an inmate's accounts?

In Rice v. State, 95 P.3d 994 (Kan. 2004), the Supreme Court of Kansas held that a ban on gift publications was reasonably related to the penological objective of rehabilitating inmates. The court noted that prison officials had developed an incentive system to induce prisoners to behave while in prison. Prisoners in a higher "incentive level" were afforded more opportunities to purchase publications with funds in their inmate accounts, while inmates in a lower incentive level had fewer such opportunities. The court found that the ban on gift subscriptions helped to prevent inmates from circumventing this incentive program and undermining its rehabilitative objectives.

The prison officials in *Rice* also contended that the publication ban prevented inmates from "strong-arming" other prisoners in an effort to obtain gift publications. While the Kansas Supreme Court found that this argument was not supported by the facts and did not, by itself, provide adequate grounds for upholding the publication ban, the court added that the strong-arming concern augmented somewhat the case for upholding the ban's constitutionality. Compare Crofton v. Roe, 170 F.3d 957 (9th Cir. 1999) (holding that a blanket ban on gift publications violated the First Amendment).

TURNER v. SAFLEY

Supreme Court of the United States, 1987.
482 U.S. 78, 107 S.Ct. 2254, 96 L.Ed.2d 64.

JUSTICE O'CONNOR delivered the opinion of the Court.

* * *

I

Respondents brought this class action for injunctive relief and damages in the United States District Court for the Western District of Missouri. The regulations challenged in the complaint were in effect at all prisons within the jurisdiction of the Missouri Division of Corrections. This litigation focused, however, on practices at the Renz Correctional Institution (Renz), located in Cedar City, Missouri. The Renz prison population includes both male and female prisoners of varying security levels. * * * Renz is used on occasion to provide protective custody for inmates from other prisons in the Missouri system. * * *

Two regulations are at issue here. The first of the challenged regulations relates to correspondence between inmates at different institutions. It permits such correspondence "with immediate family members who are inmates in other correctional institutions," and it permits correspondence between inmates "concerning legal matters." Other correspondence between inmates, however, is permitted only if "the classification/treatment team of each inmate deems it in the best interest of the parties involved." * * * At Renz, the District Court found that the rule "as practiced is that inmates may not write non-family inmates."

The challenged marriage regulation * * * permits an inmate to marry only with the permission of the superintendent of the prison, and provides that such approval should be given only "when there are compelling reasons to do so." The term "compelling" is not defined, but prison officials testified at trial that generally only a pregnancy or the birth of an illegitimate child would be considered a compelling reason. * * *

* * *

The District Court issued a memorandum opinion and order finding both the correspondence and marriage regulations unconstitutional. The court, relying on *Procunier v. Martinez,* applied a strict scrutiny standard. * * *

The Court of Appeals for the Eighth Circuit affirmed. * * *

* * *

II

* * *

Our task * * * is to formulate a standard of review for prisoners' constitutional claims that is responsive both to the "policy of judicial restraint regarding prisoner complaints and [to] the need to protect constitutional rights." * * * The *Martinez* Court based its ruling striking down the content-based regulation on the First Amendment rights of those who are not prisoners * * *. We expressly reserved the question of the proper standard of review to apply in cases "involving questions of 'prisoners' rights.' "

In four cases following *Martinez,* this Court has addressed such "questions of 'prisoners' rights.' " [The Court's opinion then discusses *Pell v. Procunier, Jones v. North Carolina Prisoners' Labor Union, Bell v. Wolfish,* and *Block v. Rutherford,* infra page 509.]

In none of these four "prisoners' rights" cases did the Court apply a standard of heightened scrutiny, but instead inquired whether a prison regulation that burdens fundamental rights is "reasonably related" to legitimate penological objectives, or whether it represents an "exaggerated response" to those concerns. The Court of Appeals in this case nevertheless concluded that *Martinez* provided the closest analogy for determining the appropriate standard of review for resolving respondents' constitutional complaints. The Court of Appeals distinguished this Court's decisions in *Pell, Jones, Bell,* and *Block* as variously involving "time, place, or manner" regulations, or regulations that restrict "presumptively dangerous" inmate activities. * * *

We disagree with the Court of Appeals that the reasoning in our cases subsequent to *Martinez* can be so narrowly cabined. In *Pell,* for example, it was found "relevant" to the reasonableness of a restriction on face-to-face visits between prisoners and news reporters that prisoners had other means of communicating with members of the general public. These alternative means of communication did not, however, make the prison regulation a "time, place, or manner" restriction in any ordinary sense of the term. As *Pell* acknowledged, the alternative methods of personal communication still available to prisoners would have been "unimpressive" if offered to justify a restriction on personal communication among members of the general public. Nevertheless, they were relevant in determining the scope of the burden placed by the regulation on inmates' First Amendment rights. *Pell* thus simply teaches that it is appropriate to consider the extent of this burden when "we [are] called upon to balance First Amendment rights against [legitimate] governmental interests."

Nor, in our view, can the reasonableness standard adopted in *Jones* and *Bell* be construed as applying only to "presumptively dangerous" inmate activities. To begin with, the Court of Appeals did not indicate how it would identify such "presumptively dangerous" conduct, other than to conclude that the group meetings in *Jones,* and the receipt of hardback books in *Bell,* both fall into that category. The Court of Appeals found that correspondence between inmates did not come within this grouping because the court did "not think a letter presents the same sort of 'obvious security problem' as does a hardback book." It is not readily apparent, however, why hardback books, which can be scanned for contraband by electronic devices and fluoroscopes are qualitatively different in this respect from inmate correspondence, which can be written in codes not readily subject to detection; or why coordinated inmate activity within the same prison is categorically different from inmate activity coordinated by mail among different prison institutions. * * *

If *Pell, Jones,* and *Bell* have not already resolved the question posed in *Martinez,* we resolve it now: when a prison regulation impinges on inmates' constitutional rights, the regulation is valid if it is reasonably related to legitimate penological interests. In our view, such a standard is necessary if "prison administrators . . ., and not the courts, [are] to make the difficult judgments concerning institutional operations." Subjecting the day-to-day judgments of prison officials to an inflexible strict scrutiny analysis would seriously hamper their ability to anticipate security problems and to adopt innovative solutions to the intractable problems of prison administration. The rule would also distort the decisionmaking process, for every administrative judgment would be subject to the possibility that some court somewhere would conclude that it had a less restrictive way of solving the problem at hand. Courts inevitably would become the primary arbiters of what constitutes the best solution to every administrative problem, thereby "unnecessarily perpetuat[ing] the involvement of the federal courts in affairs of prison administration."

As our opinions in *Pell, Bell,* and *Jones* show, several factors are relevant in determining the reasonableness of the regulation at issue. First, there must be a "valid, rational connection" between the prison regulation and the legitimate governmental interest put forward to justify it. Thus, a regulation cannot be sustained where the logical connection between the regulation and the asserted goal is so remote as to render the policy arbitrary or irrational. Moreover, the governmental objective must be a legitimate and neutral one. We have found it important to inquire whether prison regulations restricting inmates' First Amendment rights operated in a neutral fashion, without regard to the content of the expression.

A second factor relevant in determining the reasonableness of a prison restriction, as *Pell* shows, is whether there are alternative means of exercising the right that remain open to prison inmates. Where "other avenues" remain available for the exercise of the asserted right, courts should be particularly conscious of the "measure of judicial deference owed to corrections officials . . . in gauging the validity of the regulation."

A third consideration is the impact accommodation of the asserted constitutional right will have on guards and other inmates, and on the allocation of prison resources generally. In the necessarily closed environment of the correctional institution, few changes will have no ramifications on the liberty of others or on the use of the prison's limited resources for preserving institutional order. When accommodation of an asserted right will have a significant "ripple effect" on fellow inmates or on prison staff, courts should be particularly deferential to the informed discretion of corrections officials.

Finally, the absence of ready alternatives is evidence of the reasonableness of a prison regulation. By the same token, the existence of obvious, easy alternatives may be evidence that the regulation is not reasonable, but is an "exaggerated response" to prison concerns. This is not a "least restrictive alternative" test: prison officials do not have to set up and then shoot down every conceivable alternative method of accommodating the claimant's constitutional complaint. But if an inmate claimant can point to an alternative that fully accommodates the prisoner's rights at *de minimis* cost to valid penological interests, a court may consider that as evidence that the regulation does not satisfy the reasonable relationship standard.

III

* * *

A

According to the testimony at trial, the Missouri correspondence provision was promulgated primarily for security reasons. Prison officials testified that mail between institutions can be used to communicate escape plans and to arrange assaults and other violent acts. Witnesses stated that the Missouri Division of Corrections had a growing problem with prison gangs, and that restricting communications among gang members, both by transferring gang members to different institutions and by restricting their correspondence, was an important element in combating this problem. Officials also testified that the use of Renz as a facility to provide protective custody for certain inmates could be compromised by permitting correspondence between inmates at Renz and inmates at other correctional institutions.

The prohibition on correspondence between institutions is logically connected to these legitimate security concerns. * * * Moreover, the correspondence regulation does not deprive prisoners of all means of expression. Rather, it bars communication only with a limited class of other people with whom prison officials have particular cause to be concerned—inmates at other institutions within the Missouri prison system.

We also think that the Court of Appeals' analysis overlooks the impact of respondents' asserted right on other inmates and prison personnel. Prison officials have stated that in their expert opinion, correspondence between prison institutions facilitates the development of informal organizations that threaten the core functions of prison administration, maintaining safety and internal security. As a result, the correspondence rights asserted by respondents, like the organizational activities at issue in *Jones v. North Carolina Prisoners' Union,* can be exercised only at the cost of significantly less liberty and safety for everyone else, guards and other prisoners alike. Indeed, the potential "ripple effect" is even broader here than in *Jones,* because exercise of the right affects the inmates and staff of more than one institution. Where exercise of a right requires this kind of tradeoff, we think that the choice made by corrections officials—which is, after all, a judgment "peculiarly within [their] province and professional expertise"—should not be lightly set aside by the courts.

Finally, there are no obvious, easy alternatives to the policy adopted by petitioners. Other well-run prison systems, including the Federal Bureau of Prisons, have concluded that substantially similar restrictions on inmate correspondence were necessary to protect institutional order and security. As petitioners have shown, the only alternative proffered by the claimant prisoners, the monitoring of inmate correspondence, clearly would impose more than a *de minimis* cost on the pursuit of legitimate corrections goals. Prison officials testified that it would be impossible to read every piece of inmate-to-inmate correspondence, and consequently there would be an appreciable risk of missing dangerous messages. In any event, prisoners could easily write in jargon or codes to prevent detection of their real messages. The risk of missing dangerous communications, taken together with the sheer burden on staff resources required to conduct item-by-item censorship, supports the judgment of prison officials that this alternative is not an adequate alternative to restricting correspondence.

The prohibition on correspondence is reasonably related to valid corrections goals. * * * On that basis, we conclude that the regulation does not unconstitutionally abridge the First Amendment rights of prison inmates.

B

In support of the marriage regulation, petitioners first suggest that the rule does not deprive prisoners of a constitutionally protected right. They concede that the decision to marry is a fundamental right under *Zablocki v. Redhail,* 434 U.S. 374 (1978), and *Loving v. Virginia,* 388 U.S. 1 (1967), but they imply that a different rule should obtain "in ... a prison forum." * * *

We disagree with petitioners that *Zablocki* does not apply to prison inmates. It is settled that a prison inmate "retains those [constitutional] rights that are not inconsistent with his status as a prisoner or with the legitimate penological objectives of the corrections system." The right to marry, like many other rights, is subject to substantial restrictions as a result of incarceration. Many important attributes of marriage remain, however, after taking into account the limitations imposed by prison life. First, inmate marriages, like others, are expressions of emotional support and public commitment. * * * In addition, many religions recognize marriage as having spiritual significance; for some inmates and their spouses, therefore, the commitment of marriage may be an exercise of religious faith as well as an expression of personal dedication. Third, most inmates eventually will be released by parole or commutation, and therefore most inmate marriages are formed in the expectation that they ultimately will be fully consummated. Finally, marital status often is a precondition to the receipt of government benefits (*e.g.,* Social Security benefits), property rights (*e.g.,* tenancy by the entirety, inheritance rights), and other, less tangible benefits (*e.g.,* legitimation of children born out of wedlock). These incidents of marriage, like the religious and personal aspects of the marriage commitment, are unaffected by the fact of confinement or the pursuit of legitimate corrections goals.

Taken together, we conclude that these remaining elements are sufficient to form a constitutionally protected marital relationship in the prison context. * * *

The Missouri marriage regulation prohibits inmates from marrying unless the prison superintendent has approved the marriage after finding that there are compelling reasons for doing so. As noted previously, generally only pregnancy or birth of a child is considered a "compelling reason" to approve a marriage. In determining whether this regulation impermissibly burdens the right to marry, we note initially that the regulation prohibits marriages between inmates and civilians, as well as marriages between inmates. Although not urged by respondents, this implication of the interests of nonprisoners may support application of the *Martinez* standard, because the regulation may entail a "consequential restriction on the [constitutional] rights of those who are not prisoners." We need not reach this question, however, because even under the reasonable relationship test, the marriage regulation does not withstand scrutiny.

Petitioners have identified both security and rehabilitation concerns in support of the marriage prohibition. The security concern emphasized by petitioners is that "love triangles" might lead to violent confrontations between inmates. With respect to rehabilitation, prison officials testified that female prisoners often were subject to abuse at home or were overly dependent on male figures, and that this dependence or abuse was connected to the crimes they had committed. The superintendent at Renz, petitioner William Turner, testified that in his view, these women prisoners needed to concentrate on developing skills of self-reliance and that the prohibition on marriage furthered this rehabilitative goal. * * *

We conclude that on this record, the Missouri prison regulation, as written, is not reasonably related to these penological interests. No doubt legitimate security concerns may require placing reasonable restrictions upon an inmate's right to marry, and may justify requiring approval of the superintendent. The Missouri regulation, however, represents an exaggerated response to such security objectives. There are obvious, easy alternatives to the Missouri regulation that accommodate the right to marry while imposing a *de minimis* burden on the pursuit of security objectives. See, *e.g.,* 28 CFR § 551.10 (1986)(marriage by inmates in federal prison generally permitted, but not if warden finds that it presents a threat to security or order of institution, or to public safety). We are aware of no place in the record where prison officials testified that such ready alternatives would not fully satisfy their security concerns. Moreover, with respect to the security concern emphasized in petitioners' brief—the creation of "love triangles"—petitioners have pointed to nothing in the record suggesting that the marriage regulation was viewed as preventing such entanglements. Common sense likewise suggests that there is no logical connection between the marriage restriction and the formation of love triangles: surely in prisons housing both male and female prisoners, inmate rivalries are as likely to develop without a formal marriage ceremony as with one. Finally, this is not an instance where the "ripple effect" on the security of fellow inmates and prison staff justifies a broad restriction on inmates' rights * * *.

Nor, on this record, is the marriage restriction reasonably related to the articulated rehabilitation goal. First, in requiring refusal of permission absent a finding of a compelling reason to allow the marriage, the rule sweeps much more broadly than can be explained by petitioners' penological objectives. Missouri prison officials testified that generally they had experienced no problem with the marriage of male inmates, and the District Court found that such marriages had routinely been allowed as a matter of practice at Missouri correctional institutions prior to adoption of the rule. The proffered justification thus does not explain the adoption of a rule banning marriages by these inmates. Nor does it account for the prohibition on inmate marriages to civilians. Missouri prison officials testified that generally they had no objection to inmate-civilian marriages, and Superintendent Turner testified that he usually did not object to the marriage of either male or female prisoners to civilians. The rehabilitation concern appears from the record to have been centered almost exclusively on female inmates marrying other inmates or ex-felons; it does not account for the ban on inmate-civilian marriages.

* * *

It is undisputed that Missouri prison officials may regulate the time and circumstances under which the marriage ceremony itself takes place. On this record, however, the almost complete ban on the decision to marry is not reasonably related to legitimate penological objectives. We conclude, therefore, that the Missouri marriage regulation is facially invalid.

* * *

JUSTICE STEVENS, with whom JUSTICE BRENNAN, JUSTICE MARSHALL, and JUSTICE BLACKMUN join, concurring in part and dissenting in part.

How a court describes its standard of review when a prison regulation infringes fundamental constitutional rights often has far less consequence for the inmates than the actual showing that the court demands of the State in order to uphold the regulation. This case provides a prime example.

There would not appear to be much difference between the question whether a prison regulation that burdens fundamental rights in the quest for security is "needlessly broad"—the standard applied by the District Court and the Court of Appeals—and this Court's requirement that the regulation must be "reasonably related to legitimate penological interests" and may not represent "an 'exaggerated response' to those concerns." But if the standard can be satisfied by nothing more than a "logical connection" between the regulation and any legitimate penological concern perceived by a cautious warden, it is virtually meaningless. Application of the standard would seem to permit disregard for inmates' constitutional rights whenever the imagination of the warden produces a plausible security concern and a deferential trial court is able to discern a logical connection between that concern and the challenged regulation. Indeed, there is a logical connection between prison discipline and the use of bullwhips on prisoners; and security is logically furthered by a total ban on inmate communication, not only with other inmates but also with outsiders who conceivably might be interested in arranging an attack within the prison or an escape from it. Thus, I dissent from Part II of the Court's opinion.

I am able to join Part III–B because the Court's invalidation of the marriage regulation does not rely on a rejection of a standard of review more stringent than the one announced in Part II. The Court in Part III–B concludes after careful examination that, even applying a "reasonableness" standard, the marriage regulation must fail because the justifications asserted on its behalf lack record support.[15] * * *

QUESTIONS AND POINTS FOR DISCUSSION

1. In Thornburgh v. Abbott, 490 U.S. 401, 109 S.Ct. 1874 (1989), the Supreme Court considered the constitutionality of certain regulations promulgated by the Federal Bureau of Prisons (BOP). According to these regulations, prisoners could receive publications from outside the prison, but the warden retained the authority to withhold a publication deemed "detrimental to the security, good order, or discipline of the institution" or that might "facilitate criminal activity." The regulations, excerpts of which are set forth below, delineated some of the instances when censorship would be appropriate:

---

[15]. The Court's bifurcated treatment of the mail and marriage regulations leads to the absurd result that an inmate at Renz may marry another inmate, but may not carry on the courtship leading to the marriage by corresponding with him or her beforehand because he or she would not then be an "immediate family member."

Publications which may be rejected by a Warden include but are not limited to publications which meet one of the following criteria:

(1) It depicts or describes procedures for the construction or use of weapons, ammunition, bombs or incendiary devices;

(2) It depicts, encourages, or describes methods of escape from correctional facilities, or contains blueprints, drawings or similar descriptions of Bureau of Prisons institutions;

(3) It depicts or describes procedures for the brewing of alcoholic beverages, or the manufacture of drugs;

(4) It is written in code;

(5) It depicts, describes or encourages activities which may lead to the use of physical violence or group disruption;

(6) It encourages or instructs in the commission of criminal activity;

(7) It is sexually explicit material which by its nature or content poses a threat to the security, good order, or discipline of the institution, or facilitates criminal activity.

The regulations also restricted a warden's power to prohibit a prisoner from receiving a publication. The warden, for example, could not reject a publication "solely because its content is religious, philosophical, political, social or sexual, or because its content is unpopular or repugnant." Nor could the warden set up a "hit list" of publications absolutely barred from distribution within the prison. Instead, the warden had to review each issue of a publication to determine whether some portion of that particular issue posed a threat to institutional security or would facilitate a crime. If any part of the issue met any of the censorship criteria, the BOP practice was to bar the entire publication from the prison.

The federal prisoners and the publishers who were the plaintiffs in this case contended that the BOP regulations governing incoming publications violated the First Amendment on their face. The plaintiffs additionally challenged, on First Amendment grounds, the way in which these regulations had been applied to a number of incoming publications.

Applying a deferential reasonableness standard, the district court upheld the challenged regulations. The Court of Appeals for the District of Columbia reversed. Because the case involved not just the First Amendment rights of prisoners, but also of nonprisoners—the publishers who wanted to circulate their publications within federal prisons, the court of appeals concluded that the constitutionality of the regulations had to be analyzed under the more stringent standard of Procunier v. Martinez, 416 U.S. 396, 94 S.Ct. 1800 (1974), supra page 474. The Supreme Court, however, distinguished *Procunier v. Martinez*:

> [A] careful reading of *Martinez* suggests that our rejection of the regulation at issue resulted not from a least restrictive means requirement, but from our recognition that the regulated activity centrally at issue in that case—outgoing personal correspondence from prisoners—did not, by its very nature, pose a serious threat to prison order and security. * * * We deal here with incoming publications, material requested by an individual

inmate but targeted to a general audience. Once in the prison, material of this kind reasonably may be expected to circulate among prisoners, with the concomitant potential for coordinated disruptive conduct. Furthermore, prisoners may observe particular material in the possession of a fellow prisoner, draw inferences about their * * * beliefs, sexual orientation, or gang affiliations from that material, and cause disorder by acting accordingly.

Id. at 411–12, 109 S.Ct. at 1880–81.

The Supreme Court concluded that when assessing the constitutionality of prison regulations governing incoming publications, the standard to be applied is that set forth in *Turner v. Safley.* Under this standard, the regulations would be valid as long as they were "reasonably related to legitimate penological interests." To the extent that *Martinez* suggested that a different standard should apply, it was overruled. The *Martinez* standard was to be applied only to "outgoing correspondence." Id. at 413, 109 S.Ct. at 1881.

In *Thornburgh*, the Supreme Court asserted that the *Turner* reasonableness test is not "toothless." Id. at 414, 109 S.Ct. at 1882. After applying this test to the censorship regulations before it, however, the Court concluded that the regulations, on their face, were constitutional. The Court's application of the four *Turner* factors to the facts of the case is instructive:

The first *Turner* factor is multifold: we must determine whether the governmental objective underlying the regulations at issue is legitimate and neutral, and that the regulations are rationally related to that objective. * * *

The legitimacy of the Government's purpose in promulgating these regulations is beyond question. The regulations are expressly aimed at protecting prison security * * *.

As to neutrality, "[w]e have found it important to inquire whether prison regulations restricting inmates' First Amendment rights operated in a neutral fashion, without regard to the content of the expression." The ban on *all* correspondence between certain classes of inmates at issue in *Turner* clearly met this "neutrality" criterion, as did the restrictions at issue in *Pell* and *Wolfish.* The issue, however, in this case is closer.

On their face, the regulations distinguish between rejection of a publication "solely because its content is religious, philosophical, political, social or sexual, or because its content is unpopular or repugnant" (prohibited) and rejection because the publication is detrimental to security (permitted). Both determinations turn, to some extent, on content. But the Court's reference to "neutrality" in *Turner* was intended to go no further than its requirement in *Martinez* that "the regulation or practice in question must further an important or substantial governmental interest unrelated to the suppression of expression." Where, as here, prison administrators draw distinctions between publications solely on the basis of their potential implications for prison security, the regulations are "neutral" in the technical sense in which we meant and used that term in *Turner.*

We also conclude that the broad discretion accorded prison wardens by the regulations here at issue is rationally related to security interests. We reach this conclusion for two reasons. The first has to do with the kind of security risk presented by incoming publications. * * *

Second, we are comforted by the individualized nature of the determinations required by the regulation. Under the regulations, no publication may be excluded unless the warden himself makes the determination that it is "detrimental to the security, good order, or discipline of the institution or ... might facilitate criminal activity." This is the controlling standard. A publication which fits within one of the "criteria" for exclusion *may* be rejected, but only if it is determined to meet that standard under the conditions prevailing at the institution at the time. Indeed, the regulations expressly reject certain shortcuts that would lead to needless exclusions. See [28 CFR] § 540.70(b)(non-delegability of power to reject publications); § 540.71(c)(prohibition against establishing an excluded list of publications). We agree that it is rational for the Bureau to exclude materials that, although not necessarily "likely" to lead to violence, are determined by the warden to create an intolerable risk of disorder under the conditions of a particular prison at a particular time.

A second factor the Court in *Turner* held to be "relevant in determining the reasonableness of a prison restriction ... is whether there are alternative means of exercising the right that remain open to prison inmates." As has already been made clear in *Turner* and *O'Lone* [*v. Estate of Shabazz,* 482 U.S. 342 (1987), on page 520], "the right" in question must be viewed sensibly and expansively. * * * As the regulations at issue in the present case permit a broad range of publications to be sent, received, and read, this factor is clearly satisfied.

The third factor to be addressed under the *Turner* analysis is the impact that accommodation of the asserted constitutional right will have on others (guards and inmates) in the prison. * * * Where, as here, the right in question "can be exercised only at the cost of significantly less liberty and safety for everyone else, guards and other prisoners alike," the courts should defer to the "informed discretion of corrections officials."

Finally, *Turner* held that "the existence of obvious, easy alternatives may be evidence that the regulation is not reasonable, but is an 'exaggerated response' to prison concerns." * * * We agree with the District Court that these regulations, on their face, are not an "exaggerated response" to the problem at hand: no obvious, easy alternative has been established.

Regarding the all-or-nothing rule, we analyze respondents' proposed alternatives to that rule as alternative means of accommodating respondents' asserted rights. The District Court discussed the evidence and found, on the basis of testimony in the record, that petitioners' fear that tearing out the rejected portions and admitting the rest of the publication would create more discontent than the current practice was "reasonably founded." * * *

* * * In our view, when prison officials are able to demonstrate that they have rejected a less restrictive alternative because of reasonably founded fears that it will lead to greater harm, they succeed in demonstrating that the alternative they in fact selected was not an "exaggerated response" under *Turner*. Furthermore, the administrative inconvenience of this proposed alternative is also a factor to be considered, and adds additional support to the District Court's conclusion that petitioners were not obligated to adopt it.

Id. at 414–19, 109 S.Ct. at 1882–85.

In a footnote, the Supreme Court indicated that just because a publication is admitted in one prison does not mean that its exclusion from another prison is irrational and hence in contravention of the first *Turner* factor. The Court explained:

[W]hat may appear to be inconsistent results are not necessarily signs of arbitrariness or irrationality. Given the likely variability within and between institutions over time, greater consistency might be attainable only at the cost of a more broadly restrictive rule against admission of incoming publications. Any attempt to achieve greater consistency by broader exclusions might itself run afoul of the second *Turner* factor, *i.e.*, the presence or absence of "alternative means of exercising the right" in question.

Id. at 417 n. 15, 109 S.Ct. at 1883 n. 15.

After holding that the Bureau of Prison regulations were constitutional on their face, the Court remanded the case to the lower courts for application of the reasonableness test to each of the publications whose exclusion from a federal prison had been challenged by the plaintiffs. In an opinion joined by Justices Brennan and Marshall, Justice Stevens concurred in part and dissented in part. Justice Stevens agreed with the Court's decision to send the case back for consideration of the constitutionality of the actions of prison officials in rejecting particular publications. On the broader question of the standard to be applied when assessing the constitutionality of prison-censorship regulations on their face and as applied, however, Justice Stevens disagreed with the majority. The majority's limitation of the holding of *Martinez* to outgoing correspondence was, in his opinion, "disingenuous"; the language of *Martinez* did not suggest, nor its reasoning support, such a constrained interpretation of its scope. Id. at 425, 109 S.Ct. at 1888 (Stevens, J., concurring and dissenting).

Justice Stevens also disagreed with the majority's conclusion that the BOP regulations were constitutional on their face. In Justice Stevens's opinion, the regulations were unconstitutional, whatever the test applied to them—the *Martinez* standard or the *Turner* reasonableness test. Justice Stevens first disputed the majority's conclusion that the regulations were content-neutral. Words like "detrimental to the security, good order, or discipline" of the prison and references to publications that "might facilitate criminal activity" were content-oriented, he asserted, and they were also so vague that they encouraged censorship based on the personal biases of the censor.

Justice Stevens then lambasted the majority for contending that prisoners had alternative means of exercising the First Amendment right in question because they had a number of other publications to which they could gain access. To this argument, Justice Stevens responded: "Some of the rejected publications may represent the sole medium for conveying and receiving a particular unconventional message; thus it is irrelevant that the regulations permit many other publications to be delivered to prisoners." Id. at 430, 109 S.Ct. at 1890.

Finally, Justice Stevens attacked the Bureau of Prisons' "all-or-nothing rule" under which a publication was either distributed in its entirety to a prisoner or totally banned from the institution. Justice Stevens described this rule as "a meat-ax abridgement of the First Amendment rights of either a free citizen or a prison inmate." Id. at 433, 109 S.Ct. at 1892. Because no evidence, in Justice Stevens's opinion, supported the conclusion that admitting part of a publication into a prison would threaten institutional security, the justification for the rule was really administrative convenience. But this purported justification for the "all-or-nothing rule" was unconvincing to Justice Stevens. Assuming that the prison officials individually scrutinized the publications as they were supposed to do, the additional time needed to rip an article out of the publication was infinitesimal, certainly of no "constitutional significance." Id.

2. *Pell v. Procunier, Bell v. Wolfish,* and *Jones v. North Carolina Prisoners' Labor Union* also involved the constitutionality, under the First Amendment, of prison regulations restricting communications of nonprisoners with prisoners. Did these cases necessitate the Court's refusal to apply the *Martinez* standard in *Thornburgh*? Can the regulations at issue in *Thornburgh* be distinguished from those reviewed by the Court in *Pell, Bell,* and *Jones*?

3. Is *Thornburgh* consistent with the Supreme Court's rejection of the "presumptively dangerous" test in *Turner v. Safley*?

4. Could an article in a magazine describing deficiencies in the medical care afforded federal prisoners and charging that one federal prisoner was "murdered by neglect" because his medical needs were not attended to be excluded constitutionally from a federal prison? Could a letter written by a prisoner to an outsider containing such allegations be censored? Could a prisoner be lawfully disciplined for making such a statement to another prisoner or to a correctional officer?

What if the article, letter, or statement described the criminal-justice system as racist? What if it described correctional officers as "racist pigs"? Or what if the article, letter, or statement denounced people of other races and advocated racism and racial purity? Compare Chriceol v. Phillips, 169 F.3d 313, 316 (5th Cir.1999) (withholding publications espousing hatred of persons of other races, religions, and nationalities in a way that creates "a serious danger of violence" is constitutional) with McCabe v. Arave, 827 F.2d 634, 638 (9th Cir.1987) (publications that advocate racial purity but not violence or any other illegal activity cannot constitutionally be banned unless they are "so racially inflammatory as to be reasonably likely to cause violence at the prison").

5. In *Thornburgh*, the Supreme Court upheld a regulation barring publications containing "sexually explicit material which by its nature or content poses a threat to the security, good order, or discipline of the institution, or facilitates criminal activity." Many lower courts have found other bans on pornographic materials to be constitutional. For example, courts have upheld regulations, laws, and policies prohibiting prisoners confined at a special facility for sex offenders from having access to "sexually oriented and obscene materials," Waterman v. Farmer, 183 F.3d 208 (3d Cir.1999); banning publications depicting sexual penetration, Frost v. Symington, 197 F.3d 348 (9th Cir.1999); and excluding pictures that are "sexually explicit" or "feature nudity" other than nudity "illustrative of medical, educational, or anthropological content." Amatel v. Reno, 156 F.3d 192 (D.C.Cir.1998). And in Mauro v. Arpaio, 188 F.3d 1054 (9th Cir.1999), the Ninth Circuit Court of Appeals rejected the First Amendment claim of a pretrial detainee barred from receiving *Playboy* magazine under a jail's policy banning pictures and drawings depicting "frontal nudity." Significantly, the jail policy upheld in *Mauro* contained no exemption for medical, educational, or anthropological materials.

Correctional officials typically have cited one or more of three governmental interests when defending the constitutionality of pornography bans. The first is the interest in promoting rehabilitation. See, e.g., Amatel v. Reno, 156 F.3d at 199 ("Common sense tells us that prisoners are more likely to develop the now-missing self-control and respect for others if prevented from poring over pictures that are themselves degrading and disrespectful."). The second is the interest in curbing the sexual harassment of female correctional officers. See, e.g., Mauro v. Arpaio, 188 F.3d at 1057 (before the adoption of the jail's policy banning materials depicting frontal nudity, male inmates would compare the anatomy of female detention officers with that of the nude women displayed in publications such as *Playboy* magazine). And the third is the interest in protecting institutional security. See, e.g., Jones v. Salt Lake County, 503 F.3d 1147, 1156 & n.8 (10th Cir. 2007) (citing jail official's testimony that sexually explicit materials may "excite" inmates and lead them to sexually assault other inmates); Mauro, 188 F.3d at 1060 (inmates' comparisons of nude women depicted in publications with other inmates' girlfriends, wives, and mothers have triggered fights between inmates). Do you agree with the courts that each of the pornography bans described above is reasonably related to one or more of these interests?

BEARD v. BANKS

Supreme Court of the United States, 2006.
548 U.S. 521, 126 S.Ct. 2572, 165 L.Ed.2d 697.

JUSTICE BREYER announced the judgment of the Court, and delivered an opinion, in which THE CHIEF JUSTICE, JUSTICE KENNEDY, and JUSTICE SOUTER join.

* * *

I

A

The prison regulation at issue applies to certain prisoners housed in Pennsylvania's Long Term Segregation Unit. The LTSU is the most restrictive of the three special units that Pennsylvania maintains for difficult prisoners. * * * The third such unit, the LTSU, is reserved for the Commonwealth's "most incorrigible, recalcitrant inmates."

LTSU inmates number about 40. * * * The LTSU is divided into two levels. All inmates are initially assigned to the most restrictive level, level 2. After 90 days, depending upon an inmate's behavior, an individual may graduate to the less restrictive level 1, although in practice most do not.

The RHU [Restricted Housing Unit], SMU [Special Management Unit], and LTSU all seriously restrict inmates' ordinary prison privileges. At all three units, residents are typically confined to cells for 23 hours a day, have limited access to the commissary or outside visitors, and (with the exception of some phases of the SMU) may not watch television or listen to the radio.

Prisoners at level 2 of the LTSU face the most severe form of the restrictions listed above. * * * In addition they (unlike all other prisoners in the Commonwealth) are restricted in the manner at issue here: They have no access to newspapers, magazines, or personal photographs. They are nonetheless permitted legal and personal correspondence, religious and legal materials, two library books, and writing paper. If an inmate progresses to level 1, he enjoys somewhat less severe restrictions, including the right to receive one newspaper and five magazines. The ban on photographs is not lifted unless a prisoner progresses out of the LTSU altogether.

B

In 2001, plaintiff Ronald Banks, respondent here, then a prisoner confined to LTSU level 2, filed this federal-court action against Jeffrey Beard, the Secretary of the Pennsylvania Department of Corrections. Banks claimed that the level 2 Policy forbidding inmates all access to newspapers, magazines, and photographs bears no reasonable relation to any legitimate penological objective and consequently violates the First Amendment. * * *

* * * [T]he Secretary filed a motion for summary judgment. He also filed a "Statement of Material Facts Not in Dispute," with a copy of the deputy superintendent's deposition attached as an appendix.

Banks (who was represented by counsel throughout) filed no opposition to the Secretary's motion, but instead filed a cross-motion for summary judgment. * * * [B]y failing specifically to challenge the facts identified in the defendant's statement of undisputed facts, Banks is deemed to have admitted the validity of the facts contained in the Secretary's statement.

* * *

[The district court granted the Secretary's motion for summary judgment. On appeal, the Third Circuit Court of Appeals reversed.]

II

* * *

This case has arrived in this Court in the context of the Secretary's motion for summary judgment. Thus we must examine the record to see whether the Secretary, in depositions, answers to interrogatories, admissions, affidavits and the like, has demonstrated "the absence of a genuine issue of material fact" and his entitlement to judgment as a matter of law.

If the Secretary has done so, then we must determine whether Banks, the plaintiff, who bears the burden of persuasion, has "by affidavits or as otherwise provided" in Rule 56 (*e.g.* through depositions, etc.) "*set forth specific facts showing that there is a genuine issue for trial.*" Rule 56(e) (emphasis added). If not, the law requires entry of judgment in the Secretary's favor.

We recognize that at this stage we must draw "all justifiable inferences" in Banks' "favor." In doing so, however, we must distinguish between evidence of disputed facts and disputed matters of professional judgment. In respect to the latter, our inferences must accord deference to the views of prison authorities. Unless a prisoner can point to sufficient evidence regarding such issues of judgment to allow him to prevail on the merits, he cannot prevail at the summary judgment stage.

III

The Secretary in his motion set forth several justifications for the prison's policy, including the need to motivate better behavior on the part of particularly difficult prisoners, the need to minimize the amount of property they control in their cells, and the need to assure prison safety, by, for example, diminishing the amount of material a prisoner might use to start a cell fire. We need go no further than the first justification, that of providing increased incentives for better prison behavior. * * *

* * *

As we have said we believe that the first rationale itself satisfies *Turner*'s requirements. First, the statement and deposition set forth a " 'valid, rational connection' " between the Policy and " 'legitimate penological objectives.' " The deputy superintendent stated in his deposition that prison authorities are "very limited ... in what we can and cannot deny or give to [a level 2] inmate [who typically has already been deprived of almost all privileges] and these are some of the items that we feel are legitimate as incentives for inmate growth." * * *

* * * The articulated connections between newspapers and magazines, the deprivation of virtually the last privilege left to an inmate, and a significant incentive to improve behavior, are logical ones. Thus, the first factor supports the Policy's "reasonableness."

As to the second factor, the statement and deposition make clear that, as long as the inmate remains at level 2, *no* "alternative means of exercising the right" remain open to him. * * * The absence of any alternative thus provides "some evidence that the regulations [a]re unreasonable," but is not "conclusive" of the reasonableness of the Policy.

As to the third factor, the statement and deposition indicate that, were prison authorities to seek to "accommodat[e] ... the asserted constitutional right," the resulting "impact" would be negative. * * * If the Policy (in the authorities' view) helps to produce better behavior, then its absence (in the authorities' view) will help to produce worse behavior, *e.g.*, "backsliding" (and thus the expenditure of more "resources" at level 2).

Similarly, as to the fourth factor, neither the statement nor the deposition describes, points to, or calls to mind any "alternative method of accommodating the claimant's constitutional complaint ... that fully accommodates the prisoner's rights at *de minimis* cost to valid penological interests."

In fact, the second, third, and fourth factors, being in a sense logically related to the Policy itself, here add little, one way or another, to the first factor's basic logical rationale. The fact that two of these latter three factors seem to support the Policy does not, therefore, count in the Secretary's favor. The real task in this case is not balancing these factors, but rather determining whether the Secretary shows more than simply a logical relation, that is, whether he shows a *reasonable* relation. We believe the material presented here by the prison officials is sufficient to demonstrate that the Policy is a reasonable one.

* * *

We recognize that the Court of Appeals reached a contrary conclusion. But in doing so, it placed too high an evidentiary burden upon the Secretary. In respect to behavior-modification incentives, for example, the court wrote that the "District Court did not examine ... whether the ban was implemented in a way that could modify behavior, or inquire into whether the [Department of Corrections'] deprivation theory of behavior modification had any basis in real human psychology, or had proven effective with LTSU inmates." * * * The court's statements and conclusions here also offer too little deference to the judgment of prison officials about such matters. The court, for example, offered no apparent deference to the deputy prison superintendent's professional judgment that the Policy deprived "particularly difficult" inmates of a last remaining privilege and that doing so created a significant behavioral incentive.

Contrary to Justice Ginsburg's suggestion, we do not suggest that the deference owed prison authorities makes it impossible for prisoners or others attacking a prison policy like the present one ever to succeed or to survive summary judgment. After all, the constitutional interest here is an important one. *Turner* requires prison authorities to show more than a formalistic logical connection between a regulation and a penological objective. A prisoner may be able to marshal substantial evidence that, given the importance of the interest, the Policy is not a reasonable one. Cf. [*Turner*] (striking down prison policy prohibiting prisoner marriages). And * * * it is not inconceivable that a plaintiff's counsel, through rigorous questioning of officials by means of depositions, could demonstrate genuine issues of fact for trial. Finally, * * * we agree that "the restriction here is severe," and "if faced with evidence that [it were] a *de facto* permanent ban ... we might well reach a different conclusion in a challenge to a particular application of the regulation." * * *

Here prison authorities responded adequately through their statement and deposition to the allegations in the complaint. And the plaintiff failed to point to " 'specific facts' " in the record that could "lead a rational trier of fact to find" in his favor.

* * *

JUSTICE ALITO took no part in the consideration or decision of this case.

JUSTICE THOMAS, with whom JUSTICE SCALIA joins, concurring in the judgment.

* * *

* * * *Turner* and its progeny "rest on the unstated (and erroneous) presumption that the Constitution contains an implicit definition of incarceration." Because the Constitution contains no such definition, "States are free to define and redefine all types of punishment, including imprisonment, to encompass various types of deprivations—*provided only that those deprivations are consistent with the Eighth Amendment*."

Respondent has not challenged Pennsylvania's prison policy as a violation of the Eighth Amendment, and thus the sole inquiry in this case is whether respondent's sentence deprived him of the rights he now seeks to exercise. [Justice Thomas then concluded that Pennsylvania's definition of incarceration terminated the privilege to have "unfettered access" to newspapers, magazines, and photographs.]

* * *

JUSTICE STEVENS, with whom JUSTICE GINSBURG joins, dissenting.

By ratifying the Fourteenth Amendment, our society has made an unmistakable commitment to apply the rule of law in an evenhanded manner to all persons, even those who flagrantly violate their social and legal obligations. Thus, it is well settled that even the " 'worst of the worst'" prisoners retain constitutional protection, specifically including their First Amendment rights. * * *

* * *

Petitioner does not dispute that the prohibition at issue infringes upon rights protected by the First Amendment. Instead, petitioner posits two penological interests, which, in his view, are sufficient to justify the challenged rule notwithstanding these constitutional infringements: prison security and inmate rehabilitation. * * *

* * *

* * * As the Court of Appeals emphasized, LTSU–2 inmates "are not requesting unlimited access to innumerable periodicals," rather, they are seeking "the ability to have *one* newspaper or magazine and some small number of photographs in their cells at one time." In light of the quantity of materials that LTSU–2 inmates are entitled to have in their cell, it does not follow, as a matter of logic, that preventing inmates from possessing a single copy of a secular, nonlegal newspaper, newsletter, or magazine will have any measurable effect on the likelihood that inmates will start fires, hide contraband, or engage in other dangerous actions.[1]

* * *

The second rationale posited by petitioner in support of the prohibitions on newspapers, newsletters, magazines, and photographs is rehabilitation. According to petitioner, the ban "provides the [l]evel 2 inmates with the prospect of earning a privilege through compliance with orders and remission of various negative behaviors and serves to encourage the progress and discourage backsliding by the level 1 inmates." * * *

* * * [P]etitioner advances a deprivation theory of rehabilitation: Any deprivation of something a prisoner desires gives him an added incentive to improve his behavior. This justification has no limiting principle; if sufficient, it would provide a "rational basis" for any regulation that deprives a prisoner of a constitutional right so long as there is at least a theoretical possibility that the prisoner can regain the right at some future time by modifying his behavior. * * *

* * *

* * * [R]ehabilitation is a valid penological interest, and deprivation is undoubtedly one valid tool in promoting rehabilitation. Nonetheless, to ensure that *Turner* continues to impose meaningful limits on the promulgation of rules that infringe upon inmates' constitutional rights, courts must be especially cautious in evaluating the constitutionality of prison regulations that are supposedly justified primarily on that basis. When, as here, a reasonable factfinder could conclude that challenged deprivations

---

1. Even less apparent is the security risk that would be posed by respondent's alternative suggestion, which is that LTSU–2 inmates be able to access news periodicals in the LTSU mini-law library, where inmates are already permitted to go to view legal materials during 2–hour blocks of time pursuant to a first-come, first-serve roster of requests.

have a tenuous logical connection to rehabilitation, or are exaggerated responses to a prison's legitimate interest in rehabilitation, prison officials are not entitled to judgment as a matter of law.

Petitioner argues that, because the various deprivations in the levels of disciplinary confinement short of LTSU–2 are also severe, prison officials have no choice but to deprive inmates of core constitutional rights in LTSU–2 in order to make LTSU–2 more unattractive than other types of segregation. The fact that most States and the Federal Government run their prisons without resorting to the type of ban at issue in this case casts serious doubt upon the need for the challenged constitutional deprivations.

In any event, if we consider the severity of the other conditions of confinement in LTSU–2, it becomes obvious that inmates have a powerful motivation to escape those conditions irrespective of the ban on newspapers, magazines, and personal photographs. Inmates in LTSU–2 face 23 hours a day in solitary confinement, are allowed only one visitor per month, may not make phone calls except in cases of emergency, lack any access to radio or television, may not use the prison commissary, are not permitted General Educational Development (GED) or special education study, and may not receive compensation under the inmate compensation system if they work as a unit janitor. Although conditions in LTSU–1 are also harsh, * * * they are far more appealing than the conditions in LTSU–2. LTSU–1 inmates may have two visitors and may make one phone call per month; they have access to the commissary; they are permitted in-cell GED or special education study; they are permitted a wider range of counseling services; and they are eligible to obtain compensation under the inmate compensation system. * * *

In addition, prisoners in LTSU–1 do *not* regain access to personal photographs, which means that the ban on photographs cannot be justified by petitioner's " 'hope' " that inmates will respond to the constitutional deprivations in LTSU–2 by improving their behavior so they may graduate into LTSU–1. * * *

In sum, the logical connection between the ban on newspapers and (especially) the ban on personal photographs, on one hand, and the rehabilitation interests posited by petitioner, on the other, is at best highly questionable. Moreover, petitioner did not introduce evidence that his proposed theory of behavior modification has any basis in human psychology, or that the challenged rule has in fact had any rehabilitative effect on LTSU–2 inmates.[4] Accordingly, at least based on the present state of the record, a reasonable factfinder could conclude that prisoners

---

4. I emphasize the lack of evidentiary support for petitioner's position because I believe that, in light of the record currently before the Court, the logical connection between petitioner's stated interest in rehabilitation and the prohibition on newspapers and photographs is exceedingly tenuous. When the logical connection between prison officials' stated interests and the restrictions on prisoners' constitutional rights is not self-evident, we have considered whether prison officials proffered any evidence that their regulations served the values they identified. See, *e.g., Turner v. Safley,* 482 U.S. 78, 98 (1987) (discussing lack of evidence in the record to support a ban on marriage as related to prison officials' stated objectives).

would have a sufficiently powerful incentive to graduate out of LTSU–2 even absent the challenged rule, such that the rule is not likely to have any appreciable behavior modification effect.

The temporal character of LTSU–2 status further undermines petitioner's argument that the ban on newspapers and photographs at issue in this case is reasonably related to a legitimate penological interest. * * * Petitioner acknowledges that "[a]n inmate in the LTSU can remain on Level 2 status indefinitely." Indeed, as of August 2002, which is the most recent date for which there is record evidence, roughly three-quarters of inmates placed in LTSU–2 had remained in that status since the inception of the LTSU program over two years earlier. * * *

* * * It would be a different case if prison officials had promulgated a regulation that deprived LTSU–2 inmates of certain First Amendment rights for a short period of time in response to specific disciplinary infractions. The indefinite deprivations at issue here, however, obviously impose a much greater burden on inmates' ability to exercise their constitutional rights. Absent evidence that these indefinite deprivations will be more effective in achieving rehabilitation than shorter periods of deprivation, a reasonable factfinder could conclude that the challenged regulation "sweeps much more broadly than can be explained by [prison officials'] penological objectives," and is hence an exaggerated response to petitioner's legitimate interest in rehabilitation.

In short, as with regard to the current state of the record concerning the connection between the challenged regulation and its effect on prison security, the record is insufficient to conclude, as a matter of law, that petitioner has established a reasonable relationship between his valid interest in inmate rehabilitation and the prohibition on newspapers, magazines, and personal photographs in LTSU–2.

* * *

JUSTICE GINSBURG, dissenting.

* * *

* * * [T]he plurality effectively tells prison officials they will succeed in cases of this order, and swiftly, while barely trying. It suffices for them to say, in our professional judgment the restriction is warranted. * * *

* * *

QUESTIONS AND POINTS FOR DISCUSSION

1. After *Beard v. Banks*, what restrictions on prisoners would violate the First Amendment? Would a rule prohibiting the "worst of the worst" prisoners from having access to the Bible, Koran, or other religious materials until they move out of a restrictive housing unit be constitutional? Consider this question anew after reviewing the materials in Section C of this chapter on the scope of prisoners' right to religious freedom.

2. If you represented a prisoner asserting a First Amendment claim, what strategies would you employ in an effort to avert the granting of a defendant's motion for summary judgment on that claim?

B. FREEDOM OF ASSOCIATION

Subsumed within the First Amendment and the Due Process Clauses of the Fifth and Fourteenth Amendments is what has come to be known as the freedom of association. Despite the generality of the term "association," the Constitution does not extend its protection to all contemplated encounters between individuals. See, e.g., Dallas v. Stanglin, 490 U.S. 19, 109 S.Ct. 1591 (1989) (restriction on the ages of persons who can be admitted to certain recreational dances does not implicate the First Amendment). The constitutionally protected freedom of association is rather a more narrow concept.

As described by the Supreme Court in Roberts v. United States Jaycees, 468 U.S. 609, 104 S.Ct. 3244 (1984), the right to freedom of association has two dimensions. First, the right prevents the government from unduly encroaching on "choices to enter into and maintain certain intimate human relationships." Id. at 617, 104 S.Ct. at 3249. Family relationships, for example, are protected by this right to "intimate association," according to the Supreme Court, because they are marked by such characteristics as "relative smallness, a high degree of selectivity in decisions to begin and maintain the affiliation, and seclusion from others in critical aspects of the relationship." Id. at 620, 104 S.Ct. at 3250.

The Court in Roberts explained the reasoning for affording constitutional protection to certain intimate associations:

> The Court has long recognized that, because the Bill of Rights is designed to secure individual liberty, it must afford the formation and preservation of certain kinds of highly personal relationships a substantial measure of sanctuary from unjustified interference by the State. Without precisely identifying every consideration that may underlie this type of constitutional protection, we have noted that certain kinds of personal bonds have played a critical role in the culture and traditions of the Nation by cultivating and transmitting shared ideals and beliefs; they thereby foster diversity and act as critical buffers between the individual and the power of the State. Moreover, the constitutional shelter afforded such relationships reflects the realization that individuals draw much of their emotional enrichment from close ties with others. Protecting these relationships from unwarranted state interference therefore safeguards the ability independently to define one's identity that is central to any concept of liberty.

Id. at 618–19, 104 S.Ct. at 3249–50.

In addition to protecting the freedom of "intimate association," the Constitution, through the First Amendment, protects what the Supreme

Court has described as "expressive association." "Expressive association" encompasses the right to gather together with others in order to engage in the activities protected by the First Amendment, such as speaking, worshiping, and petitioning the government for a redress of grievances. Id. at 618, 104 S.Ct. at 3249. "Expressive association," according to the Court, safeguards cultural and political diversity and prevents minority viewpoints from being quashed by the majority. The Court has been careful to note, however, that not all encounters during which words or ideas are exchanged are considered "associational" within the meaning of the First Amendment. Nowhere in the Constitution, said the Court in *Dallas v. Stanglin,* is there "a generalized right of 'social association.' " 490 U.S. at 25, 109 S.Ct. at 1595.

In the prison context, two questions arise concerning the freedom of association: First, do prisoners retain any associational rights under either the First Amendment or other constitutional provisions? And second, assuming that they do, to what extent can those associational rights be curbed? As you read the case below, which concerns the associational rights of pretrial detainees, consider these two questions.

BLOCK v. RUTHERFORD

Supreme Court of the United States, 1984.
468 U.S. 576, 104 S.Ct. 3227, 82 L.Ed.2d 438.

CHIEF JUSTICE BURGER delivered the opinion of the Court.

We granted certiorari to decide whether pretrial detainees have a right guaranteed by the United States Constitution to contact visits * * *.

Los Angeles County Central Jail is one of seven principal facilities operated by the Sheriff of Los Angeles County. The three-story jail complex, located in downtown Los Angeles, is the largest jail in the country, with a capacity of over 5,000 inmates. It is the primary facility in Los Angeles County for male pretrial detainees, the vast majority of whom remain at the facility at most a few days or weeks while they await trial.

In 1975, respondents, pretrial detainees at Central Jail, brought a class action under 42 U.S.C. §§ 1983, 1985, against the County Sheriff, certain administrators of Central Jail, and the County Board of Supervisors, challenging * * * the policy of the jail denying pretrial detainees contact visits with their spouses, relatives, children, and friends * * *.[1]

The District Court agreed with respondents that "the ability of a man to embrace his wife and his children from time to time during the weeks or months while he is awaiting trial is a matter of great importance to

---

1. When respondents instituted this suit, contact visits were not generally allowed. However, all detainees at Central Jail were allowed unmonitored noncontact visits each day between the hours of 8:30 a.m. and 8:30 p.m. It is estimated that there were over 63,000 such visits each month in an air-conditioned visiting area that accommodates 228 visitors at once. Privacy partitions separated each individual visiting location from the others, and clear glass panels separated the inmates from the visitors, who visit over telephones.

him," yet it recognized that "unrestricted contact visitation would add greatly" to security problems at the jail. * * *

* * *

The court found that the "hardship" on detainees of being unable to "embrace their loved ones" for only a few days or a few weeks could not justify imposition of these substantial burdens. However, the court believed, the factors rendering contact visitation impracticable for detainees incarcerated for short periods are considerably less compelling when detention is prolonged.

The court reasoned that "the scope, burden and dangers of [a] program [of contact visitation] would be substantially diminished" were contact visitation limited to detainees "who have been in uninterrupted custody for a month or more *and who are not determined to be drug oriented or escape risks,*" and a ceiling imposed on the total number of contact visits that the jail must provide.[2] With these limitations, the court suggested, a contact visitation program would require only "[m]odest alteration" of the existing facility. Alternatively, the court said, the Sheriff could build or occupy a new facility for contact visits and transport inmates back and forth, as necessary.

* * *

* * * [T]he [Ninth Circuit] Court of Appeals affirmed the District Court's orders requiring that certain of the detainees be allowed contact visits * * *.

* * *

Four Terms ago, in *Bell v. Wolfish,* 441 U.S. 520 (1979), we considered for the first time * * * the scope of constitutional protection that must be accorded pretrial detainees. * * * We held that, where it is alleged that a pretrial detainee has been deprived of liberty without due process, the dispositive inquiry is whether the challenged condition, practice, or policy constitutes punishment, "[f]or under the Due Process Clause, a detainee must not be punished prior to an adjudication of guilt in accordance with due process of law."

* * * Specifically, we observed that "[a] court must decide whether the disability is imposed for the purpose of punishment or whether it is but an incident of some other legitimate governmental purpose." Absent proof of intent to punish, we noted, this determination "generally will turn on 'whether an alternative purpose to which [the restriction] may rationally be connected is assignable for it, and whether it appears excessive in relation to the alternative purpose assigned [to it].' " We concluded:

---

[2].   The District Court ordered that petitioners "make available a contact visit once each week to each pretrial detainee that has been held in the jail for one month or more, and concerning whom there is no indication of drug or escape propensities; provided, however, that no more than fifteen hundred such visits need be allowed in any one week." * * *

"[I]f a particular condition or restriction of pretrial detention is reasonably related to a legitimate governmental objective, it does not, without more, amount to 'punishment.' Conversely, if a restriction or condition is not reasonably related to a legitimate goal—if it is arbitrary or purposeless—a court permissibly may infer that the purpose of the governmental action is punishment that may not constitutionally be inflicted upon detainees *qua* detainees."

In setting forth these guidelines, we reaffirmed the very limited role that courts should play in the administration of detention facilities. In assessing whether a specific restriction is "reasonably related" to security interests, we said, courts should

"heed our warning that '[s]uch considerations are peculiarly within the province and professional expertise of corrections officials, and, in the absence of substantial evidence in the record to indicate that the officials have exaggerated their response to these considerations courts should ordinarily defer to their expert judgment in such matters.'" *Id.*, at 540–541, n. 23 (quoting *Pell v. Procunier,* 417 U.S. 817, 827 (1974)).

* * *

Petitioners' first contention is that it was error to conclude that even low risk detainees incarcerated for more than a month are constitutionally entitled to contact visits from friends and relatives. * * * The District Court did not find, nor did the Court of Appeals suggest, that the purpose of petitioners' policy of denying contact visitation is to punish the inmates. * * *

The question before us, therefore, is narrow: whether the prohibition of contact visits is reasonably related to legitimate governmental objectives. More particularly, because there is no dispute that internal security of detention facilities is a legitimate governmental interest, our inquiry is simply whether petitioners' blanket prohibition on contact visits at Central Jail is reasonably related to the security of that facility.

That there is a valid, rational connection between a ban on contact visits and internal security of a detention facility is too obvious to warrant extended discussion. * * * Contact visits invite a host of security problems. They open the institution to the introduction of drugs, weapons, and other contraband. Visitors can easily conceal guns, knives, drugs, or other contraband in countless ways and pass them to an inmate unnoticed by even the most vigilant observers. And these items can readily be slipped from the clothing of an innocent child, or transferred by other visitors permitted close contact with inmates.

Contact visitation poses other dangers for a detention facility, as well. Detainees—by definition persons unable to meet bail—often are awaiting trial for serious, violent offenses, and many have prior criminal convictions. Exposure of this type person to others, whether family, friends, or jail administrators, necessarily carries with it risks that the safety of innocent individuals will be jeopardized in various ways. They may, for example, be taken as hostages or become innocent pawns in escape attempts. It is no answer, of course, that we deal here with restrictions on pretrial detainees rather than convicted criminals. For, as we observed in *Wolfish,* in this context, "[t]here is no basis for concluding that pretrial detainees pose any lesser security risk than convicted inmates." Indeed, we said, "it may be that in certain circumstances [detainees] present a greater risk to jail security and order."

The District Court and Court of Appeals held that totally disallowing contact visits is excessive in relation to the security and other interests at stake. We reject this characterization. There are many justifications for denying contact visits entirely, rather than attempting the difficult task of establishing a program of limited visitation such as that imposed here. It is not unreasonable to assume, for instance, that low security risk detainees would be enlisted to help obtain contraband or weapons by their fellow inmates who are denied contact visits. Additionally, identification of those inmates who have propensities for violence, escape, or drug smuggling is a difficult if not impossible task, and the chances of mistaken identification are substantial. The burdens of identifying candidates for contact visitation—glossed over by the District Court—are made even more difficult by the brevity of detention and the constantly changing nature of the inmate population. Or a complete prohibition could reasonably be thought necessary because selectively allowing contact visits to some—even if feasible—could well create tension between those allowed contact visits and those not.[9]

* * *

On this record, we must conclude that the District Court simply misperceived the limited scope of judicial inquiry under *Wolfish.* When the District Court found that many factors counseled against contact visits, its inquiry should have ended. The court's further "balancing" resulted in an impermissible substitution of its view on the proper administration of Central Jail for that of the experienced administrators of that facility. * * *

In rejecting the District Court's order, we do not in any sense denigrate the importance of visits from family or friends to the detainee. Nor do we intend to suggest that contact visits might not be a factor contributing to the ultimate reintegration of the detainee into society. We hold only that the Constitution does not require that detainees be allowed contact visits when responsible, experienced administrators have deter-

---

[9]. The reasonableness of petitioners' blanket prohibition is underscored by the costs—financial and otherwise—of the alternative response ordered by the District Court. Jail personnel, whom the District Court recognized are now free from the "complicated, expensive, and time-consuming process[es]" of interviewing, searching, and processing visitors, would have to be reassigned to perform these tasks, perhaps requiring the hiring of additional personnel. Intrusive strip searches after contact visits would be necessary. Finally, as the District Court noted, at the very least, "modest" improvements of existing facilities would be required to accommodate a contact visitation program if the county did not purchase or build a new facility elsewhere. These are substantial costs that a facility's administrators might reasonably attempt to avoid.

mined, in their sound discretion, that such visits will jeopardize the security of the facility.

JUSTICE BLACKMUN, concurring in the judgment. [Opinion omitted.]

JUSTICE MARSHALL, with whom JUSTICE BRENNAN and JUSTICE STEVENS join, dissenting.

* * * Guided by an unwarranted confidence in the good faith and "expertise" of prison administrators and by a pinched conception of the meaning of the Due Process Clauses and the Eighth Amendment, a majority of the Court increasingly appears willing to sanction any prison condition for which the majority can imagine a colorable rationale, no matter how oppressive or ill-justified that condition is in fact. * * *

* * *

* * * [R]espondents can and do point to a fundamental right abridged by the jail's policy—namely, their freedom to engage in and prevent the deterioration of their relationships with their families.

The importance of the right asserted by respondents was acknowledged by the District Court. * * *[2] Denial of contact visitation, the court concluded, is "very traumatic treatment." Substantial evidence in the record supports the District Court's findings. William Nagel, an expert in the field of corrections, testified that contact visitation was crucial in allowing prisoners to maintain their familial bonds. Similarly, Dr. Terry Kupers, a psychiatrist, testified that denial of contact visitation contributes to the breakup of prisoners' marriages and generally threatens their mental health. The secondary literature buttresses these assertions, as do the conclusions reached by other courts.[4]

The significant injury to familial relations wrought by the jail's policy of denying contact visitation means that that policy must be tested against a legal standard more constraining than the rule announced in *Wolfish*. * * *

* * * [I]t could be argued that the "withdrawal or limitation of many privileges and rights" that necessarily accompanies incarceration, combined with the fact that the inmates' familial bonds are not altogether severed by such a ban, means that something less than a "compelling" government interest would suffice to legitimate the impairment of the inmates' rights.[8] On the other hand, * * * even persons lawfully incarcerated after being convicted of crimes retain important constitutional rights;

---

2. It should be stressed that, while most of the jail inmates are detained for only brief periods of time (and thus are not covered by the District Court's order), some are detained for very substantial periods. For example, plaintiffs Rutherford and Taylor were held in the jail pending their trials for 38 months and 32 months, respectively.

4. See *Boudin v. Thomas*, 533 F.Supp. 786, 792–793 (S.D.N.Y.1982) (pointing out, *inter alia*, that, when an inmate's child is too young to talk, denial of contact visitation is the equivalent of denial of any visitation whatsoever).

8. Cf. *Schall v. Martin*, 467 U.S. 253, 291, n. 15 (1984) (Marshall, J., dissenting) (suggesting a test under which "the strength of the state interest needed to legitimate a statute [would depend] upon the *degree* to which the statute encroaches upon fundamental rights") (emphasis in original).

presumptively innocent persons surely are entitled to no less. * * * [A] sensitive balancing of these competing considerations is unnecessary to resolve the case before us. At a minimum, petitioners, to prevail, should be required to show that the jail's policy materially advances a substantial government interest. * * *

It should be emphasized that what petitioners must defend is not their reluctance to allow *unlimited* contact visitation, but rather their refusal to adopt the specific reforms ordered by the lower courts. * * *

* * * [P]etitioners contend that a ban on contact visitation is necessary to prevent the introduction into the jail of drugs and weapons. It must be admitted that this is a legitimate and important goal. However, petitioners fail to show that its realization would be materially impaired by adoption of the reforms ordered by the District Court. Indeed, evidence adduced at trial establishes the contrary. Several witnesses testified that security procedures could be implemented that would make importation of contraband very difficult. Among the precautions effectively used at other institutions are: searches of prisoners before and after visits; dressing of prisoners in special clothes for visitation; examination of prisoners and visitors with metal detectors and fluoroscopes; exclusion of parcels from the visiting area; rejection of visitors who do not comply with visiting rules; and continuous observation of the visiting area by guards.[13] * * * Further protection against the transmission of contraband from visitors to inmates is provided by the District Court's restriction of its order to inmates who have been classified as low risk. In short, there is no reason to think that compliance with the lower courts' directive would result in more than a negligible increase in the flow of drugs or weapons into the jail.[14]

Second, petitioners contend that allowance of contact visitation would endanger innocent visitors who are placed in near proximity to dangerous detainees. Again, though the importance of the objective is apparent, the nexus between it and the jail's current policy is not. As indicated above, the District Court's order applies only to detainees who are unlikely to try to escape. And security measures could be employed by petitioners that would make it very difficult for inmates to hurt or take advantage of visitors. Finally, the administrators of other institutions that have long permitted contact visits between inmates and their families testified at trial that violent incidents resulting from such visitation are rare, apparently because inmates value their visitation privileges so highly.

* * * In an effort to discredit the limitations on the District Court's order, the majority argues that determination of which inmates have a

13. The majority implies that the intrusiveness of some of these measures provides an additional justification for petitioners' refusal to allow any contact visitation. It is possible that some inmates or visitors might decide to forgo visitation rather than submit to such procedures, but surely the choice should be left to them.

14. It should be pointed out that drugs and weapons enter the jail in significant quantities through several other routes. It would thus be a mistake to think that the jail is currently free of contraband, and that the small amounts that might enter the facility through contact visitation would infect the facility for the first time.

sufficiently low propensity to misbehave would be difficult and time-consuming, especially in light of "the brevity of detention and the constantly changing nature of the inmate population." This contention is rebutted by the District Court's finding that, after an inmate has been incarcerated for a month, jail officials have considerable information regarding his background and behavior patterns, and by evidence in the record that the jail already has a classification system that, with some modification and improvement, could be used to evaluate detainees' propensities for escape and drug abuse. Next, the majority contends that compliance with the District Court's order would be expensive. Again, the District Court's findings are decisive; the court found that only "modest" changes in the jail facilities would be required. More fundamentally, a desire to run a jail as cheaply as possible is not a legitimate reason for abridging the constitutional rights of its occupants. Finally, the majority suggests that the District Court's order might cause some dissension in the jail, because inmates denied visitation privileges would resent those granted such privileges. There is no evidence whatsoever in the record to support this speculative observation.

In sum, neither petitioners nor the majority have shown that permitting low-risk pretrial detainees who have been incarcerated for more than a month occasionally to have contact visits with their spouses and children would frustrate the achievement of any substantial state interest.[17] Because such visitation would significantly alleviate the adverse impact of the jail's current policies upon respondents' familial rights, its deprivation violates the Due Process Clause.

* * *

QUESTIONS AND POINTS FOR DISCUSSION

1. Was the Supreme Court's repudiation of "balancing" in *Block v. Rutherford* consistent with its decisions you have read thus far? Without such balancing, how is a court to determine whether officials have "exaggerated their response" to security concerns? And without such balancing, what happens to the protection ostensibly afforded inmates by the Constitution? See Valentine v. Englehardt, 474 F.Supp. 294, 300–01 (D.N.J.1979) ("A naked man in chains poses no risk. From that point on, every increase in freedom brings at least some decrease in security.")

2. Assume that correctional officials banned not only contact visits, but all noncontact visits with family members and friends. Would such a total ban on visitation with these individuals be constitutional as applied to convicted inmates? As applied to pretrial detainees? In answering these questions, of

---

17. The feasibility of the limited contact visitation program ordered by the District Court is further suggested by the number of other institutions that have similar programs. Approximately 80% of the inmates in the California prison system are permitted contact visitation. It appears that the current policy of the Federal Bureau of Prisons is to allow visitation privileges to both convicted inmates and pretrial detainees. In New York City, all except identifiably dangerous pretrial detainees are permitted contact visits with their families. * * *

what significance are the following observations about associational rights made by the Supreme Court in Jones v. North Carolina Prisoners' Labor Union, 433 U.S. 119, 97 S.Ct. 2532 (1977), supra page 481:

> [N]umerous associational rights are necessarily curtailed by the realities of confinement. They may be curtailed whenever the institution's officials, in the exercise of their informed discretion, reasonably conclude that such associations, whether through group meetings or otherwise, possess the likelihood of disruption to prison order or stability, or otherwise interfere with the legitimate penological objectives of the prison environment.

Id. at 132, 97 S.Ct. at 2541.

Consider also the import of Kentucky Dep't of Corrections v. Thompson, 490 U.S. 454, 109 S.Ct. 1904 (1989), infra page 609, to the question whether inmates have constitutionally protected associational rights. In that case, the Supreme Court held that prisoners do not have a liberty interest stemming from the Constitution to visit with a particular person. Consequently, a prisoner's visiting privileges with a specific individual can be withdrawn without affording the prisoner any due process—any procedural safeguards, such as those outlined in *Procunier v. Martinez* on page 478, to ensure that the withdrawal of visiting privileges is not based on erroneous information or the arbitrary actions of correctional officials.

In a concurring opinion in *Thompson,* Justice Kennedy emphasized that the case did not involve a general ban on the visitation privileges of some or all prisoners. In addition, the visiting privileges of the visitors in *Thompson* were only temporarily, not permanently, suspended. Underscoring the limited nature of the Court's holding, Justice Kennedy observed: "Nothing in the Court's opinion forecloses the claim that a prison regulation permanently forbidding all visits to some or all prisoners implicates the protections of the Due Process Clause in a way that the precise and individualized restrictions at issue here do not." Id. at 465, 109 S.Ct. at 1911 (Kennedy, J., concurring). In your opinion, do prisoners retain a limited constitutional right to visitation?

3. Even after assuming or deciding that inmates retain associational rights protected by the First Amendment or some other constitutional provision, courts often have found restrictions on visiting privileges with particular individuals to be reasonable and therefore constitutional. See, e.g., Caraballo–Sandoval v. Honsted, 35 F.3d 521, 525 (11th Cir.1994) (constitutional to deny visiting privileges to prisoner's wife, a former prison employee with knowledge of security procedures); Smith v. Coughlin, 748 F.2d 783, 788 (2d Cir.1984) (permitting inmate on death row to only visit with family members, but not friends, was constitutional); Robinson v. Palmer, 841 F.2d 1151, 1157 (D.C.Cir.1988) (permanently suspending visiting privileges of inmate's wife after she attempted to smuggle marijuana into the prison did not violate any First Amendment rights of the inmate or his wife).

4. In Overton v. Bazzetta, 539 U.S. 126, 123 S.Ct. 2162 (2003), the Supreme Court confronted questions regarding the constitutionality of much broader restrictions on visitation privileges than those that were at issue in *Thompson.* The Michigan prisoners who, along with family members and friends, filed a § 1983 suit in *Overton* were classified at the highest security

level and consequently were limited to noncontact visits. The plaintiffs challenged the constitutionality of several additional restrictions on their visiting privileges, alleging violations of substantive due process, the First Amendment, and the Eighth Amendment. These restrictions included, among others: a prohibition on visits from minors younger than eighteen unless they were the prisoner's children, stepchildren, grandchildren, or siblings; a requirement that a child be accompanied by an immediate family member or a legal guardian when visiting a prisoner; a bar on visits from former prisoners unless the prospective visitor was a member of the inmate's immediate family and the warden had authorized the former prisoner's placement on the approved visitor list; and termination, for at least two years, of the visitation privileges of inmates who had violated the correctional department's substance-abuse policies two or more times.

In an opinion written by Justice Kennedy, the Supreme Court skirted the question whether the constitutional right of association survives incarceration at least to some extent, holding that the restrictions on visiting privileges were constitutional in any event because they had a rational relation to legitimate penological interests. The Court noted, for example, that limiting the children authorized to visit prisoners reduced the overall number of visitors, making it easier for correctional officials to monitor visits and maintain institutional security. In addition, these restrictions were rationally connected to the interest in minimizing the disruption caused by children in the visiting area. Although the Court did not elaborate on this point, one of the commonly asserted justifications for restrictions on children's visits in prisons is that they become restless and roam around during the visits, distracting the correctional officers charged with monitoring the visiting room and detracting from the quality of the visits enjoyed by other inmates. The Court also stated that curtailing visits by children to prisons would protect the children from the harm that could ensue from prisoner misconduct or an accident. See, e.g., Bazzetta v. McGinnis, 148 F.Supp.2d 813, 822 (E.D. Mich. 2001) (describing the molestation of a three-year-old girl by an inmate whom the girl's mother was visiting).

In summary fashion, the Court also concluded that it was reasonable to require that a child visiting a prisoner be accompanied by someone, whether an immediate family member or a legal guardian, entrusted with the responsibility of acting in the child's best interests. And the Court invoked the governmental interests in preserving institutional security and averting future crimes as justifications for the general ban on visits from former prisoners.

The Court more closely scrutinized the two-year ban on visiting privileges when a prisoner had two or more substance-abuse violations. The Court acknowledged that the across-the-board ban on visiting privileges was "severe," at least in part because restoration of the privileges after the two-year period had elapsed fell within the warden's discretion. Id. at 134, 123 S.Ct. at 2169. But in finding the restriction rationally connected to the goal of discouraging inmates from using drugs or drinking alcohol while in prison, the Court noted: "Withdrawing visitation privileges is a proper and even necessary management technique to induce compliance with the rules of inmate behavior, especially for high-security prisoners who have few other privileges to lose." Id., 123 S.Ct. at 2168–69. The Court added, though, that if, in a different case, the Court determined that the regulation limiting the visiting privileges of inmates with substance-abuse violations was being implemented in a way that made it "a *de facto* permanent ban on all visitation for certain inmates," it might not find the requisite connection between the regulation and a legitimate penological interest. Id., 123 S.Ct. at 2169.

The other part of the Court's application of the *Turner* test in *Overton* that bears highlighting is its discussion of the extent to which inmates had alternative means of communicating with the persons prohibited from visiting them. The Court cited what it considered one viable alternative—sending messages through individuals who were permitted to visit the inmate. While the Court acknowledged that prisoners whose visiting privileges had been totally curtailed because of substance-abuse violations could not avail themselves of this alternative, the Court said that they still could communicate with friends and family members via letters and telephone calls. To the plaintiffs' argument that these alternatives were infeasible for illiterate prisoners and for communications with young children, the Court responded: "Alternatives to visitation need not be ideal, however; they need only be available." Id. at 135, 123 S.Ct. at 2169.

Do you agree with the Supreme Court's analysis in *Overton* and with its conclusions? Would an across-the-board ban on visits, both contact and noncontact, with children under the age of eighteen in a prison be constitutional? In a jail? Cf. N.E.W. v. Kennard, 952 F.Supp. 714, 720 (D. Utah 1997) (policy generally prohibiting children under eight from having noncontact visits with pretrial detainees, the only kind of visits allowed at the jail, is reasonably related to penological and administrative interests and therefore comports with due process).

5. Assume that officials at a prison permit the formation of an Afro–American Culture Organization and a Latin Studies Group. However, they deny the request of white inmates to form a "white ethnic club." Have the prison officials violated the constitutional rights of the white inmates? See Thomas v. United States Sec'y of Def., 730 F.Supp. 362 (D.Kan.1990).

6. Would a prison policy permitting heterosexual, but not homosexual, inmates to visit with their boyfriends or girlfriends be constitutional? See Doe v. Sparks, 733 F.Supp. 227 (W.D.Pa.1990).

7. Researchers have found that the maintenance of family ties while inmates are incarcerated decreases recidivism rates upon their release. Solangel Maldonado, Recidivism and Paternal Engagement, 40 Fam. L.Q. 191, 196–97 (2006). If you were to draft a regulation for a state's correctional agency governing visiting privileges in the state's prisons, would these research findings affect the regulation's content? How? Would you provide for conjugal visits in the regulation? Why or why not? If you did provide for conjugal visits, would they be restricted to spouses? For several proposals on visitation rights, see American Bar Association Standards for Criminal Justice: Legal Status of Prisoners, Standards 23–6.2 to 6.4 (1981); Uniform Law Commissioners' Model Sentencing and Corrections Act, §§ 4–115 to –116, 4–118 (1978).

8. In your opinion, does the right of prisoners to marry, which was recognized in *Turner v. Safley*, entitle male inmates to have the opportunity

to inseminate their wives through artificial means? See Gerber v. Hickman, 291 F.3d 617, 621 (9th Cir. 2002) (the right to procreate is fundamentally inconsistent with, and does not survive, incarceration); Goodwin v. Turner, 908 F.2d 1395, 1398–400 (8th Cir.1990) (assuming the right to procreate survives incarceration, artificial-insemination ban is reasonably related to legitimate interest in treating male and female inmates equally).

9. Studies have found that children whose mothers or fathers are criminals are much more likely to commit crimes themselves. Joseph Murray & David P. Farrington, The Effects of Parental Imprisonment on Children, 37 Crime & Just. 133, 163 (2008). When both parents have criminal histories, the risk that the children will become delinquent is extremely high. Kevin N. Wright & Karen E. Wright, U.S. Dep't of Justice, Family Life, Delinquency, and Crime: A Policymaker's Guide 23 (1994). One explanation for this enhanced risk of delinquency is that parents with criminal histories are less likely to closely supervise and monitor the activities of their children, increasing the chances that the children will become involved in delinquent activities. Id. at 24. Another theory is that children learn maladaptive values and behaviors from the example set by their parents. Murray & Farrington, supra, at 163–64; J. David Hawkins et al., A Review of Predictors of Youth Violence, in Serious & Violent Juvenile Offenders: Risk Factors and Successful Interventions 134 (Rolf Loeber & David P. Farrington eds., 1998).

If you were charged with the responsibility of devising prison programs for a department of corrections, what, if any, bearing would these research findings have on your programming decisions? See Ann Booker Loper & Elena Hontorio Tuerk, Parenting Programs for Incarcerated Parents: Current Research and Future Directions, 17 Crim. Just. Pol'y Rev. 407 (2006) (describing prison parenting programs and measures of their effectiveness). Would you offer the same programming to male and female prisoners? See Elise Zealand, Protecting the Ties that Bind from Behind Bars: A Call for Equal Opportunities for Incarcerated Fathers and Their Children to Maintain the Parent–Child Relationship, 31 Colum. J.L. & Soc. Probs. 247, 255–60 (1998) (describing the dearth of parenting programs for male inmates). For a discussion of equal-protection constraints on differential programming for male and female inmates, see pages 661–73.

C. FREEDOM OF RELIGION

The First Amendment provides in part that "Congress shall make no law respecting an establishment of religion, or prohibiting the free exercise thereof." The Supreme Court confirmed in Cruz v. Beto, 405 U.S. 319, 92 S.Ct. 1079 (1972) that inmates retain rights to religious freedom. In that case, a Buddhist prisoner had filed a § 1983 suit in which he claimed that he was not afforded the same opportunities to practice his religion as were prisoners of other faiths. His complaint alleged, for example, that while other prisoners were allowed to use the prison chapel, he was not. The plaintiff also contended that the state encouraged prisoners to join orthodox religions, and not his own; he alleged, for example, that the state funded Catholic, Jewish, and Protestant chaplains in the prison and provided inmates free Bibles.

Holding that the district court had erred in dismissing the plaintiff's complaint, the Supreme Court observed: "If Cruz was a Buddhist and if he was denied a reasonable opportunity of pursuing his faith comparable to the opportunity afforded fellow prisoners who adhere to conventional religious precepts, then there was palpable discrimination by the State against the Buddhist religion * * *." Id. at 322, 92 S.Ct. at 1081. In an important footnote, the Court added:

> We do not suggest, of course, that every religious sect or group within a prison—however few in number—must have identical facilities or personnel. A special chapel or place of worship need not be provided for every faith regardless of size; nor must a chaplain, priest, or minister be provided without regard to the extent of the demand. But reasonable opportunities must be afforded to all prisoners to exercise the religious freedom guaranteed by the First and Fourteenth Amendments without fear of penalty.

Id. at 322 n. 2, 92 S.Ct. at 1081 n. 2.

Fifteen years later, in the case set forth below, the Supreme Court returned to the subject of the scope of inmates' right to religious freedom.

O'LONE v. ESTATE OF SHABAZZ

Supreme Court of the United States, 1987.
482 U.S. 342, 107 S.Ct. 2400, 96 L.Ed.2d 282.

CHIEF JUSTICE REHNQUIST delivered the opinion of the Court.

* * * Respondents, members of the Islamic faith, were prisoners in New Jersey's Leesburg State Prison. They challenged policies adopted by prison officials which resulted in their inability to attend Jumu'ah, a weekly Muslim congregational service regularly held in the main prison building and in a separate facility known as "the Farm." Jumu'ah is commanded by the Koran and must be held every Friday after the sun reaches its zenith and before the Asr, or afternoon prayer. * * *

Inmates at Leesburg are placed in one of three custody classifications. Maximum security and "gang minimum" security inmates are housed in the main prison building, and those with the lowest classification—full minimum—live in "the Farm." * * *

* * * In April 1983, the New Jersey Department of Corrections issued Standard 853 * * *. * * * Because of serious overcrowding in the main building, Standard 853 * * * mandated that gang minimum inmates ordinarily be assigned jobs outside the main building. These inmates work in details of 8 to 15 persons, supervised by one guard. Standard 853 also required that full minimum inmates work outside the main institution, whether on or off prison grounds, or in a satellite building such as the Farm.

* * *

Significant problems arose with those inmates assigned to outside work details. Some avoided reporting for their assignments, while others found reasons for returning to the main building during the course of the workday (including their desire to attend religious services). Evidence showed that the return of prisoners during the day resulted in security risks and administrative burdens that prison officials found unacceptable. Because details of inmates were supervised by only one guard, the whole detail was forced to return to the main gate when one prisoner desired to return to the facility. The gate was the site of all incoming foot and vehicle traffic during the day, and prison officials viewed it as a high security risk area. When an inmate returned, vehicle traffic was delayed while the inmate was logged in and searched.

In response to these burdens, Leesburg officials took steps to ensure that those assigned to outside details remained there for the whole day. Thus, arrangements were made to have lunch and required medications brought out to the prisoners, and appointments with doctors and social workers were scheduled for the late afternoon. These changes proved insufficient, however, and prison officials began to study alternatives. After consulting with the director of social services, the director of professional services, and the prison's imam and chaplain, prison officials in March 1984 issued a policy memorandum which prohibited inmates assigned to outside work details from returning to the prison during the day except in the case of emergency.

The prohibition of returns prevented Muslims assigned to outside work details from attending Jumu'ah. Respondents filed suit under 42 U.S.C. § 1983, alleging that the prison policies unconstitutionally denied them their Free Exercise rights under the First Amendment, as applied to the States through the Fourteenth Amendment. The District Court * * * concluded that no constitutional violation had occurred. * * *

The Court of Appeals, *sua sponte* hearing the case en banc, decided that * * * prison policies could be sustained only if:

> "the state . . . show[s] that the challenged regulations were intended to serve, and do serve, the important penological goal of security, and that no reasonable method exists by which [prisoners'] religious rights can be accommodated without creating bona fide security problems. * * * "

In considering whether a potential method of accommodation is reasonable, the court added, relevant factors include cost, the effects of overcrowding, understaffing, and inmates' demonstrated proclivity to unruly conduct. The case was remanded to the District Court for reconsideration under the standards enumerated in the opinion. * * *

* * *

* * * To ensure that courts afford appropriate deference to prison officials, we have determined that prison regulations alleged to infringe constitutional rights are judged under a "reasonableness" test less restric-

tive than that ordinarily applied to alleged infringements of fundamental constitutional rights. We recently restated the proper standard: "[W]hen a prison regulation impinges on inmates' constitutional rights, the regulation is valid if it is reasonably related to legitimate penological interests." *Turner v. Safley.* * * *

We think the Court of Appeals decision in this case was wrong when it established a separate burden on prison officials to prove "that no reasonable method exists by which [prisoners'] religious rights can be accommodated without creating bona fide security problems." * * * Though the availability of accommodations is relevant to the reasonableness inquiry, we have rejected the notion that "prison officials . . . have to set up and then shoot down every conceivable alternative method of accommodating the claimant's constitutional complaint." By placing the burden on prison officials to disprove the availability of alternatives, the approach articulated by the Court of Appeals fails to reflect the respect and deference that the United States Constitution allows for the judgment of prison administrators.

Turning to consideration of the policies challenged in this case, we think the findings of the District Court establish clearly that prison officials have acted in a reasonable manner. *Turner v. Safley* drew upon our previous decisions to identify several factors relevant to this reasonableness determination. First, a regulation must have a logical connection to legitimate governmental interests invoked to justify it. The policies at issue here clearly meet that standard. The requirement that full minimum and gang minimum prisoners work outside the main facility was justified by concerns of institutional order and security, for the District Court found that it was "at least in part a response to a critical overcrowding in the state's prisons, and . . . at least in part designed to ease tension and drain on the facilities during that part of the day when the inmates were outside the confines of the main buildings." * * *

The subsequent policy prohibiting returns to the institution during the day also passes muster under this standard. Prison officials testified that the returns from outside work details generated congestion and delays at the main gate, a high risk area in any event. Return requests also placed pressure on guards supervising outside details, who previously were required to "evaluate each reason possibly justifying a return to the facilities and either accept or reject that reason." Rehabilitative concerns further supported the policy; corrections officials sought a simulation of working conditions and responsibilities in society. Chief Deputy Ucci testified: "One of the things that society demands or expects is that when you have a job, you show up on time, you put in your eight hours, or whatever hours you are supposed to put in, and you don't get off. . . . If we can show inmates that they're supposed to show up for work and work a full day, then when they get out at least we've done something." These legitimate goals were advanced by the prohibition on returns; it cannot seriously be maintained that "the logical connection between the regulation and the asserted goal is so remote as to render the policy arbitrary or irrational."

Our decision in *Turner* also found it relevant that "alternative means of exercising the right ... remain open to prison inmates." There are, of course, no alternative means of attending Jumu'ah; respondents' religious beliefs insist that it occur at a particular time. * * * In *Turner,* we did not look to see whether prisoners had other means of communicating with fellow inmates, but instead examined whether the inmates were deprived of "all means of expression." Here, similarly, we think it appropriate to see whether under these regulations respondents retain the ability to participate in other Muslim religious ceremonies. The record establishes that respondents are not deprived of all forms of religious obligations. The right to congregate for prayer or discussion is "virtually unlimited except during working hours," and the state-provided imam has free access to the prison. Muslim prisoners are given different meals whenever pork is served in the prison cafeteria. Special arrangements are also made during the month-long observance of Ramadan, a period of fasting and prayer. During Ramadan, Muslim prisoners are awakened at 4 a.m. for an early breakfast, and receive dinner at 8:30 p.m. each evening. We think this ability on the part of respondents to participate in other religious observances of their faith supports the conclusion that the restrictions at issue here were reasonable.

Finally, the case for the validity of these regulations is strengthened by examination of the impact that accommodation of respondents' asserted right would have on other inmates, on prison personnel, and on allocation of prison resources generally. Respondents suggest several accommodations of their practices, including placing all Muslim inmates in one or two inside work details or providing weekend labor for Muslim inmates. As noted by the District Court, however, each of respondents' suggested accommodations would, in the judgment of prison officials, have adverse effects on the institution. Inside work details for gang minimum inmates would be inconsistent with the legitimate concerns underlying Standard 853, and the District Court found that the extra supervision necessary to establish weekend details for Muslim prisoners "would be a drain on scarce human resources" at the prison. Prison officials determined that the alternatives would also threaten prison security by allowing "affinity groups" in the prison to flourish. Administrator O'Lone testified that "we have found out and think almost every prison administrator knows that any time you put a group of individuals together with one particular affinity interest ... you wind up with ... a leadership role and an organizational structure that will almost invariably challenge the institutional authority." Finally, the officials determined that special arrangements for one group would create problems as "other inmates [see] that a certain segment is escaping a rigorous work detail" and perceive favoritism. These concerns of prison administrators provide adequate support for the conclusion that accommodations of respondents' request to attend Jumu'ah would have undesirable results in the institution. These difficulties also make clear that there are no "obvious, easy alternatives to the policy adopted by petitioners."

* * * Here the District Court decided that the regulations alleged to infringe constitutional rights were reasonably related to legitimate penological objectives. We agree with the District Court, and it necessarily follows that the regulations in question do not offend the Free Exercise Clause of the First Amendment to the United States Constitution. * * *

JUSTICE BRENNAN, with whom JUSTICE MARSHALL, JUSTICE BLACKMUN, and JUSTICE STEVENS join, dissenting.

* * *

I

Prisoners are persons whom most of us would rather not think about. Banished from everyday sight, they exist in a shadow world that only dimly enters our awareness. They are members of a "total institution" that controls their daily existence in a way that few of us can imagine * * *.

It is thus easy to think of prisoners as members of a separate netherworld, driven by its own demands, ordered by its own customs, ruled by those whose claim to power rests on raw necessity. Nothing can change the fact, however, that the society that these prisoners inhabit is our own. Prisons may exist on the margins of that society, but no act of will can sever them from the body politic. When prisoners emerge from the shadows to press a constitutional claim, they invoke no alien set of principles drawn from a distant culture. Rather, they speak the language of the charter upon which all of us rely to hold official power accountable. They ask us to acknowledge that power exercised in the shadows must be restrained at least as diligently as power that acts in the sunlight.

* * *

In my view, adoption of "reasonableness" as a standard of review for *all* constitutional challenges by inmates is inadequate to this task. Such a standard is categorically deferential, and does not discriminate among degrees of deprivation. From this perspective, restricting use of the prison library to certain hours warrants the same level of scrutiny as preventing inmates from reading at all. * * *

It is true that the degree of deprivation is one of the factors in the Court's reasonableness determination. This by itself does not make the standard of review appropriate, however. If it did, we would need but a single standard for evaluating all constitutional claims, as long as every relevant factor were considered under its rubric. Clearly, we have never followed such an approach. * * * The use of differing levels of scrutiny proclaims that on some occasions official power must justify itself in a way that otherwise it need not. A relatively strict standard of review is a signal that a decree prohibiting a political demonstration on the basis of the participants' political beliefs is of more serious concern, and therefore will be scrutinized more closely, than a rule limiting the number of demonstrations that may take place downtown at noon.

* * *

An approach better suited to the sensitive task of protecting the constitutional rights of inmates is laid out by Judge Kaufman in *Abdul Wali v. Coughlin,* 754 F.2d 1015 (C.A.2 1985). That approach maintains that the degree of scrutiny of prison regulations should depend on "the nature of the right being asserted by prisoners, the type of activity in which they seek to engage, and whether the challenged restriction works a total deprivation (as opposed to a mere limitation) on the exercise of that right." Essentially, if the activity in which inmates seek to engage is presumptively dangerous, or if a regulation merely restricts the time, place, or manner in which prisoners may exercise a right, a prison regulation will be invalidated only if there is no reasonable justification for official action. Where exercise of the asserted right is not presumptively dangerous, however, and where the prison has completely deprived an inmate of that right, then prison officials must show that "a particular restriction is necessary to further an important governmental interest, and that the limitations on freedoms occasioned by the restrictions are no greater than necessary to effectuate the governmental objective involved."

The court's analytical framework in *Abdul Wali* recognizes that in many instances it is inappropriate for courts "to substitute our judgments for those of trained professionals with years of firsthand experience." It would thus apply a standard of review identical to the Court's "reasonableness" standard in a significant percentage of cases. At the same time, the *Abdul Wali* approach takes seriously the Constitution's function of requiring that official power be called to account when it completely deprives a person of a right that society regards as basic. In this limited number of cases, it would require more than a demonstration of "reasonableness" to justify such infringement. To the extent that prison is meant to inculcate a respect for social and legal norms, a requirement that prison officials persuasively demonstrate the need for the absolute deprivation of inmate rights is consistent with that end. Furthermore, prison officials are in control of the evidence that is essential to establish the superiority of such deprivation over other alternatives. It is thus only fair for these officials to be held to a stringent standard of review in such extreme cases.

The prison in this case has completely prevented respondent inmates from attending the central religious service of their Muslim faith. I would therefore hold prison officials to the standard articulated in *Abdul Wali,* and would find their proffered justifications wanting. The State has neither demonstrated that the restriction is necessary to further an important objective nor proved that less extreme measures may not serve its purpose. Even if I accepted the Court's standard of review, however, I could not conclude on this record that prison officials have proved that it is reasonable to preclude respondents from attending Jumu'ah. * * *

II

* * * The Court in this case acknowledges that "respondents' sincerely held religious beliefs compe[l] attendance at Jumu'ah" and concedes that there are "no alternative means of attending Jumu'ah." Nonetheless, the Court finds that prison policy does not work a complete deprivation of respondents' asserted religious right, because respondents have the opportunity to participate in other religious activities. This analysis ignores the fact that, as the District Court found, Jumu'ah is the central religious ceremony of Muslims, "comparable to the Saturday service of the Jewish faith and the Sunday service of the various Christian sects." * * *

Jumu'ah therefore cannot be regarded as one of several essentially fungible religious practices. The ability to engage in other religious activities cannot obscure the fact that the denial at issue in this case is absolute * * *. If a Catholic prisoner were prevented from attending Mass on Sunday, few would regard that deprivation as anything but absolute, even if the prisoner were afforded other opportunities to pray, to discuss the Catholic faith with others, and even to avoid eating meat on Friday if that were a preference. Prison officials in this case therefore cannot show that " 'other avenues' remain available for the exercise of the asserted right."

* * *

* * * [A] reasonableness test in this case demands at least minimal substantiation by prison officials that alternatives that would permit participation in Jumu'ah are infeasible. Under the standard articulated by the Court in *Turner,* this does not mean that petitioners are responsible for identifying and discrediting these alternatives; "prison officials do not have to set up and then shoot down every conceivable alternative method of accommodating the claimant's constitutional complaint." When prisoners themselves present alternatives, however, and when they fairly call into question official claims that these alternatives are infeasible, we must demand at least some evidence beyond mere assertion that the religious practice at issue cannot be accommodated. Examination of the alternatives proposed in this case indicates that prison officials have not provided such substantiation.

Respondents' first proposal is that gang minimum prisoners be assigned to an alternative inside work detail on Friday, as they had been before the recent change in policy. Prison officials testified that the alternative work detail is now restricted to maximum security prisoners, and that they did not wish maximum and minimum security prisoners to mingle. Even the District Court had difficulty with this assertion, as it commented that "[t]he defendants did not explain why inmates of different security levels are not mixed on work assignments when otherwise they are mixed." The court found, nonetheless, that this alternative would be inconsistent with Standard 853's mandate to move gang minimum inmates to outside work details. This conclusion, however, neglects the fact that the very issue is whether the prison's policy, of which Standard

853 is a part, should be administered so as to accommodate Muslim inmates. The policy itself cannot serve as a justification for its failure to provide reasonable accommodation. The record as it now stands thus does not establish that the Friday alternative work detail would create a problem for the institution.

Respondents' second proposal is that gang minimum inmates be assigned to work details inside the main building on a regular basis. While admitting that the prison used inside details in the kitchen, bakery, and tailor shop, officials stated that these jobs are reserved for the riskiest gang minimum inmates, for whom an outside job might be unwise. Thus, concluded officials, it would be a bad idea to move these inmates outside to make room for Muslim gang minimum inmates. Respondents contend, however, that the prison's own records indicate that there are a significant number of jobs inside the institution that could be performed by inmates posing a lesser security risk. This suggests that it might not be necessary for the riskier gang minimum inmates to be moved outside to make room for the less risky inmates. Officials provided no data on the number of inside jobs available, the number of high-risk gang minimum inmates performing them, the number of Muslim inmates that might seek inside positions, or the number of staff that would be necessary to monitor such an arrangement. Given the plausibility of respondents' claim, prison officials should present at least this information in substantiating their contention that inside assignments are infeasible.

Third, respondents suggested that gang minimum inmates be assigned to Saturday or Sunday work details, which would allow them to make up any time lost by attending Jumu'ah on Friday. While prison officials admitted the existence of weekend work details, they stated that "[s]ince prison personnel are needed for other programs on weekends, the creation of additional weekend details would be a drain on scarce human resources." The record provides no indication, however, of the number of Muslims that would seek such a work detail, the current number of weekend details, or why it would be infeasible simply to reassign current Saturday or Sunday workers to Friday, rather than create additional details. The prison is able to arrange work schedules so that Jewish inmates may attend services on Saturday and Christian inmates may attend services on Sunday. Despite the fact that virtually all inmates are housed in the main building over the weekend, so that the demand on the facility is greater than at any other time, the prison is able to provide sufficient staff coverage to permit Jewish and Christian inmates to participate in their central religious ceremonies. Given the prison's duty to provide Muslims a "reasonable opportunity of pursuing [their] faith comparable to the opportunity afforded fellow prisoners who adhere to conventional religious precepts," *Cruz v. Beto*, 405 U.S. 319, 322 (1972), prison officials should be required to provide more than mere assertions of the infeasibility of weekend details for Muslim inmates.

Finally, respondents proposed that minimum security inmates living at the Farm be assigned to jobs either in the Farm building or in its immediate vicinity. Since Standard 853 permits such assignments for full minimum inmates, and since such inmates need not return to prison facilities through the main entrance, this would interfere neither with Standard 853 nor the concern underlying the no-return policy. Nonetheless, prison officials stated that such an arrangement might create an "affinity group" of Muslims representing a threat to prison authority. Officials pointed to no such problem in the five years in which Muslim inmates were permitted to assemble for Jumu'ah, and in which the alternative Friday work detail was in existence. Nor could they identify any threat resulting from the fact that during the month of Ramadan all Muslim prisoners participate in both breakfast and dinner at special times. Furthermore, there was no testimony that the concentration of Jewish or Christian inmates on work details or in religious services posed any type of "affinity group" threat. * * *

Petitioners also maintained that the assignment of full minimum Muslim inmates to the Farm or its near vicinity might provoke resentment because of other inmates' perception that Muslims were receiving special treatment. Officials pointed to no such perception during the period in which the alternative Friday detail was in existence, nor to any resentment of the fact that Muslims' dietary preferences are accommodated and that Muslims are permitted to operate on a special schedule during the month of Ramadan. Nor do they identify any such problems created by the accommodation of the religious preferences of inmates of other faiths. Once again, prison officials should be required at a minimum to identify the basis for their assertions.

* * *

* * * *Turner* directed attention to two factors of particular relevance to this case: the degree of constitutional deprivation and the availability of reasonable alternatives. The respondents in this case have been absolutely foreclosed from participating in the central religious ceremony of their Muslim faith. At least a colorable claim that such a drastic policy is not necessary can be made * * *. If the Court's standard of review is to represent anything more than reflexive deference to prison officials, any finding of reasonableness must rest on firmer ground than the record now presents.

Incarceration by its nature denies a prisoner participation in the larger human community. To deny the opportunity to affirm membership in a spiritual community, however, may extinguish an inmate's last source of hope for dignity and redemption. Such a denial requires more justification than mere assertion that any other course of action is infeasible. While I would prefer that this case be analyzed under the approach set out in Part I, I would at a minimum remand to the District Court for an analysis of respondents' claims in accordance with the standard enunciated by the Court in *Turner* and in this case. I therefore dissent.

QUESTIONS AND POINTS FOR DISCUSSION

1. Is the approach to prisoners' freedom-of-religion claims outlined in *O'Lone* consistent with the standard the Supreme Court articulated in *Cruz v. Beto?*

2. As in other cases where individuals assert free-exercise claims, a court may have to determine both whether the protection sought by the prisoner is for "religious" beliefs or practices and whether those religious beliefs are sincerely held by the prisoner. Gladson v. Iowa Dep't of Corrections, 551 F.3d 825, 831 (8th Cir. 2009). The care with which courts must embark on these inquiries is underscored by the fact that prison gangs have been known to invoke the Free Exercise Clause in seeking protection for their activities. See, e.g., Goff v. Graves, 362 F.3d 543, 547 n. 2 (8th Cir. 2004) (referring to new evidence that Church of the New Song is a sham religion that exists only in prisons and is used as a front for gang activity).

At the same time, delving deeply into the dictates of a religion to determine whether an inmate's belief is truly "religious" and "sincerely held" can pose other problems for courts. In Mack v. O'Leary, 80 F.3d 1175 (7th Cir.1996), the Seventh Circuit Court of Appeals highlighted the problems that can ensue from courts' in-depth scrutiny of religious beliefs and practices. In that case, the court considered what constitutes the "substantial burden" on religious freedom that triggers the protections of the Religious Freedom Restoration Act, which is discussed in note 3 below. In rejecting a substantial-burden test that necessitates determining whether a particular practice is required by an inmate's religion, the court stated:

> We hold, therefore, that a substantial burden on the free exercise of religion, within the meaning of the Act, is one that forces adherents of a religion to refrain from religiously motivated conduct, inhibits or constrains conduct or expression that manifests a central tenet of a person's religious beliefs, or compels conduct or expression that is contrary to those beliefs.
>
> [This] definition is also the one more sensitive to religious feeling. Many religious practices that clearly are not mandatory, such as praying the rosary, in the case of Roman Catholics, or wearing yarmulkes, in the case of Orthodox Jews (optional because while Jewish men are required to cover their heads, the form of the head covering is not prescribed), are important to their practitioners, who would consider the denial of them a grave curtailment of their religious liberty.
>
> But the decisive argument in favor of the generous definition of "substantial burden," it seems to us, is the undesirability of making judges arbiters of religious law, as required by the alternative approach. That approach * * * requires the courts to determine what practices the plaintiff's religion obligates him to follow, and this is an issue of religious law, requiring the court to determine the authoritative sources of law for the religion in question and to interpret the commands emanating from those sources. In the case of hierarchical religions such as Roman Catholicism this process of identification and interpretation * * * is feasible. In

the case of nonhierarchical religions, however, such as Islam, Judaism, and a multitude of Protestant sects, the process is infeasible, or at least very difficult and attended with a high degree of indeterminacy. The danger that courts will find themselves taking sides in religious schisms, if they must opine on matters of religious obligation, is not a trivial one.

* * *

Mack's case illustrates the superiority of the broader definition of substantial burden. It would be an exquisitely difficult undertaking for a court to determine whether the practices that he claims the defendants interfered with, such as facing Mecca while eating Ramadan meals or purifying oneself during as well as before the meals, are actually obligatory for Muslims. There are different branches of Islam, of which the Sunni and the Shiite are merely the best known, so that the court would first have to determine which branch the plaintiff considered himself to be a member of. And neither branch has a supreme leader, corresponding to the Pope or to the Patriarch of the Russian Orthodox Church, to whom a court might look for a definitive ruling on a subtle or contested article of faith. The proper and feasible question for the court is simply whether the practices in question are important to the votaries of the religion, and being factual that is not a question that can usually, or here, be resolved on the pleadings.

Id. at 1179–80. Compare Spies v. Voinovich, 173 F.3d 398, 406 (6th Cir.1999) (holding that Buddhist prisoner fed vegetarian meals had no First Amendment right to a vegan diet (vegetarian meals that include no animal-based food products, such as dairy and egg products) because the Buddhist religion only requires adherence to a vegetarian diet).

In another Seventh Circuit case, Reed v. Faulkner, 842 F.2d 960 (7th Cir.1988), the court cautioned against the intermeddling in religious affairs that also can ensue when courts improperly assess the sincerity of an inmate's asserted religious beliefs. In that case, Homer Reed, a Rastafarian inmate, claimed that prison officials abridged his First Amendment right to religious freedom when they required him to cut his hair. In rejecting this claim after a bench trial, the district court found that Reed's "protestations of religious faith" were not "sincere." The court of appeals critiqued the analysis that culminated in that conclusion:

In concluding that Reed is insincere, the district judge appears to have attached conclusive weight to Reed's "backsliding"—his eating of meat, and his (inferred) shaving of his beard. Evidence of nonobservance is relevant on the question of sincerity, and is especially important in the prison setting, for an inmate may adopt a religion merely to harass the prison staff with demands to accommodate his new faith. * * * But the fact that a person does not adhere steadfastly to every tenet of his faith does not mark him as insincere. Some religions place unrealistic demands on their adherents; others cater especially to the weak of will. It would be bizarre for prisons to undertake in effect to promote strict orthodoxy, by forfeiting the religious rights of any inmate observed backsliding, thus placing guards and fellow inmates in the role of religious police. We cannot determine from [the district court's] opinion whether he thought

Reed's backsliding merely evidence of insincerity, which would be proper, or whether he thought it conclusive evidence of insincerity, which would be improper.

Id. at 963.

3. The Supreme Court alternatively could have upheld the regulations found constitutional in *O'Lone v. Shabazz* by applying a rule that it later expounded in a case involving the freedom-of-religion claims of nonprisoners. The plaintiffs in that case, Employment Div. v. Smith, 494 U.S. 872, 110 S.Ct. 1595 (1990), had been fired from their jobs at a drug-rehabilitation center after ingesting peyote during a religious ceremony for Native Americans. When the plaintiffs later applied for unemployment-compensation benefits, their applications were denied because they had been fired for work-related misconduct. The Supreme Court rejected the plaintiffs' claim that this denial unconstitutionally impinged upon their First Amendment right to freely exercise their religion. The Court ruled that the First Amendment is simply not violated when the burden on a religious practice is "merely the incidental effect of a generally applicable and otherwise valid provision" rather than the result of a governmental regulation whose purpose is to restrict religious practices. Id. at 878, 110 S.Ct. at 1600.

Congress attempted to reverse the effects of the Supreme Court's decision in *Employment Div. v. Smith* by enacting the Religious Freedom Restoration Act of 1993 (RFRA), 42 U.S.C. §§ 2000bb–1 to –4. Under RFRA, actions taken by government officials that place a "substantial burden" on a person's exercise of religion are illegal unless the officials prove that the actions further a "compelling governmental interest" and are the "least restrictive means" of furthering that interest. Id. § 2000bb–1(a)–(b).

Despite the strong opposition of many correctional officials, Congress included prisoners within the scope of RFRA's protections. In City of Boerne v. Flores, 521 U.S. 507, 117 S.Ct. 2157 (1997), however, the Supreme Court ruled that the Constitution bars applying RFRA to state officials. Compare Gonzales v. O Centro Espirita Beneficente Uniao do Vegetal, 546 U.S. 418, 424, 126 S.Ct. 1211, 1217 (2006) (applying RFRA to federal officials). The Court held that when enacting RFRA, Congress had exceeded its authority under section 5 of the Fourteenth Amendment to enforce the provisions of that amendment.

Congress responded to *City of Boerne v. Flores* by enacting the Religious Land Use and Institutionalized Persons Act (RLUIPA), 42 U.S.C. §§ 2000cc to 2000cc–5. In enacting RLUIPA, Congress invoked its authority under the Constitution's Commerce Clause and the Spending Clause, which vests Congress with the power to spend money to promote the "general welfare" of the United States. The Act, which augments the protection afforded the religious practices of certain state and local inmates, including pretrial detainees, provides in part as follows:

42 U.S.C. § 2000cc–1. Protection of religious exercise of institutionalized persons

(a) General Rule

No government shall impose a substantial burden on the religious exercise of a person residing in or confined to an institution, as defined in section 1997 of this title, even if the burden results from a rule of general applicability, unless the government demonstrates that imposition of the burden on that person—

(1) is in furtherance of a compelling governmental interest; and

(2) is the least restrictive means of furthering that compelling governmental interest.

(b) Scope of application

This section applies in any case in which—

(1) the substantial burden is imposed in a program or activity that receives Federal financial assistance; or

(2) the substantial burden affects, or removal of that substantial burden would affect, commerce with foreign nations, among the several States, or with Indian tribes.

In Cutter v. Wilkinson, 544 U.S. 709, 125 S.Ct. 2113 (2005), the Supreme Court noted that all of the states receive federal funding for their prisons, inferring that all state prisons are therefore subject to RLUIPA's requirements. In *Cutter*, the Court held that the statute, on its face, does not violate the First Amendment's Establishment Clause even though it affords heightened protection to inmates' religious, compared to nonreligious, activities. The Court viewed the statute as a permissible way to accommodate the religious needs of inmates who, because of obstacles stemming from their incarceration by the government, are encumbered in meeting those needs themselves. The Court left open the question whether Congress exceeded its authority under the Spending and Commerce Clauses of the Constitution when enacting RLUIPA.

In your opinion, should federal and state statutes that provide more protection for religious practices than required by the Constitution extend to prisoners? Why or why not?

4.   The lower courts have struggled with questions concerning the extent to which prison officials must accommodate the religious practices of inmates. Frequently litigated questions include whether, when an inmate's faith so dictates, the inmate has a First Amendment right or a federal statutory right to grow a beard, have long hair, or be provided with a special diet. A majority of the courts have upheld prison regulations restricting prisoners' hair length and their growing of beards. See, e.g., Fegans v. Norris, 537 F.3d 897, 903–08 (8th Cir. 2008) (holding policy forbidding beards and hair below the ears violated neither the First Amendment nor RLUIPA). The courts have found that the grooming restrictions are reasonably related to a number of legitimate penological interests and the least restrictive means of furthering the compelling governmental interests in safety and security. The restrictions can facilitate the identification of inmates who might otherwise attempt to alter their appearance after an escape or commission of a crime within the prison by shaving their beards or cutting their hair. The restrictions also curb the movement of drugs, weapons, and other contraband throughout the prison that can be hidden in an inmate's hair or beard. See, e.g., Flagner v.

Wilkinson, 241 F.3d 475, 485 (6th Cir.2001) (citing warden's affidavit describing items retrieved from the hair of Ohio inmates, including a razor blade, tobacco, and marijuana). And the grooming restrictions help to preserve order, in part by preventing prisoners from publicizing their gang affiliations through their hairstyles and type of beard.

More problematic for the courts has been the question whether prison officials must accommodate prisoners' requests, founded on their religious beliefs, for a special diet, such as a kosher diet for Jewish inmates or a vegetarian diet for Buddhist inmates. In some cases, courts have held that prison officials must provide prisoners with a diet that comports with their religious precepts, while in other cases, the courts have found no constitutional or statutory obligation to provide the prisoners in question with a special diet. See DeHart v. Horn, 227 F.3d 47, 60 n. 8 (3d Cir.2000) (listing First Amendment cases and emphasizing that the differing outcomes reflect a "contextual, record-sensitive analysis"). What facts should bear on the resolution of this question? Should it matter whether prison officials at a particular prison are providing special meals to prisoners for medical reasons or how many of those health-prescribed meals are served each day?

5. Courts also have been asked to decide the extent to which, if at all, correctional officials must accommodate inmates who, for religious reasons, want to change their names. See, e.g., Hakim v. Hicks, 223 F.3d 1244 (11th Cir.2000). Consider this question under both the First Amendment and the federal statutes that protect religious freedom.

6. Would a ban on group worship services in prison be constitutional? Would such a ban violate RFRA or RLUIPA? Why or why not? Compare Salahuddin v. Coughlin, 993 F.2d 306, 308 (2d Cir.1993) (inmates have a constitutional right to participate in group worship services) with Counts v. Newhart, 951 F.Supp. 579, 589–90 (E.D.Va.1996), aff'd, 116 F.3d 1473 (4th Cir.1997) (barring inmates from participating in group worship services in this case contravened neither the First Amendment nor RFRA).

7. Does the Establishment Clause permit a prison to have a faith-based prison unit designed to provide prisoners who want to live in the unit with "intense opportunities for spiritual growth and deepening their religious roots"? Fed. Bureau of Prisons, U.S. Dep't of Justice, Residential Re–Entry Program: Life Connections (2002). In Americans United for Sep. of Church & St. v. Prison Fellowship Ministries, 509 F.3d 406, 425–26 (8th Cir. 2007), the Eighth Circuit Court of Appeals held that a faith-based prison unit run by a private nonprofit, "The InnerChange Freedom Initiative," and subsidized by government funds violated the Establishment Clause. InnerChange had described its faith-based program in the Iowa prison as a "24–hour–a–day, Christ-centered, biblically based, program that promotes personal transformation of prisoners through the power of the Gospel." Id. at 418.

The Eighth Circuit did not find that faith-based prison units are *per se* unconstitutional and, in fact, emphasized that the district court had not enjoined InnerChange from ever operating in the state of Iowa. In your opinion, under what circumstances, if any, does the Establishment Clause permit a prison to have a faith-based unit? For differing perspectives on this question, see Symposium, The Constitutionality of Faith–Based Prison Units,

6 Ave Maria L.Rev. 341 (2008). If you were charged with the task of setting up these units in a way that both meets inmates' faith-based needs but avoids constitutional concerns, what steps would you take? For a discussion of this question, see Lynn S. Branham, "Go and Sin No More": The Constitutionality of Governmentally Funded Faith–Based Prison Units, 37 U. Mich. J. L. Ref. 291, 343–50 (2004).

8. Consider the following problem:

The plaintiff, an inmate at a maximum-security prison in Illinois, has filed a § 1983 suit in a federal district court against various prison officials claiming that his rights to religious freedom under the First and Fourteenth Amendments and the Religious Land Use and Institutionalized Persons Act have been abridged. According to the plaintiff, he is a Muslim and therefore has a religious duty to make charitable contributions. To meet that obligation, he has asked that money be withdrawn from his prison trust-fund account and sent to "Sister" Zubaydah Maydun, the trustee of what is called the "Fellowship Trust Fund." The defendants have refused to transfer the funds as requested.

The defendants have filed a motion for summary judgment. They contend that they are entitled to summary judgment because, as required by Rule 56(c) of the Federal Rules of Civil Procedure, there is no "genuine issue" of "material fact" and they are entitled to judgment as a matter of law. In support of their motion, the defendants have submitted the affidavit of an assistant warden recounting the prison's policy regarding the withdrawal of funds from inmates' trust accounts. Under this policy, a prisoner's request to have money withdrawn from his account can be denied for three reasons: (1) if the request is involuntary due to pressure exerted on the prisoner by another inmate; (2) if the designated recipient of the money is not "authentic, legitimate, and accountable"; and (3) if the designated recipient is related to another inmate in the prison. The purpose of this policy, according to the affidavit, is to ward off disputes and tension between inmates. The policy applies to all inmates, regardless of their religious affiliation.

The assistant warden has further stated in her affidavit that the plaintiff's disbursement request was denied for two reasons: one, because "Sister" Maydun is the wife of another inmate; and two, because the "Fellowship Trust Fund" is not connected with an "authentic" religion since the American Muslim Mission exercises no authority over the fund. The plaintiff has filed an affidavit attempting to demonstrate the authenticity of the fund.

Should the defendants' motion for summary judgment be granted?

CHAPTER 12

RIGHT OF ACCESS TO THE COURTS

■ ■ ■

Prisoners file lawsuits for a variety of reasons. Prisoners who file petitions for habeas corpus and other types of postconviction complaints are seeking release from what they contend is illegal confinement. Habeas corpus petitions, for example, frequently allege that prisoners' constitutional rights were violated at trial, nullifying the convictions subsequently obtained. Other prisoners file civil-rights suits for damages or equitable relief, most commonly under 42 U.S.C. § 1983. In these suits, the prisoners challenge, generally on constitutional grounds, the way in which they have been treated by prison officials or the conditions of their confinement. Finally, prisoners, like ordinary citizens, may turn to the courts to resolve everyday civil disputes; prisoners, for example, may be involved in divorce proceedings, disputes about parental rights, or personal-injury suits.

Some prisoners file lawsuits for less laudable reasons. The filing of a lawsuit, for example, may offer a welcome diversion from the boredom of prison life, the opportunity to harass prison officials, or the chance to leave the correctional institution for an appearance in court. But while the legal claims of some prisoners are nonmeritorious and even frivolous, others have valid claims but never file them, because they are too intimidated to do so, or do not know how and have no access to legal services.

Of particular note is the type of prisoner lawsuit that seeks to enforce a prisoner's right of access to the courts. As some courts have recognized, this right is of fundamental importance to inmates. For example, a habeas corpus action is a vehicle through which innocent persons wrongfully convicted of a crime may obtain their release from prison. And unconstitutional conditions often will continue unabated in a correctional facility without court intervention. As the Seventh Circuit Court of Appeals observed in Adams v. Carlson, 488 F.2d 619, 630 (7th Cir.1973), "An inmate's right of unfettered access to the courts is as fundamental a right as any other he may hold.... All other rights of an inmate are illusory without it." Mindful of the central importance of court access to prisoners seeking to enforce their constitutional rights, but also aware of the abusive use of litigation by some prisoners, courts have wrestled with questions concerning the extent to which a prisoner's access to the courts may be restricted constitutionally.

A. COURT APPEARANCES AND COMMUNICATIONS

EX PARTE HULL

Supreme Court of the United States, 1941.
312 U.S. 546, 61 S.Ct. 640, 85 L.Ed. 1034.

MR. JUSTICE MURPHY delivered the opinion of the Court.

* * *

In November, 1940, petitioner prepared a petition for writ of habeas corpus and exhibits to file in this Court. He took the papers to a prison official and requested him to notarize them. The official refused and informed petitioner that the papers and a registered letter to the clerk of this Court concerning them would not be accepted for mailing. Although the papers were not notarized, petitioner then delivered them to his father for mailing outside the prison but guards confiscated them. Several days later, petitioner again attempted to mail a letter concerning his case to the clerk of this Court. It was intercepted and sent to the legal investigator for the state parole board.[1] Apparently neither of the letters was returned to the petitioner, and the papers taken from his father were not returned until late in December.

* * *

Petitioner then prepared another document which he somehow managed to have his father, as "agent," file with the clerk of this Court on December 26, 1940. In this document petitioner detailed his efforts to file the papers confiscated by prison officials, contended that he was therefore unlawfully restrained, and prayed that he be released.

On January 6, 1941, we issued a rule to show cause why leave to file a petition for writ of habeas corpus should not be granted. The warden filed a return to the rule * * *. In justification of the action preventing petitioner from filing his papers or communicating with this Court, the warden alleged that in November, 1940, he had published a regulation providing that: "All legal documents, briefs, petitions, motions, habeas corpus proceedings and appeals will first have to be submitted to the institutional welfare office and if favorably acted upon be then referred to Perry A. Maynard, legal investigator to the Parole Board, Lansing, Michi-

---

1. About a week later petitioner received the following reply from the legal investigator: "Your letter of November 18, 1940, addressed to the Clerk of the United States Supreme Court, has been referred to the writer for reply. In the first place your application in its present form would not be acceptable to that court. You must file a petition for whatever relief you are seeking and state your reasons therefor, together with a memorandum brief. Your petition must be verified under oath and supported by proper affidavits, if any you have. Your letter was, no doubt, intercepted for the reason that it was deemed to be inadequate and which undoubtedly accounts for the fact that it found its way to my desk."

gan. Documents submitted to Perry A. Maynard, if in his opinion are properly drawn, will be directed to the court designated or will be referred back to the inmate."

* * *

The first question concerns the effect of the regulation quoted in the warden's return.

The regulation is invalid. The considerations that prompted its formulation are not without merit, but the state and its officers may not abridge or impair petitioner's right to apply to a federal court for a writ of habeas corpus. Whether a petition for writ of habeas corpus addressed to a federal court is properly drawn and what allegations it must contain are questions for that court alone to determine.

[The Court then turned to the substantive issues raised by the habeas corpus petition, rejecting the petitioner's argument that he was unconstitutionally confined.]

QUESTIONS AND POINTS FOR DISCUSSION

1. *Ex Parte Hull*, as it was later described by Justice Rehnquist, was a "bare-bones holding." Bounds v. Smith, 430 U.S. 817, 838, 97 S.Ct. 1491, 1503 (1977) (Rehnquist, J., dissenting). The Court in *Hull* never identified the source of the right not to have a habeas corpus petition screened and approved by prison officials prior to transmittal to a court. Only in subsequent cases did the Supreme Court identify what it considered the source of the constitutional right of access to the courts. That right, according to the Court, is embodied in the Due Process Clauses of the Fifth and Fourteenth Amendments. See, e.g., Procunier v. Martinez, 416 U.S. 396, 419, 94 S.Ct. 1800, 1814 (1974), on page 474. In addition, the Court has said that the right to have access to the courts is subsumed within the First Amendment right to petition the government for a redress of grievances. California Motor Transport Co. v. Trucking Unlimited, 404 U.S. 508, 510, 92 S.Ct. 609, 612 (1972).

2. When prison officials refuse to forward a prisoner's legal documents to a court, other rights may be infringed. For example, in Cochran v. Kansas, 316 U.S. 255, 257–58, 62 S.Ct. 1068, 1069–70 (1942), the Supreme Court held that if state prison officials had prevented a prisoner from filing documents necessary to appeal his conviction, depriving him of the appeal privileges accorded to others, he was denied the equal protection of the law guaranteed by the Fourteenth Amendment.

3. Inmates' access to the courts can be impeded not only by a refusal to send mail to a court, but also by the withholding of mail from a court. For example, in Simkins v. Bruce, 406 F.3d 1239, 1243 (10th Cir. 2005), the Tenth Circuit Court of Appeals held that the intentional failure of the supervisor of a prison mail room to forward what was marked as legal mail to the addressee, a prisoner confined in a jail to which he had been transferred, abridged his right of access to the courts. Because of this failure, the prisoner missed the deadline for appealing an order granting the defendants' motion for summary judgment in a conditions-of-confinement suit. In addition, the

prisoner did not respond to this motion of which he was unaware. The court in *Simkins*, like other courts, held that to give rise to a constitutional violation, the interference with a prisoner's legal mail must be intentional, though it need not be malicious; mere negligence in the processing of the mail will not suffice. See id. at 1242 (listing cases).

4. While correctional officials cannot censor inmate mail to courts, can they read, or at least inspect, such mail before mailing it? Why or why not? Compare Royse v. Superior Court, 779 F.2d 573, 575 (9th Cir.1986) (upholding the constitutionality of a court order requiring inspection, but forbidding reading, of prisoner mail to courts that was adopted after a judge in an adjoining county died when a bomb mailed to his office exploded) with Stone–El v. Fairman, 785 F.Supp. 711, 716–17 (N.D.Ill.1991) (prison officials cannot open inmate mail to courts).

Do the same constitutional constraints that apply to prison officials' handling of outgoing mail to the courts apply to incoming mail from courts to prisoners? In McCain v. Reno, 98 F.Supp.2d 5, 8 (D.D.C.2000), the District Court for the District of Columbia concluded that a prison policy permitting prison officials to open, read, and copy mail received from courts does not have an unconstitutional chilling effect on inmates' right of access to the courts. The court reasoned that court mail typically is filed on the court's docket and is a matter of public record. In addition, the defendants sued by prisoners receive copies of all court orders. By contrast, the Sixth Circuit Court of Appeals stated in Sallier v. Brooks, 343 F.3d 868, 877 (6th Cir. 2003) that it disagreed that mail sent from a court to an inmate always will be in the public record. The court noted that court correspondence may concern a complaint that has not been filed, perhaps because a requirement for the filing of a complaint, such as payment of a filing fee or the signing of the complaint, has yet to be met. In order to safeguard inmates' right of access to the courts and avert a chilling effect on their First Amendment rights, the court held that incoming court mail cannot be opened outside the presence of an inmate who has asked to be present when legal mail is opened.

5. Some lower courts have held that the right of prison inmates to have access to, and communicate with, the courts does not necessarily include the right to have particular witnesses appear at trial or even the right to personally appear themselves at a hearing or trial. For example, in Holt v. Pitts, 619 F.2d 558, 561 (6th Cir.1980), the Sixth Circuit Court of Appeals held that the district court properly had exercised its discretion under 28 U.S.C. § 1651(a), which authorizes the issuance of writs of habeas corpus *ad testificandum* to secure inmates' presence at judicial proceedings. The district court had refused to issue a writ of habeas corpus ordering federal prison officials in California to bring the plaintiff to Tennessee for a pretrial hearing in a § 1983 suit challenging the treatment of the plaintiff while previously incarcerated in a Tennessee jail. Two facts were central to the decision of the court of appeals: one, the distance between the place where the plaintiff was incarcerated and the place where the pretrial hearing was to be held, and two, the fact that the writ was sought for a pretrial stage of the litigation.

By contrast, the district court in Hawks v. Timms, 35 F.Supp.2d 464 (D.Md.1999) directed the U.S. Marshal's Office to transport the prisoner-plaintiff to the court for a trial of his claim that several police officers had used excessive force when arresting him. The court noted that the plaintiff's claim hinged on his credibility and that he would be at a substantial disadvantage if the police officers, but not he, could testify before the jury. The court also factored feedback it had received from the Marshal's Office into its decision: transporting the plaintiff to the court and temporarily housing him away from the prison posed no "particular problem of security," and the expense of transporting him 135 miles to the courthouse would not be "excessive." Finally, the court concluded that deferring the trial until the plaintiff's release from prison was not a viable option because he had served only five years of his 26–year sentence.

6. Many of the lower-court cases in which the courts have either refused to grant, or approved the refusal to grant, a prisoner's petition for a writ of habeas corpus directing the bringing of the prisoner to court for trial or for a pretrial hearing have relied on Price v. Johnston, 334 U.S. 266, 68 S.Ct. 1049 (1948). In *Price,* the Supreme Court held that prisoners have no "absolute right" to either argue their own appeals or to be present during oral arguments before the appellate court. The Court observed that the decision whether to issue a writ of habeas corpus directing prison officials to bring a prisoner before the appellate court is one falling within the appellate court's discretion. As long as there was a "reasonable necessity" for not issuing the writ, the appellate court's exercise of its discretion should be sustained. Id. at 286, 68 S.Ct. at 1060.

7. In refusing to issue a writ of habeas corpus directing that a prisoner be brought to court for a trial, some courts have cited another alternative to the prisoner's in-court appearance—videoconferencing. See, e.g., Pryor v. District of Columbia, 2000 WL 1788112, *2 (D.D.C.2000). Videoconferencing is becoming more commonplace in some courts. In 1996, Congress enacted the Prison Litigation Reform Act, one provision of which requires pretrial proceedings in conditions-of-confinement cases brought by prisoners under 42 U.S.C. § 1983 or "other federal law" to be conducted, "[t]o the extent practicable," via videoconference, telephone conference, or some other telecommunications medium. 42 U.S.C. § 1997e(f). In addition, Federal Rule of Civil Procedure 43(a) sets forth an exception to its directive that witnesses normally testify in person: when there are "compelling circumstances" establishing "good cause" for contemporaneously transmitting a witness's testimony from off-site and the court has put into place "appropriate safeguards."

Rule 43 is silent on the question whether an entire civil trial can be conducted via videoconference. In Thornton v. Snyder, 428 F.3d 690, 698–99 (7th Cir. 2005), the Seventh Circuit Court of Appeals held that a district court did not violate the prisoner-plaintiff's due-process rights or abuse its discretion when it conducted the trial of the prisoner's civil-rights suit by videoconference. The court of appeals highlighted the following facts, among others, in support of its conclusion: First, the plaintiff was serving a life sentence, was deemed by prison officials to be an "extremely high escape risk," and had a "moderate aggression level." Second, two correctional officers would have been needed to transport the prisoner to the federal courthouse, which was 120 miles from the prison. Third, the approximately twenty witnesses in the case—inmates and correctional officials—were "scattered all over the state."

Fourth, four-way screens enabled the plaintiff and the jury to observe at the same time the judge, the plaintiff, the defendants' attorney (who also was not in the courtroom), and the witness testifying from off-site. Fifth, the plaintiff's claim—that he was subjected to cruel and unusual punishment when he was barred from exercising in the prison yard for over seven months—was "relatively straightforward." Finally, the court emphasized that since the prisoner-plaintiff was representing himself, his attorney did not have to choose between being in the courtroom with the judge and jury or being at the prison, where the attorney could confer with the plaintiff during the trial.

In the trial context, what are the potential advantages and disadvantages of employing videoconferencing in prisoners' cases? See Lynn S. Branham, Limiting the Burdens of *Pro Se* Inmate Litigation: A Technical–Assistance Manual for Courts, Correctional Officials, and Attorneys General 202–08 (1997). If you were a judge, when, if at all, would you employ this technology in the trial of a prisoner's civil lawsuit?

B. COMMUNICATIONS WITH ATTORNEYS

PROCUNIER v. MARTINEZ

Supreme Court of the United States, 1974.
416 U.S. 396, 94 S.Ct. 1800, 40 L.Ed.2d 224.

MR. JUSTICE POWELL delivered the opinion of the Court.

This case concerns the constitutionality of certain regulations promulgated by appellant Procunier in his capacity as Director of the California Department of Corrections. Appellees brought a class action on behalf of themselves and all other inmates of penal institutions under the Department's jurisdiction to challenge * * * the ban against the use of law students and legal paraprofessionals to conduct attorney-client interviews with inmates. * * *

* * *

The District Court * * * enjoined continued enforcement of Administrative Rule MV–IV–02, which provides in pertinent part:

"Investigators for an attorney-of-record will be confined to not more than two. Such investigators must be licensed by the State or must be members of the State Bar. Designation must be made in writing by the Attorney."

By restricting access to prisoners to members of the bar and licensed private investigators, this regulation imposed an absolute ban on the use by attorneys of law students and legal paraprofessionals to interview inmate clients. In fact, attorneys could not even delegate to such persons the task of obtaining prisoners' signatures on legal documents. The District Court reasoned that this rule constituted an unjustifiable restriction on the right of access to the courts. We agree.

The constitutional guarantee of due process of law has as a corollary the requirement that prisoners be afforded access to the courts in order to challenge unlawful convictions and to seek redress for violations of their constitutional rights. This means that inmates must have a reasonable opportunity to seek and receive the assistance of attorneys. Regulations and practices that unjustifiably obstruct the availability of professional representation or other aspects of the right of access to the courts are invalid.

The District Court found that the rule restricting attorney-client interviews to members of the bar and licensed private investigators inhibited adequate professional representation of indigent inmates. The remoteness of many California penal institutions makes a personal visit to an inmate client a time-consuming undertaking. The court reasoned that the ban against the use of law students or other paraprofessionals for attorney-client interviews would deter some lawyers from representing prisoners who could not afford to pay for their traveling time or that of licensed private investigators. And those lawyers who agreed to do so would waste time that might be employed more efficaciously in working on the inmates' legal problems. Allowing law students and paraprofessionals to interview inmates might well reduce the cost of legal representation for prisoners. The District Court therefore concluded that the regulation imposed a substantial burden on the right of access to the courts.

As the District Court recognized, this conclusion does not end the inquiry * * *. The extent to which that right is burdened by a particular regulation or practice must be weighed against the legitimate interests of penal administration and the proper regard that judges should give to the expertise and discretionary authority of correctional officials. In this case the ban against the use of law students and other paraprofessional personnel was absolute. Its prohibition was not limited to prospective interviewers who posed some colorable threat to security or to those inmates thought to be especially dangerous. Nor was it shown that a less restrictive regulation would unduly burden the administrative task of screening and monitoring visitors.

Appellants' enforcement of the regulation in question also created an arbitrary distinction between law students employed by practicing attorneys and those associated with law school programs providing legal assistance to prisoners. While the Department flatly prohibited interviews of any sort by law students working for attorneys, it freely allowed participants of a number of law school programs to enter the prisons and meet with inmates. These largely unsupervised students were admitted without any security check other than verification of their enrollment in a school program. Of course, the fact that appellants have allowed some persons to conduct attorney-client interviews with prisoners does not mean that they are required to admit others, but the arbitrariness of the distinction between the two categories of law students does reveal the absence of any real justification for the sweeping prohibition of Administrative Rule MV–IV–02. We cannot say that the District Court erred in invalidating this regulation.

* * *

QUESTIONS AND POINTS FOR DISCUSSION

1. Courts periodically have had to consider whether prison officials constitutionally can open, inspect, read, censor, or withhold mail to and from inmates and their attorneys. In Wolff v. McDonnell, 418 U.S. 539, 94 S.Ct. 2963 (1974), the Supreme Court addressed the constitutionality of opening and inspecting mail from an attorney to an inmate. This legal mail was opened in the inmate's presence. In upholding the constitutionality of the inspection scheme, which was designed to thwart the entry of contraband into the prison, the Court observed:

> As to the ability to open the mail in the presence of inmates, this could in no way constitute censorship, since the mail would not be read. Neither could it chill such communications, since the inmate's presence insures that prison officials will not read the mail. * * * [W]e think that petitioners, by acceding to a rule whereby the inmate is present when mail from attorneys is inspected, have done all, and perhaps even more, than the Constitution requires.

Id. at 577, 94 S.Ct. at 2985.

Although the Supreme Court in *Wolff* intimated that the prison officials might have exceeded the requirements of the Constitution by deciding to refrain from opening and inspecting mail from an attorney to an inmate unless the inmate was present, the lower courts generally have required the inmate to be present or be given the option of being present before mail from an attorney can be opened and inspected for contraband. See Al–Amin v. Smith, 511 F.3d 1317, 1329 & n.27 (11th Cir. 2008); Jones v. Brown, 461 F.3d 353, 363–64 (3d Cir. 2006) (legitimate interest in protecting prisons from anthrax contamination did not justify opening letters from lawyers and courts outside inmates' presence). But see Brewer v. Wilkinson, 3 F.3d 816, 825 (5th Cir.1993) (opening incoming legal mail outside inmate's presence does not violate First Amendment or right of access to the courts).

2. Can prison officials read correspondence between attorneys and inmates? If so, under what circumstances? The majority of the courts that have addressed this issue have held that inmates have a general constitutional right not to have their attorney-inmate mail read. See, e.g., Shatner v. Page, 2009 WL 260788, *20 (S.D. Ill. 2009) (describing correctional official's reading of prisoner's letter to his attorney as an "egregious violation" of the prisoner's constitutional rights). At the same time, some courts have intimated that attorney-inmate mail can be read, without violating the Constitution, when security concerns about a particular piece of mail reach a certain level. See, e.g., Cody v. Weber, 256 F.3d 764, 769 (8th Cir.2001) (reading of inmate's correspondence to and from attorney abridges right of access to the courts unless the prison officials demonstrate the intrusion was "reasonably related to a legitimate penological interest"); Lemon v. Dugger, 931 F.2d 1465, 1468 (11th Cir.1991) (alluding to an "affirmative defense of probable cause"); Proudfoot v. Williams, 803 F.Supp. 1048, 1053 (E.D.Pa.1992) (noting absence of "reason to believe" letters posed a threat to security).

In addition, some courts have held that prison officials, in some circumstances, can "scan" legal mail to confirm that the mail is indeed to or from an attorney. For example, in Bell–Bey v. Williams, 87 F.3d 832, 838–40 (6th Cir.1996), the court upheld a prison policy requiring prison officials to inspect certain outgoing legal mail to confirm, through docket numbers, case titles, and the like, that it concerned a pending lawsuit. The policy applied to legal mail sent by indigent inmates who had spent all of their "indigent allowance" and now sought a postage loan to send more legal mail. See also Lemon v. Dugger, 931 F.2d 1465, 1467 (11th Cir.1991) (citing, with approval, a prison rule providing that if the inspection of an envelope cannot confirm incoming correspondence's legal nature, prison officials can, in the inmate's presence, read the letterhead and signature to verify that incoming mail concerns a legal matter).

Do you agree with the observation of one court that drawing a distinction between scanning and reading legal mail is "rife with the potential for abuse?" Marquez v. Miranda, 1998 WL 57000, *2 (N.D.Cal.1998) (holding that scanning of legal documents during cell searches was unconstitutional). Do institutional-security and public-safety concerns, in any event, justify the drawing of this distinction? See State v. Mason, 986 P.2d 387 (Kan. 1999) (pretrial detainee had solicited his girlfriend's murder in a letter that he had falsely labeled as legal mail).

3.   If prison officials can read, at least in some circumstances, an inmate's mail to or from an attorney, presumably they can, in some instances, refuse to forward the mail to the addressee. See, e.g., Wright v. McMann, 460 F.2d 126, 131–32 (2d Cir.1972) (censorship or withholding of attorney-inmate mail justified when attorney or inmate has used access privilege to the other to transmit contraband or communicate plans for engaging in illegal activities). Certain procedural safeguards, however, would have to attend this censorship process. See Procunier v. Martinez, 416 U.S. 396, 417–19, 94 S.Ct. 1800, 1814 (1974), on page 474.

4.   Individuals charged with a crime generally have a Sixth Amendment right to the assistance of an attorney at their trial and during certain "critical stages" preceding the trial. Reading the mail of pretrial detainees to or from their attorneys therefore may pose special constitutional problems by interfering with this right to counsel.

Maine v. Moulton, 474 U.S. 159, 106 S.Ct. 477 (1985) arguably supports the proposition that potential Sixth Amendment problems would not be obviated by the security interests ostensibly furthered by the reading of mail between attorneys and pretrial detainees. In *Moulton,* the Supreme Court considered whether police officers violated a defendant's Sixth Amendment right to counsel when, after he had been indicted, they electronically monitored a conversation he had with a codefendant. The police monitored this conversation for two reasons—to protect the codefendant should the defendant discover that the codefendant was cooperating with the police and to discover whether the defendant was going to follow up on a threat to kill a witness. Despite these legitimate reasons for monitoring the defendant's conversation with his codefendant, the Supreme Court concluded that the police had abridged the defendant's Sixth Amendment right to "rely on counsel as a 'medium' between him and the State." Id. at 176, 106 S.Ct. at 487.

Consider the practical repercussions in the jail context if the Sixth Amendment right to counsel were deemed violated even when correctional officials have legitimate and important reasons for monitoring a criminal defendant's communications with her attorney. If jail officials reasonably believe that communications between a pretrial detainee and her attorney will threaten the jail's security or result in the planning of another crime, how should they respond? Should they read the mail between the detainee and the attorney, exposing themselves to liability for violating the detainee's civil rights, or refrain from reading the mail, possibly jeopardizing the jail's security or facilitating the commission of a crime? Is there another alternative?

5. Shortly after the attacks on the World Trade Center and the Pentagon on September 11, 2001, the Federal Bureau of Prisons promulgated a regulation governing the monitoring of inmates' communications with their attorneys. The regulation, which applies to inmates, including pretrial detainees, confined in BOP facilities and contract facilities, provides in part as follows:

> (d) In any case where the Attorney General specifically so orders, based on information from the head of a federal law enforcement or intelligence agency that reasonable suspicion exists to believe that a particular inmate may use communications with attorneys or their agents to further or facilitate acts of terrorism, the Director, Bureau of Prisons, shall * * * provide appropriate procedures for the monitoring or review of communications between that inmate and attorneys or attorneys' agents who are traditionally covered by the attorney-client privilege, for the purpose of deterring future acts that could result in death or serious bodily injury to persons, or substantial damage to property that would entail the risk of death or serious bodily injury to persons.

* * *

> (2) Except in the case of prior court authorization, the Director, Bureau of Prisons, shall provide written notice to the inmate and to the attorneys involved, prior to the initiation of any monitoring or review under this paragraph (d). The notice shall explain:
>
> > (i) That * * * all communications between the inmate and attorneys may be monitored, to the extent determined to be reasonably necessary for the purpose of deterring future acts of violence or terrorism;
> >
> > (ii) That communications between the inmate and attorneys or their agents are not protected by the attorney-client privilege if they would facilitate criminal acts or a conspiracy to commit criminal acts, or if those communications are not related to the seeking or providing of legal advice.
>
> (3) The Director, Bureau of Prisons, with the approval of the Assistant Attorney General for the Criminal Division, shall employ appropriate procedures to ensure that all attorney-client communications

are reviewed for privilege claims and that any properly privileged materials (including, but not limited to, recordings of privileged communications) are not retained during the course of the monitoring. To protect the attorney-client privilege and to ensure that the investigation is not compromised by exposure to privileged material relating to the investigation or to defense strategy, a privilege team shall be designated, consisting of individuals not involved in the underlying investigation. The monitoring shall be conducted pursuant to procedures designed to minimize the intrusion into privileged material or conversations. Except in cases where the person in charge of the privilege team determines that acts of violence or terrorism are imminent, the privilege team shall not disclose any information unless and until such disclosure has been approved by a federal judge.

28 C.F.R. § 501.3(d). Analyze the constitutionality of this regulation. How if at all, would you revise it?

C. JAILHOUSE LAWYERS, LAW LIBRARIES, AND OTHER LEGAL ASSISTANCE

JOHNSON v. AVERY

Supreme Court of the United States, 1969.
393 U.S. 483, 89 S.Ct. 747, 21 L.Ed.2d 718.

MR. JUSTICE FORTAS delivered the opinion of the Court.

Petitioner is serving a life sentence in the Tennessee State Penitentiary. In February 1965 he was transferred to the maximum security building in the prison for violation of a prison regulation which provides:

> "No inmate will advise, assist or otherwise contract to aid another, either with or without a fee, to prepare Writs or other legal matters. It is not intended that an innocent man be punished. When a man believes he is unlawfully held or illegally convicted, he should prepare a brief or state his complaint in letter form and address it to his lawyer or a judge. A formal Writ is not necessary to receive a hearing. False charges or untrue complaints may be punished. Inmates are forbidden to set themselves up as practitioners for the purpose of promoting a business of writing Writs."

In July 1965 petitioner filed in the United States District Court for the Middle District of Tennessee a "motion for law books and a typewriter," in which he sought relief from his confinement in the maximum security building. The District Court treated this motion as a petition for a writ of habeas corpus and, after a hearing, ordered him released from disciplinary confinement and restored to the status of an ordinary prisoner. The District Court held that the regulation was void because it in effect barred illiterate prisoners from access to federal habeas corpus and conflicted with 28 U.S.C. § 2242.[1]

* * *

The State appealed. The Court of Appeals for the Sixth Circuit reversed, concluding that the regulation did not unlawfully conflict with the federal right of habeas corpus. According to the Sixth Circuit, the interest of the State in preserving prison discipline and in limiting the practice of law to licensed attorneys justified whatever burden the regulation might place on access to federal habeas corpus.

This Court has constantly emphasized the fundamental importance of the writ of habeas corpus in our constitutional scheme, and the Congress has demonstrated its solicitude for the vigor of the Great Writ. The Court has steadfastly insisted that "there is no higher duty than to maintain it unimpaired."

Since the basic purpose of the writ is to enable those unlawfully incarcerated to obtain their freedom, it is fundamental that access of prisoners to the courts for the purpose of presenting their complaints may not be denied or obstructed. For example, the Court has held that a State may not validly make the writ available only to prisoners who could pay a $4 filing fee. *Smith v. Bennett,* 365 U.S. 708 (1961). * * *

Tennessee urges, however, that the contested regulation in this case is justified as a part of the State's disciplinary administration of the prisons. There is no doubt that discipline and administration of state detention facilities are state functions. They are subject to federal authority only where paramount federal constitutional or statutory rights supervene. It is clear, however, that in instances where state regulations applicable to inmates of prison facilities conflict with such rights, the regulations may be invalidated.

* * *

There can be no doubt that Tennessee could not constitutionally adopt and enforce a rule forbidding illiterate or poorly educated prisoners to file habeas corpus petitions. Here Tennessee has adopted a rule which, in the absence of any other source of assistance for such prisoners, effectively does just that. The District Court concluded that "[f]or all practical purposes, if such prisoners cannot have the assistance of a 'jailhouse lawyer,' their possibly valid constitutional claims will never be heard in any court." The record supports this conclusion.

Jails and penitentiaries include among their inmates a high percentage of persons who are totally or functionally illiterate, whose educational attainments are slight, and whose intelligence is limited. This appears to be equally true of Tennessee's prison facilities.

---

1. 28 U.S.C. § 2242 provides in part: "Application for a writ of habeas corpus shall be in writing signed and verified by the person for whose relief it is intended or by someone acting in his behalf."

In most federal courts, it is the practice to appoint counsel in post-conviction proceedings only after a petition for post-conviction relief passes initial judicial evaluation and the court has determined that issues are presented calling for an evidentiary hearing.

* * * Accordingly, the initial burden of presenting a claim to post-conviction relief usually rests upon the indigent prisoner himself with such help as he can obtain within the prison walls or the prison system. In the case of all except those who are able to help themselves—usually a few old hands or exceptionally gifted prisoners—the prisoner is, in effect, denied access to the courts unless such help is available.

It is indisputable that prison "writ writers" like petitioner are sometimes a menace to prison discipline and that their petitions are often so unskillful as to be a burden on the courts which receive them. But, as this Court held in *Ex parte Hull,* in declaring invalid a state prison regulation which required that prisoners' legal pleadings be screened by state officials:

> "The considerations that prompted [the regulation's] formulation are not without merit, but the state and its officers may not abridge or impair petitioner's right to apply to a federal court for a writ of habeas corpus."

Tennessee does not provide an available alternative to the assistance provided by other inmates. The warden of the prison in which petitioner was confined * * * indicated that he sometimes allowed prisoners to examine the listing of attorneys in the Nashville telephone directory so they could select one to write to in an effort to interest him in taking the case, and that "on several occasions" he had contacted the public defender at the request of an inmate. There is no contention, however, that there is any regular system of assistance by public defenders. In its brief the State contends that "[t]here is absolutely no reason to believe that prison officials would fail to notify the court should an inmate advise them of a complete inability, either mental or physical, to prepare a habeas application on his own behalf," but there is no contention that they have in fact ever done so.

This is obviously far short of the showing required to demonstrate that, in depriving prisoners of the assistance of fellow inmates, Tennessee has not, in substance, deprived those unable themselves, with reasonable adequacy, to prepare their petitions, of access to the constitutionally and statutorily protected availability of the writ of habeas corpus. By contrast, in several States, the public defender system supplies trained attorneys, paid from public funds, who are available to consult with prisoners regarding their habeas corpus petitions. At least one State employs senior law students to interview and advise inmates in state prisons. Another State has a voluntary program whereby members of the local bar association make periodic visits to the prison to consult with prisoners concerning their cases.[10] We express no judgment concerning these plans, but their existence indicates that techniques are available to provide alternatives if the State elects to prohibit mutual assistance among inmates.

Even in the absence of such alternatives, the State may impose reasonable restrictions and restraints upon the acknowledged propensity of prisoners to abuse both the giving and the seeking of assistance in the preparation of applications for relief: for example, by limitations on the time and location of such activities and the imposition of punishment for the giving or receipt of consideration in connection with such activities. But unless and until the State provides some reasonable alternative to assist inmates in the preparation of petitions for post-conviction relief, it may not validly enforce a regulation such as that here in issue, barring inmates from furnishing such assistance to other prisoners.[11]

* * *

MR. JUSTICE DOUGLAS, concurring. [Opinion omitted.]

MR. JUSTICE WHITE, with whom MR. JUSTICE BLACK joins, dissenting.

* * *

The majority admits that it "is indisputable" that jailhouse lawyers like petitioner "are sometimes a menace to prison discipline and that their petitions are often so unskillful as to be a burden on the courts which receive them." That is putting it mildly. The disciplinary problems are severe, the burden on the courts serious, and the disadvantages to prisoner clients of the jailhouse lawyer are unacceptable.

Although some jailhouse lawyers are no doubt very capable, it is not necessarily the best amateur legal minds which are devoted to jailhouse lawyering. Rather, the most aggressive and domineering personalities may predominate. And it may not be those with the best claims to relief who are served as clients, but those who are weaker and more gullible. Many assert that the aim of the jailhouse lawyer is not the service of truth and justice, but rather self-aggrandizement, profit, and power. According to prison officials, whose expertise in such matters should be given some consideration, the jailhouse lawyer often succeeds in establishing his own power structure, quite apart from the formal system of warden, guards, and trusties which the prison seeks to maintain. Those whom the jailhouse lawyer serves may come morally under his sway as the one hope of their release, and repay him not only with obedience but with what minor gifts and other favors are available to them. When a client refuses to pay,

---

10. One State has designated an inmate as the official prison writ-writer.

11. In reversing the District Court, the Court of Appeals relied on the power of the State to restrict the practice of law to licensed attorneys as a source of authority for the prison regulation. The power of the States to control the practice of law cannot be exercised so as to abrogate federally protected rights. In any event, the type of activity involved here—preparation of petitions for post-conviction relief—though historically and traditionally one which may benefit from the services of a trained and dedicated lawyer, is a function often, perhaps generally, performed by laymen. Title 28 U.S.C. § 2242 apparently contemplates that in many situations petitions for federal habeas corpus relief will be prepared by laymen.

violence may result, in which the jailhouse lawyer may be aided by his other clients.

* * *

* * * [S]ome jailhouse clients are illiterate; and whether illiterate or not, there are others who are unable to prepare their own petitions. They need help, but I doubt that the problem of the indigent convict will be solved by subjecting him to the false hopes, dominance, and inept representation of the average unsupervised jailhouse lawyer.

I cannot say, therefore, that petitioner Johnson, who is a convicted rapist serving a life sentence and whose prison conduct the State has wide discretion in regulating, cannot be disciplined for violating a prison rule against aiding other prisoners in seeking post-conviction relief, particularly when there is no showing that any prisoner in the Tennessee State Penitentiary has been denied access to the courts, that Johnson has confined his services to those who need it, or that Johnson is himself competent to give the advice which he offers. * * *

* * *

QUESTIONS AND POINTS FOR DISCUSSION

1. In Wolff v. McDonnell, 418 U.S. 539, 94 S.Ct. 2963 (1974), the Supreme Court extended its holding in *Johnson v. Avery,* concluding that the right to assistance from a jailhouse lawyer or to some other "reasonable alternative" assistance is not limited to assistance in preparing habeas corpus petitions; in *Wolff,* the Court held that the right to assistance also extends to prisoners preparing civil-rights complaints.

The litigation in *Wolff* was prompted by a prison regulation authorizing the warden to appoint one prisoner purportedly versed in the law to advise other prisoners on legal matters. The regulation barred prisoners from obtaining assistance in preparing legal documents from inmates other than this designated inmate unless the warden gave his written approval. Because the warden had denied permission to seek advice from inmates other than the appointed legal advisor, the question arose whether a single inmate advisor for all the prisoners in the prison constituted "reasonable alternative" assistance within the meaning of *Johnson v. Avery.*

In resolving that question, the Eighth Circuit Court of Appeals directed the district court to consider the inmates' need for assistance not only in preparing habeas corpus petitions, but civil-rights complaints as well. When the case reached the Supreme Court, the prison officials argued that the court of appeals had erred—that the adequacy of the available assistance is to be evaluated only in light of the need for assistance in preparing habeas corpus petitions. But the Supreme Court rejected the prison officials' narrow construction of *Johnson v. Avery:*

[W]hile it is true that only in habeas actions may relief be granted which will shorten the term of confinement, it is more pertinent that both actions serve to protect basic constitutional rights. The right of access to the courts, upon which *Avery* was premised, is founded in the Due Process Clause and assures that no person will be denied the opportunity to present to the judiciary allegations concerning violations of fundamental constitutional rights. It is futile to contend that the Civil Rights Act of 1871 has less importance in our constitutional scheme than does the Great Writ. The recognition by this Court that prisoners have certain constitutional rights which can be protected by civil rights actions would be diluted if inmates, often "totally or functionally illiterate," were unable to articulate their complaints to the courts.

Id. at 579, 94 S.Ct. at 2984.

2. An illiterate inmate might seek the assistance of a jailhouse lawyer for a variety of reasons having nothing to do with filing a constitutional claim. The inmate, for example, might want help with a divorce proceeding or a tort suit for personal injuries sustained before or during confinement. Does the illiterate inmate have a constitutional right to consult a jailhouse lawyer about such ordinary civil matters if no "reasonable alternative assistance" has been made available to the inmate? Why or why not? After reading Lewis v. Casey, 518 U.S. 343, 116 S.Ct. 2174 (1996), on page 553, consider how, if at all, that case has a bearing on this question.

3. In determining whether inmates at a particular prison have available to them the assistance needed to prepare court documents with "reasonable adequacy," not only are the types of claims for which there is a constitutional right of assistance relevant, but also the number of inmates entitled to assistance and the number of persons rendering assistance. See, e.g., Disciplinary Counsel v. Cotton, 873 N.E.2d 1240, 1243 (Ohio 2007) (four inmate law clerks for prison population of 2153 inmates not a "reasonable alternative" to assistance from jailhouse lawyer); Walters v. Thompson, 615 F.Supp. 330, 336 (N.D.Ill.1985) (two inmate clerks and two inmate trainees insufficient for prison population of over 1200).

Courts have spurned the suggestion that only completely illiterate inmates have the right to the assistance expounded on in *Johnson v. Avery*, noting that *Johnson* also evinced a concern for functionally illiterate and "poorly educated" prisoners. See, e.g., Wainwright v. Coonts, 409 F.2d 1337, 1338 (5th Cir.1969). Most prisoners function at the two lowest literacy levels, able to decipher, at best, the information in simple and short documents. Nat'l Ctr. for Educ. Statistics, Literacy Behind Prison Bars: Results From the 2003 National Assessment of Adult Literacy Prison Survey 2–8, 13 (2007). But if the entitlement to assistance were predicated on the inability to perform legal research and writing competently, even more prisoners would be entitled to some form of assistance, at least when filing suits involving constitutional claims. In Battle v. Anderson, 457 F.Supp. 719, 731 (E.D.Okl.1978), the court observed that 70% of the inmates at one prison lacked the intelligence or education to do legal research, while in Walters v. Thompson, 615 F.Supp. 330, 336 (N.D.Ill.1985), the court said that fully 90% of the inmates at another prison were incapable of doing their own legal research or writing.

A study on prisoners' literacy levels conducted by the National Center for Education Statistics corroborates these courts' observations. According to this study, over 95% of prisoners are unable to read and understand complex documents or perform tasks that require "integrating, synthesizing, and analyzing multiple pieces of information" located in such documents. Nat'l Ctr. for Educ. Statistics, supra, at 4–5, 13. It therefore seems unlikely that most prisoners have the capacity to conduct legal research, which requires the distillation of information from court opinions, other legal materials, and documents produced during discovery.

4.　The ban on inmate-to-inmate correspondence at issue in Turner v. Safley, 482 U.S. 78, 107 S.Ct. 2254 (1987), supra page 487, exempted correspondence "concerning legal matters." In an amicus brief filed with the Supreme Court in *Turner,* the state of Texas recounted prison gangs' use of what purported to be legal correspondence to transmit messages, including directives to kill other inmates:

> Throughout the document legal terms such as "plaintiff" and "plaintiff-class" are used to refer to the gang and its members. Investigation has revealed that other legal phrases, as well as all types of other innocuous words and phrases, have been added to the underground vocabulary of the AB and other gangs. "File a brief," "file an affidavit," "file a writ," "file a suit," in AB parlance, are all instructions to kill another inmate. Depending on how it is used in a sentence and what is already known about an individual, "give our regards to John Doe" could mean that the inmate is to be killed, or that the inmate has been approved for AB membership. TDC's list of gang phraseology now includes in excess of 100 phrases, and of course many have not been uncovered.

Brief for the State of Texas at 13.

In Shaw v. Murphy, 532 U.S. 223, 121 S.Ct. 1475 (2001), the Supreme Court considered the standard to be applied when assessing the constitutionality of restrictions placed on correspondence between inmates concerning legal matters. The plaintiff in that case, an inmate law clerk, had sent a letter to a fellow inmate who had been charged with assaulting a correctional officer. In the letter, the plaintiff had urged the inmate not to plead guilty to the charge. The letter stated that the plaintiff could locate at least a hundred witnesses who would testify that the correctional officer repeatedly harassed prisoners and made homosexual advances towards them.

Prison officials intercepted the plaintiff's letter and, because of its content, charged him with multiple disciplinary infractions. He was ultimately found guilty of violating two prison rules, those prohibiting insolence and interference with due-process hearings. As sanctions, the plaintiff received a suspended sentence of ten days in segregation and demerits that could adversely affect his custody level and, in turn, his prison privileges.

The issue before the Supreme Court in *Shaw* was whether the *Turner* test or a more rigorous test should be applied in adjudicating the plaintiff's claim that disciplining him violated his First Amendment right to correspond with other inmates about legal matters. The Court refused to modulate the constitutional protection afforded prisoners' correspondence based on its content. The Court added that even if it were inclined to elevate the scope of the protection afforded prisoners' speech because of its content, it would not provide augmented protection to prisoners' legal advice. Reiterating that jailhouse lawyers can be " 'a menace to prison discipline,' " id. at 231, 121 S.Ct. at 1480 (quoting Johnson v. Avery, 393 U.S. 483, 488, 89 S.Ct. 747, 751 (1969)), the Court noted that legal correspondence can be used by prisoners to pass contraband and instructions for the making of drugs and weapons. The Court also expressed concern that legal correspondence "could be an excuse for making clearly inappropriate comments, which 'may be expected to circulate among prisoners.' " Id. (quoting Thornburgh v. Abbott, 490 U.S. 401, 412, 109 S.Ct. 1874, 1881 (1989)).

Do you agree with the Supreme Court's holding and analysis in *Shaw*? Would the ban on jailhouse lawyers deemed unconstitutional in *Johnson v. Avery* have survived the Supreme Court's scrutiny under the *Turner* test? What are the practical ramifications of the Court's holding in *Shaw*? For one case, decided before *Shaw*, in which the *Turner* test was applied to prisoners' legal correspondence, see Goff v. Nix, 113 F.3d 887, 891 (8th Cir.1997) (prohibition on correspondence between prisoners in different prison units that prevented co-plaintiffs from corresponding about a pending lawsuit meets the *Turner* test).

5. Retaliating against a prisoner for pursuing litigation is unconstitutional, violating the First Amendment right to petition the government for a redress of grievances and the related or derivative right of access to the courts. Retaliating against a prisoner for filing an administrative grievance also violates the right of access to the courts, because 42 U.S.C. § 1997e(a) requires prisoners to exhaust administrative remedies before filing a federal claim challenging the conditions of their confinement. DeWalt v. Carter, 224 F.3d 607, 618 (7th Cir.2000). Cases abound in which prisoners allege that they have been taunted, threatened, transferred to other prisons, removed from coveted work assignments, beaten, and otherwise hassled because of lawsuits they brought against prison officials. Such retaliatory measures have been directed or allegedly directed against both the inmates bringing suit and the jailhouse lawyers willing to assist with the litigation. Examples of cases containing allegations of retaliation include: Espinal v. Goord, 558 F.3d 119, 129–30 (2d Cir. 2009) (severe beating of prisoner for over thirty minutes by correctional officers, one of whom was a defendant in a prior lawsuit filed by the prisoner); Gomez v. Vernon, 255 F.3d 1118, 1122–23 (9th Cir.2001) (prisoners fired from prison jobs and transferred to other prisons); DeWalt v. Carter, 224 F.3d 607, 618–19 (7th Cir.2000) (prisoner removed from prison job and falsely charged with disciplinary infractions); Allah v. Seiverling, 229 F.3d 220, 225 (3d Cir.2000) (prisoner confined in administrative segregation); and Thaddeus–X v. Blatter, 175 F.3d 378, 384 (6th Cir.1999) (prisoner transferred to section of the prison housing mentally ill inmates who threw feces and urine on each other and the correctional officers).

To prevail on a retaliation claim, a prisoner must prove that she engaged in activities protected by the Constitution or a statute; that the defendant took an adverse action against the plaintiff that would dissuade a person of "ordinary firmness" from engaging in the protected activity; and that the adverse action was motivated, at least in part, by the protected conduct. Siggers–El v. Barlow, 412 F.3d 693, 699 (6th Cir. 2005). A number of courts have held that once the prisoner proves that the protected conduct precipitated the adverse action, such as a transfer to a prison with a higher security level, the burden shifts to the defendant to prove that the same action would have been taken even in the absence of the protected activity. See Leland v. Parramore, 2009 WL 320698, *9 & n.7 (N.D. Fla. 2009) (listing cases). Other courts, however, put the burden on the plaintiff of proving that the adverse action would not have been taken were it not for the retaliatory motive. See, e.g., Peterson v. Shanks, 149 F.3d 1140, 1144 (10th Cir.1998).

6. Prison officials are not the only ones who have not looked kindly on the activities of jailhouse lawyers. In an acerbic dissent in Cruz v. Beto, 405 U.S. 319, 92 S.Ct. 1079 (1972), Justice Rehnquist argued that because of what he considered prisoners' abuse of the right of access, a different standard should be applied to prisoners' complaints when determining whether they state a claim upon which relief can be granted. To support his argument, Justice Rehnquist quoted from a Law Review article discussing jailhouse lawyers:

> When decisions do not help a writ-writer, he may employ a handful of tricks which damage his image in the state courts. Some of the not too subtle subterfuges used by a small minority of writ-writers would tax the credulity of any lawyer. One writ-writer simply made up his own legal citations when he ran short of actual ones. In one action against the California Adult Authority involving the application of administrative law, one writ-writer used the following citations: Aesop v. Fables, First Baptist Church v. Sally Stanford, Doda v. One Forty-four Inch Chest, and Dogood v. The Planet Earth. The references to the volumes and page numbers of the nonexistent publications were equally fantastic, such as 901 Penal Review, page 17,240. To accompany each case, he composed an eloquent decision which, if good law, would make selected acts of the Adult Authority unconstitutional. In time the "decisions" freely circulated among other writ-writers, and several gullible ones began citing them also.

Id. at 327 n. 7, 92 S.Ct. at 1084 n. 7 (quoting Charles Larsen, A Prisoner Looks at Writ–Writing, 56 Cal.L.Rev. 343, 355 (1968)).

Has an illiterate or uneducated inmate whose jailhouse lawyer is citing *Doda v. One Forty-four Inch Chest* received the "meaningful access" to the courts to which, according to the Supreme Court case below, he is entitled? Can an inmate who has had the assistance of a jailhouse lawyer still assert a violation of the right of access to the courts on the grounds that the jailhouse lawyer or lawyers in the prison are not sufficiently competent? In answering these questions, consider the implications of the following Supreme Court case.

LEWIS v. CASEY

Supreme Court of the United States, 1996.
518 U.S. 343, 116 S.Ct. 2174, 135 L.Ed.2d 606.

JUSTICE SCALIA delivered the opinion of the Court.

In *Bounds v. Smith*, 430 U.S. 817 (1977), we held that "the fundamental constitutional right of access to the courts requires prison authorities to assist inmates in the preparation and filing of meaningful legal papers by providing prisoners with adequate law libraries or adequate assistance from persons trained in the law." Petitioners, who are officials of the Arizona Department of Corrections (ADOC), contend that the United States District Court for the District of Arizona erred in finding them in violation of *Bounds,* and that the court's remedial order exceeded lawful authority.

I

Respondents are 22 inmates of various prisons operated by ADOC. In January 1990, they filed this class action "on behalf of all adult prisoners who are or will be incarcerated by the State of Arizona Department of Corrections," alleging that petitioners were "depriving [respondents] of their rights of access to the courts and counsel protected by the First, Sixth, and Fourteenth Amendments." Following a 3–month bench trial, the District Court ruled in favor of respondents, finding that "[p]risoners have a constitutional right of access to the courts that is adequate, effective and meaningful," citing *Bounds,* and that "[ADOC's] system fails to comply with constitutional standards." The court identified a variety of shortcomings of the ADOC system, in matters ranging from the training of library staff, to the updating of legal materials, to the availability of photocopying services. In addition to these general findings, the court found that two groups of inmates were particularly affected by the system's inadequacies: "[l]ockdown prisoners" (inmates segregated from the general prison population for disciplinary or security reasons), who "are routinely denied physical access to the law library" and "experience severe interference with their access to the courts," and illiterate or non-English-speaking inmates, who do not receive adequate legal assistance.

Having thus found liability, the court appointed a special master "to investigate and report about" the appropriate relief—that is (in the court's view), "how best to accomplish the goal of constitutionally adequate inmate access to the courts." Following eight months of investigation, and some degree of consultation with both parties, the special master lodged with the court a proposed permanent injunction, which the court proceeded to adopt, substantially unchanged. The 25–page injunctive order mandated sweeping changes designed to ensure that ADOC would "provide meaningful access to the Courts for all present and future prisoners." It specified in minute detail the times that libraries were to be kept open, the number of hours of library use to which each inmate was entitled (10 per week), the minimal educational requirements for prison librarians (a library science degree, law degree or paralegal degree), the content of a videotaped legal-research course for inmates (to be prepared by persons appointed by the special master but funded by ADOC) and similar matters. The injunction addressed the court's concern for lockdown prisoners by ordering that "ADOC prisoners in all housing areas and custody levels shall be provided regular and comparable visits to the law library," except that such visits "may be postponed on an individual basis because of the prisoner's documented inability to use the law library without creating a threat to safety or security, or a physical condition if determined by medical personnel to prevent library use." With respect to illiterate and non-English-speaking inmates, the injunction declared that they were entitled to "direct assistance" from lawyers, paralegals or "a sufficient number of at least minimally trained prisoner Legal Assistants"; it enjoined ADOC that "[p]articular steps must be taken to locate and train bilingual prisoners to be Legal Assistants."

* * * The Ninth Circuit affirmed both the finding of a *Bounds* violation and, with minor exceptions not important here, the terms of the injunction. * * *

II

Although petitioners present only one question for review, namely whether the District Court's order "exceeds the constitutional requirements set forth in *Bounds,*" they raise several distinct challenges, including renewed attacks on the court's findings of *Bounds* violations with respect to illiterate, non-English-speaking and lockdown prisoners, and on the breadth of the injunction. But their most fundamental contention is that the District Court's findings of injury were inadequate to justify the finding of system-wide injury and hence the granting of system-wide relief. * * * We agree that the success of respondents' systemic challenge was dependent on their ability to show widespread actual injury, and that the court's failure to identify anything more than isolated instances of actual injury renders its finding of a systemic *Bounds* violation invalid.

A

The requirement that an inmate alleging a violation of *Bounds* must show actual injury derives ultimately from the doctrine of standing, a constitutional principle that prevents courts of law from undertaking tasks assigned to the political branches. It is the role of courts to provide relief to claimants, in individual or class actions, who have suffered, or will imminently suffer, actual harm; it is not the role of courts, but that of the political branches, to shape the institutions of government in such fashion as to comply with the laws and the Constitution. In the context of the present case: It is for the courts to remedy past or imminent official interference with individual inmates' presentation of claims to the courts; it is for the political branches of the State and Federal Governments to manage prisons in such fashion that official interference with the presentation of claims will not occur. Of course the two roles briefly and partially coincide when a court, in granting relief against actual harm that has been suffered, or that will imminently be suffered, by a particular individual or class of individuals, orders the alteration of an institutional organization or procedure that causes the harm. But the distinction between the two roles would be obliterated if, to invoke intervention of the courts, no actual or imminent harm were needed, but merely the status of being subject to a governmental institution that was not organized or managed properly. If—to take another example from prison life—a healthy inmate who had suffered no deprivation of needed medical treatment were able to claim violation of his constitutional right to medical care, see *Estelle v. Gamble,* 429 U.S. 97, 103 (1976), simply on the ground that the prison medical facilities were inadequate, the essential distinction between judge and executive would have disappeared: it would have become the function of the courts to assure adequate medical care in prisons.

The foregoing analysis would not be pertinent here if, as respondents seem to assume, the right at issue—the right to which the actual or threatened harm must pertain—were the right to a law library or to legal assistance. But *Bounds* established no such right, any more than *Estelle* established a right to a prison hospital. The right that *Bounds* acknowledged was the (already well-established) right of *access to the courts.* * * * Although it affirmed a court order requiring North Carolina to make law library facilities available to inmates, it stressed that that was merely "one constitutionally acceptable method to assure meaningful access to the courts," and that "our decision here ... does not foreclose alternative means to achieve that goal." In other words, prison law libraries and legal assistance programs are not ends in themselves, but only the means for ensuring "a reasonably adequate opportunity to present claimed violations of fundamental constitutional rights to the courts."

Because *Bounds* did not create an abstract, free-standing right to a law library or legal assistance, an inmate cannot establish relevant actual injury simply by establishing that his prison's law library or legal assistance program is sub-par in some theoretical sense. That would be the precise analogue of the healthy inmate claiming constitutional violation because of the inadequacy of the prison infirmary. Insofar as the right vindicated by *Bounds* is concerned, "meaningful access to the courts is the touchstone," and the inmate therefore must go one step further and demonstrate that the alleged shortcomings in the library or legal assistance program hindered his efforts to pursue a legal claim. He might show, for example, that a complaint he prepared was dismissed for failure to satisfy some technical requirement which, because of deficiencies in the prison's legal assistance facilities, he could not have known. Or that he had suffered arguably actionable harm that he wished to bring before the courts, but was so stymied by inadequacies of the law library that he was unable even to file a complaint.

Although *Bounds* itself made no mention of an actual-injury requirement, it can hardly be thought to have eliminated that constitutional prerequisite. * * * Moreover, the assumption of an actual-injury requirement seems to us implicit in the opinion's statement that "we encourage local experimentation" in various methods of assuring access to the courts. One such experiment, for example, might replace libraries with some minimal access to legal advice and a system of court-provided forms such as those that contained the original complaints in two of the more significant inmate-initiated cases in recent years, *Sandin v. Conner,* 515 U.S. 472 (1995), and *Hudson v. McMillian,* 503 U.S. 1 (1992)—forms that asked the inmates to provide only the facts and not to attempt any legal analysis. We hardly think that what we meant by "experimenting" with such an alternative was simply announcing it, whereupon suit would immediately lie to declare it theoretically inadequate and bring the experiment to a close. We think we envisioned, instead, that the new program would remain in place at least until some inmate could demonstrate that a nonfrivolous[3] legal claim had been frustrated or was being impeded.

It must be acknowledged that several statements in *Bounds* went beyond the right of access recognized in the earlier cases on which it relied, which was a right to bring to court a grievance that the inmate wished to present. These statements appear to suggest that the State must enable the prisoner to *discover* grievances, and to *litigate effectively* once in court. These elaborations upon the right of access to the courts have no antecedent in our pre-*Bounds* cases, and we now disclaim them. To demand the conferral of such sophisticated legal capabilities upon a mostly uneducated and indeed largely illiterate prison population is effectively to demand permanent provision of counsel, which we do not believe the Constitution requires.

Finally, we must observe that the injury requirement is not satisfied by just any type of frustrated legal claim. * * * In other words, *Bounds* does not guarantee inmates the wherewithal to transform themselves into litigating engines capable of filing everything from shareholder derivative actions to slip-and-fall claims. The tools it requires to be provided are those that the inmates need in order to attack their sentences, directly or collaterally, and in order to challenge the conditions of their confinement. Impairment of any *other* litigating capacity is simply one of the incidental (and perfectly constitutional) consequences of conviction and incarceration.

B

Here the District Court identified only two instances of actual injury. * * * (lawsuit of inmate Bartholic dismissed with prejudice), (inmate Harris unable to file a legal action).

Petitioners contend that "any lack of access experienced by these two inmates is not attributable to unconstitutional State policies," because ADOC "has met its constitutional obligations." The claim appears to be that all inmates, including the illiterate and non-English-speaking, have a right to nothing more than "physical access to excellent libraries, *plus* help from legal assistants and law clerks." This misreads *Bounds,* which as we have said guarantees no particular methodology but rather the conferral of a capability—the capability of bringing contemplated challenges to sentences or conditions of confinement before the courts. When

---

3. Justice Souter believes that *Bounds* guarantees prison inmates the right to present frivolous claims—the determination of which suffices to confer standing, he says * * *. * * * Depriving someone of an arguable (though not yet established) claim inflicts actual injury because it deprives him of something of value—arguable claims are settled, bought and sold. Depriving someone of a frivolous claim, on the other hand, deprives him of nothing at all, except perhaps the punishment of Rule 11 sanctions.

any inmate, even an illiterate or non-English-speaking inmate, shows that an actionable claim of this nature which he desired to bring has been lost or rejected, or that the presentation of such a claim is currently being prevented, because this capability of filing suit has not been provided, he demonstrates that the State has failed to furnish "*adequate* law libraries or *adequate* assistance from persons trained in the law." Of course, we leave it to prison officials to determine how best to ensure that inmates with language problems have a reasonably adequate opportunity to file nonfrivolous legal claims challenging their convictions or conditions of confinement. But it is that capability, rather than the capability of turning pages in a law library, that is the touchstone.

C

Having rejected petitioners' argument that the injuries suffered by Bartholic and Harris do not count, we turn to the question whether those injuries, and the other findings of the District Court, support the injunction ordered in this case. The actual-injury requirement would hardly serve the purpose we have described above—of preventing courts from undertaking tasks assigned to the political branches—if once a plaintiff demonstrated harm from one particular inadequacy in government administration, the court were authorized to remedy *all* inadequacies in that administration. The remedy must of course be limited to the inadequacy that produced the injury-in-fact that the plaintiff has established.

* * *

After the trial in this case, the court found actual injury on the part of only one named plaintiff, Bartholic; and the cause of that injury—the inadequacy which the suit empowered the court to remedy—was failure of the prison to provide the special services that Bartholic would have needed, in light of his illiteracy, to avoid dismissal of his case. At the outset, therefore, we can eliminate from the proper scope of this injunction provisions directed at special services or special facilities required by non-English-speakers, by prisoners in lockdown, and by the inmate population at large. If inadequacies of this character exist, they have not been found to have harmed any plaintiff in this lawsuit, and hence were not the proper object of this District Court's remediation.

As to remediation of the inadequacy that caused Bartholic's injury, a further question remains: Was that inadequacy widespread enough to justify systemwide relief? The only findings supporting the proposition that, in all of ADOC's facilities, an illiterate inmate wishing to file a claim would be unable to receive the assistance necessary to do so were (1) the finding with respect to Bartholic, at the Florence facility, and (2) the finding that Harris, while incarcerated at Perryville, had once been "unable to file [a] legal actio[n]." These two instances were a patently inadequate basis for a conclusion of systemwide violation and imposition of systemwide relief.

To be sure, the District Court also noted that "the trial testimony ... indicated that there are prisoners who are unable to research the law because of their functional illiteracy." As we have discussed, however, the Constitution does not require that prisoners (literate or illiterate) be able to conduct generalized research, but only that they be able to present their grievances to the courts—a more limited capability that can be produced by a much more limited degree of legal assistance. Apart from the dismissal of Bartholic's claim with prejudice, and Harris's inability to file his claim, there is no finding, and as far as we can discern from the record no evidence, that in Arizona prisons illiterate prisoners cannot obtain the minimal help necessary to file particular claims that they wish to bring before the courts. The constitutional violation has not been shown to be systemwide, and granting a remedy beyond what was necessary to provide relief to Harris and Bartholic was therefore improper.[7]

III

There are further reasons why the order here cannot stand. We held in *Turner v. Safley,* 482 U.S. 78 (1987), that a prison regulation impinging on inmates' constitutional rights "is valid if it is reasonably related to legitimate penological interests." * * *

* * * [W]e think it quite obvious that *Bounds* and *Turner* must be read in *pari materia*.

The District Court here failed to accord adequate deference to the judgment of the prison authorities in at least three significant respects. First, in concluding that ADOC's restrictions on lockdown prisoners' access to law libraries were unjustified. *Turner*'s principle of deference has special force with regard to that issue, since the inmates in lockdown include "the most dangerous and violent prisoners in the Arizona prison system" and other inmates presenting special disciplinary and security concerns. The District Court made much of the fact that lockdown prisoners routinely experience delays in receiving legal materials or legal assistance, some as long as 16 days, but so long as they are the product of prison regulations reasonably related to legitimate penological interests, such delays are not of constitutional significance, even where they result in actual injury (which, of course, the District Court did not find here).

Second, the injunction imposed by the District Court was inordinately—indeed, wildly—intrusive. There is no need to belabor this point. One need only read the order to appreciate that it is the *ne plus ultra* of what our opinions have lamented as a court's "in the name of the Constitution, becom[ing] ... enmeshed in the minutiae of prison operations."

Finally, the order was developed through a process that failed to give adequate consideration to the views of state prison authorities. We have said that "[t]he strong considerations of comity that require giving a state

---

7. Our holding regarding the inappropriateness of systemwide relief for illiterate inmates does not rest upon the application of standing rules, but rather, like Justice Souter's conclusion, upon "the respondents' failure to prove that denials of access to illiterate prisoners pervaded the State's prison system." * * *

court system that has convicted a defendant the first opportunity to correct its own errors ... also require giving the States the first opportunity to correct errors made in the internal administration of their prisons." *Preiser v. Rodriguez,* 411 U.S. 475, 492 (1973). For an illustration of the proper procedure in a case such as this, we need look no further than *Bounds* itself. There, after granting summary judgment for the inmates, the District Court refrained from " 'dictat[ing] precisely what course the State should follow.' " Rather, recognizing that "determining the 'appropriate relief to be ordered ... presents a difficult problem,' " the court " 'charge[d] the Department of Correction with the task of devising a Constitutionally sound program' to assure inmate access to the courts." The State responded with a proposal, which the District Court ultimately approved with minor changes, after considering objections raised by the inmates. We praised this procedure, observing that the court had "scrupulously respected the limits on [its] role," by "not ... thrust[ing] itself into prison administration" and instead permitting "[p]rison administrators [to] exercis[e] wide discretion within the bounds of constitutional requirements."

As *Bounds* was an exemplar of what should be done, this case is a model of what should not. The District Court totally failed to heed the admonition of *Preiser*. Having found a violation of the right of access to the courts, it conferred upon its special master, a law professor from Flushing, New York, rather than upon ADOC officials, the responsibility for devising a remedial plan. * * * The State was entitled to far more than an opportunity for rebuttal, and on that ground alone this order would have to be set aside.

* * *

JUSTICE THOMAS, concurring.

* * *

In the end, I agree that the Constitution affords prisoners what can be termed a right of access to the courts. That right, rooted in the Due Process Clause and the principle articulated in *Ex parte Hull,* is a right not to be arbitrarily prevented from lodging a claimed violation of a federal right in a federal court. The State, however, is not constitutionally required to finance or otherwise assist the prisoner's efforts, either through law libraries or other legal assistance. Whether to expend state resources to facilitate prisoner lawsuits is a question of policy and one that the Constitution leaves to the discretion of the States.

* * *

JUSTICE SOUTER, with whom JUSTICE GINSBURG and JUSTICE BREYER join, concurring in part, dissenting in part, and concurring in the judgment.

I agree with the Court on certain, fundamental points: The case before us involves an injunction whose scope has not yet been justified by the factual findings of the district court, one that was imposed through a "process that failed to give adequate consideration to the views of state prison authorities," and that does not reflect the deference we accord to state prison officials under *Turner v. Safley*. Although I therefore concur in the judgment and in portions of the Court's opinion, reservations about the Court's treatment of standing doctrine and about certain points unnecessary to the decision lead me to write separately.

The question accepted for review was a broadside challenge to the scope of the District Court's order of systemic or class-wide relief * * *, not whether proof of actual injury is necessary to establish standing to litigate a *Bounds* claim. * * *

While we are certainly free ourselves to raise an issue of standing as going to Article III jurisdiction, and must do so when we would lack jurisdiction to deal with the merits, there is no apparent question that the standing of at least one of the class-action plaintiffs suffices for our jurisdiction and no dispute that standing doctrine does not address the principal issue in the case. * * *

* * *

Although application of standing doctrine may for our purposes dispose of the challenge to remedial orders insofar as they touch non-English speakers and lockdown prisoners, standing principles cannot do the same job in reviewing challenges to the orders aimed at providing court access for the illiterate prisoners. One class representative has standing, as the Court concedes * * *. * * *

* * *

While the propriety of the order of systemic relief for illiterate prisoners does not turn on the standing of class members, and certainly need not turn on class-action rules, it clearly does turn on the respondents' failure to prove that denials of access to illiterate prisoners pervaded the State's prison system. * * * [T]he state of the evidence simply left the District Court without an adequate basis for the exercise of its equitable discretion in issuing an order covering the entire system.

* * *

Even if I were to reach the standing question, however, I would not adopt the standard the Court has established. * * *

* * *

* * * I would go no further than to hold (in a case not involving substantial, systemic deprivation of access to court)[2] that Article III

---

2. Dispensing with any underlying claim requirement in such instances would be consistent with the rule of equity dealing with threatened injury. See, e.g., *Farmer v. Brennan*, 511 U.S. 825, 845 (1994) (holding that a prisoner need not suffer physical injury before obtaining relief because " '[o]ne does not have to await the consummation of threatened injury to obtain preventive relief' "); *Helling v. McKinney*, 509 U.S. 25, 33 (1993) (observing that prisoners may obtain relief "even though it was not alleged that the likely harm would occur immediately and even though the possible [harm] might not affect all of those [at risk]"). If the state denies prisoners all access

requirements will normally be satisfied if a prisoner demonstrates that (1) he has a complaint or grievance, meritorious or not,[3] about the prison system or the validity of his conviction that he would raise if his library research (or advice, or judicial review of a form complaint or other means of "access" chosen by the State) were to indicate that he had an actionable claim; and (2) that the access scheme provided by the prison is so inadequate that he cannot research, consult about, file, or litigate the claim, as the case may be.

* * *

There are, finally, two additional points on which I disagree with the Court. First, I cannot concur in the suggestion that *Bounds* should be overruled to the extent that it requires States choosing to provide law libraries for court access to make them available for a prisoner's use in the period between filing a complaint and its final disposition. *Bounds* stated the obvious reasons for making libraries available for these purposes * * *.[a]

Second, I see no reason at this point to accept the Court's view that the *Bounds* right of access is necessarily restricted to attacks on sentences or challenges to conditions of confinement. It is not clear to me that a State may force a prisoner to abandon all opportunities to vindicate rights outside these two categories no matter how significant. * * * One can imagine others that would arguably entitle a prisoner to some limited

---

to the courts, it is hardly implausible for a prisoner to claim a protected stake in opening some channel of access.

3. See *Harris v. Young,* 718 F.2d 620, 622 (CA4 1983) ("It is unfair to force an inmate to prove that he has a meritorious claim which will require access until after he has had an opportunity to see just what his rights are.").

a. In explaining in *Bounds* why states must take steps to ensure that prisoners have a "reasonably adequate opportunity to present claimed violations of fundamental constitutional rights to the courts," the Supreme Court stated:

> Although it is essentially true, as petitioners argue, that a habeas corpus petition or civil right complaint need only set forth facts giving rise to the cause of action, it hardly follows that a law library or other legal assistance is not essential to frame such documents. It would verge on incompetence for a lawyer to file an initial pleading without researching such issues as jurisdiction, venue, standing, exhaustion of remedies, proper parties plaintiff and defendant, and types of relief available. Most importantly, of course, a lawyer must know what the law is in order to determine whether a colorable claim exists, and if so, what facts are necessary to state a cause of action.

> If a lawyer must perform such preliminary research, it is no less vital for a *pro se* prisoner. Indeed, despite the "less stringent standards" by which a *pro se* pleading is judged, *Haines v. Kerner,* 404 U.S. 519, 520 (1972), it is often more important that a prisoner complaint set forth a nonfrivolous claim meeting all procedural prerequisites, since the court may pass on the complaint's sufficiency before allowing filing in *forma pauperis* and may dismiss the case if it is deemed frivolous. See 28 U.S.C. § 1915. Moreover, if the State files a response to a *pro se* pleading, it will undoubtedly contain seemingly authoritative citations. Without a library, an inmate will be unable to rebut the State's argument. It is not enough to answer that the court will evaluate the facts pleaded in light of the relevant law. Even the most dedicated trial judges are bound to overlook meritorious cases without the benefit of an adversary presentation.

430 U.S. at 825–26, 97 S.Ct. at 1496–97. Since *Bounds,* the procedures governing the processing of prisoners' federal lawsuits and claims have been changed. Courts now must screen prisoners' incoming complaints and dismiss those claims that are frivolous, fail to state a claim on which relief can be granted, or seek damages from a defendant with immunity from that relief. See 28 U.S.C. § 1915(e)(2)(B); id. § 1915A(a)–(b); 42 U.S.C. § 1997e(c)(1).

right of access to court. See, e.g., *Lassiter v. Department of Social Servs. of Durham Cty.*, 452 U.S. 18 (1981) (parental rights); *Boddie v. Connecticut*, 401 U.S. 371 (1971) (divorce); cf. *Wong Yang Sung v. McGrath*, 339 U.S. 33, 49–50 (1950) (deportation). This case does not require us to consider whether, as a matter of constitutional principle, a prisoner's opportunities to vindicate rights in these spheres may be foreclosed, and I would not address such issues here.

I therefore concur in Parts I and III of the Court's opinion, dissent from Part II, and concur in the judgment.

Justice Stevens, dissenting.

[After noting, as had Justice Souter, that the majority of the Court had unnecessarily addressed the subject of standing, Justice Stevens proffered his views on this subject.]

At first glance, the novel approach adopted by the Court today suggests that only those prisoners who have been refused the opportunity to file claims later found to have arguable merit should be able to challenge a rule as clearly unconstitutional as the one addressed in *Hull*. * * * [B]ecause prisoners are uniquely subject to the control of the State, and because unconstitutional restrictions on the right of access to the courts—whether through nearly absolute bars like that in *Hull* or through inadequate legal resources—frustrate the ability of prisoners to identify, articulate, and present to courts injuries flowing from that control, I believe that any prisoner who claims to be impeded by such barriers has alleged constitutionally sufficient injury-in-fact.

[In subsequent portions of his opinion, Justice Stevens agreed with the other members of the Court that the court-ordered relief in this case was overly broad. Justice Stevens objected, however, to the Court's discussion of issues upon which the parties' debate had not focused: whether the "*Bounds* right" extends beyond attacks on sentences and conditions of confinement and whether the right includes the right to "discover" grievances or "litigate effectively" a claim already lodged with a court.]

Questions and Points for Discussion

1. *Lewis v. Casey* has been criticized for creating a "cruel catch–22." Stephen B. Bright, Neither Equal Nor Just: The Rationing and Denial of Legal Services to the Poor When Life and Liberty are at Stake, 1997 Ann. Surv. Am. L. 783, 798 (1999). Without access to attorneys or law libraries, prisoners, it has been argued, will be unable to prove that they suffered the actual injury needed to state a viable claim for denial of access to the courts. On the other hand, Seventh Circuit Judge Richard Posner has spotlighted what he considers the "paradox" that a prisoner's ability to litigate a right-of-access claim is evidence that the inmate has no such claim. Walters v. Edgar, 163 F.3d 430, 436 (7th Cir.1998). Do you concur with either or both of these observations? Does *Lewis v. Casey* provide adequate assurance that inmates deprived of their right to have "meaningful access" to the courts will obtain redress for the violation of this constitutional right?

2. When analyzing the scope of inmates' right to legal assistance, two of the Supreme Court cases that should be considered are Pennsylvania v. Finley, 481 U.S. 551, 107 S.Ct. 1990 (1987) and Murray v. Giarratano, 492 U.S. 1, 109 S.Ct. 2765 (1989). In both cases, the Court addressed whether indigent inmates have the constitutional right to have an attorney appointed to assist them when challenging the validity of their convictions in a state postconviction proceeding. Relying on Ross v. Moffitt, 417 U.S. 600, 94 S.Ct. 2437 (1974), the Court in *Finley* rejected the argument that the due-process and equal-protection provisions of the Constitution accord inmates this right. In *Ross,* the Court had held that while indigent inmates challenging their convictions may have the right to an appointed attorney when first appealing their convictions, they have no right to appointed counsel when seeking the discretionary review of their convictions by a state supreme court or the United States Supreme Court.

The inmate in *Finley* was serving time for a noncapital crime, so the question still remained after *Finley* whether inmates sentenced to death have the right to appointed counsel to assist them during postconviction proceedings. In *Murray v. Giarratano*, the Supreme Court, in a 5–4 decision, answered this question in the negative. In a plurality opinion, Chief Justice Rehnquist, joined by Justices White, O'Connor, and Scalia, observed that *Finley* was controlling. The plurality considered it inconsequential that the Virginia prisoner in this case was faced with the ultimate sanction—death. According to the plurality, safeguards surrounding capital cases at the trial stage provide sufficient assurance that the death penalty is imposed only in appropriate cases. Consequently, the failure to appoint counsel to assist death-row inmates in collaterally attacking their convictions violates neither the Due Process Clause of the Fourteenth Amendment nor the prohibition of cruel and unusual punishments found in the Eighth Amendment.

Justice Kennedy's concurring opinion, in which he was joined by Justice O'Connor, provided the critical fifth vote for the Court, so his opinion is of especial significance. Justice Kennedy emphasized that there was no evidence that any Virginia inmate on death row had ever been unable to procure the assistance of an attorney during postconviction proceedings. Justice Kennedy also noted that in Virginia, lawyers were assigned to the prisons to assist inmates in drafting petitions for postconviction relief. The emphasis Justice Kennedy placed on these facts suggests that the Court might reach a different result in a case where an indigent inmate on death row had no access to an attorney for help in preparing a petition for postconviction relief and to represent the inmate during the postconviction proceeding.

Justice Stevens wrote a dissenting opinion in *Murray v. Giarratano* in which Justices Brennan, Marshall, and Blackmun joined. Justice Stevens underscored the constitutional requirement that a prisoner's access to the courts be "meaningful." By no means, said Justice Stevens, could the access of an indigent death-row inmate to the postconviction review process be considered "meaningful" when that inmate was not provided with an attorney to draft the petition for postconviction relief and represent the inmate throughout the postconviction proceeding. In support of his conclusion, Justice Stevens cited a number of factors, including the following: (1) the limited time that an inmate often has to file a postconviction petition; (2) the inordinate complexity of the issues in capital cases; (3) the difficulty of preparing legal documents when faced with the pressures of an impending death; and (4) the large number of capital cases in which a collateral attack has been successful.

3.   In Jackson v. State, 732 So.2d 187, 191 (Miss.1999), the Supreme Court of Mississippi distinguished *Murray v. Giarratano*. Holding that the failure to appoint counsel to represent indigent inmates on death row in state postconviction proceedings deprived them of meaningful access to the courts, the court noted that death-row inmates in Mississippi had been unable to procure counsel on their own to represent them. The court considered this lack of assistance a particularly grave concern because claims that an inmate received ineffective assistance of counsel at trial, in violation of the Sixth Amendment, are often asserted, for the first time, in postconviction proceedings. For a discussion of the dimensions of the problem of ineffective assistance of counsel in capital cases, see pages 330–32.

In *Jackson*, the Mississippi Supreme Court also acknowledged what it described as "the reality" that inmates on death row are utterly incapable of effectively representing themselves. Id. at 190. An evaluation conducted in 1997 of prisoners on death row in Mississippi seems to buttress this conclusion. The study found that while understanding the documents relevant to postconviction proceedings requires reading comprehension between the 12.8 and 15.2 grade levels, the average reading-comprehension level of inmates on death row measured at the 5.13 grade level. Mark D. Cunningham & Mark P. Vigen, Without Appointed Counsel in Capital Postconviction Proceedings, 26 Crim. Just. & Beh. 293, 301–02 (1999).

4.   Apart from the question of the assistance to which an inmate is constitutionally entitled when litigating a court case is the question of the right to assistance that should be accorded by statutes or court rules. Rule 8(c) of the Rules Governing Section 2254 Cases in the United States District Courts (federal habeas corpus actions involving state prisoners), 28 U.S.C. foll. § 2254, for example, requires that counsel be appointed to represent an indigent inmate once the decision is made to hold an evidentiary hearing on the merits of the inmate's habeas corpus petition.

The decision whether to appoint an attorney to represent an indigent prisoner bringing a § 1983 suit in federal court presently falls within the court's discretion. 28 U.S.C. § 1915(e)(1). Most inmates' civil-rights suits, however, proceed without the inmates being assisted by lawyers. See Roger A. Hanson & Henry W.K. Daley, Challenging the Conditions of Prisons and Jails: A Report on Section 1983 Litigation 21 (1995) (96% of prisoners bringing § 1983 suits proceed *pro se*). Nor can this void be filled by legal-services programs that provide legal assistance to the poor, in part because Congress has, since 1996, forbidden legal-services programs that receive federal funds from representing prisoners. See Omnibus Consolidated Rescissions and Appropriations Act of 1996, Pub. L. No. 104–134, § 504(a)(15), 110 Stat. 1321 (1996); 45 C.F.R. § 1637.3 (2009). The prison officials being sued, on the other hand, usually are represented by an attorney. The prison officials normally do not have to pay for their attorneys because the attorneys typically are employees of, and paid by, the government.

5.   Even if a prisoner is fully capable of utilizing a prison law library, the existence of a library will not alone satisfy constitutional requirements. If the library lacks certain books or materials needed to afford the prisoner a "reasonably adequate opportunity" to file a nonfrivolous constitutional claim, a prisoner actually harmed by this deficiency will have been deprived of the constitutional right of access to the courts. In a number of cases preceding *Lewis v. Casey,* courts held prison law libraries constitutionally deficient because of books not included in the library collection. See, e.g., Gilmore v. Lynch, 319 F.Supp. 105, 110–11 (N.D.Cal.1970), aff'd sub nom., Younger v. Gilmore, 404 U.S. 15, 92 S.Ct. 250 (1971) (regulation listing books to be included in state prison law libraries omitted *U.S. Supreme Court Reports,* other federal reporters, the *United States Code,* annotated copies of the state's codes, many local federal district court rules, and *U.S. Law Week*); Ramos v. Lamm, 639 F.2d 559, 584 (10th Cir.1980) (prison law library lacked most volumes of the Federal Reporter Second and the Federal Supplement); Wade v. Kane, 448 F.Supp. 678, 684 (E.D.Pa.1978), aff'd, 591 F.2d 1338 (3d Cir.1979) (library did not contain the *U.S. Supreme Court Reports,* the Federal Reporter Second, Federal Rules Decisions, the annotated versions of 28 U.S.C. §§ 2254 and 2255, which deal with habeas corpus relief, the annotated state statutes on criminal procedure, the Atlantic Reporter Second, many state reporters, the Federal Rules of Criminal Procedure, the Federal Rules of Civil Procedure, and the local rules of the federal district courts located in the state). It bears repeating though that after *Lewis v. Casey,* a prisoner also must prove an "actual injury" stemming from deficiencies in a library's book collection.

6.   Even if a prison law library is "adequate" as far as the books in that library, constitutional problems may remain if prisoners are encumbered in filing nonfrivolous constitutional claims because they are not provided with sufficient access to those books. Those problems may result from restrictions on the number of inmates that can use the law library at any one time or the number of hours that an inmate can use the library during a particular visit. See, e.g., Ramos v. Lamm, 639 F.2d 559, 582, 586 (10th Cir.1980) (regulation confining use of the library to thirteen inmates a day for three-hour sessions, which may result in inmates having access to the law library only three hours every thirteen weeks, violates right of access to the courts). Or limits on the total amount of time that the law library is open may lead to a deprivation of court access. See, e.g., Taylor v. Perini, 413 F.Supp. 189, 203, 205 (N.D.Ohio 1976) (law-library hours extending from 6 to 8:30 p.m. Mondays through Fridays and 9 a.m. to 3 p.m. on Saturdays are constitutionally inadequate). The specific times that the library is open also may be a factor contributing to the denial of the right of access to the courts, since some inmates may be unable to use the prison law library because of the library's hours. For example, prisoners who have work and school assignments during the day may not have access, as a practical matter, to the library if it is only open during the day and the inmates are unable to leave their assignments to use the library.

7.   Implementing the right of access to the courts poses special problems for county and city jails and similar short-term detention facilities. Many jails are small and cannot afford the costs of maintaining a law library. In addition,

because of the transient nature of jail populations, jailhouse lawyers may not be available to render assistance to other persons incarcerated in the jail.

Effectuating an inmate's right of access to the courts also may be difficult when the inmate has been placed in disciplinary segregation, protective custody, or some type of administrative segregation designed to protect correctional officers and other inmates from a particularly disruptive or violent prisoner. Releasing the prisoner from restrictive confinement for a visit to the prison law library may not be feasible. Release may precipitate the security problems that the restrictive confinement was designed to avert or may undermine the punitive and deterrent purposes of disciplinary confinement.

It is evident from *Lewis v. Casey* that a restriction that impairs segregated inmates' access to legal materials is not unconstitutional if the restriction is "reasonably related to legitimate penological interests." An inmate's right of access to the courts, however, is not abnegated by restrictive confinement. In fact, an inmate isolated from the general prison population may have a particularly pressing reason for pursuing a court action since conditions of confinement in segregation units may be especially onerous, not meeting basic needs as to space, exercise, or sanitation. What options might a warden pursue to ensure that segregated inmates' right of access to the courts is preserved? What are the drawbacks of the options you have identified?

8. In recent years, some states have eliminated their prison libraries, supplanting them with other forms of legal assistance. Evan R. Seamone, *Fahrenheit 451* on Cell Block D: A Bar Examination to Safeguard America's Jailhouse Lawyers from the Post–*Lewis* Blaze Consuming Their Law Libraries, 24 Yale L. & Pol'y Rev. 91, 91–92 (2006). Some states, for example, utilize paralegals to help prisoners draft civil-rights complaints and habeas corpus petitions. Jill Schachner Chanen, Banned in the Bighouse, A.B.A. J., March, 1998, at 26, while others use attorneys. See Carper v. DeLand, 54 F.3d 613, 617 (10th Cir.1995) (using two attorneys to provide legal assistance to prisoners in lieu of a library meets constitutional requirements). This assistance often does not extend beyond the preparation of pleadings. By contrast, North Carolina has a contract with a legal-services provider that specializes in prisoner litigation under which more extensive assistance is provided to inmates. Prisoners receive legal advice and representation in habeas corpus actions, other postconviction proceedings, and civil suits brought under state or federal law concerning the conditions of confinement in the state's prisons or other governmental actions affecting North Carolina inmates.

As a policy matter, what kind of legal-assistance program would you advise prison officials to establish? For what types of cases would assistance be available, and for what stages of the litigation would assistance be rendered? Would the program include prisoner access to law libraries? For a discussion of several legal-assistance programs for prisoners and recommendations regarding the development of an "access to the courts" plan by correctional departments, see Lynn S. Branham, Limiting the Burdens of *Pro Se* Inmate Litigation: A Technical–Assistance Manual for Courts, Correctional Officials, and Attorneys General 98–138 (1997). For a summary of problems encountered with some legal-assistance alternatives—contract attorneys, paralegals, standardized complaint forms, and law-school clinics—and recommended steps, including the adoption of a "Jailhouse Lawyer Bar Exam," to improve the quality of legal services provided by jailhouse lawyers, see Seamone, supra, at 115–45.

9. In his dissenting opinion in *Bounds,* Chief Justice Burger distinguished between interfering with inmates' access to the courts and subsidizing that access. According to the Chief Justice, while prison officials may be prohibited from unduly obstructing court access, they need not, as a constitutional matter, provide "affirmative assistance" to facilitate that access. Do you agree with this viewpoint, one to which Justice Thomas subscribed in *Lewis v. Casey*? If so, do indigent inmates then have no right to free paper and pens needed to communicate with a court? Do they have a right to free photocopies of documents that they need to file with a court? To free stamps needed to mail the documents to the court? Where would you draw the line on the scope of the right of access and why?

10. Judges, some of whom have seen inmate complaints written on sacks and toilet paper, have been hospitable to claims that prison officials must provide indigent inmates with free paper and pens to prepare legal documents. The district court in Wade v. Kane, 448 F.Supp. 678, 685 (E.D.Pa. 1978), aff'd, 591 F.2d 1338 (3d Cir.1979), for example, held that the failure to provide indigent inmates with free paper and pens abridges not only their constitutional right of access to the courts, but also their right to equal protection of the law. According to the court in *Wade,* this latter right is infringed, because inmates with money have these basic litigation tools available to them.

11. Although "typed papers may leap more vividly than handwritten ones to the watery judicial eye," United States ex rel. Wolfish v. Levi, 439 F.Supp. 114, 131 (S.D.N.Y.1977), courts concur that inmates generally have no right to use or possess typewriters or word processors to prepare court documents. See, e.g., Roberts v. Cohn, 63 F.Supp. 2d 921, 924 (N.D.Ind.1999), aff'd, 215 F.3d 1330 (7th Cir.2000). But prison officials must provide inmates with "some means of preparing documents that comply with the rules of the court." Phillips v. Hust, 477 F.3d 1070, 1077 (9th Cir. 2007). Thus, if a court's rules required that certain documents filed with the court be typed, the failure to take steps to enable an inmate to meet this requirement could abridge the right of access to the courts. See Armstrong v. Scribner, 2008 WL 268974, *18 (S.D. Cal. 2008) (denying motion to dismiss prisoner's claim that failure to afford access to computer needed to format certiorari petition in conformance with Supreme Court rules violated right of access to the courts).

12. An inmate who is preparing or litigating a court case may want to use a photocopying machine to duplicate documents to be filed with the court or to duplicate cases, statutes, and other materials that may be relevant to the litigation. Whether denial of access to a photocopier culminates in an abridgment of the right of access to the courts depends, in part, on the extent to which the inmate has access to a typewriter as well as other supplies for writing or typing, such as carbon paper and paper. The amount of time that inmates are permitted to stay in the law library and the permissibility of taking law books to cells also may affect whether an inmate must be provided

access to photocopying equipment. In addition, the feasibility of sending papers to family members and friends for photocopying may be considered when determining whether access to a photocopier is needed to effectuate the right of access to the courts. See Harrell v. Keohane, 621 F.2d 1059, 1060–61 (10th Cir.1980). After *Lewis v. Casey,* are there any other factors that bear on the extent to which the Constitution dictates that an inmate be afforded access to a photocopier? What if the documents that the prisoner wants to copy are needed to respond to the defendant's motion for summary judgment?

13. If inmates are afforded access to a photocopying machine, are indigent inmates entitled to free photocopies or photocopies at reduced rates? When, if ever? See, e.g., Giles v. Tate, 907 F.Supp. 1135, 1138 (S.D.Ohio 1995) (charging indigent inmate thirty-five cents a page to photocopy medical records and other discoverable documents needed to litigate his lawsuit and not permitting him to pay for photocopies on a credit basis violated his right of access to the courts). If prisoners have a right, in certain circumstances, to free photocopies, to how many free photocopies are they entitled? See Walters v. Thompson, 615 F.Supp. 330, 340 (N.D.Ill.1985) (noting the "severe effect" on segregation inmates, who had no direct access to law books, of limiting free photocopies to three hundred a year).

CHAPTER 13

PRISON DISCIPLINARY PROCEEDINGS

■ ■ ■

A. PROCEDURAL DUE PROCESS

To correctional officials, the disciplining of inmates for their misconduct while in prison is critical to the maintenance of security and order within the institution. And to prisoners, the disciplinary system is of inordinate importance. In a place where privileges are few and freedom is curtailed, prisoners have a heightened interest in retaining the privileges they are allotted in the prison environment.

To penalize inmates for having violated a prison rule or regulation, one or more sanctions might be imposed. The inmates, for example, might not be permitted to use the commissary, watch television, or enjoy certain other privileges for a certain number of days. Alternatively, the inmates might be placed in the disciplinary segregation unit, where privileges are drastically curtailed and the prisoners spend most of the day in their cells. Or prisoners might lose accumulated good-time credits as a result of a disciplinary infraction, thereby prolonging their confinement in prison.

As is true when a person is charged with a crime, there is always the possibility that a prisoner charged with violating a prison rule or regulation is innocent of wrongdoing. The question then arises as to what steps, if any, must be taken by prison officials to minimize the risk of punishing an inerrant prisoner. The Supreme Court addressed this question in the case which follows.

WOLFF v. McDONNELL
Supreme Court of the United States, 1974.
418 U.S. 539, 94 S.Ct. 2963, 41 L.Ed.2d 935.

MR. JUSTICE WHITE delivered the opinion of the Court.

[The respondent, an inmate incarcerated in the Nebraska Penal and Correctional Complex in Lincoln, Nebraska, filed a class-action suit under § 1983 claiming, among other things, that the disciplinary proceedings at the prison failed to meet the requirements of due process of law. The district court rejected this claim, but on appeal, the Eighth Circuit Court of Appeals reversed. The Supreme Court then agreed to review the case.]

* * *

Section 16 of the Nebraska Treatment and Corrections Act provides that the chief executive officer of each penal facility is responsible for the discipline of inmates in a particular institution. * * *

* * *

The only statutory provision establishing procedures for the imposition of disciplinary sanctions which pertains to good time merely requires that an inmate be "consulted regarding the charges of misconduct" in connection with the forfeiture, withholding, or restoration of credit. But prison authorities have framed written regulations dealing with procedures and policies for controlling inmate misconduct. By regulation, misconduct is classified into two categories: major misconduct is a "serious violation" and must be formally reported to an Adjustment Committee, composed of the Associate Warden Custody, the Correctional Industries Superintendent, and the Reception Center Director. This Committee is directed to "review and evaluate all misconduct reports" and, among other things, to "conduct investigations, make findings, [and] impose disciplinary actions." If only minor misconduct, "a less serious violation," is involved, the problem may either be resolved informally by the inmate's supervisor or it can be formally reported for action to the Adjustment Committee. Repeated minor misconduct must be reported. The Adjustment Committee has available a wide range of sanctions. "Disciplinary action taken and recommended may include but not necessarily be limited to the following: reprimand, restrictions of various kinds, extra duty, confinement in the Adjustment Center [the disciplinary cell], withholding of statutory good time and/or extra earned good time, or a combination of the elements listed herein."

Additional procedures have been devised by the Complex governing the actions of the Adjustment Committee. Based on the testimony, the District Court found that the following procedures were in effect when an inmate is written up or charged with a prison violation:

"(a) The chief correction supervisor reviews the 'write-ups' on the inmates by the officers of the Complex daily;

"(b) the convict is called to a conference with the chief correction supervisor and the charging party;

"(c) following the conference, a conduct report is sent to the Adjustment Committee;

"(d) there follows a hearing before the Adjustment Committee and the report is read to the inmate and discussed;

"(e) if the inmate denies [the] charge he may ask questions of the party writing him up;

"(f) the Adjustment Committee can conduct additional investigations if it desires;

"(g) punishment is imposed."

* * *

Petitioners assert that the procedure for disciplining prison inmates for serious misconduct is a matter of policy raising no constitutional issue. If the position implies that prisoners in state institutions are wholly without the protections of the Constitution and the Due Process Clause, it is plainly untenable. Lawful imprisonment necessarily makes unavailable many rights and privileges of the ordinary citizen, a "retraction justified by the considerations underlying our penal system." But though his rights may be diminished by the needs and exigencies of the institutional environment, a prisoner is not wholly stripped of constitutional protections when he is imprisoned for crime. There is no iron curtain drawn between the Constitution and the prisons of this country. * * *

Of course, as we have indicated, the fact that prisoners retain rights under the Due Process Clause in no way implies that these rights are not subject to restrictions imposed by the nature of the regime to which they have been lawfully committed. Prison disciplinary proceedings are not part of a criminal prosecution, and the full panoply of rights due a defendant in such proceedings does not apply. * * *

We also reject the assertion of the State that whatever may be true of the Due Process Clause in general or of other rights protected by that Clause against state infringement, the interest of prisoners in disciplinary procedures is not included in that "liberty" protected by the Fourteenth Amendment. It is true that the Constitution itself does not guarantee good-time credit for satisfactory behavior while in prison. But here the State itself has not only provided a statutory right to good time but also specifies that it is to be forfeited only for serious misbehavior. * * *

* * *

We think a person's liberty is equally protected, even when the liberty itself is a statutory creation of the State. The touchstone of due process is protection of the individual against arbitrary action of government. Since prisoners in Nebraska can only lose good-time credits if they are guilty of serious misconduct, the determination of whether such behavior has occurred becomes critical, and the minimum requirements of procedural due process appropriate for the circumstances must be observed.

* * * The State contends that the procedures already provided are adequate. The Court of Appeals held them insufficient and ordered that the due process requirements outlined in *Morrissey* [v. *Brewer*, 408 U.S. 471 (1972)] and [*Gagnon v.*] *Scarpelli*, [411 U.S. 778 (1973)] be satisfied in serious disciplinary cases at the prison.

Morrissey held that due process imposed certain minimum procedural requirements which must be satisfied before parole could finally be revoked. These procedures were:

"(a) written notice of the claimed violations of parole; (b) disclosure to the parolee of evidence against him; (c) opportunity to be heard in person and to present witnesses and documentary evidence; (d) the right to confront and cross-examine adverse witnesses (unless the hearing officer specifically finds good cause for not allowing confrontation); (e) a 'neutral and detached' hearing body such as a traditional parole board, members of which need not be judicial officers or lawyers; and (f) a written statement by the factfinders as to the evidence relied on and reasons for revoking parole."

* * * Following the decision in *Morrissey,* in *Gagnon v. Scarpelli,* the Court held the requirements of due process established for parole revocation were applicable to probation revocation proceedings. The Court added to the required minimum procedures of *Morrissey* the right to counsel, where a probationer makes a request, "based on a timely and colorable claim (i) that he has not committed the alleged violation of the conditions upon which he is at liberty; or (ii) that, even if the violation is a matter of public record or is uncontested, there are substantial reasons which justified or mitigated the violation and make revocation inappropriate, and that the reasons are complex or otherwise difficult to develop or present." In doubtful cases, the agency was to consider whether the probationer appeared to be capable of speaking effectively for himself, and a record was to be made of the grounds for refusing to appoint counsel.

We agree with neither petitioners nor the Court of Appeals: the Nebraska procedures are in some respects constitutionally deficient but the *Morrissey–Scarpelli* procedures need not in all respects be followed in disciplinary cases in state prisons.

We have often repeated that "[t]he very nature of due process negates any concept of inflexible procedures universally applicable to every imaginable situation." "[C]onsideration of what procedures due process may require under any given set of circumstances must begin with a determination of the precise nature of the government function involved as well as of the private interest that has been affected by governmental action." * * *

* * * For the prison inmate, the deprivation of good time is not the same immediate disaster that the revocation of parole is for the parolee. The deprivation, very likely, does not then and there work any change in the conditions of his liberty. It can postpone the date of eligibility for parole and extend the maximum term to be served, but it is not certain to do so, for good time may be restored. Even if not restored, it cannot be said with certainty that the actual date of parole will be affected * * *. The deprivation of good time is unquestionably a matter of considerable importance. * * * But it is qualitatively and quantitatively different from the revocation of parole or probation.

In striking the balance that the Due Process Clause demands, however, we think the major consideration militating against adopting the full range of procedures suggested by *Morrissey* for alleged parole violators is the very different stake the State has in the structure and content of the prison disciplinary hearing. That the revocation of parole be justified and based on an accurate assessment of the facts is a critical matter to the State as well as the parolee; but the procedures by which it is determined whether the conditions of parole have been breached do not themselves threaten other important state interests, parole officers, the police, or witnesses—at least no more so than in the case of the ordinary criminal trial. Prison disciplinary proceedings, on the other hand, take place in a closed, tightly controlled environment peopled by those who have chosen to violate the criminal law and who have been lawfully incarcerated for doing so. Some are first offenders, but many are recidivists who have repeatedly employed illegal and often very violent means to attain their ends. They may have little regard for the safety of others or their property or for the rules designed to provide an orderly and reasonably safe prison life. Although there are very many varieties of prisons with different degrees of security, we must realize that in many of them the inmates are closely supervised and their activities controlled around the clock. Guards and inmates co-exist in direct and intimate contact. Tension between them is unremitting. Frustration, resentment, and despair are commonplace. Relationships among the inmates are varied and complex and perhaps subject to the unwritten code that exhorts inmates not to inform on a fellow prisoner.

* * * The reality is that disciplinary hearings and the imposition of disagreeable sanctions necessarily involve confrontations between inmates and authority and between inmates who are being disciplined and those who would charge or furnish evidence against them. Retaliation is much more than a theoretical possibility; and the basic and unavoidable task of providing reasonable personal safety for guards and inmates may be at stake, to say nothing of the impact of disciplinary confrontations and the resulting escalation of personal antagonisms on the important aims of the correctional process.

Indeed, it is pressed upon us that the proceedings to ascertain and sanction misconduct themselves play a major role in furthering the institutional goal of modifying the behavior and value systems of prison inmates sufficiently to permit them to live within the law when they are released. Inevitably there is a great range of personality and character among those who have transgressed the criminal law. Some are more amenable to suggestion and persuasion than others. Some may be incorrigible and would merely disrupt and exploit the disciplinary process for their own ends. With some, rehabilitation may be best achieved by simulating procedures of a free society to the maximum possible extent; but with others, it may be essential that discipline be swift and sure. In any event, it is argued, there would be great unwisdom in encasing the disciplinary procedures in an inflexible constitutional straitjacket that would necessarily call for adversary proceedings typical of the criminal trial, very likely raise the level of confrontation between staff and inmate, and make more difficult the utilization of the disciplinary process as a tool to advance the rehabilitative goals of the institution. This consideration, along with the necessity to maintain an acceptable level of personal security in the institution, must be taken into account as we now examine in more detail the Nebraska procedures that the Court of Appeals found wanting.

Two of the procedures that the Court held should be extended to parolees facing revocation proceedings are not, but must be, provided to prisoners in the Nebraska Complex if the minimum requirements of procedural due process are to be satisfied. These are advance written notice of the claimed violation and a written statement of the factfinders as to the evidence relied upon and the reasons for the disciplinary action taken. * * *

Part of the function of notice is to give the charged party a chance to marshal the facts in his defense and to clarify what the charges are, in fact. Neither of these functions was performed by the notice described by the Warden. Although the charges are discussed orally with the inmate somewhat in advance of the hearing, the inmate is sometimes brought before the Adjustment Committee shortly after he is orally informed of the charges. Other times, after this initial discussion, further investigation takes place which may reshape the nature of the charges or the evidence relied upon. In those instances, under procedures in effect at the time of trial, it would appear that the inmate first receives notice of the actual charges at the time of the hearing before the Adjustment Committee. We hold that written notice of the charges must be given to the disciplinary-action defendant in order to inform him of the charges and to enable him to marshal the facts and prepare a defense. At least a brief period of time after the notice, no less than 24 hours, should be allowed to the inmate to prepare for the appearance before the Adjustment Committee.

We also hold that there must be a "written statement by the factfinders as to the evidence relied on and reasons" for the disciplinary action. Although Nebraska does not seem to provide administrative review of the action taken by the Adjustment Committee, the actions taken at such proceedings may involve review by other bodies. They might furnish the basis of a decision by the Director of Corrections to transfer an inmate to another institution because he is considered "to be incorrigible by reason of frequent intentional breaches of discipline" and are certainly likely to be considered by the state parole authorities in making parole decisions. Written records of proceedings will thus protect the inmate against collateral consequences based on a misunderstanding of the nature of the original proceeding. Further, as to the disciplinary action itself, the provision for a written record helps to insure that administrators, faced with possible scrutiny by state officials and the public, and perhaps even the courts, where fundamental constitutional rights may have been abridged, will act fairly. Without written records, the inmate will be at a severe disadvantage in propounding his own cause to or defending himself from others. It may be that there will be occasions when personal or institutional safety is so implicated that the statement may properly exclude certain items of evidence, but in that event the statement should indicate the fact of the omission. Otherwise, we perceive no conceivable rehabilitative objective or prospect of prison disruption that can flow from the requirement of these statements.

We are also of the opinion that the inmate facing disciplinary proceedings should be allowed to call witnesses and present documentary evidence in his defense when permitting him to do so will not be unduly hazardous to institutional safety or correctional goals. Ordinarily, the right to present evidence is basic to a fair hearing; but the unrestricted right to call witnesses from the prison population carries obvious potential for disruption and for interference with the swift punishment that in individual cases may be essential to carrying out the correctional program of the institution. We should not be too ready to exercise oversight and put aside the judgment of prison administrators. It may be that an individual threatened with serious sanctions would normally be entitled to present witnesses and relevant documentary evidence; but here we must balance the inmate's interest in avoiding loss of good time against the needs of the prison, and some amount of flexibility and accommodation is required. Prison officials must have the necessary discretion to keep the hearing within reasonable limits and to refuse to call witnesses that may create a risk of reprisal or undermine authority, as well as to limit access to other inmates to collect statements or to compile other documentary evidence. Although we do not prescribe it, it would be useful for the Committee to state its reason for refusing to call a witness, whether it be for irrelevance, lack of necessity, or the hazards presented in individual cases. Any less flexible rule appears untenable as a constitutional matter, at least on the record made in this case. * * *

Confrontation and cross-examination present greater hazards to institutional interests. If confrontation and cross-examination of those furnishing evidence against the inmate were to be allowed as a matter of course, as in criminal trials, there would be considerable potential for havoc inside the prison walls. Proceedings would inevitably be longer and tend to unmanageability. These procedures are essential in criminal trials where the accused, if found guilty, may be subjected to the most serious deprivations, or where a person may lose his job in society. But they are not rights universally applicable to all hearings. Rules of procedure may be shaped by consideration of the risks of error and should also be shaped by the consequences which will follow their adoption. Although some States do seem to allow cross-examination in disciplinary hearings, we are not apprised of the conditions under which the procedure may be curtailed; and it does not appear that confrontation and cross-examination are generally required in this context. We think that the Constitution should not be read to impose the procedure at the present time and that adequate bases for decision in prison disciplinary cases can be arrived at without cross-examination.

Perhaps as the problems of penal institutions change and correctional goals are reshaped, the balance of interests involved will require otherwise. But in the current environment, where prison disruption remains a serious concern to administrators, we cannot ignore the desire and effort of many States, including Nebraska, and the Federal Government to avoid situations that may trigger deep emotions and that may scuttle the disciplinary process as a rehabilitation vehicle. To some extent, the American adversary trial presumes contestants who are able to cope with the pressures and aftermath of the battle, and such may not generally be the case of those in the prisons of this country. At least, the Constitution, as we interpret it today, does not require the contrary assumption. * * *

We recognize that the problems of potential disruption may differ depending on whom the inmate proposes to cross-examine. If he proposes to examine an unknown fellow inmate, the danger may be the greatest, since the disclosure of the identity of the accuser, and the cross-examination which will follow, may pose a high risk of reprisal within the institution. Conversely, the inmate accuser, who might freely tell his story privately to prison officials, may refuse to testify or admit any knowledge of the situation in question. Although the dangers posed by cross-examination of known inmate accusers, or guards, may be less, the resentment which may persist after confrontation may still be substantial. Also, even where the accuser or adverse witness is known, the disclosure of third parties may pose a problem. There may be a class of cases where the facts are closely disputed, and the character of the parties minimizes the dangers involved. However, any constitutional rule tailored to meet these situations would undoubtedly produce great litigation and attendant costs in a much wider range of cases. Further, in the last analysis, even within the narrow range of cases where interest balancing may well dictate cross-examination, courts will be faced with the assessment of prison officials as to the dangers involved, and there would be a limited basis for upsetting such judgments. The better course at this time, in a period where prison practices are diverse and somewhat experimental, is to leave these matters to the sound discretion of the officials of state prisons.

As to the right to counsel, the problem as outlined in *Scarpelli* with respect to parole and probation revocation proceedings is even more pertinent here:

"The introduction of counsel into a revocation proceeding will alter significantly the nature of the proceeding. If counsel is provided for the probationer or parolee, the State in turn will normally provide its own counsel; lawyers, by training and disposition, are advocates and bound by professional duty to present all available evidence and arguments in support of their clients' positions and to contest with vigor all adverse evidence and views. The role of the hearing body itself, aptly described in *Morrissey* as being 'predictive and discretionary' as well as factfinding, may become more akin to that of a judge at a trial, and less attuned to the rehabilitative needs of the individual probationer or parolee. In the greater self-consciousness of its quasi-judicial role, the hearing body may be less tolerant of marginal deviant behavior and feel more pressure to reincarcerate than to continue nonpunitive rehabilitation. Certainly, the decisionmaking process will be prolonged, and the financial cost to the State—for appointed counsel, counsel for the State, a longer record, and the possibility of judicial review—will not be insubstantial."

The insertion of counsel into the disciplinary process would inevitably give the proceedings a more adversary cast and tend to reduce their utility as a means to further correctional goals. There would also be delay and very practical problems in providing counsel in sufficient numbers at the time and place where hearings are to be held. At this stage of the development of these procedures we are not prepared to hold that inmates have a right to either retained or appointed counsel in disciplinary proceedings.

Where an illiterate inmate is involved, however, or where the complexity of the issue makes it unlikely that the inmate will be able to collect and present the evidence necessary for an adequate comprehension of the case, he should be free to seek the aid of a fellow inmate, or if that is forbidden, to have adequate substitute aid in the form of help from the staff or from a sufficiently competent inmate designated by the staff. * * *

Finally, we decline to rule that the Adjustment Committee which conducts the required hearings at the Nebraska Prison Complex and determines whether to revoke good time is not sufficiently impartial to satisfy the Due Process Clause. The Committee is made up of the Associate Warden Custody as chairman, the Correctional Industries Superintendent, and the Reception Center Director. * * * The Committee is not left at large with unlimited discretion. It is directed to meet daily and to operate within the principles stated in the controlling regulations, among which is the command that "[f]ull consideration must be given to the causes for the adverse behavior, the setting and circumstances in which it occurred, the man's accountability, and the correctional treatment goals," as well as the direction that "disciplinary measures will be taken only at such times and to such degrees as are necessary to regulate and control a man's behavior within acceptable limits and will never be rendered capriciously or in the nature of retaliation or revenge." We find no warrant in the record presented here for concluding that the Adjustment Committee presents such a hazard of arbitrary decisionmaking that it should be held violative of due process of law.

Our conclusion that some, but not all, of the procedures specified in *Morrissey* and *Scarpelli* must accompany the deprivation of good time by state prison authorities[19] is not graven in stone. As the nature of the

---

19. Although the complaint put at issue the procedures employed with respect to the deprivation of good time, under the Nebraska system, the same procedures are employed where disciplinary confinement is imposed. The deprivation of good time and imposition of "solitary" confinement are reserved for instances where serious misbehavior has occurred. This appears a realistic approach, for it would be difficult for the purposes of procedural due process to distinguish between the procedures that are required where good time is forfeited and those that must be extended when solitary confinement is at issue. The latter represents a major change in the conditions of confinement and is normally imposed only when it is claimed and proved that there has been a major act of misconduct. Here, as in the case of good time, there should be minimum procedural safeguards as a hedge against arbitrary determination of the factual

prison disciplinary process changes in future years, circumstances may then exist which will require further consideration and reflection of this Court. It is our view, however, that the procedures we have now required in prison disciplinary proceedings represent a reasonable accommodation between the interests of the inmates and the needs of the institution.

MR. JUSTICE MARSHALL, with whom MR. JUSTICE BRENNAN joins, concurring in part and dissenting in part.

* * *

* * * I fully support the Court's holding that the interest of inmates in freedom from imposition of serious discipline is a "liberty" entitled to due process protection. But, in my view, the content which the Court gives to this due process protection leaves these noble holdings as little more than empty promises. To be sure, the Court holds that inmates are constitutionally entitled to advance written notice of the charges against them and a statement of the evidence relied on, the facts found, and the reasons supporting the disciplinary board's decision. Apparently, an inmate is also constitutionally entitled to a hearing and an opportunity to speak in his own defense. These are valuable procedural safeguards, and I do not mean for a moment to denigrate their importance.

But the purpose of notice is to give the accused the opportunity to prepare a defense, and the purpose of a hearing is to afford him the chance to present that defense. Today's decision deprives an accused inmate of any enforceable constitutional right to the procedural tools essential to the presentation of any meaningful defense, and makes the required notice and hearing formalities of little utility. * * *

* * *

* * * Our decisions flatly reject the Court's view of the dispensability of confrontation and cross-examination. We have held that "[i]n almost every setting where important decisions turn on questions of fact, due process requires an opportunity to confront and cross-examine adverse witnesses." * * * Surely confrontation and cross-examination are as crucial in the prison disciplinary context as in any other, if not more so. Prison disciplinary proceedings will invariably turn on disputed questions of fact, and, in addition to the usual need for cross-examination to reveal mistakes of identity, faulty perceptions, or cloudy memories, there is a significant potential for abuse of the disciplinary process by "persons motivated by malice, vindictiveness, intolerance, prejudice, or jealousy," whether these be other inmates seeking revenge or prison guards seeking to vindicate their otherwise absolute power over the men under their control. I can see no rational means for resolving these disputed questions of fact without providing confrontation and cross-examination.

---

predicate for imposition of the sanction. We do not suggest, however, that the procedures required by today's decision for the deprivation of good time would also be required for the imposition of lesser penalties such as the loss of privileges.

* * * The Court cites concern for administrative efficiency in support of its holding: "Proceedings would inevitably be longer and tend to unmanageability." I can only assume that these are makeweights, for I refuse to believe that the Court would deny fundamental rights in reliance on such trivial and easily handled concerns.

A more substantial problem with permitting the accused inmate to demand confrontation with adverse witnesses is the need to preserve the secrecy of the identity of inmate informers and protect them from the danger of reprisal. I am well aware of the seriousness of this problem, and I agree that in some circumstances this confidentiality must prevail over the accused's right of confrontation. "But this concern for the safety of inmates does not justify a wholesale denial of the right to confront and cross-examine adverse witnesses." The need to keep the identity of informants confidential will exist in only a small percentage of disciplinary cases. Whether because of the "inmates' code" or otherwise, the disciplinary process is rarely initiated by a fellow inmate and almost invariably by a correctional officer. I see no legitimate need to keep confidential the identity of a prison guard who files charges against an inmate; indeed, Nebraska, like most States, routinely informs accused prisoners of the identity of the correctional officer who is the charging party, if he does not already know. In the relatively few instances where inmates press disciplinary charges, the accused inmate often knows the identity of his accuser, as, for example, where the accuser was the victim of a physical assault.

Thus, the Court refuses to enforce prisoners' fundamental procedural rights because of a legitimate concern for secrecy which must affect only a tiny fraction of disciplinary cases. This is surely permitting the tail to wag the constitutional dog. When faced with a similar problem in *Morrissey v. Brewer,* we nonetheless held that the parolee had the constitutional right to confront and cross-examine adverse witnesses, and permitted an exception to be made "if the hearing officer determines that an informant would be subjected to risk of harm if his identity were disclosed." In my view, the same approach would be appropriate here.

* * * The Court apparently accepts petitioners' arguments that there is a danger that such cross-examination will produce hostility between inmate and guard, or inmate and inmate, which will eventually lead to prison disruption; or that cross-examination of a guard by an inmate would threaten the guard's traditional role of absolute authority; or that cross-examination would somehow weaken the disciplinary process as a vehicle for rehabilitation.

I do not believe that these generalized, speculative, and unsupported theories provide anything close to an adequate basis for denying the accused inmate the right to cross-examine his accusers. The State's arguments immediately lose most of their potential force when it is observed that Nebraska already permits inmates to question the correctional officer who is the charging party with respect to the charges.

Moreover, by far the greater weight of correctional authority is that greater procedural fairness in disciplinary proceedings, including permitting confrontation and cross-examination, would enhance rather than impair the disciplinary process as a rehabilitative tool.

> "Time has proved ... that blind deference to correctional officials does no real service to them. Judicial concern with procedural regularity has a direct bearing upon the maintenance of institutional order; the orderly care with which decisions are made by the prison authority is intimately related to the level of respect with which prisoners regard that authority. There is nothing more corrosive to the fabric of a public institution such as a prison than a feeling among those whom it contains that they are being treated unfairly." *Palmigiano v. Baxter,* 487 F.2d 1280, 1283 (C.A.1 1973).

As The Chief Justice noted in *Morrissey v. Brewer,* "fair treatment ... will enhance the chance of rehabilitation by avoiding reactions to arbitrariness."

Significantly, a substantial majority of the States do permit confrontation and cross-examination in prison disciplinary proceedings, and their experience simply does not bear out the speculative fears of Nebraska authorities. The vast majority of these States have observed "no noticeable effect on prison security or safety. Furthermore, there was general agreement that the quality of the hearings had been 'upgraded' and that some of the inmate feelings of powerlessness and frustration had been relieved." The only reported complaints have been, not the theoretical problems suggested by petitioners, but that these procedures are time consuming and have slowed down the disciplinary process to some extent. These are small costs to bear to achieve significant gains in procedural fairness.

Thus, in my view, we should recognize that the accused prisoner has a constitutional right to confront and cross-examine adverse witnesses, subject to a limited exception when necessary to protect the identity of a confidential inmate informant. This does not mean that I would not permit the disciplinary board to rely on written reports concerning the charges against a prisoner. Rather, I would think this constitutional right sufficiently protected if the accused had the power to compel the attendance of an adverse witness so that his story can be tested by cross-examination. Again, whenever the right to confront an adverse witness is denied an accused, I would require that this denial and the reasons for it be noted in writing in the record of the proceeding. I would also hold that where it is found necessary to restrict the inmate's right of confrontation, the disciplinary board has the constitutional obligation to call the witness before it *in camera* and itself probe his credibility, rather than accepting the unchallenged and otherwise unchallengeable word of the informer.
* * *

The Court next turns to the question of an accused inmate's right to counsel, and quotes a long passage from our decision last Term in *Gagnon* *v. Scarpelli,* 411 U.S. 778 (1973), in support of its conclusion that appointed counsel need not be provided and retained counsel need not be permitted in prison disciplinary proceedings at this time. The Court seemingly forgets that the holding of *Scarpelli* was that fundamental fairness requires the appointment of counsel in some probation revocation or parole revocation proceedings * * *.

* * * I think it is clear that, at least in those serious disciplinary cases meeting the *Scarpelli* requirements, any inmate who seeks assistance in the preparation of his defense must be constitutionally entitled to have it. But, although for me the question is fraught with great difficulty, I agree with the Court that it would be inappropriate at this time to hold that this assistance must be provided by an appointed member of the bar.[2] * * * At least 41 States already provide such counsel substitutes, reflecting the nearly universal recognition that for most inmates, this assistance with the preparation of a defense, particularly as disciplinary hearings become more complex, is absolutely essential. Thus, I would hold that any prisoner is constitutionally entitled to the assistance of a competent fellow inmate or correctional staff member—or, if the institution chooses, such other alternatives as the assistance of law students—to aid in the preparation of his defense.

Finally, the Court addresses the question of the need for an impartial tribunal to hear these prison disciplinary cases. We have recognized that an impartial decisionmaker is a fundamental requirement of due process in a variety of relevant situations, and I would hold this requirement fully applicable here. But in my view there is no constitutional impediment to a disciplinary board composed of responsible prison officials like those on the Adjustment Committee here. While it might well be desirable to have persons from outside the prison system sitting on disciplinary panels, so as to eliminate any possibility that subtle institutional pressures may affect the outcome of disciplinary cases and to avoid any appearance of unfairness, in my view due process is satisfied as long as no member of the disciplinary board has been involved in the investigation or prosecution of the particular case, or has had any other form of personal involvement in the case. * * *

Thus, it is my conclusion that the Court of Appeals was substantially correct in its holding that the minimum due process procedural requirements of *Morrissey v. Brewer* are applicable in the context of prison disciplinary proceedings. To the extent that the Court is willing to tolerate reduced procedural safeguards for accused inmates facing serious punishment which do not meet the standards set out in this opinion, I respectfully dissent.

---

2. * * * I would reserve for another day the questions whether the Constitution requires that an inmate able to afford counsel be permitted to bring counsel into the disciplinary hearing, or whether the Constitution allows a State to permit the presence of retained counsel when counsel is not appointed for indigents.

MR. JUSTICE DOUGLAS, dissenting in part, concurring in the result in part.

* * *

I would start with the presumption that cross-examination of adverse witnesses and confrontation of one's accusers are essential rights which ought always to be available absent any special overriding considerations. * * * The decision as to whether an inmate should be allowed to confront his accusers should not be left to the unchecked and unreviewable discretion of the prison disciplinary board. The argument offered for that result is that the danger of violent response by the inmate against his accusers is great, and that only the prison administrators are in a position to weigh the necessity of secrecy in each case. But it is precisely this unchecked power of prison administrators which is the problem that due process safeguards are required to cure. "Not only the principle of judicial review, but the whole scheme of American government, reflects an institutionalized mistrust of any such unchecked and unbalanced power over essential liberties. That mistrust does not depend on an assumption of inveterate venality or incompetence on the part of men in power. . . ." Likewise the prisoner should have the right to cross-examine adverse witnesses who testify at the hearing. * * *

* * *

* * * In some circumstances it may be that an informer's identity should be shielded. Yet in criminal trials the rule has been that if the informer's information is crucial to the defense, then the government must choose between revealing his identity and allowing confrontation, or dismissing the charges. *Roviaro v. United States,* 353 U.S. 53 [(1957)]. And it is the court, not the prosecutor, who determines the defendant's need for the information. We should no more place the inmate's constitutional rights in the hands of the prison administration's discretion than we should place the defendant's right in the hands of the prosecutor.

* * *

QUESTIONS AND POINTS FOR DISCUSSION

1. In Sandin v. Conner, 515 U.S. 472, 115 S.Ct. 2293 (1995), the Supreme Court concluded, in a 5–4 decision, that prison officials did not have to afford a prisoner the procedural safeguards outlined in *Wolff v. McDonnell* during disciplinary proceedings which resulted in his confinement in the prison's disciplinary segregation unit for thirty days. In contrast to the dictum in *Wolff* (see footnote 19 on page 578), the Court in *Sandin* reasoned that the disciplinary confinement did not deprive the prisoner of the liberty that triggers due-process protections. Excerpts from the Court's opinion, in which it revamped its approach to state-created liberty interests, at least in the prison context, can be found in Chapter 14, beginning on page 610.

2. Since *Wolff* was decided, a recurring question before the lower courts has been what is a constitutionally adequate statement of the evidence relied

on and reasons for the disciplinary action taken. Seeming vacillations in the decisions of the Seventh Circuit Court of Appeals reflect the difficulty courts have had resolving this question. In a series of decisions, different panels of the Seventh Circuit deemed the following statements of the disciplinary decisionmaker to be constitutionally inadequate:

1. "Based on our review of the violation report and the report by the special investigator it is our motion that we find Mr. Hayes guilty as charged. We find that Mr. Hayes is guilty of conspiracy to incite to riot and commit mutinous acts." Hayes v. Walker, 555 F.2d 625, 631–33 (7th Cir.1977).

2. "We recognize and consider the resident[']s statement[,] however[,] we accept the reporting officer[']s charges." Chavis v. Rowe, 643 F.2d 1281, 1286–87 (7th Cir.1981).

3. "All evidence presented has convinced the committee the resident is guilty of forging a pass or altering a pass, giving false information to a [sic] employee and disobeying a prison rule." Redding v. Fairman, 717 F.2d 1105, 1115–16 (7th Cir.1983).

According to these decisions, simply referring to unspecified "evidence" as the basis for a guilty finding or, without elaboration, to the charge filed by the reporting officer or an investigator's report does not fulfill the purposes described in *Wolff* of the written statement.

Subsequent decisions rendered by panels comprised of different Seventh Circuit judges, however, held that the following statements satisfied due process:

1. [Guilty finding based] "on statements in C.R. (conduct report) by Staff in guilt finding that inmate was disrespectful" and "caused disruption by his actions." Culbert v. Young, 834 F.2d 624, 630–31 (7th Cir.1987).

2. "Officer Fabry's written statement supports the finding of guilt that an attempt was made by Inmate Saenz to commit battery upon the (other) inmate." Saenz v. Young, 811 F.2d 1172, 1173–74 (7th Cir.1987).

In *Culbert,* the court said that "the kind of statements that will satisfy the constitutional minimum will vary from case to case depending on the severity of the charges and the complexity of the factual circumstances and proof offered by both sides." 834 F.2d at 631. Because the inmate in that case was found guilty of charges that were not complex and because the only evidence pointing to his lack of guilt was his own protestation of innocence, the disciplinary committee's statement, according to the court, met the requirements of due process.

In *Saenz,* the court proffered another rationale for its conclusion that the disciplinary committee's statement comported with due process:

A statement of reasons has no particular value in itself. It is instrumental to the goal of making sure that prisoners are not subjected through sloppy procedures to an undue risk of being disciplined for things they have not actually done. As that risk did not materialize here, we find no denial of due process * * *.

811 F.2d at 1174.

Do you agree with the reasoning of the court and the results in the *Culbert* and *Saenz* cases? If not, how should the decision of the disciplinary decisionmaker be written in order to comply with the requirements of due process?

3. In *Wolff v. McDonnell,* the Supreme Court observed that prisoners found guilty of a disciplinary infraction are entitled to a " 'written statement by the factfinders as to the evidence relied on *and* reasons' for the disciplinary action." 418 U.S. at 564, 94 S.Ct. at 2979 (quoting Morrissey v. Brewer, 408 U.S. 471, 489, 92 S.Ct. 2593, 2604 (1972) (emphasis added)). The lower courts have differing views on the significance of the Court's reference to the reasons for the disciplinary action taken. Some courts have suggested that the disciplinary decisionmaker must explain why the particular penalty imposed is considered appropriate and warranted. See, e.g., Redding v. Fairman, 717 F.2d 1105, 1115 n. 4 (7th Cir.1983) (statement must reveal reasons for type, as well as amount, of punishment imposed). Other courts have required such an explanation only when the sanction imposed on the prisoner is much more severe than the penalty imposed on other prisoners found guilty of committing the same offense. See, e.g., Ivey v. Wilson, 577 F.Supp. 169, 173 (W.D.Ky.1983). Still other courts do not require the disciplinary decisionmaker to explain and defend the actual penalty imposed. These courts consider the constitutional requirement that the disciplinary decisionmaker explain in writing why the disciplinary action was taken satisfied as long as the written decision recounts the factual basis for the guilty finding, *i.e.,* what it is that the prisoner actually did that constituted a violation of the prison's rules or regulations. See, e.g., Harmon v. Auger, 768 F.2d 270, 276 (8th Cir.1985).

4. Is a prison policy under which an inmate's requested witnesses generally are barred from appearing at a disciplinary hearing, but written statements obtained from the witnesses are admitted in evidence constitutional? Most courts have held that such an across-the-board ban on live testimony violates due process. See Brown v. Braxton, 373 F.3d 501, 507 (4th Cir. 2004) (listing cases). According to many of these courts, the disciplinary decisionmaker must make an individualized assessment of an inmate's witness request. See, e.g., Ramer v. Kerby, 936 F.2d 1102, 1104 (10th Cir.1991) (prison policy prohibiting inmates from calling staff members as witnesses, but providing for the collection of their written statements, violates due process). At least some courts though have indicated that a rule prohibiting a discrete category of witnesses from testifying in person at a disciplinary hearing is, in some circumstances, constitutional. Noting that such a categorical exclusion is "presumptively disfavored," the Seventh Circuit Court of Appeals has held that to rebut this presumption, prison officials would have to demonstrate that the reasons for barring the group as a whole from testifying in person apply to each individual within that group. Whitlock v. Johnson, 153 F.3d 380, 387 (7th Cir. 1998).

Assume that disciplinary charges are pending against a prisoner confined in a segregation unit where inmates awaiting a disciplinary hearing are housed. The prisoner has asked that three inmates confined in general population be permitted to testify about the altercation between the prisoner and a correctional officer that gave rise to the filing of the charges. According to the prisoner, the inmate-witnesses would corroborate his claim that the correctional officer instigated the altercation by pushing him. Whenever a general-population inmate enters the segregation unit, the inmate must be strip-searched and accompanied by two correctional officers. Because of the demands these security measures place on staff, a prison policy forbids inmates in the general population from testifying at disciplinary hearings held in the segregation unit. Is this policy constitutional? See McGuinness v. Dubois, 75 F.3d 794 (1st Cir.1996).

5.   In *Wolff*, the Supreme Court indicated that "lack of necessity" would be a justifiable reason for denying an inmate's request to have a witness testify at a disciplinary hearing. Would the exclusion of the inmate witnesses from the disciplinary hearing in the case described above be constitutional on the independent ground that their testimony would duplicate that of the prisoner charged with the disciplinary infraction? Consider the observations of the Eighth Circuit Court of Appeals in Graham v. Baughman, 772 F.2d 441, 445 (8th Cir.1985): "[A]s is many times the case with disciplinary proceedings, this was a swearing contest between the inmate and the charging officer. * * * 'Merely corroborative' evidence is many times the most probative for it may substantiate and make credible an otherwise bald and self-serving position."

6.   In Pino v. Dalsheim, 605 F.Supp. 1305 (S.D.N.Y.1984), the inmate-plaintiff challenged, on due-process grounds, a hearing officer's refusal to permit several inmates to testify on the plaintiff's behalf at a disciplinary hearing. The plaintiff had been charged with a number of disciplinary offenses after yelling at and threatening a correctional officer. According to the plaintiff, his witnesses would have testified that he was provoked by the correctional officer, who had been taunting and hassling him. Written statements recounting this provocation were obtained from the witnesses and admitted at the disciplinary hearing.

The district court found no due-process violation. After noting that the witnesses' expected testimony concerned the question whether there were mitigating circumstances surrounding the plaintiff's commission of the disciplinary offense, the court observed that the right to call witnesses at disciplinary hearings is confined to witnesses who can testify on the issue of the inmate's guilt or innocence of the disciplinary infraction. The right does not encompass witnesses whose testimony only bears on the question of the appropriate penalty to be imposed. Obtaining a written statement from the latter type of witness will, according to the court, normally satisfy due process.

7.   Even if a disciplinary decisionmaker erred in denying an inmate's request to call a witness to testify at the disciplinary hearing, the error is, according to many courts, subject to harmless-error review. See Grossman v. Bruce, 447 F.3d 801, 805 (10th Cir. 2006) (listing cases). Unless the inmate demonstrates that the witness's testimony would have affected the case's outcome, the inmate is not entitled to redress. Courts have reasoned that since they typically apply the harmless-error rule when determining whether a constitutional error requires the reversal of a conviction, they likewise

should apply the rule in the prison disciplinary context. Can you construct a contrary argument?

8. In Ponte v. Real, 471 U.S. 491, 105 S.Ct. 2192 (1985), the Supreme Court revisited an issue that had been addressed at least partially in *Wolff*: whether due process requires support or reasons in the administrative record for a disciplinary committee's decision not to permit a witness to testify before it. The Court reaffirmed its conclusion in *Wolff* that a disciplinary committee does not have to explain, at the time of the disciplinary hearing, its reason for not calling a witness. Nor need the administrative record otherwise contain support for the disciplinary committee's decision. However, if a prisoner later contests in a lawsuit the decision not to permit a witness to testify at the disciplinary hearing, due process requires that the committee then explain, at least "in a limited manner," the basis for its decision. Id. at 497, 105 S.Ct. at 2196. If necessary to protect institutional security or other "paramount interests," the reasons for not calling a witness before the disciplinary committee can be presented to the court *in camera*.

The Court in *Ponte* added the following observation:

> The requirement that contemporaneous reasons for denying witnesses and evidence be given admittedly has some appeal, and it may commend itself to prison officials as a matter of choice: recollections of the event will be fresher at the moment, and it seems a more lawyer-like way to do things. But the primary business of prisons is the supervision of inmates, and it may well be that those charged with this responsibility feel that the additional administrative burdens which would be occasioned by such a requirement detract from the ability to perform the principal mission of the institution.

Id. at 497–98, 105 S.Ct. at 2196–97.

Justice Marshall, joined by Justice Brennan in a dissenting opinion, disagreed that due process permits a disciplinary committee to decide whether to give contemporaneous reasons for refusing to call a witness to testify before the committee. Concluding that "*post hoc* court-room rationalizations" could not possibly satisfy due process, Justice Marshall emphasized the ease with which a disciplinary committee could record its reasons for not calling a witness at the time the decision was made. And if institutional security would be imperiled by divulging this reason to the inmate charged with a disciplinary infraction, that part of the record could be kept confidential. With whose views do you agree—the majority's or the dissenters'?

9. In *Wolff,* the Supreme Court outlined two instances when an inmate has a right to assistance in preparing and presenting a defense to a disciplinary charge: (1) when the inmate is illiterate; and (2) when the case is sufficiently complex that it is unlikely that the inmate could adequately mount a defense without such assistance. Are there any other circumstances, in your opinion, that would trigger a constitutional right to assistance?

10. In Redding v. Fairman, 717 F.2d 1105 (7th Cir.1983), the Seventh Circuit Court of Appeals discussed prisoners' due-process right to have their guilt or innocence of a disciplinary infraction adjudicated by a "sufficiently impartial" decisionmaker. The prisoner-plaintiff in that case contended that

this right was violated automatically when the Adjustment Committee that found him guilty of a number of disciplinary offenses included one member who was a defendant in a pending civil-rights suit filed by the plaintiff. The court of appeals disagreed:

> Although the requirement of a "neutral and detached" decisionmaker must not be impaired, disqualification is not necessary in every case. * * * A prisoners' rights lawsuit often includes several defendants, some of whom may not know the plaintiff. Moreover, if an Adjustment Committee member is a defendant in the unrelated action named in her or his administrative capacity for performing ministerial duties, then the Committee member may have little personal involvement in the case. Under these circumstances, the Committee member's ability to serve as a neutral and detached decisionmaker at a hearing involving the plaintiff-prisoner may not be impaired, and disqualification may not be necessary. From a practical standpoint, requiring each staff member who is the subject of a separate lawsuit to disqualify himself from sitting in judgment of that inmate would heavily tax the working capacity of the prison staff. Additionally, prisoners may file many lawsuits naming multiple defendants. If every named defendant in a prisoners' rights lawsuit must be disqualified from sitting on the Adjustment Committee, such a litigation strategy would vest too much control in a prisoner to determine the Committee make-up. For these reasons, the disqualification issue should be decided on a case-by-case basis.

Id. at 1112–13.

The following remarks of Judge George Fagg, rendered in his concurring and dissenting opinion in the case of Malek v. Camp, 822 F.2d 812 (8th Cir.1987), reflect a different approach to the problem discussed in *Redding*:

> Malek's discipline was upheld by an appeals board. While such a circumstance would be irrelevant in a case involving a court adjudication, I do not believe the same conclusion should follow in the case of prison disciplinary proceedings. The Supreme Court has recognized that "one cannot automatically apply procedural rules designed for free citizens in an open society * * * to the very different situation presented by a [prison] disciplinary proceeding."

> I believe a prison disciplinary hearing and the accompanying administrative review should be considered a unitary proceeding. Due process would then depend not on the internal integrity of distinct trial and appellate tiers but on the fairness of prison disciplinary procedures taken as a whole. Specifically, there would be no prejudice from a biased decisionmaker, and no constitutional violation, if a neutral appeals board found in the record the minimal "some evidence" needed to sustain the prison disciplinary action.

Id. at 817 (Fagg, J., concurring and dissenting).

How would you reconcile the due-process right to a relatively unbiased disciplinary decisionmaker with the reality that some prisoners, many of whom appear with regularity before disciplinary decisionmakers whom they subsequently sue, are litigious? More fundamentally, do you agree with the premise of *Wolff* that a disciplinary committee comprised of prison employees selected by the warden can be "sufficiently impartial" to meet the requirements of due process? If not, how could and would you structure the disciplinary process to meet those requirements? See James E. Robertson, Impartiality and Prison Disciplinary Tribunals, 17 New Eng. J. on Crim. & Civ. Confinement 301, 328–333 (1991) (advocating the use of "outsiders," such as administrative law judges, boards of visitors, or hearing officers employed by the central office of the department of corrections rather than the prison, to adjudicate disciplinary charges).

Eleven years after the Supreme Court decided *Wolff v. McDonnell*, the Court recognized another procedural safeguard to which prisoners have a constitutional right when prison disciplinary proceedings result in a loss of good-time credits. In *Superintendent, Mass. Correctional Institution at Walpole v. Hill*, the case which follows, the Court discussed that right.

SUPERINTENDENT, MASSACHUSETTS CORRECTIONAL INSTITUTION AT WALPOLE v. HILL

Supreme Court of the United States, 1985.
472 U.S. 445, 105 S.Ct. 2768, 86 L.Ed.2d 356.

JUSTICE O'CONNOR delivered the opinion of the Court.

* * *

Respondents Gerald Hill and Joseph Crawford are inmates at a state prison in Walpole, Mass. In May 1982, they each received prison disciplinary reports charging them with assaulting another inmate. At separate hearings for each inmate, a prison disciplinary board heard testimony from a prison guard, Sergeant Maguire, and received his written disciplinary report. According to the testimony and report, Maguire heard an inmate twice say loudly, "What's going on?" The voice came from a walkway that Maguire could partially observe through a window. Maguire immediately opened the door to the walkway and found an inmate named Stephens bleeding from the mouth and suffering from a swollen eye. Dirt was strewn about the walkway, and Maguire viewed this to be further evidence of a scuffle. He saw three inmates, including respondents, jogging away together down the walkway. There were no other inmates in the area, which was enclosed by a chain link fence. Maguire concluded that one or more of the three inmates had assaulted Stephens and that they had acted as a group. Maguire also testified at Hill's hearing that a prison "medic" had told him that Stephens had been beaten. Hill and Crawford each declared their innocence before the disciplinary board, and Stephens gave written statements that the other inmates had not caused his injuries.

After hearing the evidence in each case, the disciplinary board found respondents guilty of violating prison regulations based on their involvement in the assault. The board recommended that Hill and Romano each lose 100 days of good time and be confined in isolation for 15 days. Respondents unsuccessfully appealed the board's action to the superintendent of the prison. They then filed a complaint in the Superior Court, State of Massachusetts, alleging that the decisions of the board violated their constitutional rights because "there was no evidence to confirm that the incident took place nor was there any evidence to state that if the incident did take place the [respondents] were involved." After reviewing the record, the Superior Court concluded that "the Board's finding of guilty rested, in each case, on no evidence constitutionally adequate to support that finding." The Superior Court granted summary judgment for respondents and ordered that the findings of the disciplinary board be voided and the lost good time restored.

The Massachusetts Supreme Judicial Court affirmed. * * *

* * *

The issue we address is whether findings of a prison disciplinary board that result in the loss of good time credits must be supported by a certain amount of evidence in order to satisfy due process. * * *

* * *

The requirements of due process are flexible and depend on a balancing of the interests affected by the relevant government action. Where a prisoner has a liberty interest in good time credits, the loss of such credits threatens his prospective freedom from confinement by extending the length of imprisonment. Thus the inmate has a strong interest in assuring that the loss of good time credits is not imposed arbitrarily. This interest, however, must be accommodated in the distinctive setting of a prison, where disciplinary proceedings "take place in a closed, tightly controlled environment peopled by those who have chosen to violate the criminal law and who have been lawfully incarcerated for doing so." Consequently, in identifying the safeguards required by due process, the Court has recognized the legitimate institutional needs of assuring the safety of inmates and prisoners, avoiding burdensome administrative requirements that might be susceptible to manipulation, and preserving the disciplinary process as a means of rehabilitation.

Requiring a modicum of evidence to support a decision to revoke good time credits will help to prevent arbitrary deprivations without threatening institutional interests or imposing undue administrative burdens. * * * Because the written statement mandated by *Wolff* requires a disciplinary board to explain the evidence relied upon, recognizing that due process requires some evidentiary basis for a decision to revoke good time credits will not impose significant new burdens on proceedings within the prison. Nor does it imply that a disciplinary board's factual findings or decisions with respect to appropriate punishment are subject to second-guessing upon review.

We hold that the requirements of due process are satisfied if some evidence supports the decision by the prison disciplinary board to revoke good time credits. This standard is met if "there was some evidence from which the conclusion of the administrative tribunal could be deduced. . . ." Ascertaining whether this standard is satisfied does not require examination of the entire record, independent assessment of the credibility of witnesses, or weighing of the evidence. Instead, the relevant question is whether there is any evidence in the record that could support the conclusion reached by the disciplinary board. We decline to adopt a more stringent evidentiary standard as a constitutional requirement. Prison disciplinary proceedings take place in a highly charged atmosphere, and prison administrators must often act swiftly on the basis of evidence that might be insufficient in less exigent circumstances. The fundamental fairness guaranteed by the Due Process Clause does not require courts to set aside decisions of prison administrators that have some basis in fact. Revocation of good time credits is not comparable to a criminal conviction, and neither the amount of evidence necessary to support such a conviction nor any other standard greater than some evidence applies in this context.

Turning to the facts of this case, we conclude that the evidence before the disciplinary board was sufficient to meet the requirements imposed by the Due Process Clause. The disciplinary board received evidence in the form of testimony from the prison guard and copies of his written report. That evidence indicated that the guard heard some commotion and, upon investigating, discovered an inmate who evidently had just been assaulted. The guard saw three other inmates fleeing together down an enclosed walkway. No other inmates were in the area. The Supreme Judicial Court found that this evidence was constitutionally insufficient because it did not support an inference that more than one person had struck the victim or that either of the respondents was the assailant or otherwise participated in the assault. This conclusion, however, misperceives the nature of the evidence required by the Due Process Clause.

The Federal Constitution does not require evidence that logically precludes any conclusion but the one reached by the disciplinary board. Instead, due process in this context requires only that there be some evidence to support the findings made in the disciplinary hearing. Although the evidence in this case might be characterized as meager, and there was no direct evidence identifying any one of three inmates as the assailant, the record is not so devoid of evidence that the findings of the disciplinary board were without support or otherwise arbitrary. Respondents relied only upon the Federal Constitution, and did not claim that the disciplinary board's findings failed to meet evidentiary standards imposed by state law. Because the determination of the disciplinary board was not so lacking in evidentiary support as to violate due process, the judgment of the Supreme Judicial Court is reversed, and the case is remanded for further proceedings not inconsistent with this opinion.

* * *

[Justice Stevens, joined by Justices Brennan and Marshall, wrote an opinion concurring in part and dissenting in part. While Justice Stevens disagreed with the Court's decision to review this case, he agreed that the "some evidence" standard adopted by the Court was the appropriate one.]

QUESTIONS AND POINTS FOR DISCUSSION

1. Assume that a disciplinary committee found an inmate guilty of possessing six homemade weapons. The weapons were found in a vent running next to a cell that the inmate shared with three other prisoners. The four prisoners in an adjoining cell also had ready access to the area in the vent where the weapons were found. Was there "some evidence" to support the disciplinary committee's finding of guilt? See Hamilton v. O'Leary, 976 F.2d 341, 346 (7th Cir.1992) (what the majority considered a 25% chance of guilt satisfied the "some evidence" standard). Compare Broussard v. Johnson, 253 F.3d 874, 877 (5th Cir.2001) (insufficient evidence prisoner was guilty of possession of contraband intended for use in an escape when bolt cutters were found in an area to which a hundred inmates had access); Cardenas v. Wigen, 921 F.Supp. 286, 289 n. 4 (E.D.Pa.1996) (8.3% chance that a prisoner possessed contraband discovered in area shared by twelve inmates did not constitute "some evidence" of guilt).

2. Assume that a regulation authorizes the revocation of good-time credits when the disciplinary factfinder determines that there is "some evidence" that the inmate committed what is considered "major misconduct" under the disciplinary rules. Does Hill mean that this regulation comports with due process?

The Supreme Court has described Hill as setting forth the "standard of review" to be applied by courts considering the evidence adduced at a disciplinary hearing, not the "standard of proof" that the disciplinary factfinder must apply. See Hamdi v. Rumsfeld, 542 U.S. 507, 537, 124 S.Ct. 2633, 2651 (2004). The question still remains then as to what is the constitutional standard of proof that must be met at the disciplinary hearing itself. The courts are split on this question. Compare Carrillo v. Fabian, 701 N.W.2d 763, 777 (Minn. 2005) (guilt must be established by a preponderance of the evidence) with Goff v. Dailey, 991 F.2d 1437, 1441–42 (8th Cir. 1993) ("some evidence" standard applies).

In Carrillo, the Minnesota Supreme Court explained why, in its opinion, due process requires application of a higher standard of proof by the disciplinary factfinder than "some evidence":

> To determine whether a standard of proof in a particular type of proceeding satisfies due process, the Supreme Court has prescribed a three-factor test that examines: (1) the private interest affected, (2) the risk of an erroneous deprivation of such interest, and (3) the government's interest. Mathews v. Eldridge, 424 U.S. 319, 335, 96 S.Ct. 893 (1976).

* * * The Supreme Court has acknowledged that when an inmate has a liberty interest in good time credits, he also has a strong interest in assuring that the loss of his good time credits is not imposed arbitrarily because such a loss threatens his prospective freedom from confinement by extending the length of imprisonment. * * *

Under the second factor, the risk of erroneous deprivation of an interest is high when the fact finder uses the "some evidence" standard. * * * Under the "some evidence" standard, a fact finder could conclude that an inmate has committed a disciplinary offense even when the greater weight of the evidence indicates that he did not. Indeed, the fact finder could reach this conclusion even when significantly more than the greater weight of evidence indicates that the inmate is not guilty. * * * Under this standard of proof, the benefits of certain procedural safeguards provided by the DOC's rules, such as notice and opportunity to respond, are of no value when prison authorities can extend an inmate's term of incarceration for an alleged violation of a disciplinary rule even when the balance of the evidence fails to prove that the inmate committed the charged offense.

We turn now to the third and final factor, the government's interest. The * * * government has an interest in assuring the safety of inmates and employees, as well as avoiding burdensome administrative requirements that might be susceptible to manipulation. But the government also has an interest in promoting fair procedures, and the government derives no benefit from disciplining inmates who have committed no offense. The institution's goals of preparing and rehabilitating inmates for re-entry into society are better achieved if they have been treated fairly. * * * The "some evidence" standard sends the message to prison inmates as well as society at large that once an individual is convicted of a crime, he is presumed guilty of every subsequent allegation. This message runs contrary to fundamental principles of criminal law in the United States.

Taking the Supreme Court's three factors into consideration, we conclude that the "some evidence" standard is inappropriate for use by the DOC at the fact-finding level. We conclude that the preponderance of the evidence standard better protects against an erroneous deprivation of an inmate's liberty interest in his supervised release date and does not impose an unacceptable burden on the DOC. * * *

Id. at 776–77. Do you agree or disagree with the court's analysis and conclusion?

3. Assume that an inmate was charged with a number of disciplinary infractions, including extortion. The notice apprising the inmate of the charges stated as follows: "Information has been received from various confidential sources that during the months of June, July and August, 1980, while confined in [Marion] you pressured other inmates to pay you commissary and perform homosexual acts with you. You applied this pressure by threat of harm to their person or their friends." The inmate was not provided with any additional details about the alleged offenses on the grounds that to do so would jeopardize the lives and safety of the informants.

A prison investigator spoke with the informants and submitted an unsworn report to the disciplinary committee summarizing their statements to the investigator. The informants themselves did not appear before the committee.

Relying on the investigator's report, the disciplinary committee found the inmate guilty of the offenses charged. After essentially repeating the contents of the notice previously given to the inmate, the committee added in its report finding the inmate guilty: "Information received from confidential sources has proven reliable in the past."

Was the inmate afforded due process of law? The Seventh Circuit Court of Appeals addressed this question in McCollum v. Miller, 695 F.2d 1044 (7th Cir.1982) (*McCollum I*). Pertinent portions of the court's analysis are set forth below:

> Ramirez–Rodriguez argues that he should have received both a more detailed notice of the charges against him and more safeguards against erroneous findings at the hearing. The notice he received was so general that it was difficult for him to prepare any defense. But unfortunately the costs of additional notice would have been great. The essential information that Ramirez–Rodriguez needed to prepare his defense was the time and place of each alleged act of extortion. Any information falling short of this would have added nothing of value to the uninformative statement of charges he did receive. But the additional information would have tipped him off to the names of all or most of the informants, whether the informants were the alleged victims of extortion, or witnesses to the alleged acts of extortion, or some of each. Such a tip-off could be lethal. Marion is the successor to Alcatraz as the maximum-security federal penitentiary. Not only does it have the most dangerous federal offenders, but it takes in, by way of assistance to the very overcrowded state prisons of the area, some of the most dangerous state offenders. Violent crime directed at other inmates is a common experience in our prisons today, and "rats" are frequent targets. In the short run revealing the names of informants against a gang of extortionists and homosexual molesters could lead to the death or serious injury of some or all of the informants; in the long run it would dry up the supply of informants and allow extortion to rage unchecked through Marion.

> These costs outweigh in our judgment the benefits, substantial as they would be, of giving inmates accused of serious offenses the information they need to prepare an effective defense. But without such notice the adversary hearing so prized in American procedure is likely to have little meaning. The inmates will not know what the evidence is against them, so they will not be able to counter it with evidence of their own. The disciplinary proceeding will be inquisitorial. The conditions in Marion today make that inescapable and it is therefore consistent with due process. But if the usual safeguards of an adversary procedure are unavailable it is all the more important that there be other safeguards, and we find none in this case. The report of the investigator is persuasive in its detail, but an investigative report, however vivid and apparently true, is not, as the magistrate thought, self-validating. The investigator

was not called as a witness, although his identity is not confidential. He was not asked to swear to the truth of the report. None of the informants testified before, or were interviewed by, the Institution Discipline Committee. The Committee would not even vouch for the credibility of the investigator or his informants. All it said was that information received from confidential sources had proved reliable in the past—not necessarily information from these sources, compiled by this investigator. Not all prison inmates who inform on other inmates are telling the truth; some are enacting their own schemes of revenge; and though it is unlikely that all or most of the informants interviewed for the investigative report were lying, if some were that could have affected the severity of the sanction that the Committee meted out to Ramirez–Rodriguez.

Since the procedures used by the Committee in this case carried with them a significant risk of error, and the consequences of error in this setting are serious for Ramirez–Rodriguez, it remains only to consider the costs of extending to him some additional procedural safeguards. We cannot determine these costs on the scanty record before us. One safeguard Ramirez–Rodriguez is seeking is to let his lawyer read the investigative report. We have no reason to believe that his counsel would give Ramirez–Rodriguez the names of the informants, or information from which those names could be deduced, but we do not know whether it would be safe to allow inmates' counsel access to such reports as a general rule and we do not think that courts or prison officials should try to decide which lawyers are trustworthy. It should be perfectly feasible to insist that the Institution Disciplinary Committee require that its investigative reports be under oath and that the investigator appear in person and be available for cross-examination; but we are not sure whether it is feasible to go further and require the Committee to interview—*in camera*, of course—some or all of the informants. Maybe that is too dangerous. Maybe the prison grapevine is so efficient that Ramirez–Rodriguez would learn who had been interviewed by the Committee—or maybe whether or not it is that efficient, informants would be afraid to give testimony other than through the investigator. You need a better feel for Marion than we have to make judgments in these sensitive matters; and they happen to be matters of life and death.

Id. at 1048–49.

The court of appeals remanded the case to the district court to consider the feasibility of providing additional procedural safeguards when a prison disciplinary committee's guilty finding is based substantially on information received from a confidential informant. The district court concluded that requiring the disciplinary committee to interview confidential informants in person was not a viable option. However, the court found that as long as the investigator's report was submitted under oath, due process was afforded by the following new procedures that had been instituted at the Marion penitentiary:

1) The disciplinary committee's finding of guilt must be supported by more than one reliable confidential source. If there is only one source, the confidential informant information must be corroborated by independent-

ly verified factual evidence linking the inmate charged to the prohibited act. Uncorroborated information from a single informant is insufficient unless the peculiar circumstances of the incident and the peculiar knowledge possessed by the informant convince the committee that the informant's information must be reliable. The committee report should include a statement giving the committee's rationale for deciding that uncorroborated single informant information is reliable.

2) The reliability of the informant must be established before informant-based information can be used to support a finding by the Disciplinary Committee. Reliability may be determined by a record of past reliability or other factors which convince the IDC [Institutional Disciplinary Committee] of the informant's reliability. The staff member providing the information must include a written statement of the frequency with which the confidential informant has provided information, the period of time during which the confidential informant has provided information, and the degree of accuracy of that information. If reliability is based on other factors, then such factors should clearly be specified. Staff have an affirmative obligation to determine whether there is any basis for concluding that the confidential informant is providing false information. The IDC may not consider information obtained in exchange for the promise of a favor to support its finding.

3) All confidential information presented to the Disciplinary Committee must be in writing and state facts and the manner in which the informant arrived at knowledge of those facts.

4) The identity of the confidential informant must be known, at a minimum, by the chairman of the Disciplinary Committee and at the chairman's discretion, may be revealed to the other committee members. The substance of the confidential informant information must be known to all members of the Disciplinary Committee. The Committee chairman shall include, in the record of the hearing, a statement of the basis for finding the information provided by the confidential informant reliable.

5) Confidential informant's statements shall, at a minimum, be incorporated into the committee report by reference. The committee shall document, ordinarily in the report, the finding as to the reliability of each informant and the factual basis for that finding, unless such information would reveal the identity of the informant. In such a case, the chairman shall prepare a separate report documenting the committee's findings as to the reliability of each informant relied on, the factual basis for that finding, the specific information relied on and the factual basis for that reliance. This report must be available for later administrative or judicial review.

McCollum v. Williford, 793 F.2d 903, 907–08 n. 3 (7th Cir.1986) (*McCollum II*). On appeal, the Seventh Circuit Court of Appeals affirmed the decision of the district court. Id.

Like the Seventh Circuit, most courts require the disciplinary decision-maker to take some steps to verify the reliability of a confidential informant's tip on which a guilty finding rests rather than simply rely on a correctional officer's or an investigator's assurance in a written report that the information relayed is reliable. Broussard v. Johnson, 253 F.3d 874, 876 (5th Cir. 2001). How would you balance the interest in averting the imposition of sanctions on inmates innocent of any wrongdoing and the need to keep confidential the identity of certain informants?

4. Consider the Fourth Circuit's decision in Baker v. Lyles, 904 F.2d 925 (4th Cir.1990). In that case, Lieutenant Elijah Thomas reported in a letter to the prison's chief of security that a "very reliable source" had informed Thomas that inmate Russell Baker possessed tools to be used in an escape. According to the letter, this informant later provided Lieutenant Thomas with a hacksaw blade the informant claimed he had gotten from Baker. On the basis of this letter, a hearing officer found Baker guilty of possession of escape tools and recommended that Baker forfeit fifteen days of good-time credits and be confined in the punitive-segregation unit for 210 days. The warden approved the guilty finding and the recommended sanctions. In holding that the guilty finding was supported by "some evidence," the court of appeals emphasized additional facts about the case that came to light and were provided to the warden after the disciplinary hearing: Some grill gate bars had been sawed in the prison chapel in an apparent escape attempt, and Baker had a prior escape conviction. Do you agree with the court's analysis and conclusion?

5. Some lower courts have held that prisoners have rights during prison disciplinary proceedings in addition to those delineated in *Wolff*. Several courts, for example, have concluded that prisoners have a constitutional right to be apprised of the rules or regulations whose violation will lead to the imposition of punishment. See, e.g., Reeves v. Pettcox, 19 F.3d 1060, 1062 (5th Cir.1994) (punishing prisoner for putting his food tray outside his cell violated due process because he was not given a copy of the rule requiring prisoners in solitary confinement to keep their trays in their cells until they are picked up nor given the chance to read notices of the rule posted on the bulletin board in the unit). Others have recognized a general due-process right to be informed by the disciplinary committee of exculpatory information of which it is aware and to have the committee consider that information before rendering its decision. See, e.g., Whitford v. Boglino, 63 F.3d 527, 536 (7th Cir.1995) (disciplinary committee cannot refuse to consider exculpatory evidence simply because there is already "some evidence" of the inmate's guilt in the record); Chavis v. Rowe, 643 F.2d 1281, 1285–86 (7th Cir.1981) (Adjustment Committee should have disclosed to plaintiff-inmate, who was charged with stabbing a correctional officer, the results of a polygraph test administered to another inmate, who apparently was telling the truth when he identified someone other than the plaintiff as the assailant).

In your opinion, what other constitutional rights, if any, extend to prisoners during disciplinary proceedings? For additional information on the rights of inmates during prison disciplinary proceedings, see Daniel E. Manville, Disciplinary Self–Help Litigation Manual (2004).

6. There are other government-created rights that inmates have during prison disciplinary proceedings that go beyond the constitutional baseline. See, e.g., Mich.Comp.Laws § 791.251(6) (hearing officer must be an attorney); 28 C.F.R. § 541.15(i) (all inmates have the right to assistance from a staff

representative at disciplinary hearings). Apart from rights accorded by the United States Constitution, what additional rights, if any, do you believe inmates should have during prison disciplinary proceedings?

The American Bar Association's Standards for Criminal Justice: Legal Status of Prisoners (1981) call for the following procedural safeguards during prison disciplinary proceedings:

Standard 23–3.1. Rules of conduct

(a) Correctional authorities should promulgate clear written rules for prisoner conduct. These rules and implementing criteria should include:

(i) a specific definition of offenses, a statement that the least severe punishment appropriate to each offense should be imposed, and a schedule indicating the minimum and maximum possible punishment for each offense, proportionate to the offense; and

(ii) specific criteria and procedures for prison discipline and classification decisions, including decisions involving security status and work and housing assignments.

(b) A personal copy of the rules should be provided to each prisoner upon entry to the institution. For the benefit of illiterate and foreign-language prisoners, a detailed oral explanation of the rules should be given. In addition, a written translation should be provided in any language spoken by a significant number of prisoners.

Standard 23–3.2. Disciplinary Hearing Procedures

(a) At a hearing where a minor sanction is imposed, the prisoner should be entitled to:

(i) written notice of the charge, in a language the prisoner understands, within [seventy-two][a] hours of the time he or she is suspected of having committed an offense; within another [twenty-four] hours the prisoner should be given copies of any further written information the tribunal may consider;

(ii) a hearing within [three] working days of the time the written notice of the charge was received;

(iii) be present and speak on his or her own behalf;

(iv) a written decision based upon a preponderance of the evidence, with specified reasons for the decision. The decision should be rendered promptly and in all cases within [five] days after conclusion of the hearing; and

(v) appeal, within [five] days, to the chief executive officer of the institution, and the right to a written decision by that officer within [thirty] days, based upon a written summary of the hearing, any documentary evidence considered at the hearing, and the prisoner's written reason for appealing. The chief executive officer should either affirm or reverse the determination of misconduct and decrease or

---

a. The time limits specified in the ABA standards are bracketed because they are "suggestions to be adapted to institutional needs." Standard 23–3.2 commentary.

approve the punishment imposed. Execution of the punishment should be suspended during the appeal unless individual safety or individual security will be adversely affected thereby.

(b) At a hearing where a major sanction is imposed, in addition to the requirements of paragraph (a), the prisoner should be entitled to have in attendance any person within the local prison community who has relevant information, and to examine or cross-examine such witnesses except when the hearing officer(s):

(i) exclude testimony as unduly cumulative; or

(ii) receive testimony outside the presence of the prisoner pursuant to a finding that the physical safety of a person would be endangered by the presence of a particular witness or by disclosure of his or her identity.

(c) Disciplinary hearings should be conducted by one or more impartial persons.

(d) Unless the prisoner is found guilty, no record relating to the charge should be retained in the prisoner's file or used against the prisoner in any way.

* * *

(f) In the event of a situation requiring the chief executive officer to declare all, or a part, of an institution to be in a state of emergency, the rights provided in this standard may be temporarily suspended for up to [twenty-four] hours after the emergency has terminated.

Standard 23–3.3. Criminal Misconduct

(a) Where a prisoner is alleged to have engaged in conduct that would be a criminal offense under state or federal law, the prosecutor should be notified and, in consultation with the chief executive officer, should determine promptly whether to charge the prisoner. Institutional proceedings arising from the same conduct need not be suspended while the decision to charge is being made or while resolution of the charge is pending. However, correctional authorities should exercise caution in conducting institutional proceedings so that the right of the public and of the prisoner to a fair criminal trial is not infringed.

* * *

(c) After disposition of the criminal charge, the prisoner may be reclassified. He or she also may be subjected to disciplinary proceedings if they were suspended during the prosecution.

B. *MIRANDA* AND THE PRIVILEGE AGAINST SELF–INCRIMINATION

1. *MIRANDA* RIGHTS

In Miranda v. Arizona, 384 U.S. 436, 86 S.Ct. 1602 (1966), the Supreme Court held that for statements obtained during custodial interrogation to be admissible in a criminal prosecution, individuals questioned by a governmental official must be apprised before the interrogation that they have the right to remain silent, that anything they say can be used later against them in a court of law, that they have the right to consult an attorney and to have the attorney present during the interrogation, and that if they cannot afford an attorney, one will be appointed to represent them.

The question arises whether an inmate must be given these *Miranda* warnings before being questioned about a disciplinary offense the inmate is suspected of having committed that is also a crime, such as an assault or a theft. In Baxter v. Palmigiano, 425 U.S. 308, 96 S.Ct. 1551 (1976), the Supreme Court noted that the failure to comply with the requirements of *Miranda* only affects the admissibility of statements in criminal cases. If an inmate is questioned by a correctional officer or disciplinary committee about the circumstances surrounding the inmate's suspected or alleged commission of a disciplinary offense, the inmate's responses properly can be considered during a disciplinary hearing, regardless of whether the inmate was given *Miranda* warnings before the questioning began.

More difficult is the question whether the inmate's answers are admissible in court to prove that the inmate is guilty of a crime with which he or she is charged. In answering this question, the Supreme Court's decision in Mathis v. United States, 391 U.S. 1, 88 S.Ct. 1503 (1968) must be considered. *Mathis* concerned an inmate who, while incarcerated in a state prison for a state crime, was questioned by an IRS agent about suspected criminal tax violations. The IRS agent did not apprise the inmate of his *Miranda* rights before questioning him, and the inmate made incriminating statements to the agent. His statements later were admitted in evidence to help secure his conviction for criminal tax fraud.

The Supreme Court held that since the inmate was in custody when he was questioned by the IRS agent, the interrogation should have been preceded by the giving of *Miranda* warnings. Consequently, the inmate's statements should not have been admitted during his criminal trial.

The Supreme Court distinguished *Mathis* in Illinois v. Perkins, 496 U.S. 292, 110 S.Ct. 2394 (1990). In *Perkins,* an undercover police officer was placed in the same jail cell with the defendant, who was awaiting trial for aggravated battery. The undercover agent then questioned the defendant about a murder that the defendant was suspected of having committed, and the defendant made some incriminating statements. The Supreme Court held that the defendant's statements could be used against him in his subsequent trial for murder even though the undercover agent did not give the defendant *Miranda* warnings before questioning him. The Court held that the concerns that prompted the Court's ruling in *Miranda*—that a defendant's will might be overborne by the coercive influences exerted on him in a "police-dominated atmosphere"—simply were not present when the defendant was being asked questions by someone whom he believed to be just a fellow inmate. Id. at 296, 110 S.Ct. at 2397.

In *Perkins,* the Supreme Court made the following potentially telling observation: "The bare fact of custody may not in every instance require a warning even when the suspect is aware that he is speaking to an official, but we do not have occasion to explore that issue here." Id. at 299, 110 S.Ct. at 2398. Some lower courts have agreed with this observation, holding that inmates need not invariably be given *Miranda* warnings when prison staff members question them about criminal conduct. See, e.g., United States v. Conley, 779 F.2d 970 (4th Cir.1985) (no right to *Miranda* warnings when two correctional officers questioned prisoner in a conference room about fatal stabbing of another inmate). According to these courts, in order to be in "custody" within the meaning of *Miranda,* a prisoner must be subjected to some "added imposition" on his or her freedom of movement beyond the restrictions that normally attend confinement at the correctional facility. See State v. Conley, 574 N.W.2d 569, 573 (N.D.1998) (listing cases); Laurie Magid, Questioning the Question–Proof Inmate: Defining Miranda Custody for Incarcerated Suspects, 58 Ohio St. L.J. 883, 939–47 (1997). Many of the courts applying what is often called the "additional restraint test" have distinguished *Mathis* on the grounds that the inmate in that case was subjected to coercive pressures sufficient to trigger the protections of *Miranda* because he was questioned by an outside governmental investigator about a matter not under investigation within the prison. Cervantes v. Walker, 589 F.2d 424, 428 (9th Cir.1978).

State v. Conley, 574 N.W.2d 569 (N.D.1998) is another example of the additional restraints on a prisoner that can give rise to the "custody" that triggers the need to give *Miranda* warnings before interrogating a prisoner about a suspected crime. In that case, the following combination of facts led the Supreme Court of North Dakota to conclude that the defendant was "in custody" for *Miranda* purposes when a prison official questioned him about his possession, in violation of a criminal statute, of contraband to be used to facilitate an escape: First, the defendant was the only suspect. Second, he was handcuffed throughout the interview. Third, the questioning occurred in the prison official's office rather than in the prisoner's cell or in an open area. Fourth, the interview was not spontaneous on-the-scene questioning. Fifth, during the interrogation session, the defendant was confronted with evidence of his guilt. And sixth, the defendant was being held at the time in administrative segregation while prison officials investigated his culpability of the crime with which he eventually was charged.

The court in *Conley* also held that the defendant was "in custody" within the meaning of *Miranda* at the time of his disciplinary hearing. Consequently, his incriminating statements made in response to the disciplinary committee's questions, which were not prefaced by *Miranda* warnings, were inadmissible in the later criminal trial. Do you agree with either or both of the court's findings of custody in this case?

2. THE PRIVILEGE AGAINST SELF–INCRIMINATION: INMATES' SILENCE DURING DISCIPLINARY HEARINGS

The Supreme Court has held that a disciplinary committee can consider an inmate's silence during a disciplinary hearing as evidence of the inmate's guilt without abridging the privilege against self-incrimination subsumed within the Fifth Amendment and applicable to the states via the Fourteenth Amendment's Due Process Clause. Baxter v. Palmigiano, 425 U.S. 308, 317–20, 96 S.Ct. 1551, 1557–59 (1976). In *Baxter,* the disciplinary committee had informed the inmate, who was charged with violating prison rules by participating in a prison disturbance, that his silence could be used against him. The Supreme Court observed that not all pressures placed by the government upon an individual to speak violate the privilege against self-incrimination. At the same time, the Court emphasized that under the law of the state in which the inmate was incarcerated, an inmate's silence was not enough evidence, by itself, to support a guilty finding.

The Supreme Court also mentioned in *Baxter* that no criminal charges were pending against the inmate at the time of the disciplinary hearing or later filed. Should these facts have any bearing on the constitutionality of drawing an adverse inference from an inmate's silence at a disciplinary hearing that the inmate is guilty of a disciplinary infraction?

Do you agree with the Court's ruling in *Baxter?* How will it affect inmates confronted with disciplinary charges? After reading the Supreme Court's decision in McKune v. Lile, 536 U.S. 24, 122 S.Ct. 2017 (2002), on page 639, reconsider the Fifth Amendment implications of drawing an inference of guilt from an inmate's silence during a prison disciplinary hearing.

CHAPTER 14

TRANSFERS, CLASSIFICATION, AND PRISON PROGRAMMING

■ ■ ■

A. PROCEDURAL DUE PROCESS

After an individual is sentenced to prison, correctional officials must make a number of decisions concerning that individual. To what prison should the individual be sent? In what section of that prison should the individual be housed? To what work, school, or other programs, if any, should the individual be assigned? And the list goes on.

Throughout a person's incarceration in prison, decisions will continue to be made that affect both the location and the conditions of the inmate's confinement. The inmate, for example, may be transferred from one prison to another, perhaps to a prison where inmates have far fewer privileges and are subject to much worse conditions than at the prison where the inmate was confined initially. Or the inmate may be placed in an administrative-segregation unit, where privileges are sparse and confinement in one's cell for almost twenty-four hours a day is the norm. Or the inmate may be removed from a work assignment or lose other privileges because of a concern that the inmate will abuse the privileges, causing disruption within the institution.

As with all decisions, there is the risk that correctional officials will make mistakes when rendering decisions adversely affecting a prisoner. Perhaps a decision will be grounded on misinformation or even no information; or perhaps a decision will stem from personal animosity directed against a particular prisoner. One question which therefore arises is whether prison officials are constitutionally obliged to take steps to reduce the risk of error when making decisions having an immediate and adverse impact on individual prisoners. The Supreme Court addressed this question in the case which follows.

MEACHUM v. FANO

Supreme Court of the United States, 1976.
427 U.S. 215, 96 S.Ct. 2532, 49 L.Ed.2d 451.

MR. JUSTICE WHITE delivered the opinion of the Court.

[After a number of fires were started at the Massachusetts Correctional Institution at Norfolk, a medium-security prison, several prisoners were transferred to Bridgewater, a prison with both maximum and medium-security units, and Walpole, a maximum-security prison with much more draconian conditions of confinement than those at Norfolk. The prisoners then filed a § 1983 suit, contending that their transfers were effected without due process of law. The district court agreed, holding that the prisoners were entitled to the procedural safeguards set forth in *Wolff v. McDonnell,* 418 U.S. 539 (1974), supra page 570, before their transfers. The First Circuit Court of Appeals affirmed.]

* * *

The Fourteenth Amendment prohibits any State from depriving a person of life, liberty, or property without due process of law. The initial inquiry is whether the transfer of respondents from Norfolk to Walpole and Bridgewater infringed or implicated a "liberty" interest of respondents within the meaning of the Due Process Clause. Contrary to the Court of Appeals, we hold that it did not. We reject at the outset the notion that *any* grievous loss visited upon a person by the State is sufficient to invoke the procedural protections of the Due Process Clause. In *Board of Regents v. Roth,* 408 U.S. 564 (1972), a university professor was deprived of his job, a loss which was surely a matter of great substance, but because the professor had no property interest in his position, due process procedures were not required in connection with his dismissal. We there held that the determining factor is the nature of the interest involved rather than its weight.

Similarly, we cannot agree that *any* change in the conditions of confinement having a substantial adverse impact on the prisoner involved is sufficient to invoke the protections of the Due Process Clause. The Due Process Clause by its own force forbids the State from convicting any person of [a] crime and depriving him of his liberty without complying fully with the requirements of the Clause. But given a valid conviction, the criminal defendant has been constitutionally deprived of his liberty to the extent that the State may confine him and subject him to the rules of its prison system so long as the conditions of confinement do not otherwise violate the Constitution. The Constitution does not require that the State have more than one prison for convicted felons; nor does it guarantee that the convicted prisoner will be placed in any particular prison if, as is likely, the State has more than one correctional institution. The initial decision to assign the convict to a particular institution is not subject to audit under the Due Process Clause, although the degree of confinement in one prison may be quite different from that in another. The conviction has sufficiently extinguished the defendant's liberty interest to empower the State to confine him in *any* of its prisons.

Neither, in our view, does the Due Process Clause in and of itself protect a duly convicted prisoner against transfer from one institution to another within the state prison system. Confinement in any of the State's institutions is within the normal limits or range of custody which the conviction has authorized the State to impose. That life in one prison is much more disagreeable than in another does not in itself signify that a Fourteenth Amendment liberty interest is implicated when a prisoner is transferred to the institution with the more severe rules.

* * * [T]o hold as we are urged to do that *any* substantial deprivation imposed by prison authorities triggers the procedural protections of the Due Process Clause would subject to judicial review a wide spectrum of discretionary actions that traditionally have been the business of prison administrators rather than of the federal courts.

Transfers between institutions, for example, are made for a variety of reasons and often involve no more than informed predictions as to what would best serve institutional security or the safety and welfare of the inmate. Yet under the approach urged here, any transfer, for whatever reason, would require a hearing as long as it could be said that the transfer would place the prisoner in substantially more burdensome conditions tha[n] he had been experiencing. We are unwilling to go so far.

Wolff v. McDonnell * * * is not to the contrary. Under that case, the Due Process Clause entitles a state prisoner to certain procedural protections when he is deprived of good-time credits because of serious misconduct. But the liberty interest there identified did not originate in the Constitution, which "itself does not guarantee good-time credit for satisfactory behavior while in prison." The State itself, not the Constitution, had "not only provided a statutory right to good time but also specifies that it is to be forfeited only for serious misbehavior." * * *

Here, Massachusetts law conferred no right on the prisoner to remain in the prison to which he was initially assigned, defeasible only upon proof of specific acts of misconduct. Insofar as we are advised, transfers between Massachusetts prisons are not conditioned upon the occurrence of specified events.[7] On the contrary, transfer in a wide variety of circumstances is vested in prison officials. The predicate for invoking the protection of the Fourteenth Amendment as construed and applied in *Wolff v. McDonnell* is totally nonexistent in this case.

Even if Massachusetts has not represented that transfers will occur only on the occurrence of certain events, it is argued that charges of

---

7. At the time the transfers in this case occurred, Massachusetts General Laws Annotated, c. 127, § 97 (1974) provided as follows:

* * *

"The commissioner may transfer any sentenced prisoner from one correctional institution of the commonwealth to another * * *."

serious misbehavior, as in this case, often initiate and heavily influence the transfer decision and that because allegations of misconduct may be erroneous, hearings should be held before transfer to a more confining institution is to be suffered by the prisoner. That an inmate's conduct, in general or in specific instances, may often be a major factor in the decision of prison officials to transfer him is to be expected unless it be assumed that transfers are mindless events. A prisoner's past and anticipated future behavior will very likely be taken into account in selecting a prison in which he will be initially incarcerated or to which he will be transferred to best serve the State's penological goals.

A prisoner's behavior may precipitate a transfer; and absent such behavior, perhaps transfer would not take place at all. But, as we have said, Massachusetts prison officials have the discretion to transfer prisoners for any number of reasons. Their discretion is not limited to instances of serious misconduct. * * * Whatever expectation the prisoner may have in remaining at a particular prison so long as he behaves himself, it is too ephemeral and insubstantial to trigger procedural due process protections as long as prison officials have discretion to transfer him for whatever reason or for no reason at all.

Holding that arrangements like this are within reach of the procedural protections of the Due Process Clause would place the Clause astride the day-to-day functioning of state prisons and involve the judiciary in issues and discretionary decisions that are not the business of federal judges. We decline to so interpret and apply the Due Process Clause. The federal courts do not sit to supervise state prisons, the administration of which is of acute interest to the States. The individual States, of course, are free to follow another course, whether by statute, by rule or regulation, or by interpretation of their own constitutions. They may thus decide that prudent prison administration requires pretransfer hearings. Our holding is that the Due Process Clause does not impose a nationwide rule mandating transfer hearings.

* * *

MR. JUSTICE STEVENS, with whom MR. JUSTICE BRENNAN and MR. JUSTICE MARSHALL join, dissenting.

The Court's rationale is more disturbing than its narrow holding. If the Court had merely held that the transfer of a prisoner from one penal institution to another does not cause a sufficiently grievous loss to amount to a deprivation of liberty within the meaning of the Due Process Clause of the Fourteenth Amendment, I would disagree with the conclusion but not with the constitutional analysis. The Court's holding today, however, appears to rest on a conception of "liberty" which I consider fundamentally incorrect.

The Court indicates that a "liberty interest" may have either of two sources. According to the Court, a liberty interest may "originate in the Constitution," or it may have "its roots in state law." * * *

If man were a creature of the State, the analysis would be correct. But neither the Bill of Rights nor the laws of sovereign States create the liberty which the Due Process Clause protects. * * *

I had thought it self-evident that all men were endowed by their Creator with liberty as one of the cardinal unalienable rights. It is that basic freedom which the Due Process Clause protects, rather than the particular rights or privileges conferred by specific laws or regulations.

A correct description of the source of the liberty protected by the Constitution does not, of course, decide this case. For, by hypothesis, we are dealing with persons who may be deprived of their liberty because they have been convicted of criminal conduct after a fair trial. We should therefore first ask whether the deprivation of liberty which follows conviction is total or partial.

At one time the prevailing view was that the deprivation was essentially total. The penitentiary inmate was considered "the slave of the State." * * *

* * *

* * * [I]f the inmate's protected liberty interests are no greater than the State chooses to allow, he is really little more than the slave described in the 19th century cases. I think it clear that even the inmate retains an unalienable interest in liberty—at the very minimum the right to be treated with dignity—which the Constitution may never ignore.

* * *

* * * While custody denies the inmate the opportunity to offend, it also gives him an opportunity to improve himself and to acquire skills and habits that will help him to participate in an open society after his release. Within the prison community, if my basic hypothesis is correct, he has a protected right to pursue his limited rehabilitative goals, or at the minimum, to maintain whatever attributes of dignity are associated with his status in a tightly controlled society. It is unquestionably within the power of the State to change that status, abruptly and adversely; but if the change is sufficiently grievous, it may not be imposed arbitrarily. In such case due process must be afforded.

That does not mean, of course, that every adversity amounts to a deprivation within the meaning of the Fourteenth Amendment.[4] There must be grievous loss, and that term itself is somewhat flexible. I would certainly not consider every transfer within a prison system, even to more onerous conditions of confinement, such a loss. * * * In view of the Court's basic holding, I merely note that I agree with the Court of Appeals

---

4. * * * "Moreover, in determining whether to require due process, we need not choose between the 'full panoply' of rights accorded a defendant in a criminal prosecution, on the one hand, and no safeguards whatsoever, on the other. Rather, the requirements of due process may be shaped to fit the needs of a particular situation."

that the transfer involved in this case was sufficiently serious to invoke the protection of the Constitution.[5]

* * *

QUESTIONS AND POINTS FOR DISCUSSION

1. In Olim v. Wakinekona, 461 U.S. 238, 103 S.Ct. 1741 (1983), the prisoner-plaintiff also challenged, on due-process grounds, his transfer to another prison. In *Olim,* the prisoner was transferred from his home state of Hawaii to a prison over 2500 miles away in California. Nonetheless, the Supreme Court concluded that scrutiny of the transfer under the Due Process Clause was foreclosed because the transfer did not deprive the plaintiff of any protected liberty interest.

In explaining why it found no constitutionally-derived liberty interest at stake, the Court said:

> Just as an inmate has no justifiable expectation that he will be incarcerated in any particular prison within a State, he has no justifiable expectation that he will be incarcerated in any particular State. Often, confinement in the inmate's home State will not be possible. A person convicted of a federal crime in a State without a federal correctional facility usually will serve his sentence in another State. Overcrowding and the need to separate particular prisoners may necessitate interstate transfers. For any number of reasons, a State may lack prison facilities capable of providing appropriate correctional programs for all offenders.

* * *

> In short, it is neither unreasonable nor unusual for an inmate to serve practically his entire sentence in a State other than the one in which he was convicted and sentenced, or to be transferred to an out-of-state prison after serving a portion of his sentence in his home State. Confinement in another State * * * is "within the normal limits or range of custody which the conviction has authorized the State to impose." Even when, as here, the transfer involves long distances and an ocean crossing, the confinement remains within constitutional limits. The difference between such a transfer and an intrastate or interstate transfer of shorter distance is a matter of degree, not of kind, and *Meachum* instructs that "the determining factor is the nature of the interest involved rather than its weight." The reasoning of *Meachum* and *Montanye* compels the conclusion that an interstate prison transfer, including one from Hawaii to California, does not deprive an inmate of any liberty interest protected by the Due Process Clause in and of itself.

Id. at 245–48, 103 S.Ct. at 1745–47.

---

5. There is no question that respondents in this case suffered loss because of the transfer. Hathaway lost his laundry business—a source of income—which he had been running at Norfolk; Dussault lost his job as a plumber, in which he had been performing "a difficult job especially well"; Royce was separated from counselors with whom he had a "good relationship" which had helped him in his effort "to get himself together." These losses were in addition to the generally more restrictive conditions inherent in a maximum-security institution as compared to a medium-security institution.

The Supreme Court also held that no state-created liberty interest was implicated by the plaintiff's transfer. Although the state had set up an elaborate procedural mechanism to govern such interstate transfers, the Court emphasized that the ultimate decision whether to transfer a prisoner out of state fell within the unlimited discretion of the warden.

2.   In Hewitt v. Helms, 459 U.S. 460, 103 S.Ct. 864 (1983), the Supreme Court considered whether an inmate's transfer from the general-population unit of a prison to administrative segregation deprived him of liberty, thereby triggering the protections of due process. The Court began by rejecting the argument that the inmate had been deprived of liberty derived from the Constitution itself:

> It is plain that the transfer of an inmate to less amenable and more restrictive quarters for nonpunitive reasons is well within the terms of confinement ordinarily contemplated by a prison sentence. The phrase "administrative segregation," as used by the state authorities here, appears to be something of a catchall: it may be used to protect the prisoner's safety, to protect other inmates from a particular prisoner, to break up potentially disruptive groups of inmates, or simply to await later classification or transfer. Accordingly, administrative segregation is the sort of confinement that inmates should reasonably anticipate receiving at some point in their incarceration. This conclusion finds ample support in our decisions regarding parole and good-time credits. Both these subjects involve release from institutional life altogether, which is a far more significant change in a prisoner's freedoms than that at issue here, yet in *Greenholtz* [*v. Nebraska Penal Inmates,* 442 U.S. 1 (1979)] and *Wolff* [*v. McDonnell,* 418 U.S. 539 (1974)], we held that neither situation involved an interest independently protected by the Due Process Clause. These decisions compel an identical result here.

Id. at 468, 103 S.Ct. at 869–70.

The Supreme Court went on to hold, however, that the state had created a liberty interest of which the inmate was deprived when he was transferred to administrative segregation. The Court pointed to language in a state statute and regulations that circumscribed the discretion of correctional officials to place inmates in administrative segregation. Inmates could be transferred to administrative segregation only if certain "substantive predicates" were met, such as the "need for control" or "the threat of a serious disturbance." Id. at 472, 103 S.Ct. at 871.

3.   In Kentucky Dep't of Corrections v. Thompson, 490 U.S. 454, 109 S.Ct. 1904 (1989), the Supreme Court discussed further how liberty interests are created in the prison context. *Thompson* involved a civil-rights suit initiated after the visiting privileges of several prisoners at the Kentucky State Penitentiary were curtailed without a hearing. One inmate was not permitted to see his mother for six months because she brought someone to the prison who previously had been involved in smuggling contraband into the prison. The mother and girlfriend of another prisoner were forbidden from visiting at the prison for a while after the inmate was found with contraband after one of their visits.

The district court held that before a visitor could be excluded from the penitentiary, a prisoner had to be provided with notice of, and the reasons for, the exclusion and be afforded the opportunity to present his views as to why the exclusion order was unwarranted. The Sixth Circuit Court of Appeals affirmed.

The Supreme Court first dismissed the argument that the Due Process Clause itself creates a liberty interest in unrestricted visiting privileges. The Court explained that "[t]he denial of prison access to a particular visitor 'is well within the terms of confinement ordinarily contemplated by a prison sentence' and therefore is not independently protected by the Due Process Clause." Id. at 461, 109 S.Ct. at 1909. In a brief concurring opinion, Justice Kennedy emphasized that the case did not involve a general ban on prison visitors.

The dissenting Justices in the case—Justices Marshall, Brennan, and Stevens—disagreed with the Court's summary rejection of the notion that a prisoner could have a constitutionally-derived liberty interest in retained visiting privileges. "[T]he 'within the sentence' test," they observed, "knows few rivals for vagueness and pliability, not the least because a typical prison sentence says little more than that the defendant must spend a specified period of time behind bars." Id. at 466–67, 109 S.Ct. at 1912.

The majority of the Court also found that the plaintiffs had no state-created liberty interest in visiting with people from outside the prison. The Court noted that one of the Kentucky prison regulations governing visiting privileges listed examples of when it would be appropriate to exclude a visitor from the prison, such as when a visitor is under the influence of alcohol or drugs. The regulation specifically indicated that the list of reasons was not all-inclusive. The Supreme Court consequently concluded that an inmate could not "reasonably form an objective expectation that a visit would necessarily be allowed absent the occurrence of one of the listed conditions." Id. at 465, 109 S.Ct. at 1911.

Six years after its decision in *Thompson,* the Supreme Court once again revisited, in the case set forth below, the subject of state-created liberty interests, this time substantially modifying its analysis of how these interests are created in the prison setting.

SANDIN v. CONNER

Supreme Court of the United States, 1995.
515 U.S. 472, 115 S.Ct. 2293, 132 L.Ed.2d 418.

CHIEF JUSTICE REHNQUIST delivered the opinion of the Court.

[The plaintiff in this case, DeMont Conner, was incarcerated in a maximum-security prison in Hawaii, serving a prison sentence of thirty years to life for a number of crimes, including murder. In August of 1987, Conner cursed when told that he would have to undergo a strip search. He then was charged with numerous disciplinary infractions, including the "high misconduct" of obstructing a correctional officer in the performance of his duties.

At Conner's disciplinary hearing, the disciplinary committee denied his request to call several staff witnesses to confirm his innocence. The committee then found Conner guilty of all of the disciplinary infractions with which he had been charged and sentenced him to thirty days in the disciplinary-segregation unit for impeding a correctional officer's performance of his duties.

Conner subsequently filed an administrative appeal in which he contested the disciplinary committee's findings. He also filed a civil-rights suit under 42 U.S.C. § 1983 in which he claimed that the disciplinary committee's refusal to hear testimony from the witnesses he had requested violated his right to due process of law. While the lawsuit was pending, the administrative appeal process concluded, largely in Conner's favor. A deputy administrator reversed the disciplinary committee's finding of guilt on the obstruction charge and ordered all references to this guilty finding expunged from Conner's prison records.

The federal district court entered summary judgment for the prison officials in this case, finding that Conner was not deprived of the liberty protected by the Due Process Clause when he was transferred to disciplinary segregation. The Ninth Circuit Court of Appeals reversed. The court of appeals found that Conner's transfer out of the general-population unit deprived him of a state-created liberty interest stemming from a prison regulation that required a finding of guilt whenever a misconduct charge was supported by "substantial evidence."

The Supreme Court began its analysis in this case by discussing its decisions in *Wolff v. McDonnell*, 418 U.S. 539 (1974), supra page 570, and Meachum v. Fano, 427 U.S. 215 (1976), supra page 604.]

Shortly after *Meachum,* the Court embarked on a different approach to defining state-created liberty interests. * * *

* * *

As this methodology took hold, no longer did inmates need to rely on a showing that they had suffered a " 'grievous loss' " of liberty retained even after sentenced to terms of imprisonment. For the Court had ceased to examine the "nature" of the interest with respect to interests allegedly created by the State. In a series of cases since *Hewitt,* the Court has wrestled with the language of intricate, often rather routine prison guidelines to determine whether mandatory language and substantive predicates created an enforceable expectation that the state would produce a particular outcome with respect to the prisoner's conditions of confinement.

* * *

By shifting the focus of the liberty interest inquiry to one based on the language of a particular regulation, and not the nature of the deprivation, the Court encouraged prisoners to comb regulations in search of mandatory language on which to base entitlements to various state-conferred privileges. Courts have, in response, and not altogether illogically, drawn negative inferences from mandatory language in the text of prison regulations. The Court of Appeals' approach in this case is typical: it inferred from the mandatory directive that a finding of guilt "shall" be imposed under certain conditions the conclusion that the absence of such conditions prevents a finding of guilt.

Such a conclusion may be entirely sensible in the ordinary task of construing a statute defining rights and remedies available to the general public. It is a good deal less sensible in the case of a prison regulation primarily designed to guide correctional officials in the administration of a prison. Not only are such regulations not designed to confer rights on inmates, but the result of the negative implication jurisprudence is not to require the prison officials to follow the negative implication drawn from the regulation, but is instead to attach procedural protections that may be of quite a different nature. Here, for example, the Court of Appeals did not hold that a finding of guilt could *not* be made in the *absence* of substantial evidence. Instead, it held that the "liberty interest" created by the regulation entitled the inmate to the procedural protections set forth in *Wolff*.

Hewitt has produced at least two undesirable effects. First, it creates disincentives for States to codify prison management procedures in the interest of uniform treatment. Prison administrators need be concerned with the safety of the staff and inmate population. Ensuring that welfare often leads prison administrators to curb the discretion of staff on the front line who daily encounter prisoners hostile to the authoritarian structure of the prison environment. Such guidelines are not set forth solely to benefit the prisoner. They also aspire to instruct subordinate employees how to exercise discretion vested by the State in the warden, and to confine the authority of prison personnel in order to avoid widely different treatment of similar incidents. The approach embraced by *Hewitt* discourages this desirable development: States may avoid creation of "liberty" interests by having scarcely any regulations, or by conferring standardless discretion on correctional personnel.

Second, the *Hewitt* approach has led to the involvement of federal courts in the day-to-day management of prisons, often squandering judicial resources with little offsetting benefit to anyone. * * * See, *e.g., Segal v. Biller*, 1994 WL 594705 (C.A.9 Oct.31, 1994) (claiming liberty interest in a waiver of the travel limit imposed on prison furloughs); *Burgin v. Nix*, 899 F.2d 733, 735 (C.A.8 1990) (claiming liberty interest in receiving a tray lunch rather than a sack lunch); *Spruytte v. Walters*, 753 F.2d 498, 506–508 (C.A.6 1985) (finding liberty interest in receiving a paperback dictionary due to a rule that states a prisoner " 'may receive any book . . . which does not present a threat to the order or security of the institution' "); *Lyon v. Farrier*, 727 F.2d 766, 766–769 (C.A.8 1984) (claiming liberty interest in freedom from transfer to a smaller cell without electrical outlets for televisions and liberty interest in a prison job); *United*

States v. Michigan, 680 F.Supp. 270, 277 (W.D.Mich.1988) (finding liberty interest in not being placed on food loaf diet).

In light of the above discussion, we believe that the search for a negative implication from mandatory language in prisoner regulations has strayed from the real concerns undergirding the liberty protected by the Due Process Clause. The time has come to return to the due process principles we believe were correctly established and applied in *Wolff* and *Meachum*.[5] Following *Wolff,* we recognize that States may under certain circumstances create liberty interests which are protected by the Due Process Clause. See also *Board of Pardons v. Allen,* 482 U.S. 369 (1987). But these interests will be generally limited to freedom from restraint which, while not exceeding the sentence in such an unexpected manner as to give rise to protection by the Due Process Clause of its own force, see, *e.g., Vitek* [*v. Jones*], 445 U.S. [480], at 493 [1980](transfer to mental hospital), and *Washington* [*v. Harper*], 494 U.S. [210], at 221–222 [1990](involuntary administration of psychotropic drugs), nonetheless imposes atypical and significant hardship on the inmate in relation to the ordinary incidents of prison life.

Conner asserts, incorrectly, that any state action taken for a punitive reason encroaches upon a liberty interest under the Due Process Clause even in the absence of any state regulation. * * *

* * *

The punishment of incarcerated prisoners * * * effectuates prison management and prisoner rehabilitative goals. * * * Discipline by prison officials in response to a wide range of misconduct falls within the expected parameters of the sentence imposed by a court of law.

This case, though concededly punitive, does not present a dramatic departure from the basic conditions of Conner's indeterminate sentence. Although Conner points to dicta in cases implying that solitary confinement automatically triggers due process protection, this Court has not had the opportunity to address in an argued case the question whether disciplinary confinement of inmates itself implicates constitutional liberty interests. We hold that Conner's discipline in segregated confinement did not present the type of atypical, significant deprivation in which a state might conceivably create a liberty interest. The record shows that, at the time of Conner's punishment, disciplinary segregation, with insignificant exceptions, mirrored those conditions imposed upon inmates in administrative segregation and protective custody. We note also that the State expunged Conner's disciplinary record with respect to the "high misconduct" charge 9 months after Conner served time in segregation. Thus, Conner's confinement did not exceed similar, but totally discretionary

---

5. Such abandonment of *Hewitt's* methodology does not technically require us to overrule any holding of this Court. * * * Although it did locate a liberty interest in *Hewitt,* it concluded that due process required no additional procedural guarantees for the inmate. As such, its answer to the anterior question of whether the inmate possessed a liberty interest at all was unnecessary to the disposition of the case. * * *

confinement in either duration or degree of restriction. Indeed, the conditions at Halawa involve significant amounts of "lockdown time" even for inmates in the general population.[8] Based on a comparison between inmates inside and outside disciplinary segregation, the State's actions in placing him there for 30 days did not work a major disruption in his environment.

Nor does Conner's situation present a case where the State's action will inevitably affect the duration of his sentence. Nothing in Hawaii's code requires the parole board to deny parole in the face of a misconduct record or to grant parole in its absence, even though misconduct is by regulation a relevant consideration. The decision to release a prisoner rests on a myriad of considerations. And, the prisoner is afforded procedural protection at his parole hearing in order to explain the circumstances behind his misconduct record. The chance that a finding of misconduct will alter the balance is simply too attenuated to invoke the procedural guarantees of the Due Process Clause. The Court rejected a similar claim in *Meachum* (declining to afford relief on the basis that petitioner's transfer record might affect his future confinement and possibility of parole).[10]

We hold, therefore, that neither the Hawaii prison regulation in question, nor the Due Process Clause itself, afforded Conner a protected liberty interest that would entitle him to the procedural protections set forth in *Wolff*. The regime to which he was subjected as a result of the misconduct hearing was within the range of confinement to be normally expected for one serving an indeterminate term of 30 years to life.

JUSTICE GINSBURG, with whom JUSTICE STEVENS joins, dissenting.

* * *

Unlike the Court, I conclude that Conner had a liberty interest, protected by the Fourteenth Amendment's Due Process Clause, in avoiding the disciplinary confinement he endured. As Justice Breyer details, Conner's prison punishment effected a severe alteration in the conditions of his incarceration. Disciplinary confinement as punishment for "high misconduct" not only deprives prisoners of privileges for protracted periods; unlike administrative segregation and protective custody, disciplinary confinement also stigmatizes them and diminishes parole prospects. Those immediate and lingering consequences should suffice to qualify such confinement as liberty-depriving for purposes of Due Process Clause protection.

I see the Due Process Clause itself, not Hawaii's prison code, as the wellspring of the protection due Conner. Deriving protected liberty interests from mandatory language in local prison codes would make of the

---

8. General population inmates are confined to cells for anywhere between 12 and 16 hours a day, depending on their classification.

10. Again, we note that Hawaii expunged Conner's record with respect to the "high misconduct" charge, so he personally has no chance of receiving a delayed release from the parole board as a direct result of that allegation.

fundamental right something more in certain States, something less in others. Liberty that may vary from Ossining, New York, to San Quentin, California, does not resemble the "Liberty" enshrined among "unalienable Rights" with which all persons are "endowed by their Creator." Declaration of Independence.[2]

Deriving the prisoner's due process right from the code for his prison, moreover, yields this practical anomaly: a State that scarcely attempts to control the behavior of its prison guards may, for that very laxity, escape constitutional accountability; a State that tightly cabins the discretion of its prison workers may, for that attentiveness, become vulnerable to constitutional claims. An incentive for ruleless prison management disserves the State's penological goals and jeopardizes the welfare of prisoners.

* * *

Justice Breyer, with whom Justice Souter joins, dissenting.

* * *

* * * [I]t seems fairly clear * * * that the prison punishment here at issue deprived Conner of constitutionally protected "liberty." For one thing, the punishment worked a fairly major change in Conner's conditions. In the absence of the punishment, Conner, like other inmates in Halawa's general prison population would have left his cell and worked, taken classes, or mingled with others for eight *hours* each day. As a result of disciplinary segregation, however, Conner, for 30 days, had to spend his entire time alone in his cell (with the exception of 50 *minutes* each day on average for brief exercise and shower periods, during which he nonetheless remained isolated from other inmates and was constrained by leg irons and waist chains).

Moreover, irrespective of whether this punishment amounts to a deprivation of liberty *independent* of state law, here the prison's own disciplinary rules severely cabin the authority of prison officials to impose this kind of punishment. * * *

* * * The majority believes that the Court's present "cabining of discretion" standard reads the Constitution as providing procedural protection for trivial "rights," as, for example, where prison rules set forth specific standards for the content of prison meals. * * * It therefore imposes a minimum standard, namely that a deprivation falls within the Fourteenth Amendment's definition of "liberty" only if it "imposes atypical and significant hardship on the inmate in relation to the ordinary incidents of prison life."

---

2. The Court describes a category of liberty interest that is something less than the one the Due Process Clause itself shields, something more than anything a prison code provides. The State may create a liberty interest, the Court tells us, when "atypical and significant hardship [would be borne by] the inmate in relation to the ordinary incidents of prison life." What design lies beneath these key words? The Court ventures no examples, leaving consumers of the Court's work at sea, unable to fathom what would constitute an "atypical, significant deprivation," and yet not trigger protection under the Due Process Clause directly.

I am not certain whether or not the Court means this standard to change prior law radically. If so, its generality threatens the law with uncertainty * * *. There is no need, however, for a radical reading of this standard, nor any other significant change in present law, to achieve the majority's basic objective, namely to read the Constitution's Due Process Clause to protect inmates against deprivations of freedom that are important, not comparatively insignificant. * * *

Three sets of considerations, taken together, support my conclusion that the Court need not (and today's generally phrased minimum standard therefore does not) significantly revise current doctrine by deciding to remove minor prison matters from federal-court scrutiny. First, * * * there is a broad middle category of imposed restraints or deprivations that, considered by themselves, are neither obviously so serious as to fall within, nor obviously so insignificant as to fall without, the Clause's protection.

Second, the difficult line-drawing task that this middle category implies helps to explain why this Court developed its additional liberty-defining standard, which looks to local law (examining whether that local law creates a "liberty" by significantly limiting the discretion of local authorities to impose a restraint). * * *

* * * The fact that a further deprivation of an inmate's freedom takes place under local rules that cabin the authorities' discretionary power to impose the restraint suggests, *other things being equal,* that the matter is more likely to have played an important role in the life of the inmate. It suggests, other things being equal, that the matter is more likely of a kind to which procedural protections historically have applied, and where they normally prove useful, for such rules often *single out* an inmate and condition a deprivation upon the existence, or nonexistence, of particular facts. It suggests, other things being equal, that the matter will not involve highly judgmental administrative matters that call for the wise exercise of discretion—matters where courts reasonably should hesitate to second-guess prison administrators. It suggests, other things being equal, that the inmate will have thought that he himself, through control of his own behavior, could have avoided the deprivation, and thereby have believed that (in the absence of his misbehavior) the restraint fell outside the "sentence imposed" upon him. Finally, courts can identify the presence or absence of cabined discretion fairly easily and objectively, at least much of the time. These characteristics of "cabined discretion" mean that courts can use it as a kind of touchstone that can help them, when they consider the broad middle category of prisoner restraints, to separate those kinds of restraints that, in general, are more likely to call for constitutionally guaranteed procedural protection, from those that more likely do not. * * *

Third, there is, therefore, no need to apply the "discretion-cabining" approach—the basic purpose of which is to provide a somewhat more objective method for identifying deprivations of protected "liberty" within a broad middle-range of prisoner restraints—where a deprivation is unimportant enough (or so similar in nature to ordinary imprisonment) that it rather clearly falls *outside* that middle category. Prison, by design, restricts the inmates' freedom. And, one cannot properly view unimportant matters that happen to be the subject of prison regulations as substantially aggravating a loss that has already occurred. Indeed, a regulation about a minor matter, for example, a regulation that seems to cabin the discretionary power of a prison administrator to deprive an inmate of, say, a certain kind of lunch, may amount simply to an instruction to the administrator about how to do his job, rather than a guarantee to the inmate of a "right" to the status quo. Cf. *Colon v. Schneider,* 899 F.2d 660, 668 (C.A.7 1990) (rules governing use of Mace to subdue inmates "directed toward the prison staff, not the inmates").* * *

I recognize that, as a consequence, courts must separate the unimportant from the potentially significant, without the help of the more objective "discretion-cabining" test. Yet, making that judicial judgment seems no more difficult than many other judicial tasks. See *Goss v. Lopez,* 419 U.S. 565, 576 (1975) (*"de minimis"* line defining property interests under the Due Process Clause). It seems to me possible to separate less significant matters such as television privileges, "sack" versus "tray" lunches, playing the state lottery, attending an ex-stepfather's funeral, or the limits of travel when on prison furlough from more significant matters, such as the solitary confinement at issue here. Indeed, prison regulations themselves may help in this respect, such as the regulations here which separate (from more serious matters) "low moderate" and "minor" misconduct.

* * *

* * * I disagree with the majority's assertion about the relevance of the expungement. * * * How can a later expungement restore to Conner the liberty that, in fact, he had already lost? * * *

In sum, expungement or no, Conner suffered a deprivation that was significant, not insignificant. And, that deprivation took place under disciplinary rules that * * * do cabin official discretion sufficiently. I would therefore hold that Conner was deprived of "liberty" within the meaning of the Due Process Clause.

* * *

QUESTIONS AND POINTS FOR DISCUSSION

1. *Sandin* is not without its critics. In Leslie v. Doyle, 896 F.Supp. 771 (N.D.Ill.1995), Judge Milton Shadur criticized the Supreme Court's decision:

> [T]he consequence of taking *Sandin* at its word (as this Court is obliged to do) is to arm prison authorities, who have heretofore possessed uncircumscribed powers over the inmates within their custody only to a limited extent, with now-unrestrained power to punish those inmates by

arbitrary reassignment to the meaningfully more restrictive environment of segregated confinement. * * * That result—which effectively treats wrongful commitment to segregation as an inherent consequence, a sort of assumed risk, of being in prison to begin with—strikes this Court as one more befitting a totalitarian regime than our own, and it is hard to credit that outcome as flowing from a principled Supreme Court decision.

Id. at 773–74.

Do you agree or disagree with the Supreme Court's view of the way in which liberty interests are created in the prison context? After *Sandin v. Conner,* would an inmate's confinement in administrative segregation under any circumstances deprive the inmate of a liberty interest? Would the transfer of an inmate to a disciplinary-segregation unit under any circumstances deprive the inmate of a liberty interest? If so, identify the relevant circumstances. Consider these questions again after reading the Supreme Court's decision in Wilkinson v. Austin, 545 U.S. 209, 125 S.Ct. 2384 (2005), which can be found on page 625.

2. The time period that inmates are subject to segregated confinement can vary greatly and sometimes extend for years. See, e.g., Williams v. Norris, 277 Fed. Appx. 647, 648 (8th Cir. 2008) (prisoner had been confined twelve years in administrative segregation); Shoats v. Horn, 213 F.3d 140, 144 (3d Cir.2000) (eight years in administrative segregation). In Spence v. Senkowski, 1997 WL 394667, at *8 (N.D.N.Y.1997), the district court observed that considering the length of segregated confinement when determining whether that confinement deprived a prisoner of a liberty interest will inevitably produce inconsistent decisions because of judges' differing perceptions of the length of time needed for the segregated confinement to be considered "atypical and significant." Compare, e.g., Jones v. Baker, 155 F.3d 810, 812 (6th Cir.1998) (administrative segregation for 2½ years of prisoner implicated in correctional officer's murder during a prison riot did not deprive him of a liberty interest) and Colon v. Howard, 215 F.3d 227, 231–232 (2d Cir.2000) (305 days in disciplinary segregation deprived prisoner of a liberty interest). Is there a time period beyond which, in your opinion, segregated confinement presumptively effectuates a deprivation of a liberty interest? In answering that question, consider the results of research on the effects of solitary confinement on prisoners:

[S]trikingly similar negative psychological effects have been uncovered in a wide variety of studies of solitary confinement itself. The case studies reported anxiety, panic, rage, loss of control, appetite and sleep disturbances, self-mutilations, and other recurring themes and symptoms. Direct studies of the effects of prison isolation have documented a wide range of harmful psychological effects, including increases in negative attitudes and affect, insomnia, anxiety, panic, withdrawal, hypersensitivity, ruminations, cognitive dysfunction, hallucinations, loss of control, aggression, rage, paranoia, hopelessness, lethargy, depression, emotional breakdowns, self-mutilation, and suicidal impulses. Among the correlational studies of the relationship between housing type and various incident reports, self-mutilation is prevalent in isolated housing, as is deterioration of mental and physical health, other-directed violence, such as stabbings, attacks on staff, and property destruction, and collective violence. In addition, many of the negative effects of solitary confinement are analogous to the acute reactions of trauma victims and the psychiatric sequelae fit the common diagnostic criteria for victims of deprivation and constraint torture techniques.

There is not a single study of solitary confinement wherein non-voluntary confinement that lasted for longer than 10 days failed to result in negative psychological effects. The deleterious effects varied in severity and included hypertension, uncontrollable anger, hallucinations, psychosis, chronic depression, and suicidal thoughts and behavior.

Craig Haney & Mona Lynch, Regulating Prisons of the Future: A Psychological Analysis of Supermax and Solitary Confinement, 23 N.Y.U. Rev. L. & Soc. Change 477, 530 (1997).

3. Whether or not segregated confinement inflicts an "atypical and significant hardship" on a prisoner may depend on the prisons or parts of a prison with which conditions in the segregation unit are compared. The lower courts are divided on what is the proper comparative reference point. Wilkinson v. Austin, 545 U.S. 209, 223, 125 S.Ct. 2384, 2394 (2005) (listing cases). Some courts compare the conditions in segregation with those in the general-population unit; other courts compare conditions in disciplinary segregation with those that normally attend administrative segregation; and some courts compare conditions of segregation with segregation conditions in other prisons throughout the state. Compare, e.g., Hatch v. District of Columbia, 184 F.3d 846, 857 (D.C.Cir. 1999) (more onerous conditions at other prisons serve as a comparative baseline only if it is likely that prisoners serving sentences like those of the plaintiff both would be transferred to those prisons and subjected to those conditions) with Wagner v. Hanks, 128 F.3d 1173, 1175 (7th Cir.1997) (conditions should be compared with those in the most restrictive form of nondisciplinary confinement in any prison in the state). What, in your opinion, is the appropriate point of comparison under the Supreme Court's "atypical and significant hardship test" and why?

4. Most courts have concluded that *Sandin* does not apply to pretrial detainees. Surprenant v. Rivas, 424 F.3d 5, 17 (1st Cir. 2005) (listing cases). In other words, a pretrial detainee who allegedly violated jail rules is constitutionally entitled to certain procedural safeguards before being placed in disciplinary segregation. The courts have reasoned that since pretrial detainees have not been sentenced, the possibility of segregated confinement cannot implicitly fall within the terms of any prison or jail sentence. In addition, affording pretrial detainees such due-process protection can prevent veiled attempts to unconstitutionally punish detainees for crimes of which they have not been convicted.

5. Although the absence of a protected liberty interest often might preclude a prisoner from challenging a transfer to another prison or part of a prison on procedural-due-process grounds, could there be other constitutional bases for such a challenge? See, e.g., Allah v. Seiverling, 229 F.3d 220, 224 (3d Cir.2000) (*Sandin* does not foreclose claim, rooted in the right of access to the courts, that prisoner was placed in administrative segregation in retaliation for filing civil-rights suits against prison officials). For a case in which the

Supreme Court considered a prisoner's claim that his transfer to a maximum-security prison abridged his Fifth Amendment privilege against compelled self-incrimination, see McKune v. Lile, 536 U.S. 24, 122 S.Ct. 2017 (2002), on page 639.

6. Once a court concludes that certain actions of correctional officials deprived an inmate of liberty within the meaning of the Due Process Clause, the next question is what procedural safeguards must have been in place to protect the inmate from being deprived arbitrarily of that liberty. In Hewitt v. Helms, 459 U.S. 460, 103 S.Ct. 864 (1983), the Supreme Court addressed this question. *Hewitt* involved an inmate who was suspected of participating in a prison riot and transferred to the prison's administrative-segregation unit to await the completion of an investigation by prison officials and state police and the adjudication of disciplinary charges. While the Supreme Court in *Sandin v. Conner* discarded the test for state-created liberty interests applied in *Hewitt,* the second portion of the Court's opinion in *Hewitt*—its analysis of what "process" was "due" the plaintiff when he was transferred to administrative segregation—is still instructive. Pertinent excerpts from the Court's opinion, written by Justice Rehnquist, are set forth below:

> Under *Mathews v. Eldridge,* 424 U.S. 319, 335 (1976), we consider the private interests at stake in a governmental decision, the governmental interests involved, and the value of procedural requirements in determining what process is due under the Fourteenth Amendment. Respondent's private interest is not one of great consequence. He was merely transferred from one extremely restricted environment to an even more confined situation. Unlike disciplinary confinement the stigma of wrongdoing or misconduct does not attach to administrative segregation under Pennsylvania's prison regulations. Finally, there is no indication that administrative segregation will have any significant effect on parole opportunities.

> Petitioners had two closely related reasons for confining Helms to administrative segregation prior to conducting a hearing on the disciplinary charges against him. First, they concluded that if housed in the general population, Helms would pose a threat to the safety of other inmates and prison officials and to the security of the institution. Second, the prison officials believed that it was wiser to separate respondent from the general population until completion of state and institutional investigations of his role in the December 3 riot and the hearing on the charges against him. Plainly, these governmental interests are of great importance. The safety of the institution's guards and inmates is perhaps the most fundamental responsibility of the prison administration. Likewise, the isolation of a prisoner pending investigation of misconduct charges against him serves important institutional interests relating to the insulating of possible witnesses from coercion or harm.

> Neither of these grounds for confining Helms to administrative segregation involved decisions or judgments that would have been materially assisted by a detailed adversary proceeding. * * * In assessing the seriousness of a threat to institutional security, prison administrators necessarily draw on more than the specific facts surrounding a particular

incident; instead, they must consider the character of the inmates confined in the institution, recent and longstanding relations between prisoners and guards, prisoners *inter se,* and the like. In the volatile atmosphere of a prison, an inmate easily may constitute an unacceptable threat to the safety of other prisoners and guards even if he himself has committed no misconduct; rumor, reputation, and even more imponderable factors may suffice to spark potentially disastrous incidents. The judgment of prison officials in this context, like that of those making parole decisions, turns largely on "purely subjective evaluations and on predictions of future behavior;" indeed, the administrators must predict not just one inmate's future actions, as in parole, but those of an entire institution. Owing to the central role of these types of intuitive judgments, a decision that an inmate or group of inmates represents a threat to the institution's security would not be appreciably fostered by the trial-type procedural safeguards suggested by respondent.[7] * * *

Likewise, confining respondent to administrative segregation pending completion of the investigation of the disciplinary charges against him is not based on an inquiry requiring any elaborate procedural safeguards. * * *

* * *

We think an informal, nonadversary evidentiary review is sufficient both for the decision that an inmate represents a security threat and the decision to confine an inmate to administrative segregation pending completion of an investigation into misconduct charges against him. An inmate must merely receive some notice of the charges against him and an opportunity to present his views to the prison official charged with deciding whether to transfer him to administrative segregation. Ordinarily a written statement by the inmate will accomplish this purpose, although prison administrators may find it more useful to permit oral presentations in cases where they believe a written statement would be ineffective. So long as this occurs, and the decisionmaker reviews the charges and then-available evidence against the prisoner, the Due Process Clause is satisfied.[8] This informal procedure permits a reasonably accurate assessment of probable cause to believe that misconduct occurred, and the "value [of additional 'formalities and safeguards'] would be too slight to justify holding, as a matter of constitutional principle" that they must be adopted.[9]

---

7. Indeed, we think an administrator's judgment probably would be hindered. Prison officials, wary of potential legal liability, might well spend their time mechanically complying with cumbersome, marginally helpful procedural requirements, rather than managing their institution wisely.

8. The proceeding must occur within a reasonable time following an inmate's transfer, taking into account the relatively insubstantial private interest at stake and the traditionally broad discretion of prison officials.

[9]. Of course, administrative segregation may not be used as a pretext for indefinite confinement of an inmate. Prison officials must engage in some sort of periodic review of the confinement of such inmates. This review will not necessarily require that prison officials permit the submission of any additional evidence or statements. The decision whether a prisoner remains a security risk will be based on facts relating to a particular prisoner—which will have been ascertained when determining to confine the inmate to administrative segregation—and on the

Id. at 473–76, 103 S.Ct. at 872–74.

In a dissenting opinion in which Justices Brennan, Marshall, and Blackman joined, Justice Stevens disagreed that the procedural safeguards outlined by the majority satisfied the requirements of due process:

> The "touchstone of due process," as we pointed out in *Wolff v. McDonnell,* is "protection of the individual against arbitrary action of government." Pennsylvania may not arbitrarily place a prisoner in administrative segregation. The majority agrees with this general proposition, but I believe its standards guarding against arbitrariness fall short of what the Constitution requires.

> First, the majority declares that the Constitution is satisfied by an initial proceeding[16] with minimal participation by the inmate who is being transferred into administrative custody. * * *

> I agree with the Court that the Constitution does not require a hearing with all of the procedural safeguards set forth in *Wolff v. McDonnell* when prison officials initially decide to segregate an inmate to safeguard institutional security or to conduct an investigation of an unresolved misconduct charge. But unlike the majority, I believe that due process does require that the inmate be given the opportunity to present his views in person to the reviewing officials. As many prisoners have little education, limiting an inmate to a written statement is unlikely to provide a "meaningful opportunity to be heard" in accordance with due process principles.

> Of greater importance, the majority's due process analysis fails to provide adequate protection against arbitrary continuation of an inmate's solitary confinement.[18] * * *

* * *

officials' general knowledge of prison conditions and tensions, which are singularly unsuited for "proof" in any highly structured manner. Likewise, the decision to continue confinement of an inmate pending investigation of misconduct charges depends upon circumstances that prison officials will be well aware of—most typically, the progress of the investigation. In both situations, the ongoing task of operating the institution will require the prison officials to consider a wide range of administrative considerations; here, for example, petitioners had to consider prison tensions in the aftermath of the December 3 riot, the ongoing state criminal investigation, and so forth. The record plainly shows that on January 2 a Program Review Committee considered whether Helms' confinement should be continued. This review, occurring less than a month after the initial decision to confine Helms to administrative segregation, is sufficient to dispel any notions that the confinement was a pretext.

16. The Court of Appeals recognized that, in the emergency conditions on December 3, 1978, prison officials were justified in placing respondent in administrative segregation without a hearing. * * * The Due Process Clause allows prison officials flexibility to cope with emergencies. But petitioners acknowledge that the disturbance was "quelled" the same day and that, within a day or two after the December 3, 1978, prison riot, conditions had returned completely to normal. At that point the emergency rationale for administrative segregation without a hearing had expired. The Due Process Clause then required a prompt proceeding to determine whether continued administrative segregation was justified. Yet Helms was not accorded any procedural safeguards whatsoever until five days after the riot—another violation of his due process rights.

18. Unlike disciplinary custody, which is imposed for a fixed term, in practice administrative custody sometimes continues for lengthy or indefinite periods. See *Ruiz v. Estelle,* 503 F.Supp. 1265, 1365, 1367 (S.D.Tex.1980) ("months or even years"); *Mims v. Shapp,* 457 F.Supp. 247, 249 (W.D.Pa.1978) (five years); *United States ex rel. Hoss v. Cuyler,* 452 F.Supp. 256 (E.D.Pa.1978)

At each periodic review, I believe due process requires that the prisoner be allowed to make an oral statement about the need for and the consequences of continued confinement. Concededly some of the information relevant to a decision whether to continue confinement will be beyond the reach of a prisoner who has been held in segregated custody, including conditions in the general prison population and the progress of an ongoing investigation. But the prisoner should have the right to be present in order to explain his current attitude toward his past activities and his present circumstances, and the impact of solitary confinement on his rehabilitation program and training. These factors may change as the period of confinement continues.

Further, if the decisionmaker decides to retain the prisoner in segregation, I believe he should be required to explain his reasons in a brief written statement which is retained in the file and given to the prisoner. As Justice Marshall has written in a related prison context, this requirement would direct the decisionmaker's focus "to the relevant ... criteria and promote more careful consideration of the evidence. It would also enable inmates to detect and correct inaccuracies that could have a decisive impact. And the obligation to justify a decision publicly would provide the assurance, critical to the appearance of fairness, that the Board's decision is not capricious." A written statement of reasons would facilitate administrative and judicial review and might give the prisoner an opportunity to improve his conduct.

Neither a right to personal appearance by the prisoner nor a requirement of written reasons would impose an undue burden on prison officials. It is noteworthy that these procedural safeguards are provided in regulations governing both the Pennsylvania and federal prison systems. Given the importance of the prisoner's interest in returning to the general prison population, the benefits of additional procedural safeguards, and the minimal burden on prison officials, I am convinced that the Due Process Clause requires more substantial periodic reviews than the majority acknowledges.

Id. at 488–90, 494–96, 103 S.Ct. at 880–81, 883–84.

7. The Supreme Court in *Hewitt* purported to apply the three-pronged balancing test previously applied by the Court in Mathews v. Eldridge, 424 U.S. 319, 96 S.Ct. 893 (1976). In *Mathews*, the Court described the factors to be balanced as follows:

First, the private interest that will be affected by the official action; second, the risk of an erroneous deprivation of such interest through the procedures used, and the probable value, if any, of additional or substitute procedural safeguards; and finally, the Government's interest, including the function involved and the fiscal and administrative burdens that the additional or substitute procedural requirement would entail.

Id. at 335, 96 S.Ct. at 903. Did the Supreme Court in *Hewitt* apply the same balancing test described in *Mathews*?

(more than five years); *Wright v. Enomoto,* 462 F.Supp. 397, 403–404 (N.D.Cal.1976) (various instances up to a year).

8. Assuming that a transfer to administrative segregation implicates due process in some circumstances, questions remain about the process "due" an inmate confined in administrative segregation. Some of those questions include:

a. How specific must the notice of the reason for an inmate's transfer to administrative segregation be to pass constitutional muster? Compare Bills v. Henderson, 631 F.2d 1287, 1295 (6th Cir.1980) (notice to inmate that there was "sufficient cause to believe that his presence in the general population would constitute a threat to the welfare of other residents and to the good of the institution" was inadequate) with Shango v. Jurich, 608 F.Supp. 931, 937 (N.D.Ill.1985) (notice that inmate was being investigated for "extortion, sexual assault and trafficking, etc." was sufficient even though the specific instances when the inmate allegedly was involved in such misconduct were not revealed).

b. When must the reason for initially confining a prisoner in administrative segregation be reviewed to satisfy due process? Compare Soto v. Walker, 44 F.3d 169, 172 (2d Cir.1995) (7–day delay states due-process claim) with Sourbeer v. Robinson, 791 F.2d 1094, 1099 (3d Cir.1986) (35–day delay before hearing where inmate was permitted to present his views did not violate due process). Cf. Standard 4–4250 of the American Correctional Association's Standards for Adult Correctional Institutions (4th ed.2003) (although an inmate can immediately be placed in segregation when "necessary to protect the inmate or others," the "appropriate authority" must then review, within 72 hours, the propriety of the inmate's confinement in segregation).

c. How frequently must periodic reviews of an inmate's administrative confinement be conducted? Cf. Standard 4–4253 of the American Correctional Association's Standards for Adult Correctional Institutions (4th ed.2003) (review every seven days for first two months and then every thirty days). Some guidance to answer this question can be found in Wilkinson v. Austin, 545 U.S. 209, 125 S.Ct. 2384 (2005), infra page 624. One of the due-process issues the Supreme Court addressed in that case was the permissible amount of time that could elapse between periodic reviews of the appropriateness of a prisoner's confinement in a supermaximum prison.

d. Must any steps be taken to guard against perfunctory periodic reviews of an inmate's confinement in administrative segregation? See McClary v. Coughlin, 87 F.Supp.2d 205, 214–15 (W.D.N.Y.2000), aff'd, 237 F.3d 185 (2d Cir.2001) (repeated references over a four-year period to the "notoriety" of the inmate's crime—he murdered a police officer—as a justification for his confinement in administrative segregation did not provide him with the "meaningful" periodic review to which he was constitutionally entitled); United States ex rel. Hoss v. Cuyler, 452 F.Supp. 256, 295 (E.D.Pa.1978) (inmate has a right to "more than a periodical *ipse dixit* pronouncement that he is a 'security case' "). Some courts have held that the periodic-review process is not a "sham" when "some evidence" with "some indicia of reliability" is adduced to support the prisoner's continued detention in segregation. See, e.g., Williams v. Cambra, 1998 WL 387617, at *3 (N.D.Cal.1998).

9. Assuming that a prisoner's confinement in disciplinary segregation can, in some circumstances, deprive the inmate of a liberty interest, to what procedural safeguards would an inmate confined in disciplinary segregation be entitled in your opinion? The procedural safeguards set forth in *Hewitt v. Helms*? The procedural safeguards required in *Wolff v. McDonnell*? Some other mixture of procedural safeguards?

In applying the *Mathews* balancing test to a prisoner's disciplinary confinement, consider the observations made by one attorney, who was representing correctional officials, about how the state's interest in promoting institutional security is better protected by incorporating procedural safeguards into the decision-making process preceding disciplinary confinement:

> To have an inmate and just put him in [a] special housing unit because he doesn't have a per se liberty interest would cause such an unrest within the prison system that it would be unlivable and would not be able to function as a prison. * * * It is a way to make sure that innocent people are not going, spending significant time in punitive segregation.... You can't run a prison like that. It would be impossible from an inmate's point of view to not have these kind of Tier E [III] hearings.

Lee v. Coughlin, 26 F.Supp.2d 615, 636 (S.D.N.Y.1998). Consider also what import the following Supreme Court case has to the question of what procedural safeguards a prisoner is entitled to when confinement in a disciplinary-segregation unit effects a deprivation of liberty within the meaning of due process.

WILKINSON v. AUSTIN

Supreme Court of the United States, 2005.
545 U.S. 209, 125 S.Ct. 2384 162 L.Ed.2d 174.

JUSTICE KENNEDY delivered the opinion of the Court.

This case involves the process by which Ohio classifies prisoners for placement at its highest security prison, known as a "Supermax" facility. Supermax facilities are maximum-security prisons with highly restrictive conditions, designed to segregate the most dangerous prisoners from the general prison population. We must consider what process the Fourteenth Amendment to the United States Constitution requires Ohio to afford to inmates before assigning them to Supermax. * * *

I

* * * In 1998, Ohio opened its only Supermax facility, the Ohio State Penitentiary (OSP), after a riot in one of its maximum-security prisons. OSP has the capacity to house up to 504 inmates in single-inmate cells and is designed to " 'separate the most predatory and dangerous prisoners from the rest of the ... general [prison] population.' "

Conditions at OSP are more restrictive than any other form of incarceration in Ohio, including conditions on its death row or in its administrative control units. * * * In the OSP almost every aspect of an inmate's life is controlled and monitored. Inmates must remain in their cells, which measure 7 by 14 feet, for 23 hours per day. A light remains on in the cell at all times, though it is sometimes dimmed, and an inmate who attempts to shield the light to sleep is subject to further discipline. During the one hour per day that an inmate may leave his cell, access is limited to one of two indoor recreation cells.

Incarceration at OSP is synonymous with extreme isolation. In contrast to any other Ohio prison, including any segregation unit, OSP cells have solid metal doors with metal strips along their sides and bottoms which prevent conversation or communication with other inmates. All meals are taken alone in the inmate's cell instead of in a common eating area. Opportunities for visitation are rare and in all events are conducted through glass walls. It is fair to say OSP inmates are deprived of almost any environmental or sensory stimuli and of almost all human contact.

Aside from the severity of the conditions, placement at OSP is for an indefinite period of time, limited only by an inmate's sentence. For an inmate serving a life sentence, there is no indication how long he may be incarcerated at OSP once assigned there. Inmates otherwise eligible for parole lose their eligibility while incarcerated at OSP.

Placement at OSP is determined in the following manner: Upon entering the prison system, all Ohio inmates are assigned a numerical security classification from level 1 through level 5, with 1 the lowest security risk and 5 the highest. The initial security classification is based on numerous factors (*e.g.*, the nature of the underlying offense, criminal history, or gang affiliation) but is subject to modification at any time during the inmate's prison term if, for instance, he engages in misconduct or is deemed a security risk. Level 5 inmates are placed in OSP * * *.

Ohio concedes that when OSP first became operational, the procedures used to assign inmates to the facility were inconsistent and undefined. * * * Haphazard placements were not uncommon, and some individuals who did not pose high-security risks were designated, nonetheless, for OSP. * * * After forming a committee to study the matter and retaining a national expert in prison security, Ohio promulgated the New Policy in early 2002. The New Policy provided more guidance regarding the factors to be considered in placement decisions and afforded inmates more procedural protection against erroneous placement at OSP.

* * * The New Policy appears to operate as follows: A classification review for OSP placement can occur either (1) upon entry into the prison system if the inmate was convicted of certain offenses, *e.g.*, organized crime, or (2) during the term of incarceration if an inmate engages in specified conduct, *e.g.*, leads a prison gang. The review process begins when a prison official prepares a "Security Designation Long Form" (Long Form). This three-page form details matters such as the inmate's recent violence, escape attempts, gang affiliation, underlying offense, and other pertinent details.

A three-member Classification Committee (Committee) convenes to review the proposed classification and to hold a hearing. At least 48 hours before the hearing, the inmate is provided with written notice summarizing the conduct or offense triggering the review. At the time of notice, the inmate also has access to the Long Form, which details why the review was initiated. The inmate may attend the hearing, may "offer any pertinent information, explanation and/or objections to [OSP] placement," and may submit a written statement. He may not call witnesses.

If the Committee does not recommend OSP placement, the process terminates. If the Committee does recommend OSP placement, it documents the decision on a "Classification Committee Report" (CCR), setting forth "the nature of the threat the inmate presents and the committee's reasons for the recommendation," as well as a summary of any information presented at the hearing. The Committee sends the completed CCR to the warden of the prison where the inmate is housed or, in the case of an inmate just entering the prison system, to another designated official.

If, after reviewing the CCR, the warden (or the designated official) disagrees and concludes that OSP is inappropriate, the process terminates and the inmate is not placed in OSP. If the warden agrees, he indicates his approval on the CCR, provides his reasons, and forwards the annotated CCR to the Bureau of Classification (Bureau) for a final decision. (The Bureau is a body of Ohio prison officials vested with final decisionmaking authority over all Ohio inmate assignments.) The annotated CCR is served upon the inmate, notifying him of the Classification Committee's and warden's recommendations and reasons. The inmate has 15 days to file any objections with the Bureau of Classification.

After the 15–day period, the Bureau of Classification reviews the CCR and makes a final determination. If it concludes OSP placement is inappropriate, the process terminates. If the Bureau approves the warden's recommendation, the inmate is transferred to OSP. The Bureau's chief notes the reasons for the decision on the CCR, and the CCR is again provided to the inmate.

Inmates assigned to OSP receive another review within 30 days of their arrival. That review is conducted by a designated OSP staff member, who examines the inmate's file. If the OSP staff member deems the inmate inappropriately placed, he prepares a written recommendation to the OSP warden that the inmate be transferred to a lower security institution. If the OSP warden concurs, he forwards that transfer recommendation to the Bureau of Classification for appropriate action. If the inmate is deemed properly placed, he remains in OSP and his placement is reviewed on at least an annual basis according to the initial three-tier classification review process outlined above.

II

This action began when a class of current and former OSP inmates brought suit under Rev. Stat. § 1979, 42 U.S.C. § 1983, in the United

States District Court for the Northern District of Ohio against various Ohio prison officials. * * *

The inmates' complaint alleged that Ohio's Old Policy, which was in effect at the time the suit was brought, violated due process. * * * The inmates' suit sought declaratory and injunctive relief. On the eve of trial Ohio promulgated its New Policy and represented that it contained the procedures to be followed in the future. The District Court and Court of Appeals evaluated the adequacy of the New Policy, and it therefore forms the basis for our determination here.

* * * [T]he District Court found Ohio had denied the inmates due process by failing to afford a large number of them notice and an adequate opportunity to be heard before transfer; failing to give inmates sufficient notice of the grounds serving as the basis for their retention at OSP; and failing to give the inmates sufficient opportunity to understand the reasoning and evidence used to retain them at OSP. * * *

* * * The following are some of the procedural modifications the District Court ordered:

(1) Finding that the notice provisions of Ohio's New Policy were inadequate, the District Court ordered Ohio to provide the inmates with an exhaustive list of grounds believed to justify placement at OSP and a summary of all evidence upon which the Classification Committee would rely. Matters not so identified, the District Court ordered, could not be considered by the Committee.

(2) The District Court supplemented the inmate's opportunity to appear before the Committee and to make an oral or written statement by ordering Ohio to allow inmates to present documentary evidence and call witnesses before the Committee, provided that doing so would not be unduly hazardous or burdensome. The District Court further ordered that Ohio must attempt to secure the participation of any witness housed within the prison system.

(3) Finding the New Policy's provision of a brief statement of reasons for a recommendation of OSP placement inadequate, the District Court ordered the Classification Committee to summarize all evidence supporting its recommendation. Likewise, the District Court ordered the Bureau of Classification to prepare a "detailed and specific" statement "set [ting] out all grounds" justifying OSP placement including "facts relied upon and reasoning used." The statement shall "not use conclusory," "vague," or "boilerplate language," and must be delivered to the inmate within five days.

(4) The District Court supplemented the New Policy's 30–day and annual review processes, ordering Ohio to notify the inmate twice per year both in writing and orally of his progress toward a security level reduction. Specifically, that notice must "advise the inmate what specific conduct is necessary for that prisoner to be reduced from

Level 5 and the amount of time it will take before [Ohio] reduces the inmate's security level classification.''

* * * The Court of Appeals * * * affirmed the District Court's procedural modifications in their entirety. * * *

* * *

III

* * * We need reach the question of what process is due only if the inmates establish a constitutionally protected liberty interest, so it is appropriate to address this threshold question at the outset.

* * *

We have held that the Constitution itself does not give rise to a liberty interest in avoiding transfer to more adverse conditions of confinement. *Meachum v. Fano,* 427 U.S. 215, 225 (1976). We have also held, however, that a liberty interest in avoiding particular conditions of confinement may arise from state policies or regulations, subject to the important limitations set forth in *Sandin v. Conner,* 515 U.S. 472 (1995).

* * *

The *Sandin* standard requires us to determine if assignment to OSP "imposes atypical and significant hardship on the inmate in relation to the ordinary incidents of prison life." In *Sandin*'s wake the Courts of Appeals have not reached consistent conclusions for identifying the baseline from which to measure what is atypical and significant in any particular prison system. * * * We need not resolve the issue here, however, for we are satisfied that assignment to OSP imposes an atypical and significant hardship under any plausible baseline.

For an inmate placed in OSP, almost all human contact is prohibited, even to the point that conversation is not permitted from cell to cell; the light, though it may be dimmed, is on for 24 hours; exercise is for 1 hour per day, but only in a small indoor room. Save perhaps for the especially severe limitations on all human contact, these conditions likely would apply to most solitary confinement facilities, but here there are two added components. First is the duration. Unlike the 30–day placement in *Sandin*, placement at OSP is indefinite and, after an initial 30–day review, is reviewed just annually. Second is that placement disqualifies an otherwise eligible inmate for parole consideration. While any of these conditions standing alone might not be sufficient to create a liberty interest, taken together they impose an atypical and significant hardship within the correctional context. It follows that respondents have a liberty interest in avoiding assignment to OSP.

* * *

IV

A liberty interest having been established, we turn to the question of what process is due an inmate whom Ohio seeks to place in OSP. * * *

* * *

Applying the three factors set forth in *Mathews* [*v. Eldridge*, 424 U.S. 319 (1976)], we find Ohio's New Policy provides a sufficient level of process. We first consider the significance of the inmate's interest in avoiding erroneous placement at OSP. Prisoners held in lawful confinement have their liberty curtailed by definition, so the procedural protections to which they are entitled are more limited than in cases where the right at stake is the right to be free from confinement at all. See, *e.g.,* *Wolff* [*v. McDonnell*], 418 U.S. 539 [1974]. The private interest at stake here, while more than minimal, must be evaluated, nonetheless, within the context of the prison system and its attendant curtailment of liberties.

The second factor addresses the risk of an erroneous placement under the procedures in place, and the probable value, if any, of additional or alternative procedural safeguards. The New Policy provides that an inmate must receive notice of the factual basis leading to consideration for OSP placement and a fair opportunity for rebuttal. * * * Requiring officials to provide a brief summary of the factual basis for the classification review and allowing the inmate a rebuttal opportunity safeguards against the inmate's being mistaken for another or singled out for insufficient reason. In addition to having the opportunity to be heard at the Classification Committee stage, Ohio also invites the inmate to submit objections prior to the final level of review. This second opportunity further reduces the possibility of an erroneous deprivation.

* * *

If the recommendation is OSP placement, Ohio requires that the decisionmaker provide a short statement of reasons. This requirement guards against arbitrary decisionmaking while also providing the inmate a basis for objection before the next decisionmaker or in a subsequent classification review. The statement also serves as a guide for future behavior.

As we have noted, Ohio provides multiple levels of review for any decision recommending OSP placement, with power to overturn the recommendation at each level. In addition to these safeguards, Ohio further reduces the risk of erroneous placement by providing for a placement review within 30 days of an inmate's initial assignment to OSP.

The third *Mathews* factor addresses the State's interest. In the context of prison management, and in the specific circumstances of this case, this interest is a dominant consideration. * * * The State's first obligation must be to ensure the safety of guards and prison personnel, the public, and the prisoners themselves.

Prison security, imperiled by the brutal reality of prison gangs, provides the backdrop of the State's interest. Clandestine, organized, fueled by race-based hostility, and committed to fear and violence as a means of disciplining their own members and their rivals, gangs seek nothing less than to control prison life and to extend their power outside prison walls. Murder of an inmate, a guard, or one of their family members on the outside is a common form of gang discipline and control, as well as a condition for membership in some gangs. * * * It is worth noting in this regard that for prison gang members serving life sentences, some without the possibility of parole, the deterrent effects of ordinary criminal punishment may be substantially diminished.

The problem of scarce resources is another component of the State's interest. The cost of keeping a single prisoner in one of Ohio's ordinary maximum-security prisons is $34,167 per year, and the cost to maintain each inmate at OSP is $49,007 per year. We can assume that Ohio, or any other penal system, faced with costs like these will find it difficult to fund more effective education and vocational assistance programs to improve the lives of the prisoners. It follows that courts must give substantial deference to prison management decisions before mandating additional expenditures for elaborate procedural safeguards when correctional officials conclude that a prisoner has engaged in disruptive behavior.

The State's interest must be understood against this background. Were Ohio to allow an inmate to call witnesses or provide other attributes of an adversary hearing before ordering transfer to OSP, both the State's immediate objective of controlling the prisoner and its greater objective of controlling the prison could be defeated. This problem, moreover, is not alleviated by providing an exemption for witnesses who pose a hazard, for nothing in the record indicates simple mechanisms exist to determine when witnesses may be called without fear of reprisal. The danger to witnesses, and the difficulty in obtaining their cooperation, make the probable value of an adversary-type hearing doubtful in comparison to its obvious costs.

A balance of the *Mathews* factors yields the conclusion that Ohio's New Policy is adequate to safeguard an inmate's liberty interest in not being assigned to OSP. Ohio is not, for example, attempting to remove an inmate from free society for a specific parole violation, see, *e.g., Morrissey* [*v. Brewer*], 408 U.S. [471, 481 (1972)], or to revoke good time credits for specific, serious misbehavior, see, *e.g., Wolff,* 418 U.S., at 539, where more formal, adversary-type procedures might be useful. Where the inquiry draws more on the experience of prison administrators, and where the State's interest implicates the safety of other inmates and prison personnel, the informal, nonadversary procedures set forth in *Greenholtz v. Inmates of Neb. Penal and Correctional Complex,* 442 U.S. 1 (1979), and *Hewitt v. Helms,* 459 U.S. 460, provide the appropriate model. *Greenholtz, supra,* at 16 (level of process due for inmates being considered for release on parole includes opportunity to be heard and notice of any adverse decision); *Hewitt, supra,* at 473–476 (level of process due for inmates being considered for transfer to administrative segregation includes some notice of charges and an opportunity to be heard). Although *Sandin* abrogated *Greenholtz*'s and *Hewitt*'s methodology for establishing the liberty interest, these cases remain instructive for their discussion of the appropriate level of procedural safeguards. * * *

* * *

* * * We now hold that the New Policy as described in this opinion strikes a constitutionally permissible balance between the factors of the *Mathews* framework. If an inmate were to demonstrate that the New Policy did not in practice operate in this fashion, resulting in a cognizable injury, that could be the subject of an appropriate future challenge. * * *

VITEK v. JONES

Supreme Court of the United States, 1980.
445 U.S. 480, 100 S.Ct. 1254, 63 L.Ed.2d 552.

[The plaintiff in this case, a prisoner incarcerated in Nebraska, brought a § 1983 suit claiming that he was deprived of liberty without due process of law when he was transferred to a state mental hospital. The plaintiff was transferred under a Nebraska statute, Neb.Rev.Stat. § 83–180(1), which provided in part as follows:

When a physician designated by the Director of Correctional Services finds that a person committed to the department suffers from a physical disease or defect, or when a physician or psychologist designated by the director finds that a person committed to the department suffers from a mental disease or defect, the chief executive officer may order such person to be segregated from other persons in the facility. If the physician or psychologist is of the opinion that the person cannot be given proper treatment in that facility, the director may arrange for his transfer for examination, study, and treatment to any medical-correctional facility, or to another institution in the Department of Public Institutions where proper treatment is available.

The Supreme Court discussed the plaintiff's due-process claim in an opinion written by Justice White. Parts I, II, III, IV–A, and V of Justice White's opinion constituted the Court's majority opinion. Excerpts from Parts III, IV, and V of that opinion are set forth below.]

III

* * *

* * * Section 83–180(1) * * * gave Jones a liberty interest that entitled him to the benefits of appropriate procedures in connection with determining the conditions that warranted his transfer to a mental hospital. * * *

* * *

The District Court was also correct in holding that independently of § 83–180(1), the transfer of a prisoner from a prison to a mental hospital must be accompanied by appropriate procedural protections. The issue is whether after a conviction for robbery, Jones retained a residuum of liberty that would be infringed by a transfer to a mental hospital without complying with minimum requirements of due process.

* * * The loss of liberty produced by an involuntary commitment is more than a loss of freedom from confinement. It is indisputable that commitment to a mental hospital "can engender adverse social consequences to the individual" and that "[w]hether we label this phenomena 'stigma' or choose to call it something else . . . we recognize that it can occur and that it can have a very significant impact on the individual." Also, "[a]mong the historic liberties" protected by the Due Process Clause is the "right to be free from, and to obtain judicial relief for, unjustified intrusions on personal security." Compelled treatment in the form of mandatory behavior modification programs, to which the District Court found Jones was exposed in this case, was a proper factor to be weighed by the District Court.

* * *

Appellants maintain that the transfer of a prisoner to a mental hospital is within the range of confinement justified by imposition of a prison sentence, at least after certification by a qualified person that a prisoner suffers from a mental disease or defect. We cannot agree. None of our decisions holds that conviction for a crime entitles a State not only to confine the convicted person but also to determine that he has a mental illness and to subject him involuntarily to institutional care in a mental hospital. Such consequences visited on the prisoner are qualitatively different from the punishment characteristically suffered by a person convicted of crime. * * * [I]nvoluntary commitment to a mental hospital is not within the range of conditions of confinement to which a prison sentence subjects an individual. A criminal conviction and sentence of imprisonment extinguish an individual's right to freedom from confinement for the term of his sentence, but they do not authorize the State to classify him as mentally ill and to subject him to involuntary psychiatric treatment without affording him additional due process protections.

In light of the findings made by the District Court, Jones' involuntary transfer to the Lincoln Regional Center pursuant to § 83–180, for the purpose of psychiatric treatment, implicated a liberty interest protected by the Due Process Clause. * * * [T]he stigmatizing consequences of a transfer to a mental hospital for involuntary psychiatric treatment, coupled with the subjection of the prisoner to mandatory behavior modification as a treatment for mental illness, constitute the kind of deprivations of liberty that requires procedural protections.

IV

The District Court held that to afford sufficient protection to the liberty interest it had identified, the State was required to observe the following minimum procedures before transferring a prisoner to a mental hospital:

"A.   Written notice to the prisoner that a transfer to a mental hospital is being considered;

"B.   A hearing, sufficiently after the notice to permit the prisoner to prepare, at which disclosure to the prisoner is made of the evidence being relied upon for the transfer and at which an opportunity to be heard in person and to present documentary evidence is given;

"C.   An opportunity at the hearing to present testimony of witnesses by the defense and to confront and cross-examine witnesses called by the state, except upon a finding, not arbitrarily made, of good cause for not permitting such presentation, confrontation, or cross-examination;

"D.   An independent decisionmaker;

"E.   A written statement by the factfinder as to the evidence relied on and the reasons for transferring the inmate;

"F.   Availability of legal counsel, furnished by the state, if the inmate is financially unable to furnish his own; and

"G.   Effective and timely notice of all the foregoing rights."

A

We think the District Court properly identified and weighed the relevant factors in arriving at its judgment. Concededly the interest of the State in segregating and treating mentally ill patients is strong. The interest of the prisoner in not being arbitrarily classified as mentally ill and subjected to unwelcome treatment is also powerful, however; and as the District Court found, the risk of error in making the determinations required by § 83–180 is substantial enough to warrant appropriate procedural safeguards against error.

We recognize that the inquiry involved in determining whether or not to transfer an inmate to a mental hospital for treatment involves a question that is essentially medical. The question whether an individual is mentally ill and cannot be treated in prison "turns on the meaning of the facts which must be interpreted by expert psychiatrists and psychologists." The medical nature of the inquiry, however, does not justify dispensing with due process requirements. It is precisely "[t]he subtleties and nuances of psychiatric diagnoses" that justify the requirement of adversary hearings.

Because prisoners facing involuntary transfer to a mental hospital are threatened with immediate deprivation of liberty interests they are currently enjoying and because of the inherent risk of a mistaken transfer, the District Court properly determined that procedures similar to those required by the Court in *Morrissey v. Brewer*, 408 U.S. 471 (1972), were appropriate in the circumstances present here.

The notice requirement imposed by the District Court no more than recognizes that notice is essential to afford the prisoner an opportunity to challenge the contemplated action and to understand the nature of what is happening to him. Furthermore, in view of the nature of the determinations that must accompany the transfer to a mental hospital, we think each of the elements of the hearing specified by the District Court was appropriate. The interests of the State in avoiding disruption was recognized by limiting in appropriate circumstances the prisoner's right to call witnesses, to confront and cross examine. The District Court also avoided unnecessary intrusion into either medical or correctional judgments by providing that the independent decisionmaker conducting the transfer hearing need not come from outside the prison or hospital administration.

B*

The District Court did go beyond the requirements imposed by prior cases by holding that counsel must be made available to inmates facing transfer hearings if they are financially unable to furnish their own. We have not required the automatic appointment of counsel for indigent prisoners facing other deprivations of liberty, *Gagnon v. Scarpelli,* 411 U.S., at 790 [probation revocation]; *Wolff v. McDonnell,* [418 U.S.] at 569–570 [revocation of good-time credits]; but we have recognized that prisoners who are illiterate and uneducated have a greater need for assistance in exercising their rights. *Gagnon v. Scarpelli, supra,* at 786–787; *Wolff v. McDonnell, supra,* at 570. A prisoner thought to be suffering from a mental disease or defect requiring involuntary treatment probably has an even greater need for legal assistance, for such a prisoner is more likely to be unable to understand or exercise his rights. In these circumstances, it is appropriate that counsel be provided to indigent prisoners whom the State seeks to treat as mentally ill.

V

Because Mr. Justice Powell, while believing that Jones was entitled to competent help at the hearing, would not require the State to furnish a licensed attorney to aid him, the judgment below is affirmed as modified to conform with the separate opinion filed by Mr. Justice Powell.

* * *

MR. JUSTICE POWELL, concurring in part.

I join the opinion of the Court except for Part IV–B. I agree with Part IV–B insofar as the Court holds that qualified and independent assistance must be provided to an inmate who is threatened with involuntary transfer to a state mental hospital. I do not agree, however, that the requirement of independent assistance demands that a licensed attorney be provided.

* * *

---

* This part is joined only by Mr. Justice Brennan, Mr. Justice Marshall, and Mr. Justice Stevens.

The essence of procedural due process is a fair hearing. I do not think that the fairness of an informal hearing designed to determine a medical issue requires participation by lawyers. Due process merely requires that the State provide an inmate with qualified and independent assistance. Such assistance may be provided by a licensed psychiatrist or other mental health professional. Indeed, in view of the nature of the issue involved in the transfer hearing, a person possessing such professional qualifications normally would be preferred. * * * I would not exclude, however, the possibility that the required assistance may be rendered by competent laymen in some cases. The essential requirements are that the person provided by the State be competent and independent, and that he be free to act solely in the inmate's best interest.

In sum, although the State is free to appoint a licensed attorney to represent an inmate, it is not constitutionally required to do so. Due process will be satisfied so long as an inmate facing involuntary transfer to a mental hospital is provided qualified and independent assistance.

[Four Justices—Stewart, Burger, Rehnquist, and Blackmun—dissented on the grounds that the case was mooted by the plaintiff's release on parole.]

QUESTIONS AND POINTS FOR DISCUSSION

1. Compare the procedural safeguards required by the Supreme Court in *Wilkinson v. Austin*, *Vitek v. Jones*, and *Wolff v. McDonnell*, supra page 570. Can you reconcile the three cases? If so, how? In your opinion, did any of the cases incorrectly construe the scope of the procedural safeguards to which inmates are constitutionally entitled?

2. In Washington v. Harper, 494 U.S. 210, 110 S.Ct. 1028 (1990), the Supreme Court addressed procedural-due-process issues stemming from the involuntary administration of psychotropic drugs to mentally ill prisoners. The pertinent facts of the case were described by Justice Kennedy in his opinion for the Court:

Policy 600.30 * * * has several substantive and procedural components. First, if a psychiatrist determines that an inmate should be treated with antipsychotic drugs but the inmate does not consent, the inmate may be subjected to involuntary treatment with the drugs only if he (1) suffers from a "mental disorder" and (2) is "gravely disabled" or poses a "likelihood of serious harm" to himself, others, or their property. Only a psychiatrist may order or approve the medication. Second, an inmate who refuses to take the medication voluntarily is entitled to a hearing before a special committee consisting of a psychiatrist, psychologist, and the Associate Superintendent of the Center, none of whom may be, at the time of the hearing, involved in the inmate's treatment or diagnosis. If the committee determines by a majority vote that the inmate suffers from a mental disorder and is gravely disabled or dangerous, the inmate may be medicated against his will, provided the psychiatrist is in the majority.

Third, the inmate has certain procedural rights before, during, and after the hearing. He must be given at least 24 hours' notice of the Center's intent to convene an involuntary medication hearing, during which time he may not be medicated. In addition, he must receive notice of the tentative diagnosis, the factual basis for the diagnosis, and why the staff believes medication is necessary. At the hearing, the inmate has the right to attend; to present evidence, including witnesses; to cross-examine staff witnesses; and to the assistance of a lay advisor who has not been involved in his case and who understands the psychiatric issues involved. Minutes of the hearing must be kept, and a copy provided to the inmate. The inmate has the right to appeal the committee's decision to the Superintendent of the Center within 24 hours, and the Superintendent must decide the appeal within 24 hours after its receipt. The inmate may seek judicial review of a committee decision in state court by means of a personal restraint petition or extraordinary writ.

Fourth, after the initial hearing, involuntary medication can continue only with periodic review. When respondent first refused medication, a committee, again composed of a non-treating psychiatrist, a psychologist, and the Center's Associate Superintendent, was required to review an inmate's case after the first seven days of treatment. If the committee reapproved the treatment, the treating psychiatrist was required to review the case and prepare a report for the Department of Corrections medical director every 14 days while treatment continued.

In this case, respondent was absent when members of the Center staff met with the committee before the hearing. The committee then conducted the hearing in accordance with the Policy, with respondent being present and assisted by a nurse practitioner from another institution. The committee found that respondent was a danger to others as a result of a mental disease or disorder, and approved the involuntary administration of antipsychotic drugs. On appeal, the Superintendent upheld the committee's findings. Beginning on November 23, 1982, respondent was involuntarily medicated for about one year. Periodic review occurred in accordance with the Policy.

In November 1983, respondent was transferred from the Center to the Washington State Reformatory. While there, he took no medication, and as a result, his condition deteriorated. He was retransferred to the Center after only one month. Respondent was the subject of another committee hearing in accordance with Policy 600.30, and the committee again approved medication against his will. Respondent continued to receive antipsychotic drugs, subject to the required periodic reviews, until he was transferred to the Washington State Penitentiary in June 1986.

Id. at 215–17, 110 S.Ct. at 1033–34.

In February of 1985, the respondent filed a § 1983 suit in which he claimed that the compulsory administration of antipsychotic drugs violated a number of his rights, including his right to procedural due process under the Fourteenth Amendment. In addressing this claim, the Supreme Court first observed that when the respondent was given antipsychotic medication over his objection, he was deprived of both a constitutionally-derived and a state-created liberty interest. The source of the latter interest was the written prison policy dictating the circumstances under which inmates could be treated involuntarily with antipsychotic drugs.

The Court then rejected the respondent's argument that before being deprived of the liberty interest in not being involuntarily medicated with antipsychotic drugs, the decision had to be approved by a judge after a judicial hearing. The Court acknowledged that antipsychotic drugs can cause serious adverse side effects and even death. (Some of these side effects are listed in an excerpt on page 760 from the dissenting opinion of Justice Stevens.) The Court opined, however, that "an inmate's interests are adequately protected, and perhaps better served, by allowing the decision to medicate to be made by medical professionals rather than a judge," since medical professionals might be better able to assess the need for, and the risks posed by, certain medications. Id. at 231–33, 110 S.Ct. at 1042–43. Due process therefore was satisfied as long as the decision to medicate a prisoner involuntarily was reviewed by "independent" medical professionals. Id. at 233, 110 S.Ct. at 1043. In this particular case, this requirement was met, according to the Court, because the review panel was comprised of a psychiatrist, a psychologist, and an associate warden, none of whom at the time of the review were involved in the respondent's treatment. But elsewhere in its opinion, the Court emphasized that under state law, an inmate could seek judicial review of a review panel's decision by filing a personal restraint petition or a petition for an extraordinary writ.

The Court also held that the respondent had no right to be represented by an attorney during the review process. Because the purpose of the review was to unearth any errors in a medical judgment, due process required no more than that the respondent be afforded assistance from "an independent lay advisor who understands the psychiatric issues involved." Id. at 236, 110 S.Ct. at 1044.

Finally, the Court summarily rejected the respondent's argument that due process required the state to establish the need for the antipsychotic medication by "clear, cogent, and convincing evidence." The Court simply noted that "[t]his standard is neither required nor helpful when medical personnel are making the judgment required by the regulations here." Id. at 235, 110 S.Ct. at 1044.

Justice Stevens, joined by Justices Brennan and Marshall, dissented from the Court's resolution of the respondent's constitutional claims. Leaving open the question whether antipsychotic drugs ever can be administered involuntarily to a mentally ill prisoner who has not been declared incompetent by a court, Justice Stevens stated that, in any event, the compulsory-treatment decision would have to be made by an "impartial professional." Id. at 250, 110 S.Ct. at 1052. This requirement, according to Justice Stevens, was not met here, in part because there was too great a risk that the review panels, comprised of prison staff members, deferred to the recommendation of the treating physician or psychiatrist in return for similar deference to recommendations concerning their own patients. Justice Stevens also was unconvinced that the advisors appointed by prison officials to assist inmates contesting antipsychotic-medication orders were sufficiently "qualified" and "independent" to satisfy the requirements of due process. Id. at 256, 110 S.Ct. at 1055. Finally, Justice Stevens criticized the majority for concluding that the need to involuntarily administer antipsychotic medication need not be established by clear and convincing evidence, noting that this standard of proof is required for the involuntary civil confinement of an individual in a mental hospital. See Addington v. Texas, 441 U.S. 418, 433, 99 S.Ct. 1804, 1813 (1979).

In your opinion, what procedural safeguards must attend the involuntary administration of antipsychotic drugs to an inmate? For the Supreme Court's discussion of another claim asserted by the respondent in *Harper*—a substantive-due-process claim, see pages 757–62.

B.   THE FIFTH AMENDMENT PRIVILEGE AGAINST SELF–INCRIMINATION

McKUNE v. LILE

Supreme Court of the United States, 2002.
536 U.S. 24, 122 S.Ct. 2017, 153 L.Ed.2d 47.

JUSTICE KENNEDY announced the judgment of the Court and delivered an opinion, in which THE CHIEF JUSTICE, JUSTICE SCALIA, and JUSTICE THOMAS join.

In 1982, respondent lured a high school student into his car as she was returning home from school. At gunpoint, respondent forced the victim to perform oral sodomy on him and then drove to a field where he raped her. * * * Although respondent maintained that the sexual intercourse was consensual, a jury convicted him of rape, aggravated sodomy, and aggravated kidnapping. * * *

In 1994, a few years before respondent was scheduled to be released, prison officials ordered him to participate in a Sexual Abuse Treatment Program (SATP). As part of the program, participating inmates are required to complete and sign an "Admission of Responsibility" form, in which they discuss and accept responsibility for the crime for which they have been sentenced. Participating inmates also are required to complete a sexual history form, which details all prior sexual activities, regardless of whether such activities constitute uncharged criminal offenses. A polygraph examination is used to verify the accuracy and completeness of the offender's sexual history.

While information obtained from participants advances the SATP's rehabilitative goals, the information is not privileged. Kansas leaves open the possibility that new evidence might be used against sex offenders in future criminal proceedings. In addition, Kansas law requires the SATP staff to report any uncharged sexual offenses involving minors to law enforcement authorities. * * *

Department officials informed respondent that if he refused to participate in the SATP, his privilege status would be reduced from Level III to Level I. As part of this reduction, respondent's visitation rights, earnings, work opportunities, ability to send money to family, canteen expenditures, access to a personal television, and other privileges automatically would be curtailed. In addition, respondent would be transferred to a maximum-security unit, where his movement would be more limited, he would be moved from a two-person to a four-person cell, and he would be in a potentially more dangerous environment.

Respondent refused to participate in the SATP on the ground that the required disclosures of his criminal history would violate his Fifth Amendment privilege against self-incrimination. He brought this action under 42 U.S.C. § 1983 against the warden and the secretary of the Department, seeking an injunction to prevent them from withdrawing his prison privileges and transferring him to a different housing unit.

After the parties completed discovery, the United States District Court for the District of Kansas entered summary judgment in respondent's favor. The District Court noted that because respondent had testified at trial that his sexual intercourse with the victim was consensual, an acknowledgement of responsibility for the rape on the "Admission of Guilt" form would subject respondent to a possible charge of perjury. After reviewing the specific loss of privileges and change in conditions of confinement that respondent would face for refusing to incriminate himself, the District Court concluded that these consequences constituted coercion in violation of the Fifth Amendment.

The Court of Appeals for the Tenth Circuit affirmed. * * *

* * *

When convicted sex offenders reenter society, they are much more likely than any other type of offender to be rearrested for a new rape or sexual assault. See [U.S. Dept. of Justice, Bureau of Justice Statistics, Sex Offenses and Offenders 27 (1997)]. States thus have a vital interest in rehabilitating convicted sex offenders.

Therapists and correctional officers widely agree that clinical rehabilitative programs can enable sex offenders to manage their impulses and in this way reduce recidivism. See U.S. Dept. of Justice, Nat. Institute of Corrections, A Practitioner's Guide to Treating the Incarcerated Male Sex Offender xiii (1988) ("[T]he rate of recidivism of treated sex offenders is fairly consistently estimated to be around 15%," whereas the rate of recidivism of untreated offenders has been estimated to be as high as 80%. "Even if both of these figures are exaggerated, there would still be a significant difference between treated and untreated individuals"). An important component of those rehabilitation programs requires participants to confront their past and accept responsibility for their misconduct. * * * Research indicates that offenders who deny all allegations of sexual abuse are three times more likely to fail in treatment than those who admit even partial complicity.

* * *

* * * The SATP lasts for 18 months and involves substantial daily counseling. It helps inmates address sexual addiction; understand the

thoughts, feelings, and behavior dynamics that precede their offenses; and develop relapse prevention skills. Although inmates are assured of a significant level of confidentiality, Kansas does not offer legal immunity from prosecution based on any statements made in the course of the SATP. According to Kansas, however, no inmate has ever been charged or prosecuted for any offense based on information disclosed during treatment. There is no contention, then, that the program is a mere subterfuge for the conduct of a criminal investigation.

As the parties explain, Kansas' decision not to offer immunity to every SATP participant serves two legitimate state interests. First, the professionals who design and conduct the program have concluded that for SATP participants to accept full responsibility for their past actions, they must accept the proposition that those actions carry consequences. Although no program participant has ever been prosecuted or penalized based on information revealed during the SATP, the potential for additional punishment reinforces the gravity of the participants' offenses and thereby aids in their rehabilitation. If inmates know society will not punish them for their past offenses, they may be left with the false impression that society does not consider those crimes to be serious ones. The practical effect of guaranteed immunity for SATP participants would be to absolve many sex offenders of any and all cost for their earlier crimes. This is the precise opposite of the rehabilitative objective.

Second, while Kansas as a rule does not prosecute inmates based upon information revealed in the course of the program, the State confirms its valid interest in deterrence by keeping open the option to prosecute a particularly dangerous sex offender. * * *

* * *

The SATP does not compel prisoners to incriminate themselves in violation of the Constitution. The Fifth Amendment Self–Incrimination Clause, which applies to the States via the Fourteenth Amendment, provides that no person "shall be compelled in any criminal case to be a witness against himself." The "Amendment speaks of compulsion," and the Court has insisted that the "constitutional guarantee is only that the witness not be *compelled* to give self-incriminating testimony." The consequences in question here—a transfer to another prison where television sets are not placed in each inmate's cell, where exercise facilities are not readily available, and where work and wage opportunities are more limited—are not ones that compel a prisoner to speak about his past crimes despite a desire to remain silent. The fact that these consequences are imposed on prisoners, rather than ordinary citizens, moreover, is important in weighing respondent's constitutional claim.

The privilege against self-incrimination does not terminate at the jailhouse door, but the fact of a valid conviction and the ensuing restrictions on liberty are essential to the Fifth Amendment analysis. * * *

* * *

* * * [T]he Court in *Sandin* [*v. Conner*, 515 U.S. 472, 484 (1995)] held that challenged prison conditions cannot give rise to a due process violation unless those conditions constitute "atypical and significant hardship[s] on [inmates] in relation to the ordinary incidents of prison life." The determination under *Sandin* whether a prisoner's liberty interest has been curtailed may not provide a precise parallel for determining whether there is compelled self-incrimination, but it does provide useful instruction for answering the latter inquiry. * * * The compulsion inquiry must consider the significant restraints already inherent in prison life and the State's own vital interests in rehabilitation goals and procedures within the prison system. A prison clinical rehabilitation program, which is acknowledged to bear a rational relation to a legitimate penological objective, does not violate the privilege against self-incrimination if the adverse consequences an inmate faces for not participating are related to the program objectives and do not constitute atypical and significant hardships in relation to the ordinary incidents of prison life.

* * *

In the present case, respondent's decision not to participate in the Kansas SATP did not extend his term of incarceration. Nor did his decision affect his eligibility for good-time credits or parole. Respondent instead complains that if he remains silent about his past crimes, he will be transferred from the medium-security unit—where the program is conducted—to a less desirable maximum-security unit.

No one contends, however, that the transfer is intended to punish prisoners for exercising their Fifth Amendment rights. Rather, the limitation on these rights is incidental to Kansas' legitimate penological reason for the transfer: Due to limited space, inmates who do not participate in their respective programs will be moved out of the facility where the programs are held to make room for other inmates. As the Secretary of Corrections has explained, "it makes no sense to have someone who's not participating in a program taking up a bed in a setting where someone else who may be willing to participate in a program could occupy that bed and participate in a program."

* * *

Respondent also complains that he will be demoted from Level III to Level I status as a result of his decision not to participate. * * * An essential tool of prison administration, however, is the authority to offer inmates various incentives to behave. The Constitution accords prison officials wide latitude to bestow or revoke these perquisites as they see fit. * * *

* * *

Determining what constitutes unconstitutional compulsion involves a question of judgment: Courts must decide whether the consequences of an inmate's choice to remain silent are closer to the physical torture against which the Constitution clearly protects or the *de minimis* harms against which it does not. The *Sandin* framework provides a reasonable means of assessing whether the response of prison administrators to correctional and rehabilitative necessities are so out of the ordinary that one could sensibly say they rise to the level of unconstitutional compulsion.

* * *

The cost to respondent of exercising his Fifth Amendment privilege—denial of certain perquisites that make his life in prison more tolerable—is much less than that borne by the defendant in *McGautha* [*v. California*, 402 U.S. 183, 213 (1971)]. There, the Court upheld a procedure that allowed statements, which were made by a criminal defendant to mitigate his responsibility and avoid the death penalty, to be used against him as evidence of his guilt.[a] The Court likewise has held that plea bargaining does not violate the Fifth Amendment, even though criminal defendants may feel considerable pressure to admit guilt in order to obtain more lenient treatment. See, *e.g., Bordenkircher v. Hayes*, 434 U.S. 357 (1978); *Brady* [*v. United States*], 397 U.S., at 751 [(1970)].

* * *

Respondent is mistaken as well to concentrate on the so-called reward/penalty distinction and the illusory baseline against which a change in prison conditions must be measured. The answer to the question whether the government is extending a benefit or taking away a privilege rests entirely in the eye of the beholder. * * * The prison warden in this case stated that it is largely a matter of chance where in a prison an inmate is assigned. Even if Inmates A and B are serving the same sentence for the same crime, Inmate A could end up in a medium-security unit and Inmate B in a maximum-security unit based solely on administrative factors beyond their control. Under respondent's view, however, the Constitution allows the State to offer Inmate B the opportunity to live in the medium-security unit conditioned on his participation in the SATP, but does not allow the State to offer Inmate A the opportunity to live in that same medium-security unit subject to the same conditions. The consequences for Inmates A and B are identical: They may participate and live in medium security or refuse and live in maximum security. Respondent, however, would have us say the Constitution puts Inmate A in a superior position to Inmate B solely by the accident of the initial assignment to a medium-security unit.

This reasoning is unsatisfactory. The Court has noted before that "[w]e doubt that a principled distinction may be drawn between 'enhancing' the punishment imposed upon the petitioner and denying him the 'leniency' he claims would be appropriate if he had cooperated." *Roberts v. United States*, 445 U.S. 552, 557, n. 4 (1980). Respondent's reasoning would provide States with perverse incentives to assign all inmates con-

---

a. In *McGautha*, the Supreme Court rejected the defendant's claim that the jury's adjudication of his guilt and punishment in a single trial violated his privilege against self-incrimination.

victed of sex offenses to maximum security prisons until near the time of release, when the rehabilitation program starts. * * *

* * *

The Kansas SATP represents a sensible approach to reducing the serious danger that repeat sex offenders pose to many innocent persons, most often children. The State's interest in rehabilitation is undeniable. There is, furthermore, no indication that the SATP is merely an elaborate ruse to skirt the protections of the privilege against compelled self-incrimination. Rather, the program allows prison administrators to provide to those who need treatment the incentive to seek it.

* * *

JUSTICE O'CONNOR, concurring in the judgment.

The Court today is divided on the question of what standard to apply when evaluating compulsion for the purposes of the Fifth Amendment privilege against self-incrimination in a prison setting. I write separately because, although I agree with Justice Stevens that the Fifth Amendment compulsion standard is broader than the "atypical and significant hardship" standard we have adopted for evaluating due process claims in prisons, I do not believe that the alterations in respondent's prison conditions as a result of his failure to participate in the Sexual Abuse Treatment Program (SATP) were so great as to constitute compulsion for the purposes of the Fifth Amendment privilege against self-incrimination. I therefore agree with the plurality that the decision below should be reversed.

* * *

I do not believe the consequences facing respondent in this case are serious enough to compel him to be a witness against himself. * * * These changes in living conditions seem to me minor. Because the prison is responsible for caring for respondent's basic needs, his ability to support himself is not implicated by the reduction in wages he would suffer as a result. While his visitation is reduced as a result of his failure to incriminate himself, he still retains the ability to see his attorney, his family, and members of the clergy. The limitation on the possession of personal items, as well as the amount that respondent is allowed to spend at the canteen, may make his prison experience more unpleasant, but seems very unlikely to actually compel him to incriminate himself.

Justice Stevens also suggests that the move to the maximum-security area of the prison would itself be coercive. Although the District Court found that moving respondent to a maximum-security section of the prison would put him "in a more dangerous environment occupied by more serious offenders," there was no finding about how great a danger such a placement posed. Because it is respondent's burden to prove compulsion, we may assume that the prison is capable of controlling its inmates so that respondent's personal safety is not jeopardized by being placed in the maximum-security area of the prison, at least in the absence of proof to the contrary.

* * *

JUSTICE STEVENS, with whom JUSTICE SOUTER, JUSTICE GINSBURG, and JUSTICE BREYER join, dissenting.

* * *

Our holding in *Malloy v. Hogan*, 378 U.S. 1 (1964), that the privilege applies to the States through the Fourteenth Amendment, determined that the right to remain silent is itself a liberty interest protected by that Amendment. We explained that "[t]he Fourteenth Amendment secures against state invasion the same privilege that the Fifth Amendment guarantees against federal infringement—the right of a person to remain silent unless he chooses to speak in the unfettered exercise of his own will, and to suffer no penalty ... for such silence." Since *Malloy*, we have construed the text to prohibit not only direct orders to testify, but also indirect compulsion effected by comments on a defendant's refusal to take the stand, *Griffin v. California*, 380 U.S. 609, 613–614 (1965) * * *. Without requiring the deprivation of any other liberty interest, we have found prohibited compulsion in the threatened loss of the right to participate in political associations, *Lefkowitz v. Cunningham*, 431 U.S. 801 (1977), forfeiture of government contracts, *Lefkowitz v. Turley*, 414 U.S. [70], at 82 [1973], loss of employment, *Uniformed Sanitation Men Ass'n, Inc. v. Commissioner of Sanitation of City of New York*, 392 U.S. 280 (1968), and disbarment, *Spevack v. Klein*, 385 U.S. 511, 516 (1967). None of our opinions contains any suggestion that compulsion should have a different meaning in the prison context. * * *

* * *

Respondent was directly ordered by prison authorities to participate in a program that requires incriminating disclosures * * *. Like a direct judicial order to answer questions in the courtroom, an order from the State to participate in the SATP is inherently coercive. Moreover, the penalty for refusing to participate in the SATP is automatic. * * *

The plurality and Justice O'Connor hold that the consequences stemming from respondent's invocation of the privilege are not serious enough to constitute compulsion. * * *

It took respondent several years to acquire the status that he occupied in 1994 when he was ordered to participate in the SATP. Because of the nature of his convictions, in 1983 the Department initially placed him in a maximum-security classification. Not until 1989 did the Department change his "security classification to 'medium by exception' because of his good behavior." Thus, the sanction at issue threatens to deprive respondent of a status in the prison community that it took him six years to earn and which he had successfully maintained for five more years when he was ordered to incriminate himself. Moreover, abruptly "busting" his custody back to Level I would impose the same stigma on him as would a disciplinary conviction for any of the most serious offenses described in petitioners' formal statement of Internal Management Policy and Procedure (IMPP). * * * This same loss of privileges is considered serious enough by prison authorities that it is used as punishment for theft, drug abuse, assault, and possession of dangerous contraband.

The punitive consequences of the discipline include not only the dignitary and reputational harms flowing from the transfer, but a serious loss of tangible privileges as well. Because he refused to participate in the SATP, respondent's visitation rights will be restricted. He will be able to earn only $0.60 per day, as compared to Level III inmates, who can potentially earn minimum wage. His access to prison organizations and activities will be limited. He will no longer be able to send his family more than $30 per pay period. He will be prohibited from spending more than $20 per payroll period at the canteen, rather than the $140 he could spend at Level III, and he will be restricted in what property he can keep in his cell. In addition, because he will be transferred to a maximum-security unit, respondent will be forced to share a cell with three other inmates rather than one, and his movement outside the cell will be substantially curtailed. The District Court found that the maximum-security unit is "a more dangerous environment occupied by more serious offenders."[9] Perhaps most importantly, respondent will no longer be able to earn his way back up to Level III status through good behavior during the remainder of his sentence. ("To complete Level I, an inmate must ... demonstrate a willingness to participate in recommended programs and/or work assignments for a full review cycle").

* * *

* * * We have recognized that the government can extend a benefit in exchange for incriminating statements, but cannot threaten to take away privileges as the cost of invoking Fifth Amendment rights, see *e.g., Turley*, 414 U.S., at 82; *Spevack*, 385 U.S., at 516. * * *[10]

* * * The plurality contends that the transfer from medium to maximum security and the associated loss of Level III status is not intended to punish prisoners for asserting their Fifth Amendment rights, but rather is merely incidental to the prison's legitimate interest in making room for participants in the program. Of course, the Department could still house participants together without moving those who refuse to

---

9. Respondent attested to the fact that in his experience maximum security "is a very hostile, intimidating environment because most of the inmates in maximum tend to have longer sentences and are convicted of more serious crimes, and, as a consequence, care less how they act or treat others." He explained that in the maximum-security unit "there is far more gang activity," "reported and unreported rapes and assaults of inmates are far more prevalent," and "sex offenders ... are seen as targets for rape and physical and mental assault[s]," whereas in medium security, "because the inmates want to maintain their medium security status, they are less prone to breaking prison rules or acting violently."

10. * * * While it is true that in some cases the line between enhancing punishment and refusing leniency may be difficult to draw, that does not mean the distinction is irrelevant for Fifth Amendment purposes. * * *

participate to more restrictive conditions of confinement and taking away their privileges. Moreover, petitioners have not alleged that respondent is taking up a bed in a unit devoted to the SATP; therefore, all the Department would have to do is allow respondent to stay in his current medium-security cell. If need be, the Department could always transfer respondent to another medium-security unit. Given the absence of evidence in the record that the Department has a shortage of medium-security beds, or even that there is a separate unit devoted to participants in the SATP, the only plausible explanation for the transfer to maximum security and loss of Level III status is that it serves as punishment for refusing to participate in the program.

* * *

* * * The benefits of obtaining confessions from sex offenders may be substantial, but "claims of overriding interests are not unusual in Fifth Amendment litigation," and until today at least "they have not fared well." The State's interests in law enforcement and rehabilitation are present in every criminal case. If those interests were sufficient to justify impinging on prisoners' Fifth Amendment right, inmates would soon have no privilege left to invoke.

The plurality's willingness to sacrifice prisoners' Fifth Amendment rights is also unwarranted because available alternatives would allow the State to achieve the same objectives without impinging on inmates' privilege. The most obvious alternative is to grant participants use immunity. Petitioners have not provided any evidence that the program's therapeutic aims could not be served equally well by granting use immunity. * * * In fact, the program's rehabilitative goals would likely be furthered by ensuring free and open discussion without the threat of prosecution looming over participants' therapy sessions.

The plurality contends that requiring immunity will undermine the therapeutic goals of the program because once "inmates know society will not punish them for their past offenses, they may be left with the false impression that society does not consider those crimes to be serious ones." The idea that an inmate who is confined to prison for almost 20 years for an offense could be left with the impression that his crimes are not serious or that wrongdoing does not carry consequences is absurd. Moreover, the argument starts from a false premise. Granting use immunity does not preclude prosecution; it merely prevents the State from using an inmate's own words, and the fruits thereof, against him in a subsequent prosecution. * * * Nor is a State *required* to grant use immunity in order to have a sex offender treatment program that involves admission of responsibility.

Alternatively, the State could continue to pursue its rehabilitative goals without violating participants' Fifth Amendment rights by offering inmates a voluntary program. * * * Indeed, there is reason to believe successful rehabilitation is more likely for voluntary participants than for those who are compelled to accept treatment. See Abel, Mittelman, Becker, Rathner & Rouleau, Predicting Child Molesters' Response to Treatment, 528 Annals N.Y. Acad. of Sciences 223 (1988) (finding that greater perceived pressure to participate in treatment is strongly correlated with the dropout rate).

Through its treatment program, Kansas seeks to achieve the admirable goal of reducing recidivism among sex offenders. In the process, however, the State demands an impermissible and unwarranted sacrifice from the participants. No matter what the goal, inmates should not be compelled to forfeit the privilege against self-incrimination simply because the ends are legitimate or because they have been convicted of sex offenses. Particularly in a case like this one, in which respondent has protested his innocence all along and is being compelled to confess to a crime that he still insists he did not commit, we ought to ask ourselves—what if this is one of those rare cases in which the jury made a mistake and he is actually innocent? And in answering that question, we should consider that even members of the Star Chamber thought they were pursuing righteous ends.

I respectfully dissent.

QUESTIONS AND POINTS FOR DISCUSSION

1. Do you agree with the majority of the Court in *McKune* that the respondent was not faced with compulsion to incriminate himself within the meaning of the Fifth Amendment? If so, are there circumstances under which a mandated prison transfer following a prisoner's refusal to discuss past crimes as part of a treatment program would violate the Fifth Amendment privilege? Would it be constitutional, in your opinion, to condition parole release on participation in a treatment program in which the discussion of past crimes is required?

2. Since *McKune*, courts have wrestled with the questions of if and when the prolongation of confinement due to a prisoner's refusal to participate in a sex-offender treatment program violates the Fifth Amendment privilege against self-incrimination. In Ainsworth v. Stanley, 317 F.3d 1, 3, 5–6 (1st Cir. 2002), the First Circuit Court of Appeals held that although nonparticipation in a sex-offender treatment program "almost always" resulted in the denial of parole in the state, the reduced likelihood of parole did not constitute compulsion to make incriminating statements, in part because parole was a "benefit" in that state. By contrast, the Minnesota Supreme Court found the requisite compulsion when two prisoners' refusal to participate in a sex-offender treatment program in which they were supposed to admit committing the sex crimes of which they were convicted led to the imposition of disciplinary sanctions that extended their imprisonment by forty-five days. Johnson v. Fabian, 735 N.W.2d 295, 309 (Minn. 2007).

It is important to remember that compulsion alone does not give rise to a Fifth Amendment claim. To prevail on such a claim, the person asserting it must face a "real and appreciable" risk of incrimination. Hiibel v. Sixth Judicial Dist. Court of Nev., Humboldt Cty., 542 U.S. 177, 190, 124 S.Ct.

2451, 2460 (2004). In *Johnson v. Fabian*, the Minnesota Supreme Court found that both prisoners were confronted with this risk. One prisoner's criminal case was pending on appeal at the time he refused to participate in the treatment program. And the other prisoner faced a genuine risk of incriminating himself during the treatment program of the crime of perjury because at trial, he had denied committing the sex offense that he was supposed to admit committing as part of his treatment. For a discussion of the Fifth Amendment privilege against self-incrimination in the probation context, see pages 382–385.

C. EQUAL PROTECTION OF THE LAW

In the volatile confines of the nation's prisons, the threat of violence is ever present. Most prisoners are bored, frustrated, and resentful; deep down, many are also afraid—afraid of being sexually assaulted and afraid of being killed. Adding to the tension pervading the prisons is deep-seated animosity between some prisoners of different races. At times, some correctional officials have responded to the threats that racial tensions pose to security and order within prisons by separating black prisoners from white prisoners. In the case below, the Supreme Court considered the constitutionality of one state's segregation policies.

JOHNSON v. CALIFORNIA

Supreme Court of the United States, 2005.
543 U.S. 499, 125 S.Ct. 1141, 160 L.Ed.2d 949.

JUSTICE O'CONNOR delivered the opinion of the Court.

The California Department of Corrections (CDC) has an unwritten policy of racially segregating prisoners in double cells in reception centers for up to 60 days each time they enter a new correctional facility. We consider whether strict scrutiny is the proper standard of review for an equal protection challenge to that policy.

I

A

CDC institutions house all new male inmates and all male inmates transferred from other state facilities in reception centers for up to 60 days upon their arrival. During that time, prison officials evaluate the inmates to determine their ultimate placement. Double-cell assignments in the reception centers are based on a number of factors, predominantly race. In fact, the CDC has admitted that the chances of an inmate being assigned a cellmate of another race are " '[p]retty close' " to zero percent. The CDC further subdivides prisoners within each racial group. Thus, Japanese-Americans are housed separately from Chinese-Americans, and Northern California Hispanics are separated from Southern California Hispanics.

The CDC's asserted rationale for this practice is that it is necessary to prevent violence caused by racial gangs. It cites numerous incidents of racial violence in CDC facilities and identifies five major prison gangs in the State: Mexican Mafia, Nuestra Familia, Black Guerilla Family, Aryan Brotherhood, and Nazi Low Riders. The CDC also notes that prison-gang culture is violent and murderous. An associate warden testified that if race were not considered in making initial housing assignments, she is certain there would be racial conflict in the cells and in the yard. Other prison officials also expressed their belief that violence and conflict would result if prisoners were not segregated. The CDC claims that it must therefore segregate all inmates while it determines whether they pose a danger to others.

With the exception of the double cells in reception areas, the rest of the state prison facilities—dining areas, yards, and cells—are fully integrated. After the initial 60–day period, prisoners are allowed to choose their own cellmates. The CDC usually grants inmate requests to be housed together, unless there are security reasons for denying them.

B

Garrison Johnson is an African–American inmate in the custody of the CDC. * * * Upon his arrival at Folsom prison in 1987, and each time he was transferred to a new facility thereafter, Johnson was double-celled with another African–American inmate.

Johnson filed a complaint *pro se* * * * alleging that the CDC's reception-center housing policy violated his right to equal protection under the Fourteenth Amendment by assigning him cellmates on the basis of his race. * * *

* * *

* * * The District Court granted summary judgment to the defendants on grounds that they were entitled to qualified immunity because their conduct was not clearly unconstitutional. The Court of Appeals for the Ninth Circuit affirmed. * * *

* * *

II

A

We have held that "*all* racial classifications [imposed by government] ... must be analyzed by a reviewing court under strict scrutiny." Under strict scrutiny, the government has the burden of proving that racial classifications "are narrowly tailored measures that further compelling governmental interests." We have insisted on strict scrutiny in every context, even for so-called "benign" racial classifications, such as race-conscious university admissions policies, race-based preferences in government contracts, and race-based districting intended to improve minority representation.

The reasons for strict scrutiny are familiar. Racial classifications raise special fears that they are motivated by an invidious purpose. Thus, we have admonished time and again that, "[a]bsent searching judicial inquiry into the justification for such race-based measures, there is simply no way of determining ... what classifications are in fact motivated by illegitimate notions of racial inferiority or simple racial politics." * * *

The CDC claims that its policy should be exempt from our categorical rule because it is "neutral"—that is, it "neither benefits nor burdens one group or individual more than any other group or individual." In other words, strict scrutiny should not apply because all prisoners are "equally" segregated. The CDC's argument ignores our repeated command that "racial classifications receive close scrutiny even when they may be said to burden or benefit the races equally." Indeed, we rejected the notion that separate can ever be equal—or "neutral"—50 years ago in *Brown v. Board of Education,* 347 U.S. 483 (1954), and we refuse to resurrect it today.

We have previously applied a heightened standard of review in evaluating racial segregation in prisons. In *Lee v. Washington,* 390 U.S. 333 (1968) *(per curiam),* we upheld a three-judge court's decision striking down Alabama's policy of segregation in its prisons. Alabama had argued that desegregation would undermine prison security and discipline, but we rejected that contention. Three Justices concurred "to make explicit something that is left to be gathered only by implication from the Court's opinion"—"that prison authorities have the right, acting in good faith and in *particularized circumstances,* to take into account racial tensions in maintaining security, discipline, and good order in prisons and jails." *Ibid.* (emphasis added). * * *

The need for strict scrutiny is no less important here, where prison officials cite racial violence as the reason for their policy. As we have recognized in the past, racial classifications "threaten to stigmatize individuals by reason of their membership in a racial group and to *incite racial hostility.*" Indeed, by insisting that inmates be housed only with other inmates of the same race, it is possible that prison officials will breed further hostility among prisoners and reinforce racial and ethnic divisions. By perpetuating the notion that race matters most, racial segregation of inmates "may exacerbate the very patterns of [violence that it is] said to counteract." See also Brief for Former State Corrections Officials as *Amici Curiae* 19 (opinion of former corrections officials from six States that "racial integration of cells tends to diffuse racial tensions and thus diminish interracial violence" and that "a blanket policy of racial segregation of inmates is contrary to sound prison management").

* * * Virtually all other States and the Federal Government manage their prison systems without reliance on racial segregation. Federal regulations governing the Federal Bureau of Prisons (BOP) expressly prohibit racial segregation. 28 CFR § 551.90 (2004). * * * Indeed, the United States argues, based on its experience with the BOP, that it is possible to address "concerns of prison security through individualized consideration

without the use of racial segregation, unless warranted as a necessary and temporary response to a race riot or other serious threat of race-related violence." As to transferees, in particular, whom the CDC has already evaluated at least once, it is not clear why more individualized determinations are not possible.

* * * We therefore hold that the Court of Appeals erred when it failed to apply strict scrutiny to the CDC's policy and to require the CDC to demonstrate that its policy is narrowly tailored to serve a compelling state interest.

B

The CDC invites us to make an exception to the rule that strict scrutiny applies to all racial classifications, and instead to apply the deferential standard of review articulated in *Turner v. Safley,* 482 U.S. 78 (1987), because its segregation policy applies only in the prison context. We decline the invitation. * * *

* * * [W]e * * * have applied *Turner*'s reasonable-relationship test *only* to rights that are "inconsistent with proper incarceration." Thus, for example, we have relied on *Turner* in addressing First Amendment challenges to prison regulations, including restrictions on freedom of association, *Overton* [*v. Bazzetta,* 539 U.S. 126 (2003)]; limits on inmate correspondence, *Shaw v. Murphy,* 532 U.S. 223 (2001); restrictions on inmates' access to courts, *Lewis v. Casey,* 518 U.S. 343 (1996); restrictions on receipt of subscription publications, *Thornburgh v. Abbott,* 490 U.S. 401 (1989); and work rules limiting prisoners' attendance at religious services, [*O'Lone v. Estate of*] *Shabazz,*[482 U.S. 342 (1987)]. We have also applied *Turner* to some due process claims, such as involuntary medication of mentally ill prisoners, *Washington v. Harper,* 494 U.S. 210 (1990); and restrictions on the right to marry, *Turner, supra.*

The right not to be discriminated against based on one's race is not susceptible to the logic of *Turner.* It is not a right that need necessarily be compromised for the sake of proper prison administration. On the contrary, compliance with the Fourteenth Amendment's ban on racial discrimination is not only consistent with proper prison administration, but also bolsters the legitimacy of the entire criminal justice system. Race discrimination is "especially pernicious in the administration of justice." * * * When government officials are permitted to use race as a proxy for gang membership and violence without demonstrating a compelling government interest and proving that their means are narrowly tailored, society as a whole suffers. For similar reasons, we have not used *Turner* to evaluate Eighth Amendment claims of cruel and unusual punishment in prison. * * * This is because the integrity of the criminal justice system depends on full compliance with the Eighth Amendment. * * *

* * *

We did not relax the standard of review for racial classifications in prison in *Lee,* and we refuse to do so today. Rather, we explicitly reaffirm what we implicitly held in *Lee:* The "necessities of prison security and discipline" are a compelling government interest justifying only those uses of race that are narrowly tailored to address those necessities.

Justice Thomas would subject race-based policies in prisons to *Turner*'s deferential standard of review * * *. But *Turner* is too lenient a standard to ferret out invidious uses of race. *Turner* requires only that the policy be "reasonably related" to "legitimate penological interests." *Turner* would allow prison officials to use race-based policies even when there are race-neutral means to accomplish the same goal, and even when the race-based policy does not in practice advance that goal.

* * * Indeed, under Justice Thomas' view, there is no obvious limit to permissible segregation in prisons. It is not readily apparent why, if segregation in reception centers is justified, segregation in the dining halls, yards, and general housing areas is not also permissible. Any of these areas could be the potential site of racial violence. * * *

* * *

The fact that strict scrutiny applies "says nothing about the ultimate validity of any particular law; that determination is the job of the court applying strict scrutiny." At this juncture, no such determination has been made. On remand, the CDC will have the burden of demonstrating that its policy is narrowly tailored with regard to new inmates as well as transferees. Prisons are dangerous places, and the special circumstances they present may justify racial classifications in some contexts. * * *

* * *

THE CHIEF JUSTICE [REHNQUIST] took no part in the decision of this case.

JUSTICE GINSBURG, with whom JUSTICE SOUTER and JUSTICE BREYER join, concurring. [Opinion omitted.]

JUSTICE STEVENS, dissenting.

In my judgment a state policy of segregating prisoners by race during the first 60 days of their incarceration, as well as the first 60 days after their transfer from one facility to another, violates the Equal Protection Clause of the Fourteenth Amendment. The California Department of Corrections (CDC) has had an ample opportunity to justify its policy during the course of this litigation, but has utterly failed to do so whether judged under strict scrutiny or the more deferential standard set out in *Turner v. Safley.* * * * I therefore agree with the submission of the United States as *amicus curiae* that the Court should hold the policy unconstitutional on the current record.

* * * Proclivity toward racial violence unquestionably varies from inmate to inmate, yet the CDC applies its blunderbuss policy to *all* new and transferred inmates housed in double cells regardless of their criminal histories or records of previous incarceration. Under the CDC's policy, for example, two car thieves of different races—neither of whom has any

history of gang involvement, or of violence, for that matter—would be barred from being housed together during their first two months of prison. This result derives from the CDC's inflexible judgment that such integrated living conditions are simply too dangerous. This Court has never countenanced such racial prophylaxis.

* * *

In support of its policy, the CDC offers poignant evidence that its prisons are infested with violent race-based gangs. The most striking of this evidence involves a series of riots that took place between 1998 and 2001 at Pelican Bay State Prison. * * * The riots involved both interracial and intraracial violence. * * *

* * * But even if the incidents cited by the CDC, which occurred in the general prison population, were relevant to the conditions in the reception centers, they provide no support for the CDC's decision to apply its segregation policy to *all* of its reception centers, without regard for each center's security level or history of racial violence. Nor do the incidents provide any support for a policy applicable only to cellmates, while the common areas of the prison in which the disturbances occurred remain fully integrated.

* * *

Specifically, the CDC has failed to explain why it could not, as an alternative to automatic segregation, rely on an individualized assessment of each inmate's risk of violence when assigning him to a cell in a reception center. The Federal Bureau of Prisons and other state systems do so without any apparent difficulty. For inmates who are being transferred from one facility to another—who represent approximately 85% of those subject to the segregation policy—the CDC can simply examine their prison records to determine if they have any known gang affiliations or if they have ever engaged in or threatened racial violence. * * * For new inmates, assignments can be based on their presentence reports, which contain information about offense conduct, criminal record, and personal history—including any available information about gang affiliations. In fact, state law requires the county probation officer to transmit a presentence report to the CDC along with an inmate's commitment papers.

Despite the rich information available in these records, the CDC considers these records only rarely in assigning inmates to cells in the reception centers. The CDC's primary explanation for this is administrative inefficiency—the records, it says, simply do not arrive in time. * * * Similarly, with regard to transferees, counsel stated that their prison records do not arrive at the reception centers in time to make cell assignments. Even if such inefficiencies might explain a temporary expedient in some cases, they surely do not justify a system-wide policy. When the State's interest in administrative convenience is pitted against the Fourteenth Amendment's ban on racial segregation, the latter must prevail. When there has been no "serious, good faith consideration of workable race-neutral alternatives that will achieve the [desired goal],'' and when "obvious, easy alternatives" are available, *Turner,* 482 U.S., at 90, the conclusion that CDC's policy is unconstitutional is inescapable regardless of the standard of review that the Court chooses to apply.

* * * Race is an unreliable and necessarily underinclusive predictor of violence. Without the inmate-specific information found in the records, there is a risk that corrections officials will, for example, house together inmates of the same race who are nevertheless members of rival gangs, such as the Bloods and Crips.[4]

Accordingly, while I agree that a remand is appropriate for a resolution of the issue of qualified immunity, I respectfully dissent from the Court's refusal to decide, on the basis of the record before us, that the CDC's policy is unconstitutional.

JUSTICE THOMAS, with whom JUSTICE SCALIA joins, dissenting.

The questions presented in this case require us to resolve two conflicting lines of precedent. On the one hand, as the Court stresses, this Court has said that " '*all* racial classifications reviewable under the Equal Protection Clause must be strictly scrutinized.' " *Gratz v. Bollinger*, 539 U.S. 244 (2003) (emphasis added). On the other, this Court has no less categorically said that "the [relaxed] standard of review we adopted in *Turner* [*v. Safley*, 482 U.S. 78 (1987),] applies to *all* circumstances in which the needs of prison administration implicate constitutional rights." *Washington v. Harper*, 494 U.S. 210, 224 (1990) (emphasis added).

* * *

To understand this case, one must understand just how limited the policy at issue is. * * *

When an inmate like Johnson is admitted into the California prison system or transferred between the CDC's institutions, he is housed initially for a brief period—usually no more than 60 days—in one of California's prison reception centers for men. In 2003, the centers processed more than 40,000 newly admitted inmates, almost 72,000 inmates returned from parole, over 14,000 inmates admitted for other reasons, and some portion of the 254,000 inmates who were transferred from one prison to another.

At the reception center, prison officials have limited information about an inmate, "particularly if he has never been housed in any CDC facility." The inmate therefore is classified so that prison officials can place the inmate in appropriate permanent housing. During this process, the CDC evaluates the inmate's "physical, mental and emotional health." The CDC also reviews the inmate's criminal history and record in jail to

---

4. The CDC's policy may be counterproductive in other ways. For example, an official policy of segregation may initiate new arrivals into a corrosive culture of prison racial segregation, lending credence to the view that members of other races are to be feared and that racial alliances are necessary. While integrated cells encourage inmates to gain valuable cross-racial experiences, segregated cells may well facilitate the formation of race-based gangs.

assess his security needs and classification level. Finally, the CDC investigates whether the inmate has any enemies in prison. This process determines the inmate's ultimate housing placement and has nothing to do with race.

While the process is underway, the CDC houses the inmate in a one-person cell, a two-person cell, or a dormitory. The few single cells available at reception centers are reserved for inmates who present special security problems, including those convicted of especially heinous crimes or those in need of protective custody. At the other end of the spectrum, lower risk inmates are assigned to dormitories. Placement in either a single cell or a dormitory has nothing to do with race, except that prison officials attempt to maintain a racial balance within each dormitory. Inmates placed in single cells or dormitories lead fully integrated lives: The CDC does not distinguish based on race at any of its facilities when it comes to jobs, meals, yard and recreation time, or vocational and educational assignments.

Yet some prisoners, like Johnson, neither require confinement in a single cell nor may be safely housed in a dormitory. The CDC houses these prisoners in double cells during the 60–day period. In pairing cellmates, race is indisputably the predominant factor. California's reason is simple: Its prisons are dominated by violent gangs. And as the largest gangs' names indicate—the Aryan Brotherhood, the Black Guerrilla Family, the Mexican Mafia, the Nazi Low Riders, and La Nuestra Familia—they are organized along racial lines.

According to the State, housing inmates in double cells without regard to race threatens not only prison discipline, but also the physical safety of inmates and staff. That is because double cells are especially dangerous. The risk of racial violence in public areas of prisons is high, and the tightly confined, private conditions of cells hazard even more violence. Prison staff cannot see into the cells without going up to them, and inmates can cover the windows to prevent the staff from seeing inside the cells. The risk of violence caused by this privacy is grave, for inmates are confined to their cells for much of the day.

* * *

The problem of prison gangs is not unique to California, but California has a history like no other. * * * California has the largest number of gang-related inmates of any correctional system in the country, including the Federal Government.

* * * Interracial murders and assaults among inmates perpetrated by these gangs are common.[8] And, again, that brutality is particularly severe in California's prisons.

---

8. See, e.g., United States v. Silverstein, 732 F.2d 1338, 1341–1342 (C.A.7 1984) (describing murder of a black inmate by members of the Aryan Brotherhood); State v. Kell, 61 P.3d 1019, 1024–1025 (Utah 2002) (describing fatal stabbing of a black inmate by two white supremacists); State v. Farmer, 617 P.2d 521, 522–523 (1980) (en banc) (describing murder of a black inmate by members and recruits of the Aryan Brotherhood).

* * * Viewed in that context and in light of the four factors enunciated in *Turner,* California's policy is constitutional * * *.

First, the policy is reasonably related to a legitimate penological interest. The protection of inmates and staff is undeniably a legitimate penological interest. * * *

California's policy bears a valid, rational connection to this interest. The racial component to prison violence is impossible for prison administrators to ignore. Johnson himself testified that he is afraid of violence—based solely on the color of his skin. In combating that violence, an inmate's arrival or transfer into a new prison setting is a critical time for inmate and staff alike. The policy protects an inmate from other prisoners, and they from him, while prison officials gather more information, including his gang affiliation, about his compatibility with other inmates. * * *

Second, alternative means of exercising the restricted right remain open to inmates like Johnson. The CDC submits, and Johnson does not contest, that all other facets of prison life are fully integrated: work, vocational, and educational assignments; dining halls; and exercise yards and recreational facilities. And after a brief detention period at the reception center, inmates may select their own cellmates regardless of race in the absence of overriding security concerns. * * *

Third, Johnson fails to establish that the accommodation he seeks—*i.e.,* assigning inmates to double cells without regard to race—would not significantly impact prison personnel, other inmates, and the allocation of prison resources. Prison staff cannot see into the double cells without going up to them, and inmates can cover the windows so that staff cannot see inside the cells at all. Because of the limited number of staff to oversee the many cells, it "would be very difficult to assist inmates if the staff were needed in several places at one time." Coordinated gang attacks against nongang cellmates could leave prison officials unable to respond effectively. In any event, diverting prison resources to monitor cells disrupts services elsewhere.

Then, too, fights in the cells are likely to spill over to the exercise yards and common areas. * * * *White v. Morris,* 832 F.Supp. 1129, 1130 (S.D.Ohio 1993) (racially integrated double celling contributed to a race riot in which 10 people were murdered). * * *

Finally, Johnson has not shown that there are "obvious, easy alternatives" to the CDC's policy. Johnson contends that, for newly admitted inmates, prison officials need only look to the information available in the presentence report that must accompany a convict to prison. But prison officials already do this to the extent that they can. Indeed, gang affiliation, not race, is the first factor in determining initial housing assignments. Race becomes the predominant factor only because gang affiliation is often not known, especially with regard to newly admitted inmates. * * * Even if the CDC had the manpower and resources to prescreen the more than 40,000 new inmates it receives yearly, leafing through presentence reports would not tell prison officials what they need to know.

Johnson presents a closer case with regard to the segregation of prisoners whom the CDC transfers between facilities. As I understand it, California has less need to segregate prisoners about whom it already knows a great deal (since they have undergone the initial classification process and been housed for some period of time). However, this does not inevitably mean that racially integrating transferred inmates, while obvious and easy, is a true alternative. For instance, an inmate may have affiliated with a gang since the CDC's last official assessment, or his past lack of racial violence may have been due to the absence of close confinement with members of other races. * * * In short, applying the policy to transfers is not "arbitrary or irrational," requiring that we set aside the considered contrary judgment of prison administrators.

* * *

Lee said nothing about the applicable standard of review, for there was no need. Surely Alabama's wholesale segregation of its prisons was unconstitutional even under the more deferential standard of review that applies within prisons. * * *

Yet even if *Lee* had announced a heightened standard of review for prison policies that pertain to race, *Lee* also carved out an exception to the standard that California's policy would certainly satisfy. As the *Lee* concurrence explained without objection, the Court's exception for "the necessities of prison security and discipline" meant that "prison authorities have the right, acting in *good faith* and in *particularized circumstances,* to take into account racial tensions in maintaining security, discipline, and good order in prisons and jails."

California's policy—which is a far cry from the wholesale segregation at issue in *Lee*—would fall squarely within *Lee*'s exception. Johnson has never argued that California's policy is motivated by anything other than a desire to protect inmates and staff. And the "particularized" nature of the policy is evident: It applies only to new inmates and transfers, only in a handful of prisons, only to double cells, and only then for a period of no more than two months. * * *

* * *

The majority offers various other reasons for applying strict scrutiny. None is persuasive. The majority's main reason is that "*Turner*'s reasonable-relationship test [applies] *only* to rights that are 'inconsistent with proper incarceration.'" According to the majority, the question is thus whether a right "need necessarily be compromised for the sake of proper prison administration." This inconsistency-with-proper-prison-administration test begs the question at the heart of this case. For a court to know whether any particular right is inconsistent with proper prison administration, it must have some implicit notion of what a proper prison ought to look like and how it ought to be administered. But the very issue in this case is whether such second-guessing is permissible.

The majority's test eviscerates *Turner*. Inquiring whether a given right is consistent with "proper prison administration" calls for precisely the sort of judgments that *Turner* said courts were ill equipped to make. * * *

* * *

The majority also mentions that California's policy may be the only one of its kind, as virtually all other States and the Federal Government manage their prison systems without racially segregating inmates. This is * * * irrelevant because the number of States that have followed California's lead matters not to the applicable standard of review (the only issue the Court today decides), but to whether California satisfies whatever standard applies, a question the majority leaves to be addressed on remand. In other words, the uniqueness of California's policy might show whether the policy is reasonable or narrowly tailored* * *.

* * *

The majority also observes that we have already carved out an exception to *Turner* for Eighth Amendment claims of cruel and unusual punishment in prison. In that context, we have held that "[a] prison official's 'deliberate indifference' to a substantial risk of serious harm to an inmate violates the Eighth Amendment." *Farmer v. Brennan,* 511 U.S. 825, 828 (1994). * * * If anything, that standard is *more* deferential to the judgments of prison administrators than *Turner*'s reasonable-relationship test: It subjects prison officials to liability only when they are subjectively aware of the risk to the inmate, and they fail to take reasonable measures to abate the risk. * * *

Moreover, the majority's decision subjects prison officials to competing and perhaps conflicting demands. In this case, California prison officials have uniformly averred that random double-celling poses a substantial risk of serious harm to the celled inmates. If California assigned inmates to double cells without regard to race, knowing full well that violence might result, that would seem the very definition of deliberate indifference. See *Robinson v. Prunty,* 249 F.3d 862, 864–865 (C.A.9 2001) (prisoner alleged an Eighth Amendment violation because administrators had *failed* to consider race when releasing inmates into the yards). * * *

Finally, the majority presents a parade of horribles designed to show that applying the *Turner* standard would grant prison officials unbounded discretion to segregate inmates throughout prisons. But we have never treated *Turner* as a blank check to prison officials. Quite to the contrary, this Court has long had "confidence that . . . a reasonableness standard is not toothless." [*Thornburgh v.*] *Abbott,* 490 U.S. [401], at 414 [1989]. California prison officials segregate only double cells, because only those cells are particularly difficult to monitor—unlike "dining halls, yards, and general housing areas." * * * The majority does not say why *Turner*'s standard ably polices all other constitutional infirmities, just not racial discrimination. * * *

* * *

* * * Johnson concedes that California's prisons are racially violent places, and that he lives in fear of being attacked because of his race. Perhaps on remand the CDC's policy will survive strict scrutiny, but in the event that it does not, Johnson may well have won a Pyrrhic victory.

QUESTIONS AND POINTS FOR DISCUSSION

1. In your opinion, is the Supreme Court's approach to questions concerning the constitutionality of racial segregation in prisons consistent with its analysis of other constitutional claims asserted by prisoners? If not, how would you eliminate that inconsistency?

2. Under a strict-scrutiny test, when would it be constitutional to segregate inmates in a prison or jail on the basis of race? Cf. Robinson v. Prunty, 249 F.3d 862, 867 (9th Cir.2001) (questions of material fact precluded the entry of summary judgment for prison officials on prisoner's Eighth Amendment claim depicting a "gladiator-like scenario" in which correctional officers were aware of the substantial risk of violence when inmates of different races were released onto the exercise yard at the same time).

In White v. Morris, 832 F.Supp. 1129 (S.D. Ohio 1993), a federal district court upheld the temporary modification of a consent decree in which prison officials had agreed to eliminate race-based double ceiling. Prison officials sought modification of the consent decree after a riot sparked in part by racial tensions exacerbated by interracial cell assignments made to comply with the terms of the consent decree. In the course of the riot, which culminated in the deaths of nine inmates and one correctional officer, prison records needed to assess the security risks posed by individual inmates were destroyed.

The district court, obviously quite reluctantly, agreed to temporarily modify the consent decree's provision for random cell assignments to permit race-based cell assignments for four months, while security records were being reconstructed. However, the court underscored that prison officials were faced with an emergency situation and that the court would not countenance long-term segregation by race.

3. Even when there is a specific basis for fearing racial conflict, segregation is impermissible if there are other means of maintaining institutional security. Depending on the circumstances, potentially viable alternatives may include closer supervision of the inmates, disciplining and removing troublemakers from the general prison population, and decreasing the number of prisoners in the prison. Blevins v. Brew, 593 F.Supp. 245, 248 (W.D.Wis. 1984). See also McClelland v. Sigler, 456 F.2d 1266, 1267 (8th Cir.1972) ("We think it is incumbent upon the officials in charge to make other provisions for housing those who would commit assaults or aggravations on other inmates, white or black, and thus only penalize those guilty of offending the personal and constitutional rights of others.").

4. In *Johnson v. California*, the Supreme Court observed that prisoners in California, as a general rule, were permitted to choose their own cellmates after completing the screening and classification process at a reception center. In fact, according to Justice Thomas, Johnson had had "by his own choice" African–American cellmates for sixteen of the seventeen years he had been incarcerated. 543 U.S. at 550, 125 S.Ct. at 1172 (Thomas, J., dissenting). In your opinion, would segregation resulting from the "voluntary" choices of inmates as to where they want to live be constitutional?

One such segregation scheme was before the Fifth Circuit Court of Appeals in Jones v. Diamond, 636 F.2d 1364 (5th Cir.1981). At the jail in question in that case, inmates could choose in which of two bull pens they would be confined. All of the white inmates chose one bull pen, and all of the black inmates chose another. The court of appeals held the resulting segregation to be unconstitutional:

> At least 48 prisoners—those in the two bull pens—were segregated by race with the explanation that this was the result of their choice. In prisons, where hostility of every kind is rampant, freedom of choice is but a gauze for discrimination. In the inherently coercive setting of a jail, the failure of officials properly to supervise their wards is an abdication of responsibility. A black person newly admitted to the crowded jail and ordered to choose between confinement in a cell crowded with white prisoners, some convicted of major felonies, could hardly find the "choice" to be aught but illusory. A white prisoner would be equally unlikely voluntarily to enter a cell full of black prisoners in preference to one occupied by whites. The defendants do not suggest any justification for the policy. While it was disguised in terms of choice, the practice was racially discriminatory and, hence, unconstitutional.

Id. at 1373.

5. In your opinion, what other constitutional protections are consistent with "proper incarceration" such that their infringement triggers more rigorous judicial scrutiny than allowed under *Turner*? What standard, for example, should be employed when adjudicating a § 1983 claim filed by female prisoners who allege that they are being deprived of the equal protection of the law because programs and services are sub-par compared to those afforded male prisoners in the state? Should the court apply the same standard in a suit brought by a male prisoner who claims that his equal-protection rights are being violated because female officers have assignments that enable them to see him nude, while female prisoners are not subject to such cross-gender monitoring? For a discussion of the constitutionality of differing policies governing cross-gender monitoring and searches of male, versus female, inmates, see 712–14.

In recent years, courts have confronted, with increasing frequency, claims of female inmates that they are not treated as well as male inmates and, on occasion, the claims of male inmates that female inmates receive more favorable treatment. See, e.g., Yates v. Stalder, 217 F.3d 332, 333 (5th Cir.2000) (male prisoners claimed that they were treated more harshly than female inmates, who were confined in air-conditioned facilities and did not have to work in agricultural fields). One of the female inmates' more common complaints has been that male inmates in the jurisdiction in which they are incarcerated are afforded a variety of prison-industry jobs and educational and vocational-training programs from which to choose while the female inmates are consigned to training programs and jobs involving low-paying work traditionally performed by women, such as cooking and clerical tasks. In the case set forth below, the Court of Appeals for the District of Columbia Circuit addressed such claims.

WOMEN PRISONERS OF THE DISTRICT OF COLUMBIA DEPARTMENT OF CORRECTIONS v. DISTRICT OF COLUMBIA

Court of Appeals, District of Columbia Circuit, 1996.
93 F.3d 910.

BUCKLEY, CIRCUIT JUDGE:

In this case, appellants raise a number of challenges to a district court judgment ordering them to improve conditions at various District of Columbia ("District" or "D.C.") facilities in which women are imprisoned. * * *

* * *

* * * The District * * * houses them in three facilities: the Lorton Minimum Security Annex ("Annex"), the Correctional Treatment Facility ("CTF"), and the Central Detention Facility ("Jail"). * * *

* * *

The district court found that female inmates at CTF and the Annex did not have access to educational, vocational, work, recreational, and religious programs equal to those made available by the District to similarly situated men. In reaching this conclusion, the court compared the programs offered to the women with those available to men in facilities that had "similar custody levels, sentence structures and purposes of incarceration." Specifically, the court compared the programs available to women at the Annex with those available to the men at Minimum; and it compared the programs available to women at CTF with those available to inmates at three men's prisons: the Occoquan Facility ("Occoquan"), the Central Facility ("Central"), and the Medium Facility ("Medium").

* * * Because appellants agree that Title IX applies to the educational and vocational training programs offered inmates at District prisons, we will only summarize the court's findings with respect to those programs that, in their view, lie outside the scope of Title IX.

Work Details. The district court described work details as "support duties needed for the running of the jail." At the Annex, women could participate in a variety of such details, including work as receptionists, housekeepers, and librarians. At CTF, women could choose among thirteen work details, including clerical, housekeeping, and culinary assignments. The court found, however, that similarly situated male inmates had access to better and more numerous programs than the "stereotypical" ones available to the women. [Here the court of appeals cited the district court's findings that men at Minimum could participate in details involving carpentry, electrical, and mechanical work and that men at Central could participate in such work as bricklaying, mechanics, and welding.]

Prison Industries. "A prison industry is a business run out of a prison where goods are produced with inmate labor and then sold to government agencies." At the Annex, women could work in a garment shop and a print shop; at Minimum, men could engage in agriculture and landscape work. The court found that these programs were comparable and held that the women at the Annex and men at Minimum had equal access to industrial programs. At CTF, women could participate in only one program that was "remotely" akin to a prison industry. Because the men enjoyed access to a greater number of industries, *i.e.*, one at Occoquan, two at Medium, and ten at Central, the court found that the women at CTF had been denied an "equivalent opportunity in the area of industries" * * *.

Recreation. At the Annex, women had access to "a recreation trailer which contains a pool table, a ping pong table, exercise bikes and a weight machine." Furthermore, the women were escorted twice a week to recreation areas at Minimum, where they could play volleyball, basketball, and handball. The court found that the men at Minimum had greater recreational opportunities: they had access to a gymnasium and a ball field for approximately six hours a day, Monday through Friday, as well as for three hours on several nights each week; they could use a weight trailer seven days a week; and they could participate in a variety of organized intramural team sports, as well as in a "Renaissance Drama Class."

At CTF, women could participate in scheduled recreation for an hour a day, five days a week, and had access to a gymnasium for two hours, three days a week; they were able to play basketball and volleyball in a small outside area; and they could take part in "low-impact aerobics" two days a week for an hour each day. The district court found that the men had far greater opportunities for recreation. For example, the men at Central could play cards or engage in sports or other outdoor activities between 7 a.m. and 10 p.m.; those at Medium could "have recreation all day long"; and at Occoquan, they had between five and seven hours of recreation per day, depending on the season.

Religion. While women at the Annex had "Catholic and Protestant services on a weekly basis and a Bible Study Program," the court concluded that they did not have access to the same religious activities as the men at Minimum. [The court of appeals then cited the district court's finding that religious services at the Annex were not as frequent as those at Minimum.] The court made no findings with respect to religious programs at CTF.

* * *

* * * Part III [of the district court's order] requires appellants to improve the quality of the academic, vocational, work, recreational, and religious programs available to female inmates. Its purpose is to ensure that the women have access to the same opportunities and programs that are available to similarly situated men at other prisons.

With regard to academic programs, appellants are ordered to provide the women with greater access to adult education and college-level programs. They must also make a variety of vocational, pre-vocational, and work programs available to them. The Order requires appellants to provide the women at CTF with 25 hours of recreation per week and those at the Annex with access to a recreation trailer "8 hours a day, 7 days a week." Appellants must also "improve the Annex grounds by adding a basketball court, volleyball pit, and outdoor tables." Finally, appellants must provide chaplaincy service to female inmates five days a week, including "evening hours during the week to accommodate those women working on details, industry, or in the community."

* * *

Appellants do not challenge the provisions that relate to educational (academic and vocational) programs. They ask us, however, to vacate those paragraphs of the Order that require them to upgrade the work, recreational, and religious programs available to female inmates * * *. * * *

* * * [T]he "[d]issimilar treatment of dissimilarly situated persons does not violate equal protection." *Klinger v. Department of Corrections*, 31 F.3d 727, 731 (8th Cir.1994) ("*Klinger 1*"). The threshold inquiry in evaluating an equal protection claim is, therefore, "to determine whether a person is similarly situated to those persons who allegedly receive favorable treatment." * * *

In reviewing the district court's conclusions, we begin, as indicated above, by addressing its assumption that the prisoners at the several facilities were similarly situated "by virtue of their similar custody levels, sentence structures and purposes of incarceration." Appellants argue that these are only three of a number of factors that must be considered when determining whether two groups of inmates are sufficiently similarly situated to render meaningful a comparison of the programs available to each.

* * * *Pargo v. Elliott*, 894 F.Supp. 1243, 1254–62 (S.D.Iowa 1995), *aff'd*, 69 F.3d 280 (8th Cir.1995), illustrates the variables that must be taken into consideration. In concluding that the female inmates were not similarly situated to the male inmates with whom they sought to be compared, the district court in *Pargo* placed particular stress on five factors: population size of the prison, security level, types of crimes, length of sentence, and special characteristics. *See also* testimony of Regina Gilmore, Acting Female Program Coordinator at DCDC, and of Dr. T.A. Ryan, expert witness (programming needs of inmates are gauged by their classification, which takes the following factors into account: custody level; medical, educational, and employment histories; substance abuse information; impending factors relating to pre-release; results of psychological testing; social services reports; and security risks).

Here, the district court acknowledged that 82 percent of women incarcerated in the facilities operated by the District were single-parent primary caretakers, and that only seven percent were serving sentences for violent crimes. It failed, however, to make any findings regarding the types of crimes for which male inmates had been convicted, or other "special characteristics" of male inmates. Nor did it take into account the striking disparities between the sizes of the prison populations that were being compared.

The district court found that the female inmates at the Annex were similarly situated to the men at Minimum. Yet Minimum had a population of 936 prisoners in contrast to the 167 at the Annex. It is hardly surprising, let alone evidence of discrimination, that the smaller correctional facility offered fewer programs than the larger one. We doubt, for example, that tuition-paying parents who entrust their daughters to the all-women Smith College in Northampton, Massachusetts, would raise an eyebrow (let alone accuse the college of sex discrimination) on learning that Smith offers its 2,800 students approximately 1,000 courses while Harvard University provides its 6,600 undergraduates with three times as many.

Even if the women at the Annex had access to a third or half the number of work and religious programs as the men at Minimum, because of the six-to-one difference in their respective populations, on a per inmate basis, the women had access to two or three times the number of programs as did the men. We do not suggest that these mechanical ratios are a test of comparability; merely that, standing alone, the difference in the number of programs provided by prisons having vastly different numbers of inmates cannot be taken as evidence that those in small institutions that offer fewer programs have been denied equal protection. More than that is required.

As regards the women at CTF, the district court found that they were similarly situated to male inmates at the Occoquan, Central, and Medium facilities. [The court then discussed differences between the female and male inmates at these facilities, including the extended length of the men's sentences compared to the women's.] The female inmates at CTF are, therefore, foreclosed from making an equal protection challenge.

The dissent contends that our analysis errs because we have ignored "how the prisoners came to be segregated," with women typically assigned to smaller prisons than the men. As an initial matter, we note that the segregation of inmates by sex is unquestionably constitutional. The District's decision to imprison women in smaller facilities than the typical male prison is the obvious result of an undisputed fact: there are far fewer female inmates. As of January 1994, the total number of female inmates incarcerated in all of the District's jails was 606; this is considerably less than the total population at the smallest male facility (Minimum, pop. 936) discussed in this case. It would be difficult for one facility to house all these female inmates because they range from minimum to maximum custody, from those awaiting immediate release to those serving long sentences.

Furthermore, our decision here is altogether consistent with the Supreme Court's most recent articulation of equal protection principles in *United States v. Virginia* 518 U.S. 515 (1996) (*"VMI"*). In *VMI*, the Supreme Court compared the programs available at the all-female Mary Baldwin College, where the Virginia Women's Institute for Leadership ("VMIL") is located, with the programs available at the all-male Virginia Military Institute ("VMI"). The enrollment at Mary Baldwin College is 1,327 students, of whom 650 actually live on the campus; the enrollment at VMI is 1,124. Despite their comparable sizes, the two colleges offered vastly different educational and athletic programming. The Court noted:

> Mary Baldwin does not offer a VMIL student the range of curricular choices available to a VMI cadet. VMI awards baccalaureate degrees in liberal arts, biology, chemistry, civil engineering, electrical and computer engineering, and mechanical engineering. VMIL students attend a school "that does not have a math and science focus"; they cannot take at Mary Baldwin any courses in engineering or the advanced math and physics courses VMI offers.

In addition, the Court noted the extreme discrepancy in the financial resources available to Mary Baldwin and VMI. Here, while appellees have alleged that the District provides inferior programs, they have not alleged that the District allocates fewer resources per female inmate, nor was any evidence apparently introduced at trial to that effect. Appellees' claim, therefore, would appear to be that appellants have mismanaged the resources allocated to female inmates by failing to provide them with the identical programs offered to the men. In effect, appellees are inviting this court to find that the District's decision to provide male (but not female) inmates with access to any given program violates equal protection principles.

We decline this invitation. While certain programs (such as a work detail in auto mechanics) may be available only to male inmates, other programs (such as a life skills class) may be available only to female inmates. Under the program-by-program method of comparison embraced by the dissent, any divergence from an identity of programs gives rise to equal protection liability. Thus, if male inmates have access to a work detail that is unavailable to women, that violates equal protection. If men can spend an extra hour a day in a gymnasium, that violates equal protection. Conversely, if women had access to a parenting class unavailable to men, that violates equal protection. Such an approach completely eviscerates the deference that federal courts are obliged to give prison administrators. As the Eighth Circuit has observed, as between any two prisons, there will always be stark differences in programming. * * * Thus, female inmates always can point out ways in which male prisons are "better" than theirs, just as male inmates can point out *other* ways in which female prisons are "better" than theirs.

Klinger, 31 F.3d at 732.

* * * If federal courts could find equal protection liability whenever male and female inmates have access to different sets of programs, budget-strapped prison administrators may well respond by reducing, to a constitutional minimum, the number of programs offered to all inmates. * * *

Given these significant differences in the situations of the women at the Annex and CTF and those of the men at the facilities with which the court compared them, and given the fact that the court's Title IX and equal protection analyses both depend on findings that they were similarly situated, we need not examine the programs themselves in order to vacate the program-related provisions that appellants have challenged. * * *

* * *

ROGERS, CIRCUIT JUDGE, concurring in part and dissenting in part:

* * *

The court's equal protection analysis is * * * flawed. Two people commit the same crime. Each is similarly convicted by a District of Columbia court. In all respects—criminal history, family circumstances, education, drug use, favorite baseball team—they are identical. All save one, that is: they are of different sexes. Solely because of that difference, they are sent to different facilities at which the man enjoys superior programming options. Rather than examine whether the District can justify its separate and unequal treatment of the sexes, however, the court concludes that equal protection principles do not even apply: these two identical prisoners are not "similarly situated."

Not surprisingly, there are flaws in an analysis that concludes that identical people are not similar. The court errs because it starts in the middle, rather than at the beginning. The District consigns similarly situated men and women to separate facilities having different characteristics, acting expressly on the basis of their sex. The court relies on the different characteristics of *the facilities* to conclude that the otherwise identical men and women incarcerated therein are not similarly situated, and on that basis holds that there can be no judicial comparison of the differences in the treatment accorded to them. The anomalous result is that the more unequal the men's and women's prisons are, the less likely it is that this court will consider differences in the prison experiences of men and women unconstitutional. Indeed, by maintaining drastically unequal prisons for the two sexes, the government could foreclose any comparison of the rehabilitative programs it provides for the benefit of men and women. This analysis stands the concept of equal protection on its head. The District may not treat men and women dissimilarly and then rely on the very dissimilarity it has created to justify discrimination in the provision of benefits. * * *

* * * Because the prisoners have not challenged sex segregation, the court must assume that such segregation is lawful: in other words, that this facial sex-based classification "serves important governmental objectives and . . . the discriminatory means employed are substantially related to the achievement of those objectives." *United States v. Virginia,* 518 U.S. 515, 524 (1996) ("*VMI*"). * * * Even if the District may properly segregate prisoners by sex, it does not follow that it may segregate them by sex *into unequal facilities.* Put in doctrinal terms, the "important governmental objectives" served by the physical separation of the sexes are not necessarily served by providing different benefits to the segregated populations. Thus, to justify depriving women of the programming choices available to men, the District must explain how the deprivation substantially relates to the achievement of an important governmental objective.

* * * Under the court's rationale, it would almost seem that the District could send men to a country club and women to the Black Hole of Calcutta; a difference in treatment the women received there would be ascribed to their dissimilar situation and would require no further justification. Less fancifully perhaps, the District could provide only stereotypically feminine programming at the women's prisons, such as cooking and sewing classes, while providing men with training in stereotypically masculine pursuits such as construction and carpentry. Or the District could simply cease providing any programming at all at the women's prisons. In any of these cases, the court apparently would not examine the differences in treatment accorded to men and women. The court's holding that male and female prisoners are dissimilarly situated would preclude constitutional comparison of programming no matter how vast the differences in programming were.

This is not to suggest that population size is completely irrelevant to equal protection analysis. Because women comprise a fairly small (but rising) percentage of felons, it is not reasonable to expect that the menu of programs at a women's prison will be exactly the same as that at a men's prison. This, however, is properly accounted for in determining whether the benefits afforded to women are substantially equivalent to those afforded to men. The court errs by using different population sizes to avoid making a comparison at all. Nor does a "per inmate" numerical comparison suffice. As the district court recognized, the programs available to men are often different in kind, not only in number, from those available to women.[15]

* * *

---

15. *See, e.g., Women Prisoners I,* 877 F.Supp. at 657 (noting that work details at the Annex are limited to such things as housekeeping and library work, while men at Minimum have access to work details in carpentry, plumbing, and other skilled tasks); *id.* at 659 (women at CTF have

The Supreme Court's sex discrimination cases make it clear that the government may not rely on generalizations—even somewhat accurate ones—about women to justify different treatment of the sexes. *VMI*, 518 U.S. at 541; *J.E.B. v. Alabama ex rel. T.B.*, 511 U.S. 127, 139 n. 11 (1994).[b] Yet that is what the court permits the District to do, in the guise of requiring the district court to consider "special characteristics" of the male and female prison populations as a whole. For an idea of what "special characteristics" might be, the district court should presumably have consulted the opinion in *Pargo v. Elliott*, 894 F.Supp. 1243 (S.D.Iowa 1995), cited with evident approval by this court. *Pargo* noted the following programs devoted to the "special characteristics" of the female prison population in Iowa: "[p]rograms about domestic violence, prostitution, and incest survivors"; "a family preservation program" apparently devoted to the needs of prisoners who had been custodial parents; "counseling for postpartum depression"; "classes in anger management and self-esteem"; and unspecified programs for inmates with eating disorders. Assuming that the "special characteristics" identified by *Pargo* are more common among women than men, it is unclear why that fact should prohibit a particular woman from choosing to work on a carpentry detail over receiving counseling for post-partum depression.[18] "[E]stimates of what is appropriate for most women[ ] no longer justify denying opportunity to women whose talent and capacity place them outside the average description." *VMI*, 518 U.S. at 550.

What the Constitution commands, rather, is that the District address directly the differences among *individuals* that pertain to the purposes of its prison programs, rather than using sex as a proxy for such differences. If, for example, the purposes of prison programs would be served by providing special programs for prisoners with substance abuse problems, the District could offer such programs to drug-addicted prisoners of both sexes. It would not be permissible, however, for the District to presume that women as a group were more likely to have such problems and therefore offer drug-related programming only at women's facilities.[19]

* * *

---

access to associate degree programs, while men at Central, Medium, and Occoquan can earn bachelor's degrees). "Visiting American prisons in the 1990s is like taking a time machine back to the high schools of the '50s, where the boys took Shop, and the girls learned cooking, baking, and sewing—glorified under the name of Home Economics." Stephen J. Schulhofer, *The Feminist Challenge in Criminal Law*, 43 Penn.L.Rev. 2151, 2198 (1995). Another commentator has observed that differences in population do not "account for the inferior quality of the programming. Only discrimination explains why male prisoners are assigned to apprenticeships that lead to well-paying and secure jobs outside of prison while female prisoners are relegated to those which require little to no training." Stefanie Fleischer Seldin, *A Strategy for Advocacy on Behalf of Women Offenders*, 5 Colum. J. Gender & L. 1, 3 (1995).

b. In *J.E.B.*, the Supreme Court held that gender-based peremptory challenges of prospective jurors violate equal protection.

18. Nor, for that matter, why a man lacking in confidence should be denied the opportunity to take classes in self-esteem just because men in general may hold themselves in higher esteem than do women.

19. The District asserted that women had more acute substance abuse problems than men, but the district court rejected the assertion as unfounded in the record. As *J.E.B.* and *VMI* make

[T]he court also misconceives what it means for persons to be "similarly situated" for purposes of equal protection analysis. Whether two people (or classes of people) treated differently by the government are similarly situated depends on the purpose for which the government is acting. *Cf. Klinger v. Department of Corrections,* 31 F.3d 727, 734–35 (8th Cir.1994) (McMillian, J., dissenting) (noting that men and women are imprisoned for the same purpose and are similarly situated "with respect to the goal of rehabilitation"). * * * [T]he court fixates on such irrelevancies as the size of the various facilities, which have everything to do with the cost of administering programs and nothing to do with determining which inmates are similarly capable of benefiting from them. Notably, this was not an error into which the district court fell. *See, e.g., Women Prisoners I,* 877 F.Supp. at 675 (finding women at the Annex similarly situated to men at Minimum with respect to the purposes of programming because "[b]oth of these populations are preparing for release into the community and therefore [ ] have the same need to fully prepare themselves for this stage of their lives").

* * *

Even assuming the government may constitutionally provide separate programs for the sexes, the programs must be substantially equivalent. This does not mean, however, that all women must have access to the programming choices that are available to any man. Rational sex-neutral criteria, applied evenhandedly to men and women, may be used to determine eligibility for programs. If custody level is such a criterion, for example, then medium-custody women would not be entitled to programs made available only to minimum-custody men. However, if the District chooses to house minimum-and medium-custody women in the same facility, it cannot use that fact to deny the programs to minimum-custody women. That is, the District may not treat differently men and women who are identical but for sex * * *.

When the sexes are permissibly segregated, "substantial equivalence" may not require perfectly identical treatment. Some differences may be unavoidable because of the physical separation. Moreover, the peculiar circumstances of prison administration may require different programs for prisoners housed in different facilities. While programming decisions are to be made by the District and not by the court, the District must show that the important penological interests implicated by the policies of its various facilities have a substantial relationship to the denial of access by a female prisoner to a program available to male prisoners.[28]

* * *

clear, however, even if the assertion were true, it would not justify using sex as a proxy for drug addiction.

28. Thus, the court mischaracterizes the analysis of the dissent as tantamount to a conclusion that "if male inmates have access to a work detail that is unavailable to women," or "[i]f men can spend an extra hour a day in a gymnasium," then there is a violation of equal protection. Rather, consistent with due deference to District officials that is consistent with constitutional protec-

* * * The district court correctly found that women imprisoned at the Annex and CTF receive inferior programming because of their sex. None of the arguments mustered by the court can change the inescapable fact that the District's policies would, solely on the basis of sex, send two otherwise identical people, convicted of the same crime, facing the same sentence, and imprisoned for the same purpose, to facilities offering substantially unequal programming. The court, by ignoring this fact, does not require the District to take even the most minimal steps to assure parity of access to opportunities between the sexes. Equal protection requires more. * * *

* * *

QUESTIONS AND POINTS FOR DISCUSSION

1.   When analyzing the claims of female inmates grounded on their constitutional right to equal protection of the law, courts have faced three pivotal questions:

a.   Are the female inmates "similarly situated" to the male inmates whom they contend are treated more favorably? If the court, like the court of appeals in *Women Prisoners of the Dist. of Columbia Dep't of Corrections*, finds that the female inmates are not "similarly situated," they will not prevail on their equal-protection claims, because differential treatment of dissimilar persons is not unconstitutional. See also Klinger v. Department of Corrections, 31 F.3d 727, 731–32 (8th Cir.1994) (female prisoners at Nebraska Center for Women (NCW) are not "similarly situated" to male prisoners at Nebraska State Penitentiary (NSP) because (1) NSP has six times more inmates; (2) the male prisoners are incarcerated two to three times longer than the female inmates; (3) NCW is a lower-security prison; (4) female prisoners are more likely to be single parents with the "primary responsibility for child rearing"; (5) female inmates are more likely to be victims of sexual or physical abuse; and (6) male inmates tend to be more violent and predatory than female inmates). How, in your opinion, should courts determine whether certain male and female inmates are "similarly situated" for equal-protection purposes?

b.   What test is to be applied when determining whether the differential treatment of "similarly situated" female inmates violates their right to equal protection of the law? Some courts have demanded what they call "parity of treatment" between male and female inmates. Ashann–Ra v. Virginia, 112 F.Supp.2d 559, 571 (W.D. Va. 2000). While male and female inmates need not be treated identically under this standard, the facilities, programs, and privileges made available to each group of inmates must be "substantially equivalent ... in substance if not form." Glover v. Johnson, 478 F.Supp. 1075, 1079 (E.D.Mich.1979). If they are not "substantially equivalent," government officials must prove that the

tions, the District must explain the governmental purpose behind such differences for similarly situated prisoners. This imposes no liability as a result of program-by-program comparisons but only recognizes that District officials are subject to the Constitution in its treatment of prisoners.

differential treatment of female inmates is "substantially related to the achievement of important government objectives" to avoid a finding that the equal-protection rights of the female inmates have been violated. Pitts v. Thornburgh, 866 F.2d 1450, 1455 (D.C. Cir.1989).

What test do you believe should be applied when assessing the equal-protection claims of female inmates? Should the *Turner* test apply? Compare Pitts v. Thornburgh, 866 F.2d at 1453–54 (the *Turner* test applies to regulations affecting "the day-to-day operation of prisons," not to the "general budgetary and policy choices" that resulted in the confinement of female, but not male, inmates in federal facilities far from the District of Columbia) with Glover v. Johnson, 35 F.Supp.2d 1010, 1021 (E.D.Mich.1999) (even if differences in vocational programs offered to female inmates do not constitute "parity of treatment," they are constitutionally permissible under the *Turner* test because they are reasonably related to legitimate penological interests, such as the need to place a cap on the number of programs in a prison in order to maintain security and order).

c. Do the facts of the case before the court reveal an equal-protection violation under the test being applied by the court? In Jeldness v. Pearce, 30 F.3d 1220 (9th Cir.1994), a case involving claims of gender discrimination under Title IX of the Education Amendments of 1972, 20 U.S.C. §§ 1681–1688, Judge Kleinfeld highlighted in a dissenting opinion what he considered the conundrum faced by courts presented with gender-discrimination claims in the prison context:

> The difficulty in applying the law against discrimination in educational programs to prisons arises from the separation of the sexes into separate male and female prisons, and the much lower number of females sent to prison. If Oregon offers educational programs with anything like equal opportunity for men and women to enroll, and limits mobility and residential options of prisoners, then the twenty-to-one sex ratio of prisoners will generate some classes available to men and not to women. This is the lack of "equality" which troubles the majority. But numbers matter. Requiring as many programs in the female prison as in the male prison is like saying that there should be as much opera in Ketchikan as in New York. If both sexes had "equality" in the availability of courses, then the female prisoners would have twenty times as many courses per prisoner available to them as the male prisoners. This vast inequality in courses per prisoner is not required by a statute which prohibits exclusion, denial of benefits, or discrimination "on the basis of sex." Nor does "equality," in any meaningful sense, require that prisoners of one sex have twenty times the freedom of choice as prisoners of the other sex. There cannot be equality of courses per prisoner, and equality of availability of courses, to males and females, where far more males than females are incarcerated. Equality of one variable forces inequality of the other. Equality is an arithmetic impossibility.

Id. at 1234–35. How would you address the quandary faced by courts and policymakers striving to provide male and female inmates with parity or equality of treatment?

2. Title IX provides in part that "[n]o person in the United States shall, on the basis of sex, be excluded from participation in, be denied the benefits of, or be subjected to discrimination under any education program or activity receiving Federal financial assistance...." 20 U.S.C. § 1681(a). In Jeldness v. Pearce, 30 F.3d 1220, 1225 (9th Cir.1994), the Ninth Circuit Court of Appeals held that Title IX applies to educational programs in state prisons. The court also held that Title IX affords female inmates greater protection than the Equal Protection Clause—that Title IX requires, not just "parity of treatment," but "equality." Id. at 1228. In defining what "equality" means in the prison context, however, the court said that female inmates need not be afforded access to the identical number or types of programs offered male inmates. Instead, female inmates simply must be provided with "reasonable opportunities for similar studies" and an "equal opportunity" to take part in programs of "comparable quality." Id. at 1229.

D. LEGAL RESTRICTIONS ON PRISON INDUSTRY PROGRAMS

STEVEN D. LEVITT, THE ECONOMICS OF INMATE LABOR PARTICIPATION

National Symposium on the Economics of Inmate Labor Force Participation, 1999. Reprinted with the permission of the author.

* * *

*Fact * * *: Prison labor, on average, is relatively unproductive due both to the composition of the prisoner pool and the structural impediments that prisons pose as workplaces.*

While many prisoners are no doubt highly motivated and productive workers, prisoners are not an ideal work force. Prisoners tend to have less education than the U.S. workforce as a whole. They also tend to have uneven past work histories and labor-force attachment. As a consequence, the pool of prison labor is a relatively unskilled one, making it an unattractive workforce for employers, at least at prevailing wages.

Also, there are important structural impediments to producing goods in prisons. First, turnover rates among prison workers are high due to release from prison: roughly forty percent of the prison population is released each year. In private sector manufacturing, a turnover rate of production workers above twenty percent annually would be deemed unacceptable. Such turnover is costly to employers and also discourages training since the employer will have less time to recoup any investment made. There are also disruptions to production as a result of periodic lockdowns.

Given these facts, it is not surprising that prison labor, on average, is not very productive. By my rough calculations, output per prisoner-hour worked is about one third as great as for the typical American worker. Because of this low productivity level, prison industries tend not to be profitable. * * *

*Fact * * *: The current system of prison industry is characterized by a non-level playing field.*

When an economist speaks of a "level playing field," it means that all competitors have access to the same set of rules, resources, and markets for their products. A level playing field also requires keeping the government out of decisions that can be made by the market, such as determining who will produce a particular good or be given access to a particular set of workers. As a general economic proposition, a level playing field is an important ingredient of economic efficiency.

It is clear that the current situation with respect to prison labor is not characterized by a level playing field. Prisoners are not covered by the same set of labor laws as the rest of the work force. Prisoners are exempt from the Fair Standards Labor Act (FLSA) that dictates a minimum hourly wage and imposes other constraints on employer behavior. Prison-made products are often given preferential treatment with respect to government purchases. At the same time, in many states prison industries are restricted as to the markets they are allowed to serve. Finally, it is unclear how or why certain private companies are granted access to prison laborers and others are not. Because there is no free market for prisoner labor, allocation of such labor is likely to be governed primarily by political rather than economic considerations.

* * *

IV. How might prison labor policies be designed to create the greatest economic benefits?

* * *

Economic efficiency begins with production being done by the lowest-cost producer. For instance, if the government allows one producer access to prison labor that is subsidized by virtue of the government paying the costs of the physical plant and requiring prisoners to work for extremely low wages, then that producer may be able to sell output more cheaply than a competitor. But it may be economically inefficient because the producer is being subsidized by taxpayer dollars spent on maintaining the prison. It also may be inefficient because a second producer, given access to cheap prison labor, could have produced at even lower cost. Finally, it may be inefficient because different producers spend money attempting to lobby the government for the right to gain access to the cheap prison labor.

The current system of prison labor regulation has all of these potential inefficiencies built into it. * * * [B]y giving preferences to prison-made goods in some cases (e.g., government purchases), and restricting the sale of prison-made goods in other instances, the present set of rules further distorts economic choices in ways that are likely to adversely affect economic efficiency. My advice, therefore, would be to dismantle the current set of regulations, put all competitors on a level-playing field, and let the market dictate the outcome.

Putting all competitors on a level-playing field would entail the following four changes. It is important to note that I view each of the four elements as critical to a successful transition to a more rational utilization of prison labor. If any one of the elements were to be omitted, the program would be unlikely to be completely successful.

First, I would privatize prison industry. As long as the government is in charge of prison industries, it will be difficult if not impossible to avoid decisions being made with political rather than economic justifications. Furthermore, the difficulty in allocating costs between prison overhead and the prison industry will be impossible to solve.

Second, every prison system that wants to have inmates employed in prison industries should put the rights to use those workers out to a competitive bid of prospective employers. The prison would stipulate certain conditions (e.g., the length of contract, types of training required, wages to be paid, etc.), and subject to agreeing to those terms, the highest bidder would obtain the rights to access the prison labor. Individual prisoners would have the right to choose whether or not they wanted to participate in the prison labor force, just as individuals who are not incarcerated have this choice. It would be incumbent on the private company to provide wages and working conditions that are attractive enough that prisoners would choose to accept the jobs. Voluntary partic- ipation on the part of prisoners is especially important given the potential exploitation of prison labor that has sometimes occurred in the past.

In my opinion, this competitive bidding system is critical to any proposal to liberalize the regulation of prison labor. This system has a number of attractive features: no company can complain that another company has an unfair advantage because of access to prison labor since the complaining company had their chance to bid, it brings revenue directly to the state via bids, and if it is economically inefficient to use prison labor then there will be no bidders and production will not occur. Under this system it would be fine for the government to pay the cost of guards and the physical structure. If they do so, private companies will bid higher for the right to use the prison labor, so in the end the market will take care of it.

The third change that would be useful in leveling the playing field would be to extend current civilian labor laws to cover prisoners. In particular, I think minimum wages dictated by the Fair Labor Standards Act (FLSA) should apply, as should employer requirements concerning workers comp, contributions to Social Security, etc. * * * It is quite reasonable for the government to garnish prisoner wages to pay for maintaining prisons, providing support to dependents of those incarcerat- ed * * *, or victim compensation. The key point is not to pay the inmates a particular wage, but rather to put the choice between prison labor and civilian labor on an equal footing. If the prison labor is more profitable given the same set of rules, then the prison labor should be used rather than civilian labor and vice versa.

The fourth and final change that I propose would be to eliminate all preferences and restrictions with respect to prison-made goods. No one should be required to buy prison-made goods and no one should be prohibited from doing so if they want to. Since prison industries would be producing on the same terms as all others, they should be able to sell their goods on the same terms.

* * *

V. Beyond narrow economic considerations: does prison labor reduce recidivism?

* * *

[E]xisting estimates of the social costs of crime committed by prisoners when free are on the order of $30,000 a year. If working a prison job has even a relatively small impact on recidivism, the social benefits could be enormous. For instance, if working a prison job resulted in 10 percent of prisoners dropping out of crime upon their release, then the annual social benefit from reduced crime would be $6.1 billion.

My reading of the (very limited) existing literature on recidivism and prison labor, however, leads me to believe that working in prison industry is unlikely to yield a large recidivism benefit. Although there are a handful of studies * * * that find lower recidivism rates among prison workers relative to non-workers, the critical concern in interpreting these studies is whether the prisoners who worked are in fact comparable to those who did not work. In particular, one worries that the workers were more motivated than the non-workers and that motivation is itself an important determinant of recidivism likelihood. Consequently, the impact of having a prison job on later recidivism may not be causal. * * *

It is surprising that so little research has been devoted to this important question. The ideal way to attempt to answer this question in the future is through randomized experiments in which prisoners are divided into two pools: one that is eligible to participate in prison industry and another which is not. By comparing future recidivism across these two groups, an estimate of the independent contribution of prison labor in determining future criminal involvement could be obtained.

QUESTIONS AND POINTS FOR DISCUSSION

1. Do you agree with economist Levitt's analysis and recommendations? Do you agree, for example, that inmate participation in work programs should be voluntary? Do Dr. Levitt's recommendations comport with his factual premises?

In developing policies governing the adoption and implementation of inmate work programs, of what relevance is the potential impact of these programs on recidivism rates to the economic calculus? Are there any other arguable benefits of inmate work programs that should be assessed and potentially incorporated into that calculus? See Making Federal Prison Industries Subject to Competitive Bidding: Hearing on S. 346 Before the Subcomm. on Fin. Mgmt., the Budget, and Int'l Sec. of the S. Comm. on Governmental Affairs, 108th Cong. (2004) (statement of Harley G. Lappin, Director, Fed. Bureau of Prisons) (prisoners working in federal prison industries are much less likely to violate prison rules than comparable nonemployed inmates).

2.   The Fair Labor Standards Act (FLSA) requires employers to pay their employees a minimum wage prescribed by the Act. 29 U.S.C. § 206. But as Dr. Levitt mentioned in his paper, prisoners participating in work programs typically are not paid the minimum wage. Nat'l Correctional Industries Ass'n, 2008 Directory 116 (2008) (reporting that the majority of states pay some prisoners less than fifty cents an hour, with Louisiana paying as little as two cents and no more than twenty cents an hour). Courts generally have rejected the FLSA claims of prisoners and pretrial detainees for work performed producing goods or providing services used within a correctional facility. See Loving v. Johnson, 455 F.3d 562, 563 (5th Cir. 2006) (listing cases). Citing the Act's purpose of ensuring that workers are able to maintain a minimum standard of living, courts have emphasized that the basic needs of inmates for food, shelter, clothing, and medical care are met while they are incarcerated.

At the same time, most courts have concluded that inmates are not categorically exempt from the protections of the FLSA. See Barnett v. Young Men's Christian Ass'n, 175 F.3d 1023 (8th Cir.1999) (Table) (listing cases). In finding that inmates can be, in at least some circumstances, employees within the meaning of the FLSA, courts have cited another central purpose of the Act—the prevention of the unfair competition that results when employers pay employees subminimum wages. These courts have noted that such unfair competition can result when inmate-produced goods or services compete with goods or services produced outside the correctional facility. See, e.g., Danneskjold v. Hausrath, 82 F.3d 37, 44 (2d Cir.1996) (FLSA applies when a prisoner's work for a private employer "would tend to undermine the FLSA wage scale"); Watson v. Graves, 909 F.2d 1549, 1556 (5th Cir.1990) (FLSA applies to jail inmates paid twenty dollars a day to work for construction company owned by the sheriff's daughter and son-in-law). But courts have been disinclined to find such unfair competition when prisoners are working in state prison industries. See Gambetta v. Prison Rehabilitative Indus. & Diversified Enter., 112 F.3d 1119, 1124 (11th Cir.1997) (listing cases). In the opinion of these courts, the Ashurst–Sumners Act, 18 U.S.C. §§ 1761–62, which is discussed subsequently in note 5, averts such unfair competition by limiting the interstate transportation of inmate-produced goods.

As a policy matter, should the FLSA, in your opinion, require the payment of minimum wages to inmates? If so, in what circumstances? When inmates are working in a prison kitchen or doing custodial work in the prison? When inmates are working in a government-run industry program that produces goods used only by the prison and other governmental entities? When inmates are working in a government-run industry program that produces goods that are sold in the general marketplace? When inmates are working for a private employer producing goods or providing services, such as tutoring, that are used only in the prison? When inmates are working for a private employer producing goods or providing services that are sold in the general marketplace?

3. The American Bar Association supports "fairly" compensating inmate laborers and paying them "at least" the minimum wage if they work for a private employer. Am. Bar Ass'n, Rep. 101B, 2002 Midyear Meeting (2002), available at http://www.abanet.org/crimjust/policy/cjpol.html; ABA Standards for Criminal Justice, Legal Status of Prisoners, Standard 23–4.5(a)(1985). The ABA further calls for increasing inmate wages until they reach the prevailing wage rate paid nonprisoners working in the same industry. Standard 23–4.5(b). These recommendations on inmate compensation include a caveat: taxes should be deducted from inmates' wages, and inmates should be required to contribute a "commensurate proportion" of their income to defray the costs of their incarceration, meet family-support obligations, and pay victim restitution.

4. Although inmates may or may not have a statutory right to receive compensation for their labor, they generally have no constitutional right to receive such compensation. The Thirteenth Amendment explicitly exempts prisoners who are forced to labor as part of their punishment from its prohibition of involuntary servitude. Ali v. Johnson, 259 F.3d 317, 318 n. 2 (5th Cir.2001) (noting that it is irrelevant, for Thirteenth Amendment purposes, whether a prisoner was specifically sentenced to "hard labor"). Requiring pretrial detainees to perform certain kinds of jobs in a correctional facility, such as cleaning a housing unit or assisting in food service, also contravenes neither the Thirteenth Amendment nor the Fourteenth Amendment's prohibition on punishing persons not yet convicted of a crime. Tourscher v. McCullough, 184 F.3d 236, 242 (3d Cir.1999); Bijeol v. Nelson, 579 F.2d 423, 424 (7th Cir.1978) ("A pretrial detainee has no constitutional right to order from a menu or have maid service."). According to the courts, assigning detainees chores that are reasonably related to the operation of the facility does not reflect the punitive intent needed to trigger a Thirteenth Amendment or due-process violation. Hause v. Vaught, 993 F.2d 1079, 1085 (4th Cir.1993).

5. Congress generally has banned the interstate transportation of inmate-produced goods, authorizing the imposition of criminal sanctions for flouting this ban. 18 U.S.C. § 1761(a). Congress has exempted some pilot projects certified under the Prison Industry Enhancement (PIE) Certification Program from this ban, provided that the wages of inmates participating in those projects are not lower than the wages paid for comparable work in the community. Id. § 1761(c). In addition, goods produced for nonprofit organizations and federal, state, and local governments are not subject to the ban. Id. § 1761(b). Despite these exemptions, the ban as a whole has hindered the development and expansion of prison-industry programs. See The 2002 Corrections Yearbook: Adult Corrections 119 (Camille Graham Camp, ed., 2003) (only 7.8% of prisoners were assigned to work in prison industries in 2002).

The adverse effect of this ban on the federal prison industries program, known as UNICOR, has been dissipated somewhat over the years by federal legislation mandating that most federal agencies purchase goods produced by

UNICOR if the goods meet the agencies' requirements and do not exceed market prices. 18 U.S.C. § 4124(a). The statute directs UNICOR's Board of Directors to diversify the products produced by federal prisoners and to take other steps to ensure that UNICOR garners no more that a "reasonable share" of the market within the federal government for a particular product and reduces "to a minimum" competition with private industries. Id. § 4122(b)(1)–(3). Nonetheless, the mandatory-source rule has sparked controversy, inciting charges that it is hurting domestic manufacturers. In response, Congress passed an appropriations bill in 2004 prohibiting federal agencies in fiscal year 2005 and thereafter from purchasing goods or services from the federal prison industries program unless they provide the "best value" to the purchasing agency. Consolidated Appropriations Act, 2005, Pub. L. No. 108–447, § 637, 118 Stat. 3281.

6. What steps do you believe Congress should take to avert unfair competition caused by inmate-produced goods without thwarting the adoption and expansion of programs that can both decrease institutional management problems caused by inmate idleness and provide inmates with work skills that may facilitate their successful reentry into society upon their release from prison? Do you support the enactment of legislation designed to facilitate or require the development and expansion of prison industry programs that produce products currently manufactured only in other countries? Why or why not? If you favor this general concept, what specific provisions would you include in the legislation? Would it extend to both privately and governmentally operated prison industry programs? What impact, if any, does the federal law generally prohibiting the importation of goods produced by inmates in other countries have on your analysis and conclusions? See 19 U.S.C. § 1307 (prohibiting the importation of goods produced by "convict labor" unless the domestic demand for these goods is not being met by manufacturers and producers within the United States).

CHAPTER 15

SEARCHES, SEIZURES, AND PRIVACY RIGHTS

■ ■ ■

A. THE FOURTH AMENDMENT

The Fourth Amendment to the United States Constitution provides in part that "[t]he right of the people to be secure in their persons, houses, papers, and effects, against unreasonable searches and seizures, shall not be violated * * *." The language of the amendment raises two questions: One, when has a search or seizure occurred, triggering the protections of the Fourth Amendment? And two, when is a search or seizure prohibitively unreasonable? The Supreme Court discussed the first question in the case that follows.

HUDSON v. PALMER

Supreme Court of the United States, 1984.
468 U.S. 517, 104 S.Ct. 3194, 82 L.Ed.2d 393.

CHIEF JUSTICE BURGER delivered the opinion of the Court.

The facts underlying this dispute are relatively simple. Respondent Palmer is an inmate at the Bland Correctional Center in Bland, Va., serving sentences for forgery, uttering, grand larceny, and bank robbery convictions. On September 16, 1981, petitioner Hudson, an officer at the Correctional Center, with a fellow officer, conducted a "shakedown" search of respondent's prison locker and cell for contraband. During the "shakedown," the officers discovered a ripped pillowcase in a trash can near respondent's cell bunk. Charges against Palmer were instituted under the prison disciplinary procedures for destroying state property. After a hearing, Palmer was found guilty on the charge and was ordered to reimburse the State for the cost of the material destroyed; in addition, a reprimand was entered on his prison record.

[Palmer filed a § 1983 suit, contending that Hudson had violated his Fourth Amendment right not to be subjected to unreasonable searches and seizures; Palmer also alleged that Hudson had deprived him of his property without due process of law. The Supreme Court's disposition of this latter claim is discussed on page 736.

The district court rejected Palmer's Fourth Amendment claim, granting Hudson's motion for summary judgment. On appeal, the Fourth Circuit Court of Appeals reversed. The court of appeals held that the Fourth Amendment accords inmates a "limited privacy right" to be protected from searches designed solely to harass them. To ensure that inmates are not subjected to such searches, a cell search, according to the court, either had to be based on the "reasonable belief" that a particular inmate possesses contraband or be conducted pursuant to an "established program of random searches" that reasonably could be expected to detect or deter inmates' possession of contraband. The Supreme Court then granted certiorari.]

The first question we address is whether respondent has a right of privacy in his prison cell entitling him to the protection of the Fourth Amendment against unreasonable searches. * * * Petitioner contends that the Court of Appeals erred in holding that respondent had even a limited privacy right in his cell, and urges that we adopt the "bright line" rule that prisoners have no legitimate expectation of privacy in their individual cells that would entitle them to Fourth Amendment protection.

* * *

* * * [W]hile persons imprisoned for crime enjoy many protections of the Constitution, it is also clear that imprisonment carries with it the circumscription or loss of many significant rights. * * * The curtailment of certain rights is necessary, as a practical matter, to accommodate a myriad of "institutional needs and objectives" of prison facilities, chief among which is internal security. Of course, these restrictions or retractions also serve, incidentally, as reminders that, under our system of justice, deterrence and retribution are factors in addition to correction.

* * * The applicability of the Fourth Amendment turns on whether "the person invoking its protection can claim a 'justifiable,' a 'reasonable,' or a 'legitimate expectation of privacy' that has been invaded by government action." We must decide * * * whether a prisoner's expectation of privacy in his prison cell is the kind of expectation that "society is prepared to recognize as 'reasonable.'"

Notwithstanding our caution in approaching claims that the Fourth Amendment is inapplicable in a given context, we hold that society is not prepared to recognize as legitimate any subjective expectation of privacy that a prisoner might have in his prison cell and that, accordingly, the Fourth Amendment proscription against unreasonable searches does not apply within the confines of the prison cell. The recognition of privacy rights for prisoners in their individual cells simply cannot be reconciled with the concept of incarceration and the needs and objectives of penal institutions.

Prisons, by definition, are places of involuntary confinement of persons who have a demonstrated proclivity for antisocial criminal, and often violent, conduct. * * * During 1981 and the first half of 1982, there were over 120 prisoners murdered by fellow inmates in state and federal prisons. A number of prison personnel were murdered by prisoners during this period. Over 29 riots or similar disturbances were reported in these facilities for the same time frame. And there were over 125 suicides in these institutions. * * *

Within this volatile "community," prison administrators are to take all necessary steps to ensure the safety of not only the prison staffs and administrative personnel, but also visitors. They are under an obligation to take reasonable measures to guarantee the safety of the inmates themselves. They must be ever alert to attempts to introduce drugs and other contraband into the premises which, we can judicially notice, is one of the most perplexing problems of prisons today; they must prevent, so far as possible, the flow of illicit weapons into the prison; they must be vigilant to detect escape plots, in which drugs or weapons may be involved, before the schemes materialize. In addition to these monumental tasks, it is incumbent upon these officials at the same time to maintain as sanitary an environment for the inmates as feasible, given the difficulties of the circumstances.

The administration of a prison, we have said, is "at best an extraordinarily difficult undertaking." But it would be literally impossible to accomplish the prison objectives identified above if inmates retained a right of privacy in their cells. Virtually the only place inmates can conceal weapons, drugs, and other contraband is in their cells. Unfettered access to these cells by prison officials, thus, is imperative if drugs and contraband are to be ferreted out and sanitary surroundings are to be maintained.

Determining whether an expectation of privacy is "legitimate" or "reasonable" necessarily entails a balancing of interests. The two interests here are the interest of society in the security of its penal institutions and the interest of the prisoner in privacy within his cell. The latter interest, of course, is already limited by the exigencies of the circumstances: A prison "shares none of the attributes of privacy of a home, an automobile, an office, or a hotel room." We strike the balance in favor of institutional security, which we have noted is "central to all other corrections goals." A right of privacy in traditional Fourth Amendment terms is fundamentally incompatible with the close and continual surveillance of inmates and their cells required to ensure institutional security and internal order.[8] We are satisfied that society would insist that the prison-

---

8. Respondent contends also that the destruction of his personal property constituted an unreasonable *seizure* of that property violative of the Fourth Amendment. Assuming that the Fourth Amendment protects against the destruction of property, in addition to its mere seizure, the same reasons that lead us to conclude that the Fourth Amendment's proscription against unreasonable searches is inapplicable in a prison cell, apply with controlling force to seizures. Prison officials must be free to seize from cells any articles which, in their view, disserve legitimate institutional interests.

That the Fourth Amendment does not protect against seizures in a prison cell does not mean that an inmate's property can be destroyed with impunity. We note, for example, that even apart

er's expectation of privacy always yield to what must be considered the paramount interest in institutional security. * * *

The Court of Appeals was troubled by the possibility of searches conducted solely to harass inmates; it reasoned that a requirement that searches be conducted only pursuant to an established policy or upon reasonable suspicion would prevent such searches to the maximum extent possible. Of course, there is a risk of maliciously motivated searches, and of course, intentional harassment of even the most hardened criminals cannot be tolerated by a civilized society. However, we disagree with the court's proposed solution. The uncertainty that attends random searches of cells renders these searches perhaps the most effective weapon of the prison administrator in the constant fight against the proliferation of knives and guns, illicit drugs, and other contraband. * * *

A requirement that even random searches be conducted pursuant to an established plan would seriously undermine the effectiveness of this weapon. It is simply naive to believe that prisoners would not eventually decipher any plan officials might devise for "planned random searches," and thus be able routinely to anticipate searches. * * *

Respondent acknowledges that routine shakedowns of prison cells are essential to the effective administration of prisons. He contends, however, that he is constitutionally entitled not to be subjected to searches conducted only to harass. The crux of his claim is that "because searches and seizures to harass are unreasonable, a prisoner has a reasonable expectation of privacy not to have his cell, locker, personal effects, [or] person invaded for such a purpose." This argument, which assumes the answer to the predicate question whether a prisoner has a legitimate expectation of privacy in his prison cell at all, is merely a challenge to the reasonableness of the particular search of respondent's cell. Because we conclude that prisoners have no legitimate expectation of privacy and that the Fourth Amendment's prohibition on unreasonable searches does not apply in prison cells, we need not address this issue.

Our holding that respondent does not have a reasonable expectation of privacy enabling him to invoke the protections of the Fourth Amendment does not mean that he is without a remedy for calculated harassment unrelated to prison needs. Nor does it mean that prison attendants can ride roughshod over inmates' property rights with impunity. The Eighth Amendment always stands as a protection against "cruel and unusual punishments." By the same token, there are adequate state tort and common-law remedies available to respondent to redress the alleged destruction of his personal property.

* * *

We hold that the Fourth Amendment has no applicability to a prison cell. * * *

* * *

_____

from inmate grievance procedures, respondent has adequate state remedies for the alleged destruction of his property.

JUSTICE O'CONNOR, concurring. [Opinion omitted.]

JUSTICE STEVENS, with whom JUSTICE BRENNAN, JUSTICE MARSHALL, and JUSTICE BLACKMUN join, concurring in part and dissenting in part.

This case comes to us on the pleadings. We must take the allegations in Palmer's complaint as true. Liberally construing this *pro se* complaint as we must, it alleges that after examining it, prison guard Hudson maliciously took and destroyed a quantity of Palmer's property, including legal materials and letters, for no reason other than harassment.

* * *

Measured by the conditions that prevail in a free society, neither the possessions nor the slight residuum of privacy that a prison inmate can retain in his cell, can have more than the most minimal value. From the standpoint of the prisoner, however, that trivial residuum may mark the difference between slavery and humanity. * * *

Personal letters, snapshots of family members, a souvenir, a deck of cards, a hobby kit, perhaps a diary or a training manual for an apprentice in a new trade, or even a Bible—a variety of inexpensive items may enable a prisoner to maintain contact with some part of his past and an eye to the possibility of a better future. Are all of these items subject to unrestrained perusal, confiscation, or mutilation at the hands of a possibly hostile guard? Is the Court correct in its perception that "society" is not prepared to recognize *any* privacy or possessory interest of the prison inmate no matter how remote the threat to prison security may be?

* * *

Even if it is assumed that Palmer had no reasonable expectation of privacy in most of the property at issue in this case because it could be inspected at any time, that does not mean he was without Fourth Amendment protection.[5] For the Fourth Amendment protects Palmer's possessory interests in this property entirely apart from whatever privacy interest he may have in it.

* * *

The Court suggests that "the interest of society in the security of its penal institutions" precludes prisoners from having any legitimate possessory interests. That contention is fundamentally wrong for at least two reasons.

First, Palmer's possession of the material was entirely legitimate as a matter of state law. There is no contention that the material seized was contraband or that Palmer's possession of it was in any way inconsistent

---

5. Though I am willing to assume that for purposes of this case * * * the Court's holding concerning most of Palmer's privacy interests is correct, that should not be taken as an endorsement of the Court's new "bright line" rule that a prisoner can have no expectation of privacy in his papers or effects. I cannot see any justification for applying this rule to minimum security facilities in which inmates who pose no realistic threat to security are housed. I also see no justification for reading the mail of a prisoner once it has cleared whatever censorship mechanism is employed by the prison and has been received by the prisoner.

with applicable prison regulations. Hence, he had a legal right to possess it. * * *

Second, the most significant of Palmer's possessory interests are protected as a matter of substantive constitutional law, entirely apart from the legitimacy of those interests under state law or the Due Process Clause. The Eighth Amendment forbids "cruel and unusual punishments." Its proscriptions are measured by society's "evolving standards of decency." The Court's implication that prisoners have no possessory interests that by virtue of the Fourth Amendment are free from state interference cannot, in my view, be squared with the Eighth Amendment. To hold that a prisoner's possession of a letter from his wife, or a picture of his baby, has no protection against arbitrary or malicious perusal, seizure, or destruction would not, in my judgment, comport with any civilized standard of decency.

There are other substantive constitutional rights that also shed light on the legitimacy of Palmer's possessory interests. The complaint alleges that the material at issue includes letters and legal materials. This Court has held that the First Amendment entitles a prisoner to receive and send mail, subject only to the institution's right to censor letters or withhold delivery if necessary to protect institutional security, and if accompanied by appropriate procedural safeguards.[13] We have also held that the Fourteenth Amendment entitles a prisoner to reasonable access to legal materials as a corollary of the constitutional right of access to the courts.[14] Thus, these substantive constitutional rights affirmatively protect Palmer's right to possess the material in question free from state interference. It is therefore beyond me how the Court can question the legitimacy of Palmer's possessory interests which were so clearly infringed by Hudson's alleged conduct.

Once it is concluded that Palmer has adequately alleged a "seizure," the question becomes whether the seizure was "unreasonable." Questions of Fourth Amendment reasonableness can be resolved only by balancing the intrusion on constitutionally protected interests against the law enforcement interests justifying the challenged conduct.

* * * There can be no penological justification for the seizure alleged here. * * * When, as here, the material at issue is not contraband it simply makes no sense to say that its seizure and destruction serve "legitimate institutional interests." Such seizures are unreasonable.

The Court's holding is based on its belief that society would not recognize as reasonable the possessory interests of prisoners. * * * The Court itself acknowledges that "intentional harassment of even the most hardened criminals cannot be tolerated by a civilized society." That being the case, I fail to see how a seizure that serves no purpose except

---

13. See *Procunier v. Martinez,* 416 U.S. 396 (1974). A prisoner's possession of other types of personal property relating to religious observance, such as a Bible or a crucifix, is surely protected by the Free Exercise Clause of the First Amendment.

14. See *Bounds v. Smith,* 430 U.S. 817 (1977).

harassment does not invade an interest that society considers reasonable, and that is protected by the Fourth Amendment.

The Court rests its view of "reasonableness" almost entirely upon its assessment of the security needs of prisons. * * * I am unaware that any responsible prison administrator has ever contended that there is a need to take or destroy noncontraband property of prisoners; the Court certainly provides no evidence to support its conclusion that institutions require this sort of power. To the contrary, it appears to be the near-universal view of correctional officials that guards should neither seize nor destroy noncontraband property. * * *

Depriving inmates of any residuum of privacy or possessory rights is in fact plainly *contrary* to institutional goals. Sociologists recognize that prisoners deprived of any sense of individuality devalue themselves and others and therefore are more prone to violence toward themselves or others. At the same time, such an approach undermines the rehabilitative function of the institution: "Without the privacy and dignity provided by fourth amendment coverage, an inmate's opportunity to reform, as small as it may be, will further be diminished. It is anomalous to provide a prisoner with rehabilitative programs and services in an effort to build self-respect while simultaneously subjecting him to unjustified and degrading searches and seizures."

To justify its conclusion, the Court recites statistics concerning the number of crimes that occur within prisons. * * * The Court's homicide rate of 80 per year yields an annual prison homicide rate of 18.26 persons per 100,000 inmates. In 1982, the homicide rate in Miami was 51.98 per 100,000; in New York it was 23.50 per 100,000; in Dallas 31.53 per 100,000; and in the District of Columbia 30.70 per 100,000. Thus, the prison homicide rate, it turns out, is significantly lower than that in many of our major cities. I do not suggest this type of analysis provides a standard for measuring the reasonableness of a search or seizure within prisons, but I do suggest that the Court's use of statistics is less than persuasive.[30]

* * *

QUESTIONS AND POINTS FOR DISCUSSION

1. It is clear from *Hudson v. Palmer* and other Supreme Court cases that even when government officials have conducted a search from a layper-

---

30. I cannot help but think that the Court's holding is influenced by an unstated fear that if it recognizes that prisoners have any Fourth Amendment protection this will lead to a flood of frivolous lawsuits. Of course, this type of burden is not sufficient to justify a judicial modification of the requirements of law. "Frivolous cases should be treated as exactly that, and not as occasions for fundamental shifts in legal doctrine. Our legal system has developed procedures for speedily disposing of unfounded claims; if they are inadequate to protect [defendants] from vexatious litigation, then there is something wrong with those procedures, not with the [Fourth Amendment]." *Hoover v. Ronwin,* 466 U.S. 558, 601 (1984) (Stevens, J., dissenting). In fact, the lower courts have permitted such suits to be brought for some time now, without disastrous results. Moreover, costs can be awarded against the plaintiff when frivolous cases are brought. Even modest assessments against prisoners' accounts could provide an effective weapon for deterring truly groundless litigation.

son's perspective, a "search" within the meaning of the Fourth Amendment may not have occurred. See, e.g., California v. Greenwood, 486 U.S. 35, 108 S.Ct. 1625 (1988) (no "search" occurred when police officers examined the contents of garbage bags left at the curbside for pickup); Oliver v. United States, 466 U.S. 170, 104 S.Ct. 1735 (1984) (search of open field does not implicate the Fourth Amendment). Not unless there has been a governmental intrusion into an area in which an individual has a "legitimate" or "reasonable" expectation of privacy will a "search" have occurred triggering the protections of the Fourth Amendment.

While the Supreme Court in *Hudson* explained why it believed a cell shakedown in a prison is not a "search" as that term is used in the Fourth Amendment, did the Court fully explain why the confiscation of a prisoner's noncontraband property is not a "seizure" of the prisoner's "effects" and, in some cases, "papers"? Do you agree with this portion of the Court's decision? Compare Soldal v. Cook County, Illinois, 506 U.S. 56, 113 S.Ct. 538 (1992) (rejecting argument that removal of a trailer from a trailer park did not constitute a seizure because it did not invade any legitimate expectation of privacy and holding that a seizure of property occurs within the meaning of the Fourth Amendment whenever "there is some meaningful interference with an individual's possessory interests in that property"). If not, what requirements would have to be met for the seizure of a prisoner's property to be reasonable under the Fourth Amendment?

2. According to *Hudson,* claims contesting cell searches in prisons, no matter how abusive and unwarranted the searches, are not actionable under the Fourth Amendment. At times, though not frequently, courts have found that abusive cell searches violated the Eighth Amendment. In one such case, after a prisoner had reported that a correctional officer was pressuring him to obtain illicit weapons, his cell was searched in retaliation ten times in nineteen days, with everything left strewn about the cell after three of those searches. See Scher v. Engelke, 943 F.2d 921 (8th Cir. 1991). See also Teahan v. Wilhelm, 2007 WL 5041440, at *5 (S.D. Cal. 2007) (listing cases in which prisoners contesting cell searches had and had not stated a valid Eighth Amendment claim).

3. Is the Fourth Amendment implicated if correctional officials search a prisoner's cell at the request of law-enforcement officials for evidence of a crime unrelated to institutional security? The Second Circuit Court of Appeals has answered that question in the negative, noting that the Supreme Court's conclusion in *Hudson* that prisoners have no legitimate expectation of privacy in their cells was grounded not only on the need to safeguard prison security, but on the interest in advancing the retributive and deterrent purposes of incarceration. Willis v. Artuz, 301 F.3d 65, 68–69 (2d Cir. 2002).

What if the police-initiated search targets a pretrial detainee's cell? How, if at all, would that fact affect your Fourth Amendment analysis? Cf. Rogers v. State, 783 So.2d 980, 992 (Fla. 2001) (warrantless search of pretrial detainee's cell conducted by prosecutor's investigators for reasons unrelated to jail security and directly related to the criminal charges pending against the detainee violated the Fourth Amendment).

The courts are divided on the extent to which, if at all, pretrial detainees have a legitimate expectation of privacy in their cells. See People v. Davis, 115 P.3d 417, 428–29 (Cal. 2005) (listing cases). Some courts have held that the Fourth Amendment affords pretrial detainees, like prisoners, no protection when their cells are searched. Other courts have carved out a limited exception to this general rule, holding that the Fourth Amendment places restrictions on cell searches unrelated to protecting institutional security.

4. Searches of prisoners' cells have uncovered almost every type of contraband imaginable, including liquor, drugs, knives, bomb-making instructions, and guns. The photograph on this page depicts some of the kinds of weapons confiscated from cells in prisons. Prison officials have taken steps to reduce the presence of weapons in prisons, but as the photograph demonstrates, the problem of disarming prisoners still persists.

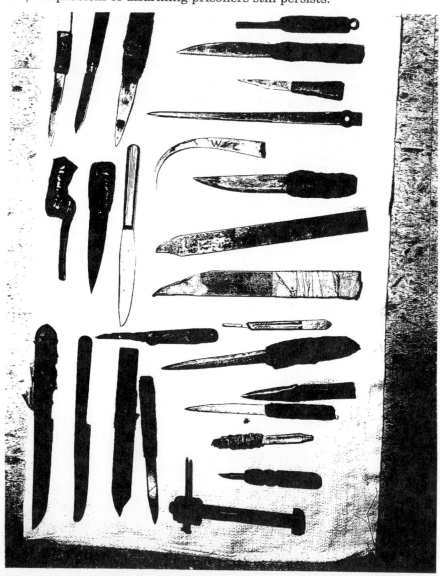

Photograph reprinted with the permission of the American Correctional Association.

5. In addition to not being able to contest cell searches and property seizures on Fourth Amendment grounds, prisoners have no constitutional right to observe a search of their cells to help ensure that their property is not wrongfully confiscated, stolen, or destroyed. The Supreme Court has indicated on two different occasions that even pretrial detainees have no such right. See Block v. Rutherford, 468 U.S. 576, 589–91, 104 S.Ct. 3227, 3235 (1984); Bell v. Wolfish, 441 U.S. 520, 555–57, 99 S.Ct. 1861, 1883–84 (1979).

In *Bell v. Wolfish,* the Court observed that even assuming that the Fourth Amendment provides protection to pretrial detainees, refusing to permit pretrial detainees to observe searches of their cells does not contravene the Fourth Amendment. Not allowing detainees to be present during cell searches is "reasonable," and hence in conformance with the Fourth Amendment, for at least two reasons. First, permitting detainees to observe a search of their cells might lead to friction between the detainees and the correctional officers conducting the search, friction which might erupt into violence. Second, detainees near the area being searched might be able to move contraband from one cell to another, frustrating the objectives of the search.

In the lower-court proceedings in *Block v. Rutherford,* the district court had tried to allay the latter concern by allowing jail officials to bring detainees one at a time from a holding room to watch the search of their cells. Under this approach, the risk that the detainees would be wrongfully dispossessed of their property could be diminished without detainees undermining the purpose of cell searches by passing contraband from one cell to another.

The Supreme Court adhered to its decision in *Bell v. Wolfish,* emphasizing that detainees have neither a Fourth Amendment nor a due-process right to observe searches of their cells. To the argument that *Wolfish* was distinguishable because the detainees here, under the district court's order, could not pass contraband from cell to cell ahead of the searchers, the Court responded:

> This factual distinction is without legal significance. In effect, the order here merely attempts to impose on officials the least restrictive means available for accomplishment of their security objectives. We reaffirm that administrative officials are not obliged to adopt the least restrictive means to meet their legitimate objectives. *Wolfish,* 441 U.S. at 542, n. 25.

468 U.S. at 591 n. 11, 104 S.Ct. at 3235 n. 11.

Even if a least-restrictive-alternative requirement were applied when analyzing Fourth Amendment and due-process claims of inmates and pretrial detainees, would a rule barring inmates or detainees from observing cell searches be unconstitutional?

———

When a search or seizure triggering the protections of the Fourth Amendment has occurred, the Fourth Amendment has not necessarily been violated. The search or seizure must have been unreasonable to fall within the prohibitions of the Fourth Amendment. The question still remains as to when a search or seizure is unreasonable from a constitutional perspective, a question the Supreme Court addressed in the case that follows.

BELL v. WOLFISH

Supreme Court of the United States, 1979.
441 U.S. 520, 99 S.Ct. 1861, 60 L.Ed.2d 447.

[This case arose as a class-action suit filed by pretrial detainees and inmates housed at the Metropolitan Correctional Center (MCC) in New York City. The detainees and inmates contested the constitutionality of the conditions of their confinement on a number of grounds. The claim discussed below is a Fourth Amendment challenge to visual body-cavity inspections conducted on persons incarcerated at MCC after they had had a contact visit.]

MR. JUSTICE REHNQUIST delivered the opinion of the Court.

* * *

Inmates at all Bureau of Prisons facilities, including the MCC, are required to expose their body cavities for visual inspection as a part of a strip search conducted after every contact visit with a person from outside the institution.[39] Corrections officials testified that visual cavity searches were necessary not only to discover but also to deter the smuggling of weapons, drugs, and other contraband into the institution. The District Court upheld the strip-search procedure but prohibited the body-cavity searches, absent probable cause to believe that the inmate is concealing contraband. Because petitioners proved only one instance in the MCC's short history where contraband was found during a body-cavity search, the Court of Appeals affirmed. In its view, the "gross violation of personal privacy inherent in such a search cannot be outweighed by the government's security interest in maintaining a practice of so little actual utility."

Admittedly, this practice instinctively gives us the most pause. However, assuming for present purposes that inmates, both convicted prisoners and pretrial detainees, retain some Fourth Amendment rights upon commitment to a corrections facility, we nonetheless conclude that these searches do not violate that Amendment. The Fourth Amendment prohibits only unreasonable searches, and under the circumstances, we do not believe that these searches are unreasonable.

The test of reasonableness under the Fourth Amendment is not capable of precise definition or mechanical application. In each case it requires a balancing of the need for the particular search against the

---

39. If the inmate is a male, he must lift his genitals and bend over to spread his buttocks for visual inspection. The vaginal and anal cavities of female inmates are also visually inspected. The inmate is not touched by security personnel at any time during the *visual* search procedure.

invasion of personal rights that the search entails. Courts must consider the scope of the particular intrusion, the manner in which it is conducted, the justification for initiating it, and the place in which it is conducted. A detention facility is a unique place fraught with serious security dangers. Smuggling of money, drugs, weapons, and other contraband is all too common an occurrence. And inmate attempts to secrete these items into the facility by concealing them in body cavities are documented in this record and in other cases. That there has been only one instance where an MCC inmate was discovered attempting to smuggle contraband into the institution on his person may be more a testament to the effectiveness of this search technique as a deterrent than to any lack of interest on the part of the inmates to secrete and import such items when the opportunity arises.[40]

We do not underestimate the degree to which these searches may invade the personal privacy of inmates. Nor do we doubt, as the District Court noted, that on occasion a security guard may conduct the search in an abusive fashion. Such abuse cannot be condoned. The searches must be conducted in a reasonable manner. But we deal here with the question whether visual body-cavity inspections as contemplated by the MCC rules can *ever* be conducted on less than probable cause. Balancing the significant and legitimate security interests of the institution against the privacy interests of the inmates, we conclude that they can.

[The Court also held that the visual body-cavity searches of pretrial detainees did not constitute "punishment" proscribed by the Due Process Clause, since the searches were reasonably related to the legitimate governmental interests in institutional security and order.]

MR. JUSTICE POWELL, concurring in part and dissenting in part.

I join the opinion of the Court except the discussion and holding with respect to body-cavity searches. In view of the serious intrusion on one's privacy occasioned by such a search, I think at least some level of cause, such as a reasonable suspicion, should be required to justify the anal and genital searches described in this case. I therefore dissent on this issue.

MR. JUSTICE MARSHALL, dissenting.

[Justice Marshall first observed that for a restriction on a pretrial detainee to be constitutional, the government must at least establish that the restriction is "substantially necessary to jail administration." If the

---

40. The District Court indicated that in its view the use of metal detection equipment represented a less intrusive and equally effective alternative to cavity inspections. We noted in *United States v. Martinez–Fuerte,* 428 U.S. 543, 556–557, n. 12 (1976), that "[t]he logic of such elaborate less-restrictive-alternative arguments could raise insuperable barriers to the exercise of virtually all search-and-seizure powers." However, assuming that the existence of less intrusive alternatives is relevant to the determination of the reasonableness of the particular search method at issue, the alternative suggested by the District Court simply would not be as effective as the visual inspection procedure. Money, drugs, and other non-metallic contraband still could easily be smuggled into the institution. Another possible alternative, not mentioned by the lower courts, would be to closely observe inmate visits. But MCC officials have adopted the visual inspection procedure as an alternative to close and constant monitoring of contact visits to avoid the obvious disruption of the confidentiality and intimacy that these visits are intended to afford. That choice has not been shown to be irrational or unreasonable. * * *

restriction impinges on a fundamentally important interest or causes "significant" injury to a detainee, a higher standard is to be applied: the restriction must further a "compelling necessity" to pass constitutional scrutiny. Justice Marshall then applied the standards he had enunciated to the practice of conducting visual body-cavity searches in a correctional facility.]

In my view, the body-cavity searches of MCC inmates represent one of the most grievous offenses against personal dignity and common decency. After every contact visit with someone from outside the facility, including defense attorneys, an inmate must remove all of his or her clothing, bend over, spread the buttocks, and display the anal cavity for inspection by a correctional officer. Women inmates must assume a suitable posture for vaginal inspection, while men must raise their genitals. And, as the Court neglects to note, because of time pressures, this humiliating spectacle is frequently conducted in the presence of other inmates.

The District Court found that the stripping was "unpleasant, embarrassing, and humiliating." A psychiatrist testified that the practice placed inmates in the most degrading position possible, a conclusion amply corroborated by the testimony of the inmates themselves. There was evidence, moreover, that these searches engendered among detainees fears of sexual assault, were the occasion for actual threats of physical abuse by guards, and caused some inmates to forgo personal visits.

Not surprisingly, the Government asserts a security justification for such inspections. These searches are necessary, it argues, to prevent inmates from smuggling contraband into the facility. In crediting this justification despite the contrary findings of the two courts below, the Court overlooks the critical facts. As respondents point out, inmates are required to wear one-piece jumpsuits with zippers in the front. To insert an object into the vaginal or anal cavity, an inmate would have to remove the jumpsuit, at least from the upper torso. Since contact visits occur in a glass-enclosed room and are continuously monitored by corrections officers,[18] such a feat would seem extraordinarily difficult. There was medical testimony, moreover, that inserting an object into the rectum is painful and "would require time and opportunity which is not available in the visiting areas," and that visual inspection would probably not detect an object once inserted. Additionally, before entering the visiting room, visitors and their packages are searched thoroughly by a metal detector, fluoroscope, and by hand. Correction officers may require that visitors leave packages or handbags with guards until the visit is over. Only by blinding itself to the facts presented on this record can the Court accept the Government's security rationale.

Without question, these searches are an imposition of sufficient gravity to invoke the compelling-necessity standard. It is equally indisput-

---

18. To facilitate this monitoring, MCC officials limited to 25 the number of people in the visiting room at one time. Inmates were forbidden to use the locked lavatories, and visitors could use them only by requesting a key from a correctional officer. The lavatories, as well, contain a built-in window for observation.

able that they cannot meet that standard. Indeed, the procedure is so unnecessarily degrading that it "shocks the conscience." *Rochin v. California,* 342 U.S. 165, 172 (1952). * * * Here, the searches are employed absent any suspicion of wrongdoing. It was this aspect of the MCC practice that the Court of Appeals redressed, requiring that searches be conducted only when there is probable cause to believe that the inmate is concealing contraband. The Due Process Clause, on any principled reading, dictates no less.

[The dissenting opinion of Justice Stevens, in which Justice Brennan joined, is omitted.]

QUESTIONS AND POINTS FOR DISCUSSION

1. In *Bell v. Wolfish,* the Supreme Court assumed, without deciding, that visual body-cavity examinations are "searches" within the meaning of the Fourth Amendment. After *Hudson v. Palmer,* how do you think the Supreme Court would and should resolve the question left open in *Bell?* What about strip searches of inmates or pretrial detainees not involving anal or vaginal examinations? Would and should such searches be considered searches under the Fourth Amendment? Would pat-down frisks? Should they?

2. Most of the courts that have addressed the question whether prisoners retain some residual Fourth Amendment rights after incarceration have concluded that they do. See, e.g., Hutchins v. McDaniels, 512 F.3d 193, 196 (5th Cir. 2007). The Fourth Amendment, according to these courts, places at least some constraints on searches of prisoners' bodies. See, e.g., Peckham v. Wisconsin Dep't of Corrections, 141 F.3d 694, 697 (7th Cir.1998) (prisoners have Fourth Amendment rights, although strip searches would rarely violate those rights); Bonitz v. Fair, 804 F.2d 164, 173 (1st Cir.1986), overruled on other grounds by Unwin v. Campbell, 863 F.2d 124 (1st Cir.1988) ("clearly established" Fourth Amendment right violated by digital body-cavity searches of female inmates conducted by female police officers, rather than medical personnel, in the presence of male officers, and with only one pair of gloves used for multiple searches).

3. Assuming that searches of prisoners' bodies implicate the Fourth Amendment, the next question is: What constraints does the Fourth Amendment place on such searches? In other words, what requirements must be met in order for such searches to be considered reasonable?

a. *Probable cause.* The Supreme Court has often held that searches must be based on probable cause to be reasonable. For example, the Court generally has required the presence of probable cause before police can search a home for evidence of a crime. In the prison context, imposition of a probable-cause requirement would mean that before searching a prisoner's body, correctional officers would have to have probable cause to believe that the search would uncover contraband or some evidence of a crime or violation of a prison regulation. Probable cause would exist if, considering all of the circumstances, there was a "fair probability" that the search would yield contraband or inculpatory evidence. See Illinois v. Gates, 462 U.S. 213, 238, 103 S.Ct. 2317, 2332 (1983).

b. *Reasonable suspicion.* The Supreme Court has condoned some searches based on a degree of suspicion not rising to the level of probable cause. For example, the Court has held that a frisk of an unincarcerated person for weapons is constitutional as long as two requirements are met: one, the search is grounded on a reasonable and articulable suspicion that the person is armed and dangerous, and two, the search is limited in scope to what is reasonably necessary to locate weapons. See Terry v. Ohio, 392 U.S. 1, 88 S.Ct. 1868 (1968).

In arriving at its conclusion that frisks for weapons are reasonable even though probable cause for the frisks may be absent, the Supreme Court applied a balancing test, like the one later applied by the Court in *Bell v. Wolfish.* The Court said that when a police officer has a reasonable suspicion that an individual is armed and dangerous, the need to conduct a limited search for weapons outweighs the intrusion resulting from the search. The interest of the police officer in protecting himself or herself and the public from armed violence, plus the societal interests in the prevention and detection of crimes, warrant what the Court acknowledged to be a "serious intrusion upon the sanctity of the person," one that may involve the touching of genital areas. Id. at 17, 88 S.Ct. at 1877. See also United States v. Knights, 534 U.S. 112, 122 S.Ct. 587 (2001), discussed in note 1 on page 389, in which the Supreme Court upheld the warrantless search of a probationer's apartment that was predicated only on reasonable suspicion that the apartment contained evidence of a crime.

c. *No Individualized Suspicion.* In some cases, one of which is *Bell v. Wolfish,* the Supreme Court has upheld searches or seizures unsupported by any individualized suspicion, whether probable cause or even reasonable suspicion. See, e.g., Board of Educ. of Indep. Sch. Dist. No. 92 v. Earls, 536 U.S. 822, 122 S.Ct. 2559 (2002) (mandatory urinalysis drug tests administered to middle-school and high-school students before they can participate in school-related extracurricular activities and administered randomly while engaging in those activities); Colorado v. Bertine, 479 U.S. 367, 107 S.Ct. 738 (1987) (search of containers found in a car during an inventory search); Illinois v. Lafayette, 462 U.S. 640, 103 S.Ct. 2605 (1983) (inventory search of arrestee's shoulder bag before his confinement in jail). The Court often has condoned such searches and seizures when "special needs," besides the "normal need for law enforcement," have made application of the traditional Fourth Amendment requirements of a warrant and probable cause, in its opinion, impractical. Bd. of Educ. of Indep. Sch. Dist. No. 92 v. Earls, 536 U.S. at 829, 122 S.Ct. at 2564. The line between "special needs" searches and seizures and those to which traditional rules apply is somewhat obscure. But at least as a general rule, the principal, immediate purpose of searches and seizures falling within the "special needs" category is to further some legitimate governmental objective other than those of capturing criminals or discovering evidence to be used in criminal prosecutions. See, e.g., Ferguson v. City of Charleston, 532 U.S. 67, 82–84, 86, 121 S.Ct. 1281, 1291–93 (2001) (holding that even though the "ultimate goal" of a nonconsensual drug-testing program for pregnant patients ostensibly was to funnel women who tested positive into drug-treatment programs, the tests conducted without probable cause or a warrant violated the Fourth Amendment because their "immediate objective" was to obtain evidence to be turned over to police).

In approving administrative searches and seizures not grounded on probable cause or even reasonable suspicion, the Supreme Court often has emphasized that the searches or seizures were conducted in accordance with prescribed, standardized procedures. See, e.g., Colorado v. Bertine, 479 U.S. 367, 374 n. 6, 107 S.Ct. 738, 742 n. 6 (1987) ("We emphasize that, in this case, the trial court found that the Police Department's procedures mandated the opening of closed containers and the listing of their contents. Our decisions have always adhered to the requirement that inventories be conducted according to standardized criteria."). Because of these standardized procedures, the discretion of government officials as to whether and how a search or seizure would be conducted was confined, thereby limiting the intrusiveness of the search or seizure.

In Samson v. California, 547 U.S. 843, 126 S.Ct. 2193 (2006), which can be found on page 389, the Supreme Court upheld a suspicionless search of a parolee observed by a police officer walking down the street. The Court specifically refrained from applying a special-needs analysis to the search that had led to the discovery of methamphetamine in the parolee's breast pocket. The Court instead applied what it called a "totality of the circumstances" approach under which it balanced the need to conduct suspicionless searches of parolees against the intrusiveness of such searches. Id. at 848, 126 S.Ct. at 2197. In concluding that this balancing of interests pointed to the reasonableness of the suspicionless searches of parolees authorized by a California statute, the Court emphasized that the parolee in the case before it had signed a form indicating that he was aware that he could be searched "at any time" by parole or police officers and that he had assented to this condition of his parole release. But since the Court found that the search of the parolee did not violate the Fourth Amendment, the Court did not resolve whether he had waived his Fourth Amendment rights by acquiescing to this condition.

In light of Supreme Court precedents, what, if any, Fourth Amendment limitations would or should be placed, in your opinion, on pat-down frisks, strip searches, and visual body-cavity searches of prisoners? What about manual body-cavity searches, ones that entail an actual touching of the body cavities of an inmate? Supreme Court precedents aside, what restrictions, if any, do you believe the Fourth Amendment places on the searches of prisoners' bodies?

4.   In your opinion, should the Fourth Amendment standards that apply to prisoners differ at all for pretrial detainees? If, as *Bell v. Wolfish* held, a pretrial detainee can be subjected to a visual body-cavity inspection after a contact visit, can a detainee undergo such an inspection during the intake process at a jail? Should the answer to that question depend on the offense for which the detainee was arrested? Cf. Atwater v. City of Lago Vista, 532 U.S. 318, 121 S.Ct. 1536 (2001) (warrantless arrest for a "minor criminal offense," such as violating a seatbelt law, does not violate the Fourth Amendment). Should the answer hinge on the frequency with which individuals being processed into a jail have been caught trying to smuggle contraband into the facility? Should it depend on the kinds of contraband that these individuals

have secreted on or in their bodies? See Bull v. City and County of San Francisco, 539 F.3d 1193, 1210–12 (Tallman, J., dissenting) (citing examples of incoming detainees hiding drugs and other contraband in their buttocks or body cavities, including a female arrested for traffic violations who had a crack pipe and case in her vagina).

Most courts, thus far, have required that strip searches and body-cavity inspections conducted when detainees arrested for "minor crimes" are admitted into a jail be predicated on reasonable suspicion that the detainee is carrying a weapon or contraband. See, e.g., Roberts v. Rhode Island, 239 F.3d 107, 112 (1st Cir.2001) (listing cases). And the broad language of some courts' opinions seems to suggest that the reasonable-suspicion requirement applies to all detainees at intake, regardless of the reason for their arrest. See Powell v. Barrett, 541 F.3d 1298, 1306–07 (11th Cir. 2008) (listing and critiquing some of these cases). By contrast, the Eleventh Circuit Court of Appeals has held that all arrestees being booked into a jail, including those arrested for "relatively minor" offenses, can be strip searched without any reasonable suspicion that they are carrying contraband. Id. at 1300–01 (upholding suspicionless strip searches at intake of individuals arrested, for example, for a traffic violation and for failure to pay child support). The court of appeals opined that *Bell v. Wolfish* dictated this result. The court noted that the Supreme Court upheld in that case even more intrusive, suspicionless searches—visual body-cavity inspections—and did not differentiate between detainees based on the kind of crime for which they were being detained.

If the majority of the lower courts are correct that reasonable suspicion must preface strip and body-cavity searches of some or all pretrial detainees at intake, in what circumstances, if any, would the crime for which the detainee was arrested establish the requisite reasonable suspicion? See Roberts v. Rhode Island, 239 F.3d 107, 112 (1st Cir.2001) (an arrest for a violent felony satisfies the reasonable-suspicion standard); Foote v. Spiegel, 118 F.3d 1416, 1426 (10th Cir.1997) (unreasonable to assume that persons arrested for driving under the influence of drugs "routinely carry a personal stash in a body cavity").

5. Virtually all federal and state courts have upheld the constitutionality of compulsory blood tests and saliva swabs administered to inmates to obtain DNA samples to be stored in DNA databases used to solve crimes. State v. Bartylla, 755 N.W.2d 8, 15–17 (Minn. 2008). Do you agree that these tests comport with the Fourth Amendment? Why or why not? For a discussion of DNA-testing laws that apply, not just to prisoners, but to other convicted felons, see note 3 on page 394.

6. According to the Supreme Court in *Bell v. Wolfish,* a search under the Fourth Amendment may be reasonable even though there are less intrusive means of meeting the governmental objectives served by the search. Do you agree? Is the existence of less intrusive means of accomplishing the governmental objectives at all relevant to the question of the reasonableness of the governmental intrusion?

7. The Supreme Court's refusal to find a least-restrictive-alternative requirement subsumed in the Fourth Amendment is due, at least in part, to a concern about "unrealistic second-guessing" by judges. United States v.

Sharpe, 470 U.S. 675, 686, 105 S.Ct. 1568, 1575 (1985). In *Sharpe,* the Court made some observations about judicial oversight of police conduct under the Fourth Amendment that presumably the Court would hold equally true in the prison context:

> A creative judge engaged in post-hoc evaluation of police conduct can almost always imagine some alternative means by which the objectives of the police might have been accomplished. But "[t]he fact that the protection of the public might, in the abstract, have been accomplished by 'less intrusive' means does not, by itself, render the search unreasonable." The question is not simply whether some other alternative was available, but whether the police acted unreasonably in failing to recognize or to pursue it.

Id. at 686–87, 105 S.Ct. at 1575–76.

8.   Professional standards have urged correctional officials, as a matter of policy, to place certain limits not required by case law on searches. The Model Sentencing and Corrections Act, for example, recommends that examinations of confined persons' body cavities, other than visual inspections of their mouths, noses, or ears, be conducted by medical personnel in the medical unit of a correctional facility. National Conference of Commissioners on Uniform State Laws, Model Sentencing and Corrections Act § 4–119(e)(1978).

Rodriguez v. Ames, 287 F. Supp. 2d 213 (W.D.N.Y. 2003) is one of many cases that have held constitutional prison practices that stand in stark contrast with this recommendation. In that case, a prisoner contested the constitutionality of a visual rectal examination conducted in his cell and in front of his cellmate by a prison doctor. The examination was conducted after the prisoner complained of an intestinal ailment. The district court found that the examination abridged neither the prisoner's right to privacy nor his Eighth Amendment right to be free from cruel and unusual punishment. The court considered the examination to be "cursory"—in its words, "a rather minor inconvenience and embarrassment in the context of prison life full of such things." Id. at 219. The court also emphasized that the doctor, nurse, and cellmate present during the examination were all males, just like the plaintiff, and that the plaintiff's bowel problem was not the kind of medical condition whose disclosure to other inmates would likely subject him to discrimination and violence. Furthermore, the court added, allowing certain medical examinations to be performed in prisoners' cells promoted institutional security by limiting the movement of prisoners to and from the infirmary.

As a matter of policy, what limitations, in your opinion, should be placed on searches of prisoners and pretrial detainees, their belongings, and their living quarters?

B.   RIGHT OF PRIVACY

Nowhere in the Constitution is a right of privacy specifically mentioned. But privacy interests are clearly protected and promoted by the Fourth Amendment, which restricts governmental intrusions into our homes, seizures of our property, and searches and seizures of our bodies.

According to the Supreme Court, the constitutional protection of privacy interests is not confined to the Fourth Amendment. The Court has recognized a constitutional right of privacy that extends beyond the strictures of the Fourth Amendment; this right limits, for example, the extent to which the government can interfere with personal decisions involving such matters as marriage and contraception. See, e.g., Zablocki v. Redhail, 434 U.S. 374, 98 S.Ct. 673 (1978) (holding unconstitutional a law requiring a court's permission before a person, under court order to provide child support for a minor child, can marry); Griswold v. Connecticut, 381 U.S. 479, 85 S.Ct. 1678 (1965) (striking down state statute barring the use of contraceptive devices and prohibiting doctors from giving advice on the use of such devices). In *Zablocki v. Redhail,* the Court observed that this "fundamental right of privacy" is part of the "liberty" protected by the Due Process Clause of the Fourteenth Amendment. 434 U.S. at 384, 98 S.Ct. at 679.

One question concerning the right of privacy is whether it extends to prisoners. If it does, the ensuing question is: To what extent must that right give way when it collides with other important governmental and individual interests? The courts frequently have encountered these questions in cases pitting inmates' asserted right to privacy against the equal-employment rights of individuals of the opposite gender who are working or wish to work in correctional facilities. One of these cases is set forth below.

TIMM v. GUNTER

Court of Appeals, Eighth Circuit, 1990.
917 F.2d 1093.

BOWMAN, CIRCUIT JUDGE.

This is a class action brought by inmates of the Nebraska State Penitentiary (hereinafter "NSP"). They complain that for the prison administrators to allow female guards to perform pat searches and to see them nude or partially nude violates their right to privacy. The female guards counter with equal employment claims. * * *

I.

NSP is an all-male maximum security prison designed to house prisoners who have been classified as requiring medium or maximum security. * * * Housing at NSP is comprised of four main housing units numbered 1–4 (hereinafter "Units 1–4"); a maximum security unit (hereinafter "Unit 5"); and a dormitory-style medium security unit (hereinafter "Unit 6"). * * *

Each of the housing units in Units 1–4 contains two control rooms, one for each two-story wing in the unit. There is always an officer on duty in the control room. Besides having visual access to the two-story wing, the control room officer is responsible for monitoring the two shower rooms on the wing. This is done through the use of two small windows which look into the shower rooms. One window looks into the lower shower room, one into the upper room. Monitoring of the shower rooms is performed by occasionally glancing through the windows.

Each unit in Units 1–4 has four shower rooms, with three shower heads in each. There are no curtains in the shower room, although there is a curtain separating the shower room from an outer vestibule, which opens into the hallway. There is no door between the vestibule and the hallway. The rooms are situated so that the vestibule cannot be viewed from the control rooms, and the showers cannot be viewed from the hall.

Each cell in Units 1–4 contains an unenclosed toilet that is located immediately inside the cell door. When the door is opened inward, the toilet is in direct view from the hall. The solid cell doors contain a small window approximately five feet from the ground.

At fixed times throughout the day, the staff checks all cells by looking through the windows in order to determine that all inmates are present. The staff is required to see "living flesh" during this procedure to ascertain that inmates are in their cells. If the guard cannot see the inmate through the window, the guard knocks on the door. If there is no response, the door is opened. The hallways are subject to patrolling at all times. Unannounced room checks and "shakedowns" are also performed.

Unit 5 consists of three galleries, which contain single-inmate cells. It is the most secure unit at NSP. Each cell contains a toilet in the rear of the cell, which is visible through the window on the cell door. Strip searches are performed routinely in the "bullpen" area of the unit, a secured area in the hallway enclosed by open bars. The bullpen is visible from the hallway.

There are five individual shower stalls in Unit 5, located in the galleries' hallways. The shower heads are located on the wall opposite the cells, with a partial wall running parallel to the wall. The sides of each shower stall are open. Guards observe the showering inmates from approximately thirty feet away, through two sets of open bars.

Unit 6 is a dormitory-style unit which houses only medium-custody inmates. It contains three open sleeping "bays," with single beds arranged in rows in a large room. Inmates dress and undress next to their bed in the sleeping bay; there is no dressing screen available or permitted. The bathrooms in Unit 6 can be viewed from a window in a hallway. Toilets are visible from the window; some have partitions but none have doors. The showers in these bathrooms are visible from either the window or the doorway. Some of the showers have curtains; the prison plans to install curtains on all showers in Unit 6. The bays and bathrooms are subject to continual visual surveillance, counts, and shakedowns.

The outside recreation "yard" contains a urinal located under the guard tower, which is approximately thirty feet above the urinal. The urinal is screened on three sides by a waist-high wall. Inmates are also permitted to leave the yard to use the toilets in the housing units at certain times.

Pat searches are conducted routinely at NSP: during shakedowns, when inmates move between certain areas of the penitentiary, and when it is deemed necessary for security purposes. The pat searches performed at NSP are clothed searches of the body, and involve the guard running his or her hands over the inmate's clothing. It takes approximately ten seconds to perform a pat search. Strip searches are performed when inmates enter and leave the visitors' area, and at other times when deemed necessary. Strip searches are performed on a routine basis only in Unit 5.

In 1983, prison administrators opened all jobs at NSP to applicants on a sex-neutral basis. Female employees were allowed to conduct pat searches on the same basis as male employees, and were put in positions which allowed observation of inmates showering and using toilet facilities, but were not permitted to conduct strip searches.

This policy was challenged by two inmates in 1985. In *Nielsen v. Gunter,* No. CV83–L–682 (Mag.Neb. July 15, 1985), the Magistrate ruled that inmates be given access to showers not visible to female guards and that an inmate, when subject to a pat search, be allowed to demand that the search of his groin area be performed only by a male guard.

In response to this ruling prison administrators developed a new policy which requires that female guards, before pat-searching an inmate, ask the inmate if he would prefer to be searched by a male guard. If the inmate so desires, the pat search is delayed until a male guard arrives. Female officers currently are not assigned to one-person posts as a result of this policy. The policy also excludes female officers from second-shift assignments, so that inmates have the option to shower without being viewed by female guards. Female guards are also not assigned to posts in Unit 5.

Seeking damages and injunctive relief, the inmates filed this suit under 42 U.S.C. § 1983 against the prison administrators, asserting a constitutional claim that their right of privacy was being violated as the result of being viewed while partially or totally nude while showering, using toilet facilities, dressing and undressing, and sleeping.[4] This viewing occurs in the cells, the sleeping bays, the shower rooms, and the bathrooms. The inmates also claimed that the pat searches performed by female guards similarly violated their right of privacy. Finally, the plaintiffs alleged that, as a result of more privacy protections afforded female inmates at the Nebraska Center for Women (hereinafter "NCW"), the female counterpart to NSP, their equal protection rights were violated.[5]

---

4. We proceed in our analysis of this case on the assumption that inmates possess a constitutional right to privacy. For purposes of this case, it is not necessary for us to decide whether this unenumerated right exists or to define its constitutional foundation or scope, and we expressly decline to do so.

5. At NCW, male guards are not assigned routinely to monitor shower rooms, and the showers are equipped with curtains. Cell-door windows have covering flaps that are usually left down,

The female employees, who were brought in as a defendant class, claimed that as a result of being required to obtain inmate consent before performing pat searches, being excluded from second-shift and one-officer posts, and being excluded from all posts at Unit 5, they were denied equal employment opportunities in violation of 42 U.S.C. § 2000e–2(a) (Title VII). They sought injunctive relief.

* * *

The District Court rejected the inmates' equal protection claims, but granted them partial relief on their privacy claims. Specifically, the Court ordered the following accommodations: 1) all guards are to be instructed to refrain from deliberately searching an inmate's genital and anal areas while conducting a pat search; 2) female guards shall be allowed to perform pat searches on the same basis as male guards; 3) inmates, upon request, shall be pat searched by male guards, if the attending female guard decides that such a request is not disruptive and does not pose an undue security risk; 4) female guards shall be instructed to make "minor accommodations of courtesy" when patrolling rooms and galleries to avoid viewing inmates who are using toilet facilities or in a state of undress; and 5) prison administrators shall make various physical and schedule modifications at NSP to accommodate prisoner privacy interests.[6] The court found that the prison policy of staffing Unit 5 with male employees only did not violate Title VII. * * *

* * *

For the reasons set forth below, we reverse the District Court's orders concerning pat searches. We also reverse the court's order requiring physical and staffing modifications at NSP, its order that female guards make "minor accommodations of courtesy" while monitoring inmates, and the award of attorney fees and expenses. Finally, we affirm the court's denial of the inmates' equal protection claims and its denial of the female employees' equal employment claims with respect to Unit 5.

II.

* * *

The case at hand is an excellent example of the difficult, multi-faceted balancing that must be performed by prison administrators. The administrators at NSP must weigh the rights of the prisoners, the equal employment rights of both the female guards and the male guards, and the institutional need for internal security. * * *

---

except when lifted by a guard to view the room. Further, the cell toilets have portable screens to block the view of the monitoring guards. Also, male officers do not perform cross-sex pat searches on a routine basis.

6. These modifications include a window shade for the shower monitoring window in the control centers in Units 1–4, a partial door between the shower vestibule and the hallway in Units 1–4, toilet doors for the bathrooms in Unit 6, a privacy screen for dressing in Unit 6, and staffing of the control centers in Units 1–4 by male guards only for a minimum of two hours a day.

In considering a case of this sort, we use the standard of review set forth by the Court in *Turner* [*v. Safley*, 482 U.S. 78, 107 S.Ct. 2254 (1987)]. Specifically, "when a prison regulation impinges on inmates' constitutional rights, the regulation is valid if it is reasonably related to legitimate penological interests." * * *

A.

Pat searches serve two purposes in a correctional institution: they detect contraband, and they deter the movement of contraband within the institution. * * * Although pat searches are necessary, the question remains whether the pat searches performed by female guards on male inmates at NSP can be considered unreasonable. * * *

The record shows that all NSP employees are trained to perform pat searches in a professional manner, conforming to the generally accepted practices in the field. * * *

The District Court found that any touching of the genital and anal areas is brief and incidental. Several female officers also stated that they have never intentionally touched an inmate's genital or anal areas. In fact, the representative of the plaintiff class, James Timm, testified that he never had experienced being touched in those areas by a female guard.

The District Court found that at NSP most inmates do not reject opposite-sex pat searches with "great frequency." It also found that "[t]he invasion of inmates' privacy in the performance of a pat search is not substantial" * * *.

* * * Although an inmate may very well retain some privacy rights when entering a prison, such rights, when balanced against the legitimate equal employment rights of male and female guards, and against the internal security needs of the prison, must give way to the use of pat searches on a sex-neutral basis as performed at NSP.

The first *Turner* factor, the connection between the prison regulation (sex-neutral pat searches) and the government interests justifying it (internal security and equal employment opportunities), is clear and requires no further explanation. While there may not be an alternative method available for an inmate to exercise his right of privacy while being pat searched, the search is of such short duration and of such minimum obtrusiveness that this factor is of minimum importance. Further, accommodating a right to be free from opposite-sex searches would greatly burden guards and prison resources. There was abundant testimony at trial indicating the problems that arise when female guards are prohibited from conducting pat searches on the same basis as male guards.[10] Finally,

---

10. As a result of the current policy, female officers have not been assigned to one-officer posts, because resources do not permit the creation of a "roving" male guard position to assist in pat searches. The District Court found that this policy created scheduling difficulties, as well as resentment by male guards, tension among male and female employees, deterioration of morale, and a potential decrease in internal security. The current policy could also result in ineffective female supervisors as a result of their lack of experience in certain posts. Further, allowing inmates to "override" female guards by requesting that a male guard search them tends to

the alternatives available impose more than a *de minimis* cost to the prison administration's objectives of maximizing internal security, providing equal employment opportunities, and containing costs.

Thus, we believe the District Court erred in requiring prison administrators to accommodate inmates' rights to be free from opposite-sex pat searches. * * *

B.

Many of the considerations in the opposite-sex pat search analysis apply with equal force to the issue of visual surveillance of male inmates by female guards. Like pat searches, visual surveillance is an essential factor in maintaining prison security. * * *

* * *

None of these techniques involves constant, intrusive observation. For instance, a guard monitoring the shower rooms in Units 1–4 must watch two shower rooms at the same time, through small steam-and-water-covered windows positioned in such a way as to hinder the guard's attempt to see every showering inmate's body in full. Guards monitoring inmates in Units 1–4 pass by the cells while on patrol, occasionally peering through a small window in the cell door which likewise does not afford the guard a full view of the inmate at all times. The view through a cell window of an inmate using the toilet is restricted by the size and position of the window. Guards occasionally open the cell door without notice to the inmate, to pass along a message or to observe the inmate.

In Unit 5, officers observe showering inmates from thirty feet away, through two sets of bars. There is also a partial wall partly enclosing the showers in Unit 5. Some of the showers in Unit 6 are equipped with partitions and curtains; the prison plans to install curtains on all Unit 6 showers. When inmates use these, only their feet are visible to a guard. Inmates using the urinal in the "yard" are monitored from the guard tower thirty feet above the urinal. The urinal is protected by a three-sided wall which, as the District Court found, permits an inmate the opportunity to minimize the view of his genital area from the guard tower.

In circumstances such as these, we are convinced that opposite-sex surveillance of male inmates, performed on the same basis as same-sex surveillance, is not "unreasonable" under the *Turner* analysis. Whatever minimal intrusions on an inmate's privacy may result from such surveillance, whether the inmate is using the bathroom, showering, or sleeping in the nude, are outweighed by institutional concerns for safety and equal employment opportunities. * * *

---

decrease the female guards' authority over the inmates, and causes the female guards to feel like inferior officers. These factors can severely impede overall internal security. As to the possibility that female guards be restricted to conducting pat searches while excluding the groin area completely, the testimony indicates that such a practice would severely diminish the effectiveness of the search.

This observation is borne out by application of the *Turner* test. There is undoubtedly a rational connection between sex-neutral visual surveillance of inmates and the goal of prison security. Second, there are alternative means available for inmates to retain their privacy. The use of a covering towel while using the toilet or while dressing and body positioning while showering or using a urinal allow the more modest inmates to minimize invasions of their privacy. Third, the accommodations prescribed by the District Court adversely affect the guards and prison resources to a significant degree, by requiring many staffing adjustments (which have a particularly adverse effect on the female guards) and not insubstantial expenditures. Finally, these adjustments have more than a *de minimis* cost to prison objectives, by increasing costs and jeopardizing internal security.

As with the pat search policy, prison administrators are in the best position to balance the competing interests present in the context of visual surveillance techniques. Absent a showing that the resultant plan unequally balances such interests so as to violate a constitutional or a federal equal employment opportunity mandate, we must defer to their expertise.

* * * None of these measures—sex-neutral assignments in all areas of the prison except for Unit 5, male-only staff assignments in Unit 5, and maintaining the physical condition of the prison with no additional privacy measures—are prohibited. They neither impermissibly violate the inmates' privacy rights nor impermissibly violate the guards' equal employment rights.

III.

Turning to the inmates' claim that differences in privacy protections afforded male and female inmates in the Nebraska penal system violate the equal protection clause of the fourteenth amendment, we are persuaded that the analysis of this issue by the District Court is correct. The District Court found that male inmates and female inmates "are not similarly situated." * * *

The District Court ruled that differences in security concerns at NSP and NCW (reflecting differences in the number and age of the inmates, the kinds of crimes committed by them, the length of sentences, and the frequency of incidents involving violence, escapes, or contraband) justified the differences in the security measures taken in the two prisons. We agree.

* * *

BRIGHT, SENIOR CIRCUIT JUDGE, dissenting.

To treat men and women as equals does not require that courts ignore that differences exist. Even prisoners, men or women, are entitled to a modicum of privacy and are entitled not to be embarrassed by needlessly requiring that they expose their nakedness and private parts to guards who are of the opposite sex. * * *

* * *

My colleagues have stripped the prisoners of these limited rights, and in doing so, have undertaken the fact finding function of the district judge. * * *

Assuming the *Turner* test applies, the fourth element is crucial, *i.e.,* whether an alternative is available at only a *de minimis* cost to prison objectives. In this case, the evidence evinces several alternatives, as adopted by the district court, which protect prisoners' privacy rights at only a *de minimis* cost to prison objectives. For example, when fashioning relief with respect to pat searches, the district court expressly stated:

> However, the institution can provide a limited accommodation to the plaintiffs' privacy interests *without significant disruption.* Accordingly, women will be permitted to perform pat searches under all circumstances in which men can perform them, and may be assigned one-officer posts, provided that, whenever more than one officer is assigned to a post, the officers assigned must be all male or male and female. Inmates shall be allowed the choice of being searched by a male or female when both are on duty. Such a practice does not discriminate against women and offers nominal intrusion of the inmate's privacy. Likewise, if a male officer is in the immediate vicinity of an inmate who is about to be pat searched by a female officer and the male officer can perform the search without disruption of his duties in the opinion of the female officer, the search should be performed by the male officer upon request. An inmate should also be permitted to wait a reasonable period of time for the male officer to arrive, when doing so would not create an undue security risk in the judgment of the female officer on duty. *In these circumstances, at least, the inmates will have an alternative open to them which will have de minimis impact on the institution, in contrast to the current procedures that exclude women.*

(emphasis added).

Likewise, with regard to relief in the housing units, the district court found that:

> The best solution is one that alters the physical facilities in a manner that protects both security and privacy interests. Such a solution would have no adverse effects upon employment rights of male or female staff and would ensure privacy protections in the future.... I am persuaded that reasonable accommodations to inmate privacy in the showers can be made *at minimal cost to valid penological objectives or employees' interests in equal employment experiences and options.*

(emphasis added).

Here, the district court examined the policies and considered the alternatives in light of the evidence. The result reached is supportable by the evidence and application of existing law.

I would affirm the district court in all respects.

QUESTIONS AND POINTS FOR DISCUSSION

1. The tension between protecting the privacy of inmates and affording equal-employment opportunities to correctional employees, regardless of their gender, becomes a nonissue from a constitutional perspective if inmates have no constitutionally protected privacy interests. The Supreme Court's decision in Turner v. Safley, 482 U.S. 78, 107 S.Ct. 2254 (1987), on page 487, at least arguably suggests that inmates do have a constitutionally based right to privacy. In *Turner,* the Court concluded that a rule restricting inmate marriages violated what the Court described as a fundamental right to marry. Although the Court did not allude to a constitutional right to privacy, the right to marry commonly has been recognized as one subsumed within the more general right to privacy. See, e.g., Zablocki v. Redhail, 434 U.S. 374, 385, 98 S.Ct. 673, 680 (1978).

In Houchins v. KQED, Inc., 438 U.S. 1, 98 S.Ct. 2588 (1978), then Chief Justice Burger wrote an opinion, in which Justices White and Rehnquist joined, that did refer to inmates' "fundamental rights to privacy." In that case, a television and radio broadcasting company had sought, but been denied, permission to photograph parts of a jail after an inmate confined in the jail had committed suicide. Four of the seven Justices of the Supreme Court who participated in the decision concluded that members of the media generally have no greater right of access to jails than members of the public. In the opinion announcing the Court's judgment, Chief Justice Burger dropped a potentially telling footnote in which he stated: "Inmates in jails, prisons, or mental institutions retain certain fundamental rights of privacy; they are not like animals in a zoo to be filmed and photographed at will by the public or by media reporters, however 'educational' the process may be for others." Id. at 5 n. 2, 98 S.Ct. at 2592 n. 2.

Most of the lower courts have either assumed or decided that inmates enjoy a limited right to privacy under the Constitution, one that includes a right to bodily privacy. See, e.g., Boxer X v. Harris, 437 F.3d 1107, 1111 (11th Cir. 2006) (holding that prisoner's allegations that a correctional officer forced him to strip and masturbate himself stated a claim for violation of his constitutional right to bodily privacy). The courts are divided though on the source of inmates' residual privacy rights. Some find these rights rooted in the Fourth Amendment, others in the Eighth Amendment, still others in substantive due process, and others in more that one of these constitutional provisions. Compare Oliver v. Scott, 276 F.3d 736, 743 n. 9, 744–45 (5th Cir. 2002) challenge to cross-gender surveillance of inmates when showering or going to the bathroom should be analyzed as a right-to-privacy claim grounded on substantive due process, not under the Eighth Amendment); Moore v. Carwell, 168 F.3d 234, 237 (5th Cir.1999) (constitutionality of cross-gender strip and body-cavity searches should be analyzed under the Fourth, not the

Eighth, Amendment); and Peckham v. Wisconsin Dep't of Corrections, 141 F.3d 694, 697 (7th Cir.1998) (although the Fourth Amendment affords some protection to prisoners, constitutionality of strip searches is "more properly" analyzed under the Eighth Amendment).

2. Pretrial detainees can contest the constitutionality of correctional practices that encroach on their privacy interests on grounds unavailable to convicted inmates, asserting that the practices constitute the punishment of pretrial detainees proscribed by due process. For example, in Demery v. Arpaio, 378 F.3d 1020 (9th Cir. 2004), pretrial detainees challenged the use of webcams to stream live images worldwide of detainees in the jail being photographed, fingerprinted, frisked, and confined in the holding area. The website transmitting these images received six million hits from around the world during the first few days after it opened. Finding that "turning pretrial detainees into the unwilling objects of the latest reality show" serves no legitimate, nonpunitive governmental objectives, the Ninth Circuit Court of Appeals held that the use of the webcams effectively punished pretrial detainees in violation of due process. Id. at 1031.

3. The courts have struggled in defining the scope of inmates' right to privacy. Some courts have concluded that inmates have the right to be protected from the unrestricted viewing of their genitals or their use of the toilet by members of the opposite sex. See Baker v. Welch, 2003 WL 22901051, at *15–17 (S.D.N.Y. 2003) (listing cases). Other courts, however, have disagreed or expressed doubts regarding the existence of such a right. See, e.g., Somers v. Thurman, 109 F.3d 614, 622 (9th Cir.1997) ("highly questionable" whether inmates have a right to be free from the viewing of their naked bodies by correctional officers of the opposite gender); Johnson v. Phelan, 69 F.3d 144, 150–51 (7th Cir.1995).

The conflict between the courts regarding the scope of inmates' right to privacy reflects, in part, judges' differing perspectives regarding the impact of being seen naked by a member of the opposite sex with whom one does not have an intimate relationship. These differing perspectives were highlighted in *Johnson v. Phelan*, a Seventh Circuit case in which a pretrial detainee protested the monitoring of naked male inmates by female correctional officers. In analyzing the viability of the plaintiff's claim under the Eighth Amendment, Judge Easterbrook, writing for the majority, observed:

> How odd it would be to find in the eighth amendment a right not to be seen by the other sex. Physicians and nurses of one sex routinely examine the other. In exotic places such as California people regularly sit in saunas and hot tubs with unclothed strangers. Most persons' aversion to public nudity pales compared with the taboo against detailed inspections of body cavities, yet the Court found no constitutional obstacle to these in *Wolfish*; the Constitution does not require prison managers to respect the social conventions of free society. * * * More to the point, the clash between modesty and equal employment opportunities has been played out in sports. Women reporters routinely enter locker rooms after games. How could an imposition that male athletes tolerate be deemed cruel and unusual punishment?

Id. at 148.

Dissenting from the majority's rejection of the plaintiff's Eighth Amendment claim, Judge Posner remonstrated:

> There are different ways to look upon the inmates of prisons and jails in the United States * * *. One way is to look upon them as members of a different species, indeed as a type of vermin, devoid of human dignity and entitled to no respect; and then no issue concerning the degrading or brutalizing treatment of prisoners would arise. * * * The parading of naked male inmates in front of female guards, or of naked female inmates in front of male guards, would be no more problematic than "cross-sex surveillance" in a kennel.

> I do not myself consider the 1.5 million inmates of American prisons and jails in that light. * * * A substantial number of these prison and jail inmates, including the plaintiff in this case, have not been convicted of a crime. They are merely charged with [a] crime, and awaiting trial. Some of them may actually be innocent. Of the guilty, many are guilty of sumptuary offenses, or of other victimless crimes uncannily similar to lawful activity (gambling offenses are an example), or of esoteric financial and regulatory offenses (such as violation of the migratory game laws) some of which do not even require a guilty intent. It is wrong to break even foolish laws, or wise laws that should carry only civil penalties. It is wrongful to break the law even when the lawbreaker is flawed, weak, retarded, unstable, ignorant, brutalized, or profoundly disadvantaged, rather than violent, vicious, or evil to the core. But we should have a realistic conception of the composition of the prison and jail population before deciding that they are a scum entitled to nothing better than what a vengeful populace and a resource-starved penal system choose to give them. We must not exaggerate the distance between "us," the lawful ones, the respectable ones, and the prison and jail population; for such exaggeration will make it too easy for us to deny that population the rudiments of humane consideration.

> The nudity taboo retains great strength in the United States. It should not be confused with prudery. It is a taboo against being seen in the nude by strangers, not by one's intimates. * * * There are radical feminists who regard "sex" as a social construction and the very concept of "the opposite sex," implying as it does the dichotomization of the "sexes" (the "genders," as we are being taught to say), as a sign of patriarchy. For these feminists the surveillance of naked male prisoners by female guards and naked female prisoners by male guards are way stations on the road to sexual equality. If prisoners have no rights, the reconceptualization of the prison as a site of progressive social engineering should give us no qualms. Animals have no right to wear clothing. Why prisoners, if they are no better than animals? There is no answer, if the premise is accepted. But it should be rejected, and if it is rejected, and the duty of a society that would like to think of itself as civilized to treat its prisoners humanely therefore acknowledged, then I think that the interest of a prisoner in being free from unnecessary cross-sex surveillance has priority over the unisex-bathroom movement and requires us to reverse the judgment of the district court throwing out this lawsuit.

Id. at 151–52 (Posner, J., concurring and dissenting).

Do you agree with Judge Easterbrook's or Judge Posner's views?

4. The courts concur that inadvertent or infrequent cross-gender viewings of an inmate who is naked or using the toilet are *de minimis* incursions on inmates' privacy interests, not rising to the level of a constitutional violation. See, e.g., Michenfelder v. Sumner, 860 F.2d 328, 334 (9th Cir.1988). In addition, inmates' privacy interests are not invaded unconstitutionally when someone of a different gender will be in the inmates' living area a set, but short, amount of time. The courts reason that if inmates are aware of the impending arrival at a specified time of someone of the other sex, they can take steps to avoid being seen naked or using the toilet. See, e.g., Avery v. Perrin, 473 F.Supp. 90, 92 (D.N.H.1979).

5. Another question concerning the scope of inmates' privacy rights, assuming that they have such rights, is whether correctional officers of one gender can conduct pat-down searches or strip searches of inmates of the opposite gender. Like the court of appeals in *Timm v. Gunter,* many courts have condoned cross-gender pat-down searches, even when they include the touching of genital areas. See, e.g., Rice v. King County, 243 F.3d 549 (Table), 2000 WL 1716272, at *3 (9th Cir. 2000). But see Jordan v. Gardner, 986 F.2d 1521 (9th Cir.1993), discussed on page 712 (distinguishing between cross-gender frisks of male and female inmates and holding the latter searches to be cruel and unusual punishment). Some courts, however, have treated strip searches differently, holding that these types of searches generally should be conducted only by, and in the presence of, correctional officers of the same gender. See, e.g., Canedy v. Boardman, 16 F.3d 183, 187 (7th Cir.1994) (listing cases); Lee v. Downs, 641 F.2d 1117, 1119–20 (4th Cir.1981). By contrast, other courts have held that strip searches conducted for legitimate penological reasons in front of correctional officers of the opposite sex are constitutional, provided that they are not conducted in a way that is designed to harass and humiliate a prisoner. See, e.g., Calhoun v. DeTella, 319 F.3d 936, 938–40 (7th Cir. 2003) (while strip searches of male inmates conducted for legitimate penological reasons in the presence of female correctional officers do not constitute cruel and unusual punishment, the plaintiff stated a cognizable Eighth Amendment claim in his complaint alleging that the female officers were "invited spectators" who joined with the male officers in making lurid comments about him and pointing their sticks towards his rectum while he bent over and spread his buttocks). Compare Roden v. Sowders, 84 Fed. Appx. 611, 612–13 (6th Cir. 2003) (although female correctional officer allegedly laughed during the strip search of the plaintiff conducted after he reportedly was seen smoking marijuana, the search violated neither the Fourth or the Eighth Amendments).

In your opinion, are cross-gender pat-down searches constitutional? Are cross-gender strip searches?

6. All of the courts agree that in emergency situations, correctional officers of the opposite sex can pat down inmates' genital areas and view or conduct strip or even body-cavity searches. Thus in Lee v. Downs, 641 F.2d 1117 (4th Cir.1981), the Fourth Circuit Court of Appeals held that a female inmate had suffered no abridgement of her right to privacy when two male

correctional officers restrained her arms and legs while a female nurse searched her vagina for matches shortly after she had set her paper dress on fire. The court found that although female correctional officers worked in the prison, the male correctional officers' presence during the body-cavity search was reasonable. The female correctional officers could not be removed from their posts within a "reasonable period of time" to restrain the inmate, and in any event, the female correctional officers would have had greater difficulty restraining the inmate, a large and strong woman, increasing the risk that someone would get injured. Id. at 1120.

Whether an emergency existed justifying a particular incursion on an inmate's privacy by a correctional official of the opposite sex will often be the subject of dispute. And even when it is evident that an emergency situation existed at some point, courts may have to determine whether the emergency had abated at the time of the cross-gender monitoring or search. The Eighth Circuit's decision in Hill v. McKinley, 311 F.3d 899 (8th Cir. 2002) is a case in point. In that case, a female jail detainee was extremely drunk, with a blood-alcohol level of over .3 three hours after her arrest. When she became violent and unruly, pounding and kicking at the holding-cell door, several officers decided that she must be placed in a padded cell and removed her clothes for her own safety. When she continued beating on the walls and door in that cell, she was moved to another room where she was placed facedown and spread-eagled on a restraining board. The court of appeals concluded that employing male correctional officers to escort the nude plaintiff from the padded cell did not violate her Fourth Amendment rights because there were not enough female officers on duty to perform this task. But the court held that her Fourth Amendment rights were violated when she remained strapped, legs apart, on the restraining board without any covering to limit the exposure of her genitals to the male officers who were present.

7. A number of courts have striven to accommodate both the interest of prisoners in their bodily privacy and the interest in affording equal-employment opportunities to both men and women. See, e.g., Robino v. Iranon, 145 F.3d 1109, 1110 (9th Cir.1998). Examples of cases where the courts have attempted to protect the privacy rights of inmates while limiting the impact on the equal-employment rights of others include: Hardin v. Stynchcomb, 691 F.2d 1364 (11th Cir.1982) (deputy-sheriff positions cannot be reserved for males; job responsibilities in county jail can be rearranged so female deputy sheriffs do not conduct strip searches of male inmates or watch them use the toilet or take showers); Gunther v. Iowa State Men's Reformatory, 612 F.2d 1079 (8th Cir.1980) (policy of refusing to promote women at men's prison violates Title VII; might be permissible to limit exclusively male positions to those where correctional officers mostly monitor toilets and showers and conduct strip searches); Forts v. Ward, 621 F.2d 1210 (2d Cir.1980) (appropriate sleepwear must be provided to female inmates so that male correctional officers cannot see them scantily clad or nude while sleeping); MacDonald v. Angelone, 69 F.Supp.2d 787 (E.D. Va. 1999) (female correctional officers' observation of male inmate using the toilet did not abridge his right to privacy, in part because he could cover his genitals with a sheet or towel).

8. Accommodations that may be feasible in one prison may be infeasible in another. For example, a policy permitting inmates in one prison to cover

the window on their cell door when they are using the toilet or undressing might protect their privacy without curbing the employment opportunities of others. However, in another prison, where the inmates are more violent or unruly, covered windows might pose a serious threat to the security of the prison. In addition, some accommodations may be impractical because of the way in which a prison has been built. For example, covering windows to protect inmates' privacy would not be a viable option where inmates are housed in cells with bars in the front of the cells rather than solid doors with windows.

9. *Timm v. Gunter* illustrates the difficulty of balancing inmates' right to privacy, the equal-employment rights of others, and the need to maintain institutional security. Other interests may also be implicated when correctional officials are deciding whether to hire members of the opposite sex to work in a particular prison or in certain parts of a prison. For example, some courts and commentators have argued that having correctional officers of the opposite sex work within a prison contributes to prisoners' rehabilitation. This viewpoint was expressed in a witness's affidavit submitted to the court in Bagley v. Watson, 579 F.Supp. 1099 (D.Or.1983):

> [W]omen clearly contribute to the normality of the prison. Prisoners are often people who have great difficulty dealing with women, especially when they do not have an intimate relationship with that woman. Their rehabilitation will not, therefore, be fostered by our creating artificial environments without women. To do this, is merely to ignore the problem during the time of incarceration. The period of incarceration would be a time for men to learn to relate to women in a nonaggressive and non-intimate way. Such a capacity could only serve to enhance their chances for a successful parole adjustment.

Id. at 1101.

Other courts have argued that having members of the opposite sex work in at least some positions in a prison is anti-rehabilitative. For example, in Bowling v. Enomoto, 514 F.Supp. 201 (N.D.Cal.1981), the court said:

> Defendants do not argue, and indeed they could not convincingly argue, that the practice of allowing female officers to view male inmates in the nude furthers the penological interest in rehabilitation. On the contrary, in the normal social setting which prison inmates are ostensibly being rehabilitated to function within, people do not undress, bathe, or defecate in the presence of strangers of the opposite sex.

Id. at 203–04. See also Hudson v. Goodlander, 494 F.Supp. 890, 893 (D.Md. 1980) ("While the Court defers to the Commissioner's judgment that normalization of the prison environment is a desirable policy, it finds that policy cannot be furthered rationally by subjecting male prisoners who are using the showers or toilet facilities to the scrutiny of female officers. Such a practice aggravates, rather than mitigates, the disparity between the prison environment and society at large."); Torres v. Wisconsin Dep't of Health & Soc. Servs., 859 F.2d 1523 (7th Cir.1988) (presence of male correctional officers in a women's prison may be anti-rehabilitative because women prisoners, so many of whom have been physically and sexually abused by males, may need to be insulated from male authority figures to rehabilitate themselves).

10. In *Timm v. Gunter,* the court cited differences in the security threats posed by male and female inmates in rejecting the male inmates' claim that their equal-protection rights were violated since they were subjected to intrusions on their privacy, such as cross-gender pat-down searches, to which female inmates were not subjected. In Madyun v. Franzen, 704 F.2d 954 (7th Cir.1983), the Seventh Circuit Court of Appeals rejected a similar equal-protection claim, but for different reasons:

> Here the State of Illinois, in order to provide opportunities for women to serve as guards in its male prisons, has allowed women guards to frisk search male inmates, while male guards may not frisk search female inmates. This differentiation serves the important state interest of equal job opportunity for women, since women prison guards cannot be truly effective unless they can perform the full range of prison security tasks. Conversely, there is no indication that males have suffered a lack of opportunity to serve as prison guards because they are precluded from frisk searching female inmates. In the interest of being able to equalize opportunities for women to serve as guards in male prisons, therefore, the gender-based distinction that allows women guards to search male prisoners substantially advances an important state interest.

Id. at 962.

Still another reason for allowing the differential treatment of male and female inmates was propounded by the Ninth Circuit Court of Appeals in Jordan v. Gardner, 986 F.2d 1521 (9th Cir.1993). In *Jordan,* the court first described the cross-gender searches whose constitutionality was at issue in the case:

> During the cross-gender clothed body search, the male guard stands next to the female inmate and thoroughly runs his hands over her clothed body starting with her neck and working down to her feet. According to the prison training material, a guard is to "[u]se a flat hand and pushing motion across the [inmate's] crotch area." The guard must "[p]ush inward and upward when searching the crotch and upper thighs of the inmate." All seams in the leg and the crotch area are to be "squeez[ed] and knead[ed]." Using the back of the hand, the guard is to search the breast area in a sweeping motion, so that the breasts will be "flattened." Superintendent Vail estimated that a typical search lasts forty-five seconds to one minute. A training film, viewed by the court, gave the impression that a thorough search would last several minutes.

Id. at 1523.

The court then explained why it considered these cross-gender searches of female inmates to be different from the cross-gender pat-down searches of male inmates that the court had upheld in Grummett v. Rushen, 779 F.2d 491 (9th Cir.1985):

> The record in this case, including the depositions of several inmates and the live testimony of one, describes the shocking histories of verbal, physical, and, in particular, sexual abuse endured by many of the inmates prior to their incarceration at WCCW. For example, S.H., who gave live trial testimony, described rapes by strangers (twice) and by husbands or

boyfriends. She described how she had been beaten by various men in her life. Two deprived her of adequate food; one pushed her out of a moving car. S.H.'s story is not unique. Eighty-five percent of the inmates report a history of serious abuse to WCCW counselors, including rapes, molestations, beatings, and slavery.

Another inmate, K.D., testified by deposition that her second husband beat her, strangled her, and ran her over with a truck. As T.D., another inmate, grew up, she was frequently strapped or handcuffed to a bed by her half-brother, who beat or raped her; T.D.'s mother told her that there was nothing wrong with her half-brother's conduct. T.D.'s mother once directed her to masturbate her stepfather, and in her later teens T.D. was pushed into sexual liaisons by her mother, who would then blackmail the men. Another inmate's hand was broken by one of her two wife-beating husbands. Another, S.E., was sixteen when her uncle impregnated her; after the failure of the uncle's attempts to induce an abortion using a broom handle, screwdriver, bleach, and Lysol, the uncle paid a man to marry her. During that marriage, S.E. was frequently raped by her husband and his friends, one time ending up in the hospital after they beat her and "ripped [her] behind."

The inmates presented testimony from ten expert witnesses on the psychological impact of forced submission to these searches by male guards, and related issues. The experts included WCCW staff members, social workers, psychologists, an anthropologist, and the former Director of Corrections for four different states at various times. The testimony described the psychological fragility of and disorders found in abused women. A psychologist specializing in psychotherapy for women testified that the unwilling submission to bodily contact with the breasts and genitals by men would likely leave the inmate "revictimiz[ed]," resulting in a number of symptoms of post-traumatic stress disorder. Although there was some expert testimony that expressed uncertainty as to the magnitude of the harm suffered by the inmates, the inmates' experts, many of whom were employed by WCCW, were unanimously of the view that some would suffer substantially.

* * *

The record in this case supports the postulate that women experience unwanted intimate touching by men differently from men subject to comparable touching by women. Several witnesses, including experts in psychology and anthropology, discussed how the differences in gender socialization would lead to differences in the experiences of men and women with regard to sexuality.[5] *Grummett* is simply not controlling in this case.

---

5. We do not chart new territory in upholding the district court's finding that men and women may experience unwanted intimate touching by members of the opposite gender differently. In the Title VII context, we concluded:

[B]ecause women are disproportionately victims of rape and sexual assault, women have a stronger incentive to be concerned with sexual behavior.... Men, who are rarely victims of sexual assault, may view sexual conduct in a vacuum without a full appreciation of the social setting or the underlying threat of violence that a woman may perceive.

Ellison v. Brady, 924 F.2d 872, 879 (9th Cir.1991).

Id. at 1525–26.

11. In *Jordan v. Gardner*, the Ninth Circuit invoked the Eighth Amendment in striking down the prison policy requiring male correctional officers to conduct pat-down searches of female prisoners. Chapter 17 discusses the standards applied by the courts when determining whether prisoners have been subjected to the cruel and unusual punishment proscribed by the Eighth Amendment. After reading this chapter, consider anew the question of when the monitoring or searching of prisoners contravenes this constitutional provision.

12. Do you agree with any or all of the reasons asserted by the courts for differentiating, as a constitutional matter, between cross-gender searches of male and female inmates? Should the documented sexual misconduct of some male correctional officers in women's correctional facilities factor into the constitutional calculus? See Amnesty International, "Not Part of My Sentence": Violations of the Human Rights of Women in Custody 38–61 (1999) (identifying prisons and jails in the United States in which male correctional officers have traded food, cosmetics, and money for sexual services from female inmates, impregnated inmates, and raped them); Human Rights Watch, All Too Familiar: Sexual Abuse of Women in U.S. State Prisons (1996). Cf. Everson v. Michigan Dep't of Corrections, 391 F.3d 737, 760–61 (6th Cir. 2004) (citing the "endemic problem of sexual abuse" of female prisoners by male correctional officers in Michigan in holding that barring males from working in the housing units of women's prisons does not violate the equal-employment rights protected by Title VII). Do statistics revealing that females comprise a significant percentage of the staff involved in the sexual victimization of inmates have a bearing on this latter question? See Bureau of Justice Statistics, U.S. Dep't of Justice, Sexual Violence Reported by Correctional Authorities, 2006, at 8 (2007) (reporting that in 2006, 40% of the staff perpetrators of sexual misconduct and harassment were females).

13. Some commentators have objected to what they consider the "sexual profiling" that can limit men's employment opportunities and have reverberating effects on women. Amy Kapczynski, Same–Sex Privacy and the Limits of Antidiscrimination Law, 112 Yale L.J. 1257, 1281 (2003). Professor Teresa Miller has articulated her fundamental concern:

> [W]hen judges presume the sexual vulnerability of female prisoners, they conversely presume that male guards are sexually aggressive. When judges employ gendered stereotypes of men as sexually aggressive, and therefore limit the assignment of male guards within the housing units of women's prisons, they are accepting as a given that male guards are unable to respect the human dignity of women when observing them nude in the act of toileting, showering, and undressing. In accepting this duality of aggression and vulnerability, judges are not just rationalizing outcomes they can feel comfortable with on the basis of presumed traits. They are actually constructing a reality within prisons. They are ultimately writing rules around the fact that "boys will be boys" rather than facilitating a culture change within prisons that requires male guards to conduct themselves professionally, and in the process, to respect the basic human dignity of women prisoners.

Teresa A. Miller, Keeping the Government's Hands Off Our Bodies: Mapping a Feminist Legal Theory Approach to Privacy in Cross–Gender Prison Searches, 4 Buff. Crim. L. Rev. 861, 870–71 (2001).

14.   Does, as Professor Miller has charged, a "heterosexist bias" pervade cases interpreting the scope of inmates' privacy rights—an assumption that all correctional officers and prisoners are heterosexual? Teresa A. Miller, Sex & Surveillance: Gender, Privacy & the Sexualization of Power in Prison, 10 Geo. Mason U. Civ. Rts. L.J. 291, 351 n. 231 (2000). If so, is there any way to effectively remove this bias? Consider the implications of Judge Easterbrook's comments in *Johnson v. Phelan*:

> [T]he prison may assign homosexual male guards to monitor male prisoners, heterosexual male guards to monitor effeminate male homosexual prisoners, and so on. There are too many permutations to place guards and prisoners into multiple classes by sex, sexual orientation, and perhaps other criteria, allowing each group to be observed only by the corresponding groups that occasion the least unhappiness.

69 F.3d 144, 147 (7th Cir.1995).

15.   The courts have been much less hospitable to inmates' bodily-privacy claims not involving correctional officials of the opposite sex. For example, in Michenfelder v. Sumner, 860 F.2d 328 (9th Cir.1988), the prisoner-plaintiff objected to routine strip searches of prisoners housed in the section of the prison reserved for the most dangerous prisoners and those most likely to escape. These strip searches occurred whenever the prisoners left their cells, even though they were handcuffed and manacled when outside their cells. After observing that the prisoner had failed to demonstrate that he would not have an opportunity to obtain contraband or a weapon while outside his cell, the court of appeals concluded that the strip-search policy was reasonably related to a legitimate penological purpose.

The court in *Michenfelder* furthermore rejected the prisoner's argument that the strip searches were unconstitutional because they were conducted out on the tier where nine other inmates could observe the inmate as he stripped. Unlike the district court, which had observed that "[t]his situation is no more offensive than the usual nudity found in a locker room in a school or YMCA," Michenfelder v. Sumner, 624 F.Supp. 457, 463 (D.Nev.1985), the court of appeals found some substance to the prisoner's claim. The court ultimately concluded, however, that the practice of searching inmates in the hallway was constitutional because searching the inmates in their cells or moving them to be searched elsewhere posed dangers to the correctional officer or officers who were to conduct the search. See also Thompson v. Souza, 111 F.3d 694, 701 (9th Cir.1997) (visual body-cavity inspections conducted in front of other inmates did not violate any clearly established Fourth Amendment right; moving inmates to a more private place for inspections might enable contraband to be handed to other inmates); Lile v. McKune, 24 F.Supp.2d 1152, 1164 (D.Kan.1998) (penile plethysmograph testing of prisoner, a convicted rapist, which measured changes in his penis size during the playing of audio recordings of varied sex acts, including depicted rapes, did not violate his right to privacy).

While, as discussed earlier, the interest in rehabilitation has been asserted as a reason for assigning women to work in male prisons, the government's interest in maintaining prison security has been asserted as a reason for excluding women from certain prisons or positions within prisons. In the case which follows, the Supreme Court considered the legality of excluding women from certain prison jobs for institutional-security reasons.

DOTHARD v. RAWLINSON

Supreme Court of the United States, 1977.
433 U.S. 321, 97 S.Ct. 2720, 53 L.Ed.2d 786.

MR. JUSTICE STEWART delivered the opinion of the Court.

Appellee Dianne Rawlinson sought employment with the Alabama Board of Corrections as a prison guard, called in Alabama a "correctional counselor." After her application was rejected, she brought this class suit under Title VII of the Civil Rights Act of 1964 and under 42 U.S.C. § 1983, alleging that she had been denied employment because of her sex in violation of federal law. * * *

I

At the time she applied for a position as correctional counselor trainee, Rawlinson was a 22–year–old college graduate whose major course of study had been correctional psychology. She was refused employment because she failed to meet the minimum 120–pound weight requirement established by an Alabama statute. The statute also establishes a height minimum of 5 feet 2 inches.

After her application was rejected because of her weight, Rawlinson filed a charge with the Equal Employment Opportunity Commission, and ultimately received a right-to-sue letter. She then filed a complaint in the District Court on behalf of herself and other similarly situated women, challenging the statutory height and weight minima as violative of Title VII and the Equal Protection Clause of the Fourteenth Amendment. * * * While the suit was pending, the Alabama Board of Corrections adopted Administrative Regulation 204, establishing gender criteria for assigning correctional counselors to maximum-security institutions for "contact positions," that is, positions requiring continual close physical proximity to inmates of the institution. Rawlinson amended her class-action complaint by adding a challenge to Regulation 204 as also violative of Title VII and the Fourteenth Amendment.

Like most correctional facilities in the United States, Alabama's prisons are segregated on the basis of sex. * * * The Julia Tutwiler Prison for Women and the four male penitentiaries are maximum-security institutions. Their inmate living quarters are for the most part large dormitories, with communal showers and toilets that are open to the dormitories and hallways. The Draper and Fountain penitentiaries carry on extensive farming operations, making necessary a large number of strip searches for contraband when prisoners re-enter the prison buildings.

* * *

At the time this litigation was in the District Court, the Board of Corrections employed a total of 435 people in various correctional counselor positions, 56 of whom were women. * * * Because most of Alabama's prisoners are held at the four maximum-security male penitentiaries, 336 of the 435 correctional counselor jobs were in those institutions, a majority of them concededly in the "contact" classification. Thus, even though meeting the statutory height and weight requirements, women applicants could under Regulation 204 compete equally with men for only about 25% of the correctional counselor jobs available in the Alabama prison system.

II

In enacting Title VII, Congress required "the removal of artificial, arbitrary, and unnecessary barriers to employment when the barriers operate invidiously to discriminate on the basis of racial or other impermissible classification." The District Court found that the minimum statutory height and weight requirements that applicants for employment as correctional counselors must meet constitute the sort of arbitrary barrier to equal employment opportunity that Title VII forbids. The appellants assert that the District Court erred both in finding that the height and weight standards discriminate against women, and in its refusal to find that, even if they do, these standards are justified as "job related."

A

* * *

Although women 14 years of age or older compose 52.75% of the Alabama population and 36.89% of its total labor force, they hold only 12.9% of its correctional counselor positions. * * * When the height and weight restrictions are combined, Alabama's statutory standards would exclude 41.13% of the female population while excluding less than 1% of the male population. Accordingly, the District Court found that Rawlinson had made out a prima facie case of unlawful sex discrimination.

* * *

* * * [W]e cannot say that the District Court was wrong in holding that the statutory height and weight standards had a discriminatory impact on women applicants.

B

We turn, therefore, to the appellants' argument that they have rebutted the prima facie case of discrimination by showing that the height and weight requirements are job related. These requirements, they say, have a relationship to strength, a sufficient but unspecified amount of which is essential to effective job performance as a correctional counselor. In the District Court, however, the appellants produced no evidence correlating the height and weight requirements with the requisite amount of strength thought essential to good job performance. Indeed, they failed to offer evidence of any kind in specific justification of the statutory standards.

If the job-related quality that the appellants identify is bona fide, their purpose could be achieved by adopting and validating a test for applicants that measures strength directly. Such a test, fairly administered, would fully satisfy the standards of Title VII because it would be one that "measure[s] the person for the job and not the person in the abstract." But nothing in the present record even approaches such a measurement.

For the reasons we have discussed, the District Court was not in error in holding that Title VII of the Civil Rights Act of 1964, as amended, prohibits application of the statutory height and weight requirements to Rawlinson and the class she represents.

III

Unlike the statutory height and weight requirements, Regulation 204 explicitly discriminates against women on the basis of their sex. In defense of this overt discrimination, the appellants rely on § 703(e) of Title VII, 42 U.S.C. § 2000e–2(e), which permits sex-based discrimination "in those certain instances where ... sex ... is a bona fide occupational qualification reasonably necessary to the normal operation of that particular business or enterprise."

The District Court rejected the bona-fide-occupational-qualification (bfoq) defense, relying on the virtually uniform view of the federal courts that § 703(e) provides only the narrowest of exceptions to the general rule requiring equality of employment opportunities. * * *

We are persuaded—by the restrictive language of § 703(e), the relevant legislative history, and the consistent interpretation of the Equal Employment Opportunity Commission—that the bfoq exception was in fact meant to be an extremely narrow exception to the general prohibition of discrimination on the basis of sex.[20] In the particular factual circumstances of this case, however, we conclude that the District Court erred in rejecting the State's contention that Regulation 204 falls within the narrow ambit of the bfoq exception.

The environment in Alabama's penitentiaries is a peculiarly inhospitable one for human beings of whatever sex. Indeed, a Federal District Court has held that the conditions of confinement in the prisons of the

---

20. In the case of a state employer, the bfoq exception would have to be interpreted at the very least so as to conform to the Equal Protection Clause of the Fourteenth Amendment. The parties do not suggest, however, that the Equal Protection Clause requires more rigorous scrutiny of a State's sexually discriminatory employment policy than does Title VII. There is thus no occasion to give independent consideration to the District Court's ruling that Regulation 204 violates the Fourteenth Amendment as well as Title VII.

State, characterized by "rampant violence" and a "jungle atmosphere," are constitutionally intolerable. *Pugh v. Locke,* 406 F.Supp. 318, 325 (M.D.Ala.). The record in the present case shows that because of inadequate staff and facilities, no attempt is made in the four maximum-security male penitentiaries to classify or segregate inmates according to their offense or level of dangerousness—a procedure that, according to expert testimony, is essential to effective penological administration. Consequently, the estimated 20% of the male prisoners who are sex offenders are scattered throughout the penitentiaries' dormitory facilities.

In this environment of violence and disorganization, it would be an oversimplification to characterize Regulation 204 as an exercise in "romantic paternalism." In the usual case, the argument that a particular job is too dangerous for women may appropriately be met by the rejoinder that it is the purpose of Title VII to allow the individual woman to make that choice for herself. More is at stake in this case, however, than an individual woman's decision to weigh and accept the risks of employment in a "contact" position in a maximum-security male prison.

The essence of a correctional counselor's job is to maintain prison security. A woman's relative ability to maintain order in a male, maximum-security, unclassified penitentiary of the type Alabama now runs could be directly reduced by her womanhood. There is a basis in fact for expecting that sex offenders who have criminally assaulted women in the past would be moved to do so again if access to women were established within the prison. There would also be a real risk that other inmates, deprived of a normal heterosexual environment, would assault women guards because they were women. In a prison system where violence is the order of the day, where inmate access to guards is facilitated by dormitory living arrangements, where every institution is understaffed, and where a substantial portion of the inmate population is composed of sex offenders mixed at random with other prisoners, there are few visible deterrents to inmate assaults on women custodians.

Appellee Rawlinson's own expert testified that dormitory housing for aggressive inmates poses a greater security problem than single-cell lock-ups, and further testified that it would be unwise to use women as guards in a prison where even 10% of the inmates had been convicted of sex crimes and were not segregated from the other prisoners.[23] The likelihood that inmates would assault a woman because she was a woman would pose a real threat not only to the victim of the assault but also to the basic control of the penitentiary and protection of its inmates and the other security personnel. The employee's very womanhood would thus directly undermine her capacity to provide the security that is the essence of a correctional counselor's responsibility.

---

23. Alabama's penitentiaries are evidently not typical. Appellee Rawlinson's two experts testified that in a normal, relatively stable maximum-security prison—characterized by control over the inmates, reasonable living conditions, and segregation of dangerous offenders—women guards could be used effectively and beneficially. Similarly, an *amicus* brief filed by the State of California attests to that State's success in using women guards in all-male penitentiaries.

There was substantial testimony from experts on both sides of this litigation that the use of women as guards in "contact" positions under the existing conditions in Alabama maximum-security male penitentiaries would pose a substantial security problem, directly linked to the sex of the prison guard. On the basis of that evidence, we conclude that the District Court was in error in ruling that being male is not a bona fide occupational qualification for the job of correctional counselor in a "contact" position in an Alabama male maximum-security penitentiary.[24]

The judgment is accordingly affirmed in part and reversed in part, and the case is remanded to the District Court for further proceedings consistent with this opinion.

* * *

MR. JUSTICE REHNQUIST, with whom THE CHIEF JUSTICE and MR. JUSTICE BLACKMUN join, concurring in the result and concurring in part.

I agree with, and join, Parts I and III of the Court's opinion in this case and with its judgment. While I also agree with the Court's conclusion in Part II of its opinion, holding that the District Court was "not in error" in holding the statutory height and weight requirements in this case to be invalidated by Title VII, the issues with which that Part deals are bound to arise so frequently that I feel obliged to separately state the reasons for my agreement with its result. * * *

* * *

Appellants, in order to rebut the prima facie case under the statute, had the burden placed on them to advance job-related reasons for the qualification. * * * The District Court was confronted, however, with only one suggested job-related reason for the qualification—that of strength. Appellants argued only the job-relatedness of actual physical strength; they did not urge that an equally job-related qualification for prison guards is the *appearance* of strength. As the Court notes, the primary job of correctional counselor in Alabama prisons "is to maintain security and control of the inmates . . . ," a function that I at least would imagine is aided by the psychological impact on prisoners of the presence of tall and heavy guards. If the appearance of strength had been urged upon the District Court here as a reason for the height and weight minima, I think that the District Court would surely have been entitled to reach a different result than it did. For, even if not perfectly correlated, I would think that Title VII would not preclude a State from saying that anyone under 5'2" or 120 pounds, no matter how strong in fact, does not have a sufficient appearance of strength to be a prison guard.

* * *

---

24. The record shows, by contrast, that Alabama's minimum-security facilities, such as work-release centers, are recognized by their inmates as privileged confinement situations not to be lightly jeopardized by disobeying applicable rules of conduct. Inmates assigned to these institutions are thought to be the "cream of the crop" of the Alabama prison population.

MR. JUSTICE MARSHALL, with whom MR. JUSTICE BRENNAN joins, concurring in part and dissenting in part.

I agree entirely with the Court's analysis of Alabama's height and weight requirements for prison guards, and with its finding that these restrictions discriminate on the basis of sex in violation of Title VII. * * * I must, however, respectfully disagree with the Court's application of the bfoq exception in this case.

The Court properly rejects two proffered justifications for denying women jobs as prison guards. It is simply irrelevant here that a guard's occupation is dangerous and that some women might be unable to protect themselves adequately. Those themes permeate the testimony of the state officials below, but as the Court holds, "the argument that a particular job is too dangerous for women" is refuted by the "purpose of Title VII to allow the individual woman to make that choice for herself." Some women, like some men, undoubtedly are not qualified and do not wish to serve as prison guards, but that does not justify the exclusion of all women from this employment opportunity. * * * The highly successful experiences of other States allowing such job opportunities confirm that absolute disqualification of women is not, in the words of Title VII, "reasonably necessary to the normal operation" of a maximum-security prison.

What would otherwise be considered unlawful discrimination against women is justified by the Court, however, on the basis of the "barbaric and inhumane" conditions in Alabama prisons, conditions so bad that state officials have conceded that they violate the Constitution. To me, this analysis sounds distressingly like saying two wrongs make a right. It is refuted by the plain words of § 703(e). The statute requires that a bfoq be "reasonably necessary to the normal operation of that particular business or enterprise." But no governmental "business" may operate "normally" in violation of the Constitution. * * * A prison system operating in blatant violation of the Eighth Amendment is an exception that should be remedied with all possible speed, as Judge Johnson's comprehensive order in *Pugh v. Locke* is designed to do. In the meantime, the existence of such violations should not be legitimatized by calling them "normal." Nor should the Court accept them as justifying conduct that would otherwise violate a statute intended to remedy age-old discrimination.

The Court's error in statutory construction is less objectionable, however, than the attitude it displays toward women. Though the Court recognizes that possible harm to women guards is an unacceptable reason for disqualifying women, it relies instead on an equally speculative threat to prison discipline supposedly generated by the sexuality of female guards. There is simply no evidence in the record to show that women guards would create any danger to security in Alabama prisons significantly greater than that which already exists. All of the dangers—with one exception discussed below—are inherent in a prison setting, whatever the gender of the guards.

The Court first sees women guards as a threat to security because "there are few visible deterrents to inmate assaults on women custodians." In fact, any prison guard is constantly subject to the threat of attack by inmates, and "invisible" deterrents are the guard's only real protection. No prison guard relies primarily on his or her ability to ward off an inmate attack to maintain order. Guards are typically unarmed and sheer numbers of inmates could overcome the normal complement. Rather, like all other law enforcement officers, prison guards must rely primarily on the moral authority of their office and the threat of future punishment for miscreants. As one expert testified below, common sense, fairness, and mental and emotional stability are the qualities a guard needs to cope with the dangers of the job. Well qualified and properly trained women, no less than men, have these psychological weapons at their disposal.

The particular severity of discipline problems in the Alabama maximum-security prisons is also no justification for the discrimination sanctioned by the Court. The District Court found in *Pugh v. Locke* that guards "must spend all their time attempting to maintain control or to protect themselves." If male guards face an impossible situation, it is difficult to see how women could make the problem worse, unless one relies on precisely the type of generalized bias against women that the Court agrees Title VII was intended to outlaw. For example, much of the testimony of appellants' witnesses ignores individual differences among members of each sex and reads like "ancient canards about the proper role of women." The witnesses claimed that women guards are not strict disciplinarians; that they are physically less capable of protecting themselves and subduing unruly inmates; that inmates take advantage of them as they did their mothers, while male guards are strong father figures who easily maintain discipline, and so on. Yet the record shows that the presence of women guards has not led to a single incident amounting to a serious breach of security in any Alabama institution. And, in any event, "[g]uards rarely enter the cell blocks and dormitories," *Pugh v. Locke,* 406 F.Supp., at 325, where the danger of inmate attacks is the greatest.

It appears that the real disqualifying factor in the Court's view is "[t]he employee's very womanhood." The Court refers to the large number of sex offenders in Alabama prisons, and to "[t]he likelihood that inmates would assault a woman because she was a woman." In short, the fundamental justification for the decision is that women as guards will generate sexual assaults. With all respect, this rationale regrettably perpetuates one of the most insidious of the old myths about women—that women, wittingly or not, are seductive sexual objects. The effect of the decision, made I am sure with the best of intentions, is to punish women because their very presence might provoke sexual assaults. It is women who are made to pay the price in lost job opportunities for the threat of depraved conduct by prison inmates. Once again, "[t]he pedestal upon which women have been placed has ..., upon closer inspection, been revealed as a cage." * * *

The Court points to no evidence in the record to support the asserted "likelihood that inmates would assault a woman because she was a woman." Perhaps the Court relies upon common sense, or "innate recognition." But the danger in this emotionally laden context is that common sense will be used to mask the " 'romantic paternalism' " and persisting discriminatory attitudes that the Court properly eschews. To me, the only matter of innate recognition is that the incidence of sexually motivated attacks on guards will be minute compared to the "likelihood that inmates will assault" a *guard* because he or she is a *guard*.

The proper response to inevitable attacks on both female and male guards is not to limit the employment opportunities of law-abiding women who wish to contribute to their community, but to take swift and sure punitive action against the inmate offenders. Presumably, one of the goals of the Alabama prison system is the eradication of inmates' anti-social behavior patterns so that prisoners will be able to live one day in free society. Sex offenders can begin this process by learning to relate to women guards in a socially acceptable manner[5] * * *.

Although I do not countenance the sex discrimination condoned by the majority, it is fortunate that the Court's decision is carefully limited to the facts before it. I trust the lower courts will recognize that the decision was impelled by the shockingly inhuman conditions in Alabama prisons, and thus that the "extremely narrow [bfoq] exception" recognized here will not be allowed "to swallow the rule" against sex discrimination. Expansion of today's decision beyond its narrow factual basis would erect a serious roadblock to economic equality for women.

MR. JUSTICE WHITE, dissenting. [Opinion omitted.]

QUESTIONS AND POINTS FOR DISCUSSION

1. Several courts have distinguished *Dothard v. Rawlinson,* rejecting the contentions of correctional officials that for security reasons, being a male is a bona fide occupational qualification to work in certain men's prisons. See, e.g., Gunther v. Iowa State Men's Reformatory, 612 F.2d 1079, 1085 (8th Cir.1980) (Iowa prison "is no rose garden; neither is it the stygian spectre which faced the Supreme Court in *Dothard*"); Griffin v. Michigan Dep't of Corrections,

---

5. The appellants argue that restrictions on employment of women are also justified by consideration of inmates' privacy. It is strange indeed to hear state officials who have for years been violating the most basic principles of human decency in the operation of their prisons suddenly become concerned about inmate privacy. It is stranger still that these same officials allow women guards in contact positions in a number of nonmaximum-security institutions, but strive to protect inmates' privacy in the prisons where personal freedom is most severely restricted. I have no doubt on this record that appellants' professed concern is nothing but a feeble excuse for discrimination.

As the District Court suggested, it may well be possible, once a constitutionally adequate staff is available, to rearrange work assignments so that legitimate inmate privacy concerns are respected without denying jobs to women. Finally, if women guards behave in a professional manner at all times, they will engender reciprocal respect from inmates, who will recognize that their privacy is being invaded no more than if a woman doctor examines them. The suggestion implicit in the privacy argument that such behavior is unlikely on either side is an insult to the professionalism of guards and the dignity of inmates.

654 F.Supp. 690, 700–01 (E.D.Mich.1982) (probability of sexual assaults on female correctional officers less than in the "jungle-like" conditions in the Alabama prisons at issue in *Dothard*).

2.   In Everson v. Michigan Dep't of Corrections, 391 F.3d 737 (6th Cir. 2004), the Sixth Circuit Court of Appeals held that being female is a bona fide occupational qualification for employment as a correctional or residential unit officer in the housing units of women's prisons in Michigan. Citing the "endemic problem of sexual abuse" in that state's prisons, the court of appeals said that it concurred with the views of the director of the Michigan Department of Corrections (MDOC), who testified that "the [MDOC's] plan to assign only females in the housing units ... challenges the thinking of the past 15 years or so that officers are officers and prisoners are prisoners no matter what their gender, but the [MDOC's] staff and prisoners have paid a high price for going along with this conventional wisdom...." Id. at 760–61. How might, as the court asserted, this conventional wisdom exact a toll on prison staff?

3.   *Class Exercise*: Discuss and debate the following questions:

    a.   What limitations, if any, should be placed on the employment of female correctional officers in men's prisons?

    b.   What limitations, if any, should be placed on the employment of male correctional officers in women's prisons?

CHAPTER 16

DUE-PROCESS CLAIMS FOR PERSONAL INJURIES AND PROPERTY DEPRIVATIONS

■ ■ ■

As discussed in earlier chapters, the Due Process Clause of the Fourteenth Amendment prohibits a state from depriving a person of life, liberty, or property without due process of law. A similar prohibition, applicable to the federal government, can be found in the Fifth Amendment. To prevail on a due-process claim asserted against a government official, there generally must have been a loss of life, liberty, or property; the loss must constitute a deprivation within the meaning of the Due Process Clause; and the deprivation caused by the official must have occurred without due process of law.

The question of when a person has been deprived of a "liberty" interest falling within the scope of the Due Process Clause was discussed in Chapter 14. This chapter will focus on two questions: (1) what constitutes a "deprivation" within the meaning of the Due Process Clause; and (2) when has a prisoner whose property has been lost, damaged, or destroyed or who has suffered personal injuries because of a prison official's actions or inaction been afforded due process?

The Supreme Court addressed both of these questions in Parratt v. Taylor, 451 U.S. 527, 101 S.Ct. 1908 (1981), infra page 733. In *Parratt,* a prisoner brought a § 1983 suit to recover damages for the loss, due to the alleged negligence of several prison officials, of a hobby kit worth $23.50. The Supreme Court held that the negligence of a government official could effect a deprivation of property within the meaning of the Due Process Clause, although the Court ultimately concluded that the prisoner in that case had been afforded due process. Five years later, in *Daniels v. Williams,* the case below, the Court reexamined the question whether negligence will suffice to trigger the requirements of due process.

DANIELS v. WILLIAMS

Supreme Court of the United States, 1986.
474 U.S. 327, 106 S.Ct. 662, 88 L.Ed.2d 662.

JUSTICE REHNQUIST delivered the opinion of the Court.

* * *

In this § 1983 action, petitioner seeks to recover damages for back and ankle injuries allegedly sustained when he fell on a prison stairway. He claims that, while an inmate at the city jail in Richmond, Virginia, he slipped on a pillow negligently left on the stairs by respondent, a correctional deputy stationed at the jail. Respondent's negligence, the argument runs, "deprived" petitioner of his "liberty" interest in freedom from bodily injury; because respondent maintains that he is entitled to the defense of sovereign immunity in a state tort suit, petitioner is without an "adequate" state remedy. Accordingly, the deprivation of liberty was without "due process of law."

The District Court granted respondent's motion for summary judgment. * * * [On appeal, the Fourth Circuit Court of Appeals affirmed.]

* * *

In *Parratt,* before concluding that Nebraska's tort remedy provided all the process that was due, we said that the loss of the prisoner's hobby kit, "even though negligently caused, amounted to a deprivation [under the Due Process Clause]." Justice Powell, concurring in the result, criticized the majority for "pass[ing] over" this important question of the state of mind required to constitute a "deprivation" of property. He argued that negligent acts by state officials, though causing loss of property, are not actionable under the Due Process Clause. To Justice Powell, mere negligence could not "wor[k] a deprivation in the *constitutional sense.*" Not only does the word "deprive" in the Due Process Clause connote more than a negligent act, but we should not "open the federal courts to lawsuits where there has been no affirmative abuse of power." * * * Upon reflection, we agree and overrule *Parratt* to the extent that it states that mere lack of due care by a state official may "deprive" an individual of life, liberty, or property under the Fourteenth Amendment.

The Due Process Clause of the Fourteenth Amendment provides: "[N]or shall any State deprive any person of life, liberty, or property, without due process of law." Historically, this guarantee of due process has been applied to *deliberate* decisions of government officials to deprive a person of life, liberty, or property. *E.g., Davidson v. New Orleans,* 96 U.S. 97 (1878) (assessment of real estate); *Rochin v. California,* 342 U.S. 165 (1952) (stomach pumping); *Bell v. Burson,* 402 U.S. 535 (1971) (suspension of driver's license); *Ingraham v. Wright,* 430 U.S. 651 (1977) (paddling student); *Hudson v. Palmer,* 468 U.S. 517 (1984) (intentional destruction of inmate's property). No decision of this Court before *Parratt* supported the view that negligent conduct by a state official, even though causing injury, constitutes a deprivation under the Due Process Clause. This history reflects the traditional and common-sense notion that the Due Process Clause, like its forebear in the Magna Carta was " 'intended to secure the individual from the arbitrary exercise of the powers of government.' " By requiring the government to follow appropriate procedures when its agents decide to "deprive any person of life, liberty, or property," the Due Process Clause promotes fairness in such decisions. And by barring certain government actions regardless of the fairness of the procedures used to implement them, it serves to prevent governmental power from being "used for purposes of oppression."

We think that the actions of prison custodians in leaving a pillow on the prison stairs, or mislaying an inmate's property, are quite remote from the concerns just discussed. Far from an abuse of power, lack of due care suggests no more than a failure to measure up to the conduct of a reasonable person. To hold that injury caused by such conduct is a deprivation within the meaning of the Fourteenth Amendment would trivialize the centuries-old principle of due process of law.

The Fourteenth Amendment is a part of a Constitution generally designed to allocate governing authority among the Branches of the Federal Government and between that Government and the States, and to secure certain individual rights against both State and Federal Government. When dealing with a claim that such a document creates a right in prisoners to sue a government official because he negligently created an unsafe condition in the prison, we bear in mind Chief Justice Marshall's admonition that "we must never forget, that it is *a constitution* we are expounding," *McCulloch v. Maryland,* 4 Wheat. 316, 407 (1819) (emphasis in original). Our Constitution deals with the large concerns of the governors and the governed, but it does not purport to supplant traditional tort law in laying down rules of conduct to regulate liability for injuries that attend living together in society. We have previously rejected reasoning that " 'would make of the Fourteenth Amendment a font of tort law to be superimposed upon whatever systems may already be administered by the States,' " *Paul v. Davis,* 424 U.S. 693, 701 (1976).

* * *

That injuries inflicted by governmental negligence are not addressed by the United States Constitution is not to say that they may not raise significant legal concerns and lead to the creation of protectible legal interests. * * * It is no reflection on either the breadth of the United States Constitution or the importance of traditional tort law to say that they do not address the same concerns.

In support of his claim that negligent conduct can give rise to a due process "deprivation," petitioner makes several arguments, none of which we find persuasive. He states, for example, that "it is almost certain that *some* negligence claims are within § 1983," and cites as an example the failure of a State to comply with the procedural requirements of *Wolff v.*

McDonnell before depriving an inmate of good-time credit. We think the relevant action of the prison officials in that situation is their deliberate decision to deprive the inmate of good-time credit, not their hypothetically negligent failure to accord him the procedural protections of the Due Process Clause. But we need not rule out the possibility that there are other constitutional provisions that would be violated by mere lack of care in order to hold, as we do, that such conduct does not implicate the Due Process Clause of the Fourteenth Amendment.

Petitioner also suggests that artful litigants, undeterred by a requirement that they plead more than mere negligence, will often be able to allege sufficient facts to support a claim of intentional deprivation. In the instant case, for example, petitioner notes that he could have alleged that the pillow was left on the stairs with the intention of harming him. This invitation to "artful" pleading, petitioner contends, would engender sticky (and needless) disputes over what is fairly pleaded. What's more, requiring complainants to allege something more than negligence would raise serious questions about what "more" than negligence—intent, recklessness, or "gross negligence"—is required,[3] and indeed about what these elusive terms mean. But even if accurate, petitioner's observations do not carry the day. In the first place, many branches of the law abound in nice distinctions that may be troublesome but have been thought nonetheless necessary:

> "I do not think we need trouble ourselves with the thought that my view depends upon differences of degree. The whole law does so as soon as it is civilized." *LeRoy Fibre Co. v. Chicago, M. & St. P.R. Co.,* 232 U.S. 340, 354 (1914) (Holmes, J., partially concurring).

More important, the difference between one end of the spectrum—negligence—and the other—intent—is abundantly clear. In any event, we decline to trivialize the Due Process Clause in an effort to simplify constitutional litigation.

Finally, petitioner argues that respondent's conduct, even if merely negligent, breached a sheriff's "special duty of care" for those in his custody. * * *

* * * Jailers may owe a special duty of care to those in their custody under state tort law, see Restatement (Second) of Torts § 314A(4) (1965), but for the reasons previously stated we reject the contention that the Due Process Clause of the Fourteenth Amendment embraces such a tort law concept. Petitioner alleges that he was injured by the negligence of respondent, a custodial official at the city jail. Whatever other provisions of state law or general jurisprudence he may rightly invoke, the Fourteenth Amendment to the United States Constitution does not afford him a remedy.

---

3. Despite his claim about what he might have pleaded, petitioner concedes that respondent was at most negligent. Accordingly, this case affords us no occasion to consider whether something less than intentional conduct, such as recklessness or "gross negligence," is enough to trigger the protections of the Due Process Clause.

[Justices Marshall, Blackmun, and Stevens concurred in the Court's judgment. Excerpts from Justice Stevens's opinion, in which he concurred in the judgments in both *Daniels v. Williams* and Davidson v. Cannon, 474 U.S. 344, 106 S.Ct. 668 (1986), can be found in note 1 below and note 1 on page 735.]

Questions and Points for Discussion

1. In a companion case to *Daniels v. Williams*, Davidson v. Cannon, id., the Supreme Court reiterated that negligence cannot effect a deprivation within the meaning of the Due Process Clause. In *Davidson,* the plaintiff, a prisoner, had warned prison officials that he had been threatened by another inmate. The prison officials took no steps to protect the plaintiff, who was housed in the same unit with the inmate who had threatened him, and the plaintiff subsequently was attacked by that inmate and seriously injured.

In reaffirming its holding in *Daniels,* the Court emphasized that the plaintiff did not contend that the prison officials had been anything other than negligent in their failure to protect him. A claim of negligence, said the Court, "is quite different from one involving injuries caused by an unjustified attack by prison guards themselves or by another prisoner where officials simply stood by and permitted the attack to proceed." Id. at 348, 106 S.Ct. at 670–71.

In a separate opinion concurring in the judgments in both *Davidson* and *Daniels,* Justice Steven wrote:

> I would not reject these claims, as the Court does, by attempting to fashion a new definition of the term "deprivation" and excluding negligence from its scope. * * * "Deprivation," it seems to me, identifies, not the actor's state of mind, but the victim's infringement or loss. The harm to a prisoner is the same whether a pillow is left on a stair negligently, recklessly, or intentionally; so too, the harm resulting to a prisoner from an attack is the same whether his request for protection is ignored negligently, recklessly, or deliberately. In each instance, the prisoner is losing—being "deprived" of—an aspect of liberty as the result, in part, of a form of state action.

Id. at 340–41, 106 S.Ct. at 679–80 (Stevens, J., concurring in judgments). Justice Stevens nonetheless concurred in the Court's judgments because he believed that the prisoners in *Daniels* and *Davidson* had been afforded due process. See note 1 on page 735.

Justice Blackmun, joined by Justice Marshall, dissented in *Davidson,* making the following observations:

> When the State of New Jersey put Robert Davidson in its prison, it stripped him of all means of self-protection. It forbade his access to a weapon. N.J. Dept. of Corrections Standards 251.4.a.201 and .202. It forbade his fighting back. Standards 251.4.a.002, .003, and .004. It blocked all avenues of escape. The State forced Davidson to rely solely on its own agents for protection. When threatened with violence by a fellow inmate, Davidson turned to the prison officials for protection, but they

ignored his plea for help. As a result, Davidson was assaulted by another inmate. He suffered stab wounds on his face and body as well as a broken nose that required surgery.

* * *

The Court appears to recognize that the injuries to Davidson (as well as that to Daniels in the companion case) implicates the "liberty" protected by the Fourteenth Amendment. It is well established that this liberty includes freedom from unjustified intrusions on personal security. In particular, it includes a prisoner's right to safe conditions and to security from attack by other inmates. * * *

Although Daniels' and Davidson's liberty interests were infringed, the Court holds that they were not "deprived" of liberty in the constitutional sense. * * * I agree that mere negligent activity *ordinarily* will not amount to an abuse of state power. Where the Court today errs, in my view, is in elevating this sensible rule of thumb to the status of inflexible constitutional dogma. The Court declares that negligent activity can *never* implicate the concerns of the Due Process Clause. I see no justification for this rigid view. In some cases, by any reasonable standard, governmental negligence is an abuse of power. This is one of those cases.

It seems to me that when a State assumes sole responsibility for one's physical security and then ignores his call for help, the State cannot claim that it did not know a subsequent injury was likely to occur. Under such circumstances, the State should not automatically be excused from responsibility. In the context of prisons, this means that once the State has taken away an inmate's means of protecting himself from attack by other inmates, a prison official's negligence in providing protection can amount to a deprivation of the inmate's liberty, at least absent extenuating circumstances. Such conduct by state officials seems to me to be the "arbitrary action" against which the Due Process Clause protects. The officials' actions in such cases thus are not remote from the purpose of the Due Process Clause and § 1983.

Moreover, this case does not raise the concern noted in *Daniels* that "[t]he only tie between the facts ... and anything governmental in nature" is the identity of the parties. In *Daniels,* the negligence was only coincidentally connected to an inmate-guard relationship; the same incident could have occurred on any staircase. Daniels in jail was as able as he would have been anywhere else to protect himself against a pillow on the stairs. The State did not prohibit him from looking where he was going or from taking care to avoid the pillow.

In contrast, where the State renders a person vulnerable and strips him of his ability to defend himself, an injury that results from a state official's negligence in performing his duty is peculiarly related to the governmental function. Negligence in such a case implicates the " '[m]isuse of power, possessed by virtue of state law and made possible only because the wrongdoer is clothed with the authority of state law.' " *Monroe v. Pape,* 365 U.S. 167, 184, 81 S.Ct. 473, 482 (1961), quoting *United States v. Classic,* 313 U.S. 299, 326, 61 S.Ct. 1031, 1043 (1941).

Id. at 349, 352–56, 106 S.Ct. at 671–74.

Justice Blackmun also dissented in *Davidson* because he felt that a due-process deprivation could occur, in any event, through the recklessness or deliberate indifference of government officials. In this case, he believed that there was sufficient evidence of recklessness for this question to be considered on remand.

Justice Brennan wrote a dissenting opinion in *Davidson* because he too felt that the prison officials probably had been reckless, thereby depriving Davidson of a liberty interest. Justice Brennan agreed with the majority though that negligence alone would not support the finding of a due-process violation.

2. Rowe v. DeBruyn, 17 F.3d 1047 (7th Cir. 1994) further highlights the conundrum that inmates in some prisons may face if they try to protect themselves from a violent attack by another inmate. In that case, the prisoner-plaintiff received a note from another prisoner named Evans. The note forewarned the plaintiff that Evans planned to have sex with him the next day and that if the plaintiff did not cooperate "someone will get hurt and perhaps even die." When Evans entered the plaintiff's cell the next morning and tried to rape him, the plaintiff hit him over the head with an unheated hot pot. Since prisoners in the state could not invoke the defense of self-defense to a disciplinary charge, the disciplinary committee found the plaintiff guilty of battery. The committee, however, did treat the fact that the plaintiff had acted in self-defense as a mitigating factor when imposing the penalty for the disciplinary infraction.

The Seventh Circuit Court of Appeals held that prisoners have no constitutional right to assert the defense of self-defense in a prison disciplinary hearing. See also Scruggs v. Jordan, 485 F.3d 934 (7th Cir. 2007) (prisoner who lost ninety days of earned credit time, was confined in disciplinary segregation for three months, and was punished in other ways after striking a prisoner on the back with his cane in an attempt to stop him from continuing to stab another prisoner had no constitutional right to assert a defense-of-others defense during disciplinary proceedings). If the court is correct in this conclusion, should it, in your opinion, have any bearing on the question of when prison officials' failure to protect prisoners from attacks by other inmates amounts to a "deprivation" triggering due-process protections? If you were drafting prison disciplinary rules, would you permit inmates to use force to defend themselves or others? Why or why not?

3. Although the Supreme Court in *Daniels* and *Davidson* treated the question whether unintentional conduct can ever violate due process as an open one, the Court had held in an earlier case that correctional officials' deliberate indifference to the serious medical needs of pretrial detainees abridges their due-process rights. City of Revere v. Massachusetts Gen. Hosp., 463 U.S. 239, 244, 103 S.Ct. 2979, 2983 (1983). For the Supreme Court's definition of "deliberate indifference," a term often equated with reckless-ness, see Farmer v. Brennan, 511 U.S. 825, 114 S.Ct. 1970 (1994) on page 779. In later explaining why deliberate indifference can give rise, in some circum-stances, to a due-process violation in the correctional context, the Supreme Court underscored the responsibility of correctional officials to attend to the

basic needs of those whom the government has rendered incapable of meeting their own needs. County of Sacramento v. Lewis, 523 U.S. 833, 851, 118 S.Ct. 1708, 1719 (1998) (holding that a police officer's deliberate indifference when conducting a high-speed chase does not violate substantive due process). The Court furthermore noted:

> [L]iability for deliberate indifference to inmate welfare rests upon the luxury enjoyed by prison officials of having time to make unhurried judgments, upon the chance for repeated reflection, largely uncomplicated by the pulls of competing obligations. When such extended opportunities to do better are teamed with protracted failure even to care, indifference is truly shocking.

Id. at 853, 118 S.Ct. at 1720.

4. The Supreme Court cases mentioned above did not involve procedural due process—the safeguards to which a person constitutionally is entitled before being deprived of an interest protected by the Due Process Clause. But do the Court's holdings or reasoning in those cases, in your opinion, have any bearing on the question whether the recklessness or gross negligence of a government official can trigger the right to those procedural protections?

Most of the lower courts agree that recklessness can effect a "deprivation" within the meaning of the Due Process Clause, although they are divided on the question whether gross negligence will suffice. See Michael K. Cantwell, Constitutional Torts and the Due Process Clause, 4 Temp. Pol. & Civ. Rts. L.Rev. 311, 329–30 (1995) (listing cases). Do you believe that gross negligence reflects the abuse of governmental power that gives rise to due-process concerns? If you were representing a prisoner asserting a deprivation of procedural due process stemming from the gross negligence of a correctional official, how would you respond to the following argument of the Seventh Circuit Court of Appeals for rejecting gross negligence as the basis for due-process liability:

> Gross negligence blends into negligence; there is an indistinct and unusually invisible line between benefits exceeding the cost of precautions (negligence) and benefits substantially exceeding the costs (gross negligence). The malleable quality of these terms has produced scoffing among many, who see gross negligence as simply negligence "with the addition of a vituperative epithet." A line that cannot be policed is not a line worth drawing in constitutional law.

Archie v. City of Racine, 847 F.2d 1211, 1219 (7th Cir. 1988).

Because the Supreme Court concluded in *Daniels* and *Davidson* that the plaintiffs had not suffered any deprivation of their liberty when they were injured, it did not have to address the question whether the plaintiffs had been afforded due process. In *Parratt v. Taylor,* pertinent excerpts of which are set forth below, the Court discussed how the requirements of due process can be satisfied.

PARRATT v. TAYLOR

Supreme Court of the United States, 1981.
451 U.S. 527, 101 S.Ct. 1908, 68 L.Ed.2d 420.

Jᴜsᴛɪᴄᴇ Rᴇʜɴǫᴜɪsᴛ delivered the opinion of the Court.

[The plaintiff in this case, an inmate in a Nebraska prison, brought a § 1983 suit to recover damages for a hobby kit that was lost because of the alleged negligence of several prison officials. As discussed earlier in this chapter, the Supreme Court held that the negligence of government officials could cause a "deprivation" within the meaning of the Due Process Clause, a holding subsequently overruled in *Daniels v. Williams*, supra page 726. The Court then turned to the question whether the deprivation of the plaintiff's property had occurred without due process of law.]

This Court has never directly addressed the question of what process is due a person when an employee of a State negligently takes his property. In some cases this Court has held that due process requires a predeprivation hearing before the State interferes with any liberty or property interest enjoyed by its citizens. In most of these cases, however, the deprivation of property was pursuant to some established state procedure and "process" could be offered before any actual deprivation took place. For example, * * * in *Bell v. Burson,* 402 U.S. 535 (1971), we reviewed a state statute which provided for the taking of the driver's license and registration of an uninsured motorist who had been involved in an accident. We recognized that a driver's license is often involved in the livelihood of a person and as such could not be summarily taken without a prior hearing. * * *

We have, however, recognized that postdeprivation remedies made available by the State can satisfy the Due Process Clause. In such cases, the normal predeprivation notice and opportunity to be heard is pretermitted if the State provides a postdeprivation remedy. In *North American Cold Storage Co. v. Chicago,* 211 U.S. 306 (1908), we upheld the right of a State to seize and destroy unwholesome food without a preseizure hearing. The possibility of erroneous destruction of property was outweighed by the fact that the public health emergency justified immediate action and the owner of the property could recover his damages in an action at law after the incident. * * * Similarly, in *Fahey v. Mallonee,* 332 U.S. 245 (1947), we recognized that the protection of the public interest against economic harm can justify the immediate seizure of property without a prior hearing when substantial questions are raised about the competence of a bank's management. * * * These cases recognize that either the necessity of quick action by the State or the impracticality of providing any meaningful predeprivation process, when coupled with the availability of some meaningful means by which to assess the propriety of the State's action at some time after the initial taking, can satisfy the requirements of procedural due process. * * *

Our past cases mandate that some kind of hearing is required at some time before a State finally deprives a person of his property interests. The fundamental requirement of due process is the opportunity to be heard and it is an "opportunity which must be granted at a meaningful time and in a meaningful manner." However, as many of the above cases recognize, we have rejected the proposition that "at a meaningful time and in a meaningful manner" *always* requires the State to provide a hearing prior to the initial deprivation of property. * * *

The justifications which we have found sufficient to uphold takings of property without any predeprivation process are applicable to a situation such as the present one involving a tortious loss of a prisoner's property as a result of a random and unauthorized act by a state employee. In such a case, the loss is not a result of some established state procedure and the State cannot predict precisely when the loss will occur. It is difficult to conceive of how the State could provide a meaningful hearing before the deprivation takes place. The loss of property, although attributable to the State as action under "color of law," is in almost all cases beyond the control of the State. Indeed, in most cases it is not only impracticable, but impossible, to provide a meaningful hearing before the deprivation. That does not mean, of course, that the State can take property without providing a meaningful postdeprivation hearing. The prior cases which have excused the prior-hearing requirement have rested in part on the availability of some meaningful opportunity subsequent to the initial taking for a determination of rights and liabilities.

* * *

Application of the principles recited above to this case leads us to conclude the respondent has not alleged a violation of the Due Process Clause of the Fourteenth Amendment. Although he has been deprived of property under color of state law, the deprivation did not occur as a result of some established state procedure. Indeed, the deprivation occurred as a result of the unauthorized failure of agents of the State to follow established state procedure. There is no contention that the procedures themselves are inadequate nor is there any contention that it was practicable for the State to provide a predeprivation hearing. Moreover, the State of Nebraska has provided respondent with the means by which he can receive redress for the deprivation. The State provides a remedy to persons who believe they have suffered a tortious loss at the hands of the State. See Neb.Rev.Stat. § 81–8,209 *et seq.* (1976). Through this tort claims procedure the State hears and pays claims of prisoners housed in its penal institutions. This procedure was in existence at the time of the loss here in question but respondent did not use it. It is argued that the State does not adequately protect the respondent's interests because it provides only for an action against the State as opposed to its individual employees, it contains no provisions for punitive damages, and there is no right to a trial by jury. Although the state remedies may not provide the respondent with all the relief which may have been available if he could have proceeded under § 1983, that does not mean that the state remedies are not adequate to satisfy the requirements of due process. The remedies provided could have fully compensated the respondent for the property loss he suffered, and we hold that they are sufficient to satisfy the requirements of due process.

* * * To accept respondent's argument that the conduct of the state officials in this case constituted a violation of the Fourteenth Amendment would almost necessarily result in turning every alleged injury which may have been inflicted by a state official acting under "color of law" into a violation of the Fourteenth Amendment cognizable under § 1983. It is hard to perceive any logical stopping place to such a line of reasoning. Presumably, under this rationale any party who is involved in nothing more than an automobile accident with a state official could allege a constitutional violation under § 1983. Such reasoning "would make of the Fourteenth Amendment a font of tort law to be superimposed upon whatever systems may already be administered by the States." We do not think that the drafters of the Fourteenth Amendment intended the Amendment to play such a role in our society.

* * *

QUESTIONS AND POINTS FOR DISCUSSION

1. You will recall that Justice Stevens did not join the majority's opinion in Davidson v. Cannon, 474 U.S. 344, 106 S.Ct. 668 (1986), supra page 729, because he believed, unlike the majority, that the negligence of a government employee can deprive someone of an interest protected by the Due Process Clause. Justice Stevens still concurred in the judgment in that case, however, because he believed that the state had afforded Davidson the requisite due process. Justice Stevens explained why he adhered to this conclusion despite the fact that a statute accorded immunity to state employees sued by prisoners for personal injuries inflicted by other prisoners:

Davidson puts the question whether a state policy of noncompensability for certain types of harm, in which state action may play a role, renders a state procedure constitutionally defective. In my judgment, a state policy that defeats recovery does not, in itself, carry that consequence. Those aspects of a State's tort regime that defeat recovery are not constitutionally invalid, so long as there is no fundamental unfairness in their operation. Thus, defenses such as contributory negligence or statutes of limitations may defeat recovery in particular cases without raising any question about the constitutionality of a State's procedures for disposing of tort litigation. Similarly, in my judgment, the mere fact that a State elects to provide some of its agents with a sovereign immunity defense in certain cases does not justify the conclusion that its remedial system is constitutionally inadequate. There is no reason to believe that the Due Process Clause of the Fourteenth Amendment and the legislation enacted pursuant to § 5 of that Amendment should be construed to suggest that the doctrine of sovereign immunity renders a state procedure fundamentally unfair. Davidson's challenge has been only to the fact of sovereign immunity; he has not challenged the difference in treatment of a prisoner assaulted by a prisoner and a non-prisoner assaulted by a prisoner, and I express no comment on the fairness of that differentiation.

Id. at 342–43, 106 S.Ct. at 680–81 (Stevens, J., concurring).

In a dissenting opinion in which he was joined by Justice Marshall, Justice Blackmun spurned the notion that Davidson had a meaningful postdeprivation remedy available to him even though any claim that he filed in state court would be dismissed immediately upon the assertion of a state immunity defense. Because the majority of the Court concluded that Davidson had not suffered a deprivation in the constitutional sense, it left to another day and another case the resolution of the question whether an individual is afforded due process when an immunity defense will preclude the recovery of damages. How do you believe this issue should be resolved?

2. In Hudson v. Palmer, 468 U.S. 517, 104 S.Ct. 3194 (1984), the Supreme Court extended its holding in *Parratt* to intentional property deprivations. The plaintiff in that case, a prisoner, sued the defendant, a correctional officer, after the defendant allegedly searched the plaintiff's cell and destroyed some of his personal property just to harass him. The plaintiff contended that the defendant's actions violated his rights under the Fourth Amendment and the Due Process Clause of the Fourteenth Amendment.

After rejecting the plaintiff's Fourth Amendment claim, see page 680, the Court turned to his due-process claim:

> While *Parratt* is necessarily limited by its facts to negligent deprivations of property, it is evident, as the Court of Appeals recognized, that its reasoning applies as well to intentional deprivations of property. The underlying rationale of *Parratt* is that when deprivations of property are effected through random and unauthorized conduct of a state employee, predeprivation procedures are simply "impracticable" since the state cannot know when such deprivations will occur. We can discern no logical distinction between negligent and intentional deprivations of property insofar as the "practicability" of affording predeprivation process is concerned. The state can no more anticipate and control in advance the random and unauthorized intentional conduct of its employees than it can anticipate similar negligent conduct. Arguably, intentional acts are even more difficult to anticipate because one bent on intentionally depriving a person of his property might well take affirmative steps to avoid signaling his intent.

> * * *

> Respondent * * * contends that, because an agent of the state who intends to deprive a person of his property "*can* provide predeprivation process, then as a matter of due process he must do so." This argument reflects a fundamental misunderstanding of *Parratt*. There we held that postdeprivation procedures satisfy due process because the *state* cannot possibly know in advance of a negligent deprivation of property. Whether an individual employee himself is able to foresee a deprivation is simply of

no consequence. The controlling inquiry is solely whether the state is in a position to provide for predeprivation process.

Id. at 533–34, 104 S.Ct. at 3203–04. The Court concluded by holding that when a state employee has randomly and intentionally destroyed someone's property without authorization, the requirements of due process are met as long as the state affords the aggrieved individual a "meaningful postdeprivation remedy." Id. at 533, 104 S.Ct. at 3203.

Justice Stevens, joined by Justices Brennan, Marshall, and Blackmun, concurred in the Court's disposition of the plaintiff's due-process claim in *Hudson*. Justice Stevens emphasized, however, that he did not construe the Court's decision as extending to either violations of substantive constitutional rights—those that occur regardless of the procedures employed by the government—or to deprivations effected through "established prison procedures." Id. at 541 n. 4, 104 S.Ct. at 3208 n. 4 (Stevens, J., concurring and dissenting). A majority of the Supreme Court later held in Logan v. Zimmerman Brush Co., 455 U.S. 422, 436, 102 S.Ct. 1148, 1158 (1982) that the availability of state postdeprivation remedies does not satisfy due process when a deprivation of property was effectuated through an "established state procedure." In Zinermon v. Burch, 494 U.S. 113, 110 S.Ct. 975 (1990), the case that follows, the Court further limited the scope of *Parratt*. As you read this case, consider its implications in the prison setting.

ZINERMON v. BURCH

Supreme Court of the United States, 1990.
494 U.S. 113, 110 S.Ct. 975, 108 L.Ed.2d 100.

JUSTICE BLACKMUN delivered the opinion of the Court.

I

Respondent Darrell Burch brought this suit under 42 U.S.C. § 1983 against the 11 petitioners, who are physicians, administrators, and staff members at Florida State Hospital (FSH) in Chattahoochee, and others. Respondent alleges that petitioners deprived him of his liberty, without due process of law, by admitting him to FSH as a "voluntary" mental patient when he was incompetent to give informed consent to his admission. Burch contends that in his case petitioners should have afforded him procedural safeguards required by the Constitution before involuntary commitment of a mentally ill person, and that petitioners' failure to do so violated his due process rights.

* * *

II

* * *

On December 7, 1981, Burch was found wandering along a Florida highway, appearing to be hurt and disoriented. He was taken to Apalachee Community Mental Health Services (ACMHS) in Tallahassee. ACMHS is a private mental health care facility designated by the State to receive patients suffering from mental illness. Its staff in their evaluation forms stated that, upon his arrival at ACMHS, Burch was hallucinating, confused and psychotic and believed he was "in heaven." His face and chest were bruised and bloodied, suggesting that he had fallen or had been attacked. Burch was asked to sign forms giving his consent to admission and treatment. He did so. He remained at ACMHS for three days, during which time the facility's staff diagnosed his condition as paranoid schizophrenia and gave him psychotropic medication. On December 10, the staff found that Burch was "in need of longer-term stabilization" and referred him to FSH, a public hospital owned and operated by the State as a mental health treatment facility. Later that day, Burch signed forms requesting admission and authorizing treatment at FSH. * * *

* * *

Burch remained at FSH until May 7, 1982, five months after his initial admission to ACMHS. During that time, no hearing was held regarding his hospitalization and treatment.

* * *

Burch's complaint thus alleges that he was admitted to and detained at FSH for five months under Florida's statutory provisions for "voluntary" admission. These provisions are part of a comprehensive statutory scheme under which a person may be admitted to a mental hospital in several different ways.

* * *

[U]nder a court order a person may be detained at a mental health facility for up to five days for evaluation, if he is likely "to injure himself or others" or if he is in "need of care or treatment which, if not provided, may result in neglect or refusal to care for himself and . . . such neglect or refusal poses a real and present threat of substantial harm to his well-being." * * *

[A] person may be detained as an involuntary patient, if he meets the same criteria as for evaluation, and if the facility administrator and two mental health professionals recommend involuntary placement. Before involuntary placement, the patient has a right to notice, a judicial hearing, appointed counsel, access to medical records and personnel, and an independent expert examination. * * *

Finally, a person may be admitted as a voluntary patient. Mental hospitals may admit for treatment any adult "making application by express and informed consent," if he is "found to show evidence of mental illness and to be suitable for treatment." "Express and informed consent" is defined as "consent voluntarily given in writing after sufficient explanation and disclosure . . . to enable the person . . . to make a knowing and willful decision without any element of force, fraud, deceit, duress, or other form of constraint or coercion." * * *

* * *

III

A

* * * [W]e return to the interpretation of § 1983 articulated in *Monroe v. Pape*, 365 U.S. 167 (1961). In *Monroe*, this Court rejected the view that § 1983 applies only to violations of constitutional rights that are authorized by state law, and does not reach abuses of state authority that are forbidden by the State's statutes or Constitution or are torts under the State's common law. It explained that § 1983 was intended not only to "override" discriminatory or otherwise unconstitutional state laws, and to provide a remedy for violations of civil rights "where state law was inadequate," but also to provide a federal remedy "where the state remedy, though adequate in theory, was not available in practice." * * *

Thus, overlapping state remedies are generally irrelevant to the question of the existence of a cause of action under § 1983. A plaintiff, for example, may bring a § 1983 action for an unlawful search and seizure despite the fact that the search and seizure violated the State's Constitution or statutes, and despite the fact that there are common-law remedies for trespass and conversion. As we noted in *Monroe*, in many cases there is "no quarrel with the state laws on the books"; instead, the problem is the way those laws are or are not implemented by state officials.

This general rule applies in a straightforward way to two of the three kinds of § 1983 claims that may be brought against the State under the Due Process Clause of the Fourteenth Amendment. First, the Clause incorporates many of the specific protections defined in the Bill of Rights. A plaintiff may bring suit under § 1983 for state officials' violation of his rights to, *e.g.*, freedom of speech or freedom from unreasonable searches and seizures. Second, the Due Process Clause contains a substantive component that bars certain arbitrary, wrongful government actions "regardless of the fairness of the procedures used to implement them." As to these two types of claims, the constitutional violation actionable under § 1983 is complete when the wrongful action is taken. A plaintiff, under *Monroe v. Pape*, may invoke § 1983 regardless of any state-tort remedy that might be available to compensate him for the deprivation of these rights.

The Due Process Clause also encompasses a third type of protection, a guarantee of fair procedure. A § 1983 action may be brought for a violation of procedural due process, but here the existence of state remedies *is* relevant in a special sense. In procedural due process claims, the deprivation by state action of a constitutionally protected interest in "life, liberty, or property" is not in itself unconstitutional; what is unconstitutional is the deprivation of such an interest *without due process of law*. * * * Therefore, to determine whether a constitutional violation has occurred, it is necessary to ask what process the State provided, and whether it was constitutionally adequate. * * *

* * * The claim at issue falls within the third, or procedural, category of § 1983 claims based on the Due Process Clause.

B

* * * To determine what procedural protections the Constitution requires in a particular case, we weigh several factors:

"First, the private interest that will be affected by the official action; second, the risk of an erroneous deprivation of such interest through the procedures used, and the probable value, if any, of additional or substitute procedural safeguards; and finally, the Government's interest, including the function involved and the fiscal and administrative burdens that the additional or substitute procedural requirement would entail." *Mathews v. Eldridge,* 424 U.S. 319, 335 (1976).

Applying this test, the Court usually has held that the Constitution requires some kind of a hearing *before* the State deprives a person of liberty or property.

In some circumstances, however, the Court has held that a statutory provision for a postdeprivation hearing, or a common-law tort remedy for erroneous deprivation, satisfies due process.

This is where the *Parratt* rule comes into play. *Parratt* and *Hudson* represent a special case of the general *Mathews v. Eldridge* analysis, in which postdeprivation tort remedies are all the process that is due, simply because they are the only remedies the State could be expected to provide. * * *

* * * Thus, *Parratt* is not an exception to the *Mathews* balancing test, but rather an application of that test to the unusual case in which one of the variables in the *Mathews* equation—the value of predeprivation safeguards—is negligible in preventing the kind of deprivation at issue. Therefore, no matter how significant the private interest at stake and the risk of its erroneous deprivation, the State cannot be required constitutionally to do the impossible by providing predeprivation process.

* * *

C

* * *

Burch argues that postdeprivation tort remedies are *never* constitutionally adequate for a deprivation of liberty, as opposed to property, so the *Parratt* rule cannot apply to this case. We, however, do not find support in precedent for a categorical distinction between a deprivation of liberty and one of property. * * *

* * *[T]he reasoning of *Parratt* and *Hudson* emphasizes the State's inability to provide predeprivation process because of the random and unpredictable nature of the deprivation, not the fact that only property losses were at stake. In situations where the State feasibly can provide a predeprivation hearing before taking property, it generally must do so regardless of the adequacy of a postdeprivation tort remedy to compensate for the taking. Conversely, in situations where a predeprivation hearing is unduly burdensome in proportion to the liberty interest at stake or where the State is truly unable to anticipate and prevent a random deprivation of a liberty interest, postdeprivation remedies might satisfy due process. Thus, the fact that a deprivation of liberty is involved in this case does not automatically preclude application of the *Parratt* rule.

To determine whether, as petitioners contend, the *Parratt* rule necessarily precludes § 1983 liability in this case, we must ask whether predeprivation procedural safeguards could address the risk of deprivations of the kind Burch alleges. To do this, we examine the risk involved. The risk is that some persons who come into Florida's mental health facilities will apparently be willing to sign forms authorizing admission and treatment, but will be incompetent to give the "express and informed consent" required for voluntary placement * * *. Indeed, the very nature of mental illness makes it foreseeable that a person needing mental health care will be unable to understand any proffered "explanation and disclosure of the subject matter" of the forms that person is asked to sign, and will be unable "to make a knowing and willful decision" whether to consent to admission. * * *

Persons who are mentally ill and incapable of giving informed consent to admission would not necessarily meet the statutory standard for involuntary placement, which requires either that they are likely to injure themselves or others, or that their neglect or refusal to care for themselves threatens their well-being. The involuntary placement process serves to guard against the confinement of a person who, though mentally ill, is harmless and can live safely outside an institution. Confinement of such a person not only violates Florida law, but also is unconstitutional. *O'Connor v. Donaldson*, 422 U.S. 563, 575 (1975) (there is no constitutional basis for confining mentally ill persons involuntarily "if they are dangerous to no one and can live safely in freedom"). Thus, it is at least possible that if Burch had had an involuntary placement hearing, he would not have been found to meet the statutory standard for involuntary placement and would not have been confined at FSH. * * *

* * *

We now consider whether predeprivation safeguards would have any value in guarding against the kind of deprivation Burch allegedly suffered. Petitioners urge that here, as in *Parratt* and *Hudson*, such procedures could have no value at all, because the State cannot prevent its officials from making random and unauthorized errors in the admission process. We disagree.

The Florida statutes, of course, do not allow incompetent persons to be admitted as "voluntary" patients. But the statutes do not direct any member of the facility staff to determine whether a person is competent to give consent, nor to initiate the involuntary placement procedure for every incompetent patient. * * *

* * *

This case, therefore, is not controlled by *Parratt* and *Hudson*, for three basic reasons:

First, petitioners cannot claim that the deprivation of Burch's liberty was unpredictable. Under Florida's statutory scheme, only a person competent to give informed consent may be admitted as a voluntary patient. There is, however, no specified way of determining, before a patient is asked to sign admission forms, whether he is competent. It is hardly unforeseeable that a person requesting treatment for mental illness might be incapable of informed consent, and that state officials with the power to admit patients might take their apparent willingness to be admitted at face value and not initiate involuntary placement procedures. Any erroneous deprivation will occur, if at all, at a specific, predictable point in the admission process—when a patient is given admission forms to sign.

This situation differs from the State's predicament in *Parratt*. While it could anticipate that prison employees would occasionally lose property through negligence, it certainly "cannot predict precisely when the loss will occur." Likewise, in *Hudson,* the State might be able to predict that guards occasionally will harass or persecute prisoners they dislike, but cannot "know when such deprivations will occur."

Second, we cannot say that predeprivation process was impossible here. Florida already has an established procedure for involuntary placement. The problem is only to ensure that this procedure is afforded to all patients who cannot be admitted voluntarily, both those who are unwilling and those who are unable to give consent.

* * *

Third, petitioners cannot characterize their conduct as "unauthorized" in the sense the term is used in *Parratt* and *Hudson*. The State delegated to them the power and authority to effect the very deprivation complained of here, Burch's confinement in a mental hospital, and also delegated to them the concomitant duty to initiate the procedural safeguards set up by state law to guard against unlawful confinement. In *Parratt* and *Hudson*, the state employees had no similar broad authority to deprive prisoners of their personal property, and no similar duty to initiate (for persons unable to protect their own interests) the procedural safeguards required before deprivations occur. The deprivation here is "unauthorized" only in the sense that it was not an act sanctioned by state law, but, instead, was a "depriv[ation] of constitutional rights ... by an official's abuse of his position."[20]

* * * Burch, according to the allegations of his complaint, was deprived of a substantial liberty interest without either valid consent or an involuntary placement hearing, by the very state officials charged with the

---

20. * * * *Parratt* and *Hudson* * * * do not stand for the proposition that in every case where a deprivation is caused by an "unauthorized ... departure from established practices," state officials can escape § 1983 liability simply because the State provides tort remedies. This reading of *Parratt* and *Hudson* detaches those cases from their proper role as special applications of the settled principles expressed in *Monroe* and *Mathews*.

power to deprive mental patients of their liberty and the duty to implement procedural safeguards. Such a deprivation is foreseeable, due to the nature of mental illness, and will occur, if at all, at a predictable point in the admission process. Unlike *Parratt* and *Hudson*, this case does not represent the special instance of the *Mathews* due process analysis where postdeprivation process is all that is due because no predeprivation safeguards would be of use in preventing the kind of deprivation alleged.

* * *

JUSTICE O'CONNOR, with whom THE CHIEF JUSTICE, JUSTICE SCALIA, and JUSTICE KENNEDY join, dissenting. [Opinion omitted.]

QUESTIONS AND POINTS FOR DISCUSSION

1. Assume that some of a prisoner's personal property was confiscated, in conformance with prison rules, while he was confined in the prison's segregation unit. Upon his release from segregation, prison officials failed to return the confiscated property as required by the prison's policies. Under what circumstances, if any, would this failure violate the prisoner's right to due process of law?

2. In your opinion, is *Zinermon* consistent with *Parratt* and *Hudson*? Describing these cases as "resembling the path of a drunken sailor," Easter House v. Felder, 910 F.2d 1387, 1409 (7th Cir.1990) (Easterbrook, J., concurring), Seventh Circuit Judge Frank Easterbrook concluded:

> *Zinermon v. Burch* is inconsistent with the foundations of *Parratt v. Taylor* and *Hudson v. Palmer*. *Zinermon* said that if errors in the implementation of a state's scheme for civil commitment are foreseeable, then process after the fact is inadequate, and it "distinguished" *Parratt* and *Hudson* on the ground that the wrongs committed in those cases were not foreseeable. This is no distinction at all. It is always foreseeable that there will be some errors in the implementation of any administrative system, and it is never foreseeable which occasions will give rise to these errors. It was foreseeable that some prison guards would lose the prisoners' property (*Parratt*), just as it was foreseeable that some persons would be committed without proper authorization (*Zinermon*); in neither case could the state or a court know in advance just when the errors would occur. If foreseeability of the *category* of blunders requires process in advance, then *Parratt* and *Hudson* were wrongly decided; if the inability to foresee the *particular* blunder makes subsequent remedies all the process "due", then *Zinermon* was wrongly decided. The cases cannot coexist, except perhaps by drawing a distinction between liberty and property, or between important and modest deprivations, neither of which the majority in *Zinermon* adopted.

Id. at 1408.

3. The distinction that the Supreme Court drew in *Zinermon* between substantive claims, to which the *Parratt* rule does not apply, and procedural-due-process claims, to which the rule in some circumstances does apply, also has been criticized. In explaining the basis for his concern about the substan-

tive/procedural distinction erected by the Supreme Court, Ninth Circuit Judge Joseph Sneed observed:

> [T]he line between a "substantive constitutional proscription" and procedural due process is less helpful than might appear at first glance, however. Consider, for example, an assault and battery by a state official upon, first, an ordinary citizen, and, second, a prisoner in a state prison. In both instances the victim could base his claim on a deprivation of liberty without due process of law. A threshold issue in each case would be whether [a] *Parratt* analysis was available and, if so, whether its requirements were met. The prisoner victim, however, also could couch his complaint as a violation of the Eighth Amendment's proscription against cruel and unusual punishment and in this manner render *Parratt* inapplicable. Moreover, the prisoner's complaint could state a claim under both procedural and "substantive" due process * * *. In sum, the flexible manner in which constitutional injuries can be stated strongly suggests that the procedural-substantive due process distinction has no roots in logic.

Mann v. City of Tucson, Dep't of Police, 782 F.2d 790, 796–97 (9th Cir.1986) (Sneed, J., concurring). See also Albright v. Oliver, 510 U.S. 266, 285, 114 S.Ct. 807, 819 (1994) (Kennedy, J., concurring) (referring to the "transformation" of *Parratt* into a "mere pleading exercise" in which claims are labeled substantive rather than procedural). Do you consider the criticisms of the limitations placed on the *Parratt* rule's scope well-founded?

CHAPTER 17

CRUEL AND UNUSUAL PUNISHMENT

▪ ▪ ▪

The Eighth Amendment to the United States Constitution prohibits the infliction of "cruel and unusual punishments." This amendment extends its protection to prisoners. If pretrial detainees contend that they are being treated cruelly and unusually, their claims will be assessed under another constitutional provision, usually the Due Process Clause of the Fifth or Fourteenth Amendments. As mentioned in Chapter 10, the question whether convicted, but unsentenced, inmates challenging the conditions of their confinement or their treatment while in jail are to be considered pretrial detainees or prisoners has yet to be resolved definitively for constitutional purposes. Compare Tilmon v. Prator, 368 F.3d 521, 523–24 (5th Cir. 2004) (inmate convicted, but not sentenced, has the rights of a sentenced prisoner, not a pretrial detainee) with Fuentes v. Wagner, 206 F.3d 335, 341 & n. 7 (3d Cir.2000) (due process, not Eighth Amendment, applies to excessive-force claim of convicted, but unsentenced, inmate).

Cruel and unusual punishment claims have arisen in a number of different contexts. For example, prisoners have challenged, as cruel and unusual punishment, inadequacies in the medical care they were afforded, correctional officers' use of force against them, the failure to protect them from attacks by other inmates, and the conditions of their confinement.

In the sections below, these types of cruel and unusual punishment claims are discussed. In addition, cases discussing Eighth Amendment challenges to the sentences imposed in criminal cases can be found in Chapters 6 and 7.

A. MEDICAL AND PSYCHIATRIC CARE

1. THE RIGHT TO RECEIVE MEDICAL TREATMENT

In Madrid v. Gomez, 889 F.Supp. 1146, 1200–27 (N.D.Cal.1995), the federal district court described graphic examples of deficiencies in the medical treatment of prisoners at the Pelican Bay State Prison in California that led the court to conclude that the medical-care delivery system was unconstitutional. A few of these examples are set forth below:

An example of MTA [Medical Technical Assistant] failure to refer seriously ill inmates to a physician is the case of Ralph Burke. At 2:00 a.m. on November 1, 1992, Burke notified an MTA that his back hurt and he was having trouble breathing. The MTA gave him some ibuprofen, an over-the-counter pain reliever, but refused to take him to the infirmary. At 4:30 a.m., Burke told the MTA that his neck hurt and that he could not move. The MTA still refused to take him to the clinic. Half an hour later the MTA noted that the inmate was "sleeping," but at 5:45 a.m. noticed that Burke was "breathing in a snorting mode" and took him to the infirmary for evaluation. Although Burke was semi-conscious and paralyzed, repeatedly blurting out "help me," MTAs and the infirmary nurse were convinced that he was "faking it." When Burke was finally taken to the hospital after 7:00 a.m., he was diagnosed with an intercranial hemorrhage; he entered a coma and died shortly thereafter.

* * *

Even when inmates presenting serious medical problems are put on the doctor's line by MTAs, prisoners experience delays ranging from significant to appalling before they actually see a physician. Understaffing has created a constant backlog of inmates vying for appointments. For instance, in 1991, when Pelican Bay was particularly short of doctors, inmates waited to see a doctor for as long as four to six weeks. Inmate Arturo Castillo's experience exemplifies the outrageous delays typical of Pelican Bay's early years. After suffering a serious scalp laceration, Castillo was treated with surgical staples at Sutter Coast Hospital and then returned to his cell after a week's recuperation in the prison infirmary. Castillo subsequently told an MTA that his wound had become painful, dirty, and itchy, and even filed a grievance, but the MTA merely told him he could see a doctor in two weeks. Castillo received no medical attention at all until weeks after he complained, when a piece of his scalp finally became so severely infected that it fell off.

* * *

Perhaps the most graphic example of inadequate medical care is that received by inmate Vaughn Dortch. [Dortch, a mentally ill prisoner, was placed in a bathtub of scalding water by several correctional officers, while his hands were cuffed behind his back. When he stood up, large clumps of skin from his buttocks hung around his legs.] Dortch had received second-and third-degree burns that eventually required skin grafts on his legs and buttocks, surgical excision of part of his scrotum, and extensive physical therapy. However, despite patently obvious indications that Dortch was burned, Dr. Astorga and Dr. Gard attempted to minimize or deny the full extent of his injuries, saying that Dortch merely had "dead skin" or "exfoliation." His transfer to the hospital was delayed over an hour, until he went into shock and his blood pressure became dangerously low because medical staff had not started fluid resuscitation. * * *

* * *

The record amply demonstrates defendants' unresponsiveness to the health needs of inmates at Pelican Bay. Some of defendants' comments, actions, and policies show such disregard for inmates' pain and suffering that they shock the conscience. * * * MTA logs contain unabashed notations such as "[c]omplains of chest pain. Hah!", revealing medical staff's often flippant attitudes toward inmates' pain and suffering. Occurrences like these led Dr. Start [the former director of health-care services for the Oklahoma and Texas prison systems] to state that "[b]ased on my experience in eighteen years of correctional health care, I cannot think of a prison that more completely embodies a callous indifference toward inmate health needs."

Id. at 1206–07, 1212–13.

In the case that follows, the Supreme Court discussed when the inadequate medical care of prisoners rises to the level of a constitutional violation.

ESTELLE v. GAMBLE

Supreme Court of the United States, 1976.
429 U.S. 97, 97 S.Ct. 285, 50 L.Ed.2d 251.

MR. JUSTICE MARSHALL delivered the opinion of the Court.

Respondent J.W. Gamble, an inmate of the Texas Department of Corrections, was injured on November 9, 1973, while performing a prison work assignment. On February 11, 1974, he instituted this civil rights action under 42 U.S.C. § 1983, complaining of the treatment he received after the injury. Named as defendants were the petitioners, W.J. Estelle, Jr., Director of the Department of Corrections, H.H. Husbands, warden of the prison, and Dr. Ralph Gray, medical director of the Department and chief medical officer of the prison hospital. The District Court, *sua sponte,* dismissed the complaint for failure to state a claim upon which relief could be granted. The Court of Appeals reversed and remanded with instructions to reinstate the complaint. * * *

I

Because the complaint was dismissed for failure to state a claim, we must take as true its handwritten, *pro se* allegations. According to the complaint, Gamble was injured on November 9, 1973, when a bale of cotton fell on him while he was unloading a truck. He continued to work but after four hours he became stiff and was granted a pass to the unit hospital. At the hospital a medical assistant, "Captain" Blunt, checked him for a hernia and sent him back to his cell. Within two hours the pain became so intense that Gamble returned to the hospital where he was given pain pills by an inmate nurse and then was examined by a doctor.

The following day, Gamble saw a Dr. Astone who diagnosed the injury as a lower back strain, prescribed Zactirin (a pain reliever) and Robaxin (a muscle relaxant), and placed respondent on "cell-pass, cell-feed" status for two days, allowing him to remain in his cell at all times except for showers. On November 12, Gamble again saw Dr. Astone who continued the medication and cell-pass, cell-feed for another seven days. He also ordered that respondent be moved from an upper to a lower bunk for one week, but the prison authorities did not comply with that directive. The following week, Gamble returned to Dr. Astone. The doctor continued the muscle relaxant but prescribed a new pain reliever, Febridyne, and placed respondent on cell-pass for seven days, permitting him to remain in his cell except for meals and showers. On November 26, respondent again saw Dr. Astone, who put respondent back on the original pain reliever for five days and continued the cell-pass for another week.

On December 3, despite Gamble's statement that his back hurt as much as it had the first day, Dr. Astone took him off cell-pass, thereby certifying him to be capable of light work. At the same time, Dr. Astone prescribed Febridyne for seven days. Gamble then went to a Major Muddox and told him that he was in too much pain to work. Muddox had respondent moved to "administrative segregation." On December 5, Gamble was taken before the prison disciplinary committee, apparently because of his refusal to work. When the committee heard his complaint of back pain and high blood pressure, it directed that he be seen by another doctor.

On December 6, respondent saw petitioner Gray, who performed a urinalysis, blood test, and blood pressure measurement. Dr. Gray prescribed the drug Ser–Ap–Es for the high blood pressure and more Febridyne for the back pain. The following week respondent again saw Dr. Gray, who continued the Ser–Ap–Es for an additional 30 days. The prescription was not filled for four days, however, because the staff lost it. Respondent went to the unit hospital twice more in December; both times he was seen by Captain Blunt, who prescribed Tiognolos (described as a muscle relaxant). For all of December, respondent remained in administrative segregation.

In early January, Gamble was told on two occasions that he would be sent to the "farm" if he did not return to work. He refused, nonetheless, claiming to be in too much pain. On January 7, 1974, he requested to go on sick call for his back pain and migraine headaches. After an initial refusal, he saw Captain Blunt who prescribed sodium salicylate (a pain reliever) for seven days and Ser–Ap–Es for 30 days. Respondent returned to Captain Blunt on January 17 and January 25, and received renewals of the pain reliever prescription both times. Throughout the month, respondent was kept in administrative segregation.

On January 31, Gamble was brought before the prison disciplinary committee for his refusal to work in early January. He told the committee that he could not work because of his severe back pain and his high blood pressure. Captain Blunt testified that Gamble was in "first class" medical condition. The committee, with no further medical examination or testimony, placed respondent in solitary confinement.

Four days later, on February 4, at 8 a.m., respondent asked to see a doctor for chest pains and "blank outs." It was not until 7:30 that night that a medical assistant examined him and ordered him hospitalized. The following day a Dr. Heaton performed an electrocardiogram; one day later respondent was placed on Quinidine for treatment of irregular cardiac rhythm and moved to administrative segregation. On February 7, respondent again experienced pain in his chest, left arm, and back and asked to see a doctor. The guards refused. He asked again the next day. The guards again refused. Finally, on February 9, he was allowed to see Dr. Heaton, who ordered the Quinidine continued for three more days. On February 11, he swore out his complaint.

II

The gravamen of respondent's § 1983 complaint is that petitioners have subjected him to cruel and unusual punishment in violation of the Eighth Amendment, made applicable to the States by the Fourteenth. * * *

The history of the constitutional prohibition of "cruel and unusual punishments" has been recounted at length in prior opinions of the Court and need not be repeated here. It suffices to note that the primary concern of the drafters was to proscribe "torture[s]" and other "barbar[ous]" methods of punishment. * * *

Our more recent cases, however, have held that the Amendment proscribes more than physically barbarous punishments. The Amendment embodies "broad and idealistic concepts of dignity, civilized standards, humanity, and decency . . ." against which we must evaluate penal measures. Thus, we have held repugnant to the Eighth Amendment punishments which are incompatible with "the evolving standards of decency that mark the progress of a maturing society," or which "involve the unnecessary and wanton infliction of pain."

These elementary principles establish the government's obligation to provide medical care for those whom it is punishing by incarceration. An inmate must rely on prison authorities to treat his medical needs; if the authorities fail to do so, those needs will not be met. In the worst cases, such a failure may actually produce physical "torture or a lingering death," * * * the evils of most immediate concern to the drafters of the Amendment. In less serious cases, denial of medical care may result in pain and suffering which no one suggests would serve any penological purpose. The infliction of such unnecessary suffering is inconsistent with contemporary standards of decency * * *.

We therefore conclude that deliberate indifference to serious medical needs of prisoners constitutes the "unnecessary and wanton infliction of pain" proscribed by the Eighth Amendment. This is true whether the indifference is manifested by prison doctors in their response to the prisoner's needs[10] or by prison guards in intentionally denying or delaying access to medical care or intentionally interfering with the treatment once prescribed. * * *

This conclusion does not mean, however, that every claim by a prisoner that he has not received adequate medical treatment states a violation of the Eighth Amendment. An accident, although it may produce added anguish, is not on that basis alone to be characterized as wanton infliction of unnecessary pain. * * *

Similarly, in the medical context, an inadvertent failure to provide adequate medical care cannot be said to constitute "an unnecessary and wanton infliction of pain" or to be "repugnant to the conscience of mankind." Thus, a complaint that a physician has been negligent in diagnosing or treating a medical condition does not state a valid claim of medical mistreatment under the Eighth Amendment. Medical malpractice does not become a constitutional violation merely because the victim is a prisoner. In order to state a cognizable claim, a prisoner must allege acts or omissions sufficiently harmful to evidence deliberate indifference to serious medical needs. * * *

III

Against this backdrop, we now consider whether respondent's complaint states a cognizable § 1983 claim. The handwritten *pro se* document is to be liberally construed. As the Court unanimously held in *Haines v. Kerner,* 404 U.S. 519 (1972), a *pro se* complaint, "however inartfully pleaded," must be held to "less stringent standards than formal pleadings drafted by lawyers" * * *.

Even applying these liberal standards, however, Gamble's claims against Dr. Gray, both in his capacity as treating physician and as medical director of the Corrections Department, are not cognizable under § 1983. Gamble was seen by medical personnel on 17 occasions spanning a three-month period: by Dr. Astone five times; by Dr. Gray twice; by Dr. Heaton three times; by an unidentified doctor and inmate nurse on the day of the injury; and by medical assistant Blunt six times. They treated his back injury, high blood pressure, and heart problems. Gamble has disclaimed any objection to the treatment provided for his high blood pressure and his heart problem; his complaint is "based solely on the lack of diagnosis and inadequate treatment of his back injury." The doctors diagnosed his injury as a lower back strain and treated it with bed rest, muscle relaxants, and pain relievers. Respondent contends that more should have

---

10. See, *e.g., Williams v. Vincent,* 508 F.2d 541 (C.A.2 1974) (doctor's choosing the "easier and less efficacious treatment" of throwing away the prisoner's ear and stitching the stump may be attributable to "deliberate indifference ... rather than an exercise of professional judgment"); *Thomas v. Pate,* 493 F.2d 151, 158 (CA7 [1974]) (injection of penicillin with knowledge that prisoner was allergic, and refusal of doctor to treat allergic reaction); *Jones v. Lockhart,* 484 F.2d 1192 (C.A.8 1973) (refusal of paramedic to provide treatment); *Martinez v. Mancusi,* 443 F.2d 921 (C.A.2 1970) (prison physician refuses to administer the prescribed pain killer and renders leg surgery unsuccessful by requiring prisoner to stand despite contrary instructions of surgeon).

been done by way of diagnosis and treatment, and suggests a number of options that were not pursued. The Court of Appeals agreed, stating: "Certainly an X-ray of [Gamble's] lower back might have been in order and other tests conducted that would have led to appropriate diagnosis and treatment for the daily pain and suffering he was experiencing." But the question whether an X-ray—or additional diagnostic techniques or forms of treatment—is indicated is a classic example of a matter for medical judgment. A medical decision not to order an X-ray, or like measures, does not represent cruel and unusual punishment. At most it is medical malpractice, and as such the proper forum is the state court under the Texas Tort Claims Act. * * *

* * *

MR. JUSTICE BLACKMUN concurs in the judgment of the Court.

MR. JUSTICE STEVENS, dissenting.

* * *

On the basis of Gamble's handwritten complaint it is impossible to assess the quality of the medical attention he received. As the Court points out, even if what he alleges is true, the doctors may be guilty of nothing more than negligence or malpractice. On the other hand, it is surely not inconceivable that an overworked, undermanned medical staff in a crowded prison[2] is following the expedient course of routinely prescribing nothing more than pain killers when a thorough diagnosis would disclose an obvious need for remedial treatment. Three fine judges sitting on the United States Court of Appeals for the Fifth Circuit thought that enough had been alleged to require some inquiry into the actual facts. If this Court meant what it said in *Haines v. Kerner,* 404 U.S. 519 [1972], these judges were clearly right.

* * *

* * * [B]y its repeated references to "deliberate indifference" and the "intentional" denial of adequate medical care, I believe the Court improperly attaches significance to the subjective motivation of the defendant as a criterion for determining whether cruel and unusual punishment has been inflicted. Subjective motivation may well determine what, if any, remedy is appropriate against a particular defendant. However, whether the constitutional standard has been violated should turn on the character of the punishment rather than the motivation of the individual who inflicted it.[13] Whether the conditions in Andersonville were the product of design, negligence, or mere poverty, they were cruel and inhuman.

* * *

---

2. According to a state legislative report quoted by the Court of Appeals, the Texas Department of Corrections has had at various times one to three doctors to care for 17,000 inmates with occasional part-time help.

13. * * * If a State elects to impose imprisonment as a punishment for crime, I believe it has an obligation to provide the persons in its custody with a health care system which meets minimal

QUESTIONS AND POINTS FOR DISCUSSION

1. The Supreme Court in *Estelle v. Gamble* did not define what constitutes a "serious medical need." Many lower-court cases have defined a medical need as "serious" if a physician has diagnosed the condition as one requiring medical treatment or if the need for medical treatment would be "obvious," even to a layperson. See, e.g., Williams v. Liefer, 491 F.3d 710, 714 (7th Cir. 2007). Whether the need for medical treatment is "obvious" may depend on a number of factors, including the nature of the medical problem, the likelihood that pain or injury will result if medical treatment is delayed or denied, the severity of the pain or injury that might result from the delay or denial of medical services, and the extent to which pain or other harm attributable to the delay or denial of medical care has actually occurred.

Even if a prisoner suffers no physical injury from a delay in providing medical treatment, a "serious medical need" might be implicated if the prisoner is experiencing severe pain that could be alleviated through prompt medical attention. In Williams v. Liefer, 491 F.3d 710 (7th Cir. 2007), a prisoner told several correctional officers that he was having severe chest pain, but they ignored his repeated requests for medical assistance. Only when he blacked out was he taken to the prison emergency room. The nitroglycerin administered there promptly relieved his pain, and his blood pressure, which was dangerously high, decreased. The Seventh Circuit Court of Appeals refused to set aside the judgment for the prisoner, concluding that the jury reasonably could have found that the defendants disregarded a serious medical need by prolonging the prisoner's pain and high blood pressure for six hours for "no good reason." Id. at 716.

2. Although prisoners normally may not have a "serious medical need" for certain elective operations, such as tonsillectomies, the court in Derrickson v. Keve, 390 F.Supp. 905 (D.Del.1975), found that a prisoner had a constitutional right to two elective operations—a tonsillectomy and a resectioning of his nasal septum. The operations would have relieved the discomfort the prisoner was suffering from headaches, congestion, and a sore throat. Emphasizing that the prisoner was serving a life sentence, the court noted that the prisoner, unlike most other prisoners, could not opt to have the operations when later released from prison. His need for the operations, according to the court, was consequently much greater. See also Monmouth County Correctional Institutional Inmates v. Lanzaro, 834 F.2d 326, 351 (3d Cir.1987) (in the absence of alternative means of funding elective, nontherapeutic abortions for inmates, county must pay for them).

---

standards of adequacy. As a part of that basic obligation, the State and its agents have an affirmative duty to provide reasonable access to medical care, to provide competent, diligent medical personnel, and to ensure that prescribed care is in fact delivered. For denial of medical care is surely not part of the punishment which civilized nations may impose for crime.

Of course, not every instance of improper health care violates the Eighth Amendment. Like the rest of us, prisoners must take the risk that a competent, diligent physician will make an error. Such an error may give rise to a tort claim but not necessarily to a constitutional claim. But when the State adds to this risk, as by providing a physician who does not meet minimum standards of competence or diligence or who cannot give adequate care because of an excessive caseload or inadequate facilities, then the prisoner may suffer from a breach of the State's constitutional duty.

3.　According to the courts, "serious" medical needs are not confined to physical ailments; a prisoner may also have a "serious" medical need because of a mental-health problem. See, e.g., Domino v. Texas Dep't of Criminal Justice, 239 F.3d 752, 754 (5th Cir.2001). It is felt that such problems, if left unattended, may cause pain and suffering as grave or unendurable as that experienced from physical injuries.

The question arises as to when a mental or emotional affliction will give rise to a constitutional duty to provide care. An inmate's complaint that he feels depressed will not, by itself, suffice. Partee v. Lane, 528 F.Supp. 1254, 1261 (N.D.Ill.1981). As the court pointed out in *Partee,* if such a complaint could give rise to a constitutional claim, almost all prisoners would be entitled to psychological or psychiatric treatment since almost all prisoners are, because of their incarceration, depressed some or even all of the time.

In Bowring v. Godwin, 551 F.2d 44 (4th Cir.1977), the Fourth Circuit Court of Appeals set forth a three-part test to be applied when determining whether a prisoner is constitutionally entitled to psychological or psychiatric care. A prisoner is entitled to such care under this test "if a physician or other health care provider, exercising ordinary skill and care at the time of observation, concludes with reasonable medical certainty (1) that the prisoner's symptoms evidence a serious disease or injury; (2) that such disease or injury is curable or may be substantially alleviated; and (3) that the potential for harm to the prisoner by reason of delay or the denial of care would be substantial." Id. at 47. The court added the caveat that even when these conditions are met, the right to treatment is not an unlimited one; the right only extends to treatment that can be provided on a "reasonable cost and time basis." Id. at 48. Nor, the court noted, is there a right to treatment that is "merely desirable"; the governing test is one of "medical necessity." Id.

4.　As noted by the Supreme Court in *Estelle v. Gamble,* the failure to attend to a prisoner's "serious medical needs" does not alone contravene the Eighth Amendment. For a violation of the Eighth Amendment to occur, prison officials must act more than negligently; their actions or inaction must rise to the level of "deliberate indifference." For an in-depth discussion of what constitutes "deliberate indifference," see the Supreme Court's opinion in Farmer v. Brennan, 511 U.S. 825, 114 S.Ct. 1970 (1994) on page 779.

"Deliberate indifference" can be manifested in a number of different ways. The refusal of correctional or medical personnel to provide medical treatment to a prisoner or their delay in providing such treatment, for example, may be attributable to their "deliberate indifference." See, e.g., Hayes v. Snyder, 546 F.3d 516, 523–26 (7th Cir. 2008) (jury could reasonably conclude that prisoner, who suffered muscle spasms that compressed his testicle and caused excruciating pain, had serious medical need to which the prison's medical director was deliberately indifferent when refusing to approve referral to a urologist or prescribed painkillers); Boyd v. Knox, 47 F.3d 966, 969 (8th Cir.1995) (prison dentist's three-week delay in completing referral form for a tooth extraction could constitute an Eighth Amendment violation when the defendant had observed the prisoner's swollen mouth and seen pus oozing from his infected tooth); Toombs v. Bell, 798 F.2d 297, 298 (8th Cir.1986) (prisoner, whose complaints of abdominal pain were ignored for three weeks and whose gallbladder ultimately had to be removed because of the delay in treatment, sufficiently alleged deliberate indifference). A number of lower courts also have observed that "deliberate indifference" may become apparent through a series of incidents which, if viewed in isolation, appear to involve only negligence. See, e.g., Brooks v. Celeste, 39 F.3d 125, 128–29 (6th Cir.1994) (listing cases).

In addition, courts have recognized that general systemic problems in staffing, facilities, equipment, and procedures may be so egregious, and the ensuing inability to render adequate medical care so evident, that the failure to redress these problems is tantamount to "deliberate indifference." See, e.g., Bass v. Wallenstein, 769 F.2d 1173 (7th Cir.1985) (sick-call procedures that failed to ensure prompt access to medical care; medical personnel not qualified to use cardiac life-support equipment); Wellman v. Faulkner, 715 F.2d 269 (7th Cir.1983) (two of three doctors at the prison could barely speak English; no on-site psychiatrist; failure to stock necessary medical supplies, such as colostomy bags); Ramos v. Lamm, 639 F.2d 559 (10th Cir.1980) (primary physician worked at the prison only ten hours a week, instead of the forty hours considered necessary by all of the expert witnesses; inmates used as X-ray technicians, laboratory technicians, and other medical assistants; no on-site psychiatrist or psychologist, although experts agreed prison needed one full-time psychiatrist; delay of two to five weeks before receiving mental-health treatment); Williams v. Edwards, 547 F.2d 1206 (5th Cir.1977) (about half of the inmate nurses had a fifth-grade education or less; pharmacist had neither a pharmacological license or schooling in pharmacology; "filthy" emergency equipment; live fish kept in the whirlpool bath in the physical-therapy department); Coleman v. Wilson, 912 F.Supp. 1282 (E.D.Cal.1995) (no adequate mechanism for screening inmates for mental illness; severe and chronic shortage of mental-health staff; such long delays in obtaining mental-health treatment that some inmates cut their wrists in order to obtain medication); Madrid v. Gomez, 889 F.Supp. 1146 (N.D.Cal.1995) (gross under-staffing causing lengthy delays in medical treatment and, in turn, deaths and serious injuries; inadequate screening for tuberculosis and other communicable diseases; inaccurate, incomplete, and unavailable inmate medical records due to "disastrous" medical-records system).

5. Courts have held that as long as the medical care afforded a prisoner is "adequate," which does not mean "perfect, the best obtainable, or even very good," Brown v. Beck, 481 F.Supp. 723, 726 (S.D.Ga.1980), the prisoner generally has no right to be treated by a private physician. See, e.g., Hawley v. Evans, 716 F.Supp. 601, 603–04 (N.D.Ga.1989); Gahagan v. Pennsylvania Bd. of Probation and Parole, 444 F.Supp. 1326, 1330 (E.D.Pa.1978). This is true even when the inmate is willing and able to pay the costs of obtaining private medical assistance, absent a state law or regulation affording such a right.

6. The claims of pretrial detainees that they have been deprived uncon-stitutionally of needed medical treatment are analyzed under the Due Process Clauses of the Fifth and Fourteenth Amendments rather than under the Eighth Amendment. Courts have agreed that due process affords pretrial detainees at least the amount of protection afforded convicted prisoners by the Eighth Amendment; in other words, correctional officials cannot be "deliberately indifferent" to the "serious medical needs" of pretrial detainees.

See, e.g., City of Revere v. Massachusetts Gen. Hosp., 463 U.S. 239, 244, 103 S.Ct. 2979, 2983 (1983). One question which remains is whether the constitutional standard that must be met when providing pretrial detainees with medical care exceeds the Eighth Amendment standard. How would you resolve this question and why? See, e.g., Danley v. Allen, 540 F.3d 1298, 1310 (11th Cir.2008) (applying the deliberate-indifference standard to the medical claim of a pretrial detainee).

7.　The failure to accommodate the special needs of a disabled inmate not only raises potential constitutional concerns, but may give rise to a statutory claim. For example, state and local inmates fall within the protection of the Americans with Disabilities Act (ADA), 42 U.S.C. §§ 12101–12213. Pennsylvania Dep't of Corrections v. Yeskey, 524 U.S. 206, 118 S.Ct. 1952 (1998). One section of that Act prohibits discrimination by state and local governments and other public entities against any "qualified individual with a disability" and the exclusion of such individuals, because of their disability, from services, programs, or activities provided by the public entity. Id. § 12132. A "qualified individual with a disability" is defined as "an individual with a disability who, with or without reasonable modifications to rules, policies, or practices, the removal of architectural, communication, or transportation barriers, or the provision of auxiliary aids and services, meets the essential eligibility requirements for the receipt of services or the participation in programs or activities provided by a public entity." Id. § 12131(2).

Because of the ADA, correctional officials have had to make many changes in institutional operations to ensure that disabled inmates can participate in programs or receive services available to nondisabled inmates. See, e.g., Love v. Westville Correctional Ctr., 103 F.3d 558 (7th Cir.1996) (ADA violated when quadriplegic inmate was denied access to educational, work, and substance-abuse programs, church, and other prison programs and services because of his disability). In addition, all new construction of, and alterations to, correctional facilities must comply with ADA requirements. Americans with Disabilities Act (ADA) Accessibility Guidelines for Buildings and Facilities, 36 C.F.R. § 1191.1 app. B, at 5, 57–58 (2008). See also § 504 of the Rehabilitation Act of 1973, 29 U.S.C. § 794 (prohibits discrimination against disabled individuals by federal agencies and by certain entities, including state and local agencies, that receive federal financial assistance). For a discussion of the implications of states' immunity under the Eleventh Amendment to the constitutionality of the ADA, see pages 814–16.

8.　To have a "disability" within the meaning of the Americans with Disabilities Act, a person must either have a physical or mental impairment that "substantially limits" one or more of the individual's "major life activities," have a record of such an impairment, or be perceived as having such an impairment. 42 U.S.C. § 12102(1). In Bragdon v. Abbott, 524 U.S. 624, 118 S.Ct. 2196 (1998), the Supreme Court held that a woman who was HIV-positive, but asymptomatic, had a disability triggering the protections of the ADA. The Court reasoned that the plaintiff's seropositivity substantially impeded the major life activity of reproduction—the plaintiff's ability to reproduce and bear children. Consequently, unless her infection "pose[d] a direct threat to the health or safety of others," 42 U.S.C. § 12182(b)(3), she could prevail on her ADA claim against a dentist who refused to fill her cavity in his dental office.

Would barring prisoners who are HIV-positive, but asymptomatic, from working in food services at a prison violate the ADA? Why or why not? Cf. Gates v. Rowland, 39 F.3d 1439, 1447–48 (9th Cir.1994) (prohibiting HIV-positive inmates from working in food service did not violate the Rehabilitation Act because other prisoners, unfamiliar with the modes of HIV transmission, might respond violently if HIV-positive prisoners work in food service).

9. Curtailing the spread of communicable diseases has posed special challenges to health professionals working in correctional settings, in part because of the crowded conditions in which so many inmates are confined. In 1990 through 1992, for example, tuberculosis swept through prisons in New York, killing thirty-six prisoners and one correctional officer. Theodore M. Hammett & Lynne Harrold, U.S. Dep't of Justice, Tuberculosis in Correctional Facilities 4 (1994).

Although there is a general consensus that appropriate measures should be taken to prevent the spread of communicable diseases within correctional facilities, the question of what those measures are sometimes has provoked debate. In particular, the subject of what can and should be done to curb the spread of HIV, the virus which causes AIDS, has engendered much controversy. Some of the questions upon which debate has centered are set forth below. How would you answer each question?

a. Is the mandatory HIV testing of all inmates in a correctional facility constitutional? See Dunn v. White, 880 F.2d 1188, 1196–97 (10th Cir.1989) (mandatory HIV testing of prisoners does not violate the Fourth Amendment).

b. Do inmates who wish to be tested for evidence of HIV infection have the right to such tests? See Doe v. Wigginton, 21 F.3d 733, 738–39 (6th Cir.1994) (defendants did not act with deliberate indifference in denying prisoner's request for an HIV test when he had failed to provide them with information demonstrating that he had an elevated risk of prior HIV exposure). In answering this question, consider the relevance of studies revealing that the administration of certain drugs to asymptomatic HIV-positive persons may significantly reduce HIV-related deaths. Panel on Antiretroviral Guidelines for Adults and Adolescents, Dep't of Health and Human Services, Guidelines for the Use of Antiretroviral Agents in HIV–1-Infected Adults and Adolescents 18 (Nov. 3, 2008). See also Pub. Health Serv. Task Force, Recommendations for Use of Antiretroviral Drugs in Pregnant HIV–1–Infected Women for Maternal Health and Interventions to Reduce Perinatal HIV–1 Transmissions in the United States 3 (July 8, 2008) (administration of antiretroviral drugs to HIV-infected women dramatically reduces perinatal transmission of HIV). For regularly updated treatment guidelines, see http://www.aidsinfo.nih. gov.

c. When, if ever, is the segregation of HIV-positive inmates legal? Compare Onishea v. Hopper, 171 F.3d 1289 (11th Cir.1999) (segregation of HIV-positive inmates does not violate the Rehabilitation Act); Harris v. Thigpen, 941 F.2d 1495, 1512–21 (11th Cir.1991) (segregation of HIV-positive inmates is constitutional) with Nolley v. County of Erie, 776 F.Supp. 715, 734–36 (W.D.N.Y.1991) (automatic segregation of all inmates known to be HIV-positive violates constitutional right to privacy). When is such segregation advisable? See Nat'l Comm'n on Corr. Health Care, Position Statement: Administrative Management of HIV in Corrections (2005), available at http://www.ncchc.org/resources/statements/admin_hiv2005.html.

d.　Does the Constitution require the segregation of HIV-positive inmates? See Oladipupo v. Belt, 104 F.Supp.2d 626, 635 (W.D.La.2000) (listing cases holding there is no constitutional duty to segregate HIV-positive inmates).

e.　Should condoms be made available to inmates in prisons or other correctional facilities? Why or why not? For information on condom-distribution programs in correctional facilities in the United States and other countries, see Joseph D. Tucker et al., The Catch 22 of Condoms in U.S. Correctional Facilities, 7 BMC Public Health 296 (2007).

f.　Who can be informed of an inmate's HIV status? See, e.g., Doe v. Delie, 257 F.3d 309, 317 (3d Cir.2001) (inmates have a constitutional right to privacy in their medical information, including HIV status, but right may be limited by a policy or regulation that is reasonably related to a legitimate penological interest). Who should be so informed? See American Bar Association Policy on AIDS and the Criminal Justice System 2 (1989).

g.　To what extent, if at all, should inmates' HIV status affect decisions concerning their release on parole or on furlough and other forms of community release? Id. at 2–3.

h.　Can and should inmates be required to disclose their HIV-positive status to spouses or lovers as a condition of release on parole, on a furlough, or some other form of community release? Id. at 3.

2.　THE RIGHT TO REFUSE MEDICAL TREATMENT

While *Estelle v. Gamble* dealt with the question of the right of inmates to medical treatment, the Supreme Court in Washington v. Harper, 494 U.S. 210, 110 S.Ct. 1028 (1990) discussed the opposite question: When do inmates have the right to refuse medical treatment? The plaintiff in *Harper* was a mentally ill prisoner who was forced, over his objection, to take antipsychotic medication which he claimed had caused serious adverse side effects. The prison policy under which the plaintiff was involuntarily medicated permitted such compulsory administration of antipsychotic drugs when an inmate "suffers from a mental disorder and as a result of that disorder constitutes a likelihood of serious harm to himself or others and/or is gravely disabled."

The substantive-due-process issue before the Court concerned the circumstances under which the involuntary administration of antipsychot-

ic drugs to an inmate is constitutional. Writing for the majority, Justice
Kennedy addressed this issue:

> Respondent contends that the State, under the mandate of the
> Due Process Clause, may not override his choice to refuse antipsy-
> chotic drugs unless he has been found to be incompetent, and then
> only if the factfinder makes a substituted judgment that he, if
> competent, would consent to drug treatment. We disagree. The extent
> of a prisoner's right under the Clause to avoid the unwanted adminis-
> tration of antipsychotic drugs must be defined in the context of the
> inmate's confinement. The Policy under review requires the State to
> establish, by a medical finding, that a mental disorder exists which is
> likely to cause harm if not treated. Moreover, the fact that the
> medication must first be prescribed by a psychiatrist, and then
> approved by a reviewing psychiatrist, ensures that the treatment in
> question will be ordered only if it is in the prisoner's medical inter-
> ests, given the legitimate needs of his institutional confinement.[8]
> These standards, which recognize both the prisoner's medical inter-
> ests and the State's interests, meet the demands of the Due Process
> Clause.

> * * * In Turner v. Safley, 482 U.S. 78 (1987), and O'Lone v.
> Estate of Shabazz, 482 U.S. 342 (1987), we held that the proper
> standard for determining the validity of a prison regulation claimed to
> infringe on an inmate's constitutional rights is to ask whether the
> regulation is "reasonably related to legitimate penological interests."
> This is true even when the constitutional right claimed to have been
> infringed is fundamental, and the State under other circumstances
> would have been required to satisfy a more rigorous standard of
> review. * * *

* * *

> In Turner, we considered various factors to determine the reason-
> ableness of a challenged prison regulation. Three are relevant here.
> "First, there must be a 'valid, rational connection' between the prison
> regulation and the legitimate governmental interest put forward to
> justify it." Second, a court must consider "the impact accommodation
> of the asserted constitutional right will have on guards and other
> inmates, and on the allocation of prison resources generally." Third,
> "the absence of ready alternatives is evidence of the reasonableness of
> a prison regulation."

* * *

> Applying these factors to the regulation before us, we conclude
> that the Policy comports with constitutional requirements. There can

---

8.   * * * Unlike the dissent, we will not assume that physicians will prescribe these drugs for
reasons unrelated to the medical needs of the patients; indeed, the ethics of the medical
profession are to the contrary. See Hippocratic Oath; American Psychiatric Association, Principles
of Medical Ethics With Annotations Especially Applicable to Psychiatry, in Codes of Professional
Responsibility 129–135 (R. Gorlin ed. 1986). * * *

be little doubt as to both the legitimacy and the importance of the governmental interest presented here. There are few cases in which the State's interest in combating the danger posed by a person to both himself and others is greater than in a prison environment, which, "by definition," is made up of persons with "a demonstrated proclivity for antisocial criminal, and often violent, conduct." We confront here the State's obligations, not just its interests. The State has undertaken the obligation to provide prisoners with medical treatment consistent not only with their own medical interests, but also with the needs of the institution. Prison administrators have not only an interest in ensuring the safety of prison staffs and administrative personnel, but the duty to take reasonable measures for the prisoners' own safety. These concerns have added weight when a penal institution, like the Special Offender Center, is restricted to inmates with mental illnesses. Where an inmate's mental disability is the root cause of the threat he poses to the inmate population, the State's interest in decreasing the danger to others necessarily encompasses an interest in providing him with medical treatment for his illness.

Special Offender Center Policy 600.30 is a rational means of furthering the State's legitimate objectives. Its exclusive application is to inmates who are mentally ill and who, as a result of their illness, are gravely disabled or represent a significant danger to themselves or others. The drugs may be administered for no purpose other than treatment, and only under the direction of a licensed psychiatrist. There is considerable debate over the potential side effects of antipsychotic medications, but there is little dispute in the psychiatric profession that proper use of the drugs is one of the most effective means of treating and controlling a mental illness likely to cause violent behavior.

The alternative means proffered by respondent for accommodating his interest in rejecting the forced administration of antipsychotic drugs do not demonstrate the invalidity of the State's policy. Respondent's main contention is that, as a precondition to antipsychotic drug treatment, the State must find him incompetent, and then obtain court approval of the treatment using a "substituted judgment" standard. The suggested rule takes no account of the legitimate governmental interest in treating him where medically appropriate for the purpose of reducing the danger he poses. A rule that is in no way responsive to the State's legitimate interests is not a proper accommodation, and can be rejected out of hand. Nor are physical restraints or seclusion "alternative[s] that fully accommodat[e] the prisoner's rights at *de minimis* cost to valid penological interests." Physical restraints are effective only in the short term, and can have serious physical side effects when used on a resisting inmate, as well as leaving the staff at risk of injury while putting the restraints on or tending to the inmate who is in them. Furthermore, respondent has failed to demonstrate that physical restraints or seclusion are acceptable substitutes for antipsychotic drugs, in terms of either their medical effectiveness or their toll on limited prison resources.

We hold that, given the requirements of the prison environment, the Due Process Clause permits the State to treat a prison inmate who has a serious mental illness with antipsychotic drugs against his will, if the inmate is dangerous to himself or others and the treatment is in the inmate's medical interest. Policy 600.30 comports with these requirements * * *.

Id. at 222–27, 110 S.Ct. at 1037–40.

Justice Stevens, joined by Justices Brennan and Marshall, dissented from the Court's resolution of the claim in *Harper* asserting a violation of substantive due process. Excerpts from the dissenting opinion are set forth below:

The Court acknowledges that under the Fourteenth Amendment "respondent possesses a significant liberty interest in avoiding the unwanted administration of antipsychotic drugs," but then virtually ignores the several dimensions of that liberty. They are both physical and intellectual. Every violation of a person's bodily integrity is an invasion of his or her liberty. The invasion is particularly intrusive if it creates a substantial risk of permanent injury and premature death. Moreover, any such action is degrading if it overrides a competent person's choice to reject a specific form of medical treatment. And when the purpose or effect of forced drugging is to alter the will and the mind of the subject, it constitutes a deprivation of liberty in the most literal and fundamental sense.

* * *

The record of one of Walter Harper's involuntary medication hearings at the Special Offense Center (SOC) notes: "Inmate Harper stated he would rather die th[a]n take medication."[4] That Harper would be so opposed to taking psychotropic drugs is not surprising: as the Court acknowledges, these drugs both "alter the chemical balance in a patient's brain" and can cause irreversible and fatal side effects. The prolixin injections that Harper was receiving at the time of his statement exemplify the intrusiveness of psychotropic drugs on a person's body and mind. Prolixin acts "at all levels of the central nervous system as well as on multiple organ systems." It can induce catatonic-like states, alter electroencephalographic tracings, and cause swelling of the brain. Adverse reactions include drowsiness, excitement, restlessness, bizarre dreams, hypertension, nausea, vomiting, loss of appetite, salivation, dry mouth, perspiration, headache, constipation, blurred vision, impotency, eczema, jaundice, tremors, and muscle spasms. As with all psychotropic drugs, prolixin may cause

---

4. Record, Book 8, Jan. 5, 1984, Hearing (Harper testified: "Well all you want to do is medicate me and you've been medicating me.... Haldol paral[y]zed my right side of my body.... you are burning me out of my life ... you are burning me out of my freedom").

tardive dyskinesia, an often irreversible syndrome of uncontrollable movements that can prevent a person from exercising basic functions such as driving an automobile, and neuroleptic malignant syndrome, which is 30% fatal for those who suffer from it. The risk of side effects increases over time.

* * *

The Court does not suggest that psychotropic drugs, any more than transfer for medical treatment, may be forced on prisoners as a necessary condition of their incarceration or as a disciplinary measure. Rather, it holds:

"[G]iven the requirements of the prison environment, the Due Process Clause permits the State to treat a prison inmate who has a serious mental illness with antipsychotic drugs against his will, if the inmate is dangerous to himself or others *and the treatment is in the inmate's medical interest.* * * * "

* * * Whether or not the State's alleged interest in providing medically beneficial treatment to those in its custody who are mentally ill may alone override the refusal of psychotropic drugs by a presumptively competent person, a plain reading of Policy 600.30 reveals that it does not meet the substantive standard set forth by the Court. Even on the Court's terms, the Policy is constitutionally insufficient.

* * *

Although any application of Policy 600.30 requires a medical judgment as to a prisoner's mental condition and the cause of his behavior, the Policy does not require a determination that forced medication would advance his medical interest. * * *

Policy 600.30 sweepingly sacrifices the inmate's substantive liberty interest to refuse psychotropic drugs, regardless of his medical interests, to institutional and administrative concerns. The State clearly has a legitimate interest in prison security and administrative convenience that encompasses responding to potential risks to persons and property. * * *

* * *

* * * However, the record before us does not establish that a more narrowly drawn policy withdrawing psychotropics from only those inmates who actually refuse consent[15] and who do not pose an

---

15. There is no evidence that more than a small fraction of inmates would refuse drugs under a voluntary policy. Harper himself voluntarily took psychotropics for six years, and intermittently consented to them after 1982. See e.g., Rogers v. Okin, 478 F.Supp. 1342, 1369 (Mass.1979) (only 12 of 1,000 institutionalized patients refused psychotropic drugs for prolonged periods during the two years that judicial restraining order was in effect). The efficacy of forced drugging is also marginal; involuntary patients have a poorer prognosis than cooperative patients. See Rogers & Webster, Assessing Treatability in Mentally Disordered Offenders, 13 Law and Human Behavior 19, 20–21 (1989).

imminent threat of serious harm[16] would increase the marginal costs of SOC administration. Harper's own record reveals that administrative segregation and standard disciplinary sanctions were frequently imposed on him over and above forced medication and thus would add no new costs. Similarly, intramuscular injections of psychotropics, such as those frequently forced on Harper, entail no greater risk than administration of less dangerous drugs such as tranquilizers. Use of psychotropic drugs simply to suppress an inmate's potential violence, rather than to achieve therapeutic results, may also undermine the efficacy of other available treatment programs that would better address his illness.

* * * The flaw in Washington's Policy 600.30—and the basic error in the Court's opinion today—is the failure to divorce from each other the two justifications for forced medication and to consider the extent to which the Policy is reasonably related to either interest. The State, and arguably the Court, allows the SOC to blend the state interests in responding to emergencies and in convenient prison administration with the individual's interest in receiving beneficial medical treatment. The result is a muddled rationale that allows the "exaggerated response" of forced psychotropic medication on the basis of purely institutional concerns. So serving institutional convenience eviscerates the inmate's substantive liberty interest in the integrity of his body and mind.

Id. at 237–40, 242–45, 247–50, 110 S.Ct. at 1045–46, 1048, 1050–51 (Stevens, J., concurring and dissenting).

The Supreme Court in *Harper* also addressed some procedural-due-process issues, one of which was whether a judge must approve a recommendation to administer antipsychotic drugs to an inmate before the inmate is involuntarily medicated. The Court's resolution of these issues is discussed on pages 636–39.

---

16. As the Court notes, properly used, these drugs are "one of the most effective means of treating and controlling" certain incurable mental illnesses, but they are not a panacea for long-term care of all patients.

"[T]he maintenance treatment literature ... shows that many patients (approximately 30%) relapse despite receiving neuroleptic medication, while neuroleptics can be withdrawn from other patients for many months and in some cases for years without relapse. Standard maintenance medication treatment strategies, though they are indisputably effective in group comparisons, may be quite inefficient in addressing the treatment requirements of the individual patient." Lieberman et al., Reply to Ethics of Drug Discontinuation Studies in Schizophrenia, 46 Archives of General Psychiatry 387, 387 (1989).

Indeed, the drugs appear to have produced at most minor "savings" in Harper's case. Dr. Petrich reported that "medications are not satisfactory in containing the worst excesses of his labile and irritable behavior. He is uncooperative when on medication," and a therapy supervisor reported before Harper's involuntary medication began: "during the time in which he assaulted the nurse at Cabrini he was on neuroleptic medication yet there is indication that he was psychotic. However, during his stay at SOC he has been off of all neuroleptic medications and at times has shown some preoccupation and appearance of psychosis but has not become assaultive. His problems on medication, such as the paradoxical effect from the neuroleptic medications, may be precipitated by increased doses of neuroleptic medications and may cause an exacerbation of his psychosis. Though Mr. Harper is focused on psychosomatic problems from neuroleptic medications as per the side effects, the real problem may be that the psychosis is exacerbated by neuroleptic medications."

QUESTIONS AND POINTS FOR DISCUSSION

1. In Sell v. United States, 539 U.S. 166, 123 S.Ct. 2174 (2003), the Supreme Court enunciated the standard to be applied when determining whether antipsychotic medication can be administered involuntarily, not to prevent harm to the individual being treated or to others, but to render the person to whom the drugs may be administered competent for trial on "serious" criminal charges: The treatment must be "medically appropriate," must be "substantially unlikely" to cause side effects that would compromise the trial's fairness, and must be necessary to serve the government's interests furthered by bringing the individual to trial. Id. at 179, 123 S.Ct. at 2184. One of the key distinctions between this standard and the *Harper* test is that it includes a type of least-drastic-alternative requirement; a court cannot mandate involuntary medication without first concluding that "any alternative, less intrusive treatments are unlikely to achieve substantially the same results." Id. at 181, 123 S.Ct. at 2185.

Read against the backdrop of *Sell*, do you agree with the decision of the Supreme Court to apply the *Turner* test in *Harper*, or does the Constitution require application of a more rigorous test before psychotropic drugs can be administered involuntarily to a prisoner in order to avert harm to the prisoner or others? If you consider the *Turner* test inappropriate in the *Harper* situation, what test would you apply and why?

2. In Riggins v. Nevada, 504 U.S. 127, 112 S.Ct. 1810 (1992), the Supreme Court discussed, but ultimately did not resolve, the question of when antipsychotic medication constitutionally can be administered to pretrial detainees, over their objection, in order to prevent them from harming themselves or others. How would you answer that question?

3. In Ford v. Wainwright, 477 U.S. 399, 106 S.Ct. 2595 (1986), the Supreme Court held that the Eighth Amendment prohibits the execution of an insane prisoner who had received the death penalty. See note 2 on page 315. A question left remaining after *Harper* is whether insane prisoners on death row can be medicated forcibly in order to make them competent so that they can be executed. In Louisiana v. Perry, 610 So.2d 746 (La.1992), the Louisiana Supreme Court held that such compulsory administration of antipsychotic medication violates two state constitutional rights—the right to privacy and the right not to be subjected to cruel, excessive, or unusual punishments. Would the compulsory administration of antipsychotic medication under the circumstances condoned in *Harper* be unconstitutional if the medication also would make the prisoner competent for execution? See Singleton v. Norris, 319 F.3d 1018, 1026–27 (8th Cir. 2003), discussed in note 4 on page 316.

B. CONDITIONS OF CONFINEMENT

Many of the nation's prisons and jails are crowded, holding many more inmates than they were designed or reconfigured to hold. At the end of 2007, nineteen state prison systems were operating at over 100% of their capacity. Bureau of Justice Statistics, U.S. Dep't of Justice, Prisoners in 2007, at 7 (2007) (hereinafter Prisoners in 2007). The federal system held 36% more inmates than it officially was equipped to hold. Id. Many jails, particularly in the largest jail jurisdictions, also were jam-packed with inmates, far exceeding the jails' rated capacity. Bureau of Justice Statistics, U.S. Dep't of Justice, Prison and Jail Inmates at Midyear 2007, at 4 (2008) (sixteen of the fifty largest jail systems operating at over 100% of their capacity).

The crowded conditions in correctional facilities across the country are due in large part to the continuing escalation of the size of the nation's prison and jail populations. At midyear 2007, almost 2.3 million people were confined in state or federal prisons or local jails, over a million more than at the end of 1990. Id. at 6 (2008); Bureau of Justice Statistics, U.S. Dep't of Justice, Prisoners in 2001, at 2 (2002). For statistics on the nation's per-capita incarceration rate and other information regarding the size of correctional populations in this country, see pages 3–4 and the Bureau of Justice Statistics' website at http://www.ojp.gov/bjs.

Because of the dramatic increase in the number of persons incarcerated in prisons and jails, correctional officials have had to scramble simply to find a place where each inmate can sleep. Inmates have been housed in gymnasiums, dayrooms, libraries, hallways, and other nooks and crannies throughout correctional institutions. Tents have been erected to hold prisoners, and authorities have even placed prisoners on barges—"floating prisons"—to stem their crowding problems.

Federal, state, and local governments also have undertaken massive construction programs in an attempt to make room for the increasing number of inmates. Between 1990 and 2000, for example, the states opened 351 additional correctional institutions for adults. Bureau of Justice Statistics, U.S. Dep't of Justice, Prisoners in 2000, at 9 (2001). This construction has proven to be quite costly. In 2007, the average cost of constructing a bed in a medium-security prison was $65,000. The Pew Center on the States, One in 100: Behind Bars in America 2008, at 11 (2008). In addition, almost $24,000 on average had to be spent per prisoner in 2005 to pay for the food, staff, medical care, and other operating costs associated with the running of a prison. Id. But while adding to the capacity of the nation's prisons and jails has proven enormously expensive, it has failed to eliminate the crowding problem. As mentioned earlier, the actual number of prisoners in over a third of the nation's prison systems continues to exceed even the highest measure of the capacity of those systems.

In part because of the pervasive crowding in the nation's correctional facilities and the insufficient funds made available to operate them, correctional officials often have had difficulty operating their facilities in conformance with the Constitution. The cases and materials that follow discuss when conditions of confinement transgress constitutional boundaries.

RHODES v. CHAPMAN

Supreme Court of the United States, 1981.
452 U.S. 337, 101 S.Ct. 2392, 69 L.Ed.2d 59.

JUSTICE POWELL delivered the opinion of the Court.

The question presented is whether the housing of two inmates in a single cell at the Southern Ohio Correctional Facility is cruel and unusual punishment prohibited by the Eighth and Fourteenth Amendments.

Respondents Kelly Chapman and Richard Jaworski are inmates at the Southern Ohio Correctional Facility (SOCF), a maximum-security state prison in Lucasville, Ohio. They were housed in the same cell when they brought this action in the District Court for the Southern District of Ohio on behalf of themselves and all inmates similarly situated at SOCF. Asserting a cause of action under 42 U.S.C. § 1983, they contended that "double celling" at SOCF violated the Constitution. * * *

* * *

SOCF was built in the early 1970's. In addition to 1,620 cells, it has gymnasiums, workshops, schoolrooms, "dayrooms," two chapels, a hospital ward, commissary, barbershop, and library. Outdoors, SOCF has a recreation field, visitation area, and garden. The District Court described this physical plant as "unquestionably a top-flight, first-class facility."

Each cell at SOCF measures approximately 63 square feet. Each contains a bed measuring 36 by 80 inches, a cabinet-type night stand, a wall-mounted sink with hot and cold running water, and a toilet that the inmate can flush from inside the cell. Cells housing two inmates have a two-tiered bunk bed. Every cell has a heating and air circulation vent near the ceiling, and 960 of the cells have a window that inmates can open and close. All of the cells have a cabinet, shelf, and radio built into one of the walls, and in all of the cells one wall consists of bars through which the inmates can be seen.

The "dayrooms" are located adjacent to the cellblocks and are open to inmates between 6:30 a.m. and 9:30 p.m. According to the District Court, "[t]he day rooms are in a sense part of the cells and they are designed to furnish that type of recreation or occupation which an ordinary citizen would seek in his living room or den." Each dayroom contains a wall-mounted television, card tables, and chairs. Inmates can pass between their cells and the dayrooms during a 10–minute period each hour, on the hour, when the doors to the dayrooms and cells are opened.

As to the inmate population, the District Court found that SOCF began receiving inmates in late 1972 and double celling them in 1975 because of an increase in Ohio's statewide prison population. At the time of trial, SOCF housed 2,300 inmates, 67% of whom were serving life or other long-term sentences for first-degree felonies. Approximately 1,400 inmates were double celled. Of these, about 75% had the choice of spending much of their waking hours outside their cells, in the dayrooms, school, workshops, library, visits, meals, or showers. The other double-celled inmates spent more time locked in their cells because of a restrictive classification.[3]

The remaining findings by the District Court addressed respondents' allegation that overcrowding created by double celling overwhelmed SOCF's facilities and staff. The food was "adequate in every respect," and respondents adduced no evidence "whatsoever that prisoners have been underfed or that the food facilities have been taxed by the prison population." The air ventilation system was adequate, the cells were substantially free of offensive odor, the temperature in the cellblocks was well controlled, and the noise in the cellblocks was not excessive. Double celling had not reduced significantly the availability of space in the dayrooms or visitation facilities, nor had it rendered inadequate the resources of the library or schoolrooms.[5] Although there were isolated incidents of failure to provide medical or dental care, there was no evidence of indifference by the SOCF staff to inmates' medical or dental needs. As to violence, the court found that the number of acts of violence at SOCF had increased with the prison population, but only in proportion to the increase in population. Respondents failed to produce evidence establishing that double celling itself caused greater violence, and the ratio of guards to inmates at SOCF satisfied the standard of acceptability offered by respondents' expert witness. Finally, the court did find that the SOCF administration, faced with more inmates than jobs, had "water[ed] down" jobs by assigning more inmates to each job than necessary and by reducing the number of hours that each inmate worked; it also found that SOCF had not increased its staff of psychiatrists and social workers since double celling had begun.

Despite these generally favorable findings, the District Court concluded that double celling at SOCF was cruel and unusual punishment. The court rested its conclusion on five considerations. One, inmates at SOCF are serving long terms of imprisonment. In the court's view, that fact "can only accent[uate] the problems of close confinement and overcrowding." Two, SOCF housed 38% more inmates at the time of trial than its "design capacity." In reference to this the court asserted: "Overcrowding necessarily involves excess limitation of general movement as well as physical and mental injury from long exposure." Three, the court accepted as contemporary standards of decency several studies recommending that each person in an institution have at least 50–55 square feet of living quarters.[7]

---

3. Inmates who requested protective custody but could not substantiate their fears were classified as "limited activity" and were locked in their cells all but six hours a week. Inmates classified as "voluntarily idle" and newly arrived inmates awaiting classification had only four hours a week outside their cells. Inmates housed in administrative isolation for disciplinary reasons were allowed out of their cells for two hours a week to attend religious services, a movie, or the commissary.

5. * * * [N]o inmate who was "ready, able, and willing to receive schooling has been denied the opportunity," although there was some delay before an inmate received the opportunity to attend.

7. The District Court cited, *e.g.,* American Correctional Assn., Manual of Standards for Adult Correctional Institutions, Standard No. 4142, p. 27 (1977) (60–80 square feet); National Sheriffs'

In contrast, double-celled inmates at SOCF share 63 square feet. Four, the court asserted that "[a]t the best a prisoner who is double celled will spend most of his time in the cell with his cellmate."[8] Five, SOCF has made double celling a practice; it is not a temporary condition.

On appeal, [the Sixth Circuit Court of Appeals affirmed.]

* * *

No static "test" can exist by which courts determine whether conditions of confinement are cruel and unusual, for the Eighth Amendment "must draw its meaning from the evolving standards of decency that mark the progress of a maturing society." The Court has held, however, that "Eighth Amendment judgments should neither be nor appear to be merely the subjective views" of judges. To be sure, "the Constitution contemplates that in the end [a court's] own judgment will be brought to bear on the question of the acceptability" of a given punishment. But such " 'judgment[s] should be informed by objective factors to the maximum possible extent.' " For example, when the question was whether capital punishment for certain crimes violated contemporary values, the Court looked for "objective indicia" derived from history, the action of state legislatures, and the sentencing by juries. *Gregg v. Georgia,* [428 U.S.] at 176–187 [1976]. * * *

These principles apply when the conditions of confinement compose the punishment at issue. Conditions must not involve the wanton and unnecessary infliction of pain, nor may they be grossly disproportionate to the severity of the crime warranting imprisonment. In *Estelle v. Gamble,* we held that the denial of medical care is cruel and unusual because, in the worst case, it can result in physical torture, and, even in less serious cases, it can result in pain without any penological purpose. In *Hutto v. Finney*[, 437 U.S. 678 (1978)], the conditions of confinement in two Arkansas prisons constituted cruel and unusual punishment because they resulted in unquestioned and serious deprivations of basic human needs. Conditions other than those in *Gamble* and *Hutto,* alone or in combination, may deprive inmates of the minimal civilized measure of life's necessities. Such conditions could be cruel and unusual under the contemporary standard of decency that we recognized in *Gamble.* But conditions that cannot be said to be cruel and unusual under contemporary standards are not unconstitutional. To the extent that such conditions are restrictive and even harsh, they are part of the penalty that criminal offenders pay for their offenses against society.

In view of the District Court's findings of fact, its conclusion that double celling at SOCF constitutes cruel and unusual punishment is

---

Assn., A Handbook on Jail Architecture 63 (1975) (70–80 square feet); National Council on Crime and Delinquency, Model Act for the Protection of Rights of Prisoners, § 1, 18 Crime & Delinquency 4, 10 (1972) (50 square feet).

8. The basis of the District Court's assertion as to the amount of time that inmates spend in their cells does not appear in the court's opinion. Elsewhere in its opinion, the court found that 75% of the double-celled inmates at SOCF are free to be out of their cells from 6:30 a.m. to 9 p.m. * * *

insupportable. Virtually every one of the court's findings tends to *refute* respondents' claim. The double celling made necessary by the unanticipated increase in prison population did not lead to deprivations of essential food, medical care, or sanitation. Nor did it increase violence among inmates or create other conditions intolerable for prison confinement. Although job and educational opportunities diminished marginally as a result of double celling, limited work hours and delay before receiving education do not inflict pain, much less unnecessary and wanton pain; deprivations of this kind simply are not punishments. We would have to wrench the Eighth Amendment from its language and history to hold that delay of these desirable aids to rehabilitation violates the Constitution.

The five considerations on which the District Court relied also are insufficient to support its constitutional conclusion. The court relied on the long terms of imprisonment served by inmates at SOCF; the fact that SOCF housed 38% more inmates than its "design capacity"; the recommendation of several studies that each inmate have at least 50–55 square feet of living quarters; the suggestion that double-celled inmates spend most of their time in their cells with their cellmates; and the fact that double celling at SOCF was not a temporary condition. These general considerations fall far short in themselves of proving cruel and unusual punishment, for there is no evidence that double celling under these circumstances either inflicts unnecessary or wanton pain or is grossly disproportionate to the severity of crimes warranting imprisonment.[13] At most, these considerations amount to a theory that double celling inflicts pain. Perhaps they reflect an aspiration toward an ideal environment for long-term confinement. But the Constitution does not mandate comfortable prisons, and prisons of SOCF's type, which house persons convicted of serious crimes, cannot be free of discomfort. Thus, these considerations properly are weighed by the legislature and prison administration rather than a court. There being no constitutional violation,[15] the District Court had no authority to consider whether double celling in light of these

13. Respondents and the District Court erred in assuming that opinions of experts as to desirable prison conditions suffice to establish contemporary standards of decency. As we noted in *Bell v. Wolfish,* 441 U.S. [520], at 543–544, n. 27 [1979], such opinions may be helpful and relevant with respect to some questions, but "they simply do not establish the constitutional minima; rather, they establish goals recommended by the organization in question." Indeed, generalized opinions of experts cannot weigh as heavily in determining contemporary standards of decency as "the public attitude toward a given sanction." We could agree that double celling is not desirable, especially in view of the size of these cells. But there is no evidence in this case that double celling is viewed generally as violating decency. Moreover, though small, the cells in SOCF are exceptionally modern and functional; they are heated and ventilated and have hot and cold running water and a sanitary toilet. Each cell also has a radio.

15. * * * The dissent * * * makes much of the fact that SOCF was housing 38% more inmates at the time of trial than its "rated capacity." According to the United States Bureau of Prisons, at least three factors influence prison population: the number of arrests, prosecution policies, and sentencing and parole decisions. Because these factors can change rapidly, while prisons require years to plan and build, it is extremely difficult to calibrate a prison's "rated" or "design capacity" with predictions of prison population. The question before us is not whether the designer of SOCF guessed incorrectly about future prison population, but whether the actual conditions of confinement at SOCF are cruel and unusual.

considerations was the best response to the increase in Ohio's statewide prison population.

* * *

JUSTICE BRENNAN, with whom JUSTICE BLACKMUN and JUSTICE STEVENS join, concurring in the judgment.

Today's decision reaffirms that "[c]ourts certainly have a responsibility to scrutinize claims of cruel and unusual confinement." With that I agree. I also agree that the District Court's findings in this case do not support a judgment that the practice of double celling in the Southern Ohio Correctional Facility is in violation of the Eighth Amendment. I write separately, however, to emphasize that today's decision should in no way be construed as a retreat from careful judicial scrutiny of prison conditions, and to discuss the factors courts should consider in undertaking such scrutiny.

* * *

* * * [T]his Court and the lower courts have been especially deferential to prison authorities "in the adoption and execution of policies and practices that in their judgment are needed to preserve internal order and discipline and to maintain institutional security." Many conditions of confinement, however, including overcrowding, poor sanitation, and inadequate safety precautions, arise from neglect rather than policy. There is no reason of comity, judicial restraint, or recognition of expertise for courts to defer to negligent omissions of officials who lack the resources or motivation to operate prisons within limits of decency. Courts must and do recognize the primacy of the legislative and executive authorities in the administration of prisons; however, if the prison authorities do not conform to constitutional minima, the courts are under an obligation to take steps to remedy the violations.

The first aspect of judicial decisionmaking in this area is scrutiny of the actual conditions under challenge. It is important to recognize that various deficiencies in prison conditions "must be considered together." The individual conditions "exist in combination; each affects the other; and taken together they [may] have a cumulative impact on the inmates." Thus, a court considering an Eighth Amendment challenge to conditions of confinement must examine the totality of the circumstances.[10] Even if no single condition of confinement would be unconstitutional in itself, "exposure to the cumulative effect of prison conditions may subject inmates to cruel and unusual punishment."

* * *

In determining when prison conditions pass beyond legitimate punishment and become cruel and unusual, the "touchstone is the effect upon

---

10. The Court today adopts the totality-of-the-circumstances test. (Prison conditions "*alone or in combination,* may deprive inmates of the minimal civilized measure of life's necessities") (emphasis added).

the imprisoned." The court must examine the effect upon inmates of the condition of the physical plant (lighting, heat, plumbing, ventilation, living space, noise levels, recreation space); sanitation (control of vermin and insects, food preparation, medical facilities, lavatories and showers, clean places for eating, sleeping, and working); safety (protection from violent, deranged, or diseased inmates, fire protection, emergency evacuation); inmate needs and services (clothing, nutrition, bedding, medical, dental, and mental health care, visitation time, exercise and recreation, educational and rehabilitative programming); and staffing (trained and adequate guards and other staff, avoidance of placing inmates in positions of authority over other inmates). When "the cumulative impact of the conditions of incarceration threatens the physical, mental, and emotional health and well-being of the inmates and/or creates a probability of recidivism and future incarceration," the court must conclude that the conditions violate the Constitution.

* * *

I have not the slightest doubt that 63 square feet of cell space is not enough for two men. I understand that every major study of living space in prisons has so concluded. That prisoners are housed under such conditions is an unmistakable signal to the legislators and officials of Ohio: either more prison facilities should be built or expanded, or fewer persons should be incarcerated in prisons. Even so, the findings of the District Court do not support a conclusion that the conditions at the Southern Ohio Correctional Facility—cramped though they are—constitute cruel and unusual punishment.

The "touchstone" of the Eighth Amendment inquiry is " 'the effect upon the imprisoned.' " The findings of the District Court leave no doubt that the prisoners are adequately sheltered, fed, and protected, and that opportunities for education, work, and rehabilitative assistance are available. One need only compare the District Court's description of conditions at the Southern Ohio Correctional Facility with descriptions of other major state and federal facilities to realize that this prison, crowded though it is, is one of the better, more humane large prisons in the Nation.[15]

* * *

The District Court may well be correct *in the abstract* that prison overcrowding and double celling such as existed at the Southern Ohio Correctional Facility generally results in serious harm to the inmates. But cases are not decided in the abstract. A court is under the obligation to examine the *actual effect* of challenged conditions upon the well-being of the prisoners.[16] The District Court in this case was unable to identify any

15. If it were true that any prison providing less than 63 square feet of cell space per inmate were a *per se* violation of the Eighth Amendment, then approximately two-thirds of all federal, state, and local inmates today would be unconstitutionally confined.

16. This is not to say that injury to the inmates from challenged prison conditions must be "demonstrate[d] with a high degree of specificity and certainty." Courts may, as usual, employ common sense, observation, expert testimony, and other practical modes of proof.

actual signs that the double celling at the Southern Ohio Correctional Facility has seriously harmed the inmates there; indeed, the court's findings of fact suggest that crowding at the prison has not reached the point of causing serious injury. Since I cannot conclude that the totality of conditions at the facility offends constitutional norms, and am of the view that double celling in itself is not *per se* impermissible, I concur in the judgment of the Court.

JUSTICE BLACKMUN, concurring in the judgment. [Opinion omitted.]

JUSTICE MARSHALL, dissenting.

From reading the Court's opinion in this case, one would surely conclude that the Southern Ohio Correctional Facility (SOCF) is a safe, spacious prison that happens to include many two-inmate cells because the State has determined that that is the best way to run the prison. But the facility described by the majority is not the one involved in this case. SOCF is overcrowded, unhealthful, and dangerous. * * *

* * *

In a doubled cell, each inmate has only some 30–35 square feet of floor space.[3] Most of the windows in the Supreme Court building are larger than that. The conclusion of every expert who testified at trial and of every serious study of which I am aware is that a long-term inmate must have to himself, at the very least, 50 square feet of floor space—an area smaller than that occupied by a good-sized automobile—in order to avoid serious mental, emotional, and physical deterioration.[4] The District Court found that as a fact. * * *

* * * [T]he State cannot impose punishment that violates "the evolving standards of decency that mark the progress of a maturing society." For me, the legislative judgment and the consistent conclusions by those who have studied the problem provide considerable evidence that those standards condemn imprisonment in conditions so crowded that serious harm will result. The record amply demonstrates that those conditions are present here. It is surely not disputed that SOCF is severely overcrowded. The prison is operating at 38% above its design capacity.[5] It is also

---

3. The bed alone, which is bunk-style in the doubled cells, takes up approximately 20 square feet. Thus the actual amount of floor space per inmate, without making allowance for any other furniture in the room, is some 20–24 square feet, an area about the size of a typical door.

4. See, *e.g.*, American Public Health Assn., Standards for Health Services in Correctional Institutions 62 (1976) ("a minimum of 60 sq. ft."); Commission on Accreditation for Corrections, Manual of Standards for Adult Correctional Institutions 27 (1977) ("a floor area of at least 60 square feet"; "[i]n no case should the present use of the facility exceed designed use standards"); 3 National Institute of Justice, American Prisons and Jails 85, n. 6 (1980) ("80 square feet of floor space in long-term institutions"); National Sheriffs' Assn., A Handbook on Jail Architecture 63 (1975) ("[s]ingle occupancy detention rooms should average 70 to 80 square feet in area"); U.S. Dept. of Justice, Federal Standards for Prisons and Jails 17 (1980) ("at least 60 square feet of floor space"); National Council on Crime and Delinquency, Model Act for the Protection of Rights of Prisoners, 18 Crime & Delinquency 4, 10 (1972) ("not less than fifty square feet of floor space in any confined sleeping area"). Most of these studies recommend even more space for inmates who must spend more than 10 hours per day in their cells. * * *

5. * * * Rated capacity, the majority argues, is irrelevant because of the numerous factors that influence prison population. Actually, it is the factors that influence prison population that

significant that some two-thirds of the inmates at SOCF are serving lengthy or life sentences, for, as we have said elsewhere, "the length of confinement cannot be ignored in deciding whether the confinement meets constitutional standards." *Hutto v. Finney,* 437 U.S. 678, 686 (1978). Nor is double celling a short-term response to a temporary problem. The trial court found, and it is not contested, that double celling, if not enjoined, will continue for the foreseeable future. The trial court also found that most of the double-celled inmates spend most of their time in their cells.[6]

* * *

It is simply not true, as the majority asserts, that "there is no evidence that double celling under these circumstances either inflicts unnecessary or wanton pain or is grossly disproportionate to the severity of crimes warranting imprisonment." The District Court concluded from the record before it that long exposure to these conditions will *"necessarily"* involve "excess limitation of general movement as well as physical and mental injury. . . ."[7] And of course, of all the judges who have been involved in this case, the trial judge is the only one who has actually visited the prison. That is simply an additional reason to give in this case the deference we have always accorded to the careful conclusions of the finder of fact. * * * I see no reason to set aside the concurrent conclusions of two courts that the overcrowding and double celling here in issue are sufficiently severe that they will, if left unchecked, cause deterioration in respondents' mental and physical health. These conditions in my view go well beyond contemporary standards of decency and therefore violate the Eighth and Fourteenth Amendments. * * *

* * *

QUESTIONS AND POINTS FOR DISCUSSION

1. In Bell v. Wolfish, 441 U.S. 520, 99 S.Ct. 1861 (1979), the Supreme Court also rejected a constitutional challenge to double celling. The plaintiffs

---

are irrelevant. By definition, rated capacity represents "the number of inmates that a confinement unit, facility, or entire correctional agency can hold." 3 National Institute of Justice, American Prisons and Jails 41–42 (1980). If prison population, for whatever reason, exceeds rated capacity, then the prison must accommodate more people than it is designed to hold—in short, it is overcrowded. And the greater the proportion by which prison population exceeds rated capacity, the more severe the overcrowding. I certainly do not suggest that rated capacity is the only factor to be considered in determining whether a prison is unconstitutionally overcrowded, but I fail to understand why the majority feels free to dismiss it entirely.

6. * * * I read the District Court's opinion as finding that although most inmates are permitted to be out of their cells up to 14 hours each day, conditions in the prison are such that many choose not to do so.

* * *

7. In its findings, the District Court credited expert testimony that "close quarters" would likely increase the incidence of schizophrenia and other mental disorders and that the double celling imposed in this case had led to increases in tension and in "aggressive and anti-social characteristics." There is no dispute that the prison was violent even before it became overcrowded, and that it has become more so. I do not assert that violence has increased due to *double celling.* I accept the finding of the District Court that violence has increased due to *overcrowding.* Plainly, this case involves much more than just the constitutionality of double celling *per se.* * * *

in that case were pretrial detainees incarcerated in a federal correctional center. The rooms in that facility, which had about seventy-five square feet of floor space, were designed to house one person, but when the facility became crowded, the correctional authorities instituted double celling. The plaintiffs contended in their § 1983 suit that this double celling inflicted punishment on them in violation of their due-process rights. Although the lower courts agreed with this contention, the Supreme Court, in a decision written by Justice Rehnquist, did not:

> We disagree with both the District Court and the Court of Appeals that there is some sort of "one man, one cell" principle lurking in the Due Process Clause of the Fifth Amendment. While confining a given number of people in a given amount of space in such a manner as to cause them to endure genuine privations and hardship over an extended period of time might raise serious questions under the Due Process Clause as to whether those conditions amounted to punishment, nothing even approaching such hardship is shown by this record.
>
> Detainees are required to spend only seven or eight hours each day in their rooms, during most or all of which they presumably are sleeping. The rooms provide more than adequate space for sleeping. During the remainder of the time, the detainees are free to move between their rooms and the common area. While "double-bunking" may have taxed some of the equipment or particular facilities in certain of the common areas, this does not mean that the conditions at the MCC failed to meet the standards required by the Constitution. Our conclusion in this regard is further buttressed by the detainees' length of stay at the MCC. Nearly all of the detainees are released within 60 days. We simply do not believe that requiring a detainee to share toilet facilities and this admittedly rather small sleeping place with another person for generally a maximum period of 60 days violates the Constitution.

Id. at 542–43, 99 S.Ct. at 1875–76.

2. The conditions of confinement at the correctional facilities discussed in *Rhodes v. Chapman* and *Bell v. Wolfish* are to be contrasted with the conditions in the Arkansas prisons described by the Supreme Court in Hutto v. Finney, 437 U.S. 678, 98 S.Ct. 2565 (1978):

> The routine conditions that the ordinary Arkansas convict had to endure were characterized by the District Court as "a dark and evil world completely alien to the free world." That characterization was amply supported by the evidence.[3] The punishments for misconduct not serious

---

3. The administrators of Arkansas' prison system evidently tried to operate their prisons at a profit. Cummins Farm, the institution at the center of this litigation, required its 1,000 inmates to work in the fields 10 hours a day, six days a week, using mule-drawn tools and tending crops by hand. The inmates were sometimes required to run to and from the fields, with a guard in an automobile or on horseback driving them on. They worked in all sorts of weather, so long as the temperature was above freezing, sometimes in unsuitably light clothing or without shoes.

The inmates slept together in large, 100–man barracks, and some convicts, known as "creepers," would slip from their beds to crawl along the floor, stalking their sleeping enemies. In one 18–month period, there were 17 stabbings, all but 1 occurring in the barracks. Homosexual rape

enough to result in punitive isolation were cruel, unusual, and unpredictable. It is the discipline known as "punitive isolation" that is most relevant for present purposes.

Confinement in punitive isolation was for an indeterminate period of time. An average of 4, and sometimes as many as 10 or 11, prisoners were crowded into windowless 8′ × 10′ cells containing no furniture other than a source of water and a toilet that could only be flushed from outside the cell. At night the prisoners were given mattresses to spread on the floor. Although some prisoners suffered from infectious diseases such as hepatitis and venereal disease, mattresses were removed and jumbled together each morning, then returned to the cells at random in the evening. Prisoners in isolation received fewer than 1,000 calories a day;[7] their meals consisted primarily of 4–inch squares of "grue," a substance created by mashing meat, potatoes, oleo, syrup, vegetables, eggs, and seasoning into a paste and baking the mixture in a pan.

Id. at 681–83, 98 S.Ct. at 2568–70.

The Supreme Court observed in *Hutto* that the district court was correct in concluding that the above conditions inflicted cruel and unusual punishment on Arkansas prisoners. The Court also approved the district court's order directing that inmates be confined in punitive isolation for no more than thirty days. The Court explained:

It is perfectly obvious that every decision to remove a particular inmate from the general prison population for an indeterminate period could not be characterized as cruel and unusual. If new conditions of confinement are not materially different from those affecting other prisoners, a transfer for the duration of a prisoner's sentence might be completely unobjectionable and well within the authority of the prison administrator. It is equally plain, however, that the length of confinement cannot be ignored in deciding whether the confinement meets constitutional standards. A filthy, overcrowded cell and a diet of "grue" might be tolerable for a few days and intolerably cruel for weeks or months.

* * *

The order is supported by the interdependence of the conditions producing the violation. The vandalized cells and the atmosphere of violence were attributable, in part, to overcrowding and to deep-seated enmities growing out of months of constant daily friction. The 30–day limit will help to correct these conditions.

Id. at 686–88, 98 S.Ct. at 2571–72.

Other cases discussing the types of onerous and inhumane conditions that have prevailed in many of the nation's correctional facilities include: Tillery v.

---

was so common and uncontrolled that some potential victims dared not sleep; instead they would leave their beds and spend the night clinging to the bars nearest the guards' station.

7. A daily allowance of 2,700 calories is recommended for the average male between 23 and 50. National Academy of Sciences, Recommended Dietary Allowances, Appendix (8th rev. ed. 1974). Prisoners in punitive isolation are less active than the average person; but a mature man who spends 12 hours a day lying down and 12 hours a day simply sitting or standing consumes approximately 2,000 calories a day. Id., at 27.

Owens, 907 F.2d 418 (3d Cir.1990) (cellblocks infested with vermin, bed bugs, mice, fleas, and lice; bird feces on floors and railings and "so dense" that cellblock windows are "virtually covered"; auditorium and gymnasium, where several hundred inmates are supervised by one correctional officer, are "dens of violence"; no master system for unlocking cells during a fire, as a result of which it would take at least fifteen minutes to evacuate all inmates from a cellblock, although the block would be filled with smoke within two to three minutes); Howard v. Adkison, 887 F.2d 134 (8th Cir.1989) (inmate's cell, food slot, and mattress covered with "human waste"; no cleaning supplies provided; laundry not cleaned for five months); Ramos v. Lamm, 639 F.2d 559 (10th Cir.1980) (cells with 31.5 to 49 square feet of living space; poor ventilation; sewage accumulating in cells because of leaking pipes; rodent and insect infestation; trash and decaying food on the floors in inmate living areas; soiled bedding; rotten food, dirt, and rodent droppings on the kitchen floors); Gates v. Collier, 501 F.2d 1291 (5th Cir.1974) (water supply contaminated with sewage; exposed electrical wiring; lack of sufficient fire-fighting equipment; broken windows; cells known as the "dark holes," which were devoid of lights, a sink, a toilet, or furniture and which had a hole in the floor for bodily wastes; inmates placed in the dark hole without clothes or bedding; brutal methods of discipline employed, including the forced administration of milk of magnesia to inmates and turning fans on wet and naked inmates); Carty v. Farrelly, 957 F.Supp. 727 (D.V.I.1997) (72–square–foot cells held four to six inmates; inmates had to sleep on mattresses on the floor and were urinated on by cellmates using the toilet; cockroaches caught in a cell in one night filled a container three inches high; inmates bitten by rats; correctional officers taunted mentally ill inmates, directing them to pull down their pants and grab their crotches and to crawl across the floor); Masonoff v. DuBois, 899 F.Supp. 782, 797 (D.Mass.1995) (requiring prisoners to use chamber pots during ten hours in which they were confined in their cells, resulting in a stench that caused some inmates to vomit, "call[s] to mind the muck that 'boils up and pours over' in the gloomy second river of hell, the *Styx*, described by Dante"); Anderson v. Redman, 429 F.Supp. 1105 (D.Del.1977) (because of crowding, inmates housed in the prison hospital, staff dining room, libraries, and TV rooms; receiving cells designed for eight men housing sixty during the day and twenty-four at night; inmates having to stand on mattresses while using the toilet and sometimes urinating on them; inmates having to share beds and sleep under bunk beds; homosexual rape "the norm" in the receiving rooms); Pugh v. Locke, 406 F.Supp. 318 (M.D.Ala. 1976), aff'd, 559 F.2d 283 (5th Cir.1977), rev'd in part on other grounds sub nom., Alabama v. Pugh, 438 U.S. 781, 98 S.Ct. 3057 (1978) (mattresses in hallways and next to urinals; one toilet for over two hundred men in one part of the prison; broken and unscreened windows; food infested with insects; inmates in wheelchairs left unsupervised in areas only accessible by stairway; up to six inmates housed in each "isolation cell" with thirty-two square feet of living space, no beds, no lights, no running water, and a hole in the floor for a toilet, fed only once a day and often given no utensils, and permitted to shower only every eleven days); and Costello v. Wainwright, 397 F.Supp. 20 (M.D.Fla.1975), aff'd, 525 F.2d 1239 (5th Cir.1976) (Florida prison system had a "normal capacity" of 7000 and an "emergency capacity" of 8300 inmates, but housed 10,300 inmates; as a result, four inmates were sometimes housed in one-person cells. See the photograph below which was included in the appendix to the district court's opinion).

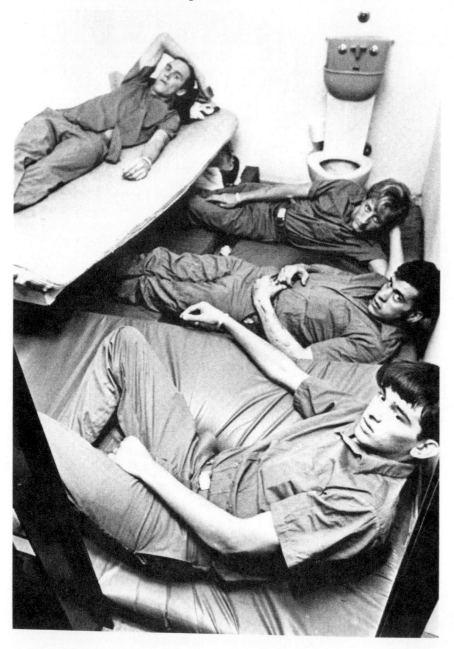

3. Prisoners' conditions of confinement raise not only a number of constitutional questions, but a number of policy questions as well. For example, some states have reinstituted the use of prisoner chain gangs. Prisoners in chain gangs are often chained together and forced to do work along public highways, such as chopping weeds, or other menial tasks, such as

bashing rocks to be used in road gravel. From a policy perspective, are chain gangs a good or a bad idea?

A majority of the states have also built "supermax" prisons where the "worst of the worst" prisoners are supposed to be confined. Jones 'El v. Berge, 164 F.Supp.2d 1096, 1099 (W.D.Wis.2001). But see Leena Kurki & Norval Morris, The Purposes, Practices, and Problems of Supermax Prisons, 28 Crime & Just. 385, 392 (2001) (citing reports that supermax prisons are housing fairly low-risk prisoners). Supermax prisons share a number of common features, including almost complete isolation of prisoners from staff and other inmates and denial of most other sensory stimuli. For example, prisoners housed at the supermax prison described in *Jones 'El v. Berge* were confined almost twenty-four hours a day in a single cell separated from the corridor by two solid steel doors. Meals were delivered through a trap door in the doors, enabling correctional staff to avoid interaction with the inmates. Inmates were not permitted to exercise outdoors and could only catch a glimpse of the sky by standing on their beds and peering through a five-inch skylight. The prisoners were not permitted to have clocks, watches, radios, cassette players, or televisions. What additional facts would you want to know about a particular supermax prison to assess its constitutionality? What additional facts would you need to assess the wisdom of utilizing supermax prisons from a policy standpoint? See Leena Kurki & Norval Morris, supra, at 385.

4.   Courts generally have held that prisoners have no constitutional right to be rehabilitated while they are in prison. See, e.g., Rizzo v. Dawson, 778 F.2d 527, 531 (9th Cir.1985). In other words, the government is not obligated to take affirmative steps to try to reform prisoners and make them better persons. Courts have therefore held that correctional officials need not make educational, vocational, and other rehabilitative programs available to inmates. See, e.g., Dillard v. DeTella, 1998 WL 111704, at *4 (N.D.Ill.1998). These cases seem in keeping with the Supreme Court's admonition in Wilson v. Seiter, 501 U.S. 294, 304, 111 S.Ct. 2321, 2327 (1991) that for conditions of confinement to inflict cruel and unusual punishment, they must deprive inmates of an "identifiable human need such as food, warmth, or exercise."

In Helling v. McKinney, 509 U.S. 25, 113 S.Ct. 2475 (1993), however, the Supreme Court rejected the argument that prisoners must already have suffered or currently be suffering injuries from their conditions of confinement in order for those conditions to be considered cruel and unusual punishment. The plaintiff in *Helling* was a nonsmoking inmate who claimed that placing him in an eight-foot-by-six-foot cell with an inmate who smoked five packs of cigarettes a day constituted cruel and unusual punishment. The lower court directed a verdict for the prison officials because the plaintiff had failed to prove that he currently was suffering any ill effects to his health caused by the involuntary exposure to cigarette smoke.

The Supreme Court held that a sufficiently high risk of future harm stemming from an inmate's conditions of confinement could give rise to an Eighth Amendment claim. The Court observed that to satisfy the objective requirement that must be met to establish an Eighth Amendment violation, the plaintiff first would have to prove that he was being exposed to unreasonably high levels of tobacco smoke. The plaintiff's burden of proof did not end there though, as the Court explained below:

> Also with respect to the objective factor, determining whether McKinney's conditions of confinement violate the Eighth Amendment requires more than a scientific and statistical inquiry into the seriousness of the potential harm and the likelihood that such injury to health will actually be caused by exposure to ETS [environmental tobacco smoke]. It also requires a court to assess whether society considers the risk that the prisoner complains of to be so grave that it violates contemporary standards of decency to expose *anyone* unwillingly to such a risk. In other words, the prisoner must show that the risk of which he complains is not one that today's society chooses to tolerate.

Id. at 36, 113 S.Ct. at 2482.

5. In Overton v. Bazzetta, 539 U.S. 126, 123 S.Ct. 2162 (2003), the Supreme Court rebuffed an Eighth Amendment claim that the punishment imposed for a second violation of a substance-abuse regulation, the loss of visiting privileges for at least two years, inflicted cruel and unusual punishment on prisoners. The Court noted that employing the withdrawal of visiting privileges as a disciplinary sanction was a common means of enforcing prison rules and hence was not a "dramatic departure from accepted standards for conditions of confinement." Id. at 137, 123 S.Ct. at 2170. Nor, according to the Court, did the denial of visiting privileges make the conditions of the inmates' confinement "inhumane," deprive them of "basic necessities," inflict pain or injury on them, or evince deliberate indifference to the risk that such pain or injury might ensue. Id. The Court, however, once again alluded to the possibility that the outcome of a case with different facts might be different— where the termination of visiting privileges was permanent, where visiting privileges were withheld for a much longer period of time, or where the sanction of withdrawn visiting privileges was applied arbitrarily—in other words, without procedural safeguards. Do you agree or disagree with the Court's analysis and disposition of the prisoners' Eighth Amendment claim?

6. In Wilson v. Seiter, 501 U.S. 294, 111 S.Ct. 2321 (1991), the Supreme Court held that even if conditions of confinement deprive inmates of a basic human need, those conditions do not rise to the level of cruel and unusual punishment unless correctional officials have acted with a sufficiently culpable state of mind in maintaining those conditions. The Court rested its conclusion on a long line of cases holding that for the unnecessary infliction of pain to be considered cruel and unusual, its infliction must be "wanton."

The Court then held that the deliberate-indifference standard is the one that has to be met to satisfy the Eighth Amendment's state-of-mind requirement in conditions-of-confinement cases. Seeing no substantial difference between claims involving the provision of inadequate medical care and claims involving other allegedly inadequate conditions of confinement, the Court found that *Estelle v. Gamble* dictated this conclusion.

Four members of the Court—Justices White, Marshall, Blackmun, and Stevens—disagreed with the proposition that prison officials must maintain prison conditions with a certain state of mind before those conditions can be considered cruel and unusual. What is important to look at when determining whether prison conditions are cruel and unusual, the dissenters argued, is the conditions' "objective severity, not the subjective intent of government officials." Id. at 309, 111 S.Ct. at 2330.

The dissenting Justices were particularly concerned that prison officials might avoid responsibility for inhumane conditions of confinement under a deliberate-indifference standard. They noted that prison officials might argue that they had done everything that they could to alleviate those conditions but were hamstrung in their efforts to rectify the problems because of the state legislature's failure to provide the funds needed to do so. To this argument, Justice Scalia, writing for the majority, responded:

> Even if that were so, it is hard to understand how it could control the meaning of "cruel and unusual punishment" in the Eighth Amendment. An intent requirement is either implicit in the word "punishment" or is not; it cannot be alternately required and ignored as policy considerations might dictate. At any rate, the validity of a "cost" defense as negating the requisite intent is not at issue in this case, since respondents have never advanced it. Nor, we might note, is there any indication that other officials have sought to use such a defense to avoid the holding of *Estelle v. Gamble*.

Id. at 301–02, 111 S.Ct. at 2326. See also Harris v. Angelina County, Texas, 31 F.3d 331, 336 (5th Cir.1994) (holding that even if there were a "cost defense" to an Eighth Amendment claim, the defense did not apply because the defendants had failed to show that additional funds could not be obtained from the taxpayers).

With whose views do you agree on the question of whether prison officials must have acted with deliberate indifference for conditions of confinement to be considered cruel and unusual punishment? How would you define "deliberate indifference"? In the case which follows, the Supreme Court addressed this latter question.

FARMER v. BRENNAN

Supreme Court of the United States, 1994.
511 U.S. 825, 114 S.Ct. 1970, 128 L.Ed.2d 811.

Justice Souter delivered the opinion of the Court.

* * *

I

The dispute before us stems from a civil suit brought by petitioner, Dee Farmer, alleging that respondents, federal prison officials, violated the Eighth Amendment by their deliberate indifference to petitioner's safety. Petitioner, who is serving a federal sentence for credit card fraud, has been diagnosed by medical personnel of the Bureau of Prisons as a transsexual, one who has "[a] rare psychiatric disorder in which a person feels persistently uncomfortable about his or her anatomical sex," and who typically seeks medical treatment, including hormonal therapy and surgery, to bring about a permanent sex change. For several years before being convicted and sentenced in 1986 at the age of 18, petitioner, who is biologically male, wore women's clothing (as petitioner did at the 1986 trial), underwent estrogen therapy, received silicone breast implants, and submitted to unsuccessful "black market" testicle-removal surgery. Petitioner's precise appearance in prison is unclear from the record before us, but petitioner claims to have continued hormonal treatment while incarcerated by using drugs smuggled into prison, and apparently wears clothing in a feminine manner, as by displaying a shirt "off one shoulder." The parties agree that petitioner "projects feminine characteristics."

The practice of federal prison authorities is to incarcerate preoperative transsexuals with prisoners of like biological sex, and over time authorities housed petitioner in several federal facilities, sometimes in the general male prison population but more often in segregation. While there is no dispute that petitioner was segregated at least several times because of violations of prison rules, neither is it disputed that in at least one penitentiary petitioner was segregated because of safety concerns.

On March 9, 1989, petitioner was transferred for disciplinary reasons from the Federal Correctional Institution in Oxford, Wisconsin (FCI–Oxford), to the United States Penitentiary in Terre Haute, Indiana (USP–Terre Haute). Though the record before us is unclear about the security designations of the two prisons in 1989, penitentiaries are typically higher security facilities that house more troublesome prisoners than federal correctional institut[ions]. After an initial stay in administrative segregation, petitioner was placed in the USP–Terre Haute general population. Petitioner voiced no objection to any prison official about the transfer to the penitentiary or to placement in its general population. Within two weeks, according to petitioner's allegations, petitioner was beaten and raped by another inmate in petitioner's cell. * * *

Acting without counsel, petitioner then filed a *Bivens* complaint, alleging a violation of the Eighth Amendment. * * * As later amended, the complaint alleged that respondents either transferred petitioner to USP–Terre Haute or placed petitioner in its general population despite knowledge that the penitentiary had a violent environment and a history of inmate assaults, and despite knowledge that petitioner, as a transsexual who "projects feminine characteristics," would be particularly vulnerable to sexual attack by some USP–Terre Haute inmates. * * *

[The federal district court granted the prison officials' motion for summary judgment on the grounds that there was no evidence that the officials had acted with deliberate indifference to petitioner's safety. On appeal, the Seventh Circuit Court of Appeals summarily affirmed.]

II

A

The Constitution "does not mandate comfortable prisons," but neither does it permit inhumane ones, and it is now settled that "the

treatment a prisoner receives in prison and the conditions under which he is confined are subject to scrutiny under the Eighth Amendment." * * *

In particular, as the lower courts have uniformly held, and as we have assumed, "[p]rison officials have a duty ... to protect prisoners from violence at the hands of other prisoners." Having incarcerated "persons [with] demonstrated proclivit[ies] for antisocial criminal, and often violent, conduct," having stripped them of virtually every means of self-protection and foreclosed their access to outside aid, the government and its officials are not free to let the state of nature take its course. Prison conditions may be "restrictive and even harsh," but gratuitously allowing the beating or rape of one prisoner by another serves no "legitimate penological objectiv[e]" any more than it squares with " 'evolving standards of decency.' " Being violently assaulted in prison is simply not "part of the penalty that criminal offenders pay for their offenses against society."

It is not, however, every injury suffered by one prisoner at the hands of another that translates into constitutional liability for prison officials responsible for the victim's safety. Our cases have held that a prison official violates the Eighth Amendment only when two requirements are met. First, the deprivation alleged must be, objectively, "sufficiently serious;" a prison official's act or omission must result in the denial of "the minimal civilized measure of life's necessities." For a claim (like the one here) based on a failure to prevent harm, the inmate must show that he is incarcerated under conditions posing a substantial risk of serious harm.[3]

The second requirement follows from the principle that "only the unnecessary and wanton infliction of pain implicates the Eighth Amendment." To violate the Cruel and Unusual Punishments Clause, a prison official must have a "sufficiently culpable state of mind." In prison-conditions cases that state of mind is one of "deliberate indifference" to inmate health or safety, a standard the parties agree governs the claim in this case. The parties disagree, however, on the proper test for deliberate indifference, which we must therefore undertake to define.

B

* * *

While *Estelle* establishes that deliberate indifference entails something more than mere negligence, the cases are also clear that it is satisfied by something less than acts or omissions for the very purpose of causing harm or with knowledge that harm will result. * * *

With deliberate indifference lying somewhere between the poles of negligence at one end and purpose or knowledge at the other, the Courts

---

3. At what point a risk of inmate assault becomes sufficiently substantial for Eighth Amendment purposes is a question this case does not present, and we do not address it.

of Appeals have routinely equated deliberate indifference with reckless-ness. * * *

That does not, however, fully answer the pending question about the level of culpability deliberate indifference entails, for the term reckless-ness is not self-defining. The civil law generally calls a person reckless who acts or (if the person has a duty to act) fails to act in the face of an unjustifiably high risk of harm that is either known or so obvious that it should be known. The criminal law, however, generally permits a finding of recklessness only when a person disregards a risk of harm of which he is aware. * * *

We reject petitioner's invitation to adopt an objective test for deliber-ate indifference. We hold instead that a prison official cannot be found liable under the Eighth Amendment for denying an inmate humane conditions of confinement unless the official knows of and disregards an excessive risk to inmate health or safety; the official must both be aware of facts from which the inference could be drawn that a substantial risk of serious harm exists, and he must also draw the inference. This approach comports best with the text of the Amendment as our cases have inter-preted it. The Eighth Amendment does not outlaw cruel and unusual "conditions"; it outlaws cruel and unusual "punishments." * * * [A]n official's failure to alleviate a significant risk that he should have per-ceived but did not, while no cause for commendation, cannot under our cases be condemned as the infliction of punishment.

* * *

We are no more persuaded by petitioner's argument that, without an objective test for deliberate indifference, prison officials will be free to ignore obvious dangers to inmates. Under the test we adopt today, an Eighth Amendment claimant need not show that a prison official acted or failed to act believing that harm actually would befall an inmate; it is enough that the official acted or failed to act despite his knowledge of a substantial risk of serious harm. We doubt that a subjective approach will present prison officials with any serious motivation "to take refuge in the zone between 'ignorance of obvious risks' and 'actual knowledge of risks.'" Whether a prison official had the requisite knowledge of a substantial risk is a question of fact subject to demonstration in the usual ways, including inference from circumstantial evidence, and a factfinder may conclude that a prison official knew of a substantial risk from the very fact that the risk was obvious. ("[I]f the risk is obvious, so that a reasonable man would realize it, we might well infer that [the defendant] did in fact realize it; but the inference cannot be conclusive, for we know that people are not always conscious of what reasonable people would be conscious of"). For example, if an Eighth Amendment plaintiff presents evidence showing that a substantial risk of inmate attacks was "long-standing, pervasive, well-documented, or expressly noted by prison offi-cials in the past, and the circumstances suggest that the defendant-official being sued had been exposed to information concerning the risk and thus 'must have known' about it, then such evidence could be sufficient to permit a trier of fact to find that the defendant-official had actual knowledge of the risk."[8]

Nor may a prison official escape liability for deliberate indifference by showing that, while he was aware of an obvious, substantial risk to inmate safety, he did not know that the complainant was especially likely to be assaulted by the specific prisoner who eventually committed the assault. The question under the Eighth Amendment is whether prison officials, acting with deliberate indifference, exposed a prisoner to a sufficiently substantial "risk of serious damage to his future health," and it does not matter whether the risk comes from a single source or multiple sources, any more than it matters whether a prisoner faces an excessive risk of attack for reasons personal to him or because all prisoners in his situation face such a risk. See Brief for Respondents 15 (stating that a prisoner can establish exposure to a sufficiently serious risk of harm "by showing that he belongs to an identifiable group of prisoners who are frequently singled out for violent attack by other inmates"). If, for example, prison officials were aware that inmate "rape was so common and uncontrolled that some potential victims dared not sleep [but] instead . . . would leave their beds and spend the night clinging to the bars nearest the guards' station," *Hutto v. Finney,* 437 U.S. 678, 681–682, n. 3 (1978), it would obviously be irrelevant to liability that the officials could not guess beforehand precisely who would attack whom.

Because, however, prison officials who lacked knowledge of a risk cannot be said to have inflicted punishment, it remains open to the officials to prove that they were unaware even of an obvious risk to inmate health or safety. That a trier of fact may infer knowledge from the obvious, in other words, does not mean that it must do so. Prison officials charged with deliberate indifference might show, for example, that they did not know of the underlying facts indicating a sufficiently substantial danger and that they were therefore unaware of a danger, or that they knew the underlying facts but believed (albeit unsoundly) that the risk to which the facts gave rise was insubstantial or nonexistent.

In addition, prison officials who actually knew of a substantial risk to inmate health or safety may be found free from liability if they responded reasonably to the risk, even if the harm ultimately was not averted. A prison official's duty under the Eighth Amendment is to ensure "reasonable safety," a standard that incorporates due regard for prison officials' "unenviable task of keeping dangerous men in safe custody under humane

---

8. While the obviousness of a risk is not conclusive and a prison official may show that the obvious escaped him, he would not escape liability if the evidence showed that he merely refused to verify underlying facts that he strongly suspected to be true, or declined to confirm inferences of risk that he strongly suspected to exist (as when a prison official is aware of a high probability of facts indicating that one prisoner has planned an attack on another but resists opportunities to obtain final confirmation; or when a prison official knows that some diseases are communicable and that a single needle is being used to administer flu shots to prisoners but refuses to listen to a subordinate who he strongly suspects will attempt to explain the associated risk of transmitting disease). * * *

conditions." Whether one puts it in terms of duty or deliberate indifference, prison officials who act reasonably cannot be found liable under the Cruel and Unusual Punishments Clause.

* * *

Accordingly, we reject petitioner's arguments and hold that a prison official may be held liable under the Eighth Amendment for denying humane conditions of confinement only if he knows that inmates face a substantial risk of serious harm and disregards that risk by failing to take reasonable measures to abate it.

III

* * *

In granting summary judgment to respondents on the ground that petitioner had failed to satisfy the Eighth Amendment's subjective requirement, the District Court may have placed decisive weight on petitioner's failure to notify respondents of a risk of harm. That petitioner "never expressed any concern for his safety to any of [respondents]" was the only evidence the District Court cited for its conclusion that there was no genuine dispute about respondents' assertion that they "had no knowledge of any potential danger to [petitioner]". But with respect to each of petitioner's claims, for damages and for injunctive relief, the failure to give advance notice is not dispositive. Petitioner may establish respondents' awareness by reliance on any relevant evidence.

* * *

IV

The judgment of the Court of Appeals is vacated, and the case is remanded for further proceedings consistent with this opinion.

[Justices Blackmun, Stevens, and Thomas wrote separate concurring opinions, which are omitted here.]

QUESTIONS AND POINTS FOR DISCUSSION

1. According to the Supreme Court in Davidson v. Cannon, 474 U.S. 344, 348, 106 S.Ct. 668, 671 (1986), which is discussed on page 729, the failure to protect an inmate from an attack by another inmate may also give rise to a due-process claim. What if a prisoner was attacked by twenty inmates and two officers in a control room failed to intervene? Would their inaction constitute either cruel and unusual punishment or a violation of due process? See Stubbs v. Dudley, 849 F.2d 83, 87 (2d Cir.1988).

2. The courts have generally agreed that the Eighth Amendment and, in the case of pretrial detainees, the Due Process Clause, can be violated not only when correctional officials are deliberately indifferent to a substantial risk that an inmate will be seriously injured or killed by others, but also when they are deliberately indifferent to a substantial risk that an inmate will commit

suicide. See, e.g., Brown v. Harris, 240 F.3d 383, 388–89, 389 n. 6 (4th Cir.2001) (listing cases). The courts' rationale is that an inmate with suicidal tendencies has a "basic human need" for medical care and protection from serious harm to which, under Estelle v. Gamble, 429 U.S. 97, 97 S.Ct. 285 (1976) and Farmer v. Brennan, 511 U.S. 825, 114 S.Ct. 1970 (1994), correctional officials cannot be deliberately indifferent. *Brown*, 240 F.3d at 388–89.

Just because an inmate kills himself, however, does not mean that correctional officials have manifested the requisite deliberate indifference. The courts have recognized that correctional facilities cannot guarantee the safety of the persons confined within them and that inmates bent on killing themselves may eventually succeed in doing so. See, e.g., Estate of Cills v. Kaftan, 105 F.Supp.2d 391, 397 (D.N.J.2000) ("states are not required to furnish prisoners with suicide-proof prisons"). Consequently, one of the prerequisites for a finding of deliberate indifference to the risk that an inmate would commit suicide is that there was, in the words of some courts, a " 'strong likelihood, rather than a mere possibility, that suicide would result from a defendant's actions or inaction.' " See, e.g., Heggs v. Grant, 73 F.3d 317, 320 (11th Cir.1996) (quoting Tittle v. Jefferson County Comm'n, 10 F.3d 1535, 1540 (11th Cir.1994)).

Some of the cases in which the courts have found sufficient evidence of deliberate indifference, at least to withstand a motion to dismiss or for summary judgment, include: Jacobs v. West Feliciana Sheriff's Dep't, 228 F.3d 388 (5th Cir.2000) (sheriff knew that decedent had tried earlier to kill herself but placed her in a cell with tie-off points—window bars—that another inmate had previously used, like the decedent did, to hang himself); Gordon v. Kidd, 971 F.2d 1087, 1095 (4th Cir.1992) (jail official, who was warned that decedent might kill himself, failed to pass the warning on to decedent's custodians and to ask a nurse, as required by jail policy, to screen the decedent for suicidal tendencies); Greason v. Kemp, 891 F.2d 829, 836 (11th Cir.1990) (mental-health professional told by decedent's parents and two inmates of decedent's prior suicide attempts took no steps to ensure that decedent would be monitored in his cell); Guglielmoni v. Alexander, 583 F.Supp. 821 (D.Conn.1984) (decedent earlier had tried unsuccessfully to hang himself in the prison); and Matje v. Leis, 571 F.Supp. 918 (S.D.Ohio 1983) (authorities were aware that the decedent had threatened to kill herself with drugs that she would smuggle into the prison behind her diaphragm, but she was not subjected to a body-cavity search upon entry into the prison).

Cases in which the courts have found insufficient allegations or evidence of deliberate indifference include: Boncher v. Brown County, 272 F.3d 484 (7th Cir.2001) (intake officers at jail where there had been five suicides in five years were poorly trained in screening inmates for suicide risk but believed that the decedent, who, unbeknownst to them, had previously tried at least three times to commit suicide, was joking when he said he had tried to kill himself several days before); Hott v. Hennepin County, 260 F.3d 901 (8th Cir.2001) (in the presence of jail officials, decedent placed his hands so tightly on his neck that he left red marks, but the officials did not know that the decedent had previously attempted suicide); Domino v. Texas Dep't of Criminal Justice, 239 F.3d 752 (5th Cir.2001) (prison psychiatrist concluded, incorrectly, that decedent was simply threatening suicide for "secondary gain"—to obtain sedatives or a move to a single cell); Jacobs v. West Feliciana Sheriff's Dep't, 228 F.3d 388 (5th Cir.2000) (deputy sheriff waited up to forty-five minutes to check on decedent, who was considered a suicide risk, rather than every fifteen minutes as required by the jail's informal policy); and Freedman v. City of Allentown, 853 F.2d 1111 (3d Cir.1988) (police officers did not realize that scars on decedent's wrists and neck were from a previous suicide attempt).

3. *Class Exercise*: Some prisoners are contesting the constitutionality of the conditions of confinement in the prison described below. Half of the class will represent them, and the other half will represent the prison officials defending the constitutionality of the prison's conditions.

The prison in question is a maximum-security penitentiary built in 1871. Designed to hold up to 1200 inmates, the prison now houses 1918 inmates. The majority of these inmates are serving lengthy sentences for serious and violent offenses—murder, rape, and armed robbery.

Fifty-six per cent of the inmates in the prison are double-celled; the rest are mostly confined in segregation or protective-custody units. Assume that a study introduced at the hearing on the prisoners' motion for injunctive relief revealed that there was single celling in 80% of the cells in state prisons and 90% of the cells in federal prisons.

The inmates who are double-celled in the prison are housed in the west and south cellblocks. The trial judge visited the prison and measured the cells in each cellblock. The dimensions of the cells in the west cellblock are about 75 inches by 124 inches, which means that there is about 64.5 square feet of living space. The cells in the south cellblock are smaller—64 inches by 125 inches—with about 55.5 square feet of living space. A state statute requires that new or renovated state institutions provide at least 50 square feet of cell space per person.

Each cell contains a bunk bed, a sink, a toilet, and a chest of drawers or cardboard boxes used for storage. Each inmate is permitted to keep twenty-five books, twelve records, a tape player, a radio, and a television set in the cell. Because of the accoutrements in each cell, inmates are often left with only nine square feet or less of room in which to stand or walk in their cells. Consequently, an inmate generally has to climb onto the bunk bed to avoid being touched when his cellmate is moving within, or attempting to leave, the cell.

The lighting in each cell is dim, because each cell only has one fluorescent bulb in the ceiling. Although each cell is fairly clean, a "borderline stench" pervades the cellblocks because of the number of people confined in such a small area. Problems with ventilation are exacerbated by the inmates, who cover the air vents in their cells to keep out roaches and dust.

The amount of time that each inmate spends in his cell varies, depending on whether the inmate has a work or school assignment. On average, inmates housed in the south cellblock spend a minimum of about twenty hours in their cells, while those in the west cellblock are confined in their cells eighteen to twenty hours a day.

Only about half of the prisoners have work or school assignments. Even when an inmate is assigned a job, the job is often a makeweight, created just to give the inmate something to do. For example, one inmate testified that he is assigned to do lawn work in a small area of the prison grounds. His job only takes about fifteen minutes to complete, and for the rest of the four-hour shift, he just pushes dirt into a pile and then rakes down the pile.

A licensed physician can be found at the prison seven days a week, twenty-four hours a day. In addition, the prison employs a full-time dentist, dental assistants, an X-ray technician, and a full-time pharmacist. The kitchen and dining rooms are clean, and the food fed the inmates is nutritious and edible.

A number of inmates testified about the problems caused by double celling, problems that were compounded by the lack of a classification program to ensure the proper placement of inmates in double cells. Some of the problems included: (1) the fear of homosexual attack by a cellmate; (2) violence or threats of violence directed against a cellmate because of his refusal to share personal property, failure to keep the cell clean and neat, or other reasons; (3) an inability to study, both because of a lack of desks and because, with so many inmates housed in the cellblock, there is a great deal of noise; (4) interference with religious practices, such as inmates turning on the television while their cellmates are praying; and (5) tension, frustration, and anger caused by the loss of privacy, particularly in the use of the toilet, and by housing together people with different religious beliefs, moral standards, gang affiliations, ages, and idiosyncrasies. One fifty-three-year-old inmate, for example, talked about his irritation with his sixteen-year-old cellmate, who frequently sat in the corner masturbating before the picture of a nude woman.

A number of experts testified at trial for the prisoners and the prison officials as did a court-appointed expert witness. Many of the experts testified that crowding increases death and illness rates, the percentage of psychiatric commitments, and institutional violence. The warden of the prison, however, testified that during his three years as warden, the number of violent incidents had decreased by fifty percent.

C.　USE OF FORCE AGAINST INMATES

JACKSON v. BISHOP

Court of Appeals, Eighth Circuit, 1968.
404 F.2d 571.

BLACKMUN, CIRCUIT JUDGE.

The three plaintiffs-appellants, inmates of the Arkansas penitentiary, in separate actions call upon us to direct the entry of an injunction barring the use of the strap as a disciplinary measure in Arkansas' penal institutions. The claim is that the district court

erred in refusing to hold that corporal punishment of prisoners is cruel and unusual punishment within the meaning of the Eighth

Amendment to the United States Constitution, and in holding that the whipping of prisoners was not unconstitutional per se.

* * *

* * * We regard the following history and facts as particularly pertinent for our review:

1.   The Arkansas penal institutions are under the general supervision of a five-man "honorary" commission known as the State Penitentiary Board. Actual day-to-day supervision is delegated by the Board to a full-time compensated superintendent. * * *

* * *

7.   Corporal punishment in the Arkansas system was authorized formally only in 1962 but evidently it had been employed for many years. At that time the Board, by resolution, authorized such punishment whenever, in the Superintendent's judgment, its infliction was necessary in order to maintain discipline. The resolution did not prescribe form or limit of punishment.

8.   In *Talley v. Stephens,* 247 F.Supp. 683 (E.D.Ark.1965), the three petitioning inmates sought injunctive relief with respect to certain prison practices including the infliction of corporal punishment. * * * Chief Judge Henley found that, at that time, there were no written rules as to whipping; that such punishment was administered in the sole discretion of the one inflicting it, subject to an informal requirement that the blows not exceed ten for a single offense; and that two of those three petitioners had been whipped and one beaten by a field-line supervisor-trusty. The judge noted that the Supreme Court of Arkansas, over 80 years ago, deplored the whipping of convicts, and that the Arkansas statutes do not themselves specifically prescribe whipping even as a punishment for crime. He observed, however, that corporal punishment had not been viewed historically as a constitutionally forbidden cruel and unusual punishment. The court concluded that it was not prepared to say that such punishment was unconstitutional per se. Nevertheless, Judge Henley said, this conclusion presupposes that the infliction of such punishment is surrounded by appropriate safeguards, that is, it must not be excessive, it must be inflicted dispassionately and by responsible people, and it must be applied under recognizable standards so that the convict knows what conduct will cause him to be whipped and how much punishment his conduct will produce. The court found that those safeguards did not exist in the Arkansas system and enjoined further corporal punishment of the petitioners until they were established.

9.   The *Talley* opinion was filed on November 15, 1965. As a result, the Board issued written rules and regulations on January 10, 1966. These were in effect until the district court decision in the present case was rendered June 3, 1967. In addition to a number of other provisions, the rules state that certain "major offenses will warrant corporal punishment." The ones listed are homosexuality, agitation, insubordination,

making or concealing weapons, refusal to work when medically certified able to work, and participating in or inciting a riot. They further state:

> No inmate shall ever be authorized to inflict any corporal punishment under color of prison authority on another inmate.

> Punishment shall not, in any case, exceed Ten lashes with the strap, the number of lashes to be administered shall be determined by a Board of Inquiry, consisting of at least two officials of the Arkansas State Penitentiary, the Superintendent or Assistant Superintendent, and the head Warden or an associate Warden. The Board of Inquiry will request that the accused inmate appear before the Board and speak in his own behalf. No Punishment will be administered in the field.

10. The straps used in Arkansas vary somewhat but all are similar. Each is of leather and from 3½ to 5½ feet in length, about 4 inches wide, and ¼ inch thick. Each has a wooden handle 8 to 12 inches long.

11. Since *Talley,* whippings are administered by wardens. The prisoner lies face down and the blows are to his buttocks. Supposedly, they are administered while the prisoner is fully clothed. Petitioners Ernst and Mask, however, testified without contradiction that they were required to lower their trousers and that they received lashes on the bare buttocks. There is corroborating and other evidence to the same effect with respect to other inmates and there was proof, some offered through the State Police, of deep bruises and bleeding.

12. Whipping is the primary disciplinary measure used in the Arkansas system. Prisoners there have few privileges which can be withheld from them as punishment. Facilities for segregation and solitary confinement are limited.

13. There is testimony that the strap hurts the inmate's pride, that it has been needed in order to preserve discipline, and that the work level improves after its administration. Contrarily, there is testimony that the whipping generates hate in the inmate who is whipped and that this hate flows toward the whipper, the institution and the system.

14. * * * The testimony of James V. Bennett, former Director of the Federal Bureau of Prisons, and that of Fred T. Wilkinson, Director of the Department of Corrections of the State of Missouri (and former Deputy Director of the Federal Bureau of Prisons) are summarized in the district court's opinion. This testimony is to the effect that, among other things, corporal punishment has not been used for disciplinary purposes in federal prisons for years and that only Mississippi, in addition to Arkansas, uses it officially. Testifying as a penologist, it was Mr. Bennett's opinion that the whippings administered to the three plaintiffs were "cruel, degrading and certainly they were unusual in this day and age." Mr. Wilkinson testified that use of the strap "is cruel and unusual and unnecessary."

15. On July 20, 1966, six months after the issuance of the January 1966 regulations, plaintiff Ernst received two whippings of ten lashes each to the bare buttocks within a period of 45 minutes.

* * *

17. The district judges concluded that the post-*Talley* rules and regulations of January 1966 still did not provide adequate safeguards. The use of the strap was therefore enjoined until further safeguards were provided. * * *.[5]

* * *

* * * [W]e have no difficulty in reaching the conclusion that the use of the strap in the penitentiaries of Arkansas is punishment which, in this last third of the 20th century, runs afoul of the Eighth Amendment; that the strap's use, irrespective of any precautionary conditions which may be imposed, offends contemporary concepts of decency and human dignity and precepts of civilization which we profess to possess * * *.

Our reasons for this conclusion include the following: (1) We are not convinced that any rule or regulation as to the use of the strap, however seriously or sincerely conceived and drawn, will successfully prevent abuse. The present record discloses misinterpretation and obvious over-narrow interpretation even of the newly adopted January 1966 rules. (2) Rules in this area seem often to go unobserved. Despite the January 1966 requirement that no inmate was to inflict punishment on another, the record is replete with instances where this very thing took place. (3) Regulations are easily circumvented. Although it was a long-standing requirement that a whipping was to be administered only when the prisoner was fully clothed, this record discloses instances of whippings upon the bare buttocks, and with consequent injury. (4) Corporal punishment is easily subject to abuse in the hands of the sadistic and the unscrupulous. (5) Where power to punish is granted to persons in lower levels of administrative authority, there is an inherent and natural difficulty in enforcing the limitations of that power. (6) There can be no argument that excessive whipping or an inappropriate manner of whipping or too great frequency of whipping or the use of studded or overlong straps all constitute cruel and unusual punishment. But if whipping were to be authorized, how does one, or any court, ascertain the point which

---

5. At oral argument we were advised that since the entry of the district court's decree other new rules and regulations have been adopted. * * * Before punishment is imposed, a full hearing before a Board of Inquiry is required. The accusing warden may not sit on the Board of Inquiry or take part in carrying out the punishment. Punishment may include solitary confinement, reduction of rations, corporal punishment, loss of mail, recreation and other privileges, loss of future good time, and recording the offense for parole purposes. Corporal punishment shall not exceed ten lashes with the strap and a period in solitary confinement. In no case may the strap be applied to the bare buttocks. An accuser or other inmate shall not administer the strap. The strap shall not be used in the fields. No inmate shall be whipped within 24 hours of any preceding whipping. Each inmate sentenced to corporal punishment has the right of appeal to the superintendent or the assistant superintendent and this official or his designee may change the sentence. * * *

* * *

would distinguish the permissible from that which is cruel and unusual? (7) Corporal punishment generates hate toward the keepers who punish and toward the system which permits it. It is degrading to the punisher and to the punished alike. It frustrates correctional and rehabilitative goals. This record cries out with testimony to this effect from the expert penologists, from the inmates and from their keepers. (8) Whipping creates other penological problems and makes adjustment to society more difficult. (9) Public opinion is obviously adverse. Counsel concede that only two states still permit the use of the strap. Thus almost uniformly has it been abolished. It has been expressly outlawed by statute in a number of states. And 48 states, including Arkansas, have constitutional provisions against cruel or unusual punishment.

We are not convinced contrarily by any suggestion that the State needs this tool for disciplinary purposes and is too poor to provide other accepted means of prisoner regulation. Humane considerations and constitutional requirements are not, in this day, to be measured or limited by dollar considerations or by the thickness of the prisoner's clothing.

* * *

We choose to draw no significant distinction between the word "cruel" and the word "unusual" in the Eighth Amendment. We would not wish to place ourselves in the position of condoning punishment which is shown to be only "cruel" but not "unusual" or vice versa. In any event, the testimony of the two expert penologists clearly demonstrates that the use of the strap in this day is unusual and we encounter no difficulty in holding that its use is cruel.

Neither do we wish to draw, in this context, any meaningful distinction between punishment by way of sentence statutorily prescribed and punishment imposed for prison disciplinary purposes. It seems to us that the Eighth Amendment's proscription has application to both.

The district court's decree is vacated and the case is remanded with directions to enter a new decree embracing the injunctive relief heretofore granted but, in addition, restraining the Superintendent of the Arkansas State Penitentiary and all personnel of the penitentiary system from inflicting corporal punishment, including the use of the strap, as a disciplinary measure.

QUESTIONS AND POINTS FOR DISCUSSION

1. As was discussed in Chapter 6, the Supreme Court has condoned imposition of the death penalty in some circumstances. If it is not cruel and unusual punishment to sometimes kill a prisoner, why is it cruel and unusual punishment to whip the prisoner?

2. In Ingraham v. Wright, 430 U.S. 651, 97 S.Ct. 1401 (1977), the Supreme Court addressed the constitutionality of paddling students as a form of discipline. Such paddling, the Court observed, does not inflict cruel and

unusual punishment, because the Eighth Amendment generally only protects those convicted of crimes. Nor does the paddling of students, according to the Court, violate their due-process rights unless the amount of force used is excessive under the circumstances. If paddling children can be constitutional, why isn't it constitutional in some circumstances to whip, or at least paddle, convicted criminals?

3. If the majority of states authorized the corporal punishment of prisoners who had committed certain disciplinary infractions, would such punishment violate the Eighth Amendment? Why or why not?

HUDSON v. McMILLIAN

Supreme Court of the United States, 1992.
503 U.S. 1, 112 S.Ct. 995, 117 L.Ed.2d 156.

JUSTICE O'CONNOR delivered the opinion of the Court.

* * *

At the time of the incident that is the subject of this suit, petitioner Keith Hudson was an inmate at the state penitentiary in Angola, Louisiana. Respondents Jack McMillian, Marvin Woods, and Arthur Mezo served as corrections security officers at the Angola facility. During the early morning hours of October 30, 1983, Hudson and McMillian argued. Assisted by Woods, McMillian then placed Hudson in handcuffs and shackles, took the prisoner out of his cell, and walked him toward the penitentiary's "administrative lockdown" area. Hudson testified that, on the way there, McMillian punched Hudson in the mouth, eyes, chest, and stomach while Woods held the inmate in place and kicked and punched him from behind. He further testified that Mezo, the supervisor on duty, watched the beating but merely told the officers "not to have too much fun." As a result of this episode, Hudson suffered minor bruises and swelling of his face, mouth, and lip. The blows also loosened Hudson's teeth and cracked his partial dental plate, rendering it unusable for several months.

Hudson sued the three corrections officers in Federal District Court under 42 U.S.C. § 1983, alleging a violation of the Eighth Amendment's prohibition on cruel and unusual punishments and seeking compensatory damages. [He prevailed on his claim and was awarded $800 in damages. On appeal, the Fifth Circuit Court of Appeals reversed. Although the court found that the correctional officers' conduct constituted the "unnecessary and wanton infliction of pain," the court concluded that Hudson had not been subjected to any cruel and unusual punishment since his injuries were "minor."]

In *Whitley v. Albers,* 475 U.S. 312 (1986), the principal question before us was what legal standard should govern the Eighth Amendment claim of an inmate shot by a guard during a prison riot. We based our answer on the settled rule that " 'the unnecessary and wanton infliction of pain ... constitutes cruel and unusual punishment forbidden by the Eighth Amendment.' "

What is necessary to establish an "unnecessary and wanton infliction of pain," we said, varies according to the nature of the alleged constitutional violation. For example, the appropriate inquiry when an inmate alleges that prison officials failed to attend to serious medical needs is whether the officials exhibited "deliberate indifference." See *Estelle v. Gamble,* 429 U.S. 97, 104 (1976). This standard is appropriate because the State's responsibility to provide inmates with medical care ordinarily does not conflict with competing administrative concerns.

By contrast, officials confronted with a prison disturbance must balance the threat unrest poses to inmates, prison workers, administrators, and visitors against the harm inmates may suffer if guards use force. Despite the weight of these competing concerns, corrections officials must make their decisions "in haste, under pressure, and frequently without the luxury of a second chance." We accordingly concluded in *Whitley* that application of the deliberate indifference standard is inappropriate when authorities use force to put down a prison disturbance. Instead, "the question whether the measure taken inflicted unnecessary and wanton pain and suffering ultimately turns on 'whether force was applied in a good faith effort to maintain or restore discipline or maliciously and sadistically for the very purpose of causing harm.' "

Many of the concerns underlying our holding in *Whitley* arise whenever guards use force to keep order. Whether the prison disturbance is a riot or a lesser disruption, corrections officers must balance the need "to maintain or restore discipline" through force against the risk of injury to inmates. Both situations may require prison officials to act quickly and decisively. Likewise, both implicate the principle that " '[p]rison administrators ... should be accorded wide-ranging deference in the adoption and execution of policies and practices that in their judgment are needed to preserve internal order and discipline and to maintain institutional security.' " In recognition of these similarities, we hold that whenever prison officials stand accused of using excessive physical force in violation of the Cruel and Unusual Punishments Clause, the core judicial inquiry is that set out in *Whitley*: whether force was applied in a good-faith effort to maintain or restore discipline, or maliciously and sadistically to cause harm.

* * *

Under the *Whitley* approach, the extent of injury suffered by an inmate is one factor that may suggest "whether the use of force could plausibly have been thought necessary" in a particular situation, "or instead evinced such wantonness with respect to the unjustified infliction of harm as is tantamount to a knowing willingness that it occur." In determining whether the use of force was wanton and unnecessary, it may also be proper to evaluate the need for application of force, the relationship between that need and the amount of force used, the threat "reasonably perceived by the responsible officials," and "any efforts made to temper the severity of a forceful response." The absence of serious injury is therefore relevant to the Eighth Amendment inquiry, but does not end it.

Respondents nonetheless assert that a significant injury requirement of the sort imposed by the Fifth Circuit is mandated by what we have termed the "objective component" of Eighth Amendment analysis. See *Wilson v. Seiter,* 501 U.S. 294, 298 (1991). *Wilson* extended the deliberate indifference standard applied to Eighth Amendment claims involving medical care to claims about conditions of confinement. In taking this step, we suggested that the subjective aspect of an Eighth Amendment claim (with which the Court was concerned) can be distinguished from the objective facet of the same claim. Thus, courts considering a prisoner's claim must ask both if "the officials act[ed] with a sufficiently culpable state of mind" and if the alleged wrongdoing was objectively "harmful enough" to establish a constitutional violation.

* * * What is necessary to show sufficient harm for purposes of the Cruel and Unusual Punishments Clause depends upon the claim at issue * * *.

The objective component of an Eighth Amendment claim is therefore contextual and responsive to "contemporary standards of decency." For instance, extreme deprivations are required to make out a conditions-of-confinement claim. Because routine discomfort is "part of the penalty that criminal offenders pay for their offenses against society," "only those deprivations denying 'the minimal civilized measure of life's necessities' are sufficiently grave to form the basis of an Eighth Amendment violation." A similar analysis applies to medical needs. Because society does not expect that prisoners will have unqualified access to health care, deliberate indifference to medical needs amounts to an Eighth Amendment violation only if those needs are "serious."

In the excessive force context, society's expectations are different. When prison officials maliciously and sadistically use force to cause harm, contemporary standards of decency always are violated. This is true whether or not significant injury is evident. Otherwise, the Eighth Amendment would permit any physical punishment, no matter how diabolic or inhuman, inflicting less than some arbitrary quantity of injury. * * *

That is not to say that every malevolent touch by a prison guard gives rise to a federal cause of action. See *Johnson v. Glick,* 481 F.2d, at 1033 ("Not every push or shove, even if it may later seem unnecessary in the peace of a judge's chambers, violates a prisoner's constitutional rights"). The Eighth Amendment's prohibition of "cruel and unusual" punishment necessarily excludes from constitutional recognition *de minimis* uses of physical force, provided that the use of force is not of a sort " 'repugnant to the conscience of mankind.' "

In this case, the Fifth Circuit found Hudson's claim untenable because his injuries were "minor." Yet the blows directed at Hudson, which caused bruises, swelling, loosened teeth, and a cracked dental plate, are not *de minimis* for Eighth Amendment purposes. The extent of Hudson's injuries thus provides no basis for dismissal of his § 1983 claim.

* * *

The dissent's argument that claims based on excessive force and claims based on conditions of confinement are no different in kind is likewise unfounded. * * * To deny, as the dissent does, the difference between punching a prisoner in the face and serving him unappetizing food is to ignore the " 'concepts of dignity, civilized standards, humanity, and decency' " that animate the Eighth Amendment.

* * *

JUSTICE STEVENS, concurring in part and concurring in the judgment. [Opinion omitted. Justice Stevens believed that the malicious-and-sadistic standard only should be applied when injuries were inflicted during a prison disturbance "that indisputably poses significant risks to the safety of inmates and prison staff." He wrote a concurring opinion, however, because he believed that even this elevated Eighth Amendment standard was satisfied by the facts of this case.]

JUSTICE BLACKMUN, concurring in the judgment.

The Court today appropriately puts to rest a seriously misguided view that pain inflicted by an excessive use of force is actionable under the Eighth Amendment only when coupled with "significant injury," *e.g.*, injury that requires medical attention or leaves permanent marks. Indeed, were we to hold to the contrary, we might place various kinds of state-sponsored torture and abuse—of the kind ingeniously designed to cause pain but without a tell-tale "significant injury"—entirely beyond the pale of the Constitution. In other words, the constitutional prohibition of "cruel and unusual punishments" then might not constrain prison officials from lashing prisoners with leather straps, whipping them with rubber hoses, beating them with naked fists, shocking them with electric currents, asphyxiating them short of death, intentionally exposing them to undue heat or cold, or forcibly injecting them with psychosis-inducing drugs. * * *

* * *

I do not read anything in the Court's opinion to limit injury cognizable under the Eighth Amendment to physical injury. It is not hard to imagine inflictions of psychological harm—without corresponding physical harm—that might prove to be cruel and unusual punishment. See, *e.g.*, *Wisniewski v. Kennard,* 901 F.2d 1276, 1277 (CA5 1990) (guard placing a revolver in inmate's mouth and threatening to blow prisoner's head off).

* * *

To be sure, as the Court's opinion intimates, *de minimis* or nonmeasurable pain is not actionable under the Eighth Amendment. But psychological pain can be more than *de minimis*. Psychological pain often may be clinically diagnosed and quantified through well established methods, as in the ordinary tort context where damages for pain and suffering are regularly awarded. I have no doubt that to read a "physical pain" or "physical injury" requirement into the Eighth Amendment would be no less pernicious and without foundation than the "significant injury" requirement we reject today.

[Justice Blackmun also opposed extending the *Whitley* standard outside the prison-riot context.]

JUSTICE THOMAS, with whom JUSTICE SCALIA joins, dissenting.

* * *

In my view, a use of force that causes only insignificant harm to a prisoner may be immoral, it may be tortious, it may be criminal, and it may even be remediable under other provisions of the Federal Constitution, but it is not "cruel and unusual punishment." In concluding to the contrary, the Court today goes far beyond our precedents.

* * *

We made clear in *Estelle* that the Eighth Amendment plays a very limited role in regulating prison administration. The case involved a claim that prison doctors had inadequately attended an inmate's medical needs. We rejected the claim because the inmate failed to allege "acts or omissions sufficiently harmful to evidence *deliberate indifference* to *serious* medical needs." From the outset, thus, we specified that the Eighth Amendment does not apply to every deprivation, or even every unnecessary deprivation, suffered by a prisoner, but *only* that narrow class of deprivations involving "serious" injury inflicted by prison officials acting with a culpable state of mind. We have since described these twin elements as the "objective" and "subjective" components of an Eighth Amendment prison claim.

* * *

Perhaps to compensate for its elimination of the *objective* component in excessive force cases, the Court simultaneously makes it harder for prisoners to establish the *subjective* component. As we explained in *Wilson,* "deliberate indifference" is the baseline mental state required to establish an Eighth Amendment violation. Departure from this baseline is justified where, as in *Whitley,* prison officials act in response to an emergency; in such situations their conduct cannot be characterized as "wanton" unless it is taken "maliciously and sadistically for the very purpose of causing harm." The Court today extends the heightened mental state applied in *Whitley* to *all* excessive force cases, even where no competing institutional concerns are present. The Court simply asserts that "[m]any of the concerns underlying our holding in *Whitley* arise *whenever* guards use force to keep order." I do not agree. Many excessive force cases do not arise from guards' attempts to "keep order." (In this very case, the basis for petitioner's Eighth Amendment claim is that the guards hit him when there was no need for them to use any force at all.) The use of excessive physical force is by no means invariably (in fact, perhaps not even predominantly) accompanied by a "malicious and sadistic" state of mind. I see no justification for applying the extraordinary *Whitley* standard to *all* excessive force cases, without regard to the constraints facing prison officials. * * *

* * *

QUESTIONS AND POINTS FOR DISCUSSION

1. In Hope v. Pelzer, 536 U.S. 730, 122 S.Ct. 2508 (2002), an Alabama prisoner filed a lawsuit under § 1983 after he was handcuffed two different times to a hitching post, once after having a verbal argument with another inmate on his chain gang and another time after not responding quickly enough to an order to get off the bus upon its arrival at a worksite. The plaintiff's hands were shackled close together and raised, with the hitching post slightly above his shoulders. One of the times the plaintiff was handcuffed to the hitching post, his shirt was removed, and he stood in the baking sun for seven hours. During that time, he was allowed some water only once or twice, and he was never unhitched to use the bathroom. The denial of bathroom breaks apparently was common when inmates were tied to the hitching post. The Supreme Court cited, for example, an instance when another prisoner defecated on himself while tied to the hitching post.

The Supreme Court held that the tying of the plaintiff to the hitching post was an "obvious" violation of the Eighth Amendment. Id. at 738, 122 S.Ct. at 2514. In concluding that the plaintiff had been subjected to the "unnecessary and wanton infliction of pain," the Court applied a deliberate-indifference standard. Id. at 737–38, 122 S.Ct. at 2514. Does the Court's application of a deliberate-indifference standard in this context demonstrate that the closely divided Court in *Hudson* was correct or incorrect in extending application of the *Whitley* standard beyond situations involving a prison disturbance?

2. A provision of the Prison Litigation Reform Act, which was enacted in 1996, prohibits persons confined in prisons, jails, and other correctional facilities from bringing civil suits in federal court for mental or emotional injuries sustained while in custody unless they can show that they also suffered some type of "physical injury." 42 U.S.C. § 1997e(e). Is this statute, in your opinion, constitutional? Is it wise? For a list of cases reflecting the view of the majority of the courts that the physical-injury requirement does not abridge inmates' constitutional rights, see Searles v. Van Bebber, 251 F.3d 869, 876–77 (10th Cir.2001).

3. According to the Supreme Court, a pretrial detainee against whom excessive force has been used cannot assert an Eighth Amendment claim. However, excessive force used against a pretrial detainee that is tantamount

to punishment violates due process. Graham v. Connor, 490 U.S. 386, 395 n. 10, 109 S.Ct. 1865, 1871 n. 10 (1989).

In adjudicating the excessive-force claims of pretrial detainees, some of the lower courts have collapsed the distinction between pretrial detainees and convicted prisoners, applying the *Hudson* analysis to the detainees' due-process claims. See, e.g., Fennell v. Gilstrap, 559 F.3d 1212, 1217 (11th Cir. 2009) (applying the *Hudson* test in determining whether force used against pretrial detainee "shocks the conscience"). In your opinion, should the scope of the protection afforded pretrial detainees by the Due Process Clause in this context mirror the protection afforded prisoners under the Eighth Amendment?

4. Excessive-force claims have arisen outside the prison context. For example, in Tennessee v. Garner, 471 U.S. 1, 105 S.Ct. 1694 (1985), a § 1983 suit was brought after the decedent was shot in the head and killed by a police officer when fleeing the scene of a burglary. The Supreme Court concluded that the use of deadly force, under the circumstances, subjected the decedent to an "unreasonable seizure" in violation of the Fourth Amendment. The Court outlined three of the requirements that must be met before deadly force can be employed to prevent the escape of a fleeing felon: first, the force must be necessary to avert the escape; second, the officer must have "probable cause to believe that the suspect poses a significant threat of death or serious bodily injury to the officer or others"; and third, if it is possible to do so, the police officer must provide the person against whom deadly force is about to be employed with some type of warning before using the force.

The Supreme Court has left unresolved the question whether pretrial detainees and convicted prisoners can, like free citizens, assert a Fourth Amendment claim when challenging the excessive use of force. Graham v. Connor, 490 U.S. 386, 395 n. 10, 109 S.Ct. 1865, 1871 n. 10 (1989). If an escaping prisoner has managed to scale the wall or a fence surrounding a prison, under what circumstances can deadly force constitutionally be used to apprehend the prisoner? What standard or standards will be applied when assessing the constitutionality of the force employed? See, e.g., Gravely v. Madden, 142 F.3d 345, 348–49 (6th Cir.1998) (applying the Eighth Amendment, not the *Garner* standard, to the use of deadly force against an escaped prisoner).

PART 3

PRISONERS' RIGHTS LITIGATION

■ ■ ■

CHAPTER 18

THE MECHANICS OF LITIGATING INMATES' § 1983 SUITS

■ ■ ■

A. THE FILING AND PROCESSING OF THE COMPLAINT

1. ELEMENTS OF A CAUSE OF ACTION UNDER § 1983

The statute under which state and local inmates customarily challenge the constitutionality of their treatment while in a prison or jail or the conditions of their confinement, 42 U.S.C. § 1983, provides in part as follows:

> Every person who, under color of any statute, ordinance, regulation, custom, or usage, of any State or Territory or the District of Columbia, subjects, or causes to be subjected, any citizen of the United States or other person within the jurisdiction thereof to the deprivation of any rights, privileges, or immunities secured by the Constitution and laws, shall be liable to the party injured in an action at law, suit in equity, or other proper proceeding for redress * * *.

The elements that must be established by an inmate asserting a § 1983 cause of action are outlined below. (For samples of complaints and other documents typically filed by prisoners bringing claims under § 1983, see John Boston & Daniel E. Manville, Prisoners' Self–Help Litigation Manual app. C (4th ed. 2009).)

1. *Person*—According to the Supreme Court, the word "person" in § 1983 is not confined to human beings. At the time Congress enacted § 1 of the Civil Rights Act of 1871, 17 Stat. 13, which was the predecessor to § 1983, another statute, known as the Dictionary Act, provided that "in all acts hereafter passed ... the word 'person' may extend and be applied to bodies politic and corporate ... unless the context shows that such words were intended to be used in a more limited sense." Act of Feb. 25, 1871, § 2, 16 Stat. 431. Relying on the terms of the Dictionary Act as well as the legislative history of § 1983, the Supreme Court concluded in Monell v. Department of Soc. Servs., 436 U.S. 658, 98 S.Ct. 2018 (1978) that municipalities, as well as other local governing bodies, are "persons"

within the meaning of § 1983. See also Hampton Co. Nat'l Sur., LLC v. Tunica County, Miss., 543 F.3d 221, 224 (5th Cir.2008) (counties are "persons" that can be sued under § 1983).

In Will v. Michigan Dep't of State Police, 491 U.S. 58, 109 S.Ct. 2304 (1989), the Supreme Court held, however, in a 5–4 decision, that states are not "persons" within the meaning of § 1983. The Court grounded its decision on the Eleventh Amendment immunity of states when they are sued in federal court. See pages 813–816. The Court reasoned that when Congress enacted § 1983, it would have been aware of this immunity and could not have intended that a state be subject to a § 1983 suit brought in a state court while it was insulated from § 1983 liability in a lawsuit filed in federal court. See also Ngiraingas v. Sanchez, 495 U.S. 182, 110 S.Ct. 1737 (1990) (a territory is not a "person" within the meaning of § 1983).

The Supreme Court in *Will* also addressed the question whether a state official sued in his or her official capacity is a "person" against whom a § 1983 suit can be brought. The Court answered this question in the negative:

> Obviously, state officials literally are persons. But a suit against a state official in his or her official capacity is not a suit against the official but rather is a suit against the official's office. As such, it is not different from a suit against the State itself.

Id. at 71, 109 S.Ct. at 2312.

In a footnote, however, the Court added: "Of course a State official in his or her official capacity, when sued for injunctive relief, would be a person under § 1983 because 'official-capacity actions for prospective relief are not treated as actions against the State.'" Id. at 71 n. 10, 109 S.Ct. at 2311 n. 10 (quoting Kentucky v. Graham, 473 U.S. 159, 167 n. 14, 105 S.Ct. 3099, 3106 n. 14 (1985)). When state officials are sued in their official capacity, they therefore are "persons" within the meaning of § 1983 for some purposes, but not for others.

When state officials are sued for damages in their individual, rather than their official, capacities, they are considered "persons" within the meaning of § 1983. Hafer v. Melo, 502 U.S. 21, 112 S.Ct. 358 (1991). Because the cognizability of a § 1983 suit for damages against a state official depends on whether the official is being sued in an official or individual capacity, the distinction between official-capacity and personal-capacity suits needs to be understood. In Kentucky v. Graham, 473 U.S. 159, 105 S.Ct. 3099 (1985), the Supreme Court discussed this distinction:

> Personal-capacity suits seek to impose personal liability upon a government official for actions he takes under color of state law. Official-capacity suits, in contrast, "generally represent only another way of pleading an action against an entity of which an officer is an agent." As long as the government entity receives notice and an opportunity to respond, an official-capacity suit is, in all respects other than name, to be treated as a suit against the entity. It is *not* a

suit against the official personally, for the real party in interest is the entity. Thus, while an award of damages against an official in his personal capacity can be executed only against the official's personal assets, a plaintiff seeking to recover on a damages judgment in an official-capacity suit must look to the government entity itself.[11]

On the merits, to establish *personal* liability in a § 1983 action, it is enough to show that the official, acting under color of state law, caused the deprivation of a federal right. More is required in an official-capacity action, however, for a governmental entity is liable under § 1983 only when the entity itself is a " 'moving force' " behind the deprivation; thus, in an official-capacity suit the entity's "policy or custom" must have played a part in the violation of federal law. When it comes to defenses to liability, an official in a personal-capacity action may, depending on his position, be able to assert personal immunity defenses, such as objectively reasonable reliance on existing law. In an official-capacity action, these defenses are unavailable.[13] The only immunities that can be claimed in an official-capacity action are forms of sovereign immunity that the entity, *qua* entity, may possess, such as the Eleventh Amendment. While not exhaustive, this list illustrates the basic distinction between personal-and official-capacity actions.[14]

Id. at 165–67, 112 S.Ct. at 3105–06.

2. *"Under Color of" State Law*—To be liable under § 1983, a person must have acted "under color of" a "statute, ordinance, regulation, custom, or usage" of a state, United States territory, or the District of Columbia. In Monroe v. Pape, 365 U.S. 167, 81 S.Ct. 473 (1961), which was discussed in Chapter 10 beginning on page 468, the Supreme Court elaborated on the meaning of "under color of" state law. In that case, some of the defendants sued under § 1983 were Chicago police officers who allegedly had entered the plaintiffs' home without a warrant and forced the plaintiffs to stand nude while their home was searched. Portions of the Illinois Constitution and certain state statutes prohibited such conduct by police officers. Nonetheless, the Court concluded that the officers had acted "under color of" state law because of their alleged " '[m]isuse of power, possessed by virtue of state law and made possible

---

11.   The "government entity" here could be a municipality, but not a state agency. Should the official die pending final resolution of a personal-capacity action, the plaintiff would have to pursue his action against the decedent's estate. In an official-capacity action in federal court, death or replacement of the named official will result in automatic substitution of the official's successor in office. See Fed.Rule Civ.Proc. 25(d)(1).

13.   In addition, punitive damages are not available under § 1983 from a municipality, *Newport v. Fact Concerts, Inc.,* 453 U.S. 247 (1981), but are available in a suit against an official personally, see *Smith v. Wade,* 461 U.S. 30 (1983).

14.   There is no longer a need to bring official-capacity actions against local government officials, for under *Monell,* local government units can be sued directly for damages and injunctive or declaratory relief. Unless a State has waived its Eleventh Amendment immunity or Congress has overridden it, however, a State cannot be sued directly in its own name regardless of the relief sought. Thus, implementation of state policy or custom may be reached in federal court only because official-capacity actions for prospective relief are not treated as actions against the State. See *Ex parte Young,* 209 U.S. 123 (1908).

only because the wrongdoer is clothed with the authority of state law.' " Id. at 184, 81 S.Ct. at 482 (quoting United States v. Classic, 313 U.S. 299, 326, 61 S.Ct. 1031, 1043 (1941)). To the Court, it did not matter that the police officers' actions were unlawful under state law, because Congress enacted § 1983 in large part due to a concern about the failure of southern states after the Civil War to enforce their own laws against the Ku Klux Klan. The need for, and existence of, a federal remedy under § 1983 when federal rights were violated therefore did not hinge on the existence of state-law provisions that might or might not be enforced.

One of the more salient questions concerning § 1983's under-color-of-state-law requirement is whether a private contractor who provides services, such as medical care or food preparation, to a correctional facility acts "under color of" state law. In West v. Atkins, 487 U.S. 42, 108 S.Ct. 2250 (1988), the Supreme Court addressed this question. The defendant in that case was a private physician who had contracted with the state of North Carolina to provide medical services to inmates two days a week. The doctor was sued under § 1983 by a prisoner who claimed that the doctor had been deliberately indifferent to his serious medical needs in violation of the Eighth Amendment.

The Supreme Court, in a unanimous decision, held that the defendant had acted "under color of" state law. Writing for the Court, Justice Blackmun explained its conclusion:

> It is the physician's function within the state system, not the precise terms of his employment, that determines whether his actions can fairly be attributed to the State. Whether a physician is on the state payroll or is paid by contract, the dispositive issue concerns the relationship among the State, the physician, and the prisoner. Contracting out prison medical care does not relieve the State of its constitutional duty to provide adequate medical treatment to those in its custody, and it does not deprive the State's prisoners of the means to vindicate their Eighth Amendment rights. The State bore an affirmative obligation to provide adequate medical care to West; the State delegated that function to respondent Atkins; and respondent voluntarily assumed that obligation by contract.
>
> Nor does the fact that Doctor Atkins' employment contract did not require him to work exclusively for the prison make him any less a state actor than if he performed those duties as a full-time, permanent member of the state prison medical staff. It is the physician's function while working for the State, not the amount of time he spends in performance of those duties or the fact that he may be employed by others to perform similar duties, that determines whether he is acting under color of state law.

Id. at 55–56, 108 S.Ct. at 2259.

The Supreme Court's decision in *West* is of particular significance because jurisdictions frequently rely on private contractors, not only to provide selected services to correctional facilities, but to operate entire correctional facilities. For an overview of issues raised by the privatization of corrections and research on the cost-effectiveness of private prisons, see James Austin & Garry Coventry, U.S. Dep't of Justice, Emerging Issues on Privatized Prisons (2001); Richard Harding, Private Prisons, 28 Crime & Just. 265 (2001).

3. *Causation*—Liability under § 1983 is extended only to a "person" who "subjects" an individual to a violation of federal rights or "causes" the individual "to be subjected" to such a violation. In the past, the Supreme Court has said that § 1983 "should be read against the background of tort liability that makes a man responsible for the natural consequences of his actions." Monroe v. Pape, 365 U.S. 167, 187, 81 S.Ct. 473, 484 (1961). Consequently, § 1983 liability may ensue even though the person sued had no intent to deprive the plaintiff of a federal right. Id. In fact, the Court has observed that § 1983 contains no state-of-mind requirement whatsoever. Daniels v. Williams, 474 U.S. 327, 329–30, 106 S.Ct. 662, 664 (1986). For there to be a violation of the federal right underlying the § 1983 action, the defendant may need to have acted with a certain state of mind, see, e.g., Estelle v. Gamble, 429 U.S. 97, 97 S.Ct. 285 (1976), but § 1983 itself imposes no such requirement.

The Supreme Court has refrained from finding that certain other basic principles of tort law were incorporated implicitly into § 1983. A classic example of such a principle is the doctrine of *respondeat superior.* Under this doctrine, an employer can generally be held liable for torts committed by an employee if the employee's actions fell within the scope of the employee's employment. W. Page Keeton, et al., Prosser and Keeton on the Law of Torts 499–501 (5th ed. 1984). The employer is considered responsible for the injury for which suit is brought because the employer employed a tortfeasor.

The Supreme Court has rejected application of this doctrine in § 1983 suits. In Monell v. Department of Soc. Servs., 436 U.S. 658, 98 S.Ct. 2018 (1978), the Supreme Court held that a municipality cannot be held liable under § 1983 simply because of the unconstitutional conduct of one of its employees. The Court said that the original language of § 1983, which referred to "any person who . . . shall subject, or cause to be subjected," as well as § 1983's legislative history, supported its conclusion.

Deciding that an employer-employee relationship will not suffice for § 1983 liability has proven easier for the Court than deciding what will suffice for municipal liability under § 1983. In *Monell* itself, the Court described in general terms when municipal liability under § 1983 would ensue:

> Local governing bodies, therefore, can be sued directly under § 1983 for monetary, declaratory, or injunctive relief where, as here, the action that is alleged to be unconstitutional implements or executes a policy statement, ordinance, regulation, or decision officially adopted and promulgated by that body's officers. Moreover, although the touchstone of the § 1983 action against a government body is an

allegation that official policy is responsible for a deprivation of rights protected by the Constitution, local governments, like every other § 1983 "person," by the very terms of the statute, may be sued for constitutional deprivations visited pursuant to governmental "custom" even though such a custom has not received formal approval through the body's official decisionmaking channels.

Id. at 690–91, 98 S.Ct. at 2035–36. Elsewhere in its opinion, the Court indicated that the official policy or custom had to be the "moving force" behind a constitutional violation for the municipality to be liable under § 1983. Id. at 694, 98 S.Ct. at 2037.

Particularly troubling to the Supreme Court since *Monell* was decided has been the question of what constitutes a municipal "policy" to which a constitutional violation is attributable. The Supreme Court's opinions discussing municipal policies are, for the most part, a morass of plurality, concurring, and dissenting opinions. See St. Louis v. Praprotnik, 485 U.S. 112, 108 S.Ct. 915 (1988); Pembaur v. Cincinnati, 475 U.S. 469, 106 S.Ct. 1292 (1986); Oklahoma City v. Tuttle, 471 U.S. 808, 105 S.Ct. 2427 (1985). However, the Court did reach a consensus in Canton v. Harris, 489 U.S. 378, 109 S.Ct. 1197 (1989) as to when a municipality's failure to properly train its employees can lead to municipal liability under § 1983.

In *Canton,* the plaintiff brought a § 1983 suit against the city of Canton, Ohio in which she claimed that she had been denied needed medical treatment after her arrest. Her claim against the city rested on her belief that, with proper training, the municipal employees would have recognized her need for treatment. In an opinion written by Justice White, the Court observed:

> We hold today that the inadequacy of police training may serve as the basis for § 1983 liability only where the failure to train amounts to deliberate indifference to the rights of persons with whom the police come into contact. This rule is most consistent with our admonition in *Monell,* and Polk County v. Dodson, 454 U.S. 312, 326 (1981), that a municipality can be liable under § 1983 only where its policies are the "moving force [behind] the constitutional violation." Only where a municipality's failure to train its employees in a relevant respect evidences a "deliberate indifference" to the rights of its inhabitants can such a shortcoming be properly thought of as a city "policy or custom" that is actionable under § 1983. As Justice Brennan's opinion in Pembaur v. Cincinnati, 475 U.S. 469, 483–484 (1986)(plurality) put it: "[M]unicipal liability under § 1983 attaches where—and only where—a deliberate choice to follow a course of action is made from among various alternatives" by city policymakers. Only where a failure to train reflects a "deliberate" or "conscious" choice by a municipality—a "policy" as defined by our prior cases—can a city be liable for such a failure under § 1983.

> * * * It may seem contrary to common sense to assert that a municipality will actually have a policy of not taking reasonable steps

to train its employees. But it may happen that in light of the duties assigned to specific officers or employees the need for more or different training is so obvious, and the inadequacy so likely to result in the violation of constitutional rights, that the policymakers of the city can reasonably be said to have been deliberately indifferent to the need.[10] In that event, the failure to provide proper training may fairly be said to represent a policy for which the city is responsible, and for which the city may be held liable if it actually causes injury.

In resolving the issue of a city's liability, the focus must be on adequacy of the training program in relation to the tasks the particular officers must perform. That a particular officer may be unsatisfactorily trained will not alone suffice to fasten liability on the city, for the officer's shortcomings may have resulted from factors other than a faulty training program. It may be, for example, that an otherwise sound program has occasionally been negligently administered. Neither will it suffice to prove that an injury or accident could have been avoided if an officer had had better or more training, sufficient to equip him to avoid the particular injury-causing conduct. Such a claim could be made about almost any encounter resulting in injury, yet not condemn the adequacy of the program to enable officers to respond properly to the usual and recurring situations with which they must deal. And plainly, adequately trained officers occasionally make mistakes; the fact that they do says little about the training program or the legal basis for holding the city liable.

Moreover, for liability to attach in this circumstance the identified deficiency in a city's training program must be closely related to the ultimate injury. Thus in the case at hand, respondent must still prove that the deficiency in training actually caused the police officers' indifference to her medical needs. Would the injury have been avoided had the employee been trained under a program that was not deficient in the identified respect? Predicting how a hypothetically well-trained officer would have acted under the circumstances may not be an easy task for the factfinder, particularly since matters of judgment may be involved, and since officers who are well trained are not free from error and perhaps might react very much like the untrained officer in similar circumstances. But judge and jury, doing their respective jobs, will be adequate to the task.

Id. at 388–91, 109 S.Ct. at 1204–06. See also Oklahoma City v. Tuttle, 471 U.S. 808, 105 S.Ct. 2427 (1985) (holding that proof of one unconstitutional act by a lower-level police officer does not, by itself, support an inference that the constitutional violation was caused by a municipal policy of inadequate training).

---

10. * * * It could also be that the police, in exercising their discretion, so often violate constitutional rights that the need for further training must have been plainly obvious to the city policymakers, who, nevertheless, are "deliberately indifferent" to the need.

In Board of the County Comm'rs v. Brown, 520 U.S. 397, 117 S.Ct. 1382 (1997), the Supreme Court further fleshed out the circumstances that will give rise to municipal liability under § 1983. The plaintiff in that case had alleged that the county was liable under § 1983 because of the excessive force used by a deputy sheriff when effecting an arrest. The plaintiff's claim against the county rested on the sheriff's failure to thoroughly review the deputy sheriff's record, which included criminal convictions for assault and battery, resisting arrest, and public drunkenness, before hiring the deputy sheriff.

The Supreme Court held that the touchstone for municipal liability under § 1983 due to a hiring decision is not the indifference to a job applicant's record evident from a summary or incomplete review of the applicant's background. What is required is deliberate indifference to the obvious risk, based on that record, that a constitutional violation will ensue if the applicant is hired. "Only where adequate scrutiny of an applicant's background would lead a reasonable policymaker to conclude that the plainly obvious consequence of the decision to hire the applicant would be the deprivation of a third party's federally protected right can the official's failure to adequately scrutinize the applicant's background constitute 'deliberate indifference.'" Id. at 411, 117 S.Ct. at 1392. And in this case, the Court did not believe that the deputy sheriff's prior misdemeanor convictions, all of which stemmed from a "single fraternity fracas," made his use of excessive force a "plainly obvious consequence" of hiring him. Consequently, the sheriff, in making the hiring decision, did not act with the kind of deliberate indifference required for municipal liability under § 1983.

4. *Violation of Federal Rights*—To be liable under § 1983, the "person" sued must have caused the violation of another's federal rights—either rights under the United States Constitution or rights under other federal laws. Many of the constitutional rights that inmates seek to vindicate in § 1983 suits were discussed in previous chapters in this book.

2. *BIVENS* ACTIONS

Section 1983 only extends liability to persons who, while acting under the color of state law, violated the federal rights of others. No similar statute extends liability to federal officials who, for example, violate others' constitutional rights. Does the absence of such a statute mean that inmates confined in federal prisons are without recourse if their constitutional rights are violated?

The answer to that question, according to the Supreme Court, is no. In Bivens v. Six Unknown Fed. Narcotics Agents, 403 U.S. 388, 91 S.Ct. 1999 (1971), the Court concluded that an individual could sue FBI agents for damages incurred as a result of an allegedly unlawful arrest and search of his home. According to the Court, this damages remedy was conferred implicitly by the Fourth Amendment itself. In subsequent cases, the Court has upheld the bringing of a *"Bivens* suit" for violations of the Fifth Amendment's Due Process Clause, see Davis v. Passman, 442 U.S. 228, 99 S.Ct. 2264 (1979), as well as the Eighth Amendment's prohibition of cruel and unusual punishment. See Carlson v. Green, 446 U.S. 14, 100 S.Ct. 1468 (1980).

Bivens actions can only be brought against federal officials, not federal agencies. Federal Deposit Ins. Corp. v. Meyer, 510 U.S. 471, 486, 114 S.Ct. 996, 1006 (1994). Nor can a *Bivens* action be brought against a private corporation with which the federal Bureau of Prisons has contracted to house federal inmates. Correctional Servs. Corp. v. Malesko, 534 U.S. 61, 122 S.Ct. 515 (2001). Since private corporations currently can be sued under § 1983 for violations of constitutional rights, should Congress, as a policy matter, enact a law to provide parallel treatment of state and federal inmates? If so, should private corporations be uniformly exempt from, or subject to, lawsuits brought by state and federal inmates to enforce constitutional rights?

A debate now has arisen as to whether a *Bivens* action can be brought by a federal prisoner against an individual, such as a correctional officer or prison doctor, employed at a privately run prison. Courts refusing to recognize a *Bivens* cause of action in this context have emphasized what they believe is the need for judicial restraint when interpreting the scope of a remedy implied by the courts, rather than created by Congress, for a constitutional violation. At the same time, these courts have underscored that the prisoners in the cases before them could secure relief by bringing state-law claims, such as for negligence, against the employees in state court. See, e.g., Alba v. Montford, 517 F.3d 1249, 1252–56 (11th Cir. 2008).

Courts concluding that a *Bivens* action can be brought against an employee of a private prison, on the other hand, have cited the anomalies that would result from a contrary holding. See, e.g., Sarro v. Cornell Corrections, Inc., 248 F.Supp.2d 52, 63 (D.R.I. 2003). A federal prisoner housed in a federal prison could bring a *Bivens* action against a prison official for violating a constitutional right, but a federal prisoner housed in a private prison could not sue an employee of that prison for violating the same constitutional right. In addition, state prisoners confined in a private prison could seek redress against individual employees under § 1983 for a violation of their constitutional rights. But federal prisoners confined in a private prison could not pursue the same constitutional claim against the employees. For additional arguments both for and against the cognizability of *Bivens* actions against individual employees at private prisons, see the majority and dissenting opinions in Peoples v. CCA Detention Centers, 422 F.3d 1090 (10th Cir. 2005). Upon rehearing en banc in that case, an equally divided court affirmed the decision of the panel of the Tenth Circuit Court of Appeals that *Bivens* actions cannot be brought against individuals employed by private prisons. See Peoples v. CCA Detention Centers, 449 F.3d 1097, 1099 (10th Cir. 2006).

3. JURISDICTION

When a complaint is filed in a federal court, the complaint must identify the source of the court's jurisdiction over the case. Fed.R.Civ.P. 8(a)(1). Federal district courts have jurisdiction over § 1983 suits under 28 U.S.C. § 1331 and 28 U.S.C. § 1343(a)(3). These statutory provisions are set forth below:

28 U.S.C. § 1331

The district courts shall have original jurisdiction of all civil actions arising under the Constitution, laws, or treaties of the United States.

28 U.S.C. § 1343(a)(3)

The district courts shall have original jurisdiction of any civil action authorized by law to be commenced by any person:

* * *

(3) To redress the deprivation, under color of any State law, statute, ordinance, regulation, custom or usage, of any right, privilege or immunity secured by the Constitution of the United States or by any Act of Congress providing for equal rights of citizens or of all persons within the jurisdiction of the United States.

Because the jurisdiction of the federal courts under both § 1331 and § 1343(a)(3) is not exclusive, § 1983 suits can be filed in state courts. Felder v. Casey, 487 U.S. 131, 139, 108 S.Ct. 2302, 2307 (1988). Whether a lawsuit should be filed in a federal or state court will depend on a number of factors, including the procedural rules, particularly the discovery rules, governing civil litigation in the state and federal courts; the speed with which the case can be processed through the courts because of their docket loads; the location of the courts; and the perceived receptivity of the state court to federal-law-based claims. For an in-depth discussion of the factors to be considered when deciding whether to file a § 1983 suit in a state or federal court, see Steven H. Steinglass, Section 1983 Litigation in State Courts, ch. 8, Tactical Choice of Forum Considerations (2008).

4. THE ROLE OF FEDERAL MAGISTRATE JUDGES IN THE PROCESSING OF PRISONERS' COMPLAINTS

Federal magistrate judges can and do play a significant role in the processing of inmates civil-rights complaints. The Federal Magistrates Act authorizes federal district judges to refer "prisoner petitions challenging conditions of confinement" to magistrate judges for a hearing, including an evidentiary hearing. 28 U.S.C. § 636(b)(1)(B). After the hearing, the magistrate judge proposes findings of fact and makes recommendations to the district judge regarding how to rule in the case. The district judge then has the option of adopting, rejecting, or modifying the magistrate judge's findings and recommendations.

In McCarthy v. Bronson, 500 U.S. 136, 111 S.Ct. 1737 (1991), the Supreme Court broadly construed the type of "prisoner petitions" appropriately referable to a magistrate under 28 U.S.C. § 636(b)(1)(B), unanimously holding that the phrase generally encompasses all prisoner § 1983 suits, including those alleging a single episode of unconstitutional conduct. The only time when a referral would be barred would be when the inmate has a constitutional right to a jury trial because the inmate has asserted a claim for damages and the right has not been waived. Id. at 144, 111 S.Ct. at 1743. However, with the consent of both parties, a jury trial can be held before a magistrate judge charged by the district court with the authority to preside at such a trial. 28 U.S.C. § 636(c)(1).

5.   FILING FEES

An indigent inmate often will not have the money to pay the filing fee required when filing a lawsuit or an appeal in a federal court. The inmate then can file a petition with the court under 28 U.S.C. § 1915(a) seeking leave to proceed *in forma pauperis.* However, even if the court determines that the inmate lacks the funds to prepay the full filing fee, the court must normally require the inmate to pay a partial filing fee before proceeding *in forma pauperis*—20% of the greater of the average monthly deposits in the inmate's prison trust-fund account or the average monthly balance in the account in the six months preceding the filing of the complaint or appeal. 28 U.S.C. § 1915(b)(1). Only if the prisoner has no means with which to pay even a partial filing fee is the prisoner permitted to proceed with the suit or appeal *in forma pauperis* without prepaying at least some of the filing fee. Id. § 1915(b)(4). Even then, each month after a suit or appeal is filed *in forma pauperis,* 20% of the preceding month's income credited to an inmate's account must be debited for payment of the filing fee until the fee is paid in full. Id. § 1915(b)(2).

Nonprisoners are not subject to the same filing-fee requirements as prisoners. If, due to their indigency, nonprisoners are unable to pay the full filing fee up front, the court can allow them to proceed with their lawsuit or appeal *in forma pauperis* without having to pay an initial partial filing fee or subsequent installment payments. Id. § 1915 (a)(1).

The courts of appeals have held that the differential treatment of prisoners under 28 U.S.C. § 1915(b) does not violate their right to the equal protection of the law. See, e.g., Tucker v. Branker, 142 F.3d 1294, 1299–1300 (D.C.Cir.1998) (listing cases). From a policy perspective, should the filing-fee requirements applicable to prisoners and nonprisoners who bring civil-rights suits be the same or different?

6.   THREE–STRIKES PROVISION

The special filing-fee requirements applicable to prisoners were one of many changes in the standards and procedures governing inmates' lawsuits wrought by the "Prison Litigation Reform Act" (PLRA), which was enacted in 1996. The PLRA also contained what is known as the "three-strikes provision." Under 28 U.S.C. § 1915(g), prisoners who have had complaints or appeals dismissed on three or more occasions because they were frivolous, malicious, or failed to state a claim for which relief can be granted generally are prohibited from bringing further civil actions or appeals *in forma pauperis*. An indigent prisoner subject to the three-strikes provision can file suit *in forma pauperis* only if the prisoner is facing "imminent" and "serious" physical injury. The practical effect of this provision is that indigent inmates who have accrued three "strikes" and do not have the funds to prepay the full filing fee are foreclosed from bringing constitutional claims, such as First Amendment claims, that do not involve the threat of physical injury.

One of the constitutional claims leveled against the three-strikes provision is that it violates inmates' right to the equal protection of the law, because it effectively bars indigent prisoners from filing nonfrivolous claims while leaving unaffected the ability of nonindigent prisoners who have filed frivolous suits or appeals in the past to bring new claims to the court. But after applying a rational-basis test when assessing the constitutionality of the three-strikes provision, most courts have found no equal-protection violation. See, e.g., Higgins v. Carpenter, 258 F.3d 797, 799 (8th Cir.2001) (listing cases). To pass constitutional muster under this test, there need only be some "reasonably conceivable state of facts that could provide a rational basis for the classification" at issue. FCC v. Beach Communications, Inc., 508 U.S. 307, 313, 113 S.Ct. 2096, 2101 (1993). Courts have found such a rational basis for the three-strikes provision. Noting that Congress could have believed that prisoners are more likely than nonprisoners to file frivolous lawsuits, in part because prisoners have so much more free time than nonprisoners, the courts have concluded that the three-strikes provision is rationally related to the legitimate governmental interest in curbing the filing of frivolous lawsuits by prisoners.

Some commentators have insisted that a strict-scrutiny test should be applied when evaluating the constitutionality of the three-strikes provision because the provision substantially burdens inmates' fundamental right of access to the courts. See, e.g., Randal S. Jeffrey, Restricting Prisoners' Equal Access to the Federal Courts: The Three Strikes Provision of the Prison Litigation Reform Act and Substantive Equal Protection, 49 Buff. L. Rev. 1099, 1138 (2001); Joseph T. Lukens, The Prison Litigation Reform Act: Three Strikes and You're Out of Court—It May Be Effective, But Is It Constitutional?, 70 Temp. L. Rev. 471, 498–501 (1997). Under this test, a classification, to pass constitutional muster, must be "necessary" to further a "compelling" governmental interest.

What test would you apply when assessing the constitutionality of the three-strikes provision? Why? Is the three-strikes provision constitutional under the strict-scrutiny test? Under the rational-basis test? Why or why not?

7. SUFFICIENCY OF THE COMPLAINT

a. Sua Sponte Dismissals

The PLRA also modified the procedures governing the screening of complaints filed by indigent plantiffs—both prisoners and nonprisoners. Before the PLRA's enactment, the law provided that when a federal court determined that an inmate seeking leave to proceed *in forma pauperis* actually could prepay the necessary filing fee or found that the inmate's claim was "frivolous" or "malicious," the court "may" dismiss the case. A court now must dismiss a claim in a complaint filed *in forma pauperis* not only when the claim is "frivolous" or "malicious," but also when the plaintiff has failed to state a claim for which relief can be granted or when the plaintiff seeks monetary relief from a defendant who is immune from such relief. 28 U.S.C. § 1915(e)(2). Even when prisoners are not proceeding *in forma pauperis* and have paid the full filing fee, their claims are subject to *sua sponte* dismissal—dismissal on the court's own motion—for any of the above reasons. These latter screening requirements apply to prisoners' complaints contesting the legality of the conditions of their confinement under § 1983 or any other "[f]ederal law," 42 U.S.C § 1997e(c)(1), as well as to other civil actions brought by prisoners against government entities or employees. 28 U.S.C. § 1915A(a)–(b).

Were these changes in the law advisable? Why or why not?

b. Factual Frivolousness

In Denton v. Hernandez, 504 U.S. 25, 112 S.Ct. 1728 (1992), the Supreme Court considered when factual allegations in a complaint can be considered "frivolous." The plaintiff in *Denton,* a prisoner, had filed several complaints in which he alleged that while he was sleeping, he was drugged and then raped a total of twenty-eight times by correctional officers and inmates at two prisons. Because of needle marks that the plaintiff claimed to have found on his body and fecal matter and semen that he allegedly found on his clothes, the plaintiff was able, he said, to deduce that he had been sexually assaulted.

The Supreme Court did not resolve whether, as the prison officials argued, the plaintiff's claims were the fanciful imaginings of a mentally ill inmate. But the Court did enunciate principles to be applied by the lower courts in this and other cases when determining whether factual allegations in a complaint are "frivolous." The Court concluded that just because it is unlikely that the events recounted in a complaint occurred, a complaint cannot be deemed factually frivolous. The factual allegations must instead be "clearly baseless" to warrant dismissal. Id. at 32, 112 S.Ct. at 1733. However, a complaint whose facts are "wholly incredible," such as those stemming from a mentally ill plaintiff's delusions, can be dismissed as "clearly baseless" even when the complaint's allegations cannot be rebutted by facts so universally true that a court can take judicial notice of them (such as the fact that prison officials cannot be letting little green Martians steal her legal mail, as a prisoner is alleging). Id. at 33, 112 S.Ct. at 1733.

8. APPOINTMENT OF COUNSEL TO REPRESENT AN INDIGENT INMATE

Title 28 U.S.C. § 1915(e)(1) provides that a federal court "may request" an attorney to represent a party in a federal lawsuit who cannot afford to hire an attorney. Whether to appoint counsel under § 1915(e)(1) falls within the court's discretion. Pruitt v. Mote, 503 F.3d 647, 654 (7th Cir. 2007). The Seventh Circuit Court of Appeals has articulated a two-part test to guide a district court in the exercise of that discretion: First, has the indigent plaintiff made a "reasonable attempt" to secure counsel or been prevented from doing so? And second, if so, does the plaintiff appear competent to litigate the case given its complexity? Id.

A district court's decision not to appoint an attorney will be reversed only if it abused its discretion. The Seventh Circuit Court of Appeals has underscored that its task on appeal is not to determine if the trial court was "right" in making the two determinations outlined above, but "reasonable." Id. at 659. And even if the appellate court concludes that the denial of the motion for appointed counsel was an abuse of discretion, the judgment below will not be reversed unless the plaintiff was prejudiced by this denial—unless the plaintiff demonstrates that there is a "reasonable likelihood" that representation by counsel would have affected the lawsuit's outcome. Id.

Although a federal court can ask an attorney to represent an indigent litigant in a civil suit for free, the Supreme Court has held that the court has no power under the statutory provision now codified at 28 U.S.C. § 1915(e)(1) to require the attorney to provide such free assistance. Mallard v. United States Dist. Court, 490 U.S. 296, 109 S.Ct. 1814 (1989). Left unresolved by the Court in *Mallard* were the questions whether courts have inherent authority to make such compulsory assignments and whether such compulsory assignments would be constitutional.

B. AFFIRMATIVE DEFENSES

To avoid liability in a § 1983 suit, a defendant can assert a number of defenses. Set forth below is a discussion of a few of the defenses most commonly invoked in a § 1983 case.

1. IMMUNITY

a. Eleventh Amendment

The Eleventh Amendment to the United States Constitution provides that "[t]he Judicial power of the United States shall not be construed to extend to any suit in law or equity, commenced or prosecuted against one of the United States by Citizens of another State, or by Citizens or Subjects of any Foreign State." Despite the literal language of the amendment, the Supreme Court has held that a state also cannot be sued in federal court by one of its own citizens. Hans v. Louisiana, 134 U.S. 1, 10 S.Ct. 504 (1890).

The Supreme Court has recognized several exceptions or limitations to the general rule that a state is immune from suit in federal court. First, a state can consent to be sued, waiving its Eleventh Amendment immunity. Alabama v. Pugh, 438 U.S. 781, 782, 98 S.Ct. 3057, 3057 (1978). The fact that a state can consent to be sued, however, will not help a § 1983 plaintiff who wishes to sue a state, because the Supreme Court has held that a state cannot be sued in any event under § 1983 because it is not a "person" within the meaning of the statute. See Will v. Michigan Dep't of State Police, 491 U.S. 58, 71, 109 S.Ct. 2304, 2312 (1989), discussed on page 801.

Second, the Supreme Court has held that Congress has the power under § 5 of the Fourteenth Amendment to abrogate states' Eleventh Amendment immunity in order to effectuate the provisions of the Fourteenth Amendment. Fitzpatrick v. Bitzer, 427 U.S. 445, 456, 96 S.Ct. 2666, 2671 (1976). According to the Court, however, when Congress enacted § 1983, it did not intend to exercise this power. Quern v. Jordan, 440 U.S. 332, 341, 99 S.Ct. 1139, 1145 (1979). The significance of the Court's holding in *Fitzpatrick* is that Congress potentially could amend § 1983 to include states as suable defendants who cannot raise a sovereign-immunity defense.

The Supreme Court's decision in Board of Trustees of the University of Alabama v. Garrett, 531 U.S. 356, 121 S.Ct. 955 (2001) poses special challenges to Congress in the exercise of its authority under § 5 of the Fourteenth Amendment. The issue before the Court in that case was whether Congress had exceeded its authority under § 5 in enacting Title I of the Americans with Disabilities Act (ADA). 42 U.S.C. §§ 12111–12117. Title I authorizes lawsuits for damages against states, as well as other employers, who discriminate against "qualified" prospective and current employees who are disabled. Id. §§ 12112(a), 12111(2), (5), (7).

Writing for the majority in a closely divided 5–4 decision, Chief Justice Rehnquist stated that more than a congressional intent to abrogate the states' Eleventh Amendment immunity is needed to sustain legislation under § 5. In addition, the federal statute must be directed against an established "pattern of irrational state discrimination," in this case, state discrimination against the disabled. Id. at 368, 121 S.Ct. at 965. And even in the face of such entrenched state discrimination, the federal remedy must be "congruent and proportional" to the states' constitutional violations in order to fall within the boundaries of Congress's authority under § 5. Id. at 374, 121 S.Ct. at 967–68.

The Court then held that, for two reasons, Title I exceeded Congress's authority under § 5. First, Congress had adduced insufficient evidence of the pattern of state discrimination against the disabled needed to support Title I's enactment. The legislative record contained at most, according to the majority, only fifty anecdotal accounts of state discrimination against the disabled and no legislative findings confirming the existence of a pattern of state discrimination. Second, even if Congress had established the existence of such a pattern of discrimination, Title I was not narrowly tailored to remedy it. The Court noted, for example, that Title I exceeded constitutional requirements by forbidding state actions that have a disparate, adverse impact on the disabled. See 42 U.S.C. § 12112(b)(3)(A). But if there were a "rational basis" for the disparity in treatment, the states' actions would not transgress the requirements of equal protection. 531 U.S. at 372–73, 121 S.Ct. at 967.

In a scathing dissent, Justice Breyer, joined by Justices Stevens, Souter, and Ginsburg, decried the majority's review of Title I's legislative history "as if it were an administrative agency record." Id. at 376, 121 S.Ct. at 969 (Breyer, J., dissenting). According to the dissent, the legislative record recounted literally hundreds of examples of states' discrimination against the disabled, surely enough evidence to confirm that Title I was an "appropriate" means of implementing the Fourteenth Amendment, which is all that § 5 requires. See U.S. Const. amend. XIV, § 5 ("The Congress shall have the power to enforce, by appropriate legislation, the provisions of this article."). The dissent also castigated the Court for the way in which it assessed the congruence and proportionality of Title I: "[I]t is difficult to understand why the Court, which applies 'minimum "rational-basis" review' to statutes that *burden* persons with disabilities, subjects to far stricter scrutiny a statute that seeks to *help* those same individuals." Id. at 387–88, 121 S.Ct. at 975 (Breyer, J., dissenting) (quoting the majority opinion, id. at 366, 121 S.Ct. at 963–64).

The Supreme Court in *Board of Trustees of the University of Alabama* specifically left open the question whether Congress exceeded its authority under § 5 when it enacted other parts of the ADA that purport to abrogate the states' Eleventh Amendment immunity. One of the ADA provisions whose constitutionality was left unresolved was Title II, 42 U.S.C. §§ 12131–12165, which prohibits state and local governments from discriminating against the disabled in the provision of services, programs, and activities. In Tennessee v. Lane, 541 U.S. 509, 124 S.Ct. 1978 (2004), the Court held that Title II represented a valid exercise of the authority § 5 vested in Congress, at least when, as in that case, the statute was being implemented to ensure that disabled persons have access to the courts. While the Court purported to limit its holding to the court-access context, it also noted that there was abundant evidence presented to Congress about pervasive discrimination in the providing of public services to the disabled and in affording them access to public facilities.

In United States v. Georgia, 546 U.S. 151, 126 S.Ct. 877 (2006), the Supreme Court confronted the specific question whether the enforcement of Title II in a state prison is a usurpation of state power. The paraplegic prisoner who brought the ADA claims in that case alleged that he was confined twenty-three hours or longer a day in a cell so small—twelve by three feet—that he could not maneuver his wheelchair to the toilet. He furthermore claimed that the prison officials often ignored his requests for assistance in using the toilet, which then led him to have to defecate or urinate in his pants. The prisoner also asserted an array of other claims grounded on the alleged denial of access to prison programs and services due to his disability. The Supreme Court held that to the extent the prisoner's ADA claims for damages were grounded on actual violations of the Fourteenth Amendment, Title II validly abrogated the state's sovereign immunity. But the Court left open the question whether Congress had the power to repeal the states' immunity when a Title II claim for damages involved conduct that did not violate the Fourteenth Amendment.

While states sued under § 1983 in federal court presently retain their Eleventh Amendment immunity, the Supreme Court has held that they sometimes may have to pay for the plaintiff's attorney's fees incurred in the course of litigating a § 1983 suit. In Hutto v. Finney, 437 U.S. 678, 98 S.Ct. 2565 (1978), the Court held that the Civil Rights Attorney's Fees Awards Act of 1976, 42 U.S.C. § 1988(b), overrides the Eleventh Amendment immunity of states. That Act provides that "[i]n any action or proceeding" to enforce certain civil-rights statutes, including 42 U.S.C. § 1983, "the court, in its discretion, may allow the prevailing party, other than the United States, a reasonable attorney's fee as part of the costs." Although the Act, on its face, does not mention the liability of states for the attorney's fees awarded a prevailing plaintiff, the Court in *Hutto* emphasized that the Senate and House Reports discussing the Act made it clear that Congress contemplated that such fee awards would be leveled against states.

When will a state have to pay a prevailing plaintiff's attorney's fees even though the state was not, and according to the Supreme Court could not, presently be a defendant in a § 1983 action? As was mentioned earlier, in a footnote in Will v. Michigan Dep't of State Police, 491 U.S. 58, 109 S.Ct. 2304 (1989), the Court mentioned that while state officials sued in their official capacities are not "persons" within the meaning of § 1983 when damages are sought as relief, they are subject to suit when the plaintiff seeks injunctive relief. Id. at 71 n. 10, 109 S.Ct. at 2311 n. 10. And in *Hutto v. Finney*, the Court observed that when state officials sued in their official capacities have litigated a § 1983 suit in good faith but lost, Congress intended that the state bear the financial burden of paying the plaintiff's attorney's fees. Consequently, in § 1983 suits seeking injunctive relief against state officials sued in their official capacities, the states ultimately may be liable for a prevailing plaintiff's attorney's fees.

b. Sovereign Immunity—The United States

It is now well-established that the United States cannot be sued without its consent. United States v. Mitchell, 463 U.S. 206, 212, 103 S.Ct.

2961, 2965 (1983). Congress, however, has consented to the bringing of constitutional claims against the federal government. See 28 U.S.C. § 1346(a)(2). Under the Federal Tort Claims Act (FTCA), the United States also can be held liable for the negligent acts of its employees. See id. § 1346(b)(1). There are many exceptions and limitations to this Act with which an attorney contemplating or litigating a claim under the FTCA should become familiar. See id. § 2680. Persons convicted of felonies, for example, are not permitted to sue for damages under the FTCA for mental or emotional injuries suffered while in custody without first showing that they also have suffered a physical injury. Id. § 1346(b)(2). And prisoners cannot sue the United States for the negligent loss of property by prison officials. Ali v. Federal Bureau of Prisons, 128 S.Ct. 831 (2008).

c. Official Immunity—Absolute and Qualified

CLEAVINGER v. SAXNER

Supreme Court of the United States, 1985.
474 U.S. 193, 106 S.Ct. 496, 88 L.Ed.2d 507.

MR. JUSTICE BLACKMUN delivered the opinion of the Court.

[The plaintiffs in this case, two inmates incarcerated at the Federal Correctional Institution in Terre Haute, Indiana, filed a *Bivens* action against three members of a prison disciplinary committee that had found them guilty of disciplinary infractions. A jury found that the defendants had violated the plaintiffs' due-process rights under the Fifth Amendment and awarded each plaintiff $1500 in compensatory damages from each of the three defendants. Thus, each plaintiff was awarded a total of $4500, and each defendant was held liable for a total of $3000 in damages.

The defendants moved for a judgment notwithstanding the verdict, arguing that they were absolutely immune from damages liability. The trial court rejected this argument as did the Seventh Circuit Court of Appeals on appeal. The Supreme Court then granted certiorari.]

A.   This Court has observed: "Few doctrines were more solidly established at common law than the immunity of judges from liability for damages for acts committed within their judicial jurisdiction." *Pierson v. Ray,* 386 U.S. 547, 553–554 (1967). * * * In *Pierson v. Ray,* the Court held that absolute immunity shielded a municipal judge who was sued for damages under 42 U.S.C. § 1983 by clergymen who alleged that he had convicted them unconstitutionally for a peaceful protest against racial segregation. The Court stressed that such immunity was essential to protect the integrity of the judicial process. * * *

With this judicial immunity firmly established, the Court has extended absolute immunity to certain others who perform functions closely associated with the judicial process. The federal hearing examiner and administrative law judge have been afforded absolute immunity. "There can be little doubt that the role of the modern federal hearing examiner or administrative law judge ... is 'functionally comparable' to that of a judge." *Butz v. Economou,* 438 U.S. 478, 513 (1978). * * *

* * *

B. The Court has extended absolute immunity to the President when damages liability is predicated on his official act. *Nixon v. Fitzgerald,* 457 U.S. 731, 744–758 (1982). "For executive officials in general, however, our cases make plain that qualified immunity represents the norm." See *Scheuer v. Rhodes,* 416 U.S. 232 (1974)(State Governor and his aides); *Harlow v. Fitzgerald* [, 457 U.S. 800 (1982)] (Presidential aides); *Butz v. Economou* (Cabinet member * * *); *Procunier v. Navarette,* 434 U.S. 555 (1978)(state prison officials); *Wood v. Strickland,* 420 U.S. 308 (1975)(school board members); *Pierson v. Ray* (police officers). * * * In any event, "federal officials who seek absolute exemption from personal liability for unconstitutional conduct must bear the burden of showing that public policy requires an exemption of that scope."

C. * * * "[O]ur cases clearly indicate that immunity analysis rests on functional categories, not on the status of the defendant." Absolute immunity flows not from rank or title or "location within the Government," but from the nature of the responsibilities of the individual official. And in *Butz* the Court mentioned the following factors, among others, as characteristic of the judicial process and to be considered in determining absolute as contrasted with qualified immunity: (a) the need to assure that the individual can perform his functions without harassment or intimidation; (b) the presence of safeguards that reduce the need for private damages actions as a means of controlling unconstitutional conduct; (c) insulation from political influence; (d) the importance of precedent; (e) the adversary nature of the process; and (f) the correctability of error on appeal.

* * *

Petitioners, in response, and seemingly in order to negate the significance of certain of the specified factors, point out that grand jury proceedings possess few procedural safeguards that are associated with court proceedings, and are largely immune from any type of judicial review. Petitioners also observe that prosecutorial decisionmaking is not subject to the formalities of trials; instead, the prosecutor exercises broad and generally unreviewable discretion. Yet grand jurors and prosecutors enjoy absolute immunity. Petitioners finally argue that the Court's cases teach that absolute immunity shields an official if (a) the official performs an adjudicatory function comparable to that of a judge, (b) the function is of sufficient public importance, and (c) the proper performance of that function would be subverted if the official were subjected to individual suit for damages.

* * * The committee members, in a sense, do perform an adjudicatory function in that they determine whether the accused inmate is guilty or innocent of the charge leveled against him; in that they hear testimony

and receive documentary evidence; in that they evaluate credibility and weigh evidence; and in that they render a decision. We recognize, too, the presence of some societal importance in this dispute-resolution function. The administration of a prison is a difficult undertaking at best, for it concerns persons many of whom have demonstrated a proclivity for antisocial, criminal, and violent conduct. We also acknowledge that many inmates do not refrain from harassment and intimidation. The number of nonmeritorious prisoners' cases that come to this Court's notice is evidence of this. * * * And we do not underestimate the fact, stressed by petitioners, that committee members usually are persons of modest means and, if they are suable and unprotected, perhaps would be disinclined to serve on a discipline committee.

We conclude, nonetheless, that these concerns, to the extent they are well grounded, are overstated in the context of constitutional violations. We do not perceive the discipline committee's function as a "classic" adjudicatory one * * *. Surely, the members of the committee, unlike a federal or state judge, are not "independent"; to say that they are is to ignore reality. They are not professional hearing officers, as are administrative law judges. They are, instead, prison officials, albeit no longer of the rank and file, temporarily diverted from their usual duties. They are employees of the Bureau of Prisons and they are the direct subordinates of the warden who reviews their decision. They work with the fellow employee who lodges the charge against the inmate upon whom they sit in judgment. The credibility determination they make often is one between a co-worker and an inmate. They thus are under obvious pressure to resolve a disciplinary dispute in favor of the institution and their fellow employee. * * *

* * *

We relate this committee membership, instead, to the school board service the Court had under consideration in *Wood v. Strickland,* 420 U.S. 308 (1975). The school board members were to function as "adjudicators in the school disciplinary process," and they were to "judge whether there have been violations of school regulations and, if so, the appropriate sanctions for the violations." Despite the board's adjudicative function of that extent, the Court concluded that the board members were to be protected by only qualified immunity. After noting the suggestion of the presence of a deterrence-from-service factor, the Court concluded that "absolute immunity would not be justified since it would not sufficiently increase the ability of school officials to exercise their discretion in a forthright manner to warrant the absence of a remedy for students subjected to intentional or otherwise inexcusable deprivations."

That observation and conclusion are equally applicable here. * * * If qualified immunity is sufficient for the schoolroom, it should be more than sufficient for the jailhouse where the door is closed, not open, and where there is little, if any, protection by way of community observation.

Petitioners assert with some vigor that procedural formality is not a prerequisite for absolute immunity. They refer to well-known summary and *ex parte* proceedings, such as the issuance of search warrants and temporary restraining orders, and the setting of bail. * * * In any event, it is asserted, committee proceedings contain ample safeguards to ensure the avoidance or correction of constitutional errors. Among these are the qualifications for committee service; prior notice to the inmate; representation by a staff member; the right to present certain evidence at the hearing; the right to be present; the requirement for a detailed record; the availability of administrative review at three levels * * *; and the availability of ultimate review in federal court under 28 U.S.C. § 2241.[a] Finally, it is said that qualified immunity would provide insufficient protection for committee members.

We are not persuaded. To be sure, the line between absolute immunity and qualified immunity often is not an easy one to perceive and structure. That determination in this case, however, is not difficult, and we readily conclude that these committee members fall on the qualified-immunity side of the line.

Under the Bureau's disciplinary policy in effect at the time of respondents' hearings, few of the procedural safeguards contained in the Administrative Procedure Act under consideration in *Butz* were present. The prisoner was to be afforded neither a lawyer nor an independent nonstaff representative. There was no right to compel the attendance of witnesses or to cross-examine. There was no right to discovery. There was no cognizable burden of proof. No verbatim transcript was afforded. Information presented often was hearsay or self-serving. The committee members were not truly independent. In sum, the members had no identification with the judicial process of the kind and depth that has occasioned absolute immunity.

Qualified immunity, however, is available to these committee members. That, we conclude, is the proper point at which to effect the balance between the opposing considerations. This less-than-absolute protection is not of small consequence. As the Court noted in *Butz,* insubstantial lawsuits can be recognized and be quickly disposed of, and firm application of the Federal Rules of Civil Procedure "will ensure that federal officials are not harassed by frivolous lawsuits." All the committee members need to do is to follow the clear and simple constitutional requirements of *Wolff v. McDonnell;* they then should have no reason to fear substantial harassment and liability. Qualified immunity has been widely imposed on executive officials who possess greater responsibilities. "[I]t is not unfair to hold liable the official who knows or should know he is acting outside the law, and ... insisting on an awareness of clearly established constitutional limits will not unduly interfere with the exercise of official judgment." * * *

* * *

---

a. 28 U.S.C. § 2241(c)(3) authorizes federal courts to issue writs of habeas corpus to prisoners whose custody is unconstitutional or in violation of federal laws or treaties.

We likewise are not impressed with the argument that anything less than absolute immunity will result in a flood of litigation and in substantial procedural burdens and expense for committee members. This argument, too, has been made before. But this Court's pronouncements in *Harlow v. Fitzgerald,* 457 U.S., at 813–820, place the argument in appropriate perspective, for many cases may be disposed of without the necessity of pretrial discovery proceedings. Our experience teaches us that the vast majority of prisoner cases are resolved on the complaint alone. Of those prisoners whose complaints survive initial dismissal, few attempt discovery and fewer still actually obtain it. And any expense of litigation largely is alleviated by the fact that a Government official who finds himself as a defendant in litigation of this kind is often represented, as in this case, by Government counsel. If the problem becomes acute, the Government has alternatives available to it: it might decide to indemnify the defendant official; Congress could make the claim a subject for the Federal Tort Claims Act; and Congress could even consider putting in place administrative law judges to preside at prison committee hearings.

The judgment of the Court of Appeals is affirmed.

JUSTICE REHNQUIST, with whom THE CHIEF JUSTICE and JUSTICE WHITE join, dissenting. [Opinion omitted.]

QUESTIONS AND POINTS FOR DISCUSSION

1. When looking at the language of § 1983, one might wonder, not whether officials sued in their individual capacity under § 1983 should enjoy absolute or qualified immunity from damages liability, but whether the officials should be afforded any immunity whatsoever. On its face, § 1983 does not exempt any culpable officials from liability; it says that "[e]*very* person" who violates another's constitutional rights when acting under the color of state law "*shall* be liable."

The Supreme Court, however, has repeatedly observed that § 1983 must be read in light of the immunities afforded by the common law at the time of § 1983's enactment. See, e.g., the cases cited in Newport v. Fact Concerts, Inc., 453 U.S. 247, 258 & n. 18, 101 S.Ct. 2748, 2755 & n. 18 (1981). According to the Court, because there is no indication (other than, of course, the plain language of § 1983) that Congress intended to abolish these long-standing common-law immunities when government officials were sued, § 1983 defendants enjoy the same immunities they enjoyed at common law unless recognition of the immunity defense would conflict with the policies underlying § 1983. Id. at 258–59, 101 S.Ct. at 2755–56.

2. In Procunier v. Navarette, 434 U.S. 555, 98 S.Ct. 855 (1978), the Supreme Court concluded that state prison officials sued under § 1983 for alleged unconstitutional interference with a prisoner's mail could assert the defense of qualified immunity. Prison officials can prevail on such a defense unless they violated "clearly established statutory or constitutional rights of which a reasonable person would have known." Harlow v. Fitzgerald, 457 U.S. 800, 818, 102 S.Ct. 2727, 2738 (1982).

In Anderson v. Creighton, 483 U.S. 635, 107 S.Ct. 3034 (1987), the Supreme Court addressed the question of when a right is "clearly established" so as to expose a defendant who violates the right to liability. The plaintiffs in *Anderson* had filed a *Bivens* action against an FBI agent who had participated in a warrantless search of the plaintiffs' home. The plaintiffs contended that the agent could not invoke the defense of qualified immunity because the right to be protected from warrantless searches of one's home, absent exigent circumstances or consent to the warrantless search, was "clearly established" at the time of the search. The Supreme Court, in an opinion written by Justice Scalia, responded as follows:

> The operation of this [the *Harlow*] standard, however, depends substantially upon the level of generality at which the relevant "legal rule" is to be identified. For example, the right to due process of law is quite clearly established by the Due Process Clause, and thus there is a sense in which any action that violates that Clause (no matter how unclear it may be that the particular action is a violation) violates a clearly established right. Much the same could be said of any other constitutional or statutory violation. But if the test of "clearly established law" were to be applied at this level of generality, it would bear no relationship to the "objective legal reasonableness" that is the touchstone of *Harlow*. Plaintiffs would be able to convert the rule of qualified immunity that our cases plainly establish into a rule of virtually unqualified liability simply by alleging violation of extremely abstract rights. *Harlow* would be transformed from a guarantee of immunity into a rule of pleading. Such an approach, in sum, would destroy "the balance that our cases strike between the interests in vindication of citizens' constitutional rights and in public officials' effective performance of their duties," by making it impossible for officials "reasonably [to] anticipate when their conduct may give rise to liability for damages." It should not be surprising, therefore, that our cases establish that the right the official is alleged to have violated must have been "clearly established" in a more particularized, and hence more relevant, sense: The contours of the right must be sufficiently clear that a reasonable official would understand that what he is doing violates that right. This is not to say that an official action is protected by qualified immunity unless the very action in question has previously been held unlawful, but it is to say that in the light of pre-existing law the unlawfulness must be apparent.

Id. at 639–40, 107 S.Ct. at 3038–39. The Court concluded with the observation that "[t]he relevant question in this case ... is the objective (albeit fact-specific) question whether a reasonable officer could have believed Anderson's warrantless search to be lawful, in light of clearly established law and the information the searching officers possessed. Anderson's subjective beliefs about the search are irrelevant." Id. at 641, 107 S.Ct. at 3039.

3. In Hope v. Pelzer, 536 U.S. 730, 122 S.Ct. 2508 (2002), the Supreme Court further elaborated on the prerequisites for finding that a right was "clearly established," putting a reasonable person on notice of the unlawfulness of certain conduct. The plaintiff in that case, an Alabama prisoner, filed a § 1983 lawsuit alleging that correctional officers subjected him to cruel and unusual punishment when they stripped him of his shirt, handcuffed him to a

hitching post, and left him outside on a very hot summer day for seven hours. The Eleventh Circuit Court of Appeals affirmed the entry of summary judgment for the defendants on the grounds that they were entitled to qualified immunity. The court of appeals noted that although the defendants had violated the plaintiff's rights under the Eighth Amendment, there were no cases with "materially similar" facts that would have alerted them to the illegality of their conduct. Id. at 733, 122 S.Ct. at 2512.

The Supreme Court rejected the notion that when a case involves novel facts, defendants are entitled to qualified immunity. According to the Court, the "salient question" rather was whether "the state of the law" at the time of the defendants' actions provided them with "fair warning" that the way in which they were treating the plaintiff was unconstitutional. Id. at 741, 122 S.Ct. at 2516. The Court ultimately concluded that the defendants in this case had received that warning. The Court noted that the violation of the Eighth Amendment was so patent that the Court's own cases arguably provided the requisite "fair warning." But the Court said that, in any event, decisions binding within the Eleventh Circuit and rendered before the incident in question, a regulation of the Alabama Department of Corrections placing constraints on the use of the hitching post, and a report of the United States Department of Justice condemning the use of the hitching post in Alabama as unconstitutional would have put a reasonable correctional officer on notice of the unlawfulness of the conditions the plaintiff was forced to endure.

4. Do you agree with the qualified-immunity test adopted by the Supreme Court and the way in which the Court has applied that test? When, if ever, do you believe that correctional officials who have violated an inmate's constitutional rights should be immune from damages liability? What about parole-board members? See Montero v. Travis, 171 F.3d 757, 761 (2d Cir. 1999) (holding that parole-board members sued under § 1983 are entitled to absolute immunity from damages liability). If damages liability is limited to when an official has violated a "clearly established" right, what effect will that limitation have on an individual's willingness to bring suit to redress the violation of a right not yet "clearly established"?

5. In determining whether a defendant is entitled to qualified immunity, a court may undertake a two-step inquiry under which it first considers whether the defendant violated a constitutional right and, if so, whether the right violated was "clearly established." But the Supreme Court has said that courts, exercising their "sound discretion," can skip directly to the second question of whether an argued right was "clearly established." Pearson v. Callahan, 129 S.Ct. 808, 818 (2009). If the court concludes that an asserted right was not "clearly established," the defendant is entitled to qualified immunity whether or not the defendant acted illegally. In your opinion, what are the potential benefits and drawbacks of not resolving the question whether a defendant actually violated a constitutional right?

6. Because an immunity defense is designed to protect government officials not only from the burden of paying damages, but also from the costs and hassles of litigation, the question of an official's entitlement to immunity normally should be resolved before discovery in a case commences. Harlow v. Fitzgerald, 457 U.S. 800, 818, 102 S.Ct. 2727, 2738 (1982). For the same

reason, if a judge denies a defendant's motion to dismiss on immunity grounds, the defendant can often, but not always, immediately appeal that order. Mitchell v. Forsyth, 472 U.S. 511, 530, 105 S.Ct. 2806, 2817 (1985). If the issue to be resolved is the purely legal one of whether the law allegedly violated was "clearly established" at the time of the alleged violation, an interlocutory appeal from the trial judge's order finding the law "clearly established" is permissible. Johnson v. Jones, 515 U.S. 304, 312–13, 115 S.Ct. 2151, 2156 (1995). On the other hand, if the qualified-immunity dispute is essentially a factual one, no interlocutory appeal will lie. Id. at 316, 115 S.Ct. at 2158. Such a factual dispute would exist, for example, when a defendant concedes that a right was "clearly established" but claims that there is no or insufficient evidence that he violated the right. Consequently, if a prisoner sues a correctional officer under § 1983 for his involvement in a brutal beating of the prisoner and the trial judge denies the defendant's motion for summary judgment, rejecting his argument that there is insufficient evidence that he was involved in, or even knew of, the beating, the defendant cannot immediately appeal the judge's order.

7. In Harlow v. Fitzgerald, 457 U.S. 800, 102 S.Ct. 2727 (1982), the Supreme Court abandoned the subjective prong of what was once a two-part test for qualified immunity. Under that subjective prong, defendants could not avail themselves of the qualified-immunity defense if they had acted with the malicious intent to violate someone's constitutional rights or cause injury to a person. Wood v. Strickland, 420 U.S. 308, 322, 95 S.Ct. 992, 1001 (1975). According to the Court, application of this subjective prong undermined the purposes of the qualified-immunity defense since the state of mind with which a defendant acted often cannot be determined until after discovery, and sometimes trial, thereby subjecting the defendant to the burdens of litigation that the qualified-immunity defense was designed to avoid.

In Crawford–El v. Britton, 523 U.S. 574, 118 S.Ct. 1584 (1998), the Supreme Court faced a conundrum stemming from the fact that some constitutional violations require a defendant to have acted with a particular state of mind. The plaintiff in that case, a prisoner, had been very outspoken in complaining to the press about the conditions of his confinement. In his § 1983 suit, he claimed that the defendant had refused to deliver boxes of his personal property to a prison to which he had been transferred in order to retaliate against him for exercising his First Amendment rights.

Since the law is "clearly established" that it is unconstitutional for a government official to retaliate against someone for having exercised his constitutional rights, the prisoner argued that the defendant could not invoke the qualified-immunity defense. The defendant, however, insisted that the plaintiff should not be able to avoid the qualified-immunity defense by simply alleging that the defendant acted with an unconstitutional motive. The defendant argued that when a particular state of mind is an element that must be proven to establish a constitutional violation, the plaintiff must adduce clear and convincing evidence of this mental state to avoid dismissal of the claim on qualified-immunity grounds.

In a 5–4 decision, the Supreme Court refused to, in its words, put "a thumb on the defendant's side of the scales" by heightening the burden of proof in unconstitutional-intent cases. Id. at 593, 118 S.Ct. at 1594. The Court noted that there are other tools, already at the disposal of district judges, that can be used to limit the burdens of litigation on government officials in such cases. For example, before permitting the parties to engage in discovery, the judge can require the plaintiff, under Federal Rule of Civil Procedure 7(a), to reply to the defendant's answer or can grant a defendant's motion for a more definite statement under Rule 12(e). And if the case does progress to the discovery stage, Rule 26 authorizes the judge to limit the scope of discovery, define the time, place, and manner of discovery, control the order and timing of discovery, and even prohibit discovery when needed to protect the defendant from "annoyance, embarrassment, oppression, or undue burden or expense."

In a dissenting opinion, Chief Justice Rehnquist, joined by Justice O'Connor, proposed adoption of a new immunity rule for cases involving allegations that a defendant acted with an unconstitutional state of mind. Under this rule, a defendant who could cite a legitimate reason for his or her challenged actions would be entitled to qualified immunity unless the plaintiff could establish, through "objective evidence," that the asserted reason was in fact a pretext. Id. at 602, 118 S.Ct. at 1599.

In a separate dissent, Justice Scalia, joined by Justice Thomas, urged the Court to go even further in insulating government officials from intent-based constitutional claims. Justice Scalia argued that once it has been determined that the asserted reason for a challenged action was "objectively valid" (e.g., that a prisoner was transferred to a maximum-security prison for security reasons), then the exploration and consideration of "objective evidence" (such as remarks of the defendant) to determine if that reason was actually a pretext to hide unconstitutional retaliation should be foreclosed. Id. at 612, 118 S.Ct. at 1604.

Whose views do you find more persuasive—the majority's, Chief Justice Rehnquist's, or Justice Scalia's? Why?

8. In a 5–4 decision, the Supreme Court held in Richardson v. McKnight, 521 U.S. 399, 117 S.Ct. 2100 (1997) that correctional officers employed by Corrections Corporation of America, a private company that operates prisons and other correctional facilities, are not entitled to qualified immunity from suit. The Court first noted that there was no " 'firmly rooted' tradition" in existence at the time § 1983 was enacted into law of according immunity to correctional officers employed by the private sector. Id. at 404, 117 S.Ct. at 2104.

The Court was also unpersuaded that privately employed correctional officers should be accorded qualified immunity simply because they perform the same functions as correctional officers employed by the government. The Court stated that while it had, in the past, applied a functional analysis in cases presenting immunity questions, it had utilized this functional approach only when deciding what *type* of immunity a public official was entitled to— absolute or qualified. The Court noted that to use this functional approach when also identifying the dividing line between liability for damages under § 1983 and qualified immunity would insulate many individuals from liability who work in companies that perform functions similar to those performed by the government, such as the production of electricity, waste disposal, and the delivery of mail.

At the end of its opinion, the Supreme Court added a potentially significant caveat. The Court emphasized that it had not resolved whether a private corrections company or its employees could assert a good-faith defense to a § 1983 claim—a defense that, unlike the defense of qualified immunity, might hinge on the defendant's subjective state of mind.

Because the question whether private parties sued under § 1983 can invoke a qualified-immunity defense is a question of statutory interpretation, Congress, of course, has the ultimate say on how this question should be resolved. Should § 1983 be amended to include a qualified-immunity defense for private prison and jail contractors and their employees? Why or why not?

9. Municipalities are not protected by the sovereign immunity accorded by the Eleventh Amendment. Will v. Michigan Dep't of State Police, 491 U.S. 58, 70, 109 S.Ct. 2304, 2312 (1989). In addition, the Supreme Court has held that municipalities sued under § 1983 cannot invoke the good faith of their officials and employees as a defense. Owen v. City of Independence, 445 U.S. 622, 100 S.Ct. 1398 (1980). According to the Court, this type of municipal immunity was not "firmly rooted" in the common law at the time § 1983 was enacted. Id. at 637–50, 100 S.Ct. at 1408–15. In addition, refusing to insulate municipalities from § 1983 liability through an immunity defense furthers the compensatory and deterrent aims of § 1983.

The Supreme Court, however, has construed § 1983 to preclude an award of punitive damages against a municipality. Newport v. Fact Concerts, Inc., 453 U.S. 247, 101 S.Ct. 2748 (1981). According to the Court, municipalities were immune from punitive-damages awards under the common law. In addition, the Court has opined that, while it is fair to spread the loss suffered by an individual whose constitutional rights were violated across the community, it would be unfair to go beyond that and penalize innocent taxpayers, through a punitive-damages award, for the wrongdoing of others.

2. STATUTES OF LIMITATIONS

Section 1983 itself does not specify a time limit for filing a § 1983 suit, nor does any other federal statute. In the absence of a controlling federal statute of limitations, 42 U.S.C. § 1988(a) directs courts to apply the statute of limitations in effect in the state where the suit is brought unless application of the statute would conflict with the Constitution or federal law. The Supreme Court has held that the state statute of limitations to be applied in a § 1983 suit is the one governing personal-injury actions. Wilson v. Garcia, 471 U.S. 261, 105 S.Ct. 1938 (1985). If the state has two statutes of limitations, one governing certain intentional torts and the other covering all other personal-injury actions, the more general statute of limitations applies. Owens v. Okure, 488 U.S. 235, 109 S.Ct. 573 (1989).

In Hardin v. Straub, 490 U.S. 536, 109 S.Ct. 1998 (1989), the Supreme Court considered whether a tolling provision for prisoners in a state statute of limitations conflicted with the Constitution. Because of the tolling provision, Michigan prisoners did not have to bring suit within three years after their cause of action accrued, as was generally required by the state's statute of limitations; the tolling provision permitted the prisoners to defer filing suit until up to a year after their release from prison.

The Court unanimously concluded that this tolling provision comported with the Constitution. The Court noted that the tolling provision was not only consistent with, but furthered, § 1983's goal of compensating individuals whose constitutional rights have been violated. Nor did the Court believe that the tolling provision would undermine another purpose of § 1983—that of deterring constitutional violations. Prisoners, who as plaintiffs have the burden of proof in § 1983 suits, would still have an incentive to promptly file § 1983 suits, because evidence that might support their claims could be lost if their suits were unduly delayed. In addition, prison officials might be more inclined to refrain from violating the civil rights of prisoners if they knew that prisoners could wait to file a § 1983 suit until after they were released from prison and free from the practical impediments that hinder the litigation of a lawsuit while in prison.

3. MOOTNESS

Even if a civil-rights suit is filed within the time allotted under the applicable statute of limitations, the case can and must be dismissed at any stage of the litigation, including on appeal, if the case becomes moot. Mootness questions arise with some frequency when a prisoner who is challenging the conditions of confinement or treatment at a particular prison is transferred to another prison or released on parole. See, e.g., Hewitt v. Helms, 482 U.S. 755, 107 S.Ct. 2672 (1987); Board of Pardons v. Allen, 482 U.S. 369, 107 S.Ct. 2415 (1987); Vitek v. Jones, 445 U.S. 480, 100 S.Ct. 1254 (1980). To avoid a dismissal for mootness, therefore, an attorney bringing a civil-rights suit on behalf of a prisoner should consider what can and should be done to avoid potential mootness problems.

A prisoner's transfer or release normally will not moot the case if the prisoner has sought damages relief. Boag v. MacDougall, 454 U.S. 364, 102 S.Ct. 700 (1982) (per curiam). Nor will the case be mooted if the prisoner has filed a class-action suit, and the class has been certified. Sosna v. Iowa, 419 U.S. 393, 95 S.Ct. 553 (1975). Even when a court has refused to certify a class and the prisoner bringing the civil-rights suit is then released from prison, the prisoner's claim on appeal that a class should have been certified is not mooted. United States Parole Comm'n v. Geraghty, 445 U.S. 388, 100 S.Ct. 1202 (1980).

4. EXHAUSTION OF REMEDIES

The Prison Litigation Reform Act amended 42 U.S.C. § 1997e(a) to require all prisoners, pretrial detainees, and juveniles confined for alleged or adjudicated delinquency to exhaust "available" administrative remedies before bringing a lawsuit under § 1983 or any other "Federal law" challenging the legality of the conditions of their confinement. Failure to exhaust administrative remedies is an affirmative defense to be pleaded and proven by the defendant. Jones v. Bock, 549 U.S. 199, 212–16, 127 S.Ct. 910, 919–21 (2007). If a prisoner's complaint contains both exhausted and unexhausted claims, the court should dismiss only the unexhausted claims. Id. at 220–24, 127 S.Ct. at 923–26.

In Booth v. Churner, 532 U.S. 731, 121 S.Ct. 1819 (2001), the Supreme Court considered whether § 1997e(a) requires prisoners seeking damages for the allegedly unconstitutional conditions of their confinement to first process their claims through prison grievance procedures when monetary relief cannot be recovered under those procedures. The Court held that as long as a prisoner can receive some other kind of relief from the grievance process, or grievance officials have the authority to take "some responsive action" to the prisoner's grievance, the exhaustion requirement applies. Id. at 736 & n. 4, 121 S.Ct. at 1822–23 & 1823 n. 4.

Prisoners in most states cannot obtain damages through their prison grievance processes or can obtain monetary relief for only limited types of claims, such as for lost or damaged property or miscalculated medical co-payments. See Lynn S. Branham, The Prison Litigation Reform Act's Enigmatic Exhaustion Requirement: What It Means and What Congress, Courts and Correctional Officials Can Learn from It, 86 Cornell L.Rev. 483, 518 (2001) (summarizing survey results in which only six states reported that their prison grievance processes had the authority to award damages for deficient medical care and none had the authority to award monetary relief for a correctional officer's excessive use of force or other unconstitutional conditions of confinement). As a policy matter, do you think that the exhaustion requirement should apply when a grievance procedure does not afford the monetary relief the prisoner seeks? Why or why not?

Prison officials typically set very short deadlines for the filing of a grievance, sometimes as little as two to five days after the incident giving rise to the grievance. In your opinion, under what circumstances, if any, should a prisoner who tardily files a grievance be deemed to have exhausted his or her administrative remedies? Some of the questions whose answers might bear on your analysis of this issue include the following: What are the various reasons why a prisoner might file a late grievance? Do those reasons argue for or against the adoption of a procedural-default rule that bars access to the courts if an inmate did not comply with grievance procedures? What are the purposes of the exhaustion requirement? Is a procedural-default rule in keeping with and needed to effectuate those purposes? Does a procedural-default rule comport with the purposes of 42 U.S.C. § 1983 and other civil-rights statutes, and is the enforcement of such a rule, in this context, constitutional?

In Woodford v. Ngo, 548 U.S. 81, 126 S.Ct. 2378 (2006), the Supreme Court held that a prisoner who files an untimely grievance or one that otherwise fails to conform with grievance procedures has not satisfied the PLRA's exhaustion requirement. The Court disagreed with the view of several courts of appeals that as long as a prisoner pursues a grievance through all levels of the grievance process, the exhaustion requirement is met even though the prisoner may not have filed the grievance within the short timelines often set by prison officials. See, e.g., Thomas v. Woolum, 337 F.3d 720, 733 (6th Cir. 2003). According to these courts, prison officials then have the opportunity, whether or not they choose to avail themselves of it, to consider a prisoner's grievance before the prisoner turns to a court for redress.

The Supreme Court's decision in *Woodford v. Ngo* has sparked calls to amend the PLRA's exhaustion requirement. The American Bar Association, for example, has proposed that if a prisoner did not exhaust administrative remedies before filing a conditions-of-confinement claim, the court should stay the case for up to ninety days while the claim is processed administratively. Do you favor or oppose this proposed change in the exhaustion requirement? For the resolution and report outlining this and other recommended changes to the PLRA, see http://www.abanet.org/leadership/2007/midyear/docs/SUMMARYOFRECOMMENDATIONS/hundredtwob.doc.

CHAPTER 19

REMEDIES

■ ■ ■

A. § 1983 ACTIONS

1. DAMAGES

CAREY v. PIPHUS

Supreme Court of the United States, 1978.
435 U.S. 247, 98 S.Ct. 1042, 55 L.Ed.2d 252.

MR. JUSTICE POWELL delivered the opinion of the Court.

[After two students were summarily suspended from school for misconduct—one for allegedly smoking marijuana and the other for wearing an earring while at school, they and their mothers filed § 1983 suits against various school officials contending that their suspensions violated their procedural-due-process rights. The federal district court agreed that their constitutional rights had been violated but refused to award the plaintiffs any damages because they had failed to present any evidence demonstrating that they were harmed by the suspensions.

On appeal, the Seventh Circuit Court of Appeals reversed. The court held that if the suspensions were justified, though effected without due process of law, the plaintiffs could not recover damages for the value of the time that they missed in school because of their suspensions. The court held, however, that they could still recover "substantial non-punitive damages" just for having been deprived of their due-process rights. The Supreme Court then granted certiorari.]

* * *

Respondents seem to make two different arguments in support of the holding below. First, they contend that substantial damages should be awarded under § 1983 for the deprivation of a constitutional right *whether or not* any injury was caused by the deprivation. This, they say, is appropriate both because constitutional rights are valuable in and of themselves, and because of the need to deter violations of constitutional rights. * * * Second, respondents argue that even if the purpose of a § 1983 damages award is, as petitioners contend, primarily to compensate persons for injuries that are caused by the deprivation of constitutional rights, every deprivation of procedural due process may be *presumed* to cause some injury. This presumption, they say, should relieve them from the necessity of proving that injury actually was caused.

Insofar as petitioners contend that the basic purpose of a § 1983 damages award should be to compensate persons for injuries caused by the deprivation of constitutional rights, they have the better of the argument. Rights, constitutional and otherwise, do not exist in a vacuum. Their purpose is to protect persons from injuries to particular interests, and their contours are shaped by the interests they protect.

* * *

The Members of the Congress that enacted § 1983 did not address directly the question of damages, but the principle that damages are designed to compensate persons for injuries caused by the deprivation of rights hardly could have been foreign to the many lawyers in Congress in 1871. * * * To the extent that Congress intended that awards under § 1983 should deter the deprivation of constitutional rights, there is no evidence that it meant to establish a deterrent more formidable than that inherent in the award of compensatory damages.

* * *[O]ver the centuries the common law of torts has developed a set of rules to implement the principle that a person should be compensated fairly for injuries caused by the violation of his legal rights. These rules, defining the elements of damages and the prerequisites for their recovery, provide the appropriate starting point for the inquiry under § 1983 as well.

It is not clear, however, that common-law tort rules of damages will provide a complete solution to the damages issue in every § 1983 case. In some cases, the interests protected by a particular branch of the common law of torts may parallel closely the interests protected by a particular constitutional right. In such cases, it may be appropriate to apply the tort rules of damages directly to the § 1983 action. In other cases, the interests protected by a particular constitutional right may not also be protected by an analogous branch of the common law of torts. In those cases, the task will be the more difficult one of adapting common-law rules of damages to provide fair compensation for injuries caused by the deprivation of a constitutional right.

Although this task of adaptation will be one of some delicacy—as this case demonstrates—it must be undertaken. The purpose of § 1983 would be defeated if injuries caused by the deprivation of constitutional rights went uncompensated simply because the common law does not recognize an analogous cause of action. * * *

The Due Process Clause of the Fourteenth Amendment provides:

"[N]or shall any State deprive any person of life, liberty, or property, without due process of law...."

This Clause "raises no impenetrable barrier to the taking of a person's possessions," or liberty, or life. Procedural due process rules are meant to protect persons not from the deprivation, but from the mistaken or unjustified deprivation of life, liberty, or property. * * *

In this case, the Court of Appeals held that if petitioners can prove on remand that "[respondents] would have been suspended even if a proper hearing had been held," then respondents will not be entitled to recover damages to compensate them for injuries caused by the suspensions. The court thought that in such a case, the failure to accord procedural due process could not properly be viewed as the cause of the suspensions. The court suggested that in such circumstances, an award of damages for injuries caused by the suspensions would constitute a windfall, rather than compensation, to respondents. We do not understand the parties to disagree with this conclusion. Nor do we.

The parties do disagree as to the further holding of the Court of Appeals that respondents are entitled to recover substantial—although unspecified—damages to compensate them for "the injury which is 'inherent in the nature of the wrong,'" even if their suspensions were justified and even if they fail to prove that the denial of procedural due process actually caused them some real, if intangible, injury. Respondents, elaborating on this theme, submit that the holding is correct because injury fairly may be "presumed" to flow from every denial of procedural due process. Their argument is that in addition to protecting against unjustified deprivations, the Due Process Clause also guarantees the "feeling of just treatment" by the government. They contend that the deprivation of protected interests without procedural due process, even where the premise for the deprivation is not erroneous, inevitably arouses strong feelings of mental and emotional distress in the individual who is denied this "feeling of just treatment." They analogize their case to that of defamation *per se,* in which "the plaintiff is relieved from the necessity of producing any proof whatsoever that he has been injured" in order to recover substantial compensatory damages.

Petitioners do not deny that a purpose of procedural due process is to convey to the individual a feeling that the government has dealt with him fairly, as well as to minimize the risk of mistaken deprivations of protected interests. They go so far as to concede that, in a proper case, persons in respondents' position might well recover damages for mental and emotional distress caused by the denial of procedural due process. Petitioners' argument is the more limited one that such injury cannot be presumed to occur, and that plaintiffs at least should be put to their proof on the issue, as plaintiffs are in most tort actions.

We agree with petitioners in this respect. * * *

First, it is not reasonable to assume that every departure from procedural due process, no matter what the circumstances or how minor, inherently is as likely to cause distress as the publication of defamation *per se* is to cause injury to reputation and distress. Where the deprivation of a protected interest is substantively justified but procedures are deficient in some respect, there may well be those who suffer no distress over the procedural irregularities. Indeed, in contrast to the immediately distressing effect of defamation *per se,* a person may not even know that procedures *were* deficient until he enlists the aid of counsel to challenge a perceived substantive deprivation.

Moreover, where a deprivation is justified but procedures are deficient, whatever distress a person feels may be attributable to the justified deprivation rather than to deficiencies in procedure. But as the Court of Appeals held, the injury caused by a justified deprivation, including distress, is not properly compensable under § 1983. This ambiguity in causation, which is absent in the case of defamation *per se,* provides additional need for requiring the plaintiff to convince the trier of fact that he actually suffered distress because of the denial of procedural due process itself.

Finally, we foresee no particular difficulty in producing evidence that mental and emotional distress actually was caused by the denial of procedural due process itself. Distress is a personal injury familiar to the law, customarily proved by showing the nature and circumstances of the wrong and its effect on the plaintiff.[20] In sum, then, although mental and emotional distress caused by the denial of procedural due process itself is compensable under § 1983, we hold that neither the likelihood of such injury nor the difficulty of proving it is so great as to justify awarding compensatory damages without proof that such injury actually was caused.

* * *

Even if respondents' suspensions were justified, and even if they did not suffer any other actual injury, the fact remains that they were deprived of their right to procedural due process. * * *

Common-law courts traditionally have vindicated deprivations of certain "absolute" rights that are not shown to have caused actual injury through the award of a nominal sum of money. By making the deprivation of such rights actionable for nominal damages without proof of actual injury, the law recognizes the importance to organized society that those rights be scrupulously observed; but at the same time, it remains true to the principle that substantial damages should be awarded only to compensate actual injury or, in the case of exemplary or punitive damages, to deter or punish malicious deprivations of rights.

Because the right to procedural due process is "absolute" in the sense that it does not depend upon the merits of a claimant's substantive assertions, and because of the importance to organized society that procedural due process be observed, we believe that the denial of procedural

---

20. We use the term "distress" to include mental suffering or emotional anguish. Although essentially subjective, genuine injury in this respect may be evidenced by one's conduct and observed by others. * * *

due process should be actionable for nominal damages without proof of actual injury. We therefore hold that if, upon remand, the District Court determines that respondents' suspensions were justified, respondents nevertheless will be entitled to recover nominal damages not to exceed one dollar from petitioners.

* * *

MR. JUSTICE MARSHALL concurs in the result.

QUESTIONS AND POINTS FOR DISCUSSION

1. Consider the implications of *Carey v. Piphus* to prisoners' § 1983 suits. When could a prisoner recover compensatory damages for a violation of procedural-due-process rights during a disciplinary hearing? See Redding v. Fairman, 717 F.2d 1105, 1117–18 (7th Cir.1983). Now consider this question in light of the provision of the Prison Litigation Reform Act (PLRA) discussed in note 2 on page 797 of this casebook that prohibits persons confined in prisons, jails, and other correctional facilities from bringing federal claims for mental or emotional injuries suffered while in custody unless they can show that they also suffered some type of "physical injury." 42 U.S.C. § 1997e(e).

2. The PLRA's physical-injury requirement only applies to, and potentially bars, claims seeking damages for mental or emotional injuries. In some cases in which this requirement has been at issue, courts have concluded that the prisoners were seeking recompense for other kinds of harm not subject to the physical-injury requirement. For example, in Cassidy v. Indiana Dep't of Corrections, 199 F.3d 374 (7th Cir. 2000), a blind inmate filed suit under the Americans with Disabilities Act and the Rehabilitation Act of 1973, 29 U.S.C. § 794, alleging that he had been denied access to educational, vocational-training, recreational, and other programs and services afforded nondisabled inmates. The Seventh Circuit Court of Appeals concluded that the physical-injury requirement barred the plaintiff's claim for damages for mental and emotional injuries. But the court held that the prisoner could proceed with his claims for other types of damages, such as damages for the loss of freedom of movement and social contact, a diminished quality of life, and the opportunity to secure an early release from prison through rehabilitative efforts. See also Mitchell v. Horn, 318 F.3d 523, 534 n.10 (3d Cir. 2003) (holding that claims, stemming from allegedly unconstitutional disciplinary confinement, for loss of "status, custody level, and any chance at commutation" are not claims for mental or emotional injury and hence not subject to the physical-injury requirement).

3. Some constitutional violations, such as violations of the First Amendment, equal protection, and procedural due process, typically do not cause any physical injury. The courts are divided on the impact of the physical-injury requirement on claims for redress for these kinds of constitutional infractions. Most courts have held that the physical-injury requirement bars the recovery of compensatory damages for these kinds of constitutional violations. See, e.g., Geiger v. Jowers, 404 F.3d 371, 375 & n.11 (5th Cir. 2005) (listing cases). These courts have construed the prisoners' claims in the cases before them as seeking relief only for mental or emotional harm.

Other courts have held that the physical-injury requirement does not necessarily foreclose the recovery of compensatory damages for violations of First and Fourteenth Amendment rights. See, e.g., Canell v. Lightner, 143 F.3d 1210, 1213 (9th Cir. 1998) (holding that physical-injury requirement doesn't apply to prisoner's claims under the First Amendment's Free Exercise and Establishment Clauses). If you were writing the majority opinion in one of these cases, how would you articulate your reasoning for this conclusion?

4. The physical-injury requirement does not apply to claims for injunctive or declaratory relief. Royal v. Kautzky, 375 F.3d 720, 723 (8th Cir. 2004). The majority of the courts also concur that a prisoner barred by the requirement from recovering compensatory damages still can recover nominal and punitive damages. See Hutchins v. McDaniels, 512 F.3d 193, 197–98 (5th Cir. 2007) (listing cases).

5. In Smith v. Wade, 461 U.S. 30, 103 S.Ct. 1625 (1983), the Supreme Court described when an award of punitive damages in a § 1983 action would be appropriate. To be liable for punitive damages, a defendant need not have acted with a malicious intent to harm the plaintiff. "[R]eckless or callous indifference to the federally protected rights of others," as well as an "evil motive or intent," will support an award of punitive damages. Id. at 56, 103 S.Ct. at 1640.

The courts have held that a § 1983 plaintiff who is awarded only nominal damages can still recover punitive damages. See, e.g., Walker v. Bain, 257 F.3d 660, 674 (6th Cir.2001). See also Carlson v. Green, 446 U.S. 14, 22 n. 9, 100 S.Ct. 1468, 1473 n. 9 (1980) (punitive damages can be awarded even if the plaintiff is unable to prove compensable injury).

6. Can, and in your opinion should, government officials be permitted to utilize some or all of the damages recovered by prisoners in § 1983 suits to defray the costs of their incarceration? See Hankins v. Finnel, 964 F.2d 853, 861 (8th Cir.1992) (holding that state statute under which 90% of a money judgment awarded a prisoner could be appropriated to pay incarceration costs conflicted with § 1983's compensatory and deterrent objectives and was therefore unenforceable under the Supremacy Clause). What if the money is to be used to pay restitution to a victim? See Beeks v. Hundley, 34 F.3d 658 (8th Cir.1994) (concluding that seizing prisoners' damages awards to pay their crime victims does not frustrate the compensatory and deterrent aims of § 1983 and that § 1983 therefore does not preempt state's victim-restitution statute). See also 18 U.S.C. § 3626 note (requiring compensatory damages awarded to inmates in civil actions against correctional officials to be paid first to satisfy any outstanding restitution orders before the balance of the award, if any is left, is remitted to the inmates, and requiring "reasonable efforts" to notify crime victims of compensatory damages awarded to a prisoner in a suit against correctional officials before payment is made to the prisoner).

2. EQUITABLE RELIEF

a. General Rules

Plaintiffs filing § 1983 suits frequently seek declaratory or injunctive relief. When entering a declaratory judgment, a court may, for example, declare a state statute or regulation unconstitutional. Through injunctive relief, a court goes further in providing redress to plaintiffs—prohibiting defendants from engaging in certain unconstitutional conduct in the future or mandating that they take certain steps to avoid further violations of the Constitution.

Injunctive relief may be afforded in the form of a temporary restraining order, a preliminary injunction, or a permanent injunction. Standards governing the issuance of these types of injunctive orders are described in 1 Dan B. Dobbs, Law of Remedies, 223–76 (2d ed. 1993).

Courts can issue a broad array of injunctive orders in § 1983 suits after finding conditions at a prison or jail unconstitutional. To limit any unnecessary intrusion by the federal courts into states' operations of their prisons or jails though, courts must, at least generally, afford state or local officials the opportunity to develop a plan to bring conditions into compliance with the Constitution. See, e.g., Lewis v. Casey, 518 U.S. 343, 363, 116 S.Ct. 2174, 2186 (1996), on page 553; Taylor v. Freeman, 34 F.3d 266, 270–71, 274 (4th Cir.1994) (trial court erred in ordering reduction in inmate population instead of first providing correctional officials with the opportunity to develop a plan to alleviate allegedly unconstitutional conditions of confinement). The officials' failure to develop or implement such a plan then may lead the court to take more intrusive steps to rectify unconstitutional conditions, including placing a population cap on the correctional facility, appointing a receiver to run the facility, or even ordering the release of some inmates. See, e.g., Harris v. Angelina County, Texas, 31 F.3d 331, 336 (5th Cir.1994) (noting the appropriateness of a population cap as a remedy but encouraging district court to revisit the need for the cap if circumstances at the jail, such as insufficient staff and inadequate classification system, change); Plata v. Schwarzenegger, 2005 WL 2932253, at *1 (N.D. Cal. 2005) (imposing the "drastic but necessary remedy" of appointing a receiver to control the delivery of medical services to California prisoners); Duran v. Elrod, 713 F.2d 292, 298 (7th Cir.1983) (affirming order directing the release of pretrial detainees incarcerated simply because they could not pay low bonds).

The Supreme Court's decision in Missouri v. Jenkins, 495 U.S. 33, 110 S.Ct. 1651 (1990) suggests that a court may go even further to ensure that government officials take the steps necessary to remedy unconstitutional conditions of confinement in a correctional facility. In that case, a federal district court had concluded that the Kansas City, Missouri, School District (KCMSD) had unconstitutionally maintained a segregated school system. To remedy this constitutional violation, the district court approved a magnet-school program proposed by the school district that would cost over $380 million to implement. The court recognized that the school district lacked the resources to pay for its share of the costs of this plan and that the state constitution placed limits on the school district's ability to raise property taxes to pay for the desegregation plan. The court therefore ordered that property taxes be raised to cover the costs of desegregation.

The State of Missouri, which the district court had held jointly and severally liable for the costs of the plan, challenged this desegregation remedy on appeal, contending that the district court had exceeded its equitable powers by raising taxes. The Supreme Court agreed, but at the same time, confirmed that the equitable powers of the court to remedy a constitutional violation are quite broad:

We turn to the tax increase imposed by the District Court. The State urges us to hold that the tax increase violated Article III, the Tenth Amendment, and principles of federal/state comity. We find it unnecessary to reach the difficult constitutional issues, for we agree with the State that the tax increase contravened the principles of comity that must govern the exercise of the District Court's equitable discretion in this area.

It is accepted by all the parties, as it was by the courts below, that the imposition of a tax increase by a federal court was an extraordinary event. In assuming for itself the fundamental and delicate power of taxation the District Court not only intruded on local authority but circumvented it altogether. Before taking such a drastic step the District Court was obliged to assure itself that no permissible alternative would have accomplished the required task. We have emphasized that although the "remedial powers of an equity court must be adequate to the task, * * * they are not unlimited," and one of the most important considerations governing the exercise of equitable power is a proper respect for the integrity and function of local government institutions. Especially is this true where, as here, those institutions are ready, willing, and—but for the operation of state law curtailing their powers—able to remedy the deprivation of constitutional rights themselves.

The District Court believed that it had no alternative to imposing a tax increase. But there was an alternative, the very one outlined by the Court of Appeals: it could have authorized or required KCMSD to levy property taxes at a rate adequate to fund the desegregation remedy and could have enjoined the operation of state laws that would have prevented KCMSD from exercising this power. The difference between the two approaches is far more than a matter of form. Authorizing and directing local government institutions to devise and implement remedies not only protects the function of those institutions but, to the extent possible, also places the responsibility for solutions to the problems of segregation upon those who have themselves created the problems.

* * *

* * * [T]he State argues that an order to increase taxes cannot be sustained under the judicial power of Article III. Whatever the merits of this argument when applied to the District Court's own order increasing taxes, a point we have not reached, a court order directing a local government body to levy its own taxes is plainly a

judicial act within the power of a federal court. We held as much in Griffin v. Prince Edward County School Bd., 377 U.S., at 233, 84 S.Ct., at 1234, where we stated that a District Court, faced with a county's attempt to avoid desegregation of the public schools by refusing to operate those schools, could "require the [County] Supervisors to exercise the power that is theirs to levy taxes to raise funds adequate to reopen, operate, and maintain without racial discrimination a public school system...." * * *

The State maintains, however, that even under these cases, the federal judicial power can go no further than to require local governments to levy taxes *as authorized under state law*. In other words, the State argues that federal courts cannot set aside state-imposed limitations on local taxing authority because to do so is to do more than to require the local government "to exercise the power *that is theirs.*" We disagree. * * *

* * * Here the KCMSD may be ordered to levy taxes despite the statutory limitations on its authority in order to compel the discharge of an obligation imposed on KCMSD by the Fourteenth Amendment. To hold otherwise would fail to take account of the obligations of local governments, under the Supremacy Clause, to fulfill the requirements that the Constitution imposes on them. However wide the discretion of local authorities in fashioning desegregation remedies may be, "if a state-imposed limitation on a school authority's discretion operates to inhibit or obstruct the operation of a unitary school system or impede the disestablishing of a dual school system, it must fall; state policy must give way when it operates to hinder vindication of federal constitutional guarantees." Even though a particular remedy may not be required in every case to vindicate constitutional guarantees, where (as here) it has been found that a particular remedy is required, the State cannot hinder the process by preventing a local government from implementing that remedy.

Id. at 50–51, 55–57, 110 S.Ct. at 1662–63, 1665–66. What is the potential significance of this decision in the correctional context?

b. The PLRA's Restrictions on Equitable Relief

The Prison Litigation Reform Act (PLRA) enacted in 1996 dramatically changed the way in which prisoners' and pretrial detainees' civil-rights suits are to be processed by the courts. Some of the more significant changes wrought by the Act place limitations on the equitable relief awarded in conditions-of-confinement cases involving jails, prisons, or other correctional facilities. Pertinent portions of those limitations, found in 18 U.S.C. § 3626, are set forth below:

§ 3626. Appropriate remedies with respect to prison conditions.

(a) Requirements for relief.—

(1) Prospective relief.—

(A) Prospective relief in any civil action with respect to prison conditions shall extend no further than necessary to correct the violation of the Federal right of a particular plaintiff or plaintiffs. The court shall not grant or approve any prospective relief unless the court finds that such relief is narrowly drawn, extends no further than necessary to correct the violation of the Federal right, and is the least intrusive means necessary to correct the violation of the Federal right. The court shall give substantial weight to any adverse impact on public safety or the operation of a criminal justice system caused by the relief.

(B) The court shall not order any prospective relief that requires or permits a government official to exceed his or her authority under State or local law or otherwise violates State or local law, unless—

    (i) Federal law requires such relief to be ordered in violation of State or local law;

    (ii) the relief is necessary to correct the violation of a Federal right; and

    (iii) no other relief will correct the violation of the Federal right.

(C) Nothing in this section shall be construed to authorize the courts, in exercising their remedial powers, to order the construction of prisons or the raising of taxes, or to repeal or detract from otherwise applicable limitations on the remedial powers of the courts.

(2) Preliminary injunctive relief.—In any civil action with respect to prison conditions, to the extent otherwise authorized by law, the court may enter a temporary restraining order or an order for preliminary injunctive relief. Preliminary injunctive relief must be narrowly drawn, extend no further than necessary to correct the harm the court finds requires preliminary relief, and be the least intrusive means necessary to correct that harm. The court shall give substantial weight to any adverse impact on public safety or the operation of a criminal justice system caused by the preliminary relief and shall respect the principles of comity set out in paragraph (1)(B) in tailoring any preliminary relief. Preliminary injunctive relief shall automatically expire on the date that is 90 days after its entry, unless the court makes the findings required under subsection (a)(1) for the entry of prospective relief and makes the order final before the expiration of the 90-day period.

(3) Prisoner release order.—

    (A) In any civil action with respect to prison conditions, no court shall enter a prisoner release order unless—

(i) a court has previously entered an order for less intrusive relief that has failed to remedy the deprivation of the Federal right sought to be remedied through the prisoner release order; and

(ii) the defendant has had a reasonable amount of time to comply with the previous court orders.

(B) In any civil action in Federal court with respect to prison conditions, a prisoner release order shall be entered only by a three-judge court in accordance with section 2284 of title 28,[a] if the requirements of subparagraph (E) have been met.

* * *

(E) The three-judge court shall enter a prisoner release order only if the court finds by clear and convincing evidence that—

(i) crowding is the primary cause of the violation of a Federal right; and

(ii) no other relief will remedy the violation of the Federal right.

(F) Any State or local official including a legislator or unit of government whose jurisdiction or function includes the appropriation of funds for the construction, operation, or maintenance of prison facilities, or the prosecution or custody of persons who may be released from, or not admitted to, a prison as a result of a prisoner release order shall have standing to oppose the imposition or continuation in effect of such relief and to seek termination of such relief, and shall have the right to intervene in any proceeding relating to such relief.

* * *

(c) Settlements.—

(1) Consent decrees.—In any civil action with respect to prison conditions, the court shall not enter or approve a consent decree unless it complies with the limitations on relief set forth in subsection (a).

(2) Private settlement agreements.—

(A) Nothing in this section shall preclude parties from entering into a private settlement agreement that does not comply with the limitations on relief set forth in subsection (a), if the terms of that agreement are not subject to court enforcement other than the reinstatement of the civil proceeding that the agreement settled.

---

a. At least one of the judges on the three-judge court must be a circuit-court judge. 28 U.S.C. § 2284(h)(2).

(B) Nothing in this section shall preclude any party claiming that a private settlement agreement has been breached from seeking in State court any remedy available under State law.

(d) State law remedies.—The limitations on remedies in this section shall not apply to relief entered by a State court based solely upon claims arising under State law.

* * *

(g) Definitions.—As used in this section—

* * *

(3) the term "prisoner" means any person subject to incarceration, detention, or admission to any facility who is accused of, convicted of, sentenced for, or adjudicated delinquent for, violations of criminal law or the terms and conditions of parole, probation, pretrial release, or diversionary program;

(4) the term "prisoner release order" includes any order, including a temporary restraining order or preliminary injunctive relief, that has the purpose or effect of reducing or limiting the prison population, or that directs the release from or nonadmission of prisoners to a prison;

(5) the term "prison" means any Federal, State, or local facility that incarcerates or detains juveniles or adults accused of, convicted of, sentenced for, or adjudicated delinquent for, violations of criminal law;

* * *

(7) the term "prospective relief" means all relief other than compensatory monetary damages;

* * *

———————

As a precondition to granting equitable relief in a conditions-of-confinement case, 18 U.S.C. § 3626(a)(1)(A) requires a court to find that the defendants have violated a federal right. This requirement also extends to consent decrees, which are court orders that reflect the terms of the parties' settlement agreements. See id. § 3626(c)(1). The Commission on Safety and Abuse in America's Prisons has called for the repeal of the requirement that correctional officials admit that they have violated the law before a court can enter a consent decree. Comm'n on Safety & Abuse in Am. Prisons, Confronting Confinement 86 (2006). The Commission has argued that this requirement impedes the settlement of cases. Before the PLRA's enactment, correctional officials could resolve lawsuits, through consent decrees, without admitting their liability and potentially inviting a deluge of lawsuits filed by individual prisoners for damages.

The American Bar Association has gone further in advocating changes to the PLRA, recommending that the courts' full authority to grant equitable relief in conditions-of-confinement cases be restored. See Rep. 102B, Summary of Action of the House of Delegates, 2007 Midyear Meeting, available at http://www.abanet.org/leadership/2007/midyear/docs/SUMMARYOFRECOMMENDATIONS/hundredtwob.doc. How, if at all, do you believe the PLRA's limitations on the granting of equitable relief in these cases should be modified?

c. Injunctive Relief to Secure Release From Confinement

i. *Preiser v. Rodriguez*

Ordering prisoners released from prison as a remedy in a suit challenging unconstitutional crowding must be distinguished from the situation where a prisoner is challenging, not the conditions of confinement, but the fact or duration of the prisoner's confinement and, as a remedy, is seeking an immediate or earlier release from confinement. In Preiser v. Rodriguez, 411 U.S. 475, 93 S.Ct. 1827 (1973), the plaintiffs, prisoners confined in a New York prison, brought suit under § 1983 claiming that they had lost good-time credits as a result of disciplinary proceedings that did not meet due-process requirements. For relief, the plaintiffs sought an injunction directing that their good-time credits be restored. The restoration of those credits would have led to the plaintiffs' immediate release from prison.

The Supreme Court concluded in *Preiser* that when a state prisoner is challenging the fact or duration of his or her confinement and seeking immediate or an earlier release from confinement, the prisoner must assert the claim in a habeas corpus action brought under 28 U.S.C. § 2254. That statute generally requires that individuals exhaust available state court remedies before seeking a writ of habeas corpus from a federal court directing that they be released from unconstitutional custody. One purpose of this exhaustion requirement is to avoid, whenever possible, the conflict that would result between federal and state courts if a federal court, rather than a state court, set aside a state conviction. But the Court in *Preiser* observed that the federal-state comity considerations underlying § 2254(c)'s exhaustion requirement extend beyond the conviction context and would be undermined by permitting federal courts to intercede in the operation of a state's prison by issuing an injunction in a § 1983 suit directing an inmate's release from the prison sooner than prison officials have authorized.

ii. *Heck v. Humphrey*

In a series of cases following *Preiser*, the Supreme Court has attempted to further clarify the line between habeas corpus and § 1983 relief. In

Heck v. Humphrey, 512 U.S. 477, 114 S.Ct. 2364 (1994), the Court held that state prisoners challenging the fact or duration of their confinement also cannot seek damages stemming from their allegedly unconstitutional confinement in a § 1983 suit unless and until one of three events has occurred: the conviction or sentence has been reversed or set aside by a state court order; the conviction or sentence has been expunged by an executive order; or a federal court has issued a writ of habeas corpus, thereby raising doubts about the validity of the conviction or sentence. The Court read § 1983 in light of its common-law backdrop and concluded that, like a tort action for malicious prosecution, a civil-rights action for damages stemming from an unlawful conviction cannot be brought until the criminal proceeding has terminated in the accused's favor.

iii. *Edwards v. Balisok*

In Edwards v. Balisok, 520 U.S. 641, 117 S.Ct. 1584 (1997), the Supreme Court extended its ruling in *Heck v. Humphrey* to a case in which a prisoner sought a declaratory judgment and damages because of constitutionally deficient procedures allegedly utilized during a prison disciplinary hearing. The prisoner did not seek restoration of the good-time credits revoked during the disciplinary proceeding. Nonetheless, the Supreme Court underscored that a finding in favor of the prisoner would "necessarily imply the invalidity of the deprivation of his good-time credits." Id. at 646, 117 S.Ct. at 1588. The Court held that the prisoner's claims for damages and declaratory relief consequently were not cognizable, at least yet, in a § 1983 suit and therefore should have been dismissed.

The prisoner's complaint in *Balisok* also included a request for an injunction requiring prison officials to follow certain procedures in future disciplinary hearings. After observing that the granting of prospective relief does not "ordinarily" imply that a prior revocation of good-time credits was invalid, the Court remanded this claim for consideration by the lower courts. Id. at 648, 117 S.Ct. at 1589.

iv. *Spencer v. Kemna*

In Spencer v. Kemna, 523 U.S. 1, 118 S.Ct. 978 (1998), the Supreme Court considered whether a court could adjudicate a habeas corpus petition challenging the constitutionality of procedures utilized during the revocation of the petitioner's parole. Because the petitioner had, since filing his petition, completed serving his sentence, the Court concluded that his petition had become moot and should therefore be dismissed.

In *dicta*, five members of the Court noted that the petitioner still could seek damages in a § 1983 suit for the allegedly unconstitutional parole revocation. (Souter, J., with O'Connor, Ginsburg, and Breyer, J.J., concurring; Stevens, J., dissenting). These Justices agreed that the favorable-termination requirement set forth in *Heck v. Humphrey* does not have to be met when it would be impossible to meet that requirement.

Otherwise, individuals who had been unconstitutionally convicted or confined would, in cases such as this one, often be left remediless.

v.   *Muhammad v. Close*

In Muhammad v. Close, 540 U.S. 749, 124 S.Ct. 1303 (2004), the Supreme Court further elaborated on the import of *Heck v. Humphrey*. The inmate-plaintiff in *Muhammad* alleged that he had been charged by a correctional officer with "threatening behavior" in retaliation for previous lawsuits and grievances. Under prison rules, this particular offense required prehearing detention. The plaintiff ultimately was convicted of the lesser-included disciplinary offense of insolence, a charge that he conceded was justified. A charge of insolence, however, did not justify prehearing detention. The plaintiff did not seek to have his disciplinary record expunged, but sought only compensatory and punitive damages for the six days that he spent in prehearing detention, which he attributed to the officer's retaliatory motive.

The Supreme Court rejected what it termed the "mistaken view ... that *Heck* applies categorically to all suits challenging prison disciplinary proceedings." Id. at 754, 124 S.Ct. at 1306. In discussing when the *Heck* rule applies to § 1983 claims stemming from prison disciplinary proceedings, the Court stated:

> [T]hese administrative determinations do not as such raise any implication about the validity of the underlying conviction, and although they may affect the duration of time to be served (by bearing on the award or revocation of good-time credits) that is not necessarily so. The effect of disciplinary proceedings on good-time credits is a matter of state law or regulation, and in this case, the Magistrate expressly found or assumed that no good-time credits were eliminated by the prehearing action Muhammad called in question. His § 1983 suit challenging this action could not therefore be construed as seeking a judgment at odds with his conviction or with the State's calculation of time to be served in accordance with the underlying sentence. That is, he raised no claim on which habeas relief could have been granted on any recognized theory, with the consequence that *Heck*'s favorable termination requirement was inapplicable.

Id. at 754–755, 124 S. Ct. at 1306.

vi.   *Wilkinson v. Dotson*

Finally, in Wilkinson v. Dotson, 544 U.S. 74, 125 S.Ct. 1242 (2005), the Supreme Court addressed a claim by two Ohio prisoners who alleged that Ohio's parole procedures were unconstitutional. By way of relief, the inmates sought new parole hearings and injunctive relief that would affect the procedures to be followed at their hearings. The state argued that the inmates had brought these claims in the hope that a favorable outcome would mean their speedier release from prison and that their claims were therefore a challenge to the duration of their confinement.

The Supreme Court noted that the state's argument "jump[ed] from a true premise (that in all likelihood the prisoners hope these actions will help bring about earlier release) to a faulty conclusion (that habeas is their sole avenue for relief)." Id. 78, 125 S.Ct. at 1246. The Court further observed:

> Throughout the legal journey from *Preiser* to *Balisok*, the Court has focused on the need to ensure that state prisoners use only habeas corpus (or similar state) remedies when they seek to invalidate the duration of their confinement—either *directly* through an injunction compelling speedier release or *indirectly* through a judicial determination that necessarily implies the unlawfulness of the State's custody. Thus, *Preiser* found an implied exception to § 1983's coverage where the claim seeks—not where it simply "relates to"—"core" habeas corpus relief, *i.e.*, where a state prisoner requests present or future release. *Wolff* makes clear that § 1983 remains available for procedural challenges where success in the action *would not necessarily* spell immediate or speedier release for the prisoner. *Heck* specifies that a prisoner cannot use § 1983 to obtain damages where success *would necessarily* imply the unlawfulness of a (not previously invalidated) conviction or sentence. And *Balisok*, like *Wolff*, demonstrates that habeas remedies do not displace § 1983 actions where success in the civil rights suit would not necessarily vitiate the legality of (not previously invalidated) state confinement. These cases, taken together, indicate that a state prisoner's § 1983 action is barred (absent prior invalidation)—no matter the relief sought (damages or equitable relief), no matter the target of the prisoner's suit (state conduct leading to conviction or internal prison proceedings)—*if* success in that action would necessarily demonstrate the invalidity of confinement or its duration.

Id. at 81–82, 125 S.Ct. at 1247–48.

Applying the principles from these earlier cases, the Court found that, while the inmate plaintiffs were seeking to invalidate certain state procedures governing parole decisions, neither inmate sought injunctive relief that would necessarily lead to their immediate, or speedier, release from confinement. At most, they would receive new hearings relating to their eligibility or suitability for parole. Since the decision whether to release a prisoner on parole fell within the parole board's discretion, the hearings would not invariably result in a reduction in the length of their confinement. Consequently, the inmates could use § 1983 as a vehicle to challenge the parole procedures.

Assume that you are a member of Congress considering whether to redraw the current line between habeas corpus and § 1983 relief. What claims stemming from prison disciplinary, parole-release, and parole-revocation proceedings do you believe prisoners should be able to bring under § 1983?

3. ATTORNEY'S FEES

a. General Rules

The Civil Rights Attorney's Fees Awards Act of 1976, which is codified at 42 U.S.C. § 1988(b), provides that in § 1983 suits, as well as certain other suits to enforce federal statutes, "the court, in its discretion, may allow the prevailing party, other than the United States, a reasonable attorney's fee as part of the costs." The Religious Land Use and Institutionalized Persons Act, 42 U.S.C. §§ 2000cc to 2000cc–5, and the Religious Freedom Restoration Act, id. §§ 2000bb–2000bb–4, which were discussed on pages 531–33, are two of the federal statutes for whose enforcement a prevailing party can recover attorney's fees under § 1988. The Americans with Disabilities Act also authorizes a court, in its discretion, to award attorney's fees to the prevailing party. Id. § 12205. Finally, the Equal Access to Justice Act provides for the award of attorney's fees to the prevailing party in suits against the federal government and federal officials sued in their official capacity, unless a fee award is prohibited by another statute. 28 U.S.C. § 2412(b).

i. *Prevailing Party*

Section 1988 does not, on its face, require an award of attorney's fees to the prevailing party. Whether to award fees falls within the court's discretion. However, absent "special circumstances" that would make an award of fees "unjust," a prevailing plaintiff normally should be awarded attorney's fees. Hensley v. Eckerhart, 461 U.S. 424, 429, 103 S.Ct. 1933, 1937 (1983).

Despite § 1988's reference to prevailing parties, rather than prevailing plaintiffs, the Supreme Court has held that prevailing defendants sued under § 1983 normally should not recover attorney's fees from the plaintiff. Hughes v. Rowe, 449 U.S. 5, 14–15, 101 S.Ct. 173, 178–79 (1980) (per curiam). To permit fee awards against plaintiffs who bring suit under § 1983 would discourage the bringing of those suits and undermine the intent of § 1988 to encourage private enforcement of the civil-rights laws. Consequently, just because a plaintiff lost the case is not reason enough to award the defendant attorney's fees. Fees should be assessed against the plaintiff only when the plaintiff's case was " 'frivolous, unreasonable, or without foundation, even though not brought in subjective bad faith.' " Id. at 14, 101 S.Ct. at 178 (quoting Christiansburg Garment Co. v. EEOC, 434 U.S. 412, 421, 98 S.Ct. 694, 700 (1978)). And the Court has counseled special hesitancy before attorney's fees are assessed against prisoners who filed *pro se* civil-rights actions, because prisoners often will have particular difficulty understanding the factual and legal nuances of litigation. *Hughes*, 449 U.S. at 15, 101 S.Ct. at 178.

Proper application of § 1988 requires that the terms "prevailing party" and "reasonable attorney's fee" be defined. In Texas State Teachers Ass'n v. Garland Indep. Sch. Dist., 489 U.S. 782, 109 S.Ct. 1486 (1989), the Supreme Court concluded that a plaintiff should be considered a prevailing party if the plaintiff succeeded on " 'any significant issue in litigation which achieve[d] some of the benefit the parties sought in bringing suit.' " Id. at 791–92, 109 S.Ct. at 1493 (quoting Nadeau v. Helgemoe, 581 F.2d 275, 278–79 (1st Cir.1978)). The Court rejected the notion that the plaintiff must have prevailed on the "central issue" in the case in order to be considered the prevailing party.

Nor is it necessary for there to be a trial in the case for the plaintiff to be considered a prevailing party. In Maher v. Gagne, 448 U.S. 122, 100 S.Ct. 2570 (1980), the Supreme Court concluded that the plaintiffs were entitled to attorney's fees even though the case was settled through the entry of a consent decree. This holding is of especial significance to prisoners and their attorneys who litigate § 1983 suits, because a number of lawsuits challenging the conditions of confinement in correctional facilities culminate in the entry of consent decrees.

However, in Buckhannon Bd. & Care Home, Inc. v. West Virginia Dep't of Health & Human Res., 532 U.S. 598, 121 S.Ct. 1835 (2001), the Supreme Court rejected the so-called "catalyst theory" for awarding attorney's fees. The plaintiff, a corporation that operated assisted-living homes, brought an action to enjoin enforcement of portions of the West Virginia Code requiring that residents of such facilities be capable of "self-preservation"—capable of moving themselves from situations of imminent danger. The plaintiff claimed that these provisions violated several federal statutes, including the Americans with Disabilities Act. While the lawsuit was pending, the West Virginia legislature amended the relevant state statutes to eliminate the "self-preservation" requirement. The district court subsequently granted the state agency's motion to dismiss the complaint as moot. The plaintiff then moved for attorney's fees under the "catalyst theory," arguing that it was the "prevailing party" because its lawsuit had prompted the statutory modifications.

In a 5–4 opinion, the Supreme Court held that to be a "prevailing party" the plaintiff had to be awarded "some relief by the court," whether through a judgment on the merits or a settlement culminating in a judicially enforceable consent judgment. Id. at 603, 121 S.Ct. at 1839. Consequently, since one party's voluntary decision to alter its conduct did not constitute a "court-ordered 'chang[e] [in] the legal relationship' " between the parties, this conduct did not entitle the opposing party to obtain attorney's fees. Id. at 604, 121 S.Ct. at 1840.

The Court in *Buckhannon* noted that it interprets the various federal fee-shifting statutes similarly. The lower courts therefore have rejected application of the catalyst theory to support an award of attorney's fees in § 1983 suits. See, e.g., New York State Fed'n of Taxi Drivers, Inc. v. Westchester County Taxi & Limousine Comm'n, 272 F.3d 154, 158–59 (2d Cir. 2001). In your opinion, would incorporation of the catalyst theory into fee-shifting statutes aid or hamper the private enforcement of civil-rights laws?

ii. Reasonable Attorney's Fee

In calculating what constitutes a "reasonable attorney's fee" within the meaning of § 1988, what is known as the "lodestar" figure must first be computed. Hensley v. Eckerhart, 461 U.S. 424, 433, 103 S.Ct. 1933, 1939 (1983). This figure is derived from multiplying the hours "reasonably expended" on the litigation times a "reasonable" hourly rate. Id. If the parties cannot agree on the amount of fees to be paid the prevailing party, the party seeking fees has the burden of establishing the reasonableness of the hours expended on the case and the reasonableness of the hourly rate. Id. at 437, 103 S.Ct. at 1941.

After calculating the lodestar figure, a court can shift the fee award either upwards or downwards, depending on a number of factors. In Missouri v. Jenkins, 491 U.S. 274, 109 S.Ct. 2463 (1989), the Supreme Court held, for example, that in calculating a fee award under § 1988, a court can adjust the fee award to compensate the plaintiff's attorneys for any delay in receiving payment. In that case, the trial court had made this adjustment by using current market rates when calculating the lodestar figure rather than the prevailing hourly rates in effect when the attorneys had performed the work for their clients.

According to the Supreme Court, the risk of nonpayment that an attorney assumes when representing a client on a contingent-fee basis will not justify an upwards adjustment in a fee award. City of Burlington v. Dague, 505 U.S. 557, 112 S.Ct. 2638 (1992). But while the uncertainty that the attorney will recover fees will not justify enhancing the fee award, recovery of attorney's fees under § 1988 also is not limited by the amount that an attorney can recover under a contingent-fee agreement with the client. Blanchard v. Bergeron, 489 U.S. 87, 109 S.Ct. 939 (1989). What is a "reasonable" fee within the meaning of § 1988 might be more than, less than, or the same as the amount the attorney can recover under the fee agreement. At the same time, because of the terms of a contingent-fee agreement, a prevailing plaintiff in a § 1983 suit may have to pay the attorney more in fees than the plaintiff recovered under § 1988. Venegas v. Mitchell, 495 U.S. 82, 110 S.Ct. 1679 (1990) (plaintiff, who obtained a judgment for 2.08 million dollars and was awarded $117,000 in attorney's fees under § 1988, was bound by contingent-fee contract under which he had agreed to pay his attorney 40% of the gross amount of any money judgment awarded in his favor).

The Supreme Court has stated that the plaintiff's degree of success or lack of success in a case may warrant an increase or decrease in the fee award. *Hensley*, 461 U.S. at 434–36, 103 S.Ct. at 1940–41. Thus, in Farrar v. Hobby, 506 U.S. 103, 113 S.Ct. 566 (1992), the Court held that if a plaintiff recovers only nominal damages, the plaintiff, though technically a prevailing party, usually should not be awarded attorney's fees under § 1988. In a concurring opinion that provided the critical fifth vote for denying the fee award in *Farrar,* however, Justice O'Connor emphasized that not every award of nominal damages is *de minimis,* thereby warranting a denial of attorney's fees. In determining whether a plaintiff who has been awarded nominal damages should receive a fee award, Justice O'Connor said that courts must look at other factors besides the difference between the amount of damages the plaintiff sought and the nominal damages awarded. Two other factors that she identified were the significance of the legal issue on which the plaintiff had prevailed and the public purposes furthered by the lawsuit, such as the deterrence of future unconstitutional conduct.

A prevailing plaintiff can be compensated for the work of some nonlawyers as part of the attorney's fees awarded under § 1988. In *Missouri v. Jenkins,* 491 U.S. 274, 285, 109 S.Ct. 2463, 2470 (1989), the Supreme Court held that the work of paralegals and law clerks is compensable under § 1988. The fee award can also reimburse the plaintiff for the services of expert witnesses who helped in the successful preparation or presentation of the plaintiff's case. 42 U.S.C. § 1988(c).

b. Restrictions Under the Prison Litigation Reform Act

The Prison Litigation Reform Act placed special restrictions on the attorney's fees that can be awarded prisoners and pretrial detainees under 42 U.S.C. § 1988. See *Armstrong v. Davis,* 318 F.3d 965, 974 (9th Cir. 2003) (PLRA does not limit fees awarded under the Americans with Disabilities Act or the Rehabilitation Act, both of which contain their own fee-award provisions) For example, before the PLRA's enactment, the amount of attorney's fees awarded under § 1988 did not necessarily have to be proportionate to the amount of damages recovered by the plaintiff. See *City of Riverside v. Rivera,* 477 U.S. 561, 106 S.Ct. 2686 (1986) (rejecting proportionality requirement and approving $245,456.25 fee award in a case where the plaintiffs recovered $33,350 in damages). The PLRA now requires that the attorney's fees awarded inmates under § 1988 be "proportionately related" to the relief awarded. 42 U.S.C. § 1997e(d)(1)(B)(i).

In addition, the PLRA puts two specific caps on the attorney's fees awarded inmates under § 1988. First, when prisoners or pretrial detainees obtain a judgment for monetary relief, the fee award cannot exceed 150% of the monetary judgment. Id. § 1997e(d)(2). Thus, if a prisoner files a § 1983 suit for damages and is awarded $100, the fee award cannot exceed $150. In addition, a portion of the damages awarded the plaintiff—but no more that 25%—must be applied to the award of attorney's fees. Id. The defendant then pays the remainder of the fee award, up to the limit of 150% of the judgment. However, some courts have concluded that the 150% cap in 42 U.S.C. § 1997e(d)(2) does not constitute an absolute limit on attorney's fees when the prisoner has obtained *both* damages and injunctive relief. See *Dannenberg v. Valadez,* 338 F.3d 1070, 1075 (9th Cir. 2003) (listing cases).

The PLRA also caps the hourly rate utilized under § 1988 when calculating the lodestar figure in cases brought by inmates, including pretrial detainees. 42 U.S.C. § 1997e(d)(3). The hourly rate cannot exceed 150 percent of the hourly rate "established" under the Criminal Justice Act's (CJA) provisions in 18 U.S.C. § 3006A(d)(1) for the payment of court-appointed counsel in federal criminal cases. Under this statutory formula, the hourly rate used when computing the fee award cannot exceed $169.50. Gomez v. Reinke, 2008 WL 3200794, at *9 n.5 (D. Idaho 2008).

In your opinion, is the disparate treatment of prisoners compared to nonprisoners in the awarding of attorney's fees under § 1988 constitutional? Most courts have upheld the constitutionality of the PLRA's fee restrictions. See Johnson v. Daley, 339 F.3d 582, 583 (7th Cir. 2003) (listing cases). If the PLRA's fee restrictions are constitutional, are they advisable from a policy perspective?

B. MODIFYING COURT ORDERS

Like other types of lawsuits, many prisoners' civil-rights suits are settled before trial. In class-action suits, many of these settlement agreements are embodied in consent decrees, which, as mentioned earlier, are court orders that incorporate the terms of the parties' settlement agreements.

It is clear that consent decrees, like other court orders and judgments, sometimes can be modified. See Fed.R.Civ.P. 60(b). In the case that follows, the Supreme Court discussed when such modification would be appropriate in cases involving prisons, jails, or other public institutions.

RUFO v. INMATES OF THE SUFFOLK COUNTY JAIL

Supreme Court of the United States, 1992.
502 U.S. 367, 112 S.Ct. 748, 116 L.Ed.2d 867.

JUSTICE WHITE delivered the opinion of the Court.

* * *

I

This litigation began in 1971 when inmates sued the Suffolk County Sheriff, the Commissioner of Correction for the State of Massachusetts, the Mayor of Boston, and nine city councilors, claiming that inmates not yet convicted of the crimes charged against them were being held under unconstitutional conditions at what was then the Suffolk County Jail. * * *

The court permanently enjoined the government defendants: "(a) from housing at the Charles Street Jail after November 30, 1973 in a cell with another inmate, any inmate who is awaiting trial and (b) from housing at the Charles Street Jail after June 30, 1976 any inmate who is awaiting trial." The defendants did not appeal.

In 1977, with the problems of the Charles Street Jail still unresolved, the District Court ordered defendants, including the Boston City Council, to take such steps and expend the funds reasonably necessary to renovate another existing facility as a substitute detention center. The Court of Appeals agreed that immediate action was required. * * * The Court of Appeals ordered that the Charles Street Jail be closed on October 2, 1978, unless a plan was presented to create a constitutionally adequate facility for pretrial detainees in Suffolk County.

Four days before the deadline, the plan that formed the basis for the consent decree now before this Court was submitted to the District Court. * * * The court therefore allowed Suffolk County to continue housing its pretrial detainees at the Charles Street Jail.

Seven months later, the court entered a formal consent decree * * *. The decree specifically incorporated the provisions of the Suffolk County Detention Center, Charles Street Facility, Architectural Program, which— in the words of the consent decree—"sets forth a program which is both constitutionally adequate and constitutionally required."

Under the terms of the Architectural Program, the new jail was designed to include a total of 309 "[s]ingle occupancy rooms" of 70 square feet * * *. The size of the jail was based on a projected decline in inmate population, from 245 male prisoners in 1979 to 226 at present.

Although the Architectural Program projected that construction of the new jail would be completed by 1983, work on the new facility had not been started by 1984. During the intervening years, the inmate population outpaced population projections. Litigation in the state courts ensued, and defendants were ordered to build a larger jail. Thereupon, plaintiff prisoners, with the support of the sheriff, moved the District Court to modify the decree to provide a facility with 435 cells. Citing "the unanticipated increase in jail population and the delay in completing the jail," the District Court modified the decree to permit the capacity of the new jail to be increased in any amount, provided that:

> "(a) single-cell occupancy is maintained under the design for the facility;

* * *

> "(d) defendants act without delay and take all steps reasonably necessary to carry out the provisions of the Consent Decree according to the authorized schedule."

The number of cells was later increased to 453. Construction started in 1987.

In July 1989, while the new jail was still under construction, the sheriff moved to modify the consent decree to allow the double bunking of male detainees in 197 cells, thereby raising the capacity of the new jail to 610 male detainees * * *.

The District Court refused to grant the requested modification, holding that the sheriff had failed to meet the standard of *United States v. Swift & Co.,* 286 U.S. 106, 119 (1932):

> "Nothing less than a clear showing of grievous wrong evoked by new and unforeseen conditions should lead us to change what was decreed after years of litigation with the consent of all concerned." * * *

The District Court briefly stated that, even under the flexible modification standard adopted by other Courts of Appeals, the sheriff would not be entitled to relief because "[a] separate cell for each detainee has always been an important element of the relief sought in this litigation—perhaps even the most important element." * * *

The new Suffolk County Jail opened shortly thereafter.

The Court of Appeals affirmed * * *.

II

In moving for modification of the decree, the sheriff relied on Federal Rule of Civil Procedure 60(b), which in relevant part provides:

> "On motion and upon such terms as are just, the court may relieve a party or a party's legal representative from a final judgment, order, or proceeding for the following reasons: . . . (5) the judgment has been satisfied, released, or discharged, or a prior judgment upon which it is based has been reversed or otherwise vacated, or it is no longer equitable that the judgment should have prospective application; or (6) any other reason justifying relief from the operation of the judgment. . . ."

* * *

There is * * * little basis for concluding that Rule 60(b) * * * intended that modifications of consent decrees in all cases were to be governed by the standard actually applied in *Swift*. That Rule, in providing that, on such terms as are just, a party may be relieved from a final judgment or decree where it is no longer equitable that the judgment have prospective application, permits a less stringent, more flexible standard.

The upsurge in institutional reform litigation since *Brown v. Board of Education,* 347 U.S. 483 (1954), has made the ability of a district court to modify a decree in response to changed circumstances all the more important. Because such decrees often remain in place for extended periods of time, the likelihood of significant changes occurring during the life of the decree is increased.

* * *

III

Although we hold that a district court should exercise flexibility in considering requests for modification of an institutional reform consent decree, it does not follow that a modification will be warranted in all circumstances. Rule 60(b)(5) provides that a party may obtain relief from a court order when "it is no longer equitable that the judgment should have prospective application," not when it is no longer convenient to live with the terms of a consent decree. Accordingly, a party seeking modification of a consent decree bears the burden of establishing that a significant change in circumstances warrants revision of the decree. If the moving party meets this standard, the court should consider whether the proposed modification is suitably tailored to the changed circumstance.[7]

A

A party seeking modification of a consent decree may meet its initial burden by showing either a significant change in factual conditions or in law.

1

Modification of a consent decree may be warranted when changed factual conditions make compliance with the decree substantially more onerous. Such a modification was approved by the District Court in this litigation in 1985 when it became apparent that plans for the new jail did not provide sufficient cell space. Modification is also appropriate when a decree proves to be unworkable because of unforeseen obstacles, *New York State Assn. for Retarded Children, Inc. v. Carey*, 706 F.2d [956], at 969 [CA2 1983] (modification allowed where State could not find appropriate housing facilities for transfer patients); or when enforcement of the decree without modification would be detrimental to the public interest, *Duran v. Elrod*, 760 F.2d 756, 759–761 (C.A.7 1985) (modification allowed to avoid pretrial release of accused violent felons).

Respondents urge that modification should be allowed only when a change in facts is both "unforeseen and unforeseeable." Such a standard would provide even less flexibility than the exacting *Swift* test; we decline to adopt it. Litigants are not required to anticipate every exigency that could conceivably arise during the life of a consent decree.

Ordinarily, however, modification should not be granted where a party relies upon events that actually were anticipated at the time it entered into a decree. If it is clear that a party anticipated changing conditions that would make performance of the decree more onerous but

---

7. The standard we set forth applies when a party seeks modification of a term of a consent decree that arguably relates to the vindication of a constitutional right. Such a showing is not necessary to implement minor changes in extraneous details that may have been included in a decree (*e.g.*, paint color or design of a building's facade) but are unrelated to remedying the underlying constitutional violation. Ordinarily, the parties should consent to modifying a decree to allow such changes. If a party refuses to consent and the moving party has a reasonable basis for its request, the court should modify the decree. * * * Of course, the necessity of changing a decree to allow insignificant changes could be avoided by not entering an overly detailed decree.

nevertheless agreed to the decree, that party would have to satisfy a heavy burden to convince a court that it agreed to the decree in good faith, made a reasonable effort to comply with the decree, and should be relieved of the undertaking under Rule 60(b).

Accordingly, on remand the District Court should consider whether the upsurge in the Suffolk County inmate population was foreseen by the petitioners. * * *

Even if the decree is construed as an undertaking by petitioners to provide single cells for pretrial detainees, to relieve petitioners from that promise based on changed conditions does not necessarily violate the basic purpose of the decree. That purpose was to provide a remedy for what had been found, based on a variety of factors, including double celling, to be unconstitutional conditions obtaining in the Charles Street Jail. If modification of one term of a consent decree defeats the purpose of the decree, obviously modification would be all but impossible. That cannot be the rule. * * *

2

A consent decree must of course be modified if, as it later turns out, one or more of the obligations placed upon the parties has become impermissible under federal law. But modification of a consent decree may be warranted when the statutory or decisional law has changed to make legal what the decree was designed to prevent.

* * *

Petitioner Rapone urges that, without more, our 1979 decision in *Bell v. Wolfish,* 441 U.S. 520 (1979), was a change in law requiring modification of the decree governing construction of the Suffolk County Jail. We disagree. *Bell* made clear what the Court had not before announced: that double celling is not in all cases unconstitutional. But it surely did not cast doubt on the legality of single celling, and petitioners were undoubtedly aware that *Bell* was pending when they signed the decree. Thus, the case must be judged on the basis that it was immaterial to petitioners that double celling might be ruled constitutional, *i.e.,* they preferred even in that event to agree to a decree which called for providing only single cells in the jail to be built.

Neither *Bell* nor the Federal Constitution forbade this course of conduct. Federal courts may not order States or local governments, over their objection, to undertake a course of conduct not tailored to curing a constitutional violation that has been adjudicated. But we have no doubt that, to "save themselves the time, expense, and inevitable risk of litigation," petitioners could settle the dispute over the proper remedy for the constitutional violations that had been found by undertaking to do more than the Constitution itself requires (almost any affirmative decree beyond a directive to obey the Constitution necessarily does that), but also more than what a court would have ordered absent the settlement. Accordingly, the District Court did not abuse its discretion in entering the agreed-upon decree, which clearly was related to the conditions found to offend the Constitution.

To hold that a clarification in the law automatically opens the door for relitigation of the merits of every affected consent decree would undermine the finality of such agreements and could serve as a disincentive to negotiation of settlements in institutional reform litigation. * * *

While a decision that clarifies the law will not, in and of itself, provide a basis for modifying a decree, it could constitute a change in circumstances that would support modification if the parties had based their agreement on a misunderstanding of the governing law. For instance, * * * in *Nelson v. Collins,* 659 F.2d 420, 428–429 (C.A.4 1981) (en banc), the Fourth Circuit vacated an equitable order that was based on the assumption that double bunking of prisoners was *per se* unconstitutional.

Thus, if the Sheriff and Commissioner could establish on remand that the parties to the consent decree believed that single celling of pretrial detainees was mandated by the Constitution, this misunderstanding of the law could form a basis for modification. * * *

B

Once a moving party has met its burden of establishing either a change in fact or in law warranting modification of a consent decree, the District Court should determine whether the proposed modification is suitably tailored to the changed circumstance. In evaluating a proposed modification, three matters should be clear.

Of course, a modification must not create or perpetuate a constitutional violation. Petitioners contend that double celling inmates at the Suffolk County Jail would be constitutional under *Bell.* Respondents counter that *Bell* is factually distinguishable and that double celling at the new jail would violate the constitutional rights of pretrial detainees. If this is the case—the District Court did not decide this issue—modification should not be granted.

A proposed modification should not strive to rewrite a consent decree so that it conforms to the constitutional floor. Once a court has determined that changed circumstances warrant a modification in a consent decree, the focus should be on whether the proposed modification is tailored to resolve the problems created by the change in circumstances. A court should do no more, for a consent decree is a final judgment that may be reopened only to the extent that equity requires. * * *

Within these constraints, the public interest and "[c]onsiderations based on the allocation of powers within our federal system" require that the district court defer to local government administrators, who have the "primary responsibility for elucidating, assessing, and solving" the problems of institutional reform, to resolve the intricacies of implementing a decree modification.[14] Although state and local officers in charge of

14. The concurrence mischaracterizes the nature of the deference that we would accord local government administrators. As we have stated, the moving party bears the burden of establishing

institutional litigation may agree to do more than that which is minimally required by the Constitution to settle a case and avoid further litigation, a court should surely keep the public interest in mind in ruling on a request to modify based on a change in conditions making it substantially more onerous to abide by the decree. To refuse modification of a decree is to bind all future officers of the State, regardless of their view of the necessity of relief from one or more provisions of a decree that might not have been entered had the matter been litigated to its conclusion. The District Court seemed to be of the view that the problems of the fiscal officers of the State were only marginally relevant to the request for modification in this case. Financial constraints may not be used to justify the creation or perpetuation of constitutional violations, but they are a legitimate concern of government defendants in institutional reform litigation and therefore are appropriately considered in tailoring a consent decree modification.

IV

To conclude, we hold that the *Swift* "grievous wrong" standard does not apply to requests to modify consent decrees stemming from institutional reform litigation. Under the flexible standard we adopt today, a party seeking modification of a consent decree must establish that a significant change in facts or law warrants revision of the decree and that the proposed modification is suitably tailored to the changed circumstance. * * *

JUSTICE O'CONNOR, concurring in the judgment.

I agree that these cases should be remanded so that the District Court may reconsider whether to modify the decree. I write separately to emphasize the limited nature of our review; to clarify why, despite our limited review, the cases should be returned to the District Court; and to explain my concerns with certain portions of the Court's opinion.

I

A court may modify a final judgment, such as the judgment embodied in the consent decree at issue, where the court finds that "it is no longer equitable that the judgment should have prospective application." Fed. Rule Civ.Proc. 60(b)(5). Determining what is "equitable" is necessarily a task that entails substantial discretion, particularly in a case like this one, where the District Court must make complex decisions requiring the sensitive balancing of a host of factors. As a result, an appellate court should examine primarily the *method* in which the District Court exercises its discretion, not the substantive outcome the District Court reaches. If the District Court takes into account the relevant considerations (all of

---

that a significant change in circumstances warrants modification of a consent decree. No deference is involved in this threshold inquiry. However, once a court has determined that a modification is warranted, we think that principles of federalism and simple common sense require the court to give significant weight to the views of the local government officials who must implement any modification.

which are not likely to suggest the same result), and accommodates them in a reasonable way, then the District Court's judgment will not be an abuse of its discretion, regardless of whether an appellate court would have reached the same outcome in the first instance.

Our deference to the District Court's exercise of its discretion is heightened where, as in this litigation, the District Court has effectively been overseeing a large public institution over a long period of time. Judge Keeton has been supervising the implementation of this decree since 1979; he has developed an understanding of the difficulties involved in constructing and managing a jail that an appellate court, even with the best possible briefing, could never hope to match. * * *

* * *

II

In my view, the District Court took too narrow a view of its own discretion. The court's reasoning, as expressed in its opinion, was flawed by three different errors of law, each of which excised a portion of the range of options available to the court. I believe the sum of these erroneously self-imposed limits constituted an abuse of the court's discretion.

First, * * * that overcrowding was foreseen should not have been a dispositive factor in the court's decision. Modification could conceivably still be "equitable" under Rule 60(b)(5) even if the rise in inmate population had been foreseen; the danger to the community from the pretrial release of inmates, for example, might outweigh the petitioners' failure to accommodate even a foreseen increase in the inmate population.

Second, the District Court concluded that it lacked the authority to consider the petitioners' budget constraints in determining whether modification would be equitable. * * * While the lack of resources can never excuse a failure to obey constitutional requirements, it *can* provide a basis for concluding that continued compliance with a decree obligation is no longer "equitable," if, for instance, the obligation turns out to be significantly more expensive than anyone anticipated.

Third, although the District Court purported to apply the "flexible standard" proposed by the petitioners, the court denied modification because "[t]he type of modification sought here would not comply with the overall purpose of the consent decree; it would set aside the obligations of that decree." Taken literally, this conclusion deprives the "flexible standard" of any meaning; every modification, by definition, will alter an obligation of a decree. * * *

* * *

III

* * * Portions of the Court's opinion might be read to place new constraints on the District Court's discretion that are, in my view, just as

misplaced as the ones with which the District Court fettered itself the first time.

* * *

* * * It may be that the modification of one term of a decree does not *always* defeat the purpose of the decree. But it hardly follows that the modification of a single term can *never* defeat the decree's purpose, especially if that term is "the most important element" of the decree. If, for instance, the District Court finds that the respondents would never have consented to the decree (and a decade of delay in obtaining relief) without a guarantee of single celling, I should think that the court would not abuse its discretion were it to conclude that modification to permit double celling would be inequitable. Similarly, were the court to find that the jail was constructed with small cells on the assumption that each cell would hold but one inmate, I doubt that the District Court would exceed its authority under Rule 60(b)(5) by concluding that it would be inequitable to double cell the respondents. To the extent the Court suggests otherwise, it limits the District Court's discretion in what I think is an unwarranted and ill-advised fashion.

The same is true of the Court's statement that the District Court should "defer to local government administrators ... to resolve the intricacies of implementing a decree modification." To be sure, the courts should defer to prison administrators in resolving the day-to-day problems in managing a prison; these problems fall within the expertise of prison officials. But I disagree with the notion that courts must defer to prison administrators in resolving whether and how to modify a consent decree. These questions may involve details of prison management, but at bottom they require a determination of what is "equitable" to all concerned. Deference to one of the parties to a lawsuit is usually not the surest path to equity; deference to these particular petitioners, who do not have a model record of compliance with previous court orders in this case, is particularly unlikely to lead to an equitable result. * * *

JUSTICE STEVENS, with whom JUSTICE BLACKMUN joins, dissenting.

Today the Court endorses the standard for modification of consent decrees articulated by Judge Friendly in *New York State Association for Retarded Children, Inc. v. Carey,* 706 F.2d 956 (C.A.2 1983). I agree with that endorsement, but under that standard I believe the findings of the District Court in this action require affirmance of its order refusing to modify this consent decree.

* * *

From respondents' point of view, even though they had won their case, they might reasonably be prepared to surrender some of the relief to which they were unquestionably entitled—such as enforcing the deadline on closing the Charles Street Jail—in exchange for other benefits to be included in an appropriate remedy, even if each such benefit might not be constitutionally required. * * * In fact, in this action it is apparent that the two overriding purposes that informed both the District Court's interim remedy and the respondents' negotiations were the prohibition against double celling and the closing of the old jail. * * *

* * *

The increase in the average number of pretrial detainees is, of course, a change of fact. Because the size of that increase had not been anticipated in 1979, it was appropriate to modify the decree in 1985. But in 1985, the steady progression in the detainee population surely made it foreseeable that this growth would continue. The District Court's finding that "the overcrowding problem faced by the Sheriff is neither new nor unforeseen" is amply supported by the record.

Even if the continuing increase in inmate population had not actually been foreseen, it was reasonably foreseeable. Mere foreseeability in the sense that it was an event that "could conceivably arise" during the life of the consent decree should not, of course, disqualify an unanticipated development from justifying a modification. But the parties should be charged with notice of those events that reasonably prudent litigants would contemplate when negotiating a settlement. * * *

Other important concerns counsel against modification of this consent decree. Petitioners' history of noncompliance after the 1973 injunction provides an added reason for insisting that they honor their most recent commitments. * * *

The strong public interest in protecting the finality of court decrees always counsels against modifications. In the context of a consent decree, this interest is reinforced by the policy favoring the settlement of protracted litigation. To the extent that litigants are allowed to avoid their solemn commitments, the motivation for particular settlements will be compromised, and the reliability of the entire process will suffer.

It is particularly important to apply a strict standard when considering modification requests that undermine the central purpose of a consent decree. * * * [T]o recognize that *some* terms are so critical that their modification would thwart the central purpose of the decree does not render the decree immutable, but rather assures that a modification will frustrate neither the legitimate expectations of the parties nor the core remedial goals of the decree.

After a judicial finding of [a] constitutional violation, petitioners were ordered in 1973 to place pretrial detainees in single cells. In return for certain benefits, petitioners committed themselves in 1979 to continued compliance with the single-celling requirement. They reaffirmed this promise in 1985. It was clearly not an abuse of discretion for the District Court to require petitioners to honor this commitment.

* * *

QUESTIONS AND POINTS FOR DISCUSSION

1. In recent years, many government officials have tried to extricate themselves from obligations assumed or imposed in consent decrees or other court judgments. In the following article, a litigator who represents inmates in civil-rights suits discusses steps that inmates' attorneys can take to thwart such modification attempts:

The *Rufo* decision makes clearer what most institutional litigators have already begun to realize: the outcome of a motion to modify may have more to do with what happens during the formulation and entry of the judgment than with the modification proceedings themselves. Whether a changed circumstance was foreseen, whether a decree provision "relates to the vindication of a constitutional right" or is an "extraneous detail," and whether the parties proceeded on a "misunderstanding of the governing law" are all questions that refer back to the parties' intentions and state of knowledge when the decree was agreed to.

Plaintiffs' counsel should therefore proceed with the dangers of modification in mind and make the record necessary to defend future motions to modify. This should be done both with consent decrees and with injunctions entered after trial and decision.

Ideally, a consent judgment should itself address some of these issues, stating the relationship of the remedial provisions to claimed constitutional violations insofar as practicable, and identifying those compliance problems that are foreseeable. For example, some consent judgments specifically identify population increases as foreseen contingencies that do not justify modification; others address the possibility that affected populations will be transferred to different or newly constructed facilities.

In most cases it will be difficult to negotiate, or even draft, a judgment that adequately addresses all these issues, so counsel will need another forum in which to do so.

Most institutional reform cases are class actions. An appropriate forum for making a record sufficient to oppose modification is created by Rule 23(e), Fed.R.Civ.Pro., which provides that class actions "shall not be dismissed or compromised without the approval of the court." The Rule is silent concerning the requirements for such approval, but case law indicates that the district court must determine whether the proposed settlement is "fair, adequate, and reasonable" to class members, and the trend appears to be towards more formal proceedings and more thorough explorations of those questions.

The Rule 23(e) proceeding and the "fair, adequate and reasonable" inquiry neatly fit the need of plaintiffs' counsel to create a sort of "legislative history" of the consent judgment to inform future modification proceedings. The word "inform" is used advisedly, since such proceedings will often take place before a different judge from the one who approved the settlement and may be conducted by different counsel on both sides as well. Plaintiffs' counsel should present the court with an explanation of the judgment's terms, in writing or orally on the record, combining argument and evidence as required to make the point. An affidavit or declaration by counsel, supported by excerpts of depositions, documents obtained during discovery, and an expert's report, prepared either for trial or specifically in support of the consent judgment, is probably the most appropriate vehicle. A rationale should be presented for each provision of the consent judgment, explaining its relationship to the protection of constitutional rights. In particular, provisions that might seem "extraneous detail" to someone with less familiarity with the institution and its problems than plaintiffs' counsel should be explained. Counsel should also state their understanding of the relevant law, but do so in the most general terms with which they are comfortable, to avoid future claims that the parties proceeded under a "misunderstanding" of the applicable law or that subsequent decisions represent more than a "clarification" of that law. Counsel should also "foresee" everything they can, discussing the possibility of population increases and disavowing any reliance on the defendants' Pollyannish predictions, and identifying the possibility or likelihood of cost overruns, construction delays, and the other predictable disasters that prison officials like to pretend that they never thought about. One would think that such a pose by defendants would seem untenable on a subsequent motion to modify if there is a contemporaneous document in the case file predicting the kind of scenario from which the defendants seek relief.

The same principle applies to cases that are tried on the merits, though the existence of a trial record makes the job easier. In some cases, the court's findings of fact and conclusions of law may be sufficient support for an adequate remedy. But that is rarely true in cases involving technical issues or large institutions. For example, most institutional litigators understand that reforming a medical care system generally requires some form of quality assurance or other self-auditing procedure. Similarly, the control of misuse of force or the maintenance of sanitary conditions may require changes in staffing patterns, administrative reporting requirements, or other devices that may seem unnecessarily intrusive if unexplained.

Some courts may require an evidentiary hearing on remedy, resulting in the creation of the necessary remedial record. Even if a hearing is not required, plaintiffs' counsel should consider asking for one if the evidence to support plaintiffs' remedial proposals is not already in the trial record. (In some cases this purpose may be accomplished by submitting additional documentation or affidavits.) If the trial record is sufficient, counsel should marshall it appropriately to support the remedial terms sought. A handy device for this purpose is the annotated proposal order, in which every remedial paragraph is followed by an explanation of its necessity, supported by citations to relevant parts of the record.

All this makes for more work for the plaintiffs' attorney, especially in cases that are settled. In reality, though, the work will probably have to be done sometime, and it's easier to do it when the case is fresh than to engage in reconstruction years later.

John Boston, Case Law Report, 7 National Prison Project Journal, No. 2, at 8 (Spring 1992) (Reprinted with the permission of the Journal of the ACLU National Prison Project).

2. Many of the court orders designed to rectify unconstitutional conditions in a correctional facility govern numerous aspects of the facility's operations. When correctional officials bring a facility into compliance with the Constitution in certain areas, a court may properly withdraw its supervision of those areas while continuing to oversee facets of the facility's operations that do not yet satisfy constitutional standards.

In Freeman v. Pitts, 503 U.S. 467, 112 S.Ct. 1430 (1992), the Supreme Court approved such partial withdrawal of court supervision in a case involving enforcement of a court's desegregation decree. The Court emphasized, however, that a court's discretion to partially withdraw its supervision "must be exercised in a manner consistent with the purposes and objectives of its equitable power." Id. at 491, 112 S.Ct. at 1446. Factors to be considered by a court contemplating partial withdrawal of judicial supervision include: whether compliance with the court's orders in areas in which supervision is to be withdrawn has been "full and satisfactory"; whether judicial supervision in these areas is a necessary or practicable way of ensuring compliance with the court's orders in other areas; and whether government officials have demonstrated a commitment to operate their facilities in conformance with the Constitution. Id.

In a concurring opinion in *Freeman,* Justice Souter emphasized that when a court decides to end its active supervision of some areas covered by a court decree, the court still retains jurisdiction in the case. If constitutional problems later develop in the areas in which judicial supervision has been withdrawn, the court can then reassume active supervision of those areas.

3. A court can go one step further than withdrawing its supervision over some aspects of a case by dissolving an injunction and terminating the court's jurisdiction over the case. In Board of Educ. v. Dowell, 498 U.S. 237, 111 S.Ct. 630 (1991), another school-desegregation case, the Supreme Court observed that dissolution of a court decree would be appropriate when the purposes of the litigation, as reflected in the court's decree, had been "fully achieved." Id. at 247, 111 S.Ct. at 636–37. This requirement would be met, according to the Court, if the district court found both that the institution in question now was being operated in conformance with the Constitution and that it was unlikely that the defendants would resume their unconstitutional conduct. On this latter issue, the Supreme Court cautioned that a district court need not necessarily believe the protestations of defendants that they will desist from future unconstitutional conduct. Instead, the district court can, and should, examine the extent to which, thus far, the defendants have complied in good faith with the court's orders.

4. The Prison Litigation Reform Act modified the standards governing the termination of equitable relief in conditions-of-confinement cases. The new standards, found in 18 U.S.C. § 3626, are set forth below:

§ 3626.　Appropriate remedies with respect to prison conditions.

(b) Termination of relief.—

(1) Termination of prospective relief.—

(A) In any civil action with respect to prison conditions in which prospective relief is ordered, such relief shall be terminable upon the motion of any party or intervener—

(i) 2 years after the date the court granted or approved the prospective relief;

(ii) 1 year after the date the court has entered an order denying termination of prospective relief under this paragraph; or

(iii) in the case of an order issued on or before the date of enactment of the Prison Litigation Reform Act, 2 years after such date of enactment.

(B) Nothing in this section shall prevent the parties from agreeing to terminate or modify relief before the relief is terminated under subparagraph (A).

(2) Immediate termination of prospective relief.—In any civil action with respect to prison conditions, a defendant or intervener shall be entitled to the immediate termination of any prospective relief if the relief was approved or granted in the absence of a finding by the court that the relief is narrowly drawn, extends no further than necessary to correct the violation of the Federal right, and is the least intrusive means necessary to correct the violation of the Federal right.

(3) Limitation.—Prospective relief shall not terminate if the court makes written findings based on the record that prospective relief remains necessary to correct a current and ongoing violation of the Federal right, extends no further than necessary to correct the violation of the Federal right, and that the prospective relief is narrowly drawn and the least intrusive means to correct the violation.

(4) Termination or modification of relief.—Nothing in this section shall prevent any party or intervener from seeking modification or termination before the relief is terminable under paragraph (1) or (2), to the extent that modification or termination would otherwise be legally permissible.

* * *

(e) Procedure for motions affecting prospective relief.—

(1) Generally.—The court shall promptly rule on any motion to modify or terminate prospective relief in a civil action with respect to prison conditions. Mandamus shall lie to remedy any failure to issue a prompt ruling on such a motion.

(2) Automatic stay.—Any motion to modify or terminate prospective relief made under subsection (b) shall operate as a stay during the period—

(A) (i) beginning on the 30th day after such motion is filed, in the case of a motion made under paragraph (1) or (2) of subsection (b); or

(ii) beginning on the 180th day after such motion is filed, in the case of a motion made under any other law; and

(B) ending on the date the court enters a final order ruling on the motion.

(3) Postponement of automatic stay.— The court may postpone the effective date of an automatic stay specified in subsection (e)(2)(A) for not more than 60 days for good cause. No postponement shall be permissible because of general congestion of the court's calendar.

* * *

Are any parts of § 3626, in your opinion, unconstitutional? When you read the following Supreme Court case, consider whether your views are altered or affirmed by the Supreme Court's analysis of the constitutionality of the PLRA's automatic-stay provision.

MILLER v. FRENCH

Supreme Court of the United States, 2000.
530 U.S. 327, 120 S.Ct. 2246, 147 L.Ed.2d 326.

JUSTICE O'CONNOR delivered the opinion of the Court.

The Prison Litigation Reform Act * * * establishes standards for the entry and termination of prospective relief in civil actions challenging prison conditions. If prospective relief under an existing injunction does not satisfy these standards, a defendant or intervenor is entitled to "immediate termination" of that relief. 18 U.S.C. § 3626(b)(2). And under the PLRA's "automatic stay" provision, a motion to terminate prospective relief "shall operate as a stay" of that relief during the period beginning 30 days after the filing of the motion (extendable to up to 90 days for "good cause") and ending when the court rules on the motion. §§ 3626(e)(2), (3). The superintendent of the Pendleton Correctional Facility, which is currently operating under an ongoing injunction to remedy violations of the Eighth Amendment regarding conditions of confinement, filed a motion to terminate prospective relief under the PLRA. Respondent prisoners moved to enjoin the operation of the automatic stay provision of § 3626(e)(2), arguing that it is unconstitutional. The District Court enjoined the stay, and the Court of Appeals for the Seventh Circuit affirmed. We must decide whether a district court may enjoin the operation of the PLRA's automatic stay provision and, if not, whether that provision violates separation of powers principles.

* * *

II

We address the statutory question first. Both the State and the prisoner class agree, as did the majority and dissenting judges below, that

§ 3626(e)(2) precludes a district court from exercising its equitable powers to enjoin the automatic stay. The Government argues, however, that § 3626(e)(2) should be construed to leave intact the federal courts' traditional equitable discretion to "stay the stay" * * *. * * *

* * *

Such an interpretation, however, would subvert the plain meaning of the statute, making its mandatory language merely permissive. Section 3626(e)(2) states that a motion to terminate prospective relief *"shall operate* as a stay *during"* the specified time period from 30 (or 90) days after the filing of the § 3626(b) motion *until* the court rules on that motion. Thus, not only does the statute employ the mandatory term "shall," but it also specifies the points at which the operation of the stay is to begin and end. * * * To allow courts to exercise their equitable discretion to prevent the stay from "operating" during this statutorily prescribed period would be to contradict § 3626(e)(2)'s plain terms. * * *

* * *

III

* * *

Respondent prisoners contend that § 3626(e)(2) encroaches on the central prerogatives of the Judiciary and thereby violates the separation of powers doctrine. * * * According to the prisoners, the remedial order governing living conditions at the Pendleton Correctional Facility is a final judgment of an Article III court, and § 3626(e)(2) constitutes an impermissible usurpation of judicial power because it commands the district court to suspend prospective relief under that order, albeit temporarily. * * * See *Plaut,* [*v. Spendthrift Farm, Inc.,* 514 U.S. 211], at 226 [1995] (quoting *Hayburn's Case,* [2 Dall. 409], 413 [1792] (opinion of Iredell, J., and Sitgreaves, D.J.) (" '[N]o decision of any court of the United States can, under any circumstances, . . . be liable to a revision, or even suspension, by the [l]egislature itself, in whom no judicial power of any kind appears to be vested' ")). In *Plaut,* we held that a federal statute that required federal courts to reopen final judgments that had been entered before the statute's enactment was unconstitutional on separation of powers grounds. The plaintiffs had brought a civil securities fraud action seeking money damages. While that action was pending, we ruled in *Lampf, Pleva, Lipkind, Prupis & Petigrow v. Gilbertson,* 501 U.S. 350 (1991), that such suits must be commenced within one year after the discovery of the facts constituting the violation and within three years after such violation. In light of this intervening decision, the *Plaut* plaintiffs' suit was untimely, and the District Court accordingly dismissed the action as time barred. After the judgment dismissing the case had become final, Congress enacted a statute providing for the reinstatement of those actions, including the *Plaut* plaintiffs', that had been dismissed under *Lampf* but that would have been timely under the previously applicable statute of limitations.

We concluded that this retroactive command that federal courts reopen final judgments exceeded Congress' authority. The decision of an inferior court within the Article III hierarchy is not the final word of the department (unless the time for appeal has expired), and "[i]t is the obligation of the last court in the hierarchy that rules on the case to give effect to Congress's latest enactment, even when that has the effect of overturning the judgment of an inferior court, since each court, at every level, must 'decide according to existing laws.'" But once a judicial decision achieves finality, it "becomes the last word of the judicial department." And because Article III "gives the Federal Judiciary the power, not merely to rule on cases, but to *decide* them, subject to review only by superior courts in the Article III hierarchy," the "judicial Power is one to render dispositive judgments," and Congress cannot retroactively command Article III courts to reopen final judgments.

Plaut, however, was careful to distinguish the situation before the Court in that case—legislation that attempted to reopen the dismissal of a suit seeking money damages—from legislation that "altered the prospective effect of injunctions entered by Article III courts." We emphasized that "nothing in our holding today calls ... into question" Congress' authority to alter the prospective effect of previously entered injunctions. Prospective relief under a continuing, executory decree remains subject to alteration due to changes in the underlying law. This conclusion follows from our decisions in *Pennsylvania v. Wheeling & Belmont Bridge Co.*, 54 U.S. (13 How.) 518 (1851) (*Wheeling Bridge I*) and *Pennsylvania v. Wheeling & Belmont Bridge Co.*, 59 U.S. (18 How.) 421 (1855) (*Wheeling Bridge II*).

In *Wheeling Bridge I*, we held that a bridge across the Ohio River, because it was too low, unlawfully "obstruct[ed] the navigation of the Ohio," and ordered that the bridge be raised or permanently removed. Shortly thereafter, Congress enacted legislation declaring the bridge to be [a] "lawful structur[e]," establishing the bridge as a " 'post-roa[d] for the passage of the mails of the United States,' " and declaring that the Wheeling and Belmont Bridge Company was authorized to maintain the bridge at its then-current site and elevation. After the bridge was destroyed in a storm, Pennsylvania sued to enjoin the bridge's reconstruction, arguing that the statute legalizing the bridge was unconstitutional because it effectively annulled the Court's decision in *Wheeling Bridge I*. * * * Because the intervening statute altered the underlying law such that the bridge was no longer an unlawful obstruction, we held that it was "quite plain the decree of the court cannot be enforced." The Court explained that had *Wheeling Bridge I* awarded money damages in an action at law, then that judgment would be final, and Congress' later action could not have affected plaintiff's right to those damages. But because the decree entered in *Wheeling Bridge I* provided for prospective relief—a continuing injunction against the continuation or reconstruction of the bridge—the ongoing validity of the injunctive relief depended on "whether or not [the bridge] interferes with the right of navigation." When Congress altered the underlying law such that the bridge was no longer an unlawful obstruction, the injunction against the maintenance of the bridge was not enforceable.

Applied here, the principles of *Wheeling Bridge II* demonstrate that the automatic stay of § 3626(e)(2) does not unconstitutionally "suspend" or reopen a judgment of an Article III court. Section § 3626(e)(2) does not by itself "tell judges when, how, or what to do." Instead, § 3626(e)(2) merely reflects the change implemented by § 3626(b), which does the "heavy lifting" in the statutory scheme by establishing new standards for prospective relief. Section 3626 prohibits the continuation of prospective relief that was "approved or granted in the absence of a finding by the court that the relief is narrowly drawn, extends no further than necessary to correct the violation of the Federal right, and is the least intrusive means to correct the violation," § 3626(b)(2), or in the absence of "findings based on the record that prospective relief remains necessary to correct a current and ongoing violation of a Federal right, extends no further than necessary to correct the violation of the Federal right, and that the prospective relief is narrowly drawn and the least intrusive means necessary to correct the violation," § 3626(b)(3). Accordingly, if prospective relief under an existing decree had been granted or approved absent such findings, then that prospective relief must cease unless and until the court makes findings on the record that such relief remains necessary to correct an ongoing violation and is narrowly tailored. The PLRA's automatic stay provision assists in the enforcement of §§ 3626(b)(2) and (3) by requiring the court to stay any prospective relief that, due to the change in the underlying standard, is no longer enforceable, *i.e.*, prospective relief that is not supported by the findings specified in §§ 3626(b)(2) and (3).

* * *

* * * We note that the constitutionality of § 3626(b) is not challenged here; we assume, without deciding, that the new standards it pronounces are effective. As *Plaut* and *Wheeling Bridge II* instruct, when Congress changes the law underlying a judgment awarding prospective relief, that relief is no longer enforceable to the extent it is inconsistent with the new law. Although the remedial injunction here is a "final judgment" for purposes of appeal, it is not the "last word of the judicial department." The provision of prospective relief is subject to the continuing supervisory jurisdiction of the court, and therefore may be altered according to subsequent changes in the law. See *Rufo v. Inmates of Suffolk County Jail*, 502 U.S. 367, 388 (1992). Prospective relief must be "modified if, as it later turns out, one or more of the obligations placed upon the parties has become impermissible under federal law."

* * * [T]he stay merely reflects the changed legal circumstances—that prospective relief under the existing decree is no longer enforceable, and remains unenforceable unless and until the court makes the findings required by § 3626(b)(3).

* * *

Finally, the prisoners assert that * * * § 3626(e)(2) * * * still offends the principles of separation of powers because it places a deadline on judicial decisionmaking, thereby interfering with core judicial functions. Congress' imposition of a time limit in § 3626(e)(2), however, does not in itself offend the structural concerns underlying the Constitution's separation of powers. For example, if the PLRA granted courts 10 years to determine whether they could make the required findings, then certainly the PLRA would raise no apprehensions that Congress had encroached on the core function of the Judiciary to decide "cases and controversies properly before them." Respondents' concern with the time limit, then, must be its relative brevity. But whether the time is so short that it deprives litigants of a meaningful opportunity to be heard is a due process question, an issue that is not before us. We leave open, therefore, the question whether this time limit, particularly in a complex case, may implicate due process concerns.

In contrast to due process, which principally serves to protect the personal rights of litigants to a full and fair hearing, separation of powers principles are primarily addressed to the structural concerns of protecting the role of the independent Judiciary within the constitutional design. In this action, we have no occasion to decide whether there could be a time constraint on judicial action that was so severe that it implicated these structural separation of powers concerns. The PLRA does not deprive courts of their adjudicatory role, but merely provides a new legal standard for relief and encourages courts to apply that standard promptly.

* * *

JUSTICE SOUTER, with whom JUSTICE GINSBURG joins, concurring in part and dissenting in part.

I agree that 18 U.S.C. § 3626(e)(2) is unambiguous and join Parts I and II of the majority opinion. I also agree that applying the automatic stay may raise the due process issue, of whether a plaintiff has a fair chance to preserve an existing judgment that was valid when entered. But I believe that applying the statute may also raise a serious separation-of-powers issue if the time it allows turns out to be inadequate for a court to determine whether the new prerequisite to relief is satisfied in a particular case. I thus do not join Part III of the Court's opinion * * *. * * *

* * *

Congress has the authority to change rules of this sort by imposing new conditions precedent for the continuing enforcement of existing, prospective remedial orders and requiring courts to apply the new rules to those orders. If its legislation gives courts adequate time to determine the applicability of a new rule to an old order and to take the action necessary to apply it or to vacate the order, there seems little basis for claiming that Congress has crossed the constitutional line to interfere with the performance of any judicial function. But if determining whether a new rule applies requires time (say, for new factfinding) and if the statute provides insufficient time for a court to make that determination before the statute invalidates an extant remedial order, the application of the statute raises a serious question whether Congress has in practical terms assumed the judicial function. In such a case, the prospective order suddenly turns unenforceable not because a court has made a judgment to terminate it due to changed law or fact, but because no one can tell in the time allowed whether the new rule requires modification of the old order. One way to view this result is to see the Congress as mandating modification of an order that may turn out to be perfectly enforceable under the new rule, depending on judicial factfinding. * * *

* * * I would not decide the separation-of-powers question, but simply remand for further proceedings. If the District Court determined both that it lacked adequate time to make the requisite findings in the period before the automatic stay would become effective, and that applying the stay would violate the separation of powers, the question would then be properly presented.

Jᴜsᴛɪᴄᴇ Bʀᴇʏᴇʀ, with whom Jᴜsᴛɪᴄᴇ Sᴛᴇᴠᴇɴs joins, dissenting.

The Solicitor General * * * argues that the statute is silent as to whether the district court can modify or suspend the operation of the automatic stay. He would find in that silence sufficient authority for the court to create an exception to the 90–day time limit where circumstances make it necessary to do so. As so read, the statute would neither displace the courts' traditional equitable authority nor raise significant constitutional difficulties.

I agree with the Solicitor General and believe we should adopt that " 'reasonable construction' " of the statute.

At the outset, one must understand why a more flexible interpretation of the statute might be needed. To do so, one must keep in mind the extreme circumstances that at least some prison litigation originally sought to correct, the complexity of the resulting judicial decrees, and the potential difficulties arising out of the subsequent need to review those decrees in order to make certain they follow Congress' PLRA directives. A hypothetical example based on actual circumstances may help.

In January 1979, a Federal District Court made 81 factual findings describing extremely poor—indeed "barbaric and shocking"—prison conditions in the Commonwealth of Puerto Rico. *Morales Feliciano v. Romero Barcelo*, 497 F.Supp. 14, 32 (D.P.R.1979). These conditions included prisons typically operating with twice the number of prisoners they were designed to hold; inmates living in 16 square feet of space (*i.e.*, only 4 feet by 4 feet); inmates without medical care, without psychiatric care, without beds, without mattresses, without hot water, without soap or towels or toothbrushes or underwear; food prepared on a budget of $1.50 per day and "tons of food ... destroyed because of ... rats, vermin, worms, and spoilage"; "no working toilets or showers," "urinals [that] flush into the sinks," "plumbing systems ... in a state of collapse," and a "stench" that was "omnipresent"; "exposed wiring ... no fire extinguisher, ... [and] poor ventilation"; "calabozos," or dungeons, "like cages with bars on the top" or with two slits in a steel door opening onto a central corridor, the floors of which were "covered with raw sewage" and which contained prisoners with severe mental illnesses, "caged like wild animals," sometimes for months; areas of a prison where mentally ill inmates were "kept in cells naked, without beds, without mattresses, without any private possessions, and most of them without toilets that work and without drinking water." These conditions had led to epidemics of communicable diseases, untreated mental illness, suicides, and murders.

The District Court held that these conditions amounted to constitutionally forbidden "cruel and unusual punishment." It entered 30 specific orders designed to produce constitutionally mandated improvement by requiring the prison system to, for example, screen food handlers for communicable diseases, close the "calabozos," move mentally ill patients to hospitals, fix broken plumbing, and provide at least 35 square feet (*i.e.*, 5 feet by 7 feet) of living space to each prisoner.

The very pervasiveness and seriousness of the conditions described in the court's opinion made those conditions difficult to cure quickly. Over the next decade, the District Court entered further orders embodied in 15 published opinions, affecting 21 prison institutions. These orders concerned, *inter alia*, overcrowding, security, disciplinary proceedings, prisoner classification, rehabilitation, parole, and drug addiction treatment. Not surprisingly, the related proceedings involved extensive evidence and argument consuming thousands of pages of transcript. Their implementation involved the services of two monitors, two assistants, and a Special Master. Along the way, the court documented a degree of "administrative chaos" in the prison system and entered findings of contempt of court against the Commonwealth, followed by the assessment and collection of more than $74 million in fines.

* * * [M]y brief summary of the litigation should illustrate the potential difficulties involved in making the determination of continuing necessity required by the PLRA. Where prison litigation is as complex as the litigation I have just described, it may prove difficult for a district court to reach a fair and accurate decision about which orders remain necessary, and are the "least intrusive means" available, to prevent or correct a continuing violation of federal law. The orders, which were needed to resolve serious constitutional problems and may still be needed where compliance has not yet been assured, are complex, interrelated, and applicable to many different institutions. Ninety days might not provide sufficient time to ascertain the views of several different parties, including monitors, to allow them to present evidence, and to permit each to respond to the arguments and evidence of the others.

It is at least possible, then, that the statute, as the majority reads it, would sometimes terminate a complex system of orders entered over a period of years by a court familiar with the local problem—perhaps only to reinstate those orders later, when the termination motion can be decided. Such an automatic termination could leave constitutionally prohibited conditions unremedied, at least temporarily. Alternatively, the threat of termination could lead a district court to abbreviate proceedings that fairness would otherwise demand. At a minimum, the mandatory automatic stay would provide a recipe for uncertainty, as complex judicial orders that have long governed the administration of particular prison systems suddenly turn off, then (perhaps selectively) back on. So read, the statute directly interferes with a court's exercise of its traditional equitable authority, rendering temporarily ineffective pre-existing remedies aimed at correcting past, and perhaps ongoing, violations of the Constitution. That interpretation, as the majority itself concedes, might give rise to serious constitutional problems.

* * *

QUESTIONS AND POINTS FOR DISCUSSION

1. How would you resolve the due-process question the Supreme Court left open in *Miller v. French*?

2. Thus far, the courts of appeals have upheld the constitutionality of the PLRA provisions providing for the termination, in certain circumstances, of prospective relief ordered in conditions-of-confinement cases. See Gilmore v. California, 220 F.3d 987, 990 n. 3 (9th Cir.2000) (listing cases). From a constitutional standpoint, is there any way to distinguish the automatic-stay provision upheld by the Supreme Court in *Miller v. French* and the PLRA's immediate-termination provision found in 18 U.S.C. § 3626(b)(2)? Would you modify the PLRA's termination provisions or any other part of § 3626 for policy reasons? For a historical analysis raising questions regarding the soundness of the constitutional distinction courts have erected between congressional termination of prospective relief and congressional termination of final judgments awarding monetary relief, see Lynn S. Branham, Keeping the "Wolf Out of the Fold": Separation of Powers and Congressional Termination of Equitable Relief, 26 J. Legis. 185 (2000). See also Theodore K. Cheng, Invading an Article III Court's Inherent Equitable Powers: Separation of Powers and the Immediate Termination Provisions of the Prison Litigation Reform Act, 56 Wash. & Lee L. Rev. 969 (1999).

3. In your opinion, which side should bear the burden of proof when a state seeks the termination of prospective relief in a prison-conditions case? See Guajardo v. Texas Dep't of Criminal Justice, 363 F.3d 392, 395–96 (5th Cir. 2004) (burden of proof rests upon inmate plaintiffs to show the existence of ongoing violations of constitutional or other federal rights and that the prospective relief is narrowly drawn and is the least intrusive means to remedy the violation).

C. ENFORCING COURT ORDERS THROUGH CONTEMPT PROCEEDINGS AND OTHER MEANS

BADGLEY v. SANTACROCE

Court of Appeals, Second Circuit, 1986.
800 F.2d 33.

JON O. NEWMAN, CIRCUIT JUDGE:

More than two years ago, this Court characterized as a "disaster" the persistent violation by the Nassau County Sheriff and the Warden of the Nassau County Correctional Center ("NCCC") of a consent judgment limiting inmate population at the NCCC. *Badgley v. Varelas,* 729 F.2d 894, 902 (2d Cir.1984) ("*Badgley I*"). We now confront a situation of continuing violation of an amended consent judgment and discover that, since we last saw this case, little if any meaningful action has been taken to alleviate the overcrowding at the NCCC. * * *

* * *

The amended consent judgment slightly increases the inmate population limit * * *. Paragraph 4 provides that "the actual maximum in-house population of the NCCC shall not exceed 710 [the maximum allowable in cells] plus the number of inmates actually housed in [newly constructed] dormitories." Paragraph 3 establishes the maximum capacity of the new dormitory housing as 157. Thus, the judgment contemplates a maximum in-house population of 867. * * * Paragraph 32 allows the defendants to accept, "without regard to the in-house population cap," persons charged with class A or B felonies and persons held without bail or with bail of $100,000 or more.

Beginning on October 7, 1985, the county defendants began housing inmates at the NCCC above the in-cell limit of 710. Since that time, the defendants' record of compliance with the amended consent judgment has been abysmal. * * * On March 17, 1986, the in-cell population rose to a high of 781; that same day, the total in-house population (including inmates in dormitories) was 961. Overcrowding in violation of the amended consent judgment has been the rule and compliance the rare exception.

On October 17, 1985, the plaintiffs moved for an order holding the county defendants in contempt of court for violation of * * * the amended consent judgment. After a series of hearings, the District Court on January 6, 1986, concluded that the county defendants had not willfully violated the judgment, that they had made every reasonable effort to comply with the population limit, and that it was impossible for them to comply with the judgment without the assistance of state officials. The Court therefore denied the contempt motion, and the inmates appealed. We now reverse.

The purpose of civil contempt, broadly stated, is to compel a reluctant party to do what a court requires of him. Because compliance with a court's directive is the goal, an order of civil contempt is appropriate "only when it appears that obedience is within the power of the party being coerced by the order." *Maggio v. Zeitz,* 333 U.S. 56, 69 (1948). A court's power to impose coercive civil contempt is limited by an individual's ability to comply with the court's coercive order. A party may defend against a contempt by showing that his compliance is "factually impossible." In raising this defense, the defendant has a burden of production that may be difficult to meet, particularly in cases such as this where the defendants have a long history of delay and the plaintiffs' needs are urgent.

A classic application of the factual impossibility defense arises when a court orders an individual to produce documents that are not in his possession or control. * * * And an inability to comply with an order requiring the payment of money because of poverty or insolvency will generally be a defense to contempt. In all these situations, the contempt is excused because compliance is literally impossible and, as a result, any attempts at coercion are pointless.

By contrast, on the undisputed facts of this case, nothing makes it factually impossible for the Sheriff to cease delivering persons to the NCCC or for the Warden to refuse to accept such persons until the population requirements of the amended consent judgment are met. As we noted in *Badgley I,* if a natural disaster such as fire or disease required the NCCC to be closed, the county defendants would place the inmates elsewhere and would not deliver or accept new prisoners until the crisis ended. The continued violation of the amended consent judgment is a legal crisis of equal gravity, and it is obvious that the defendants are just as able to decline to deliver and accept new prisoners until this crisis is ended. The terms of the amended consent judgment automatically operate, whenever the population limit is exceeded, to close the jail's doors as tightly as would fire or disease.

* * *

The defendants also suggested to the District Court that compliance might place them in contempt of the state courts that send them prisoners. Justice Arthur D. Spatt, Administrative Judge for Nassau County, told the District Court that, if the Sheriff refused to accept prisoners committed to his custody by local criminal courts, he would be in contempt of those courts. Significantly, however, he added that state judges do not commit prisoners to specific facilities and would not direct the Sheriff to take prisoners to the NCCC in light of the federal court's order barring delivery and acceptance of additional inmates. Compliance with the amended consent judgment has not been shown to pose a risk of contempt of state courts.

Even if a state court would hold the defendants in contempt for refusing to house inmates at the NCCC, or if compliance would otherwise violate state law, Supremacy Clause considerations require that the judgment of the federal court be respected. In any attempt by a state court to hold defendants in contempt for taking actions required by the judgment of the District Court, that judgment would provide a complete defense.

The respect due the federal judgment is not lessened because the judgment was entered by consent. * * * When the defendants chose to consent to a judgment, rather than have the District Court adjudicate the merits of the plaintiffs' claims, the result was a fully enforceable federal judgment that overrides any conflicting state law or state court order. The strong policy encouraging settlement of cases requires that the terms of a consent judgment, once approved by a federal court, be respected as fully as a judgment entered after trial.

* * *

Compliance with the amended consent judgment must now occur, and the remedial provisions of that judgment must be put into effect. We will allow a delay of thirty days only to permit necessary notification to the appropriate court, agency, and police officials.

* * * The District Court is also directed to hold the county defendants in civil contempt in the event of any subsequent failure to implement * * * the amended consent judgment and, in that event, to assess compensatory damages in favor of the plaintiffs of not less than $5,000 for each person admitted to the NCCC in violation of the amended consent judgment and to order any additional remedies that may be appropriate. * * *

Questions and Points for Discussion

1. Failure to comply with a court order may result in the institution of either civil or criminal contempt proceedings against the defendant. As was discussed in *Badgley v. Santacroce*, the purposes of the sanction imposed if a defendant is found in civil contempt are coercive and remedial—to induce the defendant to provide the plaintiff with the relief to which the plaintiff is entitled under a prior court order. Thus, if a court orders that a defendant found in civil contempt be confined in jail, the defendant can avoid the confinement or obtain release from the jail by complying with the court order. If the defendant is ordered to pay a fine for not complying with the court's order, the fine is typically, though not always, payable to the plaintiff. But see New York State Nat'l Org. for Women v. Terry, 159 F.3d 86, 94–95 (2d Cir.1998) (contempt fine that would be purged upon compliance with the court's order was civil even though it was payable to the state and counties).

The purpose of criminal contempt, by contrast, is punishment—to punish the defendant for disobeying a court order. If a defendant is held in criminal contempt and, as a result, sentenced to jail, the defendant cannot avoid the penalty by complying with the court's order. And any fine leveled against the defendant is payable to the court, since the purpose of the finding of contempt is to vindicate the court's authority.

The Supreme Court has acknowledged that the distinction between civil and criminal contempt is "somewhat elusive." International Union, United Mine Workers of Am. v. Bagwell, 512 U.S. 821, 830, 114 S.Ct. 2552, 2559 (1994). It is still important to determine whether the contempt proceedings instituted against a defendant are civil or criminal because if they are criminal, the defendant is entitled to the constitutional protections afforded individuals charged with a crime, including the requirement that guilt be established beyond a reasonable doubt. Hicks on Behalf of Feiock v. Feiock, 485 U.S. 624, 632, 108 S.Ct. 1423, 1429–1430 (1988). See also *Bagwell*, 512 U.S. at 838–39, 114 S.Ct. at 2563 (recognizing a right to jury trial in criminal contempt proceedings in which nonpetty sanctions are imposed). If ability to comply with the court's order is an element of the offense of contempt, the plaintiff has the burden of proof on this question. By contrast, in civil contempt proceedings, some courts place the burden on the defendant of demonstrating that compliance with the court's order is not possible. See, e.g., Loftus v. Southeastern Pa. Transp. Auth., 8 F.Supp.2d 464, 468–69 (E.D. Pa. 1998). Other courts place the burden of proving the defendant's ability to comply with the court's order on the plaintiff. This burden shifts to the plaintiff once the defendant has produced evidence of this incapacity to comply. See, e.g., Bilzerian v. Securities & Exch. Comm'n, 276 B.R. 285, 288, 299–300 (M.D. Fla. 2002).

2. A prisoner who has prevailed in a § 1983 lawsuit can recover attorney's fees under 42 U.S.C. § 1988 for efforts undertaken to secure a defendant's compliance with a court order or judgment. 42 U.S.C. § 1997e(d)(1)(B)(ii); Cody v. Hillard, 304 F.3d 767, 774 (8th Cir. 2002). The fees recoverable for monitoring and enforcement work include those incurred during contempt proceedings brought to compel such compliance. See, e.g., Webb v. Ada County, 285 F.3d 829, 834–35 (9th Cir.2002).

3. To assist in the enforcement of a court's order entered in a complex prison-conditions case, a federal court occasionally will exercise its authority under 18 U.S.C. § 3626(f) and Rule 53 of the Federal Rules of Civil Procedure and appoint what is called a "special master." The special master generally is charged with reporting to the court at periodic intervals about the defendant's compliance with the court's decree. The master may also be responsible for assisting in the development of a remedial plan.

D. OTHER REMEDIES

Some federal statutes provide inmates with rights and remedies that go beyond the constitutional minima. Two examples are the Religious Land Use and Institutionalized Persons Act, 42 U.S.C. §§ 2000cc to 2000cc–5, discussed on page 531, and the Americans with Disabilities Act, §§ 12101–12213, discussed on page 755. In addition, a state or local inmate's treatment while in prison or jail or the conditions of confinement at a correctional facility may give rise to state common-law claims for such torts as assault, battery, or negligence. Inmates may also be able to assert state statutory claims or claims under the state's constitution. These state claims may be asserted in a lawsuit filed in state court or possibly as pendent claims in a § 1983 suit filed in federal court. But one of the impediments to a prisoner's prevailing on a state-law claim is the existence, in some states, of immunity statutes limiting the liability of correctional officials against whom inmates have asserted state-law-based claims. See, e.g., 745 Ill. Comp. Stat. 10/4–103 ("Neither a local public entity nor a public employee is liable for failure to provide a jail, detention, or correctional facility, or if such facility is provided, for failure to provide sufficient equipment, personnel, supervision or facilities therein. Nothing in this Section requires the periodic inspection of prisoners.")

States, as well as the Federal Bureau of Prisons, have also set up administrative processes through which a prisoner may pursue a grievance against correctional officials and secure at least some forms of relief. For a discussion of the need to exhaust administrative remedies before bringing a conditions-of-confinement suit under § 1983 or other "Federal law" and of limits government officials place on the recovery of monetary relief in grievance processes, see pages 828–29.

INDEX

References are to Pages

References are to Pages

MUNICIPAL LIABILITY—Cont'd
"Person" under § 1983, 800–01
Policy, 805–06
Punitive damages, 802, 826
Qualified immunity, 826
Respondeat-superior liability, 804

PARALEGALS
Attorney's fees, 849
Interviews of prisoners, 540–41
Law libraries, in lieu of, 567

PAROLE RELEASE
See also Probation; Supervised Release
Generally, 70, 396–413
Conditions,
Castration, 368
Sex-offender treatment, 648
Ex post facto laws, 219–20
Guidelines, 173
Liberty interest, 398–400, 402–04, 408–09
Process due, 400–08, 411–12

PAROLE REVOCATION
See also Probation; Supervised Release
Generally, 270–71, 371–96
Counsel, right to, 376–79
Due process,
Liberty interest, 373–74
Preliminary hearings, 374–75, 379
Revocation hearings, 375–80
Exclusionary rule, 395–96
Standard of proof, 380

PERSONAL PROPERTY
Seizure or destruction of,
Due process, 725, 733–37
Fourth Amendment, 682–87

PLEA BARGAINS
Generally, 41–42, 62–80
Admissibility, statements made during plea negotiations, 44–45
Appeal, waiver of, 41, 76–77
Benefits, 34–35
Breach,
Defendant, by, 66–67
Prosecutor, by, 62–66
Codefendant, reduced charge, 70, 74
Criticisms, 33–34
Inducements,
Legislative, 77–78
Prosecutorial, 67–77
Judges' participation in, 79
Release-dismissal agreements, 74–75

POSTCONVICTION PROCEEDINGS
See also Habeas Corpus
Attorney, assistance of, 564–65

PRESENTENCE INVESTIGATION REPORT
Defendant interviews in preparing, 98–100, 134
Federal cases, 133–36
Right of access to, 93–96, 135
Right to respond to, 94, 135–36

PRESENTENCE INVESTIGATION REPORT—Cont'd
Sample, 86–92

PRETRIAL DETAINEES
Attorneys, monitoring communications with, 543–45
Body searches, 690–93, 695–96
Cell searches,
Fourth Amendment, applicability of, 687–88
Right to observe, 689
Contact visits, 509–16
Credit for time incarcerated, 178–79
Cruel and unusual punishment, 745, 754–55, 797–98
Definition of, 460, 745
Disciplinary segregation, 619
Double celling, 772–73
First Amendment, 485–86
Force used against, 797–98
Medical care, 754–55, 763
Privacy of, 706–09
Punishment proscribed, 510–11

PRISON LITIGATION REFORM ACT
Attorney's fees, restrictions on, 849–50
Court appearances, restrictions on, 539
Equitable relief,
Restrictions on, 838–42
Stay of, 863–71
Termination of, 862–64, 871
Filing fees, 810–11
Physical-injury requirement, 797, 817, 834–35
Remedies, exhaustion of, 828–29
Sua sponte dismissals, 812
Three strikes, 810–11

PRISONS
Crowding, 26–30, 215, 763–64
Incarceration, increase in, 3–4, 764
Programs,
Gender discrimination, 661–73
Parenting, 519
Prison industry, 673–79
Supermaximum-security, 625–32, 777

PRIVACY, RIGHT OF
See also Fourth Amendment
Generally, 697–715, 723
Bodily functions, view of, 699–701, 703–04, 707, 710–11
Body-cavity searches, 697, 709–10
Emergencies, 709–10
Equal employment opportunities, correctional personnel, 698–706, 710–11, 714–24
Genitals, view of, 698–701, 703–11, 715
Marriage, 706
Patdown searches, 698, 700–03, 705, 709–10
Source of, 697–98, 706–07
Strip searches, 709–10, 715

PRIVATE CONTRACTORS
Bivens actions, 808
Immunity, 825–26
Section 1983 liability, 803–04

†